W9-BPN-700

Statistical Techniques in Business and Economics

THE IRWIN SERIES

PRODUCTION OPERATIONS MANAGEMENT

Aquilano, Chase, and Davis
Fundamentals of Operations Management
Second Edition

Chase and Aquilano
Production and Operations Management: Manufacturing and Services
Seventh Edition

Hill
Manufacturing Strategy: Text and Cases
Second Edition

Hopp and Spearman
Factory Physics
First Edition

Lambert and Stock
Strategic Logistics Management
Third Edition

Leenders and Fearon
Purchasing and Materials Management
Tenth Edition

Lotfi and Pegels
Decision Support Systems for Operations and Management Sciences
Third Edition

Nahmias
Production and Operations Analysis
Second Edition

Niebel
Motion and Time Study
Ninth Edition

Schonberger and Knod
Operations Management: Continuous Improvement
Fifth Edition

Stevenson
Production/Operations Management
Fifth Edition

Vollmann, Berry, and Whybark
Manufacturing Planning and Control Systems
Third Edition

Zimmerman
ABC Operations Software
Beta Edition

STATISTICS

Aczel
Statistics: Concepts and Applications
First Edition

Aczel
Complete Business Statistics
Third Edition

Bryant and Smith
Practical Data Analysis: Case Studies in Business Statistics, Volumes I and II
First Edition

Duncan
Quality Control and Industrial Statistics
Fifth Edition

Cooper and Emory
Business Research Methods
Fifth Edition

Gitlow, Oppenheim, and Oppenheim
Quality Management: Tools and Methods for Improvement
Second Edition

Hall
Computerized Business Statistics
Fourth Edition

Hanke and Reitsch
Understanding Business Statistics
Second Edition

Lind and Mason
Basic Statistics for Business and Economics
First Edition

Mason and Lind
Statistical Techniques in Business and Economics
Ninth Edition

Neter, Kutner, Nachtsheim, and Wasserman
Applied Linear Statistical Models
Fourth Edition

Neter, Kutner, Nachtsheim, and Wasserman
Applied Linear Regression Models
Third Edition

Shin
The Irwin Statistical Software Series: Minitab, SAS, SPSS, Statgraphics Guides

Siegel
Practical Business Statistics
Second Edition

Webster
Applied Statistics for Business and Economics
Second Edition

Wilson and Keating
Business Forecasting
Second Edition

QUANTITATIVE METHODS AND MANAGEMENT SCIENCE

Bierman, Bonini, and Hausman
Quantitative Analysis for Business Decisions
Eighth Edition

Knowles
Management Science: Building and Using Models
First Edition

Lotfi and Pegels
Decision Support Systems for Operations and Management Science
Third Edition

Stevenson
Introduction to Management Science
Second Edition

Turban and Meredith
Fundamentals of Management Science
Sixth Edition

Statistical Techniques in Business and Economics

Ninth Edition

Robert D. Mason
Douglas A. Lind
Both of the University of Toledo

IRWIN

Chicago • Bogotá • Boston • Buenos Aires • Caracas
London • Madrid • Mexico City • Sydney • Toronto

Cover photos: *John Gajda/FPG International; Color Box/FPG International; Telegraph Color Library/FPG International; Gerald French/FPG International; and Raymond A. Bock*

Trademark Acknowledgments:

Minitab is a registered trademark of Minitab, Inc.
IBM and IBM PC are registered trademarks of International Business Machines Corporation.

Irwin Book Team

Senior sponsoring editor: *Richard T. Hercher, Jr.*
Developmental editor: *Gail Korosa*
Marketing manager: *Brian Kibby*
Project editor: *Waivah Clement*
Production supervisor: *Laurie Kersch*
Designer: *Heidi J. Baughman*
Interior designer: *Maureen McCutcheon*
Cover designer: *Maureen McCutcheon*
Photo researcher: *Randall Nicholas/Nicholas Communications Inc.*
Art studio: *Weimer Graphics, Inc.*
Graphics supervisor: *Heather D. Burbridge*
Compositor: *Weimer Graphics, Inc.*
Typeface: *9.5/12 Helvetica*
Printer: *Von Hoffmann Press, Inc.*

Times Mirror
Higher Education Group

Library of Congress Cataloging-in-Publication Data

Mason, Robert Deward
Statistical techniques in business and economics / Robert D. Mason, Douglas A. Lind. — 9th ed.
p. cm.
Includes index.
ISBN 0-256-13901-6. — ISBN 0-256-18904-8 (instructor's ed.)
1. Social sciences—Statistical methods. 2. Economics—-Statistical methods. 3. Commercial statistics. I. Lind, Douglas A. II. Title.
HA29.M268 1996
519.5—dc20 95–16497

Printed in the United States of America
2 3 4 5 6 7 8 9 0 VH 2 1 0 9 8 7 6

To Anita and Jane

PREFACE TO THE STUDENT

As the name implies, the major objective of this book is to assist you in developing an understanding of the skills needed for future success in marketing, accounting, management, finance, and other fields of business administration and economics. *Statistical Techniques in Business and Economics* also provides an excellent background for more advanced courses in statistics.

We have designed this book to assist you in approaching this basic course without the anxiety often associated with statistics. To accomplish this we have developed a large number of very effective learning aids. We list and comment on some of these below.

LEARNING AIDS

Goals. Each chapter opens with a set of goals. They state what you should be able to do after completing the chapter. When you have finished the chapter, make sure you have accomplished these objectives.

Example and solution. After a brief discussion of a statistical technique there is a simple example followed by the detailed solution. These examples/solutions are continued throughout the chapter.

Self-review problems. A number of self-review problems are interspersed throughout each chapter. They are designed to give you an opportunity to work problems similar to the preceding examples. The objective is to reinforce an understanding of the material just covered. The answer and method of solution are given at the end of the chapter. We urge you to do these review problems because they continue to give learning reinforcement as you progress through the chapter.

Exercises. Throughout a chapter, and at the end of a chapter, are a large number of exercises that may be assigned by your instructor. The answers to the odd-numbered exercises are given at the end of the book. Again, we urge you to work these exercises to give you practice in the various statistical computations.

Definitions and formulas. Definitions of new terms and formulas used for the first time are boxed and highlighted in color for emphasis. Refer to them when appropriate.

Chapter outline. This learning aid gives you a chance to summarize the material in the chapter.

Computer data exercises. The last few exercises in most chapters are based on three large data sets found at the end of the book. One involves the sale of homes in Sarasota, Florida, another involves baseball statistics, and the third concerns sales of magazines such as *Ebony, Good Housekeeping,* and *National Geographic.* We urge you to solve these exercises using MINITAB or some other software.

Chapter examination. There is an examination at the end of each chapter covering all the material in the chapter. It allows you to quickly evaluate your comprehension of the subject matter. The answers and methods of solution for the examination questions are also given at the end of the chapter.

Section review. After each logical group of chapters there is an overall summary of the contents of these chapters. This gives you an overview of the material covered in those chapters.

STUDY GUIDE

There is a Study Guide available for the text, written by the authors. Each chapter includes the chapter goals, an introduction, a discussion of the statistical tools, a glossary, and chapter problems with solutions done step by step with explanations. Following each chapter problem is an exercise to do, with the answer given at the end of the guide. If it is not available in your bookstore, ask the bookstore manager about ordering it.

Bob Mason
Doug Lind

PREFACE FOR THE STUDENT (by a student)

Statistical Techniques in Business and Economics is an excellent tool for understanding statistical concepts. The chapters are well organized and the examples relate to the "real world." The best part, however, is its readability. While many statistical terms and concepts are confusing and sometimes intimidating, this book presents them in a clear and concise manner.

Jeffrey Long
University of Toledo

ACKNOWLEDGMENTS

The ninth edition of *Statistical Techniques in Business and Economics* is the product of the effort of many people: students, colleagues, reviewers, and the staff at Richard D. Irwin, Inc. We thank them all. We wish to express our gratitude to the reviewers:

Mark P. Karscig
Central Missouri State University

Denise L. Kummer
St. Louis Community College—Meramec

Louis A. Patille
University of Phoenix—Colorado Division

J. Burdeane Orris
Butler University

Mary Jo Boehms
Jackson State Community College

Charles E. Lienert
Metropolitan State College

Christopher W. Rogers
Miami-Dade Community College

David A. Parmenter
Governors State University

Judson Faurer
Metro State College of Denver

Janice Roe
University of Toledo

Frank Goulard
Portland Community College

Abraham Axelrud
Queensborough Community College

David R. Hoffman
University of Phoenix

Creig R. Kronstedt
Cardinal Stritch College

A. Eugene Hileman
Northeastern State University

Barry Morris
University of North Alabama

Their suggestions and thorough reviews of the previous edition and the manuscript for this edition made this a better text.

Special thanks go to a number of people. Louis A. Patille, of the University of Phoenix, and Wendy McGuire, of Santa Fe Community College, each solved all of the exercises and checked our answers for accuracy. Jeffrey Lind provided help with the Lotus software, and Natalie Anderson helped with the formula card.

Lloyd Landau of Mercy College prepared the Test Bank. Lloyd Jaisingh, of Morehead State University, prepared the PowerPoint Presentation and Lecture Guide. These supplements take a great deal of work to write, and we appreciate their efforts.

We also would like to thank the staff at Richard D. Irwin, Inc.: Richard T. Hercher, Jr., the senior sponsoring editor; Gail Korosa, the developmental editor; Waivah Clement, the project editor; Heidi Baughman, the designer; and Laurie Kersch, the production supervisor.

R.D.M.
D.A.L.

CONTENTS IN BRIEF

CONTENTS

CHAPTER 4

Measures of Dispersion and Skewness 113

CHAPTER 5

A Survey of Probability Concepts 167

CHAPTER 6

Discrete Probability Distributions 217

CHAPTER 7

The Normal Probability Distribution 255

CHAPTER 8

Sampling Methods and Sampling Distributions 293

CHAPTER 9

Tests of Hypotheses: Large Samples 343

CHAPTER 10

Tests of Hypotheses: Small Samples 399

CHAPTER 11

Analysis of Variance 433

CHAPTER 16

Statistical Quality Control 655

CHAPTER 17

Index Numbers 691

CHAPTER 18

Time Series and Forecasting 727

CHAPTER 19

An Introduction to Decision Making under Uncertainty 767

APPENDIXES:

INDEX *863*

Chapter 1

What Is Statistics?

GOALS

When you have completed this chapter, you will be able to:

1
Define what is meant by statistics.

2
Cite some uses of statistics in business and other areas.

3
Explain what is meant by descriptive statistics and inferential statistics.

4
Cite the published sources of some of the more commonly used business data.

5
Explain the purpose of questionnaires.

6
Distinguish between nominal, ordinal, interval, and ratio levels of measurement.

How would a marketing manager proceed in making recommendations about the location of an amusement park? (See Goal 2 and Exercise 5.)

INTRODUCTION

About 100 years ago H. G. Wells noted that "statistical thinking will one day be as necessary for efficient citizenship as the ability to read and write." He made no mention of business simply because the Industrial Revolution was still in its infancy. Were he to comment on statistical thinking today he would probably say that "statistical thinking is necessary not only for efficient citizenship, but also for effective decision making in various facets of business."

A recent article in the *Washington Post* by Michael Schrage emphasizes the importance of statistics.[1] He stated that America is not going to have a quality revolution until its managers and workers get some grasp of probability and statistics. Schrage points out that corporate statistical literacy is, unfortunately, abysmally low. Brian Joyner, a Wisconsin-based consultant, agrees. To his dismay, he finds that much of his consulting time is spent on remedial statistical education. Author Andrea Gabor points out in the same article that "Japanese students are inundated with statistics in high school. You realize that statistics is now part of their culture. Just as our bookstores have sections on science and technology, their bookstores have sections on quality control and statistics." No doubt the emphasis on quality control, statistics, and probability has played a major part in the huge success of their Toyotas, Hondas, Sonys, Minoltas, and other manufactured product brands.

The late W. Edwards Deming, noted statistician and quality control expert, insisted that we should start statistics education before high school. He liked to tell the story of an 11-year-old who devised a quality control chart to track the on-time performance of his school bus. Deming commented, "He's got a good start in life." It is hoped that this book will give you a solid foundation in statistics for your future life in marketing, accounting, management, or some other facet of business.

WHAT IS MEANT BY STATISTICS?

Whether you are listening to your favorite local radio station, watching the Cubs play the Dodgers on television, or reading *USA Today, The Wall Street Journal,* or *Sports Illustrated,* you are the target of a barrage of assorted figures commonly referred to as "statistics." These statistics might pertain to sports, the stock market, employment information, agricultural production, health, religion, retail or wholesale sales, and so forth. Some examples of statistics follow:

- The results of a recent Harris poll indicated that 60 percent of the respondents thought that small business owners have good moral and ethical standards. In addition, 25 percent thought that lawyers and 19 percent thought that members of Congress have good moral and ethical standards.
- The National Center for Educational Statistics stated that of the 64,465,000 students who use computers, 28,262,000 are in high school and 10,661,000 are college undergraduates.
- In the *Jackson Hole News,* June 8, 1994, a real estate company in Jackson Hole, Wyoming, offered a home located on 6.1 acres with a view of the Tetons for $1,450,000.

[1]Michael Schrage, "If Statistics Are the Key to Quality, Our Students Need Some Chance Encounters," *Washington Post* (March 15, 1991).

- Stocks rose yesterday because investors were encouraged by a rebound in the dollar and lower interest rates. Advancing issues outnumbered decliners on the New York Stock Exchange. The Dow Jones industrial average rose 5.53 to 4,198.15. The Standard & Poor's 500 stock index rose 0.59 to 507.01, and the NASDAQ composite index rose 6.57 to 821.26.

Each of the preceding figures is called a **statistic.** The price of the Jackson Hole property for sale ($1,450,000) is a statistic. The 19 percent of the survey respondents who felt that members of Congress have good moral and ethical standards is a statistic.

Statistics

A collection of more than one figure is referred to as **statistics.** For example, a collection of data such as 55,200 flower orders for Father's Day, 30,000 travel agencies in the United States, 2.2 percent of the labor force employed in farming, and $10,000 for a fly rod is commonly referred to as statistics.

However, the subject of statistics as we will explore it in this text has a much broader meaning than just collecting and publishing numerical facts and figures. Statistics is defined as:

Statistics defined

> **Statistics** The science of collecting, organizing, presenting, analyzing, and interpreting numerical data for the purpose of assisting in making a more effective decision.

Just as attorneys have "rules of evidence" and accountants have "commonly accepted practices," persons dealing with numerical data follow some standard guidelines. Some of the basic statistical techniques they use in decision problems are presented in the following chapters.

Many first approach the application of numerical data to solve a problem with some trepidation. They have heard such often-quoted phrases as "statistics lie." Statistics "lie" only if they are not applied correctly. For illustration, suppose the sales of Chicago Carpet World for the past 20 years were depicted as in Chart 1–1. Initially, you might conclude that sales increased at a very rapid rate since 1975 (the lie).

CHART 1–1 **Sales of Chicago Carpet World since 1975**

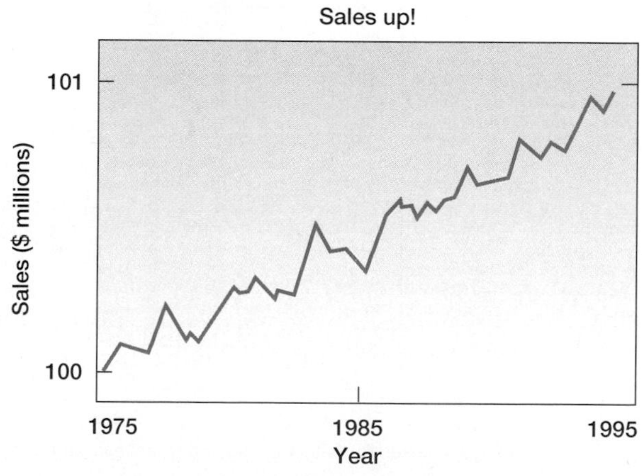

A closer look at Chart 1–1, however, reveals that sales increased only about 1 percent—from $100 million to $101 million (the truth). The designer of the chart—intentionally or unintentionally—scaled the vertical (sales) axis incorrectly, leaving us with the wrong impression regarding the trend of sales since 1975. Graphic representation is covered in Chapter 2.

Our objectives in this book are many. One, of course, is to alert you of possible misuses of charts, averages, correlation and regression techniques, and other statistical tools. Another is to introduce you to the usefulness of statistical techniques in marketing, accounting, finance, international trade, economics, law enforcement, and other fields. Specifically, who uses statistics?

WHO USES STATISTICS?

Use in business and other fields

As noted, statistical techniques are used extensively by marketing, accounting, quality control, and other departments; consumers; professional sports people; hospital administrators; educators; political parties; physicians; and others involved in making decisions. The following examples suggest the wide use of statistics in decision problems.

- Health researchers are currently concerned about protecting persons of all ages from catastrophic bills for hospital charges. Statistics are needed regarding how many persons will require medical care during the year, what the cost will be, and so on.
- The Census Bureau did some research and reported the percentage of people in each age group who are not covered by health insurance. Surprisingly, only 12.9 percent of persons 55 to 64 are not covered and 28.9 percent of those 18 to 24 are not covered. See Chart 1–2.

CHART 1–2 **Who Isn't Covered by Health Insurance (by percent of age group)**

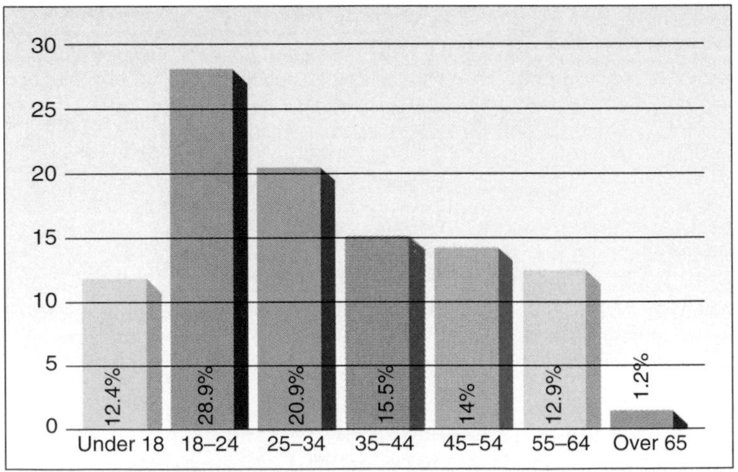

Source: Census Bureau (1992 figures, latest available).

To further explore the health insurance dilemma, the answers to several questions will be needed. Who will pay the bills, and where will the money come from? Can employers afford it? Does the state and the federal government have the funds to cover these huge expenses? Facts and figures (statistics) are needed to answer these questions. This is the job of the researcher.

Some other uses of statistics in decision making are as follows:

Some specific uses of statistics in problem solving

- The research analysts for such firms as Merrill Lynch evaluate many facets of a particular stock before making a "buy" or "sell" recommendation. They collect the past sales data of the company and estimate future earnings. Other factors, such as projected worldwide demand for the company's products, the strength of the competition, and the effect of the new management-union contract, are also considered before a recommendation is made.
- The Republican party wants to determine its chances of winning at least five of the seven contested seats in the Senate. How can the chances of challenger A. J. Farley in Oklahoma be assessed? A sample survey of potential voters in the state could be conducted. The party could hire pollsters, such as Gallup or Harris; or the party could undertake the survey. Scientifically selecting, say, 2,000 registered voters in Oklahoma and evaluating the results require a knowledge of the techniques of probability and sampling (covered in Chapters 5–8).

Statistics imperative in quality assurance

- Management must make decisions on the quality of current production. For example, automatic drill presses do not produce a perfect hole 1.3000 inches in diameter each time a hole is drilled (because of drill wear, vibration of the machine, and other factors). Slight tolerances are permitted, but when the hole is too small or too large, production is considered defective (not usable). The quality assurance department is charged with continually monitoring production using sampling and other standard statistical techniques (covered in Chapter 16).

Use of statistical techniques by government

- The federal government is particularly concerned with the present condition of our economy and with predicting future economic trends. The government conducts a large number of surveys to determine consumer confidence and the outlook of management regarding sales and production for the next 12 months. Indexes, such as the Consumer Price Index (covered in Chapter 17), are constructed each month to assess the trend of inflation. Department store sales, housing starts, money turnover, and industrial production statistics are just a few of the hundreds of economic indicators evaluated monthly. These evaluations are used to make decisions regarding the prime rate charged by banks and are used by the Federal Reserve Board to decide the level of control to place on the money supply.

Statistics use in marketing

- The marketing department of a soap manufacturer has the responsibility of making recommendations regarding the potential profitability of a newly developed group of face soaps having fruit smells, such as pineapple, orange, and lime. Likewise, the marketing department of a nationally known soft drink bottler must make a similar decision regarding a newly developed group of drinks having such unique tastes as avocado and plum. Both departments will conduct consumer tests and make profit projections based on sample results.

In the foregoing examples of the use of statistics in quality control, sales, and so on, the collecting, analyzing, and interpretation of data play an important role in decision making. The quality assurance department might take measurements on five piston rings and, based on these measurements and commonly used statistical techniques, make a decision to either accept or reject the output of the last two hours. (Quality control is discussed in Chapter 16.) The IBM sales manager is interested in both seasonal and long-term sales. Past records are analyzed and, using standard statistical techniques, estimates of December sales and long-term sales for 1998 are developed. (Trend analysis is covered in Chapter 18.) A basic knowledge regarding quality control, trend analysis, and the other statistical tools is necessary to be successful in today's business.

The knowledge of these basic techniques is more crucial today than 30 years ago. Business is changing rapidly. Today there is significantly more competition from Europe, Japan, and the Far East, as well as other areas of the globe. Our economy now has a significant number of mergers, new businesses starting up, and old businesses failing. Pollution is now a major problem, and so is the pressure on wildlife. Statistics are needed to evaluate the probability that a new business or merger will survive.

What is needed, therefore, is a knowledge of statistics, including probability, sampling, the techniques needed to project sales or production into future periods, correlation analysis (determining the relationship between two or more variables, discussed in Chapters 12 and 13), and so on.

TYPES OF STATISTICS

Descriptive Statistics

The definition of statistics given earlier referred to "organizing, presenting, and analyzing numerical data." This facet of statistics is commonly referred to as **descriptive statistics.** What is descriptive statistics?

Descriptive statistics

> **Descriptive statistics** Statistical methods used to describe data that have been collected.

Following are some examples of statistics intended to describe something.

- Gallup makes ongoing studies of America's knowledge of the Bible. Gallup found that 49 percent (49 out of every 100 persons) knew the name of the first book of the Bible. The statistic 49 describes the number out of every 100 persons who got the correct answer.
- According to J. D. Powers, Lexus LS400 owners reported 32 problems per 100 cars during 1994. The statistic 32 describes the number of problems out of every 100 cars.
- Al Unser, Jr., averaged 160.872 miles per hour in the 1994 Indianapolis 500 race. The statistic 160.872 describes Unser's speed. It does not indicate that this speed is fast or slow.
- The *Monthly Labor Review* reported that the average hourly wage in the retail trade for May 1994 was $8.03. The figure $8.03 describes the hourly earnings of a typical (average) employee working in such firms as Heitel Jewelers, Wal-Mart, Sears, Dayton-Hudson, and other retail stores.

Masses of unorganized numerical data—such as the census of population, the weekly earnings of thousands of computer programmers, and the individual responses of 2,340 registered voters regarding their choice for President of the United States—are of little value as is. However, statistical techniques are available to organize this type of data into a meaningful form. Some data can be organized into a **frequency distribution.** (The procedure for doing this is covered in Chapter 2.) Various **charts** may be used to describe data; several basic chart forms are also presented in Chapter 2.

Median—another descriptive tool

Specialized averages, such as the *median,* may be computed to describe the central value of a group of numerical data. These averages are presented in Chapter 3. A number of statistical measures may be used to describe how closely the data are clustered about an average. These measures are examined in Chapter 4.

Inferential Statistics

Another facet of statistics is **inferential statistics**—also called **statistical inference** and **inductive statistics.** Our main concern regarding inferential statistics is finding out something about a population based on a sample taken from that population. For example, based on a sample survey by the federal government reported in *USA Today,* only 46 percent of high school seniors can solve problems involving fractions, decimals, and percentages. And only 77 percent of high school seniors correctly totaled the cost of soup, a burger, fries, and a cola on a restaurant menu. Since these are inferences about the population (all high school seniors) based on sample data, we refer to them as inferential statistics.

Inferential statistics

> **Inferential statistics** The methods used to find out something about a population, based on a sample.

Note the words "population" and "sample" in the definition of inferential statistics. We often make reference to the population living in the United States or the 1 billion population of China. However, in statistics the word *population* has a broader meaning. A **population** may consist of *individuals*—such as all the students enrolled at Utah State University, all the students in Accounting 201, or all the inmates at Attica prison. A population may also consist of *objects,* such as all the XB-70 tires produced during the week at the Cooper Tire and Rubber Company in Findlay, Ohio, or all the trout in a stock pond. A population may also consist of a group of *measurements,* such as all the weights of the defensive linemen on the Penn State University football team or all the heights of the basketball players in the Southeastern Conference. Thus, a population in the statistical sense of the word does not necessarily refer to people.

Population

Population A collection of all possible individuals, objects, or measurements of interest.

To infer something about a population, we usually take a **sample** from the population.

Sample

Sample A portion, or part, of the population of interest.

Reasons for sampling

Why take a sample instead of studying every member of the population? A sample of registered voters is necessary because of the prohibitive cost of contacting millions of voters before an election. Testing wheat for moisture content destroys the wheat, thus making a sample imperative. If the wine testers tested all the wine, none would be available for sale. It would be physically impossible for a few marine biologists to capture and tag all the seals in the ocean. (These and other reasons for sampling are discussed in Chapter 8.)

As noted, taking a sample to find out something about a population is done extensively in business, agriculture, politics, and government, as cited in the following examples:

Specific uses of sampling

- Before an election, such professional polling organizations as Gallup and Harris sample only about 2,000 registered voters out of the millions eligible to vote. Based on sample results, certain inferences are made regarding how all voters will cast their ballots on election day. Historically, the actual election results have been remarkably close to the sample results. The following figures are based on Gallup's predictions; for Roosevelt (1944), 51.5 percent estimated versus 53.3 percent actual; for Reagan (1984), 59.0 percent of the total vote prior to the election versus 59.2 percent actual; for Bush (1988), 52.9 percent estimated versus 53.4 percent actual; for Clinton (1992), 50.2 percent estimated versus 52.1 percent actual.
- A small scoop of wheat is taken from a truck as it waits to be unloaded at Anderson's grain elevator in Maumee, Ohio. Based on the results of this sample, a price is established for the whole truckload.
- Television networks constantly monitor the popularity of their programs by hiring Nielsen and other organizations to sample the preferences of TV

viewers. These program ratings are used to set advertising rates and to cancel programs.

- Wine tasters sip a few drops of wine to make a decision with respect to all the wine waiting to be released for sale.
- The accounting department checks only a few invoices to find out something about the accuracy of all the invoices.

Risks of sampling

There are certain risks involved in using sample results to infer something about an unknown population. Five pinion gears selected at random by the quality assurance department from all the pinion gears manufactured during the past hour might be acceptable. Thus, it might be inferred from the sample of five that all the gears produced were satisfactory. However, since this inference was based on only a portion of the population, there is a chance that not all gears are satisfactory. In fact, it might be that the five gears chosen at random were the only acceptable ones produced during the hour! Pollsters such as Gallup and Harris might predict that John Corrigan will win the vacant House seat by a landslide. However, there is a chance that Sue Bronner might win.

We strongly suggest you do the Self-Review exercises

Following is a self-review problem. There are a number of them interspersed throughout each chapter. They test your comprehension of the preceding material. The answer and method of solution are given at the end of the chapter. We recommend that you solve each one and then check your answer.

SELF-REVIEW 1–1

The answers are at the end of the chapter.

Chicago-based Market Facts asked a sample of 1,960 consumers to try a newly developed frozen fish dinner by Morton called Fish Delight. Out of the 1,960 sampled, 1,176 said they would purchase the dinner if it is marketed.

1. What would Market Facts report to Morton Foods regarding acceptance of Fish Delight in the population?
2. Is this an example of descriptive statistics or inferential statistics? Explain.

TYPES OF VARIABLES

Qualitative variable

There are two basic types of data: (1) those obtained from a qualitative population and (2) those obtained from a quantitative population. When the characteristic or variable being studied is nonnumeric, it is called a **qualitative variable** or an **attribute.** Examples of qualitative variables are gender, religious affiliation, type of automobile owned, state of birth, and eye color. When the data being studied are qualitative, we are usually interested in how many or what proportion fall in each category. For example, what percent of the population have blue eyes? How many Catholics and how many Protestants are there in the United States? What percent of the total number of cars sold last month were Buicks? Qualitative data are often summarized in charts and bar graphs (Chapter 2).

Quantitative variable

When the variable studied can be reported numerically, the variable is called a **quantitative variable,** and the population is called a quantitative population. Examples of quantitative variables are the balance in your checking account, the ages of company presidents, the life of a battery (such as 42 months), the speeds of automobiles traveling along Interstate 5 near Seattle, and the number of children in a family.

Discrete variable

Quantitative variables are either discrete or continuous. **Discrete variables** can assume only certain values, and there are usually "gaps" between the values. Examples of discrete variables are the number of bedrooms in a house (1, 2, 3, 4, etc.), the number of cars arriving at a tollbooth on I-75 at Berea, Kentucky, over an hour (16, 19, 30, etc.), and the number of students in each section of a statistics course (25 in section A, 42 in section B, and 18 in section C). Notice that a home can have 3 or 4 bedrooms, but it cannot have 3.56 bedrooms. Thus, there is a "gap" between possible values. Typically, discrete variables result from counting. We count, for example, the number of cars arriving at the Berea exit on I-75, and we count the number of statistics students in each section.

Continuous variable

Observations of a **continuous variable** can assume any value within a specific range. Examples of continuous variables are the air pressure in a tire and the weight of a shipment of grain (which, depending on the accuracy of the scales, could be 15.0 tons, 15.01 tons, 15.03 tons, etc.). The amount of raisin bran in a box and the time it took to fly from Orlando to San Diego are other variables of a continuous nature. The Orlando–San Diego flight could take 7 hours and 30 minutes; or 7 hours, 30 minutes, and 45 seconds; or 7 hours, 30 minutes, and 45.1 seconds, depending on the accuracy of the timing device. Typically, continuous variables result from measuring something.

The types of variables are summarized in the diagram.

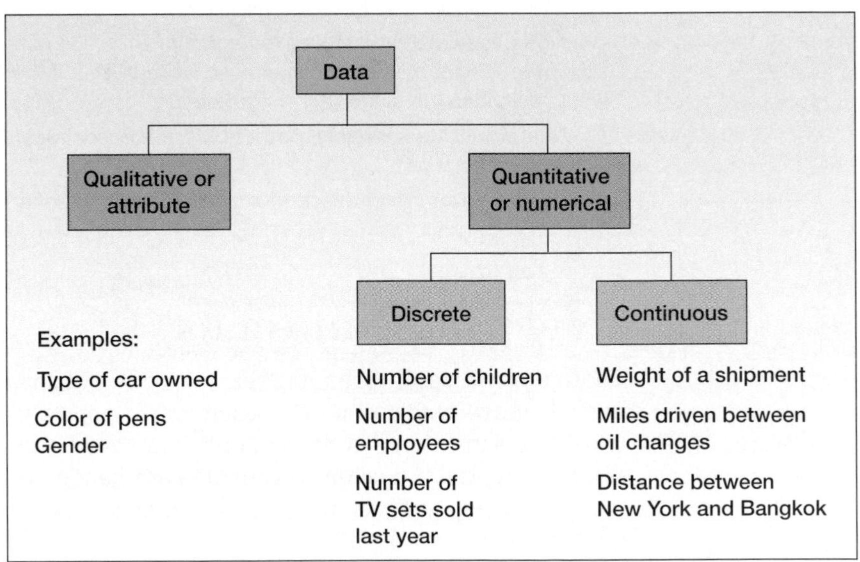

SOURCES OF STATISTICAL DATA

Researching problems involving such topics as crime, health, imports and exports, production, and hourly wages generally requires published data. We may want figures on the number of abortions last year (1,529,000), the assets of Citicorp

($213,701,000,000), the state with the largest number of inmates in prisons (California, with 109,409), and countries projected to have more than 2 million persons age 65 and over in the year 2020 (China, India, and the United States). These and thousands of other assorted statistics can be found in publications such as the *Statistical Abstract of the United States* and the *World Almanac and Book of Facts.*

What if we wanted to know the hourly wages of employees in manufacturing, mining, and retail trade since 1975? We would find these in the *Monthly Labor Review,* published monthly by the U.S. Department of Labor. These and other historical data are released regularly by the federal government, each state, and the United Nations.

In addition to regularly published data, prestigious publications such as *Fortune, Business Week,* and *The Wall Street Journal* contain a multitude of statistics with emphasis on business and economic topics. In addition to these publications, which come out on a regular basis, Gallup and other pollsters release studies on the popularity of political candidates. Alan Guttmacher's Institute, which studies reproductive issues, just released the preceding statistic on the number of abortions last year.

Published data are not always available on the particular subject of interest. Persons may be contacted in a shopping mall, at their homes, over the telephone, or by mail. The respondents' answers are usually tabulated either by hand or using a computer. You have probably seen and completed many questionnaires. Perhaps you will be presented with such a questionnaire at the end of this course. Here are the results from surveys in the recent literature.

Midsized manufacturers were surveyed by the Grant Thornton Survey of Manufacturers. One question asked was, "Do you plan to add full-time employees next year?" The choices were "Yes," "No," and "Undecided." Sixty-three percent of the manufacturers responding said yes. Another question from the same survey was, "Are you hiring extra part-time employees?" Forty-two percent indicated yes.

Working Mother just commissioned Gallup to study how satisfied working mothers are with their dual role. Gallup polled 1,000 working mothers nationwide. Some of the findings were:

1. Seven out of 10 women said they work to feel good about themselves, regardless of the job they do or the amount of money they make.
2. Eight out of 10 working mothers were "extremely satisfied" or "very satisfied" with the job they are doing as mothers.
3. Ninety percent said their children are happy.
4. Three quarters said they "like" or "love" their jobs.
5. Four percent said they hate their work.

The study concerning knowledge of the Bible was cited previously. While testing respondents on their biblical and religious knowledge, Gallup asked these questions:

1. What country ruled Jerusalem during the time of Jesus? (Thirty-five percent knew it was Rome.)
2. What is the Holy Trinity? (Forty percent knew the answer.)
3. Who delivered the sermon on the Mount? (Thirty-four percent knew it was Jesus.)

The sponsor of the questionnaire (Princeton Religion Research Center) learned that about one out of three respondents could answer questions similar to these.

Following are two examples of questionnaires. The first is a portion of a survey of consumer satisfaction with the service of Lexus automobiles. The second is a survey by the Hertz Corporation regarding customer satisfaction with car rentals.

16. Since you have owned your 1990 car, how satisfied have you been with the SERVICE you received on it? (Including all service received from a dealership and/or other service outlets.)

Very Satisfied	Somewhat Satisfied	Neither Satisfied Nor Dissatisfied	Somewhat Dissatisfied	Very Dissatisfied
☐	☐	☐	☐	☐

17. Overall, how satisfied have you been with your 1990 CAR?

Very Satisfied	Somewhat Satisfied	Neither Satisfied Nor Dissatisfied	Somewhat Dissatisfied	Very Dissatisfied
☐	☐	☐	☐	☐

---

19. Which of the following features were included with your 1990 car AT THE TIME YOU PURCHASED IT?

☐ Automatic transmission
 ☐ 3-speed ☐ 4-speed/overdrive
☐ Manual transmission
 ☐ 3-speed ☐ 4-speed ☐ 5-speed/overdrive
 ☐ 6-speed

☐ Air conditioning
☐ Power steering
☐ Anti-lock brake system (ABS)
☐ Power seats
☐ Power windows
☐ Power radio antenna
☐ Electric door locks
☐ Trailer towing package

☐ AM radio
☐ AM-FM radio
☐ AM-FM stereo
☐ AM-FM stereo with tape player and/or CD player
} **Check One Only**

☐ Clock
☐ Intermittent windshield wipers
☐ Speed/cruise control
☐ Optional gauges
☐ Tilt/adjustable steering wheel
☐ Automatic leveling control

☐ Rear window defogger
☐ Vinyl top
☐ Sun roof/T-top
☐ Rustproofing
☐ Protective paint coating
☐ Manufacturer's extended warranty service policy. (General Motors Protection Plan, Ford ESP, etc.)
☐ An independent extended warranty policy (American Warranty, General Warranty, etc.)

20. Have the brakes/brake lining pads been replaced? ☐ Yes ☐ No

How Do We Rate?

City where car was:

Rented ______________________

Date __________ Time __________

☐ Airport ☐ Downtown ☐ Other

City where car was:

Returned ______________________

Date __________ Time __________

☐ Airport ☐ Downtown ☐ Other

Rental record number? ______________

Did you make a reservation? ☐ Yes ☐ No

If yes; through a travel agent? ☐

Or direct with Hertz? ☐

Name and address (optional)

____
Name

____
Company

____
Street address

____
City

__________ __________
State Zip code

Day telephone: ( ) ______-______

Evening telephone: ( ) ______-______

Hertz rents Fords and other fine cars.

1. Type of service used this rental?

At rental:	At return:	Used Hertz courtesy bus:
☐ #1 Club Gold–Canopy	☐ Instant (at car)	☐ Yes
☐ #1 Club Gold–Counter	☐ Express (box)	☐ No
☐ Standard	☐ Self service	
	☐ Standard	

2. Speed of service this rental?

	Excellent	Good	Fair	Poor
At rental	☐	☐	☐	☐
At return	☐	☐	☐	☐
Courtesy bus pickup	☐	☐	☐	☐

3. Vehicle condition this rental?

	Excellent	Good	Fair	Poor
Cleanliness	☐	☐	☐	☐
Mechanical	☐	☐	☐	☐

4. Courtesy and friendliness of Hertz personnel this rental?

	Excellent	Good	Fair	Poor
At reservation	☐	☐	☐	☐
At rental	☐	☐	☐	☐
At return	☐	☐	☐	☐
On courtesy bus	☐	☐	☐	☐

5. Competence of Hertz personnel this rental?

	Excellent	Good	Fair	Poor
At reservation	☐	☐	☐	☐
At rental	☐	☐	☐	☐
At return	☐	☐	☐	☐
On courtesy bus	☐	☐	☐	☐

6. Overall experience?

	Excellent	Good	Fair	Poor
This rental	☐	☐	☐	☐
Prior rentals	☐	☐	☐	☐

7. Additional comments?

____

Thank you for your time.

LEVELS OF MEASUREMENT

"Level of measurement" will be mentioned frequently in the following chapters. The four general types, or levels, of measurement are nominal, ordinal, interval, and ratio.

Nominal Level

The information presented in Table 1–1 and Table 1–2 represents nominal measurement. This level is considered the most "primitive," the "lowest," or the most limited type of measurement.

TABLE 1–1 Religion Reported by the Population of the United States 14 Years Old and Older

Religion	Total
Protestant	78,952,000
Roman Catholic	30,669,000
Jewish	3,868,000
Other religion	1,545,000
No religion	3,195,000
Religion not reported	1,104,000
Total	119,333,000

Source: U.S. Department of Commerce, Bureau of the Census, *Current Population Reports,* series P-20, no. 79.

TABLE 1–2 Top Seven New Passenger Car Sales in Canada, by Company

Company	Annual sales (number of units)
General Motors	379,159
Ford	193,000
Chrysler	156,078
Honda	72,976
Toyota	68,753
Hyundai	50,648
Volkswagen	41,470
All others	187,648

Source: Member companies of the Motor Vehicle Manufacturers Association and the Automobile Importers of Canada.

Nominal level: Data can only be classified into categories

The terms **nominal level of measurement** and **nominal-scaled** are commonly used to refer to data that can *only be classified into categories.* In the strict sense of the words, however, there are no measurements and no scales involved. Instead, there are just counts.

The arrangement of the religions in Table 1–1 could have been changed. Roman Catholic could have been listed first, Jewish second, and so on. This essentially indicates that for the nominal level of measurement, *there is no particular order for the groupings.* Further, the categories are considered to be **mutually exclusive,** meaning, for example, that a person could not be a Protestant and have no religion at the same time. In the case of Table 1–2, a car could not be a Ford and a Hyundai at the same time.

Mutually exclusive

Mutually exclusive An individual, object, or measurement is included in only one category.

It should be noted that the categories in Table 1–1 and Table 1–2 are **exhaustive,** meaning that every member of the population, or sample, must appear in one of the categories. If a person refused to give her religion, she would be included in the category "religion not reported." If she embraced Buddhism, her religion would be included in the category "other religion." In Table 1–2, a Mercedes-Benz would fall in the category "all others."

Exhaustive

Exhaustive Each individual, object, or measurement must appear in one category.

Don't try to add 1 + 2

In order to process data on religious preference, sex, employment by industry, and so forth, the categories are often coded 1, 2, 3, . . . with, say, 1 representing Protestant, 2 representing Roman Catholic, and so on. This facilitates counting when a computer or other counting device is used. It is not permissible, however, to manipulate these numbers algebraically. For example, 1 + 2 does not equal 3; that is, a Protestant plus a Roman Catholic does not equal a person of the Jewish religion. Likewise, if a General Motors car was coded 1, a Ford 2, and so on, a GM plus a Ford does not equal a Chrysler.

Tests applied to nominal-scaled data do not make any assumptions regarding the underlying distribution of the population from which the sample was selected. Thus, these tests are called *distribution-free* or *nonparametric* tests. Some of these tests will be discussed starting with Chapter 14.

Ordinal Level

Ordinal level means ranking

Table 1–3, which lists the ratings of the company commander by the nurses under her command, is an illustration of the **ordinal level of measurement.** One category is higher than the next one; that is, "superior" is a higher rating than "good," "good" is higher than "average," and so on.

If 1 is substituted for "superior," 2 substituted for "good," and so on, a 1 ranking is obviously higher than a 2 ranking, and a 2 ranking is higher than a 3 ranking. However, it cannot be said that (as an example) a company commander rated good is twice as competent as one rated average, or that a company commander rated superior is twice as competent as one rated good. It can only be said that a rating of superior is greater than a rating of good, and a good rating is greater than an average rating.

TABLE 1–3 **Ratings of the Company Commander**

Rating	Number of nurses
Superior	6
Good	28
Average	25
Poor	17
Inferior	0

In review, the major difference between a nominal level and an ordinal level of measurement is the "greater than" relationship between the ordinal-level categories. Otherwise, the ordinal scale of measurement has the same characteristics as the nominal scale, namely, the categories are mutually exclusive and exhaustive.

Interval Level

The **interval scale of measurement** is the next higher level. It includes all the characteristics of the ordinal scale, but in addition, the distance between values is a constant size. Temperature on the Fahrenheit scale is an example. Suppose the high temperatures for three consecutive days in January in North Platte, Nebraska, are 28, 31, and 20. These temperatures can easily be ranked, but we can also determine the differences between the temperatures. This is possible because 1 degree Fahrenheit represents a constant unit of measurement. It is important to note that the zero point is arbitrary—just another point on the Fahrenheit scale. Zero degrees Fahrenheit does not represent the absence of heat, just that it is cold! Suppose that the August temperature of 96 degrees is to be compared with the three North Platte January temperatures of about 30 degrees. We can say that it is more than 60 degrees warmer on an August day than on a day in January, but we cannot say that it is three times as hot. Scores on an SAT examination and scores on a history or a math examination are also examples of the interval scale of measurement.

The interval scale of measurement has mutually exclusive and exhaustive properties. An August high temperature, for example, cannot be both 88 and 76. Hence, the mutually exclusive feature is met. We can list the high temperatures for all days in August. Thus, the exhaustive feature is met.

Ratio Level

Ratio level is the "highest" level of measurement. This level has all the characteristics of interval level: the distances between numbers are of a known, constant size; the categories are mutually exclusive; and so on. The major differences between interval and ratio levels of measurement are these: (1) Ratio-level data has a *meaningful* zero point, and (2) the ratio between two numbers is meaningful. Money is a good illustration. Having zero dollars has meaning—you have none! Weight is another ratio-level measurement. If the dial on a scale is zero, there is a complete absence of weight. Also, if you earn $40,000 a year and Keith earns $10,000, you earn four times what he does. Likewise, if you weigh 240 pounds and Pat weighs 80 pounds, you weigh three times what she does. We can say that you earn $30,000 a year more than Keith does and weigh 160 pounds more than Pat does. Other examples of the ratio level of measurement are the number of years doctors spend in medical practice and the number of Hondas sold last month by the salespeople at Westgate Honda.

SELF-REVIEW 1–2

The answers are at the end of the chapter.

1. *Canadian Statistics* reported these populations:

Province or territory	Number of people
Newfoundland	567,681
Nova Scotia	847,442
New Brunswick	691,403
Northwest Territories	45,741
Yukon	23,153

   What level of measurement is reflected by these data? Why?

2. Test scores on a special examination given to Army enlisted personnel interested in attending Officer Candidate School are:

Scores	Number of applicants
90–99	42
80–89	19
70–79	7
60–69	4
Below 60	3

   What level of measurement do these data represent? Explain.

SOME LEARNING AIDS

Valuable learning aids

As you progress through each chapter, you will notice a number of learning aids designed to help you determine immediately whether or not you have grasped the preceding subject matter. Among these are:

- **Self-review problems** scattered throughout every chapter. We suggest that you solve each of these review problems and check your answers against those provided at the end of the chapter.
- **Exercises** interspersed throughout each chapter. The answers and methods of solution to the odd-numbered exercises are at the end of the book.
- The **chapter outline.** It summarizes the key points of the chapter, gives definitions of the key terms, and repeats most of the formulas.

- A section entitled **Computer Data Exercises** at the end of most chapters and each major review section. It contains more challenging problems and larger data sets. A computer is essential to solve them.
- An **examination** at the end of each chapter. Included are objective-type questions and problems covering the entire chapter. This test allows you to pull together the main ideas presented in the chapter. The answers are at the end of the chapter.
- A **review section** after a group of chapters consisting of the highlights of the preceding chapters, a glossary, a comprehensive group of exercises, and the Century Bank case.

A word of encouragement

Such symbols as χ^2, Σ, σ, and ρ are used in this text. So are formulas such as:

$$\overline{X} = \frac{\Sigma X}{n} \quad \text{and} \quad \chi^2 = \Sigma\frac{(f_o - f_e)^2}{f_e}$$

They should not intimidate or discourage you! These symbols and formulas are merely a way of condensing the subject matter.

COMPUTER APPLICATIONS

Computers are now available for student use at most colleges and universities, as are such software systems as MINITAB, SAS, Computerized Business Statistics (CBS), and the Statistical Package for the Social Sciences (SPSS). We chose MINITAB for most of the statistical applications in this text. It is user-friendly, meaning that it is easy to operate and does not require learning a special programming language. To help you, we've given the MINITAB commands at the top of each computer output.

To illustrate the use of a computer and the applications of MINITAB (a statistical software package), starting in Chapter 2 we examine the annual salary of full professors at four-year universities. The following MINITAB output in $000, used in Chapters 2, 3, and 4, reveals among other things that: (1) 160 universities were included in the study, (2) the mean (average) salary was $54,030, and (3) the annual salaries ranged from a low of $26,000 to a high of $96,500 (Harvard). The various headings will be explained later, starting with Chapter 2.

```
MTB > Describe 'Salary'.

                 N      MEAN     MEDIAN     TRMEAN     STDEV    SEMEAN
Salary         160     54.03      52.55      53.55     13.76      1.09

               MIN       MAX         Q1         Q3
Salary       26.00     96.50      44.65      61.80
```

Had we used a calculator to arrive at these measures and others needed to fully analyze the salary amounts, many hours of calculations would be required. The likelihood of an error in arithmetic is very high when a large number of values are considered. MINITAB can provide us with the needed information in just seconds.

At the option of your instructor, and depending on the operating system and equipment available, we urge you to apply a statistical computer package to the exercises having large data sets. It will relieve you of tedious manipulations and allow you to concentrate on data analysis.

CHAPTER OUTLINE

I. Definition of statistics.
   A. *Statistics* may be thought of as a collection of numerical data.
   B. As used in a broader sense, statistics refers to the statistical tools used to collect, present, analyze, and interpret data for the purpose of making more effective decisions.

II. Statistics is divided into two categories.
   A. *Descriptive statistics* deals with presenting data in a graph or a frequency distribution and applying various measures of central tendancy and dispersion.
   B. *Inferential statistics* deals with taking a sample from a population and making estimates about a characteristic of that population based on the sample results.

III. Types of variables.
   A. *Qualitative variables* are nonnumeric, such as make of motorcycle (Harley-Davidson, Yamaha).
   B. *Quantitative variables* can be measured, such as weight (110 pounds, 304 pounds) or annual sales ($10.1 million, $7.6 million).

IV. Sources of data: Making a decision to merge with another company, to relocate, to introduce a new product, and so on often requires published data or taking a survey.

V. Levels of measurement.
   A. *Nominal level of measurement* refers to data that can only be counted and put into categories. There is no particular order to the categories.
   B. *Ordinal level of measurement* presumes that one category is higher than another. Freshman, sophomore, junior, and senior illustrates this kind of ranking.
   C. *Interval level of measurement* includes the ranking characteristics of the ordinal measurement and specifies that the distance between numbers is the same.
   D. *Ratio level of measurement* has all the characteristics of the interval level of measurement. In addition, the zero point is meaningful, and the ratio between two numbers is meaningful.

EXERCISES

The answers to the odd-numbered exercises are at the end of the book.

1. One definition of statistics is that they are a collection of facts and figures. In business and other fields, statistics is thought of as a science. Discuss the difference between the two concepts.
2. Distinguish between *descriptive statistics* and *inferential statistics.*
3. An actual study of 200 executives revealed that 60 of them had some degree of hypertension due in part to their jobs. What could be inferred about all executives? Why?
4. Numerous complaints have been received by the management of the food-processing plant where you work part-time. It is claimed that there is an excessive amount of liquid in some cans of cherries. The plant has no systematic quality assurance program. If you

were named the quality assurance manager, what steps would you take to check production?

5. You have just been appointed the chief marketing executive for Fun Enterprise, a company that specializes in designing and erecting amusement parks near large cities. F.E. is primarily interested in a location in the Southeast. Once the site has been selected, you must recommend whether the park should be oriented toward persons of all ages, just children, or just retired persons. How would you proceed with making recommendations regarding (1) the location of the park and (2) the group orientation (all ages, young, old)?

6. The average annual salaries for full professors at selected universities and colleges in California and Arkansas are (in $ thousands):

California

University	Average salary
Azusa Pacific University	$43.7
California Institute of Technology	93.3
California Maritime Academy	52.0
California Lutheran University	47.3
Cal. State University–Long Beach	60.2

Source: The Annual Report on the Economic Status of the Profession 1992–1993, *Academie,* pages 34–35.

Arkansas

University	Average salary
Arkansas College	$47.7
Arkansas State University–Main Campus	50.2
Hendrix College	46.2
University of Arkansas–Fayetteville	54.7
University of the Ozarks	30.5

a. Are these two listings samples or populations? Explain.
b. Are the categories considered to be mutually exclusive? Explain.
c. What approximate salary would you choose to be a typical salary for these two states? Explain.

7. You are studying the price movements of a selected group of stocks listed on the New York Stock Exchange. Referring to the Sarasota *Herald-Tribune,* you found:

Movement of Stock	Number
Increased	69
Decreased	32
Stayed the same	11

a. Are the 112 stocks considered a sample or a population? Explain.
b. What is the level of measurement? Explain.
c. Are the categories mutually exclusive? Explain.
d. In your study IBM increased 2¼. What is that one figure called?

8. Prior to the 1992 Democratic National Convention Gordon S. Black Corp. made a telephone poll of 906 adults nationwide regarding these Democrats as presidential candidates. Totals do not sum to 100 due to rounding.

A LOOK AT POLITICIANS AND THE PRESIDENCY

Opinions of These Democrats as Presidential Candidates

	Favorable	Not favorable	Undecided	Not enough information
Mario Cuomo	26%	23%	16%	35%
Jerry Brown	17	28	13	42
Tom Harkin	9	8	8	75
Bob Kerrey	10	7	10	73
Paul Tsongas	9	8	9	73
Douglas Wilder	11	10	11	68
Bill Clinton	9	6	9	76

Data collected by Gordon S. Black Corp. Telephone poll of 906 adults nationwide on December 9–10. Margin of error: 3.5%.

Source: *USA Today,* December 12, 1991, p. 4A.

a. Is this a sample or a population?
b. What level of measurement are the candidate opinions? Explain.
c. Write an analysis of the results of the poll.

9. A survey of U.S. households regarding satisfaction in the American economy revealed the following data portrayed graphically. Note that 1989 = 100. The 100 represents an "average" satisfaction of Americans during a given year. A figure such as 75.0 would indicate that consumer satisfaction in the economy for that year is 25 percent below normal.

   Write an analysis of consumer satisfaction in the economy for the years 1984 to 1995.

CONSUMER SATISFACTION

From a Survey of U.S. Households, 1989 = 100

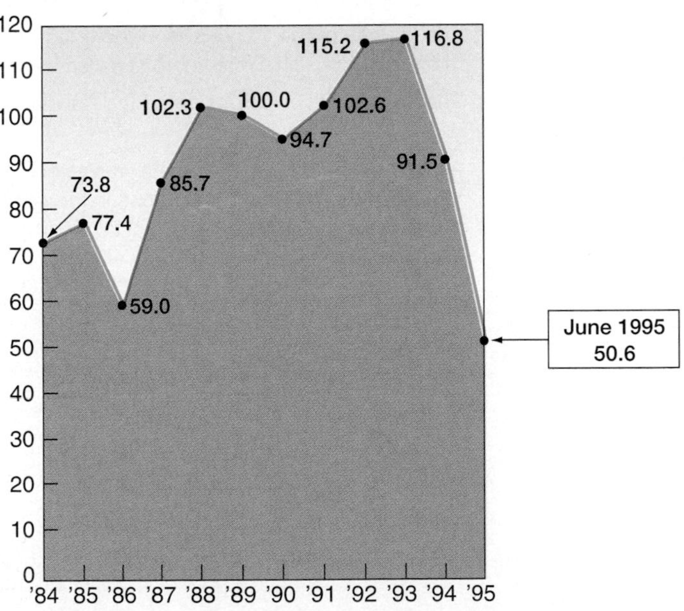

10. Although this chapter did not cover published data and questionnaire construction in depth, select a problem in the area of business, state the problem in specific terms, and suggest the data needed to solve the problem. A library search might be necessary to locate potential sources of pertinent statistics. As a suggestion, the problem might involve moving the headquarters of a national firm from one state to another. What data would you want to consider? Some examples might be the rate of unemployment, the tax rates, and labor costs.

CHAPTER 1 EXAMINATION

The answers are at the end of the chapter.

Indicate whether each of the following 10 statements is true or false. If false, give the correct answer.

1. Another name for inferential statistics is descriptive statistics.
2. A sample of consumers tasted a new cheese chip and rated it either excellent, very good, fair, or poor. The level of measurement for this market research problem is ordinal.
3. The Pipe Fitters and Plumbers Union consists of 5,020 members. A representative group of 248 members was selected and asked questions. The 248 is considered the population.
4. A total of 9,386 unmarried women under 15 had a baby last year, there were 6,950 accidental deaths in January, and the record Atlantic halibut weighed 250 pounds. This collection of facts and figures is called statistics.
5. The method used to find out something about the cutthroat trout population in Yellowstone National Park based on a sample of 40 trout is called inferential statistics.
6. Gallup and other pollsters seldom employ sampling methods because the populations they work with are so large.
7. The chamber of commerce asked a sample of persons sunbathing on Siesta Beach, Sarasota, Florida, if they lived in Sarasota or within 30 miles of the beach, lived out of state, or lived in a foreign country. This research project involved nominal-level data.
8. The Bureau of the Census reported that there are 12,955,000 production workers in manufacturing. This one figure is called a statistic.
9. The nominal level is considered the "lowest" level of data, and the data must be mutually exclusive.
10. A sample of 3,014 steelworkers was selected to find out if they will go on strike on Monday. Over 50 percent of those in the sample said they would go out on strike. Since the number sampled is large and those advocating a strike constitute over 50 percent, we can assume that the majority of all the steelworkers favor a strike.

CHAPTER 1 Answers

Self-Review

1–1

1. Based on the sample of 1,960 consumers, we estimate that, if it is marketed, 60 percent of all consumers will purchase Fish Delight $(1{,}176/1{,}960) \times 100 = 60$ percent.
2. Inferential statistics, because a sample was used to make an inference about how all consumers in the population would react if Fish Delight were marketed.

1–2

1. Nominal level. There is no particular order to the provinces and territories. Yukon, for example, could have been listed first. And the categories are mutually exclusive, meaning that a person could not be a resident of the Yukon and Nova Scotia at the same time.
2. The scores can be ranked, but in addition, we can determine the differences between the scores. These differences are of a known, constant size. The score of 95 is 10 points higher than a score of 85, a score of 85 is 10 points higher than a score of 75, and so on. Hence, the level of measurement is interval.

Examination

1. False. Inductive or inferential statistics.
2. True.
3. False. A sample.
4. True.
5. True.
6. False. Most of their polls and surveys involve a sample selected from the population of interest.
7. True.
8. True.
9. True.
10. False. There is always a chance that the sample results will not accurately reflect the characteristics of the population.

Chapter 2

Summarizing Data: Frequency Distributions and Graphic Presentation

GOALS

When you have completed this chapter, you will be able to:

1
Organize raw data into a frequency distribution.

2
Portray the frequency distribution in a histogram, a frequency polygon, and cumulative frequency polygons.

3
Develop a stem-and-leaf display.

4
Present data using such common graphic techniques as line charts, bar charts, and pie charts.

Given a list of select companies and their number of shareholders, how would you graphically portray their distribution? (See Goal 2 and Exercise 27.)

INTRODUCTION

Dr. Beth McPherson, president of Duval University, recently received an inquiry from the local teachers union regarding the pay scale of the teaching staff at Duval. The union claims that the annual salaries of professors at Duval are significantly lower than those paid at other colleges. How should she explore this accusation? What information should she collect? How should she report her findings?

One approach to the problem is to collect salary data from some other schools, organize it in some meaningful way, and then summarize it. Recall from Chapter 1 that this facet of statistics is referred to as **descriptive statistics.**

CONSTRUCTION OF A FREQUENCY DISTRIBUTION

What is the first step?

Logically, the president's first step is to collect salary data from other colleges. Fortunately, the Association of University Professors publishes this information annually in *Academe* for all two-year and four-year universities. Instead of including all schools in her study, she selected 160 four-year colleges and recorded the average annual salaries for professors, associate professors, assistant professors, and instructors. These unorganized observations are referred to as **raw data.** This step and others to follow are shown schematically in the following diagram.

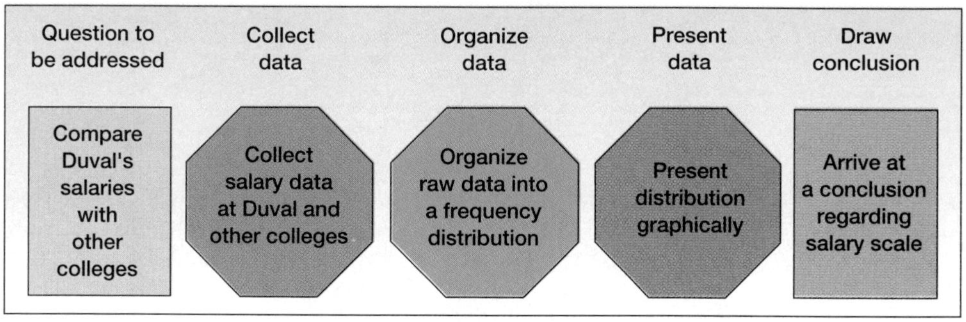

EXAMPLE

Dr. McPherson collected sample information from 160 colleges and universities. These raw data are shown in Table 2–1. Data in this form are *ungrouped data.* Once we organize the data into a frequency distribution, which we will do shortly, we will have *grouped data.*

Summarize the data so that her study of the salaries at other universities can be forwarded to the union. Give the lowest and the highest salaries, determine how much a typical professor earns, and so on.

Solution ► A perusal of the average annual salaries at the 160 colleges does not give much insight into the salary structure of professors. About all we can do is locate the highest average salary ($96,500, at Harvard) and the lowest average salary ($26,000). What is needed is a grouping of the incomes so that we can see not only low and high incomes but other characteristics of the data, such as where the incomes are

TABLE 2–1 Average Annual Incomes of Professors at 160 Universities (in $ thousands)

59.6	50.2	43.8	30.5	93.3	60.5	59.7	61.1	35.8	79.2
74.8	65.3	62.0	67.0	75.9	91.2	70.1	52.2	77.9	46.1
63.2	57.9	43.1	39.1	44.8	45.2	59.2	54.7	48.0	39.6
61.8	44.8	49.8	73.4	28.1	47.1	55.3	44.2	28.0	37.0
56.1	55.5	40.2	44.6	37.8	41.9	77.9	46.4	63.4	41.3
50.0	61.2	65.0	36.8	64.8	49.5	64.5	49.2	57.8	32.3
53.3	43.9	30.6	75.8	60.0	48.5	66.4	60.8	72.8	90.2
49.2	41.4	53.8	49.2	37.1	63.3	60.7	72.2	43.9	37.9
43.6	35.5	82.6	50.8	52.1	65.7	49.9	61.7	59.1	40.7
41.2	34.3	43.3	53.2	54.0	50.7	45.6	50.2	29.7	61.5
57.7	44.4	47.4	56.9	70.2	84.2	57.2	50.6	76.8	57.1
53.1	66.3	26.0	52.8	96.5	72.6	62.3	50.5	69.2	37.5
51.2	73.1	52.0	53.9	52.1	39.7	52.7	60.2	45.3	62.2
50.1	56.7	40.2	50.0	45.4	34.7	63.5	76.4	48.7	57.5
70.1	64.0	37.0	47.6	52.4	45.8	55.1	47.2	33.0	39.1
44.8	45.2	61.5	58.4	45.1	56.1	54.7	39.6	61.8	58.3
		Low		High					

Source: *Academe,* Special Salary Issue; "The Annual Report on the Economic Status of the Profession, 1992–1993," pp. 34–81.

clustered. When the incomes are tabulated in this way, we refer to it as a **frequency distribution.** (It is sometimes referred to as a frequency table.)

> **Frequency distribution** A grouping of the data into categories showing the number of observations in each of the nonoverlapping classes.

The steps in constructing a frequency distribution are as follows.

What is a class?

Step 1. The first step in designing a frequency distribution is to set up groupings called classes. In this problem the first class might contain all the average annual salaries of professors from $20,000 up to $30,000, the next class would be $30,000 up to $40,000, and so on.

$20,000 up to $30,000 ← a class

$30,000 up to $40,000 ← a class

Lower and upper class limits

Each class (category) has two limits, a lower limit and an upper limit. The usual practice is to let the lowest class limit be a number slightly below the lowest observation ($26,000). We could have let the lowest class limit be $25,000 rather than $20,000. The classes must be **mutually exclusive,** meaning in this example that a particular salary, such as $43,200, can occur in only one class ($40,000 up to $50,000).

Tally the data into classes

Step 2. After setting up the classes, we *tally the incomes into their appropriate classes.* A tally mark (/) represents an income. The average annual income of professors at Southwestern North Dakota University ($59,600), which is in the upper left- hand corner of Table 2–1, is tallied in the "$50,000 up to $60,000" class. The next number in that column ($74,800) is tallied in the "$70,000 up to $80,000" class, and so forth. When all the salaries are tallied, the table would appear as:

Class	Tallies
$20,000 up to $ 30,000	////
30,000 up to 40,000	//// //// //// ////
40,000 up to 50,000	//// //// //// //// //// //// //// //// /
50,000 up to 60,000	//// //// //// //// //// //// //// //// ////
60,000 up to 70,000	//// //// //// //// //// ////
70,000 up to 80,000	//// //// //// /
80,000 up to 90,000	//
90,000 up to 100,000	////

Class frequency: number of observations in a class

Step 3. Next we count the number of tallies in each class. The number of observations in a class is called the **class frequency.** In the "$20,000 up to $30,000" class there are 4 observations, and there are 20 observations in the "$30,000 up to $40,000" class. Therefore, the class frequency for the $20,000 up to $30,000 class is 4, and the class frequency for the $30,000 up to $40,000 class is 20. The president of Duval sampled 160 schools, which is the total number of class frequencies. (See Table 2–2.)

TABLE 2–2 **Frequency Distribution: Average Annual Incomes of College Professors**

Income ($ thousands)	Frequency
$20 up to $ 30	4
30 up to 40	20
40 up to 50	41
50 up to 60	44
60 up to 70	29
70 up to 80	16
80 up to 90	2
90 up to 100	4
Total	160

Now that we have organized the data into a frequency distribution, we can begin to summarize the pattern of the annual incomes of college professors in four-year universities. In Table 2–2 note that the lowest average annual income at a school is about $20,000 and the highest about $100,000. Furthermore, the highest concentration of incomes is in the $50,000–$60,000 interval. Over half of the colleges (85 out of the 160 schools selected) have average annual salaries between $40,000 and $60,000. If we wanted just one income to represent the income of a full professor in a four-year school, it would be $55,000, which is the midpoint of the "$50,000 up to $60,000" class.

Again we want to call your attention to the self-review problems. They appear in each chapter following the discussion of a major topic. By solving each one of them, you can immediately test your comprehension of the preceding text material. The answers are given at the end of the chapter.

Important: Do each self-review

SELF-REVIEW 2–1

The answers are at the end of the chapter.

Employees assembling a sample of fishing reels are paid 20 cents for each reel assembled. The numbers produced last week by 14 assemblers were 1,540, 1,611, 1,421, 1,780, 1,799, 1,462, 1,500, 1,559, 1,698, 1,674, 1,701, 1,500, 1,650, and 1,599, respectively.

1. What are the numbers 1,540, 1,611, and so on called?
2. Using 1,400 up to 1,500 as the first class, 1,500 up to 1,600 as the second class, and so forth, organize the weekly productions into a frequency distribution.
3. What are the numbers in the right column of your frequency distribution called?
4. Describe the distribution of weekly production.

CLASS INTERVALS AND MIDPOINTS

Midpoint—halfway between the lower and upper class limits

We will use two other concepts quite frequently. One is the **midpoint,** and the other is the **class interval.** The midpoint, also called a **class mark,** is determined by going halfway between the lower class limit and the upper class limit. It can be computed by adding the lower and upper limits of a class and dividing the total by 2. Referring to Table 2–2, we find the midpoint of the "$20,000 up to $30,000" class by adding $20,000 and $30,000 and dividing the total ($50,000) by 2 to give $25,000. The midpoint $25,000 best represents, or is typical of, the average annual salaries in that class.

How is the class interval determined?

The class interval for a frequency distribution having classes of the same size can be determined by subtracting the lower limit of a class from the lower limit of the next higher class. For example, using the distribution of the salaries of professors:

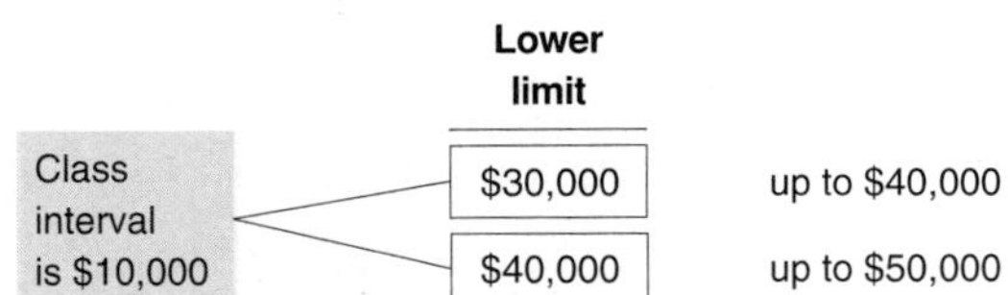

Assuming that the classes in a distribution are the same size, the class interval may also be determined by finding the distance between any two successive midpoints. For this example, $45,000 − $35,000 gives a class interval of $10,000.

SUGGESTIONS ON CONSTRUCTING A FREQUENCY DISTRIBUTION

Try to have equal class intervals

1. *Use equal-size class intervals.* Whenever possible, the class intervals used in a frequency distribution should be equal. Unequal class intervals present problems when the distribution is portrayed graphically. Unequal class intervals, however, may be necessary in certain situations in order to avoid a large number of empty, or almost empty, classes. Such is the case in the following example. The Internal Revenue Service used unequal-size class intervals to give the distribution of adjusted gross incomes of individuals. (See Table 2–3). Had the IRS used an equal-size class inter-

val of $1,000, more than 1,000 classes would have been required to encompass all the incomes! It would, of course, be almost impossible to analyze this large a frequency distribution.

TABLE 2–3 Adjusted Gross Income for Individuals Filing Income Tax Returns

Adjusted gross income	Number of returns (in thousands)
Under $ 2,000	135
$ 2,000 up to 3,000	3,399
3,000 up to 5,000	8,175
5,000 up to 10,000	19,740
10,000 up to 15,000	15,539
15,000 up to 25,000	14,944
25,000 up to 50,000	4,451
50,000 up to 100,000	699
100,000 up to 500,000	162
500,000 up to 1,000,000	3
$1,000,000 and over	1

2. *Find the suggested class interval.* Suppose you have a mass of raw data to organize into a frequency distribution and you want to use the same interval for each class. What class interval should you use? The following formula gives a suggested common class interval. (Note the number (2–1) to the right of the formula. We will refer to these formula numbers in future discussions.)

Determining class interval

$$\text{Suggested class interval} = \frac{\text{Highest value} - \text{Lowest value}}{\text{Number of classes}} \qquad (2\text{–}1)$$

Note from the data in Table 2–1 that the highest average annual salary of professors at four-year schools is $96,500 and the lowest is $26,000. Suppose we want to condense the raw data into eight classes. What is the suggested class interval?

$$\text{Suggested class interval} = \frac{\$96{,}500 - \$26{,}000}{8} = \$8{,}813$$

A class interval of $8,813 would be very awkward to work with. It would be much easier to tally the annual incomes into a frequency distribution if the interval were rounded to, say, $9,000 or $10,000. We used $10,000 in Table 2–2.

If you are uncertain about the size of the class interval to use, the following formula will help.

$$\text{Suggested class interval} = \frac{\text{Highest observed value} - \text{Lowest observed value}}{1 + 3.322(\text{logarithm of total frequencies})} \qquad (2\text{–}2)$$

To find the logarithm of 160 on your calculator, depress 160 and then `log`. The logarithm of 160 is 2.204119983. (Some calculators do not have the log feature. In that case a table of logarithms can be used.)

Inserting the values for the Duval University problem into formula (2–2):

$$\text{Suggested class interval} = \frac{\$96{,}500 - \$26{,}000}{1 + 3.322(2.204119983)}$$

$$= \frac{\$70{,}500}{8.3220863} = \$8{,}471$$

Again, we rounded \$8,471 to \$10,000 to facilitate the calculations.

3. *Choose an appropriate number of classes.* Normally, your personal judgment can influence the selection of the number of classes. Too many or too few classes, however, might not reveal the basic shape of the distribution. In the problem concerning the annual salaries of professors, for example, a class interval of \$40,000 (instead of the \$10,000 we used) would not give much insight into the pattern of salaries. Notice in Table 2–4 that with a class interval of \$40,000, about all we could say is that two thirds of the colleges pay professors less than \$60,000 and one third pay more than \$60,000. As a general rule, no fewer than 5 or more than 15 classes should be used in the construction of a frequency distribution.

TABLE 2–4 **An Example of Too Few Classes**

Too few classes

Annual income	Number of colleges
\$20,000 up to \$ 60,000	109
60,000 up to 100,000	51
Total	160

Guideline for determining the number of classes

One guideline to determine the number of classes is to use the smallest integer k such that $2^k \geq n$, where n is the total number of observations. Using the 160 annual salaries of professors at four-year universities, let us try the integer 7. Thus, $2^7 = 128$, which is not equal to or greater than 160. With eight classes, $2^8 = 256$, which is equal to or greater than 160. So the recommended number of classes is at least eight, which is the number we used in Table 2–2. Based on this guideline, the following table gives the number of classes recommended for a specified number of observations.

Total number of observations	Recommended number of classes
9–16	4
17–32	5
33–64	6
65–128	7
129–256	8
257–512	9
513–1,024	10

Usually, the lower limit of the first class is an even multiple of the class interval. Suppose, for example, a class interval was selected to be \$200. Multiplying this by 3.0 (an even multiple) gives \$600 as the lower limit of the first class. As another example, suppose that some price data range from \$23 (low) to \$69 (high), and we compute a class interval to be $10. The lower limit of the first class would be $20, found by multiplying 2.0 (the even multiple) by $10, the class interval.

Avoid overlapping class limits

Avoid overlapping class limits, such as $1,300–$1,400, $1,400–$1,500, and $1,500–$1,600. Classes established in this way are not mutually exclusive, violating the definition of a frequency distribution. With overlapping classes it would not be clear where to tally $1,400, for example. Does it belong in the $1,300–$1,400 class or the $1,400–$1,500 class? Stating the classes as $1,300–$1,399, $1,400–$1,499, and $1,500–$1,599 avoids this problem; or we could state a class as "$1,300 up to but not including $1,400" or just "$1,300 up to $1,400."

Avoid open-ended classes

Try not to include *open-ended* classes. The classes "Under $2,000" and "$1,000,000 and over" used by the IRS in Table 2–3 are examples of open-ended classes. They cause problems in graphing, described in the next section, and in using certain measures of central tendency and dispersion, covered in Chapters 3 and 4.

RELATIVE FREQUENCY DISTRIBUTION

A relative frequency is a percent

It may be desirable to convert class frequencies to **relative class frequencies** to show the percent of the total number of observations in each class. In our salary analysis, for example, we may want to know what percent of the universities are in the "$20,000 up to $30,000" class. In another study we may want to know what percent of our employees are absent from work between one and three days a year due to illness.

To convert the class frequencies in a frequency distribution to **relative frequencies,** each of the class frequencies is divided by the total number of frequencies. Using the distribution of the annual salaries of professors from Table 2–2, the relative frequency for the "$20,000 up to $30,000" class is computed as 4 ÷ 160 = 0.025. That is, 2.5 percent of the colleges pay full professors between $20,000 and $30,000 per year on the average. Similarly, 12.5 percent of the schools have annual salaries between $30,000 and $40,000, found by 20 ÷ 160. See Table 2–5.

TABLE 2–5 **Annual Salaries of Professors, Class Frequencies, and Relative Frequencies**

Average annual salary ($ thousands)	Class frequency	Relative frequency	Found by
$20 up to $ 30	4	0.025 ←	4 ÷ 160
30 up to 40	20	0.125 ←	20 ÷ 160
40 up to 50	41	0.256	41 ÷ 160
50 up to 60	44	0.275	44 ÷ 160
60 up to 70	29	0.181	29 ÷ 160
70 up to 80	16	0.100	16 ÷ 160
80 up to 90	2	0.013	2 ÷ 160
90 up to 100	4	0.025	4 ÷ 160
Total	160	1.000*	

*The relative frequencies must total 1.000.

SELF-REVIEW 2–2

The answers are at the end of the chapter.

1. The monthly salaries of a sample of the 87 employees of Acklin Stamping were rounded to the nearest dollar. They ranged from a low of $2,041 to a high of $3,548.

a. Suppose we want to condense the data into seven classes. Using the same interval for each class, determine a suggested class interval.

b. What class interval would be easier to work with?

c. What is the lower class limit for the first class? The next class?

2. Suppose classes are written as:

40–60
60–90
90–150
150 and greater

These classes illustrate two practices that should be avoided. What are they?

EXERCISES

The answers to the odd-numbered exercises are at the end of the book.

1. What is meant by the raw data?
2. What is meant by a frequency distribution?
3. In a frequency distribution the classes must be mutually exclusive. Explain.
4. A set of raw data contains 53 observations. The lowest value is $42, the highest $142. The data have to be organized into a frequency distribution. Starting with 40, how many classes would you suggest?
5. The director of the honors program at Western University has 16 applications for admission next fall. The composite ACT scores of the applicants are:

27	27	27	28	27	25	25	28
26	28	26	28	31	30	26	26

The ACT scores are to be organized into a frequency distribution.

a. How many classes would you recommend?
b. What class interval would you suggest?
c. What lower limit would you recommend for the first class?
d. Organize the scores into a frequency distribution and determine the relative frequency distribution.
e. Comment on the shape of the distribution.

6. The Quick Change Oil Company has a number of outlets in the metropolitan area. No appointment is required. The numbers of oil changes at the Oak Street outlet in the past 20 days are:

65	98	55	62	79	59	51	90	72	56
70	62	66	80	94	79	63	73	71	85

The data are to be organized into a frequency distribution.

a. How many classes would you recommend?

b. What class interval would you suggest?
c. What lower limit would you recommend for the first class?
d. Organize the number of oil changes into a frequency distribution.
e. Comment on the shape of the frequency distribution. Also determine the relative frequency distribution.

7. The local manager of Food Queen is interested in the number of times a customer shops at her store during a two-week period. The responses of 51 customers were:

5	3	3	1	4	4	5	6	4	2	6	6	6	7	1
1	14	1	2	4	4	4	5	6	3	5	3	4	5	6
8	4	7	6	5	9	11	3	12	4	7	6	5	15	1
1	10	8	9	2	12									

a. Starting with 0 as the lower limit of the first class and using a class interval of 3, organize the data into a frequency distribution.
b. Describe the distribution. Where do the data tend to cluster?
c. Convert the distribution to a relative frequency distribution.

8. Moore Travel Agency, a nationwide travel agency, offers special rates on certain Caribbean cruises to senior citizens. The president of Moore Travel wants additional information on the ages of those people taking cruises. A random sample of 40 customers taking a cruise last year revealed these ages.

77	18	63	84	38	54	50	59	54	56	36	26	50	34	44
41	58	58	53	51	62	43	52	53	63	62	62	65	61	52
60	60	45	66	83	71	63	58	61	71					

a. Organize the data into a frequency distribution, using seven classes and 15 as the lower limit of the first class. What class interval did you select?

b. Where do the data tend to cluster?
c. Describe the distribution.
d. Determine the relative frequency distribution.

GRAPHIC PRESENTATION OF A FREQUENCY DISTRIBUTION

USA Today, Fortune, Business Week, and other publications emphasize the importance of graphs (also called charts). Their purpose is to give executives, hospital administrators, or other readers a quick view of the important facets of the statistical data being presented. We will concentrate on three commonly used graphic forms: a **histogram,** a **frequency polygon,** and a **cumulative frequency polygon** (often called an **ogive**).

Histogram

How is a histogram constructed?

A histogram is one of the most widely used charts and one of the easiest to understand. It describes a frequency distribution in terms of a series of bars each used to represent the number of class frequencies in a particular class. We will illustrate its construction by reintroducing the distribution of the average annual salaries of professors at 160 four-year schools.

EXAMPLE

The annual salary data are repeated below.

Average annual salary ($ thousands)	Midpoint	Number of universities
$20 up to $ 30	$25	4
30 up to 40	35	20
40 up to 50	45	41
50 up to 60	55	44
60 up to 70	65	29
70 up to 80	75	16
80 up to 90	85	2
90 up to 100	95	4
Total		160

How is a histogram constructed for the distribution of salaries?

Solution ► To construct a histogram, the class frequencies are scaled on the vertical axis (the *Y*-axis) and either the class limits or the class midpoints are scaled on the horizontal axis (the *X*-axis). We will use the class limits and show only the lower class limits. To illustrate the construction of the histogram, only the first two classes are included in Chart 2–1.

What does the height of a bar represent?

CHART 2–1 **Construction of a Histogram**

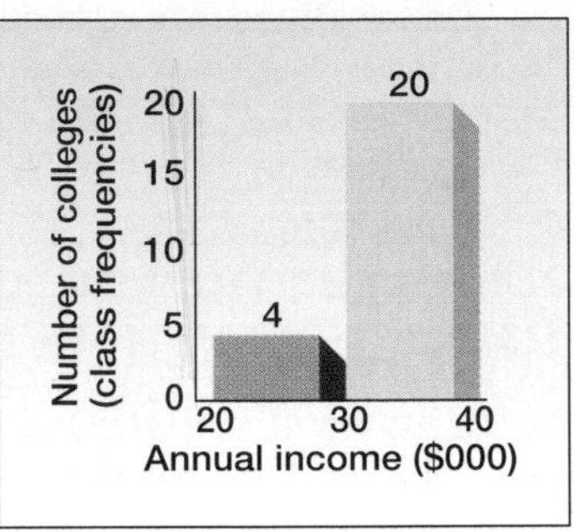

Note from the distribution of annual salaries that there are 4 colleges in the "$20,000 up to $30,000" class. Therefore, the height of the column for that class is 4. There are 20 colleges in the next class ($30,000 up to $40,000), and logically the height of that column is 20. (See Chart 2–1.) Note that the height of each bar represents the number of observations (colleges) in that class.

As shown in Chart 2–2, this procedure is continued for all classes. Note that there is no space between the bars. This is one feature of a histogram. In bar charts, which are discussed in a later section, the bars are separated slightly.

What does 4 + 20 + 41 . . . equal?

CHART 2–2 **Histogram Showing the Average Annual Salaries of Professors at 160 Colleges**

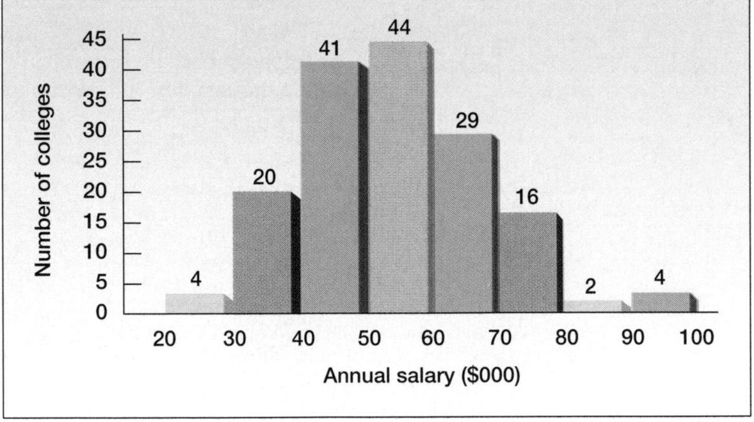

Based on the histogram in Chart 2–2, the following features are readily apparent: (1) The lowest average salary at these 160 universities is about $20,000. (2) The highest income is about $100,000. (3) The largest concentration of the annual salaries is between $50,000 and $60,000. (4) A large proportion of the salaries are between $40,000 and $70,000. Thus, this histogram provides an easily interpreted visual representation of the distribution of average annual salaries. Had we plotted relative frequencies instead of the class frequencies, the general shape of the histogram would be the same.

In recent years the computer has become an integral part of data analysis. There are many software packages that will output a histogram. The following example is from Version 10.0 of the MINITAB statistical software system. This software package is used extensively in this text. The class midpoints are shown on the *X*-axis and the class frequencies (numbers of universities) on the *Y*-axis.

CHART 2–3 **MINITAB Histogram of Professor Salaries**

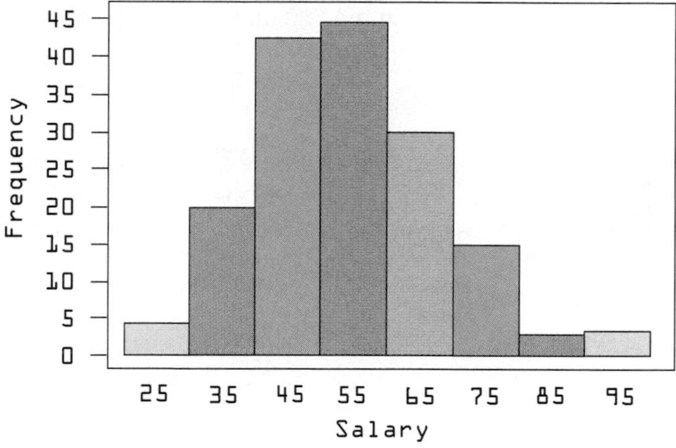

SELF-REVIEW 2–3

The answers are at the end of the chapter.

The total years on the pro tennis circuit for a group of male professionals are: 1, 6, 9, 2, 11, 13, 6, 5, 10, 7, 4 and 2 respectively. Letting the lower limit of the first class be one year and the class interval be three years:

a. Construct a frequency distribution.

b. Portray the years on the circuit in the form of a histogram.

c. What are the raw data?

d. What is the class frequency for the lowest class?

e. Interpret the distribution.

Stem-and-Leaf Display

In the previous sections, we showed how to organize data into a frequency distribution in order to summarize the raw data into some meaningful form. A disadvantage of that approach is the loss of some information when tallying. For example, it is not clear from the following distribution of the ages of new employees at the Young Foundry how the ages in the 20 to 30 age group are distributed. Are they clustered close to 20 years or somewhat evenly distributed throughout the class?

Ages of new employees	Tally	Frequency
20 to 30	~~////~~ //	7
30 to 40	~~////~~ ~~////~~ ~~////~~ ~~////~~ /	21
40 to 50	////	4
50 to 60	//	2
60 to 70	/	1

Stem-and-leaf display

A technique that has gained popularity in recent years offsets the loss of information that occurs from summarizing raw data. It is called a **stem-and-leaf display.** To construct such a display using the ages of the new employees at Young Foundry, a tally is replaced by the last digit of an employee's age. Thus, the ages of the seven employees in the "20 up to 30" class might appear as:

2 | 3 4 5 5 7 8 9

We can see that the ages are spread somewhat evenly through the "20 to 30" age class. Note that the values within a class are ordered from smallest to largest. The first value is 23, the second is 24, and so on.

The following example shows the steps needed to construct a stem-and-leaf display.

EXAMPLE

The selling prices of 45 single-family two-bedroom homes in Cartersville, Georgia, are given in Table 2–6. How are the price data organized into a stem-and-leaf display?

TABLE 2–6 Selling Prices of Single-Family Two-Bedroom Homes, Cartersville, Georgia ($ thousands)

$ 96	$ 93	$ 88	$117	$127
95	113	96	108	94
148	156	139	142	94
107	125	155	155	103
112	127	117	120	112
135	132	111	125	104
106	139	134	119	97
89	118	136	125	143
120	103	113	124	138

Solution ▶

Stem is leading digit. Leaf is trailing digit.

The **stem** is the *leading digit or digits.* The **leaf** is the *trailing digit.* The stem is placed to the left of a vertical line and the leaf (trailing digit) to the right of the line. For example, note in Table 2–6 that the sale price at the upper left is $96,000. The stem is 9 and the leaf 6. The vertical line merely separates the two parts of each number.

Stem, or leading digit	Leaf, or trailing digit
9	6

The leading digits for the raw data in Table 2–6 are 9, 10, 11, . . . , 15. The trailing digit for each sale price is recorded on the same line as its leading digit (stem). Thus, the first three prices in the left column of Table 2–6 would appear as:

Stem	**Leaf**	
9	6	5
•		
•		
•		
14	8	

Organizing all the sale prices:

Stem					**Leaf**				
8	9	8							
9	6	5	3	6	4	4	7		
10	7	6	3	8	3	4			
11	2	3	8	7	1	3	7	9	2
12	0	5	7	0	5	5	4	7	
13	5	2	9	9	4	6	8		
14	8	2	3						
15	6	5	5						

The trailing digits in each row are then rank-ordered to form a stem-and-leaf display. The first row would appear as:

Stem	**Leaf**	
8	8	9

The leaves for each row when ranked from low to high are:

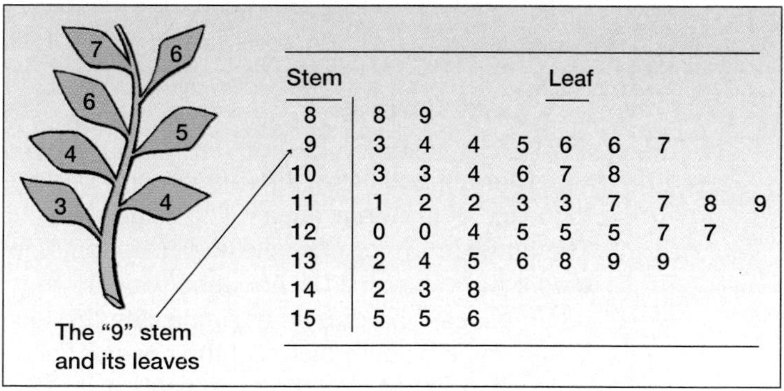

Stem				Leaf					
8	8	9							
9	3	4	4	5	6	6	7		
10	3	3	4	6	7	8			
11	1	2	2	3	3	7	7	8	9
12	0	0	4	5	5	5	7	7	
13	2	4	5	6	8	9	9		
14	2	3	8						
15	5	5	6						

Each row in this display has a stem and a leaf. The "9" stem has seven leaves and could be pictured as shown above.

The stem-and-leaf approach is very flexible. For example, following are the number of Kentucky Fried Chicken Drummer Boys (dinners containing drumstick. mashed potatoes, and slaw) sold during a four-week period: 2,463, 2,412, 2,543, and 2,488. The stem-and-leaf display would be

Stem	Leaf		
24	1	6	8
25	4		

The stem includes the hundreds and thousands digits. The units digit is dropped. The leaf therefore becomes the tens digit.

The output from the MINITAB system for the procedure called "stem" is shown below. The data are from Table 2–6. In this book the material entered by the computer user is shaded in color, and the output by the computer is in black. The MINITAB system will offer the prompt MTB>. When you see this prompt, MINITAB is asking what procedure you would like to run. In this case, the desired procedure is called "stem," and the subcommand is called "increment." Here the desired increment is 10. The data are located in a column, which is called c1. The variable is called "Price." The output follows.

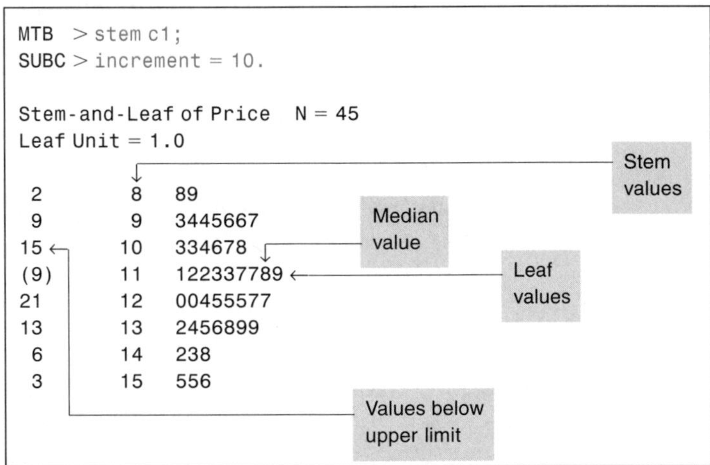

```
MTB  > stem c1;
SUBC > increment = 10.

Stem-and-Leaf of Price   N = 45
Leaf Unit = 1.0

  2       8   89
  9       9   3445667
 15      10   334678
(9)      11   122337789
 21      12   00455577
 13      13   2456899
  6      14   238
  3      15   556
```


There is additional information provided by the MINITAB solution in the column to the left of the stem values. The values 2, 9, 15, and so on are the cumulative totals. The number 15, for example, indicates that a total of 15 observations have occurred *before* the value of 110. About halfway down that column, the number 9 appears in parentheses. The parentheses indicate the location of the middle observation. That is, the value below which half the observations occur is in this row. There are a total of 45 observations, so the middle value, if the data were arranged in an array, would be the 23rd value. In this example, 15 observations fall below 110. The value 9 in parentheses indicates that there are 9 observations in the row with a stem of 110. The middle value would be the 23rd observation, or the 8th value in this row. Hence, the middle value, or the *median,* as it is called, is 118, found by counting over 8 values in the 110 row. *After the median row, the values decline.* These values represent the "more than" cumulative totals. That is, there are 21 observations of 120 or more, 13 of 130 or more, and so on.

The following MINITAB output also employs the data in Table 2–6 with respect to the selling prices of two-bedroom homes in Cartersville, Georgia. Note, however, that the increments are 5 instead of 10 as used before. The median, or middle value, is still 118, found by noting that 20 observations are 114 or less and that there are 4 observations between 115 and 119. We are looking for the third observation, which is 118.

```
MTB > stem c1

Stem-and-leaf of price   N = 45
Leaf unit = 1.0

  2       8 89
  5       9 344
  9       9 5667
 12      10 334
 15      10 678
 20      11 12233
(4)      11 7789
 21      12 004
 18      12 55577
 13      13 24
 11      13 56899
  6      14 23
  4      14 8
  3      15
  3      15 556
```

Indicates 100–104 105–109

Median value

SELF-REVIEW 2–4

The answers are at the end of the chapter.

The price-earnings ratios for 20 selected stocks are:

8.3, 9.6, 9.5, 9.1, 8.8, 11.2, 7.7, 10.1, 9.9, 10.8, 10.2, 8.0, 8.4, 8.1, 11.6, 9.6, 8.8, 8.0, 10.4, 9.8

1. Design a stem-and-leaf display.

2. Interpret the display.

EXERCISES

The answers to the odd-numbered exercises are at the end of the book.

9. The first row of a stem-and-leaf chart appears as 62 | 1 3 3 7 9. Explain.
10. The following stem-and-leaf chart represents the daily production of VCRs.
    a. What is the smallest number of VCRs produced during a day?
    b. How many observations are in the first class?
    c. What is the middle value of the production data?
    d. During how many days was production less than 95 VCRs?
    e. During how many days were 105 or more VCRs produced?

```
Stem-and-leaf of production  N = 80
Leaf unit = 1

        Stem      Leaf
  5       8       12334
 15       8       5566667899
 30       9       011111233333344
(10)      9       5556667777778888888899999
 25      10       00111223334444
 11      10       5566678
  4      11       2334
```

11. A survey of the number of calls received by a sample of Southern Phone Company subscribers last week revealed the following. Develop a stem-and-leaf chart.

52	43	30	38	30	42	12	46	39	37
34	46	32	18	41	5				

12. Citizens Banking is studying the number of times their automatic teller, located in a Loblaws Supermarket, is used daily. Following is a list of the number of times the teller was used during the last 30 days. Develop a stem-and-leaf chart.

83	64	84	76	84	54	75	59	70	61
63	80	84	73	68	52	65	90	52	77
95	36	78	61	59	84	95	47	87	60

The Frequency Polygon

A **frequency polygon** is similar in shape to the histogram. It consists of line segments connecting the points formed by the intersection of the *class midpoint* and the *class frequency.*

X is the midpoint of a class, *Y* the class frequency

Construction of a frequency polygon is illustrated using the average annual salaries of professors in four-year colleges. The midpoint of each class is scaled on the *X*-axis and the class frequencies on the *Y*-axis. Recall that a class midpoint is a value that represents the class and a class frequency is the number of observations in that class. Reintroducing the distribution of annual salaries of the professors:

Annual salary ($ thousands)	Midpoint	Number of universities
$20 up to $ 30	$25	4
30 up to 40	35	20
40 up to 50	45	41
50 up to 60	55	44
60 up to 70	65	29
70 up to 80	75	16
80 up to 90	85	2
90 up to 100	95	4

As noted, the "$20,000 up to $30,000" class is represented by its midpoint, $25,000. Move horizontally on the graph to the midpoint ($25) and then vertically to

4, the class frequency, and place a dot. The X- and Y- values that form this dot are known as its *coordinates.* The coordinates of the next dot are $X = \$35$, $Y = 20$. This process is continued until all the income classes are accounted for. Then *the dots are connected in order.* That is, the point representing the lowest class is joined to the one representing the second class, and so forth.

Note in Chart 2–4 that to complete the frequency polygon, midpoints of $15,000 and $105,000 were added on the X-axis to "anchor" the polygon at zero frequencies. These two values, $15 and $105, were derived by subtracting the class interval of $10 from the lowest midpoint ($25) and by adding $10 to the highest midpoint in the distribution ($95).

CHART 2–4 **Frequency Polygon: Average Annual Salaries of Professors at 160 Universities**

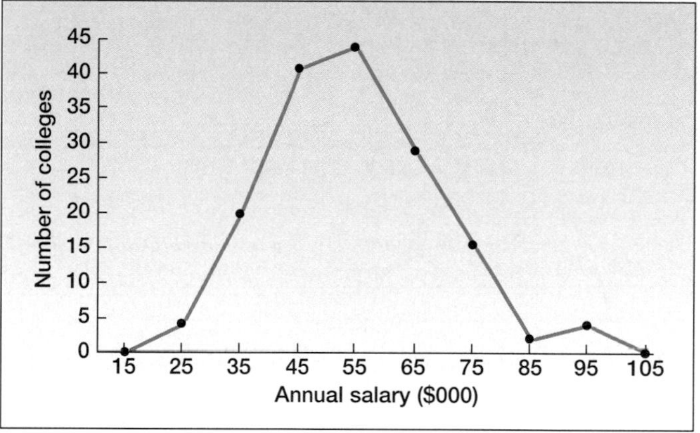

Frequency polygon preferred when comparing distributions

Both the histogram and frequency polygon allow us to get a quick picture of the main characteristics of the data (highs, lows, point of concentration, etc.). Although the two representations are similar in purpose, the histogram has the advantage of depicting each class as a rectangle, with the area of each rectangular bar representing the total number of frequencies in the class. The frequency polygon, in turn, has an advantage over the histogram. It allows us to compare directly two or more frequency distributions. Suppose, for example, that the president of Duval University wants to compare the average annual salaries of professors at other four-year schools with the average annual salaries of assistant professors at those same 160 schools. It is obvious from Chart 2–5 that the salaries of assistant professors at those same schools are significantly lower than those of full professors. (See Chart 2–5.)

Why convert to relative frequencies?

The number of class frequencies for each of the groups portrayed in Chart 2–5 is the same. If the difference in the total number of class frequencies is quite large, say, 160 professors and 42 assistant professors, converting the class frequencies *to relative frequencies* and then plotting the two distributions would allow for a clearer comparison.

CHART 2–5 **Frequency Polygons: Average Annual Salaries of Full Professors and Assistant Professors at 160 Universities**

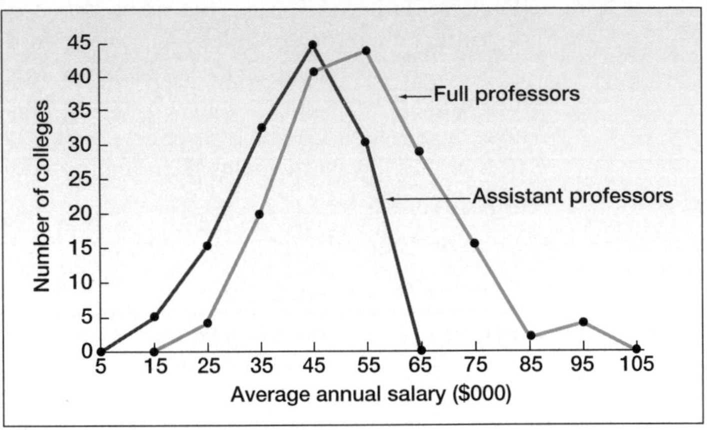

SELF-REVIEW 2–5

The answers are at the end of the chapter.

The annual imports of a selected group of electronic suppliers are shown in the following frequency distribution.

Imports ($ millions)	Number of suppliers
$ 2 up to $ 5	6
5 up to 8	13
8 up to 11	20
11 up to 14	10
14 up to 17	1

1. Portray the imports in the form of a histogram.
2. Portray the imports in the form of a relative frequency polyon.
3. Summarize the important facets of the distribution (such as low and high, concentration, etc.)

Before we continue, it should be noted that there are several ways of specifying the classes. We cited one way with respect to the annual salaries of professors, namely, $20,000 up to $30,000, $30,000 up to $40,000, and so forth. They could have been stated as:

$20,000 but under $30,000

$30,000 but under $40,000

or

$20,000–$29,999

$30,000—$39,999

The second form assumes that the annual salaries are rounded to the nearest dollar.

The National Center for Health Statistics recorded the number of new AIDS cases for males as:

Age	Number
20–29 years	6,292
30–39 years	17,795
40–49 years	10,317

and so on. The class interval is computed the same as before, namely, by subtracting the lower limit of a class from the lower limit of the next class. For example, 40 years − 30 years = 10 years, the class interval. What are the midpoints for this frequency distribution? We add the lower limit of a class to the upper limit and divide by 2. Thus, the midpoint of the first class is (20 + 29) / 2 = 24.5. The remaining midpoints are found the same way, or we could add 10 to successive midpoints.

EXERCISES

The answers to the odd-numbered exercises are at the end of the book.

13. The following frequency distribution represents the number of days during a year that employees at the Robinson Manufacturing Company were absent from work due to illness.

Number of days absent	Number of employees
0 up to 4	5
4 up to 8	12
8 up to 12	23
12 up to 16	8
16 up to 20	2
Total	50

a. Assuming that this is a sample, what is the sample size?
b. What is the midpoint of the first class?
c. Construct a histogram.
d. A frequency polygon is to be drawn. What are the coordinates of the plot for the first class?
e. Construct a frequency polygon.
f. Summarize the rate of employee absenteeism using the two charts.

14. A large retailer is studying the lead time (elapsed time between when an order is placed and when it is filled) for a sample of recent orders. The lead times are reported in days.

Lead time (days)	Frequency
0 up to 5	6
5 up to 10	7
10 up to 15	12
15 up to 20	8
20 up to 25	7
Total	40

a. How many orders were studied?
b. What is the midpoint of the first class?
c. What are the coordinates of the first class?
d. Draw a histogram.
e. Draw a frequency polygon.
f. Summarize the lead times using the two charts.

15. A study is being conducted with respect to the time it takes to assemble a plug-in unit using the Carter method versus the Manelli method. The times using the Carter method were stored in the computer, and it was a simple job to organize them into a frequency distribution. However, considerable effort had to be expended to determine the assembly times using the Manelli method, so only 50 were selected. The two distributions are:

Time, in minutes	Number studied	
	Carter method	Manelli method
5 up to 8	120	4
8 up to 11	426	11
11 up to 14	1,060	25
14 up to 17	286	7
17 up to 20	108	3

In order to compare the two methods using frequency polygons, it is first necessary to convert the class frequencies to relative frequencies (because the number studied for the Carter method is so much greater than for the Manelli method).
a. Convert the class frequencies for both distributions to relative frequencies.
b. On one chart portray the two polygons representing the assembly times.
c. Draw conclusions regarding the assembly times.

16. The Western Insurance Company is studying automobile damage claims for cars five years old and older and those less than five years old. The raw data were tabulated into the following frequency distributions.

Amount of claim	Number of claims	
	Autos five years old and older	Autos less than five years old
\$ 200 up to \$ 500	30	86
500 up to 800	129	212
800 up to 1,100	20	368
1,100 up to 1,400	10	480
1,400 up to 1,700	6	1,806
1,700 up to 2,000	2	898
2,000 up to 2,300	3	150

The distributions are to be portrayed on one chart to facilitate comparison.
a. What is the class interval?
b. What is the midpoint of the first class?
c. Convert the class frequencies for each distribution to relative frequencies.
d. Depict the relative frequencies for both distributions on one chart.
e. Summarize the chart.

CUMULATIVE FREQUENCY POLYGONS

What is an ogive?

We return to the distribution of the average annual salaries paid at 160 universities (Table 2–2). Suppose we are interested in how many schools pay the professors $55,000 a year or less. Also, how many schools have average salaries of $72,000 or more? The answers to these queries can be approximated by developing a **cumulative frequency distribution** and portraying it graphically in a **cumulative frequency polygon,** often called an **ogive.** These two statistical techniques are applicable when we want to determine how many observations lie below or above a certain value.

Less-than Cumulative Frequency Polygon

A **less-than cumulative frequency polygon** can be used to answer such questions as: What percent of the average salaries of the professors are less than $55,000? How many schools pay less than $46,000 on the average?

EXAMPLE

The frequency distribution for the annual salaries at the 160 colleges is repeated below from Table 2–2.

Income ($ thousands)	Number of colleges
$20 up to $ 30	4
30 up to 40	20
40 up to 50	41
50 up to 60	44
60 up to 70	29
70 up to 80	16
80 up to 90	2
90 up to 100	4
Total	160

Construct a less-than cumulative frequency polygon. Answer these questions: Fifty percent of the colleges have average annual salaries equal to or less than what amount? Seventy-five percent of the salaries are equal to or less than what amount?

Solution ▶ As the name implies, a cumulative frequency distribution and a cumulative frequency polygon require cumulative frequencies. To construct a less-than cumulative frequency distribution, refer to the preceding table. Note that 4 colleges have average annual salaries of less than $30,000. Those 4 colleges plus the 20 colleges in the next higher class, or 24 colleges, have annual salaries less than $40,000. The cumulative number of class frequencies for the next higher class is 65, found by 4 + 20 + 41. This process for finding the cumulative frequencies is continued for all the classes. Note that all schools pay their professors less than $100,000. (See Table 2–7.)

To plot a less-than cumulative frequency polygon, the upper class limits are scaled on the *X*-axis and the cumulative frequencies on the *Y*-axis. (See Chart 2–6.)

TABLE 2–7 Less-than Cumulative Frequency Distribution for the Average Annual Salaries of Professors

Average annual salary ($ thousands)	Number of universities		Cumulative frequency	Found by
$20 up to $ 30	4	Add	4	
30 up to 40	20	down	24	← 4 + 20
40 up to 50	41	↓	65	← 4 + 20 + 41
50 up to 60	44		109	← 4 + 20 + 41 + 44
60 up to 70	29		138	
70 up to 80	16		154	
80 up to 90	2		156	
90 up to 100	4		160	
Total	160			

Since four schools have average annual salaries less than $30,000, the first plot is X = $30,000 and $Y = 4$. The coordinates of the next plot are X = $40,000, $Y = 24$. These points and the remaining ones are connected in order to form the less-than cumulative frequency polygon. Note that the curve is extended to the X-axis. Also note that the cumulative frequencies are scaled on the left vertical axis and the percent of the total on the right vertical axis. We can use either axis to answer the following questions: Half, or 50 percent, of the schools have average annual incomes of what amount or less? Three out of four schools (75 percent) pay what amount or less? To answer the first question, we could go up to 80 schools on the left axis ($160 / 2 = 80$) or to 50 percent on the right Y-axis, draw a dashed line to the polygon, and then continue on down to the X-axis and read the salary. It is about $52,000. We find the top salary paid by 75 percent of universities by moving to 75 percent on the right vertical axis, moving horizontally to the cumulative frequency polygon, dropping down to the X-axis, and approximating the salary. It is about $65,000. We conclude that about 75 percent of the professors earn a salary of $65,000 or less.

CHART 2–6 Less-than Cumulative Frequency Polygon: Average Annual Salaries of Full Professors

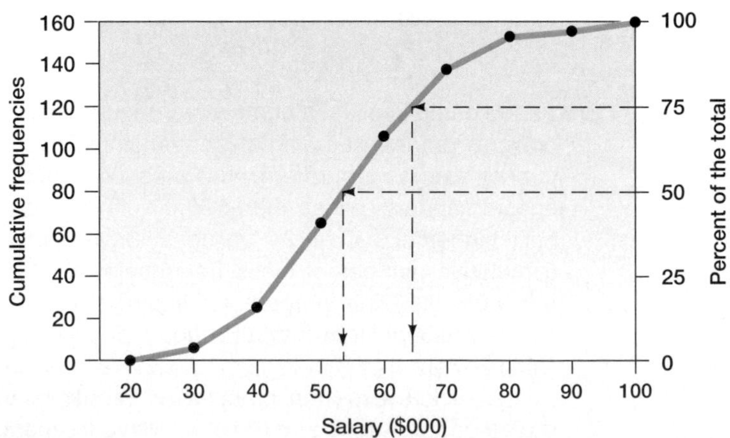

More-than Cumulative Frequency Polygon

A **more-than cumulative frequency distribution** is constructed by starting with the highest class and working backward, that is, adding the frequencies *up* from the highest class to the lowest class. To draw a more-than cumulative frequency polygon we use the *lower limit* of a class and the corresponding cumulative frequency. The details are presented in the table below.

Average annual salary ($ thousands)	Class frequency		Cumulative frequency	Found by
$20 up to $ 30	4		160	
30 up to 40	20		156	
40 up to 50	41		136	
50 up to 60	44		95	
60 up to 70	29		51	← 4 + 2 + 16 + 29
70 up to 80	16	↑	22	← 4 + 2 +16
80 up to 90	2	*Add*	6	← 4 + 2
90 up to 100	4	*up*	4	

As before, we plot the cumulative frequencies on the *Y*-axis and the salaries on the *X*-axis. (See Chart 2–7.)

CHART 2–7 **More-than Cumulative Frequency Polygon: Average Annual Salaries of Professors**

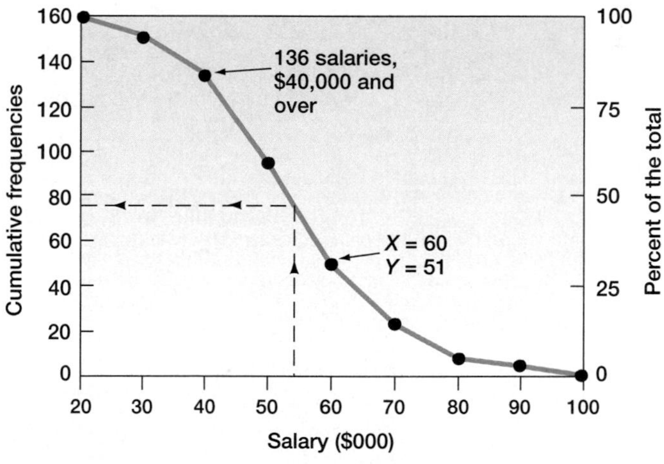

To determine how many average annual salaries at the 160 colleges are equal to or greater than $55,000, we draw a dashed line vertically from $55,000 as shown in Chart 2–7 to the more-than cumulative frequency polygon and left to the *Y*- axis. The corresponding number on the *Y*-axis is about 75, meaning that about 75 schools have average annual salaries of $55,000 or more.

SELF-REVIEW 2–6

The answers are at the end of the chapter.

A study is to be made of the price-earnings (PE) ratios of firms listed on the New York Stock Exchange. The price-earnings ratios of a sample of firms were organized into the following table.

PE ratio	Number of firms
4 up to 7	7
7 up to 10	13
10 up to 13	20
13 up to 16	11
16 up to 19	6
19 up to 22	3

1. What is the table called?

2. Develop a less-than cumulative frequency distribution and portray it in a less-than cumulative frequency polygon.

3. Develop a more-than cumulative frequency distribution and draw an appropriate frequency polygon.

4. Based on the frequency distribution and the two frequency polygons, how many firms have PE ratios of 10 up to 13? About how many firms have price-earnings ratios of 16 or less? How many firms have PE ratios of 11 or more?

EXERCISES

The answers to the odd-numbered exercises are at the end of the book.

17. The lead times it took to fill an order (from the time the order was placed by a customer to the time it was shipped out) were organized into the following frequency table.

Lead time (working days)	Number of orders
0 up to 5 days	6
5 up to 10 days	7
10 up to 15 days	24
15 up to 20 days	11
20 up to 25 days	9
25 up to 30 days	3

a. How many orders were filled in less than 10 days?
b. Convert the distribution to a less-than cumulative frequency distribution. Then draw a less-than cumulative frequency polygon.
c. Based on the less-than cumulative frequency polygon, how many orders took less than 6 days to fill?

18. A soft drink bottling machine is tested periodically to determine if it is functioning within certain limits. The frequency distribution below gives the results for 100 observations measured to the nearest hundredth of an ounce.

Class	Frequency
5.00 up to 5.50	1
5.50 up to 6.00	1
6.00 up to 6.50	2
6.50 up to 7.00	5
7.00 up to 7.50	13
7.50 up to 8.00	36
8.00 up to 8.50	31
8.50 up to 9.00	10
9.00 up to 9.50	1

a. Construct a less-than cumulative frequency distribution for these data.
b. Draw a less-than cumulative frequency polygon.
c. Based on the graph, about one fourth of the time the machine will yield less than what amount?

19. The frequency distribution representing the number of days annually the employees at the Robinson Manufacturing Company were absent from work due to illness is repeated from Exercise 13.

Number of days absent	Frequency
0 up to 4	5
4 up to 8	12
8 up to 12	23
12 up to 16	8
16 up to 20	2
Total	50

a. How many employees were absent less than four days annually? How many were absent less than eight days due to illness?
b. Convert the frequency distribution to a less-than cumulative frequency distribution.
c. Portray the cumulative distribution in the form of a less-than cumulative frequency polygon.
d. About three out of four employees were absent for how many days or less due to illness?

20. A psychologist is studying the length of time it takes mice to go through a maze and reach a reward at the end. Time is measured to the nearest tenth of a second, with the results given in the table below.

Time	Frequency
2.0 up to 3.0	3
3.0 up to 4.0	7
4.0 up to 5.0	15
5.0 up to 6.0	29
6.0 up to 7.0	81
7.0 up to 8.0	50
8.0 up to 9.0	10
9.0 up to 10.0	5

a. Construct a more-than cumulative frequency distribution for these data.
b. Draw a more-than cumulative frequency polygon.
c. Based on the graph, about 90 percent of the mice take more than what amount of time to complete the maze?

OTHER GRAPHIC REPRESENTATIONS OF DATA

The histogram, the frequency polygon, and the two cumulative frequency polygons have strong visual appeal. That is, they are designed to capture the attention of the reader. In this section we will examine some of the other graphical forms, namely the line chart, the bar chart, and the pie chart. These charts are seen extensively in *USA Today,* other newspapers, magazines, and governmental reports.

Charts 2–8 and 2–9 are examples of **line charts.** Chart 2–8 shows the sales of the Johnson & Johnson Company, which manufactures Band-Aids and other medical supplies, since 1983. Note that sales have increased steadily during the period. In fact, they have increased more than two and one half times, from $6 billion in 1983 to over $15 billion in 1994. Chart 2–9 depicts the net income for General Motors for the same 12-year period. For 3 of the 12 years the company suffered a loss. In a line chart, time is always scaled on the horizontal axis. Sales, income, costs, or a similar variable is scaled on the vertical axis.

CHART 2–8 **Total Sales of Johnson & Johnson, 1983–1994**

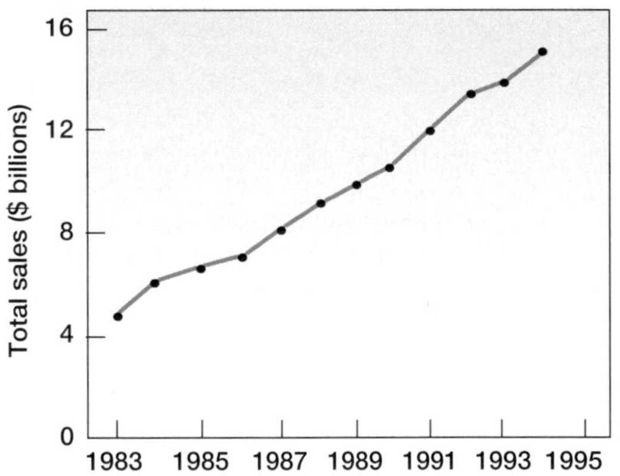

Source: Johnson & Johnson, *Annual Report,* 1993, p. 42. (1994 estimated.)

Quite often two or more series of figures are plotted on one line chart. Thus one chart can show the trends of several series. This allows for a quick comparison of several series over a period of time. Chart 2–10 is an illustration. Four series are portrayed at one time for 90 years. For example, in 1900, male children born to black and other races had a life expectancy of about 33 years. This means that half of these males born in 1900 did not live to be 33 years old. By the year 2000 it is expected that this same group will have a life expectancy of about 68 years. So the life expectancy for this group has doubled. What about white females? Their life expectancy has also increased, but the rate of increase is not as dramatic—from about 49 years to more than 80 years. Thus, one line chart allows us to compare the life expectancies of four groups at once.

CHART 2–9 **Net Income of General Motors**

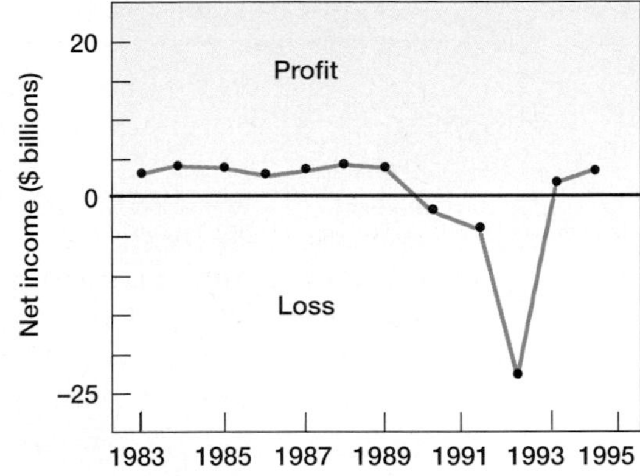

Source: General Motors, *Annual Report,* 1993, p. 54. (1994 estimated.)

CHART 2–10 **Life Expectancy at Birth, by Race and Sex, 1900 to 2000**

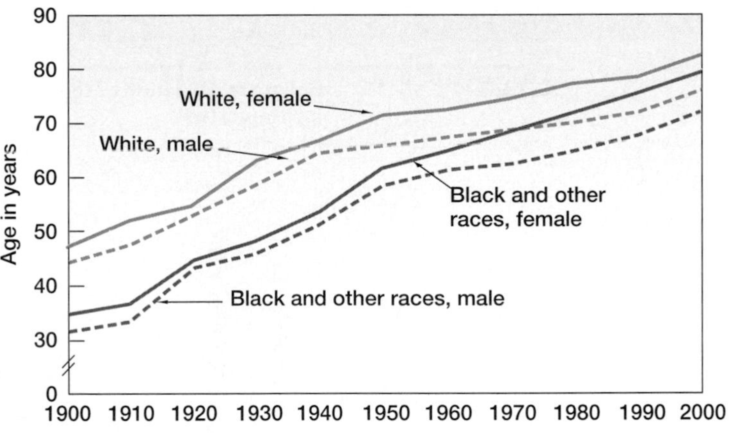

Source: National Center for Health Statistics, U.S. Department of Health and Human Services.

A **bar chart** can be used to depict any of the levels of measurement—nominal ordinal, interval, or ratio. (We discussed levels of measurement at some length in Chapter 1.) Suppose we want to portray the percentage increase for selected civilian jobs (nominal level of data) from 1988 to the year 2000. The need for medical assistants is projected to be up by 70 percent by the year 2000, travel agents up by 54 percent, computer employees up by 53 percent, and so on. We plot these figures in the form of a *horizontal bar chart.* We extend the bar for medical assistants from 0 percent in 1988 to 70 percent in the year 2000. This process is continued for all the civilian jobs as shown in Chart 2–11.

CHART 2–11 **Percentage Increases in Civilian Jobs for Selected Occupations, 1988 to 2000**

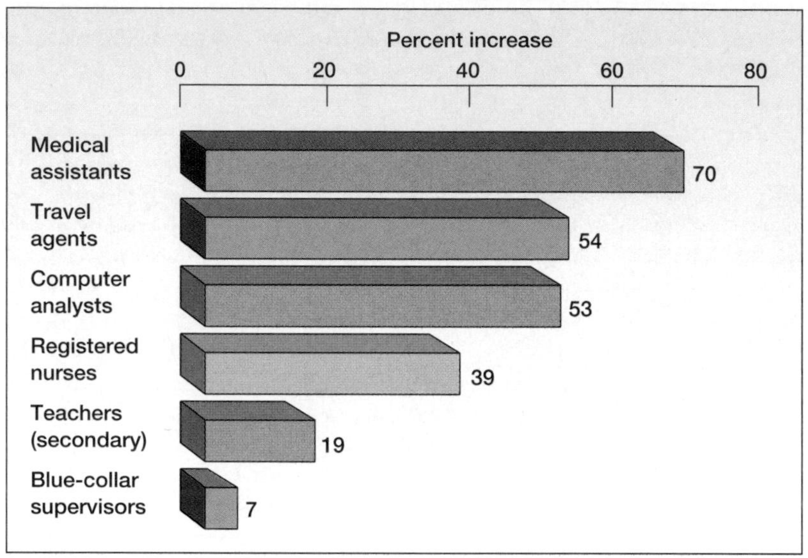

Source: *The Universal Almanac,* 1991, p. 223.

CHART 2–12 **Religious Affiliation of the U.S. Population 14 Years Old and Over (self-reported)**

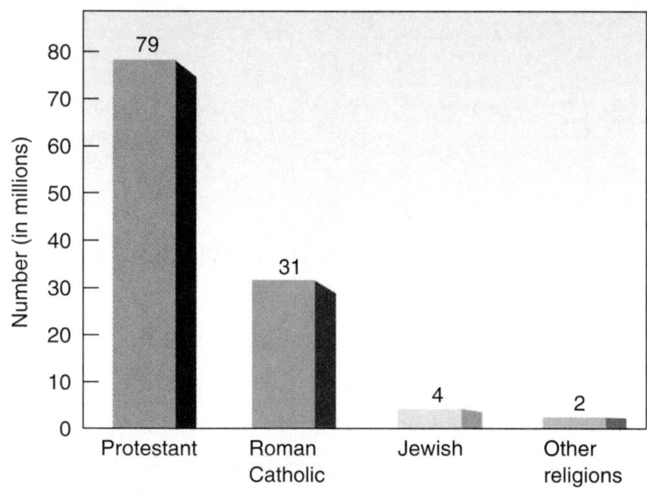

Source: *Yearbook of American and Canadian Churches,* 1993.

Suppose we want to show the religious affiliation of the U.S. population in the form of a **vertical bar chart.** From the *Yearbook of American and Canadian Churches,* we find that 79 million persons of age 14 years and older stated that their religion is Protestant, 31 million stated that their religion is Roman Catholic, 4 million identified themselves as Jewish, and 2 million had other religions. This information is depicted in Chart 2–12. It shows clearly, for example, that there are more than twice as many Protestants as Roman Catholics. Note that there is space between the bars representing the various groups. This is one of the ways in which a histogram and a vertical bar chart differ. There is no space between the bars of a histogram because the data are continuous, but this is not the case for the data in a bar chart. Protestants and Roman Catholics separate groups; therefore, the bars are separated.

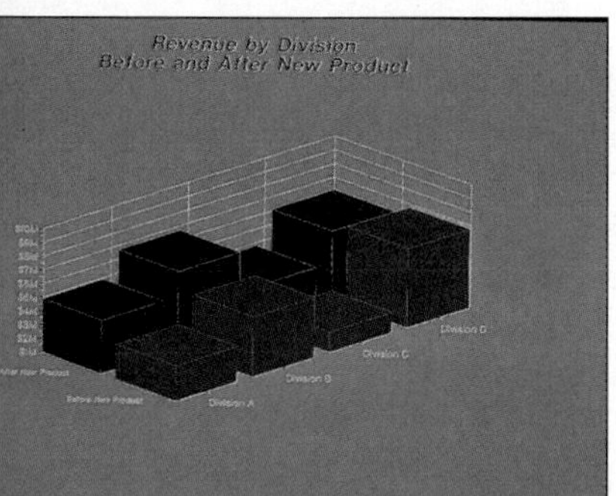

We pointed out that there are several types of line charts. Likewise, there are many types of bar charts. Only one will be discussed in detail. It is called a *two-directional bar chart* and is appropriate for showing profit and loss, above-normal and below-normal activity, and percentage changes from one period of time to another. To illustrate, suppose that the CEO of Monsanto wants to present graphically to the board of directors the *percent changes* in selected financial statistics found in the annual report to the shareholders. The items from the financial summary (in millions) for 1993 and 1988 are:

Item	1993	1988	Percent change
Shareholders' equity	$2,855	$3,800	−25
Research and development	626	556	+13
Cash provided by operations	731	1,304	−44
Stock price (high)	75	46¼	+62
Price-earnings ratio	18	10	+80
Employees (year-end)	30,019	45,635	−34

Source: Monsanto, *1993 Annual Report to Shareowners,* 1993, p. 52.

The usual procedure followed to develop a two-directional bar chart is to first divide the percent changes into two groups: percent increases and percent decreases. The percent increases are then arranged from highest to lowest, and the percent decreases are arranged in ascending order. The percent increases are plotted to the right of the origin (0) and the decreases to the left of the origin. (See Chart 2–13.)

CHART 2–13 **Two-Directional Bar Chart: Percent Changes in Financial Highlights, for Monsanto, 1988 to 1993**

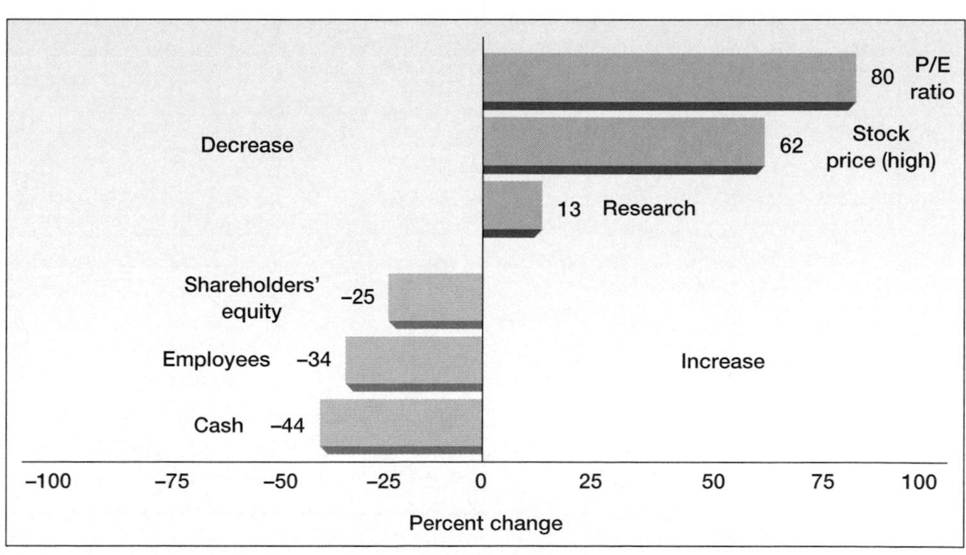

A **pie chart** is especially useful for depicting a relative frequency distribution. The procedure followed in constructing a pie chart will be described using the data in Table 2–8, provided by the FBI.

TABLE 2–8 **Arrests, by Age**

Age	Number of arrests	Relative frequency
Under 20	2,734,756	26.3%
20 up to 30	4,201,950	40.4
30 up to 40	2,122,973	20.4
40 up to 50	790,535	7.6
50 and over	541,963	5.3
Total	10,392,177	100.0

Source: Federal Bureau of Investigation, *Uniform Crime Reports for the United States.*

As shown in Chart 2–14, the percents 0, 5, 10, 15, and so on are scaled evenly around the circumference of the circle. To plot the 26.3 percent for the "Under 20" age group, a line is drawn from 0 to the center of the circle and another line from the center to 26.3 percent on the circle. Then, adding 26.3 percent to 40.4 percent for the "20 up to 30" age group, we get 66.7 percent. A line is drawn from the center of the circle to 66.7 percent. Thus, the area of the circle between 26.3 percent and 66.7

CHART 2–14 **Arrests by Age Group**

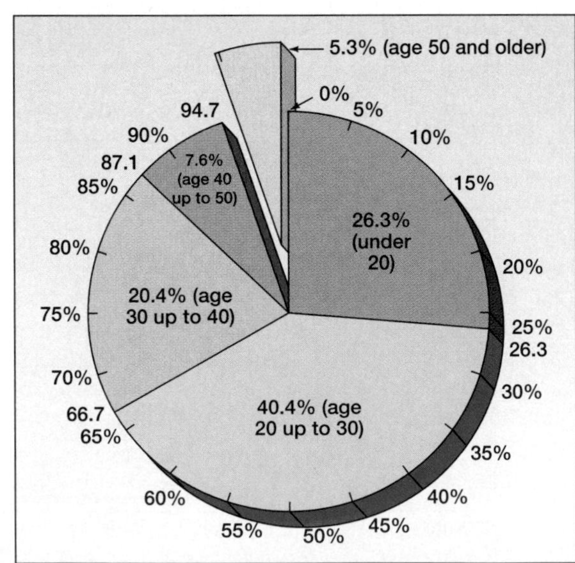

percent represents the percent of the total number of arrests attributed to the "20 up to 30" age group. Continuing, we add 20.4 percent to 66.7 percent, which gives 87.1 percent. A line is drawn from the center to 87.1 percent. The area between 66.7 and 87.1, or 20.4 percent, shows the percent of the total number of arrests attributed to the "30 up to 40" age group. This procedure is continued until all the age groups are accounted for. (See Chart 2–14.) This type of chart has a distinct advantage. Since the areas in the circle correspond directly to the relative frequencies, we can quickly grasp which area is the largest—in this case, 40.4 percent, representing the "20 up to 30" age group—and which sector is the smallest (5.3 percent, for the "50 and over" age group).

SELF-REVIEW 2–7

The Clayton County Commissioners want to design a chart to show the taxpayers attending the forthcoming meeting what happens to their tax dollars. The total amount of taxes collected is $2 million. Expenditures were; $440,000 for schools, $1,160,000 for roads, $320,000 for administration, and $80,000 for supplies. A pie chart seems ideal to show the portion of each tax dollar going for schools, roads, administration, and supplies. Convert the dollar amounts to percents of the total, and portray the percents in the form of a pie chart.

MISUSES OF STATISTICS

When you purchase a computer for your home or office, it usually includes some graphics packages. These packages will produce some very effective charts and graphs. However, you must be careful not to mislead or misrepresent. In this section we present several examples of charts and graphs that are misleading. Whenever you see a chart or graph, study it carefully. Ask yourself: What is the writer trying to show me? Could the writer have any bias?

One of easiest ways to mislead the reader is to make the range of the *Y*-axis very small in terms of the units used for that axis. In the chart below it looks like there has been a dramatic increase in sales from 1985 to 1996. However, during the period sales increased only 2 percent (from $5.0 million to $5.1 million)!

Sales of Matsui Nine-Passenger Vans 1985–1996

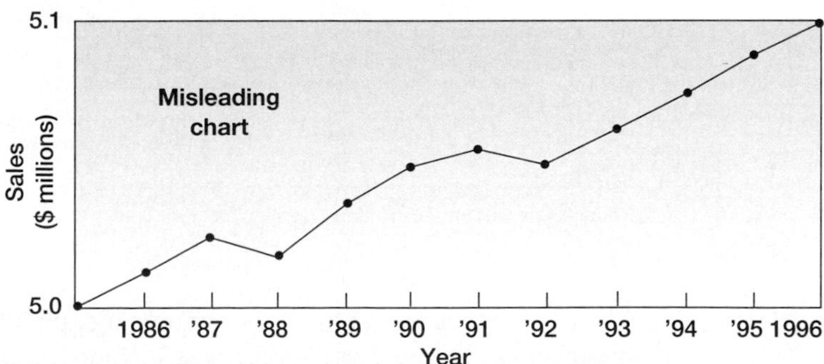

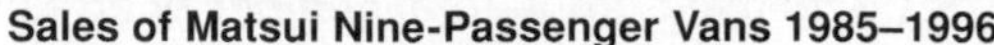

Sales of Matsui Nine-Passenger Vans 1985–1996

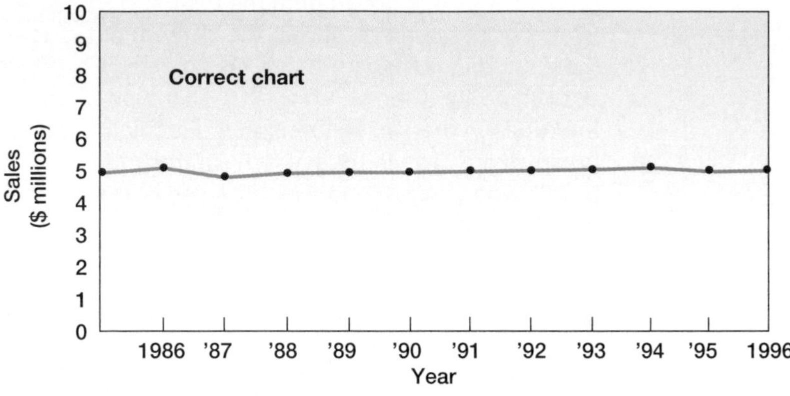

The chart above gives the correct impression of the trend in sales. Sales are almost "flat" from 1985 to 1996; that is, there was practically no change in sales during the 10-year period.

Without much comment we ask that you review each of the following charts and decide whether the intended message is accurate.

1. The following chart was adapted from an advertisement for the new Wilson ULTRA DISTANCE golf ball. The chart shows that the new ball gets the longest distance, but what is the scale for the horizontal axis? How was the test conducted?

Maybe everybody can't hit a ball like John Daly. But everybody wants to. That's why Wilson® is introducing the new ULTRA® DISTANCE ball. ULTRA DISTANCE is the longest, most accurate ball you'll ever hit.

Wilson has totally redesigned this ball from the inside out, making ULTRA DISTANCE a major advancement in golf technology.

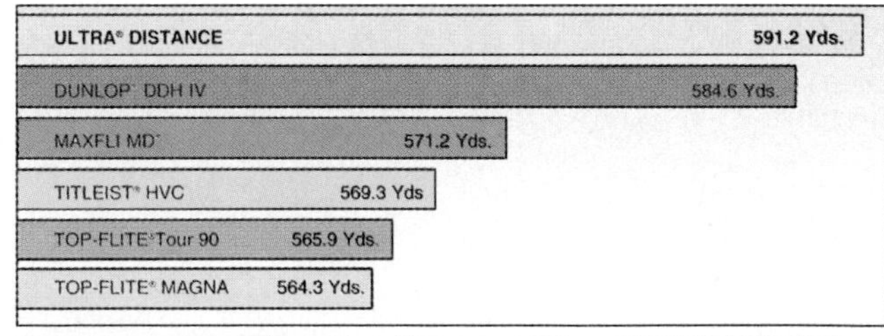

Combined yardage with a driver, #5 iron and #9 iron, ULTRA DISTANCE is clearly Measurably Longer.

Source: Adapted from *Golf,* March 1994, p. 56.

2. Fibre Tech, in Largo, Florida, makes and installs fiberglass coatings for swimming pools. The following chart was included in a brochure. Is the comparison fair? What is the scale for the vertical axis? Is the scale in dollars or in percent?

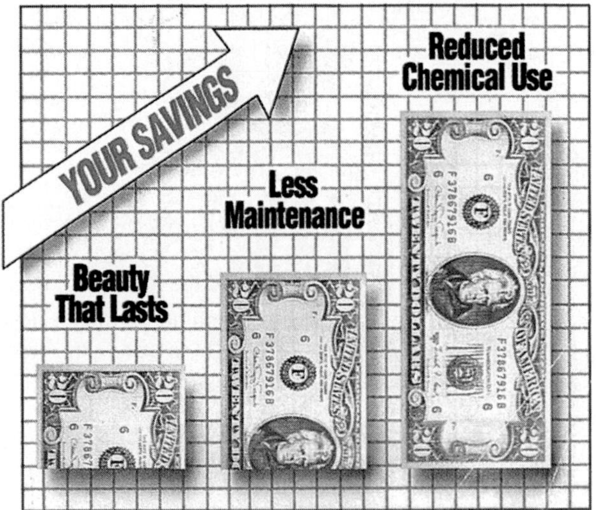

Again, we caution you. When you see a chart or graph, particularly as a part of an advertisement, be careful. Look at the scales used on the X-axis and the Y-axis.

EXERCISES

The answers to the odd-numbered exercises are at the end of the book.

21. The short-term debt of the Chevron Corporation for the years 1983–1994, in millions of dollars, is:

Year	Short-term debt ($ millions)	Year	Short-term debt ($ millions)
1983	124	1989	126
1984	2,025	1990	59
1985	1,841	1991	1,706
1986	619	1992	2,888
1987	915	1993	3,456
1988	469	1994	3,500*

*Estimate.

Source: Chevron Corporation, *Annual Report,* 1993, pp. 60–66.

Portray the trend of Chevron's short-term debt since 1983 in the form of a chart. You select the appropriate chart.

22. The high and the low common stock prices for the Chevron Corporation since 1983 are:

Year	Price High	Price Low	Year	Price High	Price Low
1983	40⅞	30⅞	1989	72	45¾
1984	40¼	30	1990	81⅝	63⅛
1985	40¾	29¼	1991	80⅛	63½
1986	48	34	1992	75⅜	60⅛
1987	64⅝	32	1993	98⅜	67¾
1988	51¾	39⅝	1994	99*	70*

*Estimate.

Source: Chevron Corporation, *Annual Report,* 1993, pp. 60–66.

Compare the high and the low common stock prices since 1983 in a chart of your choice.

23. The marketing research department is investigating the performance of several corporations in the coal, oil, and gas industries. The fourth-quarter sales (in millions of dollars) for these corporations are:

Corporation	Fourth-quarter sales ($ millions)
Americada Hess	$ 1,645.2
Atlantic Richfield	4,757.0
Chevron	8,913.0
Diamond Shamrock	627.1
Exxon	24,612.0
Quaker State	191.9

Source: The Corporate Scoreboard, *Business Week,* March 7, 1994, p. 117.

The research department wants to include in their report a chart comparing the fourth-quarter sales of the six corporations.

a. Use a pie chart to compare the fourth-quarter sales of these corporations.

b. Write a brief interpretation of the main features of the data portrayed in the chart.

24. We are interested in the percent change in the number of new passenger cars imported into the United States from 1964 to 1994.

Country	Imported cars 1964	Imported cars 1994
Japan	16,023	1,867,794
West Germany	364,683	245,286
Italy	10,843	11,045
United Kingdom	77,548	27,271
Sweden	18,562	93,084
France	39,532	1,976
Canada	9,201	1,220,221
Total	536,392	3,466,677

We want to show in graphic form the percent change in these imports, by country of origin, from 1964 to 1994. Rearrange the data, compute the percent changes, and portray these percent changes in a graph. Briefly interpret the percent changes.

CHAPTER OUTLINE

I. Frequency distributions.
   A. A frequency distribution is a grouping of data into nonoverlapping categories showing the number of observations in each category. Its purpose is to show the data in some meaningful form.
   B. Steps in developing a frequency distribution.
      1. Decide on the size of the class interval. If the number of classes has been established, a suggested class interval can be determined by

$$\frac{\text{Highest value} - \text{Lowest value}}{\text{Number of classes}} \qquad (2\text{–}1)$$

If the number of classes is uncertain, a suggested class interval can be found by

$$\frac{\text{Highest value} - \text{Lowest value}}{1 + 3.322(\text{logarithm of the total frequencies})} \qquad (2\text{–}2)$$

Alternatively, to determine the suggested number of classes, find the smallest integer k such that $2^k \geq n$, where n is the total number of observations.
      2. Tally the raw data into the classes to arrive at the frequency distribution.
   C. Criteria in constructing a frequency distribution.
      1. Avoid having fewer than 5 or more than 15 classes.
      2. Avoid open-ended classes.
      3. Keep the class intervals the same size.
      4. Do not have overlapping classes.

II. Graph of a frequency distribution.
   A. A histogram depicts the number of frequencies in each class in the form of bars.
   B. A frequency polygon and a relative frequency polygon have the classes scaled on the *X*-axis and the class frequencies on the *Y*-axis. The midpoint of a class and its corresponding class frequency are plotted using a dot. The dots are connected to form the polygon. The area under the polygon, as for the histogram, is equal to the total number of frequencies.

III. Relative frequency distribution: Similar to the frequency distribution, but instead of giving the number of observations in each class, it gives the percent of the total number of observations in each class.

IV. Stem-and-leaf displays.
   A. The purpose of a stem-and-leaf display is to organize ungrouped (raw) data into some meaningful form.
   B. Data are partitioned into a stem and a leaf. The first digit (digits) of a number is the stem. The trailing digit (digits) is the leaf.

V. Cumulative frequency polygons.
   A. A less-than cumulative frequency polygon allows us to determine how many, or what percent, of the observations are equal to or less than a certain value.
   B. A more-than cumulative frequency polygon is constructed by accumulating the class frequencies starting with the highest class. Each of the lower class limits and the cumulative frequencies is plotted. From the polygon we can determine how many, or what percent, of the values are equal to or more than a selected amount.

VI. Other graphs.

A. Line charts are ideal for portraying the trend of data over a period of time.
B. Bar charts are also used to show the long-term trend of sales, production, and other business and economic series. The bars are separated with space.
C. A two-directional bar chart is used to portray changes from one period to another.
D. Pie charts can be effectively used to portray the components of the total.

EXERCISES

The answers to the odd-numbered exercises are at the end of the book.

25. A chain of sport shops catering to beginning skiers, headquartered in Aspen, Colorado, plans to conduct a study of how much a beginning skier spends on his or her initial purchase of equipment and supplies. Based on these figures, they want to explore the possibility of offering combinations, such as a pair of boots and a pair of skis, to induce customers to buy more. A sample of their cash register receipts revealed these initial purchases:

$140	$ 82	$265	$168	$ 90	$114	$172	$230	$142
86	125	235	212	171	149	156	162	118
139	149	132	105	162	126	216	195	127
161	135	172	220	229	129	87	128	126
175	127	149	126	121	118	172	126	

a. Arrive at a suggested class interval. Use five classes, and let the lower limit of the first class be $80.
b. What would be a better class interval?
c. Organize the data into a frequency distribution.
d. Interpret your findings.

26. A 100-bed hospital in Biloxi, Mississippi, had 1,820 patients during the last year for an annual turnover rate of 18.2 patients per bed (1,820/100 = 18.2). The hospital administrator believes turnover is too low—that is, patients are remaining in the hospital beds too long. Other staff members think that the turnover rate is about average compared with those of other hospitals in the South and Southwest. In order to compare the turnover rate of 18.2 patients per bed with experience in other states, the following data from the American Hospital Association were secured.

State	Turnover rate	State	Turnover rate
Alabama	29	Missouri	29
Arizona	33	Nebraska	26
Arkansas	31	New Mexico	28
District of Columbia	22	North Carolina	26
Florida	29	Oklahoma	29
Georgia	30	South Carolina	28
Kentucky	34	Tennessee	29
Louisiana	30	Texas	31
Maryland	22	Virginia	24
Mississippi	27	West Virginia	27

a. Using formula (2–2), determine the size of the class interval.
b. Tally the turnover rates into a frequency distribution.
c. Draw a histogram.
d. Construct a less-than cumulative frequency polygon.
e. Summarize your findings.

27. The numbers of shareholders for a selected group of large companies (in thousands) are:

Company	Number of shareholders (thousands)	Company	Number of shareholders (thousands)
Pan American World Airways	144	Northeast Utilities	200
General Public Utilities	177	Standard Oil (Indiana)	173
Occidental Petroleum	266	Atlantic Richfield	195
Middle South Utilities	133	Detroit Edison	220
Chrysler Corporation	209	Eastman Kodak	251
Standard Oil of California	264	Dow Chemical	137
Bethlehem Steel	160	Pennsylvania Power	150
Long Island Lighting	143	American Electric Power	262
RCA	246	Ohio Edison	158
Greyhound Corporation	151	Transamerica Corporation	162
Pacific Gas & Electric	239	Columbia Gas System	165
Niagara Mohawk Power	204	International Telephone & Telegraph	223
E. I. du Pont de Nemours	204	Union Electric	158
Westinghouse Electric	195	Virginia Electric and Power	162
Union Carbide	176	Public Service Electric & Gas	225
BankAmerica	175	Consumers Power	161

The numbers of shareholders are to be organized into a frequency distribution and several graphs drawn to portray the distribution.

a. Using seven classes and a lower limit of 130, construct a frequency distribution.
b. Portray the distribution in the form of a frequency polygon.
c. Portray the distribution in a less-than cumulative frequency polygon.
d. Based on the polygon, three out of four (75 percent) of the companies have how many shareholders or less?
e. Write a brief analysis of the number of shareholders based on the frequency distribution and graphs.

28. The scores on a mechanical aptitude test were organized into the following distribution.

Test score	Number of scores
100 up to 120	6
120 up to 140	17
140 up to 160	38
160 up to 180	15
180 up to 200	4

a. Portray the distribution in the form of a histogram.
b. Portray the distribution in the form of a frequency polygon.
c. Using the two charts, interpret the distribution of test scores.

29. The weights of 75 ears of Growfast, an eating corn, were recorded and condensed into the following distribution.

Weight in ounces	Number of ears
16 up to 18	12
18 up to 20	36
20 up to 22	14
22 up to 24	8
24 up to 26	4
26 up to 28	1

a. Portray the weights in a histogram.
b. Show the weights in a frequency polygon.
c. Based on the charts, interpret the distribution of weights.

30. Following are the numbers of games won by each of the 28 major league baseball teams during the 1993 season.

85	80	71	94	76	85	84	69
71	88	68	82	86	95	104	84
73	67	64	85	81	94	59	97
75	87	61	103				

Develop a stem-and-leaf chart.

31. Refer to the numbers of wins in the previous problem.
    a. Organize the data into a frequency distribution. Use a class interval of 10, and let 55 be the lower limit of the first class.
    b. How many games did a typical team win?
    c. Develop a less-than cumulative frequency distribution. How many games did half or more of the teams win?
32. The salaries (in thousands of dollars) of the baseball players on the 1993 opening-day roster and the disabled list of the Cleveland Indians are:

$1,700	$1,600	$1,300	$1,200	$975	$950	$750	$725
625	610	542	500	450	425	400	350
350	335	325	325	300	145	143	130
123	114	109	109	109			

    a. Organize the salary data into a frequency distribution.
    b. Comment on the shape of the distribution.
    c. About 10 percent of the players earn more than what amount? What percent of the players earn less than $150,000?
33. There has been a substantial increase in enrollment at the University of Toledo over the last 15 years. The president has asked Dr. Patsy Scott, Director of Institutional Research, to provide student enrollment figures. Full-time and part-time enrollment figures are shown in the following table. What long- term trends, if any, are indicated? What group

Year	Full-time	Part-time	Total
1979	10,127	8,112	18,239
1980	11,684	8,586	20,270
1981	12,173	8,944	21,117
1982	12,540	8,846	21,386
1983	12,748	8,841	21,589
1984	12,612	8,427	21,039
1985	12,725	8,513	21,238
1986	12,826	8,350	21,176
1987	13,341	8,399	21,740
1988	14,433	8,373	22,806
1989	15,430	8,498	23,928
1990	16,227	8,554	24,781
1991	16,811	8,158	24,989
1992	16,878	7,663	24,541
1993	16,786	7,402	24,188

Source: University of Toledo, Department of Institutional Research, *Resource and Consumption Report,* January 1994, p. 10

accounts for the increase? Draw appropriate charts and graphs to depict the enrollment data.

34. Continuing Exercise 33, Dr. Scott has also been asked by the president to study the ethnicity of the students. The following information is obtained.

Ethnic group	1986 enrollment	1993 enrollment
Unknown	441	392
Native American/Alaskan native	109	172
Asian or Pacific Islander	195	251
Black/non-Hispanic	1,253	1,684
Hispanic	260	365
White/non-Hispanic	8,313	9,843
Nonresident alien	1,297	1,070

Source: The University of Toledo, Department of Institutional Research, *Resource and Consumption Report,* January 1994, p. 25.

a. Draw an appropriate chart showing the percent changes in the various categories from 1986 to 1994. Which groups changed the most?
b. Has there been a change in the makeup of the student body from 1986 to 1993? Compare the percent of each ethnic group for the two years.

35. The number of persons with AIDS per 100,000 population for selected metropolitan areas as of July 1990 were:

	Number with AIDS (per 100,000 population)
Atlanta, Ga.	922
Austin, Tex.	245
Dallas, Tex.	711
Houston, Tex.	1,245
New York, N.Y.	6,565
San Francisco, Calif.	1,935
Washington, D.C.	1,059
West Palm Beach, Fla.	353

Source: Department of Health and Human Services, *HIV/AIDS Surveillance Report.*

Rearrange the AIDS data, and portray them in either a vertical or a horizontal bar chart.

COMPUTER DATA EXERCISES

36. Refer to data set 1, which reports information on homes sold in Florida during the year.
a. Select an appropriate class interval and organize the selling prices into a frequency distribution.
b. Construct a stem-and-leaf chart for the selling prices. What is the typical selling price of a home?
c. Draw a less-than cumulative frequency distribution for the selling price. About what percent of the homes sold for more than $140,000?

37. Refer to data set 2 which reports information on the 28 major league baseball teams for the 1993 season.

a. Organize the information on total team salaries into a frequency distribution. Select an appropriate class interval.
b. What is the "typical" team paying in total salary?
c. Draw a less-than cumulative frequency distribution. Forty percent of the teams are paying less than what amount in total salary? About what percent of teams are paying less than $25,000,000 in salary?
d. Comment on the shape of the distribution. Does it appear that some teams are "out of line" on the high and low sides?
e. Develop a graph that reports the number of games won on the *Y*-axis and the salary on the *X*-axis. Comment on the graph.

38. Refer to data set 3, which reports information on the circulation of 48 magazines.
a. Select an appropriate class interval and organize the information on the circulation of the magazines into a frequency distribution.
b. Comment on the concentration of the data. What is the circulation of a typical magazine? About 75 percent of magazines have a circulation of what amount or less? Comment on the information on the circulation of magazines.

CHAPTER 2 EXAMINATION

The answers are at the end of the chapter.

For Questions 1–10, indicate whether the statement is true or false.

1. The raw data are a listing of all the values.
2. The number of observations in each class is called a frequency distribution.
3. A sample of 85 observations is to be organized into a frequency distribution. The suggested number of classes is 7.
4. Generally speaking, we should construct a frequency distribution with at least 20 classes.
5. A histogram is a graph representing the corresponding frequency distribution.
6. The class midpoint is obtained by adding the lower and upper class limits and dividing by 2.
7. To construct a frequency polygon, we need the class midpoints and the class frequencies.
8. A frequency polygon and a relative frequency distribution are similar in that they are both based on a frequency distribution.
9. The class interval is obtained by subtracting the lower stated limit of a class from the lower stated limit of the next higher class.
10. Relative frequency distributions are developed by dividing each class frequency by the total number of observations.

For questions 11–25, give the letter that represents the correct answer.

11. We constructed the following by tallying the ages of our employees into classes and counting the number of employees in each class.

Age	Number of ages
20 up to 30	16
30 up to 40	25
40 up to 50	51
50 up to 60	80
60 up to 70	20
70 up to 80	8

This arrangement is called:
a. A histogram. *b.* A frequency polygon.
c. An ogive. *d.* A frequency distribution.
e. None of the above.

12. Refer to Question 11. What is the class interval?
a. 50, found by 70 − 20. *b.* 59, found by 79 − 20.
c. 10, found by 30 − 20. *d.* 9, found by 29 − 20.
e. None of the above.

13. Refer to Question 11. What are the lower class limits?
a. 20, 30, 40, etc. *b.* 19.5, 29.5, 39.5, etc.
c. 29, 39, 49, etc. *d.* 24.5, 34.5, 44.5, etc.
e. 25, 35, 45, etc.

14. Refer to Question 11. What is the relative class frequency for the lowest class (20 up to 30)?
a. 16. *b.* 0.08, or 8 percent.
c. 100 percent *d.* 200
e. None of the above.

15. Refer to Question 11. What is the class frequency for the first class?
a. 20 up to 30 *b.* 16.
c. 20 and 29. *d.* Less than 20 and more than 30.
e. None of the above.

16. Using the data in Question 11, the following picture was drawn. The picture is called:
a. A histogram.
b. A frequency polygon.
c. A less-than cumulative frequency polygon.
d. A more-than cumulative frequency polygon.
. None of the above.

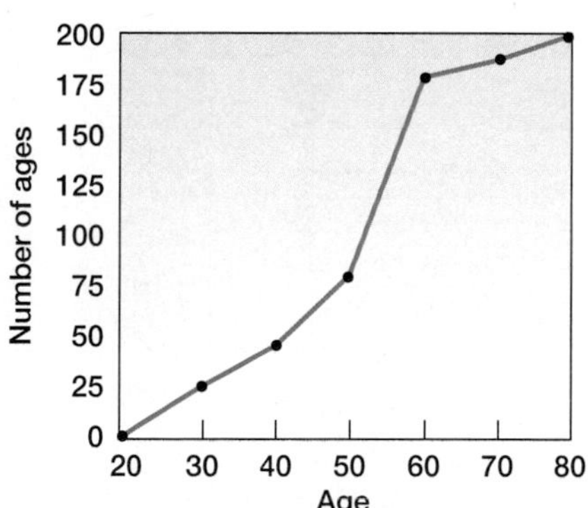

17. Refer to the picture in Question 16. About half of the employees are:
a. 79 or older. *b.* 20 or younger.
c. 51 or younger. *d.* 40 or younger.
e. None of the above.

18. Refer to the picture in Question 16. About 25 percent of the employees are what age or less?
a. 20. *b.* 80.
c. 41. *d.* 52.
e. None of the above.

19. Two distributions are plotted in the following chart. What are the two pictures called?
    a. Frequency polygons. *b.* Relative frequency polygons.
    c. Ogives. *d.* Histograms.
    e. None of the above.

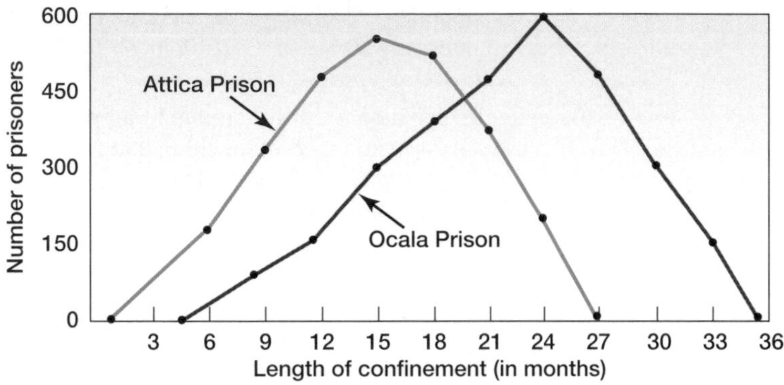

20. Refer to Question 19. In general, is the length of confinement longer in Attica Prison or in Ocala Prison?
    a. Attica Prison. *b.* Ocala Prison.
    c. Cannot tell based on the picture. *d.* None of the above.

We did not examine the following type of chart. It is called a component-part bar chart. Study the chart and then answer Questions 21 and 22 with respect to it.

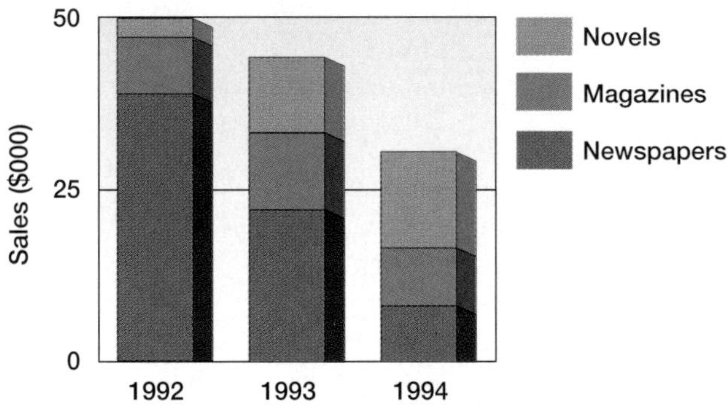

21. Regarding total sales from 1992 to 1994:
    a. Total sales increased. *b.* Total sales decreased.
    c. Total sales stayed about the same. *d.* None of the above.
22. With respect to sales of newspapers from 1992 to 1994:
    a. Newspaper sales declined but in 1994 were a larger proportion of the total compared with 1992.
    b. Newspaper sales declined and in 1994 were a smaller proportion of the total compared with 1992.
    c. Newspaper sales increased from 1992 to 1994.
    d. None of the above.

The following chart depicts the percent changes in CD sales for country-western, symphony, jazz, rock, and background music from 1988 to 1994.

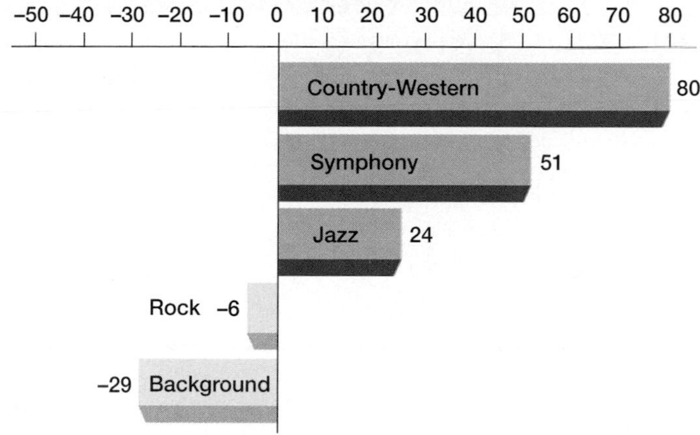

23. What type of music had the largest percent increase in sales from 1988 to 1994?
    a. Country-western.
    b. Jazz.
    c. Rock.
    d. Background.
    e. None of these is correct.
24. Sales of which type of music showed the largest percent decrease?
    a. Rock.
    b. Country-western.
    c. Jazz.
    d. Background.
    e. None of these is correct.
25. Total sales of CDs:
    a. Increased from 1988 to 1994.
    b. Decreased from 1988 to 1994.
    c. Stayed about the same from 1988 to 1994.
    d. Cannot be determined from this chart.
26. Suppose the percentages of the total annual sales of shirts, ties, socks, and robes for 1994 are shown in the following pie chart. Which clothing item had the highest annual sales?
    a. Shirts. *b.* Ties.
    c. Socks. *d.* Robes.
    e. None of the above.

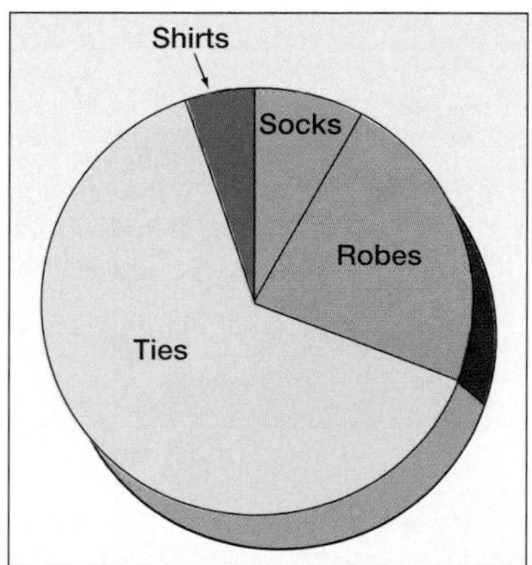

CHAPTER 2 Answers

Self-Review

2–1 1. The raw data.

2.

Production	Number of assemblers
1,400 up to 1,500	2
1,500 up to 1,600	5
1,600 up to 1,700	4
1,700 up to 1,800	3
Total	14

3. Class frequencies.
4. The largest concentration of production is between 1,500 and 1,600 reels. However, 9 out of 14 assemblers produced between 1,500 and 1,700 reels during the week.

2–2 1. *a.* \$215.29, found by (\$3,548 − 2,041) / 7.

b. \$200 (although 8 classes will be needed)

c. \$2,000
\$2,200

2. Unequal size class intervals. Open-ended class.

2–3 1. *a.*

Number of years on circuit	Number of professionals
1 up to 4	3
4 up to 7	4
7 up to 10	2
10 up to 13	2
13 up to 16	1

b.

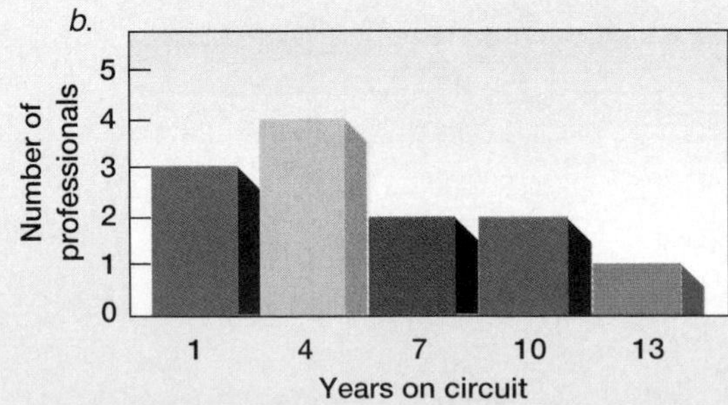

c. 1, 6, 9, 2, and so on.

d. 3.

e. About one third of the tennis professionals have been on the circuit from 4 up to 7 years ($4/12 = 0.33$). More than half have been on the circuit less than 7 years and only one player more than 13 years.

2–4 1.

Stem	Leaf
7	7
8	0 0 1 3 4 8 8
9	1 5 6 6 8 9
10	1 2 4 8
11	2 6

2. The price-earnings ratios are concentrated in the 8 and 9 percent classes. For each class, the price-earnings ratios are distributed somewhat evenly throughout the class.

2–5 1.

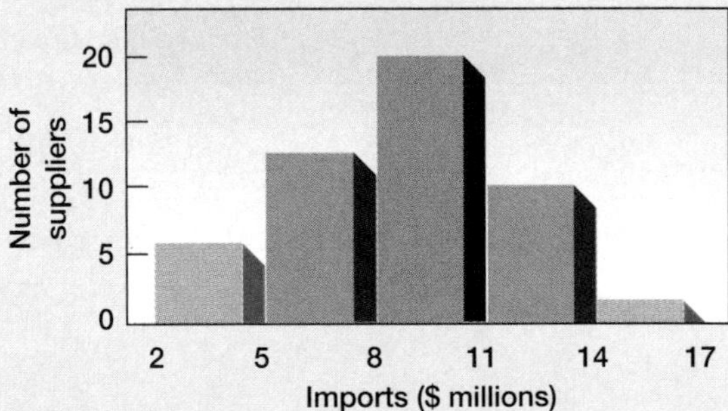

2.

Percent of total
0
10
20
30
40
2
5
8
11
14
17
Imports (\$ millions)

3. The smallest annual sales volume of imports by a supplier is about $2 million, the highest about $17 million. The concentration is between $8 million and $11 million.

2–6

1. A frequency distribution.
2. The cumulative frequency distribution is:

PE ratio	Cumulative number of firms
4 up to 7	7 less than 7
7 up to 10	20 less than 10
10 up to 13	40 less than 13
13 up to 16	51 less than 16
16 up to 19	57 less than 19
19 up to 22	60 less than 22

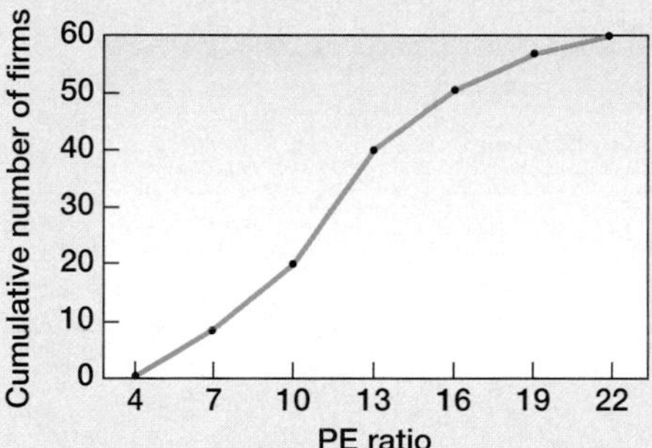

3.

PE ratio	Cumulative number of firms
4 up to 7	60 more than 4
7 up to 10	53 more than 7
10 up to 13	40 more than 10
13 up to 16	20 more than 13
16 up to 19	9 more than 16
19 up to 22	3 more than 19
	0 more than 22

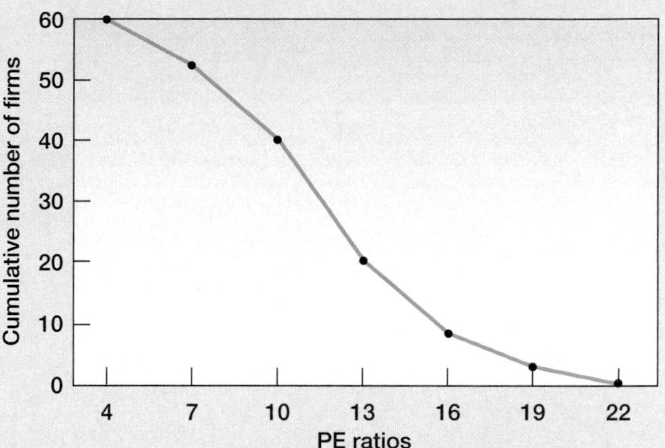

2–7

4. 20, about 51. About 38.

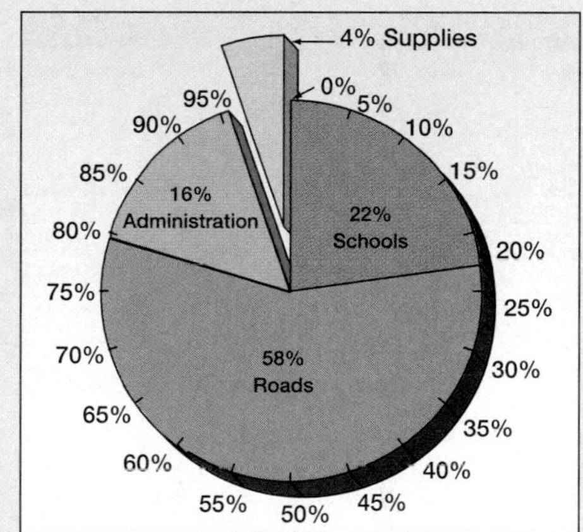

Examination

1. True.
2. False.
3. True.
4. False.
5. True.
6. True.
7. True.
8. True.
9. True.
10. True.
11. *d.*
12. *c.*
13. *a.*
14. *b.*
15. *b.*
16. *c.*
17. *c.*
18. *c.*
19. *a.*
20. *b.*
21. *b.*
22. *b.*
23. *a.*
24. *d.*
25. *d.*
26. *b.*

Chapter 3

Describing Data—Measures of Central Tendency

GOALS

When you have completed this chapter, you will be able to:

1
Calculate the arithmetic mean, median, mode, weighted mean, and the geometric mean.

2
Explain the characteristics, use, advantages, and disadvantages of each measure of central tendency.

3
Identify the position of the arithmetic mean, median, and mode for both a symmetrical distribution and a skewed distribution.

The Merrill Lynch Global Bond Fund specializes in long-term obligations of foreign countries. Given a sample of interest rates earned, what is the arithmetic mean? (See Goal 1 and Example on page 77.)

INTRODUCTION

Chapter 2 began our study of descriptive statistics. In order to transform a mass of raw data into some meaningful form, we organized it into a frequency distribution and portrayed it graphically in a histogram and a frequency polygon. We also examined other tools used to describe data, including line, bar, and pie charts.

This chapter is concerned with yet another way of describing numerical data, namely, a **measure of central tendency,** commonly referred to as an **average.**

As the name implies, a measure of central tendency pinpoints the center of a set of observations. That is, it is a typical value that represents all the values.

> **Measure of central tendency** A single value that represents a set of data. It pinpoints the center of the values.

You are familiar with averages. If you follow the sports scene, you are bombarded with them. For example, the TV announcer notes that Wilt Chamberlain of the Philadelphia 76ers averaged 50.4 points during the 1962 NBA basketball season. Michael Jordan of the Chicago Bulls averaged 32.6 points and led all scorers for seven years prior to his retirement after the 1993 season, according to the *World Almanac.* Some other references to averages:

- According to *Academe,* professors in business and management in the United States have an average annual salary of $75,392, associate professors $59,079, and assistant professors $55,273.
- According to the College Entrance Examination Board, the average mathematics SAT score for Alabama for the past year was 526, for California 484, and for Wisconsin 551. The national average was 478.
- Johnson & Johnson, manufacturers of medical supplies, had an average market price for its common stock last year of $44⅞ compared with $9 in 1984.
- The average cost per mile to operate a motor vehicle is 38.2 cents, according to *Automobile Facts and Figures.*
- Hertz Corporation reports that the annual maintenance and repair cost is $269 for a new car and $565 for a car older than one year.

There is not just one measure of central tendency. We will consider five of them: the arithmetic mean, the weighted mean, the median, the mode, and the geometric mean. We will first calculate the arithmetic mean, also known simply as the mean, of a population and then calculate the mean of a sample selected from a population.

THE POPULATION MEAN

Many studies involve all the population values. For example, if a study were concerned with all the weekly commissions earned by the full-time salespeople employed by New York Carpet World, the entire set of weekly commissions would be considered as a population. Other examples of a population are all the football players on the University of Wisconsin team, all the rainbow trout netted during the

Wyoming Big Sky fishing tournament, all the Mercury Sables coming off the assembly line during the week of October 7–11, and all the students at BYU earning at least a 3.5 grade point average during the past academic year. That is, a population includes all objects or persons being studied.

For raw data, that is, ungrouped data, the population mean is the sum of all the population values divided by the total number of population values. To find the population mean, use the following formula.

$$\text{Population mean} = \frac{\text{Sum of all the values in the population}}{\text{Number of values in the population}}$$

Instead of writing out in words the full directions for computing the population mean (or any other measure), it is more convenient to use the shorthand notation of algebra. The mean of a population in terms of symbols is:

$$\mu = \frac{\Sigma X}{N} \qquad (3\text{–}1)$$

To determine μ: Total the population values and divide by the number of values

where

- μ stands for the population mean. It is mu, the Greek letter for lowercase *m.*
- N is the total number of observations in the population.
- X stands for a particular value.
- Σ is the Greek capital sigma and indicates the operation of adding.
- ΣX stands for the sum of all the Xs.

A parameter is a population value

Any measurable characteristic of a population, such as the mean, is called a **parameter.**

Parameter A measurable characteristic of a population.

EXAMPLE

You are considering purchasing one of several new luxury automobiles priced over $95,000. The 10 automobiles you selected and their prices, top speeds, and EPA-estimated fuel economies are:

Automobile	Price as listed	Top speed	EPA fuel economy (mpg)
Bently Turbo RL	$228,330	137	11
Dinan 850I	123,734	170	11
Ferrari F 40	471,375	197	12
Ferrari 348 Spider	131,000	154	13
Ferrari 512 TR	212,160	187	11
Jaguar XJ 220	608,500	N/A	N/A
Lamborghini Diablo	272,935	204	9
Lotus Esprit, Jim Clark Edition	95,995	158	17
Mercedes-Benz 600 SEL	143,333	156	11
Porsche 911 Turbo 3.6	109,644	174	13

Source: *Car and Driver,* February 1994, pp. 118–119.

These automobiles are the only ones you are considering. So we can think of them as a population (meaning that they consist of all the cars you are interested in).

1. What is the arithmetic mean price?
2. What is the arithmetic mean EPA-estimated fuel economy (miles per gallon) of this population?
3. If you purchased all 10, what would be the total cost?
4. Is this value considered a population parameter?

Solution ▸

1. The arithmetic mean price is \$239,700.60, found by

$$\mu = \frac{\Sigma X}{N} = \frac{\$2,397,006}{10} = \$239,700.60$$

   Because the prices were recorded to the nearest dollar, we should report the population mean as \$239,701.

2. The arithmetic mean number of miles per gallon is 12, found by (note that there are now only nine in the population):

$$\mu = \frac{\Sigma X}{N} = \frac{108}{9} = 12$$

3. \$2,397,006 is the total price of the 10 automobiles.
4. Yes. Because we are considering all the cars of interest, this is a population parameter.

THE SAMPLE MEAN

As explained in Chapter 1, frequently we select a sample from the population in order to find out something about a specific characteristic of the population. The quality assurance department, for example, needs to be assured that the ball bearings being produced have an acceptable outside diameter. It would be very expensive and time-consuming to check the outside diameter of all the bearings being mass-produced. Therefore, a sample of five bearings might be selected and the mean outside diameter of the five bearings calculated in order to estimate the mean diameter of all the bearings produced.

For raw data, that is, ungrouped data, *the mean is the sum of all the values divided by the total number of values.* To find the mean for a sample:

Mean of ungrouped sample data

$$\text{Sample mean} = \frac{\text{Sum of all the values in the sample}}{\text{Number of values in the sample}}$$

The mean of a sample and the mean of a population are computed in the same way, but the shorthand notation used is different. The formula for the mean of a *sample* is:

$$\overline{X} = \frac{\Sigma X}{n} \qquad (3\text{–}2)$$

To determine $\overline{X}$: Sum the sample values and divide by the number of values

where

$\overline{X}$ stands for the sample mean—it is read "X bar."
X stands for a particular value.
Σ is the Greek capital sigma and indicates the operation of adding.

So

ΣX stands for the sum of all the Xs.
n is the total number of values in the sample.

A statistic is a sample value

The mean of a sample, or any other measure based on sample data, is called a **statistic.** If the mean outside diameter of a sample of ball bearings is computed to be 0.625 inches, that sample value is a statistic.

Statistic A measurable characteristic of a sample.

EXAMPLE

The Merrill Lynch Global Bond Fund specializes in long-term obligations of foreign countries. We are interested in the interest rate earned on these obligations. A sample of seven revealed the following.

Issue	Interest rate
Australian government bonds	9.50%
Belgium government bonds	7.25
Canadian government bonds	6.50
French government "B-TAN"	4.75
Buoni Poliennali de Tesora (Italian government bonds)	12.00
Bonos del Estado (Spanish government bonds)	8.30
UK gilts	6.00

Source: *Merrill Lynch Global Bond Fund,* March 31, 1994, pp. 6–7.

What is the arithmetic mean interest rate on this sample of long-term obligations?

Solution ▸ Using formula (3–2), the sample mean is

$$\text{Sample mean} = \frac{\text{Sum of all the values in the sample}}{\text{Number of values in the sample}}$$

$$\overline{X} = \frac{\Sigma X}{n}$$

$$= \frac{9.50 + 7.25 + 6.50 + 4.75 + 12.00 + 8.30 + 6.00}{7}$$

$$= \frac{54.3}{7}$$

$$= 7.76$$

Mean of ungrouped sample data is 7.76 percent

The arithmetic mean of this sample of long-term obligations is 7.76 percent.

Again, we recommend you solve these self-review problems.

SELF-REVIEW 3–1

The answers are at the end of the chapter.

1. The annual incomes of a sample of several middle-management employees at Westinghouse are (to the nearest $100): $42,900, $49,100, $38,300, and $56,800.
  a. Give the formula for the sample mean.
  b. Find the sample mean rounded to the nearest $100.
  c. Is the mean you computed in *b* a statistic or a parameter? Why?
  d. What is your best estimate of the population mean?

2. All the students in advanced Computer Science S411 are considered the population. Their course grades are 92, 96, 61, 86, 79, and 84.
  a. Give the formula for the population mean.
  b. Compute the mean course grade.
  c. Is the mean you computed in *b* a statistic or a parameter? Why?

THE PROPERTIES OF THE ARITHMETIC MEAN

Properties of the mean

The arithmetic mean is a widely used measure of central tendency. It has several properties:

1. Every set of interval-level and ratio-level data has a mean. (Recall from Chapter 1 that interval- and ratio-level data include such measurable data as ages, incomes, and weights, with the distance between numbers being constant.)
2. All the values are included in computing the mean.
3. A set of data has only one mean. The mean is unique. (Later in the chapter we will discover an average that might appear twice, or more than twice, in a set of data.)
4. The mean is a very useful measure for comparing two or more populations. It can, for example, be used to compare the performance of the production employees on the first shift at the Chrysler transmission plant with the performance of those on the second shift.
5. The arithmetic mean is the only measure of central tendency where *the sum of the deviations of each value from the mean will always be zero.* Expressed symbolically:

$$\Sigma(X - \overline{X}) = 0 \qquad (3\text{–}3)$$

Sum of deviations from mean = 0

As an example, the mean of 3, 8, and 4 is 5. Then:

$$\begin{aligned}\Sigma(X - \overline{X}) &= (3 - 5) + (8 - 5) + (4 - 5)\\ &= -2 + 3 - 1\\ &= 0\end{aligned}$$

Mean as a balance point

Thus, we can consider the mean as a balance point for a set of data. To illustrate, suppose we had a long board with the numbers 1, 2, 3, . . . , *n* evenly spaced on it. Suppose three gold bars of equal weight were placed on the board at numbers 3, 4, and 8, and the balance point was set at 5, the mean of the three numbers. We would find that the board balanced perfectly! The deviations below the mean (−3) are equal to the deviations above the mean (+3). Shown schematically:

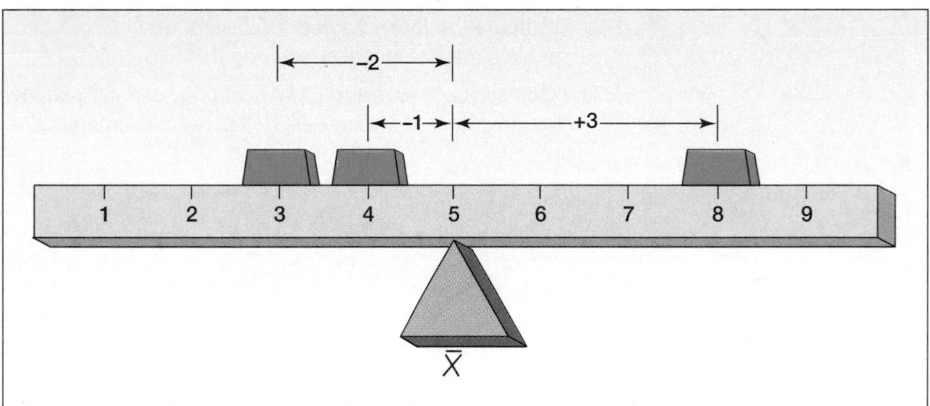

Mean unduly affected by unusually large or small values

The mean does have several disadvantages, however. Recall that the mean uses the value of every item in a sample, or population, in its computation. If one or two of these items is either extremely large or extremely small, the mean might not be an appropriate average to represent the data. For example, suppose the annual incomes of a small group of stockbrokers at Merrill Lynch are $62,900, $61,600, $62,500, $60,800, and $1.2 million. The mean income is $289,560. Obviously, it is not representative of this group because all but one broker has an income in the $60,000 to $63,000 range. One income ($1.2 million) is unduly affecting the mean.

Cannot determine mean for open-ended data

The mean is also inappropriate if there is an *open-ended class* for data tallied into a frequency distribution. If a frequency distribution has the open-ended class "$100,000 and more," and there are 10 persons in that class, we really do not know whether their incomes are close to $100,000, $500,000, or $16 million. Since we lack information about their incomes, the arithmetic mean income for this open-ended distribution cannot be determined.

EXERCISES

The answers to the odd-numbered exercises are at the end of the book.

1. What are the differences between a sample mean and a population mean?
2. List the characteristics of the mean.
3. *a.* Compute the mean of the following sample values: 5, 9, 4, 10.
   b. Show that $\Sigma(X - \bar{X}) = 0$.
4. *a.* Compute the mean of the following sample values: 1.3, 7.0, 3.6, 4.1, 5.0.
   b. Show that $\Sigma(X - \bar{X}) = 0$.
5. Compute the mean of the following sample values: 16.25, 12.91, 14.58.
6. Compute the mean hourly wage paid to carpenters who earned the following wages: $15.40, $20.10, $18.75, $22.76, $30.67, $18.00, respectively.

7. There are 10 salespeople employed by Midtown Ford. The numbers of new cars sold last month by the respective salespeople were: 15, 23, 4, 19, 18, 10, 10, 8, 28, 19.
   a. Compute the mean number of cars sold.
   b. Is this a sample statistic or a population parameter?
8. The accounting department at a mail-order company counted the following numbers of incoming calls per day to the company's toll-free number during a seven-day period: 14, 24, 19, 31, 36, 26, 17.
   a. Compute the mean number of calls per day.
   b. Is this a sample statistic or a population parameter?
9. The Cambridge Power and Light Company selected 20 residential customers. Following are the amounts, to the nearest dollar, the customers were charged for electrical service last month:

54	48	58	50	25	47	75	46	60	70
67	68	39	35	56	66	33	62	65	67

   a. Compute the mean monthly charge.
   b. Is this a sample statistic or a population parameter?
10. The personnel director at Mercy Hospital began a study of the overtime hours of the registered nurses. Fifteen RNs were selected at random, and these overtime hours during June were noted:

13	13	12	15	7	15	5	12
6	7	12	10	9	13	12	

   a. Compute the mean number of overtime hours.
   b. Is this a sample statistic or a population parameter?
11. The National Safety Council released these figures on the principal types of accidental death.

Year	Motor vehicle	Falls	Firearms
1970	54,633	16,926	2,406
1975	45,853	14,896	2,380
1980	53,172	13,294	1,955
1985	45,901	12,001	1,649
1990	45,300	12,400	1,400
1991	43,500	12,200	1,400
1992	40,300	12,400	1,400
1995*	41,000	12,500	1,350

*Estimated.

   a. Calculate the annual arithmetic mean number of accidental deaths due to motor vehicles.
   b. Calculate the annual arithmetic mean number of accidental deaths caused by firearms.
12. The worldwide airline fatalities since 1980, according to the National Safety Council, are:

Year	Number of passenger deaths	Year	Number of passenger deaths
1980	814	1987	890
1981	362	1988	699
1982	764	1989	817
1983	809	1990	440
1984	223	1991	510
1985	1,066	1992	990
1986	331		

What is the annual arithmetic mean number of passenger deaths worldwide since 1980?

THE MEDIAN

It has been pointed out that for data containing one or two very large or very small values, the arithmetic mean may not be representative. The center point for such problems can be better described using a measure of central tendency called the **median.**

Median of ungrouped data

To illustrate the need for a measure of central tendency other than the arithmetic mean, suppose you are seeking to buy a condominium in Palm Aire. Your real estate agent said that the average price of the units currently available is $110,000. Would you still want to look? If you had budgeted your maximum purchase price between $60,000 and $75,000, you might think they were out of your price range. However, checking the individual prices of the units might change your mind. They are $60,000, $65,000, $70,000, $80,000, and a superdeluxe penthouse costs $275,000. The arithmetic mean price is $110,000, as the real estate agent reported, but one price ($275,000) is pulling the arithmetic mean upward, causing it to be an unrepresentative average. It does seem that a price between $65,000 and $75,000 is a more typical or representative average, and it is. In cases such as this, the median provides a more accurate measure of central tendency.

Median: Value of middle item

> **Median** The midpoint of the values after they have been ordered from the smallest to the largest, or the largest to the smallest. There are as many values above the median as below it in the data array.

The median price of the units available is $70,000. To determine this, the prices were ordered from low ($60,000) to high ($275,000) and the middle value ($70,000) selected.

Prices ordered from low to high		Prices ordered from high to low
$ 60,000		$275,000
65,000		80,000
70,000	←Median→	70,000
80,000		65,000
275,000		60,000

Median unaffected by extreme values

Note that there are the same number of prices below the median of $70,000 as above it. The median is, therefore, unaffected by extremely low or high observations. Had the highest price been $90,000, or $300,000, or even $1 million, the median price would still be $70,000. Likewise, had the lowest price been $20,000 or $50,000, the median price would still be $70,000.

In the previous illustration there is an *odd* number of observations (five). How is the median determined for an *even* number of observations? As before, the observations are ordered. Then the usual practice is to find the arithmetic mean of the two middle observations. Note that for an even number of observations, the median may not be one of the given values.

EXAMPLE

The five-year annualized total returns of the six top-performing stock mutual funds with emphasis on aggressive growth are:

Name of fund	Annualized total return
PBHG Growth	28.5%
Dean Witter Developing Growth	17.2
AIM Aggressive Growth	25.4
Twentieth Century Giftrust	28.6
Robertson Stevens Emerging Growth	22.6
Seligman Frontier A	21.0

Source: *Kiplinger's Personal Finance Magazine,* May 1994, p. 18.

What is the median annualized total return?

Solution ► Note that the number of returns is *even* (6). As before, the returns are first ordered from low to high. Then the two middle returns are identified. The arithmetic mean of the two middle observations gives us the median return. Arranging from low to high:

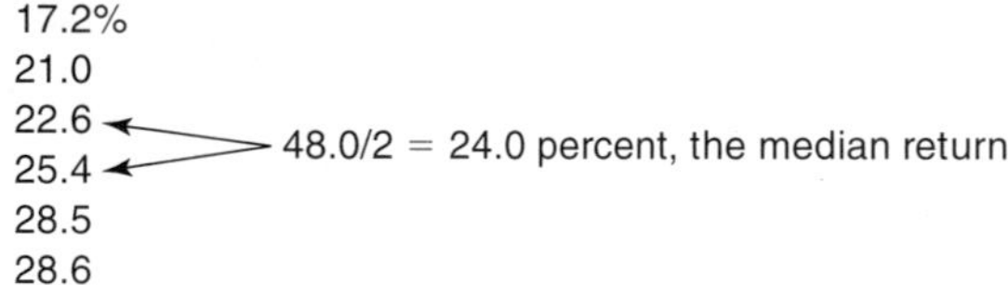

Notice that the median is not one of the values. Also, half of the returns are below the median and half are above it.

Properties of the Median

1. The median is unique; that is, like the mean, there is only one median for a set of data.
2. To determine the median, arrange the data from low to high, and find the value of the middle observation.
3. It is not affected by extremely large or small values and is therefore a valuable measure of central tendency when such values do occur.

4. It can be computed for an open-ended frequency distribution if the median does not lie in an open-ended class. (We will show the computations for the median of data grouped in a frequency distribution shortly.)

Median can be determined for all levels of data except nominal

5. It can be computed for ratio-level, interval-level, and ordinal-level data. (Recall from Chapter 1 that ordinal-level data can be ranked from low to high—such as the responses "excellent," "very good," "good," "fair," and "poor" to a question on a marketing survey.) To use a simple illustration, suppose five people rated a new fudge bar. One person thought it was excellent, one rated it very good, one called it good, one rated it fair, and one considered it poor. The median response is "good." Half of the responses are above "good"; the other half are below it.

SELF-REVIEW 3–2

The answers are at the end of the chapter.

1. A sample of single persons in Towson, Texas, receiving social security payments revealed these monthly benefits: $426, $299, $290, $687, $480, $439, and $565.
   a. What is the median monthly benefit?
   b. How many observations are below the median? Above it?
2. The numbers of work stoppages in the automobile industry for selected months are 6, 0, 10, 14, 8, and 0.
   a. What is the median number of stoppages?
   b. How many observations are below the median? Above it?

THE MODE

The **mode** is another measure of central tendency.

Mode The value of the observation that appears most frequently.

EXAMPLE

Mode of ungrouped data

The annual salaries of quality-control managers in selected states are:

Arizona	$35,000	Illinois	$58,000	Ohio	$50,000
California	49,100	Louisiana	60,000	Tennessee	60,000
Colorado	60,000	Maryland	60,000	Texas	71,400
Florida	60,000	Massachusetts	40,000	West Virginia	60,000
Idaho	40,000	New Jersey	65,000	Wyoming	55,000

What is the modal annual salary?

Solution ▶ A perusal of the salaries reveals that the annual salary of $60,000 appears more often (six times) than any other salary. The mode is, therefore, $60,000.

The mode is especially useful in describing nominal and ordinal levels of measurement. As an example of its use for nominal-level data, a company has developed five bath oils. Chart 3–1 shows the results of a marketing survey designed to find out which bath oil consumers prefer. The largest number of respondents favored Lamoure, as evidenced by the highest bar. Thus, Lamoure is the mode.

CHART 3–1 **Number of Respondents Favoring Various Bath Oils**

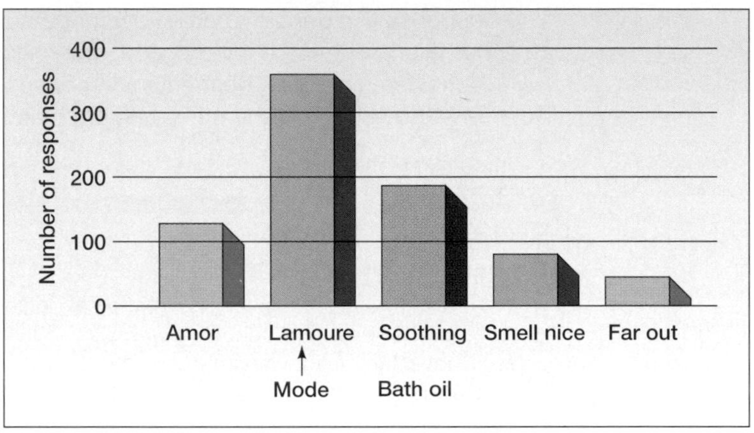

In summary, we can determine the mode for all levels of data—nominal, ordinal, interval, and ratio. The mode also has the advantage of not being affected by extremely high or low values. Like the median, it can be used as a measure of central tendency for open-ended distributions.

Disadvantages of the mode

The mode does have a number of disadvantages, however, that cause it to be used less frequently than the mean or median. For many sets of data, there is no mode because no value appears more than once. For example, there is no mode for this set of price data: $19, $21, $23, $20, and $18. Since every value is different, however, it could be argued that every value is the mode. Conversely, for some data sets there is more than one mode. Suppose the ages of a group are 22, 26, 27, 27, 31, 35, and 35. Both the ages 27 and 35 are modes. Thus, this grouping of ages is referred to as *bimodal* (having two modes). One would question the use of two modes to represent the central tendency of this set of age data.

A COMPUTER SOLUTION

A computer can be used to organize a mass of raw data and determine various measures of central tendency.

EXAMPLE

What are the mean and the median annual salaries for professors in the 160 colleges selected for study in Chapter 2?

Solution ▸

The mean and the median annual salaries of professors from Chapter 2, Table 2–1, are computed using the MINITAB statistical software system. Recall that there are 160 observations, so the calculation by hand or even with a calculator would be tedious. The MINITAB procedure required is "describe" or just "desc." The salaries of the professors are located in the column labeled 'Salary.' We can see that the sample mean salary is $54,030 and the median salary is $52,550. There is other information given in the following computer output that will be discussed in Chapter 4.

```
MTB > desc 'Salary'

              N      MEAN     MEDIAN     TRMEAN     STDEV     SEMEAN
Salary      160     54.03      52.55      53.55     13.76       1.09

            MIN       MAX         Q1         Q3
Salary    26.00     96.50      44.65      61.80
```

WEIGHTED MEAN

The importance and calculation of the weighted mean can be best described using an example.

EXAMPLE

Carter Construction pays hourly employees either $6.50, $7.50, or $8.50 an hour. It might be concluded that the arithmetic mean hourly wage is $7.50, found by ($6.50 + $7.50 + $8.50)/3. However, this is true only if there are the *same* number of employees earning $6.50, $7.50, and $8.50 an hour. However, suppose 14 employees earn $6.50 an hour, 10 are paid $7.50, and 2 get $8.50. To find the mean, $6.50 is *weighted,* or multiplied, by 14; $7.50 is weighted by 10; and $8.50 is weighted by 2. The resulting average is aptly called the **weighted mean.**

Weighted mean: Each value weighted according to its importance

In general, the weighted mean of a set of numbers designated $X_1, X_2, X_3, \ldots, X_n$ with corresponding weights $w_1, w_2, w_3, \ldots, w_n$ is computed by:

$$\overline{X}_w = \frac{w_1X_1 + w_2X_2 + w_3X_3 + \cdots + w_nX_n}{w_1 + w_2 + w_3 + \cdots + w_n} \qquad (3\text{–}4)$$

This may be shortened to:

$$\overline{X}_w = \frac{\Sigma(w \cdot X)}{\Sigma w}$$

What is the weighted mean hourly wage?

Solution ► For the Carter Construction problem:

$$\overline{X}_w = \frac{14(\$6.50) + 10(\$7.50) + 2(\$8.50)}{14 + 10 + 2}$$

$$= \frac{\$183}{26}$$

$$= \$7.038$$

The weighted mean hourly wage is $7.04.

SELF-REVIEW 3–3

The answers are at the end of the chapter.

Springers sold 95 Antonelli men's suits for the regular price of $400. For the spring sale the suits were reduced to $200, and 126 were sold. At the final clearance, the price was reduced to $100, and the remaining 79 suits were sold.

a. What was the weighted mean price of an Antonelli suit?

b. Springers paid $200 a suit for the 300 suits. Comment on the store's profit on the suits if a salesperson receives a $25 commission for each one sold.

EXERCISES

The answers to the odd-numbered exercises are at the end of the book.

13. Calico Pizza sells colas in three sizes: small, medium, and large. The small size costs $0.50, the medium $0.75, and the large $1.00. Yesterday 20 small, 50 medium, and 30 large colas were sold. What was the weighted mean price per cola?
14. A specialty bookstore concentrates mainly on used books. Paperbacks are $1.00 each, and hardcover books are $3.50. Of the 50 books sold Tuesday morning, 40 were paperback and the rest were hardcover. What was the weighted mean price of a book?
15. Metropolitan Hospital employs 200 persons on the nursing staff. Fifty are nurse's aides, 50 are practical nurses, and 100 are registered nurses. Nurse's aides receive $8 an hour, practical nurses $10 an hour, and registered nurses $14 an hour. What is the weighted mean hourly wage?
16. Andrews and Associates specialize in corporate law. They charge $100 an hour for researching a case, $75 an hour for consultations, and $200 an hour for writing a brief. Last week one of the associates spent 10 hours consulting with her client, 10 hours researching the case, and 20 hours writing the brief. What was the weighted mean hourly charge for her legal services?

THE GEOMETRIC MEAN

Two uses of the geometric mean

There are two main uses of the geometric mean: (1) to average percents, indexes, and relatives; and (2) to determine the average percent increase in sales, production, or other business or economic series from one time period to another.

The **geometric mean** of a set of n positive numbers is defined as the nth root of the product of the n numbers. Thus, the formula for the geometric mean is written:

$$GM = \sqrt[n]{(X_1)(X_2)(X_3)\cdots(X_n)} \quad (3\text{–}5)$$

Note: If one of the numbers is zero or negative, the geometric mean cannot be computed.

EXAMPLE

To illustrate the use of the geometric mean in averaging percents, suppose the profits earned by the Atkins Construction Company on four projects were 3, 2, 4, and 6 percent, respectively. What is the geometric mean profit? (Note: $n = 4$, the number of observations.)

Solution ►

$$GM = \sqrt[n]{(X_1)(X_2)(X_3) \cdots (X_n)}$$
$$= \sqrt[4]{(3)(2)(4)(6)}$$
$$= \sqrt[4]{144}$$

A calculator is very useful

The geometric mean percent is therefore the fourth root of 144. If a calculator with either a $\sqrt[x]{y}$ or y^x key is available, the geometric mean can be quickly determined:

		Display
	Multiply 3 x 2 x 4 x 6	144
	Depress $\sqrt[x]{y}$ *or* y^x key*	
Number of observations	Depress 4[†] =	3.464101615

*On some calculators you must depress the 2nd function mode before depressing y^x.

[†]If the key is y^x, the reciprocal of n must be used. The reciprocal of 4 is $\frac{1}{4}$ = .25.

The geometric mean profit is 3.46 percent.

Geometric mean—a more conservative average

The arithmetic mean profit is 3.75 percent, found by $(3 + 2 + 4 + 6)/4$. Although the profit of 6 percent is not extremely large, it is weighting the arithmetic mean upward. The geometric mean of 3.46 gives a more conservative profit figure because it is not so heavily weighted by extreme values. It will be, in fact, either equal to or less than the arithmetic mean.

EXAMPLE

As another example, suppose the prices of five computer stocks increased by 37.1, 1140.0, 0.927, 2.7, and 842.0 percent, respectively, since 1991. What is the geometric mean percent increase in the price of the five stocks?

Solution ► Using a calculator:

	Display
Multiply 37.1 × 1,140 × .927 × 2.7 × 842	89132143
Depress $\sqrt[x]{y}$ or y^x key*	
Depress 5[†] =	38.9051299

*On some calculators you must depress the 2nd function mode before depressing y^x.

[†]Use the reciprocal of 5, or ⅕ = .20, if y^x key is used.

The geometric mean percent increase is 38.9 percent. Contrast the geometric mean of 38.9 percent with the arithmetic mean of 404.5 percent, found by 2,022.727/5. Again, it is evident that the geometric mean is not so highly influenced by extreme values as is the arithmetic mean.

Geometric mean gives the correct average percent increase

Now to explore the second application of the geometric mean: determining the average percent increase in sales, exports, or other business series from one time period to another. The formula for the geometric mean as applied to this type of problem is:

$$GM = \sqrt[n-1]{\frac{\text{Value at end of period}}{\text{Value at beginning of period}}} - 1 \qquad (3\text{–}6)$$

EXAMPLE

The population of Haarlan, Alaska, in 1985 was 2 persons, and in 1995 it was 22. What was the average annual percentage increase during this period?

Solution ▸ Note that there is an 11-year span. Thus, $n = 11$. The 11 years are 1985, 1986, 1987, 1988, 1989, 1990, 1991, 1992, 1993, 1994, and 1995. Even though there are 11 years involved, there are only 10 annual rates of change, namely, from 1985 to 1986, from 1986 to 1987, and so forth up to the change from 1994 to 1995.

Formula (3–6) for the geometric mean as applied to this type of problem is:

$$GM = \sqrt[n-1]{\frac{\text{Population at end of period}}{\text{Population at beginning of period}}} - 1$$

$$= \sqrt[11-1]{\frac{22}{2}} - 1$$

$$= \sqrt[10]{\frac{22}{2}} - 1$$

Problem solved quickly using a calculator

Using a calculator:

	Display
$22 \div 2$	11
Depress $\sqrt[x]{y}$ or y^x key*	
Depress 10† =	1.270981615
Depress −1 =	.270981615

*On some calculators you must depress the 2nd function mode before depressing y^x.
†If y^x key is on the calculator, use the reciprocal of 10, or 1⁄10 = .1.

The final value of .270981615 is multiplied by 100 to express it as a percent. The geometric mean annual percent increase in Haarlan's population is approximately 27 percent.

SELF-REVIEW 3–4

The answers are at the end of the chapter.

1. The annual dividends, in percent, of four oil stocks are: 4.91, 5.75, 8.12, and 21.60.
   a. Find the geometric mean dividend.
   b. Find the arithmetic mean dividend.
   c. Is the arithmetic mean equal to or greater than the geometric mean? It should be.
2. Production of Cablos trucks increased from 23,000 units in 1975 to 120,520 units in 1995. Find the geometric mean annual percent increase.

EXERCISES

The answers to the odd-numbered exercises are at the end of the book.

17. *a.* Under what conditions is the geometric mean more representative of a set of data than the arithmetic mean?
    b. Under what conditions, if any, will the geometric mean be *larger* than the arithmetic mean?
18. Compute the geometric mean of the following values: 8, 12, 14, 26, 5.
19. Compute the geometric mean of the following values: 2, 8, 6, 4, 10, 6, 8, 4.
20. Seldom I. Darenfest and Associates Ltd. stated that in 1988 $3.9 billion was spent by hospitals on computer systems. It is estimated that by 1998 hospital spending on computers will rise to $13 billion. If spending does rise to $13 billion by 1998, what will be the annual geometric mean percent increase from 1988 to 1998?
21. The high common stock prices for the Chevron Corporation from 1991 to 1993 were: 1991, $80⅛; 1992, $75⅜; 1993, $98⅜. What is the geometric mean annual high price for the three years? (Source: Chevron Corporation, *Annual Report,* 1994, p. 60.)

THE MEAN, MEDIAN, AND MODE OF GROUPED DATA

Quite often data on incomes, ages, and so on are grouped and presented in the form of a frequency distribution. It is usually impossible to secure the original raw data.

Thus, if we are interested in a typical value to represent the data, we must *estimate* it based on the frequency distribution.

The Arithmetic Mean

Arithmetic mean of grouped data

To approximate the arithmetic mean of data organized into a frequency distribution, recall that the observations in each class are represented by the *midpoint* of the class. The mean of a sample of data organized in a frequency distribution is computed by:

$$\overline{X} = \frac{\Sigma fX}{n} \tag{3–7}$$

where:

- $\overline{X}$ is the designation for the arithmetic mean.
- X is the mid-value, or midpoint, of each class.
- f is the frequency in each class.
- fX is the frequency in each class times the midpoint of the class.
- ΣfX is the sum of these products.
- n is the total number of frequencies.

EXAMPLE

The computations for the arithmetic mean of data grouped into a frequency distribution will be shown using the annual salaries of professors in four-year colleges. These data are repeated below.

Average annual salary ($ thousands)	Number of colleges
$20 up to $ 30	4
30 up to 40	20
40 up to 50	41
50 up to 60	44
60 up to 70	29
70 up to 80	16
80 up to 90	2
90 up to 100	4
Total	160

What is the arithmetic mean average annual salary of the professors?

Solution

▶ It is assumed that the midpoint of the first class ($25,000) represents the four salaries of the professors in the "$20,000 up to $30,000" class. The midpoint of $25,000 was computed by ($20,000 + $30,000)/2. Because the frequency for this class is 4, to find fX we multiply 4 × $25,000 = $100,000. This process is continued for all the classes. Adding the fX column in Table 3–1 gives ΣfX = $8,700 (in $ thousands). Dividing that sum by 160 results in the arithmetic mean annual salary.

TABLE 3–1 Average Annual Salaries of Professors at 160 Universities

Average annual salary ($ thousands)	Number of universities, f	Midpoint, X	Frequency times midpoint, fX
$20 up to $ 30	4	$25	$ 100
30 up to 40	20	35	700
40 up to 50	41	45	1,845
50 up to 60	44	55	2,420
60 up to 70	29	65	1,885
70 up to 80	16	75	1,200
80 up to 90	2	85	170
90 up to 100	4	95	380
Total	$n = 160$		$\Sigma fX = \$8,700$

Solving for the arithmetic mean of the annual salaries of professors using formula (3–7):

$$\overline{X} = \frac{\Sigma fX}{n}$$

$$= \frac{\$8,700}{160}$$

$$= \$54.375 \text{ (in \$ thousands)}$$

Note that the arithmetic mean of the salary data grouped into a frequency distribution may be different from the mean calculated using the raw data in Table 3–1. This is because grouping results in some loss of information. The values in a particular class are assumed to average at the midpoint of that class, and this is usually not exactly true. Thus, the mean salary based on Table 3–1 ($54,375) is slightly different from that computed using the MINITAB system ($54,030). The difference is only 0.006 or 0.6 percent. Because of this slight discrepancy, however, we should say that the arithmetic mean of the grouped salaries ($54,375) is merely an *estimate* of the mean of the ungrouped data.

SELF-REVIEW 3–5

The answers are at the end of the chapter.

The net incomes of a sample of large importers of antiques were organized into the following table:

Net income ($ millions)	Number of importers
$ 2 up to $ 6	1
6 up to 10	4
10 up to 14	10
14 up to 18	3
18 up to 22	2

a. What is the table called?
b. Based on the distribution, what is the estimate of the arithmetic mean net income?

EXERCISES

The answers to the odd-numbered exercises are at the end of the book.

22. When we compute the mean of a frequency distribution, why do we refer to this as an *estimated* mean?
23. Determine the estimated mean of the following frequency distribution.

Class	Frequency
0 up to 5	2
5 up to 10	7
10 up to 15	12
15 up to 20	6
20 up to 25	3

24. Determine the estimated mean of the following frequency distribution.

Class	Frequency
20 up to 30	7
30 up to 40	12
40 up to 50	21
50 up to 60	18
60 up to 70	12

25. The selling prices of a sample of 60 antiques sold in Erie, Pennsylvania last month were organized into the following frequency distribution.

Selling price ($ thousands)	Frequency
$ 70 up to $ 80	3
80 up to 90	7
90 up to 100	18
100 up to 110	20
110 up to 120	12

Estimate the mean selling price.

26. FM radio station WLQR recently changed its format from easy listening to contemporary. A recent sample of 50 listeners revealed the following age distribution. Estimate the mean age of the listeners.

Age	Frequency
20 up to 30	1
30 up to 40	15
40 up to 50	22
50 up to 60	8
60 up to 70	4

The Median

Median: Half the values are above it, half below

Recall that the median is defined as the value below which half of the values lie and above which the other half of the values lie. Since the raw data have been organized into a frequency distribution, some of the information is not identifiable. As a result, we cannot determine the exact median. It can be estimated, however, by (1) locating the class in which the median lies and then (2) interpolating within that class to arrive at the median. The rationale for this approach is that the members of the median class are assumed to be evenly spaced throughout the class.

EXAMPLE

The problem involving the annual salaries of professors at 160 colleges is used again to show the procedure for estimating the median (see Table 3–2). The cumulative frequencies in the right column will be used shortly.

TABLE 3–2 **Annual Salaries of Professors**

Average annual salary ($ thousands)	Number of colleges, *f*	Cumulative frequency, *CF*
$20 up to $ 30	4	4
30 up to 40	20	24
40 up to 50	41	65
50 up to 60	44	109
60 up to 70	29	138
70 up to 80	16	154
80 up to 90	2	156
90 up to 100	4	160

What is the median annual salary?

Solution ▶ The average annual salaries of professors at 160 universities have been arranged in ascending order in Table 3–2. It is common practice to locate the middle observation by dividing the total number of observations (schools) by 2. In this case $n/2 = 160/2 = 80$.

The class containing the 80th college is located by referring to the cumulative frequency column in Table 3–2. Note that 65 colleges have an average annual salary for professors less than $50,000, and 109 colleges have an average annual salary of less than $60,000. Hence, the 80th college pays a professor in the range $50,000 up to $60,000. We have, therefore, located the median salary of professors somewhere between the two limits of $50,000 and $60,000.

To interpolate in the "$50,000 up to $60,000" class, recall that the salaries are assumed to be evenly distributed between the lower ($50,000) and upper ($60,000) class limits. There are 15 average annual salaries between the 65th and 80th salaries. The median is therefore, $15/44$ of the distance between $50,000 and $60,000. That distance is $10,000. Thus $15/44$ of $10,000 is added to the lower limit of $50,000 to give $53,409, the estimated median salary.

Shown schematically:

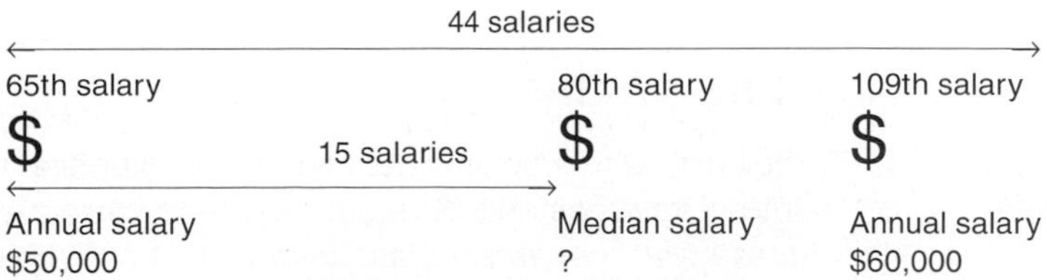

We could use the following formula to determine the median of data grouped into a frequency distribution.

$$\text{Median} = L + \frac{\frac{n}{2} - CF}{f}(i) \qquad (3\text{–}8)$$

where L is the lower limit of the class containing the median, which is \$50,000. There are 160 colleges in the sample, so $n = 160$. CF is the cumulative number of salaries preceding the median class, (65), f is the frequency in the median class (44), and i is the class interval of the class containing the median. Substituting these values,

$$\begin{aligned}\text{Median} &= L + \frac{\frac{n}{2} - CF}{f}(i)\\ &= \$50{,}000 + \frac{\frac{160}{2} - 65}{44}(\$10{,}000)\\ &= \$50{,}000 + \$3{,}409\\ &= \$53{,}409 \text{ (same as computed previously)}\end{aligned}$$

The assumption underlying the approximation of the median—that the frequencies in the median class are distributed evenly between \$50,000 and \$60,000—may not be correct. Therefore, it is safer to say that *about* half of the annual salaries are less than \$53,409 and the other half more than \$53,409. The median estimated from data grouped into a frequency distribution and the median of ungrouped data will usually differ by a small amount. In this case the median of grouped data is \$53,409 and the median of ungrouped data is \$52,550. (See the MINITAB output on page 85.) This difference is less than two percent.

Median can be determined for distributions having open ends.

A final note: The median is based only on the frequencies and the class limits of the median class. The open-ended classes that occur at the extremes are rarely needed. Therefore, the median of a frequency distribution having open ends can be determined. The arithmetic mean of a frequency distribution with an open-ended class cannot be accurately computed—unless, of course, the midpoints of the open-ended classes are estimated. Further, the median can be determined if *percentage frequencies* are given instead of the actual frequencies. This is because the median is the value with 50 percent of the distribution above it and 50 percent below it and does not depend on actual counts. The percents are considered substitutes for the actual frequencies. In a sense, they are actual frequencies whose total is 100.0. Problem 2 in Self-Review 3–6 has both open-end and percentage frequencies.

The Mode

Class midpoint—estimated mode

Recall that the mode is defined as the value that occurs most often. For data grouped into a frequency distribution, the mode can be approximated by the *midpoint of the class with the largest class frequency.* For Problem 2 in Self-Review 3–6, the modal

SELF-REVIEW 3–6

The answers are at the end of the chapter.

1. A sample of the daily production of transceivers at Scott Electronics was organized into the following distribution.

Daily production	Frequency
80 up to 90	5
90 up to 100	9
100 up to 110	20
110 up to 120	8
120 up to 130	6
130 up to 140	2

Estimate the median daily production.

2. The net sales of a sample of small stamping plants were organized into the following percentage frequency distribution.

Net sales ($ millions)	Percent of total
1 up to 4	13
4 up to 7	14
7 up to 10	40
10 up to 13	23
13 and over	10

a. What is the median net sales?
b. Interpret this sales figure.

net sales is found by first locating the class with the greatest percentage. It is the "7 up to 10" class because it has the largest percentage (40). The midpoint of that class ($8.5 million) is the estimated mode. This indicates that more stamping plants had net sales of $8.5 million than any other amount. If the raw data were available, the value appearing most often would probably be slightly different from $8.5 million.

Bimodal—having two modes

Two values may occur a large number of times. The distribution is then called *bimodal.* Suppose the ages of a sample of workers are 22, 27, 30, 30, 30, 30, 34, 58, 60, 60, 60, 60, and 65. The two modes are 30 years and 60 years. Often two points of concentration develop because the population being sampled is probably not homogeneous. In this illustration, the population might be composed of two distinct groups—one a group of relatively young employees who have been recently hired to meet the increased demand for a product, and the other a group of older employees who have been with the company a long time.

If a large number of workers were sampled, the distribution of their ages when plotted might appear as shown in Chart 3–2. Note that the two peaks need not be exactly equal in height in order for us to consider the distribution bimodal.

As shown in the chart, the median age is approximately 50 years. This would not be a representative age for those recently hired. Neither would the older group of employees consider it a typical age. Thus, a logical decision would be to divide the employees into two distinct groups before continuing the analysis of the data.

CHART 3–2 **A Bimodal Distribution**

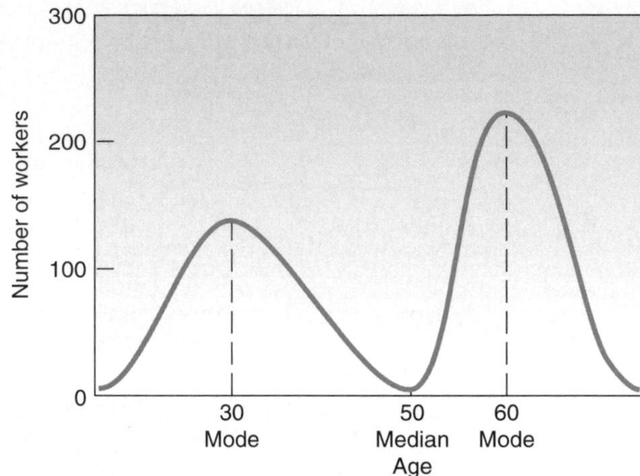

If the set of data has more than two modes, the distribution is referred to as being *multimodal.* In such cases we would probably not consider any of the modes as being representative of the central value of the data.

EXERCISES

The answers to the odd-numbered exercises are at the end of the book.

27. Refer to Exercise 23. Compute the median. What is the mode? Explain the meaning of the median.
28. Refer to Exercise 24. Compute the median. What is the mode?
29. The ages of newly hired, unskilled employees were grouped into the following distribution:

Age	Number
18 up to 21	4
21 up to 24	8
24 up to 27	11
27 up to 30	20
30 up to 33	7

a. Compute the median age. What is the meaning of this figure?
b. What is the modal age?

30. A sample of light trucks owned by Alpers Light Trucking Company revealed these mileages per gallon of diesel fuel used:

Mileage	Number of trucks
8 up to 10	2
10 up to 12	5
12 up to 14	10
14 up to 16	8
16 up to 18	3
18 up to 20	2

a. What is the median mileage per gallon of fuel used?
b. What is the modal mileage? What is the meaning of this figure?

31. We are interested in the following distribution of the number of new AIDS cases among males and females by age.

Age	Number of new cases	
	Males	Females
13 up to 20 years	635	259
20 up to 30 years	39,959	6,454
30 up to 40 years	99,956	12,128
40 up to 50 years	51,837	4,398
50 up to 60 years	16,367	1,466
60 years and over	6,227	1,221

Source: National Center for Health Statistics, U.S. Department of Health and Human Services.

a. What is the median age for all males contracting AIDS?
b. What is the modal age?

32. *a.* Refer to Exercise 31. What is the median age for all females contracting AIDS?
b. What is the modal age for females contracting AIDS?

SELECTING AN AVERAGE FOR DATA IN A FREQUENCY DISTRIBUTION

For a symmetrical distribution mean, median, and mode are equal.

Refer to the frequency polygon in Chart 3–3. It is symmetrical and bell-shaped, meaning that *the distribution has the same shape on either side of the center axis.* If the polygon were folded in half, the two halves would be identical. For a symmetric distribution, the mode, median, and mean are located at the center and are always equal. They are all 20 years in Chart 3–3.

CHART 3–3 **A Symmetric Distribution**

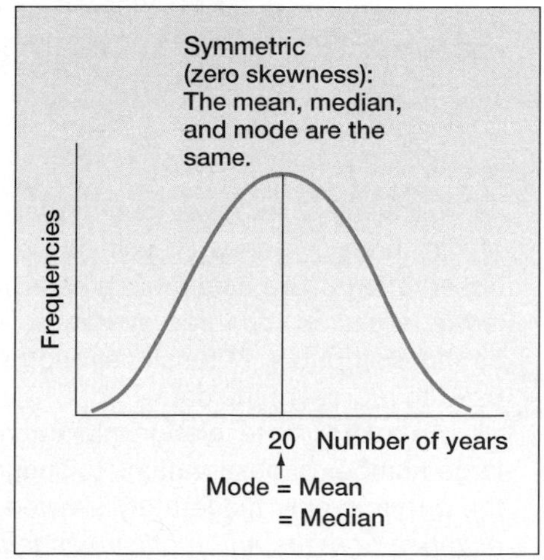

The number of years corresponding to the highest point of the curve is the *mode* (20 years). Because the frequency curve is symmetrical, the *median* corresponds to the point where the distribution is cut in half (20 years). The total number of frequencies representing many years is offset by the total number representing few years, resulting in an *arithmetic mean* of 20 years. Logically, any of the three averages would be appropriate to represent this distribution.

A skewed distribution is not symmetrical

As the distribution becomes asymmetrical, or **skewed,** the relationship among the three averages changes. In a **positively skewed distribution,** the arithmetic mean is the largest of the three averages. Why? Because the mean is influenced more than the median or mode by a few extremely high values. The median is generally the next largest average in a positively skewed frequency distribution. The mode is the smallest of the three averages.

If the distribution is highly skewed, such as the weekly incomes in Chart 3–4, the mean would not be a good average to use. The median and mode would be more representative.

CHART 3–4 **A Positively Skewed Distribution**

Extremely large values "pulling" mean upward

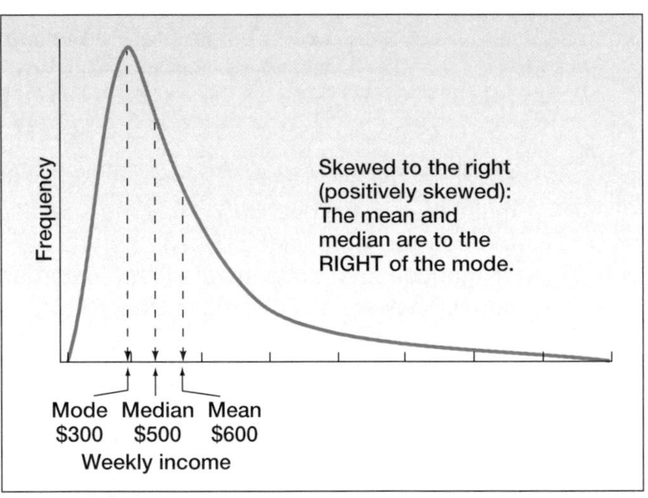

Conversely, in a distribution that is **negatively skewed,** the mean is the lowest of the three averages. The mean is, of course, influenced by a few extremely low observations. The median is greater than the arithmetic mean, and the modal value is the largest of the three averages. Again, if the distribution is highly skewed, such as the distribution of tensile strengths shown in Chart 3–5, the mean should not be used to represent the data.

An approximate relationship among the three averages is: If there is a sufficiently large number of observations to suggest a smoothed distribution and if the shape of the curve is only moderately skewed, *the median is approximately one third of the distance from the arithmetic mean to the mode.*

CHART 3–5 **A Negatively Skewed Distribution**

Extremely low values "pulling" mean downward

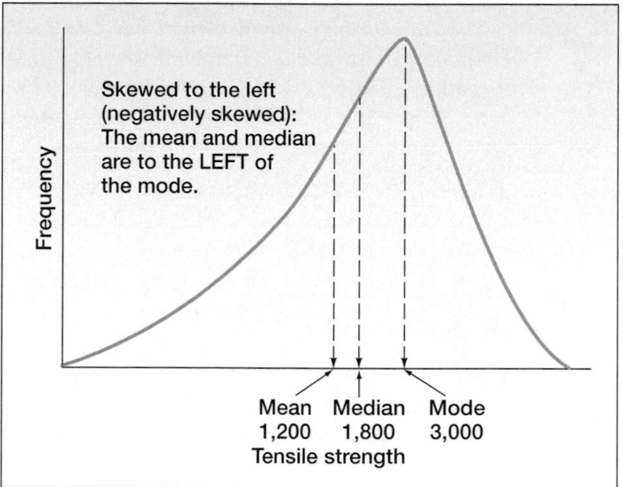

If two averages of a moderately skewed frequency distribution are known, the third can be approximated. The formulas are:

$$\text{Mode} = \text{Mean} - 3(\text{Mean} - \text{Median})$$

$$\text{Mean} = \frac{3(\text{Median}) - \text{Mode}}{2} \qquad (3\text{–}9)$$

$$\text{Median} = \frac{2(\text{Mean}) + \text{Mode}}{3}$$

We noted before that if the distribution is open-ended, the mean cannot be computed—unless the midpoint of the open-ended class, or classes, can be approximated. Consider, for example, the following distribution. Unless the midpoint of the "less than $50,000" class and the midpoint of the "$250,000 and more" class can be estimated, the mean cannot be determined.

Annual income	Number of executives
Less than $50,000	17
$50,000 up to $100,000	62
$100,000 up to $150,000	103
$150,000 up to $200,000	73
$200,000 up to $250,000	41
$250,000 and more	20

However, the median and mode could be used to represent the typical annual income of the executives.

SELF-REVIEW 3–7

The answers are at the end of the chapter.

The weekly sales from a sample of Hi-Tec electronic supply stores were organized into a frequency distribution. The mean of weekly sales was computed to be $105,900, the median $105,000, and the mode $104,500.

a. Sketch the sales in the form of a smoothed frequency polygon. Note the location of the mean, median, and mode on the *X*-axis.

b. Is the distribution symmetrical, positively skewed, or negatively skewed? Explain.

EXERCISES

The answers to the odd-numbered exercises are at the end of the book.

33. A machine weighs coal that is being loaded on barges and automatically records the total every hour. After 132 hours of operation, the total weights were organized into a frequency distribution, and based on that distribution a curve was drawn. It was approximately symmetrical in shape. The mean weight loaded per hour was computed to be 1,200 tons.
    a. What is the median? Explain.
    b. What is the mode? Explain.

34. The price-earnings ratios for a selected group of common stocks were organized into a frequency distribution, and the following frequency polygon was drawn. Three averages (mean, median, and mode) were computed. One of the three was 10.2, another 10.8, and the other 11.1.
    a. Which price-earnings ratio is the median? What does this indicate?
    b. Which price-earnings ratio is the mode? Interpret.
    c. Which price-earnings ratio is the mean?

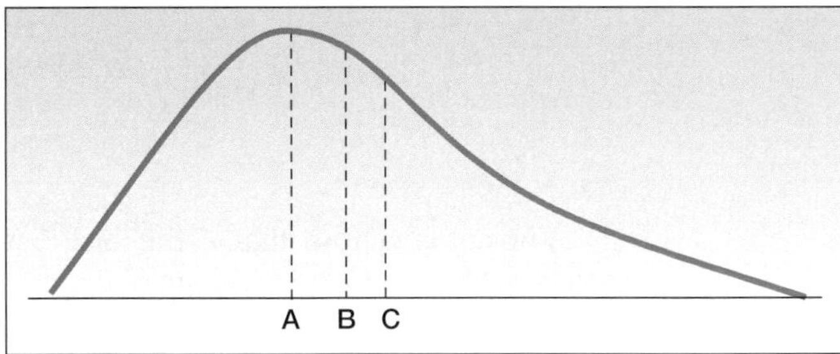

35. Idaho Trout Farm, Inc. raises trout commercially. Management is concerned about the length and weight of the trout and continually samples the ponds. A sample from Waldon Pond revealed that the modal length is 12.0 inches and the mean 12.9 inches.
    a. What is the approximate median length?
    b. Draw a picture of the distribution, and identify each of the averages.

36. The Special Education department at Coldstream University administered a test to disadvantaged children. The modal score was 72.0 and the median 78.0.
    a. What is the approximate mean score?
    b. Sketch the distribution, and identify each of the averages.

37. We are interested in the estimated fuel economy of automobiles driven mainly in the city. Based on tests done by the Environmental Protection Agency, the following information was reported in *Car and Driver.*

Model tested	EPA fuel economy (mpg)	Model tested	EPA fuel economy (mpg)
Acura Integra	25	Honda Civic de Sol	29
Alfa Romeo Spider	22	Honda Prelude S	23
Audi V8 Quattro	14	Hyundai Scoupe Turbo	26
Audi 100 CS Quattro	18	Isuzu Rodeo	16
BMW 325i convertible	19	Jaguar XJ6	17
BMW 530i	16	Jeep Grand Cherokee	15
Buick Regal	19	Lamborghini Diablo	9
Cadillac Eldorado	16	Lexus LS400	18
Cadillac Sedan de Ville	16	Lexus LC400	18
Chevrolet Camaro Z28	17	Lincoln Continental	17
Chevrolet Cavalier VL	23	Lotus Esprit	17
Chevrolet Corvette ZR-1	17	Mazda MX	22
Chevrolet 454SS	10	Mazda RX-7	17
Dinan 850	11	Mercedes-Benz C280	20
Dodge Intrepid	20	Mitsubishi Galant	22
Ferrari F40	12	Nissan Altima	21
Ferrari 348tb	13	Oldsmobile Cutlass	19
Ferrari 348 Spider	13	Plymouth Laser	18
Ford Escort RS	19	Porsche Cabrio	16
Ford Mustang GT	17	Porsche 968	16
Ford Probe	21	Saab 900SE	20
Ford Ranger Splash	18	Subaru Impreza	26
Ford Taurus SHO	18	Toyota Camry SE	19
Ford Thunderbird SC	17	Toyota Supra	19
GMC Sonoma SLS	17	Volkswagen Corrado	18
Honda Accord EX	25	Volvo 850GLT	21

Source: *Car and Driver,* February 1994, pp. 118–119.

a. Starting with 9 mpg, organize the EPA fuel economy data into a frequency distribution. Use 3 mpg as the class interval.
b. Estimate the median number of miles per gallon.
c. Estimate the modal number of miles per gallon.
d. Write a brief interpretation of the two figures you computed.

CHAPTER OUTLINE

I. A measure of central tendency is a single value used to represent a set of data.
   A. These measures include the mean, weighted mean, median, mode, and geometric mean.
   B. The arithmetic mean is the measure reported most often.

II. To compute the arithmetic mean, the values are summed, and the sum is divided by the total number of observations. For a sample, the sample mean is found by

$$\overline{X} = \frac{\Sigma X}{n} \qquad (3\text{–}2)$$

For a population, the population mean is found by

$$\mu = \frac{\Sigma X}{N} \qquad (3\text{–}1)$$

For the arithmetic mean:

A. At least the interval scale of measurement is required.
B. All the values are used in the calculation.
C. A set of data has only one mean.
D. The sum of the deviations from the mean is zero.

$$\Sigma(X - \overline{X}) = 0 \qquad (3\text{–}3)$$

For data grouped into a frequency distribution, the formula for a sample is:

$$\overline{X} = \frac{\Sigma fX}{n} \qquad (3\text{–}7)$$

III. The weighted mean is found by multiplying each observation by its corresponding weight, summing these values, then dividing by the sum of the weights.

$$\overline{X}_w = \frac{w_1X_1 + w_2X_2 + w_3X_3 + \cdots + w_nX_n}{w_1 + w_2 + w_3 + \cdots + w_n} \qquad (3\text{–}4)$$

IV. The geometric mean is the nth root of the product of n values.

A. To compute the geometric mean of a set of data:

$$\text{Geometric mean} = \sqrt[n]{(X_1)(X_2)(X_3)\cdots(X_n)} \qquad (3\text{–}5)$$

B. To measure the average annual percent increase in business or economic data from one time period to another:

$$\text{Geometric mean} = \sqrt[n-1]{\frac{\text{Value at end of period}}{\text{Value at beginning of period}}} - 1 \qquad (3\text{–}6)$$

V. The median is the middle value in a set of values ordered from smallest to largest. It can be located by

$$\frac{n+1}{2}$$

A. To determine the median, at least the ordinal scale of measurement is required.
B. It is not influenced by extreme values.
C. Fifty percent of the observations are greater than the median, and 50 percent are less than the median.
D. The median does not need to be one of the values in the data set.
E. The median is unique for a set of data; that is, there is only one median for a set of data.
F. The formula for the median of grouped data is:

$$\text{Median} = L + \frac{\frac{n}{2} - CF}{f}(i) \qquad (3\text{–}8)$$

VI. The mode is the value that occurs most often in a set of data.

A. The mode can be determined for all levels of data.
B. A set of data can have more than one mode.

VII. Skewness is the lack of symmetry in a set of data.

A. If there is no skewness in the data, the mean, median, and mode are equal. Half of the values are above these average measures and half below them. Shown graphically:

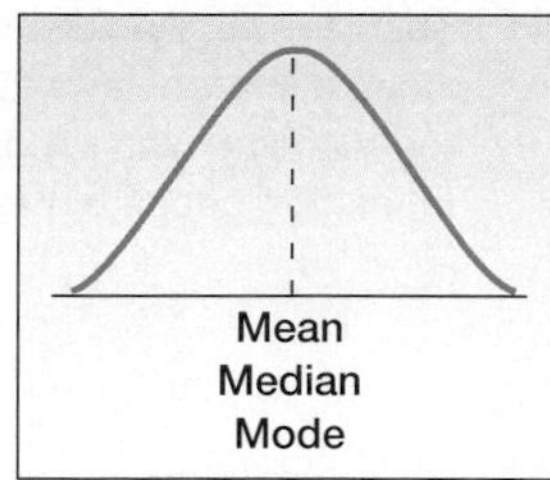

B. If the long tail of the distribution is to the right, the set of values is positively skewed.
   1. The mode is the value at the highest point of the distribution.
   2. The mean is the largest of the three averages.

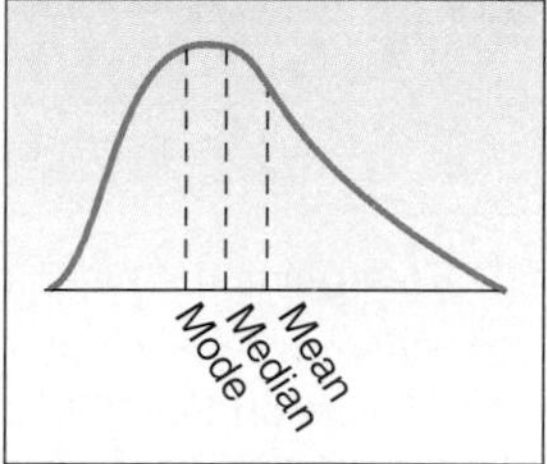

C. If the long tail of the distribution is to the left, the set of values is negatively skewed.
   1. The mode is the value at the highest point of the distribution.
   2. The mean is the smallest of the three averages.

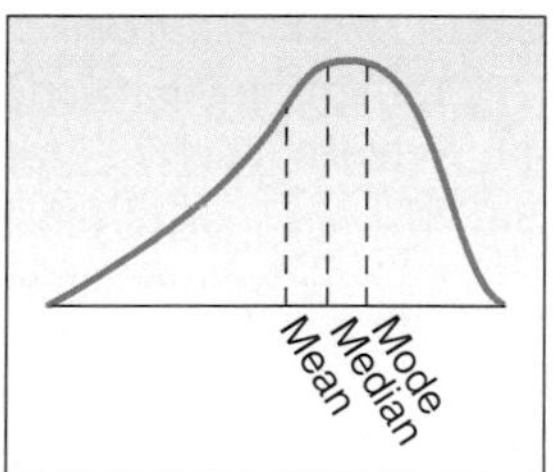

EXERCISES

The answers to the odd-numbered exercises are at the end of the book.

38. The accounting firm of Crawford and Associates has five senior partners. Yesterday the senior partners saw six, four, three, seven, and five clients, respectively.
    a. Compute the mean number and median number of clients seen by a partner.
    b. Is the mean a sample mean or a population mean?
    c. Verify that $\Sigma(X - \overline{X}) = 0$.
39. Owens Orchards sells apples in a large bag by weight. A sample of seven bags contained the following numbers of apples: 23, 19, 26, 17, 21, 24, 22.
    a. Compute the mean number and median number of apples in a bag.
    b. Verify that $\Sigma(X - \overline{X}) = 0$.
40. A sample of households that subscribe to the United Bell Phone Company revealed the following numbers of calls received last week. Determine the mean and the median numbers of calls received.

52	43	30	38	30	42	12	46	39	37
34	46	32	18	41	5				

41. The Citizens Banking Company is studying the number of times the automatic teller, located in a Loblaws Supermarket, is used per day. Following are the numbers of times the machine was used over each of the last 30 days. Determine the mean number of times the machine was used per day.

83	64	84	76	84	54	75	59	70	61
63	80	84	73	68	52	65	90	52	77
95	36	78	61	59	84	95	47	87	60

42. Refer to Problem 30 (page 64). Following are the numbers of games won by the 28 major league baseball teams during the 1993 season.

85	80	71	94	76	85	84	69
71	88	68	82	86	95	104	84
73	67	64	85	81	94	59	97
75	87	61	103				

Determine the mean and median numbers of games won.

43. Refer to Problem 32 (page 64). Repeated below are the salaries (in $ thousands) of the players on the 1993 opening-day roster and the disabled list of the Cleveland Indians.

1,700	1,600	1,300	1,200	975	950	750	725
625	610	542	500	450	425	400	350
350	335	325	325	300	145	143	130
125	114	109	109	109			

Determine the mean salary and the median salary. Which average is more representative? Why? (Source? *USA Today,* April 15, 1993, p. 3F.)

44. The numbers of Temban camcorders produced during eight-hour shifts for 50 shifts selected at random are:

348	371	360	369	376	397	368	361	374
410	374	377	335	356	322	344	399	362
384	365	380	349	358	343	432	376	347
385	399	400	359	329	370	398	352	396
366	392	375	379	389	390	386	341	351
354	395	338	390	333				

Determine the mean number of camcorders produced during an eight-hour shift.

45. The metropolitan area of Los Angeles-Long Beach, California, is the area expected to show the largest increase in the number of jobs between 1989 and 2010. The number of jobs is expected to increase from 5,164,900 to 6,286,800. What is the geometric mean expected yearly rate of increase?

46. Wells Fargo Mortgage and Equity Trust gave these occupancy rates in their annual report for various office income properties the company owns.

Pleasant Hills, California	100%
Lakewood, Colorado	90
Riverside, California	80
Scottsdale, Arizona	20
San Antonio, Texas	62

What is the geometric mean occupancy rate?

47. A recent article suggested that if you earn $25,000 a year today and the inflation rate continues at 3 percent per year, you'll need to make $33,598 in 10 years to have the same buying power. You would need to make $44,771 if the inflation rate jumped to 6 percent. Confirm that these statements are accurate by finding the geometric mean rate of increase. (Source: *Vitality Digest,* June 1994, p. 10.)
48. Wells Fargo Mortgage and Equity Trust also reported these occupancy rates for some of its industrial income properties:

Tucson, Arizona	81%
Irvine, California	100
Carlsbad, California	74
Dallas, Texas	80

What is the geometric mean occupancy rate?

49. The 12-month returns on five aggressive-growth mutual funds were 32.2 percent, 35.5 percent, 80.0 percent, 60.9 percent, and 92.1 percent. Determine the arithmetic mean and the geometric mean rates of return. (Source: *U.S. News & World Report.*)
50. In 1970 the mean salary for a major league baseball player was $29,303. In 1994 the salary increased to $1,188,679. Determine the geometric mean yearly rate of increase. (Source: *USA Today,* April 6, 1994, p. C5.)

51. Mid South University has seven defensive linemen who weigh 240 pounds each, four who weigh 212 each, three who weigh 190 each, and one who tips the scales at 314. What is the weighted mean weight of the defensive linemen?
52. A Nashville, Tennessee, bottling company offers three kinds of delivery service—instant, same day, and within five days. The profit per delivery varies according to the kind of delivery. The profit for an instant delivery is less than that for the other kinds because the driver has to go directly to a grocery store with a small load and return to the bottling plant. To find out what effect, if any, each type of delivery has on the profit picture, the company has made the following tabulation based on deliveries for the previous quarter.

Type of delivery	Number of deliveries during the quarter	Profit per delivery
Instant	100	$ 70
Same day	60	100
Within five days	40	160

a. What is the weighted mean profit per delivery?

b. Suppose the bottling company were able to eliminate instant orders through special promotions and careful planning. What would their profit per delivery be if all 100 grocery stores previously requesting instant delivery changed to same-day delivery?

53. The Oriental Star, a steamship line, is studying various facets of the business, including the length of time required to load and unload a ship and the weight of containers. The number of containers and their weights loaded on a ship bound for Hong Kong are:

Number of containers	Weight per container (pounds)
60	1,000
40	3,000
20	6,000

a. Adding 1,000, 3,000, and 6,000 gives 10,000 pounds. Dividing 10,000 pounds by 3 is 3,333 pounds, the mean weight of a container. Is that the average weight of a container on the ship bound for Hong Kong? Explain.

b. Compute the weighted mean of the 120 containers. Explain why this weight is different from the 3,333 pounds computed in *a.*

54. An automatic machine that fills containers appears to be performing erratically. A check of the weights of the contents of a number of cans revealed:

Weight (grams)	Number of cans
130 up to 140	2
140 up to 150	8
150 up to 160	20
160 up to 170	15
170 up to 180	9
180 up to 190	7
190 up to 200	3
200 up to 210	2

a. Estimate the arithmetic mean weight of the contents of a can.

b. Estimate the median weight of the contents of a can.

55. Last year 515,600 unmarried women gave birth. The ages and numbers of unmarried mothers are reported in the following frequency distribution:

Age of mother	Number (in thousands)
Under 15 years	10.1
15 up to 20	239.7
20 up to 25	168.6
25 up to 30	62.4
30 up to 35	23.7
35 up to 40	8.8
40 years and older	2.3

Estimate the median age of the unmarried mothers. Interpret.

56. The following frequency distribution shows a percentage distribution of household incomes in Alaska and Connecticut:

	Percent of households	
Incomes	Alaska	Connecticut
Less than $20,000	18.3	22.2
$20,000 up to $30,000	21.2	27.6
30,000 up to 40,000	18.4	24.1
40,000 up to 50,000	15.1	13.1
50,000 up to 60,000	11.3	6.0
$60,000 and greater	15.7	7.0

For the distribution of incomes for Alaska:

a. What is the median income?

b. What is the modal income?

57. Refer to Exercise 56. For the distribution of incomes for Connecticut:
    a. What is the median income?
    b. What is the modal income?

58. The Department of Commerce, Bureau of the Census, reported on the number of income earners in American families:

Number of earners	Number (in thousands)
0	7,083
1	18,621
2	22,414
3	5,533
4 or more	2,797

a. What is the modal number of income earners in a typical American family? Explain what this indicates.
b. Would the mean or median number of earners be a more representative average? Explain.

59. The Bureau of the Census, in *Current Population Reports,* series P-20, gave the ages of divorced males and females (in thousands of persons 18 years old and older):

Age	Males	Females
18 up to 20	5	9
20 up to 25	80	210
25 up to 30	174	303
30 up to 35	210	315
35 up to 45	385	656
45 up to 55	450	656
55 up to 65	295	409
65 up to 75	174	200
75 and older	56	69

a. Estimate the median age of divorced males. Interpret.
b. Estimate the median age of divorced females. Interpret.
c. Estimate the modal age for the males. Do the same for the females.

60. Questions *a* through *h* refer to the following measures of central tendency and the shapes of a distribution.

Measure of central tendency	Shape of distribution
Arithmetic mean	Symmetrical
Median	Positively skewed
Mode	Negatively skewed
Geometric mean	

a. Which measure of central tendency is defined as the value of the item that appears most frequently?
b. Which measure of central tendency is affected the most by extremely small or extremely large values?
c. Which measure must be used to determine the average annual percent increase in sales, for example, from 1964 to 1994?
d. How is the shape of a frequency distribution described if the three measures of central tendency are equal?

e. How is the shape of a frequency distribution described if the mean is the largest of the three measures of central tendency?
f. Which measure of central tendency is determined by summing all of the values and dividing the sum by the number of values?
g. Which measure of central tendency is defined as the point above which half of the values lie and below which the other half lie?
h. In a negatively skewed frequency distribution, which measure of central tendency is the largest?

61. An auctioneer specializes in used cars that are about 10 years old. The selling prices of a large number of automobiles were grouped into a frequency distribution, and a smoothed frequency polygon was drawn.

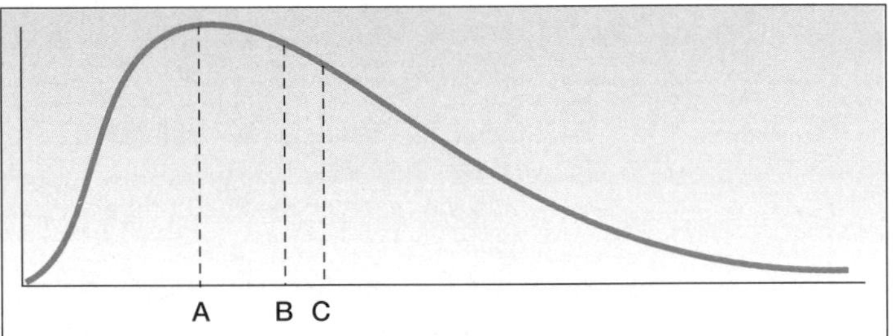

The average represented by the letter *A* was computed to be $3,000 and the average represented by *B* $3,220.
a. Approximate the average represented by the letter *C.*
b. What is the average in part *a* called, and why is it larger than the other two averages?
c. What is the modal price?
d. Is the distribution of the prices symmetrical, positively skewed, or negatively skewed? Cite evidence.

62. Each employee is given a production rating that represents her/his efficiency on the job. The ratings were organized into a frequency distribution and then portrayed in the form of a less-than cumulative frequency polygon. Based on the chart, what is the approximate median rating?

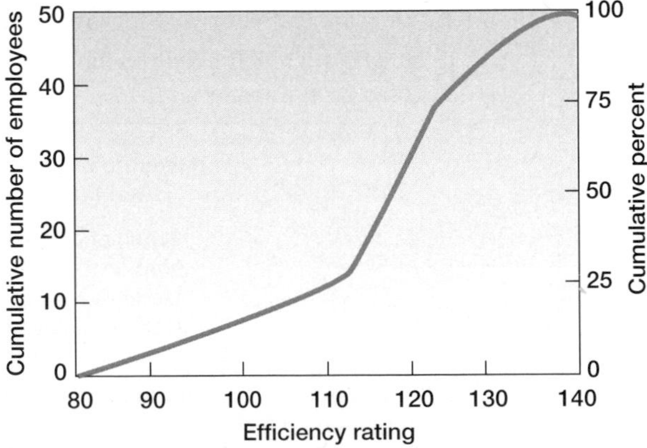

63. Motor vehicle registration in Canada increased from 22,000 in 1914 to an estimated 17,000,000 in 1994. What was the geometric mean annual percent increase in vehicle registration from 1914 to 1994? (Source: *Canadian Almanac & Directory.*)

64. Canadian fisheries production figures for 1941 and 1989 were:

Year	Production
1941	$ 62,259,000
1989	3,013,090,000

Source: *Canadian Almanac & Directory,* 1991, pp.6–81.

What was the geometric mean annual percent increase in fisheries production from 1941 to 1989?

65. Cunard's *Queen Elizabeth 2* takes a world cruise every year. The 1995 cruise is a 100-day cruise starting on January 6, 1995, from Ft. Lauderdale, Florida. It goes to South America, Australia, Hong Kong, Tokyo, Mombasa, Haifa, and other places.
    a. The price for an outside luxury double room with a veranda on the signal deck is $126,900 per person. This price is up from $88,300 per person in 1989. What is the geometric mean annual rate of increase in the cruise price from 1989 to 1995?
    b. You could join the *QE 2* in Sidney and take a 22-day partial cruise disembarking in Hong Kong. The ship stops at such places as Perth, Bali, Kota Kinabalu, Tokyo, and Taipei. The price per person for an outside room on the Mauretania deck is $8,910. This is up from $6,240 in 1989. What is the geometric mean annual rate of increase in price from 1989 to 1995? (Source: Cunard, *World Cruises and Winter Vacations.*)

66. The *Sagafjord,* a Cunard cruise-line ship, offers a full world cruise of 107 days starting January 6, 1995, from Ft. Lauderdale, Florida. It stops at such places as Lima, Punta Arenas, Rio, Zanzibar, Madras, Kuala Lumpur, and Bangkok.
    a. A luxury suite on the officers deck costs $119,900. In 1987 such a suite cost only $78,200. What is the geometric mean annual rate of increase from 1987 to 1995?
    b. If you want to take only a 46-day segment from Ft. Lauderdale to Mombasa in Africa, an outside cabin on the main deck is $16,660 per person. The corresponding 1987 price was $11,160. What is the geometric mean annual rate of increase from 1987 to 1995? What is the arithmetic mean daily cost per person in 1995 for this 46-day trip? (Source: *World Cruises and Winter Vacations.*)

COMPUTER DATA EXERCISES

67. Refer to data set 1, which reports information on homes sold in Florida during 1994.
    a. Determine the mean and the median selling prices of the 75 homes. Is one a better measure of central tendency than the other?
    b. How many bedrooms does the typical home have?
    c. How many bathrooms does a typical home have? What is the modal number of bathrooms?
    d. How many miles is the typical home from the center of the city?

68. Refer to data set 2, which reports information on the 1993 major league baseball season.
    a. Determine the mean team salary for the 28 teams. Compare this value to the median team salary. Comment on the differences and the similarities between the two values.
    b. Organize the salaries of the 28 teams into a frequency distribution and compute the mean and the median. Do the values agree exactly with those of part *a*? Comment on the differences.
    c. The information in data set 2 reports the total salary for each team. Suppose we found the salary for each player and computed the mean player salary by adding the

salaries for each of the 700 major league players (28 teams with 25 players on each team). Would you expect this mean to be exactly the same as that of part *a*? Write a brief summary of your position.

69. Refer to data set 3, which reports information on the circulation of 48 magazines.
    a. Determine the mean and the median circulation of the magazines. Comment on the two values.
    b. Select an appropriate class interval and organize the information on the circulation into a frequency distribution. Compute the mean and the median. Do the values agree with those computed in part *a*? Comment on any differences.

CHAPTER 3 EXAMINATION

The answers are at the end of the chapter.

1. What measure of central tendency is found by arranging the data from low to high and selecting the middle value?
2. What measure of central tendency cannot be computed if the frequency distribution has an open-ended class?
3. What measure of central tendency cannot be computed if one of the values is 0?

For Questions 4 through 10, fill in the blank with the correct answer.

4. If the mean is larger than the median, the distribution is ___________ skewed.
5. If the mean, median, and mode are all equal, the distribution is ___________.
6. If the mean is smaller than the median, the distribution is ___________ skewed.
7. The ___________ is not recommended if extremely large values are found in the data.
8. The ___________ is computed by adding all the values and dividing the total by the number of observations.
9. If the deviations from the mean are totaled, the result is always ___________.
10. The value that occurs most often in a set of data is called the ___________.
11. A sample of five employees from Pelton Tool and Die, Inc. revealed the following lengths of service, in years: 13, 22, 27, 24, 19.
    a. Compute the mean length of service.
    b. Determine the median length of service.
12. A sample of 50 antique dealers in the southeast United States revealed the following sales last year:

Sales ($ thousands)	Number of firms
100 up to 120	5
120 up to 140	7
140 up to 160	9
160 up to 180	16
180 up to 200	10
200 up to 220	3

    a. Estimate the mean sales.
    b. Estimate the median sales.
    c. What is the modal sales amount?

13. The mean of a frequency distribution is 230, and the mode is 200. Estimate the median.

CHAPTER 3 Answers

Self-Review

3–1

1. *a.* $\bar{X} = \frac{\Sigma X}{n}$

   b. $\bar{X} = \frac{\$187{,}100}{4}$

   $= \$46{,}775$

   $= \$46{,}800$ rounded

   c. Statistic, because it is a sample value.

   d. $46,800. The sample mean is our best estimate of the population mean.

2. *a.* $\mu = \frac{\Sigma X}{N}$

   b. $\mu = \frac{498}{6} = 83$

   c. Parameter, because it was computed using all the population values.

3–2

1. a. $439.
   b. 3, 3.
2. *a.* 7, found by (6 + 8)/2 = 7.
   b. 3, 3.

3–3

a. $237, found by:

$$\frac{(95 \times \$400) + (126 \times \$200) + (79 \times \$100)}{95 + 126 + 79}$$

$$= \frac{\$71{,}100}{300} = \$237$$

b. The profit per suit is $12, found by $237 − $200 cost − $25 commission. The total profit for the 300 suits is $3,600, found by 300 × $12.

3–4

1. *a.* About 8.39 percent.
   b. About 10.1 percent.
   c. Yes, 10.1 > 8.39.
2. About 8.63 percent.

3–5

a. Frequency distribution.

b.

f	*X*	*fX*
1	4	4
4	8	32
10	12	120
3	16	48
2	20	40
20		244

$$\bar{X} = \frac{\Sigma fX}{n} = \frac{\$244}{20} = \$12.2$$

3–6

1.

$$100 + \frac{25 - 14}{20}(10)$$

$$= 100 + 5.5 = 105.5$$

2. *a.*

Net sales	Cumulative percent
$ 1 up to $ 4	13
4 up to 7	27
7 up to 10	67
10 up to 13	90
13 and over	100

$$\$7 + \frac{50 - 27}{40}(\$3) = \$8.725 \text{ or } \$8{,}725{,}000$$

3–7 *a.*

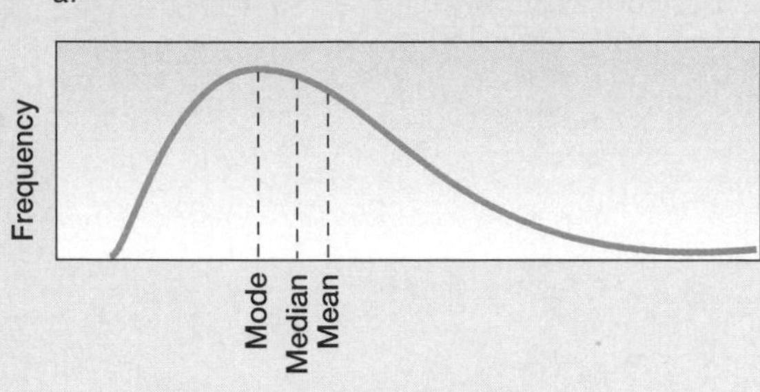

b. Positively skewed, because the mean is the largest average and the mode is the smallest.

Examination

1. Median.
2. Mean.
3. Geometric mean.
4. Positively.
5. Symmetric.
6. Negatively.
7. Mean.
8. Mean.
9. Zero.
10. Mode.
11. *a.* 21 years, found by 105/5.
    b. 22 years, found by arranging the lengths of service from low to high and selecting the middle observation.
12.

Sales	*f*	*X*	*fX*	*CF*
$100 up to $120	5	110	550	5
120 up to 140	7	130	910	12
140 up to 160	9	150	1,350	21
160 up to 180	16	170	2,720	37
180 up to 200	10	190	1,900	47
200 up to 220	3	210	630	50
			8,060	

a. $\overline{X} = \frac{8{,}060}{50} = 161.2$ or $161,200

b. Median $= \$160 + \frac{25 - 21}{16}(\$20) = \$165.0$ or $165,000

c. $170,000, which is the midpoint of the class with the largest frequency.

13. About 220, found by [2(230) + 200]/3.

Chapter 4

Measures of Dispersion and Skewness

GOALS

When you have completed this chapter, you will be able to:

1
Compute various measures of dispersion for raw data.

2
Compute various measures of dispersion for data organized in a frequency distribution.

3
Explain the characteristics, uses, advantages, and disadvantages of each measure of dispersion.

4
Explain Chebyshev's theorem and the Empirical, or Normal, Rule.

5
Compute and explain the uses of the coefficient of variation and the coefficient of skewness.

Given specific data, how would Blockbuster Video determine how many and how much variation there is in the number of videotapes a typical family rents per month? (See Goal 2 and Exercise 62.)

INTRODUCTION

Chapter 2 began our study of descriptive statistics. We organized a mass of raw data into a table called a frequency distribution and then portrayed the distribution graphically in a histogram, a frequency polygon, and a cumulative frequency polygon to further describe the shape and other important characteristics of the data. In Chapter 3 several averages were computed to describe a typical value near the center of the observations.

We will now examine several measures that describe the *dispersion, variability,* or *spread* of the data. Discussed in this chapter are the *range, average deviation, variance, standard deviation, interquartile range, quartile deviation,* and *percentile range.*

WHY STUDY DISPERSION?

An average, such as the mean or median, only pinpoints the center of the data. It is valuable from that standpoint, but it doesn't tell us anything about the spread of the data. Would you walk across a lake if you knew only that its average depth is 3 feet? What we need is a measure of dispersion (spread). A small value for a measure of dispersion indicates that the data are clustered closely, say, around the arithmetic mean. The mean is therefore considered quite representative of the data. That is, the mean is a reliable average. Conversely, a large value for a measure of dispersion indicates that the mean is not very reliable—that is, it is not very representative of the data. Such is the case in Chart 4–1. Note that the ages of the employees range from 18 to 85. This large spread results in a measure of central tendency (50) that is not very meaningful.

Average unrepresentative because of large spread

CHART 4–1 **Ages of the Employees**

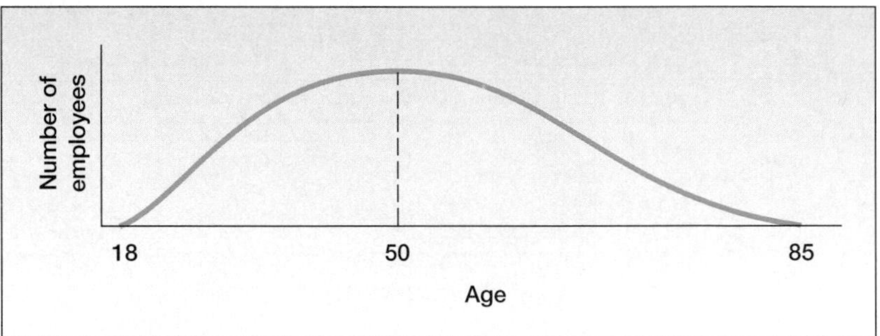

A second reason for studying the dispersion in a set of data is to compare the spread in two or more distributions. Suppose, for example, that the new PDM/3 computer is assembled in Baton Rouge and also in Tucson. The arithmetic mean daily output in the Baton Rouge plant is 50, and in the Tucson plant the mean output is also 50. Based on the two means, one might conclude that the distributions of the daily outputs are identical. Production records for nine days at the two plants, however, reveal that this conclusion is not correct. (See Chart 4–2.) Baton Rouge production varies from 48 to 52 assemblies a day. Production at the Tucson plant is more erratic, ranging from 40 to 60 a day.

A measure of dispersion can be used to evaluate the reliability of two or more averages

CHART 4–2 **Daily Production of Computers at the Baton Rouge and Tucson Plants**

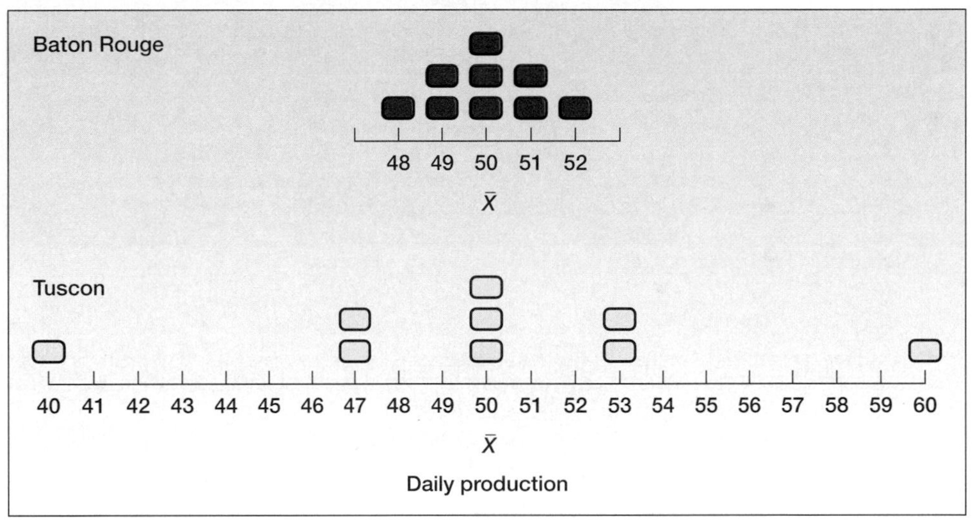

MEASURES OF DISPERSION—UNGROUPED DATA

We will apply several measures of dispersion to ungrouped (raw) data.

Range

The simplest measure of dispersion to compute and interpret is the **range.** It is the difference between the highest and lowest values in a set of data. In the form of an equation:

Definition of range

$$\text{Range} = \text{Highest value} - \text{Lowest value} \qquad (4\text{–}1)$$

The range is widely used in statistical process control (SPC) applications. For these applications see Chapter 16.

EXAMPLE

The capacities of several metal containers are 38, 20, 37, 64, and 27 liters, respectively. What is the range?

Solution ► The range is 44 liters, found by 64 − 20.

Range of ungrouped data

Returning to the example of daily production of computers in Chart 4–2, note that the range of the production in the Baton Rouge plant is 4, found by 52 − 48. The range of the daily production in the Tucson plant is 20 computers (60 − 40). It can be concluded, therefore, that (1) there is less dispersion in the daily production in the Baton Rouge plant than in the Tucson plant because the range of 4 computers is less than the range of 20 computers, and (2) the production in the Baton Rouge plant is clustered more closely about the mean of 50 than is the production in the Tucson plant (because the range of 4 is less than the range of 20). Thus, the mean production in the Baton Rouge plant (50 computers) is a more representative average than the mean of 50 computers for the Tucson plant.

SELF-REVIEW 4–1

The answers are at the end of the chapter.

The annual travel costs for executives and middle management at Trion Chemicals were organized into frequency distributions and portrayed in frequency polygons on the top of the next page.

1. What is the approximate arithmetic mean travel cost for executives? For middle management?
2. What is the range for the executives? For middle management?
3. Compare the dispersion for the two distributions, and explain what it indicates.

(continued)

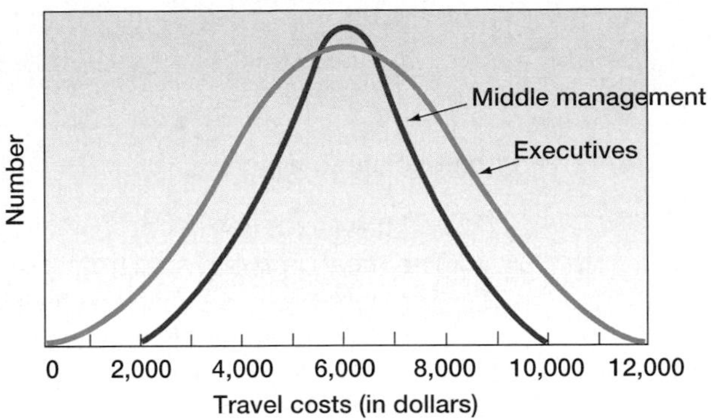

Mean Deviation

Mean deviation: arithmetic mean of the deviations from the mean

A serious defect of the range is that it is based only on two values, the highest and the lowest; it does not take into consideration all of the values. The **mean deviation** does. It measures the mean amount by which the values in a population, or sample, vary from their mean. In terms of a definition:

Mean deviation

> **Mean deviation** The arithmetic mean of the absolute values of the deviations from the arithmetic mean.

In terms of a formula, the mean deviation, designated *MD,* is computed for a sample by:

$$MD = \frac{\Sigma|X - \overline{X}|}{n} \quad (4\text{–}2)$$

where:

- X is the value of each observation.
- $\overline{X}$ is the arithmetic mean of the values.
- n is the number of observations in the sample.
- $||$ indicates the absolute value. In other words, the signs of the deviations from the mean are disregarded.

Mean absolute deviation (MAD)

Why do we ignore the signs of the deviations from the mean? If we didn't, the positive and negative deviations from the mean would exactly offset each other, and the mean deviation would always be zero. Such a measure (zero) would be a useless statistic. Because we use absolute deviations, the mean deviation is also called the **mean absolute deviation,** or **MAD,** and is usually written *MD.*

EXAMPLE

The weights of a sample of crates ready for shipment to France are (in kilograms): 103, 97, 101, 106, and 103.

1. What is the mean deviation?
2. How is it interpreted?

Solution ► The arithmetic mean weight is 102 kg, found by (103 + 97 + 101 + 106 + 103)/5.

1. To find the mean deviation:
   a. The mean is subtracted from each value.
   b. The absolute deviations are summed.
   c. The sum of the absolute deviations is divided by the number of values.

Weight (kg) X	$X - \overline{X}$		**Absolute deviation**
103	$\lvert +1 \rvert$	=	1
97	$\lvert -5 \rvert$	=	5
101	$\lvert -1 \rvert$	=	1
106	$\lvert +4 \rvert$	=	4
103	$\lvert +1 \rvert$	=	1
			12

$$MD = \frac{\Sigma \lvert X - \overline{X} \rvert}{n} = \frac{12}{5} = 2.4 \text{ kg}$$

The mean deviation of the sample is 2.4 kilograms.

2. Interpretation: The weights of the crates deviate, on the average, 2.4 kilograms from the arithmetic mean weight of 102 kilograms.

Advantages of mean deviation

Disadvantages of mean deviation

The mean deviation does have two advantages. It uses the value of every item in a set of data in its computation, and it is easy to understand—it is the average amount by which the values deviate from the mean. However, absolute values are difficult to work with, so the mean deviation is not as frequently used as other measures of dispersion, such as the standard deviation.

SELF-REVIEW 4–2

The answers are at the end of the chapter.

The weights of a group of crates being shipped to Ireland are (in kilograms): 95, 103, 105, 110, 104, 105, 112, and 90.

1. Compute the mean deviation.
2. Interpret your findings.
3. Compare the dispersion in the weights of the shipments going to France, given in the foregoing example, with the dispersion in the weights of shipments to Ireland.

A Computer Application

If there are a large number of observations, the MINITAB system can be applied to reduce computational time and ensure better accuracy. The weights of the crates going to France from the preceding example are used to show the procedure.

```
MTB > set c1
DATA > 103, 97, 101, 106, 103
DATA > end
MTB > mean c1
   MEAN      =      102.00
MTB > let c2=c1 - 102
MTB > absolute c2  c3
MTB > mean c3
   MEAN      =     2.4000
```

EXERCISES

The answers to the odd-numbered exercises are at the end of the book.

1. There were five customer service representatives on duty at the Electronic Super Store during last Friday's sale. The respective numbers of VCRs these representatives sold are: 5, 8, 4, 10, and 3.
   a. What is the range?
   b. What is the arithmetic mean?
   c. What is the mean deviation?
   d. Interpret the range.
2. The Department of Statistics at Western State University offers eight sections of basic statistics. Following are the numbers of students enrolled in these sections: 34, 46, 52, 29, 41, 38, 36, and 28.
   a. What is the range?
   b. What is the arithmetic mean number of students enrolled in a section?
   c. What is the mean deviation?
   d. Interpret the range.
3. Dave's Automatic Door installs automatic garage door openers. The following list indicates the number of minutes needed to install a sample of 10 doors: 28, 32, 24, 46, 44, 40, 54, 38, 32, and 42.
   a. What is the range?
   b. What is the arithmetic mean?
   c. What is the mean deviation?
   d. Interpret the mean deviation.
4. A sample of eight companies in the aerospace industry were surveyed as to their return on investment last year. The results are (in percent): 10.6, 12.6, 14.8, 18.2, 12.0, 14.8, 12.2, and 15.6.
   a. What is the range?
   b. What is the arithmetic mean return on investment?
   c. What is the mean deviation?
   d. Interpret the mean deviation.
5. Ten experts rated a newly developed pizza on a scale of 1 to 50. The ratings were: 34, 35, 41, 28, 26, 29, 32, 36, 38, and 40.
   a. What is the range?
   b. What is the arithmetic mean rating?
   c. What is the mean deviation? Interpret.
   d. A second group of experts rated the same pizza. The range was 8, the mean 33.9, and the mean deviation 1.9. Compare the dispersion in these ratings with that of the first group of experts.
6. A sample of the personnel files of eight male employees employed by Acme Carpet revealed that, during a six-month period, they lost the following numbers of days due to illness: 2, 0, 6, 3, 10, 4, 1, and 2.

a. What is the range?
b. What is the arithmetic mean number of days lost?
c. What is the mean deviation? Interpret.
d. A sample of the personnel files of female employees revealed that they lost 3.48 days on the average during the same six-month period due to illness. The range was computed to be 10 and the mean deviation 2.381. Compare the two groups.

Variance and Standard Deviation

Variance and standard deviation based on squared deviations

The **variance** and the **standard deviation** are also based on the deviations from the mean.

Variance The arithmetic mean of the squared deviations from the mean.

Standard deviation The positive square root of the variance.

Note in the definition of variance that the deviations from the mean are squared. The signs of the deviations (+ or −) are not ignored as they were for the mean deviation. Squaring the deviations from the mean eliminates the chance of having negative numbers because multiplying two negative numbers gives a positive number.

Population Variance The formulas for the *population variance* and the *sample variance* of ungrouped data are slightly different. The population variance is considered first. (Recall that a population is the totality of all observations being studied.) The **population variance** for ungrouped data, that is, data *not* tabulated into a frequency distribution, is found by:

$$\sigma^2 = \frac{\Sigma(X - \mu)^2}{N} \qquad (4\text{–}3)$$

where:

- σ^2 is the symbol for the population variance (σ is the lower-case Greek letter sigma).
- X is the value of an observation in the population.
- μ is the arithmetic mean of the population.
- N is the total number of observations in the population.

EXAMPLE

The ages of all the patients in the isolation ward of Yellowstone Hospital are 38, 26, 13, 41, and 22 years. What is the population variance?

Solution ▶

Age (X)	$X - \mu$	$(X - \mu)^2$
38	+10	100
26	− 2	4
13	−15	225
41	+13	169
22	− 6	36
140	0*	534

$$\mu = \frac{\Sigma X}{N} = \frac{140}{5} = 28$$

$$\sigma^2 = \frac{\Sigma(X - \mu)^2}{N} = \frac{534}{5} = 106.8$$

*Sum of the deviations from mean must equal zero.

The preceding approach for determining the population variance was used mainly to show that the variance is based on the *squared deviations from the population mean.* The mean is a whole number, and the computations for this small population of ages were relatively easy. Usually, however, the population is large, and the mean is not a whole number. For these problems a more efficient formula can be used. Note that the following formula for ungrouped data is not based on deviations from the mean, but rather on the actual values, thus eliminating a large number of subtractions.

$$\sigma^2 = \frac{\Sigma X^2}{N} - \left(\frac{\Sigma X}{N}\right)^2 \qquad (4\text{–}4)$$

Applying the formula to the previous problem:

$$\sigma^2 = \frac{(38)^2 + (26)^2 + (13)^2 + (41)^2 + (22)^2}{5} - \left(\frac{38 + 26 + 13 + 41 + 22}{5}\right)^2$$

$$= \frac{4{,}454}{5} - \left(\frac{140}{5}\right)^2$$

$$= 106.8 \text{ (which is the same answer as before)}$$

Like the range and the mean deviation, the variance can be used to compare the dispersion in two or more sets of observations. For example, the variance for the ages of the patients in isolation was just computed to be 106.8. If the variance in the ages of all the cancer patients in the hospital is 342.9, it can be said: (1) There is less dispersion in the distribution of the ages of patients in isolation than in the age distribution of all cancer patients (because 106.8 is less than 342.9). (2) The ages of the patients in isolation are clustered more closely about the mean of 28 years than are the ages of those in the cancer ward. Thus, the mean age for the patients in isolation is a more representative average than the mean for all cancer patients.

Variance: Difficult to interpret

Population Standard Deviation Both the range and the mean deviation are easy to interpret. The range is the difference between the high and low values of a set of data, and the mean deviation is the mean of the deviations from the mean. However, the variance is difficult to interpret for a single set of observations. The variance of 106.8 for the ages of the patients in isolation is not in terms of years, but rather "years squared."

Standard deviation in same units as data

There is a way out of this dilemma. By taking the square root of the population variance, we can transform it to the same unit of measurement used for the original data. The square root of 106.8 is 10.3 years. The square root of the population variance is called the **population standard deviation.** In terms of a formula for ungrouped data:

$$\sigma = \sqrt{\frac{\Sigma(X-\mu)^2}{N}} \quad \text{or} \quad \sigma = \sqrt{\frac{\Sigma X^2}{N} - \left(\frac{\Sigma X}{N}\right)^2} \qquad (4\text{–}5)$$

SELF-REVIEW 4–3

The answers are at the end of the chapter.

A population consists of the weights of all defensive tackles on St. Norbet's football team. They are: Johnson, 204 pounds; Patrick, 215 pounds; Juniors, 207 pounds; Kendron, 212 pounds; Nicko, 214 pounds; and Cochran, 208 pounds.

1. What is the population variance?

2. What is the population standard deviation?

EXERCISES

The answers to the odd-numbered exercises are at the end of the book.

7. Consider these five values a population: 8, 3, 7, 3, and 4.
   a. Compute the variance by squaring the individual deviations from the mean. [See formula (4–3).]
   b. Determine the variance by squaring the individual values as in formula (4–4).
8. These values are a population: 12, 6, 10, 4, 8, and 16.
   a. Determine the variance by squaring the individual deviations from the mean.
   b. Determine the variance by squaring each individual value as in formula (4–4).
9. The annual report of Dennis Industries cited these primary earnings per common share for the past five years: $2.68, $1.03, $2.26, $4.30, and $3.58. Considering these as population values, what is:
   a. The arithmetic mean primary earnings per common share?
   b. The variance?
10. Referring to Exercise 9, the annual report of Dennis Industries also gave these returns on stockholder equity for the same five-year period (in percent): 13.2, 5.0, 10.2, 17.5, and 12.9.
    a. What is the arithmetic mean return?
    b. What is the variance?
11. Plywood, Inc. reported these returns on stockholder equity for the past five years: 4.3, 4.9, 7.2, 6.7, and 11.6. Consider these as population values.
    a. Compute the range, the arithmetic mean, the variance, and the standard deviation.
    b. Compare the return on stockholder equity for Plywood, Inc. with that for Dennis Industries cited in Exercise 10.
12. The annual incomes of the five vice presidents of TMV industries are: $75,000; $78,000; $72,000; $83,000; and $90,000. (Consider this a population.)
    a. What is the range?

b. What is the arithmetic mean income?
c. What is the population variance? The standard deviation?
d. The annual incomes of another firm similar to TMV Industries were also studied. μ = \$79,900, and σ = \$8,612. Compare the means and dispersions in the two firms.

Sample variance used as an estimator of population variance

Sample Variance The formula for the population mean given in Chapter 3 is $\mu = \Sigma X/N$. We just change symbols for the sample mean, that is, $\overline{X} = \Sigma X/n$. Unfortunately, the conversion from the population variance to the sample variance is not quite that direct. It requires a slight change in the denominator. Instead of substituting n (number in the sample) for N (number in the population), the denominator is $n - 1$. Thus, the formula for the **sample variance** for ungrouped data used as an estimator of the population variance is:

Sample variance—ungrouped data

$$s^2 = \frac{\Sigma(X - \overline{X})^2}{n - 1} \tag{4–6}$$

where:

s^2 is the symbol used to represent the sample variance.
X is the value of the observations in the sample.
$\overline{X}$ is the mean of the sample.
n is the total number of observations in the sample.

Converting the more direct formula for the population variance σ^2 to the sample variance s^2, we have:

$$s^2 = \frac{\Sigma X^2 - \frac{(\Sigma X)^2}{n}}{n - 1} \tag{4–7}$$

Why is this seemingly insignificant change made in the denominator? It can be proven that, had the sample variance been computed using just n in the denominator, the result would *underestimate* the population variance.[1] That is, the sample variance would be a *biased* estimator of the population variance. This is especially true when the sample size is small. Using $n - 1$ compensates for this underestimation. Thus, the sample variance s^2 is considered an *unbiased estimator of the population variance.*[2]

Sample variance—an unbiased estimator

[1]To state it another way, the formula for the sample variance should be

$$\frac{\Sigma(X - \mu)^2}{n}$$

However, $\overline{X}$ is used to estimate μ. Thus, the sum in the numerator is too small. Dividing by $n - 1$ instead of n compensates for the underestimation in the numerator.

[2]If the sample variance has been computed using just n in the denominator, it can be converted to the unbiased estimator s^2 by:

$$s^2 = \frac{n}{n - 1}(\hat{s}^2)$$

where $\hat{s}^2$ is the sample variance computed using just n.

EXAMPLE

The hourly wages for a sample of part-time employees at Fruit Packers, Inc. are: \$2, \$10, \$6, \$8, and \$9. What is the sample variance?

Solution ▶ The sample variance is computed using two methods. On the left is the deviation method, using formula (4–6). On the right is the direct method, using formula (4–7).

$$\overline{X} = \frac{\Sigma X}{n} = \frac{\$35}{5} = \$7$$

Using squared deviations from the mean:

Hourly wage (X)	$X - \overline{X}$	$(X - \overline{X})^2$
\$ 2	−\$5	25
10	3	9
6	− 1	1
8	1	1
9	2	4
\$35	0	40

$$s^2 = \frac{\Sigma(X - \overline{X})^2}{n - 1} = \frac{40}{5 - 1}$$

$= 10$ in dollars squared

Using the direct formula:

Hourly wage (X)	X^2
\$ 2	4
10	100
6	36
8	64
9	81
\$35	285

$$s^2 = \frac{\Sigma X^2 - \frac{(\Sigma X)^2}{n}}{n - 1}$$

$$= \frac{285 - \frac{(35)^2}{5}}{5 - 1} = \frac{40}{5 - 1}$$

$= 10$ in dollars squared

SELF-REVIEW 4–4

The answers are at the end of the chapter.

The weights of the contents of several small aspirin bottles are (in grams): 4, 2, 5, 4, 5, 2, and 6. What is the sample variance?

Sample Standard Deviation The sample standard deviation is used as an estimator of the population standard deviation. As noted previously, the population standard deviation is the square root of the population variance. Likewise, the *sample standard deviation is the square root of the sample variance.* The sample standard deviation for ungrouped data is found by:

Formulas for the sample standard deviation

$$s = \sqrt{\frac{\Sigma(X - \overline{X})^2}{n - 1}} \quad (4\text{–}8)$$

or, using the more direct formula given in formula (4–7):

$$s = \sqrt{\frac{\Sigma X^2 - \frac{(\Sigma X)^2}{n}}{n-1}} \qquad (4\text{–}9)$$

EXAMPLE

The sample variance in the previous example involving hourly wages was computed to be 10. What is the sample standard deviation?

Solution

The sample standard deviation is \$3.16, found by $\sqrt{10}$. Note again that the sample variance is in terms of dollars squared, but taking the square root of 10 gives us \$3.16, which is in the same units (dollars) as the original data.

SELF-REVIEW 4–5

The answers are at the end of the chapter.

Refer to Self-Review 4–4.

1. What is the sample standard deviation?
2. Is the standard deviation in the same unit of measurement as the original problem? It should be!

EXERCISES

The answers to the odd-numbered exercises are at the end of the book.

13. Consider these ungrouped values a sample: 7, 2, 6, 2, and 3.
    a. Compute the sample standard deviation by squaring the individual deviations from the mean. [See formula (4–8).]
    b. Compute the variance by squaring the original values. [See formula (4–7).]
14. The following five ungrouped values are a sample: 11, 6, 10, 6, and 7.
    a. Compute the sample standard deviation by squaring the deviations from the mean.
    b. Compute the sample standard deviation by the more direct formula [formula (4–9)].
15. Dave's Automatic Door, referred to in Exercise 3, installs automatic garage door openers. Based on a sample, following are the times, in minutes, required to install 10 doors: 28, 32, 24, 46, 44, 40, 54, 38, 32, and 42.
    a. Compute the sample variance by squaring the deviations from the mean.
    b. Compute the sample variance using the more direct computational formula.
    c. Determine the standard deviation.
16. The sample of eight companies in the aerospace industry, referred to in Exercise 4, were surveyed as to their return on investment last year. The results are: 10.6, 12.6, 14.8, 18.2, 12.0, 14.8, 12.2, and 15.6.
    a. Compute the sample variance for this listing of ungrouped returns on investment by squaring the deviations from the mean.
    b. Compute the variance by using the more direct computational formula.
    c. Determine the standard deviation.
17. Trout, Inc. feeds fingerling trout in special ponds and markets them when they attain a certain weight. A sample of 10 trout were isolated in a pond and fed a special food mixture designated RT-10. At the end of the experimental period, the weights of the trout were (in grams): 124, 125, 125, 123, 120, 124, 127, 125, 126, and 121.
    a. What is the range?

b. What is the arithmetic mean of the sample?
c. Compute the sample variance.
d. Compute the standard deviation of the sample.

18. Refer to Exercise 17. Another special mixture, AB-4, was used in another pond. The mean of a sample was computed to be 126.9 grams, and the standard deviation 1.2 grams. Which food results in a more uniform weight?

MEASURES OF DISPERSION FOR DATA GROUPED INTO A FREQUENCY DISTRIBUTION

Range

Range from grouped data

Recall that the range is defined as the difference between the highest and lowest values. To estimate the range from data already grouped into a frequency distribution, subtract the lowest limit of the smallest class from the highest limit of the largest class. For example, suppose a sample of 40 hourly wages was grouped into this frequency distribution:

Hourly earnings	Number
$ 5 up to $10	10
10 up to 15	21
15 up to 20	9

The range is $15, found by $20 − $5.

SELF-REVIEW 4–6

The answers are at the end of the chapter.

Consumers reported on the number of miles the Bridgeport XCB tire traveled before it became bald. The mileages were tallied into the following distribution. What is the range in mileage?

Mileage	Number of tires
25,000 up to 30,000	16
30,000 up to 35,000	45
35,000 up to 40,000	78
40,000 up to 45,000	56
45,000 up to 50,000	21
50,000 up to 55,000	9

Standard Deviation

Recall that for *ungrouped* data, one formula for the sample standard deviation is:

$$s = \sqrt{\frac{\Sigma X^2 - \frac{(\Sigma X)^2}{n}}{n - 1}}$$

Formula for sample standard deviation—grouped data

If the data of interest are in *grouped* form (in a frequency distribution), the sample standard deviation can be approximated by substituting ΣfX^2 for ΣX^2 and ΣfX for ΣX. The formula for the *sample standard deviation* then converts to:

$$s = \sqrt{\frac{\Sigma fX^2 - \frac{(\Sigma fX)^2}{n}}{n-1}} \quad (4\text{–}10)$$

where:

- s is the symbol for the sample standard deviation.
- X is the midpoint of a class.
- f is the class frequency.
- n is the total number of sample observations.

EXAMPLE

A sample of the semimonthly amounts invested in the Dupree Paint Company's profit-sharing plan by employees was organized into a frequency distribution for further study. (See Table 4–1.)

TABLE 4–1 **A Sample of Semimonthly Amounts Invested by Employees in the Profit-Sharing Plan**

Amount invested	Number of employees
\$30 up to \$35	3
35 up to 40	7
40 up to 45	11
45 up to 50	22
50 up to 55	40
55 up to 60	24
60 up to 65	9
65 up to 70	4

What is the standard deviation of the data grouped into a frequency distribution? What is the sample variance?

Solution ▶ Following the same practice used in Chapter 3 for computing the arithmetic mean of data grouped into a frequency distribution, X represents the midpoint of each class. For example, the midpoint of the "\$30 up to \$35" class is \$32.50. (See Table 4–2.) It is assumed that the amounts invested in the "\$30 up to \$35" class are evenly distributed throughout that class and that the three amounts average about \$32.50. Similarly, the seven amounts in the "\$35 up to \$40" class are assumed to average about \$37.50, and so on.

TABLE 4–2 Calculations Needed for the Sample Standard Deviation

Amount invested	Number, f	Midpoint, X	fX	$fX \times X$ or fX^2
\$30 up to \$35	3	\$32.50	\$ 97.50	3,168.75
35 up to 40	7	37.50	262.50	9,843.75
40 up to 45	11	42.50	467.50	19,868.75
45 up to 50	22	47.50	1,045.00	49,637.50
50 up to 55	40	52.50	2,100.00	110,250.00
55 up to 60	24	57.50	1,380.00	79,350.00
60 up to 65	9	62.50	562.50	35,156.25
65 up to 70	4	67.50	270.00	18,225.00
Total	120		\$6,185.00	325,500.00

To find the standard deviation of these data grouped into a frequency distribution:

Step 1. Each class frequency is multiplied by its class midpoint. That is, multiply f times X. Thus, for the first class $3 \times \$32.50 = \$97.50$, for the second class $fX = 7 \times \$37.50 = \$262.50$, and so on.

Step 2. Calculate fX^2. This could be written $fX \times X$. For the first class it would be $\$97.50 \times \$32.50 = 3{,}168.75$, for the second class $\$262.50 \times \$37.50 = 9843.75$, and so on.

Step 3. Sum the fX and the fX^2 columns. The totals are \$6,185 and 325,500, respectively.

Inserting these sums in formula (4–10) and solving for the sample standard deviation:

$$s = \sqrt{\frac{\Sigma fX^2 - \frac{(\Sigma fX)^2}{n}}{n-1}}$$

$$= \sqrt{\frac{325{,}500 - \frac{(\$6{,}185)^2}{120}}{120 - 1}}$$

$$= \sqrt{\frac{325{,}500 - 318{,}785.2}{119}}$$

$$= \$7.51$$

The sample standard deviation is \$7.51. The sample variance is $(\$7.51)^2$, or about 56.40 (in dollars squared).

SELF-REVIEW 4–7

The answers are at the end of the chapter.

The ages of a sample of the quarter-inch drills available for rental by Tool Rental, Inc. were organized into the following table:

Age (months)	Number
2 up to 4	2
4 up to 6	5
6 up to 8	10
8 up to 10	4
10 up to 12	2

1. What is the grouping called?
2. Estimate the sample standard deviation.
3. Estimate the mean age of the drills (to the nearest tenth of a month).
4. What is the sample variance?

EXERCISES

The answers to the odd-numbered exercises are at the end of the book.

19. Refer to the following frequency distribution.

Class	Frequency
0 up to 5	2
5 up to 10	7
10 up to 15	12
15 up to 20	6
20 up to 25	3

a. Determine the range.
b. Compute the standard deviation.

20. Refer to the following frequency distribution.

Class	Frequency
20 up to 30	7
30 up to 40	12
40 up to 50	21
50 up to 60	18
60 up to 70	12

a. Determine the range.
b. Compute the standard deviation.

21. Each person who applies for an assembly job at North Carolina Furniture is given a mechanical aptitude test. One part of the test involves assembling a dresser based on numbered instructions. A sample of the lengths of time it took 42 persons to assemble the dresser was organized into the following frequency distribution.

Length of time (minutes)	Number
2 up to 4	4
4 up to 6	8
6 up to 8	14
8 up to 10	9
10 up to 12	5
12 up to 14	2

a. What is the range?
b. What is the standard deviation?
c. What is the variance?

22. A sample of the amounts paid for parking on Saturday at the Downtown Parking Garage in Toronto was organized into the following frequency distribution.

Amount paid	Number
$0.50 up to $0.75	2
0.75 up to 1.00	7
1.00 up to 1.25	15
1.25 up to 1.50	28
1.50 up to 1.75	14
1.75 up to 2.00	9
2.00 up to 2.25	3
2.25 up to 2.50	2

a. Compute the range.
b. Compute the sample standard deviation.
c. What is the sample variance?

INTERPRETATION AND USES OF THE STANDARD DEVIATION

Standard deviation used to compare dispersions

The standard deviation is commonly used as a measure to compare the spread in two or more sets of observations. For example, the standard deviation of the semi-monthly amounts invested in the Dupree Paint Company profit-sharing plan was just computed to be $7.51. Suppose these employees are located in the South. If the standard deviation for a group of employees in the West is $10.47, and the means are about the same, it indicates that the amounts invested by the southern employees are not dispersed as much as those in the West (because $7.51 < $10.47). Since the amounts invested by the southern employees are clustered more closely about the mean, the mean for the southern employees is a more reliable measure than the mean for the western group.

Chebyshev's Theorem

Chebyshev's theorem: Applies regardless of shape of distribution

We have stressed that a small standard deviation for a set of values indicates that these values are located close to the mean. Conversely, a large standard deviation reveals that the observations are widely scattered about the mean. The Russian mathematician P. L. Chebyshev (1821–1894) developed a theorem that allows us to determine the minimum proportion of the values that lie within a specified number of standard deviations of the mean. For example, based on **Chebyshev's theorem,** at least three of every four values, or 75 percent, must lie between the mean plus two standard deviations and the mean minus two standard deviations. This relationship applies regardless of the shape of the distribution. Further, at least eight of every nine values, or 89.9 percent, will lie between plus three standard deviations and minus three standard deviations of the mean. At least 24 of 25 values, or 96 percent, will lie between plus and minus five standard deviations of the mean.

Chebyshev's theorem

In general terms, Chebyshev's theorem states:

> **Chebyshev's theorem** For any set of observations (sample or population), the minimum proportion of the values that lie within k standard deviations of the mean is at least $1 - 1/k^2$, where k is any constant greater than 1.

EXAMPLE

In the previous example and solution, the arithmetic mean semimonthly amount contributed by the Dupree Paint employees to the company's profit-sharing plan was \$51.54, and the standard deviation was computed to be \$7.51. At least what percent of the contributions lie within plus two standard deviations and minus two standard deviations of the mean?

Solution ▸ About 75 percent, found by

$$1 - \frac{1}{k^2} = 1 - \frac{1}{2^2} = 1 - \frac{1}{4} = \frac{3}{4} = 0.75$$

SELF-REVIEW 4–8

The answers are at the end of the chapter.

Referring to the previous example regarding the contributions to the company's profit-sharing plan, these figures were arrived at: $\overline{X}$ = \$51.54, s = \$7.51.

1. At least what percent of the contributions to the plan lie within three standard deviations of the mean?
2. At least what percent of the contributions lie between \$34.64 and \$68.44?

The Empirical Rule

Empirical Rule: Applies only to symmetrical distributions

Chebyshev's theorem is concerned with any set of values; that is, the distribution of values can have any shape. However, for a symmetrical, bell-shaped distribution curve, such as the one in Chart 4–3, we can be more precise in explaining the dispersion about the mean. These relationships involving the standard deviation and the mean are included in the **Empirical Rule,** sometimes called the **Normal Rule.**

> **Empirical Rule** For a symmetrical, bell-shaped frequency distribution, approximately 68 percent of the observations will lie within plus and minus one standard deviation of the mean; about 95 percent of the observations will lie within plus and minus two standard deviations of the mean; and practically all (99.7 percent) will lie within plus and minus three standard deviations of the mean.

These relationships are portrayed graphically in Chart 4–3.

CHART 4–3 **A Symmetrical, Bell-Shaped Curve Showing the Relationships between the Standard Deviation and the Mean**

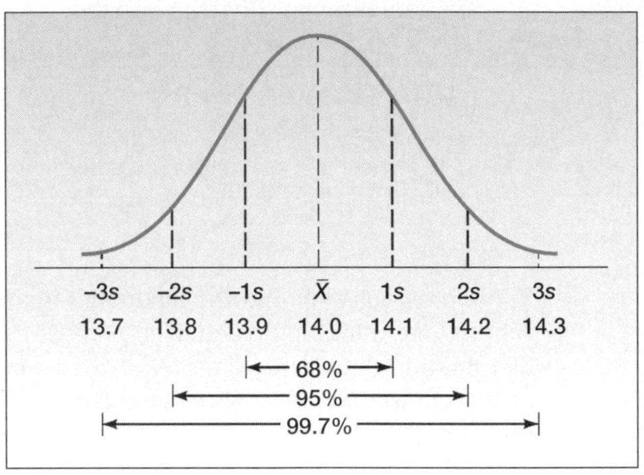

68 percent within $\bar{X} \pm 1s$; 95 percent within $\bar{X} \pm 2s$; 99.7 percent within $\bar{X} \pm 3s$

It has been noted that if a distribution is symmetrical and bell-shaped, practically all of the observations lie between the mean plus and minus three standard deviations. Thus, if $\bar{X} = 100$ and $s = 10$, practically all the observations lie between $100 + 3(10)$ and $100 - 3(10)$, or 70 and 130. The range is therefore 60, found by $130 - 70$.

Conversely, if we know that the range is 60, we can approximate the standard deviation by dividing the range by 6. For this illustration: range $\div$ 6 = 60 $\div$ 6 = 10, the standard deviation.

EXAMPLE

A sample of the monthly amounts spent for food by families of four receiving food stamps approximates a symmetrical, bell-shaped frequency distribution. The sample mean is \$150; the standard deviation is \$20. Using the empirical rule:

1. About 68 percent of the monthly food expenditures are between what two amounts?
2. About 95 percent of the monthly food expenditures are between what two amounts?
3. Almost all of the monthly expenditures are between what two amounts?

Solution ►

1. About 68 percent are between \$130 and \$170, found by $\bar{X} \pm 1s =$ \$150 ± 1(\$20).
2. About 95 percent are between \$110 and \$190, found by $\bar{X} \pm 2s =$ \$150 ± 2(\$20).
3. Almost all (99.7 percent) are between \$90 and \$210, found by $\bar{X} \pm 3s =$ \$150 ± 3(\$20).

SELF-REVIEW 4–9

The answers are at the end of the chapter.

The distribution of a sample of the outside diameters of PVC gas pipes approximates a symmetrical, bell-shaped distribution. The arithmetic mean outside diameter of the sample is 14.0 inches, and the standard deviation is 0.1 inches.

1. About 68 percent of the outside diameters lie between what two amounts?
2. About 95 percent lie between what two amounts?
3. Almost all (99.7 percent) lie between what two amounts?
4. Portray the preceding percentages and amounts graphically.

EXERCISES

The answers to the odd-numbered exercises are at the end of the book.

23. According to Chebyshev's theorem, at least what percent of any set of observations will be within 1.8 standard deviations of the mean?
24. The mean income of a group of sample observations is \$500; the standard deviation is \$40. According to Chebyshev's theorem, at least what percent of the incomes will lie between \$400 and \$600?
25. The distribution of the weights of a sample of 1,400 cargo containers is somewhat normally distributed. Based on the Empirical Rule, what percent of the weights will lie:
    a. Between $\overline{X} - 2s$ and $\overline{X} + 2s$?
    b. Between $\overline{X}$ *and* $\overline{X} + 2s$? Below $\overline{X} - 2s$?
26. The following figure portrays the symmetrical appearance of a sample distribution of efficiency ratings.

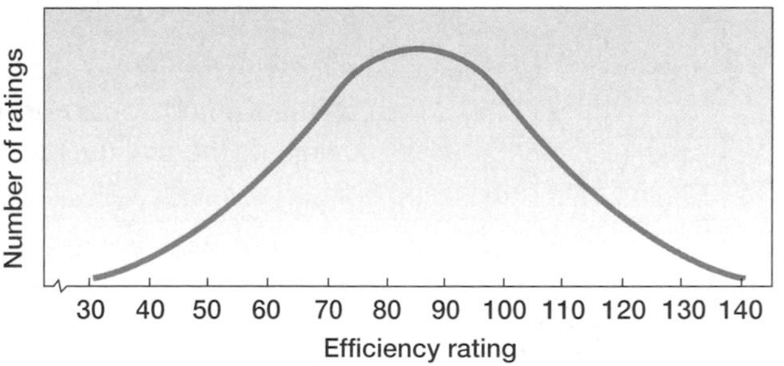

a. Estimate the mean efficiency rating.
b. Estimate the standard deviation to the nearest whole number. (Hint: Since the mean plus and minus three standard deviations encompasses practically all of the values, the range divided by 6 should give a good approximation of the standard deviation.)
c. About 68 percent of the efficiency ratings fall between what two values?
d. About 95 percent of the efficiency ratings fall between what two values?

SOME OTHER MEASURES OF DISPERSION

Three other measures of dispersion will be considered briefly. They are: the *interquartile range,* the *quartile deviation,* and the *percentile range.*

Interquartile Range

Interquartile range: Distance between Q_1 and Q_3

The **interquartile range** is the distance between the third quartile and the first quartile.

$$\text{Interquartile range} = \text{Third quartile} - \text{First quartile} = Q_3 - Q_1 \quad (4\text{–}11)$$

Recall that the median value separates the top 50 percent of a set of observations from the bottom 50 percent. In a similar fashion, the *first quartile,* Q_1, is the value corresponding to the point below which 25 percent of the observations lie. The *third quartile,* Q_3, is the value corresponding to the point above which 25 percent of the observations lie. Thus in one sense we can consider Q_1 and Q_3 measures of location. Q_1 locates the point below which 25 percent of the observations lie. Q_3 locates the point below which 75 percent of the observations are located. But they can also be considered measures of dispersion when Q_1 is subtracted from Q_3. That is, $Q_3 - Q_1$, or the interquartile range, gives us the spread (dispersion) between the third and first quartiles.

Formulas for Q_1 and Q_3

The formula for Q_1 is:

$$Q_1 = L + \frac{\frac{n}{4} - CF}{f}(i) \quad (4\text{–}12)$$

where:

- L is the lower limit of the class containing the first quartile.
- n is the total number of frequencies (not classes).
- CF is the cumulative number of frequencies in all of the classes preceding the class containing the first quartile.
- f is the frequency in the class containing the first quartile.
- i is the size of the class in which the first quartile lies.

The formula for Q_3 is:

$$Q_3 = L + \frac{\frac{3n}{4} - CF}{f}(i) \quad (4\text{–}13)$$

where:

- L is the lower limit of the class containing the third quartile.
- n is the total number of frequencies (not classes).
- CF is the cumulative number of frequencies in all of the classes preceding the class containing the third quartile.
- f is the frequency in the class containing the third quartile.
- i is the size of the class in which the third quartile lies.

EXAMPLE

What is the first quartile for the distribution of the semimonthly contributions to the Dupree Paint profit-sharing plan in Table 4–3? The cumulative frequencies in the right column are needed for the computation of Q_1.

TABLE 4–3 **Calculations Needed for the First and Third Quartiles**

Semimonthly contribution	Class frequency	Cumulative frequency
$30 up to $35	3	3
35 up to 40	7	10
40 up to 45	11	21
45 up to 50	22	43
50 up to 55	40	83
55 up to 60	24	107
60 up to 65	9	116
65 up to 70	4	120

Solution

You will no doubt notice that the procedure for determining the first and third quartiles is quite similar to that presented in Chapter 3 for the median (which is the second quartile, Q_2). Interpolating for the first quartile:

Step 1. Determine the class in which Q_1 lies. Note that there are 120 employees. One fourth of 120 is 30. Observe in the cumulative frequency column that there are 21 contributions below the upper class limit of $45 and 43 contributions below the upper limit of $50. Logically, the 30th contribution falls in the "$45 up to $50" class. So L, the lower limit of the class containing Q_1, is $45.

Step 2. Determine the cumulative number of frequencies, CF, in all of the classes immediately preceding the class containing the first quartile. Referring to Table 4–3, CF is 21.

Step 3. Determine f, the frequency in the class containing the first quartile. There are 22 observations in the "$45 up to $50" class.

Step 4. Determine i, the class interval of the class containing Q_1. The class interval is $5, found by $50 − $45.

Substituting all these values in the formula for Q_1:

$$Q_1 = L + \frac{\frac{n}{4} - CF}{f}(i)$$

$$= \$45 + \frac{\frac{120}{4} - 21}{22}(\$5)$$

$$= \$45 + \frac{9}{22}(\$5)$$

$$= \$47.05$$

The interpretation is that one fourth of the employee contributions are below \$47.05.

SELF-REVIEW 4–10

The answers are at the end of the chapter.

Refer to the distribution of the contributions to the profit-sharing plan in Table 4–3. What is the third quartile? Interpret.

Interquartile range can also be used to compare spreads

The interpretation of Q_3 from Self-Review 4–10 is that 25 percent of the observations will be larger than \$56.46 and 75 percent will be smaller than \$56.46.

Recall that the interquartile range is the distance between the third quartile and the first quartile. The interquartile range for the distribution of semimonthly amounts contributed to the company's profit-sharing plan is \$9.41, found by $Q_3 - Q_1 = \$56.46 - \$47.05$. This indicates that the middle half of the contributions by the employees is between \$47.05 and \$56.46, with the distance between these two quartiles being \$9.41.

The interquartile range can also be used to compare the dispersion between two or more distributions. For example, suppose that the interquartile range for another distribution of employee contributions is \$14.96. Two things may be said: (1) The contributions with the interquartile range of \$9.41 are clustered more closely around their mean than are the contributions with an interquartile range of \$14.96 (because $\$9.41 < \$14.96$). (2) The mean of the contributions with the interquartile range of \$9.41 is a more representative average than is the mean of the distribution of contributions with an interquartile range of \$14.96.

Quartile Deviation

Quartile deviation

The **quartile deviation** is half the distance between the third quartile, Q_3, and the first quartile, Q_1.

$$QD = \frac{Q_3 - Q_1}{2} \qquad (4\text{–}14)$$

For the semimonthly contributions to the Dupree Paint profit-sharing plan:

$$\begin{aligned} QD &= \frac{Q_3 - Q_1}{2} \\ &= \frac{\$56.46 - \$47.05}{2} \\ &= \$4.71 \end{aligned}$$

Approximating the Quartiles

The first and third quartiles may be approximated from a cumulative frequency polygon.

EXAMPLE

The annual incomes of a sample of a group of self-employed salespeople were organized into a frequency distribution. The distribution was portrayed in a less-than cumulative frequency polygon. What are the approximate first and third quartiles?

Solution

► Note that the number of salespeople is shown on the left side of the cumulative polygon, and the percent of the total is on the right side.

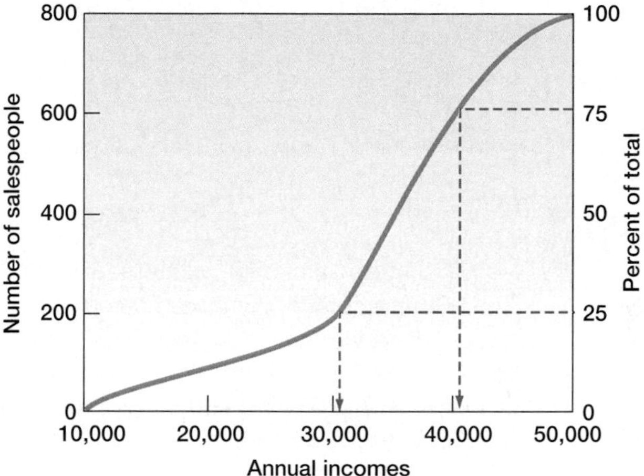

First quartile: Recall that the first quartile is the point below which 25 percent of the incomes lie. What is that point? Go to either one fourth of 800, or 200, on left side, or 25 percent on the right vertical axis. Then move horizontally to the curve and down to the X-axis, and read the income. It is about $30,000.

Third quartile: Three fourths of 800 is 600. Go either to 600 or to 75 percent on the Y-axis. Then move horizontally to the curve and down to the X-axis, and read the income. It is about $40,000.

Percentile Range

Percentile range

As noted, there are three quartiles (Q_1, Q_2, and Q_3). They divide a distribution into four parts. Likewise, the 99 *percentiles* divide a distribution into 100 parts. The 10-to-90 *percentile range* is the distance between the 10th and 90th percentiles. The percentiles are computed and interpreted in a manner similar to the quartiles. The symbol P_{10} is used to represent the 10th percentile and P_{90} the 90th percentile.

The formulas for these two percentiles are:

$$P_{10} = L + \frac{\dfrac{10n}{100} - CF}{f}(i) \tag{4–15}$$

$$P_{90} = L + \frac{\dfrac{90n}{100} - CF}{f}(i) \tag{4–16}$$

EXAMPLE

What is the 10th percentile for the distribution of Dupree Paint Company's semi-monthly profit-sharing contributions in Table 4–3?

Solution ▶

$$P_{10} = L + \frac{\frac{10n}{100} - CF}{f}(i)$$

$$= \$40.00 + \frac{\frac{10(120)}{100} - 10}{11}(\$5)$$

$$= \$40.00 + \frac{2}{11}(\$5)$$

\$40.91, the 10th percentile

$$= \$40.91$$

The 10th percentile, computed in the preceding example solution, is \$40.91. The 90th percentile, computed using formula (4–16), is \$60.56. The percentile range is the distance between the 90th and 10th percentiles. It is \$19.65, found by \$60.56 − \$40.91. Interpreting, the middle 80 percent of the employee contributions lie between \$40.91 and \$60.56 (approximately). A total of 20 percent lie either below \$40.91 or above \$60.56.

Box Plots

A **box plot** is a graphical display, based on quartiles, that helps us to picture a set of data. To construct a box plot, we need only five pieces of data: the minimum value, Q_1 (the first quartile), the median, Q_3 (the third quartile), and the maximum value. An example will help to explain.

EXAMPLE

Alexander's Pizza offers free delivery of its pizza within 15 miles. Alex, the owner, wants some information on the time it takes for delivery. How long does a typical delivery take? Within what range of times will it take for most deliveries? For a sample of 20 deliveries, he determined the following information:

$$\text{Minimum value} = 13 \text{ minutes}$$

$$Q_1 = 15 \text{ minutes}$$

$$\text{Median} = 18 \text{ minutes}$$

$$Q_3 = 22 \text{ minutes}$$

$$\text{Maximum value} = 30 \text{ minutes}$$

Develop a box plot for the delivery times. What conclusions can you make about the delivery times?

Solution ▶ The first step in drawing a box plot is to create an appropriate scale along the horizontal axis. Next, we draw a box that starts at Q_1 (15 minutes) and ends at Q_3 (22 minutes). Inside the box we place a vertical line to represent the median (18 minutes). Finally, we extend horizontal lines from the box out to the minimum value (13 minutes) and the maximum value (30 minutes).

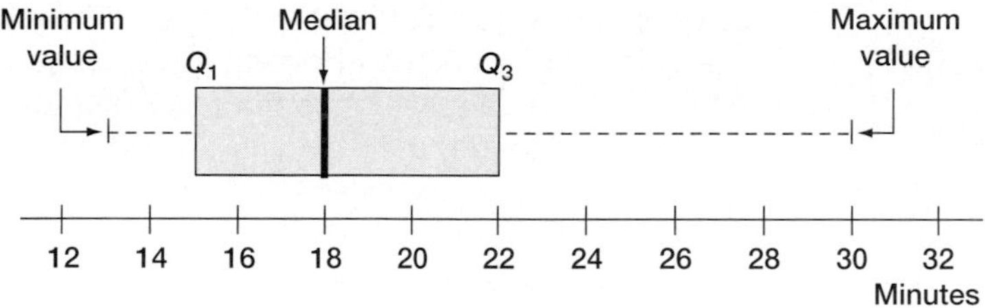

The box shows that the middle 50 percent of the deliveries take between 15 minutes and 22 minutes. The distance between the ends of the box, 7 minutes, is the *interquartile range.* So we conclude that 50 percent of the deliveries take between 15 and 22 minutes. The box plot also shows us that the distribution is positively skewed. How do we know this? The dashed line to the right of the box from 22 minutes (Q_3) to the maximum delivery time of 30 minutes is longer than the dashed line from the left of 15 minutes (Q_1) to the minimum value of 13 minutes. To put it another way, the 25 percent of the data larger than the third quartile is more spread out than the 25 percent of the data less than the first quartile. Another indication of positive skewness is that the median is not located in the center of the box. The distance from the first quartile to the median is shorter than the distance from the median to the third quartile. We know that the number of delivery times between 15 minutes and 18 minutes is the same as the number of delivery times between 18 minutes and 22 minutes.

Box plots placed next to each other are useful in comparing related data sets. The MINITAB output below shows the distribution of salaries for retail store managers in men's apparel versus electronics. The distribution of salaries, in thousands of dollars, for men's apparel is a symmetric distribution, with a median salary of about \$37,000. The salaries range from about \$17,000 to \$57,000, and 50 percent of the

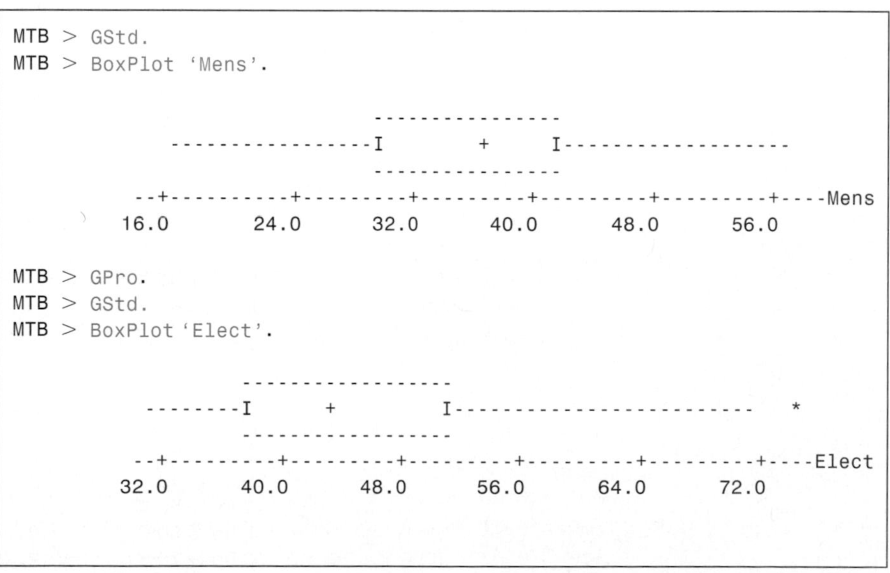

```
MTB > GStd.
MTB > BoxPlot 'Mens'.

                        ----------------
        ----------------I       +      I-------------------
                        ----------------

     --+---------+---------+---------+---------+---------+----Mens
     16.0      24.0      32.0      40.0      48.0      56.0

MTB > GPro.
MTB > GStd.
MTB > BoxPlot 'Elect'.

                 -----------------
          -------I     +         I-------------------------    *
                 -----------------

     --+---------+---------+---------+---------+---------+----Elect
     32.0      40.0      48.0      56.0      64.0      72.0
```

salaries range from $30,000 to $43,000. The electronics store managers have a typical salary of $43,000 and a range of salaries from $31,000 to about $74,000. Fifty percent of the salaries range from $37,000 to $52,000. The dashed line to the right of the box is longer than the line to the left, so we conclude that the distribution of electronics managers' salaries is positively skewed. Note that to the extreme right of this graph is an asterisk (*). This indicates that the largest salary is an **outlier.** An outlier is a value that is inconsistent with the rest of the data. Usually an outlier is more than four standard deviations from the mean. So it appears that there is one electronics store manager that earns a salary larger than the others. From the graph, the salary is about $74,000.

SELF-REVIEW 4–11

The answers are at the end of the chapter.

The following box plot is given.

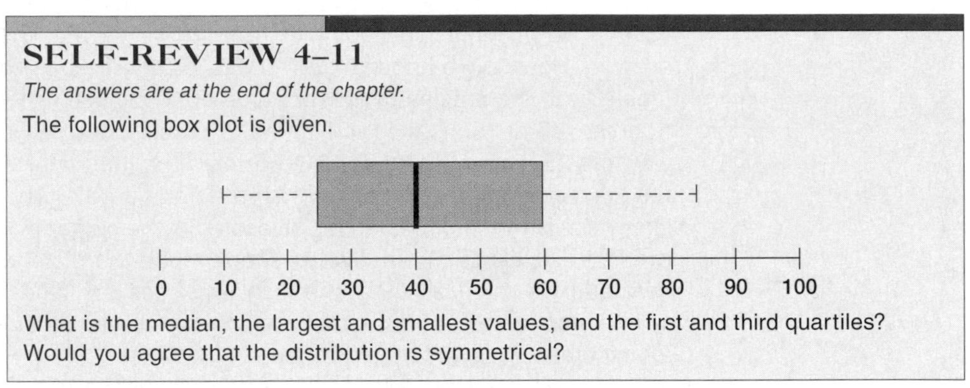

What is the median, the largest and smallest values, and the first and third quartiles? Would you agree that the distribution is symmetrical?

EXERCISES

The answers to the odd-numbered exercises are at the end of the book.

27. The data from Exercise 19 are repeated below.

Class	Frequency
0 up to 5	2
5 up to 10	7
10 up to 15	12
15 up to 20	6
20 up to 25	3

a. Compute the value of the first quartile.
b. Compute the value of the third quartile.
c. Compute the interquartile range.
d. Compute the value of the 10th percentile.
e. Compute the value of the 90th percentile.

28. The data from Exercise 20 are repeated below.

Class	Frequency
20 up to 30	7
30 up to 40	12
40 up to 50	21
50 up to 60	18
60 up to 70	12

a. Compute the value of the first quartile.
b. Compute the value of the third quartile.
c. Compute the interquartile range.
d. Compute the value of the 10th percentile.
e. Compute the value of the 90th percentile.

29. The results of the mechanical aptitude test from Exercise 21 are repeated below.

Length of time (in minutes)	Number
2 up to 4	4
4 up to 6	8
6 up to 8	14
8 up to 10	9
10 up to 12	5
12 up to 14	2

a. What is the first quartile?
b. What is the third quartile?
c. What is the interquartile range? Interpret.
d. What is the quartile deviation? Interpret.

30. In a study of the mileage of automobiles manufactured in 1994, the mean number of miles per gallon was 27.5 and the median was 26.8. The smallest value in the study was 12.70 miles per gallon, and the largest was 50.20. The first and third quartiles were 17.95 and 35.45 miles per gallon, respectively. Develop a box plot and comment on the distribution. Is it a symmetric distribution?

31. A sample of 28 hospitals in the state of Florida revealed the following daily charges for a semiprivate room. For convenience the data are ordered from largest to smallest. Construct a box plot to represent the data. Comment on the distribution. Be sure to identify the first and third quartiles and the median, and comment on the shape of the distribution of daily charges.

$116	$121	$157	$192	$207	$209	$209
229	232	236	236	239	243	246
260	264	276	281	283	289	296
307	309	312	317	324	341	353

RELATIVE DISPERSION

Coefficient of variation

A direct comparison of two or more measures of dispersion—say, the standard deviation for a distribution of annual incomes and the standard deviation of a distribution of absenteeism for this same group of employees—is impossible. Can we say that the standard deviation of $1,200 for the income distribution is greater than the standard deviation of 4.5 days for the distribution of absenteeism? Obviously not, because we cannot directly compare dollars and days absent from work. In order to make a meaningful comparison of the dispersion in incomes and absenteeism, we need to convert each of these measures to a *relative* value—that is, a percent. Karl Pearson (1857–1936), who contributed significantly to the science of statistics, developed a relative measure called the **coefficient of variation** (*CV*). It is a very useful measure when:

When to use *CV*

1. The data are in different units (such as dollars and days absent).

2. The data are in the same units, but the means are far apart (such as the incomes of the top executives and the incomes of the unskilled employees).

Coefficient of variation The ratio of the standard deviation to the arithmetic mean, expressed as a percent.

Formula for coefficient of variation

In terms of a formula for a sample:

$$CV = \frac{s}{\overline{X}}(100) \qquad (4\text{–}17)$$

← Multiplying by 100 converts the decimal to a percent

EXAMPLE

A study of the test scores for an in-plant course in management principles and the years of service of the employees enrolled in the course resulted in these statistics: The mean score was 200; the standard deviation was 40. The mean number of years of service was 20 years; the standard deviation was 2 years. Compare the relative dispersion in the two distributions using the coefficient of variation.

Solution ▸ The distributions are in different units (test scores and years of service). Therefore, they are converted to coefficients of variation.

For the test scores:

$$CV = \frac{s}{\overline{X}}(100)$$

$$= \frac{40}{200}(100)$$

$$= 20 \text{ percent}$$

The standard deviation is 20 percent of the mean.

For years of service:

$$CV = \frac{s}{\overline{X}}(100)$$

$$= \frac{2}{20}(100)$$

$$= 10 \text{ percent}$$

The standard deviation is 10 percent of the mean.

Interpreting, there is more dispersion relative to the mean in the distribution of test scores compared with the distribution of years of service (because 20 percent > 10 percent).

The same procedure is used when the data are in the same units but the means are far apart. (See the following example.)

EXAMPLE

The variation in the annual incomes of executives is to be compared with the variation in incomes of unskilled employees. For a sample of executives, $\overline{X}$ = \$500,000 and s = \$50,000. For a sample of unskilled employees, $\overline{X}$ = \$22,000, and s = \$2,200.

We are tempted to say that there is more dispersion in the annual incomes of the executives because $50,000 > $2,200. The means are so far apart, however, that we need to convert the statistics to coefficients in order to make a meaningful comparison of the variation in annual incomes.

Solution ▶ For the executives:

$$CV = \frac{s}{\overline{X}}(100)$$

$$= \frac{\$50{,}000}{\$500{,}000}(100)$$

$$= 10 \text{ percent}$$

For the unskilled employees:

$$CV = \frac{s}{\overline{X}}(100)$$

$$= \frac{\$2{,}200}{\$22{,}000}(100)$$

$$= 10 \text{ percent}$$

There is no difference in the relative dispersion of the two groups.

SELF-REVIEW 4–12

The answers are at the end of the chapter.

A large group of air force inductees was given two experimental tests—a mechanical aptitude test and a finger dexterity test. The arithmetic mean score on the mechanical aptitude test was 200, with a standard deviation of 10. The mean and standard deviation for the finger dexterity test were: $\overline{X} = 30$, $s = 6$. Compare the relative dispersion in the two groups.

EXERCISES

The answers to the odd-numbered exercises are at the end of the book.

32. For a sample of students in the College of Business Administration at Mid-Atlantic University, the mean grade point average is 3.10 with a standard deviation of 0.25. Compute the coefficient of variation. [See formula (4–17).]
33. United Airlines is studying the weight of luggage for each passenger. For a large group of domestic passengers the mean is 47 pounds with a standard deviation of 10 pounds. For a large group of overseas passengers the mean is 78 pounds and the standard deviation is 15 pounds. Compute the relative dispersion of each group. Comment on the difference in relative dispersion.
34. The research analyst for the Sidde Financial stock brokerage firm wants to compare the dispersion in the price-earnings ratios for a group of common stocks with the dispersion of their return on investment. For the price-earnings ratios, the mean is 10.9 and the standard deviation 1.8. The mean return on investment is 25 percent and the standard deviation 5.2 percent.

a. Why should the coefficient of variation be used to compare the dispersion?
b. Compare the relative dispersion for the price-earnings ratios and return on investment.

35. The spread in the annual prices of stocks selling for under $10 and the spread in prices of those selling for over $60 are to be compared. The mean price of the stocks selling for under $10 is $5.25 and the standard deviation $1.52. The mean price of those stocks selling for over $60 is $92.50 and the standard deviation $5.28.
   a. Why should the coefficient of variation be used to compare the dispersion in the prices?
   b. Compute the coefficients of variation. What is your conclusion?

SKEWNESS

Some distributions symmetrical

Some distributions positively skewed

Some distributions negatively skewed

Chapter 3 described the central tendency of a set of observations using the mean, median, and mode. This chapter has shown several measures that describe the spread in the data. Another characteristic that can be measured is the degree of **skewness** of a distribution. Recall that if a frequency distribution is *symmetrical,* it has no skewness—that is, the skewness is zero. If one or more observations are extremely large, the mean of the distribution becomes greater than the median or mode. In such cases the distribution is said to be **positively skewed.** Conversely, if one or more extremely small observations are present, the mean is the smallest of the three measures of central tendency, and the distribution is said to be **negatively skewed.** (See Chart 4–4.)

CHART 4–4 **Shapes of Frequency Polygons Depicting Skewness**

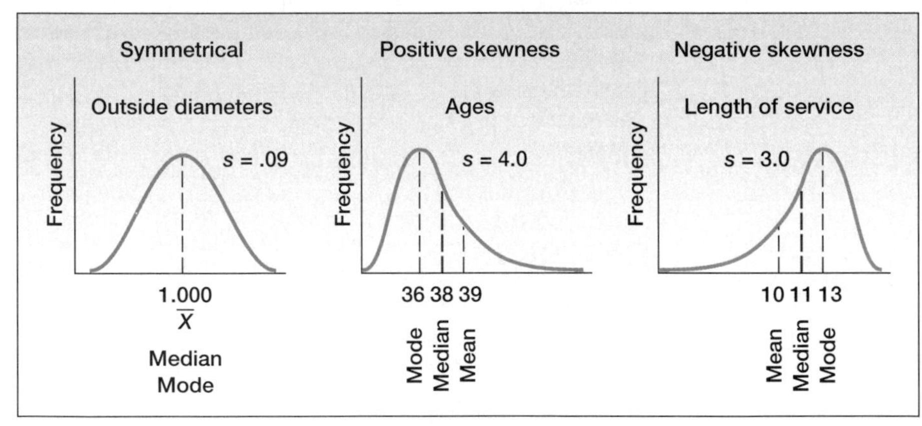

Coefficient of skewness

Karl Pearson also developed a measure to describe the degree of skewness, called the **coefficient of skewness:**

$$Sk = \frac{3(\text{mean} - \text{median})}{\text{Standard deviation}} \qquad (4\text{–}18)$$

EXAMPLE

The lengths of stay on the cancer floor of Sunnyside Hospital were organized into a frequency distribution. The mean length of stay was 28 days, the median 25 days, and the modal length 23 days. The standard deviation was computed to be 4.2 days.

1. Is the distribution symmetrical, positively skewed, or negatively skewed?
2. What is the coefficient of skewness? Interpret.

Solution ►

1. The distribution is positively skewed because the mean is the largest of the three measures of central tendency.
2. The coefficient of skewness is 2.14, found by

$$Sk = \frac{3(\text{mean} - \text{median})}{\text{Standard deviation}} = \frac{3(28 - 25)}{4.2} = \frac{9}{4.2} = 2.14$$

Interpreting, the coefficient of skewness generally lies between −3 and + 3. In this case the coefficient of + 2.14 indicates a substantial amount of positive skewness. Apparently, a few cancer patients are staying in the hospital for a long time, causing the mean to be larger than the median or mode.

SELF-REVIEW 4–13

The answers are at the end of the chapter.

A sample of experienced data entry clerks revealed that their mean typing speed is 87 words per minute and the median is 73. The standard deviation is 16.9 words per minute. What is the coefficient of skewness? Interpret.

A COMPUTER SPREADSHEET APPLICATION

In Chapters 2 and 3 we described Dr. Beth McPherson's analysis of the annual salaries of full professors for a sample of 160 schools. We developed a histogram and a frequency distribution, and we computed several descriptive measures such as the mean, the median, and the standard deviation. We showed the computer results using the MINITAB statistical software system. There are currently many spreadsheet packages available that will also do the computations and output the statistical information. Shown below is output from a Lotus 1-2-3 spreadsheet.

These results were obtained by entering the 160 salaries into the Lotus 1-2-3 spreadsheet and sorting from smallest to largest. Next the salaries were organized into groups with an interval of $10 (recall that the salaries are in thousands of dollars), and the number in each group determined. Finally, the group ranges and counts were used to create the histogram. The mean, median, and standard deviation were also output.

Professor Salary Descriptive Statistics
Midpoint of Salary Range of 10

25	35	45		55		65	75	85	95
26.0	30.5	40.2	45.2	50.0	55.3	60.0	70.1	82.6	90.2
28.0	30.6	40.2	45.3	50.0	55.5	60.2	70.1	84.2	91.2
28.1	32.3	40.7	45.4	50.1	56.1	60.5	70.2		93.3
29.7	33.0	41.2	45.6	50.2	56.1	60.7	72.2		96.5
	34.3	41.3	45.8	50.2	56.7	60.8	72.6		
	34.7	41.4	46.1	50.5	56.9	61.1	72.8		
	35.5	41.9	46.4	50.6	57.1	61.2	73.1		
	35.8	43.1	47.1	50.7	57.2	61.5	73.4		
	36.8	43.3	47.2	50.8	57.5	61.5	74.8		
	37.0	43.6	47.4	51.2	57.7	61.7	75.8		
	37.0	43.8	47.6	52.0	57.8	61.8	75.9		
	37.1	43.9	48.0	52.1	57.9	61.8	76.4		
	37.5	43.9	48.5	52.1	58.3	62.0	76.8		
	37.8	44.2	48.7	52.2	58.4	62.2	77.9		
	37.9	44.4	49.2	52.4	59.1	62.3	77.9		
	39.1	44.6	49.2	52.7	59.2	63.2	79.2		
	39.1	44.8	49.2	52.8	59.6	63.3			
	39.6	44.8	49.5	53.1	59.7	63.4			
	39.6	44.8	49.8	53.2		63.5			
	39.7	45.1	49.9	53.3		64.0			
		45.2		53.8		64.5			
				53.9		64.8			
				54.0		65.0			
				54.7		65.3			
				54.7		65.7			
				55.1		66.3			
						66.4			
						67.0			
						69.2			
Sum: 111.8	724.9		1857.5	2392.5		1830.9	1189.2	166.8	371.2
Count: 4	20		41	44		29	16	2	4

Standard Deviation: (Sample)	13.7559
Mean:	54.03
Median:	52.55

Total Salaries:	8644.8
Total Observations:	160

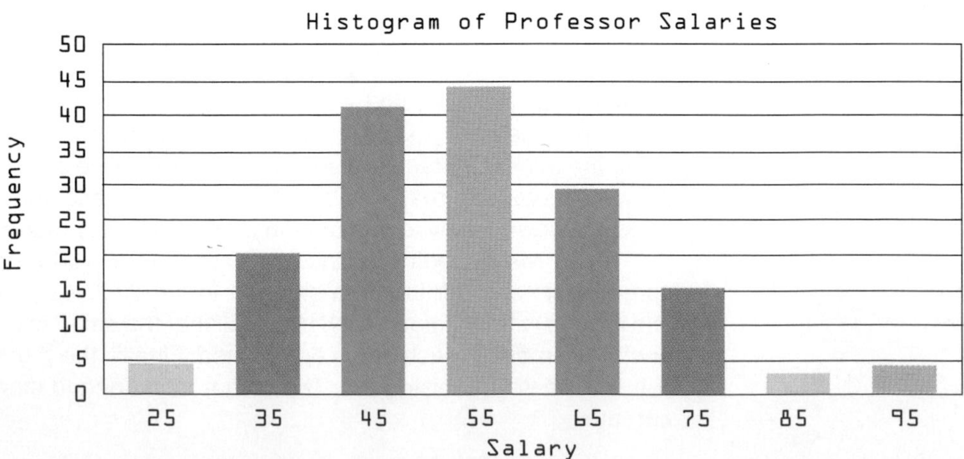

The above chart is called a histogram by the Lotus 1-2-3 spreadsheet, although technically the histogram should not have space between the vertical bars. However, the chart presents a clear picture of the distribution of professor salaries.

EXERCISES

The answers to the odd-numbered exercises are at the end of the book.

36. For a particular distribution of wages, the arithmetic mean was computed to be $25,000, the median $25,000, and the mode also $25,000. The standard deviation was $1,000. Determine the coefficient of skewness. Comment on your findings.
37. Referring to the data in Chapter 2 regarding the salaries of the 1993 Cleveland Indians, the mean salary is $542,000, and the median is $400,000. The standard deviation is $448,500. Determine the coefficient of skewness. Comment on the shape of the distribution.
38. A sample of the homes currently offered for sale in Walla Walla, Washington, revealed that the mean asking price is $75,900, the median $70,100, and the modal price $67,200. The standard deviation of the distribution is $5,900.
    a. Is the distribution of prices symmetrical, negatively skewed, or positively skewed?
    b. What is the coefficient of skewness? Interpret.
39. A study of the net sales of a sample of small corporations revealed that the mean net sales is $2.1 million, the median $2.4 million, and the modal sales $2.6 million. The standard deviation of the distribution is $500,000.
    a. Is the distribution of net sales symmetrical, negatively skewed, or positively skewed?
    b. What is the coefficient of skewness? Interpret.

CHAPTER OUTLINE

I. A measure of dispersion, such as the standard deviation, is used to evaluate a measure of central tendency. A larger amount of dispersion indicates that the data are more widely spread out from the mean.

II. The range is the difference between the largest and the smallest values.

$$\text{Range} = \text{Highest value} - \text{Lowest value} \qquad (4\text{–}1)$$

- A. It is easy to compute and easy to understand.
- B. Only two observations are used in its calculation.
- C. It is influenced by large or small values.

III. The mean deviation is the mean of the absolute differences between each observation and the mean.

$$MD = \frac{\Sigma|X - \overline{X}|}{n} \qquad (4\text{–}2)$$

- A. All the values are used in its calculation.
- B. It is not influenced by an extreme value in the way that the range is.
- C. To compute the mean deviation:
    1. Determine the mean of the values.
    2. Compute the difference between the mean and each value.
    3. Sum these differences without regard to their signs.
    4. Divide the sum of the differences by the number of observations.

IV. The variance is the mean of the squared deviations between the mean and each value. The formulas for the population variance of ungrouped data are:

$$\sigma^2 = \frac{\Sigma(X - \mu)^2}{N} \quad \text{or} \quad \frac{\Sigma X^2}{N} - \left(\frac{\Sigma X}{N}\right)^2 \qquad (4\text{–}3), (4\text{–}4)$$

For data grouped into a frequency distribution the formula is:

$$\sigma^2 = \frac{\Sigma f X^2}{N} - \left(\frac{\Sigma f X}{N}\right)^2$$

A. All the values are used in its calculation.
B. It is not influenced by large or small values.
C. The units are cumbersome to work with. (It is in the original units squared.)
D. To calculate the variance:
   1. Compute the mean.
   2. Determine the difference between each value and the mean.
   3. Square each of these differences.
   4. Sum the squared differences.
   5. If the data are a sample, divide by $n - 1$; divide by N if they represent a population.

V. The standard deviation is the square root of the variance. The formulas for a sample as applied to ungrouped data are:

$$s = \sqrt{\frac{\Sigma(X - \bar{X})^2}{n-1}} \quad \text{or} \quad \sqrt{\frac{\Sigma X^2 - \frac{(\Sigma X)^2}{n}}{n-1}} \qquad (4\text{–}8), (4\text{–}9)$$

For data grouped into a frequency distribution the formula is:

$$s = \sqrt{\frac{\Sigma f X^2 - \frac{(\Sigma f X)^2}{n}}{n-1}} \qquad (4\text{–}10)$$

A. Its value is in the same units as the original data.
B. The standard deviation is one of the most widely reported measures of dispersion.

VI. Chebyshev's theorem states that, regardless of the shape of the distribution, at least $1 - 1/k^2$ of the observations will be within k units of the mean.

VII. The quartile deviation is the difference between the first quartile and the third quartile divided by 2.

$$QD = \frac{Q_3 - Q_1}{2} \qquad (4\text{–}14)$$

where the third quartile (Q_3) and the first quartile (Q_1) are found by:

$$Q_3 = L + \frac{\frac{3n}{4} - CF}{f}(i) \qquad Q_1 = L + \frac{\frac{n}{4} - CF}{f}(i) \qquad (4\text{–}13), (4\text{–}12)$$

The distance between the first quartile and the third quartile is called the interquartile range.

$$\text{Interquartile range} = Q_3 - Q_1 \qquad (4\text{–}11)$$

A. Both of these measures are concerned with the middle 50 percent of the data.
B. They are not influenced by extreme values.

VIII. The Empirical, or Normal, Rule states that:

$\mu \pm \sigma$ encompasses about 68 percent of the values.

$\mu \pm 2\sigma$ encompasses about 95 percent of the values.

$\mu \pm 3\sigma$ encompasses about 99.7 percent of the values.

IX. The coefficient of variation is a measure of relative dispersion.
A. It is computed by dividing the standard deviation by the mean.

$$CV = \frac{s}{\overline{X}}(100) \tag{4–17}$$

B. The coefficient of variation reflects the variation in a distribution, relative to the mean. Use this measure:
   1. When there is a wide difference in the magnitude of the means being compared.
   2. When the distributions being compared are in different units.

X. The coefficient of skewness is a measure of the lack of symmetry in a distribution.

$$Sk = \frac{3(\text{mean} - \text{median})}{\text{Standard deviation}} \tag{4–18}$$

A. It may range from − 3.00 up to 3.00.
B. A value of 0 indicates a symmetric distribution.
C. If the long tail of the distribution is to the right, the distribution is positively skewed.
D. If the long tail of the distribution is to the left, the distribution is negatively skewed.

EXERCISES

The answers to the odd-numbered exercises are at the end of the book.

40. Discuss the advantages and disadvantages of the range as a measure of dispersion.

41. What are the differences in computation between the standard deviation of a population and the standard deviation of a sample?

42. If the coefficient of skewness is computed to be −2.25, describe the shape of the distribution. Include comments on the direction of the tail and whether the mean or the median is larger.

43. Two distributions are being compared. The first one has a coefficient of variation of 20 percent and the other 30 percent. Comment on the relative dispersion of the two distributions.

44. The hourly outputs of a group of employees assembling plug-in units at Zenith were selected at random. The sample outputs were: 8, 9, 8, 10, 9, 10, 12, and 10.
    a. Compute the range.
    b. Compute the mean deviation.
    c. Compute the standard deviation.

45. The ages of a sample of Canadian tourists flying from Toronto to Hong Kong were: 32, 21, 60, 47, 54, 17, 72, 55, 33, and 41.
    a. Compute the range.
    b. Compute the mean deviation.
    c. Compute the standard deviation.

46. The weights (in pounds) of a sample of five boxes being sent by UPS are: 12, 6, 7, 3, and 10.
    a. Compute the range.
    b. Compute the mean deviation.
    c. Compute the standard deviation.

47. A southern state has seven state universities in its system. The numbers of volumes (in thousands) held in their libraries are 83, 510, 33, 256, 401, 47, and 23.
    a. Is this a sample or a population?
    b. Compute the standard deviation.
    c. Compute the coefficient of variation. Interpret.

48. The heights, in inches, of the starting five for the basketball team of the University of the West are: 74, 79, 81, 80, and 78.
    a. Is this a sample or a population?

b. Compute the standard deviation.
c. Compute the coefficient of variation.

49. A recent report in *Woman's World* magazine suggested that the typical family of four with an intermediate budget spends about $96 per week on food. The following frequency distribution was included in the report.

Amount spent	Frequency
$ 80 up to $ 85	6
85 up to 90	12
90 up to 95	23
95 up to 100	35
100 up to 105	24
105 up to 110	10

a. Compute the range.
b. Compute the standard deviation.
c. Compute the interquartile range.
d. Compute the 10-to-90 percentile range. Interpret.

50. Bidwell Electronics, Inc. recently surveyed a sample of employees to determine how far they lived from corporate headquarters. The results are:

Distance (miles)	Frequency
0 up to 5	4
5 up to 10	15
10 up to 15	27
15 up to 20	18
20 up to 25	6

a. Compute the range.
b. Compute the standard deviation.
c. Compute the interquartile range.
d. Compute the 10-to-90 percentile range. Interpret.

51. Houston Memorial Hospital wants to compare its annual patient turnover rate per bed with those published by the American Hospital Association. The turnover rates for a sample of 80 beds were organized into the following frequency distribution. (An annual turnover rate of 21.0 per bed indicates that, during a year, 21 different patients occupied the same hospital bed.)

Annual turnover rate per bed	Number
17 up to 20	4
20 up to 23	9
23 up to 26	13
26 up to 29	20
29 up to 32	15
32 up to 35	7
35 up to 38	5
38 up to 41	5
41 up to 44	2

a. Compute the arithmetic mean and median turnover rate per bed.
b. Determine the standard deviation.
c. What is the coefficient of variation? Explain its meaning.
d. Is the distribution negatively or positively skewed? Cite evidence.

Exercises 52 through 55 are based on the following problem. The quality control department at GE constantly monitors three assembly lines producing built-in ovens for home use. The oven is designed to preheat to a temperature of 240 degrees Fahrenheit in four minutes and then shut off. However, the oven may not reach 240 degrees in the allotted time because of improper installation of the insulation and other reasons. Likewise, the temperature might go over 240 degrees during the four-minute preheat cycle.

A large number of ovens were sampled, and the following measures were computed on each line:

	Temperature		
Statistical measure	**Line 1**	**Line 2**	**Line 3**
Arithmetic mean	238.1	240.0	242.9
Median	240.0	240.0	240.0
Mode	241.5	240.0	239.1
Standard deviation	3.0	0.4	3.9
Mean deviation	1.9	0.2	2.2
Quartile deviation	1.0	0.1	1.7

52. The distribution of the oven readings from which line is a symmetrical, bell-shaped distribution?
    a. Line 1.
    b. Line 2.
    c. Line 3.
    d. Cannot determine based on the information given.
53. The coefficient of variation for the temperatures from line 3 is:
    a. 1.6 percent.
    b. 60.6 percent.
    c. 3.9 degrees.
    d. 242.9 degrees.
    e. Cannot be computed based on the information given.
54. According to the Empirical Rule, about 95 percent of the temperatures from line 2 were between:
    a. 238.8 and 241.2.
    b. 239.9 and 240.1.
    c. 239.2 and 240.8.
    d. 239.6 and 240.4.
    e. None of these is correct.
55. The distribution of the oven temperatures at the end of the four-minute preheat period for line 1 is:
    a. Symmetric.
    b. Negatively skewed.
    c. Positively skewed.
56. A study of households with an income of more than $75,000 reported the following percentage distribution of the ages of the heads of the households.

Age	Percent
15 up to 25	0.8
25 up to 35	16.9
35 up to 45	28.2
45 up to 55	29.3
55 up to 65	17.5
65 or older	7.3
	100.0

a. Compute the first and third quartiles.
b. Determine the quartile deviation.
c. Compute the 10th and 90th percentiles.
d. Determine the 10-to-90 percentile range.

57. The Britten Turkey Farm delivers turkeys to a distributor in the metropolitan Detroit area. The percentage distribution below shows the weights of the turkeys delivered.

Weight (pounds)	Percent
10 up to 15	4.7
15 up to 20	27.8
20 up to 25	51.6
25 or more	15.9

a. Compute the first and third quartiles.
b. Determine the quartile deviation.

58. Health issues are a concern of managers, especially as they evaluate the cost of medical insurance. In a recent survey of 150 executives at Elvers Industries, a large insurance and financial firm located in the Southwest, the numbers of pounds by which the executives were overweight were reported.

Pounds overweight	Frequency
0 up to 6	14
6 up to 12	42
12 up to 18	58
18 up to 24	28
24 up to 30	8

a. Compute the first and third quartiles.
b. Determine the quartile deviation.

59. A major airline wanted some information on those enrolled in their "frequent flyer" program. A sample of 48 members resulted in the following number of miles flown, to the nearest 1000 miles, by each participant. Develop a box plot of the data and comment on the information.

22	29	32	38	39	41	42	43	43	43	44	44
45	45	46	46	46	47	50	51	52	54	54	55
56	57	58	59	60	61	61	63	63	64	64	67
69	70	70	70	71	71	72	73	74	76	78	88

60. A large brokerage firm computed an arithmetic mean of 58.5 opening transactions per day. The standard deviation is 15.8 and the median 63.5 opening transactions.

a. Using Chebyshev's theorem, in what percent of the days will there be between 19.0 and 98.0 transactions?
b. Determine the coefficient of variation.
c. Determine the coefficient of skewness. Explain its meaning.

61. The arithmetic mean discount based on the list price of toothpaste and other such items at Merrill's Discount Drug stores is 24 percent, with a standard deviation of 2 percent. The median discount is 25.5 percent.
a. Using Chebyshev's theorem, what percent of the discounts will be between 21 and 27 percent?
b. What is the coefficient of variation? Explain what it indicates.
c. What is the coefficient of skewness? Explain its meaning.

62. The National Video Rental Association reported the following data regarding the number of videotapes rented per family unit last month.

Number rented	0	1 up to 5	5 up to 10	10 up to 20	20 up to 40	40 or more
Number of households	54	10	16	34	18	6

a. How many videos does a typical family rent per month?
b. Seventy-five percent of the households rent how many videos or less per month?
c. Determine the interquartile range.

COMPUTER DATA EXERCISES

63. Refer to data set 1, which reports information on homes sold in Sarasota, Florida, during 1994.
a. Determine the standard deviation of the selling prices of the 75 homes. Using the mean and median computed earlier, determine the coefficient of variation and the coefficient of skewness. Comment on these values.
b. Determine the standard deviation of the distance from the center of the city to the 75 homes. Using the mean and median computed earlier, determine the coefficient of variation and the coefficient of skewness. Comment on these values.

64. Refer to data set 2, which reports information on the 1993 major league baseball season.
a. Determine the mean, median, and the standard deviation for the variables salary and attendance. Determine the coefficient of variation and the coefficient of skewness for the variables. Comment on these values.
b. Determine the mean, median, and the standard deviation of the number of home runs hit by each of the 28 teams. How would you respond to the question, What is the average number of home runs hit by a team? Determine the coefficient of variation and the coefficient of skewness. Comment on these values.

65. Refer to data set 3, which reports information on the circulation of 48 magazines.
a. Determine the mean, median, and the standard deviation of the circulation of the 48 magazines. Does the distribution seem to be symmetrical? What is the range in the circulation of the 48 magazines?

The following is the first of several cases that will be presented throughout the text. You should answer the specific questions, but you should also include the solutions in a written report. The written part of your summary should not be more than a page in length.

CASE

As discussed in Chapter 2, Dr. Beth McPherson, president of Duval University, gathered data from the journal *Academe* regarding the average annual salaries of full professors at 160 four-year colleges. This information was collected in response to criticism from the Duval faculty union that salaries, particularly at the professor level, were low compared with those of other universities. The raw data were presented in Table 2–1 and were summarized into a frequency distribution in Table 3–1. In Chapter 3 various measures of central tendency were computed.

Now it is time to summarize the results and explain the meaning of these measures. Include in your report information on where the salaries tend to cluster, the various measures of central tendency, and dispersion. What is the standard deviation? Is the distribution symmetrical?

CHAPTER 4 EXAMINATION

The answers are at the end of the chapter.

Questions 1–5 are based on the following statistics. Samples of copper wire were submitted for testing by two companies. The sample pieces for each company were tested for tensile strength and the results organized into a frequency distribution. Then the mean, median, and other measures were computed. (Tensile strength are in pounds per square inch.)

	Company	
Statistic	**Tanyo**	**Artin**
Arithmetic mean	500	600
Median	500	500
Mode	500	300
Standard deviation	40	20
Mean deviation	32	16
Quartile deviation	25	14
Range	240	120
Number in sample	100	80

1. According to the Empirical Rule, the middle 95 percent of the wires from the Tanyo Company tested between approximately what two values?
2. The middle 50 percent of the wires of the Tanyo Company tested between what two values?
3. What is the coefficient of variation for the Tanyo distribution?
4. Which distribution has the larger dispersion? Explain.
5. What is the variance for the Tanyo distribution?

Questions 6 and 7 are based on the following sample weights: 7, 9, 11, 9, and 4 grams.

6. Compute the mean deviation.
7. Compute the variance and the standard deviation.

Questions 8–10 are based on the following frequency distribution.

Days absent during year	Number (f)
2 to 6	7
6 to 10	11
10 to 14	20
14 to 18	30
18 to 22	14
22 to 26	10
26 to 30	8

8. Determine the range. Explain what it indicates.
9. Determine the 10-to-90 percentile range.
10. Is the distribution symmetrical, positively skewed, or negatively skewed? (It is not necessary to compute any measures, such as the coefficient of skewness.)

CHAPTER 4 Answers

Self-Review

4–1

1. \$6,000; \$6,000.
2. \$12,000 for executives, found by \$12,000 − \$0; \$8,000 for middle management, found by \$10,000 − \$2,000.
3. There is more spread in the annual travel costs for the executives because the range for their distribution (\$12,000) is greater than the range of \$8,000 for middle management. Thus, the \$6,000 arithmetic mean for middle management is more representative of the typical travel cost.

4–2

$$\bar{X} = \frac{824}{8} = 103$$

1. 5.25 kg, found by:

X	$X - \bar{X}$	Absolute deviation
95	$\lvert -8 \rvert$	8
103	$\lvert 0 \rvert$	0
105	$\lvert +2 \rvert$	2
110	$\lvert +7 \rvert$	7
104	$\lvert +1 \rvert$	1
105	$\lvert +2 \rvert$	2
112	$\lvert +9 \rvert$	9
90	$\lvert -13 \rvert$	13
	Total	42

$$MD = \frac{42}{8} = 5.25 \text{ kg}$$

2. The weights of the crates going to Ireland deviate 5.25 kilograms on the average from the mean of 103 kilograms.
3. There is more dispersion in the crates going to Ireland compared with those going to France (because 5.25 kilograms is greater than 2.4 kilograms).

4–3

1. 15.67, found by:

X	$X - \mu$	$(X - \mu)^2$
204	−6	36
215	+5	25
207	−3	9
212	+2	4
214	+4	16
208	−2	4
	0	94

$$\mu = \frac{\Sigma X}{N} = \frac{1,260}{6} = 210 \text{ pounds}$$

$$\sigma^2 = \frac{\Sigma(X - \mu)^2}{N} = \frac{94}{6} = 15.67$$

2. 3.96 pounds, found by $\sqrt{15.67}$.

4–4

2.33, found by:

$$\bar{X} = \frac{\Sigma X}{n} = \frac{28}{7} = 4$$

X	$X - \bar{X}$	$(X - \bar{X})^2$	X^2
4	0	0	16
2	−2	4	4
5	1	1	25
4	0	0	16
5	1	1	25
2	−2	4	4
6	2	4	36
28	0	14	126

$$s^2 = \frac{\Sigma(X - \bar{X})^2}{n - 1} = \frac{14}{7 - 1} = 2.33$$

or

$$s^2 = \frac{\Sigma X^2 - \frac{(\Sigma X)^2}{n}}{n - 1} = \frac{126 - \frac{(28)^2}{7}}{7 - 1} = \frac{126 - 112}{6} = 2.33$$

4–5
1. 1.53 grams, found by $\sqrt{2.33}$.
2. Yes, the original data were in grams. The standard deviation is 1.53 grams.

4–6 30,000 miles, found by 55,000 − 25,000.

4–7
1. A frequency distribution.
2. 3.2 months, found by:

Months	f	X	fX	fX^2
2 up to 4	2	3	6	18
4 up to 6	5	5	25	125
6 up to 8	10	7	70	490
8 up to 10	4	9	36	324
10 up to 12	2	11	22	242
	23		159	1,199

$$s = \sqrt{\frac{1{,}199 - \frac{(159)^2}{23}}{23 - 1}}$$

$$= \sqrt{\frac{1{,}199 - 1{,}099.1739}{22}}$$

$$= \sqrt{4.53755}$$

$$= 2.130 \text{ months}$$

3. 6.9 months, found by 159/23.
4. 4.53753.

4–8
1. At least 88.9 percent, found by:

$$1 - \frac{1}{3^2} = 1 - \frac{1}{9} = \frac{8}{9} = 0.889$$

2. About 80.2 percent found by:

$$1 - \frac{1}{(2.25)^2} = 1 - \frac{1}{5.0625} = 1 - 0.198$$

Both $34.64 and $68.44 are 2.25 standard deviations from the mean.

4–9
1. 13.9 and 14.1 inches, found by 14.0 ± 1(0.1).
2. 13.8 and 14.2 inches, found by 14.0 ± 2(0.1).
3. 13.7 and 14.3 inches, found by 14.0 ± 3(0.1).
4.

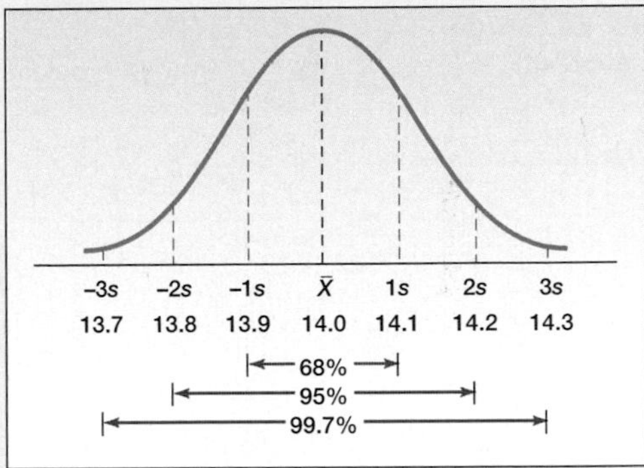

4–10 Q_3 = 56.46, found by 3/4 × 120 = 90. Q_3 lies in the "$55 up to $60" class. L = $55, CF = 83, f = 24. Solving:

$$\$55 + \frac{\frac{3(120)}{4} - 83}{24}(\$5) = \$56.46$$

One fourth of the contributions are above $56.46.

4–11 The smallest value is 10 and the largest 85; the first quartile is 25 and the third 60. About 50 percent of the values are between 25 and 60. The median value is 40. The distribution is somewhat positively skewed.

4–12 *CV* for mechanical is 5 percent, found by (10/200)(100). For finger dexterity *CV* is 20 percent, found by (6/30)(100). Thus, relative dispersion in finger dexterity scores is greater than relative dispersion in mechanical, because 20 percent > 5 percent.

4–13 2.49, found by:

$$Sk = \frac{3(87 - 73)}{16.9} = 2.49$$

There is considerable positive skewness in the distribution of the typing speeds. A few extremely fast typists are causing the mean to be greater than the median or mode.

Examination

1. About 420 and 580, found by $\bar{X} \pm 2s = 500 \pm 2(40)$.
2. About 475 and 525, found by median ± QD = 500 ± 25.
3. 8 percent, found by $(s/\bar{X})100 = (40/500)100$.
4. Tanyo. The range of 240 is greater than the range of 120. Also, standard deviation of 40 is greater than 20, and *CV* of 8 percent for Tanyo is greater than 3.3 percent for Artin.

5. 1,600, found by $(40)^2$.
6. $MD = 10/5 = 2$.
7. Variance = 28/(5 − 1) = 7. Standard deviation = $\sqrt{7} = 2.65$.

X	$X - \bar{X}$	$(X - \bar{X})^2$
7	|−1|	1
9	|+1|	1
11	|+3|	9
9	|+1|	1
4	|−4|	16
40	10	28

8. 28 (found by 30 − 2).
9. 18.1, found by 25.2 − 7.1

$$P_{10} = 6.0 + \frac{\frac{10(100)}{100} - 7}{11}(4) = 7.1$$

$$P_{90} = 22.0 + \frac{\frac{90(100)}{100} - 82}{10}(4) = 25.2$$

10. It appears to be about symmetrical.

SECTION 1 A REVIEW OF CHAPTERS 1–4

This section is a review of the major concepts and terms introduced in Chapters 1 through 4. These chapters were concerned with describing a set of data by organizing it into a *frequency distribution* and then portraying the distribution in the form of a *histogram,* a *frequency polygon,* and a *cumulative frequency polygon.* The purpose of these graphs is to visually reveal the important characteristics of the data.

Computing a central value to represent the data is another way of summarizing a mass of observations. Chapter 3 looked at several measures of central tendency, including the *mean, weighted mean, median,* and *mode.* Chapter 4 described the *dispersion,* or spread, in the data by computing the *range, standard deviation,* and other measures. Further, *skewness,* or lack of symmetry in the data, was described by determining the *coefficient of skewness.*

We stressed the importance of computer software packages, including MINITAB. Several computer outputs in these chapters demonstrated how quickly and accurately a mass of raw data can be organized into a frequency distribution and a histogram. Also, we noticed that the computer outputs present a large number of descriptive measures, including the mean, the variance, and the standard deviation.

GLOSSARY

Chapter 1

Descriptive statistics The techniques used to describe the important characteristics of a set of data. These may include organizing the values into a frequency distribution and computing measures of central tendency and measures of spread and skewness.

Exhaustive Each observation must fall into one of the categories.

Inferential statistics, also called **statistical inference** or **inductive statistics** This facet of statistics deals with estimating a population parameter based on a sample statistic. For example, if 2 out of the 10 hand calculators sampled are defective, we might infer that 20 percent of the production is defective.

Interval measurement If one observation is greater than another by a certain amount, and the zero point is arbitrary, the measurement is on at least an interval scale. For example, the difference between temperatures of 70 degrees and 80 degrees is 10 degrees. Likewise, a temperature of 90 degrees is 10 degrees more than a temperature of 80 degrees, and so on.

Mutually exclusive An observation cannot fall into more than one category.

Nominal measurement The "lowest" level of measurement. If data are classified into categories and the order of those categories is not important, it is nominal level of measurement. Examples are gender (male, female) and political affiliation (Republican, Democrat, Independent, all others). If it makes no difference whether male or female is listed first, the data are nominal-level.

Ordinal measurement Data that can be logically ranked are referred to as ordinal measures. For example, consumer response to the sound of a new speaker might be excellent, very good, fair, or poor.

Population The collection, or set, of all individuals, objects, or measurements whose properties are being studied.

Ratio measurement If the distances between numbers are of a known constant size and *there is a true zero point,* the measurement is on a ratio scale. For example, the distance between $200 and $300 is $100, and in the case of money there is a true zero point. If you have zero dollars, there is an absence of money (you have none).

Sample A portion, or subset, of the population being studied.

Statistics The science of collecting, organizing, analyzing, and interpreting numerical data for the purpose of making more effective decisions.

Chapter 2

Charts Special graphical formats used to portray a frequency distribution, including histograms, frequency polygons, and cumulative frequency polygons. Other graphical devices used to portray data are line charts, bar charts, and pie charts. They are very useful, for example, for depicting the trend in long- term debt or percent changes in profit from last year to this year.

Class The interval in which the data are tallied. For example, $4 up to $7 is a class; $7 up to $11 is another class.

Class frequency The number of observations in each class. If there are 16 observations in the "$4 up to $6" class, 16 is the class frequency.

Frequency distribution It is often difficult to analyze a large mass of raw data. To summarize the data, they can be organized into classes such as $1,000 up to $2,000 and $2,000 up to $3,000. The resulting grouping is called a frequency distribution.

Midpoint The value that divides the class into two equal parts. For the classes $10 up to $20 and $20 up to $30, the midpoints are $15 and $25, respectively.

Chapter 3

Arithmetic mean The sum of the values divided by the number of values. The symbol for the mean of a sample is $\overline{X}$, and the symbol for a population mean is μ.

Geometric mean The *n*th root of the product of all the values. It is especially useful for averaging rates of change and index numbers. It minimizes the importance of extreme values. A second use of the geometric mean is determining the mean percent change over a period of time. For example, if gross sales were $245 million in 1985 and $692 million in 1995, what is the average annual percent increase?

Measure of central tendency A number that describes the central tendency of the data. There are a number of such measures, including the arithmetic mean, weighted mean, median, mode, and geometric mean.

Median The value of the middle observation after all the observations have been arranged from low to high. For example, if observations 6, 9, 4 are rearranged to read 4, 6, 9, the middle value is 6, the median.

Mode The value of an item that appears most frequently in a set of data. For grouped data, it is the *midpoint* of the class containing the largest number of values.

Weighted mean Each value is weighted according to its relative importance. For example, if 5 shirts cost \$10 each and 20 shirts cost \$8 each, the weighted mean price is \$8.40: [(5 × \$10) + (20 × \$8)]/25 = \$210/25 = \$8.40.

Chapter 4

Coefficient of skewness A measure that describes the lack of symmetry in a distribution. For a symmetrical distribution there is no skewness, so the coefficient of skewness is zero. Otherwise, it is either positive or negative, with the limits a ± 3.0.

Coefficient of variation The standard deviation divided by the mean, expressed as a percent. It is especially useful for comparing the relative dispersion in two or more sets of data where (1) they are in different units or (2) one mean is larger than the other mean.

Dispersion or **spread** A measure of central tendency pinpoints a single value that is typical of the data. A measure of dispersion indicates how close or far apart the values are from the mean or other measure of central tendency. Such a measure of dispersion indicates how reliable the average is.

Interquartile range The distance between the third quartile and the first quartile.

Mean deviation The mean of the deviations from the mean, disregarding signs. It is abbreviated as *MD.*

Percentile range The distance between any two selected percentiles.

Quartile deviation Half the distance between the third quartile and the first quartile.

Range Difference between the highest and lowest values.

Standard deviation Square root of the variance.

Variance Mean of the squared deviations from the mean.

EXERCISES

The answers to the odd-numbered exercises are at the end of the book.

1. A small number of employees were selected from all the employees at NED Electronics and their hourly rates recorded. The rates were: \$9.50, \$9.00, \$11.70, \$14.80, and \$13.00.
   a. Are the hourly rates a sample or a population?
   b. What is the level of measurement?
   c. What is the arithmetic mean hourly rate?
   d. What is the median hourly rate? Interpret.
   e. What is the variance?
   f. What is the coefficient of skewness? Interpret.
2. The weekly overtime hours worked by all the employees at the Public Market are: 1, 4, 6, 12, 5, and 2.

a. Is this a sample or a population?
b. What is the mean number of overtime hours worked?
c. What is the median? Interpret.
d. What is the mode?
e. What is the mean deviation?
f. What is the standard deviation?
g. What is the coefficient of variation?

3. The tourist bureaus of St. Thomas and other Caribbean islands surveyed a sample of tourists as they left to return to the United States. One of the questions was: How many rolls of film did you expose when visiting our island? The sample responses were:

8	6	3	11	14	8	9	16	9	10
5	11	7	8	8	10	9	12	13	9

a. Using five classes, organize the sample data into a frequency distribution.
b. Portray the distribution in the form of a frequency polygon.
c. What is the mean number of rolls exposed?
d. What is the median?
e. What is the mode?
f. What is the range?
g. What is the sample variance?
h. What is the sample standard deviation?
i. Assuming that the distribution is symmetrical and bell-shaped, about 95 percent of the tourists exposed between ________ and ________ rolls.

4. The annual amounts spent on research and development for a sample of electronic component manufacturers are (in $ millions):

8	34	15	24	15	28	12	20	22	23
14	26	18	23	10	21	16	17	22	31
13	25	20	28	6	20	19	27	16	22

a. What is the level of measurement?
b. Using six classes, organize the expenditures into a frequency distribution.
c. Portray the distribution in the form of a histogram.
d. Portray the distribution in the form of a less-than cumulative frequency polygon.
e. Based on the less-than cumulative frequency polygon, what is the *estimated* median amount spent on research and development? Interpret.
f. What is the mean amount spent on research and development?
g. Based on the less-than cumulative frequency polygon, what is the interquartile range? The quartile deviation?

5. The rates of growth of Bardeen Chemicals for the past five years are 5.2 percent, 8.7 percent, 3.9 percent, 6.8 percent, and 19.5 percent, respectively.
a. What is the arithmetic mean annual growth rate?
b. What is the geometric mean annual growth rate?
c. Should the arithmetic mean or geometric mean be used to represent the average annual growth rate? Why?

6. The Currin Manufacturing Co. noted in its 1994 second-quarter report that as of June 30, 1994, notes payable amounted to $284.0 million. For the same date in 1984, they were $113.0 million. What is the geometric mean yearly percent increase (June to June) from June 1989 to June 1994?

7. BFI in its annual report revealed that working capital was (in billions) $4.4. $3.4, $3.0, $4.8, $7.8, and $8.3 consecutively for the years 1990–1995. Present these figures in either a simple line chart or a simple bar chart.

8. Suppose an executive of OCM wants to show graphically at the board meeting the change in selected items from the statements of income and other financial reports. From the August *Quarterly,* these items are of interest:

	Six months ended June 30 (in $ millions)	
	1994	**1995**
Income from operations	$ 74.4	$123.1
Interest income	2.7	3.3
Investments in joint ventures	118.5	105.0
Inventory of logs	21.9	6.6
Net income per common share	0.54	1.16

Present the percent changes from 1994 to 1995 in the form of a two-directional bar chart.

For exercises 9–18, fill in the blanks.

9. Employees in a company training course were asked to rate it as either outstanding, very good, good, fair, or poor. The level of measurement is ________.
10. A sample of senior citizens revealed that their mean annual retirement income is $16,900. Since the mean is based on a sample, the $16,900 is called a ________.
11. Refer to the following picture. It is called a ________. The third quartile is about ________, the first quartile ________, the interquartile range ________, the quartile deviation ________, and the range ________.

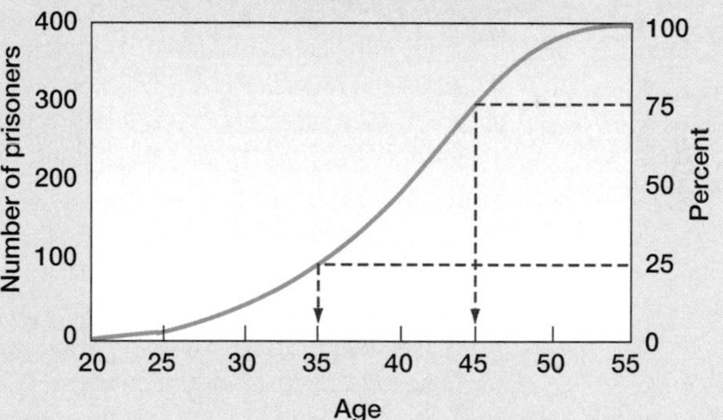

12. Refer to the following picture, which is based on a frequency distribution. It is called a ________. Describe the skewness in the distribution. Explain.

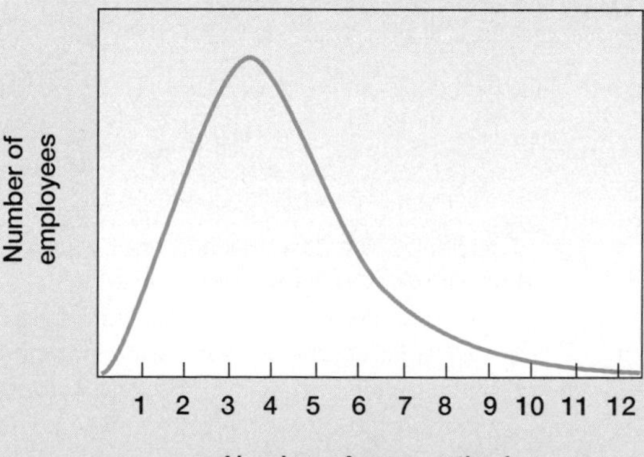

13. Mean = \$64, median = \$61, mode = \$60, standard deviation = \$6, and range = \$40. The coefficient of variation is ________.
14. Refer to Exercise 13. The coefficient of skewness is ________.
15. A useful measure to compare the relative dispersion in two or more distributions, if they are in different units, is the ________.
16. Mean = 100, median = 100, mode = 100, and $s = 4$. The range is about ________.
17. Refer to Exercise 16. About 95 percent of the values lie between ________ and ________.
18. Fine Furniture, Inc. produced 2,460 desks in 1985 and 6,520 in 1995. To find the average annual percent increase in production, the ________ should be used.

A sample of the amounts of funds customers first deposited in First Federal's MCA (miniature checking account) revealed the following.

\$124	\$ 14	\$150	\$289	\$ 52	\$156	\$203	\$ 82	\$ 27	\$248
39	52	103	58	136	249	110	298	251	157
186	107	142	185	75	202	119	219	156	78
116	152	206	117	52	299	58	153	219	148
145	187	165	147	158	146	185	186	149	140

19. Using the preceding raw data and a statistical package (such as MINITAB):
    a. Organize the data into a frequency distribution.
    b. Calculate the mean, median, and other descriptive measures. Include charts, if available. You decide on the class interval.
    c. Interpret the computer output; that is, describe the central tendency, spread, skewness, and other measures.
20. If a computer is not available, organize the miniature checking accounts into a frequency distribution. You decide on the class interval. Portray the distribution in chart form, and compute measures of central tendency, spread, and skewness. Then interpret the important characteristics of the miniature checking accounts.
21. Between 1789 and 1993, 85 judges served as associate justices of the Supreme Court of the United States. Their lengths of service are given below. Analyze the data.
    a. What is a typical length of service?
    b. What is the variation in the lengths of service?
    c. Is the distribution skewed?
    d. Develop a stem-and-leaf chart.

8	1	20	5	9	0	13	15	30	3
30	16	18	23	33	20	2	31	14	32
4	28	14	18	27	5	23	5	8	23
18	28	14	34	10	21	9	33	6	7
20	11	5	20	15	10	2	16	13	26
29	19	3	4	5	26	4	10	26	22
5	15	16	7	16	15	6	34	19	23
36	9	1	13	6	13	17	7	16	5
23	2	3	15	14					

22. The per capita personal income by state (including the District of Columbia), in thousands of dollars, follows.
    a. Organize these data into a frequency distribution.
    b. What is a "typical" per capita income for a state?
    c. How much variation in the income data is there?
    d. Is the distribution symmetrical?
    e. Summarize your findings.

11.1	17.7	13.2	10.7	16.8	15.1	19.2	15.1
18.9	14.3	13.2	14.7	11.4	15.4	12.9	13.2
14.4	11.1	11.2	12.7	16.6	17.5	14.1	14.7
9.5	13.6	11.9	13.8	15.1	15.9	18.3	11.1
17.1	12.2	12.3	13.7	12.4	12.2	13.9	14.7
11.1	11.9	11.8	13.5	10.7	12.8	15.4	14.5
10.5	13.8	13.2					

23. The following frequency distributions show the earnings of year-round full-time workers by gender. Compare the two distributions, and comment on the differences. You may want to draw some charts. Interesting comparisons might be the earnings of the highest 25 percent and the lowest 25 percent; the median, mean, and modal incomes; and the dispersion in the two distributions.

Earnings group	Women	Men
Less than $ 3,000	533	924
3,000 up to 5,000	401	422
5,000 up to 7,000	1,108	814
7,000 up to 10,000	3,218	2,233
10,000 up to 15,000	7,527	5,872
15,000 up to 20,000	5,926	6,621
20,000 up to 25,000	4,085	6,425
25,000 up to 50,000	4,297	17,489
50,000 or more	287	4,141
Total	27,382	44,941

24. Following are the ages at which the 42 U.S. presidents began their terms in office. Organize the data into a stem-and-leaf chart. Determine a typical age at the time of inauguration. Comment on the variation in age.

57	61	57	57	58	57	61	54	68	51	65
49	64	50	48	65	52	56	46	54	49	46
50	47	55	55	54	42	51	56	55	51	
54	51	60	62	43	55	56	61	52	69	

CASE

The following case will appear in the review sections. Assume that you work in the Planning Department of the Century National Bank and report to Ms. Lamberg. You will need to do some data analysis and prepare a short written report. The written part of the report should not exceed a page in length. Remember, Mr. Selig is the president of the bank, so you will want to ensure that your report is complete and accurate. A copy of the data appears in Appendix N.

The Century National Bank has offices in several cities in the Midwest and the southeastern part of the United States. Mr. Dan Selig, president and CEO, would like to know the characteristics of his checking account customers. What is the balance of a typical customer? How many other bank services do the checking account customers use? Do the customers use the ATM service and, if so, how often? What about debit cards? Who uses them, and how often are they used?

To better understand the customers, Mr. Selig asked Ms. Wendy Lamberg, Director of Planning, to select a sample of customers and prepare a report. To begin, she has appointed a team from her staff. You are the head of the team and responsible for preparing the report. You select a random sample of 60 customers. In addition to the balance in the account at the end of last month, you determine: (1) the number of ATM (automatic teller machine) transactions in the last month; (2) the number of other bank services (a savings account, a certificate of deposit, etc.) the customer uses; (3) whether the customer has a debit card (this is a relatively new bank service in which charges are made directly to the customer's account); and (4) whether or not interest is paid on the checking account. The sample included customers from the branches in Cincinnati, Ohio; Atlanta, Georgia; Louisville, Kentucky; and Erie, Pennsylvania.

1. Develop a graph or table that portrays the checking balances. What is the balance of a typical customer? Do many customers have more than $2,000 in their accounts? Does it appear that there is a difference in the distribution of the accounts among the four branches? Around what value do the account balances tend to cluster?
2. Determine the mean and median of the checking account balances. Compare the mean and the median balances for the four branches. Is there a difference among the branches? Be sure to explain the difference between the mean and the median in your report.
3. Determine the range and the standard deviation of the checking account balances. What do the first and third quartiles show? Determine the coefficient of skewness and indicate what it shows. Because Mr. Selig does not deal with statistics daily, include a brief description and interpretation of the standard deviation and other measures.

Chapter 5

A Survey of Probability Concepts

GOALS

When you have completed this chapter, you will be able to:

1
Define the term *probability*.

2
Describe the classical, the relative frequency, and the subjective approaches to probability.

3
Understand the terms *experiment*, *event*, and *outcome*.

4
Define the terms *conditional probability* and *joint probability*.

5
Calculate probabilities, applying the rules of addition and multiplication.

6
Calculate a probability using Bayes' theorem.

7
Determine the number of possible permutations and combinations.

The percentage of executives who read Time *magazine is 35; 20 percent read* Newsweek, *and 40 percent read* U.S. News & World Report *while 10 percent read both* Time *and* U.S. News. *What is the probability that a particular executive reads either* Time *or* U.S. News? *(See Goal 5 and Exercise 22.)*

INTRODUCTION

The emphasis in Chapters 2 through 4 was on descriptive statistics. In Chapter 2 professors' salaries from 160 universities were organized into a frequency distribution to show the lowest and highest salaries and where the largest concentration of data lay. We also portrayed the distribution graphically in a histogram and several polygons. In Chapters 3 and 4 a number of measures of central tendency and dispersion were used to pinpoint a typical annual salary (about $54,030) and to examine the spread in the data. The spread was described using such measures of dispersion as the range and the standard deviation. Descriptive statistics, therefore, is concerned with *describing something that has already occurred.*

We now turn to the second facet of statistics, namely, *computing the chance that something will occur.* This facet of statistics is referred to as **inferential statistics** or **statistical inference**.

Seldom does a decision maker have complete information from which to make a decision. For example:

- Toys and Things, a toy and puzzle manufacturer, has developed a new game based on sports trivia and wants to know whether or not sports buffs will purchase the game. "Slam Dunk" and "Home Run" are two of the names under consideration. One way to minimize the risk of making a wrong decision is to hire pollsters to take a sample of, say, 2,000 from the population and ask each respondent for a reaction to the new game and its proposed titles.
- The quality assurance department of Bethlehem Steel mill must assure management that the quarter-inch wire being produced has an acceptable tensile strength. Obviously, not all the wire produced can be tested for tensile strength because testing requires the wire to be stretched until it breaks—thus destroying it. So a sample is selected at random, say, 10 pieces. Based on the test results, all the wire produced is deemed to be either satisfactory or unsatisfactory.
- Other questions involving uncertainty are: Should the daytime drama "Mama Knows Best" be discontinued immediately? Should the New York Giants select Sammy Uwea or Clint Murray in the first round of the college draft? Will a newly developed mint-flavored cereal be profitable if marketed? Should I marry Jean? Should I buy a new Rolls Royce? Should I vote for Charles Linden for town commissioner?

Statistical inference deals with inferences about a population based on a sample taken from that population. (The populations for the preceding illustrations are: all consumers who like sports trivia games, all the quarter-inch steel wire produced, all television viewers who watch soaps, all the college football players to be drafted by the professional teams, and so on.)

Since there is considerable uncertainty in decision making, it is important that all the known risks involved be scientifically evaluated. Helpful in this evaluation is *probability theory,* which has often been referred to as the science of uncertainty. The use of probability theory allows the decision maker with only limited information to analyze the risks and minimize the gamble inherent, for example, in marketing a new product or accepting an incoming shipment containing defective parts.

Because probability concepts are so important in the field of statistical inference (to be discussed starting with Chapter 8), this chapter introduces the basic language of probability, including such terms as *experiment, event, subjective probability,* and *addition and multiplication rules.*

WHAT IS A PROBABILITY?

No doubt you are familiar with terms such as *probability, chance,* and *likelihood.* They are often used interchangeably. The weather forecaster announces that there is a 70 percent chance of rain for Super Bowl Sunday. Based on a survey of consumers who tested a newly developed pickle with a banana taste, the probability is .03 that, if marketed, it will be a financial success. (This means that the chance of the banana-tasting pickle being accepted by the public is rather remote.) What is a probability? In general, it is the chance that something will happen.

Probability defined

Probability A measure of the likelihood that an event in the future will happen; it can only assume a value between 0 and 1, inclusive.

Three key words are used in the study of probability: **experiment, outcome,** and **event.** These terms are used in our everyday language, but in statistics they have specific meanings.

Experiment: An observed activity

Experiment The observation of some activity or the act of taking some measurement.

This definition is more general than the one used in the physical sciences, where we picture someone manipulating test tubes or microscopes. In reference to probability, an experiment has two or more possible results, and it is uncertain which will occur.

Outcome: A particular result

Outcome A particular result of an experiment.

For example, the tossing of a coin is an experiment. You may observe the toss of the coin, but you are unsure whether it will come up "heads" or "tails." Similarly, asking 500 college students whether or not they would purchase a new Acer 486DX2/66MH_2 Multimedia at a particular price is an experiment. If the coin is tossed, one particular outcome is a "head." The alternative outcome is a "tail." In the computer purchasing experiment, one possible outcome is that 273 students indicate they would purchase the computer. Another outcome is that 317 students would purchase the computer. Still another outcome is that 423 students indicate that they would purchase it. When one or more of the experiment's outcomes are observed, we call this an event.

Event: Several outcomes

Event A collection of one or more outcomes of an experiment.

Following are some examples to clarify the definitions of the terms *experiment, outcome,* and *event.*

Experiment	Roll a die
Possible outcomes	Observe a 1
	Observe a 2
	Observe a 3
	Observe a 4
	Observe a 5
	Observe a 6
Possible events	Observe an even number
	Observe a number greater than 4
	Observe a number 3 or less

Experiment	Count the number of inmates at the Nebraska State Prison who are over 60 years of age
Possible outcomes	Counted 0 that are over 60 years
	• • •
	Counted 29 that are over 60 years
	• • •
	Counted 48 that are over 60 years
	• • •
Possible events	More than 13 are over 60 years
	Fewer than 20 are over 60 years
	• • •

In the die-rolling experiment there are six possible outcomes, but there are many possible events. As for counting the number of inmates in the Nebraska State Prison over 60 years of age, the number of possible outcomes can be anywhere from zero to the total number of inmates. There are a large number of possible events in this experiment.

How is a probability expressed?

A probability is expressed as a decimal, such as .70, .27, or .50. However, it may be given as a fraction such as 7⁄10, 27⁄100 or 1⁄2. It can assume a number from 0 to 1 inclusive. If a company has only five sales regions, and each region's name or number is written on a slip of paper and the slips put in a hat, the probability of selecting one of the five regions is 1. The probability of selecting from the hat a slip of paper that reads "Pittsburgh Steelers" is 0. Thus, the probability of 1 represents something that is certain to happen, and the probability of 0 represents something that cannot happen.

0 means no chance; 1 means certainty

The closer a probability is to 0, the more improbable it is that something will happen. The closer the probability is to 1, the more sure we are it will happen. The relationship is shown in the following diagram along with a few of our personal beliefs.

You might, however, assign a different probability to Slo Poke's chances to win the Kentucky Derby or to an increase in federal taxes.

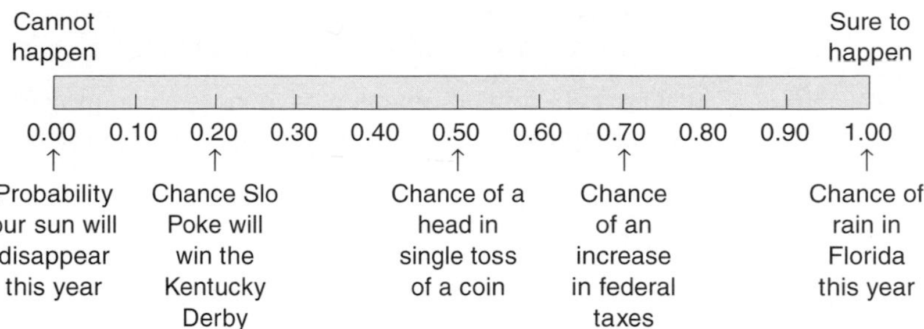

SELF-REVIEW 5–1

The answers are at the end of the chapter.

1. A new hand-held video game has been developed. Its market potential is to be tested by 80 veteran game players.
   a. What is the experiment?
   b. What is one possible outcome?

2. **a.** Suppose 65 players tried the new game and said they liked it. Is 65 a probability?
   b. The probability that the new hand-held video game will be a success is computed to be − 1. Comment.
   c. Specify one possible event.

EXERCISES

The answers to the odd-numbered exercises are at the end of the book.

1. What is the difference between an experiment and an event?
2. What is the difference between an event and an outcome?
3. Answer the following questions:
   a. What is the lowest and highest value a probability can assume?
   b. When is a probability greater than 1?
   c. When is a probability less than 0?
   d. What conclusion can be drawn if a probability is between .8 and 1.0?
4. Is it possible for a probability to assume a value of 0?
5. The Streets Department in Whitehouse, Illinois, is considering widening Indiana Avenue to three lanes. Before a final decision is made, 500 citizens are asked if they support the widening.
   a. What is the experiment?
   b. What are some of the possible events?
   c. List two possible outcomes.
6. The chairman of the board of Rudd Industries is delivering a speech to the company stockholders tomorrow explaining his position that the company should merge with Zimmerman Plastics. He has received six pieces of mail on the issue and is interested in the number of writers who agree with him.
   a. What is the experiment?
   b. What are some of the possible events?
   c. List two possible outcomes.

WHY STUDY PROBABILITY?

What role does probability have in decision making? This question can be answered by citing two cases that will be discussed in forthcoming chapters.

Case 1

Could the difference between 20 percent and 19 percent be due to sampling?

Based on past experience, a publishing company has determined that at least 20 percent of a certain group, such as musicians, must subscribe to a monthly magazine to make it a financial success. The company is considering a monthly magazine for bird-watchers. A special copy was designed and mailed to a sample of 1,000 bird-watchers. In response, 190 out of 1,000, or 19 percent, said they would subscribe to the magazine if it were published. Should we state that this proportion is less than 20 percent and make an immediate decision not to publish the magazine? Or could the difference between the required percent (20) and the sample percent (19) be attributed to sampling, that is, chance? Probability will help us arrive at a decision for this type of problem, which will be discussed in Chapter 9.

Case 2

Could the difference between 1,070 psi and 1,062 psi be due to chance?

A very large construction project requires thousands of concrete blocks. Specifications state that the blocks must stand up to pressures of 1,050 pounds per square inch (psi) on the average. Two firms manufacturing these blocks submitted samples for testing. The arithmetic mean strength of the Strong Block Company blocks was 1,070 psi; those from the Taylor Company tested at 1,062 psi. Strong Block thinks it should be awarded the contract because its blocks have a higher psi. Taylor disagrees, saying that the difference of only 8 psi could be due to sampling (chance). If Strong Block's claim is correct, it will be awarded the contract. If Taylor's statement is correct, the contract will be divided between the two companies. Probability will help us reach a decision for a problem such as this in Chapter 9.

APPROACHES TO PROBABILITY

Two approaches to probability will be discussed, namely, the *objective* and the *subjective* viewpoints. **Objective probability** can be subdivided into (1) *classical* or *a priori* probability and (2) the *relative frequency* or *a posteriori concept.*

Classical Probability

Classical probability

Classical probability is based on the assumption that the outcomes of an experiment are *equally likely.* Using the classical viewpoint, the probability of an event happening is computed by dividing the number of favorable outcomes by the total number of possible outcomes:

$$\text{Probability of an event} = \frac{\text{Number of favorable outcomes}}{\text{Total number of possible outcomes}} \qquad (5\text{–}1)$$

EXAMPLE

The experiment is to observe the "up" face on a six-sided die. What is the probability that a two spot ⚁ will appear face up?

Solution ▶ The possible events are:

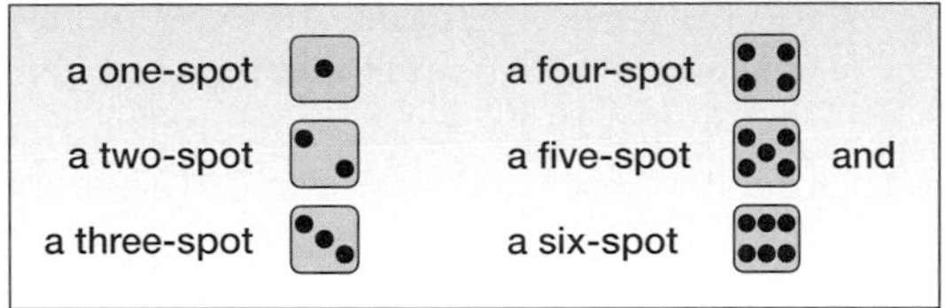

There is only one "favorable" outcome, a two-spot. All six results for the toss of the die are equally likely. Therefore:

$$\text{Probability of a two-spot} = \frac{1}{6} \quad \begin{matrix} \leftarrow \\ \leftarrow \end{matrix} \quad \boxed{\frac{\text{Number of favorable outcomes}}{\text{Total number of possible outcomes}}}$$

$$= .167$$

Mutually exclusive events

If *only one* of several events can occur at one time, we refer to the events as being **mutually exclusive.**

> **Mutually exclusive** The occurrence of any one event means that none of the others can occur at the same time.

In the die-tossing experiment, the six possible outcomes are mutually exclusive events. If a two-spot comes face up on the toss of the die, a five-spot cannot occur at the same time.

Collectively exhaustive

If an experiment has a set of events that includes every possible outcome, such as the die-tossing experiment, the set of events is called **collectively exhaustive.**

> **Collectively exhaustive** At least one of the events must occur when an experiment is conducted.

For the die-tossing experiment, the set of events consists of 1, 2, 3, 4, 5, and 6. The set is collectively exhaustive because it includes all possible outcomes.

Sum of probabilities = 1

If the set of events is collectively exhaustive and the events are mutually exclusive, the sum of the probabilities equals 1. For a coin-tossing experiment:

	Probability
Event: Head	.50
Event: Tail	.50
Total	1.00

For the classical approach to be applied, the events must have the same chance of occurring (called *equally likely* events). Also, the set of events must be mutually exclusive and collectively exhaustive.

Historically, the classical approach to probability was developed and applied in the 17th and 18th centuries to games of chance, such as cards and dice. Note that it is unnecessary to do an experiment to determine the probability of an event occurring using the classical approach; we can logically arrive, for example, at the probability of getting a tail on the toss of one coin or three heads on the toss of three coins. Nor do we have to conduct an experiment to determine the probability that your income tax return will be audited if there are 2 million returns mailed to your district office and 2,400 are to be audited. Assuming that each return has an equal chance of being audited, your probability is .0012—found by 2,400 divided by 2 million. Obviously, the chance of your return being audited is rather remote.

SELF-REVIEW 5–2

The answers are at the end of the chapter.

1. Featherstone has warehouses in four regions: southern, midwestern, Rocky Mountain, and far western. One of the regions is to be selected at random to store a seldom-used item. What is the probability that the warehouse selected would be the one in the Rocky Mountain region?
2. One card from a standard 52-card deck is to be selected at random. Express as a fraction and as a decimal:
   a. The probability the card will be a spade.
   b. The probability the card will be the jack of hearts.
   c. The probability the card will be a queen.
3. The above two examples illustrate what approach to probability?

Relative Frequency Concept

Relative frequency concept

Another probability concept is based on **relative frequencies.** The probability of an event happening in the long run is determined by observing what fraction of the time like events happened in the past. In terms of a formula:

$$\text{Probability of event happening} = \frac{\text{Number of times event occurred in past}}{\text{Total number of observations}}$$

EXAMPLE

A study of 751 business administration graduates at the University of Toledo was conducted. This is the experiment. It revealed that 383 out of the 751 were *not* employed in their major area of study in college. For illustration, a person who majored in accounting is now the marketing manager of a tomato-processing firm. What is the probability that a particular business graduate will be employed in an area other than his or her college major?

Solution ▶

$$\text{Probability of event happening} = \frac{\text{Number of times event occurred in past}}{\text{Total number of observations}}$$

$$P(A) = \frac{383}{751}$$

$$= .51$$

To simplify, letters or numbers may be used. P stands for probability, and in this case $P(A)$ stands for the probability that a graduate is not employed in his or her major area of college study.

Since 383 out of 751, or .51 in terms of a probability, are in a different field of employment from their major in college, we can use this as an estimate of the probability. In other words, based on past experience, the probability is .51 that a business graduate will be employed in a field other than his or her college major.

SELF-REVIEW 5–3

The answers are at the end of the chapter.

The National Center for Health Statistics reported that of every 883 deaths, 24 resulted from an automobile accident, 182 from cancer, and 333 from heart disease.

1. Using the relative frequency approach, approximate the probability that a particular death is due to an automobile accident. Express it as a fraction and as a decimal.
2. Using the relative frequency approach, estimate the probability that a particular death is caused by cancer. Express it as a fraction and as a decimal.

Subjective Probability

Subjective probability: Based on personal judgment and expresses degree of belief

If there is little or no past experience on which to base a probability, a probability may be arrived at subjectively. Essentially, this means evaluating the available opinions and other subjective information and then arriving at the probability. This probability is aptly called a **subjective probability.**

Subjective concept of probability The likelihood (probability) of a particular event happening that is assigned by an individual based on whatever information is available.

Illustrations of subjective probability are:

1. Estimating the likelihood that the New England Patriots will play in the Super Bowl next year.
2. Estimating the probability that General Motors Corp. will lose its number 1 ranking in total units sold to Ford Motor Co. or Chrysler Corp. within two years.
3. Estimating the likelihood that you will earn an *A* in this course.

SELF-REVIEW 5–4

The answers are at the end of the chapter.

1. What probability would you assign to the likelihood that the Dow Jones Industrial Average will climb to 5000 this year?

2. What probability would you assign to the likelihood that you will buy a new Jaguar V12 automobile this year?

In summary, there are two viewpoints regarding probability—the objective and the subjective viewpoints. We noted that a probability statement always constitutes an estimate of an unknown value that will govern an event that has not yet occurred. There is, of course, a considerable latitude in the degree of uncertainty that surrounds this estimate, based primarily on the knowledge possessed by the individual concerning the underlying process. The individual possesses a great deal of knowledge about the toss of a die and can state that the probability that a one-spot will appear face up on the toss of a true die is one sixth. But we know very little concerning the acceptance in the marketplace of a new and untested product. For example, even though a market research director tests a newly developed product in, say, 40 retail stores and states that there is a 70 percent chance that the product will have sales of more than 1 million units, she still has very little knowledge of how consumers will react when it is marketed nationally. In both cases (the case of the person rolling a die and the testing of a new product) the individual is assigning a value to an event of interest, and a difference exists only in the predictor's confidence in the precision of the estimate. However, regardless of the viewpoint, the same laws of probability (presented in the following sections) will be applied.

EXERCISES

The answers to the odd-numbered exercises are at the end of the book.

7. In each of the following cases indicate whether classical, relative frequency, or subjective probability is used.
   a. A basketball player makes 30 out of 50 foul shots. The probability is .6 that she makes the next foul shot attempted.
   b. A seven-member committee of students is formed to study environmental issues. What is the likelihood that any one of the seven is chosen as the spokesperson?

c. You purchase one of 5 million tickets sold for Lotto Canada. What is the likelihood you win the $1 million jackpot?
d. The probability of an earthquake in northern California in the next 10 years is .80.

8. Define the term *mutually exclusive* in your own words.
9. There are 52 cards in a standard deck.
   a. What is the probability that the first card selected is a spade?
   b. What is the probability that the first card selected is the jack of spades?
   c. What concept of probability do *a* and *b* illustrate?
10. A single die is rolled.
   a. What is the probability that a two-spot will show face up?
   b. What concept of probability does this illustrate?
   c. Are the events equally likely and mutually exclusive? Explain.
11. Before a nationwide survey was conducted, 40 people were selected to test the questionnaire. One question about whether or not abortions should be legal required a yes or no answer.
   a. What is the experiment?
   b. List one possible event.
   c. Ten of the 40 favored the legalization of abortions. Based on these sample responses, what is the probability that a particular person will be in favor of the legalization of abortions?
   d. What concept of probability does this illustrate?
   e. Are the events equally likely and mutually exclusive?
12. A large number of automobile drivers were selected at random, and the number of traffic violations they had, if any, were recorded.

Number of violations	Number of drivers
0	1,910
1	46
2	18
3	12
4	9
5 or more	5

   a. What is the experiment?
   b. List one possible event.
   c. What is the probability that a particular driver had exactly two violations?
   d. What concept of probability does this illustrate?

SOME BASIC RULES OF PROBABILITY

Now that we have defined probability and described the different approaches to probability, we turn our attention to combining events by applying rules of addition and multiplication.

Rules of Addition

Two mutually exclusive events cannot both happen at one time

Special Rule of Addition To apply the **special rule of addition,** the events must be mutually exclusive. Recall that *mutually exclusive* means that when one event occurs, none of the other events can occur *at the same time.* As illustrations, if a two-spot comes face up on the roll of a die, none of the other faces (1, 3, 4, 5, or 6) can be face up at the same time. And a product coming off the assembly line cannot be defective and satisfactory at the same time.

Add probability of A and B to get $P(A \text{ or } B)$

If two events A and B are mutually exclusive, the special rule of addition states that the probability of one *or* the other event's occurring equals the sum of their probabilities. This rule is expressed in the following formula.

$$P(A \text{ or } B) = P(A) + P(B) \tag{5–2}$$

For three mutually exclusive events designated A, B, and C, the rule is written:

$$P(A \text{ or } B \text{ or } C) = P(A) + P(B) + P(C)$$

EXAMPLE

An automatic Shaw machine fills plastic bags with a mixture of beans, broccoli, and other vegetables. Most of the bags contain the correct weight, but because of the slight variation in the size of the beans and other vegetables, a package might be slightly underweight or overweight. A check of 4,000 packages in the past revealed:

Weight	Event	Number of packages	Probability of occurrence	
Underweight	A	100	.025	← $\frac{100}{4,000}$
Satisfactory	B	3,600	.900	
Overweight	C	300	.075	
		4,000	1.000	

What is the probability that a particular package will be either underweight or overweight?

Solution ▶ The outcome "underweight" is the event A. The outcome "overweight" is the event C. Applying the special rule of addition:

$$\begin{aligned} P(A \text{ or } C) &= P(A) + P(C) \\ &= .025 + .075 \\ &= .10 \end{aligned}$$

Note that the events are mutually exclusive, meaning that a package of mixed vegetables cannot be underweight, satisfactory, and overweight at the same time. (Also, $P(A \text{ or } B \text{ or } C) = 1.000$.)

Venn diagram: A useful tool to depict addition or multiplication rules

English logician J. Venn (1834–1888) developed a diagram to portray graphically the outcome of an experiment. The *mutually exclusive* concept and various other rules for combining probabilities can be illustrated using this device. To construct a Venn diagram, a space is first enclosed representing the total of all possible outcomes. This space is called the *sample space,* and it is usually in the form of a rectangle. A particular outcome (for example, that the bag of mixed vegetables was overweight) is called a *sample point.* The total of all sample points equals the sample space. The following Venn diagram represents the *mutually exclusive* concept. There is no overlapping of events, meaning that the events are mutually exclusive.

Sample point, sample space

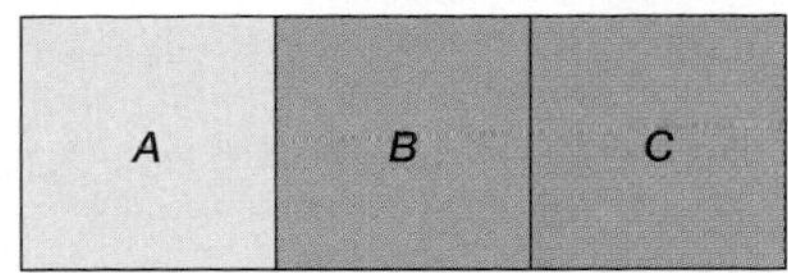

SELF-REVIEW 5–5

The answers are at the end of the chapter.

A selected group of employees of Worldwide Enterprises is to be surveyed with respect to a new pension plan. In-depth interviews are to be conducted with each employee selected in the sample. The employees are classified as follows:

Classification	Event	Number of employees
Supervisors	*A*	120
Maintenance	*B*	50
Production	*C*	1,460
Management	*D*	302
Secretarial	*E*	68

1. What is the probability that the first person selected is a maintenance employee?
2. What is the probability that the first person selected is a secretary?
3. What is the probability that the first person selected is either in maintenance or a secretary?
4. What rule of probability did you use to determine the answer to 3?
5. What is the probability that the first person chosen to be interviewed is either a supervisor or in maintenance or a production worker or a manager or a secretary?
6. Draw a Venn diagram to depict these events.
7. Are these events mutually exclusive?

The probability that a bag of mixed vegetables selected is underweight $P(A)$, plus the probability that it is not an underweight bag, written $P(\sim A)$ and read "not *A*" must logically equal 1. This is written:

$$P(A) + P(\sim A) = 1$$

This can be revised to read:

$$P(A) = 1 - P(\sim A) \qquad (5\text{–}3)$$

The complement rule

This is referred to as the **complement rule.**

The complement rule is used to determine the probability of an event occurring by subtracting the probability of the event *not* occurring from 1. A Venn diagram illustrating the complement rule might appear as:

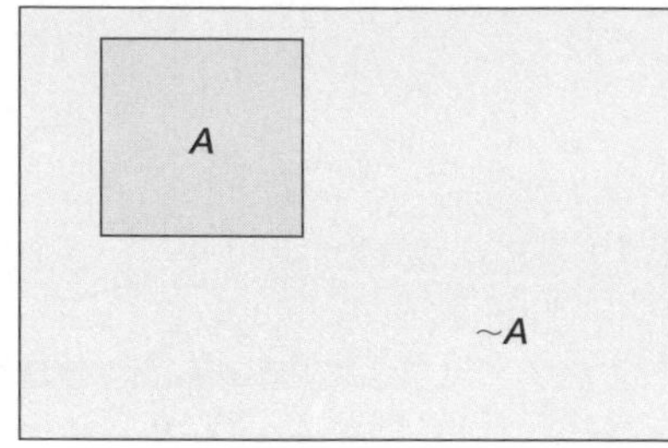

EXAMPLE

Recall that the probability that a bag of mixed vegetables is underweight is .025 and that the probability of an overweight bag is .075. Use the complement rule to show that the probability of a satisfactory bag is .900. Show the solution using a Venn diagram.

Solution

▶ The probability that the bag is unsatisfactory equals the probability that the bag is overweight plus the probability that it is underweight. That is, $P(A \text{ or } C) = P(A) + P(C) = .025 + .075 = .100$. The bag is satisfactory if it is not underweight or overweight, so $P(B) = 1 - [P(A) + P(C)] = 1 - [.025 + .075] = 0.900$. The Venn diagram portraying this situation is:

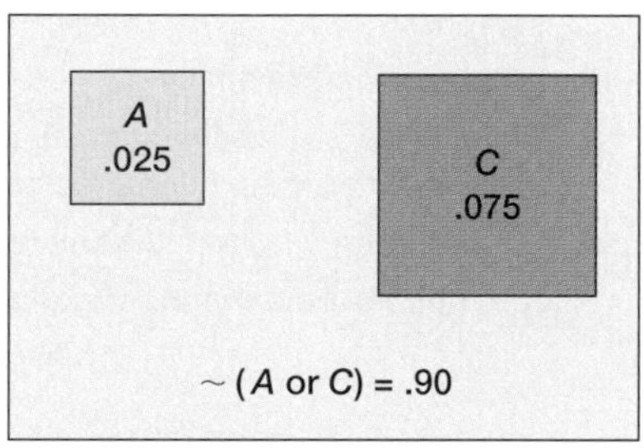

The complement rule is very important in the study of probability. Often it is more efficient to calculate the probability of an event happening by determining the probability of it not happening and subtracting the result from 1.

SELF-REVIEW 5–6

The answers are at the end of the chapter.

Refer to Self-Review 5–5. Portray the following in the form of one Venn diagram. On the first selection, what is the probability of:

1. Selecting a maintenance employee (designated event *B*)?
2. Selecting a secretary (designated event *E*)?
3. Selecting a person in management (designated event *D*)?
4. Not selecting event *B*, or *D*, or *E*?

EXERCISES

The answers to the odd-numbered exercises are at the end of the book.

13. The events *A* and *B* are mutually exclusive. Suppose $P(A) = .30$ and $P(B) = .20$. What is the probability of either *A* or *B* occurring? What is the probability that neither *A* nor *B* will happen?
14. The events *X* and *Y* are mutually exclusive. Suppose $P(X) = .05$ and $P(Y) = .02$. What is the probability of either *X* or *Y* occurring? What is the probability that neither *X* nor *Y* will happen?
15. A study of 200 grocery chains revealed these incomes after taxes:

Income after taxes	Number of firms
Under $1 million	102
$1 million to $20 million	61
$20 million or more	37

   a. What is the probability that a particular chain has under $1 million in income after taxes?
   b. What is the probability that a grocery chain selected at random has either an income between $1 million and $20 million, or an income of $20 million or more? What rule of probability was applied?

16. A study of the opinions of designers with respect to the primary color most desirable for use in executive offices showed:

Primary color	Number of opinions
Red	92
Orange	86
Yellow	46
Green	91
Blue	37
Indigo	46
Violet	2

   a. What is the experiment?
   b. What is one possible event?
   c. What is the probability of selecting a particular response and discovering that the designer prefers red or green?
   d. What is the probability that a designer does not prefer yellow?

The General Rule of Addition The outcomes of an experiment may not be mutually exclusive. Suppose, for illustration, that the Florida Tourist Commission selected a sample of 200 tourists who visited the state during the year. The survey revealed that 120 tourists went to Disney World and 100 went to Busch Gardens near Tampa. What is the probability that a person selected visited either Disney World or Busch Gardens? If the special rule of addition is used, the probability of selecting a tourist who went to Disney World is .60, found by 120/200. Similarly, the probability of a tourist going to Busch Gardens is .50. The sum of these probabilities is 1.10. We know, however, that this probability cannot be greater than 1. The explanation is that many tourists visited both attractions and are being counted twice! A check of the survey responses revealed that 60 out of the 200 sampled did, in fact, visit both attractions.

To answer our question, "What is the probability that a person selected visited either Disney World or Busch Gardens?" (1) add the probability that a tourist visited Disney World and the probability he/she visited Busch Gardens, and (2) subtract the probability of visiting both. Thus:

$$P(\text{Disney or Busch}) = P(\text{Disney}) + P(\text{Busch}) - P(\text{both Disney and Busch})$$
$$= \frac{120}{200} + \frac{100}{200} - \frac{60}{200}$$
$$= \frac{160}{200} = .80, \text{ or}$$
$$= .60 + .50 - .30 = .80$$

When two events overlap, the probability is called a **joint probability.** The probability that a tourist visits both attractions (.30) is an example of a joint probability.

Joint probability: Occurrence of two or more events at the same time

Joint probability A probability that measures the likelihood that two or more events will happen concurrently.

In summary, the general rule of addition is used to combine events that are not mutually exclusive. This rule for two events designated *A* and *B* is written:

$$P(A \text{ or } B) = P(A) + P(B) - P(A \text{ and } B) \quad (5\text{–}4)$$

For the expression $P(A \text{ or } B)$, the word *or* suggests that *A* may occur or *B* may occur. This also includes the possibility that *A* and *B* may occur. This use of *or* is sometimes called an "inclusive."

EXAMPLE

An example involving joint probability

What is the probability that a card chosen at random from a standard deck of cards will either be a king or a heart?

Solution ▸ We may be inclined to add the probability of a king and the probability of a heart. But this creates a problem. If we do that, the king of hearts is counted with the kings and also with the hearts. So, if we simply add the probability of a king (there are 4 in a deck of 52 cards) to the probability of a heart (there are 13 in a deck of 52 cards) and report that 17 out of 52 cards meet the requirement, we have counted the king of hearts twice. We need to subtract 1 card from the 17 so that the king of hearts is counted only once. Thus, there are 16 cards that are either hearts or kings. So the probability is 16/52 = .3077.

Card	Probability	Explanation
King	$P(A) = 4/52$	4 kings in a deck of 52 cards
Heart	$P(B) = 13/52$	13 hearts in a deck of 52 cards
King of hearts	$P(A \text{ and } B) = 1/52$	1 king of hearts in a deck of 52 cards

Using formula (5–4):

$$P(A \text{ or } B) = P(A) + P(B) - P(A \text{ and } B)$$
$$= 4/52 + 13/52 - 1/52$$
$$= 16/52, \text{ or } .3077$$

A Venn diagram portrays these outcomes, which are not mutually exclusive.

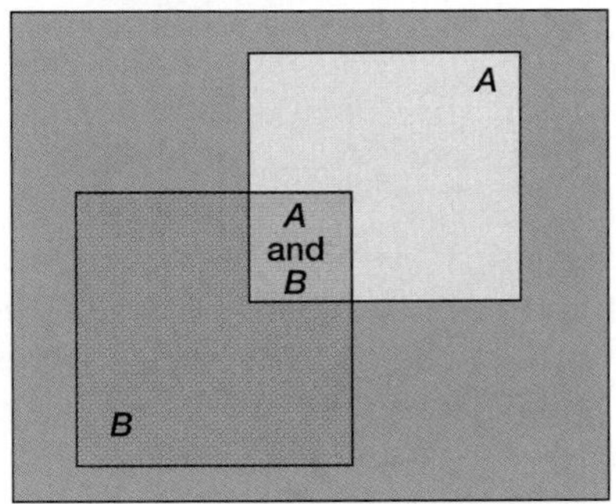

SELF-REVIEW 5–7

The answers are at the end of the chapter.

Routine physical examinations are conducted annually as part of a health service program for the General Cement employees. It was discovered that 8 percent of the employees needed corrective shoes, 15 percent needed major dental work, and 3 percent needed both corrective shoes and major dental work.

1. What is the probability that an employee selected at random will need either corrective shoes or major dental work?
2. Show this situation in the form of a Venn diagram

EXERCISES

The answers to the odd-numbered exercises are at the end of the book.

17. The probabilities of the events *A* and *B* are .20 and .30, respectively. The events are not mutually exclusive. The probability that both *A* and *B* occur is .15. What is the probability of either *A* or *B* occurring?
18. Let $P(X) = .55$ and $P(Y) = .35$. Assume that these events are not mutually exclusive and that the probability that they both occur is .20. What is the probability of either *X* or *Y* occurring?
19. Suppose the two events *A* and *B* are mutually exclusive. What is the probability of their joint occurrence?
20. A student is taking two courses, history and math. The probability that the student will pass the history course is .60, and the probability of passing the math course is .70. The probability of passing both is .50. What is the probability of passing at least one?
21. A survey of top executives revealed that 35 percent of them regularly read *Time* magazine, 20 percent read *Newsweek,* and 40 percent read *U.S. News & World Report.* Ten percent read both *Time* and *U.S. News & World Report.*
    a. What is the probability that a particular top executive reads either *Time* or *U.S. News & World Report* regularly?

   b. What is the probability .10 called?
   c. Are the events mutually exclusive? Explain.

22. A study by the National Park Service revealed that 50 percent of the vacationers going to the Rocky Mountain region visit Yellowstone Park, 40 percent visit the Tetons, and 35 percent visit both.
   a. What is the probability that a vacationer will visit at least one of these magnificent attractions?
   b. What is the probability .35 called?
   c. Are the events mutually exclusive? Explain.

Rules of Multiplication

Special Rule of Multiplication The special rule of multiplication requires that two events *A* and *B* be **independent.** Two events are independent if the occurrence of one does not alter the probability of the other. So if the events *A* and *B* are independent, the occurrence of *A* does not alter the probability of *B.*

> **Independent** The occurrence of one event has no effect on the probability of the occurrence of any other event.

For two independent events *A* and *B,* the probability that *A* and *B* will both occur is found by multiplying the two probabilities. This is called the **special rule of multiplication** and is written symbolically as:

$$P(A \text{ and } B) = P(A) \cdot P(B) \tag{5–5}$$

Raised dot means to *multiply.*

This rule for combining probabilities presumes that a second outcome is *not* affected by the first outcome. To illustrate what is meant by independence of outcomes, suppose two coins are tossed. The outcome of one coin (head or tail) is unaffected by the outcome of the other coin (head or tail). To put it another way, two events are independent if the outcome of the second event does not depend on the outcome of the first event.

For three independent events, *A, B,* and *C,* the special rule of multiplication used to determine the probability that all three events will occur is:

$$P(A \text{ and } B \text{ and } C) = P(A) \cdot P(B) \cdot P(C)$$

EXAMPLE Two coins are tossed. What is the probability that both will land tail up?

Solution ▶ The probability of a tail showing face up on one of the coins, written *P*(*A*), is one half, or .50. The probability that the other coin will land tail up, written *P*(*B*), is one half, or .50. Using formula (5–5), the probability that both will happen is one fourth, or .25, found by:

$$P(A \text{ and } B) = P(A) \cdot P(B)$$
$$= \tfrac{1}{2} \times \tfrac{1}{2}$$
$$= \tfrac{1}{4}, \text{ or } .25$$

This can be shown by listing all of the possible outcomes. Two tails is only one of the four possible outcomes:

Ⓣ Ⓣ
or Ⓣ Ⓗ
or Ⓗ Ⓣ
or Ⓗ Ⓗ

SELF-REVIEW 5–8

The answers are at the end of the chapter.

1. From long experience, Teton Tire knows that the probability is .80 that their XB-70 will last 40,000 miles before it becomes bald or fails. An adjustment is made on any tire that does not last 40,000 miles. You purchase four XB-70s. What is the probability that all four tires will last at least 40,000 miles?
2. As cited in an earlier example, an automatic Shaw machine inserts mixed vegetables into a plastic bag. Past experience revealed that some packages were underweight and some overweight, but most of them had satisfactory weight.

Weight	Probability
Underweight	.025
Satisfactory	.900
Overweight	.075

   a. What is the probability of selecting three packages from the food processing line today and finding that all three of them are underweight?
   b. What does this probability mean?

If two events are not independent, they are referred to as being *dependent.* To illustrate dependency, suppose there are 10 rolls of film in a box, and it is known that 3 are defective. A roll of film is selected from the box. Obviously, the probability of selecting a defective roll is $\tfrac{3}{10}$, and the probability of selecting a good roll is $\tfrac{7}{10}$. Then a second roll is selected from the box without the first one being returned to the box. The probability that it is defective *depends on* whether the first roll selected was defective or good. The probability that the second roll is defective is:

$\tfrac{2}{9}$, if the first roll selected was defective. (Only two defective rolls remain in the box containing nine rolls.)

$\tfrac{3}{9}$, if the first roll selected was good. (All three defective rolls are still in the box containing nine rolls.)

Conditional probability

The fraction $\tfrac{2}{9}$ (or $\tfrac{3}{9}$) is aptly called a **conditional probability** because its value is conditional on (dependent on) whether a defective or a good roll of film is chosen in the first selection from the box.

> **Conditional probability** The probability of a particular event occurring, given that another event has occurred.

If we want to determine the probability that two defective rolls of film are selected one after the other, the general rule of multiplication is applied.

General rule of multiplication

General Rule of Multiplication The **general rule of multiplication** is used to find the *joint probability* that two events will occur, such as selecting 2 defective rolls from the box of 10 rolls, one after the other. In general, the rule states that for two events A and B, the joint probability that both events will happen is found by multiplying the probability that event A will happen by the conditional probability of event B's occurring. Symbolically, the joint probability $P(A \text{ and } B)$ is found by:

$$P(A \text{ and } B) = P(A) \cdot P(B|A) \tag{5–6}$$

where $P(B|A)$ stands for the probability that B will occur *given that A has already occurred.* The vertical line means "given that."

EXAMPLE

To illustrate the formula, let's use the problem with 10 rolls of film in a box, 3 of which are defective. Two rolls are to be selected, one after the other. What is the probability of selecting a defective roll followed by another defective roll?

Solution

The first roll of film selected from the box being found defective is event A. $P(A) = 3/10$ because 3 out of the 10 are defective. The second roll selected being found defective is event B. Therefore, $P(B|A) = 2/9$, because after the first selection was found to be defective, only 2 defective rolls of film remained in the box containing 9 rolls. Determining the probability of two defectives [see formula (5–6)]:

$$\begin{aligned} P(A \text{ and } B) &= P(A) \cdot P(B|A) \\ &= \frac{3}{10} \times \frac{2}{9} \\ &= \frac{6}{90}, \text{ or about } .07 \end{aligned}$$

This means that if this experiment were repeated 100 times, in the long run seven experiments would result in defective rolls of film on both the first and second selections.

Incidentally, it is assumed that this experiment was conducted *without replacement*—that is, the defective roll of film was not thrown back in the box before the next roll was selected. It should also be noted that the general rule of multiplication can be extended to more than two events. For three events, A, B, and C, the formula would be:

$$P(A \text{ and } B \text{ and } C) = P(A) \cdot P(B|A) \cdot P(C|A \text{ and } B)$$

For illustration, the probability that the first three rolls chosen from the box will all be defective is .00833, found by:

$$P(A \text{ and } B \text{ and } C) = P(A) \cdot P(B|A) \cdot P(C|A \text{ and } B)$$
$$= \frac{3}{10} \times \frac{2}{9} \times \frac{1}{8}$$
$$= \frac{6}{720} = .00833$$

SELF-REVIEW 5–9

The answers are at the end of the chapter.

The board of directors of Tarbell Industries consists of eight men and four women. A four-member search committee is to be chosen at random to recommend a new company president.

1. What is the probability that all four members of the search committee will be women?
2. What is the probability that all four members will be men?
3. Does the sum of the probabilities for 1 and 2 equal 1? Explain.

Contingency table

Another application of the general rule of multiplication follows. A survey of executives dealt with their loyalty to the company. One of the questions asked was, "If you were given an offer by another company equal to or slightly better than your present position, would you remain with the company or take the other position?" The responses of the 200 executives in the survey were cross-classified with their length of service with the company. (See Table 5–1.) The type of table that resulted is usually referred to as a **contingency table.**

TABLE 5–1 Loyalty of Executives and Length of Service with Company

	Length of service				
Loyalty	**Less than 1 year**	**1–5 years**	**6–10 years**	**More than 10 years**	**Total**
Would remain	10	30	5	75	120
Would not remain	25	15	10	30	80
					200

EXAMPLE

What is the probability of randomly selecting an executive who is loyal to the company (would remain) and who has more than 10 years of service?

Solution

Note that two events occur at the same time—the executive would remain with the company, and he or she has more than 10 years of service.

1. Event A is an executive who would remain with the company despite an equal or slightly better offer from another company. To find the probability that event A will happen, refer to Table 5–1. Note that there are 120 executives out of the 200 in the survey who would remain with the company, so $P(A) = 120/200$, or .60.

2. Event B is an executive who has more than 10 years of service with the company. Thus, $P(B|A)$ is the conditional probability that an executive with more than 10 years of service would remain with the company despite an equal or slightly better offer from another company. Referring to the contingency table, Table 5–1, 75 of the 120 executives who would remain have more than 10 years of service, so $P(B|A) = 75/120$.

Solving for the probability that an executive randomly selected will be one who would remain with the company and who has more than 10 years of service with the company, using the general rule of multiplication in formula (5–6):

$$\begin{aligned} P(A \text{ and } B) &= P(A) \cdot P(B|A) \\ &= \frac{120}{200} \times \frac{75}{120} \\ &= \frac{9{,}000}{24{,}000} \\ &= .375 \end{aligned}$$

SELF-REVIEW 5–10

The answers are at the end of the chapter.

Refer to Table 5–1. Using the general rule of multiplication, what is the probability of selecting at random an executive who would not remain with the company and has less than one year of service?

TREE DIAGRAMS

A **tree diagram** is very useful for portraying conditional and joint probabilities. A tree diagram is particularly useful for analyzing business decisions where there are several stages to the problem. The contingency table (Table 5–1) is used to show the construction of a tree diagram.

Steps in constructing a tree diagram

1. To construct a tree diagram, we begin by drawing a heavy dot on the left to represent the trunk of the tree (see Chart 5–1).
2. For this problem, two main branches go out from the trunk, the upper one representing "would remain" and the lower one "would not remain." Their probabilities are written on the branches, namely, 120/200 and 80/200. These are $P(A)$ and $P(\sim A)$.
3. Four branches "grow" out of each of the two main branches. These branches represent the length of service—less than 1 year, 1–5 years, 6–10 years, and more than 10 years. The conditional probabilities 10/120, 30/120, 5/120, and so on are written on the appropriate branches. These are $P(B_1|A)$, $P(B_2|A)$, $P(B_3|A)$, and $P(B_4|A)$, where B_1 refers to less than 1 year of service, B_2 1 to 5 years, B_3 6 to 10 years, and B_4 more than 10 years.
4. Finally, joint probabilities, that A and B will occur together, are shown on the right side. For example, the joint probability of randomly selecting an

executive who would remain with the company and who has less than one year of service, using formula (5–6), is:

$$P(A \text{ and } B_1) = P(A) \cdot P(B_1|A)$$

$$= \left(\frac{120}{200}\right)\left(\frac{10}{120}\right) = .05$$

CHART 5–1 **Tree Diagram Showing Loyalty and Length of Service**

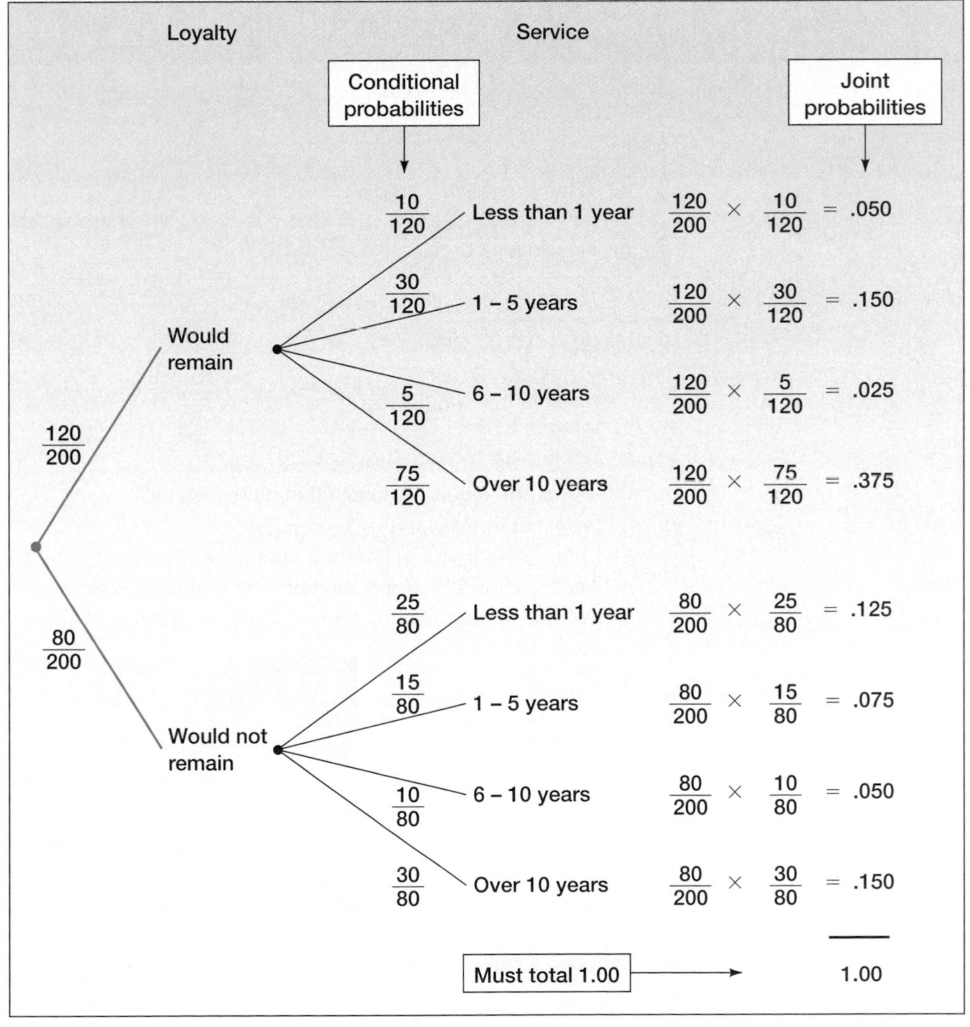

Because the joint probabilities represent all possible selections (would remain, 6–10 years service; would not remain, more than 10 years of service; etc.), they must sum to 1.00. (See Chart 5–1.)

SELF-REVIEW 5–11

The answers are at the end of the chapter.

1. Refer to the tree diagram in Chart 5–1. Explain the path you would follow to find the joint probability of selecting an executive at random who has 6–10 years' service and who would not remain with the company upon receipt of an equal or slightly better offer from another company.
2. A random sample of the employees of the Hardware Manufacturing Company was chosen in order to determine their retirement plans after age 65. Those selected in the sample were divided into management and production. The results were:

	Plans after age 65		
Employee	**Retire**	**Not retire**	**Total**
Management	5	15	20
Production	30	50	80
			100

   a. What is the table called?
   b. Draw a tree diagram, and determine the joint probabilities.
   c. Do the joint probabilities total 1.00? Why?

EXERCISES

The answers to the odd-numbered exercises are at the end of the book.

23. *a.* What is a joint probability?
    b. What is a conditional probability?
24. What is a contingency table? What does it show?
25. *a.* What is the following picture called?
    b. What is the name of the total area encompassed by the large rectangle?
    c. Are the events *D* and *H* mutually exclusive? Explain.
    d. What is the formula for arriving at the probability of *D* or *H* happening?

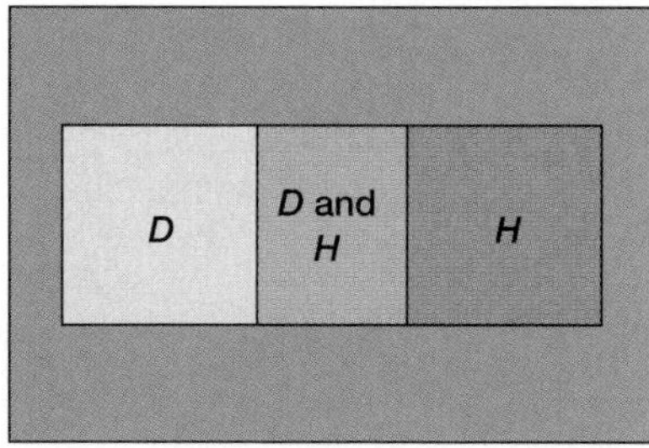

26. Suppose $P(A) = .40$ and $P(B|A) = .30$. What is the joint probability of *A* and *B*?
27. Suppose $P(X_1) = .75$ and $P(Y_2|X_1) = .40$. What is the joint probability of X_1 and Y_2?
28. Refer to the following table.

	First event			
Second event	A_1	A_2	A_3	**Total**
B_1	2	1	3	6
B_2	1	2	1	4
Total	3	3	4	10

a. Determine $P(A_1)$.
b. Determine $P(B_1|A_2)$.
c. Determine $P(B_2 \text{ and } A_3)$.

29. Three defective electric toothbrushes were accidentally shipped to a drugstore by Cleanbrush Products along with 17 nondefective ones.
    a. What is the probability that the first two electric toothbrushes sold will be returned to the drugstore because they are defective?
    b. What is the probability that the first two electric toothbrushes sold will not be defective?
30. Each salesperson at Stiles-Compton is rated either below average, average, or above average with respect to sales ability. Each salesperson is also rated with respect to his or her potential for advancement—either fair, good, or excellent. These traits for the 500 salespeople were cross-classified into the following table.

	Potential for advancement		
Sales ability	**Fair**	**Good**	**Excellent**
Below average	16	12	22
Average	45	60	45
Above average	93	72	135

a. What is this table called?
b. What is the probability that a salesperson selected at random will have above-average sales ability and excellent potential for advancement?
c. Construct a tree diagram showing all the probabilities, conditional probabilities, and joint probabilities.

BAYES' THEOREM

In the 18th century Reverend Thomas Bayes, an English Presbyterian minister, pondered this question: Does God really exist? Being interested in mathematics, he attempted to develop a formula to arrive at the probability that God does exist based on evidence that was available to him on earth. Later Laplace refined Bayes' work and gave it the name "Bayes' theorem." In a workable form, **Bayes' theorem** is:

What is the probability of *A*, given *B* has occurred?

$$P(A_1|B) = \frac{P(A_1) \cdot P(B|A_1)}{P(A_1) \cdot P(B|A_1) + P(A_2) \cdot P(B|A_2)} \quad (5\text{–}7)$$

(The meaning of each of these letters will be explained in the following example, but note that they refer to conditional probabilities.)

Consider the following problem. Suppose 5 percent of the population of Umen, a fictional Third World country, have a disease that is peculiar to that country. We will let A_1 refer to the event "has the disease" and A_2 refer to the event "does not have the disease." Thus, we know that if we select a person from Umen at random, the probability that the individual chosen has the disease is .05, or $P(A_1) = .05$. This probability, $P(A_1) = P(\text{has the disease}) = .05$, is called the **prior probability.** It is given this name because the probability is assigned before any empirical data are obtained.

Prior probability

Prior probability The initial probability based on the present level of information.

The prior probability that a person is not afflicted with the disease is therefore .95, or $P(A_2) = .95$, found by $1 - .05$.

There is a diagnostic technique to detect the disease, but it is not very accurate. Let B denote the event "test shows the disease is present." Assume that historical evidence shows that if a person actually has the disease, the probability that the test will indicate the presence of the disease is .90. Using the conditional probability definitions developed earlier in this chapter, this statement is written as:

$$P(B|A_1) = .90$$

Assume the probability is .15 that a person actually does not have the disease but the test indicates the disease is present.

$$P(B|A_2) = .15$$

Let's randomly select a person from Umen and perform the test. The test results indicate the disease is present. What is the probability that the person actually has the disease? In symbolic form, we want to know $P(A_1|B)$, which is interpreted as: P(has the disease | the test results are positive). The probability $P(A_1|B)$ is called a **posterior probability.**

Posterior probability

Posterior probability A revised probability based on the benefit of additional information.

With the help of Bayes' theorem, formula (5–7), we can determine the posterior or revised probability.

Bayes' theorem

$$P(A_1|B) = \frac{P(A_1) \cdot P(B|A_1)}{P(A_1) \cdot P(B|A_1) + P(A_2) \cdot P(B|A_2)}$$

$$= \frac{(.05)(.90)}{(.05)(.90) + (.95)(.15)}$$

$$= \frac{.0450}{.1875}$$

$$= .24$$

So the probability that a person has the disease, given that he or she tested positive, is .24. How is the result interpreted? If a person is selected at random from the population, the probability that he or she has the disease is .05. If the person is tested and the test result is positive, the probability that the person actually has the disease is increased about fivefold, from .05 to .24.

The preceding problem included only two events, A_1 and A_2, as prior probabilities. If there are more than two prior probabilities, the denominator of Bayes' theorem requires additional terms. If the prior probability distribution consists of n mutually exclusive events, Bayes' theorem, formula (5–7), becomes

$$P(A_i|B) = \frac{P(A_i) \cdot P(B|A_i)}{P(A_1) \cdot P(B|A_1) + P(A_2) \cdot P(B|A_2) + \cdots + P(A_n) \cdot P(B|A_n)}$$

where A_i refers to any of the n possible outcomes.

Using the preceding notation, the calculations for the Umen problem are summarized in the following table.

Event, A_i	Prior probability, $P(A_i)$	Conditional probability, $P(B\|A_i)$	Joint probability $P(A_i \text{ and } B)$	Posterior probability, $P(A_i\|B)$
Disease, A_1	.05	.90	.0450	.0450/.1875 = .24
No disease, A_2	.95	.15	.1425	.1425/.1875 = .76
			$P(B)$ = .1875	1.00

Another illustration of Bayes' theorem follows.

EXAMPLE

A manufacturer of VCRs purchases a particular microchip, called the LS-24, from three suppliers: Hall Electronic, Schuller Sales, and Crawford Components. Thirty percent of the LS-24 chips are purchased from Hall Electronics, 20 percent from Schuller Sales, and the remaining 50 percent from Crawford Components. The manufacturer has extensive histories on the three suppliers and knows that 3 percent of the LS-24 chips from Hall Electronics are defective, 5 percent of chips from Schuller Sales are defective, and 4 percent of the chips purchased from Crawford Components are defective.

When the LS-24 chips arrive at the manufacturer, they are placed directly in a bin and not inspected or otherwise identified by supplier. A worker selects a chip for installation in a VCR and finds it defective. What is the probability that it was manufactured by Schuller Sales?

Solution ► As a first step, let's summarize some of the information given in the problem statement.

- There are three events, that is, three suppliers.

A_1	The LS-24 was purchased from Hall Electronics
A_2	The LS-24 was purchased from Schuller Sales
A_3	The LS-24 was purchased from Crawford Components

- The prior probabilities are:

$P(A_1) = .30$	The probability the LS-24 was manufactured by Hall Electronics
$P(A_2) = .20$	The probability the LS-24 was manufactured by Schuller Sales
$P(A_3) = .50$	The probability the LS-24 was manufactured by Crawford Components

- The additional information is that the LS-24 to be assembled is defective.

B_1	The LS-24 is defective
B_2	The LS-24 is not defective

- The following conditional probabilities are given.

$P(B_1\|A_1) = .03$	The probability that an LS-24 chip produced by Hall Electronics is defective
$P(B_1\|A_2) = .05$	The probability that an LS-24 chip produced by Schuller Sales is defective
$P(B_1\|A_3) = .04$	The probability that an LS-24 chip produced by Crawford Components is defective

- A chip is selected from the bin. Because the chips are not inspected or otherwise identified by supplier, we are not certain which supplier manufactured the chip. We want to determine the probability that the defective chip was purchased from Schuller Sales. This probability is written $P(A_2|B_1)$.

Look at Schuller's quality record. It is the worst of the three suppliers. Now that we have found a defective LS-24 chip, we suspect that $P(A_2|B_1)$ is greater than $P(A_2)$. That is, we expect the revised probability to be greater than .20. But how much greater? Bayes' theorem can give us the answer. As a first step, consider the tree diagram in Chart 5–2.

CHART 5–2 **Tree Diagram of VCR Manufacturing Problem**

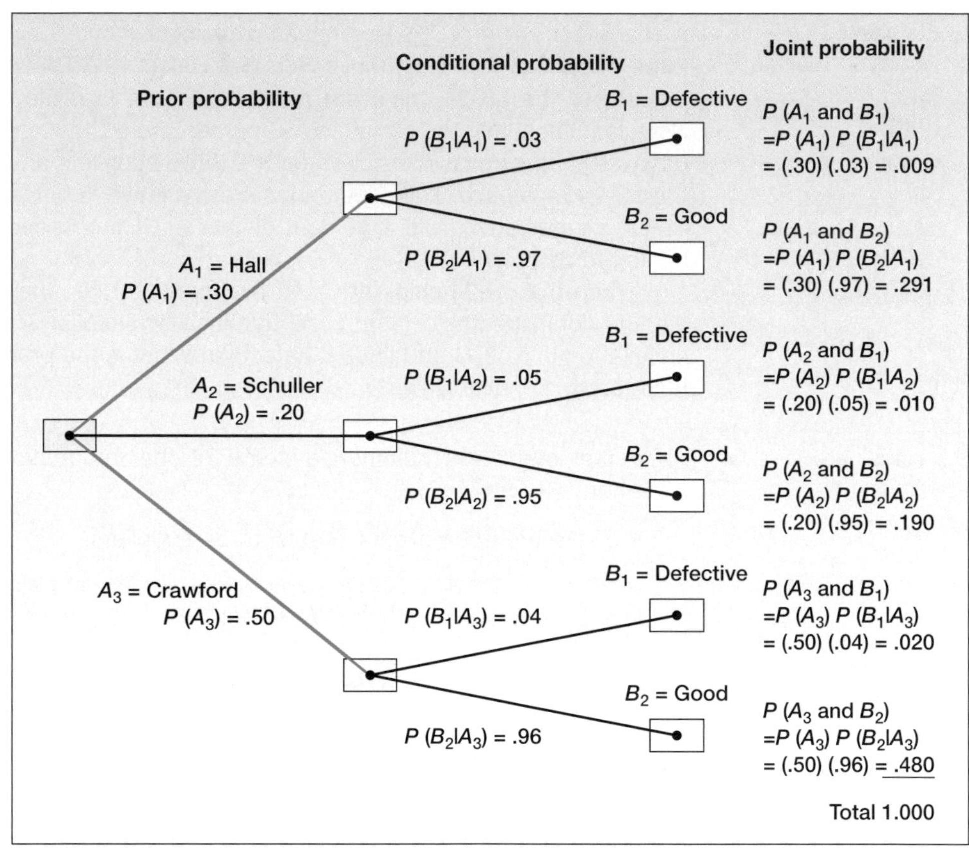

The events are dependent, so the prior probability in the first branch is multiplied by the conditional probability in the second branch to obtain the joint probability. The joint probability is reported in the last column of Chart 5–2. To construct the tree diagram of Chart 5–2, we used a time sequence that moved from the supplier to the determination of whether the chip was acceptable or unacceptable.

What we need to do is reverse the time process. That is, instead of moving from left to right in Chart 5–2, we need to move from right to left. We have a defective chip, and we want to determine the likelihood that it was purchased from Schuller Sales. How is that accomplished? We first look at the joint probabilities as relative frequencies out of 1,000 cases. For example, the likelihood of a defective LS-24 chip that was produced by Hall Electronics is .009. So out of 1,000 cases we would expect to find 9 defective chips produced by Hall Electronics. We observe that in 39 of 1,000 cases the LS-24 chip selected for assembly will be defective, found by 9 + 10 + 20. Of these 39 defective chips, 10 were produced by Schuller Sales. Thus, the probability that the defective LS-24 chip was purchased from Schuller Sales is 10/39 = .2564. We have now determined the revised probability of $P(A_2|B_1)$. Before we found the defective chip, the likelihood that it was purchased from Schuller Sales was .20. This likelihood has been increased to .2564.

This information is summarized in the following table.

Event, A_i	**Prior probability, $P(A_i)$**	**Conditional probability, $P(B_1\|A_i)$**	**Joint probability $P(A_i$ and $B_1)$**	**Posterior probability, $P(A_i\|B_1)$**
Hall	.30	.03	.009	.009/.039 = .2308
Schuller	.20	.05	.010	.010/.039 = .2564
Crawford	.50	.04	.020	.020/.039 = .5128
			$P(B_1)$ = .039	1.0000

The probability that the defective LS-24 chip came from Schuller Sales can be found by using Bayes' theorem. We want to compute $P(A_2|B_1)$, where A_2 refers to Schuller Sales and B_1 to the fact that the selected LS-24 chip was defective.

$$P(A_2|B_1) = \frac{P(A_2)P(B_1|A_2)}{P(A_1)P(B_1|A_1) + P(A_2)P(B_1|A_2) + P(A_3)P(B_1|A_3)}$$

$$= \frac{(.20)(.05)}{(.30)(.03) + (.20)(.05) + (.50)(.04)}$$

$$= \frac{.010}{.039} = .2564$$

This is the same result obtained from Chart 5–2 and from the conditional probability table.

SELF-REVIEW 5–12

The answers are at the end of the chapter.

Refer to the preceding example and solution.

1. Design a formula to find the probability that the part selected came from Crawford Components, given that it was a good chip.
2. Compute the probability using Bayes' theorem.

EXERCISES

The answers to the odd-numbered exercises are at the end of the book.

31. $P(A_1) = .60$, $P(A_2) = .40$, $P(B_1|A_1) = .05$, and $P(B_1|A_2) = .10$. Use Bayes' theorem to determine $P(A_1|B_1)$.

32. $P(A_1) = .20$, $P(A_2) = .40$, and $P(A_3) = .40$. $P(B_1|A_1) = .25$. $P(B_1|A_2) = .05$, and $P(B_1|A_3) = .10$. Use Bayes' theorem to determine $P(A_3|B_1)$.

33. The Ludlow Wildcats baseball team, a minor league team in the Cleveland Indians organization, plays 70 percent of their games at night and 30 percent during the day. The team wins 50 percent of their night games and 90 percent of their day games. According to today's newspaper, they won yesterday. What is the probability the game was played at night?
34. Dr. Stallter has been teaching basic statistics for many years. She knows that 80 percent of the students will complete the assigned problems. She has also determined that among those who do their assignments, 90 percent will pass the course. Among those students who do not do their homework, 60 percent will pass. Mike Fishbaugh took statistics last semester from Dr. Stallter and received a passing grade. What is the probability that he completed the assignments?
35. The credit department of Lion's Department Store in Anaheim, California, reported that 30 percent of their sales are cash, 30 percent are paid for by check at the time of the purchase, and 40 percent are charged. Twenty percent of the cash purchases, 90 percent of the checks, and 60 percent of the charges are for more than $50. Ms. Tina Stevens just purchased a new dress that cost $120. What is the probability that she paid cash?
36. A municipal bond rating service has three categories (A, B, and C). In the last year, of the municipal bonds issued throughout the United States, 60 percent were rated A, 30 percent B, and 10 percent C. Of the bonds rated A, 40 percent were issued by cities, 40 percent by suburbs, and 20 percent by rural areas. Of the bonds rated B, 50 percent were from cities, 30 percent from suburbs, and 20 percent from rural areas. Of the bonds rated C, 80 percent were from cities, 10 percent from suburbs, and 10 percent from rural areas. A bond is selected at random.
    a. What is the conditional probability of selecting a bond from a rural area, given that it is rated C?
    b. What is the joint probability of selecting a bond rated C that is from a rural area?
    c. What is the probability that the bond rated is C, given that it is from a rural area?

SOME PRINCIPLES OF COUNTING

Three formulas for determining the total number of events

If the number of possible outcomes in an experiment is small, it is relatively easy to list and count all of the possible events. There are six possible events, for example, resulting from the roll of a die, namely:

If, however, there are a large number of possible outcomes, such as the number of boys and girls for families with 10 children, it would be tedious to list and count all the possibilities. They could have all boys, one boy and nine girls, two boys and eight girls, and so on. To facilitate counting, three counting formulas will be examined: the **multiplication formula,** the **permutation formula,** and the **combination formula.**

The Multiplication Formula

> **Multiplication formula** If there are *m* ways of doing one thing and *n* ways of doing another thing, there are $m \times n$ ways of doing both.

In terms of a formula:

$$\text{Total number of arrangements} = m \times n \tag{5–8}$$

This can be extended to more than two events. For three events *m, n,* and *o:*

Multiplication formula for three events

$$\text{Total number of arrangements} = m \times n \times o$$

EXAMPLE

An automobile dealer wants to advertise that for $19,999 you can buy either a convertible, a two-door, or a four-door model with your choice of either wire wheel covers or solid wheel covers. How many different arrangements of models and wheel covers can the dealer offer?

Solution ▶ Of course the dealer could determine the total number of arrangements by picturing and counting them. There are six.

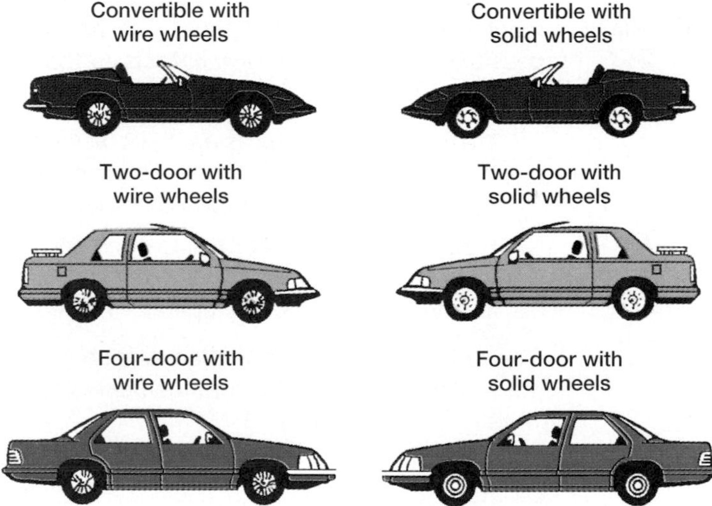

We can employ the multiplication formula as a check (where *m* is the number of models and *n* the wheel cover type). Using formula (5–8):

$$\begin{aligned}\text{Total possible arrangements} &= m \times n \\ &= 3 \times 2 \\ &= 6\end{aligned}$$

It was not difficult to list and count all the possible model and wheel cover combinations in this example. Suppose, however, that the dealer decided to offer eight models and six types of wheel covers. It would be tedious to picture and count all the possible alternatives. Instead, the multiplication formula can be used. In this case, $m \times n = 8 \times 6 = 48$ possible arrangements.

Two groups—exterior style and interior floor plan

Note in the preceding applications of the multiplication formula that there were *two or more groupings.* The automobile dealer, for example, offered a choice of models and a choice of wheel covers. If a home builder offered you four different exterior styles of a home to choose from and three interior floor plans, the multiplication formula would be used to find how many different arrangements were possible.

SELF-REVIEW 5–13

The answers are at the end of the chapter.

1. Stiffin Lamps has developed five lamp bases and four lamp shades that can be used together. How many different arrangements of base and shade can be offered?
2. Pioneer manufactures three models of stereo receivers, two cassette decks, four speakers, and three CD carousels. When the four types of compatible components are sold together, they form a "system." How many different systems can the electronics firm offer?

The Permutation Formula

Permutation applicable for one group of objects

As noted, the multiplication formula is applied to find the number of possible arrangements for two or more groups. The **permutation formula** is applied to find the possible number of arrangements when there is only *one* group of objects. As illustrations of this type of problem:

- Three electronic parts are to be assembled into a plug-in unit for a television set. The parts can be assembled in any order. The question involving counting is: In how many different ways can the three parts be assembled?
- A machine operator must make four safety checks before starting his machine. It does not matter in which order the checks are made. In how many different ways can the operator make the checks?

One order for the first illustration might be: the transistor first, the LEDs second, and the synthesizer third. This arrangement is called a **permutation.**

Permutation Any arrangement of r objects selected from n possible objects.

Permutation formula

Note that the arrangements *a, b, c,* and *b, a, c* are *different* permutations. The formula employed to count the total number of different permutations is:

$$_nP_r = \frac{n!}{(n-r)!} \tag{5–9}$$

where:

- P is the number of permutations, or ways the objects can be arranged.
- n is the total number of objects. In the first illustration, there are three electronic parts, so $n = 3$.
- r is the number of objects to be used at one time. In the electronics problem, all the objects (electronic parts) are to be assembled, so $r = 3$. If

only two out of the three electronic parts were to be inserted in the plug-in unit, r would be 2.

4! means $4 \times 3 \times 2 \times 1$

Before we solve the two problems illustrated, note that permutations and combinations (to be discussed shortly) use a notation called *n factorial.* It is written $n!$ and means the product of $n(n-1)(n-2)(n-3)\ldots[n-(n-1)]$. For instance, 5! would be found by $5(5-1)(5-2)(5-3)[5-(5-1)]$, or $5 \cdot 4 \cdot 3 \cdot 2 \cdot 1 = 120$.

As shown below, numbers can be canceled when the same numbers are included in the numerator and denominator.

$$\frac{6!3!}{4!} = \frac{6 \cdot 5 \cdot \cancel{4} \cdot \cancel{3} \cdot \cancel{2} \cdot \cancel{1}(3 \cdot 2 \cdot 1)}{\cancel{4} \cdot \cancel{3} \cdot \cancel{2} \cdot \cancel{1}} = 180$$

0! = 1

By definition, zero factorial, written 0!, is set equal to 1. That is, $0! = 1$.

EXAMPLE

Referring to the group of three electronic parts that are to be assembled in any order, in how many different ways can they be assembled?

Solution

$n = 3$ because there are three electronic parts to be assembled. $r = 3$ because all three are to be inserted in the plug-in unit. Solving using formula (5–9):

$${}_nP_r = \frac{n!}{(n-r)!} = \frac{3!}{(3-3)!} = \frac{3!}{0!} = \frac{3!}{1} = 6$$

SELF-REVIEW 5–14

The answers are at the end of the chapter.

1. What does 6! equal?
2. What does 6!2!/4!3! equal?
3. Recall that a machine operator must make four safety checks before starting to machine a part. It does not matter in which order the checks are made. In how many different ways can the operator make the checks?
4. The 10 numbers 0 through 9 are to be used in code groups of four to identify an item of clothing. Code 1083 might identify a blue blouse, size medium; the code group 2031 might identify a pair of pants, size 18; and so on. Repetitions of numbers are not permitted. That is, the same number cannot be used twice (or more) in a total sequence. For example, 2256, 2562, or 5559 would not be permitted. How many different code groups can be designed?

Another approach to the number of permutations

A check can be made to the number of permutations arrived at using the permutations formula. To check we merely determine how many spaces have to be filled and the possibilities for each space. In the problem involving three electronic parts, there are three locations in the plug-in unit for the three parts. There are three possibilities for the first space, two for the second (one has been used up), and one for the third, as follows:

$$(3)(2)(1) = 6 \text{ permutations}$$

The six ways in which the three electronic parts, lettered *A, B, C,* can be arranged are:

ABC	*BAC*	*CAB*
ACB	*BCA*	*CBA*

Another example utilizing this principle follows.

EXAMPLE

Suppose that there are eight machines but only three spaces on the floor of the machine shop for the machines. In how many different ways can eight machines be arranged in the three available spaces?

Solution ▶ There are eight possibilities for the first space, seven for the second space (one has been used up), and six for the third space. Then:

$$(8)(7)(6) = 336 \text{ permuations}$$

As before, this may also be expressed mathematically by saying that the number of permutations, P, of n items is dependent on the number of spaces, r, available:

$$_nP_r = \frac{n!}{(n-r)!} = \frac{8!}{(8-3)!} = \frac{8!}{5!} = \frac{(8)(7)(6)5!}{5!} = 336$$

SELF-REVIEW 5–15

The answers are at the end of the chapter.

A musician wants to write a score based on only five chords: B-flat, C, D, E and G. However, only three chords out of the five will be used in succession, such as C, B-flat, and E. Repetitions, such as B-flat, B-flat, and E, will not be permitted.

1. How many permutations of the five chords, taken three at a time, are possible?
2. Using formula (5–9), how many permutations are possible?

Formula for number of permutations when repetitions allowed

Permutations Allowing for Repetitions The previous discussion of permutations did not allow for any repetition. If repetitions are permitted, the permutation formula is:

$$_nP_r = n^r \qquad (5\text{–}10)$$

To illustrate the point, assume that two letters, A and B, are to be taken two at a time. With repetitions, such as AA, there are four permutations possible, found by $P = n^r = 2^2$. The four permutations are AA, AB, BA, and BB.

SELF-REVIEW 5–16

The answers are at the end of the chapter.

In Self-Review 5–15, the musician decided to use five chords taken three at a time. Repetitions—such as B-flat, B-flat, and E—were not permitted. There are 60 possible arrangements (permutations) of these chords. If repetitions are permitted, how many permutations are possible?

No repetitions allowed

In brief review of permutations, if a set of objects designated by *a, b, c, d,* and *e* can also be arranged as *a, c, d, e,* and *b*; and if they can be arranged as *c, a, e, b,* and *d*; and so on, then there are 120 permutations of these five objects taken five at a time, found by

$$_nP_r = \frac{n!}{(n-r)!} = \frac{5!}{(5-5)!} = 120$$

where:

n is the total number of objects.

r is the number of objects considered for each permutation.

If only two of the five objects were considered—such as *a, b*; *d, a*; or *c, e*—then there are a total of 20 permutations possible, found by:

$$_nP_r = \frac{n!}{(n-r)!} = \frac{5!}{(5-2)!} = 20$$

Note that in permutations *the order in which the objects are listed differs from one arrangement to the next* (that is, *a, b* differs from *b, a*; *e, a* differs from *a, e*; and so on). Each arrangement is counted.

Repetitions allowed

If repetitions are permitted, such as *a, a, a, b, b,* or *a, a, b, b, d,* the number of permutations can be determined by $_nP_r = n^r$. For the five objects ($n = 5$) taken five at a time ($r = 5$), there are 3,125 possible arrangements, found by $_nP_r = n^r = 5^5$, using formula (5–10).

The Combination Formula

In determining the number of permutations of n different things taken r at a time, the order of things is of concern. For example, in painting three color dots on a resistor, the order could be red, orange, and blue (meaning, say, a 500-ohm resistor); or the order could be orange, blue, and red (meaning a 1,000-ohm resistor); and so on. There are six permutations of the three colors, found by:

$$_nP_r = \frac{n!}{(n-r)!} = \frac{3 \cdot 2 \cdot 1}{(3-3)!} = 6$$

Combination formula

Suppose, however, it has been decided that *any combination* of red, orange, and blue will be used on a resistor to identify it as a 750-ohm resistor; *the order is not important.* In effect, the many different ways of ordering the three colors are disregarded. That is, the combination of red, blue, and orange on a resistor is considered the same as orange, blue, and red; both would identify a 750-ohm resistor. This means that the combination of red, orange, and blue can be used only once for identification purposes.

Combination The number of ways to choose r objects from a group of n objects without regard to order.

The **combination formula** is:

$$_nC_r = \frac{n!}{r!(n-r)!} \qquad (5\text{–}11)$$

EXAMPLE

The paint department has been given the assignment of designing color codes for 42 different parts. Three colors are to be used on each part, but a combination of three colors used for one part cannot be rearranged and used to identify a different part. This means that if green, yellow, and violet were used to identify a camshaft, yellow, violet, and green (or any other combination of these three colors) could not be used to identify, say, a pinion gear. Would seven colors taken three at a time be adequate to color-code the 42 parts?

Solution ▶ Using formula (5–11), there are 35 combinations, found by

$${}_7C_3 = \frac{n!}{r!(n-r)!} = \frac{7!}{3!(7-3)!} = \frac{7!}{3!4!} = 35$$

The seven colors taken three at a time (i.e., three colors to a part) would not be adequate to color-code the 42 different parts because they would provide only 35 combinations. Eight colors taken three at a time would give 56 different combinations. This would be more than adequate to color-code the 42 different parts.

SELF-REVIEW 5–17

The answers are at the end of the chapter.

1. In the preceding solution we said that eight colors taken three at a time would give 56 different combinations. Using formula (5–11), is that true?
2. As an alternative plan for color-coding the 42 different parts, it has been suggested that only two colors be placed on a part. Would 10 colors be adequate to color-code the 42 different parts? (Again, a combination of two colors could only be used once—that is, if pink and blue were coded for one part, blue and pink could not be used to identify a different part.)

Summarizing the Difference between a Permutation and a Combination

For a permutation, each different order of objects is counted

To qualify as a *permutation,* the *order of the objects for each possible outcome is different.* For three objects, *a, b,* and *c,* the order *a, b, c* is one order (permutation); *b, a, c* is another permutation; *c, a, b* is another permutation; and so on. There are six possible arrangements of these three objects taken three at a time. Using the permutation formula:

$${}_nP_r = \frac{n!}{(n-r)!} = \frac{3!}{(3-3)!} = \frac{3 \cdot 2 \cdot 1}{1} = 6$$

For a combination, order *ab* considered same as order *ba*

If the order of the objects is not important, the total number of orders is called a *combination.* For example, if executives Able, Baker, and Chauncy are to be chosen as a committee to negotiate a merger, there is only one possible combination of these three; the committee of Able, Baker, and Chauncy is the same as the committee of Baker, Chauncy, and Able. Using the combination formula:

$${}_nC_r = \frac{n!}{r!(n-r)!} = \frac{3 \cdot 2 \cdot 1}{3 \cdot 2 \cdot 1(1)} = 1$$

EXERCISES

The answers to the odd-numbered exercises are at the end of the book.

37. *a.* Describe what is meant by a permutation.
    b. Describe what is meant by a combination.
38. Solve the following:
    a. 40!/35!.
    b. ${}_7P_4$.
    c. ${}_5C_2$.
39. Solve the following:
    a. 20!/17!.
    b. ${}_9P_3$.
    c. ${}_7C_2$.
40. A pollster randomly selected 4 of 10 available people. How many different groups of 4 are possible?
41. A telephone number consists of seven digits, the first three representing the exchange. How many different numbers are possible within the 537 exchange?
42. An overnight express company must include five cities on its route. How many different routes are possible, assuming that it does not matter which order the cities are included in the routing?
43. A representative of the Environmental Protection Agency (EPA) wants to select samples from 10 landfills. He has 15 landfills from which he can collect samples. How many different samples are possible?
44. A national pollster has developed 15 questions designed to rate the performance of the president of the United States. The pollster will select 10 of these questions. How many different arrangements are there for the order of the 10 selected questions?

CHAPTER OUTLINE

I. A probability is a value between 0 and 1 that represents the likelihood that a particular event will happen.
   A. An experiment is the observation of some activity or the act of taking some measurement.
   B. An outcome is a particular result of an experiment.
   C. An event is the collection of one or more outcomes of an experiment.

II. There are three definitions of probability.
   A. The classical definition applies when there are n equally likely outcomes to an experiment.
   B. The relative frequency definition occurs when the number of times an event happens is divided by the total number of observations.
   C. A subjective probability is based on whatever information is available. It is applied only when there is not enough information for another method to be used.

III. Two events are mutually exclusive if by virtue of one event happening the other cannot happen.

IV. Events are independent if the occurrence of one event does not affect the occurrence of another event.

V. The rules of addition are used to combine events.
   A. The special rule of addition is used to combine events that are mutually exclusive.

$$P(A \text{ or } B) = P(A) + P(B) \tag{5–2}$$

B. The general rule of addition is used to combine events that are not mutually exclusive.

$$P(A \text{ or } B) = P(A) + P(B) - P(A \text{ and } B) \tag{5–4}$$

C. The complement rule is used to determine the probability of an event happening by subtracting the probability of the event not happening from 1.

$$P(A) = 1 - P(\sim A) \tag{5–3}$$

VI. The rules of multiplication are also used to combine events.

A. Events are independent if the occurrence of one event has no effect on the occurrence of any other event.

B. The special rule of multiplication is used to combine events that are independent.

$$P(A \text{ and } B) = P(A)P(B) \tag{5–5}$$

C. The general rule of multiplication is used to combine events that are not independent.

$$P(A \text{ and } B) = P(A)P(B|A) \tag{5–6}$$

D. A joint probability is the likelihood that two or more events will happen at the same time.

E. A conditional probability is the likelihood that an event will happen, given that another event has already happened.

F. Bayes' theorem is a method of revising a probability, given that additional information is obtained. For two events:

$$P(A_1|B) = \frac{P(A_1) \cdot P(B|A_1)}{P(A_1) \cdot P(B|A_1) + P(A_2) \cdot P(B|A_2)} \tag{5–7}$$

VII. There are three counting rules that are useful in determining the total number of ways in which events can occur.

A. The multiplication rule states that if there are m ways one event can happen and n ways another event can happen, then there are mn ways the two events can happen.

$$\text{Number of arrangements} = m \times n \tag{5–8}$$

B. A permutation is an arrangement in which the order of the objects is important.

$${}_nP_r = \frac{n!}{(n-r)!} \tag{5–9}$$

C. A combination is an arrangement where the order of the objects is not important.

$${}_nC_r = \frac{n!}{r!(n-r)!} \tag{5–11}$$

EXERCISES

The answers to the odd-numbered exercises are at the end of the book.

45. The marketing research department at Vernors plans to survey teenagers regarding their reactions to a newly developed soft drink. They will be asked to compare it with their favorite soft drink.
    a. What is the experiment?
    b. What is one possible event?

46. The number of times a particular event occurred in the past is divided by the total number of occurrences. What is this approach to probability called?

47. The probability that the cause and the cure of cancer will be discovered before the year 2000 is .02. What viewpoint of probability does this statement illustrate?

48. Is it true that, if there is absolutely no chance a person will recover from 50 bullet wounds, the probability assigned to this event is − 1.00? Why?

49. On the throw of one die, what is the probability that a one-spot or a two-spot or a six-spot will appear face up? What definition of probability is being used?
50. A study of the weekly offering in the envelopes at the First Baptist Church in Warren, Pennsylvania, revealed the following:

Offering in envelope	Number
$ 0 up to $ 5	200
5 up to 10	100
10 up to 20	75
20 up to 50	75
50 or more	50
Total	500

   a. What is the probability of selecting an envelope at random and finding $50 or more in it?
   b. Are the classes "$0 up to $5," "$5 up to $10," and so on considered mutually exclusive?
   c. If the probabilities associated with each class were totaled, what would the total be?
   d. What is the probability of selecting an envelope at random and finding it to contain up to $10?
   e. What is the probability of finding less than $50 in an envelope selected at random?
51. Define each of these terms:
   a. Conditional probability.
   b. Event.
   c. Joint probability.
52. The first card selected from a standard 52-card deck was a king.
   a. If it is returned to the deck, what is the probability that a king will be drawn on the second selection?
   b. If the king is not replaced, what is the probability that a king will be drawn on the second selection?
   c. What is the probability that a king will be selected on the first draw from the deck and another king on the second draw (assuming that the first king was not replaced)?
53. Armco, a manufacturer of traffic light systems, found that under accelerated-life tests, 95 percent of the newly developed systems lasted three years before failing to change the signals properly.
   a. If a city purchased four of these systems, what is the probability that all four systems would operate properly for at least three years?
   b. Which rule of probability does this illustrate?
   c. Using letters to represent the four systems, design an equation to show how you arrived at the answer to part *a.*
54. Refer to the following picture.

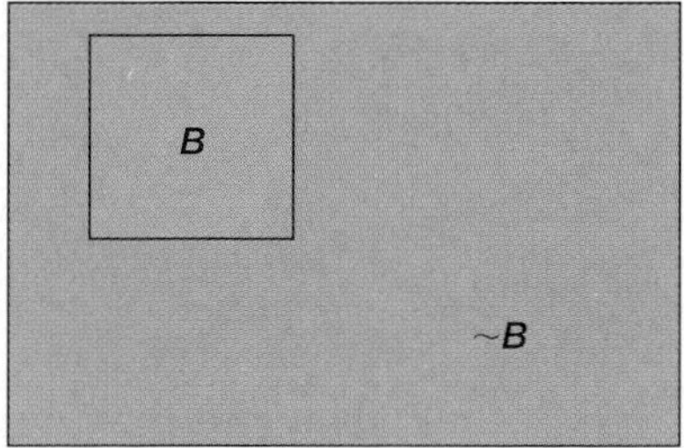

   a. What is the picture called?

b. What is the total area called?
c. What rule of probability is illustrated?
d. *B* represents the event of choosing a family that receives welfare payments. What does $P(B) + P(\sim B)$ equal?

55. In a management trainee program at Claremont Enterprises, 80 percent of the trainees are female and 20 percent male. Ninety percent of the females attended college, and 78 percent of the males attended college.
   a. A management trainee is selected at random. What is the probability that the person selected is a female who did not attend college?
   b. Construct a tree diagram showing all the probabilities, conditional probabilities, and joint probabilities.
   c. Do the joint probabilities total 1.00? Why?
56. A coin is tossed four times.
   a. What is the probability that each of the four tosses will result in a head face up?
   b. Using the letters *A, B, C,* and *D,* write the formula for the probability of this outcome.
   c. Suppose four heads did appear face up on the tosses of the coin. What is the probability that a head will appear face up on the next toss of the coin?
57. Of every 100 employees at Kiddie Carts, 57 are production workers (designated as *A*), 40 are supervisors (designated as *B*), 2 are secretaries (designated as *C*), and 1 is with either middle or top management (designated as *D*). If an employee is selected at random, what does $P(A \text{ or } B \text{ or } C)$ equal?
58. Harvey Kuenn played major league baseball from 1954 until 1966. During that time his career batting average was .308. Assume that the probability of getting a hit is .308 for each time at bat. (To put it another way, for every 1,000 times at bat, he had 308 hits.) In a particular game he batted three times.
   a. What is the probability that he had three hits?
   b. What is the probability that he did not get any hits in the game?
59. The probability that a bomber hits its target on any particular run is .80. If four bombers are sent after the same target, what is the probability that they all hit the target? What is the probability that none of the bombers hits the target?
60. Ninety students will graduate from Lima Shawnee High School this year. Out of the 90 graduates 50 are planning to attend college. Two students are selected at random to carry the flag at graduation. What is the probability that both of them are planning to attend college?
61. The board of directors of Saner Automatic Door Company consists of 12 members, 3 of whom are women. A new policy and procedures manual is to be written for the company. A committee of 3 is randomly selected from the board to do the writing.
   a. What is the probability that all members of the committee are men?
   b. What is the probability that at least 1 member of the committee is a woman?
62. A survey of undergraduate students in the School of Business at Northern University revealed the following regarding the gender and majors of the students:

	Major			
Gender	**Accounting**	**Management**	**Finance**	**Total**
Male	100	150	50	300
Female	100	50	50	200
Total	200	200	100	500

   a. What is the probability of selecting a female student?
   b. What is the probability of selecting a finance or accounting major?

c. What is the probability of selecting a female or an accounting major? Which rule of addition did you apply?
d. What is the probability of selecting an accounting major, given that the person selected is a male?
e. Suppose two students are selected randomly to attend a lunch with the president of the university. What is the probability that both of those selected are accounting majors?

63. The Wood County sheriff classifies crimes by age (in years) of the criminal and whether the crime is violent or nonviolent. As shown below, a total of 150 crimes were reported by the sheriff last year.

	Age (in years)			
Type of crime	**Under 20**	**20 to 40**	**40 or older**	**Total**
Violent	27	41	14	82
Nonviolent	12	34	22	68
Total	39	75	36	150

a. What is the probability of selecting a case to analyze and finding it involved a violent crime?
b. What is the probability of selecting a case to analyze and finding the crime was committed by someone less than 40 years old?
c. What is the probability of selecting a case that involved a violent crime or an offender less than 20 years old? Which rule of addition did you apply?
d. Given that a violent crime is selected for analysis, what is the probability the crime was committed by a person under 20 years old?
e. Two crimes are selected for review by Judge Tybo. What is the probability that both are violent crimes?

64. Mr. and Mrs. Wilhelms are both retired and living in a retirement community in Arizona. Suppose the probability that a retired man will live another 10 years is .60. The probability that a retired woman will live another 10 years is .70.
a. What is the probability that both Mr. and Mrs. Wilhelms will be alive 10 years from now?
b. What is the probability that in 10 years Mr. Wilhelms is not living and Mrs. Wilhelms is living?
c. What is the probability that in 10 years at least one is living?

65. Flashner Marketing Research, Inc. specializes in providing assessments of the prospects for women's apparel shops in shopping malls. Al Flashner, president, reports that he assesses the prospects as good, fair, or poor. Records from previous assessments show that 60 percent of the time the prospects were rated as good, 30 percent of the time fair, and 10 percent of the time poor. Of those rated good, 80 percent made a profit the first year; of those rated fair, 60 percent made a profit the first year; and of those rated poor, 20 percent made a profit the first year. Connie's Apparel was one of Flashner's clients. Connie's Apparel made a profit last year. What is the probability that it was given an original rating of poor?

66. There are 400 employees at G. G. Greene Manufacturing Co., and 100 of them smoke. There are 250 males working for the company, and 75 of them smoke. What is the probability that an employee selected at random:
a. Is a male?
b. Smokes?
c. Is male and smokes?
d. Is male or smokes?

67. With each purchase of a large pizza at Tony's Pizza the customer receives a coupon that can be scratched to see if a prize will be awarded. The odds of winning a free soft drink are 1 in 10, and the odds of winning a free large pizza are 1 in 50. You plan to eat lunch tomorrow at Tony's. What is the probability:
   a. That you will win either a large pizza or a soft drink?
   b. That you will not win a prize?
   c. That you will not win a prize on three consecutive visits to Tony's?
   d. That you will win at least one prize on one of your next three visits to Tony's?
68. For the daily lottery game in Illinois, participants select three numbers between 0 and 9. A number cannot be selected more than once, so a winning ticket could be, say, 307. Purchasing one ticket allows you to select one set of numbers. The winning numbers are announced on TV each night.
   a. How many different outcomes (three-digit numbers) are possible?
   b. If you purchase a ticket for the game tonight, what is the likelihood you will win?
   c. Suppose you purchase three tickets for tonight's drawing and select a different number for each ticket. What is the probability that you will not win with any of the tickets?

69. A new job consists of assembling four different parts. All four have different color codes, and they can be assembled in any order. The production department wants to determine the most efficient way to assemble the four parts. The supervisors are going to conduct some experiments to solve the problem. First, they plan to assemble the parts in this order—green, black, yellow, and blue—and record the time. Then the assembly will be accomplished in a different order. In how many different ways can the four parts be assembled?
70. It was found that 60 percent of the tourists to China visited the Forbidden City, the Temple of Heaven, the Great Wall, and other historical sites in or near Beijing. Forty percent visited Xi'an with its magnificent terracotta soldiers, horses, and chariots, which lay buried for over 2,000 years. Thirty percent of the tourists went to both Beijing and Xi'an. What is the probability that a tourist visited at least one of these places?

71. Two boxes of men's Arrow shirts were received from the factory. Box 1 contained 25 sport shirts and 15 dress shirts. Box 2 contained 30 sport shirts and 10 dress shirts. One of the boxes was selected at random, and a shirt was chosen at random from that box to be inspected. The shirt was a sport shirt. Given this information, what is the probability that the sport shirt came from box 1?

72. The operators of Riccardo's Restaurant want to advertise that they have a large number of different meals. They offer 4 soups, 3 salads, 12 entrees, 6 vegetables, and 5 desserts. How many different meals do they offer? In addition, Riccardo's has an "early bird" special: You may omit any part of the meal except the entrees for a reduced price. How many different meals do they have for the "early birds"?

73. Several years ago Wendy's Hamburgers advertised that there are 256 different ways to order your hamburger. You may choose to have, or omit, any combination of the following on your hamburger: mustard, ketchup, onion, pickle, tomato, relish, mayonnaise, and lettuce. Is the advertisement correct?

74. Reynolds Construction Company has agreed not to erect all "look-alike" homes in a new subdivision. Five exterior designs are offered to potential home buyers. The builder has standardized three interior plans that can be incorporated in any of the five exteriors. How many different ways can the exterior and interior plans be offered to potential home buyers?

75. A small rug weaver has decided to use seven compatible colors in her new line of rugs. However, in weaving a rug, only five spindles can be used. In her advertising she wants to indicate the number of different color groupings for sale. How many color groupings using the seven colors taken five at a time are there? (This assumes that five different colors will go into each rug—i.e., there are no repetitions of color.)

76. Consideration is being given to forming a Super Ten football conference. The top 10 football teams in the country, based on past records, would be members of the Super Ten conference. Each team would play every other team in the conference during the season. The team winning the most games would be declared the national champion. How many games would the conference commissioner have to schedule each year? (Remember, Oklahoma versus Michigan is the same as Michigan versus Oklahoma.)

77. A new chewing gum has been developed that is helpful to those who want to stop smoking. If 60 percent of those people chewing the gum are successful in stopping smoking, what is the probability that in a group of four smokers at least one quits smoking?

78. The state of Ohio has license plates with three numbers followed by three letters. How many different license plates are possible?

79. A new sports car model has defective brakes 15 percent of the time and a defective steering mechanism 5 percent of the time. Let's assume (and hope) that these problems occur independently. If one or the other of these problems is present, the car is called a "lemon." If both of these conditions are present, the car is a "hazard." Your instructor purchased one of these cars yesterday. What is the probability it is:
   a. A lemon?
   b. A hazard?

80. Tim Bleckie is the owner of Bleckie Investment and Real Estate Company. The company recently purchased four tracts of land in Holly Farms Estates and six tracts in Newburg Woods. The tracts are all equally desirable and sell for about the same amount.
   a. What is the probability that the next two tracts sold will be in Newburg Woods?
   b. What is the probability that of the next four sold at least one will be in Holly Farms?
   c. Are these events independent or dependent?

81. There are four people being considered for the position of chief executive officer of Dalton Enterprises. Three of the applicants are over 60 years of age. Two are female, of which only one is over 60. All four applicants are either over 60 years of age or female.
   a. What is the probability that a candidate is over 60 and female?
   b. Given that the candidate is male, what is the probability he is less than 60?
   c. Given that the person is over 60, what is the probability the person is female?
82. A case of 24 cans contains 1 can that is contaminated. Three cans are to be chosen randomly for testing.
   a. How many different combinations of 3 cans could be selected?
   b. What is the probability that the contaminated can is selected for testing?
83. The ages of drunk drivers in Ohio and whether the drunk drivers were first-time or repeat offenders are as follows:

Age	First-time	Repeat	Total
16–20	5,311	519	5,830
21–25	10,713	4,104	14,817
26–30	10,301	5,719	16,020
31–35	8,246	4,344	12,590
36–40	5,442	2,596	8,038
41–45	3,474	1,719	5,193
Total	43,487	19,001	62,488

   A drunk driver is selected at random.
   a. What is the probability that the driver is a repeat offender?
   b. What is the probability that the driver is under 21 or a first-time offender?
   c. What is the probability that the driver is a repeat offender, given that the driver is over 30?
   d. Is a first-time offender or a repeat offender more likely to be over 30?
   e. What is the probability of selecting two drunk drivers and finding they are both first-time offenders?
84. Betts Electronics, Inc. purchases TV picture tubes from four different suppliers. Tyson Wholesale supplies 20 percent of the tubes, Fuji Importers 30 percent, Kirkpatricks 25 percent, and Parts, Inc. 25 percent. Tyson Wholesale tends to have the best quality, as only 3 percent of their tubes arrive defective. Fuji Importers tubes are 4 percent defective, Kirkpatricks 7 percent, and Parts, Inc. 6.5 percent defective.
   a. What is the overall (average) percent defective?
   b. A defective picture tube was discovered in the latest shipment. What is the probability that it came from Tyson Wholesale?
   c. What is the probability that the defective tube came from Fuji Importers? From Kirkpatricks? From Parts, Inc.?
85. The following diagram represents a system of two components, *A* and *B,* which are in series. (Being in series means that for the system to operate, both components *A* and *B* must work.) Suppose that the probability that *A* functions is .90, and the probability that *B* functions is also .90. Assume that these two components are independent. What is the probability that the system operates?

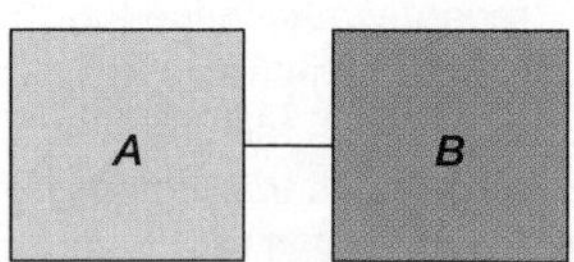

86. Refer to the system diagram above, but suppose the system works if *either A* or *B* works. What is the probability the system works under these conditions?
87. A puzzle in a newspaper presents a matching problem. The names of 10 U.S. presidents are listed in one column, and their vice presidents are listed in random order in the second column. The puzzle asks the reader to match each president with his vice president. If you make the matches randomly, how many matches are possible? What is the probability all 10 of your matches are correct?
88. To reduce theft, the Meredeth Company screens all its employees with a lie detector test that is known to be correct 90 percent of the time (for both guilty and innocent subjects). George Meredeth decides to fire all employees who fail the test. Suppose 5 percent of the employees are guilty of theft.
    a. What proportion of the workers are fired?
    b. Of the workers fired, what proportion are actually guilty?
    c. Of the workers not fired, what proportion are guilty?
    d. What do you think of George's policy?

COMPUTER DATA EXERCISES

89. Refer to data set 1, which reports information on homes sold in Sarasota, Florida, during 1994.
    a. Sort the data into a table that shows the number of homes that have a pool versus the number that don't have a pool in each of the five townships. If a home is selected at random, compute the following probabilities:
        (1) The home is in township 1 or has a pool.
        (2) Given that it is in township 3, that it has a pool.
        (3) Has a pool and is in township 3.
    b. Sort the data into a table that shows the number of homes that have a garage versus those that don't have a garage in each of the five townships. If a home is selected at random, compute the following probabilities:
        (1) The home has a garage.
        (2) Given that it is in township 5, that it does not have a garage.
        (3) The home has a garage and is in township 3.
        (4) Does not have a garage or is in township 2.
90. Refer to data set 2, which reports information on the 28 major league baseball teams for the 1993 season. Set up a variable that divides the teams into two groups, those that had a winning season and those that did not. That is, create a variable to count the teams that won 81 games or more, and those that won 80 or less. Next create a new variable for attendance using three categories: attendance less than 1,500,000 (shown in the data as 1.5), attendance of 1.5 million up to 2.5 million, and attendance of 2.5 million or more.
    a. Create a table that shows the number of teams with a winning season versus those with a losing season by the three categories of attendance. If a team is selected at random, compute the following probabilities:
        (1) Having a winning season?
        (2) Having a winning season or attendance of more than 2.5 million?
        (3) Given attendance of more than 2.5 million, having a winning season?
        (4) Having a losing season and drawing less than 1.5 million?
    b. Create a table that shows the number of teams that play on artificial turf fields by winning and losing records. If a team is selected at random, compute the following probabilities:

(1) Selecting a team with a home field that is turf.
(2) Is the likelihood of selecting a team with a winning record larger for teams with grass or turf fields?
(3) Having a winning record or playing on a turf field.

91. Refer to data set 3, which reports information on the circulation of 48 magazines. First, set up a variable that divides the magazines into two groups: those that have male readership of 50 percent or more and those that have less than 50 percent male readership. Create a second variable that divides the circulation into magazines with less than 3,000 (remember, this is in thousands) circulation and those with 3,000 or more. If a magazine is randomly selected, what is the probability that:
    a. More than half the readers are male?
    b. More than half the readers are male and the circulation is 3,000 or more?
    c. More than half the readers are male or the circulation is 3,000 or more?
    d. Given that the circulation is 3,000 or more, more than half the readers are male?

CASE

The Bell Telephone System, in 1946, set in place an area code system in which the United States and Canada were divided into 86 area codes. At the time Bell system researchers estimated that the 144 possible area codes would be used up by the year 2000. Under the original system the first digit of an area code could be any number from 2 through 9. The second digit had to be either a 0 or a 1. The third digit could be any of the 10 numbers from 0 to 9. Excluded were numbers ending in 00 or 11. (These were reserved for toll-free calls, emergencies, and special services.) Show that there were a total of 144 possible area codes.

CHAPTER 5 EXAMINATION

The answers are at the end of the chapter.

For Questions 1–7 indicate whether the statement is true or false. If false, correct the statement.

1. Two coins are tossed. The tossing of the coins is called an experiment, and one possible event is a head.
2. The outcomes must be equally likely for the relative frequency probability approach to be used.
3. The complement rule states that the probability of an event not occurring is equal to 1 minus the probability of its occurrence.
4. The classical approach to probability is based on a person's degree of belief and hunches that a particular event will happen.
5. If two events are mutually exclusive, then $P(A \text{ or } B) = P(A) + P(B)$.
6. There are five vacant parking places. Five automobiles arrive at the same time. There are 25 different ways they can park.
7. This Venn diagram shows that the events are mutually exclusive.

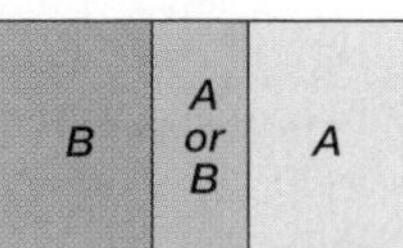

Questions 8–11 are based on the following tabulation of the status of the employees at BMD. Indicate whether the statement is true or false. If false, correct the statement.

Status	Male	Female	Total
Executive	80	20	100
Supervisors	100	300	400
Production	150	250	400
Clerical	40	60	100
Total	370	630	1,000

8. The probability of selecting at random a female executive is 20.0.
9. The probability of selecting a supervisor or a female is about .716.
10. The probability of selecting a supervisor given that a female employee is selected is .476.
11. The probability of selecting a clerical employee is .10.

Questions 12 and 13 are based on the following problem. A machine operator grinds a very thin disk the size of a dime. One side of the disk is plain, but the operator mills a slot on the other side. The disks are immediately wrapped for shipment. The operator suddenly realized that he did not machine the slot in one of the last four disks he made, but he cannot recall which one was neglected.

12. What is the probability that one of the four pieces selected at random (say, the one on the extreme right) is defective? What is this probability called?
13. As an experiment, the machine operator unwrapped the disk on the extreme right and tossed it in the air. If it lands with the slot face up, the machine operator would know it is not the defective disk. However, if the disk landed with a plain face up, the machine operator would be uncertain whether that particular disk is defective or not defective. The disk landed with a plain face up. What is the probability that it is the defective disk? What is the probability called?
14. The First National Bank has two computers. The probability that the newer one will be inoperative in any particular month is .05. The probability that the older one will be inoperative in any particular month is .10. Assuming that these events are independent, what is the probability that they both become inoperative during a month?
15. The shipping department has just received 20 orders. A shipping clerk will be given 8 orders to fill. How many different groups of 8 orders could shipping clerk Catlin be given to fill?
16. The Swatzi motorbike dealer is promoting two top-of-the line motorbikes by offering the buyer one of three free options. In how many different ways can the two bikes and three options be arranged?

CHAPTER 5 Answers

Self-Review

5–1
1. *a.* Testing of the new computer game.
   b. Seventy-three players liked the game.
2. *a.* No. Probability cannot be greater than 1. The probability that the game, if put on the market, will be successful is 65/80, or .8125.
   b. Cannot be less than 0. Perhaps a mistake in arithmetic.
   c. More than half of the persons testing the game liked it. (Of course, other answers are possible.)

5–2
1. $1/4 = .25$
2. *a.* $\dfrac{\text{13 spades in deck}}{\text{52 cards total}} = \dfrac{13}{52} = .25$
   b. $\dfrac{\text{1 jack of hearts in deck}}{\text{52 cards total}} = \dfrac{1}{52} = .0192$
   c. $\dfrac{\text{4 queens in deck}}{\text{52 cards total}} = \dfrac{4}{52} = .0769$
3. Classical.

5–3
1. $\dfrac{24}{883} = .027$
2. $\dfrac{182}{883} = .206$

5–4
1. The author's view of the chance that the DJIA will climb to 5000 is .25. You may be more optimistic or less optimistic.
2. Because it is a very expensive car the probability is quite low, say .01.

5–5
1. .025, found by 50/2,000.
2. .034, found by 68/2,000.
3. .059, found by $P(B \text{ or } E) = .025 + .034$.
4. Special rule of addition.
5. 1.
6.

A	*B*	*C*	*D*	*E*

7. Yes.

5–6 For 1, 2, 3, and 4, the Venn diagram might appear as:

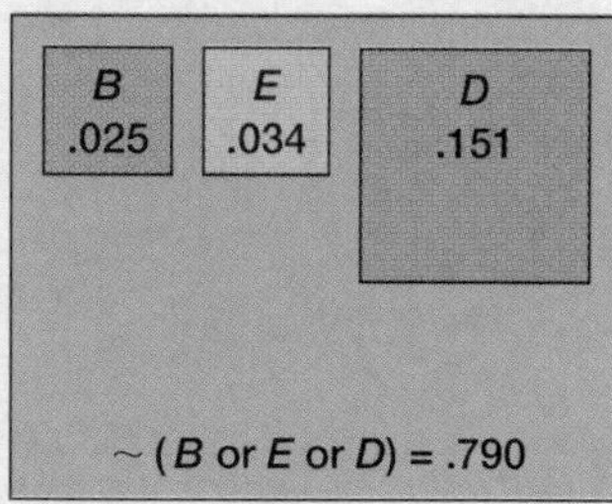

We found .790 by 1 − (.025 + .034 + .151).

5–7
1. Need for corrective shoes is event *A*. Need for major dental work is event *B*.

$$\begin{aligned} P(A \text{ or } B) &= P(A) + P(B) - P(A \text{ and } B) \\ &= .08 + .15 - .03 \\ &= .20 \end{aligned}$$

2. One possibility is:

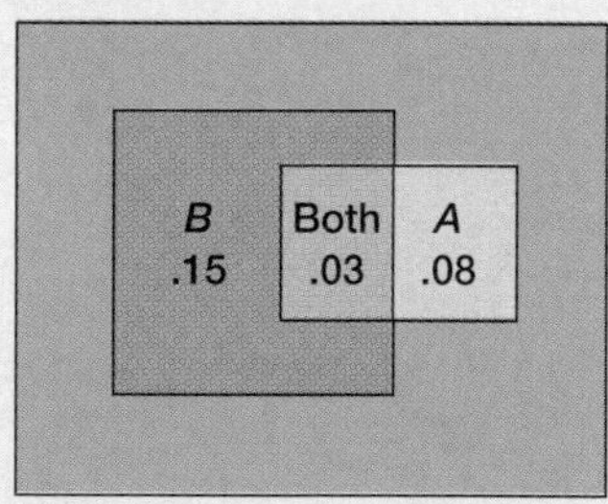

5–8
1. (.80)(.80)(.80)(.80) = .4096.
2. *a.* .0000156, found by: .025 × .025 × .025.
   b. The chance of selecting three bags and finding them all underweight is rather remote.

5–9
1. .002, found by:

$$\frac{4}{12} \times \frac{3}{11} \times \frac{2}{10} \times \frac{1}{9} = \frac{24}{11{,}880} = .002$$

2. .14, found by:

$$\frac{8}{12} \times \frac{7}{11} \times \frac{6}{10} \times \frac{5}{9} = \frac{1,680}{11,880} = .1414$$

3. No, because there are other possibilities, such as three women and one man.

5–10 $P(A \text{ and } B) = P(A) \cdot P(B|A)$

$$= \frac{80}{200} \times \frac{25}{80}$$

$$= .125$$

5–11 1. Go out from the tree trunk on the lower branch, "would not remain." The probability of that event is 80/200. Continuing on the same path, find the branch labeled "6–10 years." The conditional probability is 10/80. To get the joint probability:

$$P(A \text{ and } B) = \frac{80}{200} \times \frac{10}{80}$$

$$= \frac{800}{16,000}$$

$$= .05$$

2. *a.* Contingency table.

b.

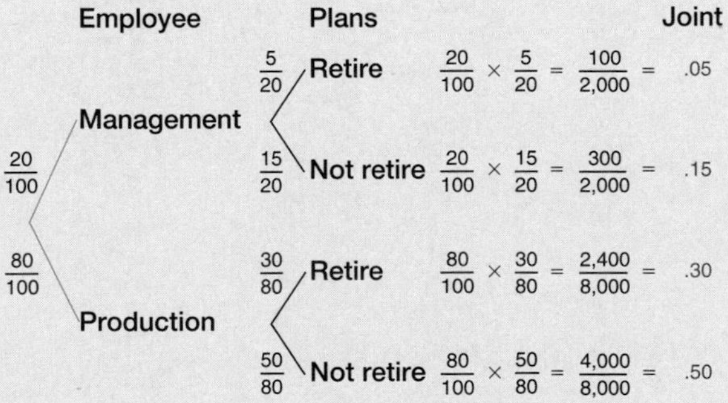

Employee	Plans		Joint
Management ($\frac{20}{100}$)	$\frac{5}{20}$ Retire	$\frac{20}{100} \times \frac{5}{20} = \frac{100}{2,000} =$	.05
	$\frac{15}{20}$ Not retire	$\frac{20}{100} \times \frac{15}{20} = \frac{300}{2,000} =$	.15
Production ($\frac{80}{100}$)	$\frac{30}{80}$ Retire	$\frac{80}{100} \times \frac{30}{80} = \frac{2,400}{8,000} =$	.30
	$\frac{50}{80}$ Not retire	$\frac{80}{100} \times \frac{50}{80} = \frac{4,000}{8,000} =$	.50

c. Yes, all possibilities are included.

5–12 1. $P(A_3|B_2) = \frac{P(A_3)P(B_2|A_3)}{P(A_1)P(B_2|A_1) + P(A_2)P(B_2|A_2) + P(A_3)P(B_2|A_3)}$

$$= \frac{.50(.96)}{(.30)(.97) + (.20)(.95) + (.50)(.96)}$$

$$= \frac{.480}{.961} = .499$$

5–13 1. There are 20, found by 5×4.
2. There are 72, found by $3 \times 2 \times 4 \times 3$.

5–14 1. 720, found by $6 \times 5 \times 4 \times 3 \times 2 \times 1$.
2. 10, found by:

$$\frac{6 \cdot 5 \cancel{\cdot 4 \cdot 3 \cdot 2 \cdot 1}(\cancel{2 \cdot 1})}{\cancel{4 \cdot 3 \cdot 2 \cdot 1}(3 \cdot \cancel{2 \cdot 1})}$$

3. 24, found by:

$$\frac{4!}{(4-4)!} = \frac{4!}{0!} = \frac{4!}{1} = \frac{4 \cdot 3 \cdot 2 \cdot 1}{1}$$

4. 5,040, found by:

$$\frac{10!}{(10-4)!} = \frac{10 \cdot 9 \cdot 8 \cdot 7 \cancel{\cdot 6 \cdot 5 \cdot 4 \cdot 3 \cdot 2 \cdot 1}}{\cancel{6 \cdot 5 \cdot 4 \cdot 3 \cdot 2 \cdot 1}}$$

5–15 1. 60, found by (5)(4)(3).
2. 60, found by:

$$\frac{5!}{(5-3)!} = \frac{5 \cdot 4 \cdot 3 \cdot \cancel{2 \cdot 1}}{\cancel{2 \cdot 1}}$$

5–16 125, found by ${}_nP_r = n^r = 5^3$.

5–17 1. 56 is correct, found by:

$${}_8C_3 = \frac{n!}{r!(n-r)!} = \frac{8!}{3!(8-3)!} = 56$$

2. Yes. There are 45 combinations, found by:

$${}_{10}C_2 = \frac{n!}{r!(n-r)!} = \frac{10!}{2!(10-2)!} = 45$$

Examination

1. True.
2. False. The outcomes are equally likely in the classical approach.
3. True.
4. False. This is the definition of the subjective approach.
5. True.
6. False. There are 120, found by 5!/0!.
7. False. The events are not mutually exclusive. That is, there is an overlapping of events.
8. False. It is .020, found by 20/1,000.
9. False. It is about .730, found by:

$$P(S \text{ or } F) = P(S) + P(F) - P(S \text{ and } F)$$

$$= \frac{400}{1,000} + \frac{630}{1,000} - \frac{300}{1,000} = .730$$

10. True.
11. True.
12. .25. Prior probability.
13. .40, found by using Bayes' theorem:

$$\frac{(.25)(1.00)}{.25(1.00) + .75(.50)}$$

The value .40 is called a posterior probability.

14. .005, found by $P(A \text{ and } B) = P(A) \cdot P(B) = (.05)(.10)$.
15. 125,970, found by 20!/8!(20 − 8)!.
16. 6, found by 2×3.

Chapter 6

Discrete Probability Distributions

GOALS

When you have completed this chapter, you will be able to:

1
Define the terms *probability distribution* and *random variable.*

2
Distinguish between a discrete probability distribution and a continuous probability distribution.

3
Calculate the mean, variance, and standard deviation of a discrete probability distribution.

4
Describe the characteristics and compute the probabilities using the binomial, the hypergeometric, and the Poisson distributions.

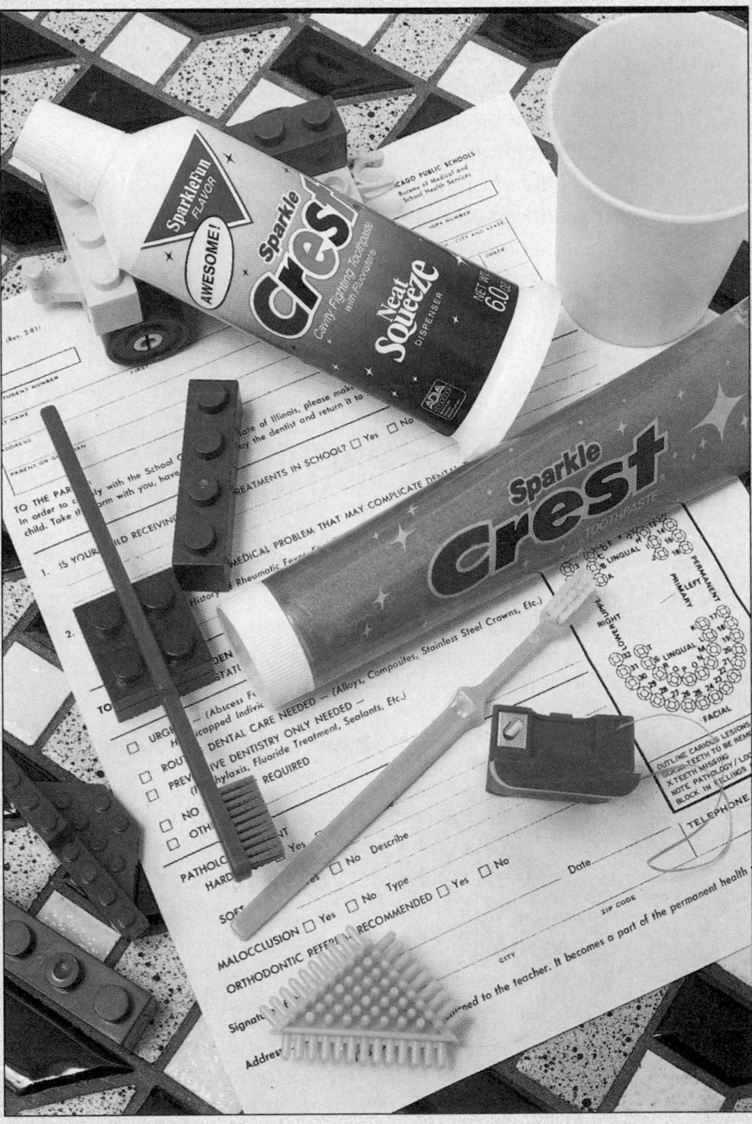

A new toothpaste was tested by ten people. Six liked it while four did not. Four of the ten are selected for in-depth interviews. What is the probability that of the four, two liked the new flavor and two did not? (See Goal 4 and Exercise 41.)

INTRODUCTION

Chapters 2 through 4 were devoted to descriptive statistics. We described raw data by organizing them into a frequency distribution and portraying the distribution in charts. Also, we computed a measure of central tendency—such as the arithmetic mean, median, or mode—to represent a typical value near the center of the distribution. The range and the standard deviation were used to describe the spread in the data. These chapters, focused on describing *something that has already happened.*

Starting with Chapter 5, the emphasis changed—we began examining *something that would probably happen.* We noted that this facet of statistics is called *statistical inference.* The objective is to make inferences (statements) about a population based on a small number of observations, called a sample, selected from the population. In Chapter 5, we stated that a probability is a value between 0 and 1 inclusive, and we examined how probabilities can be combined using rules of addition and multiplication.

This chapter will begin the study of **probability distributions.** A probability distribution gives the entire range of values that can occur based on an experiment. In this chapter we consider *discrete distributions,* where the outcome of an experiment can assume only certain values. For the toss of a die, as an example, only a one-, two-, three-, four-, five-, or six-spot can appear face up. Three discrete distributions are examined, namely, the *binomial, hypergeometric,* and *Poisson.*

WHAT IS A PROBABILITY DISTRIBUTION?

A probability distribution shows the expected outcomes of an experiment and the probability of each of these outcomes.

What is a probability distribution?

Probability distribution A listing of all the outcomes of an experiment and the probability associated with each outcome.

How can we generate a probability distribution?

EXAMPLE

Suppose we are interested in the number of heads showing face up on three tosses of a coin. This is the experiment. The possible results are: zero heads, one head, two heads, and three heads. What is the probability distribution for the number of heads?

Solution ▸ There are eight possible results. A tail might appear face up on the first toss, another tail on the second toss, and another tail on the third toss of the coin. Or we might get a tail, tail, and head, in that order. The table on top of page 219 shows the eight possibilities (H represents a head and T a tail).

Note that the outcome "zero heads" occurred only once, "1 head" occurred three times, "two heads" occurred three times, and the outcome "three heads" occurred only once. That is, "zero heads" happened one out of eight times. Thus, the probability of zero heads is one eighth, the probability of one head is three eighths, and so on. The distribution of probabilities is shown in Table 6–1. Note that the total of the probabilities of all possible events is 1.000. This is always true. The same information can be shown using a chart. (See Chart 6–1 on the facing page.)

Possible result	Coin toss			Number of heads
	First	Second	Third	
1	T	T	T	0
2	T	T	H	1
3	T	H	T	1
4	T	H	H	2
5	H	T	T	1
6	H	T	H	2
7	H	H	T	2
8	H	H	H	3

TABLE 6–1 **Probability Distribution for the Outcomes of Zero, One, Two, and Three Heads Showing Face up on Three Tosses of a Coin**

Number of heads, r	Probability of outcome, $P(r)$
0	$\frac{1}{8} = .125$
1	$\frac{3}{8} = .375$
2	$\frac{3}{8} = .375$
3	$\frac{1}{8} = .125$
Total	$\frac{8}{8} = 1.000$

CHART 6–1 **Graphical Presentation of the Number of Heads and the Associated Probability Resulting from Three Tosses of a Coin**

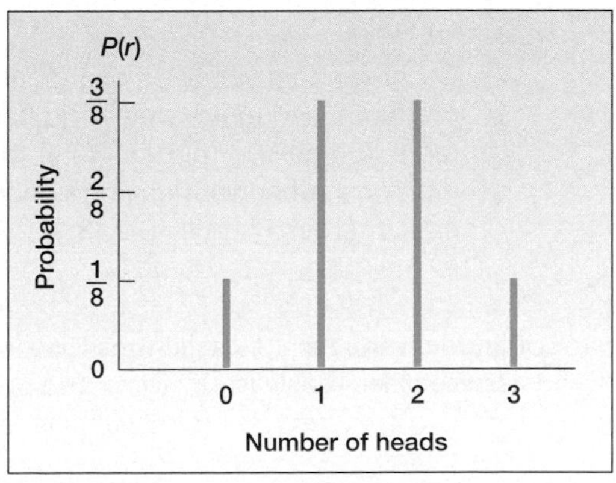

Characteristics of a probability distribution

Before continuing, we should note two important characteristics of a probability distribution.

1. The probability of a particular outcome must always be between 0 and 1 inclusive. (The probabilities of *r,* written *P*(*r*) in the coin tossing example, were .125, .375, etc.)
2. The sum of the probabilities of all mutually exclusive outcomes is 1.000. (Referring to Table 6–1, .125 + .375 + .375 + .125 = 1.000.)

SELF-REVIEW 6–1

The answers are at the end of the chapter.

The possible outcomes of an experiment involving the roll of a six-sided die are: a one-spot, a two-spot, a three-spot, a four-spot, a five-spot, and a six-spot.

1. Develop a probability distribution for these outcomes.
2. Portray the probability distribution graphically.
3. What is the total of the probabilities?

RANDOM VARIABLES

In any experiment of chance, the outcomes occur randomly. For example, rolling a single die is an experiment: any one of six possible outcomes can occur. Some experiments result in outcomes that are quantitative (such as dollars, weight, or number of children), and others result in qualitative outcomes (such as color or religious preference). A few examples will further illustrate what is meant by a **random variable.**

- If we count the number of employees absent on Monday, the number might be 0, 1, 2, 3, ... The number absent is the random variable.
- If we weigh a steel ingot, it might be 2,500 pounds, 2,500.1 pounds, 2,500.13 pounds, and so on depending on the accuracy of the scale.
- If we toss two coins and count the number of heads, there could be zero, one, or two heads. Since the exact number of heads resulting from this experiment is due to chance, the number of heads appearing is the random variable.
- Other random variables might be: the number of defective light bulbs produced during the week, the heights of the members of the girls' basketball team, the number of runners in the Boston Marathon, and the daily number of drivers charged with driving under the influence of alcohol in Texas. In the last case there may be 0, 1, 2, 3, 4, . . . drivers.

Definition of a random variable

Random variable A quantity resulting from a random experiment that, by chance, can assume different values.

A random variable may be either *discrete* or *continuous.*

Discrete Random Variable

Discrete random variable can assume only certain separated values in an interval

A discrete random variable can assume only a certain number of separated values. If there are 100 employees, then the count of the number absent on Monday can only be 0, 1, 2, 3, . . . , 100. A discrete random variable is usually the result of counting something. By way of a definition:

> **Discrete random variable** A variable that can assume only certain clearly separated values resulting from a count of some item of interest.

It should be noted that a discrete variable can, in some cases, assume fractional or decimal values. These values must be separated, that is, have distance between them. As an example, the scores awarded by judges for technical competence and artistic form in figure skating are decimal values, such as 7.2, 8.9, and 9.7. Such values are discrete because there is a distance between scores of, say, 8.3 and 8.4. A score cannot be 8.34 or 8.347, for example.

Continuous Random Variable

Continuous random variable can assume any value in an interval

If we measure something such as the width of a room, the height of a person, or the outside diameter of a bushing, the variable is called a *continuous random variable.* It can assume one of an infinitely large number of values, within certain limitations. As examples:

- The distance between Atlanta and Los Angeles could be 2,254 miles, 2,254.1 miles, 2,254.162 miles, and so on, depending on the accuracy of our measuring device.

- Tire pressure could be 28 pounds per square inch (psi), 28.6 psi, 28.62 psi, 28.624 psi, and so on, depending on the accuracy of the gauge.

Logically, if we organize a set of discrete random variables in a probability distribution, the distribution is called a **discrete probability distribution.** Several discrete probability distributions will be presented in this chapter. Chapter 7 will examine a very important continuous probability distribution—the normal probability distribution.

THE MEAN, VARIANCE, AND STANDARD DEVIATION OF A PROBABILITY DISTRIBUTION

In Chapters 3 and 4, measures of location and variation were discussed for a frequency distribution. The mean reports the central location of the data, and the variance describes the spread in the data. In a similar fashion, a probability distribution is summarized by its mean and variance. The mean of a probability distribution is denoted by the lower-case Greek letter mu (μ) and the variance by the lower-case Greek letter sigma (squared) (σ^2).

Mean

The mean is a typical value used to represent a probability distribution. It also is the long-run average value of the random variable. The mean of a probability distribution is also referred to as its expected value, $E(X)$. It is a weighted average where the possible values are weighted by their corresponding probabilities of occurrence.

The mean of a discrete probability distribution is computed by the formula:

$$\mu = E(X) = \Sigma[XP(X)] \qquad (6\text{–}1)$$

where $P(X)$ is the probability of the various outcomes X. In words, multiply each X value by its probability of occurrence, and then add these products.

Variance and Standard Deviation

As noted, the mean is a typical value used to represent a discrete probability distribution. However, it does not describe the amount of spread (variation) of a distribution. The variance does this. As explained in Chapter 4, a comparison of two variances allows you to compare the variation in two distributions having the same mean but different spreads. The formula for the variance of a probability distribution is:

$$\sigma^2 = \Sigma[(X - \mu)^2 P(X)] \qquad (6\text{–}2)$$

The computational steps are:

1. Subtract the mean from each value, and square this difference.
2. Multiply each squared difference by its probability.
3. Sum the resulting products to arrive at the variance.

The standard deviation σ of a discrete probability distribution is found by taking the square root of σ^2, that is, $\sigma = \sqrt{\sigma^2}$.

EXAMPLE

John Ragsdale sells new cars for Pelican Ford. John usually sells the largest number of cars on Saturday. He has established the following probability distribution for the number of cars he expects to sell on a particular Saturday.

Number of cars sold, X		Probability, $P(X)$
0		.10
1		.20
2		.30
3		.30
4		.10
	Total	1.00

1. What type of distribution is this?
2. On a typical Saturday, how many cars should John expect to sell?
3. What is the variance of the distribution?

Solution ▶

1. This is an example of a discrete probability distribution. Note that John expects to sell only within a certain range of cars; he does not expect to sell 5 cars or 50 cars. Further, he cannot sell half a car. He can only sell 0, 1, 2, 3, or 4 cars. Also, the outcomes are mutually exclusive—he cannot sell a total of both 3 and 4 cars on the same Saturday.
2. The mean number of cars sold is computed by weighting the number of cars sold by the probability of selling that number and totaling the products using formula (6–1):

$$\begin{aligned}\mu &= E(X) = \Sigma[XP(X)]\\ &= 0(.10) + 1(.20) + 2(.30) + 3(.30) + 4(.10)\\ &= 2.1\end{aligned}$$

These calculations are summarized in the following table.

Number of cars sold, X	Probability, $P(X)$		$X \cdot P(X)$
0	.10		0.00
1	.20		0.20
2	.30		0.60
3	.30		0.90
4	.10		0.40
	1.00	$E(X) =$	2.10

How do we interpret a mean of 2.1? This value indicates that, over a large number of Saturdays, John Ragsdale expects to sell a mean of 2.1 cars a day. (Of course, it is not possible for him to sell *exactly* 2.1 cars on any particular Saturday.)

3. Again, a table is useful for systemizing the computations for the variance. It is 1.290.

Number of cars sold, X	**Probability, $P(X)$**	$(X - \mu)$	$(X - \mu)^2$	$(X - \mu)^2 P(X)$
0	.10	0 − 2.1	4.41	0.441
1	.20	1 − 2.1	1.21	0.242
2	.30	2 − 2.1	0.01	0.003
3	.30	3 − 2.1	0.81	0.243
4	.10	4 − 2.1	3.61	0.361
				$\sigma^2 = 1.290$

Recall that the standard deviation, σ, is the square root of the variance. In this problem, $\sqrt{\sigma^2} = \sqrt{1.290} = 1.136$ cars. How do we interpret a standard deviation of 1.136 cars? If salesperson Rita Kirsch also sold a mean of 2.1 cars on Saturdays, and the standard deviation in her sales was 1.91 cars, we would conclude that there is more variability in the Saturday sales of Ms. Kirsch than in those of Mr. Ragsdale (because $1.91 > 1.136$).

SELF-REVIEW 6–2

The answers are at the end of the chapter.

The Pizza Palace offers three sizes of cola—small, medium, and large—to go with its pizza. The colas are sold for 50 cents, 75 cents, and 90 cents, respectively. Thirty percent of the orders are for small, 50 percent are for medium, and 20 percent are for the large size. Organize the size of the colas and the probability of a sale into a probability distribution.

1. Is this a discrete probability distribution? Indicate why or why not.

2. Compute the mean amount charged for a cola.

3. What is the variance of the amount charged for a cola? The standard deviation?

EXERCISES

The answers to the odd-numbered exercises are at the end of the book.

1. Describe the difference between a discrete distribution and a continuous distribution.
2. Describe the characteristics of a discrete probability distribution.
3. Compute the mean and variance of the following discrete probability distribution.

X	$P(X)$
0	.20
1	.40
2	.30
3	.10

4. Compute the mean and variance of the following discrete probability distribution.

X	$P(X)$
2	.50
8	.30
10	.20

5. Dan Woodward is the owner and manager of Dan's Truck Stop. Dan offers free refills on all coffee orders. He gathered the following information on the number of coffee refills.

Refills	Percent
0	30.0
1	40.0
2	20.0
3	10.0

Compute the mean, variance, and standard deviation for the number of refills.

6. The director of admissions at Kinzua University in Nova Scotia estimated the student admission for the fall semester based on past experience.

Admission	Probability
1,000	.60
1,200	.30
1,500	.10

What is the expected number of admissions for the fall semester? Compute the variance and the standard deviation.

BINOMIAL PROBABILITY DISTRIBUTION

The **binomial probability distribution** is an example of a discrete probability distribution. One characteristic of a binomial distribution is that there are only two possible outcomes. For example, the statement in a true/false question is either true or false. The outcomes are *mutually exclusive,* meaning that the answer to a true/false question cannot be both true and false at the same time. As other examples, a product is classified as either acceptable or not acceptable by the quality-control department, a worker is classified as employed or unemployed, and a sales call results in the customer either purchasing the product or not purchasing the product. Frequently we classify the two possible outcomes as "success" and "failure." However, this classification does *not* imply that one outcome is good and the other is bad.

Another characteristic of the binomial distribution is that the information is the result of counts. That is, we count the number of successes in the total number of trials. We flip a fair coin five times and count the number of times a head appears; we select 10 workers and count the number that are over 60 years old, or we select 20 boxes of Kellogg's Raisin Bran and count the number that weigh more than the amount indicated on the package.

Another characteristic of a binomial distribution is that the probability of a success remains the same from one trial to another. Examples:

- The probability that you will guess the first question of a true/false test correctly (a success) is one half. This is the first "trial." The probability that you will guess right on the second question (the second trial) is also one half, the probability of success on the third trial is one half, and so on.
- If past experience revealed that the drawbridge over the Gulf Intracoastal Waterway was raised one out of every five times you approach it, then the probability is one fifth that it will be raised (a success) the next time you approach it, one fifth the following time, and so on.

The final characteristic of a binomial probability distribution is that one trial is *independent* of any other trial. In effect, this is the same as saying that there is no rhythmic pattern with respect to the outcomes. As an example, the answers to a true/false test are not arranged T, T, T, F, F, F, T, T, T, and so forth.

A binomial distribution has these characteristics

In summary, a binomial distribution has these characteristics:

1. An outcome of an experiment is classified into one of two mutually exclusive categories—a success or a failure.
2. The data collected are the result of counts.
3. The probability of a success stays the same for each trial. So does the probability of a failure.
4. The trials are independent, meaning that the outcome of one trial does not affect the outcome of any other trial.

SELF-REVIEW 6–3

The answers are at the end of the chapter.

The professor teaching Horticulture 101 made an assignment involving the memorization of the Latin names of flowers. Unfortunately, none of the students studied the chapter. A pop quiz the next day consisted of 20 multiple-choice questions, each having five choices. All the students guessed the answer to each question.

1. Why would the binomial probability distribution be used to determine the probability of guessing 0, 1, 2, . . . , 20 questions correctly?
2. What is the probability that a student will guess all 20 questions correctly? (It is not necessary to calculate this probability. Instead, show in fractional form how it would be determined.)

How Is a Binomial Probability Distribution Constructed?

Formula for binomial

To construct a binomial probability distribution, we must know (1) the number of trials and (2) the probability of success on each trial. For example, if an examination at the conclusion of a management seminar consists of 20 multiple-choice questions, the number of trials is 20. If each question has five choices and only one choice is correct, the probability of success on each trial is .20. Thus, the probability is .20 that a person with no knowledge of the subject matter will guess the answer to a question correctly. So the conditions of the binomial distribution just noted are met.

The binomial probability distribution can be described using the formula:

$$P(r) = \frac{n!}{r!(n-r)!} p^r q^{n-r} \tag{6–3}$$

where:

- n is the number of trials.
- r is the number of observed successes.
- p is the probability of success on each trial.
- q is the probability of a failure, found by $1 - p$.

EXAMPLE

As we all know, the answer to a true/false question is either correct or incorrect. Assume that (1) an examination consists of four true/false questions, and (2) a student has no knowledge of the subject matter. The chance (probability) that the student will guess the correct answer to the first question is .50. Likewise, the probability of guessing each of the remaining questions correctly is .50. What is the probability of:

1. Getting exactly none out of four correct?
2. Getting exactly one out of four correct?

Solution ▶

1. The probability of guessing none out of the four correctly is .0625, found by applying formula (6–3). (Recall from Chapter 5 that 0! is equal to 1.)

$$P(r) = \frac{n!}{r!(n-r)!} p^r q^{n-r}$$

$$P(0) = \frac{4!}{0!(4-0)!}(.50)^0(1-.50)^{4-0}$$
$$= .0625$$

2. The probability of getting exactly one out of four correct is .2500, found by:

$$P(1) = \frac{4!}{1!(4-1)!}(.50)^1(1-.50)^{4-1}$$
$$= .2500$$

SELF-REVIEW 6–4

The answers are at the end of the chapter.

Refer to the preceding example and solution. Note that there are four true/false questions. Using formula (6–3), what is the probability of getting exactly two of the four questions correct?

The probabilities of getting exactly zero, one, two, three, and four true/false questions correct out of a total of four questions are shown in Table 6–2.

TABLE 6–2 Binomial Probability Distribution for $n = 4$, $p = .50$

Number of correct guesses	Probability: Fraction	Probability: Decimal
0	$\frac{1}{16}$	.0625
1	$\frac{4}{16}$	.2500
2	$\frac{6}{16}$	.3750
3	$\frac{4}{16}$	.2500
4	$\frac{1}{16}$	.0625
Total	$\frac{16}{16}$	1.000

The data in Table 6–2 have been plotted in Chart 6–2. Note that this distribution is symmetrical. This is always the case when *p,* the probability of a success, is .50.

CHART 6–2 Binomial Distribution for $n = 4$, $p = .50$

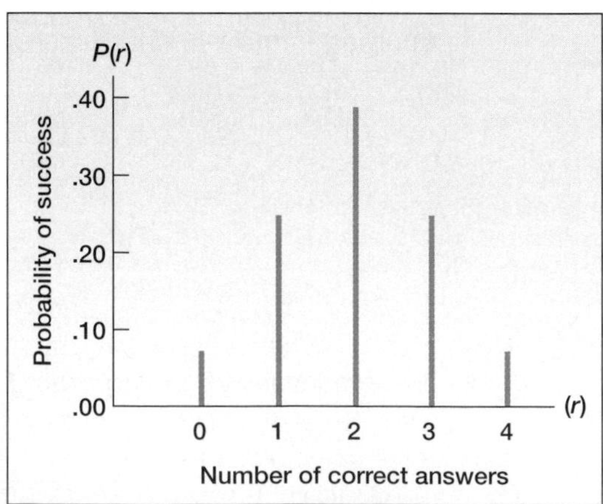

EXERCISES

The answers to the odd-numbered exercises are at the end of the book.

7. List the characteristics of the binomial distribution.
8. In a binomial situation, $n = 5$ and $p = .20$. Determine the following probabilities using formula (6–3).
   a. $r = 1$
   b. $r = 3$
9. In a binomial situation $n = 4$ and $p = .25$. Determine the following probabilities using the binomial formula.
   a. $r = 2$
   b. $r = 3$
10. In a binomial situation $n = 5$ and $p = .40$. Determine the following probabilities using the binomial formula.
    a. $r = 1$
    b. $r = 2$

Using Binomial Probability Tables

Binomial table: Quick way of determining a probability

A binomial probability distribution is a theoretical distribution that, as has been shown, can be generated mathematically. However, except for problems involving small n (say, $n = 3$ or 4), the calculations for the probabilities of 0, 1, 2, . . . successes can be rather tedious. As an aid in finding the needed probabilities, an extensive table has been developed that gives the probabilities of 0, 1, 2, 3, . . . successes for various values of n and p. This table is in Appendix A, and a small portion of the table needed for the following example is shown in Table 6–3.

TABLE 6–3 **Binomial Probabilities for $n = 6$**

r	.05	.1	.2	.3	.4	.5	.6	.7	.8	.9	.95
0	.735	.531	.262	.118	.047	.016	.004	.001	.000	.000	.000
1	.232	.354	.393	.303	.187	.094	.037	.010	.002	.000	.000
2	.031	.098	.246	.324	.311	.234	.138	.060	.015	.001	.000
3	.002	.015	.082	.185	.276	.313	.276	.185	.082	.015	.002
4	.000	.001	.015	.060	.138	.234	.311	.324	.246	.098	.031
5	.000	.000	.002	.010	.037	.094	.187	.303	.393	.354	.232
6	.000	.000	.000	.001	.004	.016	.047	.118	.262	.531	.735

EXAMPLE

Based on recent experience, 5 percent of the worm gears produced by an automatic, high-speed Carter-Bell milling machine are defective. What is the probability that out of six gears selected at random, exactly zero gears will be defective? Exactly one? Exactly two? Exactly three? Exactly four? Exactly five? Exactly six out of the six? (Note: $n = 6$, $p = .05$.)

Solution ▸ Note that the binomial conditions are met: (1) There is a constant probability of success (.05), (2) there is a fixed number of trials (6), (3) the trials are independent, and (4) there are only two possible outcomes (a particular gear is either defective or acceptable).

Binomial probability distribution

Refer to Table 6–3 for the probability of exactly zero defective gears. Go down the left margin to an r of 0. Now move horizontally to the column headed by a p of .05 to find the probability. It is .735.

The probability of exactly one defective in a sample of six worm gears is .232. The complete binomial probability distribution for $n = 6$ and $p = .05$ is:

Number of defective gears, r	**Probability of occurrence, $P(r)$**
0	.735
1	.232
2	.031
3	.002
4	.000
5	.000
6	.000

Of course, there is a slight chance of getting exactly five defective gears out of six random selections. It is .00000178, found by inserting the appropriate values in the binomial formula:

$$\begin{aligned} P(5) &= \frac{6!}{5!(6-5)!}(.05)^5(.95)^1 \\ &= (6)(.05)^5(.95) \\ &= .00000178 \end{aligned}$$

For six out of the six, the probability is .000000016. Thus, the probability is very small that five or six defective gears will be selected in a sample of six.

This problem can also be solved on the MINITAB system. The command PDF is used to access the probability density function. The subcommand BINOMIAL is used with n, the number of trials (or sample size), and p, the probability of a success. The output follows.

```
MTB > pdf;
SUBC> binomial  n=6  p=.05.
    BINOMIAL WITH N = 6   P = 0.050000
    K          P(X = K)
    0          0.7351
    1          0.2321<-- Probability of one defective
    2          0.0305
    3          0.0021
    4          0.0001
    5          0.0000
```

The output is the same as in Table 6–3 except for the difference in the number of digits after the decimal.

SELF-REVIEW 6–5

The answers are at the end of the chapter.

One of every five times you approached the drawbridge over the Gulf Intracoastal Waterway, it was raised, and you had to wait. Using the binomial probability table in Appendix A:

1. What is the probability that on your next seven approaches to the drawbridge it will not be raised?
2. What is the probability that it will be raised exactly one out of the seven approaches?
3. What is the probability that it will be raised exactly twice? Exactly three times? Exactly four times? Exactly five times? Exactly six times? All seven times?
4. What should the probabilities in Questions 1, 2, and 3 total?

Appendix A is somewhat limited in that it gives probabilities only for *n* values of 1 to 20 and 25 and *p* values of .05, .10, .20, . . . , .95. There are two methods for arriving at a binomial distribution for an *n* over 25 and/or a *p* not found in the table (say, .07): (1) The normal approximation to the binomial may be used. This will be presented in Chapter 7. (2) A computer can generate the probabilities for a specified number of successes, given an *n* and a *p*. To illustrate, following are two MINITAB outputs—one for an *n* of 40 and a *p* of .09, and the other for an *n* of 27 and a *p* of .376.

```
MTB > pdf;
SUBC> binomial  n=40  p=.09.
    BINOMIAL WITH N = 40   P = 0.090000
         K        P(X = K)
         0         0.0230
         1         0.0910
         2         0.1754
         3         0.2198
         4         0.2011
         5         0.1432
         6         0.0826
         7         0.0397
         8         0.0162
         9         0.0057
        10         0.0017
        11         0.0005
        12         0.0001
        13         0.0000
```

```
MTB > pdf;
SUBC> binomial  n=27  p=.376.
     BINOMIAL WITH N = 27   P = 0.376000
         K          P(X = K)
         1          0.0000
         2          0.0004
         3          0.0019
         4          0.0068
         5          0.0189
         6          0.0418
         7          0.0756
         8          0.1139
         9          0.1448
        10          0.1571
        11          0.1463
        12          0.1175
        13          0.0817
        14          0.0492
        15          0.0257
        16          0.0116
        17          0.0045
        18          0.0015
        19          0.0004
        20          0.0001
        21          0.0000
```

As *p* becomes closer to .50, binomial distribution becomes more symmetrical

Several additional points should be made about binomial distributions:

1. If *n* remains the same but *p* increases from .05 to .95, the shape of the distribution changes. Note in Table 6–4 that the probabilities for a *p* of .05 are positively skewed. As *p* approaches .50, the distribution approaches a symmetrical distribution. As *p* goes beyond .50 and moves toward .95, the probability distribution becomes negatively skewed. Table 6–4 gives probabilities for $n = 10$ and probabilities of success of .05, .10, .20, .50, and .70. The plots of these values are shown in Chart 6–3.

TABLE 6–4 **Probability of 0, 1, 2, . . . Successes for a *p* of .05, .10, .20, .50, and .70 and an *n* of 10**

r	.05	.1	.2	.3	.4	.5	.6	.7	.8	.9	.95
0	.599	.349	.107	.028	.006	.001	.000	.000	.000	.000	.000
1	.315	.387	.268	.121	.040	.010	.002	.000	.000	.000	.000
2	.075	.194	.302	.233	.121	.044	.011	.001	.000	.000	.000
3	.010	.057	.201	.267	.215	.117	.042	.009	.001	.000	.000
4	.001	.011	.088	.200	.251	.205	.111	.037	.006	.000	.000
5	.000	.001	.026	.103	.201	.246	.201	.103	.026	.001	.000
6	.000	.000	.006	.037	.111	.205	.251	.200	.088	.011	.001
7	.000	.000	.001	.009	.042	.117	.215	.267	.201	.057	.010
8	.000	.000	.000	.001	.011	.044	.121	.233	.302	.194	.075
9	.000	.000	.000	.000	.002	.010	.040	.121	.268	.387	.315
10	.000	.000	.000	.000	.000	.001	.006	.028	.107	.349	.599

CHART 6–3 **Chart Representing the Binomial Probability Distribution for a *p* of .05, .10, .20, .50, and .70 and an *n* of 10**

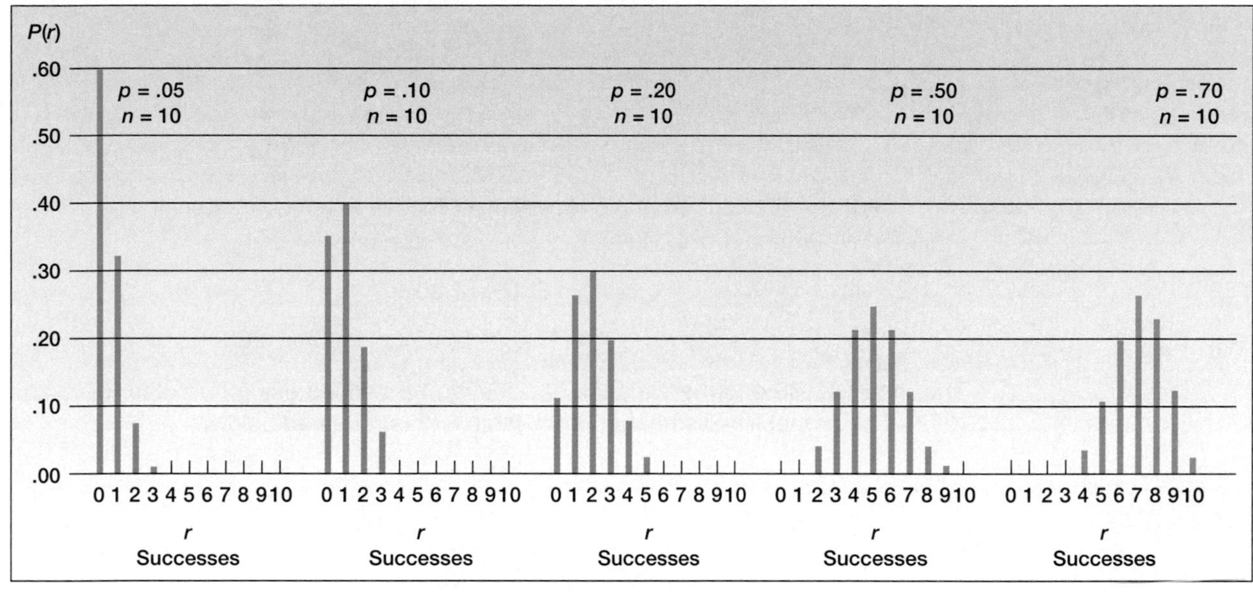

2. If *p,* the probability of success, remains the same but *n* becomes larger and larger, the shape of the binomial distribution becomes more symmetrical. Chart 6–4 shows a situation where *p* remains constant at .10 but *n* increases from 7 to 40.

CHART 6–4 **Chart Representing the Binomial Probability Distribution for a *p* of .10 and an *n* of 7, 12, 20, and 40**

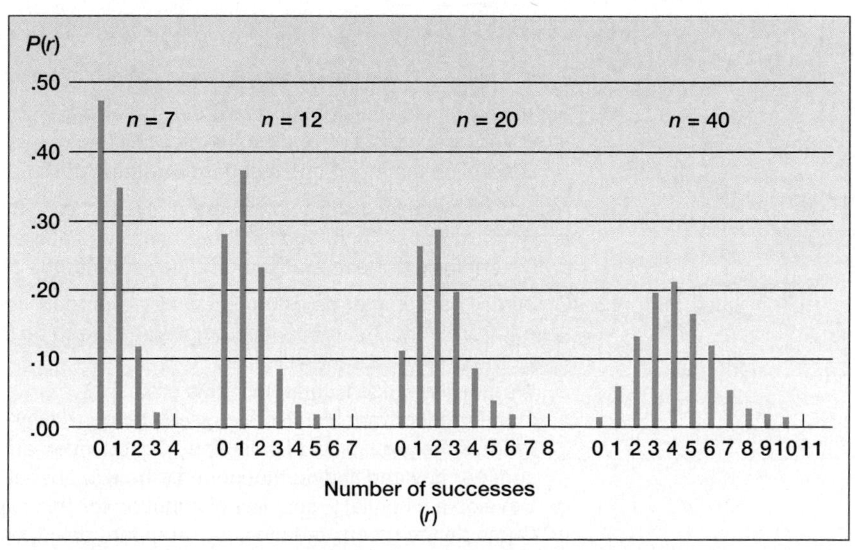

3. The mean (μ) and the variance (σ^2) of a binomial distribution can be computed by:

$$\mu = np \tag{6–4}$$

$$\sigma^2 = np(1 - p) \tag{6–5}$$

For the previous example regarding defective worm gears, recall that $p = .05$ and $n = 6$. Hence:

$$\mu = np = 6(.05) = .30$$

$$\sigma^2 = np(1 - p) = 6(.05)(1 - .05) = .285$$

The mean of .30 and the variance of .285 can be verified using formulas (6–1) and (6–2). The probability distribution from Table 6–3 is repeated below.

Number of defects, r	$P(r)$	$rP(r)$	$r - \mu$	$(r - \mu)^2$	$(r - \mu)^2P(r)$
0	.735	0	−0.30	0.09	0.06615
1	.232	0.232	0.70	0.49	0.11368
2	.031	0.062	1.70	2.89	0.08959
3	.002	0.006	2.70	7.29	0.01458
4	.000	0	3.70	13.69	0
5	.000	0	4.70	22.09	0
6	.000	0	5.70	32.49	0
		0.30			0.284*

*The slight discrepancy between .285 and .284 is due to rounding.

EXERCISES

The answers to the odd-numbered exercises are at the end of the book.

11. Assume a binomial distribution where $n = 3$ and $p = .60$.
    a. Refer to Appendix A, and list the probabilities of a success for values of r from 0 to 3.
    b. Determine the mean and standard deviation of the distribution.
12. Assume a binomial distribution where $n = 5$ and $p = .30$.
    a. Refer to Appendix A, and list the probabilities of a success for values of r from 0 to 5.
    b. Determine the mean and standard deviation of the distribution.
13. On a very hot summer day, 10 percent of the production employees at Nome Steel are absent from work. Ten production employees are to be selected at random for a special in-depth study on absenteeism.
    a. What is the random variable in this problem?
    b. Is the random variable discrete or continuous? Why?
    c. What is the probability of selecting 10 production employees at random on a hot summer day and finding that none of them is absent?
    d. Develop a binomial probability distribution for this experiment.
    e. Compute the mean, variance, and standard deviation of the distribution.

f. Portray the binomial probability distribution in the form of a chart.
g. Why is the binomial probability distribution appropriate for this type of problem?

14. The marketing department of the Kellogg Company plans to conduct a national survey to find out whether or not consumers of flake cereals can distinguish one of their favorite flake cereals from other flake cereals. To test the questionnaire and procedure to be used, eight persons were asked to cooperate in an experiment. Five very small bowls of flake cereals were placed in front of a person. The bowls were labeled A, B, C, D, and E. The person was informed that only one bowl contained his or her favorite flake cereal.
    a. Suppose a person could not identify his or her favorite cereal and just guessed that it was in bowl C. What is the probability that the person guessed correctly?
    b. What is the random variable in this problem?
    c. Is the random variable discrete or continuous? Why?
    d. Suppose that all eight persons in the experiment were unable to identify their favorite cereal and just guessed which bowl it was in. What is the probability that none of the eight guessed correctly?
    e. Develop a binomial probability distribution for this experiment.
    f. Compute the mean, variance, and standard deviation of the distribution.
    g. Portray the binomial probability distribution in the form of a chart.
    h. Suppose seven of the eight persons identified the cereal they liked best. Is it reasonable to assume that they were just guessing? Explain. What would you conclude?
    i. Why is the binomial probability distribution appropriate for this problem?

Uses and Importance of the Binomial Probability Distribution

Some uses of the binomial distribution

We have cited several examples of the use and importance of a probability distribution in this chapter. In brief, we noted that any probability distribution is a theoretical distribution showing how the outcomes of an experiment are expected to be distributed. Specifically, a binomial probability distribution shows how an experiment involving only two outcomes (a success or a failure) is expected to be distributed. In the examples, the chapter exercises, and the self-reviews, we also illustrated some uses of the binomial probability distribution. Here are two other cases:

Case 1 Suppose that past experience revealed that 5 percent of the automobile doors coming off the production line are defective. A defective door is defined by quality control as a door with an exposed sharp burr, a faulty paint, or a dent. Ten doors are to be selected at random by quality control. The binomial distribution for the number of defective doors in a sample of 10 with $p = .05$ is shown in Table 6–5.

Note that the probable number of defective doors in the sample of 10 is either 0 or 1. Three or more defective doors is quite improbable. If 6 doors were defective out of the 10, quality control would no doubt investigate the causes of the defects and take corrective action. Thus, knowledge of the distribution tells us, in advance of the experiment, what we can expect to occur and what are unusual results.

TABLE 6–5 **Binomial Probability Distribution for an *n* of 10 and a *p* of .05**

Number of defects	Probability of occurrence	
0	.599	Most probable
1	.315	
2	.075	
3	.010	Quite improbable
4	.001	
5	.000	
6	.000	
7	.000	
8	.000	
9	.000	
10	.000	

Case 2 Surveys are conducted continuously by various research groups regarding voting preference, consumer protection policies, product preference, and so on. A set of multiple-choice questions is often used, and the respondent checks what he or she considers the correct answer. The researcher is always concerned that uninformed respondents may merely guess the answers to avoid embarrassment. The researcher, therefore, generates a binomial probability distribution and matches it with the *actual responses* in order to help identify the guesses. For example, a questionnaire consists of six questions, and each question has five choices. Only one answer is correct. The binomial probability distribution for the number of correct answers arrived at *by chance* is shown in Table 6–6. If the respondents were just guessing the answers to avoid embarrassment, the probable number they would guess correctly is zero, one, or two. However, if most of the respondents had five or six correct out of six, we would assume that they knew the answers to most of the questions because the chance of guessing five or six out of six correctly is only .002, or about 2 out of 1,000.

TABLE 6–6 **Binomial Probability Distribution for an *n* of 6 and a *p* of .20**

Number of correct answers	Probability of occurrence	
0	.262	Most probable
1	.393	
2	.246	
3	.082	
4	.015	Least probable
5	.002	
6	.000	

In summary, we generate an appropriate theoretical probability distribution to identify the expected outcomes of an experiment. We then match the actual outcomes with the expected outcomes in order to evaluate the results of the experiment.

CUMULATIVE PROBABILITY DISTRIBUTIONS

We may want to know the probability of correctly guessing the answers to 6 *or more* true/false questions out of 10. Or we may be interested in the probability of selecting *less than* two defectives at random from the production during the previous hour. This sounds like we need cumulative frequency distributions similar to the ones developed in Chapter 2. The following example will illustrate.

EXAMPLE

A recent study by the American Highway Patrolman's Association revealed that 60 percent of American drivers use their seat belts. A sample of 10 drivers on the Florida Turnpike is selected.

1. What is the probability that exactly 7 were wearing seat belts?
2. What is the probability that 7 or fewer of the drivers were wearing seat belts?

Solution ▶ This situation meets the binomial requirements, namely:

- A particular driver either is wearing a seat belt or is not. There are only two possible outcomes.
- The probability of a "success" (wearing a seat belt) is the same from driver to driver: 60 percent.
- The trials are independent. If the fourth driver selected in the sample is wearing a seat belt, for example, it has no effect on whether the fifth driver selected is or is not wearing a seat belt.
- There is a fixed number of trials—10 in this case, because 10 drivers were checked.

1. To find the likelihood of *exactly* 7 drivers, we use Appendix A. Locate the page for $n = 10$. Next find the column for $p = .60$ and the row for $r = 7$. The value is .215. Thus, the probability of finding 7 out of the 10 drivers in the sample wearing their seat belts is .215. This is often written as follows:

   $$P(r = 7 \mid n = 10 \text{ and } p = .60) = .215$$

   where r refers to the number of successes, n the number of trials, and p the probability of a success. The bar "|" means "given that."
2. To find the probability of 7 or fewer of the drivers wearing seat belts, we apply the special rule of addition, formula (5–2), from Chapter 5. Because the events are mutually exclusive, we determine the probability that of the 10 drivers stopped, none was wearing a seat belt, 1 was wearing a seat belt, 2 were wearing a seat belt, and so on up to 7 drivers. The eight possible outcomes are then totaled. From Appendix A, $n = 10$, and $p = .60$:

   $$\begin{aligned} P(r \le 7 \mid n = 10 \text{ and } p = .60) &= P(r = 0) + P(r = 1) + P(r = 2) + P(r = 3) \\ &\quad + P(r = 4) + P(r = 5) + P(r = 6) + P(r = 7) \\ &= .000 + .002 + .011 + .042 + .111 + .201 \\ &\quad + .251 + .215 \\ &= .833 \end{aligned}$$

So the probability of stopping 10 cars at random and finding 7 or fewer of the drivers wearing their seat belts is .833. This value may also be determined, with less computation, using the complement rule. First, find $P(r > 7)$ given that $n = 10$ and $p = .60$. This probability is .167, found by $P(r = 8) + P(r = 9) + P(r = 10) = .121 + .040 + .006$. The probability that $r \leq 7$ is equal to $1 - P(r > 7)$, so $P(r \leq 7) = 1 - .167 = .833$, the same as computed above.

SELF-REVIEW 6–6

The answers are at the end of the chapter.

For a case where $n = 4$ and $p = .60$, determine the probability that:

a. $r = 2$.

b. $r \leq 2$.

c. $r > 2$.

EXERCISES

The answers to the odd-numbered exercises are at the end of the book.

15. In a binomial distribution $n = 8$ and $p = .30$. Find the following probabilities.
    a. $r = 2$.
    b. $r \leq 2$ (the probability that r is equal to or less than 2).
    c. $r \geq 3$ (the probability that r is equal to or greater than 3).
16. In a binomial distribution $n = 12$ and $p = .60$. Find the following probabilities.
    a. $r = 5$
    b. $r \leq 5$
    c. $r \geq 6$
17. In a recent study 90 percent of the homes in the United States were found to have color TVs. In a sample of nine homes, what is the probability that:
    a. All nine have color TVs?
    b. Less than five have color TVs?
    c. More than five have color TVs?
    d. At least seven homes have color TVs?
18. A manufacturer of window frames knows from long experience that 5 percent of the production will have some type of minor defect that will require a slight adjustment. What is the probability that in a sample of 20 window frames:
    a. None will need adjustment?
    b. At least 1 will need adjustment?
    c. More than 2 will need adjustment?

HYPERGEOMETRIC DISTRIBUTION

We pointed out that for the binomial distribution to be applied, the probability of a success must stay the same for each successive trial. For example, the probability of guessing the correct answer to a true/false question is .50. This probability remains the same for each question on an examination. Likewise, suppose that 40 percent of the registered voters in a precinct are Republicans. If 27 registered voters are to be selected at random, the probability of choosing a Republican on the first selection is .40. The chance of choosing a Republican on the next selection is also .40, assuming that the sampling is done *with replacement,* meaning that the person selected is put back in the population before the next person is selected.

Most sampling is done *without replacement.* Thus, the outcomes are not independent—meaning that the probability for each successive observation will change. For example, if the population consists of 20 items, the probability of selecting a particular item from that population is $1/20$. If the sampling is done without replacement, there are only 19 items remaining; the probability of selecting a particular item on the second selection is only $1/19$. For the third selection, the probability is $1/18$, and so on.

Finite population

This assumes that the population is **finite**—that is, the number in the population is known.

Finite population A population consisting of a fixed number of known individuals, objects, or measurements.

Examples of a finite population are 2,842 Republicans in the precinct, 9,241 applications for medical school, and the 18 Pontiac Sunbirds currently in stock at North Pontiac.

Hypergeometric distribution

Recall that one of the criteria for using the binomial distribution is that the probability of success remain the same from trial to trial. Since the probability of success does not remain the same from trial to trial when sampling is done without replacement, the binomial distribution should not be used. Instead, the **hypergeometric distribution** should be applied. Therefore, (1) if a sample is selected from a finite population without replacement and (2) if the size of the sample n is greater than 5 percent of the size of the population N, then the hypergeometric distribution is used to determine the probability of a specified number of successes or failures. It is especially appropriate when the size of the population is small.

The formula for the hypergeometric distribution is:

$$P(r) = \frac{({}_SC_r)({}_{N-S}C_{n-r})}{{}_NC_n} \qquad (6\text{–}6)$$

where:

- N is the size of the population.
- S is the number of successes in the population.
- r is the number of successes of interest. It may be 0, 1, 2, 3, ...
- n is the size of the sample or the number of trials.
- C is the symbol for a combination.

EXAMPLE

Suppose 50 transceivers were manufactured during the week ($N = 50$). Forty operated perfectly ($S = 40$), and 10 had at least one defect. A sample of 5 is selected at random ($n = 5$). Using the hypergeometric formula, what is the probability that

4 ($r = 4$) of the 5 will operate perfectly? (Note that sampling is done without replacement, and the sample size of 5 is 5/50, or 10 percent of the population. This is greater than the 5 percent requirement.)

Solution ► In this problem,

$N = 50$, the number of transceivers manufactured.

$n = 5$, the size of the sample.

$S = 40$, the number of transceivers in the population operating perfectly.

$r = 4$, the number in the sample operating perfectly.

We want to find the probability that 4 transceivers of the 5 selected will operate perfectly.

Inserting these values in formula (6–6) and solving for the probability that 4 out of 5 transceivers in the sample operate perfectly:

$$P(r) = \frac{({}_{S}C_{r})({}_{N-S}C_{n-r})}{{}_{N}C_{n}}$$

$$P(4) = \frac{({}_{40}C_{4})({}_{50-40}C_{5-4})}{{}_{50}C_{5}}$$

$$= \frac{\left(\frac{40!}{4!36!}\right)\left(\frac{10!}{1!9!}\right)}{\frac{50!}{5!45!}}$$

$$= \frac{(91{,}390)(10)}{2{,}118{,}760} = .431$$

Thus, the probability of selecting 5 transceivers at random out of 50 and finding that 4 of the 5 operate perfectly is .431.

The hypergeometric probabilities of finding 0, 1, 2, 3, 4, and 5 working transceivers of the 5 transceivers selected at random are given in Table 6–7.

TABLE 6–7 **Hypergeometric Probabilities ($n = 5$, $N = 50$, $S = 40$) that Transceivers Operate Correctly**

Number operating correctly	Probability
0	.000*
1	.004
2	.044
3	.210
4	.431
5	.311

*Actually .0001.

Hypergeometric probabilities closely approximate binomial probabilities. For comparison, Table 6–8 gives the hypergeometric and binomial probabilities for the transceiver problem. (Since 40 of the 50 transceivers operated correctly, the binomial probability of selecting a perfect transceiver is $^{40}/_{50} = .80$. The binomial probabilities for Table 6–8 come from the binomial table in Appendix A, $n = 5$, $p = .80$.)

TABLE 6–8 Hypergeometric and Binomial Probabilities for the Transceiver Problem

Number of transceivers in sample operating correctly, r	Hypergeometric probability, $P(r)$	Binomial probability* ($n = 5$, $p = 40/50 = .80$)
0	.000	.000
1	.004	.006
2	.044	.051
3	.210	.205
4	.431	.410
5	.311	.328

*From Appendix A for an n of 5 and a p of .80, found by 40/50.

We pointed out that when the binomial requirement of a constant probability of success cannot be met, the hypergeometric distribution should be used in its place. However, as Table 6–8 shows, under many conditions the results of the binomial closely approximate those of the hypergeometric. As a rule of thumb, if the selected items are not returned to the population and the sample size is less than 5 percent of the population, the binomial distribution can be used to approximate the hypergeometric distribution. That is, when $n < .05N$, the binomial approximation should suffice.

SELF-REVIEW 6–7

The answers are at the end of the chapter.

Refer to the transceiver example and Table 6–7. Verify the hypergeometric probability of .210 that three of the five randomly selected transceivers will operate correctly.

EXERCISES

The answers to the odd-numbered exercises are at the end of the book.

19. Suppose a population consists of 10 items, 6 of which are defective. A sample of 3 items is selected. What is the probability that exactly 2 are defective?
20. Suppose a population consists of 15 items, 10 of which are acceptable. A sample of 4 items is selected. What is the probability that exactly 3 are acceptable?
21. Kolzak Appliance Outlet just received a shipment of 10 TV sets. Shortly after they were received, the manufacturer called to report that he had inadvertently shipped 3 defective sets. Ms. Kolzak, the owner of the outlet, decided to test 2 of the 10 sets she received. What is the probability that neither of the 2 sets tested was defective?
22. The Computer Systems Department consists of eight faculty, six of whom are tenured. Dr. Vonder, the chairman, wants to establish a committee of three department faculty members to review the curriculum. If she selects the committee at random:
    a. What is the probability all members of the committee are tenured?
    b. What is the probability that at least one member is not tenured? (Hint: For this question use the complement rule.)

23. Keith's Florists has 15 delivery trucks, used mainly to deliver flowers and flower arrangements in the Tulsa area. Suppose 6 of the 15 trucks have brake problems. Five trucks were selected at random to be tested. What is the probability that 2 of those tested have defective brakes?
24. Professor Jon Hammer has a pool of 15 multiple-choice questions regarding probability distributions. Four of these questions involve the hypergeometric distribution. What is the probability at least 1 of these hypergeometric questions will appear on the 5-question quiz on Monday?

POISSON PROBABILITY DISTRIBUTION

Poisson probability distribution—a discrete distribution

The binomial probability distributions for probabilities of success (p) less than .05 could be computed, but the calculations would be quite time-consuming (especially for a large n of, say, 100 or more). The distribution of probabilities would become more and more skewed as the probability of success became smaller. The limiting form of the binomial distribution where the probability of success is very small and n is large is called the **Poisson probability distribution.** The distribution is named after Simeon Poisson, who described it in 1837. It is often referred to as the law of improbable events, meaning that the probability p of a particular event's happening is quite small. The Poisson distribution is a discrete probability distribution because it is formed by counting something.

This distribution has many applications. It is used as a model to describe the distribution of errors in data entry, the number of scratches and other imperfections in newly painted car panels, the number of defective parts in outgoing shipments, the number of customers waiting to be served at a restaurant or waiting to get into an attraction at Disney World, and the number of accidents on I-75 during a three-month period.

The Poisson distribution can be described mathematically using the formula:

$$P(x) = \frac{\mu^x e^{-\mu}}{x!} \qquad (6\text{–}7)$$

where

μ (mu) is the arithmetic mean number of occurrences (successes) in a particular interval of time.

e is the constant 2.71828 (base of the Naperian logarithmic system).

x is the number of occurrences (successes).

$P(x)$ is the probability to be computed for a specified value of x.

Mean of a Poisson distribution

The mean number of successes μ can be determined in binomial situations by *np,* where *n* is the total number of trials and *p* the probability of success.

$$\mu = np \qquad (6\text{–}8)$$

The variance of the Poisson is also equal to *np.* If, for example, the probability that a check cashed by a bank will bounce is .0003, and 10,000 checks are cashed, the mean number of bad checks is 3.0, found by $\mu = np = 10{,}000\,(.0003) = 3.0$.

Recall that for a binomial distribution there is a determinate number of successes. For example, for a four-question multiple-choice test there can only be zero, one, two, three, or four successes (correct answers). The random variable x for a Poisson distribution, however, can assume an *infinite number of values*—that is, 0, 1, 2, 3, 4, 5, ... However, *the probabilities become very small after the first few occurrences* (successes).

To illustrate the computation of a Poisson probability, assume that billing clerks rarely make errors in data entry on the billing statements. Many statements, of course, have no mistakes; some have one; a very few have two mistakes; rarely will a statement have three mistakes; and so on. A random sample of 1,000 statements revealed 300 errors. Thus, the arithmetic mean number of mistakes per billing statement is 0.3, found by 300/1,000. This is a sample mean, $\overline{X}$, which is used to estimate the population mean, μ, for a model (Poisson) of the process.

The probability of no (0) mistakes appearing in a statement is computed by:

$$P(x) = \frac{\mu^x e^{-\mu}}{x!}$$

Substituting:

$$P(0) = \frac{0.3^0(2.71828)^{-0.3}}{0!}$$

Use a table to determine Poisson probabilities

However, the computations of the probabilities for a Poisson distribution using the formula are time-consuming. As an aid, a table of Poisson probabilities is given in Appendix C for various values of μ.

EXAMPLE

Recall from the previous illustration that the mean number of errors per billing statement was estimated to be 0.3. That is, $\mu = 0.3$. What is the probability that no mistakes will be found on a randomly selected billing statement? What is the probability that exactly one mistake will be found?

Solution ► A portion of Appendix C is repeated in Table 6–9. To find the probability of no billing errors, first locate the column headed 0.3 and then read down that column to the row labeled 0. The probability is .7408. The probability of exactly one error is .2222, for two errors it is .0333, for three errors it is .0072, and for four errors it is .0003.

TABLE 6–9 **Poisson Table for Various Values of μ**

	μ								
x	**0.1**	**0.2**	**0.3**	**0.4**	**0.5**	**0.6**	**0.7**	**0.8**	**0.9**
0	0.9048	0.8187	0.7408	0.6703	0.6065	0.5488	0.4966	0.4493	0.4066
1	0.0905	0.1637	0.2222	0.2681	0.3033	0.3293	0.3476	0.3595	0.3659
2	0.0045	0.0164	0.0333	0.0536	0.0758	0.0988	0.1217	0.1438	0.1647
3	0.0002	0.0011	0.0033	0.0072	0.0126	0.0198	0.0284	0.0383	0.0494
4	0.0000	0.0001	0.0003	0.0007	0.0016	0.0030	0.0050	0.0077	0.0111
5	0.0000	0.0000	0.0000	0.0001	0.0002	0.0004	0.0007	0.0012	0.0020
6	0.0000	0.0000	0.0000	0.0000	0.0000	0.0000	0.0001	0.0002	0.0003
7	0.0000	0.0000	0.0000	0.0000	0.0000	0.0000	0.0000	0.0000	0.0000

These probabilities can also be found using the MINITAB system. The command required is "pdf" followed by a semicolon. The subcommand is "poisson mu = .3." The output appears below. A graph of the distribution of the number of errors is shown in Chart 6–5 at the top of the following page. Note that the distribution is severely skewed in the positive direction.

```
MTB > pdf;
SUBC> poisson mu = .3.
    POISSON WITH MEAN = 0.300
        K            P(X = K)
        0              0.7408
        1              0.2222
        2              0.0333
        3              0.0033
        4              0.0003
        5              0.0000
```

SELF-REVIEW 6–8

The answers are at the end of the chapter.

A hybrid seed grower is experiencing trouble with corn borers. A random check of 5,000 ears revealed the following: Many of the ears contained no borers; some ears had one borer; a few had two borers; and so on. The distribution of the number of borers per ear approximates the Poisson distribution. The grower counted 3,500 borers in the 5,000 ears.

1. What is the probability that an ear of corn selected at random will contain no borers?
2. Develop a Poisson probability distribution for this experiment.

CHART 6–5 **Poisson Probability Distribution for $\mu = 0.3$**

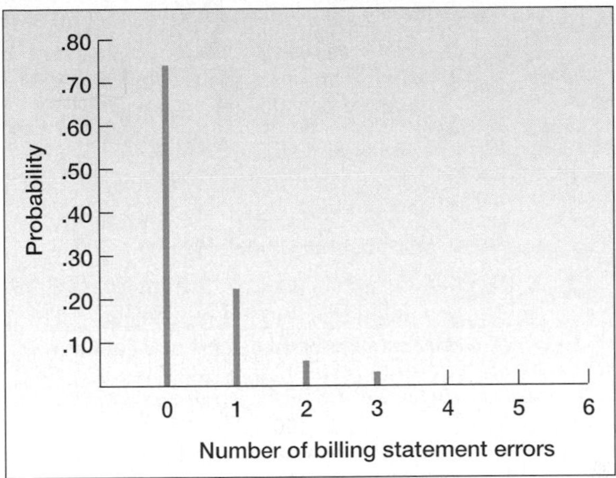

The Poisson probability distribution is always positively skewed. Also, the Poisson random variable has no specific upper limit. The Poisson distributions for the data entry illustration, where $\mu = 0.3$, and for the corn borer experiment in Self-Review 6–8, where $\mu = 0.7$, are highly skewed. As μ becomes larger, the Poisson distribution becomes almost symmetrical. For illustration, the distributions for means of 0.7, 2.0, and 6.0 are shown in Chart 6–6.

CHART 6–6 **Poisson Probability Distributions for Means of 0.7, 2.0, and 6.0**

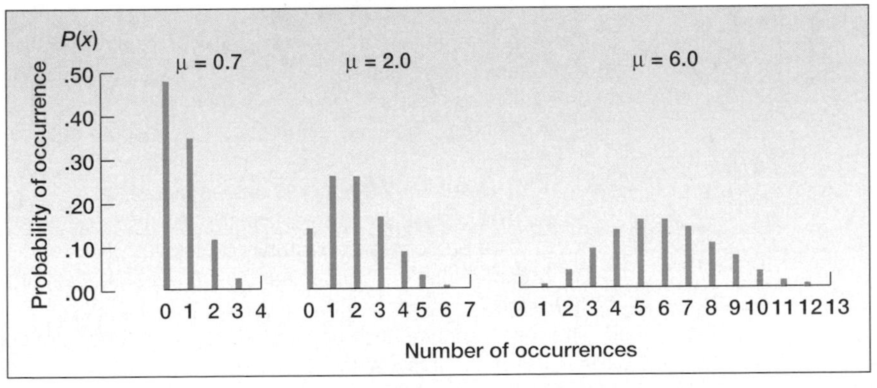

Only μ needed to construct Poisson

In brief summary, the Poisson distribution is actually a group of discrete distributions. To apply it, *n* must be large, such as 1,000 sheared pieces. Conversely, the probability *p* of a defect, error, and the like must be small. All that is needed to construct a Poisson probability distribution is the mean number of defects, errors, and so on—designated as μ. It is computed by *np*.

EXERCISES

The answers to the odd-numbered exercises are at the end of the book.

25. In a Poisson distribution $\mu = 0.4$.
    a. What is the probability that $x = 0$?
    b. What is the probability that $x > 0$?
26. In a Poisson distribution $\mu = 4$.
    a. What is the probability that $x = 2$?
    b. What is the probability that $x \leq 2$?
    c. What is the probability that $x > 2$?
27. Ms. Bergen is a loan officer at Coast Bank and Trust. Based on her years of experience she estimates that the probability is .025 that an applicant will not be able to repay his or her installment loan. Last month she made 40 loans.
    a. What is the probability that 3 loans will be defaulted?
    b. What is the probability that at least 3 loans will be defaulted?
28. Automobiles arrive at the Elkhart exit of the Indiana Toll Road at the rate of two per minute. The distribution of arrivals approximates a Poisson distribution.
    a. What is the probability that no automobiles arrive in a particular minute?
    b. What is the probability that at least one automobile arrives during a particular minute?
29. It is estimated that 0.5 percent of the callers to the billing department of the U.S. West Telephone Company will receive a busy signal. What is the probability that of today's 1,200 callers at least 5 received a busy signal?
30. Textbook authors and publishers work very hard to minimize the number of errors in a text. However, some errors are unavoidable. Mr. J. A. Carmen, statistics editor, reports that the mean number of errors per chapter is 0.8. What is the probability that there are less than 2 errors in a particular chapter?

CHAPTER OUTLINE

I. A random variable is a numerical value determined by the outcome of an experiment.

II. A probability distribution is a listing of all the outcomes of an experiment and the probability associated with each outcome.
   A. A discrete probability distribution can assume only certain values. The main features are:
      1. The sum of the possible outcomes is 1.00.
      2. The probability of a particular outcome is between 0.00 and 1.00.
      3. The outcomes are mutually exclusive.
   B. A continuous distribution can assume an infinite number of values within a specific range.

III. The mean and variance of a probability distribution are computed as follows.
   A. The mean is equal to:

$$\mu = \Sigma[XP(X)] \tag{6–1}$$

   B. The variance is equal to:

$$\sigma^2 = \Sigma[(X - \mu)^2 P(X)] \tag{6–2}$$

IV. The binomial distribution has the following characteristics.
   A. Each outcome is classified into one of two mutually exclusive categories.
   B. The probability of a success remains the same from trial to trial.
   C. Each trial is independent.

   D. The distribution results from a count of the number of successes in a fixed number of trials.
   E. A binomial probability is determined as follows.

$$P(r) = \frac{n!}{r!(n-r)!} p^r q^{n-r} \tag{6–3}$$

   F. The mean is computed as:

$$\mu = np \tag{6–4}$$

   G. The variance is

$$\sigma^2 = np(1-p) \tag{6–5}$$

V. The hypergeometric distribution has the following characteristics.
   A. There are only two possible outcomes.
   B. The trials are *not* independent, so the probability of a success is not the same on each trial.
   C. The distribution results from a count of the number of successes in a fixed number of trials.
   D. A hypergeometric probability is computed from the following equation.

$$P(r) = \frac{({}_SC_r)({}_{N-S}C_{n-r})}{{}_NC_n} \tag{6–6}$$

VI. The Poisson distribution has the following characteristics.
   A. Each outcome is classified into one of two mutually exclusive categories.
   B. The probability of a success remains the same from trial to trial.
   C. Each trial is independent.
   D. The distribution results from a count of the number of successes in a fixed number of trials.
   E. A Poisson probability is determined from the following equation.

$$P(x) = \frac{\mu^x e^{-\mu}}{x!} \tag{6–7}$$

   F. The probability of a success is usually small, and the number of trials is usually large.
   G. The mean and variance of a Poisson distribution are the same and are equal to *np*.

$$\mu = np \tag{6–8}$$

EXERCISES

The answers to the odd-numbered exercises are at the end of the book.

31. List the characteristics of the hypergeometric distribution.
32. What is a binomial distribution?
33. Under what conditions will the Poisson and the binomial distributions give roughly the same results?
34. What is a discrete probability distribution?
35. Samson Apartments has a large number of units available to rent each month. A concern of management is the number of vacant apartments each month. A recent study revealed the percent of the time that a given number of apartments are vacant.

Number of vacant units	Probability
0	.10
1	.20
2	.30
3	.40

Compute the mean and standard deviation of the number of vacant apartments.

36. An investment will be worth $1,000, $2,000, or $5,000 at the end of the year. The probabilities of these values are .25, .60, and .15, respectively. Determine the mean and variance of the worth of the investment.

37. The personnel manager of the Cumberland Pig Iron Company is studying the number of on-the-job accidents over a period of one month. He developed the following probability distribution.

Number of accidents	Probability
0	.40
1	.20
2	.20
3	.10
4	.10

Compute the mean, variance, and standard deviation of the number of accidents in a month.

38. Corso Bakery offers special decorated cakes for birthdays, weddings, and other occasions. They also have regular cakes available in their bakery. The following table gives the total number of cakes sold per day and the corresponding probability.

Number of cakes sold in a day	Probability
12	.25
13	.40
14	.25
15	.10

Compute the mean, variance, and standard deviation of the number of cakes sold per day.

39. A Tamiami shearing machine is producing 10 percent defective pieces, which is abnormally high. The quality-control engineer has been checking the output by almost continuous sampling since the abnormal condition began. What is the probability that in a sample of 10 pieces:
    a. Exactly 5 will be defective?
    b. 5 or more will be defective?

40. Thirty percent of the population in a southwestern community are Spanish-speaking Americans. A Spanish-speaking person is accused of killing a non-Spanish-speaking American. Of the first 12 potential jurors, only 2 are Spanish-speaking Americans, and 10 are not. The defendant's lawyer challenges the jury selection, claiming bias against her client. The government lawyer disagrees, saying that the probability of this particular jury composition is common. What do you think?

41. A new flavor of toothpaste has been developed. It was tested by a group of 10 people. Six of the group said they liked the new flavor, and the remaining 4 indicated they did not.

Four of the 10 are selected to participate in an in-depth interview. What is the probability that of those selected for the in-depth interview 2 liked the new flavor and 2 did not?

42. Suppose it is known that 5 out of 25 Chrysler subcompact automobiles off the assembly line require adjustment of some kind. Four subcompacts are selected at random. We are interested in the probability that exactly one will require adjustment.
    a. Solve the problem assuming that out of the 25 subcompacts, the samples are drawn without replacement.
    b. Solve the problem assuming the sampling is done with replacement.
    c. Assuming replacement, work the problem using the Poisson distribution.
    d. Compare the results in parts *a, b,* and *c.* Comment on your findings.
43. The law firm of Hagel and Hagel is located in downtown Cincinnati. There are 10 partners in the firm; 7 live in Ohio and 3 in northern Kentucky. Ms. Wendy Hagel, the managing partner, wants to appoint a committee of 3 partners to look into moving the firm to northern Kentucky. If the committee is selected at random from the 10 partners, what is the probability that:
    a. One member of the committee lives in northern Kentucky and the others live in Ohio?
    b. At least one member of the committee lives in northern Kentucky?
44. According to recent information published by the U.S. Environmental Protection Agency, four of the top nine cars in terms of fuel economy are manufactured by Honda. Determine the probability distribution for the number of Hondas in a sample of three cars chosen from the top nine. What is the likelihood that in the sample of three at least one Honda is included?
45. The position of chief of police in the city of Corry is open. The search committee, charged with the responsibility of recommending a new chief to the city council, received 12 applications for the position. Four of the 12 applicants are either female or members of a minority. The search committee decides to interview all 12 of the applicants. To begin, they randomly select 4 applicants to be interviewed on the first day, and none of the 4 is female or a member of a minority. The local newspaper, the *Corry Press,* suggests discrimination in an editorial. What is the likelihood of this occurrence?
46. A box of electric hedge trimmers contains six Cummings trimmers. Two are defective; four operate correctly. Three trimmers are selected from the box.
    a. What is the probability that exactly one of the Cummings trimmers is defective?
    b. What is the probability that two trimmers of the three selected are defective?
47. The sales of Lexus automobiles in the Detroit area follow a Poisson distribution with a mean of 3.00 per day.
    a. What is the probability that no Lexus is sold on a particular day?
    b. What is the probability that for five consecutive days at least one Lexus is sold?
48. Suppose 1.5 percent of the plastic spacers produced by a Corson high-speed mold injection machine are defective. The distribution of defectives follows a Poisson distribution. For a random sample of 200 spacers, find the probability that:
    a. None of the spacers is defective.
    b. Three or more of the spacers are defective.
49. A study of the lines at the checkout registers of Safeway Supermarket revealed that, during a certain period at the rush hour, the number of customers waiting averaged four. What is the probability that during that period:
    a. No customers were waiting?
    b. Four customers were waiting?
    c. Four or fewer were waiting?
    d. Four or more were waiting?
50. L. L. Bean advertised same-day service. Unfortunately, the movement of orders did not go as planned, and there were a large number of complaints. A complete change in the handling of incoming and outgoing orders was then made. An internal goal was set to

have fewer than five unfilled orders on hand (per picker) at the end of 95 out of every 100 working days. Frequent checks of the unfilled orders at the end of the day revealed that the distribution of the unfilled orders approximated a Poisson distribution; that is, most of the days there were no unfilled orders, some of the days there was one order, and so on. The mean number of unfilled orders per picker was 2.0.

a. Has L. L. Bean lived up to its internal goal? Cite evidence.

b. Draw a histogram representing the Poisson probability distribution of unfilled orders at the end of the day.

51. On January 29, 1986, the space shuttle *Challenger* exploded at an altitude of 46,000 feet, resulting in the death of all seven astronauts. A 1985 study published by the National Aeronautics and Space Administration (NASA) suggested that the probability of a catastrophic occurrence such as this was about 1 in 60,000. A similar report by the air force set the likelihood of a catastrophe at 1 in 35. The *Challenger* flight was the 25th mission in the shuttle program. Use the Poisson distribution to compare the probabilities of at least one disaster in 25 missions using both estimates of the probability of occurrence.

52. According to the "January theory," if the stock market is up for the month of January, it will be up for the year. If it is down in January, it will be down for the year. According to an article in *The Wall Street Journal,* this theory held for 29 out of the last 34 years. Suppose there is no truth to this theory. What is the probability this could happen by chance? (You will probably need a computer. Use the binomial distribution.)

53. During the second round of the 1989 U.S. Open golf tournament, four golfers each made a hole in one on the sixth hole. The odds of a professional golfer making a hole in one are 3,708 to 1, so the probability is 1/3709. There were 155 golfers participating in the second round that day. Estimate the probability that four golfers would score a hole in one on the sixth hole.

COMPUTER DATA EXERCISES

54. Refer to data set 1, which reports information on homes sold in Florida during 1994.
    a. Create a probability distribution for the number of bedrooms. Compute the mean and standard deviation of this distribution.
    b. Create a probability distribution for the number of bathrooms. Compute the mean and standard deviation of this distribution.

55. Refer to data set 2, which contains information on the 1993 major league baseball season. There are 28 teams in the major leagues, and 10 of them have home fields with an artificial surface. As part of the negotiations with the players' union, a study regarding injuries on grass versus artificial fields will be conducted. Five teams are to participate in the study, and the teams are to be selected at random. What is the likelihood that 2 of the 5 teams selected for study play their home games on artificial turf?

CHAPTER 6 EXAMINATION

The answers are at the end of the chapter.

For Questions 1–10 fill in the correct answer.

1. A ________ is a listing of the possible outcomes from an experiment and the probability associated with each of these outcomes.
2. In a ________ distribution the probability of a success is *not* the same for each trial.
3. In a ________ distribution the probability of a success is usually small.

4. In a ________ distribution the mean and the variance are equal.
5. In a binomial experiment there are ________ possible outcomes.
6. The Poisson distribution is an example of a (discrete, continuous) ________ probability distribution.
7. The Poisson distribution is ________ skewed.
8. A ________ population consists of a fixed number of individuals, objects, or measurements.
9. For a discrete probability distribution, the sum of the probabilities is ________.
10. For a discrete probability distribution, the outcomes must be ________.
11. Current medical studies indicate that 30 percent of the population will suffer from the flu each winter. A group of 12 people is randomly selected.
    a. What is the probability that exactly 5 in the group will have the flu this winter?
    b. What is the probability that at least 5 in the group will have the flu this winter?
    c. Compute the mean and variance of the number in the group that will suffer from the flu this winter.
12. A college basketball coach has 12 players on his roster. Eight of the players are receiving basketball scholarships, and 4 are not. Recently the team has been losing most of their games. The coach decided to draw the names of 5 players out of a hat and designate them as the starting lineup. What is the probability that 4 of the 5 players selected are on a scholarship?
13. Suppose there were 200 students in your high school graduating class. Current statistics indicate that 0.5 percent, or .005, of the population will become millionaires. What is the probability that at least one student from your class becomes a millionaire?

CHAPTER 6 Answers

Self-Review

6–1 1.

Number of spots	Probability
1	$\frac{1}{6}$
2	$\frac{1}{6}$
3	$\frac{1}{6}$
4	$\frac{1}{6}$
5	$\frac{1}{6}$
6	$\frac{1}{6}$
Total	$\frac{6}{6} = 1.00$

2.

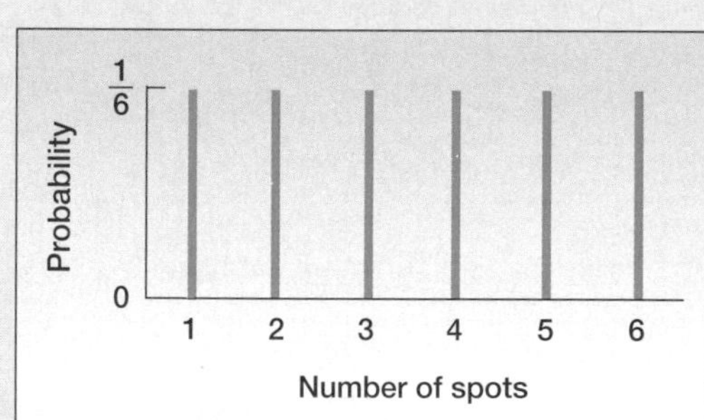

3. $\frac{6}{6}$, or 1.

6–2 1. It is discrete, because the sum of the probabilities is 1.00, and the outcomes are mutually exclusive.

2.

X	$P(X)$	$XP(X)$
50	.30	15.0
75	.50	37.5
90	.20	18.0
		70.5

The mean is 70.5 cents.

3.

X	$P(X)$	$(X - \mu)$	$(X - \mu)^2 P(X)$
50	.30	−20.5	126.075
75	.50	4.5	10.125
90	.20	19.5	76.050
			212.250

The variance is 212.25, and the standard deviation is 14.57 cents.

6–3 1. *a.* For each multiple-choice question, a student either guesses the answer correctly (a success) or does not (a failure).

b. The distribution of successes is discrete, resulting from a count of the number of successes.

c. The probability that a student will guess each question correctly is one fifth, or .20.

d. The trials are independent, meaning that a success, or failure, for any question does not affect the outcome of any other question.

2. $\left(\frac{1}{5}\right)^{20}$

6–4 .3750, found by:

$$P(2) = \frac{4!}{2!(4-2)!}(.50)^2(.50)^{4-2}$$

$$= (6)(.50)^2(.50)^2$$

$$= (6)(.25)(.25)$$

6–5 $n = 7$, $p = .20$

	r	Probability
1.	0	.210
2.	1	.367
3.	2	.275
	3	.115
	4	.029
	5	.004
	6	.000
	7	.000

4. 1.000

6–6 $n = 4, p = .60$

a. $P(r = 2) = .346$

b. $P(r \leq 2) = .526$

c. $P(r > 2) = 1 - .526$
$= .474$

6–7 .210, found by:

$$P(3) = \frac{({}_{40}C_3)({}_{10}C_2)}{{}_{50}C_5}$$

$$= \frac{\left(\frac{40 \cdot 39 \cdot 38}{3 \cdot 2 \cdot 1}\right)\left(\frac{10 \cdot 9}{2}\right)}{\left(\frac{50 \cdot 49 \cdot 48 \cdot 47 \cdot 46}{5 \cdot 4 \cdot 3 \cdot 2 \cdot 1}\right)}$$

$$= \frac{(9,880)(45)}{(2,118,760)} = .210$$

6–8 1. .4966. $\mu = 0.7$, found by 3,500/5,000. Refer to Appendix C, for a μ of 0.7 and an x of 0.

2.

Number of occurrences, x	Probability of occurrence, $P(x)$
0	.4966
1	.3476
2	.1217
3	.0284
4	.0050
5	.0007
6	.0001

Examination

1. Probability distribution.
2. Hypergeometric.
3. Poisson.
4. Poisson.
5. Two.
6. Discrete.
7. Positively.
8. Finite.
9. 1.00.
10. Mutually exclusive.
11. $n = 12, p = .30$
    a. $P(r = 5 \mid n = 12 \text{ and } p = .30) = .158$
    b. $P(r \geq 5 \mid n = 12 \text{ and } p = .30) = 1 - .724 = .276$
    c. $\mu = np = 12(.30) = 3.6$
    $\sigma^2 = np(1 - p) = 12(.30)(.70) = 2.52$
12. .354, found by:

$$P(4) = \frac{({}_8C_4)({}_4C_1)}{{}_{12}C_5} = \frac{\left(\frac{8!}{4!4!}\right)\left(\frac{4!}{3!1!}\right)}{\left(\frac{12!}{7!5!}\right)}$$

$$= \frac{\left(\frac{8 \cdot 7 \cdot 6 \cdot 5}{4 \cdot 3 \cdot 2 \cdot 1}\right)4}{\left(\frac{12 \cdot 11 \cdot 10 \cdot 9 \cdot 8}{5 \cdot 4 \cdot 3 \cdot 2 \cdot 1}\right)} = \frac{280}{792} = .354$$

13. $\mu = np = 200(.005) = 1.00.$
    $P(X \geq 1) = 1 - P(X = 0) = 1 - .3679 = .6321.$

Chapter 7

The Normal Probability Distribution

GOALS

When you have completed this chapter, you will be able to:

1
List the characteristics of a normal probability distribution.

2
Define and calculate *z* values.

3
Determine the probability that an observation will lie between two points, using the standard normal distribution.

4
Determine the probability that an observation will be above, or below, a value, using the standard normal distribution.

5
Compare two or more observations that are in different probability distributions.

6
Use the normal probability distribution to approximate the binomial probability distribution.

The price of the Blair Corporation stock is normally distributed with a mean of $42 per share and a standard deviation of $2.25 per share. What percent of the days is the price between $38 and $40? (See Goal 3 and Exercise 48.)

INTRODUCTION

Chapter 6 dealt with three *discrete* probability distributions: the binomial distribution, the hypergeometric distribution, and the Poisson distribution. Recall that these distributions are based on discrete random variables, which can assume only specified values. For example, the number of correct answers on a 10-question examination can only be 0, 1, 2, 3, . . . , 10. There cannot be a negative number of correct answers, such as −7, nor can there be 7¼ or 15 correct answers.

We will continue our study of probability distributions in this chapter by examining a very important *continuous* probability distribution, namely, the **normal probability distribution.** As noted in the preceding chapter, a continuous random variable is one that can assume an *infinite* number of possible values within a specified range. It usually results from measuring something, such as the weight of an individual. The weight might be 112.0 kilograms, 112.1 kilograms, 112.12 kilograms, and so on, depending on the accuracy of the scale. Other continuous random variables are the life expectancy of alkaline batteries, the volume of a shipping container, and the weight of impurities in a steel ingot.

The probability distributions of the life expectancies of some products, such as batteries, tires, and light bulbs, tend to follow a "normal" pattern. So do the weights of boxes of Kellogg's Special K cereal, the lengths of rolls of aluminum, and other variables measured on a continuous scale.

In this chapter the main characteristics of a normal probability distribution and the normal curve are examined first. Then the **standard normal distribution** and its uses are presented. Finally, we will look at how the normal distribution is used to estimate binomial probabilities.

CHARACTERISTICS OF A NORMAL PROBABILITY DISTRIBUTION

The normal probability distribution and its accompanying normal curve have the following characteristics:

Bell-shaped

1. The normal curve is *bell-shaped* and has a single peak at the exact center of the distribution. The arithmetic mean, median, and mode of the distribution are equal and located at the peak. Thus, half the area under the curve is above this center point, and the other half is below it.

Symmetrical

2. The normal probability distribution is *symmetrical* about its mean. If we cut the normal curve vertically at this central value, the two halves will be mirror images.

Asymptotic

3. The normal curve falls off smoothly in either direction from the central value. It is *asymptotic,* meaning that the curve gets closer and closer to the *X*-axis but never actually touches it. That is, the "tails" of the curve extend indefinitely in both directions. In real-world problems, however, this is somewhat unrealistic. The life of an alkaline battery, for example, could not be 300 years.

These characteristics are summarized in Chart 7–1.

THE FAMILY OF NORMAL PROBABILITY DISTRIBUTIONS

Family of normal distributions

There is not just one normal probability distribution, but rather a "family" of them. There is one normal probability distribution for the lengths of service of the employees in our Camden plant, where the mean is 20 years and the standard deviation is 3.1 years. There is another normal probability distribution for the lengths of service in our Dunkirk plant, where $\mu = 20$ years and $\sigma = 3.9$ years. Chart 7–2 portrays three such normal distributions, where the means are the same but the standard deviations are different.

CHART 7–1 **Characteristics of a Normal Distribution**

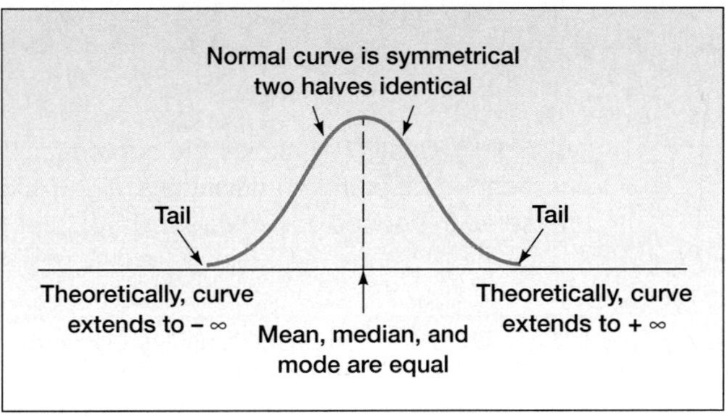

Equal means, unequal standard deviations

CHART 7–2 **Normal Probability Distributions with Equal Means but Different Standard Deviations**

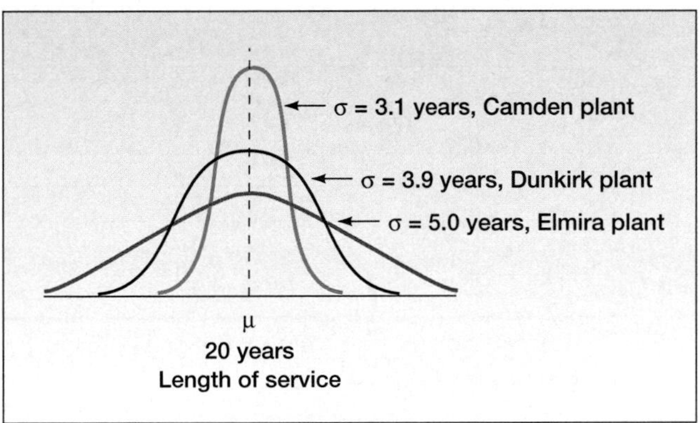

Chart 7–3 on the top of page 258 shows the weights of three different cereals. The weights are normally distributed with different means but identical standard deviations.

Unequal means, equal standard deviations

CHART 7–3 **Normal Probability Distributions Having Different Means but Equal Standard Deviations**

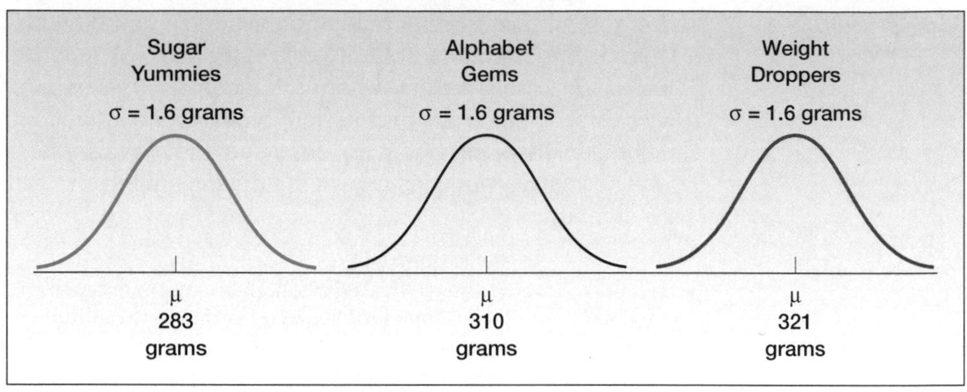

Finally, Chart 7–4 shows the curves for three normal distributions having different means and standard deviations. They show the distribution of tensile strengths, measured in pounds per square inch (psi) for three types of cables.

Unequal means, unequal standard deviations

CHART 7–4 **Normal Probability Distributions with Different Means and Standard Deviations**

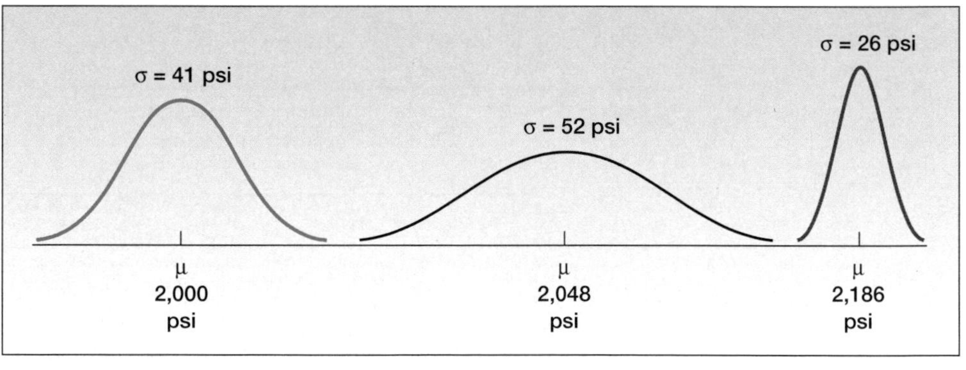

THE STANDARD NORMAL PROBABILITY DISTRIBUTION

Standard normal probability distribution

We noted that there is a family of normal distributions. Each distribution has a different mean (μ) or standard deviation (σ). The number of normal distributions is therefore unlimited. It would be physically impossible to provide a table of probabilities (such as for the binomial and Poisson) for each combination of μ and σ. Fortunately, one member of the family of normal distributions can be used for all problems where the normal distribution is applicable. It has a mean of 0 and a standard deviation of 1 and is called the **standard normal distribution.**

First it is necessary to convert, or *standardize,* the actual distribution to a standard normal distribution using a *z value,* also called a *z score,* a *z statistic,* the *standard normal deviate,* or just the *normal deviate.*

> ***z* value** The distance between a selected value, designated *X,* and the population mean, μ, divided by the population standard deviation, σ.

So, a *z* value is the distance from the mean, measured in units of the standard deviation.

In terms of a formula:

$$z = \frac{X - \mu}{\sigma} \qquad (7\text{–}1)$$

where:

- X is the value of any particular observation or measurement.
- μ is the mean of the distribution.
- σ is the standard deviation of the distribution.

As noted in the above definition, a *z* value measures the distance between a particular value of *X* and the arithmetic mean in units of the standard deviation. By determining the *z* value using formula (7–1), we can find the area or the probability under the normal curve by referring to Appendix D.

To explain, suppose we computed *z* to be 1.91. What is the area under the normal curve between the mean and *X*? A portion of Appendix D is repeated at the top of page 260 as Table 7–1. Go down the column of the table headed by the letter *z* to 1.9. Then move horizontally to the right and read the probability under the column headed 0.01. It is .4719. This means that 47.19 percent of the area under the curve is between the mean and the *X* value 1.91 standard deviations above the mean. This is also interpreted as the *probability* that an observation is between 0 and 1.91 standard deviations of the mean.

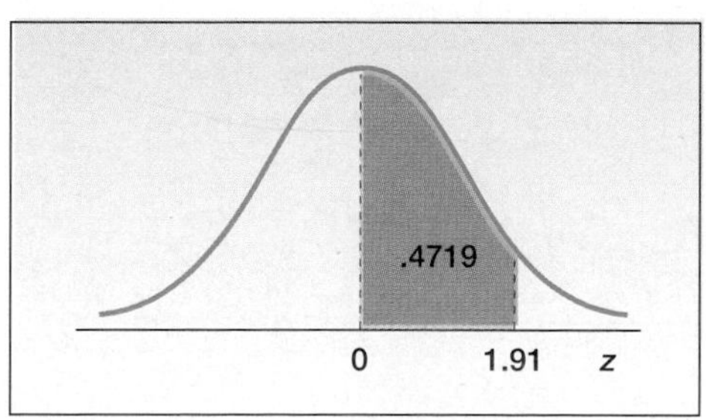

TABLE 7–1 Areas under the Normal Curve

z	0.00	0.01	0.02	0.03	0.04	0.05	...
⋮							
1.0	0.3413	0.3438	0.3461	0.3485	0.3508	0.3531	
1.1	0.3643	0.3665	0.3686	0.3708	0.3729	0.3749	
1.2	0.3849	0.3869	0.3888	0.3907	0.3925	0.3944	
1.3	0.4032	0.4049	0.4066	0.4082	0.4099	0.4115	
1.4	0.4192	0.4207	0.4222	0.4236	0.4251	0.4265	
1.5	0.4332	0.4345	0.4357	0.4370	0.4382	0.4394	
1.6	0.4452	0.4463	0.4474	0.4484	0.4495	0.4505	
1.7	0.4554	0.4564	0.4573	0.4582	0.4591	0.4599	
1.8	0.4641	0.4649	0.4656	0.4664	0.4671	0.4678	
1.9	0.4713	0.4719	0.4726	0.4732	0.4738	0.4744	
⋮							

Applications of the Standard Normal Distribution

What is the area under the curve between the mean and *X* for the following *z* values? Check your answers against those given. (Not all the values are available in Table 7–1. You will need to use Appendix D or the table located in the back inside cover of the text.)

Computed *z* value	Area under curve
2.84	.4977
1.00	.3413
0.49	.1879

Now we will compute the *z* value given the population mean, μ, the population standard deviation, σ, and a selected *X*.

EXAMPLE

The weekly incomes of a large group of middle managers are normally distributed with a mean of $1,000 and a standard deviation of $100. What is the *z* value for an income *X* of $1,100? For $900?

Solution

Using formula (7–1), the *z* values for the two *X* values ($1,100 and $900) are computed as follows:

For $X = \$1,100$:

$$z = \frac{X - \mu}{\sigma} = \frac{\$1,100 - \$1,000}{\$100} = 1.00$$

For $X = \$900$:

$$z = \frac{X - \mu}{\sigma} = \frac{\$900 - \$1,000}{\$100} = -1.00$$

The z of 1.00 indicates that a weekly income of $1,100 for a middle manager is one standard deviation above the mean, and a z of $-$ 1.00 shows that a $900 income is one standard deviation below the mean. Note that both incomes ($1,100 and $900) are the same distance ($100) from the mean.

SELF-REVIEW 7–1

The answers are at the end of the chapter.

Using the same information as in the preceding example (μ = $1,000, σ = $100), convert:

1. The weekly income of $1,225 to a standard unit (z value).
2. The weekly income of $775 to a z value.

Areas under the Normal Curve

Before examining various applications of the standard normal probability distribution, we will consider three areas under the normal curve that will be used extensively in the following chapters.

Areas under the normal curve

1. About 68 percent of the area under the normal curve is within plus one and minus one standard deviation of the mean. This can be written as $\mu \pm 1\sigma$.
2. About 95 percent of the area under the normal curve is within plus and minus two standard deviations of the mean, written $\mu \pm 2\sigma$.
3. Practically all (99.74 percent) of the area under the normal curve is within three standard deviations of the mean, written $\mu \pm 3\sigma$.

Shown diagrammatically, using more precise percentages:

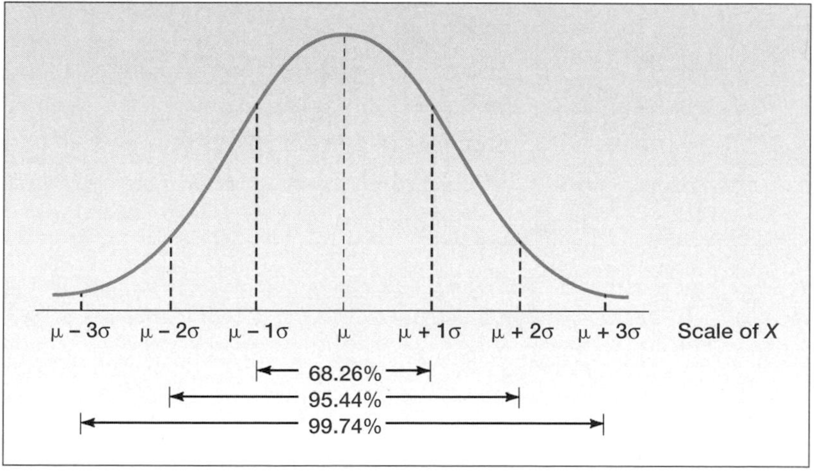

Transforming measurements to standard normal deviates changes the scale. The conversions are shown in the following graph. For example, $\mu + 1\sigma$ is converted to a z value of $+$ 1.00. Likewise, $\mu - 2\sigma$ is transformed to a z value of $-$ 2.00. Note that the center of the z distribution is zero, indicating no deviation from the mean, μ.

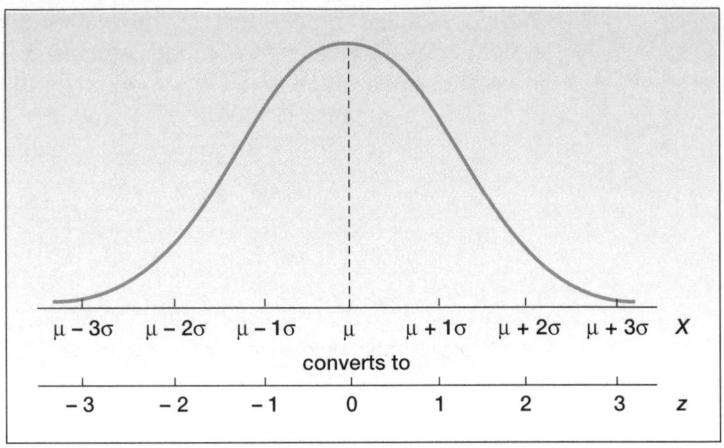

Total area under normal curve is 1

These concepts can be stated somewhat differently: The area under the normal curve within plus and minus one standard deviation of the mean is about .6826. The area within plus and minus two standard deviations of the mean is about .9544. The area within three standard deviations of the mean is about .9974. The total area under the normal curve is 1.0000.

EXAMPLE

A life test on a large number of type D alkaline batteries revealed that the mean life for a particular use before failure is 19.0 hours. The distribution of the lives approximated a normal distribution. The standard deviation of the distribution was 1.2 hours.

1. About 68.26 percent of the batteries failed between what two values?
2. About 95.44 percent of the batteries failed between what two values?
3. About 99.74 percent of the batteries failed between what two values?

Solution ▸

1. About 68.26 percent failed between 17.8 hours and 20.2 hours, found by $19.0 \pm 1(1.2)$.
2. About 95.44 percent failed between 16.6 hours and 21.4 hours, found by $19.0 \pm 2(1.2)$.
3. About 99.74 percent failed between 15.4 hours and 22.6 hours, found by $19.0 \pm 3(1.2)$.

Shown in a diagram:

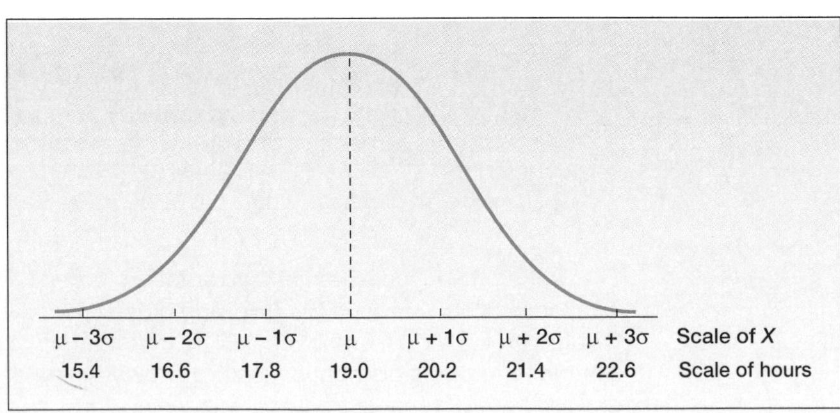

SELF-REVIEW 7–2

The answers are at the end of the chapter.

The distribution of the annual incomes of a group of middle-management employees at Compton Plastics approximates a normal distribution with a mean of $37,200 and a standard deviation of $800.

1. About 68.26 percent of the incomes lie between what two amounts?

2. About 95.44 percent of the incomes lie between what two amounts?

3. About 99.74 percent of the incomes lie between what two amounts?

4. What are the median and the modal incomes?

5. Is the distribution of incomes symmetrical?

EXERCISES

The answers to the odd-numbered exercises are at the end of the book.

1. Explain what is meant by this statement: "There is not just one normal probability distribution but a 'family' of them."
2. List the major characteristics of a normal probability distribution.
3. The mean of a normal probability distribution is 500; the standard deviation is 10.
   a. About 68 percent of the observations lie between what two values?
   b. About 95 percent of the observations lie between what two values?
   c. Practically all of the observations lie between what two values?
4. The mean of a normal probability distribution is 60; the standard deviation is 5.
   a. About what percent of the observations lie between 55 and 65?
   b. About what percent of the observations lie between 50 and 70?
   c. About what percent of the observations lie between 45 and 75?

First application of the standard normal distribution

The first application of the standard normal distribution involves the determination of the area under the normal curve between the mean and a selected value, designated *X*. Using the same problem as in the previous weekly income example (μ = $1,000, σ = $100), what is the area under the normal curve between $1,000 and $1,100?

What is area between $1,000 and $1,100?

We have already converted $1,100 to a *z* value of 1.00 using formula (7–1). To repeat:

$$z = \frac{X - \mu}{\sigma} = \frac{\$1{,}100 - \$1{,}000}{\$100} = 1.00$$

The probability associated with a *z* of 1.00 has been computed and is found in Appendix D. A small portion of that appendix table follows. To locate the area, go down the left column to 1.0. Then move horizontally to the right, and read the area under the curve in the column marked .00. It is .3413.

z	.00	.01	.02
0.7	.2580	.2611	.2642
0.8	.2881	.2910	.2939
0.9	.3159	.3186	.3212
1.0	.3413	.3438	.3461
1.1	.3643	.3665	.3686

Shown in a diagram:

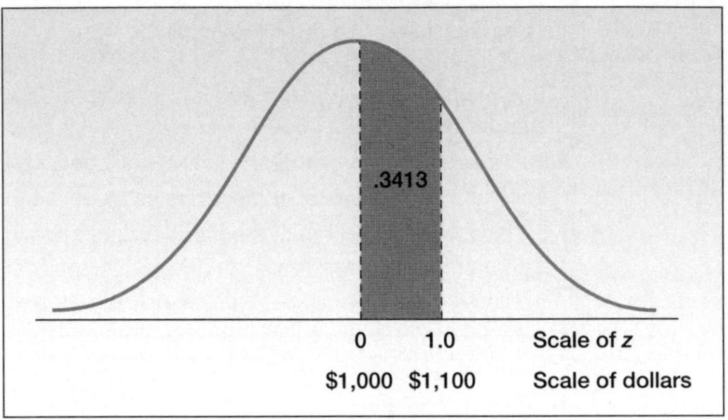

The area under the normal curve between $1,000 and $1,100 is .3413, and the total area under the curve is 1.0000. One can also say that 34.13 percent of the weekly incomes are between $1,000 and $1,100 and that the probability of a particular income being between $1,000 and $1,100 is .3413.

EXAMPLE

Refer to the previous problem (μ = $1,000, σ = $100).

1. What is the probability that a particular weekly income selected at random is between $790 and $1,000?
2. What is the probability that the income is less than $790?

Solution

▶ Computing the z value for $790 using formula (7–1):

$$z = \frac{X - \mu}{\sigma} = \frac{\$790 - \$1{,}000}{\$100} = \frac{-\$210}{\$100} = -2.10$$

1. The area under the normal curve between μ and X for a z value of -2.10 is .4821 (from Appendix D). The minus sign in front of 2.10 indicates that the area is to the left of the mean.
2. The mean divides the normal curve into two identical halves. The area under the half to the left of the mean is .5000, and the area to the right of the mean is also .5000. Since the area under the curve between $790 and $1,000 is .4821, the area below $790 can be found by subtracting .4821 from .5000. Thus, .5000 − .4821 = .0179. Shown in a diagram:

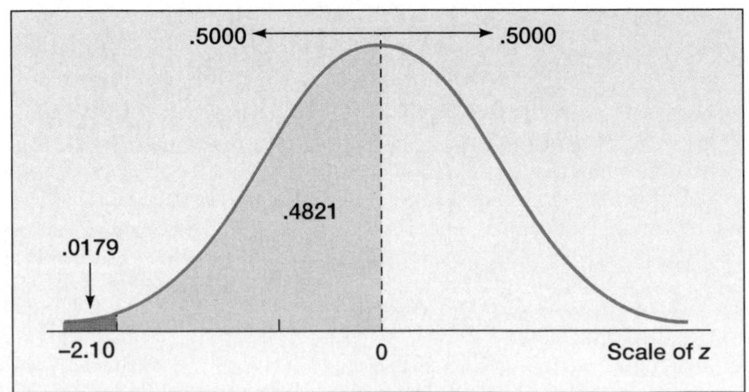

SELF-REVIEW 7–3

The answers are at the end of the chapter.

The employees of Cartwright Manufacturing are awarded efficiency ratings. The distribution of the ratings approximates a normal distribution. The mean is 400, the standard deviation 50.

1. What is the area under the normal curve between 400 and 482?

2. What is the area under the normal curve for ratings greater than 482?

3. Show the facets of this problem in a chart.

EXERCISES

The answers to the odd-numbered exercises are at the end of the book.

5. A normal population has a mean of 20.0 and a standard deviation of 4.0.
   a. Compute the *z* value associated with 25.0.
   b. What proportion of the population is between 20.0 and 25.0?
   c. What proportion of the population is less than 18.0?
6. A normal population has a mean of 12.2 and a standard deviation of 2.5.
   a. Compute the *z* value associated with 14.3.
   b. What proportion of the population is between 12.2 and 14.3?
   c. What proportion of the population is less than 10.0?
7. A recent study of the hourly wages of maintenance crews for major airlines showed that the mean hourly salary was $16.50, with a standard deviation of $3.50. If we select a crew member at random, what is the probability:
   a. The crew member earns between $16.50 and $20.00 per hour?
   b. The crew member earns more than $20.00 per hour?
   c. The crew member earns less than $15.00 per hour?

8. The mean of a normal distribution is 400 pounds. The standard deviation is 10 pounds.
   a. What is the area between 415 pounds and the mean of 400 pounds?
   b. What is the area between the mean and 395 pounds?
   c. What is the probability of selecting a value at random and discovering that it has a value of less than 395 pounds?

A second application of the standard normal distribution involves combining two areas, one to the right and the other to the left of the mean.

EXAMPLE

Another application of standard normal distribution

Returning to the distribution of weekly incomes (μ = \$1,000, σ = \$100), what is the area under the normal curve between \$840 and \$1,200?

Solution ▸ The problem is divided into two parts. For the area between \$840 and the mean of \$1,000:

$$z = \frac{\$840 - \$1{,}000}{\$100} = \frac{-\$160}{\$100} = -1.60$$

For the area between the mean of \$1,000 and \$1,200:

$$z = \frac{\$1{,}200 - \$1{,}000}{\$100} = \frac{\$200}{\$100} = 2.00$$

The area under the curve for a z of -1.60 is .4452 (from Appendix D). The area under the curve for a z of 2.00 is .4772. Adding the two areas: .4452 + .4772 = .9224.

Thus, the probability of selecting an income between \$840 and \$1,200 is .9224. In other words, 92.24 percent of the managers have weekly incomes between \$840 and \$1,200. Shown in a diagram:

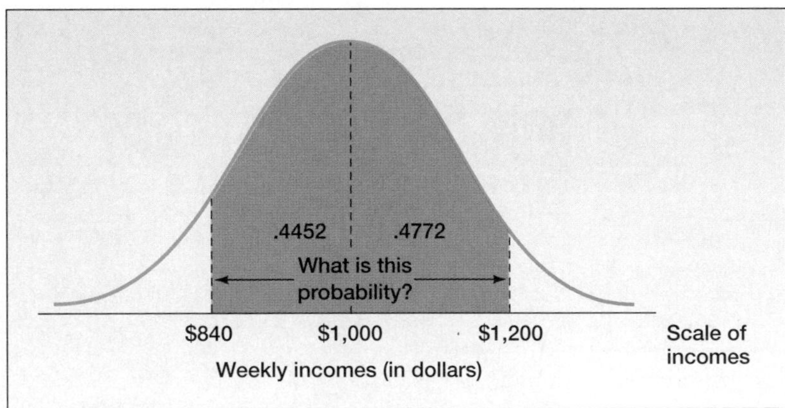

Another application of standard normal distribution

Another application of the standard normal distribution is finding the area above, or below, a specified value.

EXAMPLE

Returning again to the weekly incomes illustration (μ = \$1,000, σ = \$100), what percent of the executives earn weekly incomes of \$1,245 or more?

Solution

Find the area above $1,245

► We first need to find the area between the mean of $1,000 and an X of $1,245. We will first use formula (7–1) to find z.

$$z = \frac{X - \mu}{\sigma} = \frac{\$1,245 - \$1,000}{\$100} = \frac{\$245}{\$100} = 2.45$$

Then, referring to Appendix D, the area associated with a z of 2.45 is .4929. This is the area between $1,000 and $1,245. Logically, the area for $1,245 and beyond is found by subtracting .4929 from .5000. This area is .0071, indicating that only 0.71 percent of the executives earn weekly incomes of $1,245 or more.

The following diagram shows the various facets of this problem.

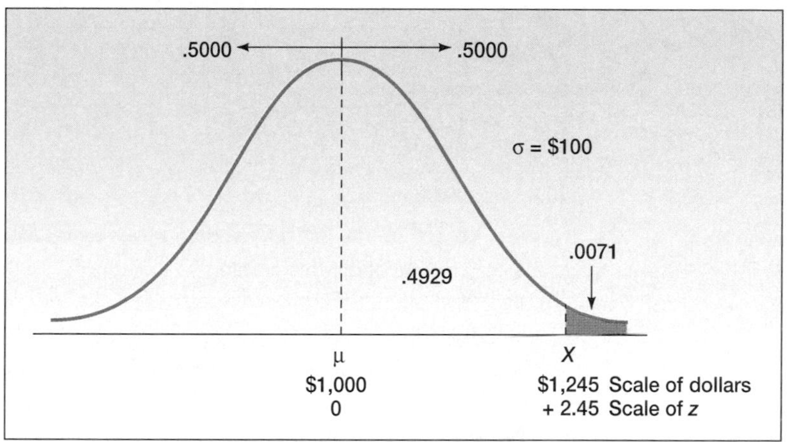

Still another application of the standard normal distribution involves determining the area between values on the *same* side of the mean.

EXAMPLE

Returning again to the weekly incomes example (μ = $1,000 and σ = $100), what is the area under the normal curve between $1,150 and $1,250?

Solution

► The problem is again separated into two parts, and formula (7–1) is used. First we find the z value associated with a weekly salary of $1,250:

$$z = \frac{\$1,250 - \$1,000}{\$100} = 2.50$$

Next we find the z value for a weekly salary of $1,150:

$$z = \frac{\$1,150 - \$1,000}{\$100} = 1.50$$

From Appendix D the area associated with a z value of 2.50 is .4938. So the probability of a weekly salary between $1,000 and $1,250 is .4938. Similarly, the area associated with a z value of 1.50 is .4332, so the probability of a weekly salary between $1,000 and $1,150 is .4332. The probability of a weekly salary between $1,150 and $1,250 is found by subtracting the area associated with a z value of 1.50 (.4332) from that associated with a z of 2.50 (.4938). Thus, the probability of a weekly salary between $1,150 and $1,250 is .0606. Shown in a diagram:

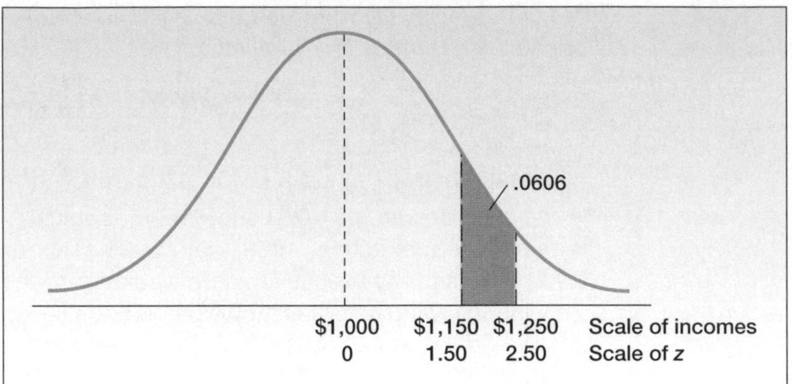

SELF-REVIEW 7–4

The answers are at the end of the chapter.

Refer to the previous example (μ = \$1,000, σ = \$100).

1. What percent of the executives earn a weekly income of \$925 or less?
2. Portray the facets of this problem in a diagram.

Another application

Previous examples required finding the percent of the observations located between two observations or the percent of the observations above, or below, a particular observation *X*. A further application of the standard normal distribution involves finding the value of the observation *X* when the percent above or below the observation is given.

EXAMPLE

Given a percent, find *X*

Suppose a tire manufacturer wants to set a mileage guarantee on its new MX100 tire. Life tests revealed that the mean mileage is 47,900 and the standard deviation of the normal distribution of mileages is 2,050 miles. The manufacturer wants to set the guaranteed mileage so that no more than 5 percent of the tires will have to be replaced. What guaranteed mileage should the manufacturer announce?

Solution

The facets of this problem are shown in the following diagram. *X* represents the guaranteed mileage.

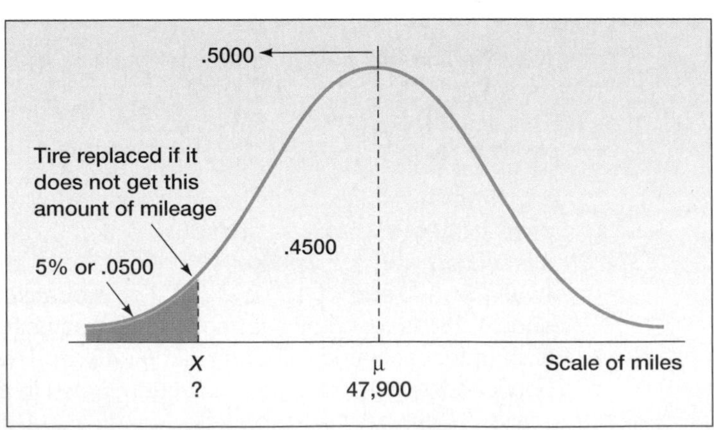

Inserting these values in formula (7–1) for *z:*

$$z = \frac{X - \mu}{\sigma} = \frac{X - 47{,}900}{2{,}050}$$

There are two unknowns, *z* and *X*. To find *z,* note that the area under the normal curve to the left of *X* is .0500. Logically, the area between μ and *X* is .4500, found by .5000 − .0500. Now refer to Appendix D. Search the body of the table for the area closest to .4500. There are two values equidistant from .4500, namely, .4505 and .4495. Move left from these values, and read the *z* values in the margin: 1.65 and 1.64. "Split the difference," and say the *z* score is 1.645. (It is really −1.645 because it is to the left of the mean.) These steps are summarized in Table 7–2.

TABLE 7–2 **Selected Areas under the Normal Curve**

z	. . .	0.03	0.04	0.05	0.06
⋮		⋮	⋮	⋮	⋮
1.5	. . .	.4370	.4382	.4394	.4406
1.6	. . .	.4484	.4495	.4505	.4515
1.7	. . .	.4582	.4591	.4599	.4608

Knowing that the distance between μ and *X* is -1.645σ, we can now solve for *X* (the guaranteed mileage):

$$z = \frac{X - 47{,}900}{2{,}050}$$

$$-1.645 = \frac{X - 47{,}900}{2{,}050}$$

$$-1.645(2{,}050) = X - 47{,}900$$

$$X = 44{,}528 \text{ miles}$$

How is the value 44,528 interpreted? If the manufacturer advertises that its tires will last 44,528 miles, only 5 percent of the tires will fail to last that long.

SELF-REVIEW 7–5

The answers are at the end of the chapter.

An analysis of the final test scores for a computer programming seminar revealed that they approximate a normal curve with a mean of 75 and a standard deviation of 8. The instructor wants to award the grade of A to the upper 10 percent of the test grades. What is the dividing point between an A and a B grade?

Final application of standard normal distribution

A fourth application of the standard normal distribution is to compare two or more observations that are on different scales or in different units. That is, the observations are in different distributions.

EXAMPLE

Comparing observations on different scales

Suppose a study of the inmates at a correctional institution is concerned with the social adjustment of the inmates in prison and their prospects for rehabilitation upon being released. Each inmate was given a test regarding social adjustment. The scores are normally distributed, with a mean of 100 and a standard deviation of 20. Prison psychologists rated each of the inmates with respect to the prospect for rehabilitation. These ratings were also normally distributed, with a mean of 500 and a standard deviation of 100.

Tora Carney scored 146 on the social adjustment test, and her rating with respect to rehabilitation is 335. How does Tora compare with the group with respect to social responsibility and the prospect for rehabilitation?

Solution ▸ Converting her social responsibility test score of 146 to a z value using formula (7–1):

$$z = \frac{X - \mu}{\sigma} = \frac{146 - 100}{20}$$

$$= \frac{46}{20} = 2.30$$

Converting her rehabilitation rating of 335 to a z value:

$$z = \frac{X - \mu}{\sigma} = \frac{335 - 500}{100}$$

$$= \frac{-165}{100} = -1.65$$

The standardized test score and the standardized rating are shown below.

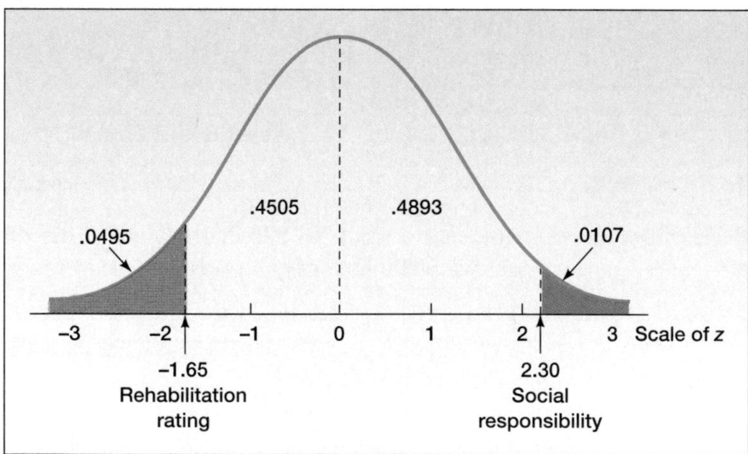

Interpretation With respect to social responsibility, Tora Carney is in the highest 1 percent of the group. However, compared with the other inmates, she is among the lowest 5 percent with regard to the prospects for rehabilitation.

Self-Review 7–6 illustrates the use of the standard normal distribution for comparing data in different units—ratios and percent changes, in this case. The ratios are in one distribution and the percent changes in another.

SELF-REVIEW 7–6

The answers are at the end of the chapter.

The price-earnings (PE) ratios and the changes in price over a three-year period for selected stocks were studied. For the PE ratios, $\mu = 10.0$ and $\sigma = 2.0$. For the price changes, $\mu = 50$ percent and $\sigma = 10$ percent. Both distributions are normally distributed. Radnor Industries had a PE of 11.2 and a 75 percent increase in price in the three-year period.

1. Convert Radnor's PE and percent change to z values.
2. Show the two z values on a standardized normal curve.
3. Compare Radnor's PE ratio and percent change with those of the other selected stocks.

EXERCISES

The answers to the odd-numbered exercises are at the end of the book.

9. A normal population has a mean of 50.0 and a standard deviation of 4.0.
   a. Compute the probability of a value between 44.0 and 55.0.
   b. Compute the probability of a value greater than 55.0.
   c. Compute the probability of a value between 52.0 and 55.0.
   d. Determine the value of X below which 95 percent of the values will occur.
10. A normal population has a mean of 80.0 and a standard deviation of 14.0.
   a. Compute the probability of a value between 75.0 and 90.0.
   b. Compute the probability of a value of 75.0 or less.
   c. Compute the probability of a value between 55.0 and 70.0.
   d. Determine the value of X above which 80 percent of the values will occur.
11. A cola-dispensing machine is set to dispense 7.00 ounces of cola per cup. The standard deviation is 0.10 ounces. What is the probability that a machine will dispense:
   a. Between 7.10 and 7.25 ounces of cola?
   b. 7.25 ounces of cola or more?
   c. Between 6.8 and 7.25 ounces of cola?
   d. How much cola is dispensed in the largest 1 percent of the drinks?
12. The amounts of money requested in home loan applications at Dawn River Federal Savings are approximately normally distributed with a mean of $70,000 and a standard deviation of $20,000. A loan application is received this morning. What is the probability that:
   a. The amount requested is $80,000 or more?
   b. The amount requested is between $65,000 and $80,000?
   c. The amount requested is $65,000 or more?
   d. Twenty percent of the loans are larger than what amount?
13. WNAE, an FM stereo station with a rock and roll format, finds that the mean length of time a person is tuned to the station is 15.0 minutes with a standard deviation of 3.5 minutes. What is the probability that a particular listener will tune in:
   a. For 20 minutes or more?
   b. For 20 minutes or less?
   c. Between 10 and 12 minutes?
   d. Seventy percent of the listeners are tuned in for how many minutes or less?
14. Landrum Airline flies the route between Chicago and Pittsburgh. The mean number of passengers per flight is 160 with a standard deviation of 20. The aircraft used for the route has 200 seats.
   a. What percent of the flights are sold out?

b. The airline must sell 150 seats to break even on this particular flight. On what percent of the flights does the airline make money?

c. The airline would like to reduce the number of flight attendants on 20% of the flights. This will be done on the flights with the fewest passengers. Below what number of passengers on a flight will the airline reduce the number of flight attendants?

THE NORMAL APPROXIMATION TO THE BINOMIAL

Normal approximation to the binomial

Chapter 6 described the binomial probability distribution, which is a discrete distribution. The table of binomial probabilities in Appendix A goes successively from an n of 1 to an n of 20, and then to $n = 25$. Suppose a problem involved taking a sample of 60. Generating a binomial distribution for that large a number would be very time-consuming—even using a computer. A more efficient approach is to apply the *normal approximation to the binomial.*

Using the normal distribution (a continuous distribution) as a substitute for a binomial distribution (a discrete distribution) for large values of n seems reasonable because as n increases, a binomial distribution gets closer and closer to a normal distribution. The change in the shape of a binomial distribution with $p = .50$ from an n of 1 to an n of 20 is depicted in Chart 7–5.

CHART 7–5 **Binomial Distributions for an n of 1, 3, and 20, Where $p = .50$**

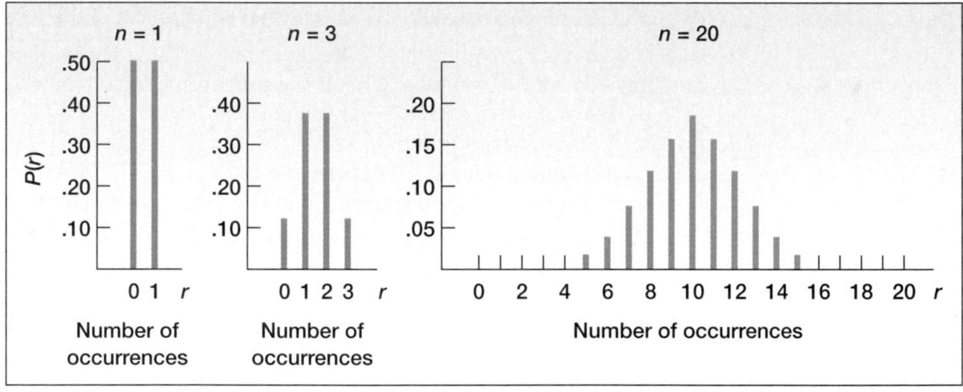

When to use the normal approximation

When can we use the normal approximation to the binomial? The normal probability distribution is generally deemed a good approximation to the binomial probability distribution when np and $n(1 - p)$ are both greater than 5. However, before we apply the normal approximation, we must make sure that our distribution of interest is in fact a binomial distribution. Recall from Chapter 6 that four criteria must be met:

1. There are only two mutually exclusive outcomes to an experiment: a "success" and a "failure."
2. A binomial distribution results from counting the number of successes.
3. Each trial is independent.

4. The probability p must remain the same from trial to trial, and there must be a fixed number of trials, n.

Continuity Correction Factor

To show the application of the normal approximation to the binomial and the need for a correction factor, suppose that the management of the Santoni Pizza Restaurant found that 70 percent of their new customers return for another meal. For a week in which 80 new (first-time) customers dined at Santoni's, what is the probability that 60 or more will return for another meal?

Notice that the binomial conditions are met: (1) There are only two possible outcomes—a customer either returns for another meal or does not return. (2) We can count the number of successes, meaning, for example, that 57 of the 80 customers return. (3) The trials are independent, meaning that if the 34th person returns for a second meal, that does not affect whether the 58th person returns. (4) The probability of a customer returning remains at .70 for all 80 customers.

Therefore, we could use the binomial formula (6–3)

$$P(r) = \frac{n!}{r!(n-r)!}(p)^r(q)^{n-r}$$

to calculate this probability. It would mean, however, computing the probabilities of 60, 61, 62, . . . , 80 and adding them to arrive at the probability of 60 or more. No doubt you will agree that using the normal approximation to the binomial is a much more efficient method of estimating the probability of 60 or more.

Since we are going to determine the binomial probability of 60 or more successes using the normal curve, we must subtract, in this case, .5 from 60. The value .5 is called the **continuity correction factor.** This small adjustment must be made because a continuous distribution (the normal distribution) is being used to approximate a discrete distribution (the binomial distribution). Subtracting, $60 - .5 = 59.5$.

Continuity correction factor

Continuity correction factor The value .5 subtracted or added, depending on the problem, to a selected value when a binomial probability distribution, which is a discrete probability distribution, is being approximated by a continuous probability distribution—the normal distribution.

To use the normal distribution to approximate the probability that 60 or more first-time Santoni customers out of 80 will return, follow the procedure shown below.

Step 1 Find the z value corresponding to an X of 59.5 using formula (7–1), and formulas (6–4) and (6–5) for the mean and variance of a binomial distribution:

$\mu = np = 80(.70) = 56.$
$\sigma^2 = np(1 - p) = 80(.70)(1 - .70) = 16.8.$
$\sigma = 4.0988$, found by $\sqrt{16.8}$.
$z = 0.85$, found by:

$$z = \frac{X - \mu}{\sigma} = \frac{59.5 - 56}{4.0988} = 0.85$$

Step 2 Determine the area under the normal curve between a μ of 56 and an X of 59.5. From step 1 we know that the z value corresponding to 59.5 is 0.85. So we go to Appendix D and read down the left margin to 0.8, and then we go horizontally to the area under the column headed by .05. That area is .3023.

Step 3 Calculate the area beyond 59.5 by subtracting .3023 from .5000 (.5000 − .3023 = .1977). Thus, .1977 is the approximate probability that 60 or more first-time Santoni customers out of 80 will return for another meal.

The facets of this problem are shown graphically:

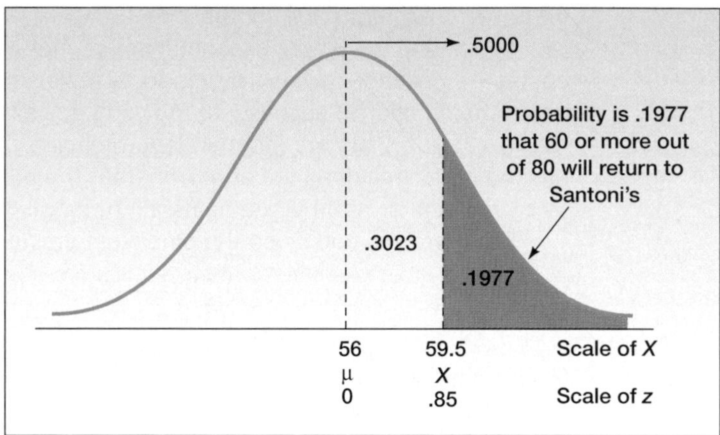

The MINITAB system can be used to check this binomial probability (.1977) by using the normal distribution. The MINITAB probability of .8034 in the following output is a cumulative probability and must be subtracted from 1.00.

```
MTB  > cdf 59.5
SUBC > normal 56 4.0988.
     59.5000     0.8034
```

Using the computed MINITAB probability of .8034, given above we can determine the probability that 60 or more customers will return for another meal. It is .1966. (The small discrepancy between .1977 and .1966 is due to rounding.)

$$\begin{aligned} P(z > 0.85) &= 1 - P(z < 0.85) \\ &= 1 - .8034 \\ &= .1966 \end{aligned}$$

SELF-REVIEW 7–7

The answers are at the end of the chapter.

A study by Great Southern Home Insurance revealed that none of the stolen goods were recovered by the homeowners in 80 percent of the reported thefts.

1. During a period in which 200 thefts occurred, what is the probability that no stolen goods were recovered in 170 or more of the robberies?
2. During a period in which 200 thefts occurred, what is the probability that no stolen goods were recovered in 150 or more robberies?

EXERCISES

The answers to the odd-numbered exercises are at the end of the book.

15. Suppose X has a binomial probability distribution with $n = 50$ and $p = .25$. Compute the following:
    a. The mean and standard deviation of the random variable.
    b. The probability that X is 15 or more.
    c. The probability that X is 10 or less.
16. Suppose X has a binomial probability distribution with $n = 40$ and $p = .55$. Compute the following:
    a. The mean and standard deviation of the random variable.
    b. The probability that X is 25 or greater.
    c. The probability that X is 15 or less.
    d. The probability that X is between 15 and 25 inclusive.
17. Theresa's Tax Service specializes in federal tax returns. A recent audit by the IRS of the returns she prepared indicated that an error was made on 10 percent of the returns she prepared last year. Assuming this rate continues into this year and she prepares 60 returns, what is the probability that she makes:
    a. More than nine errors?
    b. At least nine errors?
    c. Exactly nine errors?
18. Shorty's Muffler advertises that they can change a muffler in 30 minutes or less. However, the work standards department at corporate headquarters recently conducted a study and found that 20 percent of the mufflers were not installed in 30 minutes or less. The Maumee branch installed 50 mufflers last month. If the corporate report is correct:
    a. How many of the installations at the Maumee branch would you expect to take more than 30 minutes?
    b. What is the likelihood that fewer than eight installations took more than 30 minutes?
    c. What is the likelihood that eight or fewer installations took more than 30 minutes?
    d. What is the likelihood that exactly eight of the 50 installations took more than 30 minutes?
19. A study conducted by the nationally known Taurus Health Club revealed that 30 percent of its new members are significantly overweight. A membership drive in a metropolitan area resulted in 500 new members.
    a. It has been suggested that the normal approximation to the binomial be used to determine the probability that of the 500 new members, 175 or more are significantly overweight. Does this problem qualify as a binomial problem? Explain.
    b. What is the probability that 175 or more of the new members are overweight?
    c. What is the probability that 140 or more new members are significantly overweight?
20. Research on new juvenile delinquents who were put on probation by Judge Conners revealed that 38 percent of them committed another crime.
    a. What is the probability that of the last 100 new juvenile delinquents put on probation, 30 or more will commit another crime?
    b. What is the probability that 40 or fewer of the delinquents will commit another crime?
    c. What is the probability that between 30 and 40 of the delinquents will commit another crime?

CHAPTER OUTLINE

I. The normal distribution is a continuous probability distribution with the following major characteristics.
   A. It is bell-shaped and the mean, median, and mode are equal.

B. It is symmetrical.
C. It is asymptotic, meaning the curve approaches but never touches the X-axis.
D. It is completely described by the mean and the standard deviation.
E. There is a family of normal distributions. Each time the mean or the standard deviation changes, a new distribution is created.

II. The standard normal distribution is a particular normal distribution.
A. It has a mean of 0.00 and a standard deviation of 1.00.
B. Any normal distribution can be converted to the standard normal distribution by the following formula.

$$z = \frac{X - \mu}{\sigma} \tag{7–1}$$

C. By standardizing a normal distribution, we can report the distance from the mean in units of the standard deviation.

III. The normal distribution can be used to approximate a binomial distribution under certain conditions.
A. np and $n(1 - p)$ must both be greater than 5.
1. n is the number of observations.
2. p is the probability of a success.

B. The four conditions for a binomial distribution are:
1. There are only two possible outcomes.
2. p remains the same from trial to trial.
3. The trials are independent.
4. The distribution results from a count of the number of successes in a fixed number of trials.

C. The mean and the variance of a binomial distribution are computed as follows:

$$\mu = np$$

$$\sigma^2 = np(1 - p)$$

D. The continuity correction factor of .5 is used to extend the continuous value of X one-half unit in either direction. This correction compensates for estimating a discrete distribution by a continuous distribution.

EXERCISES

The answers to the odd-numbered exercises are at the end of the book.

21. Ball-Bearings, Inc. produces ball bearings automatically on a Kronar BBX machine. For one of the ball bearings, the arithmetic mean diameter is set at 20.00 mm (millimeters). The standard deviation of the production over a long period of time was computed to be 0.150 mm.
a. What percent of the ball bearings will have diameters between 20.00 mm and 20.27 mm?
b. What percent of the ball bearings will have diameters of 20.27 mm or more?
c. What percent of the ball bearings will have diameters between 19.85 mm and 20.30 mm?
d. What percent of the ball bearings will have diameters 19.91 mm or less?

22. The accounting department at Weston, a national manufacturer of unattached garages, reports that it takes two construction workers a mean of 32 hours and a standard deviation of 2 hours to erect the Red Barn model.
a. What percent of the garages take between 32 hours and 34 hours to erect?
b. What percent of the garages take 28.7 hours or less to erect?
c. What percent of the garages take between 29 hours and 34 hours to erect?
d. Of the garages, 5 percent take how many hours or more to erect?

23. The net sales and the number of employees for aluminum fabricators with similar characteristics were organized into frequency distributions. Both were normally distributed. For the net sales, μ = \$180 million and σ = \$25 million. For the number of employees, μ = 1,500 and σ = 120. Clarion Fabricators had sales of \$170 million and 1,850 employees.
    a. Convert Clarion's sales and number of employees to *z* values.
    b. Locate the two *z* values on a standard normal distribution.
    c. Compare Clarion's sales and number of employees with those of the other fabricators. What percent of the fabricators have more sales than Clarion? More employees?

24. A mechanical aptitude test designed for entering college students has a mean of 1,000 and a standard deviation of 150. An IQ test designed for college students has a mean of 110 and a standard deviation of 10. Shawn Bucci scored 1,310 on the mechanical aptitude test and 122 on the IQ test. Evaluate his test scores relative to those of others who took the tests.

25. A study of Furniture Wholesales, Inc. regarding the payment of invoices revealed that, on the average, an invoice was paid 20 days after it was received. The standard deviation equaled 5 days.
    a. What percent of the invoices are paid within 15 days of receipt?
    b. What is the probability of selecting any invoice and finding it was paid between 18 and 26 days after it was received?
    c. The management of Furniture Wholesales wants to encourage their customers to pay their monthly invoices as soon as possible. Therefore, it was announced that a 2 percent reduction in price would be in effect for customers who pay within 7 working days of the receipt of the invoice. Assuming the payments are normally distributed, out of 200 customers during July, how many would normally be eligible for the reduction?

26. The annual commissions per salesperson employed by Machine Products, which is a manufacturer of light machinery, averaged \$40,000, with a standard deviation of \$5,000. What percent of the salespeople earn between \$32,000 and \$42,000?

27. The weights of cans of Monarch pears are normally distributed with a mean of 1,000 grams and a standard deviation of 50 grams. Calculate the percentage of the cans that weigh:
    a. 860 grams or less.
    b. Between 1,055 and 1,100 grams.

28. Past experience with respect to the number of passengers on the *Queen Elizabeth II,* offering one-week cruises to the Caribbean, revealed that the mean number of passengers is 1,820 and the standard deviation of the normal distribution of the number of passengers is 120.
    a. What percent of the cruises will have between 1,820 and 1,970 passengers?
    b. What percent of the cruises will have 1,970 passengers or more?
    c. What percent of the Caribbean cruises will have 1,600 or fewer passengers?

29. Management at Gordon Electronics is considering adopting a bonus system to increase production. One suggestion is to pay a bonus on the highest 5 percent of production based on past experience. Past records indicate that, on the average, 4,000 units of a small assembly are produced during a week. The distribution of the weekly production is approximately normal with a standard deviation of 60 units. If the bonus is paid on the upper 5 percent of production, the bonus will be paid on how many units or more?

30. Fast Service Truck Lines uses the Ford Super 1310 exclusively. Management made a study of the maintenance costs using a sample. It revealed that the arithmetic mean number of kilometers traveled per truck during the year was 60,000. The distances

traveled during the year were normally distributed. The standard deviation of the normally distributed distances in the sample of Ford 1310s was 2,000 kilometers.

a. What percent of the Ford Super 1310s logged 65,200 kilometers or more?
b. The truck line owns 3,500 Ford Super 1310s. Based on the sample findings, how many of them traveled 55,000 kilometers or less?
c. How many of the Fords traveled 62,000 kilometers or less during the year?

31. The annual incomes of a large group of supervisors at Belco are normally distributed with a mean of $28,000 and a standard deviation of $1,200. The length of service of the same supervisors is also normally distributed with a mean of 20 years and a standard deviation of 5 years. John McMaster earns $30,400 annually and has 10 years of service.
a. Compare his income with those of the other supervisors.
b. Compare this length of service with those of the other supervisors.

32. An executive at Westinghouse drives from his home in the suburbs near Pittsburgh to his office in the center of the city. The driving times are normally distributed with a mean of 35 minutes and a standard deviation of 8 minutes.
a. In what percent of the days will it take him 30 minutes or less to drive to work?
b. In what percent of the days will it take 40 minutes or more to drive to work?
c. Explain to the executive why the probability is nearly 0 that it will take him exactly 40 minutes to get to work.
d. Since the executive didn't understand your answer to part *c,* how would you estimate the percent of days in which it takes 40 minutes to drive to work? (Hint: Within what range of values would the times be rounded to 40?)
e. Some days there will be accidents or other delays, so the trip will take longer than usual. How long will the longest 10 percent of the trips take?

33. A large retailer offers a "no hassle" returns policy. The mean number of customers returning items is 10.3 with a standard deviation of 2.25 customers per day.
a. In what percent of the days are there 8 or fewer customers returning items?
b. In what percent of the days are there between 12 and 14 customers returning items?
c. Is there any chance of a day with no returns?

34. A recent study showed that 20 percent of all employees steal from their company each year. If a company employs 50 people, what is the probability that:
a. Fewer than 5 employees steal?
b. More than 5 employees steal?
c. Exactly 5 employees steal?
d. More than 5 but fewer than 15 employees steal?

35. A recent study showed that 64 percent of American men over the age of 18 consider nutrition a top priority in their lives. A sample of 60 men is selected. What is the likelihood that:
a. 32 or more consider diet important?
b. 44 or more consider diet important?
c. More than 32 but fewer than 43 consider diet important?
d. Exactly 44 consider diet important?

36. Two-liter plastic bottles used for bottling cola are shipped in lots of 100. Suppose the lots are 5 percent defective. Some bottles leak, some are too small, and so forth.
a. What is the probability that a shipment of plastic bottles contains 8 or more defectives?
b. What is the probability that between 8 and 10 bottles are defective?
c. What is the probability that there are exactly 8 defectives?
d. What is the probability of no defectives?

37. At Casper State College 20 percent of the students drop basic statistics the first time they enroll. There are 50 students enrolled in Dr. Corbell's statistics class this semester. Compute the following probabilities.

a. What is the probability that at least 8 drop?
b. What is the probability that exactly 8 drop?
c. What is the probability that 8 or fewer drop?

38. Assume that 10 percent of those taking the statistics part of the examination to qualify as a certified public accountant fail. Sixty students are taking the exam this Saturday.
    a. What is the probability that exactly two students will fail?
    b. What is the probability at least two students will fail?
39. The Tri-State county traffic division reported that 40 percent of the high-speed chases involving automobiles result in a minor or major accident. During a month in which 50 high-speed chases occur, what is the probability that 25 or more will result in a minor or major accident?
40. Cruise ships of the Royal Viking line report that 80 percent of their rooms are occupied during September. For a cruise ship having 800 rooms, what is the probability that 665 or more are occupied in September?
41. The goal at U.S. airports handling international flights is to clear these flights within 45 minutes. Let's interpret this to mean that 95 percent of the flights are cleared in 45 minutes, so 5 percent of the flights take longer to clear. Let's also assume that the distribution of times is normal.
    a. If the standard deviation of the time to clear an international flight is 5 minutes, what is the mean time to clear a flight?
    b. Suppose the standard deviation is 10 minutes, not the 5 minutes suggested in part *a.* What is the new mean?
    c. If an executive has 30 minutes from the time her flight landed to catch her limousine, assuming the information in part *b,* what is the likelihood that she will be cleared in time?
42. Refer to Exercise 51 in Chapter 6. In this problem an air force study indicated that the probability of a disaster such as the January 28, 1986, explosion of the space shuttle *Challenger* was 1 in 35. Use the normal approximation to the binomial to compute the probability of at least one disaster in 25 missions. How does this compare with your result in Chapter 6?
43. The registrar at Elmwood University studied the grade point averages (GPAs) of students over many years. He has discovered that the distribution is approximately normal with a mean of 2.80 and a standard deviation of 0.40.
    a. What is the probability that a randomly selected student has a GPA of from 2.00 up to 3.00?
    b. What percent of the students are on probation, that is, have a GPA less than 2.00?
    c. The student population at EU is 10,000. How many students are on the dean's list, that is, have GPAs of 3.70 or higher?
    d. To qualify for a Bell scholarship, a student must be in the top 10 percent of the student body. What GPA must a student have to qualify for a Bell scholarship?
44. Mr. Jon Molnar will graduate from Eastwood High School this year. He took the American College Test (ACT) for college admission and received a score of 30. The high school principal informed him that only 2 percent of the students taking the exam receive a higher score. The mean score for all students taking the exam is 18.3. Jon's friends Karrie and George also took the test but were not given any information by the principal other than their scores. Karrie scored 25 and George 18. Based on this information, what were Karrie's and George's percentile ranks? What assumption is necessary?
45. Canned hams processed at the Henline Ham Company are normally distributed with a mean of 9.20 pounds and a standard deviation of 0.25 pounds. The label weight is given as 9.00 pounds.
    a. What proportion of the hams actually weigh less than the amount claimed on the label?

b. The owner, Glen Henline, is considering two proposals to reduce the proportion of hams below label weight. He can increase the mean weight to 9.25 and leave the standard deviation the same, or he can leave the mean weight at 9.20 and reduce the standard deviation from 0.25 pounds to 0.15. Which change would you recommend?

46. A newspaper article reported that the mean number of hours worked per week by those employed full-time is 43.9. The article further indicated that about one third of those employed full-time work less than 40 hours per week. Given this information and assuming that number of hours worked is normally distributed, what is the standard deviation of the number of hours worked? The article also indicated that 20 percent of those working full-time work more than 49 hours. Determine the standard deviation with this information. Are the two estimates of the standard deviation similar? What would you conclude if they are not?

    (Source: "Women Push up Work Hours," *The Cincinnati Enquirer,* June 12, 1994, p. F3.)

47. Most four-year automobile leases allow up to 60,000 miles. If the lessee goes beyond this amount, a penalty of 10 cents per mile is added to the lease cost. Suppose the distribution of miles driven on four-year leases is normal with a mean of 52,000 miles and a standard deviation of 5,000 miles.
    a. What percent of the leases will yield a penalty because of excess mileage?
    b. If the lessor wanted to change the terms so that 25 percent of the leases went over the limit, where should the new upper limit be set?
    c. One definition of a low-mileage car is one that is four years old and has been driven less than 45,000 miles. What percent of the cars returned are considered low-mileage?

48. The price of Blair Corporation stock is normally distributed throughout the year with a mean of $42.00 per share and a standard deviation of $2.25 per share.
    a. What percent of the days is the price over $45.00? If stock is traded 240 days out of the year, how many days is the price over $45.00?
    b. What percent of the days is the price between $38.00 and $40.00?
    c. What is the stock's value on the highest 15 days of the year? (Again assume that there are 240 trading days in a year.)

49. The annual sales of romance novels are normally distributed with an unknown mean and an unknown standard deviation. Forty percent of the time sales are more than 470,000, and 10 percent of the time sales are more than 500,000. What is the mean and the standard deviation?

50. In establishing warranties on TV sets the manufacturer wants to set the limits so that few will need repair at manufacturer expense. On the other hand, the warranty period must be long enough to make the purchase attractive to the buyer. For a new TV the mean number of months until repairs are needed is 36.84 with a standard deviation of 3.34 months. Where should the warranty limits be set so that only 10 percent of the TVs need repairs at the manufacturer's expense?

51. DeKorte Marketing, a telephone sales firm, is considering the purchase of a machine that randomly selects and automatically dials telephone numbers. DeKorte Marketing makes most of its calls during the evening, so calls to business phones are wasted. The manufacturer of the machine claims that its programming reduces the business phone calling rate to 15 percent of the calls. As a test, a sample of 150 numbers selected by the machine is checked. If the manufacturer's claim is true, what is the likelihood that more than 30 of the phone numbers selected will be for businesses?

COMPUTER DATA EXERCISES

52. Refer to data set 1, which reports information on homes sold in Florida during 1994.
    a. The mean selling price (in thousands of dollars) of the homes was computed earlier to be $166.67, with a standard deviation of $35.68. Use the normal distribution to

estimate the percent of homes selling for more than $210. Compare this to the actual percent. Does the normal distribution yield a good approximation of the actual results?

b. The mean distance from a home to the center of the city is 14.893 miles with a standard deviation of 4.892 miles. Use the normal distribution to estimate the percentages of homes within 19, 20, and 21 miles from the center of the city. Compare each result to the actual percent. Does the normal distribution yield a good approximation of the actual results?

53. Refer to data set 2, which reports information on the 28 major league baseball teams for the 1993 season.
    a. The mean attendance per team for the season (in millions) was 2.509 with a standard deviation of 0.781. Use the normal distribution to estimate the number of teams with attendance of more than 4.0. Compare this with the actual number. Comment on the accuracy of your estimate.
    b. The mean number of home runs hit per team during the season was 141.79 with a standard deviation of 23.04. Use the normal distribution to estimate the number of teams that hit more than 160 homers. Compare that estimate with the actual number. Comment on the accuracy of your estimate.

54. Refer to data set 3, which reports information on the circulation of 48 magazines.
    a. The mean circulation of the 48 magazines is 3,048 (in thousands) with a standard deviation of 3,756. Use the normal distribution to estimate the number of magazines with a circulation of more than 5,000. Compare that with the actual percent. Comment on the accuracy of the estimate.
    b. The mean percent of the magazines whose readers have a college education is 42.75 percent with a standard deviation of 13.74 percent. Use the normal distribution to estimate the number of magazines where more than 75 percent of the readership has a college education. Compare that with the actual percent. Comment on the accuracy of the estimate.

CHAPTER 7 EXAMINATION

The answers are at the end of the chapter.

For Questions 1 to 10 indicate whether the statement is true or false. If it is false, correct it.

1. The normal probability distribution is a continuous probability distribution.
2. There is only one normal distribution.
3. The normal distribution is positively skewed.
4. The curve representing a normal distribution has its tallest point at the mean.
5. The binomial distribution may be approximated by the normal distribution when np and $n(1 - p)$ are both greater than 3.
6. The z value for the area under the normal curve between 0 and 1.34 is .4099. Likewise, the z value for the area between 0 and -1.34 is also .4099.
7. For a normal distribution where $\mu = 10$, $\sigma = 2$, and $X = 13$, the corresponding z value for X is 3.00.
8. Refer to Question 7. The probability of a value of 13 or greater is .0668.
9. For a binomial random variable $p = .70$ and $n = 50$. The mean and variance are 35 and 10.5, respectively.
10. Refer to the data in Question 9. If $X = 38$, the likelihood of a value of 38 or less is .8599.
11. The seasonal output of a new experimental strain of pepper plants was carefully weighed. The mean weight per plant is 15.0 pounds, and the standard deviation is 1.75 pounds. The weights are approximately normally distributed.

a. What proportion of the plants will weigh between 13 and 16 pounds?
b. What proportion of the plants will weigh 13 or more pounds?
c. The largest 5 percent of the plants are to be studied further to evaluate why they were so large. What is the cutoff point between those plants that will be studied and those that will not be studied?

12. A new dental study reported that 40 percent of children under 10 years of age now wear braces. In a group of 30 children what is the likelihood that:
a. More than 15 wear braces?
b. Fewer than 8 wear braces?
c. Between 8 and 15 inclusive wear braces?

CHAPTER 7 Answers

Self-Review

7–1 1. 2.25, found by:

$$z = \frac{\$1,225 - \$1,000}{\$100} = \frac{\$225}{\$100} = 2.25$$

2. −2.25, found by:

$$z = \frac{\$775 - \$1,000}{\$100} = \frac{-\$225}{\$100} = -2.25$$

7–2 1. \$36,400 and \$38,000, found by \$37,200 ± 1(\$800).
2. \$35,600 and \$38,800, found by \$37,200 ± 2(\$800).
3. \$34,800 and \$39,600, found by \$37,200 ± 3(\$800).
4. \$37,200. Mean, median, and mode are equal for a normal distribution.
5. Yes, a normal distribution is symmetrical.

7–3 1. Computing z:

$$z = \frac{482 - 400}{50} = +1.64$$

Referring to Appendix D, the area is .4495
2. .0505, found by .5000 − .4495.
3.

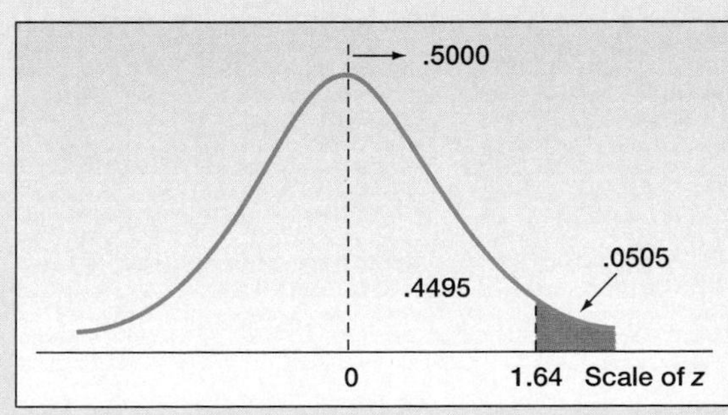

7–4 1. About 22.66 percent, found by:

$$z = \frac{\$925 - \$1,000}{\$100} = -0.75$$

Area = .2734 from Appendix D. Then .5000 − .2734 = .2266.
2.

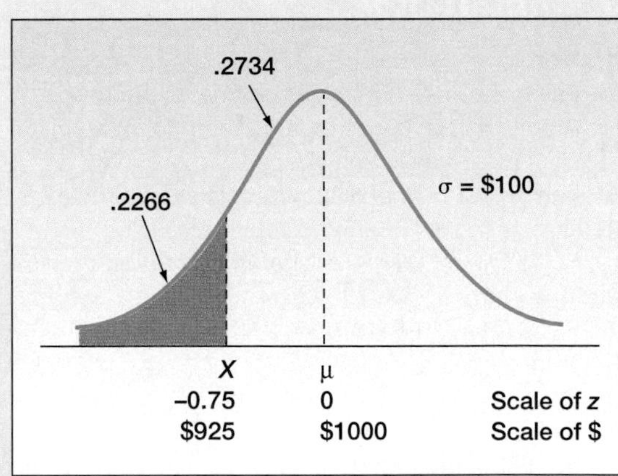

7–5 85.24 (instructor would no doubt make it 85). The closest area to .4000 is .3997; z is 1.28. Then:

$$1.28 = \frac{X - 75}{8}$$

$$10.24 = X - 75$$

$$X = 85.24$$

7–6 1. $z = 0.60$ for PE ratio, found by:

$$z = \frac{11.2 - 10.0}{2.0} = 0.60$$

$z = 2.50$ for percent change, found by:

$$z = \frac{75 - 50}{10} = 2.50$$

2.

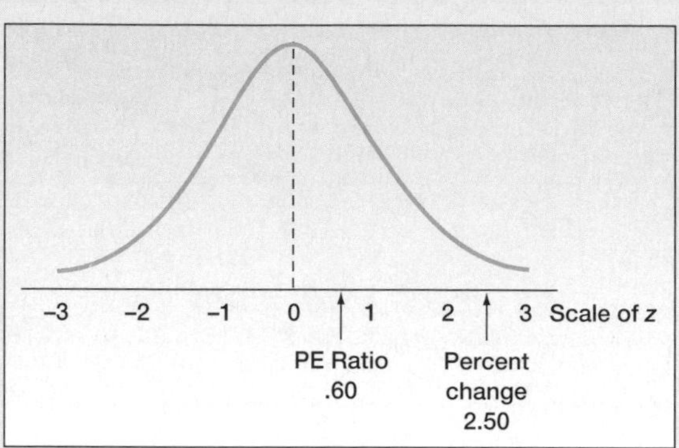

3. Compared with the other selected stocks, Radnor's PE ratio is slightly above average; the percent increase is well above average.

7–7

1. .0465, found by $\mu = np = 200(.80) = 160$, and $\sigma^2 = np(1 - p) = 200(.80)(1 - .80) = 32$. Then,

$$\sigma = \sqrt{32} = 5.66$$

$$z = \frac{169.5 - 160}{5.66} = 1.68$$

Area from Appendix D is .4535. Subtracting from .5000 gives .0465.

2. .9686, found by .4686 + .5000. First calculate z:

$$z = \frac{149.5 - 160}{5.66} = -1.86$$

Area from Appendix D is .4686.

Examination

1. True.
2. False. There is a family of normal distributions. A new distribution is created each time the mean or standard deviation changes.
3. False. The normal distribution is symmetrical.
4. True.
5. False. np and $n(1 - p)$ should be greater than 5.
6. True.
7. False. $z = (13 - 10)/2 = 1.50$.
8. True.
9. True.
10. True.
11. *a.* .5886, found by

$$z = \frac{13.0 - 15.0}{1.75} = -1.14$$

Area under the curve is .3729.

$$z = \frac{16.0 - 15.0}{1.75} = 0.57$$

Area under the curve is .2157.
Adding, .3729 + .2157 = .5886.

b. .8729, found by .5000 + .3729.

c. 17.88 pounds, found by

$$1.645 = \frac{X - 15.0}{1.75}$$

$$X = 15.0 + 1.645(1.75)$$

$$= 15.0 + 2.88 = 17.88$$

12.

$$\mu = np = 30(.40) = 12$$

$$\sigma^2 = np(1 - p) = 30(.40)(.60) = 7.2$$

$$\sigma = \sqrt{7.2} = 2.6833$$

a. .0968, found by

$$z = \frac{15.5 - 12.0}{2.6833} = 1.30$$

Area beyond 1.30 is .5000 − .4032 = .0968.

b. .0465, found by

$$z = \frac{7.5 - 12.0}{2.6833} = -1.68$$

Area less than − 1.68 is .5000 − .4535 = .0465.

c. .8567, found by .4032 + .4535.

SECTION 2 A REVIEW OF CHAPTERS 5–7

This section is a review of the major concepts, terms, symbols, and equations introduced in Chapters 5, 6, and 7. These three chapters are concerned with methods of dealing with uncertainty. As an example of the uncertainty in business, consider the role of the quality assurance department in most mass-production firms. Usually, the department has neither the personnel nor the time to check, say, all 200 plug-in modules produced during a two-hour period. Standard procedure may call for selecting a sample of 5 modules and shipping all 200 modules if the 5 operate correctly. However, if 1 or more in the sample are defective, all 200 are checked. Assuming that all 5 function correctly, quality assurance personnel cannot be absolutely certain that their action (allowing shipment of the modules) will prove to be correct. It could be that the 5 selected at random are the only ones out of the 200 that function properly! Probability theory lets us measure the uncertainty involved, in this case, of shipping out defective modules. Also, probability as a measurement of uncertainty comes into play when Gallup, Harris, and other pollsters predict that Jim Barstow will win the vacant senatorial seat in Georgia.

Chapter 5 noted that a *probability* is a number between 0 and 1 inclusive that measures one's belief that a particular event will occur. A weather forecaster might state that the probability of rain tomorrow is .20. The project director of a firm bidding on a subway station in Bangkok might assess the firm's chance of being awarded the contract at .50. We looked at the ways probabilities can be combined using rules of addition and multiplication, some principles of counting, and the importance of Bayes' theorem.

Chapter 6 presented *discrete* probability distributions—the *binomial distribution,* the *hypergeometric distribution,* and the *Poisson distribution.* Other probability distributions will be discussed in forthcoming chapters (*t* distribution, chi-square distribution, etc.). Probability distributions are listings of all the possible outcomes of an experiment and the probability associated with each outcome. A probability distribution allows us to evaluate sample results.

As an example, suppose a consumer research firm, such as National Family Opinion, conducted a survey to find out whether or not grocery shoppers can identify the brand name of a product if the name does not appear on the can, box, or package. For question 1, NFO deleted the name of a soup and gave the shopper five choices: (1) Campbell's, (2) Knorr, (3) Progresso, (4) Chalet Suzanne, and (5) Heinz.

There were six similar questions, and 1,000 shoppers participated in the experiment. There is a possibility that shoppers unfamiliar with various labels and brand names would select a name at random—that is, guess the brand name. So a binomial probability distribution is generated to see what a random distribution of choices would look like. These probabilities are in column 2 of the following table; the numbers expected are in column 3. Note that we expect only 2 of the 1,000 shoppers to *guess* five of the six questions correctly. We expect practically no shoppers to guess six out of six. The actual responses are in column 4. A comparison of columns 3 and 4 indicates that a large percentage of the shoppers can identify the brand name of the product by looking at the label. NFO would conclude that it is highly unlikely for such a large number of shoppers to select so many correct brand names by chance.

1 Number of correct identifications	2 Probability*	3 Expected number by chance	4 Actual number in survey
0	.262	262	5
1	.393	393	16
2	.246	246	10
3	.082	82	27
4	.015	15	81
5	.002	2	346
6	.000	0	515
	1.000	1,000	1,000

*Probabilities from Appendix A.

MINITAB and other computer programs can generate a binomial distribution given *n* and *p*. Following is the MINITAB output for the preceding illustration.

```
MTB  > pdf;
SUBC > binomial n = 6, p = 20.

     BINOMIAL WITH N = 6 P = 0 .200000
     K      P(X = K)
     0      0.2621
     1      0.3932
     2      0.2458
     3      0.0819
     4      0.0154
     5      0.0015
     6      0.0001
```

In Chapter 7 we described the *normal probability distribution,* which is a continuous distribution. Some phenomena, such as the tensile strength of wires and the weights of the contents of cans and bottles, approximate a normal, bell-shaped distribution. Actually, there is a family of normal distributions—each with its own mean and standard deviation. There is a normal distribution, for example, for a mean of $100 and a standard deviation of $5, another for a mean of $149 and a standard deviation of $5.26, and so on. It was noted that a normal probability distribution is bell-shaped and symmetrical about its mean and that the tails of the normal curve extend in either direction infinitely. Since there are an unlimited number of normal distributions, it is difficult to compare two or more distributions directly. Instead, the distributions of interest can be *standardized.* The distribution of these standardized values is aptly called the *standard normal distribution.* The standard normal distribution has a mean of 0 and a standard deviation of 1. It is very useful, for example, for comparing distributions in different units. The distribution of the incomes of middle managers and the distribution of their efficiency ratings is an example of distributions in different units. It is also used to compute the probability that various events will happen.

GLOSSARY

Chapter 5

Bayes' theorem Developed by Reverend Bayes in the 1700s, it is designed to find the probability of one event, *A*, occurring, given that another event, *B*, has already occurred.

Classical probability Probability based on the assumption that each of the outcomes is equally likely. On the toss of a coin, for example, a head or tail is equally likely. Using this concept of probability, if there are *n* possible outcomes, the probability of a particular outcome is $1/n$. Thus, on the toss of a coin, the probability of a head is $1/n = ½$.

Combination formula A formula used to count the number of possible outcomes. If the order *a, b, c* is considered the same as *b, a, c*, or *c, b, a*, and so on, the number of arrangements is found by:

$$_nC_r = \frac{n!}{r!(n-r)!}$$

Conditional probability The likelihood that an event will occur given that another event has already occurred.

Event A collection of one or more outcomes of an experiment. For example, an event may be three defective valves in an incoming shipment of valves for a 351 cu. in. Ford V8 engine.

Experiment An activity that is either observed or measured. An experiment may be counting the number of correct responses to a question, for example.

General rule of addition Used to combine probabilities when the events are *not* mutually exclusive.

$$P(A \text{ or } B) = P(A) + P(B) - P(A \text{ and } B)$$

General rule of multiplication Used when the events are *not* independent. Example: It is known that there are 3 defective radios in a box containing 10 radios. What is the probability of selecting 2 defective radios on the first two selections from the box?

$$P(A \text{ and } B) = P(A) \cdot P(B \mid A) = \frac{3}{10} \times \frac{2}{9} = \frac{6}{90} = .067$$

where $P(B|A)$ means the "probability of *B* occurring given that *A* has already occurred."

Independent The occurrence of one event has no effect on the probability of the occurrence of any other event.

Multiplication formula One of the formulas that can be used to count the number of possible outcomes of an experiment. It states that if there are *m* ways of doing one thing and n ways of doing another, there are $m \times n$ ways of doing both. Example: A sports shop offers two sport coats and three contrasting pants for $400. How many different outfits can there be? Answer: $m \times n = 2 \times 3 = 6$.

Outcome A particular result of an experiment.

Permutation formula A formula used to count the number of possible outcomes. If *a, b, c* is one arrangement, *b, a, c* another, *c, a, b* another, and so on, the total number of arrangements is determined by

$$_nP_r = \frac{n!}{(n-r)!}$$

Probability A value between 0 and 1 that reports the likelihood that a specific event will occur.

Relative frequency A concept of probability based on past experience. For example, the Metropolitan Life Insurance Company reported that during the year, 100.2 of every 100,000 persons in Wyoming died of accidental death (motor vehicle accidents, falls, drowning, firearms, etc.). Based on this experience, Metropolitan can estimate the probability of accidental death for a particular person in Wyoming: 100.2/100,000 = .001002.

Special rule of addition For this rule to apply, the events must be mutually exclusive. For two events, the probability of A or B occurring is found by:

$$P(A \text{ or } B) = P(A) + P(B)$$

Example: The probability of a one-spot or a two-spot occurring on the toss of one die is

$$P(A \text{ or } B) = \frac{1}{6} + \frac{1}{6} = \frac{2}{6} = \frac{1}{3}$$

Special rule of multiplication If two events are not related—that is, they are independent—this rule is applied to determine the probability of their joint occurrence.

$$P(A \text{ and } B) = P(A) \cdot P(B)$$

Example: The probability of two heads on two tosses of a coin is:

$$P(A \text{ and } B) = P(A) \cdot P(B) = \frac{1}{2} \times \frac{1}{2} = \frac{1}{4}$$

Subjective probability The chance of an event happening based on whatever information is available—hunches, personal opinion, opinions of others, rumors, and so on.

Chapter 6

Binomial probability distribution A discrete random variable with the following characteristics:

1. Each outcome is mutually exclusive, meaning that it cannot be a "success" and a "failure" at the same time. Example: The answer to a multiple-choice question is either correct or wrong.

2. The distribution is the result of counting the number of successes. The counts may be, for example, the number of correct answers to a 10-question multiple-choice test. The counts listed would be 0, 1, 2, . . . 10.
3. Each trial is independent, meaning that the answer to trial 1 (correct or wrong) in no way affects the answer to trial 2, for example.
4. The probability of a success stays the same from trial to trial. Example: For a multiple-choice quiz having four choices per question, the probability of guessing the answer to question 1 is .25, that of guessing the answer to question 2 is also .25, and so on.

Continuous random variable A random variable that may assume an infinite number of values with certain limitations. Example: The height of the power forward on Indiana's basketball team may be 78.0 inches, 78.01 inches, 78.014 inches, and so on, depending on the accuracy of the measuring device being used.

Discrete random variable A random variable that can assume only certain specific values. Example: A family can consist of 1, 2, 3, . . . persons, not −14 or 2¼ persons.

Hypergeometric probability distribution A probability distribution based on a discrete random variable. Its major characteristics are:

1. There is a fixed number of trials.
2. The probability of success is not the same from trial to trial.

Poisson distribution A distribution often used to approximate binomial probabilities when n is large and p is small. What is considered "large" or "small" is not precisely defined, but a general rule is that n should be equal to or greater than 20 and p equal to or less than .05.

Probability distribution A distribution in the form of a table listing all the possible outcomes of an experiment and the probability associated with each outcome.

Random variable A quantity obtained from an experiment that may, by chance, result in different values. For example, a count of the number of accidents (the experiment) on I-75 during a week might be 10, or 11, or 12, or some other number.

Chapter 7

Continuity correction factor Used to improve the accuracy of the approximation of a discrete distribution (binomial) by a continuous distribution (normal).

Normal probability distribution A continuous distribution that is bell-shaped and symmetrical, with the mean dividing the distribution into two equal parts. Further, the normal curve extends infinitely in either direction; that is, it never touches the X-axis. By converting a normal distribution to a *standard normal distribution,* we can, for example, compare two or more distributions having significantly different means or that are in different units (such as incomes and years of service).

***z* value** The distance between a selected value and the population mean measured in units of the standard deviation.

EXERCISES

The answers to the odd-numbered exercises are at the end of the book.

Part I—Fill in the Blanks

1. Based on your assessment of the stock market, you state that chances are 50–50 that stock prices will start to go down within two months. This concept of probability based on your belief is called ________.
2. A study of absenteeism from the classroom is being conducted. In our study of probability, this particular activity is called ________.
3. Refer to Exercise 2. It was found that 126 students were absent from Monday morning classes. This number (126) is called ________.
4. To apply this rule of addition:

$$P(A \text{ or } B \text{ or } C) = P(A) + P(B) + P(C)$$

   the events must be ________.
5. Management claims that the probability of a defective relay is only .001. The rule to use for finding the probability of the relay *not* being defective is ________. The formula for that rule is ________. The probability of a particular relay not being defective is ________.
6. For a probability distribution, the sum of all possible outcomes must equal ________.
7. Is the binomial distribution a discrete or continuous probability distribution? ________.
8. The characteristics of a binomial probability distribution are: ________, ________, ________, ________.
9. The Poisson probability distribution is (discrete or continuous?) ________.
10. To construct a Poisson distribution, you need ________.
11. The characteristics of a normal probability distribution and its accompanying normal curve are: ________, ________, ________.
12. If we convert values of a normal distribution to a distribution that has a mean of 0 and a standard deviation of 1, this probability distribution is called the ________.

Part II—Problems

13. A self-study course on management principles was offered to all employees of TMC Electronics. At the end of the time period, the employees were tested, with the following results:

Course grade	Number of employees
A	20
B	35
C	90
D	40
F	10
Withdrew	5

What is the probability that an employee selected at random:

a. Earned an A?
b. Earned a C or better?
c. Did not fail or withdraw?

14. It is claimed that Aldradine, a new medicine for acne, is 80 percent effective—that is, of every 100 persons who apply it, 80 show significant improvement. It is applied to the affected areas of a group of 15 people.
    a. What is the probability that all 15 will show significant improvement?
    b. What is the probability that fewer than 9 of the 15 will show significant improvement?
    c. What is the probability that 12 or more people will show significant improvement?
15. First National Bank thoroughly investigates its applicants for small home-improvement loans. Their default record is very impressive: the probability that a homeowner will default is only .005. The bank has approved 400 small home-improvement loans. Assuming the Poisson probability distribution applies to this problem:
    a. What is the probability that no homeowners out of the 400 will default?
    b. How many of the 400 are expected not to default?
    c. What is the probability that 3 or more homeowners will default on their small home-improvement loans?
16. A study of the attendance at the University of Toledo's basketball games revealed that the distribution of attendance is normally distributed with a mean of 10,000 and a standard deviation of 2,000.
    a. What is the probability of a particular game having an attendance of 13,500 or more?
    b. What percent of the games had an attendance between 8,000 and 11,500?
    c. Ten percent of the games had an attendance of how many or less?
17. The following table shows a breakdown of the U.S. Congress by party affiliation and branch prior to the Clinton administration.

	Party	
	Democrats	**Republicans**
House	258	177
Senate	54	46

    a. A member of Congress is selected at random. What is the probability of selecting a Republican member of Congress?
    b. Given that the person selected is a member of the House of Representatives, what is the probability of selecting a Republican?
    c. What is the probability of selecting a member of the House of Representatives or a Democrat?
18. The Internal Revenue Service has set aside 200 tax returns where the amount of charitable contributions seemed excessive. A sample of six returns is selected from the group. If two or more of this sampled group have "excessive" amounts deducted for charitable contributions, the entire group will be audited. What is the probability that the entire group will be audited, if the true proportion of "excessive" deductions is 20 percent? What if the true proportion is 30 percent?
19. The Daniel-James Insurance Company will insure an offshore Mobil Oil production platform for one year. The president of Daniel-James estimates the following losses for that platform (in millions of dollars) with the accompanying probabilities:

Amount of loss ($ millions)	**Probability of loss**
0	.98
40	.016
300	.004

    a. What is the expected amount Daniel-James will have to pay to Mobil in claims?

b. What is the likelihood that Daniel-James will actually lose less than the expected amount?

c. Given that Daniel-James suffers a loss, what is the likelihood that it is for $300 million?

d. Daniel-James has set the annual premium at $2.0 million. Does that seem like a fair premium? Will it cover their risk?

20. The distribution of the number of school-age children per family in the Whitehall Estates area of Boise, Idaho, is:

Number of children	0	1	2	3	4
Percent of families	40	30	15	10	5

a. Determine the mean and standard deviation of the number of school-age children per family in Whitehall Estates.

b. A new school is to be built in Whitehall Estates. An estimate of the number of school-age children is needed. There are 500 family units. How many children would you estimate?

c. Some additional information is needed about only the families having children. Convert the preceding distribution to one for families with children. What is the mean number of children among families that have children?

CASE

Refer to the Century National Bank Data. Does it seem reasonable that the distribution of the checking account balances approximates a normal distribution? Determine the mean and the standard deviation for the sample of 60 customers. Compare the results between the actual distribution and the theoretical distribution. Cite some specific examples and comment on your findings.

Divide the account balance into three groups, of about 20 each, with the smallest third of the balances in the first group, the middle third in the second group, and those with the largest balances in the third group. Next, develop a table that shows the categories of the account balances by branch. Does it appear that the account balances are related to the branch? Cite some examples and comment on your findings.

Chapter 8

Sampling Methods and Sampling Distributions

GOALS

When you have completed this chapter, you will be able to:

1
Explain why in many situations a sample is the only feasible way to learn something about a population.

2
Explain the various methods of selecting a sample.

3
Distinguish between probability sampling and nonprobability sampling.

4
Define and construct a sampling distribution of sample means.

5
Explain the central limit theorem and its importance in statistical inference.

6
Calculate confidence intervals for means and proportions.

7
Determine how large a sample should be for both means and proportions.

A member of Congress wants to determine her popularity in her home state. The proportion of voters who will vote for her must be estimated with plus or minus 2 percent of the population proportion. The .95 degree of confidence is to be used. How many voters should be sampled? (See Goal 7 and Example page 332.)

INTRODUCTION

Chapters 1 through 4 emphasized the techniques used to describe data. To illustrate these techniques, we organized the yearly salaries of professors into a frequency distribution and computed various averages and measures of dispersion. Such measures as the mean and the standard deviation were computed to describe the central tendency of the data and the extent of their spread. These chapters were concerned with *describing something that has already occurred.*

We started to lay the foundation in Chapter 5 for statistical inference with the study of the basic concepts of probability. Three discrete distributions—hypergeometric, binomial, and Poisson—were discussed in Chapter 6. The normal probability distribution, which is a continuous distribution, was presented in Chapter 7. Probability distributions encompass all possible outcomes of an experiment and the probability associated with each outcome. Probability distributions are generated mainly to evaluate *something that might occur.*

We are going to look at another probability distribution in this chapter, called the *sampling distribution of the means.* Before we do, however, can you discover what these four cases have in common?

Case 1: The quality-control department at USX has the job of assuring the quality of production. To check the tensile strength of drawn steel wire, five small pieces are selected every three hours, and the tensile strength of each piece is determined by stretching it until it breaks.

Case 2: The marketing department of Procter & Gamble has the responsibility of determining consumer opinion with respect to new products or products that have been changed. To assess sales potential of Ivory Soap with a new scent, 452 consumers were asked to try it for one week. At the end of one week, each consumer completed a questionnaire regarding Ivory.

Case 3: Harris Polls was hired to gather the opinion of registered voters regarding policies of the federal government. Two thousand registered voters were selected at random. Their opinions regarding our immigration policy, measures being taken to curb inflation, and other strategies were recorded.

Case 4: In a study of the migratory pattern of seals, 50 seals were tagged by marine biologists in California, and their movements were charted for a period of three years.

The cases have these common characteristics: (1) It would be very expensive, if not impossible, to contact all the registered voters in the United States, all the seals, and all the consumers. Further, checking all t he drawn wire produced at USX in a three-hour period for tensile strength would destroy it, and none would be available for sale! (2) Only a relatively small group was involved in each study. Only five pieces of wire were tested, only 50 seals tagged, and so on.

The cases illustrate one way to evaluate the quality of steel wire and the opinions of consumers about a product—namely, to take a *sample* from the *population* of interest. In Chapter 1 we noted that a *sample is a part of the population.* The populations in these cases are all the seals in the ocean, all the registered voters in the United States, all the adult consumers, and all the wire drawn in a three-hour period. Note that the population might be persons, objects, or other phenomena of interest. Making general conclusions about the entire group (the *population*) based on statistical information obtained from a small group (the *sample*) is called **statistical inference.** For example, finding that all five pieces of wire tested for tensile strength did not meet specifications, the quality-control inspector would conclude that production during the three-hour period was not satisfactory. If 403 of the 452 consumers in the sample *disliked* the new scent of Ivory, no doubt Lever Bros. would not manufacture or market the soap!

Making decisions based on incomplete information is not new. For centuries wine tasters, for example, have made predictions about the vintage based on a few sips. Many shoppers purchase a pizza at the grocery store after sampling a small wedge. (The inference is that if the small sample tastes good, the whole pizza will taste equally good.) In industry, a random sample of 50 ball bearings might result in an inference (generalization) that 5 percent of all ball bearings produced are defective. Similarly, an inventory of a few items in a department store might result in a prediction that if the present security measures remain unchanged, 8 percent of the stock will be stolen during the month. In medicine, a sample of blood might result in an inference that the patient is anemic.

This chapter will first explain why, in many cases, sampling may be the only logical way to find out something about a population. Then some of the basic methods of selecting a probability sample will be discussed. Then we will explain why sample statistics may differ from the corresponding population parameters. The central limit theorem, confidence intervals, and determining the required sample size are also covered in this chapter.

WHY SAMPLE THE POPULATION?

Why taking a sample from a population is often necessary

As noted previously, it is often not feasible to study the entire population. Some of the major reasons why sampling is necessary are:

1. **The destructive nature of certain tests.** If the wine tasters at the Sutter Home Winery in California drank all the wine to evaluate the vintage, they would consume the entire crop, and none would be available for sale. In the area of industrial production, steel plates, wires, and similar products must often have a certain minimum tensile strength. To ensure that the product meets the minimum standard, a relatively small sample is selected. Each piece is stretched until it breaks, and the breaking point (usually measured in pounds per square inch) is recorded. Obviously, if all the wire or all the plates were tested for tensile strength, none would be available for sale or use. For the same reason, only a sample of photographic film is selected to determine the quality of all the film produced, and only a few seeds are tested for germination by Burpee prior to the planting season.

2. **The physical impossibility of checking all items in the population.** The populations of fish, birds, snakes, mosquitoes, and the like are large and are constantly moving, being born, and dying. Instead of even attempting to count all the ducks in Canada or all the fish in Lake Erie, we make estimates using various techniques—such as counting all the ducks on a pond picked at random, making creel checks, or setting nets at predetermined places in the lake.

3. **The cost of studying all the items in a population is often prohibitive.** Public opinion polls and consumer testing organizations, such as Gallup Polls and Marketing Facts, located in Chicago, usually contact fewer than 2,000 families out of approximately 50 million families in the United States. One consumer panel-type organization charges about $40,000 to mail out samples and tabulate the responses in order to test a product (such as cereal, cat food, or perfume). The same product test using all 50 million families would cost about $1 billion.

4. **The adequacy of sample results.** Even if funds were available, it is doubtful whether the additional accuracy of a 100 percent sample—that is, studying the entire population—is essential in most problems. For example, the federal government uses a sample of grocery stores scattered throughout the United States to determine the monthly index of food prices. The prices of bread, beans, milk, and other major food items are included in the index. It is unlikely that the inclusion of all grocery stores in the United States would significantly affect the index, since the prices of milk, bread, and other major foods usually do not vary by more than a few cents from one chain store to another.

5. **To contact the whole population would often be time-consuming.** A candidate for a national office may wish to determine her chances for election. A sample poll using the regular staff and field interviews of a professional polling firm would take only one or two days. By using the same staff and interviewers and working seven days a week, it would take nearly 200 years to contact all the voting population!

Even if a large staff of interviewers could be assembled, the cost of contacting all of the voters would probably not be worth the expense. If the candidate were extremely popular, the sample poll might indicate that she would most certainly receive between 79 percent and 81 percent of the popular vote. The additional expense and time needed to find out that she might receive exactly 80 percent of the popular vote does not seem justified.

WHAT IS A PROBABILITY SAMPLE?

In general, there are two types of samples: a probability sample and a nonprobability sample. What is a probability sample?

> **Probability sample** A sample selected in such a way that each item or person in the population being studied has a known (nonzero) likelihood of being included in the sample.

Nonprobability sample: Results may be biased

If probability sampling is done, each item in the population has a chance of being chosen. If **nonprobability methods** are used, not all items or people have a chance of being included in the sample. In such instances the results may be **biased,** meaning that the sample results may not be representative of the population. Panel sampling and convenience sampling are two nonprobability methods. For example, a panel may consist of 2,000 cat owners or mothers of new babies. The panel is formed to solicit opinions on a newly developed cat food or a disposable baby diaper. Selection of panel members is based on the judgment of the person conducting the research, and the sample results may therefore not be representative of the entire population of cat owners or new mothers (since not all cat owners or all new mothers have a chance of being chosen). The statistical procedures used in this text to evaluate sample results are based on probability sampling. Therefore, only the methods of probability sampling will be discussed in the following section.

METHODS OF PROBABILITY SAMPLING

There is no one "best" method of selecting a probability sample from a population of interest. A method used to select a sample of invoices in a file drawer might not be the most appropriate method for choosing a national sample of voters. However, all probability sampling methods have a similar goal, namely, *to allow chance to determine the items or persons to be included in the sample.* The first method presented is **simple random sampling.**

Simple Random Sampling

Simple random sample

> **Simple random sample** A sample formulated so that each item or person in the population has the same chance of being included.

To illustrate simple random sampling and selection, suppose a population consists of 845 employees of Nitra Industries. A sample of 52 employees is to be selected from that population. One way of ensuring that every employee in the population has a chance of being chosen is to first write the name of each one on a small slip of paper and deposit all of the slips in a box. After they have been thoroughly mixed, the first selection is made. This process is repeated until the sample of size 52 is chosen.

Table of random numbers: Efficient way to select members of the sample

A more convenient method of selecting a random sample is to use the identification number of each employee and a **table of random numbers** such as the one in Appendix E. As the name implies, these numbers have been generated by a random process (in this case, by a computer). For each digit of a number, the probability of 0, 1, 2, . . . , 9 is the same. Thus, the probability that employee number 011 will be selected is the same as for employee 722 or employee 382. Bias is eliminated from the selection process.

A portion of a table of random numbers is shown in the following illustration. To use such a table to select a sample of employees you must first choose a starting point in the table. Any starting point will do. Suppose the time is 3:04. You might look at the third column and then move down to the fourth set of numbers. The number is 03759. Since there are only 845 employees, we will use the first three digits of a five-digit random number. Thus, 037 is the number of the first employee to be a member of the sample. To continue selecting employees, you could move in any direction. Suppose you decide to move right. The first three digits of the number to the right of 03759 are 447—the number of the employee selected to be the second member of the sample. The next three-digit number to the right is 961. You cannot use 961 because there are only 845 employees. You continue to the right and select employee 784, then 189, and so on. Another way of selecting the starting point is to close your eyes and point at a number in the table.

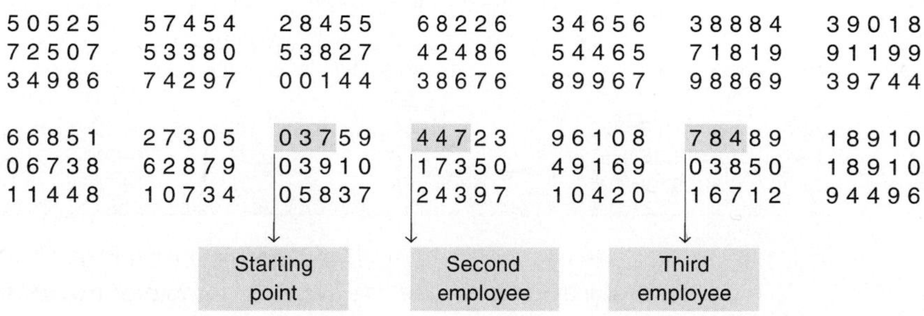

50525	57454	28455	68226	34656	38884	39018
72507	53380	53827	42486	54465	71819	91199
34986	74297	00144	38676	89967	98869	39744
66851	27305	03759	44723	96108	78489	18910
06738	62879	03910	17350	49169	03850	18910
11448	10734	05837	24397	10420	16712	94496

A study conducted by Marion Bryson and Robert Mason[1] further illustrates the use of a table of random numbers and simple random sampling.

> Located in 18 warehouses on a U.S. Army ordnance depot were 186,810 different ordnance items such as tires, nuts, bolts, tank treads, and tire irons. In each warehouse there were bays, and in each bay there were bins. For example, in warehouse 17 motor vehicle parts were stored. Bay 260, bin 2, contained Jeep cranks. Bay 260, bin 3, had Jeep radiator caps.
>
> The problem involved selecting a bin at random from a warehouse and counting all the items found in the bin. This physical count was compared with the count that computer inventory records indicated should be on hand. Thus, the problem was essentially a physical inventory problem involving sampling methods. The objective of the research project was to determine how accurate the computer records were.
>
> To ensure that each bin had an equal chance of being selected, a table of random numbers was used to choose the warehouse, bay, and bin.
>
> If warehouse 5, bay 455, and bin 6 were selected, a checker went to that location and counted the number of items in that bin.

Using a table of random numbers to prevent bias

Why was such a time-consuming method used to select the bins to sample? The alternative would have been to allow the checkers to count the items in any bins they wished. No doubt the checkers would have avoided counting the items in bins containing heavy or greasy parts. And they probably would have shunned the top bins, 20 feet from the floor of a warehouse. The omission of the items in these bins from this physical inventory research project might have biased the results—that is, their omission might have given a false picture of the accuracy of the computer records.

SELF-REVIEW 8–1

The answers are at the end of the chapter.

Following and on the top of the next page is the class roster for an introductory course in business statistics. Three students are to be randomly selected and asked various questions regarding course content and method of instruction.

1. The numbers 00 through 45 are handwritten on slips of paper and placed in a bowl. The three numbers selected were 31, 7, and 25. Which students would be included in the sample?
2. Now use the table of random digits, Appendix E, to select your own sample.
3. What would you do if you encountered the number 59 in the table of random digits?

CSPM 264 01 BUSINESS & ECONOMIC STAT

8:00 AM 9:40 AM MW ST 118 LIND D

RANDOM NUMBER	NAME	CLASS RANK	RANDOM NUMBER	NAME	CLASS RANK
00	SPILLSON, JOHN	SO	04	BOBAK, JAMES PATRICK	SO
01	ANGER, CHERYL RENEE	SO	05	BRIGHT, M. STARR	JR
02	BALL, CLAIRE JEANETTE	FR	06	CHONTOS, PAUL JOSEPH	SO
03	BERRY, CHRISTOPHER G	FR	07	DETLEV, BRIAN HANS	JR

[1]Office of Ordnance Research, *Physical Inventory Accounting Program,* Technical Report Number 1.

RANDOM NUMBER	NAME	CLASS RANK	RANDOM NUMBER	NAME	CLASS RANK
08	DUDAS, VIOLA	SO	27	NICHOLAS, ROBERT CHARLES	JR
09	DULBS, RICHARD ZALFA	JR	28	NICKENS, VIRGINIA	SO
10	EDINGER, SUSAN KEE	SR	29	PENNYWITT, SEAN PATRICK	SO
11	FINK, FRANK JAMES	SR	30	POTEAU, KRIS E	JR
12	FRANCIS, JAMES P	JR	31	PRICE, MARY LYNETTE	SO
13	GAGHEN, PAMELA LYNN	JR	32	RISTAS, JAMES	SR
14	GOULD, ROBYN KAY	SO	33	SAGER, ANNE MARIE	SO
15	GROSENBACHER, SCOTT ALAN	SO	34	SMILLIE, HEATHER MICHELLE	SO
16	HEETFIELD, DIANE MARIE	SO	35	SNYDER, LEISHA KAY	SR
17	KABAT, JAMES DAVID	JR	36	STAHL, MARIA TASHERY	SO
18	KEMP, LISA ADRIANE	FR	37	ST. JOHN, AMY J	SO
19	KILLION, MICHELLE A	SO	38	STURDEVANT, RICHARD R	SO
20	KOPERSKI, MARY ELLEN	SO	39	SWETYE, LYNN MICHELE	SO
21	KOPP, BRIDGETTE ANN	SO	40	WALASINSKI, MICHAEL	SO
22	LEHMANN, KRISTINA MARIE	JR	41	WALKER, DIANE ELAINE	SO
23	MEDLEY, CHERYL ANN	SO	42	WARNOCK, JENNIFER MARY	SO
24	MITCHELL, GREG R	FR	43	WILLIAMS, WENDY A	SO
25	MOLTER, KRISTI MARIE	SO	44	YAP, HOCK BAN	SO
26	MULCAHY, STEPHEN ROBERT	SO	45	YODER, ARLAN JAY	JR

Systematic Random Sampling

Systematic random sample: First sample member chosen at random

The simple random sampling procedure may be awkward to use in certain research situations. For example, suppose that the population of interest consists of 2,000 invoices located in file drawers. Drawing a simple random sample would first require numbering the invoices from 0000 to 1999. Using a table of random numbers, a sample of, say, 100 numbers would then have to be selected. An invoice to match each of these 100 numbers would have to be located in the file drawers. This would be a very time-consuming task. Instead, a **systematic random sample** could be selected by simply going through the file drawers and selecting every 20th invoice for study. The first invoice would be chosen using a random process—a table of random numbers, for example. If the 10th invoice were chosen, the sample would consist of the 10th, 30th, 50th, 70th, . . . invoices.

Members of sample chosen systematically

> **Systematic random sample** The items or individuals of the population are arranged in some way—alphabetically, in a file drawer by date received, or by some other method. A random starting point is selected, and then every *k*th member of the population is selected for the sample.

A systematic sample should not be used, however, if there is a predetermined pattern to the population. For example, in the physical inventory study mentioned previously, some of the warehouses in the ordnance depot have bays six bins high. In the bottom row of bins are fast-moving ordnance items, such as grease, touch-up spray paint, and hardware. These items are stored on the floor-level bins to speed the work of the pickers who must fill the requisitions. In the top row of bins are slow-moving items, such as tire rims, half-track treads, and firing pins. The middle four rows are stocked with moderately fast-moving items, such as tires, headlights, and cotter pins. If a systematic sample is used to check the inventory, then it is quite possible that a biased sample will be selected. Suppose the sampling procedure called for a selection of every third bin, and bin 1 is selected first. Then bins 1, 4, 7, 10, 13, 16, 19 and 22 would be selected systematically.

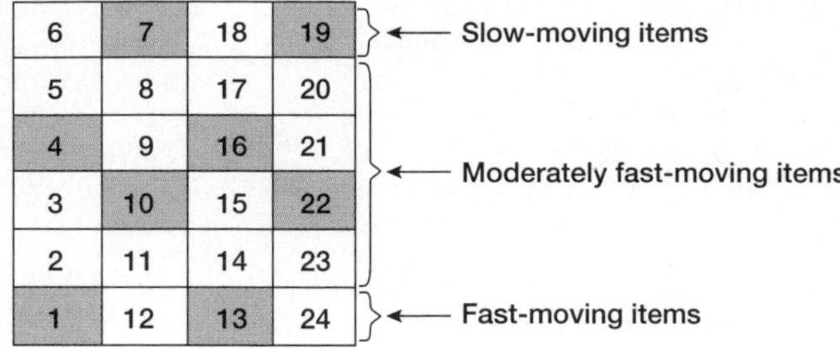

A systematic sample may produce biased results

The systematic procedure automatically selected 4 bins filled with moderately fast-moving items and a total of 4 bins filled with either fast-moving or slow-moving items. This 50-50 division of the sample does not coincide with the actual population characteristics. The population consists of 16 bins of moderately fast-moving items, 4 bins of fast-moving items, and 4 bins of slow-moving items. The sample results would undoubtedly be biased toward the slow- and fast-moving items.

SELF-REVIEW 8–2

The answers are at the end of the chapter.

Refer to Self-Review 8–1. Suppose the sample is to consist of every ninth student enrolled in the class. Initially, the fourth student down on the list was selected at random. That student is numbered 03. Remembering that the random numbers start with 00, which students will be chosen to be members of the sample?

EXERCISES

The answers to the odd-numbered exercises are at the end of the book.

1. The following is a list of Marco's Pizza stores in Lucas County. Also noted is whether the store is corporate-owned (C) or manager-owned (M). A sample of four locations is to be selected and inspected for customer convenience, safety, cleanliness, and other features.
   a. The random numbers selected are 08, 18, 11, 54, 02, 41, and 54. Which stores are selected?
   b. Use a table of random numbers to select your own sample of four locations.

Random number	Marco's Pizza store	Ownership type	Random number	Marco's Pizza store	Ownership type
00	2607 Starr Av	C	12	2040 Ottawa River Rd	C
01	309 W Alexis Rd	C	13	2116 N Reynolds Rd	C
02	2652 W Central Av	C	14	3678 Rugby Dr	C
03	630 Dixie Hwy	M	15	1419 South Av	C
04	3510 Dorr St	C	16	1234 W Sylvania Av	C
05	5055 Glendale Av	C	17	4624 Woodville Rd	M
06	3382 Lagrange St	M	18	5155 S Main	M
07	2525 W Laskey Rd	C	19	106 E Airport Hwy	C
08	303 Louisiana Av	C	20	6725 W Central & McCord	M
09	149 Main St	C	21	4252 Monroe	C
10	835 S McCord Rd	M	22	2036 Woodville Rd	C
11	3501 Monroe St	M	23	1316 Michigan Av	M

2. The following is a list of the Wendy's Old Fashioned Hamburgers store locations in the Cordon metropolitan area. Also noted is whether the location has a salad bar.
   a. A sample of five locations is to be randomly selected and inspected by the corporate quality-assurance department. The random numbers obtained were 09, 16, 00, 49, 54, 12, and 04. What locations are included in the sample?
   b. Use a table of random numbers to develop your own sample of five locations.

Random number	Wendy's Old Fashioned Hamburgers store	Salad bar	Random number	Wendy's Old Fashioned Hamburgers store	Salad bar
00	5555 Airport Hwy	S	09	3124 Monroe St	S
01	6525 Airport Hwy	S	10	27393 Helen Dr	NS
02	5166 Airport Hwy at Reynolds Rd	NS	11	4277 Monroe St	S
03	E Alexis Rd & Telegraph Rd	S	12	5804 Monroe	S
04	2124 W Alexis Rd	S	13	2866 Navarre Av	S
05	5560 W. Central Av	S	14	3435 Secor Rd	NS
06	914 Conant St	NS	15	1109 South Av	NS
07	3454 Dorr St	S	16	3465 Stickney Av	S
08	Front St & Main St	S	17	1945 Woodville Rd	S

3. Refer to Exercise 1, regarding the Marco's Pizza locations. A sample is to consist of every seventh location. The number 03 is selected as the starting point. Which locations will be contacted?
4. Refer to Exercise 2, regarding the Wendy's locations. A sample is to consist of every fifth location. A random starting point of 02 is selected. Which stores are included in the sample?

Stratified Random Sampling

Another type of probability sampling is referred to as **stratified random sampling.**

> **Stratified random sample** A population is first divided into subgroups, called strata, and a sample is selected from each stratum.

Stratified sample guarantees representation of each subgroup

After the population has been divided into strata, either a *proportional* or a *non-proportional* sample can be selected. As the name implies, a proportional sampling procedure requires that the number of items in each stratum be in the same proportion as found in the population. For instance, the problem might be to study the advertising expenditures of the 352 largest companies in the United States. Suppose that the objective of the study is to determine whether firms with high returns on equity (a measure of profitability) spent more or less of each sales dollar on advertising than firms with a low return or a deficit. Assume that the 352 firms were divided into five strata. (See Table 8–1.) If, say, 50 firms are to be selected for intensive study, then 1 firm with a level of profitability of 30 percent or more would be studied, 5 firms in the 20–30 percent stratum would be selected at random, and so on.

TABLE 8–1 Number Sampled for a Proportional Stratified Random Sample

Stratum	Profitability (return on equity)	Number of firms	Percent of total	Number sampled
1	30 percent and over	8	2	1*
2	20 up to 30 percent	35	10	5*
3	10 up to 20 percent	189	54	27
4	0 up to 10 percent	115	33	16
5	Deficit	5	1	1
Total		352	100	50

*2 percent of 50 = 1; 10 percent of 50 = 5; etc.

In a *nonproportional* stratified sample, the number of items studied in each stratum is disproportionate to the respective numbers in the population. We then weight the sample results according to the stratum's proportion of the total population. For example, if nonproportional sampling were used in the preceding case, we would weight the results of stratum 1 by 2/100, stratum 2 by 10/100, stratum 3 by 54/100, and so on. Regardless of whether a proportional or a nonproportional sampling procedure is used, every item or person in the population has a chance of being selected for the sample.

Stratified sampling has the advantage, in some cases, of more accurately reflecting the characteristics of the population than does simple random or systematic random sampling. Note in Table 8–1 that 2 percent of the firms have a return on equity of 30 percent or more (stratum 1), and 1 percent have a deficit (stratum 5). If a simple random sample of 50 were taken, we might not *by chance* select any firms in stratum 1 or 5. A stratified random sample, however, would ensure that at least one firm in stratum 1 and one firm in stratum 5 are represented in the sample.

EXERCISES

The answers to the odd-numbered exercises are at the end of the book.

5. Refer to Exercise 1, regarding Marco's Pizza. Suppose a sample is to consist of three locations, of which two are corporate-owned and one is manager-owned. Select a sample accordingly.
6. Refer to Exercise 2, regarding Wendy's. A sample of four restaurants is to consist of three locations with salad bars (S) and one without a salad bar (NS). Select the sample accordingly.

Cluster Sampling

Cluster sampling reduces sampling cost

Another common type of sampling is **cluster sampling.** It is often employed to reduce the cost of sampling a population scattered over a large geographic area. Suppose you want to conduct a survey to determine the views of industrialists in the state with respect to state and federal environmental protection policies. Selecting a random sample of industrialists in the state and personally contacting each one would be time-consuming and very expensive. Instead, you could employ cluster sampling by subdividing the state into small units—either counties or regions. These are often called *primary units.* Suppose you divided the state into 12 primary units, then selected at random four regions—2, 7, 4, and 12—and concentrated your efforts in these primary units. You could take a random sample of the industrialists in each of these regions and interview them. (Note that this is a combination of cluster sampling and simple random sampling.)

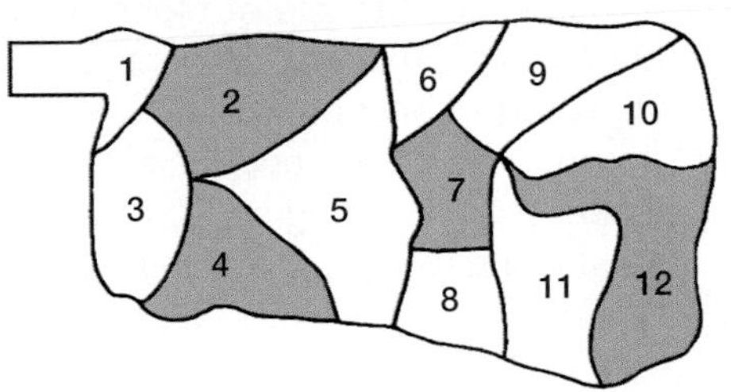

Many other sampling methods

The discussion of sampling methods in the preceding sections did not include all the sampling methods available to a researcher. Should you become involved in a major research project in marketing, finance, accounting, or other areas, you would need to consult books devoted solely to sample theory and sample design.

SAMPLING ERROR

The previous discussion stressed the importance of selecting a sample so that every item or individual in the population has a chance of being selected. To accomplish this, we could choose a simple random sample, a systematic sample, a stratified sample, a cluster sample, or a combination of these methods. Logically, it is unlikely that the mean of a sample taken from a population would be *identical* to the population mean. Likewise, the sample standard deviation or other measure computed from a sample would probably not be *exactly* equal to the corresponding population value. We can therefore expect some difference between a *sample statistic,* such as the sample mean or sample standard deviation, and the corresponding *population parameter.* The difference between a sample statistic and a population parameter is called the **sampling error.**

Sampling error defined

> **Sampling error** The difference between a sample statistic and its corresponding population parameter.

Suppose a population of five production employees had efficiency ratings of 97, 103, 96, 99, and 105. Further suppose that a sample of two ratings—97 and 105—was selected from that population to estimate the population mean rating. The mean of that sample would be 101, found by $(97 + 105)/2$. Another sample of two is selected: 103 and 96, with a sample mean of 99.5. The mean of all the ratings (the population mean) is 100, found by: $(97 + 103 + 96 + 99 + 105)/5 = 500/5 = 100.0$. The sampling error for the first sample is 1.0, determined by $\bar{X} - \mu = 101 - 100$. The second sample has a sampling error of -0.5. Each of these differences, 1.0 and

−0.5, is the error that would be made in estimating the population mean based on a sample mean, and these sampling errors are due to chance.

Now that we have discovered the possibility of a sampling error when sample results are used to estimate a population parameter, how can the marketing research department make an accurate prediction about the possible success of a newly developed toothpaste or other product, based only on sample results? How can the quality-assurance department in a mass-production firm release a shipment of microchips based only on a sample of 10 chips? How can Gallup or Harris polls make an accurate prediction about a presidential race based on a sample of 2,000 registered voters out of a voting population of nearly 90 million? To answer these questions, we must first develop a *sampling distribution of the sample means.*

SAMPLING DISTRIBUTION OF THE SAMPLE MEANS

Sample means vary from sample to sample

The efficiency rating example showed how the means for samples of a specified size vary from sample to sample. The mean efficiency rating of the first sample of two employees was 101, and the second sample mean was 99.5. A third sample would probably result in a different mean. The population mean was 100. If we organized the means of all possible samples of size 2 into a probability distribution, we would obtain the **sampling distribution of the sample means.**

Sampling distribution defined

> **Sampling distribution of the sample means** A probability distribution consisting of all possible sample means of a given sample size selected from a population, and the probability of occurrence associated with each sample mean.

The following example illustrates the construction of a sampling distribution of the sample means.

EXAMPLE

Tartus Industries has seven production employees (considered the population). The hourly earnings of each employee are given in Table 8–2.

TABLE 8–2 **Hourly Earnings of the Production Employees of Tartus Industries**

Employee	Hourly earnings
Joe	$7
Sam	7
Sue	8
Bob	8
Jan	7
Art	8
Ted	9

Suppose that all possible samples of size 2 were selected from the population

1. What is the population mean?
2. What is the sampling distribution of the sample means for a sample of size 2?

3. What is the mean of the sampling distribution?
4. What observations can be made with respect to the population and the sampling distribution?

Solution ▶

1. The population mean is \$7.7143, found by:

$$\mu = \frac{\$7 + \$7 + \$8 + \$8 + \$7 + \$8 + \$9}{7}$$

2. To arrive at the sampling distribution of the sample means, all possible samples of size 2 were selected without replacement from the population, and their means were computed. There are 21 possible samples, found by using formula (5–11) on page 201.

$$_{N}C_{n} = \frac{N!}{n!(N-n)!} = \frac{7!}{2!(7-2)!} = 21$$

where $N = 7$ is the number of items in the population and $n = 2$ is the number of items in the sample.

The 21 distinct sample means from all possible samples of size 2 that can be drawn from the population are shown in Table 8–3. This probability distribution is the sampling distribution of the sample means and is summarized in Table 8–4.

TABLE 8–3 **Sample Means for All Possible Samples of Size 2**

Sample	Employees	Hourly earnings	Sum	Mean
1	Joe, Sam	\$7, \$7	\$14	\$7.00
2	Joe, Sue	7, 8	15	7.50
3	Joe, Bob	7, 8	15	7.50
4	Joe, Jan	7, 7	14	7.00
5	Joe, Art	7, 8	15	7.50
6	Joe, Ted	7, 9	16	8.00
7	Sam, Sue	7, 8	15	7.50
8	Sam, Bob	7, 8	15	7.50
9	Sam, Jan	7, 7	14	7.00
10	Sam, Art	7, 8	15	7.50
11	Sam, Ted	7, 9	16	8.00
12	Sue, Bob	8, 8	16	8.00
13	Sue, Jan	8, 7	15	7.50
14	Sue, Art	8, 8	16	8.00
15	Sue, Ted	8, 9	17	8.50
16	Bob, Jan	8, 7	15	7.50
17	Bob, Art	8, 8	16	8.00
18	Bob, Ted	8, 9	17	8.50
19	Jan, Art	7, 8	15	7.50
20	Jan, Ted	7, 9	16	8.00
21	Art, Ted	8, 9	17	8.50

TABLE 8–4 **Sampling Distribution of the Sample Means for $n = 2$**

Sample mean	Number of means	Probability
$7.00	3	.1429
7.50	9	.4285
8.00	6	.2857
8.50	3	.1429
	21	1.0000

3. The mean of the distribution of sample means is obtained by summing the various sample means and dividing the sum by the number of samples. The mean of all the sample means is usually written, $\mu_{\bar{X}}$. The μ reminds us that it is a population value, because we have considered all possible samples. The subscript $\bar{X}$ indicates that it is a sampling distribution of means.

$$\mu_{\bar{X}} = \frac{\text{Sum of all sample means}}{\text{Total number of samples}} = \frac{\$7.00 + \$7.50 + \cdots + \$8.50}{21}$$

$$= \frac{\$162}{21} = \$7.7143$$

Refer to Chart 8–1.

CHART 8–1 **Population Values and Sample Means**

Population mean is equal to the mean of the sample means

Sample means approximate a normal distribution

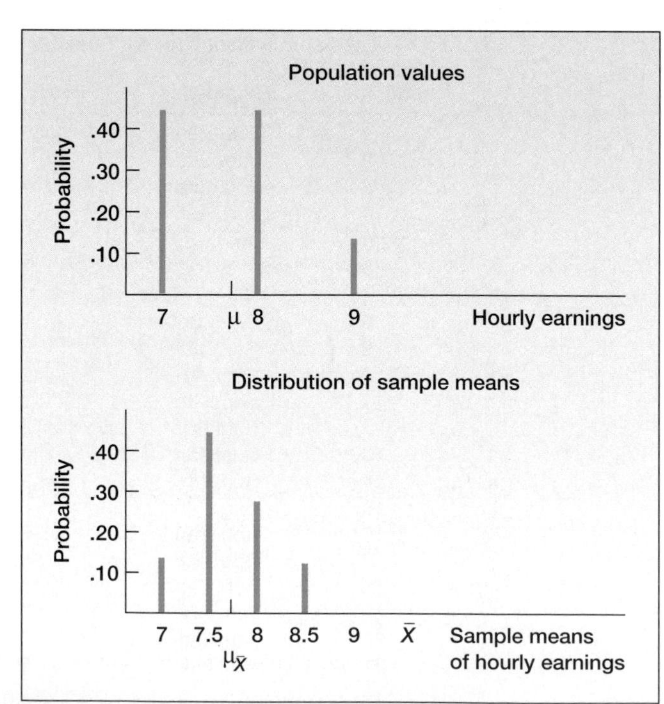

4. These observations can be made:
   a. The mean of the sample means ($7.7143) is equal to the mean of the population: $\mu = \mu_{\bar{X}}$. This is always true if all possible samples of a given size are selected from the population of interest.
   b. Note from Chart 8–1 that the dispersion in the distribution of sample means is less than the dispersion in the population. The sample means vary from $7.00 to $8.50, whereas the population values vary from $7.00 to $9.00.
   c. The graph representing the distribution of the population and that of the sample means show the change in shape from the population to the sample.

SELF-REVIEW 8–3

The answers are at the end of the chapter.

The lengths of service of all the executives employed by Standard Chemicals are:

Name	Years
Mr. Snow	20
Ms. Tolson	22
Mr. Kraft	26
Ms. Irwin	24
Mr. Jones	28

1. Using the combination formula, how many samples of size 2 are possible?
2. Select all possible samples of size 2 from the population, and compute their means.
3. Organize the means into a sampling distribution.
4. Compare the population mean and the mean of the sample means.
5. Compare the dispersion in the population with that of the distribution of sample means.
6. Following is a chart portraying the population values. Is the distribution of population values normally distributed (bell-shaped) or is it nonnormal?

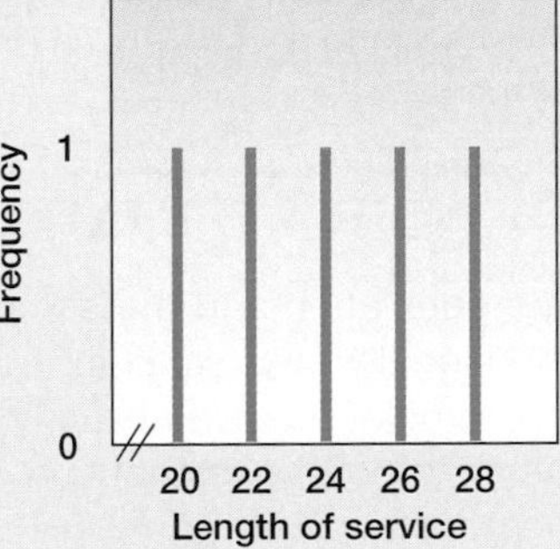

7. Is the distribution of sample means computed in Question 3 starting to show some tendency toward being bell-shaped?

EXERCISES

The answers to the odd-numbered exercises are at the end of the book.

7. A population consists of the following four values: 12, 12, 14, 16.
   a. How many samples of size 2 are possible?

b. List all possible samples of size 2, and compute the mean of each sample.
c. Compute the mean of the sample means and the population mean. Compare the two values.
d. Compare the dispersion in the population with that of the sample means.

8. A population consists of the following 5 values: 2, 2, 4, 4, 8.
   a. How many samples of size 2 are possible?
   b. List all possible samples of size 2, and compute the mean of each sample.
   c. Compute the mean of the sample means and the population mean. Compare the two values.
   d. Compare the dispersion in the population with that of the sample means.
9. In your "Introduction to College Mathematics" class last semester, the instructor gave four tests. You received scores of 90, 86, 70, and 80. Suppose the instructor offered you the option of randomly selecting two scores and basing your course grade on the mean of those two tests.
   a. How many different samples are possible?
   b. List all the possible samples, and compute the mean of each.
   c. Compare the mean of all the sample means with the mean of the population.
   d. Compare the dispersion of the sample means with that of the population by drawing a graph.
   e. Would you accept the instructor's grade offer? Explain.
10. There are five sales representatives at Mid-Motors Ford. Below are listed the five representatives and the number of cars they sold last week.

Sales representative	Cars sold
Pete Hankish	8
Connie Stallter	6
Ron Eaton	4
Ted Barnes	10
Peggy Harmon	6

   a. How many different samples of size 2 are possible?
   b. List all possible samples of size 2, and compute the mean of each sample.
   c. Compare the mean of the sample means with that of the population.
   d. On a chart similar to Chart 8–1, compare the dispersion of the sample means with that of the population.

CENTRAL LIMIT THEOREM

The population and the sample size in the preceding example and self-review were intentionally kept small in order to emphasize two concepts: first, that the mean of the sample means is exactly equal to the mean of the population, and second, that the shape of the distribution of sample means is not necessarily the same as that of the population.

- Refer to Chart 8–1. Notice the shape of the population compared with that of the sampling distribution of the means. The sampling distribution of the means more closely approximates the normal distribution.

If the population is not normally distributed, the sampling distribution will be somewhat normal

- Refer to Self-Review 8–3, where the lengths of service of executives at Standard Chemicals were reported. The sampling distribution of the means moves toward a normal distribution from a uniform distribution. See the comparison below.

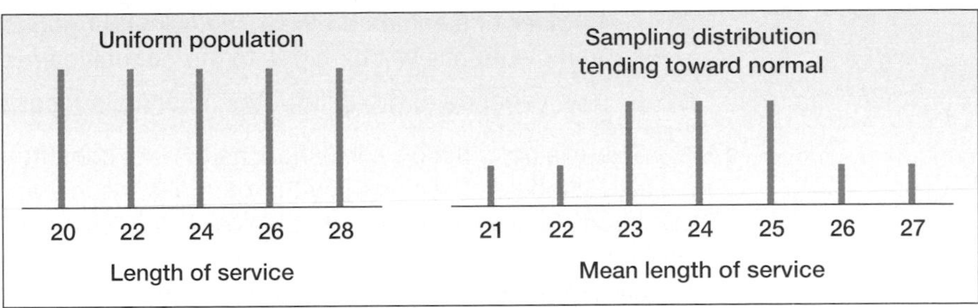

If population is normally distributed, so is the distribution of sample means

- If the population itself is normally distributed, the sampling distribution of the sample means is also normally distributed. To explain, the distribution below on the left depicts the hourly earnings of all production employees at Fulton Industries. Note that the earnings are normally distributed. Samples of size 4 were selected from this population and the mean of each sample computed. Notice that the sampling distribution of the sample means on the right is also normally distributed.

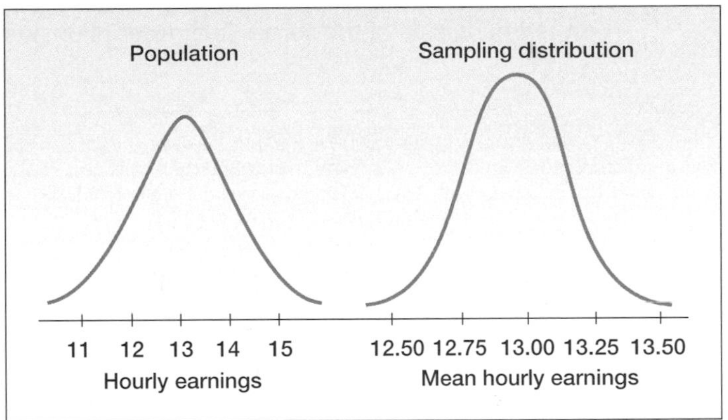

Why is this tendency toward the normal distribution so important? This is the basis of the **central limit theorem,** one of the most important theorems in statistics.

> **Central limit theorem** For a population with a mean μ and a variance σ^2, the sampling distribution of the means of all possible samples of size *n* generated from the population will be approximately normally distributed—with the mean of the sampling distribution equal to μ and the variance equal to σ^2/n—assuming that the sample size is sufficiently large.

The important facets of the central limit theorem bear repeating:

1. If the sample size *n* is sufficiently large, the sampling distribution of the sample means will be approximately normal. This is true whether or not the population is normally distributed. That is, whether the population is normally distributed, skewed, or uniform, the theorem will apply.
2. As shown earlier, the mean of the population, μ, and the mean of all possible sample means, $\mu_{\bar{X}}$, are equal. If the population is large and a large

number of samples are selected from that population, then the mean of the sample means will be close to the population mean.

3. The variance of the distribution of sample means is determined by σ^2/n.

There is no common agreement as to what constitutes a "sufficiently large" sample size. Some statisticians say 30; others go as low as 12. The example concerning the hourly earnings of all the employees at Tartus Industries given in Table 8–2 worked quite well with a sample of 2. However, unless the population is approximately normal, such small sample sizes generally do not result in a sampling distribution that is normal. As the sample size becomes larger and larger, however, the distribution of the sample means becomes closer and closer to the bell-shaped normal distribution.

Computer Simulation 1

A computer simulation will be used to illustrate the central limit theorem. Chart 8–2 shows the graph of an exponential distribution developed with the following MINITAB commands. An exponential distribution is continuous, and it is positively skewed. The range of the values is from 1 to about 20, with the concentration of the data in the left-hand side of the curve. The distribution has a mean of 5.

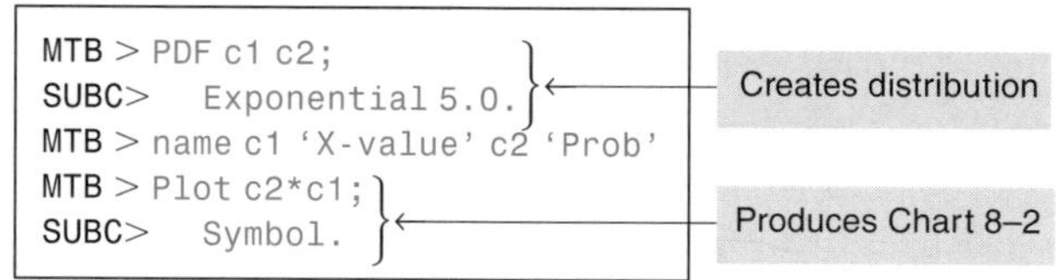

CHART 8–2 **Exponential Distribution with a Mean of 5**

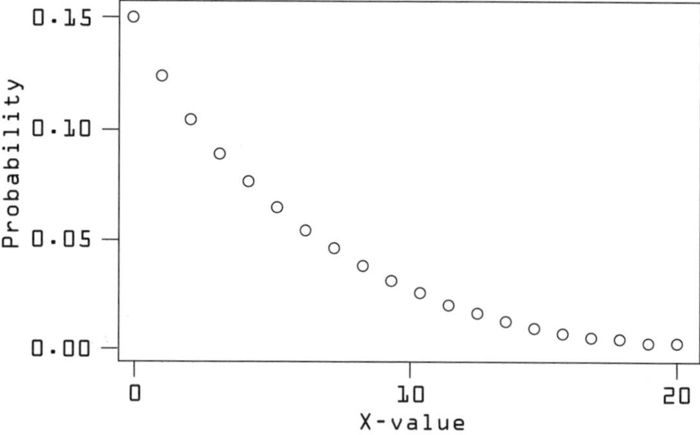

Using the MINITAB statistical software system, 50 random samples of size 10 were selected and the mean of each sample computed. The 50 sample means are summarized in a histogram, in Chart 8–3. The sample means range from 2.683 up to 8.467 (as indicated in the data below the chart). The shape of the sampling distribution as shown in the histogram is approaching normal. The mean of the 50 samples of size 10 is 4.787, which is close to the population mean of 5.00.

CHART 8–3 Sampling Distribution of the Means for 50 Samples of Size 10

```
MTB > random 50 c1-c10;
SUBC> exponential b=5.
MTB > rmean c1-c10 c11
MTB > name c11 'S-Mean'
MTB > hist c11
Histogram of S-Mean   N = 50
Midpoint  Count
     2.5      1  *
     3.0      3  ***
     3.5     10  **********
     4.0      3  ***
     4.5     10  **********
     5.0      7  *******
     5.5      4  ****
     6.0      4  ****
     6.5      5  *****
     7.0      1  *
     7.5      0
     8.0      1  *
     8.5      1  *
MTB > describe c11
              N    MEAN   MEDIAN   TRMEAN   STDEV   SEMEAN
S-Mean       50   4.787    4.608    4.709   1.291    0.183
            MIN     MAX       Q1       Q3
S-Mean    2.683   8.467    3.673    5.660
```

Computer simulation: Exponential distribution with mean of 5, 50 samples of size 10

Refer to the population in Chart 8–2. We will again take 50 random samples from that skewed population, but this time each sample will consist of 30 observations. The sample means are plotted in the form of a MINITAB histogram in Chart 8–4. Notice that the minimum and maximum values for the means of samples of size 30 are closer to the population mean than those for the samples of size 10 in Chart 8–3. Note too that the shape of the sampling distribution in Chart 8–4 on the top of the following page is more nearly normal, and the mean of the sample means is 5.159. Most important is that as the sample size increases (from 10 to 30) in this computer simulation, the distribution of sample means becomes more and more normal despite the fact that the population is highly skewed.

Computer Simulation 2

The preceding simulation dealt with a skewed population. We pointed out that as the size of a sample taken from a skewed distribution becomes larger and larger, the sampling distribution of the sample means tends toward a normal distribution.

What about a normal population? Chart 8–5 at the bottom of page 312 depicts a normal distribution. This population has a mean of 50 and a standard deviation of 5. The population ranges from about 32 to 72.

CHART 8–4 Sampling Distribution of the Means for 50 Samples of Size 30

Computer simulation: Exponential distribution with mean of 5, 50 samples of size 30

```
MTB > random 50 c21-c50;
SUBC> exponential b=5.
MTB > rmean c21-c50 c51
MTB > name c51 'S-Mean1'
MTB > hist c51

Histogram of S-Mean1   N = 50
Midpoint  Count
     3.0      2  **
     3.5      3  ***
     4.0      2  **
     4.5      9  *********
     5.0      9  *********
     5.5     12  ************
     6.0      8  ********
     6.5      2  **
     7.0      3  ***

MTB > describe c51
               N    MEAN   MEDIAN  TRMEAN   STDEV  SEMEAN
S-Mean1       50   5.159    5.249   5.178   0.929   0.131
             MIN     MAX       Q1      Q3
S-Mean1    3.156   6.939    4.598   5.801
```

CHART 8–5 Normal Distribution with $\mu = 50$ and $\sigma = 5$

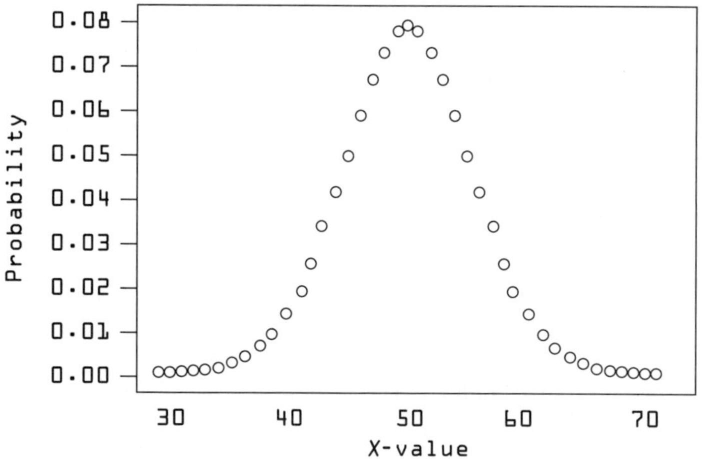

Fifty random samples of size 10 are selected from this population and the mean of each of the 50 samples computed. The sampling distribution of the means ranges from 45.628 to 52.965, and the sampling distribution, as shown in the histogram, appears normal. The mean of the sample means is 49.906, compared with the population value of 50. (See Chart 8–6 on the top of the following page.)

CHART 8–6 **Sampling Distribution of the Means for 50 Samples of Size 10, Normal Population**

```
MTB > random 50 c1-c10;
SUBC> normal mu=50 sigma=5.
MTB > rmean c1-c10 into c11
MTB > hist c11
Histogram of C11   N = 50
Midpoint  Count
      46      1  *
      47      4  ****
      48      5  *****
      49      9  *********
      50     10  **********
      51     10  **********
      52      9  *********
      53      2  **
MTB > describe c11
                  N     MEAN   MEDIAN   TRMEAN   STDEV  SEMEAN
S-Mean           50   49.906   50.176   49.956   1.769   0.250
                MIN      MAX       Q1       Q3
             45.628   52.965   48.680   51.416
```

Computer simulation: Normal population, $\mu = 50$, $\sigma = 5$, with samples of $n = 10$

When the sample size for this normal population is increased from 10 to 30, the sampling distribution of the means is even more nearly normal, the range is smaller, and the mean of the sample means is 50.009—even closer to the population mean. (See Chart 8–7.)

CHART 8–7 **Sampling Distribution of the Means for a Population, 50 Samples of Size 30**

```
MTB > random 50 c21-c50;
SUBC> normal mu=50 sigma=5.
MTB > rmean c21-c50 c51
MTB > hist c51
Histogram of C51   N = 50
Midpoint  Count
    48.5      1  *
    49.0      7  *******
    49.5     12  ************
    50.0      9  *********
    50.5     15  ***************
    51.0      4  ****
    51.5      1  *
    52.0      1  *
MTB > describe c51
                  N     MEAN   MEDIAN   TRMEAN   STDEV  SEMEAN
S-Mean           50   50.009   50.017   49.985   0.763   0.108
                MIN      MAX       Q1       Q3
             48.283   52.139   49.473   50.457
```

There are two very important observations evident from the computer simulations:

1. The shape of the sampling distribution of sample means approaches normal, regardless of the shape of the population.
2. The mean of the sample means is close to the mean of the population.

Central limit theorem: Foundation for estimation and hypothesis testing

The central limit theorem provides the theoretical foundation for statistical inference. Statistical inference is concerned with *estimation* (introduced in this chapter) and *hypothesis testing* (to be discussed starting with Chapter 9).

Managers in business, education, social work, and other fields make decisions without complete information. Automobile manufacturers do not know *exactly* how many people will purchase new cars next year. The college registrar does not know *exactly* how many students will enroll next fall. The sales manager for an automobile manufacturer, for example, must *estimate* the forthcoming sales of the new compact, the Firengia GT. She might estimate sales to be 325,000 units, but there is considerable uncertainty about consumer reaction to the GT's new styling, the economic climate of the United States and foreign countries, and what competitors will introduce. There are two kinds of estimates, *point estimates* and *interval estimates.*

POINT ESTIMATES AND INTERVAL ESTIMATES

Point Estimate

Point estimate defined

Fish and game wardens estimate the mean weight and other characteristics of the fish or game population by using creel checks and other devices. Based on these sample data, a warden might estimate that the mean weight of Coho salmon caught in Lake Michigan is 2½ pounds. A sample of five financial "experts" might result in an estimate of 5.2 percent yield on certificates of deposit by the year's end. These single numbers (2½ pounds and 5.2 percent) are estimates of an unknown population parameter and are called **point estimates.**

> **Point estimate** One value (called a *point*) that is used to estimate a population parameter.

Sample mean used as an estimate of population mean

The sample mean, $\overline{X}$, is the best estimator of the population mean, μ. Recall that the sample mean is computed by formula (3–2):

$$\overline{X} = \frac{\Sigma X}{n}$$

where X is the value of an observation and n is the total number of observations in the sample.

EXAMPLE

A study of the cold cranking power of 12-volt Longlast automobile batteries is to be conducted to estimate the number of times a 440-cubic-inch displacement engine will start before the battery fails. A sample of 40 randomly selected batteries revealed these numbers of starts:

26	27	26	20	21	42	30	22
22	21	26	9	21	22	28	26
19	16	20	32	18	23	32	28
21	41	19	31	21	22	16	23
30	21	37	28	39	30	21	23

What is the best estimate of the population mean number of starts?

Solution ▶ The sum of the 40 observations is 1,000. The mean number of starts before the battery fails is 25, found by

Best estimate of population mean is 25 starts

$$\overline{X} = \frac{\Sigma X}{n} = \frac{1{,}000}{40} = 25 \text{ starts}$$

So, the best estimate of μ, the unknown population mean, is the sample mean, which is 25.

$\overline{p}$: the sample proportion—a statistic

Likewise, the proportion of the population favoring more strict environmental protection measures can be estimated using a sample proportion. Letting p be the unknown population proportion and $\overline{p}$ be the sample proportion, the point estimate for the population proportion is:

$$\overline{p} = \frac{\text{Number of successes in sample}}{\text{Number sampled}}$$

$$= \frac{X}{n}$$

where X stands for the number of successes in the sample and n the total number sampled.

EXAMPLE

Of 2,000 persons sampled, 1,600 favored more strict environmental protection measures. What is the estimated population proportion?

Solution ▶

$$\overline{p} = \frac{\text{Number of successes in sample}}{\text{Number sampled}}$$

$$= \frac{1{,}600}{2{,}000} = .80$$

Eighty percent is an estimate of the proportion in the population who favor more strict measures.

In summary, based on the sampling distribution of the means and the central limit theorem, the sample mean can be used as a good estimator of the population mean. We assume, of course, that the size of the sample is sufficiently large. The same can be said for a population proportion (which is a special case of the sample mean), the population variance, the population standard deviation, and other population parameters. Each of these estimators is a point estimate.

Interval Estimate

We now turn to the other type of estimate, the **interval estimate.**

Interval estimate	States the range within which a population parameter probably lies.

Mean is in this interval

The interval within which a population parameter is expected to occur is called a **confidence interval.** For example, the confidence interval for the population mean is the interval that has a high probability of containing the population mean, μ. Two confidence intervals are used extensively: the 95 percent confidence interval and the 99 percent confidence interval. Other confidence intervals may also be used, such as 80 percent, 90 percent, or even a value such as 87.6 percent.

How do we interpret a 95 percent confidence interval, for example? A 95 percent confidence interval means that about 95 percent of the similarly constructed intervals will contain the parameter being estimated. If we use the 99 percent level of confidence, then we expect about 99 percent of the intervals to contain the parameter being estimated. Notice two important features of this definition. First, not *every* interval constructed includes the parameter. Second, if we construct 100 intervals and use the 95 percent level, not *exactly* 95 of the intervals will include the parameter.

Another interpretation of the 95 percent confidence interval is that 95 percent of the sample means for a specified sample size will lie within 1.96 standard deviations of the hypothesized population mean. Similarly, for a 99 percent confidence interval, 99 percent of the sample means will lie within 2.58 standard deviations of the hypothesized population mean.

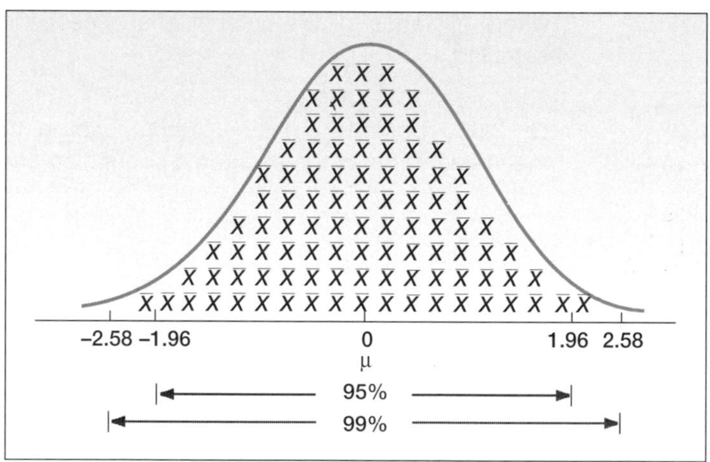

Where do the values 1.96 and 2.58 come from? The middle 95 percent of the sample means lie equally on either side of the mean and, logically, .95/2 = .4750, or 47.5 percent. Thus, the area to the right of the mean is .4750, and the area to the left of the mean is also .4750. Since these areas refer to the normal curve, we can use Appendix D to find the number of standard deviations (z values) from the mean. First, find .4750 in the body of Appendix D. Then move to the left margin and the appropriate column to find z. It is 1.96. The z to the right of the mean is designated as $+1.96$, and the z to the left is -1.96. Shown in a diagram:

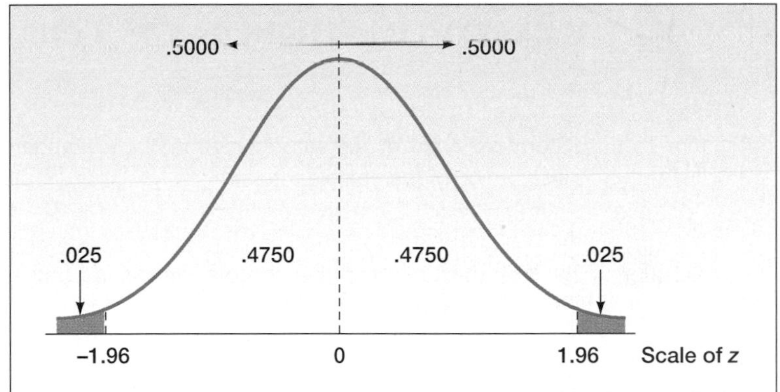

The same procedure is used to find the z of 2.58.

To expand on the confidence interval concept, suppose we had time to select 100 samples of size 256 from a population and we computed the sample means and confidence intervals for each sample. We would discover that about 95 of the 100 confidence intervals would contain the population mean, and about 5 of the intervals would not. Shown schematically:

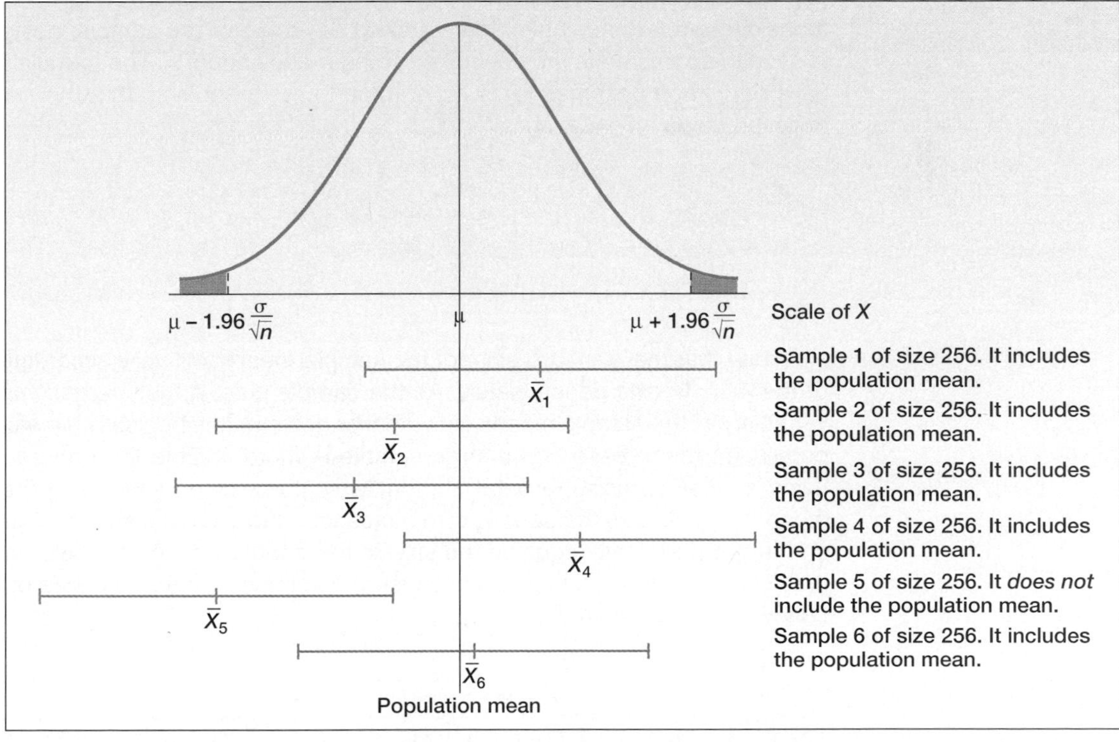

Of the intervals, 95 percent contain μ

How is a confidence interval constructed? First we need to compute the *standard error of the sample means.*

STANDARD ERROR OF THE SAMPLE MEANS

Standard error of the sample means defined

Standard error of the sample means The standard deviation of the sampling distribution of the sample means.

Formula for standard error of sample means

The standard error of the sample means is computed by:

$$\sigma_{\bar{x}} = \frac{\sigma}{\sqrt{n}} \qquad (8\text{–}1)$$

where:

$\sigma_{\bar{x}}$ is the symbol for the standard error of the sample means.

σ is the standard deviation of the population.

n is the size of the sample.

Formula (8–1) for the standard error of the sample means assumes that the population standard deviation, σ, is known. If it is not known and n = 30 or more (considered a large sample), the standard deviation of the sample, designated by s, is used to approximate the population standard deviation, σ. The formula for the standard error then becomes ($s_{\bar{x}}$ is substituted for $\sigma_{\bar{x}}$ to indicate that the standard error is based on sample statistics):

Alternative formula for standard error of sample means

$$s_{\bar{x}} = \frac{s}{\sqrt{n}} \qquad (8\text{–}2)$$

Note that the standard error of the sample means will vary according to the size of the sample (the denominator). As the sample size, n, gets larger and larger, the variability of the sample means gets smaller and smaller. Logically, an estimate of the population mean based on a large sample is more reliable than an estimate made using a small sample. To put it another way, the error in estimating the population mean decreases as the sample size increases. If the sample size kept getting larger and larger and finally equaled the size of the population, there would be no error in predicting the population mean because the sample size and the size of the population would be the same!

CONSTRUCTING THE 95 PERCENT AND THE 99 PERCENT CONFIDENCE INTERVALS

The 95 percent and the 99 percent confidence intervals are constructed as follows when $n \geq 30$.

95 percent confidence interval:

$$\bar{X} \pm 1.96\frac{s}{\sqrt{n}} \quad (8\text{–}3)$$

99 percent confidence interval:

$$\bar{X} \pm 2.58\frac{s}{\sqrt{n}} \quad (8\text{–}4)$$

As discussed earlier, the values 1.96 and 2.58 refer to the z values corresponding to the middle 95 percent or 99 percent of the observations.

Other levels of confidence can be used. For those cases, the z value changes accordingly. In general, a confidence interval for the mean is computed by:

$$\bar{X} \pm z\frac{s}{\sqrt{n}} \quad (8\text{–}5)$$

where z reflects the level of confidence. So if we want to construct the 92 percent confidence interval, the formula becomes

$$\bar{X} \pm 1.75\frac{s}{\sqrt{n}}$$

The value 1.75 is from Appendix D. The table is based on half the normal distribution, so .9200/2 = .4600. The closest number in the body of the table is .4599, and the corresponding z value is 1.75. Try looking up the following z values, and check your answers against those on the right.

Confidence interval	Closest number	z value
90 percent	.4505	1.65
96 percent	.4798	2.05

EXAMPLE

An experiment involves selecting a random sample of 256 middle managers for study. One item of interest is annual income. The sample mean is computed to be $45,420, and the sample standard deviation is $2,050.

1. What is the estimated mean income of all middle managers (the population)? That is, what is the point estimate?
2. What is the 95 percent confidence interval (rounded to the nearest $10)?
3. What are the 95 percent confidence limits?
4. What degree of confidence is being used?
5. Interpret the findings.

Solution ▶

1. The point estimate of the population mean is $45,420.
2. The confidence interval is between $45,170 and $45,670, found by:

Constructing the confidence interval

$$\overline{X} \pm 1.96 \frac{s}{\sqrt{n}} = \$45{,}420 \pm 1.96 \frac{\$2{,}050}{\sqrt{256}}$$
$$= \$45{,}420 \pm 251.125$$
$$= \$45{,}168.875 \text{ and } \$45{,}671.125$$

These endpoints are frequently rounded and, in this case, would be recorded as $45,170 and $45,670.

3. The endpoints of the confidence interval are called the *confidence limits.* In this example, $45,170 and $45,670 are the confidence limits.
4. The measure of confidence a person has is referred to as the *degree of confidence* or the *level of confidence.* In this case it is .95.
5. Interpretation: If we had time to select 100 samples of size 256 from the population of middle managers and compute the sample means and confidence intervals, the population mean annual income would be found in about 95 out of the 100 confidence intervals. Either an interval contains the population mean or it does not. About 5 out of the 100 confidence intervals would *not* contain the population mean annual income, μ.

Computer Simulation 3

The following computer simulation example reemphasizes the concept that the level of confidence represents the approximate percent of similarly constructed intervals that include the parameter being estimated.

EXAMPLE

Chart 8–5 on page 312 presented a normal distribution with a population mean of 50 and a standard deviation of 5. We will select 30 random samples of size 50 from that population and develop the 95 percent confidence interval for each sample mean. We want to find out what proportion of those intervals include the population mean of 50. Interpret the result.

Solution ▶ The first step is to generate the 30 random samples of size 50. This is accomplished in the same manner as the simulations for the skewed and the normal distributions presented in simulations 1 and 2. The MINITAB procedure used to develop the confidence interval is called ZINTERVAL. This procedure requires as input the level of confidence (95 percent in this case), the value of the population standard deviation (5 in this case), and the location of the samples. The 30 samples are stored in columns 21 through 50, and each sample has size 50.

```
MTB > random 50 c21-c50;
SUBC> normal mu=50 sigma=5.
MTB > zinterval level of confidence 95 sigma = 5 c21-c50
THE ASSUMED SIGMA = 5.00
```

	N	MEAN	STDEV	SE MEAN	95.0 PERCENT C.I.
C21	50	50.806	4.832	0.707	(49.420, 52.193)
C22	50	50.158	6.007	0.707	(48.772, 51.545)
C23	50	49.587	4.328	0.707	(48.201, 50.973)
C24	50	49.516	5.302	0.707	(48.130, 50.903)
C25	50	49.715	5.384	0.707	(48.329, 51.102)
C26	50	50.127	5.597	0.707	(48.740, 51.513)
C27	50	49.031	5.245	0.707	(47.645, 50.417)
C28	50	50.016	5.260	0.707	(48.629, 51.402)
C29	50	50.380	4.455	0.707	(48.994, 51.767)
C30	50	49.409	4.923	0.707	(48.023, 50.795)
C31	50	50.243	5.188	0.707	(48.857, 51.630)
C32	50	50.242	5.148	0.707	(48.856, 51.628)
C33	50	48.810	4.892	0.707	(47.424, 50.197)
C34	50	50.367	5.171	0.707	(48.981, 51.754)
C35	50	50.542	5.269	0.707	(49.155, 51.928)
C36	50	50.607	4.310	0.707	(49.221, 51.994)
C37	50	50.045	4.934	0.707	(48.658, 51.431)
C38	50	51.148	4.063	0.707	(49.762, 52.534)
C39	50	49.451	5.668	0.707	(48.064, 50.837)
C40	50	51.712	4.711	0.707	(50.326, 53.099)*
C41	50	50.248	4.476	0.707	(48.861, 51.634)
C42	50	48.938	5.677	0.707	(47.551, 50.324)
C43	50	50.717	5.548	0.707	(49.331, 52.103)
C44	50	49.834	5.618	0.707	(48.448, 51.221)
C45	50	50.954	4.736	0.707	(49.568, 52.341)
C46	50	49.491	5.436	0.707	(48.104, 50.877)
C47	50	50.381	5.709	0.707	(48.995, 51.768)
C48	50	49.954	5.473	0.707	(48.568, 51.341)
C49	50	48.384	5.289	0.707	(46.998, 49.770)*
C50	50	49.895	4.623	0.707	(48.508, 51.281)

***Interval that does not contain the population mean of 50.**

Out of a total of 30 confidence intervals produced, 2, or 6.7 percent, do not include the population mean of 50. Another set of 30 intervals would have a different percentage of intervals that do not include the population mean.

For the 50 sample observations in column C21, the sample mean is 50.806, and the population standard deviation is 5.0. The interval 49.420 to 52.192 is determined as follows, using formula (8–3) (but using σ instead of s). There is a slight discrepancy of just $1.00 between the calculated interval below and that of the MINITAB system.

$$\bar{X} \pm 1.96 \frac{\sigma}{\sqrt{n}} = 50.806 \pm 1.96 \frac{5}{\sqrt{50}}$$

$$= 50.806 \pm 1.386$$

$$= 49.420 \text{ up to } 52.192$$

SELF-REVIEW 8–4

The answers are at the end of the chapter.

The wildlife department has been feeding a special food to rainbow trout fingerlings in a pond. A sample of the weights of 40 trout revealed that the mean weight is 402.7 grams and the standard deviation 8.8 grams.

1. What is the estimated mean weight of the population? What is that estimate called?
2. What is the 99 percent confidence interval?
3. What are the 99 percent confidence limits?
4. What degree of confidence is being used?
5. Interpret your findings.

EXERCISES

The answers to the odd-numbered exercises are at the end of the book.

11. A sample of 49 observations is taken from a normal population. The sample mean is 55, and the standard deviation of the sample is 10. Determine the 99 percent confidence interval for the population mean.
12. A sample of 81 observations is taken from a normal population. The sample mean is 40, and the standard deviation of the sample is 5. Determine the 95 percent confidence interval for the population mean.
13. A sample of 10 observations is selected from a normal population for which the population standard deviation is known to be 5. The sample mean is 20.
    a. Determine the standard error of the mean.
    b. Explain why we can use formula (8–3) to determine the 95 percent confidence interval even though the sample is less than 30.
    c. Determine the 95 percent confidence interval for the population mean.
14. Suppose you wanted to use a 90 percent confidence level instead of the 95 percent and 99 percent intervals used in formulas (8–3) and (8–4). What value would you use to multiply the standard error of the mean?
15. A research firm conducted a survey to determine the mean amount steady smokers spend on cigarettes during a week. A sample of 49 steady smokers revealed that $\overline{X} =$ \$20 and $s =$ \$5.
    a. What is the point estimate? Explain what it indicates.
    b. Using the .95 degree of confidence, determine the confidence interval for μ. Explain what it indicates.
16. Refer to Exercise 15. Suppose that 64 smokers (instead of 49) had been surveyed, and the sample mean and the sample standard deviation remained the same (\$20 and \$5, respectively).
    a. What is the 95 percent confidence interval estimate of μ?
    b. Explain why this confidence interval is narrower than the one determined in Exercise 15.
17. Al Fishhaber is the owner of Al's Marathon gas station. Al would like to estimate the mean number of gallons of gasoline sold to his customers. From his records he selects a sample of 60 sales and finds that the mean number of gallons sold is 8.60 and the standard deviation is 2.30 gallons.
    a. What is the estimate of the population mean?
    b. Develop a 99 percent confidence interval for the population mean.
    c. Interpret the meaning of part *b.*

18. An English professor counted the number of misspelled words on an essay he recently assigned. For his class of 40 students, the mean number of misspelled words was 6.05 and the standard deviation 2.44. Construct a 95 percent confidence interval for the mean number of misspelled words in the population of students.

CONFIDENCE INTERVAL FOR A POPULATION PROPORTION

The theory and procedure for determining a point estimator and an interval estimator for a *population proportion* are quite similar to those described in the previous section. A point estimate for the population proportion is found by dividing the number of successes in the sample by the total number sampled. Suppose 100 of 400 sampled said they liked a new cola they tested better than their regular cola. The best estimate of the population proportion favoring the new cola is .25, or 25 percent, found by 100/400. Note that a proportion is based on a *count* of the number of successes relative to the total number sampled.

Constructing confidence interval for a population proportion

How is the **confidence interval for a population proportion** estimated?

$$\bar{p} \pm z\sigma_{\bar{p}} \qquad (8\text{–}6)$$

where $\sigma_{\bar{p}}$ is the standard error of the proportion:

$$\sigma_{\bar{p}} = \sqrt{\frac{\bar{p}(1-\bar{p})}{n}} \qquad (8\text{–}7)$$

Therefore, the confidence interval is constructed by:

$$\bar{p} \pm z\sqrt{\frac{\bar{p}(1-\bar{p})}{n}} \qquad (8\text{–}8)$$

where:

$\bar{p}$ is the sample proportion.
z is the z value for the degree of confidence selected.
n is the sample size.

EXAMPLE

Suppose 1,600 of 2,000 union members sampled said they plan to vote for the proposal to merge with the UMA. Using the .95 level of confidence, what is the interval estimate for the population proportion? Based on the confidence interval, what conclusion can be drawn?

Solution ▶ Using formula (8–8), the interval is computed as follows.

$$\bar{p} \pm z\sqrt{\frac{\bar{p}(1-\bar{p})}{n}} = .80 \pm 1.96\sqrt{\frac{.80(1-.80)}{2,000}}$$

$$= .80 \pm 1.96\sqrt{.00008}$$

$$= .78247 \text{ and } .81753\text{, rounded to } .782 \text{ and } .818.$$

Confidence limits: 78.2 and 81.8 percent

Assume that at least 50 percent of the union members must approve of the merger. Based on the sample results, when all 2,000 union members vote, the proposal will probably pass because .50 lies below the interval between .782 and .818.

SELF-REVIEW 8–5

The answers are at the end of the chapter.

A market survey was conducted to estimate the proportion of homemakers who could recognize the brand name of a cleanser based on the shape and color of the container. Of the 1,400 homemakers, 420 were able to identify the brand name.

1. Using the .99 degree of confidence, the population proportion lies within what interval?

2. What are the confidence limits?

3. Interpret your findings.

EXERCISES

The answers to the odd-numbered exercises are at the end of the book.

19. In Exercise 17, the owner of Al's Marathon determined the mean number of gallons of gasoline purchased by his customers. He is also interested in the proportion of women who pump their own gasoline. He surveyed 100 women and found that 80 indicated they pump their own gasoline.
    a. What is the estimated proportion of women in the population that pump their own gasoline?
    b. Develop a 95 percent confidence interval for the proportion of women who pump their own gasoline. Interpret.

20. Ms. Maria Wilson is considering running for mayor of the town of Bear Gulch, Montana. Before completing the petitions, she decides to conduct a survey of voters in Bear Gulch. A sample of 400 voters revealed that 300 would support her in the November election.
    a. What proportion of the population of voters in Bear Gulch do you estimate would support Ms. Wilson?
    b. Develop a 99 percent confidence interval for the proportion of voters in the population that would support Ms. Wilson.
    c. In part *b,* note that both of the endpoints of the confidence interval are greater than .50. What importance would she attach to this?

21. Suppose the Fox TV network is considering replacing one of its prime-time shows with a new family-oriented comedy. Before a final decision is made, a random sample of 400 prime-time viewers is conducted. After seeing a preview of the comedy, 250 indicated that they would watch it.
    a. What is your estimate of the proportion of viewers in the population who will watch the new show?
    b. Develop a 95 percent confidence interval for the proportion of viewers who will watch the new show.

22. A silkscreen printer purchases plastic cups on which to print logos for sporting events and other special occasions. The printer received a large shipment this morning and

would like to estimate the percent defective. A sample of 200 revealed 30 of the cups to be defective.

a. What proportion of the shipment is estimated to be defective?

b. Develop a 95 percent confidence interval for the proportion of defective cups.

FINITE-POPULATION CORRECTION FACTOR

Infinite population

The populations we have sampled so far have been very large, or assumed to be *infinite.* What happens if the sampled population is not infinite, or not even very large? In such instances we need to make some adjustments in the standard error of the sample means and the standard error of the sample proportions.

Finite population

A population that has a fixed upper bound is said to be **finite.** For example, there are 21,376 students enrolled at Eastern Illinois University, and the Chrysler-Jeep Corp. manufactured 917 units at the Arkansas plant last year. A finite population can be rather small; it could be all the students registered for this class. It can also be very large, such as all senior citizens living in Florida. Note in the latter example that the number of senior citizens is large. We don't know exactly what the count is, but it is a number that in theory could be determined by a statewide census.

For a finite population, where the total number of objects is N and the size of the sample is n, the following adjustment is made to the standard errors of the sample means and the proportion:

Standard error of the sample means:

$$\sigma_{\bar{x}} = \frac{\sigma}{\sqrt{n}}\sqrt{\frac{N-n}{N-1}} \qquad (8\text{–}9)$$

Standard error of the sample proportions:

$$\sigma_{\bar{p}} = \sqrt{\frac{\bar{p}(1-\bar{p})}{n}}\sqrt{\frac{N-n}{N-1}} \qquad (8\text{–}10)$$

Finite-population correction factor

This adjustment is called the **finite-population correction factor.** Why is it necessary to apply a factor, and what is its effect? Logically, if the sample is a substantial percentage of the population, then we would expect any estimates to be more precise than those for a smaller sample. Note the effect of the term $(N - n)/(N - 1)$. Suppose the population is 1,000 and the sample is 100. Then this ratio is $(1{,}000 - 100)/(1{,}000 - 1)$, or 900/999. Taking the square root gives the correction factor, .9492. Multiplying by the standard error reduces the error by about 5 percent ($1 - .9492 \cong .05$). This reduction in the size of the standard error yields a smaller range of values in estimating the population mean. If the sample is 200, the correction factor is .8949, meaning that the standard error has been reduced by more than 10 percent. Table 8–5 shows the effects of various sizes of samples on the correction factor. Note that when the sample is less than about 5 percent of the population, the impact of the correction factor is quite small. The usual rule is that if the ratio n/N is less than .05, the finite-population correction factor is ignored.

TABLE 8–5 Computation of the Finite-Population Correction Factor for Selected Sample Sizes When the Population Is 1,000

Sample size	Fraction of population	Correction factor
10	.010	.9955
25	.025	.9879
50	.050	.9752
100	.100	.9492
200	.200	.8949
500	.500	.7075

EXAMPLE

There are 250 families in the small town of Scandia. A poll of 40 families revealed that the mean annual church contribution is \$450 with a standard deviation of \$75. Construct a 95 percent confidence interval for the mean annual contribution.

Solution

First note that the population is finite. That is, there is a limit to the number of people in Scandia. Second, note that the sample constitutes more than 5 percent of the population; that is, $n/N = 40/250 = .16$. Hence, the finite-population correction factor is used. The 95 percent confidence interval is constructed as follows, using formulas (8–3) and (8–9).

$$\bar{X} \pm z\frac{s}{\sqrt{n}}\left(\sqrt{\frac{N-n}{N-1}}\right) = \$450 \pm 1.96\frac{\$75}{\sqrt{40}}\left(\sqrt{\frac{250-40}{250-1}}\right)$$

$$= \$450 \pm \$23.24(\sqrt{.8434})$$

$$= \$450 \pm \$21.34$$

$$= [\$428.66, \$471.34]$$

SELF-REVIEW 8–6

The answers are at the end of the chapter.

The same study of church contributions in Scandia revealed that 15 of the 40 families sampled attend church regularly. Construct the 95 percent confidence interval for the proportion of families attending church regularly. Should the finite-population correction factor be applied? Why or why not?

EXERCISES

The answers to the odd-numbered exercises are at the end of the book.

23. A population consists of 300 items. A sample of size 36 is selected, and the mean is 35 and the standard deviation 5. Develop a 95 percent confidence interval for the population mean.
24. A population consists of 500 items. A sample of size 49 is selected. The mean is 40 and the standard deviation 9. Develop a 99 percent confidence interval for the population mean.
25. The attendance at the Durham Bulls minor league baseball game last night was 400. A random sample of 50 of those in attendance revealed that the mean number of soft

drinks consumed was 1.86 with a standard deviation of 0.50. Develop a 99 percent confidence interval for the number of soft drinks consumed.

26. There are 300 welders employed at the Maine Shipyards Corporation. A sample of 30 welders revealed that 18 graduated from a registered welding course. Construct the 95 percent confidence interval for the proportion of all welders who graduated from a registered welding course.

SELECTING A SAMPLE SIZE

Size of sample must be determined scientifically

The sample sizes in the previous problems were always given. Now we are going to determine an appropriate sample size. Care must be taken not to select a sample too large or too small. For example, if we arbitrarily selected 400 items or individuals, and if that sample size were too large, time and money would be expended unnecessarily. If 400 were not large enough, the conclusions drawn about the population might be incorrect. Using an extreme example, suppose two persons were selected from the voting population and each asked his or her preference for president. If both persons selected for the sample were members of the Communist party, one might erroneously conclude that the next president of the United States would be a Communist.

Misconceptions about how many to sample

There are several misconceptions about the number to sample. One fallacy is that a sample consisting of 5 percent (or a similar constant percentage) is adequate for all problems. However, a sample of 3 from a population of 60 might be too small, and a sample of size 50,000 from a population of 1 million too large. Another misconception is that a larger sample of consumers or voters, for example, must be selected from a heavily populated state, such as California, than from a small state, such as New Hampshire.

There are three factors that determine the size of the sample, *none of which has any direct relationship to the size of the population.* They are:

1. **The degree of confidence selected.** This is usually .95 or .99, but it may be any level. You, the researcher, specify the degree of confidence.
2. **The maximum allowable error.** You must decide on this, too. It is the maximum error you will tolerate at a specified level of confidence.
3. **The variation of the population.** The variation of the population is measured by the standard deviation. (Of course, a population with little variation requires smaller samples.)

The role each of these factors plays in determining the sample size is now examined.

Degree of Confidence

Researcher must specify degree of confidence

Recall that the purpose of taking a sample is to estimate a population parameter. Suppose the parameter to be estimated is the arithmetic mean, and the degree of confidence selected is .90. Based on a sample, it was estimated that the population mean is in the interval between $89,050 and $91,050. Logically, if the degree of confidence (often referred to as the level of confidence) were increased to .95 or .99, the sample size would have to be increased (assuming the interval remained the same). Carrying this to the extreme, if you wanted to be 100 percent sure that the true mean was in the interval between $89,050 and $91,050, you would have to survey the entire population—that is, take a 100 percent sample. Thus, one of the factors related to the sample size is the *degree of confidence.* The higher the degree of confidence, the larger the sample required to give a certain precision.

Maximum Error Allowed

Researcher must specify allowable error

Suppose that a developer is considering building a shopping mall near several subdivisions. One important statistic needed is the mean income in the area. A leisurely drive through the subdivisions indicated that the family incomes range from a probable low of $29,000 to a high of about $49,000. On the assumption that these are reasonable estimates, does it seem likely that the developer would be satisfied with this statement resulting from a sample of area residents: "The population mean is between $33,000 and $45,000"? Probably not! Confidence limits that wide indicate little or nothing about the population mean. Instead, the developer stated: "Using the .95 probability, the total error in predicting the population mean should not exceed $200." The developer is essentially saying this: "Based on a sample of size *n,* if the estimate of the population mean is computed to be $35,000, then you will assure me that the population mean is in the interval between $34,800 and $35,200—found by $35,000 + $200 and $35,000 − $200."

For the .95 degree of confidence selected by the developer, the maximum error of ±$200 in terms of z is 1.96. To determine the value of *one* standard error of the sample means, $\sigma_{\bar{x}}$, simply divide the total error of $200 by 1.96. It is $102.04.

$$\sigma_{\bar{x}} = \frac{\$200}{1.96}$$
$$= \$102.04$$

Shown schematically:

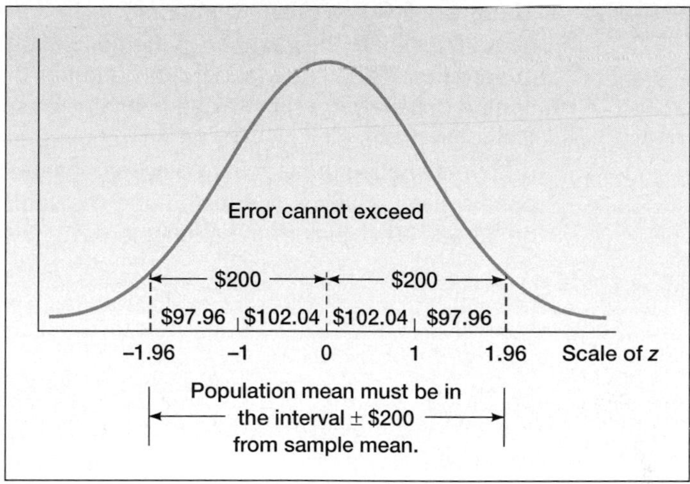

The size of the sample is computed by solving for n in the formula (note that since we are using a sample, $s_{\bar{x}}$ is substituted for $\sigma_{\bar{x}}$ and s for σ):

$$s_{\bar{x}} = \frac{s}{\sqrt{n}} \tag{8–11}$$

where:

$s_{\bar{x}}$ is the standard error of the sample means.

s is the standard deviation of the sample.

n is the sample size.

Thus far:

$$s_{\bar{x}} = \frac{s}{\sqrt{n}}$$

$$\frac{\text{Total allowable error}}{z \text{ standard deviations}} = \frac{\text{Sample standard deviation}}{\sqrt{\text{Sample size}}}$$

Letting E represent the total allowable error:

$$\frac{E}{z} = \frac{s}{\sqrt{n}}$$

$$\frac{\$200}{1.96} = \frac{s}{\sqrt{n}}$$

$$\$102.04 = \frac{s}{\sqrt{n}}$$

Variation in the Population

Pilot survey conducted to estimate variation in population

There are still two unknowns, s and n. To solve for the number to be sampled, we need to estimate the variation in the population. The standard deviation is a measure of variation. Thus, the standard deviation of the population must be estimated. This can be done either (1) by taking a small pilot survey (say, 50) and using the standard deviation of the pilot sample as an estimate of the population standard deviation or (2) by estimating the standard deviation based on knowledge of the population. Suppose a pilot survey is conducted and the sample standard deviation is computed to be \$3,000. The number to be sampled can now be estimated:

$$s_{\bar{x}} = \frac{s}{\sqrt{n}}$$

$$\frac{E}{z} = \frac{s}{\sqrt{n}}$$

$$\frac{\$200}{1.96} = \frac{\$3{,}000}{\sqrt{n}}$$

$$\$102.04\sqrt{n} = \$3{,}000$$

$$\sqrt{n} = \frac{\$3{,}000}{\$102.04}$$

$$n = 864.36$$

A more convenient computational formula for determining n is:

$$n = \left(\frac{z \cdot s}{E}\right)^2 \qquad (8\text{–}12)$$

where:

E is the allowable error.

z is the z score associated with the degree of confidence selected.

s is the sample deviation of the pilot survey.

For this problem:

$$\begin{aligned} n &= \left(\frac{z \cdot s}{E}\right)^2 \\ &= \left(\frac{1.96 \times \$3{,}000}{\$200}\right)^2 \\ &= \left(\frac{\$5{,}880}{\$200}\right)^2 \\ &= 864.36 \end{aligned}$$

which is the same answer as before. We would round it up to 865.

The sample of size 865 may or may not give the developer what he wants—an estimate of the true mean within \$200. The sample of 865 may be the correct sample size, or it may prove to be too small or too large. If it proves to be too large, the cost of surveying all 865 families was not warranted. If the sample of size 865 is too small, more families must be contacted if the error is to be reduced to within $200 (as originally specified by the developer).

Sample size seldom correct

Why isn't the sample size computed using the formula always the correct one? One reason is that it is highly unlikely for the standard deviation of the sample of 865 families to be exactly $3,000 (the same as for the pilot survey of about 50 families). If the standard deviation of the sample proved to be $2,500, the correct sample size should have been 600. This is found by solving for n in the following: $\$200/1.96 = \$2{,}500/\sqrt{n}$, or $n = [(1.96 \times \$2{,}500)/\$200]^2$. Obviously, the sample of 865 was too large.

SELF-REVIEW 8–7

The answers are at the end of the chapter.

Will you assist the college registrar in determining how many transcripts to study? The registrar wants to estimate the arithmetic mean final grade point average of all graduating seniors during the past 10 years. GPAs range between 2.0 and 4.0. The mean grade point average is to be estimated within plus and minus 0.05 of the population mean.

The .99 degree of confidence is to be used. Thus, the registrar wants to report something like this (hypothetical): "With a probability of .99, the mean grade point average of graduating seniors is in the interval between 2.45 and 2.55." The standard deviation of a small pilot survey is 0.279. How many transcripts should be sampled?

EXERCISES

The answers to the odd-numbered exercises are at the end of the book.

27. A population is estimated to have a standard deviation of 10. We want to estimate the population mean within 2, with a 95 percent level of confidence. How large a sample is required?
28. We want to estimate the population mean within 5, with a 99 percent level of confidence. The population standard deviation is estimated to be 15. How large a sample is required?
29. A survey is being planned to determine the mean amount of time corporation executives watch television. A pilot survey indicated that the mean time per week is 12 hours, with a standard deviation of 3 hours. It is desired to estimate the mean viewing time within one-quarter hour. The .95 degree of confidence is to be used. How many executives should be surveyed?
30. A processor of carrots cuts the green top off each carrot, washes the carrots, and inserts six to a package. Twenty packages are inserted in a box for shipment. To test the weight of the boxes, a few were checked. The mean weight was 20.4 pounds, the standard deviation 0.5 pounds. How many boxes must the processor sample to be 95 percent confident that the sample mean does not differ from the population mean by more than 0.2 pounds?

SAMPLE SIZE FOR PROPORTIONS

The procedure just used is applicable to determining the sample size when proportions are involved. Three things must be specified: (1) You, the researcher, must decide on the level of confidence—usually .95 or .99. (2) You must indicate how precise the estimate of the population proportion must be. (3) The population proportion, $\bar{p}$, must be either approximated from past experience (such as past elections) or approximated from a small pilot survey of, say, 50 or 100.

Proportions: Formula for sample size

The formula for determining the sample size in the case of a proportion is:

$$n = \bar{p}(1 - \bar{p})\left(\frac{z}{E}\right)^2 \qquad (8\text{–}13)$$

where:

- $\bar{p}$ is the estimated proportion, based on past experience or a pilot survey.
- z is the z value associated with the degree of confidence selected.
- E is the maximum allowable error the researcher will tolerate.

EXAMPLE

A member of Congress wants to determine her popularity in a certain part of the state. She indicates that the proportion of voters who will vote for her must be estimated within ±2 percent of the population proportion. Further, the .95 degree of confidence is to be used. In past elections she received 40 percent of the popular vote in that area of the state. She doubts whether it has changed much. How many registered voters should be sampled?

Solution

▶ The sample size should be 2,305, found by using formula (8–13):

$$\begin{aligned} n &= \bar{p}(1 - \bar{p})\left(\frac{z}{E}\right)^2 \\ &= .40(1 - .40)\left(\frac{1.96}{.02}\right)^2 \\ &= .24(98)^2 \\ &= 2{,}304.96 \end{aligned}$$

Again, the sample size of 2,305 might be too large, too small, or exactly correct, depending on the accuracy of $\bar{p} = .40$.

Note: If there is no logical estimate of $\bar{p}$ the sample size can be estimated by letting $\bar{p} = .50$. (The size of the sample will never be larger than the one obtained for n when $\bar{p} = .50$.)

SELF-REVIEW 8–8

The answers are at the end of the chapter.

The following statements refer to the example regarding the popularity of the representative. For each statement, indicate whether it is true or false, and give supporting evidence. Suppose 2,305 registered voters were surveyed.

1. If 922 of the 2,305 registered voters surveyed said they plan to vote for the representative, the sample of size 2,305 was exactly correct.
2. If 461 of the 2,305 registered voters surveyed said they planned to vote for the representative, the sample size of 2,305 was too large.

EXERCISES

The answers to the odd-numbered exercises are at the end of the book.

31. The estimate of the population proportion is to be within ± .05, with a 95 percent level of confidence. The best estimate of the population proportion is .15. How large a sample is required?
32. The estimate of the population proportion is to be within ± .10, with a 99 percent level of confidence. The best estimate of the population proportion is .45. How large a sample is required?
33. Suppose the President wants an estimate of the proportion of the population that support his current policy toward Haiti. The President wants the estimate to be within .04 of the true proportion. Assume a 95 percent level of confidence. The Secretary of State estimated the proportion supporting current policy to be .60.
    a. How large a sample is required?
    b. How large would the sample have to be if the estimate by the Secretary of State were not available?
34. Past surveys revealed that 30 percent of the tourists going to Las Vegas to gamble during a weekend spent more than $1,000. Management wants to update that percentage.
    a. Using the .90 degree of confidence, management wants to estimate the percentage of the tourists spending more than $1,000 within 1 percent. What sample size should be employed?
    b. Management said that the sample size suggested in part *a* is much too large. Suggest something that could be done to reduce the sample size. Based on your suggestion, recalculate the sample size.

CHAPTER OUTLINE

I. There are many reasons for sampling a population.
   A. Often testing destroys the sampled item and it cannot be returned to the population.
   B. It may be impossible to check or locate all the members of the population.
   C. The cost of studying all items in the population may be prohibitive.
   D. The results of a sample may adequately estimate the population parameter, thus saving time and money.
   E. It may be too time-consuming to contact all the members of the population.

II. There are two types of samples: probability and nonprobability.
   A. In a probability sample all members of the population have a chance of being selected for the sample. There are several probability sampling methods.
      1. In a simple random sample all members of the population have the same chance of being selected for the sample.
      2. In a systematic sample a random starting point is selected, and then every *k*th item is selected for the sample.
      3. In a stratified sample the population is divided into several groups, or strata, and then a sample is selected from each stratum.
      4. In cluster sampling the population is divided into primary units, and then samples are drawn from the primary units.
   B. In nonprobability sampling, inclusion in the sample is based on the judgment of the person conducting the sample. Nonprobability samples may lead to biased results.

III. The difference between the population parameter and the sample statistic is called the sampling error.

IV. The sampling distribution of the sample means is a probability distribution showing all possible sample means and their probabilities of occurrence.

A. For a given sample size, the mean of all possible means selected from the population is exactly equal to the population mean.
B. There is less dispersion in the sampling distribution of the sample means than in the population. The variation in a sampling distribution, called the standard error of the sample means, is computed by

$$\sigma_{\bar{x}} = \frac{\sigma}{\sqrt{n}} \tag{8–1}$$

C. The central limit theorem states that if the population is normal, then the sampling distribution of the sample means is also normal. If the population is not normal, the sampling distribution of the sample means approaches normal as the size of the sample increases.

V. A point estimate is a single value used to estimate a population value.

VI. An interval estimate is a range of values within which the population parameter is expected to occur.
A. The factors that make up a confidence interval for a mean are:
1. The number of observations in the sample (n).
2. The variability in the population, usually estimated by the sample standard deviation (s).
3. The level of confidence. It is represented by the z value.
B. A confidence interval for the mean is obtained using the formula

$$\bar{X} \pm z\frac{s}{\sqrt{n}} \tag{8–5}$$

C. The factors that make up a confidence interval for a proportion are:
1. The number of observations in the sample.
2. The value of $\bar{p}$, which is obtained by dividing the number of successes in the sample (X) by the number of observations in the sample (n).
3. The level of confidence. It is represented by the z value.
D. A confidence interval for a proportion is obtained using the formula

$$\bar{p} \pm z\sqrt{\frac{\bar{p}(1-\bar{p})}{n}} \tag{8–8}$$

VII. The required size of a sample can be determined for both means and proportions.
A. The factors that determine the size of the sample for a mean are:
1. The desired level of confidence (z).
2. The maximum allowable error (E).
3. The variation in the population (usually estimated by s).
B. The formula for sample size for a mean is:

$$n = \left(\frac{z \cdot s}{E}\right)^2 \tag{8–12}$$

C. The factors that determine the size of the sample for a proportion are:
1. The desired level of confidence (z).
2. The maximum allowable error (E).
3. An estimate of the population proportion. If no estimate is available, then .50 is used.
D. The formula for sample size for a proportion is:

$$n = \bar{p}(1-\bar{p})\left(\frac{z}{E}\right)^2 \tag{8–13}$$

E. The finite-population correction factor is applied if n/N is more than .05. The correction factor is shown as follows:

$$\sqrt{\frac{N-n}{N-1}}$$

EXERCISES

The answers to the odd-numbered exercises are at the end of the book.

35. Briefly explain:
    a. The purpose of sampling.
    b. Some of the reasons for using a sample instead of contacting, enumerating, or testing the entire population.
36. Identify each of the following types of sampling.
    a. Auditors may select every 20th file starting with, say, the 5th file in the top drawer. Then file numbers 25, 45, 65, 85, . . . are audited.
    b. Manufacturers were subdivided into groups by volume of sales. Those with more than $100 million in sales were classified as class A large, those from $50 to $100 million as class A medium, those between $25 and $50 million . . . , and so on. Samples were then selected from each of these groups.
37. Explain the statement: "If nonprobability sampling methods are used, the results may be biased."
38. Explain what is meant by sampling error.
39. Cite a situation in which cluster sampling might be used.
40. Briefly explain a nonprobability type of sampling called panel sampling.
41. The following is a list of family-practice physicians. Three physicians are to be randomly selected and contacted regarding their charge for a routine office visit. The 39 physicians have been coded from 00 to 38. Also noted is whether they are in practice by themselves (S), have a partner (P), or are in a group practice (G).

Random number	Physician	Type of practice	Random number	Physician	Type of practice
00	R. E. Scherbarth, M.D.	S	20	Gregory Yost, M.D.	P
01	Crystal R. Goveia, M.D.	P	21	J. Christian Zona, M.D.	P
02	Mark D. Hillard, M.D.	P	22	Larry Johnson, M.D.	P
03	Jeanine S. Huttner, M.D.	P	23	Sanford Kimmel M.D.	P
04	Francis Aona, M.D.	P	24	Harry Mayhew M.D.	S
05	Janet Arrowsmith, M.D.	P	25	Leroy Rodgers M.D.	S
06	David DeFrance, M.D.	S	26	Thomas Tafelski M.D.	S
07	Judith Furlong, M.D.	S	27	Mark Zilkoski M.D.	G
08	Leslie Jackson, M.D.	G	28	Ken Bertka, M.D.	G
09	Paul Langenkamp, M.D.	S	29	Mark DeMichiei, M.D.	G
10	Philip Lepkowski, M.D.	S	30	John Eggert, M.D.	P
11	Wendy Martin, M.D.	S	31	Jeanne Fiorito, M.D.	P
12	Denny Mauricio, M.D.	P	32	Michael Fitzpatrick, M.D.	P
13	Hasmukh Parmar, M.D.	P	33	Charles Holt, D.O.	P
14	Ricardo Pena, M.D.	P	34	Richard Koby, M.D.	P
15	David Reames, M.D.	P	35	John Meier, M.D.	P
16	Ronald Reynolds, M.D.	G	36	Douglas Smucker, M.D.	S
17	Mark Steinmetz, M.D.	G	37	David Weldy, M.D.	P
18	Geza Torok, M.D.	S	38	Cheryl Zaborowski, M.D.	P
19	Mark Young, M.D.	P			

a. If the random numbers 31, 94, 43, 36, 03, 24, 17, and 09 are obtained, which physicians should be contacted?
b. Select a random sample of size 4 using the table of random numbers (Appendix E).

42. Refer to Exercise 41. A sample is to consist of every fifth physician. The number 04 is selected as the starting point. Which physicians will be contacted?

43. Refer to Exercise 41. A sample is to consist of two physicians in solo practice (S), two in partnership (P), and one in group practice (G). Select a sample accordingly. Explain your procedure.

44. A study of motel facilities in a metropolitan area showed there were 25 facilities. The city's convention and visitors bureau is studying the number of rooms at each location. The results are as follows: 90, 72, 75, 60, 75, 72, 84, 72, 88, 74, 105, 115, 68, 74, 80, 64, 104, 82, 48, 58, 60, 80, 48, 58, and 108.
    a. Using a table of random numbers (Appendix E), select a random sample of size 5 from this population.
    b. Obtain a systematic sample by selecting a random starting point among the first five motels, and then select every fifth motel.
    c. Suppose the last five motels listed are "cut-rate" motels. Describe how you would select a random sample of three regular motels and two cut-rate motels.

45. Dr. Lamberg has five students doing special independent study this semester. To evaluate their reading progress, Dr. Lamberg gave the students a five-question true/false test. The number of correct answers for each student is given below.

Student	Number correct
Tayor	4
Hurley	3
Fowler	5
Rousche	3
Telatko	2

    a. How many samples of size 2 are possible from this population?
    b. List all possible samples of size 2, and compute the sample means.
    c. Organize the sample means into a probability distribution.
    d. Compute the mean of the sample means, and compare it with the population mean.
    e. Compare the shape of the population and the shape of the distribution of the sample means.

46. The commercial banks in region III are to be surveyed. Some of them are very large, with assets of more than \$500 million; others are medium-size, with assets between \$100 million and \$500 million; and the remaining banks have assets of less than \$100 million. Explain how you would select a sample of these banks.

47. Plastic Products is concerned about the inside diameter of the plastic PVC pipe it produces. A machine extrudes the pipe, which is then cut into 10-foot lengths. About 720 pipes are produced per machine during a two-hour period. How would you go about taking a sample from the two-hour production period?

48. The ages of the six executives of the Ace Manufacturing Company (considered the population) are:

Name	Age
Mr. Jones	54
Ms. Smith	50
Mr. Kirk	52
Ms. Small	48
Mr. Hugh	50
Mr. Sioto	52

a. How many samples of size 2 are possible?
b. Select all possible samples of size 2 from the population of executives, and compute the means.
c. Organize the means into a sampling distribution.
d. What is the mean of the population? Of the sample means?
e. What is the shape of the population?
f. What is the shape of the sampling distribution?

49. A random sample of 85 group leaders, supervisors, and similar personnel at Amana revealed that, on the average, a person spent 6.5 years on the job before being promoted. The standard deviation of the sample was 1.7 years. Using the .95 degree of confidence, construct the confidence interval within which the population mean lies.
50. Of 900 consumers surveyed, 414 said they were very enthusiastic about a new home decor scheme. Construct the 99 percent confidence interval for the population proportion.
51. It is estimated that 60 percent of U.S. households now can get cable TV. You would like to verify this statement for your class in mass communications. If you want your estimate to be with ±5 percentage points with a 95 percent level of confidence, how large a sample is required?
52. There are 20,000 eligible voters in the fifth precinct. A sample of 500 voters is selected. Of the 500 surveyed, 350 said they are going to vote for the Democratic incumbent. Using the .99 degree of confidence, set the confidence limits for the proportion who plan to vote for the Democratic incumbent.
53. The mean number of travel days per year for the outside salespeople is to be estimated. The .90 degree of confidence is to be used. The mean of a small pilot study was 150 days, with a standard deviation of 14 days. If the population mean is to be estimated within 2 days, how many outside salespeople should be sampled?
54. Ten passengers are to be selected at random from the New York–Los Angeles Delta flight and interviewed in depth regarding airport facilities, service, food, and so on. Each passenger boarding the aircraft was given a number. The numbers started with 001 and ended with 250.
    a. Select 10 numbers at random using the table of random numbers in Appendix E.
    b. The sample of 10 could have been chosen using a systematic sample. Choose the first number using Appendix E, and then list the numbers to be interviewed.
    c. Evaluate the two methods by giving the advantages and possible disadvantages.
    d. In what other way could a random sample be selected from the 250 passengers?
55. The Iowa state meat inspector has been given the assignment of estimating the actual mean net weight of packages of ground chuck labeled "3 pounds." Of course, he realizes that the weights cannot be precisely 3 pounds. A sample of 36 packages revealed the mean weight to be 3.01 pounds with a standard deviation of 0.03 pounds.
    a. What is the estimated population mean?
    b. Using the .95 degree of confidence, what are the confidence limits for the population mean?
    c. Summarize your findings.

56. Police Chief Kress of River City reports that 500 traffic citations were issued last month. A sample of 35 of these citations showed the mean amount of the fine to be $54 with a standard deviation of $4.50. Construct a 95 percent confidence interval for the mean amount of a citation in River City.

57. The First National Bank of Wilson has 650 checking account customers. A recent sample of 50 of these customers showed 26 to have a Visa card with the bank. Construct the 99 percent confidence interval for the proportion of checking account customers that have a Visa card with the bank.

58. A recent study of 50 self-service gasoline stations in the Cincinnati, Ohio, area revealed that the mean price of unleaded gas was $1.179 per gallon and the standard deviation was $0.03 per gallon. Determine a 99 percent confidence interval for the mean price per gallon of unleaded gasoline.

59. In a survey of 1,200 voters in Oklahoma, 792 were able to name their two U.S. Senators. Develop a 95 percent confidence interval for the proportion of voters in Oklahoma that can identify their senators.

60. The Badik Construction Company limits its business to repairing driveways, installing patios, and building decks. The mean time for each of these three jobs is 12 hours, but the standard deviation is 3 hours for repairing a driveway, 6 hours for a patio, and 8 hours for a deck. This information is based on samples of 40 of each type of job.

    a. Before you do any calculation, which of the three types of jobs will have the smallest range of values for a 99 percent confidence interval for mean construction time?
    b. Construct a confidence interval for the mean construction time for each type of job.

61. A recent survey of 50 unemployed male executives showed that it took a mean of 26 weeks to find another position. The standard deviation was 6.2 weeks. Find the 95 percent confidence interval for the mean time it took executives to find another job.

62. Dr. Fowler, a professor of management, is studying the relationship between work schedules and family life. In a sample of 120 people who worked the night shift only, she found the following:
    a. The mean weekly amount of time (in hours) they spent caring for their children was 27.2 hours with a standard deviation of 10.3 hours. Determine a 95 percent confidence interval for the mean number of hours spent caring for their children.
    b. A total of 18 indicated that their parents had also worked the night shift. Determine the 90 percent confidence interval for the proportion of workers whose parents also worked nights.

63. The proportion of public accountants who had changed companies within three years is to be estimated within 3 percent. The .95 degree of confidence is to be used. A study conducted several years ago revealed that the percent of public accountants changing companies within three years was 21.
    a. To update this study, the files of how many junior executives should be studied?
    b. How many junior executives would be contacted if no previous estimate were available?

64. The Hunington National Bank, like most other large banks, found that the use of automatic teller machines (ATMs) reduces the cost of routine bank transactions. Hunington installed an ATM in the corporate offices of the Fun Toy company. The ATM is for the exclusive use of Fun's 605 employees. After several months of operation, a sample of 100 employees revealed the following use of the ATM machine by Fun employees in a month.

Number of times ATM used		Frequency
0		25
1		30
2		20
3		10
4		10
5		5
	Total	100

a. What is the estimate of the proportion of employees that do not use the ATM in a month?
b. Develop a 95 percent confidence interval for this estimate. Can Hunington be sure that at least 40 percent of the employees of Fun Toy Company will use the ATM?
c. How many transactions does the average Fun employee make per month?
d. Develop a 95 percent confidence interval for the mean number of transactions per month.
e. Is it possible that the population mean is 0? Explain.

COMPUTER DATA EXERCISES

65. Refer to data set 1, which reports information on homes sold in Florida during 1994.
    a. Determine the 95 percent confidence interval for the mean selling price.
    b. Determine the 95 percent confidence interval for the mean distance from the center of the city.
    c. Determine the 95 percent confidence interval for the proportion of homes with a garage.
66. Refer to data set 2, which reports the information on the 1993 major league baseball season. Suppose you were asked to determine the 95 percent confidence interval for the mean number of home runs hit by each team. Could you provide this estimate? Would your estimate be reasonable?
67. Refer to data set 3, which reports information on the circulation of magazines.
    a. Determine the 95 percent confidence interval for the mean number of other magazines read by women. To explain, if you are a reader of *Time* and read three other magazines, you receive a 3 for this variable.
    b. Determine the 95 percent confidence interval for the mean cost of a page of black and white advertising.
    c. Determine the 95 percent confidence interval for the mean percent of subscribers who attended college.

CHAPTER 8 EXAMINATION

The answers are at the end of the chapter.

For Questions 1 through 10, indicate whether the statement is true or false. If the statement is false, correct it.

1. A sample is a part of the population.
2. In a probability sample each member of the population has a chance of being selected as part of the sample.
3. The difference between a sample statistic and the corresponding population parameter is called the sampling error.

4. The mean of all the sample means is always larger than the population mean.
5. If a population is normal, the sampling distribution of the sample means is also normal.
6. A value used to estimate a population parameter is called a sample statistic.
7. An interval estimate always contains the population parameter.
8. If the sample size for estimating a population mean is increased, the width of the confidence interval will decrease.
9. The finite-population correction factor is used when n/N is greater than .80.
10. Suppose we want to determine the confidence interval for a population proportion. If the level of confidence is increased, say, from 95 percent to 99 percent, the width of the interval will decrease.
11. It has been discovered that some of the small steel shafts stored in warehouse E have rusted and will have to be cleaned before they can be sold. To approximate the percent that need cleaning, a sample of 200 was selected at random. It was found that 80 out of the 200 need cleaning. Using a degree of confidence of .90, set confidence limits between which the population proportion should fall.
12. A random sample of size 200 was selected to estimate the mean amount of time adults over 65 years old, retired, and living in Florida listened to the radio during the day. The sample mean was calculated to be 110 minutes, and the standard deviation of the sample was 30 minutes. What are the 95 percent confidence limits for the population mean listening time?
13. A sample survey is to be conducted to determine the mean family income in an area. The question is, how many families should be sampled? In order to get more information about the area, a small pilot survey was conducted, and the standard deviation of the sample was computed to be $500. The sponsor of the survey wants you to use the .95 degree of confidence. The estimate is to be within $100. How many families should be interviewed?
14. You plan to conduct a survey to find out what proportion of the work force has two or more jobs. You decide on the .95 degree of confidence and state that the estimated proportion must be within plus or minus 2 percent of the population proportion. A pilot survey reveals that 5 out of the 50 sampled hold two or more jobs. How many in the work force should be interviewed to meet your requirements?

CHAPTER 8 Answers

Self-Review

8–1
1. Students selected are Price, Detlev, and Molter.
2. Answers will vary.
3. Drop it, and move to the next random number.

8–2 The students selected are: Berry, Francis, Kopp, Poteau, and Swetye.

8–3
1. 10, found by:

$$\frac{5!}{2!(5-2)!}$$

2.

	Service	Sample mean
Snow, Tolson	20, 22	21
Snow, Kraft	20, 26	23
Snow, Irwin	20, 24	22
Snow, Jones	20, 28	24
Tolson, Kraft	22, 26	24
Tolson, Irwin	22, 24	23
Tolson, Jones	22, 28	25
Kraft, Irwin	26, 24	25
Kraft, Jones	26, 28	27
Irwin, Jones	24, 28	26

3.

Means	Number	Probability
21	1	.10
22	1	.10
23	2	.20
24	2	.20
25	2	.20
26	1	.10
27	1	.10
	10	1.00

4. Identical: population mean, μ, is 24, and mean of sample means is also 24.
5. Sample means range from 21 to 27. Population values go from 20 to 28.
6. Nonnormal.
7. Yes.

8–4
1. 402.7 grams. The point estimate.
2. The interval is between 399.11 and 406.29 grams, found by:

$$\overline{X} \pm 2.58\frac{s}{\sqrt{n}} = 402.7 \pm 2.58\frac{8.8}{\sqrt{40}}$$

3. 399.11 and 406.29 grams.
4. .99.
5. If we were to construct 100 similar intervals, about 99 should include the population mean.

8–5
1. Between .268 and .332, found by:

$$.30 \pm 2.58\sqrt{\frac{.30(1-.30)}{1,400}} = .30 \pm 2.58(.0122474)$$

2. .268 and .332.
3. If we were to construct 100 similar intervals, about 99 should include the population proportion.

8–6 About 23.7 and 51.3 percent, found by:

$$.375 \pm 1.96\sqrt{\frac{.375(.625)}{40}}\sqrt{\frac{250-40}{250-1}}$$

$$= .375 \pm 1.96(.0765466)(.9183537)$$

$$= .375 \pm .138$$

$$= [.237, .513]$$

The correction factor was applied because $40/250 > .05$.

8–7 208, found by:

$$n = \left[\frac{(2.58)(0.279)}{0.05}\right]^2$$

$= 207.26$, which is rounded up to 208.

8–8
1. True. $\bar{p} = 922/2,305 = .40$. Substituting:

$$n = .40(1-.40)\left(\frac{1.96}{.02}\right)^2 = 2,304.96$$

$$= 2,305$$

2. True. $\bar{p} = 461/2,305 = .20$. Substituting:

$$.20(1 - .20)\left(\frac{1.96}{.02}\right)^2 = .16(98)^2$$

$$= 1{,}537$$

The sample of 2,305 was too large. Only 1,537 voters needed to be surveyed.

Examination

1. True.
2. True.
3. True.
4. False. The mean of the sample means and the population mean are equal.
5. True.
6. True.
7. False. The parameter will be included in the confidence interval about the same percent of times as the level of confidence.
8. True.
9. False. It is used when $n/N > .05$.
10. False. The width of the interval will be increased.
11. Between 34.3 and 45.7 percent, found by:

$$.40 \pm 1.645\sqrt{\frac{.40(1 - .40)}{200}}$$

$$= .40 \pm 1.645\sqrt{.0012}$$

$$= .40 \pm .057$$

12. Between 105.84 and 114.16 minutes, found by:

$$110 \pm 1.96\left(\frac{30}{\sqrt{200}}\right) = 110 \pm 1.96(2.12)$$

$$= 110 \pm 4.16$$

13. 97, found by:

$$n = \left(\frac{1.96 \times \$500}{\$100}\right)^2 = 96.04$$

rounded up to 97.

14. 865, found by

$$(.10)(.90)\left(\frac{1.96}{0.02}\right)^2 = .09(98)^2 = 864.36$$

Chapter 9

Tests of Hypotheses: Large Samples

GOALS

When you have completed this chapter, you will be able to:

1
Define what is meant by a hypothesis and hypothesis testing.

2
Describe the five-step hypothesis-testing procedure.

3
Distinguish between a one-tailed and a two-tailed test of hypothesis.

4
Conduct a test of hypothesis about a population mean or proportion.

5
Conduct a test of hypothesis about the difference between two population means or proportions.

6
Describe the statistical errors that might result in testing a hypothesis.

7
Compute the probability of a Type II error.

The efficiency ratings of Boeing employees have been normally distributed over a period of years. However, new training and production methods have been instituted. How can we test the hypothesis that the mean is still the same? (See Goal 4 and Example on page 354.)

INTRODUCTION

Chapter 8 dealt with one aspect of statistical inference—estimation. Estimation involves estimating, or predicting, the value of an unknown population parameter, such as the population mean or the population proportion.

This chapter begins our study of another aspect of statistical inference, namely, **hypothesis testing.** Some types of questions to be dealt with are:

1. Is the mean impact strength of the plate glass being produced on the production line 70 pounds per square inch?
2. Are more than 10 percent of the 50-millimeter shells in storage defective?
3. Is there a difference in the proportion of consumers who purchased Smell Sweet soap before our television advertising campaign and after the campaign?
4. Is there a difference in mean usable life between Always Ready and Hotshot type-C batteries?

This chapter and several of the following chapters are concerned with hypothesis testing. We will first examine what is meant by a *hypothesis* and *hypothesis testing.* Then we will outline the steps followed to test a hypothesis. We will conduct tests with respect to one population mean and two population means. Then we will conduct tests of hypotheses regarding one population proportion and more than one population proportion. Finally, the possible statistical errors in testing a hypothesis will be explored.

WHAT IS A HYPOTHESIS?

Hypothesis A statement about the value of a population parameter developed for the purpose of testing.

Examples of hypotheses

Examples of hypotheses, or statements, made about a population parameter are:

- The mean monthly income from all sources for systems analysts is $3,625.
- Twenty percent of all juvenile offenders ultimately are caught and sentenced to prison.
- The mean outside diameter of all the ball bearings produced during the day is 1.000 inches.
- Ninety percent of all federal income tax forms are filled out correctly.
- The mean impact strengths of the windshields produced last year by the Delaware Glass Company and Stabler-Pittsburgh Glass are the same.

May not be feasible to study entire population

All these hypotheses have one thing in common. The populations of interest are so large that for various reasons it would not be feasible to study all the items, or persons, in the population. For example, it would be almost impossible to contact every systems analyst in the United States to find out his or her monthly income. Likewise, the quality-assurance department does not have the personnel to check every ball bearing produced during the day to determine whether the mean outside diameter is in fact exactly 1.000 inches.

Sample imperative in many problems

As noted in Chapter 8, an alternative to measuring or interviewing the entire population is to take a sample from the population of interest. We can, therefore, test a statement to determine if the empirical evidence from the sample does or does not support the statement concerning the population.

WHAT IS HYPOTHESIS TESTING?

Hypothesis: Statement about a population parameter

The terms *hypothesis testing* and *testing a hypothesis* are used interchangeably. Hypothesis testing starts with a statement, or assumption, about a population parameter—such as the population mean. As noted this statement is referred to as a *hypothesis.* A hypothesis might be that the mean monthly commission of salespeople in retail computer stores, such as Computerland, is $2,000. We cannot contact all these salespeople to ascertain that the mean is in fact $2,000. The cost of locating and interviewing every computer salesperson in the United States would be exorbitant. To test the validity of the assumption (population mean = $2,000), we must select a sample from the population consisting of all computer salespeople, calculate sample statistics, and based on certain decision rules accept or reject the hypothesis. A sample mean of $1,000 for the computer salespeople would certainly cause rejection of the hypothesis. However, suppose the sample mean is $1,995. Is that close enough to $2,000 for us to accept the assumption that the population mean is $2,000? Can we attribute the difference of $5 between the two means to sampling error, or is that difference statistically significant?

Hypothesis testing defined

Hypothesis testing A procedure based on sample evidence and probability theory used to determine whether the hypothesis is a reasonable statement and should not be rejected, or is unreasonable and should be rejected.

FIVE-STEP PROCEDURE FOR TESTING A HYPOTHESIS

A systematic procedure

There is a five-step procedure that systematizes hypothesis testing; when we get to step 5, we are ready to make a decision to reject or not reject the hypothesis. However, hypothesis testing as used by statisticians does not provide proof that something is true, in the manner in which a mathematician "proves" a statement. It does provide a kind of "proof beyond a reasonable doubt," in the manner of the court system. Hence, there are specific rules of evidence, or procedures, that are followed. The steps are shown in the following diagram. We will discuss in detail each of the steps.

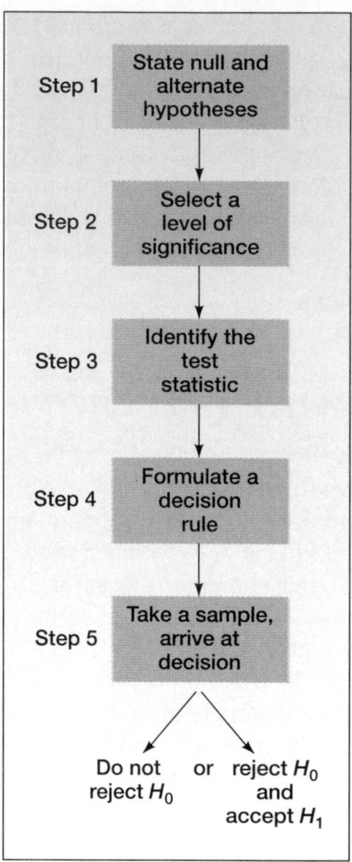

Step 1: The Null Hypothesis and the Alternate Hypothesis

The systematic procedure

The first step is to state the hypothesis to be tested. It is called the **null hypothesis,** designated H_0, and read "*H* sub-zero." The capital letter *H* stands for hypothesis, and the subscript zero implies "no difference." There is usually a *not* or a *no* term in the null hypothesis, meaning there is "no change." The null hypothesis for question 1 in the introduction would be, "The mean impact strength of the glass is *not* significantly different from 70 psi." This is the same as saying the mean (μ) impact strength of the glass is equal to 70 psi. The null hypothesis H_0 would then be written H_0: $\mu = 70$. For question 3 in the introduction, the null hypothesis would be, "There is *no* difference in the proportion of consumers who purchased Smell Sweet before and after the television advertising campaign." This is the same as saying that the two proportions are equal, written H_0: $p_1 = p_2$. Generally speaking, *the null hypothesis is set up for the purpose of testing.* We either reject or fail to reject the null hypothesis. To put it another way, the null hypothesis is a statement that is not rejected if our sample data fail to provide us with convincing evidence that it is false.

We should emphasize at this point that if the null hypothesis is not rejected based on sample data, in effect we are saying that the evidence does not allow us to reject it. We cannot state, however, that the null hypothesis is true. To put it another way, accepting the null hypothesis does not prove that H_0 is true. To prove without any doubt that the null hypothesis is true, the population parameter would have to be known. To actually determine it, we would have to test, survey, or count every item in the population. This is usually not feasible. The alternative is to take a sample from the population.

It should also be noted that we often begin the null hypothesis by stating "There is no *significant* difference between . . . ," or "The mean impact strength of the glass is not *significantly* different from. . . ." When we select a sample from a population, the sample statistic is usually different from the hypothesized population parameter. As an illustration, suppose that the hypothesized impact strength of a glass plate is 70 psi, and the mean impact strength of a sample of 12 glass plates is 69.5 psi. We must make a judgment about the difference of 0.5 psi. Is it a true difference, that is, a significant difference, or is the difference between the sample statistic (69.5) and the hypothesized population parameter (70.0) due to chance (sampling)? As noted, to answer this question we conduct a test of significance, commonly referred to as a test of hypothesis. To define what is meant by a null hypothesis:

Identify H_0

> **Null hypothesis** A statement about the value of a population parameter.

The **alternate hypothesis** describes what you will conclude if you reject the null hypothesis. It is written as H_1 and is read "*H* sub-one." It is also referred to as the research hypothesis. The alternate hypothesis is accepted if the sample data provide us with statistically significant evidence that the null hypothesis is false.

> **Alternate hypothesis** A statement that is accepted if the sample data provide evidence that the null hypothesis is false.

The following example will help clarify what is meant by the null hypothesis and the alternate hypothesis. A recent article indicated that the mean age of U.S. commercial aircraft is 15 years. To conduct a statistical test regarding this statement, the first step is to determine the null and the alternate hypotheses. The null hypothesis represents the current or reported condition. It is written H_0: $\mu = 15$. The alternate hypothesis is that the statement is not true, that is, H_1: $\mu \neq 15$. It is important to remember that no matter how the problem is stated, the null hypothesis will always contain the equal sign. The equality sign (=) will never appear in the alternate hypothesis. Why is this so? Because the null hypothesis is the statement being tested. We turn to the alternate hypothesis only if we prove the null hypothesis to be untrue.

Step 2: The Level of Significance

Select a level of significance or risk

After setting up the null hypothesis and alternate hypothesis, the next step is to state the level of significance.

> **Level of significance** The probability of rejecting the null hypothesis when it is actually true.

The level of significance is designated α, the Greek letter alpha. It is also referred to as the *level of risk.* This may be a more appropriate term because it is the risk you take of rejecting the null hypothesis when it is really true.

There is no one level of significance that is applied to all studies involving sampling. A decision must be made to use the .05 level (often stated as the 5 percent level), the .01 level, the .10 level, or any other level between 0 and 1. Traditionally, the .05 level is selected for consumer research projects, .01 for quality assurance, and .10 for political polling. You, the researcher, must decide on the level of significance *before* formulating a decision rule and collecting sample data.

To illustrate how it is possible to reject a true hypothesis, suppose a firm manufacturing home computers uses a large number of printed circuit boards. Suppliers bid on the boards, and the one with the lowest bid is awarded a sizable contract. Suppose the contract specifies that the computer manufacturer's quality-assurance department will sample all incoming shipments of circuit boards. If more than 6 percent of the boards sampled are substandard, the shipment will be rejected. The null hypothesis is that the incoming shipment of boards contains 6 percent or less substandard boards. The alternate hypothesis is that more than 6 percent of the boards are defective.

A sample of 50 circuit boards received July 21 from Allied Electronics revealed that 4 boards, or 8 percent, were substandard. The shipment was rejected because it exceeded the maximum of 6 percent substandard printed circuit boards. If the shipment was actually substandard, then the decision to return the boards to the supplier was correct. However, suppose the 4 substandard printed circuit boards selected in the sample of 50 were the only substandard boards in the shipment of 4,000 boards. Only 1⁄10 of 1 percent were defective (4/4,000 = .001). In that case, less than 6 percent of the entire shipment was substandard, and rejecting the shipment was an error. In terms of hypothesis testing, we rejected the null hypothesis that the shipment was not substandard when we should have accepted the null hypothesis. By rejecting a true hypothesis, we committed a *Type I error.* The probability of committing a Type I error is designated α.

Type I error

Type I error Rejecting the null hypothesis, H_0, when it is actually true.

Type II error

The probability of committing another type of error, called a *Type II* error, is designated by the Greek letter beta (β).

Type II error Accepting the null hypothesis when it is actually false.

The firm manufacturing home computers would commit a Type II error if, unknown to the manufacturer, an incoming shipment of printed circuit boards from Allied Electronics contained 15 percent substandard boards, yet the shipment was accepted. How could this happen? Suppose 2 of the 50 boards in the sample (4 percent) tested were substandard, and 48 of the 50 were good boards. According to the stated procedure, because the sample contained less than 6 percent substandard boards, the shipment was accepted. It could be that *by chance* the 48 good boards selected in the sample were the only acceptable ones in the entire shipment consisting of thousands of boards!

In retrospect, the researcher cannot study every item or individual in the population. Thus, there is a possibility of two types of error—a Type I error, wherein the null hypothesis is rejected when it should have been accepted, and a Type II error, wherein the null hypothesis is accepted when it should have been rejected.

Alpha error
Beta error

We often refer to these two possible errors as the *alpha error,* α, and the *beta error,* β. Alpha (α) is the probability of making a Type I error, and beta (β) is the probability of making a Type II error.

The following table summarizes the decisions the researcher could make and the possible consequences:

Null hypothesis	Researcher: Accepts H_0	Researcher: Rejects H_0
If H_0 is true and	Correct decision	Type I error
If H_0 is false and	Type II error	Correct decision

Step 3: The Test Statistic

There are many test statistics. In this chapter we use z as the test statistic. In other chapters we will use such test statistics as t, F, and χ^2, called chi-square.

Test statistic A value, determined from sample information, used to determine whether or not to reject the null hypothesis.

Use of z as the test statistic

In hypothesis testing, the test statistic z is computed by:

$$z = \frac{\overline{X} - \mu}{\sigma/\sqrt{n}} \tag{9–1}$$

The z value is based on the sampling distribution of $\overline{X}$, which is normally distributed with a mean ($\mu_{\bar{x}}$) equal to μ, and a standard deviation $\sigma_{\bar{x}}$, which is equal to $\sigma/\sqrt{n}$. We can determine if the difference between $\overline{X}$ and μ is statistically significant by finding the number of standard deviations $\overline{X}$ is from μ using formula (9–1).

Step 4: The Decision Rule

Decision rule: States condition of rejection or nonrejection

A decision rule is a statement of the conditions under which the null hypothesis is rejected and the conditions under which it is not rejected. The region or area of rejection defines the location of all those values that are so large or so small that the probability of their occurrence under a true null hypothesis is rather remote.

Chart 9–1 portrays the rejection region for a test of significance that will be conducted later in the chapter.

CHART 9–1 **Sampling Distribution for the Statistic z for a One-Tailed Test, .05 Level of Significance**

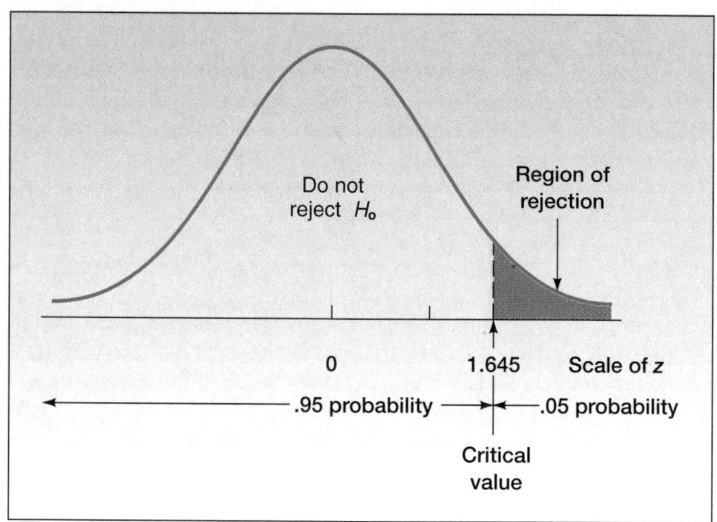

Note in the chart that:

1. The area where the null hypothesis is not rejected includes the area to the left of 1.645. We will explain how to get the 1.645 shortly.
2. The area of rejection is to the right of 1.645.
3. A one-tailed test is being applied. (This will also be explained later.)
4. The .05 level of significance was chosen.
5. The sampling distribution of the statistic z is normally distributed.
6. The value 1.645 separates the regions where the null hypothesis is rejected and where it is not rejected.
7. The value 1.645 is called the **critical value.**

Critical value The dividing point between the region where the null hypothesis is rejected and the region where it is not rejected.

Step 5: Making a Decision

The fifth and final step in hypothesis testing is making a decision to reject or not to reject the null hypothesis. Referring to Chart 9–1, if, based on sample information, z is computed to be 2.34, the null hypothesis is rejected at the .05 level of significance. The decision to reject H_0 was made because 2.34 lies in the region of rejection, that is, beyond 1.645. We would reject the null hypothesis reasoning that it is highly improbable that a computed z value this large is due to sampling variation (chance).

Had the computed value been 1.645 or less, say 0.71, the null hypothesis would not be rejected. It would be reasoned that such a small computed value could be attributed to chance, that is, sampling variation.

As noted, one of two decisions is possible in hypothesis testing—either accept or reject the null hypothesis. Instead of "accepting" the null hypothesis, H_0, some researchers prefer to phrase the decision as: "Do not reject H_0," "We fail to reject H_0," or "The sample results do not allow us to reject H_0."

It should be reemphasized that there is a possibility that the null hypothesis will be rejected when it should not have been rejected (a Type I error). Also, there is a definable chance that the null hypothesis will be accepted when it should have been rejected (a Type II error).

It should also be noted that the decision whether or not to reject is one made by the statistician conducting the research. That person could be a professional statistician, an accountant, a marketing manager, a quality-control engineer, or an executive. He or she states the null and alternate hypotheses, decides on the level of significance, selects a sample, and makes a decision whether or not to reject the null hypothesis. The statistician makes a recommendation based on this sample evidence; however, unless it is a routine decision, top management usually makes the final decision.

Before actually conducting a test of hypothesis, we will differentiate between a one-tailed test of significance and a two-tailed test.

ONE-TAILED AND TWO-TAILED TESTS OF SIGNIFICANCE

One-tailed test

Refer to Chart 9–1. It indicates that a one-tailed test is being applied. The region of rejection is only in the right (upper) tail of the curve. To illustrate, suppose that the packaging department at General Foods Corporation is concerned that some boxes of Grape Nuts are significantly overweight. The cereal is packaged in 453-gram boxes, so the null hypothesis is H_0: $\mu \leq 453$. This is read "the population mean (μ) is equal to or less than 453." The alternate hypothesis is therefore H_1: $\mu > 453$. This is read "μ is greater than 453." Note that the inequality sign in the alternate hypothesis $>$ points to the region of rejection in the upper tail. (See Chart 9–1.)

Chart 9–2 portrays a situation where the rejection region is in the left (lower) tail of the normal curve. As an illustration, consider the problem of automobile manufacturers, large automobile leasing companies, and other organizations that purchase large quantities of tires. They want the tires to average, say, 40,000 miles of wear under normal usage. They will therefore reject a shipment of tires if accelerated-life tests reveal that the life of the tires is significantly below 40,000 miles on the average. They gladly accept a shipment if the mean life is greater than 40,000 miles! They are not concerned with this possibility, however. They are concerned only if they have sample evidence to conclude that the tires will average less than 40,000 miles of useful life. Thus, the test is set up to satisfy the concern of the automobile manufacturers and others that *the mean life of the tires is less than 40,000 miles.* The null and alternate hypotheses are written H_0: $\mu \geq 40{,}000$ and H_1: $\mu < 40{,}000$.

CHART 9–2 **Sampling Distribution for the Statistic *z*, One-Tailed Test, .05 Level of Significance**

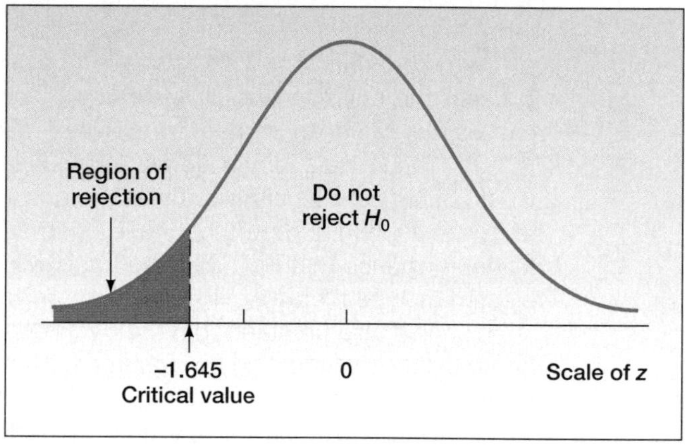

Test is one-tailed if H_1 states $\mu >$ or $\mu <$

One way to determine the location of the rejection region is to look at the direction in which the inequality sign in the alternate hypothesis is pointing (either $<$ or $>$). In this problem it is pointing to the left, and the rejection region is therefore in the left tail.

If H_1 states a direction, test is one-tailed

In summary, a test is one-tailed when the alternate hypothesis, H_1, states a direction, such as:

H_0: The mean income of females is less than or equal to the mean income of males.

H_1: The mean income of males is *greater than* the mean income of females.

Two-tailed test

If no direction is specified under the alternate hypothesis, a *two-tailed test* is being applied. Changing the previous alternate hypothesis to illustrate:

H_0: There is *no difference* between the mean income of males and the mean income of females.

Test is two-tailed if H_1 does not state a direction

H_1: There *is a difference* between the mean income of males and the mean income of females.

If the null hypothesis is rejected and H_1 accepted, the mean income of males could be greater than that of females, or vice versa. To accommodate these two possibilities, the 5 percent representing the area of rejection is divided equally into the two tails of the sampling distribution (2.5 percent each). Chart 9–3 shows the two areas and the critical values. Note that the total area under the normal curve is 1.000, found by .95 + .025 + .025.

CHART 9–3 **Regions of Nonrejection and Rejection for a Two-Tailed Test, .05 Level of Significance**

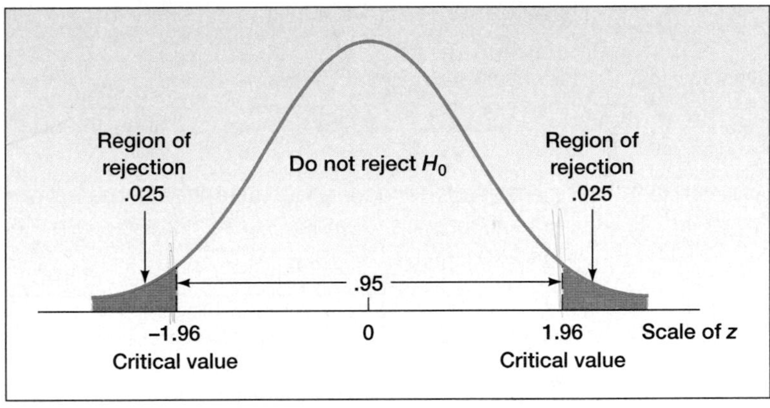

We will now test a hypothesis about the mean of a population by taking a large sample from that population. It is generally agreed that a sample of 30 or more is considered large.

TESTING FOR THE POPULATION MEAN: LARGE SAMPLE, POPULATION STANDARD DEVIATION KNOWN

Answering these questions involves a population mean:

- Is the mean income of top executives in manufacturing $325,000?
- Is the mean length of the slugs being sheared 2.0000 inches?
- Is the mean age of the inmates of federal prisons less than 40 years?
- Is the mean amount owed by credit card holders greater than $1,000?
- Is the mean efficiency rating of the production employees at Boeing, Inc. equal to 200?

We will use the five-step hypothesis-testing procedure to test the last question. The phrasing of the question suggests a two-tailed test.

A Two-Tailed Test

EXAMPLE

The efficiency ratings of Boeing employees at the Seattle plant have been normally distributed over a period of many years. The arithmetic mean (μ) of the distribution is 200, and the standard deviation (σ) is 16. Recently, however, young employees have been hired and new training and production methods inaugurated. Using the .01 level of significance, we want to test the hypothesis that the mean is still 200. (Note that the population standard deviation is known, namely, 16.)

Solution

Step 1 The null hypothesis is: "The population mean is 200." The alternate hypothesis is: "The mean is different from 200" or "The mean is not 200." The two hypotheses are written as:

$$H_0: \mu = 200$$
$$H_1: \mu \neq 200$$

Why a two-tailed test?

This is a *two-tailed test* because the alternate hypothesis does not state the direction of the difference. That is, it does not state whether the mean is greater than or less than 200.

Step 2 As noted, the .01 level of significance is to be used. This is α, the probability of committing a Type I error. That is, it is the probability of rejecting a true hypothesis.

Step 3 The test statistic for this type of problem is z. It was discussed at length in Chapter 7. Transforming the efficiency rating data to standard units (z values) permits their use not only in this problem but also in other hypothesis-testing problems. Formula (9–1) for z is repeated below with the various letters identified.

Formula for the test statistic

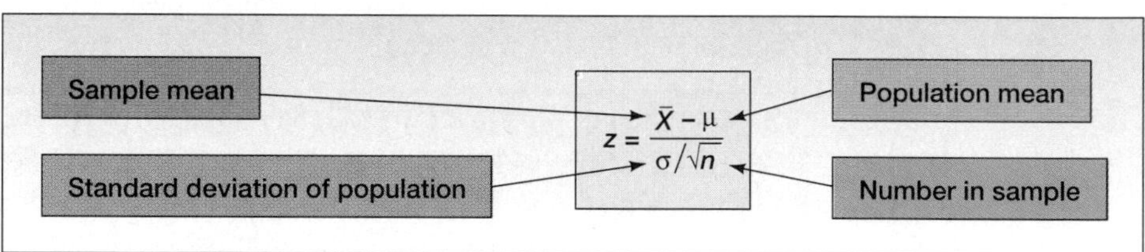

Step 4 The decision rule is formulated by finding the critical value of z from Appendix D. Since this is a two-tailed test, half of .01, or .005, is in each tail. The area where H_0 is not rejected, located between the two tails, is therefore .99. Appendix D is based on just half of the area under the curve, or .5000. Then, .5000 − .005 is .4950, so .4950 is the area between 0 and the critical value. Locate .4950 in the body of the table. The value nearest to .4950 is .4951. Then read the critical value in the row and column corresponding to .4951. It is 2.58. For your convenience Appendix D, Areas under the Normal Curve, is repeated in the inside back cover.

All the facets of this problem are shown in the form of a diagram in Chart 9–4.

CHART 9–4 Decision Rule for the .01 Significance Level

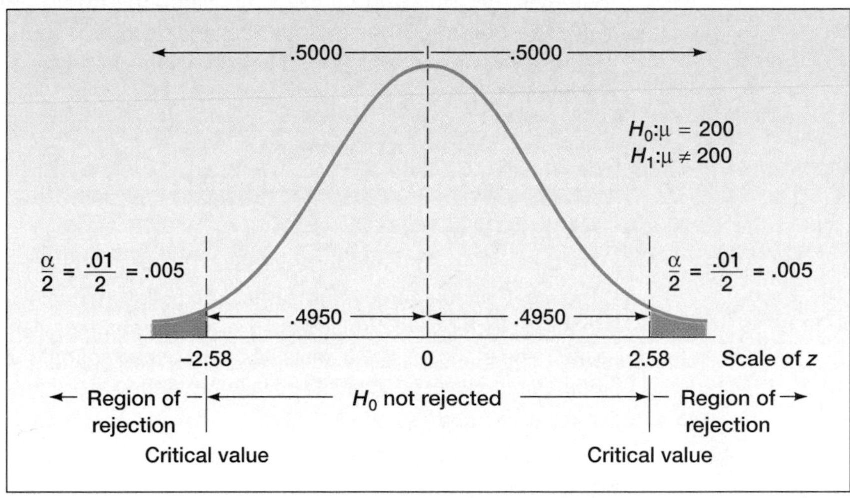

Do not reject H_0 if computed value is between −2.58 and +2.58

The decision rule is therefore: Reject the null hypothesis and accept the alternate hypothesis (which states that the population mean is not 200) if the computed value of *z* does not fall in the region between −2.58 and +2.58. Do not reject the null hypothesis if *z* falls between −2.58 and +2.58.

Step 5 Take a sample from the population (efficiency ratings); compute *z*; and, based on the decision rule, arrive at a decision to reject H_0 or not to reject H_0.

The efficiency ratings of 100 production employees were analyzed. The mean of the sample, $\overline{X}$, was computed to be 203.5. Computing *z* using formula (9–1):

$$z = \frac{\overline{X} - \mu}{\sigma/\sqrt{n}} = \frac{203.5 - 200}{16/\sqrt{100}} = \frac{3.5}{1.6} = 2.19$$

H_0 not rejected because 2.19 is less than the critical value 2.58

Since 2.19 does not fall in the rejection region, H_0 is not rejected. At the .01 level, there is not a statistically significant difference between the sample mean $\overline{X}$ and the hypothesized mean μ. So we conclude that the population mean is not different from 200. The difference between 203.5 and 200 can be attributed to chance variation.

We are concluding that our sample data *do not allow us to reject the null hypothesis.* We therefore assume that the null hypothesis is true.

We did not reject the null hypothesis that the population mean efficiency rating is 200 based on sample evidence. However, we did not prove beyond doubt that H_0 is true. The only way to prove beyond any doubt that it is 200 is to check every efficiency rating in the population—that is, take a 100 percent sample.

One further note about the hypothesis-testing procedure. This chapter has stressed the importance of selecting the level of significance *before* setting up the decision rule and sampling the population. In the example, the null hypothesis that $\mu = 200$ was *accepted* at the 1 percent level. You could have biased the later decision by not initially selecting the .01 level. Instead, you could have waited until *after* the

Reason for selecting level of significance before choosing sample

sampling and selected a level of significance that would cause the null hypothesis to be *rejected.* You could have chosen, for example, the .05 level. The critical values for that level are plus and minus 1.96. Since the computed value of z (2.19) lies beyond 1.96, the null hypothesis would be rejected, and you would conclude that the mean efficiency rating is *not* 200. This decision would be just the opposite of our earlier conclusion!

SELF-REVIEW 9–1

The answers are at the end of the chapter.

The mean annual turnover rate of a brand of allopurinol was reported 6.0. (This indicates that the stock of allopurinol turns over on the pharmacy shelves an average of six times a year.) The standard deviation is 0.5. It is suspected that the actual mean turnover is not 6.0. The .05 level of significance is to be used to test this hypothesis.

1. State H_0 and H_1.
2. What is the probability of a Type I error?
3. Give the formula for the test statistic.
4. State the decision rule.
5. A random sample of 64 bottles of allopurinol was selected. The mean turnover rate was computed to be 5.84. Shall we reject the null hypothesis at the .05 level? Interpret.

A One-Tailed Test

We emphasized previously that if the alternate hypothesis states a direction (either "greater than" or "less than"), the test is *one-tailed.* The hypothesis-testing procedure is generally the same as for a two-tailed test, except that the critical value is different. Let us change the alternate hypothesis in the previous problem, involving the efficiency rating of the production workers at Boeing, from:

$$H_1: \mu \neq 200 \text{ (a two-tailed test)}$$

to

$$H_1: \mu > 200 \text{ (a one-tailed test)}$$

The critical values for the two-tailed test were -2.58 and $+2.58$ (see Chart 9–5). The region of rejection for a one-tailed test is in the right tail (the inequality sign, $>$, points to the rejection region). For a one-tailed test, the critical value is equal to $+2.33$, found by: (1) subtracting .01 from .5000 and (2) finding the z value associated with .4900 in Appendix D.

p-VALUE IN HYPOTHESIS TESTING

In testing a hypothesis, we compare the test statistic to a critical value. A decision is made to either reject the null hypothesis or not reject it. So, for example, if the critical value of z is 1.96 and the computed value of the test statistic is 2.19, the decision is made to reject the null hypothesis.

CHART 9–5 **Rejection Regions for Two-Tailed and One-Tailed Tests, α = .01**

Critical values for a two-tailed and a one-tailed test, where $\alpha = .01$

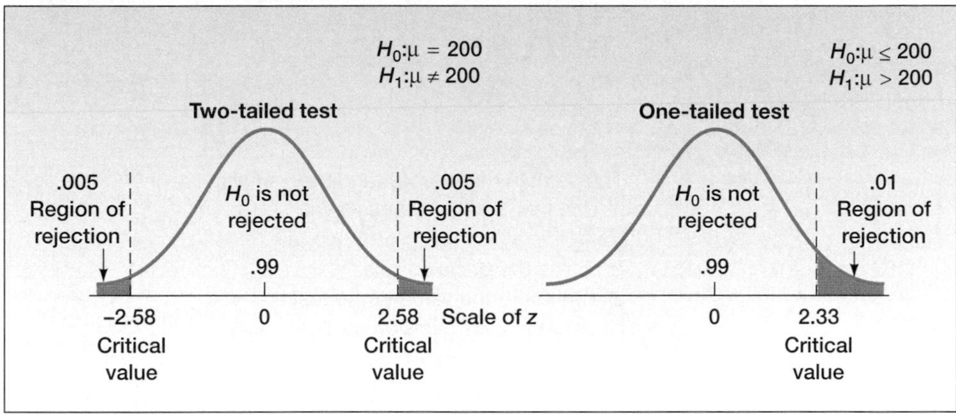

In recent years, spurred by the availability of computer software, additional information is often reported on the "strength" of the rejection, or how confident we are in rejecting the null hypothesis. This method reports the probability (assuming that the null hypothesis is true) of getting a value of the test statistic at least as extreme as that obtained. This procedure compares the probability, called the ***p*-value,** with the significance level. If the *p*-value is smaller than the significance level, H_0 is rejected. If it is larger than the significance level, H_0 is not rejected. This procedure not only results in a decision regarding H_0, but it gives us insight into the strength of the decision. A very small *p*-value, say, .001, means that there is very little likelihood that H_0 is true. On the other hand, a *p*-value of .40 means that H_0 is not rejected, and we did not come very close to rejecting it.

To explain further, recall that for the efficiency ratings at Boeing, the computed value of z was 2.19. The decision was not to reject H_0 because the z of 2.19 fell in the nonrejection region between −2.58 and +2.58. The probability of obtaining a z value of 2.19 or more is .0143, found by .5000 − .4857. That is, the probability of obtaining an $\overline{X}$ greater than 203.5 if $\mu = 200$ is .0143. To compute the *p*-value, we need to be concerned with values less than −2.19 and values greater than +2.19 (because there are rejection regions in both tails). The *p*-value is .0286, found by 2(.0143). The *p*-value of .0286 is greater than the significance level (.01) decided upon initially, so H_0 is not rejected.

SELF-REVIEW 9–2

The answers are at the end of the chapter.

Refer to Self-Review 9–1.

1. Suppose this hypothesis-testing problem was changed to a one-tailed test. How would the null hypothesis be written symbolically if it read: "The population mean is equal to or greater than 6.0"?
2. How would the alternate hypothesis be written symbolically if it read: "The population mean is less than 6.0"?
3. Show the decision rule graphically. Show the rejection region and indicate the critical value.

EXERCISES

The answers to the odd-numbered exercises are at the end of the book.

1. The following information is available.

$$H_0: \mu = 50$$
$$H_1: \mu \neq 50$$

The sample mean is 49, and the sample size is 36. The population standard deviation is 5. Use the .05 significance level.
a. Is this a one-tailed or a two-tailed test?
b. State the decision rule.
c. Compute the value of the test statistic.
d. What is your decision regarding H_0?
e. Determine the *p*-value.

2. The following information is available.

$$H_0: \mu \leq 10$$
$$H_1: \mu > 10$$

The sample mean is 12 for a sample of 36. The population standard deviation is 3. Use the .02 significance level.
a. Is this a one-tailed or a two-tailed test?
b. State the decision rule.
c. Compute the value of the test statistic.
d. What is your decision regarding H_0?
e. Determine the *p*-value.

3. The manufacturer of the X-15 steel-belted radial truck tire claims that the mean mileage the tire can be driven before the tread wears out is 60,000 miles. The standard deviation of the mileages is 5,000 miles. The Crosset Truck Company bought 48 tires and found that the mean mileage for their trucks is 59,500 miles. Is Crosset's experience different from that claimed by the manufacturer at the .05 significance level?
a. State the null hypothesis and the alternate hypothesis.
b. State the decision rule.
c. Compute the value of the test statistic.
d. What is your decision regarding H_0? Interpret the result. What is the *p*-value?

4. The MacBurger restaurant chain claims that the mean waiting time of customers for service is normally distributed with a mean of 3 minutes and a standard deviation of 1 minute. The quality-assurance department found in a sample of 50 customers at the Warren Road MacBurger that the mean waiting time was 2.75 minutes. At the .05 significance level, can we say that the mean waiting time is less than 3 minutes?
a. State the null hypothesis and the alternate hypothesis.
b. State the decision rule.
c. Compute the value of the test statistic.
d. What is your decision regarding H_0? Interpret the result. What is the *p*-value?

TESTING FOR THE POPULATION MEAN: LARGE SAMPLE, POPULATION STANDARD DEVIATION UNKNOWN

In the preceding problems, we knew σ, the population standard deviation. In most cases, however, it is unlikely that the population standard deviation would be known. Thus, σ must be based on prior studies or estimated using the sample standard deviation, s. The population standard deviation in the following example is not known, so the sample standard deviation must be used to estimate σ. As long as the sample size n is greater than 30, s can be substituted for σ as illustrated in the following formula:

$$z = \frac{\overline{X} - \mu}{s/\sqrt{n}} \qquad (9\text{–}2)$$

EXAMPLE

The Thompson's Discount Store chain issues its own credit card. The credit manager wants to find out if the mean monthly unpaid balance is more than \$400. The level of significance is set at .05. A random check of 172 unpaid balances revealed the sample mean to be \$407 and the standard deviation of the sample to be \$38. Should the credit manager conclude that the population mean is greater than \$400, or is it reasonable to assume that the difference of \$7 (\$407 − \$400 = \$7) is due to chance?

Solution

▶ The null and alternate hypotheses are stated as:

$$H_0: \mu \leq \$400$$

$$H_1: \mu > \$400$$

Because the alternate hypothesis states a direction, a one-tailed test is applied. The critical value of z is 1.645. The computed value of z is 2.42, found by using formula (9–2):

$$z = \frac{\overline{X} - \mu}{s/\sqrt{n}} = \frac{\$407 - \$400}{38/\sqrt{172}} = \frac{\$7}{\$2.8975} = 2.42$$

The decision rule is portrayed graphically in the following chart.

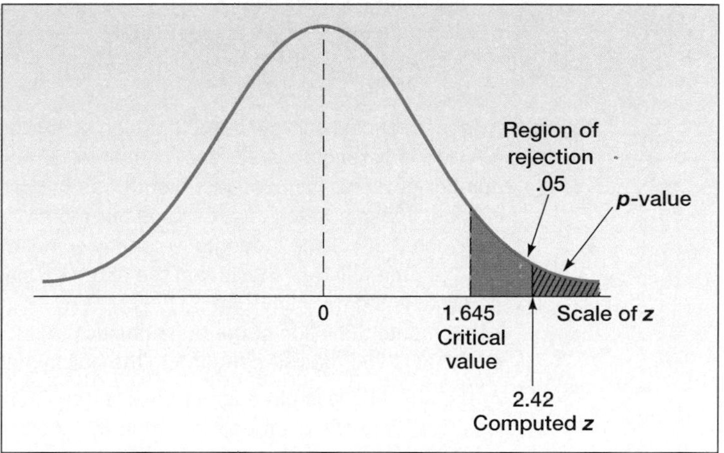

Because the computed value of the test statistic (2.42) is larger than the critical value (1.645), the null hypothesis is rejected. The credit manager can conclude that the mean unpaid balance is greater than \$400.

The p-value provides additional insight into the decision. Recall that the p-value is the probability of finding a value of the test statistic as large or larger than that obtained, given that the null hypothesis is true. So we need to find the probability of a z value greater than 2.42. From Appendix D the probability of a z value between 0 and 2.42 is .4922. We want to determine the likelihood of a value *greater than* 2.42, so $.5000 - .4922 = .0078$. We conclude that the likelihood of finding a z value of 2.42 or larger when the null hypothesis is true is 0.78 percent. It is unlikely, therefore, that the null hypothesis is true.

EXERCISES

The answers to the odd-numbered exercises are at the end of the book.

5. A sample of 36 observations is selected from a normal population. The sample mean is 21, and the sample standard deviation is 5. Conduct the following test of hypothesis using the .05 significance level.

$$H_0: \mu \leq 20$$

$$H_1: \mu > 20$$

   a. Is this a one-tailed or a two-tailed test?
   b. State the decision rule.
   c. Compute the value of the test statistic.
   d. What is your decision regarding H_0?
   e. What is the *p*-value? Interpret it.

6. A sample of 64 observations is selected from a normal population. The sample mean is 215, and the sample standard deviation is 15. Conduct the following test of hypothesis using the .03 significance level.

$$H_0: \mu \geq 220$$

$$H_1: \mu < 220$$

   a. Is this a one-tailed or a two-tailed test?
   b. State the decision rule.
   c. Compute the value of the test statistic.
   d. What is your decision regarding H_0?
   e. What is the *p*-value?

7. A recent national survey found that high school students watched an average (mean) of 6.8 videos per month. A random sample of 36 college students revealed that the mean number of videos watched last month was 6.2, with a standard deviation of 0.5. Do college students watch fewer videos per month? At the .05 significance level, can we conclude that college students watch fewer videos a month than high school students?
   a. State the null hypothesis and the alternate hypothesis.
   b. What is the decision rule?
   c. Compute the value of the test statistic.
   d. What is your decision regarding the null hypothesis? Interpret the result.

8. At the time she was hired as a server at the Grumney Family Restaurant, Beth Brigden was told, "You can average more than $20 a day in tips." Over the first 35 days she was employed at the restaurant, the mean daily amount of her tips was $24.85, with a standard deviation of $3.24. At the .01 significance level, can Ms. Brigden conclude that she is earning more than $20 in tips?
   a. State the null hypothesis and the alternate hypothesis.
   b. What is the decision rule?
   c. Compute the value of the test statistic.
   d. What is your decision regarding the null hypothesis? Interpret the result.

HYPOTHESIS TESTING: TWO POPULATION MEANS

This problem involves two means

The following illustration, involving a test of significance between two population means, typifies a practical industrial problem.

Concrete blocks are to be used in the foundations of several buildings. The specifications state that the minimum mean compressive strength of a sample of blocks must be 1,000 pounds per square inch (psi). If two companies submit samples of blocks that have mean compressive strengths over the minimum (1,000 psi), then the specifications state that one of two actions will be taken: (1) If a statistical test applied to the sampling results indicates that both samples could have come from the same, or identical, populations, the contract for the blocks will be divided equally. (2) If the sample statistics indicate that there are two populations involved, the company submitting the blocks having the higher compressive strength will be awarded the contract.

A large construction project requires a large number of concrete blocks. The Stanblock Corporation and the Hicompressive Company have supplied blocks to the builder in the past, and both are interested in providing blocks for the new construction project. Before the blocks are tested for compressive strength, null and alternate hypotheses will be stated, a level of significance selected, an appropriate statistical test decided upon, and a decision rule formulated.

Follow the usual five-step testing procedure

Step 1: The Null Hypothesis The null hypothesis is that there is *no* difference between the mean compressive strength of the concrete blocks manufactured by the Stanblock Company and the mean compressive strength of the concrete blocks manufactured by the Hicompressive Company. Thus, they constitute a single, overlapping population of concrete blocks. The alternate hypothesis, H_1, is that there *is* a significant difference between the two mean compressive strengths. Symbolically:

State H_0 and H_1

$$H_0: \mu_1 = \mu_2$$

$$H_1: \mu_1 \neq \mu_2$$

Since the alternate hypothesis does not specify a direction (such as that the mean compressive strength of the blocks from Stanblock is greater than the mean of the Hicompressive blocks), a two-tailed test is used.

$\alpha = .01$

Step 2: The Level of Significance The .01 level of significance has been chosen. This is the same as saying that the probability of committing a Type I error is .01.

Step 3: The Statistical Test At least 30 blocks (n_1) will be selected at random from the Stanblock Company, and at least 30 will be selected from Hicompressive (n_2). As noted previously, when n_1 and n_2 are 30 or more, the samples are considered large, and z can be used as the test statistic. The selection process also meets one other assumption underlying the z test, namely, independence. This means that the two populations are not related. The z test assumes that the data are at least interval-scaled. Of course, either of the two populations could be called number 1. However, once you have labeled a particular population number 1, you must continue to call it that.

The theory underlying the sampling distribution of z (the critical value) will be examined briefly. It states in part:

> If a large number of independent random samples are selected from the two populations, the distribution of the differences between the two means divided by the standard error of the difference between the two means (the critical value) will approximate a normal distribution.

The corresponding formula for z is:

The test statistic

$$z = \frac{\overline{X}_1 - \overline{X}_2}{\sqrt{\dfrac{s_1^2}{n_1} + \dfrac{s_2^2}{n_2}}} \qquad (9\text{–}3)$$

Difference between two sample means (numerator)

Standard error of the difference between the two sample means (denominator)

To illustrate this theory, assume that many samples of size 100 were taken from the Stanblock Company, and many samples of 100 blocks were taken from the Hicompressive Company. For the sake of simplicity, assume that the standard deviation for each sample was computed to be 20 psi. (The sample means are hypothetical and are included merely to show the computation of z.) Then compute the z values:

Sample	$\overline{X}_1$	$\overline{X}_2$	$\overline{X}_1 - \overline{X}_2$	$\dfrac{\overline{X}_1 - \overline{X}_2}{\sqrt{\frac{s_1^2}{n_1} + \frac{s_2^2}{n_2}}}$	z
1	1,020	1,020	0	$\frac{0}{2.8} =$	0
2	1,022	1,020	+2	$\frac{+2}{2.8} =$	+0.71
3	1,030	1,021	+9	$\frac{+9}{2.8} =$	+3.21
4	1,018	1,021	−3	$\frac{-3}{2.8} =$	−1.07

Thus, in theory, if the two population means are equal and if the z values of 0, +0.71, +3.21, −1.07, and so on were plotted, the distribution of these z values would approximate a normal distribution.

Reference to the areas under the normal curve (Appendix D) reveals that about 68 percent of the z values would fall within 0 ± 1.0; about 95 percent would fall within 0 ± 1.96; and about 99 percent would fall within 0 ± 2.58. (See Chart 9–6.)

Step 4: The Decision Rule Recall that the .01 level of significance was selected. A two-tailed test will be used (because the alternate hypothesis, H_1, does not state that the mean compressive strength of the blocks of one company is greater than the mean compressive strength of the other firm's blocks). It was noted in step 3 that about 99 percent of the computed z values will be between −2.58 and +2.58 under the assumption that there is no difference between the means of the two populations. So if the computed z value does fall within the region between plus and minus 2.58, the null hypothesis is not rejected. Thus, it would be concluded that the difference between the two sample means is due to chance.

CHART 9–6 **Distribution of z When $\mu_1 - \mu_2 = 0$**

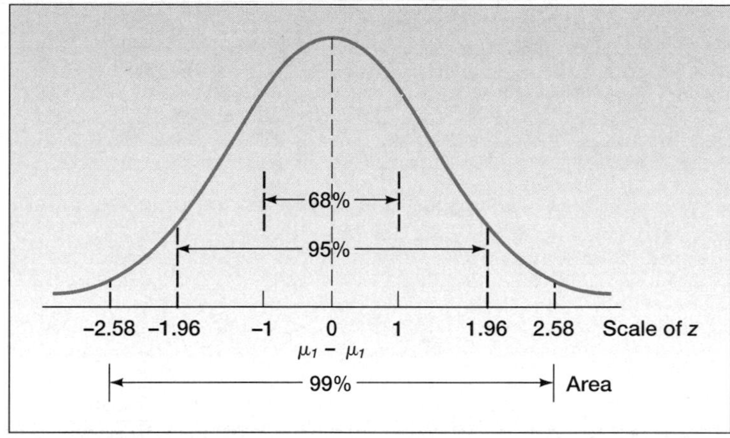

If the computed z value is greater than 2.58, the null hypothesis is *rejected.* The null hypothesis would be rejected on the basis that it is highly unlikely that a computed z value could be 2.58 or greater *by chance.* Of course, H_0 is also rejected if the computed z is to the left of −2.58. This decision rule is portrayed in Chart 9–7. (Note that we have inserted the p-value in the two tails. Computation for the p-value is shown on the next page.)

CHART 9–7 **Two-tailed Test, Areas of Nonrejection and Rejection, with a .01 Significance Level**

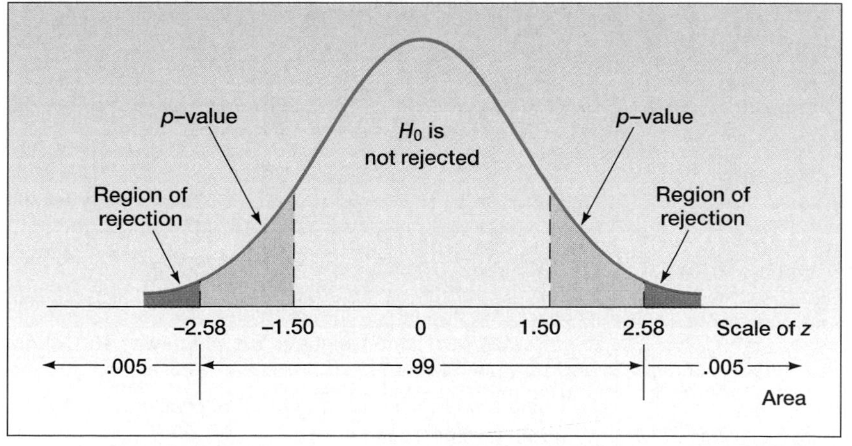

Select samples from the two populations

Step 5: The Sample Results and the Decision A total of 81 blocks were selected at random from the Stanblock Company production, and the compressive strength of each was determined. The standard deviation of the sample and the mean compressive strength were computed. Sixty-four blocks from the Hicompressive Company were selected, and the same procedure was followed. The sample statistics are:

Stanblock Company	Highcompressive Company
$\overline{X}_1 = 1{,}070$ psi	$\overline{X}_2 = 1{,}055$ psi
$n_1 = 81$	$n_2 = 64$
$s_1 = 63$ psi	$s_2 = 57$ psi

Using formula (9–3), the computed test statistic (z) is 1.50. The calculations are:

$$z = \frac{\overline{X}_1 - \overline{X}_2}{\sqrt{\dfrac{s_1^2}{n_1} + \dfrac{s_2^2}{n_2}}}$$

$$= \frac{1{,}070 - 1{,}055}{\sqrt{\dfrac{(63)^2}{81} + \dfrac{(57)^2}{64}}} = \frac{15}{9.98827} = 1.50$$

The computed z value of 1.50 falls in the area where the null hypothesis is not rejected. This means that we cannot reject the null hypothesis that the mean compression strength of the two companies is the same. The difference of 15 psi, found by 1070 − 1055, is attributed to chance.

What is the p-value for the problem? Recall that we had a two-tailed test, so we need to find the area to the left of − 1.50 and the area fo the right of 1.50. Referring to Appendix D, the area between a z value of 0 and 1.50 is .4332. So the area to the right of 1.50 is .0668, found by .5000 − .4332. The area to the left of − 1.50 is also .0668, so the p-value is .0668 + .0668 = .1336. As expected, the p-value is larger than the significance level (.01) when the null hypothesis is not rejected. The p-value is shown in "tan" in Chart 9–7 on the previous page.

SELF-REVIEW 9–3

The answers are at the end of the chapter.

Corngrow is a chemical specifically designed to add weight to corn during the growing season. Alternate acres were treated with Corngrow during the growing season. In order to determine whether or not Corngrow was effective, 400 ears of corn receiving the Corngrow treatment were selected at random. Each was weighed, and the mean weight was computed to be 16 ounces, with a standard deviation of 1 ounce. Likewise, 100 ears of untreated corn were weighed. The mean was 15.7 ounces, and the standard deviation was 1.2 ounces.

1. Using a one-tailed test and the .05 level, can we say that Corngrow was effective in adding weight to the corn?
2. Show the decision rule graphically.
3. Compute the p-value. Interpret it.

EXERCISES

The answers to the odd-numbered exercises are at the end of the book.

9. A sample of 40 observations is selected from one normal population. The sample mean is 102, and the sample standard deviation is 5. A sample of 50 observations is selected from a second normal population. The sample mean is 99, and the sample standard deviation is 6. Conduct the following test of hypothesis using the .04 significance level.

$$H_0: \mu_1 = \mu_2$$

$$H_1: \mu_1 \neq \mu_2$$

   a. Is this a one-tailed or a two-tailed test?
   b. State the decision rule.
   c. Compute the value of the test statistic.
   d. What is your decision regarding H_0?
   e. What is the *p*-value?

10. A sample of 65 observations is selected from one normal population. The sample mean is 2.67, and the sample standard deviation is 0.75. A sample of 50 observations is selected from a second normal population. The sample mean is 2.59, and the sample standard deviation is 0.66. Conduct the following test of hypothesis using the .08 significance level.

$$H_0: \mu_1 \leq \mu_2$$

$$H_1: \mu_1 > \mu_2$$

   a. Is this a one-tailed or a two-tailed test?
   b. State the decision rule.
   c. Compute the value of the test statistic.
   d. What is your decision regarding H_0?
   e. What is the *p*-value?

11. The Metro Real Estate Association is preparing a pamphlet that they feel might be of interest to prospective home buyers in the Rossford and Northwood areas of the city. One item of interest is the length of time the seller occupied the home. A sample of 40 homes sold recently in Rossford revealed that the mean length of ownership was 7.6 years, with a standard deviation of 2.3 years. A sample of 55 homes in Northwood revealed that the mean length of ownership was 8.1 years with a standard deviation of 2.9 years. At the .05 significance level, can we conclude that the Rossford residents owned their homes for a shorter period of time? Use the five-step hypothesis-testing procedure. Compute the *p*-value and interpret it.

12. A study is made comparing the cost to rent a one-bedroom apartment in Cincinnati with the corresponding cost of similar apartments in Pittsburgh. A sample of 35 apartments in Cincinnati showed the mean rental rate to be $370 with a standard deviation of $30. A sample of 40 apartments in Pittsburgh showed the mean rate to be $380 with a standard deviation of $26. At the .05 significance level, is there a difference in the mean rental rate between Cincinnati and Pittsburgh? Use the five-step hypothesis-testing procedure.

13. A financial analyst is interested in comparing the turnover rates, in percent, for shares of oil-related stocks versus other stocks, such as GE and IBM. She selected 32 oil-related stocks and 49 other stocks. The mean turnover rate of oil-related stocks is 31.4 percent and the standard deviation 5.1 percent. For the other stocks, the mean rate was computed to be 34.9 percent and the standard deviation 6.7 percent. Is there a significant

difference in the turnover rates of the two types of stock? The null and alternate hypotheses are:

$$H_0: \mu_1 = \mu_2$$

$$H_1: \mu_1 \neq \mu_2$$

a. Is this a one-tailed or a two-tailed test? What is your reasoning?
b. Using the .01 level of significance, what is the decision rule?
c. Determine the value of the test statistic, and arrive at a decision regarding H_0. Explain the meaning of your decision.

TESTS CONCERNING PROPORTIONS

The material presented so far in this chapter has used the interval or the ratio scale of measurement. That is, we used variables such as weights, incomes, distances, and ages. We now want to consider situations such as the following:

- The career services director at Southern Technical College reports that 80 percent of its graduates enter the job market in a position directly related to their field of study.
- A company representative claims that more than 45 percent of Burger King sales are made at the drive-through window.
- A large company wants to know if there is a difference in the proportions of male and female executives willing to move to a different city to gain a promotion.

These problems are illustrations of the nominal scale of measurement. Recall that for the nominal scale of measurement the observation is recorded in one of two or more categories. For example, a person is classified as being male or female. Or a potential voter is classified as Republican, Democrat, independent, or other.

Proportion A fraction, ratio, or percentage that indicates the part of the population or sample having a particular trait of interest.

As an example of a proportion, suppose 92 out of 100 surveyed favor daylight savings time during the summer. The sample proportion is 92/100, or .92, or 92 percent. If we let $\bar{p}$ stand for the sample proportion, then:

$$\bar{p} = \frac{\text{Number of successes in the sample}}{\text{Number sampled}} \qquad (9\text{–}4)$$

Some assumptions must be made and conditions met before testing a population proportion. To test a hypothesis about a population proportion, a random sample is chosen from the population. This is called the experiment. It is assumed that the binomial assumptions discussed in Chapter 6 are met: (1) the sample data collected are the result of counts; (2) an outcome of an experiment is classified into one of two mutually exclusive categories—a "success" or a "failure"; (3) the probability of a success stays the same for each trial; and (4) the trials are independent, meaning that the outcome of one trial does not affect the outcome of any other trial.

np and *n*(1 − *p*) must be greater than 5

The test we will conduct shortly is appropriate when both *np* and *n*(1 − *p*) are greater than 5. *n* is the sample size, and *p* is the population proportion. In addition, *n* should be large. Researchers disagree on how large *n* should be; some say 30, some say 50, and others say 100. For the purposes of this book, the sample size should be at least 50.

This test is introduced here because it is a special extension of the test presented earlier in this chapter and also is widely used. This test is a good example of the case wherein the normal probability distribution is applied to approximate a binomial probability distribution with a great deal of accuracy.

A One-Tailed Test

EXAMPLE

Suppose prior elections in a state indicated that it is necessary for a candidate for governor to receive at least 80 percent of the vote in the northern section of the state to be elected. The incumbent governor is interested in assessing his chances of returning to office and plans to conduct a survey consisting of 2,000 registered voters in the northern section of the state.

Will the incumbent governor be reelected?

Using the hypothesis-testing procedure, assess the governor's chances of reelection.

Solution ▸

The following test of hypothesis can be conducted because both *np* and *n*(1 − *p*) exceed 5. Also, *n* is greater than 50. In this problem $n = 2{,}000$ and $p = .80$ (*p* is the proportion of the vote in the northern part of the state, or 80 percent, needed to be elected). Thus, $np = 2{,}000(.80) = 1{,}600$ and $n(1 - p) = 2{,}000(1 - .80) = 400$. Both 1,600 and 400 are greater than 5.

We will use the five-step hypothesis-testing procedure.

Hypotheses

Step 1 The null hypothesis, H_0, is that the population proportion *p* is .80 (or more). The alternate hypothesis, H_1, is that the proportion is less than .80. From a practical standpoint, the incumbent governor is concerned only when the sample proportion is less than .80. If it is equal to or greater than .80, he will have no problem; that is, the sample data would indicate he will probably be reelected. These hypotheses are written symbolically as:

$$H_0\colon p \geq .80$$

$$H_1\colon p < .80$$

H_1 states a direction. Thus, as noted previously, the test is one-tailed, with the inequality sign pointing to the tail of the curve containing the region of rejection.

Level of significance

Step 2 The level of significance is .05. This is the likelihood that a true hypothesis will be rejected.

Test statistic is *z*

Step 3 *z* is the appropriate statistic, found by:

$$z = \frac{\bar{p} - p}{\sigma_p} \qquad (9\text{–}5)$$

where:

p is the population proportion.

$\bar{p}$ is the sample proportion.

σ_p is the standard error of the population proportion. It is computed by $\sqrt{p(1 - p)/n}$, so the formula for z becomes:

$$z = \frac{\bar{p} - p}{\sqrt{\frac{p(1 - p)}{n}}} \qquad (9\text{–}6)$$

where n is the sample size.

Critical value

Step 4 The critical value or values of z form the dividing point or points between the regions where H_0 is rejected and where it is not rejected. Since the alternate hypothesis states a direction, this is a one-tailed test. The sign of inequality points to the left, so only the left half of the curve is used. (See Chart 9–8.) Alpha was given as .05 in step 2. This probability is in the left tail and determines the region of rejection. The area between zero and the critical value is .4500, found by .5000 − .0500. Referring to Appendix D and searching for .4500, we find the critical value of z to be about 1.645. The decision rule is therefore: Reject the null hypothesis and accept the alternate hypothesis if the computed value of z falls to the left of − 1.645; otherwise do not reject H_0.

CHART 9–8 **Rejection and Nonrejection Regions for the .05 Level of Significance, One-Tailed Test**

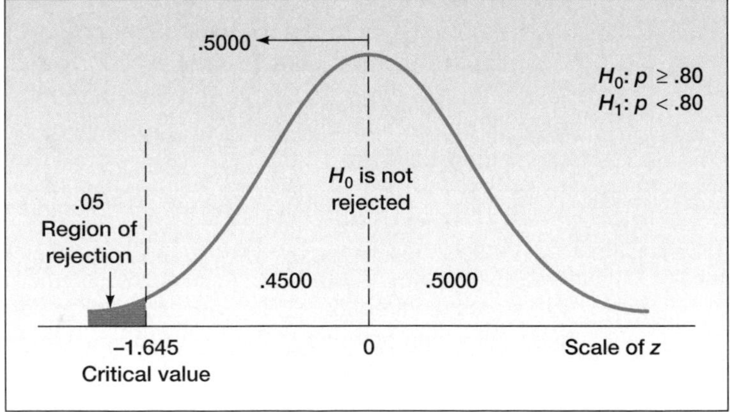

Select a sample, make a decision regarding H_0

Step 5 Select a sample and make a decision with respect to H_0. A sample survey of 2,000 potential voters in the northern part of the state revealed that 1,550 planned to vote for the incumbent governor. Is the proportion of .775 (found by 1,550/2,000) "close enough" to .80 to conclude that the difference is due to chance?

In this problem:

$\bar{p}$ is .775, the proportion in the sample who plan to vote for the governor.
n is 2,000, the number of voters surveyed.
p is .80, the hypothesized population proportion.
z is a normally distributed test statistic when the hypothesis is true and the other assumptions are true.

$\bar{p}$ = sample proportion;
p = population proportion

Using formula (9–6) and computing z:

$$z = \frac{\bar{p} - p}{\sqrt{\dfrac{p(1-p)}{n}}} = \frac{\dfrac{1{,}550}{2{,}000} - .80}{\sqrt{\dfrac{.80(1-.80)}{2{,}000}}} = \frac{.775 - .80}{\sqrt{.00008}} = \frac{-.025}{.0089443} = -2.80$$

Sample survey reveals incumbent won't be reelected.

The computed value of z (− 2.80) is in the rejection region, so the null hypothesis is rejected at the .05 level. The difference of 2.5 percentage points between the sample percent (77.5 percent) and the hypothesized population percent in the northern part of the state necessary to carry the state (80 percent) is statistically significant. It is probably not due to sampling variation. To put it another way, the evidence at this point does not support the claim that the incumbent governor will return to the governor's mansion for another four years.

The p-value is the probability of finding a z value less than −2.80. From Appendix D, the probability of a z value between 0 and −2.80 is .4974. So the p-value is .0026, found by .5000 − .4974. The governor cannot be confident of reelection.

SELF-REVIEW 9–4

The answers are at the end of the chapter.

This claim is to be investigated at the .01 level: "Forty percent or more of those persons who retired from an industrial job before the age of 60 would return to work if a suitable job were available." Seventy-four persons out of the 200 sampled said they would return to work.

1. Can the z test be used? Why or why not?
2. State the null and alternate hypotheses.
3. Show the decision rule graphically.
4. Compute z, and arrive at a decision.
5. Compute the p-value. Interpret it.

EXERCISES

The answers to the odd-numbered exercises are at the end of the book.

14. The following hypotheses are given.

$$H_0: p \leq .70$$

$$H_1: p > .70$$

A sample of 100 observations revealed that $\bar{p}$ = .75. At the .05 significance level, can the null hypothesis be rejected?

a. State the decision rule.
b. Compute the value of the test statistic.
c. What is your decision regarding the null hypothesis?

15. The following hypotheses are given.

$$H_0: p = .40$$
$$H_1: p \neq .40$$

A sample of 120 observations revealed that $\bar{p} = .30$. At the .05 significance level, can the null hypothesis be rejected?
a. State the decision rule.
b. Compute the value of the test statistic.
c. What is your decision regarding the null hypothesis?

Note: It is recommended that the five-step hypothesis-testing procedure be used in solving the following problems.

16. The National Safety Council reported in *Vitality* that 52 percent of American turnpike drivers are men. A sample of 300 cars traveling eastbound on the Ohio Turnpike yesterday revealed that 170 were driven by men. At the .01 significance level, can we conclude that a larger proportion of men were driving on the Ohio Turnpike than the national statistics indicate?
17. A recent article in *USA Today* reported that a job awaits only one in three new college graduates. The major reasons given were an overabundance of college graduates and a weak economy. A survey of 200 recent graduates from your school revealed that 80 students had jobs. At the .02 significance level, can we conclude that a larger proportion of students at your school have jobs?
18. Chicken Delight claims that 90 percent of its orders are delivered within 30 minutes of the time the order is placed. A sample of 100 orders revealed that 82 were delivered within the promised time. Is Chicken Delight's claim valid at the .10 level of significance? Let H_1 be $p < .90$.
19. Research at the University of Toledo indicates that 50 percent of the students change their major area of study after their first year in the program. A random sample of 100 students in the College of Business revealed that 48 had changed their major area of study after their first year of the program. Has there been a significant decrease in the proportion of students who change their major after the first year in the program? Test at the .05 level of significance. (Source: Unpublished study, Office of Institutional Research, University of Toledo.)

A TEST INVOLVING THE DIFFERENCE BETWEEN TWO POPULATION PROPORTIONS

Cases involving two proportions

Several typical cases involving population proportions follow.

A mock model of a proposed new automobile was shown to two groups of 150 persons each. One group consisted of a random sample of persons between 18 and 25 years of age, and the other group consisted of a random sample of persons more than 50 years old. Eighty percent of the younger group rated the styling satisfactory, but only 50 percent of the older group gave it a similar rating. In evaluating the market potential of this proposed automobile, is it reasonable to expect that it would appeal primarily to younger persons? Or is it possible that this difference of 30 percentage points could be due to sampling; that is,

might not the two age groups in the population like the proposed automobile equally well?

Two new high-speed machines designed by different companies are being considered for purchase. One factor in the final choice is the percent defective that each machine produces. A sample of the output of one of the machines revealed that 6 percent were defective. A sample of the output of the other machine indicated that 10 percent of the total were defective. Is the machine with the 6 percent scrap significantly better than the one with the 10 percent scrap? Or is there a chance that the two machines are producing an equal percent defective?

An agricultural example

Comstock hybrid corn seed was divided into two piles before planting. The seeds in one pile were soaked with a chemical claimed to significantly reduce corn borers. The other pile was not treated. The two types of seed corn were planted in alternate rows and clearly identified. Samples from each row were selected at random during the harvest season, and it was discovered that 20 percent of the treated corn had corn borers and 80 percent of the untreated sample had borers. Was the treatment effective?

A marketing example

Manelli has developed a new perfume named Heavenly. A number of comparison tests indicate that the perfume has good market potential. The marketing and advertising departments, however, want to plan their strategy so as to reach and impress the largest possible segment of the buying public. One of the questions is whether the perfume is preferred by a larger proportion of younger women or a larger proportion of older women. There are two populations, therefore—a population consisting of young women and one consisting of older women. A standard smell test is used. Women selected at random are asked to sniff several perfumes in succession, including the one they most frequently use and, of course, Heavenly. The names of the perfumes are known only to the person administering the test. Each woman selects the perfume she likes best.

A Two-Tailed Test

The procedures followed in making a statistical decision involving the difference between two proportions will now be examined. The perfume problem has been selected.

The usual five steps

Step 1: A Statement of H_0 and H_1 In this problem the null hypothesis is: "There is no difference between the proportion of young women who prefer Heavenly and the proportion of older women who prefer it." If the proportion of young women in the population is designated as p_1 and the proportion of older women is p_2, then the null hypothesis is $p_1 = p_2$. The alternate hypothesis is that the two proportions are not equal, or $p_1 \neq p_2$. (Note again that the lower-case letter p represents the population proportions.)

Step 2: The Level of Significance It was decided to use the .05 level.

Step 3: The Statistical Test Plans are to take a random sample of 100 young women, designated n_1, and a sample of 200 older women, designated by n_2. The z distribution is the appropriate test statistic. It approximates the standard normal distribution and is computed by:

$$z = \frac{\bar{p}_1 - \bar{p}_2}{\sqrt{\frac{\bar{p}_c(1-\bar{p}_c)}{n_1} + \frac{\bar{p}_c(1-\bar{p}_c)}{n_2}}} \qquad (9\text{–}7)$$

where:

n_1 is the number of young women selected in the sample.

n_2 is the number of older women selected in the sample.

$\bar{p}_c$ is the *weighted* mean of the two sample proportions, computed by:

$$\bar{p}_c = \frac{\text{Total number of successes}}{\text{Total number in samples}} = \frac{X_1 + X_2}{n_1 + n_2} \qquad (9\text{–}8)$$

X_1 is the number of young women (sample 1) who prefer Heavenly.

X_2 is the number of older women (sample 2) who prefer Heavenly.

$\bar{p}_c$ = combined (pooled) estimate

$\bar{p}_c$ is generally referred to as the *pooled estimate of the population proportion.* This is the best estimate of the proportion of women in the population who prefer Heavenly, and it does not consider whether they are old or young. Hence, it is a "pooled," or "combined," estimate.

Step 4: The Decision Rule Recall that the null hypothesis, H_0, states that $p_1 = p_2$, and the alternate hypothesis, H_1, is $p_1 \neq p_2$. Since H_1 does not state any direction (such as $p_1 < p_2$), the test is *two-tailed.* Thus, the critical values for the .05 level are -1.96 and $+1.96$. As before, if the computed z value falls in the region between +1.96 and −1.96, the null hypothesis is not rejected. If that does occur, it is assumed that any difference between the two sample proportions is due to chance variation (see Chart 9–9).

CHART 9–9 **Two-Tailed Test, Areas of Rejection and Nonrejection, .05 Level of Significance**

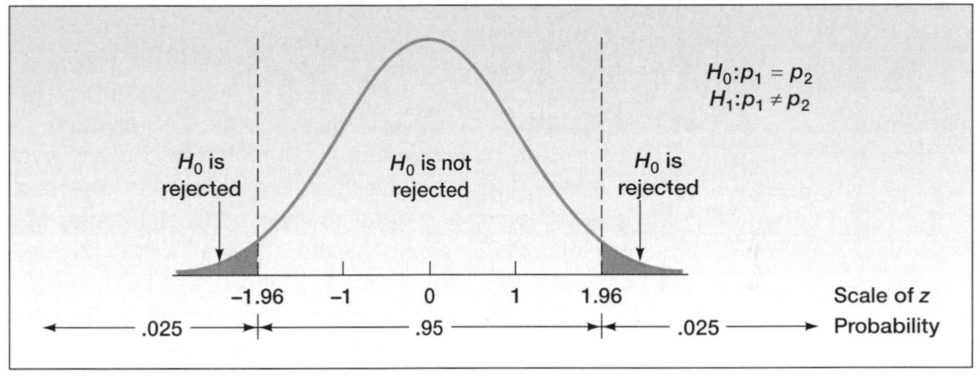

Step 5: The Decision A total of 100 young women were selected at random, and each was given the standard smell test. Twenty of the 100 young women chose Heavenly as the perfume they liked best.

Twenty percent of younger women prefer Heavenly

X_1 is the number preferring Heavenly = 20.

n_1 is the number in sample = 100.

$$\bar{p}_1 = \frac{X_1}{n_1} = \frac{20}{100} = .20$$

Two hundred older women were selected at random, and each was given the same standard smell test. Of the 200 older women, 100 preferred Heavenly.

Fifty percent of older women prefer Heavenly

X_2 is the number preferring Heavenly = 100.

n_2 is the number in sample = 200.

$$\bar{p}_2 = \frac{X_2}{n_2} = \frac{100}{200} = .50$$

The pooled or weighted proportion, $\bar{p}_c$, is computed using formula 9–8.

$$\bar{p}_c = \frac{X_1 + X_2}{n_1 + n_2} = \frac{20 + 100}{100 + 200} = \frac{120}{300} = .40$$

Pooled estimate is .40

Note that the weighted proportion of .40 is closer to .50 than to .20. (This is because more older women than younger women were sampled.)

Computing z using formula (9–7):

$$z = \frac{\bar{p}_1 - \bar{p}_2}{\sqrt{\frac{\bar{p}_c(1-\bar{p}_c)}{n_1} + \frac{\bar{p}_c(1-\bar{p}_c)}{n_2}}}$$

$$= \frac{.20 - .50}{\sqrt{\frac{.40(1-.40)}{100} + \frac{.40(1-.40)}{200}}}$$

$$= \frac{-.30}{.06} = -5.00$$

Reject H_0

The computed z of -5.00 falls in the area of rejection, that is, to the left of -1.96. Therefore, the null hypothesis is rejected at the .05 level of significance. To put it another way, the hypothesis that the proportion of young women in the population who prefer Heavenly is equal to the proportion of older women in the population who prefer Heavenly is rejected at the .05 level. It is highly unlikely that such a large difference between the two sample proportions (.30) could be due to chance (sampling).

Unlikely that difference between .20 and .50 is due to sampling error

The probability of committing a Type I error is .05, which is the same as the level of significance selected before the project started. This indicates there is a 5 percent risk of rejecting the true hypothesis that $p_1 = p_2$. The p-value is 0, because the probability of finding a z value less than -5.00 or greater than 5.00 is so small as to be virtually 0.

SELF-REVIEW 9–5

The answers are at the end of the chapter.

Of 150 adults who tried Smack Smack, a new candy, 87 rated it excellent. Of 200 children sampled, 123 rated it excellent. Using the .10 level of significance, can we conclude that there is a significant difference in the proportion of adults versus children who rate the candy excellent?

1. What is the null hypothesis? What is the alternate hypothesis?
2. What is the probability of a Type I error?
3. Is this a one-tailed test or a two-tailed test? Why?
4. What is the critical value?
5. Should the null hypothesis be rejected or not rejected?
6. What is the p-value? Explain its meaning.

EXERCISES

The answers to the odd-numbered exercises are at the end of the book.

20. The stated hypotheses are:

$$H_0: p_1 \le p_2$$

$$H_1: p_1 > p_2$$

A sample of 100 observations from the first population indicated that X_1 is 70. A sample of 150 observations from the second population revealed X_2 to be 90. Use the .05 significance level to test the hypothesis.

a. State the decision rule.
b. Compute the pooled proportion.
c. Compute the value of the test statistic.
d. What is your decision regarding the null hypothesis?

21. The hypotheses H_0 and H_1 are:

$$H_0: p_1 = p_2$$

$$H_1: p_1 \neq p_2$$

A sample of 200 observations from the first population revealed X_1 to be 170. A sample of 150 observations from the second population resulted in an X_2 of 110. Use the .05 significance level.
a. State the decision rule.
b. Compute the pooled proportion.
c. Compute the value of the test statistic.
d. What is your decision regarding the null hypothesis?

Note: It is recommended that the five-step hypothesis-testing procedure be used in solving the following problems

22. The Damon family owns a large grape vineyard in western New York state. The grapevines must be sprayed at the beginning of the growing season to protect against various insects and diseases. Two new insecticides have just been marketed: Pernod 5 and Action. To test their effectiveness, three long rows were selected and sprayed with Pernod 5, and three others were sprayed with Action. When the grapes ripened, 400 of the vines treated with Pernod 5 were checked for infestation. Likewise, a sample of 400 vines sprayed with Action were checked. The results are:

Insecticide	Number of vines checked (sample size)	Number of infested vines
Pernod 5	400	24
Action	400	40

At the .05 significance level, can we say that there is a difference in the proportion of vines infested using Pernod 5 as opposed to Action?

23. The Roper Organization conducted identical surveys in 1970 and 1990. One question asked women was, "Are most men basically kind, gentle, and thoughtful?" The 1970 survey revealed that out of the 3,000 women surveyed 2,010 said that they were. In 1990 1,530 out of the 3,000 women surveyed thought that men were kind, gentle, and thoughtful. At the .05 level, can we conclude that women think men are less kind, gentle, and thoughtful in 1990 compared with 1970? (Source: "Men Rate Less," *Detroit Free Press*, April 26, 1990, p. 15.)

24. A nationwide sample of influential Republicans and Democrats were asked as a part of a comprehensive survey whether they favored lowering the environmental standards so that high-sulfur coal could be burned in coal-fired power plants. The results were:

	Republicans	Democrats
Number sampled	1,000	800
Number in favor	200	168

At the .02 level of significance, can we conclude that there is a larger proportion of Democrats in favor of lowering the standards?

25. The research department at the home office of New Hampshire Insurance conducts ongoing research on the causes of automobile accidents, the characteristics of the

drivers, and so on. A random sample of 400 policies written on single persons was selected. It was discovered that in the previous three-year period, 120 of them had at least one accident. Similarly, a sample of 600 policies written on married persons revealed that 150 had been in at least one accident. At the .05 level, is there a significant difference in the proportions of single and married persons having an accident during a three-year period?

TYPE II ERRORS, OPERATING CHARACTERISTIC CURVES, AND POWER CURVES

Type II Errors

Recall that the risk of a Type I error, also called the alpha risk of a statistical test, is *the probability of rejecting the null hypothesis when it is really true.* This risk is the same as the level of significance selected. As noted, the most commonly used levels are .05, .01, and .10.

P (Type II error) = β

The risk of a Type II error, designated by β, is *the probability of accepting the null hypothesis as true when it is really not true.* To illustrate the computation of the probability of committing a Type II error, suppose a manufacturer purchases steel bars to

CHART 9–10 **Charts Showing Type I and Type II Errors**

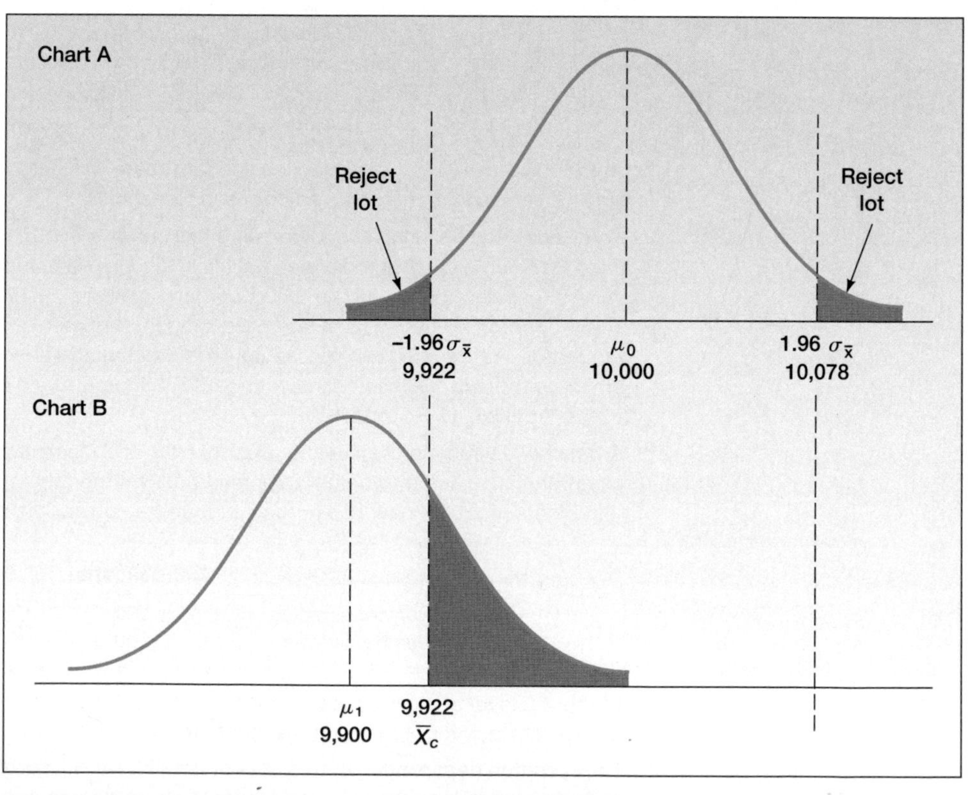

make cotter pins. Past experience revealed that the true mean tensile strength of all incoming shipments is 10,000 psi and the standard deviation (σ) 400 psi.

In order to make a decision about incoming shipments of steel bars, the manufacturer set up this rule for the quality-control inspector to follow: "Take a sample of 100 steel bars. If the sample mean ($\overline{X}$) strength falls between 9,922 psi and 10,078 psi, accept the lot. Otherwise the lot is to be rejected." Refer to Chart 9–10 and the graph labeled A. It shows the region where each lot is rejected and where it is not rejected. The mean of this distribution is designated μ_0. The tails of the curve represent the probability of making a Type I error, that is, rejecting the incoming lot of steel bars when in fact it is a good lot, with a mean of 10,000 psi.

How is the probability of a Type II error computed? (Recall it is the probability of accepting an incoming lot as a "good lot" when in fact the mean is not 10,000 psi.)

EXAMPLE

Suppose the unknown population mean of an incoming lot, designated μ_1, is really 9,900 psi. What is the probability that the quality-control inspector will fail to reject the shipment (a Type II error)?

Solution

Computations for β (Type II error)

The probability of committing a Type II error, as represented by the green area in Chart 9–10, graph B, can be computed by determining the area under the normal curve that lies above 9,922 pounds. The calculation of the areas under the normal curve was discussed in Chapter 7. Reviewing briefly, it is necessary first to determine the probability of the sample mean falling between 9,900 and 9,922. Then this probability is subtracted from .5000 (which represents all the area beyond the mean of 9,900) to arrive at the probability of making a Type II error.

The number of standard units (z values) between the mean of the incoming lot (9,900), designated μ_1, and $\overline{X}_c$, representing the critical value for 9,922 is computed by:

$$z = \frac{\overline{X}_c - \mu_1}{\sigma/\sqrt{n}} \tag{9–9}$$

With $n = 100$ and $\sigma = 400$, the value of z is 0.55:

$$z = \frac{\overline{X}_c - \mu_1}{\sigma/\sqrt{n}}$$

$$= \frac{9{,}922 - 9{,}900}{400/\sqrt{100}} = \frac{22}{40} = 0.55$$

The area under the curve between 9,900 and 9,922 (a z value of 0.55) is .2088 (from Appendix D).

The area under the curve beyond 9,922 pounds is .5000 − .2088, or .2912; this is the probability of making a Type II error—that is, accepting an incoming lot of steel bars when the population mean is 9,900 psi.

Using the methods illustrated by Charts 9–10B and 9–11C, the probability of accepting a hypothesis as true when it is actually false can be determined for any particular value of μ_1.

CHART 9–11 Type I and Type II Errors

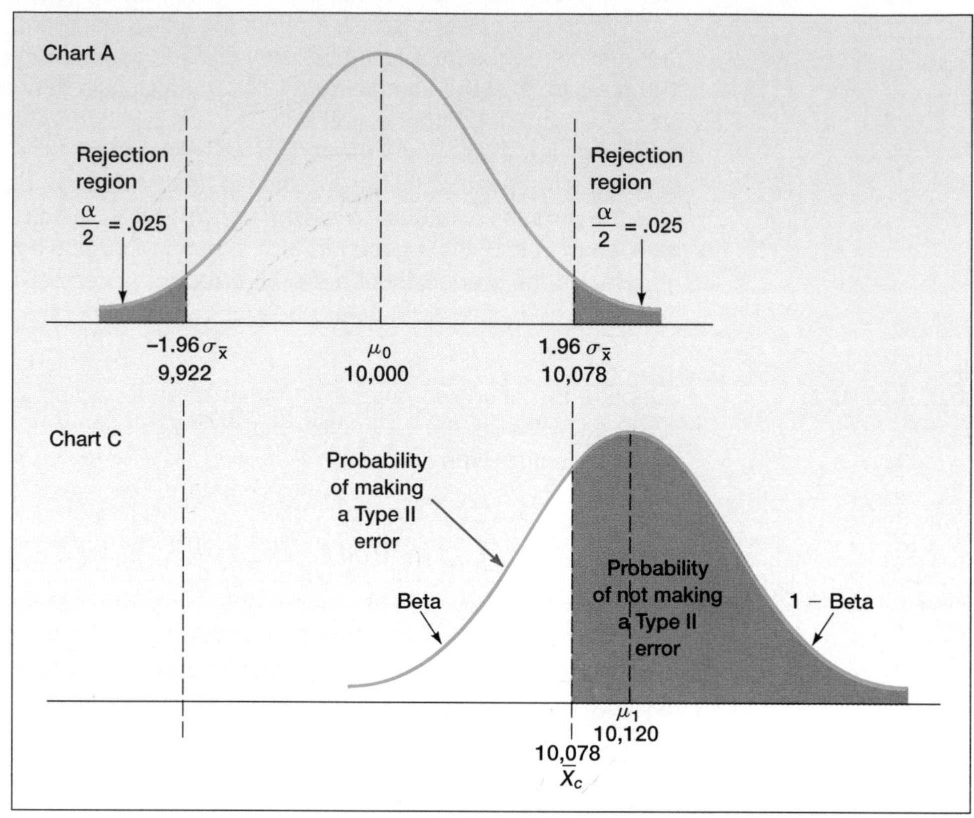

Type II error probabilities are shown in the center column of Table 9–1 for selected values of μ, given in the left column. The right column gives the probability of not making a Type II error.

TABLE 9–1 Probabilities of a Type II Error and Power Functions for μ_0 = 10,000 Pounds and Selected Alternative Means, .05 Level of Significance

Selected alternative mean (pounds)	Probability of Type II error (β)	Probability of not making a Type II error ($1 - \beta$)
9,820	.0054	.9946
9,880	.1469	.8531
9,900	.2912	.7088
9,940	.6736	.3264
9,980	.9265	.0735
10,000	—*	—
10,020	.9265	.0735
10,060	.6736	.3264
10,100	.2912	.7088
10,120	.1469	.8531
10,180	.0054	.9946

*It is not possible to make a Type II error when $\mu = \mu_0$.

SELF-REVIEW 9–6

The answers are at the end of the chapter.

Suppose the true mean of an incoming lot of steel bars is 10,120 psi. What is the probability that the quality control inspector will accept the bars as having a mean of 10,000 psi? (It sounds implausible that steel bars will be rejected if the tensile strength is higher than specified. However, it may be that the cotter pin has a dual function in an outboard motor. It may be designed not to shear off if the motor hits a small object, but to shear off if it hits a rock. Therefore, the steel should not be *too* strong.)

The white area in Chart 9–11C represents the probability of falsely accepting the hypothesis that the mean tensile strength of the incoming lot of steel is 10,000 psi. What is the probability of committing a Type II error?

EXERCISES

The answers to the odd-numbered exercises are at the end of the book.

26. Refer to Table 9–1 and the example just completed. With $n = 100$, $\sigma = 400$, $\overline{X}_c = 9{,}922$, and $\mu_1 = 9{,}880$, verify that the probability of a Type II error is .1469.
27. Refer to Table 9–1 and the example just completed. With $n = 100$, $\sigma = 400$, $\overline{X}_c = 9{,}922$, and $\mu_1 = 9{,}940$, verify that the probability of a Type II error is .6736.

Operating Characteristic Curves

The beta probabilities in column 2 of Table 9–1 are used to plot an *operating characteristic curve* (see Chart 9–12).

CHART 9–12 **Operating Characteristic Curve**

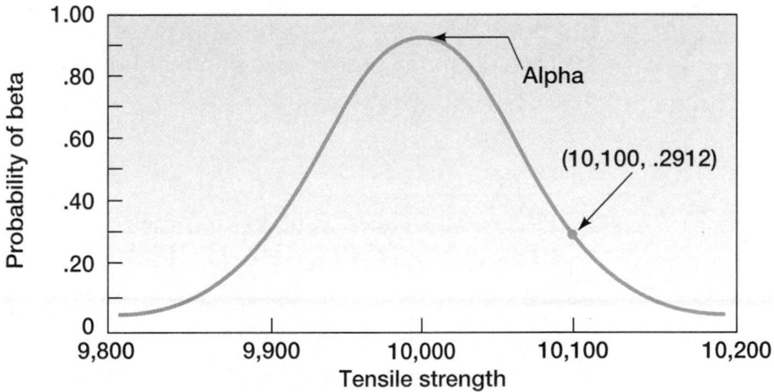

The operating characteristic (OC) curve is a convenient way of showing graphically the probability of accepting a false hypothesis. The OC curves vary according to the sample size, the standard error of the mean, and the level of significance selected.

Power Curves

Power curve

Referring to Table 9–1, the third column simply represents the probability of *not* committing a Type II error—that is, $1 - \beta$. These probabilities are the basis for the *power curve* shown in Chart 9–13.

CHART 9–13 **Power Curve**

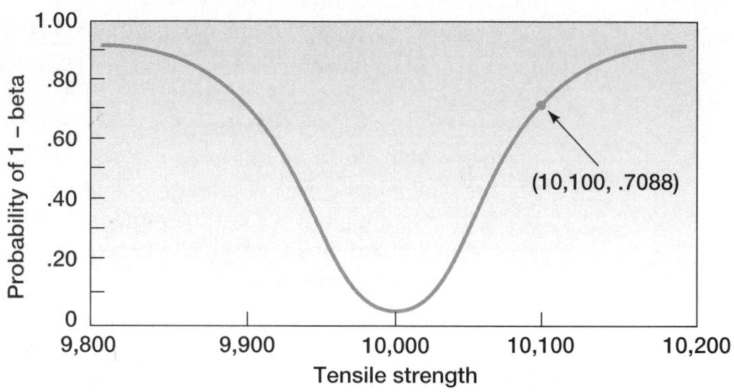

What a power curve shows

The power curve is a graphic presentation of the probabilities of not committing a Type II error. The set of $1 - \beta$ probabilities in column 3 of Table 9–1 is called the *power function* of the test. The higher the probabilities, the greater the discriminatory power of the test. To explain, suppose the mean tensile strength of an incoming shipment of steel bars is 9,880 pounds per square inch. If a large number of samples of 100 bars were tested for tensile strength, about 85.31 percent of the samples would yield the correct decision to reject the incoming shipment. It should be noted that when the mean decreases or increases slightly, we cannot detect the change as readily as we can for a substantial change in the mean.

If management wishes to be more discriminatory, one possibility is to increase the size of the sample. Suppose the sample size were increased from 100 to 200 and the probability of $1 - \beta$ computed to be .9200. It can be said that the sample of size 200 yields more power to discover that the mean of the incoming shipment is not 10,000 psi (because $.9200 > .8531$).

CHAPTER OUTLINE

I. The objective of hypothesis testing is to check the validity of statements about a population parameter.

II. The procedures used in hypothesis testing are:
   A. State the null hypothesis H_0 and the alternate hypothesis H_1.
   B. Select the level of significance. The levels .10, .05, and .01 are three of the levels most commonly used. It is the probability of rejecting a true hypothesis and is the Type I error.
   C. Decide on the test statistic. The standard normal distribution using the test statistic z is applied for large-sample tests of means and proportions.
   D. State the decision rule. This defines the region where the null hypothesis is rejected.
   E. Take a sample and make a decision regarding H_0.
   F. The *p*-value is the probability that the test statistic in a hypothesis test is as extreme as the one obtained.

III. Testing a hypothesis about the population mean.
   A. *Formula for z.* If the standard deviation of the population, σ, is known:

$$z = \frac{\bar{X} - \mu}{\sigma/\sqrt{n}} \quad (9\text{–}1)$$

B. If σ is unknown and $n \geq 30$, substitute the sample standard deviation, s, for σ.

IV. Hypothesis testing: two means, large samples.

A. *Objective.* Using the usual hypothesis-testing procedures, determine whether or not there is a difference between two population means using large samples (30 or more).

B. *Formula for z:*

$$z = \frac{\bar{X}_1 - \bar{X}_2}{\sqrt{\frac{s_1^2}{n_1} + \frac{s_2^2}{n_2}}} \quad (9\text{–}3)$$

V. Hypothesis testing about a single proportion.

A. Both np and $n(1 - p)$ must be greater than 5.

B. The formula for computing z is:

$$z = \frac{\bar{p} - p}{\sqrt{\frac{p(1 - p)}{n}}} \quad (9\text{–}6)$$

where:

$\bar{p}$ is the proportion in the sample possessing the trait.

n is the size of the sample.

p is the hypothesized population proportion.

VI. Hypothesis testing about two population proportions: The formula for z is:

$$z = \frac{\bar{p}_1 - \bar{p}_2}{\sqrt{\frac{\bar{p}_c(1 - \bar{p}_c)}{n_1} + \frac{\bar{p}_c(1 - \bar{p}_c)}{n_2}}} \quad (9\text{–}7)$$

where:

n_1 is the total number in the first sample.

n_2 is the total number in the second sample.

$\bar{p}_c$ is the pooled estimate of the population proportion, found by:

$$\bar{p}_c = \frac{X_1 + X_2}{n_1 + n_2} \quad (9\text{–}8)$$

where:

X_1 is the number in the first sample that possess the trait.

X_2 is the number in the second sample that possess the trait.

VII. Type I and Type II errors.

A. A Type I error occurs when a true null hypothesis is rejected.

1. It is equal to the level of significance.
2. It is designated as α.

B. A Type II error occurs when a false null hypothesis is not rejected.

1. It is designated as β.
2. The likelihood of a Type II error is found by:

$$z = \frac{\bar{X}_c - \mu_1}{\sigma/\sqrt{n}} \quad (9\text{–}9)$$

where:

$\overline{X}_c$ is the control limit.

μ_1 is the population mean.

σ is the population standard deviation.

n is the sample size.

EXERCISES

The answers to the odd-numbered exercises are at the end of the book.

Note: It is suggested that the five-step hypothesis-testing procedure be followed for these exercises.

28. A new weight-watching company, Weight Reducers International, advertises that those who join will lose, on the average, 10 pounds the first two weeks (H_0: $\mu \geq 10$, H_1: $\mu < 10$). A random sample of 50 people who joined the new weight reduction program revealed the mean loss to be 9 pounds. The standard deviation of the sample was computed to be 2.8 pounds. At the .05 level of significance, can we conclude that those joining Weight Reducers on average will lose less than 10 pounds? Determine the *p*-value.
29. Dole is concerned that the 16-ounce can of sliced pineapple is being overfilled. The quality-control department took a random sample of 50 cans and found that the arithmetic mean weight was 16.05 ounces, with a sample standard deviation of 0.03 ounces. At the 5 percent level of significance, can we conclude that the mean weight is greater than 16 ounces? Determine the *p*-value.
30. The Peoria Board of Education wants to consider a new academic program funded by the U.S. Department of Education. In order to be eligible for the federal grant, the arithmetic mean income per household must not be more than $15,000. The board hired a research firm to gather the required data. In its report the firm indicated that the arithmetic mean income in the district is $17,000. They further reported that 75 households were surveyed and that the standard deviation of the sample was $3,000. Can the board argue that the difference between the mean income resulting from the sample survey and the mean specified by the Department of Education is due to chance (sampling)? Use the .05 level.
31. A statewide real estate sales agency, Farm Associates, specializes in selling farm property in the state of Nebraska. Their records indicate that the mean selling time of farm property is 90 days. Because of recent drought conditions, they believe that the mean selling time is now greater than 90 days. A statewide study of 100 farms sold recently by the real estate agency is to be conducted in order to update their estimates. The random sample of 100 transactions revealed that the mean selling time was 94 days with a standard deviation of 22 days. At the .10 significance level, can we conclude that the selling time has increased?

32. The mean gross annual incomes of certified tack welders are normally distributed with a mean of $30,000 and a standard deviation of $3,000. The shipbuilding association selects a sample of 120 tack welders and finds the mean is $30,500. At the .10 significance level, can the association conclude that the mean salary does not equal $30,000? Compute the *p*-value and explain its meaning.
33. A recent article in *Vitality* magazine reported that the mean amount of leisure time per week for American men is 40.0 hours. You believe this figure is too large and decide to conduct your own test. In a random sample of 60 men you find that the mean is 37.8 hours of leisure per week and that the standard deviation of the sample is 12.2 hours. Can you conclude that the information in the article is untrue? Use the .05 significance level. Determine the *p*-value and explain its meaning.

34. NBC TV news, in a segment on the price of gasoline, reported last evening that the mean price nationwide is $1.25 per gallon for self-serve regular unleaded. A random sample of 35 stations in the Salt Lake City area revealed that the mean price was $1.27 per gallon and that the standard deviation was $0.05 per gallon. At the .05 significance level, can we conclude that the price of gasoline is higher in the Salt Lake City area? Determine the p-value.

35. The Rutter Nursery Company packages their pine bark mulch in 50-pound bags. From a long history, the packaging department reports that the standard deviation of this process is 3 pounds per bag. At the end of each day Jeff Rutter, the production manager, weighs 10 bags and computes the mean weight of the sample. Below are the weights of 10 bags from today's production.

45.6	47.7	47.6	46.3	46.2	48.5
47.4	49.2	55.8	47.5		

    a. Can Mr. Rutter conclude that the mean weight of the bags is less than 50 pounds? Use the .01 significance level.
    b. In a brief report, tell why Mr. Rutter can use the z distribution as the test statistic.
    c. Compute the p-value.

36. In a recent national survey the mean weekly allowance for a nine-year-old child from his or her parents was reported to be $3.65. A random sample of 45 nine-year-olds in northwestern Ohio revealed the mean allowance to be $3.69 with a standard deviation of $0.24. At the .05 significance level, is there a difference in the mean allowance nationally and the mean allowance in northwestern Ohio for nine-year-olds? (Source: *Vitality Digest.*)

37. The air force trains enlisted computer personnel at two bases—Cass AFB and Kingston AFB. A common final examination is administered. As part of an ongoing study of the training program, a comparison of the final test scores is to be made. Is there any significant difference in the final results of the two educational programs? Use the .04 significance level. Determine the p-value. Explain your decision to the committee studying the program.

	Cass AFB	**Kingston AFB**
Number sampled	40	50
Mean score	114.6	117.9
Sample standard deviation	9.1	10.4

38. Corrigan Industries has been awarded a large contract to supply pipeline parts to Angus Oil, a company drilling in the Scotland-Ireland area. In the past, two subcontractors specializing in steel products have provided Corrigan Industries with high-quality supplies such as nuts, bolts, steel bars, and casing. One of the concerns of Corrigan is the delivery time of the two subcontractors, Jackson Steel and Alabama Distributors. The question to be explored is whether there is a difference in the delivery times of the two subcontractors.

    Random samples from the files of Corrigan Industries revealed these statistics about delivery times:

	Jackson Steel	**Alabama Distributors**
Number in sample	45	50
Mean delivery time (days)	20	21
Sample standard deviation (days)	4	3

At the .05 significance level, is there a difference in the delivery times? Determine the *p*-value.

39. A study was conducted of the annual incomes of beginning probation officers in metropolitan areas of less than 100,000 population and in metropolitan areas having more than 500,000 population. Some sample statistics:

Sample statistic	Population less than 100,000	Population more than 500,000
Sample size	45	60
Sample mean	\$41,290	\$41,330
Sample standard deviation	\$ 1,060	\$ 1,900

Test the hypothesis that the annual incomes of beginning probation officers in areas having more than 500,000 population are significantly greater than those paid in areas of less than 100,000. Use the 5 percent level of risk.

40. Clark Heter is an industrial engineer at Lyons Products. He would like to determine if there are more units produced on the afternoon shift than on the day shift. A sample of 54 day-shift workers showed that the mean number of units produced was 345 with a standard deviation of 21. A sample of 60 afternoon-shift workers showed that the mean number of units produced was 351 with a standard deviation of 28 units. At the .05 significance level, is the number of units produced on the afternoon shift larger?

41. Fry Brothers Heating and Air Conditioning, Inc. employs Larry Clark and George Murnen to make service calls to repair furnaces and air conditioning units in homes. Tom Fry, the owner, would like to know if there is a difference in the mean number of service calls they make per day. A random sample of 40 days last year showed that Larry Clark made an average of 4.77 calls per day with a standard deviation of 1.05 calls per day. For a sample of 50 days George Murnen made an average of 5.02 calls per day with a standard deviation of 1.23 calls per day. At the .05 significance level, is there a difference in the mean number of calls per day between the two employees? What is the *p*-value?

42. A coffee manufacturer is interested in finding out if the mean daily consumption of regular-coffee drinkers is less than that of decaffeinated-coffee drinkers. A random sample of 50 regular-coffee drinkers showed a mean of 4.35 cups per day with a standard deviation of 1.20 cups per day. A sample of 40 decaffeinated-coffee drinkers showed a mean of 5.84 cups per day with a standard deviation of 1.36 cups per day. Use the .01 significance level. Compute the *p*-value.

43. The board of directors at the Anchor Pointe Marina is studying the usage of boats among its members. A sample of 30 members who have boats 10 to 20 feet in length showed that they used their boats an average of 11 days last July. The standard deviation of the sample was 3.88 days. For a sample of 40 members with boats 21 to 40 feet in length, the average number of days they used their boats in July was 7.67 with a standard deviation of 4.42 days. At the .02 significance level, can the board of directors conclude that those with the smaller boats used their crafts more frequently?

44. The *fog index* is used to measure the reading difficulty of written text. Calculating the index involves the following steps: (1) Find the mean number of words per sentence. (2) Find the percent of words with three or more syllables. (3) The fog index is 40 percent of the sum of 1 and 2.

    The fog index for a sample of 36 articles from a scientific journal showed a sample mean of 11.0 and a standard deviation of 2.65. A sample of 40 articles from trade publications showed a mean of 8.9 and a standard deviation of 1.64. At the .01 significance level, is the fog index in the scientific journals significantly higher? (Source: F. K. Shuptrine and D. D. McVicker, "Readability Levels of Magazine Advertisements," *Journal of Advertising Research,* vol. 21, no. 5.)

45. Tina Dennis is the chief accountant for Meek Industries. She believes that the current cash-flow problems of MI are due to the slow collection of accounts receivable. She believes that more than 60 percent of the accounts are in arrears more than three months. A sample of 200 accounts showed that 140 were more than three months old. At the .01 significance level, can we conclude that more than 60 percent of the accounts are in arrears for more than three months?

46. The policy of the Suburban Transit Authority is to add a bus route if more than 55 percent of the potential commuters indicate they would use the particular route. A sample of 70 commuters revealed that 42 would use a proposed route from Bowman Park to the downtown area. Does the Bowman-to-downtown route meet the STA criteria? Use the .05 significance level.

47. Past experience at the Crowder Travel Agency indicated that 44 percent of those persons who wanted the agency to plan a vacation for them wanted to go to Europe. During the most recent busy season, a sampling of 1,000 plans was selected at random from the files. It was found that 480 persons wanted to go to Europe on vacation. Has there been a significant shift upward in the percentage of persons who want to go to Europe? Test at the .05 level.

48. From past experience a television manufacturer found that 10 percent or less of its sets needed any type of repair in the first two years of operation. In a sample of 50 sets manufactured two years ago, 9 need repair. At the .05 significance level, has the percent of sets needing repair increased? Determine the p-value.

49. An urban planner claims that, nationally, 20 percent of all families renting condominiums move during a given year. A random sample of 200 families renting condominiums in Dallas revealed that 56 had moved during the past year. At the .01 significance level, does this evidence suggest that a larger proportion of condominium owners moved in the Dallas area? Determine the p-value.

50. Brayfeld Pharmaceuticals, the manufacturer of *New* Go-Away, a tablet claimed to prevent headaches, is convinced that it is more effective than the old Go-Away, which it will replace. To evaluate the manufacturer's conviction, 200 persons were asked to take *New* Go-Away. During the trial period, 180 of them did not have a headache. A different group of 300 took the old Go-Away, and 261 had no headaches during the trial period. Test the manufacturer's conviction that *New* Go-Away is more effective at the .05 level.

51. Suppose a random sample of 1,000 American-born citizens revealed that 198 favored resumption of full diplomatic relations with Cuba. Similarly, 117 of a sample of 500 foreign-born citizens favored it. At the .05 significance level, is there a difference in the proportion of American versus foreign-born citizens who favor restoring diplomatic relations with Cuba?

52. Is there a difference in the proportion of college men versus college women who smoke at least a pack of cigarettes a day? A sample of 500 men at Northern State University revealed that 70 smoked at least a pack of cigarettes a day. A sample of 400 women revealed that 72 smoked at least one pack of cigarettes a day. At the .05 significance level, is there a difference between the proportion of men and the proportion of women who smoke at least a pack of cigarettes a day, or can the difference in the proportions be attributed to sampling error?

53. One of the major U.S. automakers is studying its two-year/24,000-mile warranty policy. The warranty covers the engine, transmission, and drive train of all new cars for up to two years or 24,000 miles, whichever comes first. The manufacturer's quality-assurance department believes that the mean number of miles driven by owners is more than 24,000. A sample of 35 cars revealed that the mean number of miles driven was 24,421 with a standard deviation of 1,944 miles.
    a. At the .05 significance level, conduct the following hypothesis test.

$$H_0: \mu \leq 24{,}000$$

$$H_1: \mu > 24{,}000$$

b. Using the .05 significance level, what is the largest sample mean for which H_0 is not rejected?

c. The population mean shifts to 25,000 miles. What is the probability that this change will not be detected?

54. A cola-dispensing machine is set to dispense 9.00 ounces of cola per cup, with a standard deviation of 1.00 ounces. The manufacturer of the machine would like to set it in such a way that for samples of 36, 5 percent of the sample means will be greater than the upper control limit, and 5 percent of the sample means will be less than the lower control limit.

a. At what value should the control limit be set?

b. What is the probability that if the population mean shifts to 8.9, this change will not be detected?

c. What is the probability that if the population mean shifts to 9.3, this change will not be detected?

55. The owners of the Franklin Park Mall are studying the shopping habits of their customers. From earlier studies the owners are under the impression that a typical shopper spends 0.75 hours at the mall, with a standard deviation of 0.10 hours. Recently the mall owners have added some specialty restaurants designed to keep shoppers in the mall longer. A consulting firm, Brunner and Swanson Marketing Enterprises, has been hired to evaluate the effects of the restaurants. A sample of 45 shoppers by Brunner and Swanson revealed that the mean time spent in the mall had increased to 0.80 hours.

a. Develop a test of hypothesis to determine if the mean time spent in the mall is more than 0.75 hours. Use the .05 significance level.

b. Suppose the mean shopping time actually increased from 0.75 hours to 0.77 hours. What is the probability this increase would not be detected?

c. When Brunner and Swanson reported the information in part *b* to the mall owners, they were upset with the statement that a survey could not detect a change from 0.75 to 0.77 hours of shopping time. How could this probability be reduced?

56. The following null and alternate hypotheses are given.

$$H_0: \mu \leq 50$$

$$H_1: \mu > 50$$

Suppose the population standard deviation is 10. The probability of a Type I error is set at .01 and the probability of a Type II error at .30. Assume the population mean shifts from 50 to 55. How large a sample is necessary to meet these requirements?

COMPUTER DATA EXERCISES

57. Refer to the data set 1, which reports information on homes sold in Florida during 1994.

a. A recent article in an Arizona newspaper indicated that the mean selling price of homes in that state was $180,000. At the .05 significance level, can we conclude that homes sell for less than a mean of $180,000 in Florida? Determine the *p*-value.

b. The same article indicated that the mean size of the homes in Arizona is 2,000 square feet. Do the data indicate that the homes in Florida are larger than 2,000 square feet on the average? Use the .05 significance level.

c. Determine the proportion of homes that have a pool. At the .05 significance level, can we conclude that more than half of the homes sold have a pool?

d. Determine the proportion of homes that have an attached garage. At the .05 significance level, can we conclude that more than 50 percent of the homes sold have a garage?

58. Refer to data set 2, which reports information on the 1993 major league baseball season. Suppose you want to determine if the mean team salary for the 28 teams is greater than $30.0 million. Write a brief report indicating why, given the information in Appendix L, this is not possible.

59. Refer to data set 3, which reports information on magazines.
    a. At the .05 significance level, can we conclude that the mean number of magazines read by men is greater than 2.5?
    b. At the .05 significance level, can we conclude that the mean age of magazine readers is less than 40 years?

CHAPTER 9 EXAMINATION

The answers are at the end of the chapter.

For Questions 1–10, fill in the correct answer.

1. A statement about the value of a population parameter is called a ________.
2. If the null hypothesis is rejected, then the ________ hypothesis is accepted.
3. The level of significance is equal to the probability of a Type ________ error.
4. If a false null hypothesis is accepted, this is a Type ________ error.
5. A value calculated from the sample information and used to make a decision regarding the null hypothesis is called the ________.
6. The value that separates the region where the null hypothesis is rejected from the area where it is not rejected is called a ________.
7. If the rejection region is all in the upper right tail, a ________-tailed test is applied.
8. An operating characteristic curve is a graphic representation of the likelihood of accepting a ________ H_0.
9. The equality sign in a test of hypothesis always occurs in the ________ hypothesis.
10. A sample of 50 observations is selected from a normal population, but the population standard deviation is not known. The ________ is substituted for the population standard deviation to conduct a test of hypothesis.

For Questions 11 through 15, indicate whether the statement is true or false. If it is false, correct the statement.

11. The proportion of successes in a sample is designated $\bar{p}$.
12. To conduct a test of hypothesis about a proportion, the assumptions of the normal distribution must be met.
13. To conduct a test of hypothesis about a proportion, both np and $n(1 - p)$ must be greater than 5.
14. A pooled or weighted sample proportion is determined by adding the number of successes in both samples and dividing by the total number of items sampled.
15. Tests of proportions must be one-tailed.
16. The Department of Agriculture reports that the mean weekly amount spent on food by families of four in the United States with children less than 12 years of age is $95 with a standard deviation of $20. The distribution of the amounts spent is normal. A sample of 50 families in rural Indiana revealed that the mean amount spent was $90 per week. At the .05 significance level, is the mean amount spent less in rural Indiana?

a. State the null hypothesis and the alternate hypothesis.
b. State the decision rule.
c. Compute the value of the test statistic.
d. State your decision regarding the null hypothesis. Compute the *p*-value and interpret.

17. An official for the Iowa Department of Highways wants to compare the useful life, in months, of two brands of paint used for striping roads. The mean number of months that Cooper Paint lasted was 36.2 with a standard deviation of 1.14 months. The sample size was 35 road stripes. For King Paint, the mean number of months was 37.0 with a standard deviation of 1.3 months. The sample size was 40 stripes. At the .01 significance level, is there a difference in the useful lives of the two paints?
    a. State the null hypothesis and the alternate hypothesis.
    b. State the decision rule.
    c. Compute the value of the test statistic.
    d. State your decision regarding the null hypothesis. Compute the *p*-value and interpret.

18. The high-speed automatic Walden machine mass-produces a small washer. Past experience reveals that 70 percent of each day's production is perfect. Most of the remaining washers have a rough burr, which must be filed off before the washers can be inserted in the assembly. In an attempt to increase the percent of production that is perfect, the machine was modified somewhat. A sample of 100 washers was then checked, and it was found that 72 percent were perfect. The boss thinks that there has been no charge. The plant manager, however, believes that the production of the modified machine has definitely improved product quality; that is, the percent of perfect washers is greater than 70. Is the plant manager correct? Test at the .02 level.

19. A committee studying employer-employee relations at Carson Industries proposed that a rating system be adopted. Each employee would rate his or her immediate supervisor; in turn, the supervisor would rate each employee. In order to find out if there is a difference between the reactions of the office personnel and those of plant personnel regarding the proposal, 120 office personnel and 160 plant personnel were selected at random. Seventy-eight of the office personnel and 90 of the plant personnel were in favor of the proposal. Is there sufficient evidence to support the belief that the proportion of office personnel in favor of the proposal is greater than that of the plant personnel? Use the .05 level.

20. The Cains Pretzel Company sells its pretzels in 1-pound bags. The process that inserts the pretzels in the bags is normally distributed with a mean of 1.00 pounds and a standard deviation of 0.3 pounds. The quality-assurance department insists that the production line be stopped if the mean of a sample of 36 bags is greater than 1.098 pounds. What is the probability that if the population mean shifts from 1.00 pounds to 1.04 pounds, this change is not detected?

CHAPTER 9 Answers

Self-Review

9–1

1. H_0: $\mu = 6.0$, H_1: $\mu \neq 6.0$.
2. .05.
3. $z = \dfrac{\overline{X} - \mu}{\sigma\sqrt{n}}$
4. Do not reject the null hypothesis if the computed z value falls between -1.96 and $+1.96$.
5. Yes. Computed $z = -2.56$, found by:

$$\frac{5.84 - 6.0}{0.5/\sqrt{64}} = \frac{-0.16}{.0625} = -2.56$$

Reject H_0 at the .05 level. Accept H_1. The mean turnover rate is not equal to 6.0.

9–2

1. H_0: $\mu \geq 6.0$.
2. H_1: $\mu < 6.0$.
3. Note that the inequality sign (<) in the alternate hypothesis points in the direction of the region of rejection. To determine the critical value: $.5000 - .05 = .4500$. z from Appendix D is about 1.645.

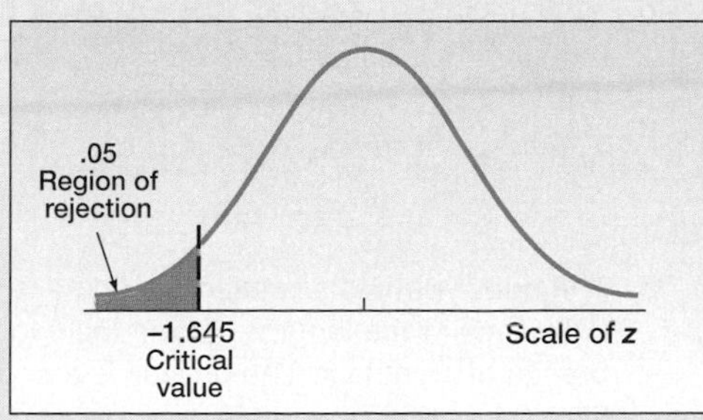

9–3

1. H_0: $\mu_1 \leq \mu_2$, H_1: $\mu_1 > \mu_2$. H_0 is rejected if computed z is > 1.645.

   Corngrow is effective. Computed z is 2.31, found by:

$$z = \frac{16.0 - 15.7}{\sqrt{\dfrac{(1)^2}{400} + \dfrac{(1.2)^2}{100}}}$$

$$= \frac{0.3}{\sqrt{.0025 + .0144}}$$

$$= \frac{0.3}{0.13}$$

$$= 2.31$$

Since 2.31 > 1.645 (critical value), the null hypothesis of $\mu_1 \leq \mu_2$ is rejected; the alternate, $\mu_1 > \mu_2$ is accepted.

2

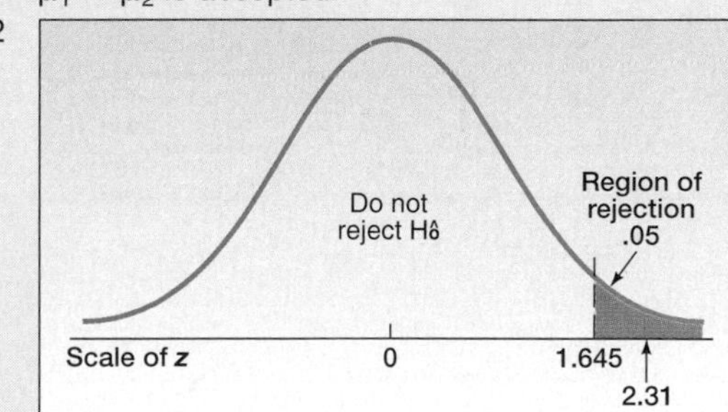

3. The p-value is .0104, found by $.5000 - .4896$.

9–4

1. Yes, because both np and $n(1 - p)$ exceed 5: $np = 200(.40) = 80$, and $n(1 - p) = 200(.60) = 120$.
2. H_0: $p \geq .40$
   H_1: $p < .40$
3.

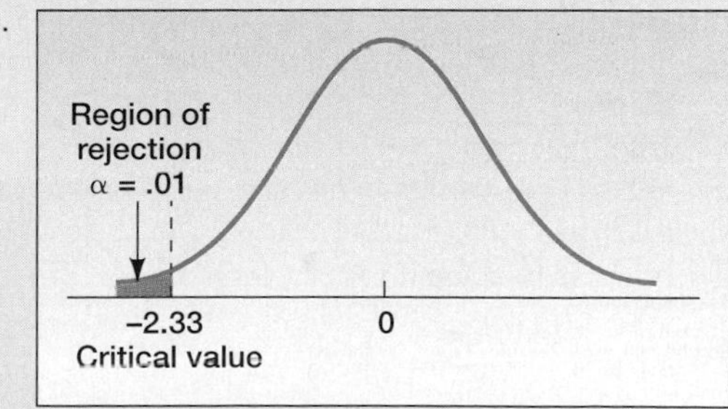

4. $z = -0.87$, found by:

$$z = \frac{.37 - .40}{\sqrt{\frac{.40(1 - .40)}{200}}}$$

$$= \frac{-.03}{\sqrt{.0012}} = -0.87$$

Do not reject H_0.

5. The *p*-value is .1922, found by .5000 − .3078.

9–5

1. H_0: $p_1 = p_2$; H_1: $p_1 \neq p_2$
2. .10.
3. Two-tailed because we are not concerned about the direction.
4. −1.645 and +1.645.
5. Not rejected. Computed $z = -0.66$.

$$\bar{p}_c = \frac{87 + 123}{150 + 200} = \frac{210}{350} = .60$$

Then:

$$z = \frac{.58 - .615}{\sqrt{\frac{.60(.40)}{150} + \frac{.60(.40)}{200}}}$$

$$= \frac{-.035}{\sqrt{.0028}} = -0.66$$

H_0 is not rejected.

6. The *p*-value is .5092. First find the area between 0 and .66; it is .2454. Then 2(.5000 − .2454) = .5092.

9–6

.1469, found by determining the area under the curve between 10,078 and 10,120 (Chart 9–11B).

$$z = \frac{\bar{X}_c - \mu_1}{\sigma/\sqrt{n}}$$

$$= \frac{10{,}078 - 10{,}120}{400/\sqrt{100}}$$

$$= -1.05$$

The area under the curve for a z of −1.05 is .3531 (Appendix D), and .5000 − .3531 = .1469.

Examination

1. Hypothesis.
2. Alternate.
3. I.
4. II.
5. Test statistic.
6. Critical value.
7. One.
8. False.
9. Null.
10. Sample standard deviation.
11. True.
12. False. The binomial assumptions must be met.
13. True.
14. True.
15. False. They can be either one-tailed or two-tailed.
16. *a.* H_0: $\mu \geq 95$, H_1: $\mu < 95$.
    b. H_0 is rejected if $z < -1.645$.
    c. $z = \frac{90 - 95}{20/\sqrt{50}} = -1.77$
    d. H_0 is rejected. Those living in rural Indiana spend less than the national average. The *p*-value is .0384, found by .5000 − .4616.
17. *a.* H_0: $\mu_c = \mu_k$, H_1: $\mu_c \neq \mu_k$.
    b. H_0 is rejected if z is less than −2.58 or greater than 2.58.
    c. $z = \frac{36.2 - 37.0}{\sqrt{\frac{(1.14)^2}{35} + \frac{(1.30)^2}{40}}} = \frac{-0.8}{0.2817} = -2.84$
    d. The null hypothesis is rejected. There is a difference in the lengths of time the two brands of paint last. The *p*-value is found by 2(.5000 − .4977) = .0046.
18. H_0: $p \leq .70$, H_1: $p > .70$. H_0 is rejected if $z > 2.05$. The computed value of z is 0.44, found by

$$z = \frac{.72 - .70}{\sqrt{\frac{(.70)(.30)}{100}}} = \frac{.02}{\sqrt{.0021}}$$

H_0 is not rejected. The evidence does not show that quality has improved.

19. H_0: $p_1 \leq p_2$; H_1: $p_1 > p_2$. Critical value is 1.645. Computed z is 1.48, found by:

$$z = \frac{.65 - .5625}{\sqrt{\dfrac{.60(1 - .60)}{120} + \dfrac{.60(1 - .60)}{160}}}$$

Pooled estimate is .60, found by (78 + 90)/(120 + 160). Since 1.48 is less than 1.645, H_0 is not rejected.

20. $$z = \frac{1.098 - 1.040}{0.3/\sqrt{36}} = \frac{0.058}{0.050} = 1.16$$

The probability that z is less than 1.16 is .8770, found by .3770 + .5000. So the probability of a Type II error is .8770.

SECTION 3 A REVIEW OF CHAPTERS 8 AND 9

Why sampling is often imperative

This section is a review of the major concepts and terms introduced in Chapters 8 and 9. Chapter 8 explored why it is almost impossible to study every item, or individual, in some populations. It would be too expensive and time-consuming, for example, to contact and record the annual incomes of all U.S. bank officers. To estimate a population parameter, therefore, we sample the population. A sample is just part of the population. Care must be taken to ensure that every member of our population has a chance of being selected; otherwise the conclusions might be biased. A number of probability-type sampling methods can be used, including *simple random, systematic, stratified,* and *cluster sampling.*

Sampling methods

Regardless of the sampling method selected, it is unlikely that a sample mean will be exactly the same as the population mean. The difference between this sample statistic and the population parameter is the *sampling error.* If the means of all possible samples of a specified size selected from a population are organized in a distribution, called the *sampling distribution of the sample means,* the mean of the sampling distribution will be equal to the population mean. If the sample size is large enough, the distribution of sample means is approximately normally distributed.

Sampling error

These concepts are the essence of the *central limit theorem,* which is the theoretical foundation of *statistical inference.* Briefly, statistical inference is concerned with inferring something about a population parameter based on a sample statistic. Chapter 8 discussed one facet of statistical inference—*estimation.* Chapter 9 concentrated on the other facet of statistical inference—*hypothesis testing.*

We may want to estimate a particular population parameter. For example, if, based on a sample, we estimate that the mean annual income of all professional house painters (the population) is $35,300, that estimate is called a *point estimate.* If we state that the population mean is probably in the interval between $35,200 and $35,400, that estimate is called an *interval estimate.* The two end points ($35,200 and $35,400) are called the *confidence limits* for the population mean.

Point estimate

Interval estimate

Confidence limits

A *hypothesis* is a statement about a population parameter or parameters. One such statement is: "The mean net weight of Campbell's canned green pea soup is 319 grams." Using a systematic procedure called *hypothesis testing,* we decide whether or not to reject this hypothesis. The procedure calls for stating the null hypothesis and the alternate hypothesis, selecting a level of significance and the appropriate test statistic, formulating a decision rule, taking a sample, and (based on the sample results) deciding whether or not to reject the null hypothesis. Chapter 9 presented tests of hypotheses about one population mean, two population means, one population proportion, and two population proportions.

Hypothesis testing: A systematic procedure followed to arrive at a decision

GLOSSARY

Chapter 8

Bias A possible consequence if certain members of the population are denied the chance to be selected for the sample. As a result, the sample may not be representative of the population.

Central limit theorem If the size of the sample is sufficiently large, the distribution of the sample means will approximate a normal distribution regardless of the shape of the population. Further, the mean of the sampling distribution will equal the population mean.

Cluster sampling A method often used to lower the cost of sampling if the population is dispersed over a wide geographic area. The area is divided in some way into smaller units (counties, precincts, blocks, etc.) called primary units. Then a few primary units are chosen, and a random sample is selected from each unit.

Interval estimate The interval within which a population parameter probably lies, based on sample information. Example: Based on sample data, we might state that the population mean probably lies in the interval between 1.9 and 2.0 pounds.

Point estimate A single number computed from a sample and used to estimate a population parameter. Example: If the sample mean is 1,020 psi, it is the best estimate of the tensile strength of the population.

Probability sample A sample of items or individuals chosen so that each member of the population has a known chance of being included in the sample.

Sampling distribution of the sample means A probability distribution consisting of all possible sample means of a given size selected from the population and their corresponding probabilities of occurrence.

Sampling error The difference between a sample statistic and the corresponding population parameter. Example: The sample mean income is $22,100; the population mean is $22,000. The sampling error is $22,100 − $22,000 = $100. This error can be attributed to sampling, that is, chance.

Simple random sampling A sampling scheme in which every member of the population has the same chance of being selected.

Stratified random sampling A population is first divided into subgroups called strata. A sample is then chosen from each stratum. If, for example, the population of interest consisted of all undergraduate students, the sample design might call for sampling 62 freshmen, 51 sophomores, 40 juniors, and 39 seniors.

Systematic random sampling Assuming that the population is arranged in some way, such as alphabetically, by height, or in a file drawer, a starting point is selected. Then every *k*th member becomes a member of the sample. If a sample design called for interviewing every ninth household on Main Street starting with 932 Main, the sample would consist of households at 932 Main, 941 Main, 950 Main, ...

Chapter 9

Critical value A value, designated *z*, that is the dividing point between the region where the null hypothesis is not rejected and the region where it is rejected. For a one-tailed test, there is only one critical value, such as −1.96. For a two-tailed test, there are two critical values—one in each tail—such as −1.96 and +1.96.

Hypothesis A statement about the value of a population parameter. Examples: 40.7 percent of all persons 65 years old and older live alone. The mean number of persons per family is 3.33.

Hypothesis testing A procedure based on sample evidence and probability theory used to determine whether the hypothesis stated is a reasonable statement and cannot be rejected or is unreasonable and should be rejected.

One-tailed test Used when the alternate hypothesis states a direction, such as H_1: $\mu > 40$. Here the rejection region is only in one tail (the right tail).

Proportion A fraction or percentage of a sample or a population having a particular trait. If 5 out of 50 in a sample liked a new cereal, the proportion is 5/50, or .10.

***p*-value** The probability of getting a value of the test statistic at least as extreme as the one found in the sample data when the null hypothesis is true.

Two-tailed test Used when the alternate hypothesis does not state a direction, such as H_1: $\mu \neq \$75$, read "the population mean is not equal to \$75." There is a region of rejection in each tail.

Type I error The probability of rejecting a true null hypothesis.

Type II error The probability of accepting a null hypothesis that is false.

EXERCISES

The answers to the odd-numbered exercises are at the end of the book.

Part I—Multiple Choice

1. Each new employee is given an identification number. The personnel files are arranged sequentially starting with employee number 0001. To sample the employees, the number 0153 was first selected. Then numbers 0253, 0353, 0453, and so on became members of the sample. This type of sampling is called:
   a. Simple random sampling.
   b. Systematic sampling.
   c. Stratified random sampling.
   d. Cluster sampling.
   e. None of these is correct.
2. You divide a precinct into blocks. Then you select 12 blocks at random and concentrate your sampling efforts in those 12 blocks. This type of sampling is called:
   a. Simple random sampling.
   b. Systematic random sampling.
   c. Stratified random sampling.
   d. Cluster sampling.
   e. Nonprobability sampling.
3. "Sampling error" as used in statistical inference:
   a. Indicates that a Type I error has been made.
   b. Indicates that a Type II error has been made.
   c. Is the difference between a sample statistic and its corresponding population parameter.
   d. Indicates that the *z* test must be used.
   e. None of these is correct.
4. Of 180 calculators sampled, 5 were defective. The proportion of defects is found by:
   a. $\dfrac{\text{Number of defects in sample}}{\text{Number sampled}}$
   b. $n = \left(\dfrac{z \cdot s}{E}\right)^2$
   c. $s/\sqrt{n}$

d. $\dfrac{X_1 + X_2}{n_1 + n_2}$

e. None of these is correct.

5. The endpoints of a confidence interval are called:
   a. Confidence levels.
   b. The test statistics.
   c. The degrees of confidence.
   d. The confidence limits.
   e. None of these is correct.
6. If a one-tailed test is used, and if the level of significance is .01, the critical value is either:
   a. -1.96 or $+1.96$.
   b. -1.645 or $+1.645$.
   e *c.* -2.58 or $+2.58$.
   d. 0 or 1.
   e. None of these is correct.
7. A Type II error is committed if we:
   a. Reject a true null hypothesis.
   b. Accept a true alternate hypothesis.
   c. Reject a true alternate hypothesis.
   d. Accept both the null and alternate hypotheses at the same time.
   e. None of these is correct.
8. The hypotheses are H_0: $\mu = 240$ inches of pressure; H_1: $\mu \neq 240$ inches of pressure.
   a. A one-tailed test is being applied.
   b. A two-tailed test is being applied.
   b *c.* A three-tailed test is being applied.
   d. The wrong test is being applied.
   e. None of these is correct.
9. The .01 level is used in an experiment, and a one-tailed test with the rejection region in the lower tail is applied. Computed z is -1.8. This indicates:
   a. H_0 should not be rejected.
   b. We should reject H_0 and accept H_1.
   c. We should take a larger sample.
   d. We should have used the .05 level of significance.
   e. None of these is correct.
10. To test a hypothesis involving proportions, both np and $n(1 - p)$ should:
   a. Exceed 30.
   b. Exceed 5.
   b *c.* Lie in the range from 0 to 1.
   d. Be at least -2.58.
   e. None of these is correct.

Part II—Problems

11. A machine is programmed to produce tennis balls so that the mean bounce is 36 inches when the ball is dropped from a platform. The supervisor suspects that the mean bounce has changed and is less than 36 inches. An experiment is to be conducted using 42 tennis balls. The 5 percent significance level is to be used to test the hypothesis. The sample mean was computed to be 35.5 inches and the standard deviation of the sample 0.9 inches. Is the supervisor correct?

12. Research by the Illinois Banking Corp. home office revealed that only 8 percent of the corporation's customers wait more than five minutes to do their banking during rush hours. They consider this a reasonable percent and will add no new part- time tellers unless the proportion becomes significantly greater than 8 percent. One branch manager believes that more than 8 percent of customers wait more than five minutes, and she requested additional help during rush hours. The home office decided to test the hypothesis at the 1 percent level. A random sample of 100 incoming customers were timed, and it was found that 10 waited more than five minutes.
    a. State the null and alternate hypotheses.
    b. State the level of significance.
    c. Give the formula for the test statistic.
    d. State the decision rule.
    e. Do the necessary calculations, and arrive at a decision with respect to the null hypothesis.
    f. Explain the difference between the sample proportion and the hypothesized population proportion.
13. You are interested in updating a study of the errors in the company's invoices. The study made several years ago revealed that 5 percent of the invoices contained at least one error. You decide to use the .05 level, and the error in your prediction is not to exceed plus or minus 2 percent of the population proportion.
    a. How many invoices should be examined?
    b. Suppose the sample size you computed in part *a* would be too time-consuming. What could you do to reduce the sample size?
14. You want to determine the mean amount sports fans spend on snacks and drinks at a professional football game. You decide to use the .01 level and estimate the mean within plus or minus 20 cents. How many fans should be sampled if the standard deviation of a pilot survey was computed to be 50 cents?
15. A firm with plants in two metropolitan areas adjusts the hourly wages paid their employees in one area if there is a significant difference between the two population mean hourly wages. Based on the following sample data, is there a difference between the two mean wages? To solve, answer these questions:
    a. What are the null and alternate hypotheses?
    b. Is this a one-tailed or a two-tailed test? Why?
    c. What is the formula for the test statistic?
    d. Using the .05 level, what is the critical value or values?
    e. What is your decision regarding the null hypothesis?

Metropolitan area	Sample mean hourly wage	Sample standard deviation	Number in sample
Bradenton	$10.92	$0.78	180
Venice	$11.05	$0.39	200

16. A wholesale automobile parts distributor has warehouses in Chicago and Dallas. Although perpetual inventories are taken, the number of items on the shelves and the number stored in the computer records are sometimes off by a few items. For example, if computer records indicate there are 122 boxes of GE #5 headlight bulbs on the shelf, but a count revealed 124, the computer record for that item is in error. An experiment is to be conducted to find out if there is a difference between the proportion of items in error in Chicago and the proportion of items in error in the Dallas warehouse.
    a. State the null and alternate hypotheses.
    b. Is this a one-tailed or a two-tailed test? Why?
    c. Give the formula for the test statistic.
    d. Using the .05 level, state the decision rule.

e. A sample of 200 automotive items in the Chicago warehouse revealed that the computer records and the count did not differ for 180 of the 200 items. A random sample of 100 items in the Dallas warehouse revealed that the computer records and the shelf count did not differ for 87 of the 100 items. What decision should be made regarding the null hypothesis? Explain.

CASE

Refer to the Century Bank Data. When Mr. Selig took over as president of Century a few years ago, the use of debit cards was just beginning. He would like an update on the use of these cards. What proportion of the customers use these cards? Develop a 95 percent confidence interval for the proportion of customers who use this service. Interpret the results.

With many other options available to customers, Mr. Selig is concerned that the mean account balance is declining. Is it reasonable to conclude now that the mean account balance is less than $1,600?

The use of ATMs, for all types of customers, has increased in recent years. When Mr. Selig took over the bank, the mean number of ATM transactions per customer per month was 8; now he believes it is more than 10. In fact, he would like to include this information in an upcoming TV commercial. Is there sufficient evidence to conclude that the mean number of ATM transactions per month is more than 10 per customer? Can he conclude that there is an average of more than 9 transactions per month?

Chapter 10

Tests of Hypotheses: Small Samples

GOALS

When you have completed this chapter, you will be able to:

1
Describe the major characteristics of Student's *t* distribution.

2
Define the terms *dependent sample* and *independent sample*.

3
Understand the differences between the *t* distribution and the *z* distribution.

4
Test a hypothesis involving one population mean.

5
Test a hypothesis involving the difference between two population means.

6
Conduct a test of hypothesis for the difference between a set of paired observations.

The manager of a package courier service believes packages shipped at the end of the month are heavier than those shipped early in the month. How can we conclude if packages shipped at the end of the month are actually heavier? (See Goal 5 and Exercise 33.)

INTRODUCTION

Chapter 9 began our study of hypothesis testing. In that chapter, the five-step hypothesis-testing procedure was described. The standard normal distribution—the *z* distribution—was used as the test statistic. To employ the *z* distribution, the population must be normal and the population standard deviation known. In many real-world situations, the population is approximately normal, but the population standard deviation is not known. In this case *s,* the sample standard deviation is substituted for σ, the population standard deviation. If the size of the sample is at least 30, the results are deemed satisfactory.

What if the sample size is less than 30 observations and σ is unknown? For these research projects, the *z* distribution is not the appropriate test statistic. The **Student *t*,** or the ***t* distribution,** as it is usually called, is used as the test statistic.

We will first examine the characteristics of the *t* distribution. Then we will discuss three hypothesis-testing situations that require the use of the *t* distribution.

CHARACTERISTICS OF STUDENT'S *t* DISTRIBUTION

Student's *t* distribution was developed by William S. Gossett. He was a brewmaster for the Guinness Brewery in Ireland and published it in 1908 using the pen name "Student." Gossett was concerned with the behavior of

$$\frac{\overline{X} - \mu}{s/\sqrt{n}}$$

when *s* had to be used as an estimator of σ. He was especially worried about the discrepancy between *s* and σ when *s* was calculated from a very small sample. The *t* distribution and the standard normal distribution are shown graphically in Chart 10–1. Note particularly that the *t* distribution is flatter, more "spread out," than the normal *z* distribution.

CHART 10–1 **The Standard Normal Distribution and Student's *t* Distribution**

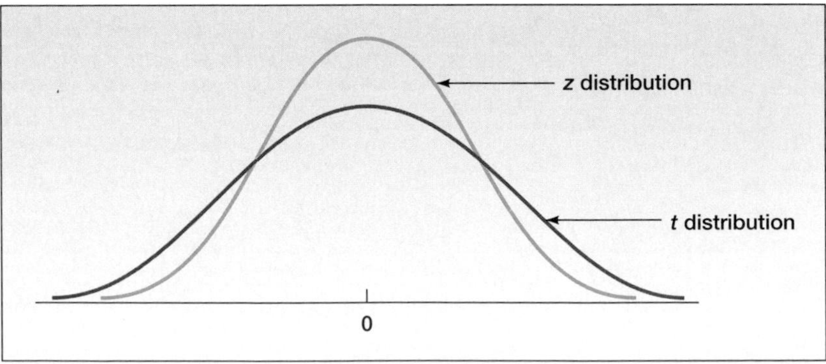

The following characteristics of the *t* distribution are based on the assumption that the population of interest is normal, or nearly normal.

Similarities between *t* and *z*

Differences between *z* and *t*

t distribution spread out more and flatter at the peak than *z*

1. It is, like the *z* distribution, a continuous distribution.
2. It is, like the *z* distribution, bell-shaped and symmetrical.
3. There is not one *t* distribution, but rather a "family" of *t* distributions. All have the same mean of zero, but their standard deviations differ according to the sample size, *n*. There is a *t* distribution for a sample size of 20, another for a sample size of 22, and so on.
4. The *t* distribution is more spread out and flatter at the center than is the standard normal distribution (see Chart 10–1). However, as the sample size increases, the curve representing the *t* distribution approaches the standard normal distribution.

As noted, Student's *t* distribution has a greater spread than the *z* distribution. As a result, the critical values of *t* for a given level of significance are larger in magnitude than the corresponding *z* critical values. Chart 10–2 shows the rejection region for a one-tailed test using the .05 level of significance. The critical value for the *z* test is 1.645, but for *t* it is 2.132. (Determining the critical *t* value of 2.132 will be discussed shortly.)

CHART 10–2 Regions of Rejection for the *z* and *t* Distributions, .05 Level of Significance, One-Tailed Test

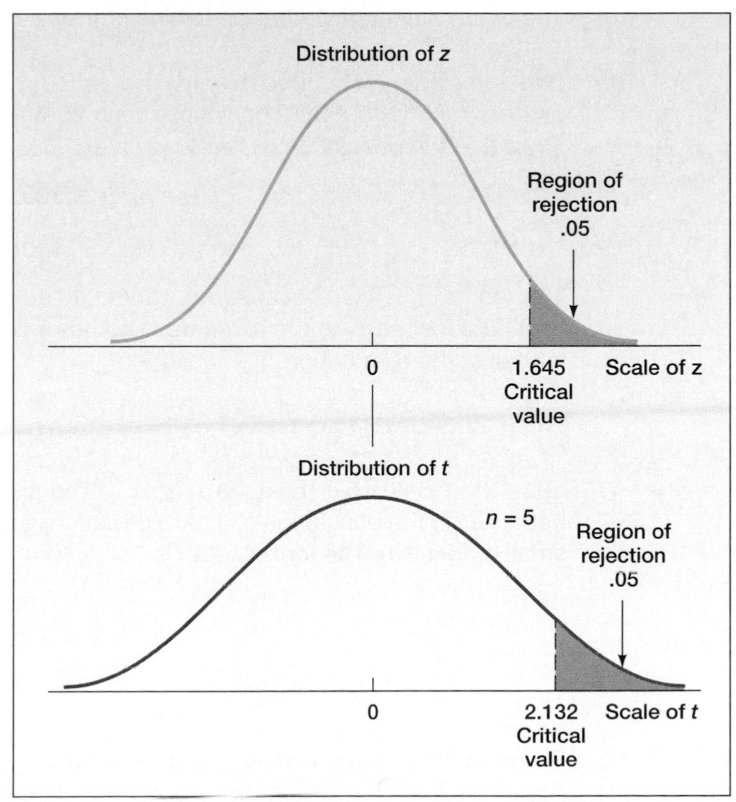

Of what importance is the fact that the critical value for a given level of significance is greater for small samples than for large samples? The following statements hold true for small samples (which employ the t distribution): (1) The confidence interval will be wider than for large samples using the z distribution. (2) The region where H_0 is not rejected is wider than for large samples using the z distribution. (3) A larger computed t value will be needed to reject the null hypothesis than for large samples using z. In other words, because there is more variability in sample means computed from smaller samples, we have less confidence in the resulting estimates and are less apt to reject the null hypothesis.

A TEST FOR THE POPULATION MEAN

EXAMPLE

Question: Has there been a reduction in cost?

Experience in investigating accident claims by the McFarland Insurance Company revealed that it costs \$60 on the average to handle the paperwork, pay the investigator, and make a decision. This cost compared with that of other insurance firms was deemed exorbitant, and cost-cutting measures were instituted. In order to evaluate the impact of these new measures, a sample of 26 recent claims was selected at random, and cost studies were made. It was found that the sample mean, $\overline{X}$, and the standard deviation, s, of the sample were \$57 and \$10, respectively. At the .01 level, is there a reduction in the mean cost, or should the difference of \$3 (\$60–\$57) be attributed to chance?

Solution ▶ The usual five-step hypothesis-testing procedure is used.

Step 1: State the Null and the Alternate Hypotheses The null hypothesis, H_0, is that the population mean is at least \$60. The alternate hypothesis, H_1, is that the population mean is less than \$60. This is written:

$$H_0: \mu \geq \$60$$

$$H_1: \mu < \$60$$

A left-tail test

The test is *one-tailed* because we want to determine if there has been a *reduction* in cost. The inequality in the alternate hypothesis points to the region of rejection in the left tail of the distribution.

Step 2: Select the Level of Significance The .01 level is to be used.

Step 3: Give the Test Statistic The test statistic is Student's t distribution because (1) the population standard deviation is unknown, and (2) the sample size is small (under 30). The formula for t is:

$$t = \frac{\overline{X} - \mu}{s/\sqrt{n}} \tag{10–1}$$

Step 4: Formulate the Decision Rule The critical values of t are given in Appendix F, and a portion of that appendix is shown in Table 10–1. (Appendix F is also repeated on the back inside cover of the text.) The far left column of the table is labeled "Degrees of freedom, *df*." For this test there are $n - 1$ degrees of freedom.[1] Move down that column to 25 ($n - 1$, or $26 - 1 = 25$). The critical value for $df = 25$, a one-tailed test, and the .01 level is 2.485.

TABLE 10–1 A Portion of the *t* Distribution Table

Degrees of freedom, *df*	Critical values of *t*					
	Level of significance for one-tailed test					
	.10	.05	.025	.01	.005	.0005
	Level of significance for two-tailed test					
	.20	.10	.05	.02	.01	.001
21	1.323	1.721	2.080	2.518	2.831	3.819
22	1.321	1.717	2.074	2.508	2.819	3.792
23	1.319	1.714	2.069	2.500	2.807	3.767
24	1.318	1.711	2.064	2.492	2.797	3.745
25	1.316	1.708	2.060	2.485	2.787	3.725
26	1.315	1.706	2.056	2.479	2.779	3.707
27	1.314	1.703	2.052	2.473	2.771	3.690
28	1.313	1.701	2.048	2.467	2.763	3.674

Rejection area only in left tail

Shown schematically in Chart 10–3, the decision rule for this one-tailed test is to reject the null hypothesis if the computed value of *t* falls in any part of the tail to the left of −2.485. Otherwise, do not reject the null hypothesis that the population mean is $60.

CHART 10–3 Rejection Region, *t* Distribution, .01 Significance Level

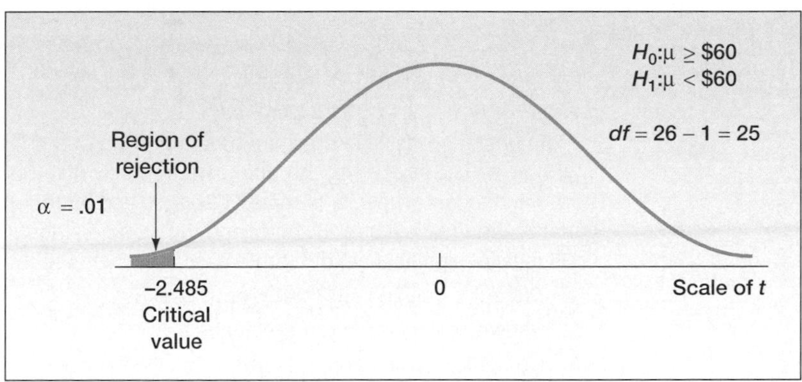

[1]In brief summary, because sample statistics are being used, it is necessary to determine the number of variables that are *free to vary*. To illustrate: If the sum of four numbers is 20, various combinations of *three* numbers can be written down, but the *fourth* number is restricted. If you select 7, 4, and 1 as three of the numbers, the fourth number *must be* 8 so that the sum of all is 20. Because of this restriction, it is said that "1 degree of freedom is lost."

For example, assume that the mean of four numbers is known to be 5. The four numbers are 7, 4, 1, and 8. The deviations of these numbers from the mean must total 0. The deviations of +2, −1, −4, and +3 do total 0. If the deviations of +2, −1, and −4 are known, then the value of +3 is fixed (restricted) in order to satisfy the condition that the sum of the deviations must equal 0. Thus, 1 degree of freedom is lost in a sampling problem involving the standard deviation of the sample because one number (the arithmetic mean) is known.

Step 5: Compute *t*, and Arrive at a Decision Recall that t is computed by using formula (10–1):

$$t = \frac{\overline{X} - \mu}{s/\sqrt{n}}$$

with $n - 1$ degrees of freedom, where:

$\overline{X}$ is the mean of the small sample.
μ is the hypothesized population mean.
s is the standard deviation of the sample.
n is the sample size.

Computing test statistic

In this problem:

$\overline{X} = \$57$, the sample mean.
$\mu = \$60$, the hypothesized population mean.
$s = \$10$, the sample standard deviation.
$n = 26$, the number of items in the sample.

The value of t is -1.530, found by:

$$t = \frac{\overline{X} - \mu}{s/\sqrt{n}} = \frac{\$57 - \$60}{\$10/\sqrt{26}} = -1.530$$

No reduction in the mean cost

Because -1.530 lies in the region to the right of the critical value of -2.485, the null hypothesis is not rejected at the .01 significance level. There is not a statistically significant difference between $\overline{X}$ and μ. This indicates that the cost-cutting measures have not reduced the mean cost per claim to less than \$60 based on the sample results.

SELF-REVIEW 10–1

The answers are at the end of the chapter.

From past records it is known that the mean life of a battery used in a digital clock is 305 days. The lives of the batteries are normally distributed. The battery was recently modified to last longer. A sample of 20 modified batteries were tested. It was discovered that the mean life was 311 days, and the sample standard deviation was 12 days. At the .05 level of significance, did the modification increase the mean life of the battery?

1. State the null and alternate hypotheses.
2. Show the decision rule graphically.
3. Compute t, and reach a decision. Briefly summarize your findings.

EXERCISES

The answers to the odd-numbered exercises are at the end of the book.

1. The following hypotheses are given:

$$H_0: \mu \leq 10$$
$$H_1: \mu > 10$$

For a random sample of 10 observations the sample mean was 12 and the sample standard deviation 3. Using the .05 significance level:

a. State the decision rule.
b. Compute the value of the test statistic.
c. What is your decision regarding the null hypothesis?

2. You are given the following hypotheses:

$$H_0: \mu = 400$$
$$H_1: \mu \neq 400$$

For a random sample of 12 observations, the sample mean was 407 and the sample standard deviation 6. Using the .01 significance level:

a. State the decision rule.
b. Compute the value of the test statistic.
c. What is your decision regarding the null hypothesis?

Note: It is recommended that the five-step hypothesis-testing procedure be used in solving the following problems.

3. The Rocky Mountain district sales manager of John C. Rath, Inc., a college book publishing company, claims that each of his sales representatives makes 40 calls on professors per week. Several reps said that this estimate is too low. To investigate, a random sample of 28 sales representatives revealed that the mean number of calls made last week was 42. The standard deviation of the sample was computed to be 2.1 calls. At the .05 level of significance, can we conclude that the mean number of calls per salesperson per week is more than 40?
4. The management of White Industries is considering a new method of assembling its three-wheel golf cart. The present method requires 42.3 minutes, on the average, to assemble a cart. The new method was introduced, and a time and motion study was conducted on a random sample of 24 carts. The mean assembly time was computed to be 40.6 minutes. The standard deviation of the sample was 2.7 minutes. Using the .10 level of significance, can it be said that the assembly time under the new method is significantly less than before?
5. The records of Yellowstone Trucks revealed that the mean life of a set of spark plugs is 22,100 miles. The distribution of the life of the plugs is approximately normal. A spark plug manufacturer claimed that its plugs have a mean life in excess of 22,100 miles. The fleet owner purchased a large number of sets. A sample of 18 sets revealed that the sample mean life was 23,400 miles and the sample standard deviation was 1,500 miles. Is there enough evidence to substantiate the manufacturer's claim at the .05 level?
6. Fast Service, a chain of automotive tune-up shops, advertises that its personnel can change the oil, replace the oil filter, and lubricate any standard automobile in 15 minutes, on the average. The National Business Bureau received complaints from customers that service takes considerably longer. To check the Fast Service claim, the bureau had service done on 21 unmarked cars. The mean service time was 18 minutes, and the standard deviation of the sample was 1 minute. Use the .05 level to check the reasonableness of the Fast Service claim.

Compute sample standard deviation

In the previous examples, the mean and standard deviation of the sample were given. The following example requires that they be computed from the sample observations.

EXAMPLE

The mean length of a small counterbalance bar is 43 millimeters. There is concern that the adjustments of the machine producing the bars have changed. The null hypothesis is that there has been no change in the mean length ($\mu = 43$). The alternate hypothesis is that there has been a change ($\mu \neq 43$). Test at the .02 level.

Twelve bars (n = 12) were selected at random and their lengths recorded. The lengths are (in millimeters) 42, 39, 42, 45, 43, 40, 39, 41, 40, 42, 43, and 42. This is now a two-tailed test. Has there been a statistically significant change in the mean length of the bars?

Solution

Note that H_1 indicates two-tailed test must be used.

The null and alternate hypotheses are:

$$H_0: \mu = 43$$

$$H_1: \mu \neq 43$$

The alternate hypothesis does not state a direction, so the test is two-tailed. There are 11 degrees of freedom, found by $n - 1 = 12 - 1 = 11$. Then—referring to Appendix F for a two-tailed test at the .02 level with 11 degrees of freedom—the critical value is 2.718. The critical values for the .02 level are shown in Chart 10–4. The decision rule is therefore to reject the null hypothesis if the computed t is to the left of -2.718 or to the right of 2.718.

CHART 10–4 Regions of Rejection, Two-Tailed Test, Student's *t* Distribution, α = .02

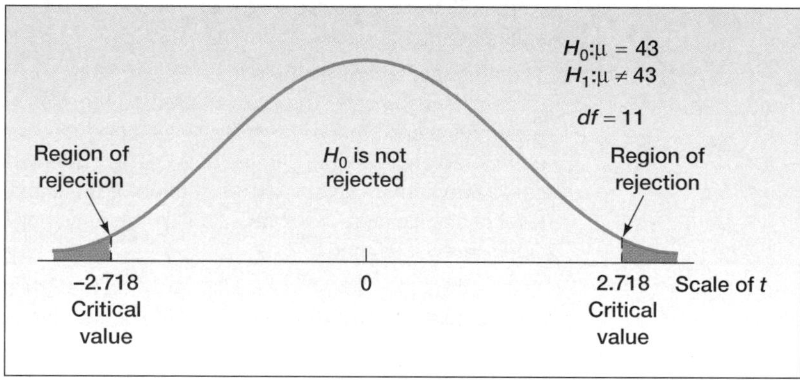

The standard deviation of the sample can be determined either by squaring the deviations from the mean or by an equivalent formula using the squares of the actual values. The two formulas from Chapter 4, (4–8) and (4–9), are:

Using squared deviations from mean	**Using squares of actual values**
$s = \sqrt{\dfrac{\Sigma(X - \overline{X})^2}{n - 1}}$	$s = \sqrt{\dfrac{\Sigma X^2 - \dfrac{(\Sigma X)^2}{n}}{n - 1}}$

The necessary calculations for these two methods are shown in Table 10–2. The mean ($\overline{X}$) is 41.5 millimeters, and the standard deviation (s) is 1.78 millimeters.

Sample standard deviation computed using two methods

TABLE 10–2 Calculations Needed for the Sample Standard Deviation

X (mm)	$X-\bar{X}$	$(X-\bar{X})^2$	$\bar{X}^2$
42	0.5	0.25	1,764
39	−2.5	6.25	1,521
42	0.5	0.25	1,764
45	3.5	12.25	2,025
43	1.5	2.25	1,849
40	−1.5	2.25	1,600
39	−2.5	6.25	1,521
41	−0.5	0.25	1,681
40	−1.5	2.25	1,600
42	0.5	0.25	1,764
43	1.5	2.25	1,849
42	0.5	0.25	1,764
498	0	35.00	20,702

$$\bar{X} = \frac{498}{12} = 41.5 \text{ mm}$$

Squared deviation method:

$$s = \sqrt{\frac{\Sigma(X-\bar{X})^2}{n-1}} = \sqrt{\frac{35}{12-1}} = 1.78$$

Squaring actual values:

$$s = \sqrt{\frac{\Sigma X^2 - \frac{(\Sigma X)^2}{n}}{n-1}} = \sqrt{\frac{20{,}702 - \frac{(498)^2}{12}}{12-1}}$$

$$= 1.78$$

Now we are ready to compute t, using formula (10–1).

$$t = \frac{\bar{X} - \mu}{s/\sqrt{n}} = \frac{41.5 - 43.0}{1.78/\sqrt{12}} = -2.92$$

The null hypothesis that the population mean is 43 millimeters is rejected at the .02 level (because the computed t of −2.92 lies in the area of the tail beyond the critical value of −2.718). The alternate hypothesis that the mean is not 43 millimeters is accepted. Based on the sample results, we can say that the machine is out of adjustment. Report this to the quality-assurance engineer and to the production manager.

A COMPUTER SOLUTION

The MINITAB statistical software system, used extensively in earlier chapters, provides an efficient way of conducting a one-sample test of hypothesis for a population mean. First the sample observations are entered into the system, using the SET command. Next, the column of data is given the identification "Length," using the NAME command. Finally, the procedure TTEST is used. The procedure TTEST requires as input the value of the null hypothesis and the column in which the data are located. Note that t (− 2.91) is approximately the same as the value determined using formula (10–1) (− 2.92). The slight difference is due to rounding.

An additional feature of MINITAB, and most other statistical software packages, is to output the p-value, which gives additional information on the null hypothesis. The p-value is the probability of a t value as large or larger than that computed, given that the null hypothesis is true. In this case, the p-value of .014 is the likelihood of a t value of −2.91 or less plus the likelihood of a t value of 2.91 or larger, given a population mean of 43. Thus, comparing the p-value to the significance level tells us whether the null hypothesis was close to being rejected, barely rejected, and so on.

```
MTB > set c1
DATA> 42,39,42,45,43,40,39,41,40,42,43,42
DATA> end
MTB > name c1 'Length'
MTB > ttest mu=43, c1
TEST OF MU = 43.000 VS MU N.E. 43.000
              N      MEAN     STDEV   SE MEAN        T   P VALUE
Length       12    41.500     1.784     0.515    -2.91     0.014
```

To explain further, refer to the following diagram, in which the *p*-value of .014 is shown in green and the significance level is the tan area plus the green area. Because the *p*-value of .014 is less than the significance level of .02, the null hypothesis is rejected. Had the *p*-value been larger than the significance level—say, .06, .19, or .57—the null hypothesis would not be rejected. If the significance level had initially been selected as .01, the null hypothesis would not be rejected. Shown schematically:

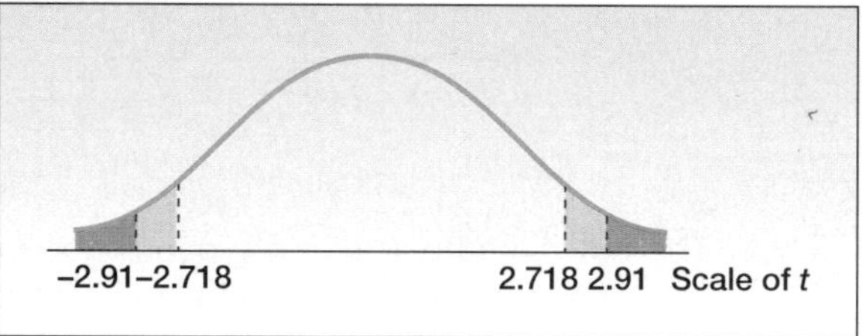

In the preceding example the alternate hypothesis was two-tailed, so there were rejection areas in both the upper and the lower tails. To determine the *p*-value, it was necessary to determine the area to the left of −2.91 for a *t* distribution with 11 degrees of freedom and add to it the value to the right of 2.91, also with 11 degrees of freedom.

What if we were conducting a one-tailed test, so that the entire rejection region would be in either the upper or the lower tail? In that case, we would report the area from only the one tail. In the counterbalance example, if H_1 were stated as $\mu < 43$, the inequality would point to the left. Thus, we would have reported the *p*-value as the area to the left of −2.91. This value is .007, found by .014/2. Thus, the *p*-value for a one-tailed test would be .007.

A computer software package such as MINITAB has extensive tables to accurately estimate *p*-values. How can we estimate a *p*-value without a computer? To explain, recall that in the Example-Solution regarding the length of a counterbalance we rejected the null hypothesis that $\mu = 43$ and accepted the alternate hypothesis that $\mu \neq 43$. The significance level was .02, so logically the *p*-value is less than .02. To estimate the *p*-value more accurately, first go to Appendix F and find the row with 11 degrees of freedom. The computed *t* value of 2.91 is between 2.718 and 3.106. (A portion of Appendix F is reproduced as Table 10–3.) The two-tailed significance level corresponding to 2.718 is .02 and for 3.106 it is .01. Therefore, the *p*-value must be between .01 and .02. The usual practice is to report that the *p*-value is *less* than the larger of the two significance levels. So we would report that "the *p*-value is less than .02." The MINITAB output reports the exact *p*-value as .014.

TABLE 10–3 **A Portion of the Student *t* Distribution**

	Level of significance for one-tailed test					
	0.100	0.050	0.025	0.010	0.005	0.0005
	Level of significance for two-tailed test					
df	0.20	0.10	0.05	0.02	0.01	0.001
⋮	⋮	⋮	⋮	⋮	⋮	⋮
6	1.440	1.943	2.447	3.143	3.707	5.959
7	1.415	1.895	2.365	2.998	3.499	5.408
8	1.397	1.860	2.306	2.896	3.355	5.041
9	1.383	1.833	2.262	2.821	3.250	4.781
10	1.372	1.812	2.228	2.764	3.169	4.587
11	1.363	1.796	2.201	2.718	3.106	4.437
12	1.356	1.782	2.179	2.681	3.055	4.318
13	1.350	1.771	2.160	2.650	3.012	4.221
14	1.345	1.761	2.145	2.624	2.977	4.140
15	1.341	1.753	2.131	2.602	2.947	4.073
	⋮	⋮	⋮	⋮	⋮	⋮

SELF-REVIEW 10–2

The answers are at the end of the chapter.

A Corkill machine is set to fill a small bottle with 9.0 grams of medicine. It is claimed that the mean weight is less than 9.0 grams. The hypothesis is to be tested at the .01 level. A sample revealed these weights (in grams): 9.2, 8.7, 8.9, 8.6, 8.8, 8.5, 8.7, and 9.0.

1. State the null and alternate hypotheses.
2. How many degrees of freedom are there?
3. Give the decision rule.
4. Compute *t*, and arrive at a decision.
5. Estimate the *p*-value.

EXERCISES

The answers to the odd-numbered exercises are at the end of the book.

7. The following null and alternate hypotheses are being considered:

$$H_0: \mu \geq 20$$

$$H_1: \mu < 20$$

A random sample of five observations was selected: 18, 15, 12, 19, and 21. At the .01 significance level, can we conclude that the population mean is less than 20?

a. State the decision rule.
b. Compute the value of the test statistic.
c. What is your decision regarding the null hypothesis?
d. Estimate the *p*-value.

8. The following null and alternate hypotheses are to be considered:

$$H_0: \mu = 100$$
$$H_1: \mu \neq 100$$

The following random sample of six observations was selected: 118, 105, 112, 119, 105, and 111. At the .05 significance level, can we conclude that the population mean is different from 100?
   a. State the decision rule.
   b. Compute the value of the test statistic.
   c. What is your decision regarding the null hypothesis?
   d. Estimate the *p*-value.

Note: It is recommended that the five-step hypothesis-testing procedure be used in solving the following problems.

9. Experience with raising New Jersey Red chickens revealed the average weight of the chickens at age five months to be 4.35 pounds. The weights are normally distributed. In an effort to increase their weight, a special additive was mixed with the chicken feed. The subsequent weights of a sample of five-month-old chickens were (in pounds): 4.41, 4.37, 4.33, 4.35, 4.30, 4.39, 4.36, 4.38, 4.40, and 4.39. At the .01 level, has the special additive increased the weight of the chickens? Estimate the *p*-value.
10. The liquid chlorine added to swimming pools to combat algae has a relatively short shelf life before it loses its effectiveness. Past records indicate that the mean shelf life of a 5-gallon jug of chlorine is 2,160 hours (90 days). As an experiment, Holdlonger was added to the chlorine to find out if it would increase the shelf life. A sample of nine jugs of chlorine gave these shelf lives (in hours): 2,159, 2,170, 2,180, 2,179, 2,160, 2,167, 2,171, 2,181, and 2,185. At the .025 level, has Holdlonger increased the shelf life of the chlorine? Estimate the *p*-value.
11. Wyoming fisheries contend that the mean number of cutthroat trout caught during a full day of fly-fishing on the Snake, Buffalo, and other rivers and streams in the Jackson Hole area is 4.0. To make their yearly update, the fishery personnel asked a sample of fly-fishermen to keep a count of the number caught during the day. The numbers were: 4, 4, 3, 2, 6, 8, 7, 1, 9, 3, 1, and 6. At the .05 level, is there convincing evidence that the number of trout caught daily has increased? Estimate the *p*-value.
12. Hugger Polls contends that an agent conducts a mean of 53 in-depth home surveys every week. A streamlined survey form has been introduced, and Hugger wants to evaluate its effectiveness. The number of in-depth surveys conducted during a week by a random sample of agents are: 53, 57, 50, 55, 58, 54, 60, 52, 59, 62, 60, 60, 51, 59, and 56. At the .05 level of significance, can we conclude that the mean number of interviews conducted by the agents is more than 53 per week? Estimate the *p*-value.

COMPARING TWO POPULATION MEANS

A test using the *t* distribution can also be applied to compare two sample means to determine if the samples were obtained from normal populations with the same mean. To conduct this test, three assumptions are required:

1. The populations must be normally distributed (or approximately normally distributed).
2. The populations must be independent.
3. The population variances must be equal.

The t statistic for the two-sample case is similar to that employed in Chapter 9, formula (9–3), for the z statistic, except that an additional calculation is required. The two sample variances must be "pooled" to form a single estimate of the unknown population variance. In essence, we will compute a weighted average of the two sample variances and use the weighted average as a pooled estimate of the population variance. Why do we pool these variances? In most cases when the samples have fewer than 30 observations, the population standard deviations are not known. So we calculate s^2 and substitute it for σ^2. Because we assume that the two populations have equal variances, the best estimate we can make of that value is to combine or pool all the information we have with respect to the population variance.

The following formula is used to pool the sample variances. Notice that two factors make up the weights: the number of observations in each sample and the sample variances themselves.

$$s_p^2 = \frac{(n_1 - 1)(s_1^2) + (n_2 - 1)(s_2^2)}{n_1 + n_2 - 2} \qquad (10\text{–}2)$$

where:

s_1^2 is the variance in the first sample.

s_2^2 is the variance in the second sample.

The value of t is then determined by:

$$t = \frac{\bar{X}_1 - \bar{X}_2}{\sqrt{s_p^2\left(\frac{1}{n_1} + \frac{1}{n_2}\right)}} \qquad (10\text{–}3)$$

where:

$\bar{X}_1$ is the mean of the first sample.

$\bar{X}_2$ is the mean of the second sample.

n_1 is the number in the first sample.

n_2 is the number in the second sample.

s_p^2 is the pooled estimate of the population variance.

The number of degrees of freedom in the test is equal to the total number of items sampled minus the number of samples. Since there are two samples, there are $n_1 + n_2 - 2$ degrees of freedom.

EXAMPLE

O'Keane Products, Inc. manufactures and assembles lawnmowers, which are shipped to dealers throughout the United States and Canada. Two different procedures have been proposed for mounting the engine on the frame of the lawnmower. The question is: Is there a difference in the mean time to mount the engines on the frames of the lawnmowers? The first procedure was developed by Welles (designated as procedure 1), and the other procedure was developed by Atkins (designated as procedure 2). To evaluate the two proposed methods, it was decided to conduct a time and motion study. A sample of five employees was timed using procedure 1, and six were timed using procedure 2. The results, in minutes, are shown below. Is there a difference in the mean mounting times? Use the .10 significance level.

Procedure 1 (minutes)	Procedure 2 (minutes)
2	3
4	7
9	5
3	8
2	4
	3

Solution ▸ The null hypothesis states that there is no difference in mean mounting time between the Welles procedure and the Atkins procedure.

$$H_0\colon \mu_1 = \mu_2$$

$$H_1\colon \mu_2 \neq \mu_2$$

The required assumptions are: (1) The observations in the Welles sample are *independent* of those observations in the Atkins sample, and of each other. (2) The two populations are approximately normal. (3) The two populations have equal variances.

Is there a difference between the assembly times using the Welles and the Atkins methods? The way the problem is stated suggests a two-tailed test. Recall that the degrees of freedom are determined by $n_1 + n_2 - 2$. Five assemblers used the Welles method and six the Atkins method. Thus, there are 9 degrees of freedom, found by $5 + 6 - 2$. The critical values of *t*, from Appendix F for $df = 9$, a two-tailed test, and the .10 level of significance, are $+1.833$ and -1.833. The decision rule is portrayed graphically in Chart 10–5. We do not reject the null hypothesis if the computed *t* value falls between -1.833 and $+1.833$. Otherwise H_0 is rejected.

CHART 10–5 **Regions of Rejection, Two-Tailed Test (9 degrees of freedom, α = .10)**

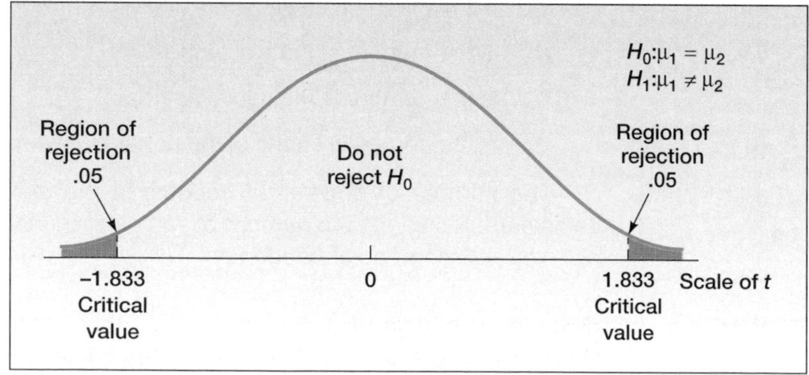

Determining Student's *t* is accomplished in three steps.

Step 1: Calculate the Sample Variances

Procedure 1		Procedure 2	
X_1	X_1^2	X_2	X_2^2
2	4	3	9
4	16	7	49
9	81	5	25
3	9	8	64
2	4	4	16
20	114	3	9
		30	172

$$s_1^2 = \frac{\sum X_1^2 - \frac{(\sum X_1)^2}{n_1}}{n_1 - 1} = \frac{114 - \frac{(20)^2}{5}}{5 - 1} = 8.5 \qquad s_2^2 = \frac{\sum X_2^2 - \frac{(\sum X_2)^2}{n_2}}{n_2 - 1} = \frac{172 - \frac{(30)^2}{6}}{6 - 1} = 4.4$$

Step 2: Pool the Variances Applying formula (10–2),

$$s_p^2 = \frac{(n_1 - 1)s_1^2 + (n_2 - 1)s_2^2}{n_1 + n_2 - 2} = \frac{(5 - 1)(8.5) + (6 - 1)(4.4)}{5 + 6 - 2} = 6.2222$$

Step 3: Determine *t* Using formula (10–3) with $\overline{X}_1 = 20/5 = 4$ and $\overline{X}_2 = 30/6 = 5$,

$$t = \frac{\overline{X}_1 - \overline{X}_2}{\sqrt{s_p^2\left(\frac{1}{n_1} + \frac{1}{n_2}\right)}} = \frac{4 - 5}{\sqrt{6.2222\left(\frac{1}{5} + \frac{1}{6}\right)}} = -0.662$$

The decision is not to reject the null hypothesis because -0.662 falls in the region between -1.833 and $+1.833$. We conclude that there is no difference in the mean time to mount the engine on the frame between the two methods.

The MINITAB output for the O'Keane Products example follows. The procedure is TWOSAMPLE, and the subcommand POOLED is required.

```
MTB > set c1
DATA> 2,4,9,3,2
DATA> end
MTB > set c2
DATA> 3,7,5,8,4,3
DATA> end
MTB > name c1 'Welles' c2 'Atkins'
MTB > twosample c1 c2;
SUBC> pooled.

TWOSAMPLE T FOR Welles VS Atkins

          N     MEAN      STDEV      SE MEAN
WELLES    5     4.00       2.92          1.3
ATKINS    6     5.00       2.10         0.86

95 PCT CI FOR MU Welles - MU Atkins: (-4.4, 2.42)         ┌p-value
                                                          ↓
TTEST MU Welles = MU Atkins (VS NE): T = -0.66  P=0.52    DF=9
POOLED STDEV =        2.49                 ↑___Test statistic
```

The computed t of -0.66 is the same as that computed using formulas (10–2) and (10–3). The p-value reported on the MINITAB output is .52. This is the probability, given that the null hypothesis is true, that we could find a t value less than -0.66 or greater than 0.66 with 9 degrees of freedom. As we would expect, the p-value of .52 is larger than the significance level of .10 when the null hypothesis is not rejected.

We can also estimate the p-value using Appendix F. Locate the row with 9 degrees of freedom and use the significance level for two-tailed tests. Find the t value, disregarding the sign, that is closest to our computed value of -0.66. It is 1.383, corresponding to a significance level of .20. So even had we used the 20 percent significance level we would not have rejected the null hypothesis of equal means. We would report that the p-value is greater than .20. This is consistent with the p-value reported by MINITAB but not as precise.

SELF-REVIEW 10–3

The answers are at the end of the chapter.

The net weights of a sample of bottles filled by a machine manufactured by Edne, and the net weights of a sample filled by a similar machine manufactured by Orno, Inc., are (in grams):

Edne: 5, 8, 7, 6, 9, 7
Orno: 8, 10, 7, 11, 9, 12, 14, 9

At the .05 level, is the mean weight of the bottles filled by the Orno machine greater than the mean weight of the bottles filled by the Edne machine? Estimate the p-values.

EXERCISES

The answers to the odd-numbered exercises are at the end of the book.

13. The null and alternate hypotheses are:

$$H_0: \mu_1 = \mu_2$$

$$H_1: \mu_1 \neq \mu_2$$

A random sample of 10 observations from the first population revealed a sample mean of 23 and a sample standard deviation of 4. A random sample of 8 observations from the second population revealed a mean of 26 with a standard deviation of 5. At the .05 significance level, is there a difference in the population means?

a. State the decision rule.
b. Compute the pooled estimate of the population variance.
c. Compute the value of the test statistic.
d. What is your decision regarding the null hypothesis?
e. Estimate the *p*-value.

14. The following hypotheses are to be tested.

$$H_0: \mu_1 = \mu_2$$

$$H_1: \mu_1 \neq \mu_2$$

A random sample of 15 observations from the first population revealed a sample mean of 350 and a sample standard deviation of 12. A random sample of 17 observations from the second population revealed a mean of 342 with a standard deviation of 15. At the .10 significance level, is there a difference in the population means?

a. State the decision rule.
b. Compute the pooled estimate of the population variance.
c. Compute the value of the test statistic.
d. What is your decision regarding the null hypothesis?
e. Estimate the *p*-value.

15. A sample of the scores on an examination given to both males and females in Statistics 201 are:

Males: 72, 69, 98, 66, 85, 76, 79, 80, 77
Females: 81, 67, 90, 78, 81, 80, 76

At the .01 significance level, is the mean grade of the females higher than that of the males?

16. The scores of two groups of inmates at Southard Prison on a rehabilitation test are:

	First offenders	Repeat offenders
Mean score	300	305
Sample variance	20	18
Sample size	16	13

Test at the .05 level that there is no difference between the mean scores of the two groups. The alternate hypothesis is that there is a difference.

17. As an experiment, the weather bureau made 22 pollen counts in the valley surrounding Wilson, Wyoming (altitude 6,200 feet). Similarly, 25 counts were made in the Teton Mountains surrounding Wilson (altitude 7,800 feet). The findings were:

	Valley	Mountains
Mean pollen count	89	87
Sample standard deviation	4	6
Sample size	22	25

At the .10 significance level, can we conclude that there is a higher pollen count in the valley around Wilson than in the nearby mountains? Find the *p*-value.

18. The Kentucky Highway Department is considering a new four-lane highway. A number of questions have been raised. One of them involves the speed of trucks on a four-lane highway with a median strip over 50 feet versus a highway with a median strip under 50 feet.

    To research the matter further, the speeds of a random sample of trucks traveling on the two types of highway were measured (speeds are in miles per hour).

Under 50 feet	Over 50 feet	
55	64	65
70	68	75
68	70	63
67	70	66
70	65	49

Based on this preliminary sample information and using the .01 level, can we say there is a significant difference in the speeds of the trucks on the two different highways? What action, if any, would you suggest the highway department take? Find the *p*-value.

HYPOTHESIS TESTING INVOLVING PAIRED OBSERVATIONS

In the previous example the difference between two population means was tested. The difference in the times required to mount the engine using the Welles method and using the Atkins method was given as an illustration. The samples were *independent,* meaning that the sample of assembly times using the Welles method was in no way related to the sample of assembly times using the Atkins method.

What to do when samples are not independent

There are situations, however, in which the samples are *not* independent. As an example, suppose the training director wishes to find out whether or not a unique training program will increase employee efficiency. He plans to take a random sample of 10 employees registered for the program and record their efficiency ratings before the training starts. After completion of the program, the efficiency ratings of the *same* sample of employees will be recorded. Thus, there will be a pair of efficiency ratings for each member of the sample. The set of sample pairs is aptly called a *paired sample.* The test of hypothesis to be conducted to find out if there is a difference between the ratings before and after the training program is called a *paired difference test.* Note that the two samples (a "before" sample and an "after" sample) depend on each other because the same employees are in both samples. Thus, they are not independent.

The paired difference test

For the test of hypothesis to be conducted now, there is essentially only one sample, not two. We are testing the hypothesis that the distribution of the differences has a mean of 0. The sample is made up of the *differences* between the efficiency ratings before the training program and the ratings after the program. If production methods before and after the training program remain the same, one could logically expect some employees to benefit from the training program and to become more efficient. Other employees would prefer the method used before the training program, and their efficiency would remain the same or even decrease. Thus, the mean of the differences in efficiency ratings, designated μ_d, would "balance out" and equal zero.

As noted, before adopting the new production techniques presented in the training program, the training director wants to know whether or not it will affect efficiency. If it does, one would reasonably assume that most of the differences would be positive—that is, increased efficiency. The null hypothesis to be tested is therefore H_0: $\mu_d \leq 0$. The alternate hypothesis is that the mean of the differences is greater than 0, written H_1: $\mu_d > 0$, signifying that the differences are positive.

H_0 and H_1

The test statistic is the Student *t*, determined by:

Test statistic for the paired difference test

$$t = \frac{\bar{d}}{s_d/\sqrt{n}} \tag{10–4}$$

with $n - 1$ degrees of freedom, where:

$\bar{d}$ is the mean difference between the paired observations.

s_d is the standard deviation of the differences between the paired observations.

n is the number of paired observations.

The standard deviation of the differences is computed using formula (4–9) except that d is substituted for X.

$$s_d = \sqrt{\frac{\Sigma d^2 - \dfrac{(\Sigma d)^2}{n}}{n - 1}}$$

The decision rule

Using the .05 significance level, the critical value of t for this one-tailed test of paired differences is 1.833, found by going to Appendix F and reading down the left column to $n - 1 = 10 - 1 = 9$ degrees of freedom.

The sample and needed calculations

These calculations are needed to determine *t*:

Sample member	Efficiency rating Before	Efficiency rating After	Difference, *d*	Difference squared, d^2
1	128	135	7	49
2	105	110	5	25
3	119	131	12	144
4	140	142	2	4
5	98	105	7	49
6	123	130	7	49
7	127	131	4	16
8	115	110	−5	25
9	122	125	3	9
10	145	149	4	16
			46	386

$$\bar{d} = \frac{\Sigma d}{n} = \frac{46}{10} = 4.60$$

$$s_d = \sqrt{\frac{\Sigma d^2 - \frac{(\Sigma d)^2}{n}}{n-1}} = \sqrt{\frac{386 - \frac{(46)^2}{10}}{10-1}} = 4.402$$

Using formula (10–4), the value of *t* is 3.30, found by:

$$t = \frac{\bar{d}}{s_d/\sqrt{n}} = \frac{4.6}{4.402/\sqrt{10}} = 3.305$$

Because the value of *t* (3.305) lies in the rejection region, that is, beyond the critical value of 1.833, the null hypothesis is rejected. We conclude that the distribution of the differences has a mean greater than 0. The training director has convincing evidence that the unique training program will be effective in increasing efficiency.

```
MTB > set c1
DATA> 128,105,119,140,98,123,127,115,122,145
DATA> end
MTB > set c2
DATA> 135,110,131,142,105,130,131,110,125,149
DATA> end
MTB > let c3=c2-c1
MTB > name c1 'before' c2 'after' c3 'diff'
MTB > ttest mu=0, c3;
SUBC> alternate =1.
TEST OF MU = 0.000 VS MU G.T. 0.000
            N      MEAN     STDEV   SE MEAN       T   P VALUE
 diff      10     4.600     4.402     1.392    3.30    0.0046
```

The MINITAB system can be used to conduct the paired difference test. First, the efficiency ratings before and after the special program are entered. Next, the differences in the ratings before and after the training program are determined by your computer. The MINITAB procedure is TTEST, with MU = 0 and the data located in column C3. The subcommand ALTERNATE = 1 is used to report the one-tailed *p*-value where the rejection region is in the upper tail.

The MINITAB output reports the same *t* value (3.30), except for rounding error, as we computed using formula (10–4). The *p*-value is also given. By using the MINITAB subcommand ALTERNATE = 1, we are able to determine the one-tailed *p*-value. Because we set up a one-tailed test, we are interested in the probability of a *t* value beyond 3.30, with 9 degrees of freedom. That value is .0046. Thus, the likelihood that we could find a *t* value of 3.30 or more with 9 degrees of freedom, given that the null hypothesis is true, is less than 0.5 percent.

SELF-REVIEW 10–4

The answers are at the end of the chapter.

An Iowa agriculture experimental station plans to test the effectiveness of two presoak solutions for corn seeds. The purpose of the experiment is to determine if there is a difference in effectiveness between the two solutions, designated solution A and solution B. Various corn seeds, such as Iowa Whopper and Tyson Gold, are to be used in the experiment. A pair of Iowa Whopper seeds is selected; one is soaked in solution A and the other in solution B. Then they are planted, and the germination and growth times (in days) are recorded. This procedure is repeated for Tyson Gold and the other seeds. The number of days needed for germination and growth to six inches are indicated for each pair in the table below.

1. State the null and alternate hypotheses using symbols.
2. Using the .05 level, show the critical values and the regions of rejection and nonrejection graphically.
3. Using the following nine pairs of sample data, compute *t*, and arrive at a decision.

	Pair								
Solution	**1**	**2**	**3**	**4**	**5**	**6**	**7**	**8**	**9**
A	16	9	21	14	26	27	18	14	30
B	18	7	26	11	26	22	19	20	28

EXERCISES

The answers to the odd-numbered exercises are at the end of the book.

19. The hypotheses are:

$$H_0: \mu_d \leq 0$$

$$H_1: \mu_d > 0$$

The following paired sample observations were obtained. The numbers represent the scores on a mechanical aptitude test before and after a special review session.

	Pair			
	1	**2**	**3**	**4**
Before	10	12	15	19
After	8	9	12	15

At the .05 significance level, can we conclude that the mean of the distribution of the differences is greater than 0?

a. State the decision rule.

b. Compute the mean and the standard deviation of differences in the "before" and "after" scores.

c. Compute the value of the test statistic.

d. What is your decision regarding the null hypothesis? Was the review session effective?

e. Estimate the *p*-value. Interpret its meaning.

20. We are given the following hypotheses:

$$H_0: \mu_d = 0$$

$$H_1: \mu_d \neq 0$$

The following paired sample observations represent the scores for five disadvantaged children chosen at random. The "before" scores represent their knowledge of the outdoors before they were shown a special movie on the subject. The "after" scores are their scores after seeing the movie.

	Pair				
	1	**2**	**3**	**4**	**5**
Before	30	22	25	19	26
After	26	19	20	15	19

At the .05 significance level, can we conclude that the mean of the distribution of the differences is not equal to 0?

a. State the decision rule.

b. Compute the mean and the standard deviation of differences in the "before" and the "after" scores.

c. Compute the value of the test statistic.

d. What is your decision regarding the null hypothesis? What does this indicate?

e. Estimate the *p*-value.

21. A survey is to be conducted at North Central University to measure the effect of the change in environment on foreign students. One of the facets of the study is a comparison of student weights upon arrival on campus with weights one year later. It is hypothesized that the richer American food will cause an increase in weight. The .01 level is to be used. A random sample of 11 foreign students is chosen for the study. What is your conclusion?

Name	Weight on arrival	Weight one year later
Nassar	124	142
O'Toole	157	157
Obie	98	96
Silverman	190	212
Kim	103	116
Gross	135	134
Farouk	149	150
Thatcher	176	184
Sambul	200	209
Onassis	180	180
Pierre	256	269

22. The management of Discount Furniture, a chain of discount furniture stores in the Northeast, designed an incentive plan for salespeople. To evaluate this innovative plan, 12 salespeople were selected at random, and their weekly incomes before and after the plan were recorded.

	Weekly income			Weekly income	
Salesperson	**Before**	**After**	**Salesperson**	**Before**	**After**
Sid Mahone	$320	$340	Peg Mancuso	$625	$631
Carol Quick	290	285	Anita Loma	560	560
Tom Jackson	421	475	John Cuso	360	365
Andy Jones	510	510	Carl Utz	431	431
Jean Sloan	210	210	A. S. Kushner	506	525
Jack Walker	402	500	Fern Lawton	505	619

Was there a significant increase in the average salesperson's weekly income due to the innovative incentive plan? Use the .05 significance level. Estimate the *p*-value, and interpret it.

23. Calorie Watchers, a national chain of exercise and diet centers, has a new weight-reduction program designed to produce dramatic results within three weeks. As a result of their advertisements, over one thousand signed up. Each was weighed before and after the initial three-week period. The results of a sample of 10 enrollees are:

	Weight			Weight	
Name	**Before**	**After**	**Name**	**Before**	**After**
Evie Gorky	190	196	Pat O'Leary	126	129
Bob Mack	250	240	Kim Dennis	186	189
Lou Brandon	345	345	Connie Kaye	116	115
Karl Unger	210	212	Tom Dama	196	194
Sue Koontz	114	113	Maxine Sims	125	124

At the .01 level of significance, can we say that the new weight-reduction program is a success?

24. A study of more than 100 high-crime locations in Miami, Florida, was conducted. The number of crimes in each of the eight sample areas during a one-year period was recorded. Then a neighborhood watch program was inaugurated. The numbers of crimes before and after the watch are indicated in the table that follows. Has there been a decrease in the number of crimes since the program was inaugurated?

	Number of crimes by area							
	A	**B**	**C**	**D**	**E**	**F**	**G**	**H**
Before watch	14	7	4	5	17	12	8	9
After watch	2	7	3	6	8	13	3	5

Use the .01 significance level. Estimate the *p*-value.

CHAPTER OUTLINE

I. The Student's *t* distribution.
   A. It is used when:
      1. The sample size is less than 30.

2. The population or populations are normally or nearly normally distributed.
3. The population standard deviation is not known.

B. Characteristics of the Student *t.*

1. It is a continuous distribution.
2. It is bell-shaped and symmetrical.
3. There is a family of *t* distributions. All have the same mean—zero—but different standard deviations, depending on the sample size.
4. It is spread out more than the standard normal distribution and is flatter at the apex of the curve.

II. The formula for a test of hypothesis about a population mean using Student's *t* distribution.

$$t = \frac{\overline{X} - \mu}{s/\sqrt{n}} \qquad (10\text{–}1)$$

with $n - 1$ degrees of freedom, where:

$\overline{X}$ is the sample mean.

μ is the hypothesized population mean.

s is the sample standard deviation.

n is the number in the sample.

III. Assumptions and formulas for a test of hypothesis involving the difference between two population means.

A. Assumptions

1. The observations in one sample are independent of those in the other sample and independent of each other.
2. The two populations are normal.
3. The two populations have equal variances.

B. Formulas.

1. The formula for pooling the variances.

$$s_p^2 = \frac{(n_1 - 1)(s_1^2) + (n_2 - 1)(s_2^2)}{n_1 + n_2 - 2} \qquad (10\text{–}2)$$

where:

n_1 is the number of observations in the first sample.

n_2 is the number of observations in the second sample.

s_1^2 is the variance of the first sample.

s_2^2 is the variance of the second sample.

2. The formula for the test statistic *t.*

$$t = \frac{\overline{X}_1 - \overline{X}_2}{\sqrt{s_p^2\left(\frac{1}{n_1} + \frac{1}{n_2}\right)}} \qquad (10\text{–}3)$$

IV. If the samples are dependent (paired):

$$t = \frac{\bar{d}}{s_d/\sqrt{n}} \qquad (10\text{–}4)$$

where:

$$\bar{d} = \frac{\Sigma d}{n} \qquad s_d = \sqrt{\frac{\Sigma d^2 - \frac{(\Sigma d)^2}{n}}{n - 1}}$$

V. A *p*-value is the likelihood of a value of *t* as large, or larger, than that computed when the null hypothesis is true.

EXERCISES

The answers to the odd-numbered exercises are at the end of the book.

25. The manufacturer of the Ososki motorcycle advertises that the cycle will average 87 miles per gallon on long trips. The mileages on eight long trips were 88, 82, 81, 87, 80, 78, 79, and 89. At the .05 level, is the mean mileage less than the advertised 87 miles per gallon?
26. The Myers Summer Casual Furniture Store tells customers that a special order will take six weeks (42 days). During recent months the owner has received several complaints that the special orders are taking longer than 42 days. A sample of 12 special orders delivered in the last month showed that the mean waiting time was 51 days with a standard deviation of 8 days. At the .05 significance level, are customers waiting an average of more than 42 days? Estimate the *p*-value.
27. A recent article in *The Wall Street Journal* reported that the prime rate for large banks now exceeds 9 percent. A sample of eight small banks in the Midwest revealed the following prime rates: 10.1, 9.3, 9.2, 10.2, 9.3, 9.6, 9.4, and 8.8. At the .01 significance level, can we conclude that the prime rate for small banks also exceeds 9 percent? Estimate the *p*-value.
28. A typical college student drinks an average of 27 gallons of coffee each year, or 2.25 gallons per month. A sample of 12 students at Northwestern State University revealed the following amounts of coffee consumed last month.

1.75	1.96	1.57	1.82	1.85	1.82
2.43	2.65	2.60	2.24	1.69	2.66

(Source: "The Typical College Student," *Vitality*, vol. 7, no. 7, July 1991, p. 3.) At the .05 significance level, is there a significant difference between the average amount consumed at Northwestern and the national average?

29. The postanesthesia care area (recovery room) at St. Luke's Hospital in Maumee, Ohio, was recently enlarged. The hope was that with the enlargment the mean number of patients per day would be more than 25. A random sample of 15 days revealed the following numbers of patients. At the .01 significance level, can we conclude that the mean number of patients per day is more than 25? Estimate the *p*-value and interpret it.

25	27	25	26	25	28	28	27
24	26	25	29	25	27	24	

30. A recent survey found that the typical grandparents live a 6½-hour drive from their grandchildren. A sample of 12 Ohio grandparents revealed the following driving times, in hours. At the .01 significance level, can we conclude that Ohio grandparents live closer to their grandchildren?

0	4	3	4	9	4
5	9	1	6	7	10

31. During recent seasons major league baseball has been criticized for the length of the games. A report indicated that the average game lasts 3 hours and 30 minutes. A sample of 17 games played during the week from August 1 to August 5, 1994, revealed

the following times to completion. (Note that the minutes have been changed to fractions of hours, so that a game that lasted 2 hours and 24 minutes is reported at 2.40 hours.)

2.98	2.40	2.70	2.25	3.23	3.17	2.93
3.18	2.80	2.38	3.75	3.20	3.27	2.52
2.58	4.45	2.45				

Do these sample data support the contention that baseball games take an average of 3½ hours to complete? Use the .05 significance level.

32. A study of the health benefits packages for employees of large and small firms was recently completed by Pohlman Associates, a management consulting firm. Among the 15 large firms studied, the benefits package costs an average of 17.6 percent of salary with a standard deviation of 2.6 percent. Among the 12 small firms studied, the benefits package averaged 16.2 percent of salary with a standard deviation of 3.3 percent. Is there a significant difference between the mean percent of the employees' salaries spent by large firms and by small firms on health benefits? Use the .05 level of significance.
33. The manager of a package courier service believes that packages shipped at the end of the month are heavier than those shipped early in the month. As an experiment, he weighed a random sample of 20 packages at the beginning of the month. He found that the mean weight was 20.25 pounds and that the standard deviation was 5.84 pounds. Ten packages randomly selected at the end of the month had a mean weight of 24.80 pounds and a standard deviation of 5.67 pounds. At the .05 significance level, can we conclude that the packages shipped at the end of the month weigh more?
34. Hamburger sales per day at two locations of the Bun 'N' Run were compared. The mean number sold for 10 randomly selected days at the Northside site was 83.55, and the standard deviation was 10.50. For a random sample of 12 days at the Southside location, the mean number sold was 78.80 and the standard deviation was 14.25. At the .05 significance level, is there a difference in the mean number of hamburgers sold at the two locations?
35. The Commercial Bank and Trust Company is studying the use of its automatic teller machines (ATMs). Of particular interest is whether young adults (under 25 years) use the machines more than senior citizens. To investigate further, samples of customers under 25 years of age and customers over 60 years of age were selected. The number of ATM transactions last month was determined for each selected individual, and the results are shown below. At the .01 significance level, can bank management conclude that younger customers use the ATMs more?

Number of transactions	
Under 25 years of age	**Over 60 years of age**
10	4
10	8
11	7
15	7
7	4
11	5
10	1
9	7
	4
	10
	5

36. The manager of Fred's Grocery is making a study of the amounts customers spend in the store. A sample of 10 weekday morning shoppers and 15 Saturday morning shoppers revealed the following amounts spent:

Weekday	Saturday
$18.88	$21.54
24.33	34.76
27.26	45.78
35.79	46.87
42.31	56.78
53.77	66.04
62.94	68.45
73.59	70.98
76.51	72.67
88.09	76.89
	81.65
	85.61
	91.87
	94.71
	95.80

Owner Fred Snead contends that Saturday morning shoppers spend an average of $10 more than weekday shoppers. Do these data substantiate his claim? Use the .05 significance level.

37. The manufacturer of a compact disc player wanted to know if a 10 percent reduction in price is enough to increase the sales of their product. To investigate, the owner randomly selected eight outlets and sold the disc player at the reduced price. At seven randomly selected outlets, the regular price was charged. Reported below are the numbers sold last month at the selected outlets. At the .01 significance level, can the manufacturer conclude that the price reduction resulted in an increase in sales?

Reduced price	Regular price
128	138
134	121
152	88
135	115
114	141
106	125
112	96
120	

38. Two boats, the *Sea Hawk* and the *Sea Queen,* are competing for a spot in the upcoming *America's* Cup race. To decide which will represent the United States, they race over a part of the course several times. Below are the sample times in minutes. At the .05 significance level, can we conclude that there is a difference in their mean times?

Sea Hawk	*Sea Queen*
12.9	14.1
12.5	14.1
11.0	14.2
13.3	17.4
11.2	15.8
11.4	16.7
11.6	16.1
12.3	13.3
14.2	13.4
11.3	13.6
	10.8
	19.0

39. A drill press operator has to do several safety checks before actually drilling holes in a steel plate. The start switch has to be held closed with one hand, and the safety checks have to be done with the other hand. The operators are on piece work and therefore want to do the job in the most efficient way. Twelve right-handed operators selected at random participated in an experiment. During a one-week period operators used the left hand to hold the start switch closed. The second week the right hand held the switch closed. The number of holes drilled each week is shown below.

	Production, by operator number											
	1	**2**	**3**	**4**	**5**	**6**	**7**	**8**	**9**	**10**	**11**	**12**
Left hand	1,240	1,137	942	1,105	846	1,216	1,190	840	892	1,115	1,260	550
Right hand	1,248	1,130	940	1,105	849	1,221	1,180	841	890	1,120	1,257	551

Do the paired sample results give us evidence to reject the statement that there is no difference between use of the left hand and use of the right hand in holding the start switch closed and doing the safety checks with the other hand? Use the .05 level.

40. A number of minor automobile accidents occur at various high-risk intersections in Teton County despite traffic lights. The traffic department claims that a modification in the type of light will reduce these accidents. The county commissioners have agreed to a proposed experiment. Eight intersections were chosen at random, and the lights at those intersections were modified. Use the .01 significance level. The numbers of minor accidents during a six-month period before and after the modifications were:

	Number of accidents, by intersection							
	A	**B**	**C**	**D**	**E**	**F**	**G**	**H**
Before modification	5	7	6	4	8	9	8	10
After modification	3	7	7	0	4	6	8	2

41. Reginald "Bud" Ownes is vice president for human resources for a large manufacturing company. In recent years he has noticed an increase in absenteeism that he thinks is related to the general health of the employees. Four years ago, in an attempt to improve the situation, he began a fitness program in which employees exercise during their lunch hour. To evaluate the program, he selected a random sample of eight participants and found the number of days each was absent in the six months before the exercise program began and in the last six months. Below are the results. At the .05 significance level, can he conclude that the number of absences has declined? Estimate the *p*-value.

Employee	Before program	After program
1	6	5
2	6	2
3	7	1
4	7	3
5	4	3
6	3	6
7	5	3
8	6	7

42. Scott Seggity, owner of Seggity Software, Inc., recently purchased a special math coprocessor chip advertised to "drastically reduce processing time." To test the chip, a sample of 12 programs was selected. The selected programs were run on two identical computers, one with the chip and the other without it. The processing times are reported below, in seconds. At the .05 significance level, can Mr. Seggity conclude that the new coprocessor will reduce the processing time? Estimate the *p*-value.

Program	Without chip	With chip
1	1.23	0.60
2	0.69	0.93
3	1.28	0.95
4	1.19	1.37
5	0.78	0.62
6	1.02	0.99
7	1.30	0.60
8	1.37	1.35
9	1.29	0.67
10	1.17	0.89
11	1.14	1.29
12	1.09	1.00

COMPUTER DATA EXERCISES

43. Refer to data set 1, which reports information on homes sold in Florida during 1994.
    a. At the .05 significance level, can we conclude that the mean selling price of a home with a pool is different from the mean selling price of a home without a pool?
    b. At the .05 significance level, can we conclude that the mean selling price of a home with a garage is different from the mean selling price of a home without a garage?
    c. At the .05 significance level, can we conclude that there is a difference in the mean selling price for a home in Township 1 versus one in Township 2?
44. Refer to data set 2, which reports information on the 28 major league baseball teams for the 1993 season.
    a. At the .05 significance level, can we conclude that teams with turf home fields hit fewer home runs than those with grass fields?
    b. At the .05 significance level, can we conclude that the mean number of stolen bases per team was higher for National League teams than for American League teams?
    c. At the .05 significance level, is there a difference in the mean attendance for American League teams versus National League teams?
45. Refer to data set 3, which reports information on the circulation of 48 magazines.
    a. Create a new variable that divides the male readership variable into two groups. The first group includes those magazines whose readership is less than 50 percent men. The second group includes magazines for which 50 percent or more of the readership

is men. Conduct a test of hypothesis to determine if the mean cost for a color advertisement is different for these two groups.

b. Using the same variable created above, is there a difference in the mean circulation between the two groups?

CHAPTER 10 EXAMINATION

The answers are at the end of the chapter.

For Questions 1 through 10, indicate whether the statement is true or false. If false, give the correct answer.

1. To apply the Student *t* to a problem involving two means, the two populations must be normal, or nearly normal.
2. A test was made about a population mean. A sample of 22 pieces of steel were selected at random. There are 22 degrees of freedom.
3. As the sample size increases, the *t* distribution tends to approximate the standard normal distribution.
4. There is only one *t* distribution, and it has a mean of zero.
5. Generally speaking, Student's *t* distribution is used when the sample is less than 30.
6. In a test of the difference between two population means, the degrees of freedom are $n_1 + n_2 - 2$.
7. The *t* test assumes that the variances of the two populations are equal, or approximately equal.

Questions 8–10 are based on the following:

$$H_0\colon \mu_1 = \mu_2 \quad H_1\colon \mu_1 \neq \mu_2$$

Sample sizes are 12 and 11. The .05 level of risk is to be used.

8. The test is two-tailed.
9. The critical values of *t* are −2.069 and +2.069.
10. If *t* were computed to be −0.999, the null hypothesis would not be rejected.
11. A radical new treatment for repairing broken leg bones has been introduced. The claim is that the amount of time a patient spends in a cast and on crutches has been reduced. Extensive records revealed that using the old method, a patient, on the average, requires 20 days to recover from a leg break. A random sample of 16 individuals receiving the new treatment revealed that the mean length of time needed for recovery was 18 days; the standard deviation of the sample was 2.5 days. Is the claim made for the new treatment supported at the .05 level? State the null and alternate hypotheses, give the critical value, and reach a decision. Estimate the *p*-value.
12. The offense of the SU football team uses a large number of complicated plays that must be learned quickly at the start of the season. The offensive coordinator wants to experiment with two methods of memorizing the plays—the Pow Wow method and the Ding Ding method. To test them, 10 pairs of players were selected at random. He paired two quarterbacks, two tight ends, and so on. One of each pair learned the plays using the Pow Wow method; the other used the Ding Ding method. Just prior to the first game against State, the 10 pairs were tested on their execution of the plays, with these results:

	Test scores by pair									
Method	**A**	**B**	**C**	**D**	**E**	**F**	**G**	**H**	**I**	**J**
Pow Wow method	100	86	82	70	82	77	80	99	86	91
Ding Ding method	91	86	94	65	91	86	60	98	89	90

Does this sample information at the .05 level of significance indicate a difference between the two methods? Answer by stating H_0 and H_1, giving the critical values, computing the appropriate statistics, and arriving at a decision to either reject or not reject H_0.

13. Two suppliers of bearings are being considered by Midland Manufacturing. Is there a difference in the quality of the bearings sold by the two suppliers? A sample of seven recent shipments from New York Supply revealed that the mean number of defects per shipment was 12 with a standard deviation of 2. A sample of six recent shipments from Discount Supply revealed the mean number of defects per shipment to be 9 with a standard deviation of 3. Use the .05 significance level to explore whether there is a difference in the quality of the bearings supplied by New York and those supplied by Discount. Estimate the p-value.

CHAPTER 10 Answers

Self-Review

10–1 1. H_0: $\mu \leq 305$, H_1: $\mu > 305$.

2. $df = 19$

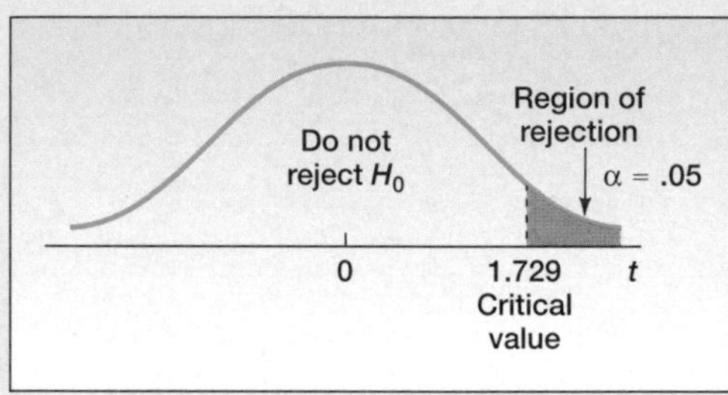

3. $$t = \frac{\overline{X} - \mu}{s/\sqrt{n}} = \frac{311 - 305}{12/\sqrt{20}} = 2.236$$

Reject H_0 because $2.236 > 1.729$. Reject H_0 and accept H_1, that the mean is greater than 305 days. It is concluded that the modification increased battery life.

10–2 1. H_0: $\mu \geq 9.0$, H_1: $\mu < 9.0$.

2. 7, found by $n - 1 = 8 - 1 = 7$.

3. Do not reject the null hypothesis if the computed value of t falls to the right of -2.998. Otherwise reject H_0 and accept H_1.

Region of rejection
Do not reject H_0
−2.998 Critical value
0
Scale of t

4. $t = -2.494$, found by:

X	$X - \overline{X}$	$(X - \overline{X})^2$	X^2
9.2	0.4	0.16	84.64
8.7	−0.1	0.01	75.69
8.9	0.1	0.01	79.21
8.6	−0.2	0.04	73.96
8.8	0.0	0.00	77.44
8.5	−0.3	0.09	72.25
8.7	−0.1	0.01	75.69
9.0	0.2	0.04	81.00
70.4	0.0	0.36	619.88

$$\overline{X} = \frac{70.4}{8} = 8.8$$

$$s = \sqrt{\frac{0.36}{8 - 1}} = 0.2268$$

or

$$s = \sqrt{\frac{619.88 - \frac{(70.4)^2}{8}}{8 - 1}} = 0.2268$$

Then

$$t = \frac{8.8 - 9.0}{0.2268/\sqrt{8}} = -2.494$$

Since −2.494 lies to the right of −2.998, H_0 is not rejected. We have not shown that the mean is less than 9.0.

5. The p-value is between .025 and .010.

10–3 H_0: $\mu_1 \geq \mu_2$, H_1: $\mu_1 < \mu_2$. H_0 is rejected if $t < -1.782$. There are 12 degrees of freedom, found by $n_1 + n_2 - 2 = 6 + 8 - 2$.

	Edne	Orno
Mean	7.00	10.00
Standard deviation	1.4142	2.2678
n	6	8

$$s_p^2 = \frac{(6 - 1)(1.4142)^2 + (8 - 1)(2.2678)^2}{6 + 8 - 2} = 3.8334$$

$$t = \frac{7.00 - 10.00}{\sqrt{3.8334\left(\frac{1}{6} + \frac{1}{8}\right)}} = \frac{-3.00}{1.0574} = -2.837$$

Because −2.837 falls in the left tail beyond −1.782, the null hypothesis is rejected at the .05 level. Orno's mean weight is greater than Edne's mean weight. The *p*-value is less than .01, because the computed value of *t* is less than −2.681.

10–4 1. H_0: $\mu_d = 0$, H_1: $\mu_d \neq 0$.

2. Two-tailed test; $n - 1 = 9 - 1 = 8$ degrees of freedom; critical values are −2.306 and +2.306.

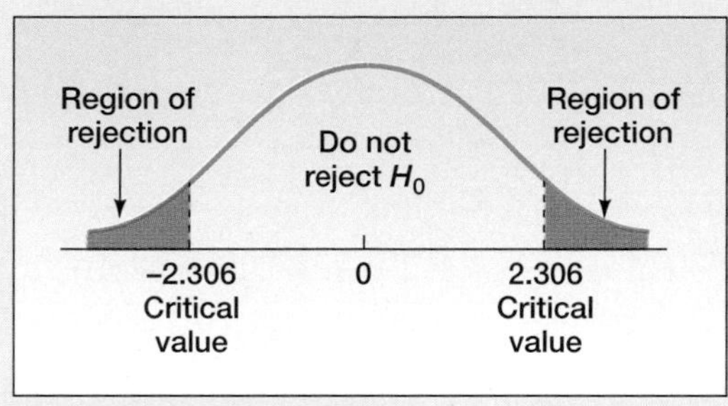

3.

Pair	A	B	$d = B - A$	d^2
1	16	18	2	4
2	9	7	−2	4
3	21	26	5	25
4	14	11	−3	9
5	26	26	0	0
6	27	22	−5	25
7	18	19	1	1
8	14	20	6	36
9	30	28	−2	4
			2	108

$$\bar{d} = \frac{\Sigma d}{n} = \frac{2}{9} = 0.22$$

$$s_d = \sqrt{\frac{108 - \frac{(2)^2}{9}}{9 - 1}} = 3.667$$

$$t = \frac{\bar{d}}{s_d/\sqrt{n}} = \frac{0.22}{3.667/\sqrt{9}} = \frac{0.22}{1.222} = 0.180$$

Since 0.180 lies between −2.306 and 2.306, the null hypothesis is not rejected. There is no difference between the effectiveness of solutions A and B.

Chapter Examination

1. True.
2. False. 21 degrees of freedom, found by $n - 1 = 22 - 1$.
3. True.
4. False. There are many *t* distributions, each with a mean of zero. The shapes of the *t* distributions vary with the sample size.
5. True.
6. True.
7. True.
8. True.
9. False, $t = \pm 2.080$. There are $n_1 + n_2 - 2 = 12 + 11 - 2 = 21$ degrees of freedom. From Appendix F, two-tailed test, .05 level, 21 degrees of freedom, the critical value of *t* is 2.080 or −2.080.
10. True.
11. H_0: $\mu \geq 20$ days, H_1: $\mu < 20$ days. $df = 15$. Computed $t = -3.20$, found by:

$$t = \frac{18 - 20}{2.5/\sqrt{16}}$$

Reject null hypothesis at the .05 level because computed *t* of −3.20 is in the region of rejection beyond −1.753. The new method significantly reduces the healing time. The *p*-value is less than .005, because the computed value of *t* is less than −2.947.

12. H_0: $\mu_d = 0$, H_1: $\mu_d \neq 0$, $df = 9$. $n = 10$. Critical values of *t* are −2.262 and +2.262 (.05 level, two-tailed values). Computed 0.099 $\bar{d} = 3/10 = 0.3$. $s_d = 9.56$. Then

$$t = \frac{0.3}{9.56/\sqrt{10}} = 0.099$$

Do not reject H_0. There is no significant difference between the two methods.

13. H_0: $\mu_1 = \mu_2$, H_1: $\mu_1 \neq \mu_2$. $df = 7 + 6 - 2 = 11$. H_0 is rejected if $t < -2.201$ or $t > 2.201$.

$$s_p^2 = \frac{(7-1)(2)^2 + (6-1)(3)^2}{7 + 6 - 2} = 6.2727$$

$$t = \frac{12.0 - 9.0}{\sqrt{6.2727\left(\frac{1}{7} + \frac{1}{6}\right)}} = \frac{3.0}{1.3934} = 2.153$$

H_0 Is not rejected. There is no difference in the mean number of defects. The *p*-value is between .05 and .10.

Chapter 11 Analysis of Variance

GOALS

When you have completed this chapter, you will be able to:

1
Discuss the general idea of analysis of variance.

2
List the characteristics of the *F* distribution.

3
Conduct a test of hypothesis to determine if two sample variances came from the same or equal populations.

4
Set up and organize data into an ANOVA table.

5
Conduct a test for a difference among three or more treatment means.

6
Conduct a test of hypothesis to determine if there is a difference between block means.

A firm that grows plants in water needs to know how often to treat plants with plant food. One group received the full treatment, another received two half-treatments and the last received monthly doses. Samples from each group were weighed. Is there a difference in the mean weights of the plants grown under the different treatments? (See Goal 5 and Case 1 on page 439.)

INTRODUCTION

In this chapter we continue our discussion of hypothesis testing. Recall that in Chapter 9 we examined the general theory of hypothesis testing and applied it to situations where a large sample was selected from a normal population. We used the standard normal distribution (z) as a basis for testing whether a sample mean came from a hypothesized population and whether two samples means were obtained from the same or equal populations. We also conducted both one- and two-sample tests for proportions, again using the standard normal distribution as the test statistic. In Chapter 10 we described methods for conducting tests of means where the populations are normal but the samples are small. In these cases we used the t distribution.

THE *F* DISTRIBUTION

In this chapter we describe the F distribution. This probability distribution is used as the test statistic for several situations. It is used to test whether two samples are from populations having equal variances, and it is also applied when we want to compare two or more population means simultaneously. The simultaneous comparison of several population means is called **analysis of variance (ANOVA).** In both of these situations, the populations must be normal, and the data must be at least interval-scale.

Characteristics of the *F* distribution

What are the major characteristics of the F distribution?

1. There is a "family" of F distributions. A particular member of the family is determined by two parameters: the degrees of freedom in the numerator and the degrees of freedom in the denominator. This is illustrated by the following graph. There is one F distribution for the combination of 29 degrees of freedom in the numerator and 28 degrees of freedom in the denominator. There is another F distribution for 19 degrees in the numerator and

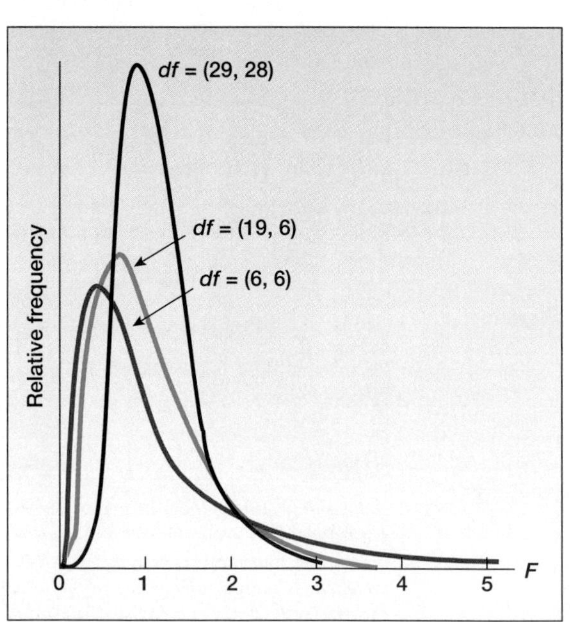

6 degrees of freedom in the denominator. Note that the shape of the curves changes as the degrees of freedom change.

2. F cannot be negative, and it is a continuous distribution.
3. The curve representing an F distribution is positively skewed.
4. Its values range from 0 to ∞. As the values of F increase, the curve approaches the X-axis, but it never touches it.

Comparing Two Population Variances

The F distribution is used in this section to test the hypothesis that the variance of one normal population equals the variance of another normal population. Thus, this test is useful for determining whether or not one normal population has more variation than another. The following examples show the use of this test:

> Two Barth shearing machines are set to produce steel bars of the same length. The bars, therefore, should have the same mean length. We want to ensure that in addition to having the same mean length, they have similar variation.
>
> The mean rate of return on investment of two types of stocks may be the same, but there may be more variation in the return of one than the other. A sample of 10 aerospace stocks and 10 utility stocks might show the same mean rate of return, but it is likely there is more variation in the rate of return of aerospace stocks.

Validating Assumptions

The F test can also be used to validate assumptions with respect to certain statistical tests. As an example, recall that the t test described in Chapter 10 is used to determine whether the means of two independent populations differ. To employ that test, it is necessary to assume that the two population variances are the same.

Regardless of whether we want to determine if one population has more variation than another population or validate an assumption with respect to a statistical test,

First state null hypothesis

we first state the null hypothesis. For either investigation, the null hypothesis is that the variance of one normal population, σ_1^2, equals the variance of the other normal population, σ_2^2. The alternate hypothesis is that the variances differ. This test of hypothesis is written:

$$H_0 : \sigma_1^2 = \sigma_2^2$$
$$H_1 : \sigma_1^2 \neq \sigma_2^2$$

To conduct the test, a random sample of n_1 observations is obtained from one population, and a sample of n_2 observations is obtained from the second population. The test statistic is s_1^2/s_2^2, where s_1^2 and s_2^2 are the respective sample variances. If the null hypothesis is true ($H_0 : \sigma_1^2 = \sigma_2^2$), the test statistic follows the F distribution with $n_1 - 1$ and $n_2 - 1$ degrees of freedom. The *larger* sample variance is placed in the numerator; hence, the F ratio is always positive and larger than 1.00. Thus, the upper-tail critical value is the only one required. The critical value of F is found by dividing the significance level in half ($\alpha/2$) and then referring to the appropriate number of degrees of freedom in Appendix G. An example will help to clarify.

EXAMPLE

Lammers Limos offers limousine service from city hall in Toledo, Ohio, to Metro Airport in Detroit. Sean Lammers, president of the company, is considering two routes. One is via U.S. 25 and the other via I-75. He wants to conduct a study of both routes and then compare the results. He recorded the following data. Using the .10 significance level, is there a difference in the variation in the two routes?

Route	Mean time (minutes)	Standard deviation (minutes)	Sample size
U.S. 25	56	12	7
I-75	59	5	8

Solution

Lammers noted that the mean times seem very similar, but there is more variation, as measured by the standard deviation, in the U.S. 25 route than in the I-75 route. This is somewhat consistent with his knowledge of the two routes; the U.S. 25 route contains more stoplights, whereas I-75 is a limited-access highway. However, the I-75 route is several miles longer. It is important that the service offered be both timely and consistent, so he decides to conduct a statistical test to determine if there really is a difference in the variation of the two routes.

The usual five-step hypothesis-testing procedure will be employed.

Step 1 The null hypothesis and the alternate hypothesis are stated. The test is two-tailed because we are looking for a difference in the variation of the two routes. We are not trying to show that one route has more variation than the other.

$$H_0 : \sigma_1^2 = \sigma_2^2$$
$$H_1 : \sigma_1^2 \neq \sigma_2^2$$

Step 2 A significance level of .10 is selected.

Step 3 The appropriate test statistic is the *F* distribution.

Step 4 The decision rule is obtained from Appendix G, a portion of which is reproduced as Table 11–1. Because we are using a two-tailed test, the significance level is .05, found by $\alpha/2 = .10/2 = .05$. There are $n_1 - 1 = 7 - 1 = 6$ degrees of freedom in the numerator, and $n_2 - 1 = 8 - 1 = 7$ degrees of freedom in the denominator. To find the critical value, move horizontally across the top portion of the *F* Table (Table 11–1 or Appendix G) for the .05 significance level to 6 degrees of freedom in the numerator. Then move down that column to the critical value opposite 7 degrees of freedom in the denominator. The critical value is 3.87. If the ratio of the sample variances, s_1^2/s_2^2, exceeds 3.87, the null hypothesis is rejected.

TABLE 11–1 **Critical Values of the *F* Distribution, $\alpha = .05$**

Degrees of freedom for denominator	Degrees of freedom for numerator			
	5	6	7	8
1	230	234	237	239
2	19.3	19.3	19.4	19.4
3	9.01	8.94	8.89	8.85
4	6.26	6.16	6.09	6.04
5	5.05	4.95	4.88	4.82
6	4.39	4.28	4.21	4.15
7	3.97	3.87	3.79	3.73
8	3.69	3.58	3.50	3.44
9	3.48	3.37	3.29	3.23
10	3.33	3.22	3.14	3.07
11	3.20	3.09	3.01	2.95
12	3.11	3.00	2.91	2.85
13	3.03	2.92	2.83	2.77
14	2.96	2.85	2.76	2.70
15	2.90	2.79	2.71	2.64

Step 5 The computed value of the test statistic is 5.76, found by $s_1^2/s_2^2 = (12)^2/(5)^2$. The null hypothesis is rejected and the alternate hypothesis accepted. The variation is not the same in the two populations.

As noted, the usual procedure is to determine the *F* ratio by putting the larger variance in the numerator. This will force the *F* ratio to be larger than the 1.00. Why is this necessary? It allows us to always use the upper tail of the *F* statistic, thus avoiding the need for more extensive *F* tables.

A question arises regarding *one-tailed tests.* How are they handled? Again, arrange the *F* ratio so that it is always greater than 1.00. Under these conditions it is not necessary to divide the level of significance in half. We are therefore restricted to the .05 or .01 significance levels (for one-tailed tests) in Appendix G. The following Self-Review gives an example of a one-tailed test.

SELF-REVIEW 11–1

The answers are at the end of the chapter.

The Treece Company assembles electrical components. For the last 10 days Mark Treece has averaged 9 rejects per day, with a standard deviation of 2 rejects. Debbie Thorton averaged 8.5 rejects per day with a standard deviation of 1.5 rejects over the same period. At the .05 significance level, can we conclude that there is more variation in the number of rejects per day attributed to Mark?

EXERCISES

The answers to the odd-numbered exercises are at the end of the book.

1. Using a two-tailed test and the .10 significance level, what is the critical F value for a sample of six observations in the numerator and four in the denominator?
2. Using a one-tailed test and the .01 significance level, what is the critical F value for a sample of four observations in the numerator and seven in the denominator?
3. The following hypotheses are given.

$$H_0 : \sigma_1^2 = \sigma_2^2$$
$$H_1 : \sigma_1^2 \neq \sigma_2^2$$

   A random sample of eight observations from the first sample resulted in a standard deviation of 10. A random sample of six observations from the second sample gave a standard deviation of 7. At the .02 significance level, is there a difference in the variation of the two populations?
4. The following hypotheses are given.

$$H_0 : \sigma_1^2 \leq \sigma_2^2$$
$$H_1 : \sigma_1^2 > \sigma_2^2$$

   A random sample of five observations from the first sample resulted in a standard deviation of 12. A random sample of seven observations from the second sample showed a standard deviation of 7. At the .01 significance level, is there more variation in the first population?
5. Stargell Research Associates conducted a study of the radio listening habits of men and women. One facet of the study involved the mean listening time. It was discovered that the mean listening time for men is 35 minutes per day. The standard deviation of the sample of the 10 men studied was 10 minutes per day. The mean listening time for the 12 women studied was also 35 minutes, but the standard deviation of the sample was 12 minutes. At the .10 significance level, can we conclude that there is a difference in the variation in the number of minutes men and women listen to the radio?
6. A stockbroker at Critical Securities reported that the mean rate of return on a sample of 10 oil stocks was 12.6 percent with a standard deviation of 3.9 percent. The mean rate of return on a sample of 8 utility stocks was 10.9 percent with a standard deviation of 3.5 percent. At the .05 significance level, can we conclude that there is more variation in the oil stocks?

UNDERLYING ASSUMPTIONS FOR ANOVA

The F distribution is also used for testing the equality of more than two means using a technique called **analysis of variance (ANOVA).** ANOVA requires the following conditions.

1. The populations being studied are normally distributed.
2. The populations have equal standard deviations (or equal variances).
3. The samples selected from these populations are independent, and the samples are selected at random.

F is the test statistic (instead of z or t) used to find out if the means of two or more populations are the same. What if one or more of these assumptions cannot be met? Then the ANOVA technique is not appropriate. Instead the Kruskal-Wallis test is used, which is discussed in Chapter 15. ANOVA had its beginnings in agriculture, and many of the terms related to that context remain. In particular, the term **treatment** is used to identify the different populations being examined.

Treatment A cause, or specific source, of variation in a set of data.

Following are two cases to expand on the meaning of a treatment.

Case 1

Do different treatments of fertilizer affect yield?

Hydroponics, Inc. is a research firm that grows tomatoes and other plants in water. The question is how often to treat newly developed tomatoes with soluble plant food. For maximum growth, should they receive a full treatment of food at the beginning of the growing season and none thereafter? Or should the plants be given one-half dose at the beginning and the other half in the middle of the four-month growing season? Or should one quarter of the soluble solution be fed to the plants every month?

As an experiment, one tank was given the full treatment, another tank received the two half-treatments, and a third tank got monthly doses. Samples of the ripe tomatoes from each of the three tanks were weighed, and the weights were recorded. A few results are shown in tabular form.

Weight (grams)		
Full treatment	Half-treatment	Monthly treatment
12.3	15.6	13.8
25.8	11.4	15.2
	14.3	

The question is, is there a difference in the mean weights of the tomatoes grown under the different treatments?

Case 2

Do different grades of gasoline affect performance?

For an automobile manufacturer, the different "treatments" may be four different grades of gasoline. Suppose, for example, that an automobile manufacturer designed a radical new lightweight engine and wants to recommend the grade of gasoline to use. The four grades, the treatments, are: leaded regular, unleaded regular, mid-grade unleaded, and premium unleaded. The test car made a number of trial runs on the test track using each of the four grades. The results are:

Kilometers per liter			
Leaded regular	**Unleaded regular**	**Mid-grade unleaded**	**Premium unleaded**
39.31	36.69	38.99	40.04
39.87	40.00	40.02	39.89
39.87	41.01	39.99	39.93
37.93		41.61	

The question to be answered by applying ANOVA is: Are the treatments (grades of gasoline) producing the same results (the same mean number of kilometers per liter)?

Why do we need to study ANOVA? Why can't we just use the *t* distribution, discussed in Chapter 10, to compare the treatment means two at a time? The major reason is the unsatisfactory buildup of Type I or α error. To explain further, suppose we have four different methods (A, B, C, and D) of training new recruits to be fire fighters. We randomly assign each of the 40 recruits in this year's class to one of the four methods. At the end of the training program, a common test to measure understanding of fire-fighting techniques is given to the four groups. The question to be explored is: Is there a difference in the mean test scores among the four groups? An answer to this question will allow us to compare the four training methods.

Using the *t* distribution to compare the four sample means, we would have to run six different *t* tests. That is, we would need to compare the mean scores for the four methods as follows: A versus B, A versus C, A versus D, B versus C, B versus D, and C versus D. If we set α at .05, the probability of a correct statistical decision is .95, found by $1 - .05$. The probability that we do *not* make an incorrect decision due to sampling in any of the six independent tests is $(.95)^6 = .735$. Thus, the probability of at least one incorrect decision due to sampling is $1 - .735 = .265$. So if we conduct six independent tests using the *t* distribution, the likelihood of at least one sampling error is increased from .05 to an unsatisfactory level of .265. It is obvious that we need a better method than conducting six *t* tests. ANOVA will allow us to compare the treatment means simultaneously and avoid the buildup of the Type I or α error.

ANALYSIS OF VARIANCE PROCEDURE

Does difference between these sample means indicate unequal population means?

The ANOVA procedure can best be illustrated using an example. Suppose the manager of the west-end branch of Appliance Stores, Inc. resigned, and three salespeople at the branch are being considered for the position. All three have about the same length of service, education, and so on. In order to make a decision, it was suggested that each of their monthly sales records be examined. The sample results of their monthly sales are shown in Table 11–2. The "treatments" in this problem are the salespeople.

TABLE 11–2 **Monthly Sales of Appliances of Three Salespeople**

	Monthly sales ($ thousands)		
	Ms. Mapes	**Mr. Sonnar**	**Mr. Mafee**
	15	15	19
	10	10	12
	9	12	16
	5	11	16
	16	12	17
Treatment means	11	12	16

The ANOVA procedure calls for the same hypothesis-testing procedure outlined in Chapter 9 and used in Chapter 10.

Null hypothesis

Step 1: The Null Hypothesis and the Alternate Hypothesis H_0 states that there is no significant difference among the mean sales of the three salespeople; that is, $\mu_1 = \mu_2 = \mu_3$. H_1 states that at least one mean is different. As before, if H_0 is rejected, H_1 will be accepted. So,

H_0: $\mu_1 = \mu_2 = \mu_3$

H_1: The treatment means are not the same.

Level of significance

Step 2: The Level of Significance The .05 level was selected.

Step 3: The Test Statistic The appropriate test statistic is the F distribution. Underlying this procedure are several assumptions: (1) The data must be at least interval-level. (2) The actual selection of the sales must be chosen using a probability-type procedure. (3) The distribution of the monthly sales for each of the populations is normal. (4) The variances of the three populations are equal, i.e., $\sigma_1^2 = \sigma_2^2 = \sigma_3^2$.

The test statistic

F is the ratio of two variances:

$$F = \frac{\text{Estimated population variance based on variation between the sample means}}{\text{Estimated population variance based on variation within samples}}$$

The common terminology for the numerator is *"between-sample variance."* For the denominator, it is *"within-sample variance."* The numerator has $k - 1$ degrees of freedom and the denominator $N - k$ degrees of freedom, where k is the number of treatments and N is the total number of observations.

The decision rule

Step 4: The Decision Rule As noted previously, the F distribution and accompanying curve are positively skewed and dependent on (1) the number of treatments, k, and (2) the total number of observations, N. For this problem involving a new store manager, there are three treatments (salespeople), so there are $k - 1 = 3 - 1 = 2$ degrees of freedom in the numerator. There are 15 observations (three samples of five each). Therefore, there are $N - k = 15 - 3 = 12$ degrees of freedom in the denominator.

Two degrees of freedom needed

The critical value of F, which is the dividing point between the region where we do not reject H_0 and the region of rejection, is found by referring to Appendix G. (*Note:* There is one page for the .05 significance level and another for the .01 significance level.) The degrees of freedom for the numerator are listed at the top of the columns. The degrees of freedom for the denominator are in the left column. Referring to the previous paragraph, we see that there are 2 degrees of freedom in the numerator and 12 degrees of freedom in the denominator. To locate the critical value of F, refer to the portion of Appendix G shown in Table 11–3 for the .05 level. Move horizontally to 2 degrees of freedom in the numerator. Then go down that column until the number opposite 12 degrees of freedom in the left column is reached. That number is 3.89 and the critical value of F for the .05 level.

TABLE 11–3 Critical Values of the *F* Statistic (.05 level of significance)

Degrees of freedom in denominator	Degrees of freedom in numerator									
	1	2	3	4	5	6	7	8	9	10
11	4.84	3.98	3.59	3.36	3.20	3.09	3.01	2.95	2.90	2.85
12	4.75	3.89	3.49	3.26	3.11	3.00	2.91	2.85	2.80	2.75
13	4.67	3.81	3.41	3.18	3.03	2.92	2.83	2.77	2.71	2.67
14	4.60	3.74	3.34	3.11	2.96	2.85	2.76	2.70	2.65	2.60
15	4.54	3.68	3.29	3.06	2.90	2.79	2.71	2.64	2.59	2.54
16	4.49	3.63	3.24	3.01	2.85	2.74	2.66	2.59	2.54	2.49

In using the predetermined .05 level, the decision rule is not to reject the null hypothesis H_0 if the computed F value is less than or equal to 3.89; we reject H_0 and accept H_1 if the computed F value is greater than 3.89. The decision rule is shown diagrammatically in Chart 11–1.

CHART 11–1 Distribution of *F* When $df_1 = 2$, $df_2 = 12$, and $\alpha = .05$

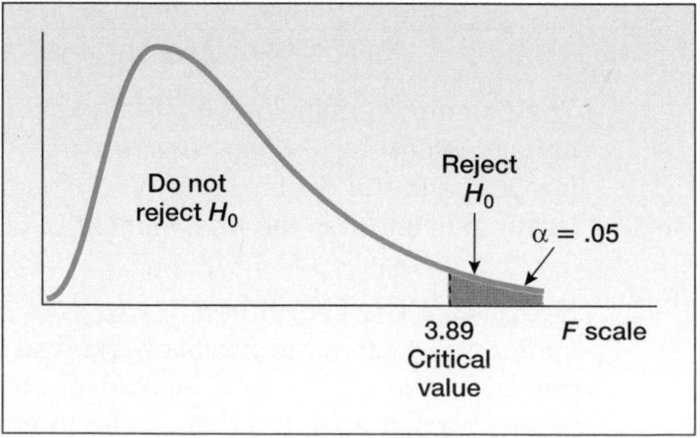

Make a decision

An ANOVA table

Step 5: Compute *F*, and Arrive at a Decision To help us compute F an *ANOVA table* is constructed. It is a convenient form to record the computations. The general format for a one-way analysis of variance problem is shown in Table 11–4.

TABLE 11–4 General Format for Analysis of Variance Table

Source of variation	(1) Sum of squares	(2) Degrees of freedom	(3) Mean square (1)/(2)
Between treatments	SST	$k - 1$	$\frac{\text{SST}}{k-1} = \text{MSTR}$
Error (within treatments)	SSE	$N - k$	$\frac{\text{SSE}}{N-k} = \text{MSE}$
Total	SS total		

Formula for F

$$F = \frac{\frac{\text{SST}}{k-1}}{\frac{\text{SSE}}{N-k}} = \frac{\text{MSTR}}{\text{MSE}}$$

Table 11–4 uses some unfamiliar abbreviations. MSTR is the *mean square between treatments.* MSE is the *mean square due to error.* It is also referred to as the *mean square within treatments.* Note that "mean square" refers to a sum of squares divided by the degrees of freedom. This is exactly how a variance is calculated. Hence, a mean square is a variance measure. SST is the abbreviation for *sum of squares treatment* and is found by:

SST

$$\text{SST} = \sum\left[\frac{T_c^2}{n_c}\right] - \frac{(\Sigma X)^2}{N} \qquad (11\text{–}1)$$

where:

T_c^2 directs one to square each column total (subscript c refers to a column).

n_c is the number of observations for each respective treatment (column). There are five sales figures for Ms. Mapes, five for Mr. Sonnar, and five for Mr. Mafee.

ΣX is the sum of all the observations (sales). It is \$195 (see Table 11–5).

k is the number of treatments (salespeople). There are three.

N is the *total* number of observations. There are 15.

Table 11–5 shows the needed calculations.

TABLE 11–5 Monthly Appliance Sales: Data Required for ANOVA Table

	Ms. Mapes		Mr. Sonnar		Mr. Mafee		
	Sales ($ thousands), X_1	Sales squared, X_1^2	Sales ($ thousands), X_2	Sales squared, X_2^2	Sales ($ thousands), X_3	Sales squared, X_3^2	
	15	225	15	225	19	361	
	10	100	10	100	12	144	
	9	81	12	144	16	256	
	5	25	11	121	16	256	
	16	256	12	144	17	289	**Total**
Column total: T_c	55		60		80		195
Sample size: n_c	5		5		5		15
Sum of squares: X^2		687		734		1,306	2,727

Computing SST:

$$\text{SST} = \sum\left[\frac{T_c^2}{n_c}\right] - \frac{(\Sigma X)^2}{N}$$

$$= \left[\frac{(55)^2}{5} + \frac{(60)^2}{5} + \frac{(80)^2}{5}\right] - \frac{(195)^2}{15}$$

$$= 2{,}605 - 2{,}535$$

$$= 70$$

SSE

Now to compute SSE, which is the abbreviation for *sum of squares error:*

$$\text{SSE} = \Sigma(X^2) - \sum\left[\frac{T_c^2}{n_c}\right] \quad (11\text{–}2)$$

where $\Sigma(X^2)$ directs one to square each monthly sales figure and then sum the squares.

$$\text{SSE} = (15)^2 + (10)^2 + (9)^2 + \cdots + (17)^2 - \left[\frac{(55)^2}{5} + \frac{(60)^2}{5} + \frac{(80)^2}{5}\right]$$

$$= 2{,}727 - 2{,}605$$

$$= 122$$

Total variation (SS total) is the sum of the between-columns and the between-rows variation; that is, SS total = SST + SSE = 70 + 122 = 192. It is computed as follows:

$$\text{SS total} = \Sigma(X^2) - \frac{(\Sigma X)^2}{N} \quad (11\text{–}3)$$

As a check:

$$\text{SS total} = \Sigma(X^2) - \frac{(\Sigma X)^2}{N}$$

$$= 2{,}727 - \frac{(195)^2}{15}$$

$$= 2{,}727 - 2{,}535$$

$$= 192$$

The three sums of squares and the calculations needed for F are transferred to the ANOVA table (Table 11–6).

k is the number of treatments (3), *N* is the total number of observations (15)

TABLE 11–6 ANOVA Table for the Store Managers Problem

Source of variation	(1) Sum of squares	(2) Degrees of freedom	(3) Mean square (1)/(2)	
Between treatments	SST = 70	$k - 1 = 3 - 1 = 2$	$\frac{SST}{k-1} = \frac{70}{2} = 35$ ←	MSTR
Error (within treatments)	SSE = 122	$N - k = 15 - 3 = 12$	$\frac{SSE}{N-k} = \frac{122}{12} = 10.17$ ←	MSE
SS total	192			

Because the ratio of two variances (mean squares) follows an F distribution, we can compute the value of F as follows:

$$F = \frac{\frac{SST}{k-1}}{\frac{SSE}{N-k}} = \frac{MSTR}{MSE} = \frac{35}{10.17} = 3.44 \qquad (11\text{–}4)$$

The decision rule states that if the computed value of F is less than or equal to the critical value of 3.89, the null hypothesis is not rejected. If the F value is greater than 3.89, H_0 is rejected and H_1 accepted. Since $3.44 < 3.89$, the null hypothesis is not rejected at the .05 level. To put it another way, the differences in the mean monthly sales ($11,000, $12,000, and $16,000) are attributed to chance (sampling). From a practical standpoint, the levels of sales of the three salespeople being considered for store manager are the same. No decision with respect to the position can be made on the basis of monthly sales.

EXERCISES

The answers to the odd-numbered exercises are at the end of the book.

7. The following is sample information. Test the hypothesis that the treatment means are equal. Use the .05 significance level.

Treatment 1	Treatment 2	Treatment 3	Treatment 4
8	3	3	5
6	2	4	4
10	4	5	4
9	3	4	5

a. State the null hypothesis and the alternate hypothesis.
b. What is the decision rule?
c. Compute SST, SSE, and SS total.
d. Complete an ANOVA table.
e. State your decision regarding the null hypothesis.

8. The following is sample information. Test the hypothesis that the treatment means are equal. Use the .05 significance level.

Treatment 1	Treatment 2	Treatment 3
9	13	10
7	20	9
11	14	15
9	13	14
12	12	15
10	14	12

a. State the null hypothesis and the alternate hypothesis.
b. What is the decision rule?
c. Compute SST, SSE, and SS total.
d. Complete an ANOVA table.
e. State your decision with respect to the null hypothesis.

9. A real estate developer is considering investing in a shopping mall on the outskirts of Atlanta, Georgia. Three parcels of land are being evaluated. Of particular importance is the income in the area surrounding the proposed mall. A random sample of four families is selected near each proposed mall. Following are the sample results. At the .05 significance level, can the developer conclude there is a difference in the mean income? Use the usual five-step hypothesis-testing procedure. (Of course, in actual practice more than four families would be selected.)

Southwyck area ($ thousands)	Franklin Park ($ thousands)	Old Orchard ($ thousands)
34	44	45
38	41	50
40	39	46
30	40	48

10. The manager of a computer software company is studying the number of hours top executives spend at their computer terminals by type of industry. A sample of five executives from each of three industries is obtained. At the .05 significance level, can the manager conclude there is a difference in the mean number of hours spent at a terminal per week by industry?

Banking	Retail	Insurance
12	8	10
10	8	8
10	6	6
12	8	8
10	10	10

The previous example and exercises had the same number of observations in each treatment. The following example of the one-way analysis of variance does not have the same number of observations in each treatment. There are four observations in rating group 1, five in rating group 2, seven in group 3, and six in group 4. However, the procedure and the formulas are the same.

EXAMPLE

A colleague had students in a large marketing class rate his performance as either 1 (excellent), 2 (good), 3 (fair), or 4 (poor). A graduate assistant collected the ratings and assured the students that the professor would not receive them until after the course grades had been filed with the student records office. The rating (the treatment) a student gave the professor was matched with his or her final course grade. Logically, one might expect that the group of students who thought the professor was excellent would have a final average course grade significantly higher than those who rated him good, fair, or poor. It would also seem that those who rated him poor would have the lowest course grades on the average. Samples from each rating group were selected. The results are:

Note unequal number of observations among treatments (ratings)

Course grades

Rating group 1 (excellent)	Rating group 2 (good)	Rating group 3 (fair)	Rating group 4 (poor)
94	75	70	68
90	68	73	70
85	77	76	72
80	83	78	65
	88	80	74
		68	65
		65	

Is there a difference among the mean scores of the four groups? Use the .01 significance level.

Solution ▶ The null hypothesis and the alternate hypothesis are:

H_0: $\mu_1 = \mu_2 = \mu_3 = \mu_4$

H_1: The treatment means are not equal.

The decision rule is: Do not reject H_0 if the computed value of F is less than the critical value. Otherwise, the null hypothesis will be rejected and H_1 accepted.

There are four treatments (ratings), so $k = 4$

Twenty-two ratings, so $N = 22$

Recall that the degrees of freedom in the numerator of the *F* ratio are found by $k - 1$, where *k* is the number of treatments (groups of faculty ratings, in this problem). There are four treatments, so there are $4 - 1 = 3$ degrees of freedom. The degrees of freedom in the denominator total 18, found by $N - k$, where *N* is the total number of students sampled. There were 22 students, so there are $22 - 4 = 18$ degrees of freedom.

Critical value is 5.09

The decision rule is portrayed in Chart 11–2. Note that the critical value of *F* is 5.09. To determine it, refer to Appendix G and the page for the .01 level of significance. Move horizontally at the top of the table to 3 degrees of freedom in the numerator. Then move down that column to the critical value opposite 18 degrees of freedom in the denominator. Do not reject the null hypothesis at the .01 level if the computed value of *F* is less than or equal to 5.09, but reject it if the computed value is greater than 5.09.

CHART 11–2 **Areas of Rejection and Nonrejection, .01 Level of Significance**

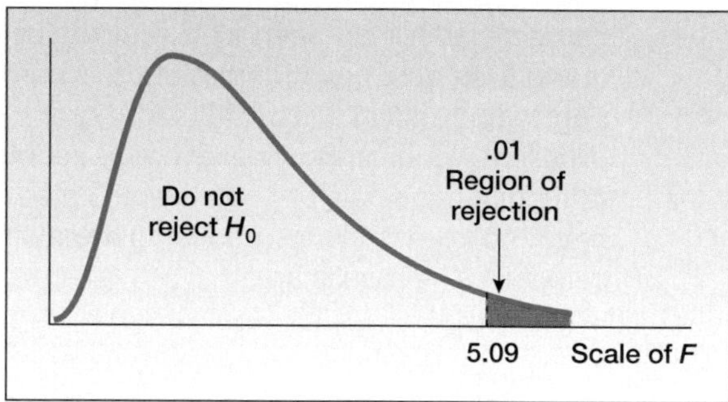

The calculations needed for the completion of the ANOVA table and the *F* ratio are shown in Table 11–7.

TABLE 11–7 **Calculations Needed for the *F* Ratio**

	Group 1 (excellent)		Group 2 (good)		Group 3 (fair)		Group 4 (poor)	
	X_1	X_1^2	X_2	X_2^2	X_3	X_3^2	X_4	X_4^2
	94	8,836	75	5,625	70	4,900	68	4,624
	90	8,100	68	4,624	73	5,329	70	4,900
	85	7,225	77	5,929	76	5,776	72	5,184
	80	6,400	83	6,889	78	6,084	65	4,225
			88	7,744	80	6,400	74	5,476
					68	4,624	65	4,225
					65	4,225		
Column total: T_c	349		391		510		414	
Sample size: n_c	4		5		7		6	
Sum of squares: X^2		30,561		30,811		37,338		28,634

Note that the sum of the column totals (ΣX) is 1,664; the total of the sample size (N) is 22; and the sum of the squares (ΣX^2) is 127,344, found by 30,561 + 30,811 + 37,338 + 28,634.

Computing SST, SSE, and SS total using formulas (11–1) and (11–2), we get:

$$\text{SST} = \sum\left[\frac{T_c^2}{n_c}\right] - \frac{(\Sigma X)^2}{N}$$

$$= \left[\frac{(349)^2}{4} + \frac{(391)^2}{5} + \frac{(510)^2}{7} + \frac{(414)^2}{6}\right] - \frac{(1{,}664)^2}{22}$$

$$= 890.68$$

$$\text{SSE} = \Sigma(X^2) - \sum\frac{T_c^2}{n_c}$$

$$= (94)^2 + (90)^2 + \cdots + (65)^2 - \left[\frac{(349)^2}{4} + \frac{(391)^2}{5} + \frac{(510)^2}{7} + \frac{(414)^2}{6}\right]$$

$$= 594.41$$

$$\text{SS total} = \text{SST} + \text{SSE} = 890.68 + 594.41 = 1{,}485.09$$

As a check, using formula (11–3):

$$\text{SS total} = \Sigma(X^2) - \frac{(\Sigma X)^2}{N}$$

$$= 127{,}344 - \frac{(1{,}664)^2}{22}$$

$$= 1{,}485.09$$

These values are inserted in the ANOVA table. (See Table 11–8.)

TABLE 11–8 ANOVA Table for the Faculty Evaluation Problem

Numerator of the F ratio is 296.89. Denominator of the F ratio is 33.02

Source of variation	(1) Sum of squares	(2) Degrees of freedom	(3) Mean square (1)/(2)
Treatment (between columns)	SST = 890.68	$k - 1 = 4 - 1 = 3$	$\frac{\text{SST}}{k-1} = \frac{890.68}{3} = 296.89$
Error (between rows)	SSE = 594.41	$N - k = 22 - 4 = 18$	$\frac{\text{SSE}}{N-k} = \frac{594.41}{18} = 33.02$

Inserting the mean squares into formula (11–4) for F, we get:

$$F = \frac{\text{MSTR}}{\text{MSE}} = \frac{296.89}{33.02} = 8.99$$

The decision: Since the computed *F* value of 8.99 is greater than the critical value of 5.09 (from Appendix G), the null hypothesis that there is no difference among the means is rejected. This indicates that it is likely that the observed differences among the means are not due to chance. It suggests that the grades students earn in a course are related to the opinions they have of the overall competency and classroom performance of the instructor.

Use MINITAB

As you noted from the previous example, the calculations become very tedious if the number of observations in each treatment is large. The MINITAB solution to the same problem is shown below. The output is in the form of an ANOVA table. To employ the MINITAB system, first enter the data. Each treatment is entered in its own column. This is accomplished using the SET command. The MINITAB procedure used is AOVONEWAY.

```
MTB > set c1
DATA> 94,90,85,80
DATA> end
MTB > set c2
DATA> 75,68,77,83,88
DATA> end
MTB > set c3
DATA> 70,73,76,78,80,68,65
DATA> end
MTB > set c4
DATA> 68,70,72,65,74,65
DATA> end                                                    Computed value of F
MTB > name c1 'Excell' c2 'Good' c3 'Fair' c4 'Poor'
MTB > aovoneway c1-c4

ANALYSIS OF VARIANCE

SOURCE     DF       SS       MS          F          P  <-- p-value
FACTOR      3    890.7    296.9       8.99      0.001
ERROR      18    594.4     33.0
TOTAL      21   1485.1
                                 INDIVIDUAL 95 PCT CI'S FOR MEAN
                                 BASED ON POOLED STDEV
 LEVEL      N     MEAN    STDEV  ---------+---------+---------+------
Excell      4   87.250    6.076                     (------*-------)
Good        5   78.200    7.662            (------*------)
Fair        7   72.857    5.490       (-----*-----)
Poor        6   69.000    3.688  (-----*-----)
                                 ---------+---------+---------+------
POOLED STDEV =   5.747                  72.0      80.0      88.0
```

The results reported in the MINITAB output are the same as in Table 11–8. The MINITAB system uses the term *factor* instead of *treatment,* with the same intended meaning. The value of *F* is the same as that reported in Table 11–8. The *p*-value is also reported. The value is located under the heading "P" and in this case is .001. How do we interpret this value? It is the probability of finding an *F* value to the right of 8.99 with 3 degrees of freedom in the numerator and 18 degrees of freedom in the denominator, given that H_0 is true. So the likelihood of committing a Type I error by rejecting a true H_0 is 0.1 percent—a very small likelihood indeed!

SELF-REVIEW 11–2

The answers are at the end of the chapter.

In an effort to determine the most effective way to teach safety principles to a group of employees at Weedco, four different methods were tried. A sample of 20 employees was randomly assigned to one of four groups. The first group was given programmed instruction booklets and worked through the course at their own pace. The second group attended lectures. The third group watched television presentations, and the fourth was divided into small discussion groups. At the end of the sessions, a test was given to the four groups. A high of 10 points was possible.

The results were:

Test grades

Programmed instruction	Lecture	TV	Group discussion
6	8	7	8
7	5	9	5
6	8	6	6
5	6	8	6
6	8	5	5

At the .05 significance level, is there a difference in the mean scores?

INFERENCES ABOUT TREATMENT MEANS

Suppose in carrying out the ANOVA procedure, we make the decision to reject the null hypothesis. This allows us to conclude that all the treatment means are not the same. Sometimes we may be satisfied with this conclusion, but in other instances we may want to know which treatment means differ. This section provides the details for such a test.

Recall in the monthly appliance sales data that there was no difference in the treatment means. In this case further analysis of the treatment means is not warranted. However, in the example regarding student opinions and grades there was a difference in the treatment means. That is, the null hypothesis was rejected and the alternate hypothesis accepted. If the student opinions do differ, the question is: Between which groups do the treatment means differ?

Several procedures are available to answer this question. Perhaps the simplest is through the use of confidence intervals. From the computer output of the previous example (see page 450), note that the mean score for those students rating the instruction excellent is 87.250, and for those rating the instruction poor it is 69.000. Thus, those students who rated the instruction excellent seemingly earned higher grades than those who rated the instruction poor. Is there enough difference to justify the conclusion that there is a difference in the mean scores of the two groups?

The t distribution, described in Chapter 10, is used as the basis for this test. Recall that one of the basic assumptions of ANOVA is that the population variances are the same for all treatments. As noted, this common population value is called the *mean square error,* or MSE, and is determined by SSE/$(N - k)$. A confidence interval for the difference between two population means is found by:

$$(\overline{X}_1 - \overline{X}_2) \pm t\sqrt{\text{MSE}\left(\frac{1}{n_1} + \frac{1}{n_2}\right)} \qquad (11\text{–}5)$$

where:

$\overline{X}_1$ is the mean of the first treatment.

$\overline{X}_2$ is the mean of the second treatment.

t is obtained from the t table. The number of degrees of freedom is equal to $N - k$.

MSE is the mean square error term obtained from the ANOVA table [SSE/$(N - k)$].

n_1 is the number of observations in the first treatment.

n_2 is the number of observations in the second treatment.

How do we find out if there is a difference in the treatment means? If the confidence interval includes zero, there is *not a* difference between the treatment means. For example, if the lower endpoint of the confidence interval has a negative sign and the upper endpoint has a positive sign, the two means do not differ. So if we developed a confidence interval from formula (11–5) and found that the difference in the treatment means was 5.00, that is $\overline{X}_1 - \overline{X}_2 = 5$, that $t\sqrt{\text{MSE}(1/n_1 + 1/n_2)} = 12$, the confidence interval would range from -7.00 up to 17.00. To put it another way:

$$\begin{aligned}(\overline{X}_1 - \overline{X}_2) &\pm t\sqrt{\text{MSE}\left(\frac{1}{n_1} + \frac{1}{n_2}\right)}\\ &= 5 \pm 12\\ &= -7.00 \text{ up to } 17.00\end{aligned}$$

Note that zero is included in this interval. Therefore, we would conclude that there is not a significant difference in the selected treatment means.

On the other hand, if the endpoints of the confidence interval have the *same* sign, this suggests that the treatment means differ. For example, if $\overline{X}_1 - \overline{X}_2 = -0.35$ and $t\sqrt{\text{MSE}(1/n_1 + 1/n_2)} = 0.25$, the confidence interval would range from -0.60 to -0.10. Because -0.60 and -0.10 have the same sign (both negative), we conclude that these two means differ.

Using the previous student opinion example and the .95 level of confidence, the endpoints of the confidence interval are 10.46 and 26.04, found by:

$$\begin{aligned}(\overline{X}_1 - \overline{X}_2) \pm t\sqrt{\text{MSE}\left(\frac{1}{n_1} + \frac{1}{n_2}\right)} &= (87.25 - 69.00) \pm 2.101\sqrt{33.0\left(\frac{1}{4} + \frac{1}{6}\right)}\\ &= 18.25 \pm 7.79\\ &= 10.46 \text{ up to } 26.04\end{aligned}$$

where:

$$\overline{X}_1 = 87.25$$
$$\overline{X}_2 = 69.00$$
$$t = 2.101 \text{ from Appendix F } (N - k = 22 - 4 = 18 \text{ degrees of freedom})$$
$$\text{MSE} = 33.0, \text{ from the ANOVA table}$$
$$n_1 = 4$$
$$n_2 = 6$$

We found that the 95 percent confidence interval ranges from 10.46 up to 26.04. Both endpoints are positive; hence, we can conclude these treatment means differ significantly. That is, students who rated the instructor excellent have significantly higher grades than those who rated the instructor as poor.

Likewise, approximate results can be obtained directly from the MINITAB output on page 450. On the bottom of the MINITAB output a confidence interval for each mean is provided. The endpoints of the dotted line indicate the endpoints of a confidence interval for each treatment mean. These endpoints are identified by the symbols (and). In those instances where the intervals overlap (that is, contain a common area) the treatment means do not differ. However, where there is not a common area, the treatment means differ. In this example, the students who rated the instructor excellent had a significantly different mean grade from that of those who rated him fair. Also, the mean grade of those who rated the instruction excellent differed from the mean of those rating it poor.

Caution: The investigation of differences in treatment means is a step-by-step process. The initial step is to conduct the ANOVA test. Only if the null hypothesis that the treatment means are equal is rejected should any analysis of the treatment means be attempted.

SELF-REVIEW 11–3

The answers are at the end of the chapter.

The following data represent the tuition charges (in thousands of dollars) for a sample of private colleges in various regions of the United States. At the .05 significance level, can we conclude there is a difference in the mean tuition charge?

Northeast ($ thousands)	**Southeast ($ thousands)**	**West ($ thousands)**
10	8	7
11	9	8
12	10	6
10	8	7
12		6

1. State the null and alternate hypotheses.
2. What is the decision rule?
3. What is the computed value of the test hypothesis?
4. What is your decision regarding the null hypothesis?
5. Could there be a significant difference between the mean tuition in the Northeast and that in the West? If so, develop a 95 percent confidence interval for that difference.

EXERCISES

The answers to the odd-numbered exercises are at the end of the book.

11. The following sample information is given. Test the hypothesis that the treatment means are equal at the .05 significance level.

Treatment 1	Treatment 2	Treatment 3
8	3	3
11	2	4
10	1	5
	3	4
	2	

a. State the null hypothesis and the alternate hypothesis.
b. What is the decision rule?
c. Compute SST, SSE, and SS total.
d. Complete an ANOVA table.
e. State your decision about the null hypothesis.
f. If H_0 is rejected, can we conclude that treatment 1 and treatment 2 differ? Use the 95 percent level of confidence.

12. The following is sample information. Test the hypothesis that the treatment means are equal at the .05 significance level.

Treatment 1	Treatment 2	Treatment 3
3	9	6
2	6	3
5	5	5
1	6	5
3	8	5
1	5	4
	4	1
	7	5
	6	
	4	

a. State the null hypothesis and the alternate hypothesis.
b. What is the decision rule?
c. Compute SST, SSE, and SS total.
d. Complete an ANOVA table.
e. State your decision about the null hypothesis.
f. If H_0 is rejected, can we conclude that treatment 2 and treatment 3 differ? Use the 95 percent level of confidence.

13. A senior accounting major at Midsouth State University has job offers from four CPA firms. To explore the offers further, she asked a sample of recent trainees how many weeks each worked for the firm before receiving a raise in salary. The sample information is:

Number of weeks before first raise in salary			
CPA, Inc.	**AB Intl.**	**Acct Ltd.**	**Pfisters**
12	14	18	12
10	12	12	14
14	10	16	16
12	10		

At the .05 level of significance, is there a difference in the mean number of weeks before a raise was granted among the four CPA firms?

14. A stock analyst wants to determine if there is a difference in the mean rate of return for three types of stock: utility, retail, and banking stocks. The following sample information is collected.

Rates of return		
Utility	**Retail**	**Banking**
14.3	11.5	15.5
18.1	12.0	12.7
17.8	11.1	18.2
17.3	11.9	14.7
19.5	11.6	18.1
		13.2

   a. Using the .05 level of significance, is there a difference in the mean rate of return among the three types of stock?
   b. Suppose the null hypothesis is rejected. Can the analyst conclude there is a difference between the mean rates of return for the utility and the retail stocks? Explain.

TWO-FACTOR ANALYSIS OF VARIANCE

In the appliance store example earlier in the chapter, we were unable to show that a difference exists among the mean sales of the three salespeople. In the computation of the *F* statistic, variation was considered from two sources. First, variation *among* the differences in the treatments means was considered. Second, variation *within* each of the treatments was considered. Thus, the variation either originated from the treatments or was considered random. There are many other sources of variation, such as the type of training the salespeople had, the days of the week on which the sample data were obtained, perhaps their gender, and so on. A two-factor analysis of variance will allow us to consider a second factor.

EXAMPLE

WARTA, the Warren Area Regional Transit Authority, is expanding bus service from the suburb of Starbrick into the central business district of Warren. There are four routes being considered from Starbrick into downtown Warren: via U.S. 6, via the west end, via the Hickory Street bridge, and via Rte. 59. WARTA conducted test runs to determine if there is a difference in the mean travel times along the four routes. The travel times, in minutes, along each of the four routes are given below.

	Travel time from Starbrick to Warren (minutes)			
Driver	**U.S. 6**	**West end**	**Hickory St.**	**Rte. 59**
Piper	18	20	20	22
Sanders	21	22	24	24
McLain	20	23	25	23
Hammons	25	21	28	25
Hoffman	26	24	28	25

At the .05 significance level, can it be concluded that there is a difference among the four routes? Is there a difference among the drivers?

Solution ▶ If the null hypothesis is that the mean travel time is the same along the four routes, this requires the one-factor ANOVA approach. The variation that occurs because of differences in the drivers is considered random and is included in the MSE term. Thus, the F ratio is reduced. If the variation due to the drivers can be removed, the denominator of the F ratio will be reduced. In this case the driver is called a **blocking variable.** Hence, we have variation due to treatment and due to blocks. The sum of squares due to blocks (SSB) is computed as follows:

Blocking variable

$$\text{SSB} = \sum\left[\frac{B_r^2}{k}\right] - \frac{(\Sigma X)^2}{N} \qquad (11\text{–}6)$$

where B_r refers to the block total, that is, the total for each row, and k refers to the number of items in each block.

The same format is used for the two-factor ANOVA table as was used for the one-factor ANOVA case. SST and SS total are computed as before. SSE is obtained by subtraction (SSE = SS total − SST − SSB). Table 11–9 shows the necessary totals.

TABLE 11–9 Calculations Needed for Two-Way ANOVA

	Travel time, by route (minutes)					
Driver	**U.S. 6**	**West end**	**Hickory St.**	**Rte. 59**	**Row sum, B_r**	
Piper	18	20	20	22	80	
Sanders	21	22	24	24	91	
McLain	20	23	25	23	91	
Hammons	25	21	28	25	99	
Hoffman	26	24	28	25	103	**Total**
Column total, T_c	110	110	125	119		464
Sum of squares	2,466	2,430	3,169	2,839		10,904
Number of blocks, b	5	5	5	5		

Analogous to the ANOVA table for a one-factor analysis, the two-factor general format is:

Source	(1) Sum of squares	(2) Degrees of freedom	(3) Mean square (1)/(2)
Treatments	SST	$k - 1$	$\frac{\text{SST}}{k-1} = \text{MSTR}$
Blocks	SSB	$b - 1$	$\frac{\text{SSB}}{b-1} = \text{MSB*}$
Error	SSE	$(k - 1)(b - 1)$	$\frac{\text{SSE}}{(k-1)(b-1)} = \text{MSE}$
Total	SS total		

*MSB = Mean square for blocks

As before, we compute SST using formula (11–1), but changing n_c to b to represent the number of blocks.

$$\text{SST} = \sum\left[\frac{T_c^2}{b}\right] - \frac{(\Sigma X)^2}{N}$$

$$= \left[\frac{(110)^2}{5} + \frac{(110)^2}{5} + \frac{(125)^2}{5} + \frac{(119)^2}{5}\right] - \frac{(464)^2}{20}$$
$$= 32.4$$

SSB is found by using formula (11–6):

$$\text{SSB} = \sum\left[\frac{B_r^2}{k}\right] - \frac{(\Sigma X)^2}{N}$$
$$= \left[\frac{(80)^2}{4} + \frac{(91)^2}{4} + \frac{(91)^2}{4} + \frac{(99)^2}{4} + \frac{(103)^2}{4}\right] - \frac{(464)^2}{20}$$
$$= 78.2$$

The remaining sum-of-squares terms are, using formula (11–3):

$$\text{SS total} = \Sigma X^2 - \frac{(\Sigma X)^2}{N}$$
$$= 10{,}904 - \frac{(464)^2}{20}$$
$$= 139.2$$

$$\text{SSE} = \text{SS total} - \text{SST} - \text{SSB}$$
$$= 139.2 - 32.4 - 78.2$$
$$= 28.6$$

The values for the various components of the ANOVA table are computed as follows:

Source of variation	(1) Sum of squares	(2) Degrees of freedom	(3) Mean square (1)/(2)
Treatments	32.4	3	10.8
Blocks	78.2	4	19.55
Error	28.6	12	2.38
Total	139.2		

There is disagreement at this point. If the purpose of the blocking variable (the drivers in this example) was only to reduce the error variation, we should not conduct a test of hypothesis for the difference in block means. That is, if our goal was to reduce the MSE term, then we should not test a hypothesis regarding the blocking variable. On the other hand, we may wish to give the blocks the same status as the treatments and conduct a test of hypothesis. In the latter case, when the blocks are important enough to be considered as a second factor, we refer to this as a **two-factor experiment.** In many cases the decision is not clear. In our example we are concerned about the differences in the travel time for the different drivers, so we will conduct the test of hypothesis. The two sets of hypotheses are:

1. H_0: The treatment means are the same ($\mu_1 = \mu_2 = \mu_3 = \mu_4$).
   H_1: The treatment means are not the same.
2. H_0: The block means are the same ($\mu_1 = \mu_2 = \mu_3 = \mu_4 = \mu_5$).
   H_1: The block means are not the same.

First we will test the hypothesis concerning the treatment means. There are $k - 1 = 4 - 1 = 3$ degrees of freedom in the numerator and $(b - 1)(k - 1) = (5 - 1)(4 - 1) = 12$ degrees of freedom in the denominator. Using the .05 significance level, the critical value of F is 3.49. The null hypothesis that the mean times for the four routes are the same is rejected if the F ratio exceeds 3.49. Using formula (11–4), F is 4.54.

$$F = \frac{\text{MSTR}}{\text{MSE}} = \frac{10.8}{2.38} = 4.54$$

The null hypothesis is rejected and the alternate accepted. It is concluded that the mean travel time is not the same for all routes. WARTA will want to conduct some tests to determine which treatment means differ.

Next, we test to find out if the travel time is the same for the various drivers. The degrees of freedom in the numerator for blocks is $b - 1 = 5 - 1 = 4$. The degrees of freedom for the denominator is the same as before: $(b - 1)(k - 1) = (5 - 1)(4 - 1) = 12$. The null hypothesis that the block means are the same is rejected if the F ratio exceeds 3.26.

$$F = \frac{\text{MSB}}{\text{MSE}} = \frac{19.55}{2.38} = 8.21$$

The null hypothesis is rejected, and the alternate is accepted. The mean time is not the same for the various drivers.

Thus, WARTA management can conclude, based on the sample results, that there is a difference in the routes and in the drivers.

A two-factor procedure called ANOVA is available on the MINITAB system. For the WARTA example of Table 11–9, the travel times are entered in column C1. The times are entered by going down the columns. So the first five values in C1 refer to the times along U.S. 6, the next five refer to the west end, and so on. We use columns C2 and C3 in MINITAB to identify the routes (C2) and the drivers (C3). We code the times along U.S. 6 as 1s, those via the west end as 2s, those via Hickory Street as 3s, and those for Rte. 59 as 4s. Therefore, the first five values in C2 are 1s, because these times were along U.S. 6. The next five times are all via the west end, so they are coded as 2s, and so on. Column C3 refers to the drivers. Driver Piper is coded as 1, so we place a 1 in the first position in C3. Next is a 2, representing driver Sanders, followed by a 3, representing driver McLain, and so on. The results are shown below.

```
MTB > set c1
DATA> 18,21,20,25,26,20,22,23,21,24,20,24,25,28,28,22,24,23,25,25
DATA> end
MTB > set c2
DATA> 1,1,1,1,1,2,2,2,2,2,3,3,3,3,3,4,4,4,4,4
MTB > set c3
DATA> 1,2,3,4,5,1,2,3,4,5,1,2,3,4,5,1,2,3,4,5
DATA> end
MTB > name c1 'Time' c2 'Routes' c3 'Drivers'
MTB > anova c1=c2 c3

Analysis of Variance for Time

Source    DF       SS       MS     F      P
Routes     3   32.400   10.800  4.53  0.024
Drivers    4   78.200   19.550  8.20  0.002
Error     12   28.600    2.383
Total     19  139.200
```

These are the same results reported earlier. An additional feature of the MINITAB output is to report the *p*-values of .024 for routes and .002 for drivers. These *p*-values confirm that the null hypotheses for treatment means and block means are both rejected at the .05 significance level.

SELF-REVIEW 11–4

The answers are at the end of the chapter.

Rudduck Shampoo sells three shampoos—for dry, normal, and oil hair. Sales, in millions of dollars, for the past five months are given in the following table.

	Sales ($ millions)		
Month	**Dry**	**Normal**	**Oily**
June	7	9	12
July	11	12	14
August	13	11	8
September	8	9	7
October	9	10	13

Using the .05 level, apply the ANOVA procedure to test whether:

1. The mean sales for dry, normal, and oily hair are the same.
2. The mean sales are the same for each of the five months.

EXERCISES

The answers to the odd-numbered exercises are at the end of the book.

15. The following data are given for a two-factor ANOVA.

	Treatment	
Block	**1**	**2**
A	46	31
B	37	26
C	44	35

Conduct a test of hypothesis to determine if the block and the treatment means differ. Use the .05 significance level.

a. State the null and alternate hypotheses for treatments.
b. State the decision rule for treatments.
c. State the null and alternate hypotheses for blocks. Also, state the decision rule for blocks.
d. Compute SST, SSB, SS total, and SSE.
e. Complete an ANOVA table.
f. What is your decision regarding the two sets of hypotheses?

16. The following data are given for a two-factor ANOVA.

	Treatment		
Block	**1**	**2**	**3**
A	12	14	8
B	9	11	9
C	7	8	8

Conduct a test of hypothesis to determine if the block and the treatment means differ. Use the .05 significance level.

a. State the null and alternate hypotheses for treatments.
b. State the decision rule for treatments.
c. State the null and alternate hypotheses for blocks. Also, state the decision rule for blocks.
d. Compute SST, SSB, SS total, and SSE.
e. Complete an ANOVA table.
f. What is your decision regarding the two sets of hypotheses?

17. The Brunner Manufacturing Company operates 24 hours a day, five days a week. The workers rotate shifts each week. Management is interested in whether there is a difference in the number of units produced when the employees work on various shifts. A sample of five workers is selected and their output recorded on each shift. At the .05 significance level, can we conclude there is a difference in the mean production by shift and in the mean production by employee?

	Units produced		
Employee	**Day**	**Afternoon**	**Night**
Skaff	31	25	35
Lum	33	26	33
Clark	28	24	30
Treece	30	29	28
Morgan	28	26	27

18. There are three hospitals in the Tulsa area. The following data show the number of outpatient surgeries performed at each hospital last week. At the .05 significance level, can we conclude that there is a difference in the mean number of surgeries performed among the three hospitals and in the mean number of surgeries by day of the week?

	Number of surgeries performed		
Day	**St. Luke's**	**St. Vincent**	**Mercy**
Monday	14	18	24
Tuesday	20	24	14
Wednesday	16	22	14
Thursday	18	20	22
Friday	20	28	24

CHAPTER OUTLINE

I. The characteristics of the *F* distribution are:
   A. It is continuous.
   B. Its values cannot be negative.
   C. It is positively skewed.
   D. There is a family of *F* distributions. Each time the degrees of freedom in either the numerator or the denominator change, a new distribution is created.

II. The *F* distribution is used to test whether two sample variances come from the same or equal populations.
   A. The sampled populations must be normal.
   B. The ratio of the two sample variances is computed and the result compared to the critical value of *F*.
   C. The larger of the two sample variances is placed in the numerator, forcing the ratio to always be greater than 1.00.

III. One-way ANOVA is used to compare three or more treatment means to determine if they came from the same or equal populations. A *treatment* is a source of variation.
   A. Assumptions underlying ANOVA.
      1. The samples are obtained from normal populations.
      2. The populations have equal standard deviations.
      3. The populations are independent.
   B. An ANOVA table is developed, which uses SS total, SST, and SSE. These values are computed as follows, where N is the total number of observations, T_c is a column total, and n_c is the number of observations in each treatment (column).
      1. SS total, the total sum of squares:

$$\text{SS total} = \Sigma X^2 - \frac{(\Sigma X)^2}{N} \tag{11–3}$$

      2. SST, the sum of squares treatment:

$$\text{SST} = \sum\left[\frac{T_c^2}{n_c}\right] - \frac{(\Sigma X)^2}{N} \tag{11–1}$$

      3. SSE, the sum of squares error:

$$\text{SSE} = \text{SS total} - \text{SST}$$

IV. Treatment means are compared to determine if they differ significantly, using the following relationship.

$$(\overline{X}_1 - \overline{X}_2) \pm t\sqrt{\text{MSE}\left(\frac{1}{n_1} + \frac{1}{n_2}\right)} \tag{11–5}$$

where:

$\overline{X}_1$ is the mean of the first treatment.

$\overline{X}_2$ is the mean of the second treatment.

t is the value obtained from the t table, where the degrees of freedom equal $N - k$.

MSE is the mean square error, found by SSE/($N - k$).

n_1 is the number of observations in the first treatment.

n_2 is the number of observations in the second treatment.

V. Two-way ANOVA considers variation due to both treatments and blocks.
   A. The same format is used as for one-way ANOVA.
   B. A blocking variable is a second source of variation. It is computed from the following formula:

$$\text{SSB} = \sum\left[\frac{B_r^2}{k}\right] - \frac{(\Sigma X)^2}{N} \tag{11–6}$$

EXERCISES

The answers to the odd-numbered exercises are at the end of the book.

19. Following is a partial ANOVA table.

Source	Sum of squares	*df*	Mean square	*F*
Treatment		2		
Error			20	
Total	500	11		

Complete the table, and answer the following questions. Use the .05 significance level.

a. How many treatments are there?
b. What was the total sample size?
c. What is the critical value of F?
d. Write out the null and alternate hypotheses.
e. What is your conclusion regarding the null hypothesis?

20. Define the terms MSE and MST. What is the difference between the two?

21. A consumer organization wants to know if there is a difference in the price of a particular toy at three different types of stores. The price of the toy was checked in a sample of five discount toy stores, five variety stores, and five department stores. The results are shown below.

Discount toy	Variety	Department
$12	$15	$19
13	17	17
14	14	16
12	18	20
15	17	19

Use the .05 significance level to conduct the test.

22. A physician who specializes in weight control has three different diets she recommends. As an experiment, she randomly selected 15 patients and then assigned 5 to each diet. After three weeks the following weight losses, in pounds, were noted. At the .05 significance level, can she conclude that there is a difference in the mean amount of weight loss among the three diets?

Plan A	Plan B	Plan C
5	6	7
7	7	8
4	7	9
5	5	8
4	6	9

23. The City of Maumee comprises four districts. Chief of Police Andy North wants determine if there is a difference in the mean number of crimes committed among the four districts. He recorded the number of crimes reported in each district for a sample of six days. At the .05 significance level, can the chief of police conclude there is a difference in the mean number of crimes?

Number of crimes			
Rec center	**Key Street**	**Monclova**	**Whitehouse**
13	21	12	16
15	13	14	17
14	18	15	18
15	19	13	15
14	18	12	20
15	19	15	18

24. The personnel director of Cander Machine Products is investigating "perfectionism" on the job. A test designed to measure perfectionism was administered to a random sample of 18 employees. The scores ranged from 20 to about 40. One of the facets of the study involved the early background of each employee. Did the employee come from a rural background, a small city, or a large city? The scores are:

Rural area	Small urban area	Large urban area
35	28	24
30	24	28
36	25	26
38	30	30
29	32	34
34	28	
31		

a. At the .05 level, can it be concluded that there is a difference in the three mean scores?

b. If the null hypothesis is rejected, can you state that the mean score of those with a rural background is different from the score of those with a large-city background?

25. It can be shown that when only two treatments are involved, ANOVA and the Student *t* test (Chapter 10) result in the same conclusions. Also, $t^2 = F$. As an example, suppose that 14 randomly selected students were divided into two groups, one consisting of 6 students and the other of 8. One group was taught using a combination of lecture and programmed instruction, the other using a combination of lecture and television. At the end of the course, each group was given a 50-item test. The following is a list of the number correct for each of the two groups.

Lecture and programmed instruction	Lecture and television
19	32
17	28
23	31
22	26
17	23
16	24
	27
	25

a. Using analysis of variance techniques, test H_0 that the two mean test scores are equal; $\alpha = .05$.

b. Using the *t* test from Chapter 10, compute *t*.

c. Interpret the results.

26. There are four radio stations in Midland. The stations have different formats (hard rock, classical, country/western, and easy listening), but each is concerned with the number of minutes of music played per hour. From a sample of 10 hours from each station, the following sample means were obtained.

$$\overline{X}_1 = 51.32 \quad \overline{X}_2 = 44.64 \quad \overline{X}_3 = 47.2 \quad \overline{X}_4 = 50.85$$

$$\text{SS total} = 650.75$$

a. Determine SST.

b. Determine SSE.

c. Complete an ANOVA table.

d. At the .05 significance level, is there a difference in the treatment means?

e. Is there a difference in the mean amount of music time between station 1 and station 4? Use the .05 significance level.

27. Listed below are the weights (in grams) of a sample of M&M Plain candies, classified according to color. Use a statistical software system to determine if there is a difference in the mean weights of candies of different colors. Use the .05 significance level.

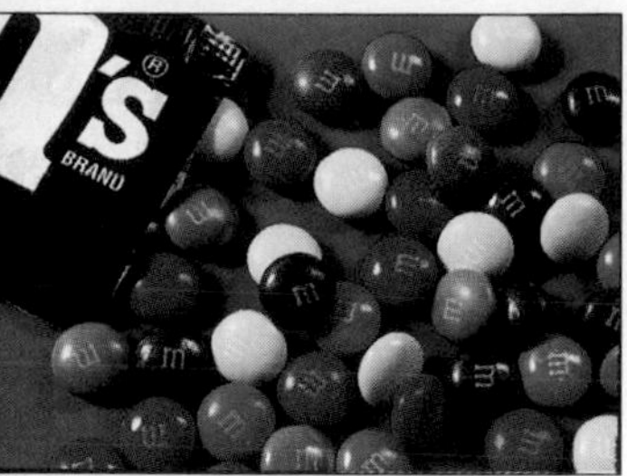

Red	Orange	Yellow	Brown	Tan	Green
0.946	0.902	0.929	0.896	0.845	0.935
1.107	0.943	0.960	0.888	0.909	0.903
0.913	0.916	0.938	0.906	0.873	0.865
0.904	0.910	0.933	0.941	0.902	0.822
0.926	0.903	0.932	0.838	0.956	0.871
0.926	0.901	0.899	0.892	0.959	0.905
1.006	0.919	0.907	0.905	0.916	0.905
0.914	0.901	0.906	0.824	0.822	0.852
0.922	0.930	0.930	0.908		0.965
1.052	0.883	0.952	0.833		0.898
0.903		0.939			
0.895		0.940			
		0.882			
		0.906			

28. Martin Motors has in stock three cars of the same make and model. The president would like to compare the gas consumption of the three cars (labeled car A, car B, and car C) using four different types of gasoline. For each trial, a gallon of gasoline was added to an empty tank, and the car was driven until it ran out of gas. The following table shows the number of miles driven in each trial.

Types of gasoline	Distance (miles)		
	Car A	Car B	Car C
Regular	22.4	20.8	21.5
Super regular	17.0	19.4	20.7
Unleaded	19.2	20.2	21.2
Premium unleaded	20.3	18.6	20.4

Using the .05 level of significance:

a. Is there a difference among types of gasoline?

b. Is there a difference in the cars?

29. Shank's, Inc., a nationwide advertising firm, wants to know if the size of an advertisement and the color of the advertisement make a difference in the response of magazine readers. A random sample of readers is shown ads of four different colors and three different sizes. Each reader is asked to give the particular combination of size and color a rating between 1 and 10. Assume that the ratings are approximately normally distributed. The rating for each combination is shown in the following table (for example, the rating for a small red ad is 2).

	Color of ad			
Size of ad	Red	Blue	Orange	Green
Small	2	3	3	8
Medium	3	5	6	7
Large	6	7	8	8

Is there a difference in the effectiveness of an advertisement by color and by size? Use the .05 level of significance.

30. There are four McBurger restaurants in the Columbus, Georgia, area. The numbers of burgers sold at the respective restaurants for each of the last six weeks are shown

below. At the .05 significance level, is there a difference in the mean number sold among the four restaurants, when the factor of week is considered?

	Restaurant			
Week	**Metro**	**Interstate**	**University**	**River**
1	124	160	320	190
2	234	220	340	230
3	430	290	290	240
4	105	245	310	170
5	240	205	280	180
6	310	260	270	205

a. Is there a difference in the treatment means?
b. Is there a difference in the block means?

31. The city of Tucson, Arizona, employs people to assess the value of homes for the purpose of establishing real estate tax. The city manager routinely sends each assessor to five homes and then compares the results. The information is given below, in thousands of dollars. Can we conclude that there is a difference in the assessors, at $\alpha = .05$?

	Assessor			
Home	**Zawodny**	**Norman**	**Cingle**	**Holiday**
A	$53.0	$55.0	$49.0	$45.0
B	50.0	51.0	52.0	53.0
C	48.0	52.0	47.0	53.0
D	70.0	68.0	65.0	64.0
E	84.0	89.0	92.0	86.0

a. Is there a difference in the treatment means?
b. Is there a difference in the block means?

32. One reads that a business school graduate with an undergraduate degree earns more than a high school graduate with no additional education, and a person with a master's degree or a doctorate earns even more. To test this, a random sample of 25 executives from companies with assets over $1 million was selected. Their incomes, classified by highest level of education, follow.

Incomes ($ thousands)		
High school or less	**Undergraduate degree**	**Master's degree or more**
45	49	51
47	57	73
53	85	82
62	73	59
39	81	94
43	84	89
54	89	89
	92	95
	62	73

Test at the .05 level of significance that there is no difference in the arithmetic mean salaries of the three groups. If the null hypothesis is rejected, conduct further tests to determine which groups differ.

33. A research firm wants to compare the miles per gallon of unleaded regular, mid-grade, and super premium gasolines. Because of differences in the performance of different automobiles, seven different automobiles were selected and treated as blocks. Therefore, each brand of gasoline is tested with each type of automobile. The results of the trials, in miles per gallon, are shown in the following table. At the .05 significance level, is there a difference in the gasolines and automobiles?

Automobile	Regular	Mid-grade	Super premium
1	21	23	26
2	23	22	25
3	24	25	27
4	24	24	26
5	26	26	30
6	26	24	27
7	28	27	32

34. Three supermarket chains in the Denver area each claim to have the lowest overall prices. As part of an investigative study on supermarket advertising, the *Denver Daily News* conducted a study. First, a random sample of nine grocery items was selected. Next, the price of each selected item was checked at each of the three chains on the same day. At the .05 significance level, is there a difference in the mean prices at the supermarkets and for the items?

Item	Super$	Ralph's	Lowblaws
1	$1.12	$1.02	$1.07
2	1.14	1.10	1.21
3	1.72	1.97	2.08
4	2.22	2.09	2.32
5	2.40	2.10	2.30
6	4.04	4.32	4.15
7	5.05	4.95	5.05
8	4.68	4.13	4.67
9	5.52	5.46	5.86

COMPUTER DATA EXERCISES

35. Refer to data set 1, which reports information on homes sold in Florida during 1994.
    a. At the .02 significance level, is there a difference in the variability of the selling prices of homes that have a pool versus those that do not have a pool?
    b. At the .02 significance level, is there a difference in the variability of the selling prices of homes that have a garage versus those that do not have a garage?
    c. At the .05 significance level, is there a difference in the mean selling price of a home among the five townships?
36. Refer to data set 2, which reports information on the 28 major league baseball teams for the 1993 season.
    a. Create a variable that classifies a team's total attendance into one of three groups: less than 2.0 (million), 2.0 up to 3.0, and 3.0 or more. At the .05 significance level, is there a difference in the mean number of games won among the three groups?

b. Using the attendance groups in part *a,* compare the number of home runs hit.
c. Using the attendance groups in part *a,* compare the number of stolen bases.

CHAPTER 11 EXAMINATION

The answers are at the end of the chapter.

For Questions 1 through 10, indicate whether the statement is true or false. If it is false, correct the statement.

1. The *F* distribution is positively skewed.
2. The *F* distribution is based on two sets of degrees of freedom.
3. A treatment is a source of variation in the data.
4. For the ANOVA procedure, the populations should be positively skewed.
5. Rejecting the null hypothesis in an ANOVA procedure indicates that all pairs of means differ.
6. If the significance level is .05 and there are 3 degrees of freedom in the numerator and 12 in the denominator, the critical value of *F* is 3.49.
7. If there are four treatments, the number of degrees of freedom in the numerator of *F* is also 4.
8. If there are four treatments and five observations in each treatment, the number of degrees of freedom in the denominator is 19.
9. A blocking variable is a source of variation similar to a treatment variable.
10. There is a "family" of *F* distributions. There is one distribution for $df = 17$ and 14, another for $df = 6$ and 4, and so on.
11. A sample of eight observations are chosen at random from population 1, and six observations are chosen from population 2. The following is the sample information. At the .10 significance level, can we conclude that there is a difference between the two population variances?

	Population 1	Population 2
Mean	15	12
Variance	10	15
Sample size	8	6

12. The Exact Machine Company uses precision grinders manufactured by four different firms. There is interest in determining if there is any overall difference in the performance of the four grinders. Sample measurements, to the nearest ten-thousandth of an inch, obtained from each of the four machines follow. At the .05 significance level, is there a difference among the four grinders?

Machine			
Deitz	Arvis	Milcron	Hunt
8	8	9	6
7	9	9	7
9	6	6	9
	5	4	4
		7	

13. The following is a two-way ANOVA table.

Source	Sum of squares	Degrees of freedom	Mean square
Treatment	50	2	25
Blocks	24	3	8
Error	48	6	8
Total	122	11	

a. How many treatments are there?
b. How many blocks are there?
c. How many samples are there in the problem?
d. Conduct a test for treatments. Is there a significant difference among the treatment means? Use the .05 significance level.
e. Conduct a test for blocks. Is there a significant difference among the block means? Use the .05 significance level.

CHAPTER 11 Answers

Self-Review

11–1 Let Mark's assemblies be population 1. Then H_0: $\sigma_1^2 \leq \sigma_2^2$; H_1: $\sigma_1^2 > \sigma_2^2$; $df_1 = 10 - 1 = 9$; and df_2 also equals 9. H_0 is rejected if $F >$ 3.18.

$$F = \frac{(2.0)^2}{(1.5)^2} = 1.78$$

H_0 is not rejected. The variation is the same for both employees.

11–2

$$\text{SS total} = 876 - \frac{(130)^2}{20} = 31$$

$$\text{SST} = \frac{(30)^2}{5} + \frac{(35)^2}{5} + \frac{(35)^2}{5} + \frac{(30)^2}{5} - \frac{(130)^2}{20} = 5$$

$$\text{SSE} = 31 - 5 = 26$$

The ANOVA table is computed as follows:

Source	Sum of squares	Degrees of freedom	Mean square
Treatment	5	3	1.667
Error	26	16	1.625
Total	31	19	

$$F = \frac{1.667}{1.625} = 1.026$$

Do not reject H_0 because 1.026 is less than the critical value of 3.24.

11–3

1. H_0: $\mu_1 = \mu_2 = \mu_3$
   H_1: Not all means are equal.
2. H_0 is rejected if $F > 3.98$.
3. $$\text{SS total} = 1{,}152 - \frac{(124)^2}{14} = 53.71$$
   $$\text{SST} = \frac{(55)^2}{5} + \frac{(35)^2}{4} + \frac{(34)^2}{5} - \frac{(124)^2}{14} = 44.16$$
   $$\text{SSE} = 53.71 - 44.16 = 9.55$$

Source	Sum of squares	*df*	Mean square	*F*
Treatment	44.16	2	22.08	25.43
Error	9.55	11	0.8682	
Total	53.71	13		

4. H_0 is rejected. The treatment means differ.
5. $(11.0 - 6.8) \pm 2.201 \sqrt{0.8682(\frac{1}{5} + \frac{1}{5})} = 4.2 \pm 1.30 = 2.90$ and 5.50.
   These treatment means differ because both endpoints of the confidence interval are of the same sign—positive in this problem.

11–4 For types:

H_0: $\mu_1 = \mu_2 = \mu_3$

H_1: The treatment means are not equal.

Reject H_0 if $F > 4.46$.

For months:

H_0: $\mu_1 = \mu_2 = \mu_3 = \mu_4 = \mu_5$

H_1: = The block means are not equal.

Reject H_0 if $F > 3.84$.

The analysis of variance table is as follows:

Source	df	SS	MS	F
Types	2	3.60	1.80	0.39
Months	4	31.73	7.93	1.71
Error	8	37.07	4.63	
Total	14	72.40		

The null hypothesis cannot be rejected for either types or months. There is no difference in the mean sales among types or by month.

Examination

1. True.
2. True.
3. True.
4. False. The populations should be normally distributed.
5. False. At least one pair of means is different.
6. True.
7. False. The number of degrees of freedom is equal to k, the number of treatments, minus 1. There are 3 degrees of freedom.
8. False. The number of degrees of freedom is equal to $N - k = 20 - 4 = 16$.
9. True.
10. True.
11. $H_0: \sigma_2^2 = \sigma_1^2$

    $H_1: \sigma_2^2 \neq \sigma_1^2$

    There are 5 degrees of freedom in the numerator and 7 in the denominator. Note that to make F greater than 1.00, the variance in population 2 is placed in the numerator. H_0 is rejected if $F > 3.97$.

    $$F = \frac{15}{10} = 1.5$$

    H_0 is not rejected. There is no difference in the population variances.
12. $H_0: \mu_1 = \mu_2 = \mu_3 = \mu_4$
    H_1: Not all means are the same.
    H_0 is rejected if the computed $F > 3.49$.

    $$\text{SS total} = 845 - \frac{(113)^2}{16} = 46.9375$$

    $$\text{SST} = \left[\frac{(24)^2}{3} + \frac{(28)^2}{4} + \frac{(35)^2}{5} + \frac{(26)^2}{4}\right] - \frac{(113)^2}{16} = 3.9375$$

    $$\text{SSE} = 46.9375 - 3.9375 = 43.0000$$

Source	SS	df	MS	F
Treatments	3.9375	3	1.3125	0.3663
Error	43.0000	12	3.5833	
Total	46.9375	15		

H_0 is not rejected. There is no difference in the mean performance of the four grinders.

13. *a.* 3 treatments.
    b. 4 blocks.
    c. 12 samples.
    d. $H_0: \mu_1 = \mu_2 = \mu_3$
    H_1: Not all treatment means are the same.
    H_0 is rejected if $F > 5.14$ (using the .05 significance level).

    $$F = \frac{25}{8} = 3.125$$

    H_0 is not rejected. There is no difference in the treatment means.
    e. $H_0: \mu_1 = \mu_2 = \mu_3 = \mu_4$
    H_1: Not all block means are the same.
    H_0 is rejected if $F > 4.76$.

    $$F = \frac{8.0}{8.0} = 1.00$$

    H_0 is not rejected. There is no difference in the block means.

SECTION 4 A REVIEW OF CHAPTERS 10 AND 11

This section is a review of the major concepts and terms introduced in Chapters 10 and 11. Chapter 10 continued the subject of hypothesis testing started in Chapter 9. Chapter 9 dealt with large samples (30 and more).

Less than 30—a small sample

Chapter 10 was concerned with small samples (less than 30). In the small-sample case, it is assumed that the standard deviation of the population is unknown. The major difference between the testing procedures for large samples (Chapter 9) and small samples (Chapter 10) is the test statistic used. For large samples it is *z*, and for small samples it is the *Student t*.

Paired difference test used for dependent samples

Testing for the reasonableness of a mean involving a small sample, or the difference between two means, also requires that the samples be *independent*. For *dependent* samples, we applied the *paired difference test*, which also uses *t* as the test statistic. One typical paired sample problem calls for recording an individual's blood pressure before administering antihypertensive medication and then again afterward in order to evaluate the effectiveness of the medication. Another typical problem using the paired difference test involves recording the production of an individual using method A and then using method B. The purpose of the experiment is to find out whether or not the difference in production between method A and method B is statistically significant.

The ANOVA procedure

Chapter 10 dealt with either one mean or the difference between two means. Chapter 11 presented a procedure called the *analysis of variance*, or *ANOVA*, used to simultaneously determine whether or not three or more populations have identical means. This is accomplished by comparing the variances of the random samples selected from these populations. The usual five-step hypothesis-testing procedure is applied, but we use a probability distribution called the *F* distribution as the test statistic. Before beginning the calculations for *F*, we set up an ANOVA table to organize the calculations into a convenient form.

As an example of the application of the analysis of variance, a test could be conducted to find out if there is any difference in effectiveness among five fertilizers on the weight of popcorn ears. This type of analysis is referred to as *one-factor ANOVA* because we are able to draw conclusions about only one factor, called a *treatment*. If we want to draw conclusions about the simultaneous effects of more than one factor or variable, the *two-factor ANOVA* technique is applied. Both the one-factor and two-factor tests use the *F distribution* as the test statistic. The *F* distribution is also the test statistic used to find out if one normal population has more variation than another. In addition, it is applied when we want to test the assumption that the variances of two populations are not equal.

GLOSSARY

Chapter 10

Degrees of freedom The number of items in a sample that are free to vary. Suppose there are two items in a sample, and we know the mean. We are free to specify only one of the two values because the other value is automatically determined (since the two values total twice the mean). Example: If the mean is \$6, we are free to choose only one value. Choosing \$4 makes the other value \$8 because \$4 + \$8 = 2(\$6). So there is 1 degree of freedom in this illustration. It could have been determined by $n - 1 = 2 - 1 = 1$ degree of freedom. If n is 4, then there are 3 degrees of freedom, found by $n - 1 = 4 - 1 = 3$.

Dependent samples Samples chosen from several populations in such a way that they are not independent of each other. Paired samples are dependent because the same individual or item is a member of both samples. Example: If the test scores of 10 individuals were recorded before a new teaching method was introduced, and then their test scores after using the new method were recorded, the two paired samples would be considered dependent.

Independent samples The samples chosen at random are in no way related to each other. A sample of the ages of 28 inmates in the Auburn maximum security prison and a sample of the ages of 19 students at Mid-South University are examples of two independent samples.

Paired difference test A test of hypothesis conducted using paired samples. It is especially useful for "before and after" problems and to test whether method A and method B are equally effective.

***t* distribution** Investigated and reported by William S. Gossett in 1908 and published under the pseudonym *Student,* it is similar to the normal distribution presented in Chapter 7. The major characteristics of t are:

1. It is a continuous distribution.
2. It can assume values between $-\infty$ and ∞.
3. It is symmetrical about its mean of zero. However, it is more spread out and flatter at the apex than the normal distribution.
4. It approaches the standard normal distribution as n gets larger.
5. There is a "family" of t distributions. One t distribution exists for a sample of 15, another for a sample of 16, and so on.

Chapter 11

Analysis of variance (ANOVA) A technique used to test simultaneously whether or not the means of three or more populations are equal. It uses the F distribution as the test statistic.

Block A second source of variation, in addition to treatments.

***F* distribution** Used as the test statistic for ANOVA problems, it has the following characteristics:

1. The value of F is always positive.

2. The F distribution is a continuous distribution approaching the X-axis but never touching it.
3. It is positively skewed.
4. Like the t distribution, there is a "family" of F distributions. There is one distribution for 17 degrees of freedom in the numerator and 9 degrees of freedom in the denominator, there is another F distribution for 7 degrees of freedom in the numerator and 12 degrees of freedom in the denominator, and so on.

Treatment A cause or specific source of variation in the data.

EXERCISES

The answers to the odd-numbered exercises are at the end of the book.

Part I—Multiple Choice

For Exercises 1 through 12, give the letter representing the correct answer.

1. The test statistic for testing a hypothesis for small sample means when the population standard deviation is not known is:
   a. z.
   b. t.
   c. F.
   d. $A > B$.
   e. None of these is correct.
2. We want to test a hypothesis for the difference between two population means. The null and alternate hypotheses are stated as H_0: $\mu_1 = \mu_2$ and H_1: $\mu_1 \neq \mu_2$.
   a. A left-tailed test should be applied.
   b. A two-tailed test should be applied.
   c. A right-tailed test should be applied.
   d. We cannot determine whether a left-, right-, or two-tailed test should be applied based on the information given.
   e. None of these is correct.
3. The F distribution:
   a. Cannot be negative.
   b. Cannot be positive.
   c. Is the same as the t distribution.
   d. Is the same as the z distribution.
   e. None of these is correct.
4. As the sample size increases, the t distribution approaches:
   a. ANOVA.
   b. The standard normal or z distribution.
   c. The Poisson distribution.
   d. Zero.
   e. None of these is correct.
5. To conduct a paired difference test, the samples must be:
   a. Infinitely large.
   b. Equal to ANOVA.
   c. Independent.
   d. Dependent.

e. None of these is correct.

6. An ANOVA test was conducted with respect to the population means. The null hypothesis was rejected. This indicates that:
   a. There were too many degrees of freedom.
   b. There is no difference between the population means.
   c. There is a difference between at least two population means.
   d. A larger sample should be selected.
   e. None of these is correct.

Use the following information for Exercises 7, 8, and 9. The Rochester Builders Association stated that the mean cost of erecting a multistory apartment building in the area is no more than \$80 per square foot. A building contractor claims that the mean cost per square foot is more than \$80. A sample of 21 apartment buildings resulted in the sample mean of \$81.

7. The alternate hypothesis is:
   a. H_1: $\mu <$ \$80.
   b. H_1: $\mu \neq$ \$80.
   c. H_1: $\mu \geq$ \$80.
   d. H_1: $\mu >$ \$80.
   e. None of these is correct.
8. The number of degrees of freedom for this problem is:
   a. 80.
   b. 0
   c. 21.
   d. 20.
   e. None of these is correct.
9. *t* was computed to be 1.90. At the .05 level, the null hypothesis is:
   a. Not rejected.
   b. Rejected.
   c. Both accepted and rejected.
   d. None of these is correct.

Exercises 10, 11, and 12 are based on the following. A preliminary study of the hourly wages paid unskilled employees in three metropolitan areas was conducted. Seven employees were included from area A, 9 from area B, and 12 from area C. The objective of the study is to find out whether there is a significant difference in the mean hourly wage in the three areas. The .01 level of significance is to be applied. The test statistic was computed to be 4.91.

10. For this type of problem we would use as the test statistic the:
    a. *z* distribution.
    b. *t* distribution.
    c. χ^2 distribution.
    d. *F* distribution.
    e. None of these is correct.
11. At the .01 level, the critical value is:
    a. 1.96.
    b. −1.96.
    c. 5,000.
    d. 5.00.
    e. None of these is correct.
12. We would conclude that:
    a. The mean hourly wages of unskilled employees in the three areas are equal.
    b. The mean hourly wages in at least two metropolitan areas are different.
    c. More degrees of freedom are needed.
    d. None of these is correct.

Part II—Problems

13. It was hypothesized that university clerical employees did not engage in productive work 20 minutes on the average out of every hour. Some claimed the time lost was greater than 20 minutes. An actual study was conducted at a midwestern university using a stopwatch and other ways of checking the work habits of the clerical employees. A random check of the employees revealed the following unproductive times, in minutes, during a one-hour period (exclusive of regularly scheduled breaks): 10, 25, 17, 20, 28, 30, 18, 23, and 18. Test at the .05 level that the mean unproductive time is 20 minutes, against the alternate hypothesis that it is greater than 20 minutes.

14. A test is to be conducted involving the mean holding power of two glues designed for plastic. First, a small plastic hook was coated at one end with Epox glue and fastened to a sheet of plastic. After it dried, weight was added to the hook until it separated from the sheet of plastic. The weight was then recorded. This was repeated until 12 hooks were tested. The same procedure was followed for Holdtite glue, but only 10 hooks were used. The sample results, in pounds, were:

	Epox	**Holdtite**
Sample mean	250	252
Sample standard deviation	5	8
Number in sample	12	10

At the .01 level, is there a difference between the holding power of Epox and that of Holdtite?

15. An additive formulated to add to the life of paints used in the South is to be tested. The top half of a piece of wood was painted using the regular paint. The bottom half was painted with the paint including the additive. The same procedure was followed for a total of 10 pieces. Then each piece was subjected to high-pressure water and brilliant light. The data, number of hours each piece lasted before it faded beyond a certain point, follow:

	Number of hours by sample									
	A	**B**	**C**	**D**	**E**	**F**	**G**	**H**	**I**	**J**
Without additive	325	313	320	340	318	312	319	330	333	319
With additive	323	313	326	343	310	320	313	340	330	315

Using the .05 level, determine if the additive is effective in prolonging the life of the paint.

16. The Buffalo, N.Y., cola distributor is featuring a super-special sale on 12-packs. She wonders where to place the cola for maximum attention. Should it be near the front door of the grocery stores, in the cola section, at the checkout registers, or near the milk and other dairy products? Four stores with similar total sales cooperated in an experiment. In one store the 12-packs were stacked near the front door, in another they were placed near the checkout registers, and so on. Sales were checked at specified times in each store for exactly four minutes. The results were:

Cola at door	**Cola in cola section**	**Cola near registers**	**Cola near dairy products**
$6	$ 5	$ 7	$10
8	10	10	9
3	12	9	6
7	4	4	11
	9	5	
		7	

The Buffalo distributor wants to find out if there is a difference in the mean sales for cola stacked at the four locations in the store. Use the .05 significance level.

17. An agriculture economist wants to determine whether soil condition and type of fertilizer have an effect on the yield of blueberries. The following results were obtained, in boxes per acre, from a study of 15 combinations of soil conditions and fertilizer types. Use the .05 significance level.

Soil conditions	Yield (boxes) by fertilizer type				
	A	B	C	D	E
Dry	15	13	7	16	9
Moderate	10	11	8	15	10
Moist	18	14	6	19	12

18. A recent study by the dean of students at Napa Valley College showed that the mean number of hours attempted by a sample of 28 engineering majors was 12.2, and the standard deviation was 2.85 hours. A study of 23 nursing arts majors at Napa Valley showed the mean number of hours attempted was nearly the same—12.8—but the standard deviation was much larger—3.9 hours. The dean speculated that this was because many nursing students were able to find part-time work at nights and weekends at a local hospital and elected to take fewer hours. Also, some of the nursing students apparently were anxious to complete their program because jobs were plentiful in the field and took an excessive number of hours. At the .05 significance level, can the dean conclude that there is more variation in the number of hours attempted by nursing majors compared with engineering majors?

CASE

Refer to the Century Bank data. The bank has branch offices in four different cities: Cincinnati, Ohio; Atlanta, Georgia; Louisville, Kentucky; and Erie, Pennsylvania. Mr. Selig would like to know if there are differences in the mean checking account balance among the four cities. If there are any differences, where do these differences occur?

Mr. Selig is also interested in the ATMs. Is there a difference in ATM use among the four cities? Also, do customers who have debit cards tend to use the ATMs differently than those who do not have debit cards? Also, is there a difference in ATM use by those with checking accounts that pay interest versus those that do not?

Chapter 12

Linear Regression and Correlation

GOALS

When you have completed this chapter, you will be able to:

1
Draw a scatter diagram.

2
Calculate Pearson's coefficient of correlation and explain its use.

3
Conduct a test of hypothesis for the coefficient of correlation.

4
Calculate and explain the meaning of the coefficient of determination.

5
Use the least squares method to determine a linear regression equation.

6
Compute the standard error of estimate and explain its use.

7
Construct a confidence interval and a prediction interval for the estimates of the dependent variable.

An agronomist experimented with different amounts of fertilizer on a sample of four equal-size lots. Given the yields, draw a scatter diagram. (See Goal 1 and Self-Review 12–1.)

INTRODUCTION

Chapters 2 through 4 dealt with *descriptive statistics.* We organized raw data into a frequency distribution, and we computed several measures of central tendency and measures of dispersion to describe the major characteristics of the data. Chapter 5 started the study of *statistical inference.* The main emphasis was on inferring something about a population parameter, such as the population mean, based on a sample. We tested for the reasonableness of a population mean or a population proportion, the difference between two population means, or whether more than two population means were equal. All of these tests involved just *one* interval- or ratio-level variable, such as the weight of a plastic soft drink bottle, the income of bank presidents, or the number of patients admitted to a particular hospital.

We shift our emphasis in this chapter. Here we are interested in studying the *relationship between two or more variables* and *developing an equation that allows us to estimate one variable based on another.* Is there a relationship between the amount a firm spends on advertising and its sales? Can we estimate the cost to heat a home in January in the upper Midwest based on the number of square feet in the home? Is there a relationship between the number of years a production worker has been on the job and the number of units produced? Note that in each of these instances there are two variables—for example, the number of years on the job and the number of units produced.

We begin this chapter by examining the meaning and purpose of **correlation analysis.** Then we look at a chart designed to portray the relationship between two variables: a **scatter diagram.** We continue our study by developing a mathematical equation that will allow us to estimate the value of one variable based on the value of another. This is called **regression analysis.** We will (1) determine the equation of the straight line that best fits the data, (2) estimate the value of one variable based on another, (3) measure the error in our estimate, and (4) establish confidence and prediction intervals for our estimate.

WHAT IS SIMPLE CORRELATION ANALYSIS?

An example will best describe what is meant by correlation analysis. Suppose the sales manager of Intrepid, Inc., which has a large sales force, wants to determine if there is a relationship between the number of sales calls made in a month and the number of units sold that month. The manager selects a sample of 10 representatives and determines the number of sales calls each representative made last month and the number of units sold. The sample information is shown in Table 12–1.

There does seem to be some relationship between the number of sales calls and the number of units sold. That is, the salespeople that made the most sales calls seem to sell the most units. The relationship is not "perfect" or exact, however. For example, Mike Keil made 12 sales calls and sold 14 units, whereas Todd Bortz made only 6 sales calls but sold more units (22).

Instead of talking in generalities, as we have been doing up to this point, we will develop some statistical measures to portray and explain more precisely the relationship between the two variables, sales calls and units sold. This group of statistical techniques is called **correlation analysis.**

TABLE 12–1 **Sales Calls and Units Sold for 10 Salespeople**

Sales representative	Number of sales calls	Number of units sold
Frank Rouses	14	28
Sue Navchek	35	66
Art Seiple	22	38
Carma Lopez	29	70
Todd Bortz	6	22
Sara Jones	15	27
Susan Welch	17	28
Carlos Ramirez	20	47
Mike Keil	12	14
Mark Reynolds	29	68

What is correlation analysis?

Correlation analysis A group of statistical techniques used to measure the strength of the relationship (correlation) between two variables.

The basic purpose of correlation analysis is to find how strong the relationship is between two variables. One measure of this relationship is the **coefficient of correlation.** It may assume any value on a scale from −1 to +1 inclusive. We can apply these measures to both interval- and ratio-scaled data.

A useful first step in looking at the relationship between two variables is to portray the information in a **scatter diagram.**

Scatter diagram

Scatter diagram A chart that portrays the relationship between the two variables of interest.

EXAMPLE

The sales manager of Intrepid, Inc. randomly selected 10 sales representatives and determined the number of sales calls each one made last month and the number of units of the product he or she sold last month. The sample information is reported in Table 12–1. Portray this information in a scatter diagram. Based on the scatter diagram, what observations can you make?

Solution ▸ Based on the information in Table 12–1, the sales manager suspects that there is a relationship between the number of calls and the number of units sold. Sue Navcheck made the most sales calls, and her number of sales is among the largest. Sales for Carma Lopez and Mark Reynolds are quite high, and they made a large number of sales calls. On the other hand, Todd Bortz and Mike Kiel did not make many sales calls and their sales are relatively low. This implies that sales *depend* on the number of sales calls. We therefore refer to sales as the **dependent variable** and the number of sales calls as the **independent variable.**

Definition of dependent and independent variables

Dependent variable The variable that is being predicted or estimated.

> **Independent variable** A variable that provides the basis for estimation. It is the predictor variable.

It is common practice to put the dependent variable (sales, in this example) on the vertical axis (Y-axis) and the independent variable (number of sales calls) on the horizontal axis (X-axis). The paired data from Table 12–1 for Frank Rouses are $X = 14$ and $Y = 28$. To plot, move right on the X-axis to 14; then go vertically to 28, and place a dot at the intersection. This process is continued until all paired data are plotted, as shown in Chart 12–1.

CHART 12–1 **Scatter Diagram Depicting Sales Calls and Units Sold**

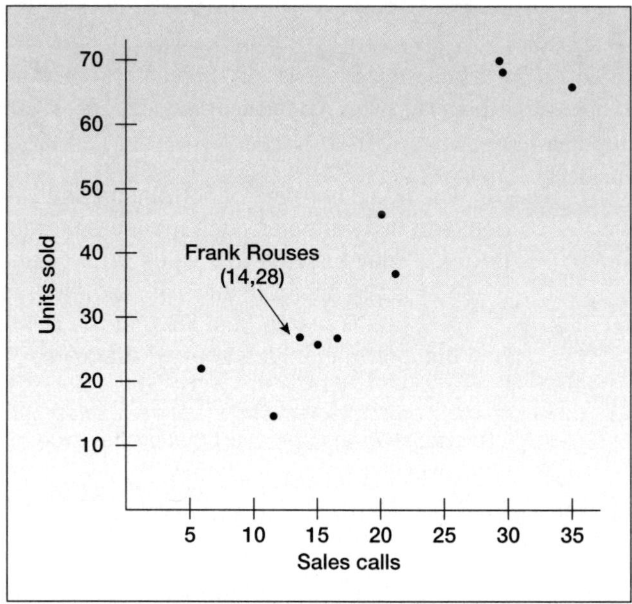

Note from the scatter diagram that as the number of sales calls increases, so does the number of units sold. It does appear, therefore, that there is a rather strong positive relationship (correlation) between sales calls and the number of units sold. The following section will measure that relationship by computing the coefficient of correlation.

THE COEFFICIENT OF CORRELATION

Interval or ratio data

Originated by Karl Pearson about 1900, the **coefficient of correlation** describes the strength of the relationship between two sets of interval-scaled or ratio-scaled

An r can assume any value between -1 and $+1$ inclusive

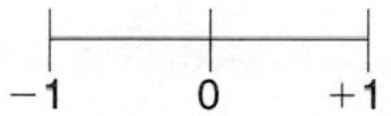

variables. Designated r, it is often referred to as *Pearson's r* and as the *Pearson product-moment correlation coefficient.* It can assume any value from -1.00 to $+1.00$ inclusive. A correlation coefficient of -1.00 or $+1.00$ indicates *perfect correlation.* For example, a correlation coefficient for the preceding example computed to be $+1.00$ would indicate that the number of sales calls was a perfect predictor of sales. That is, the number of sales calls and the number of units sold are perfectly related in a positive linear sense. A computed value of -1.00 reveals that the independent variable X and the dependent variable Y are perfectly related in a negative linear way. How the scatter diagrams would appear if the relationship between the two sets of data were linear and perfect is shown in Chart 12–2.

Coefficients of $-.87$ and $+.87$ have equal strength

If there is absolutely no relationship between the two sets of variables, Pearson's r will be zero. A coefficient of correlation r close to 0 (say, .08) shows that the relationship is quite weak. The same conclusion is drawn if $r = -.08$. Coefficients of $-.91$ and $+.91$ have equal strength; both indicate very strong correlation between the two sets of variables. Thus, *the strength of the correlation does not depend on the direction (either − or +).*

An r of -1.00 indicates an inverse relationship

CHART 12–2 Scatter Diagrams Showing Perfect Negative Correlation and Perfect Positive Correlation

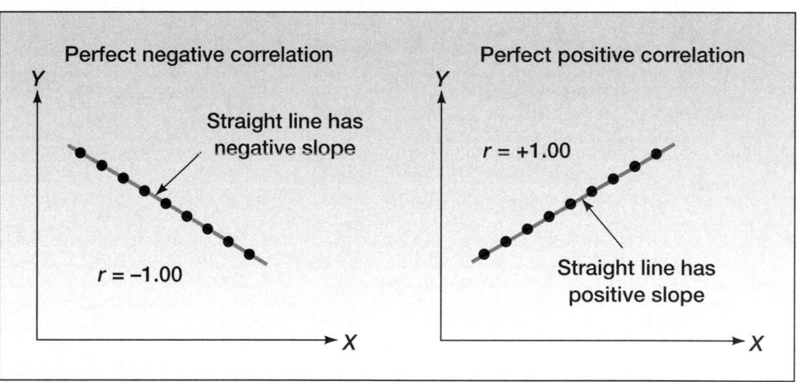

Relationship strength can be "strong," "weak," etc.

Scatter diagrams for $r = 0$, a weak r (say, $-.23$), and a strong r (say, $+.87$) are shown in Chart 12–3. Note that if the correlation is weak, there is considerable scatter about a straight line drawn through the center of the data. For the scatter diagram representing a strong relationship, there is very little scatter about the straight line. This indicates, in that example, that high school GPA is a very good predictor of performance in college.

Examples of degrees of correlation

CHART 12–3 Scatter Diagrams Depicting Zero, Weak, and Strong Correlation

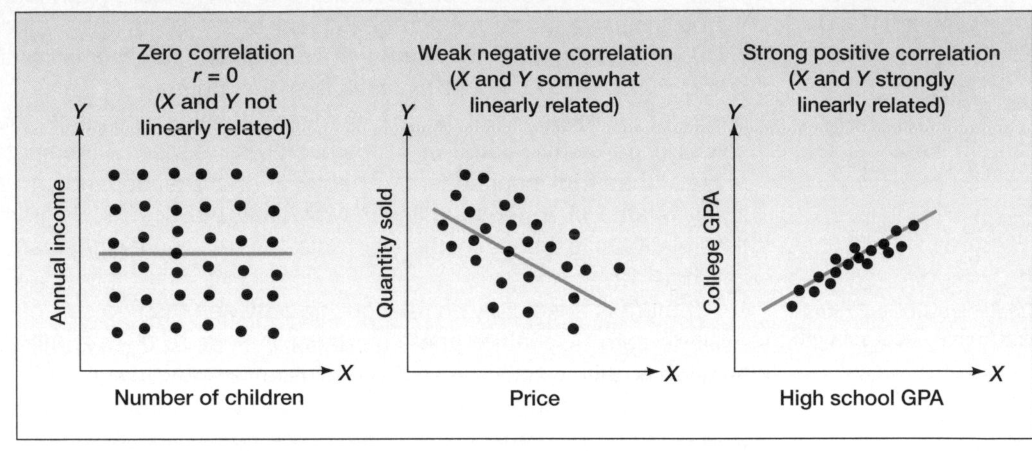

The following drawing summarizes the strength and direction of the coefficient of correlation.

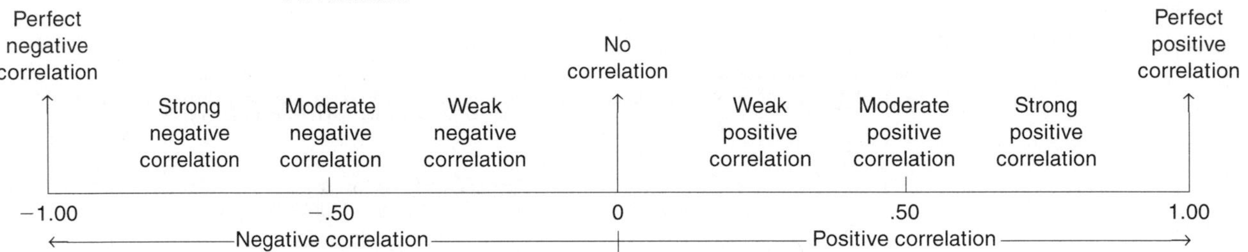

Correlation coefficient defined

Coefficient of correlation A measure of the strength of the linear relationship between two sets of variables.

Convenient formula for r

The formula for r is:

$$r = \frac{n(\Sigma XY) - (\Sigma X)(\Sigma Y)}{\sqrt{[n(\Sigma X^2) - (\Sigma X)^2][n(\Sigma Y^2) - (\Sigma Y)^2]}} \quad (12\text{–}1)$$

where:

- n is the number of paired observations.
- ΣX is the X variable summed.
- ΣY is the Y variable summed.
- (ΣX^2) is the X variable squared and the squares summed.
- $(\Sigma X)^2$ is the X variable summed and the sum squared.
- (ΣY^2) is the Y variable squared and the squares summed.
- $(\Sigma Y)^2$ is the Y variable summed and the sum squared.
- ΣXY is the sum of the products of X and Y.

EXAMPLE

The data for the problem involving the number of sales calls and the number of units sold and the calculations needed for determining the coefficient of correlation are given in Table 12–2. Determine the coefficient of correlation.

TABLE 12–2 **Sales Calls and Units Sold for 10 Salespeople**

Sales representative	Sales calls, X	Units sold, Y	X^2	XY	Y^2
Frank Rouses	14	28	196	392	784
Sue Navchek	35	66	1,225	2,310	4,356
Art Seiple	22	38	484	836	1,444
Carma Lopez	29	70	841	2,030	4,900
Todd Bortz	6	22	36	132	484
Sara Jones	15	27	225	405	729
Susan Welch	17	28	289	476	784
Carlos Ramirez	20	47	400	940	2,209
Mike Keil	12	14	144	168	196
Mark Reynolds	29	68	841	1,972	4,624
Total	199	408	4,681	9,661	20,510

Solution ► The coefficient of correlation is .924, found by using formula (12–1).

$$r = \frac{n(\Sigma XY) - (\Sigma X)(\Sigma Y)}{\sqrt{[n(\Sigma X^2) - (\Sigma X)^2)][(n(\Sigma Y^2) - (\Sigma Y)^2]}}$$

$$= \frac{10(9{,}661) - (199)(408)}{\sqrt{[10(4{,}681) - (199)^2][10(20{,}510) - (408)^2]}}$$

$$= \frac{15{,}418}{\sqrt{[7{,}209][38{,}636]}} = .924$$

How do we interpret a correlation coefficient of .924? First, it is positive, so we conclude that there is a direct relationship between the two variables. This confirms our reasoning based on the scatter diagram (Chart 12–1). The value of .924 is close to 1.00, so we conclude that the association is strong.

THE COEFFICIENT OF DETERMINATION

In the previous example regarding the relationship between the number of sales calls and the units sold, the coefficient of correlation, .924, was interpreted as being "strong." Terms such as *weak, moderate,* and *strong,* however, do not have precise meaning. A measure that has a more exact meaning is the **coefficient of determination.** It is computed by squaring the coefficient of correlation. In the example, the coefficient of determination, r^2, is .854, found by $(.924)^2$. This is a proportion or a percent; we can say that 84.5 percent of the variation in the units sold is explained, or accounted for, by the variation in the number of sales calls.

Coefficient of determination defined

Coefficient of determination The proportion of the total variation in the dependent variable Y that is explained or accounted for by the variation in the independent variable X.

Further discussion of the coefficient of determination is found later in the chapter.

A Word of Caution

If there is a strong relationship (say, .91) between two variables, we are tempted to assume that an increase or decrease in one variable *causes* a change in the other variable. For example, it can be shown that the consumption of Georgia peanuts and the consumption of aspirin have moved together. However, this does not indicate that an increase in the consumption of peanuts *caused* the consumption of aspirin to increase. Likewise, the incomes of professors and the number of inmates in mental institutions have increased proportionately. Further, as the population of donkeys has decreased, there has been an increase in the number of doctoral degrees granted. Relationships such as these are called **spurious correlations.** What we can conclude when we find two variables with a strong correlation is that there is a relationship between the two variables, not that a change in one causes a change in the other.

Self-review: A valuable learning tool

SELF-REVIEW 12–1

The answers are at the end of the chapter.

An agronomist employed by Agrico experimented with different amounts of liquid fertilizer on a sample of equal-size plots. The amounts of fertilizer and the yields are:

Plot	Amount of fertilizer (tons)	Yield (hundreds of bushels)
A	2	7
B	1	3
C	3	8
D	4	10

1. The agronomist is interested in predicting yield. What is the dependent variable? The independent variable?
2. Draw a scatter diagram.
3. Determine the coefficient of correlation.
4. Interpret the strength of r.

EXERCISES

The answers to the odd-numbered exercises are at the end of the book.

1. The following sample observations were selected.

X:	4	5	3	6	10
Y:	4	6	5	7	7

Determine the coefficient of correlation and the coefficient of determination. Interpret.

2. The following sample observations were selected.

X:	5	3	6	3	4	4	6	8
Y:	13	15	7	12	13	11	9	5

Determine the coefficient of correlation and the coefficient of determination. Interpret.

3. Bi-lo Appliance Stores has outlets in several large metropolitan areas. The general sales manager plans to air a camcorder television commercial on selected local stations at least twice prior to a gigantic sale starting on Saturday and ending Sunday. She plans to get the figures for Saturday-Sunday camcorder sales at the various outlets and pair them with the number of times the advertisement was shown on the local TV stations. The basic purpose of the research is to find out if there is any relationship between the number of times the advertisement was aired and camcorder sales. The pairings are:

Location of TV station	Number of airings	Saturday-Sunday sales ($ thousands)
Buffalo	4	15
Albany	2	8
Erie	5	21
Syracuse	6	24
Rochester	3	17

a. What is the dependent variable?
b. Draw a scatter diagram.
c. Determine the coefficient of correlation.
d. Determine the coefficient of determination.
e. Interpret these statistical measures.

4. The production department of NDB Electronics wants to explore the relationship between the number of employees who assemble a subassembly and the number produced. As an experiment, two employees were assigned to assemble the subassembly. They produced 15 during a one-hour period. Then four employees assembled it. They produced 25 during a one-hour period. The complete set of paired observations follows.

Number of assemblers	One-hour production (units)
2	15
4	25
1	10
5	40
3	30

The dependent variable is production; that is, it is assumed that the level of production depends upon the number of employees.

a. Draw a scatter diagram.
b. Based on the scatter diagram, does there appear to be any relationship between the number of assemblers and production? Explain.
c. Compute the coefficient of correlation.
d. Evaluate the strength of the relationship by computing the coefficient of determination.

TESTING THE SIGNIFICANCE OF THE CORRELATION COEFFICIENT

Recall that the sales manager of Intrepid, Inc. found that the correlation between the number of sales calls and the number of units sold was .924. This indicated a strong association between the two variables. However, only 10 salespeople were sampled. Could it be that the correlation in the population is actually 0? This would mean that the correlation of .924 was due to chance. The population in this example is all the salespeople employed by the firm.

Could the correlation in the population be zero?

Resolving this dilemma requires a test to answer the obvious question: Is there zero correlation in the population from which the sample was selected? To put it another way, did the computed r come from a population of paired observations with zero correlation? To continue our convention of allowing Greek letters to represent a population value, we will let ρ represent the correlation in the population. It is pronounced "rho."

Small Samples

We will continue with the illustration involving sales calls and units sold. The null hypothesis and the alternate hypothesis are:

H_0: $\rho = 0$ (The correlation in the population is zero.)

H_1: $\rho \neq 0$ (The correlation in the population is different from zero.)

From the way H_1 is stated, we know that the test is two-tailed.

The formula for t is:

$$t = \frac{r\sqrt{n-2}}{\sqrt{1-r^2}} \quad \text{with } n-2 \text{ degrees of freedom} \qquad (12\text{–}2)$$

Using the .05 level of significance, the decision rule states that if the computed t falls in the area between plus 2.306 and minus 2.306, the null hypothesis will not be rejected. To locate the critical value of 2.306, refer to Appendix F for $df = n - 2 = 10 - 2 = 8$. Shown schematically:

Critical values of t are −2.306 and 2.306

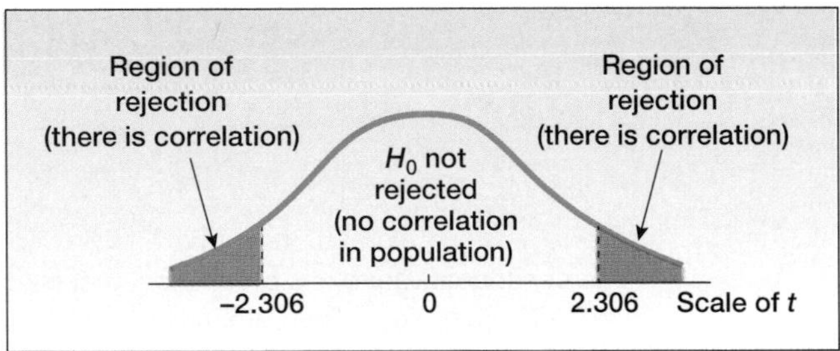

Applying formula (12–2) to the problem of sales calls and units sold:

$$t = \frac{r\sqrt{n-2}}{\sqrt{1-r^2}} = \frac{.924\sqrt{10-2}}{\sqrt{1-(.924)^2}} = 6.835$$

The computed value of t falls in the rejection region. Thus, H_0 is rejected at the .05 significance level. This means that the correlation in the population is not zero. From a practical standpoint, it indicates to the sales manager that there is correlation in the population of salespeople with respect to the number of sales calls made and the number of units sold.

What is the p-value associated with the test of hypothesis? We discussed p-values in Chapters 9 and 10. To review, it is the likelihood of finding a value of the test statistic this large or larger, when H_0 is true. To determine the p-value, go to the t distribution in Appendix F and find the row for 8 degrees of freedom. The value of the test statistic is 6.835, so in the row for 8 degrees of freedom and a two-tailed test, find the value closest to 6.835. The largest value in this row is 5.041, which is in the .001 column. Because the computed value of the test statistic is larger than 5.041, the p-value must be *less than .001.*

AN APPLICATION USING THE MINITAB SYSTEM

The computer offers substantial savings in time and greatly reduces the likelihood of a computational error. Most packages also have available some type of plot routine. The MINITAB system was used to solve the following problem.

EXAMPLE

The principal at Odessa City High School in Texas surveyed a sample of 20 students in the 1988 graduating class. She recorded the number of years of education beyond high school and the individual's yearly income last year. She wants to know if there is an association between the two variables. The sample findings are listed in Table 12–3.

TABLE 12–3 Number of Years of Education beyond High School and Annual Income

Years beyond high school	Yearly income ($ thousands)	Years beyond high school	Yearly income ($ thousands)
0	31.6	4	35.6
0	28.0	4	50.2
1	34.0	4	31.7
1	30.5	5	48.0
1	27.8	5	36.5
2	29.5	6	50.6
2	26.8	6	63.9
2	31.2	7	57.6
3	34.2	7	61.2
3	39.8	7	54.9

Solution ▸ As a first step, the principal plotted the data in Chart 12–4 using MINITAB. Note that the relationship is not exact—that is, all the points are not on a straight line—but it does appear that as the years of education increase, so does the yearly income.

CHART 12–4 **MINITAB Plot of Years of Education beyond High School and Yearly Income**

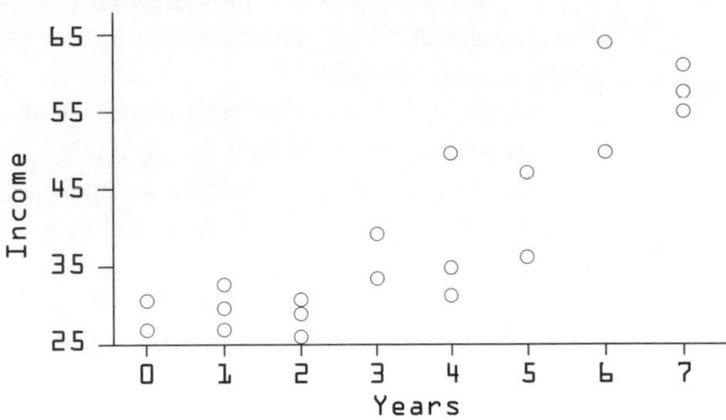

MINITAB is used to determine the coefficient of correlation, which is .868.

```
MTB > set c1
DATA> 0, 0, 1, 1, 1, 2, 2, 2, 3, 3, 4, 4, 4, 5, 5, 6, 6, 7, 7, 7
DATA> end
MTB > set c2
DATA> 31.6, 28, 34, 30.5, 27.8, 29.5, 26.8, 31.2, 34.2, 39.8, 35.6, 50.2, 31.7, 48, 36.5
DATA> 50.6, 63.9, 57.6, 61.2, 54.9
DATA> end
MTB > name c1 'Years' c2 'Income'
MTB > corr 'Income' vs 'years'

Correlation of Income and Years = 0.868 ← Coefficient of correlation
```

The normal hypothesis-testing procedure can be used to determine if the association in the population is greater than zero. In this instance, assume that the principal wants to determine if there is a positive association between years of education beyond high school and yearly income. The null and alternate hypotheses would be:

$$H_0\text{: } \rho \leq 0$$

$$H_1\text{: } \rho > 0$$

The sample size is 20, so there are $n - 2 = 20 - 2 = 18$ degrees of freedom. Using the .05 level and a one-tailed test, the decision rule is to reject the null hypothesis if the computed value of t is greater than 1.734. The computed test statistic t is 7.42, found by using formula (12–2):

$$t = \frac{r\sqrt{n-2}}{\sqrt{1-r^2}}$$

$$= \frac{.868\sqrt{20-2}}{\sqrt{1-(.868)^2}} = 7.42$$

Since the computed t value of 7.42 exceeds the critical value, the null hypothesis is rejected and the alternate hypothesis accepted. Yearly income does increase as the number of years of education beyond high school increases. There is a positive association in the population between these two variables. The p-value is less than .001. (See Appendix F, for 18 degrees of freedom.)

SELF-REVIEW 12–2

The answers are at the end of the chapter.

A sample of 25 mayoral campaigns in cities with populations larger than 50,000 showed that the correlation between the percent of the vote received and the amount spent on the campaign by the candidate was .43. At the .05 significance level, is there a positive association between the variables?

EXERCISES

The answers to the odd-numbered exercises are at the end of the book.

5. The following hypotheses are given.

$$H_0: \rho \leq 0$$
$$H_1: \rho > 0$$

A sample of 12 paired observations indicated a correlation of .32. Can we conclude that the correlation in the population is greater than zero? Use the .05 significance level.

6. The following hypotheses are given.

$$H_0: \rho \geq 0$$
$$H_1: \rho < 0$$

A sample of 15 paired observations have a correlation of −.46. Can we conclude that the correlation in the population is zero? Use the .05 significance level.

7. The Pennsylvania Refining Company is studying the relationship between the pump price of gasoline and the number of gallons sold at a particular gasoline station. For a sample of 20 stations last Tuesday, the correlation was .78. At the .01 significance level, is the correlation in the population greater than zero?
8. A study of 20 worldwide financial institutions showed the correlation between their assets and pretax profit to be .86. At the .05 significance level, can we conclude that there is positive correlation in the population?

REGRESSION ANALYSIS

We are going to develop an equation to express the relationship between two variables and estimate the value of the dependent variable Y based on a selected value of the independent variable X. The technique used to develop the equation for the straight line and make these predictions is called **regression analysis.**[1]

[1]The word *regression* was introduced by Sir Francis Galton in 1877 in his study of heredity. He found that the heights of descendants of tall parents tended to regress (i.e., go back) toward the average height of the population. The mathematical line he developed was called the line of regression. The term *line of regression* is commonly used even though *predictive equation* or *estimating equation* seems to be more appropriate.

In Table 12–1 we reported the number of sales calls and the number of units sold for a sample of 10 sales representatives at Intrepid, Inc. Chart 12–1 portrayed this information in the form of a scatter diagram. Now we want to develop an equation that expresses the relationship between the number of sales calls and the number of units sold. The equation for the straight line used to estimate *Y* based on *X* is referred to as the **regression equation.**

Regression equation used to estimate *Y* based on *X*

> **Regression equation** A mathematical equation that defines the relationship between two variables.

Straight line drawn by hand to fit scatter plots

The scatter diagram in Chart 12–1 is reproduced in Chart 12–5, with a line drawn with a ruler through the dots to illustrate that a straight line would probably fit the data best. However, the line drawn using a straight edge has one disadvantage: Its position is based on the judgment of the person drawing the line. The hand-drawn lines in Chart 12–6 represent the judgments of four people. All the lines except line *A* seem to be reasonable. Each would, however, give a different estimate of units sold.

CHART 12–5 Sales Calls and Units Sold for 10 Salespeople

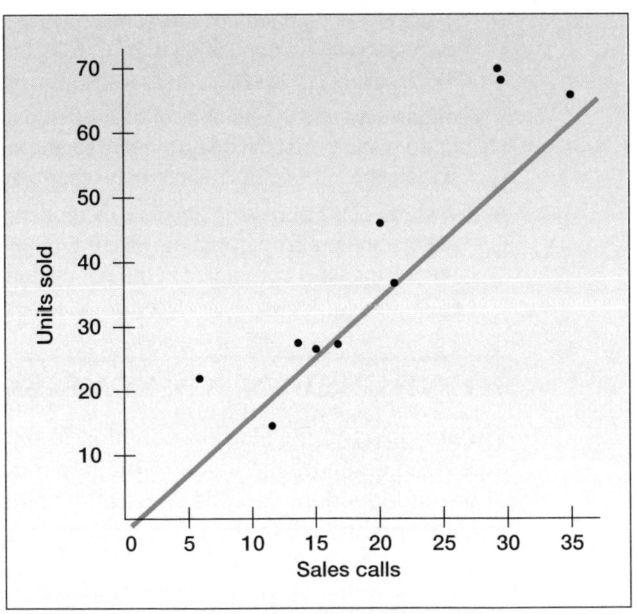

CHART 12–6 **Four Freehand Lines Superimposed on the Scatter Diagram**

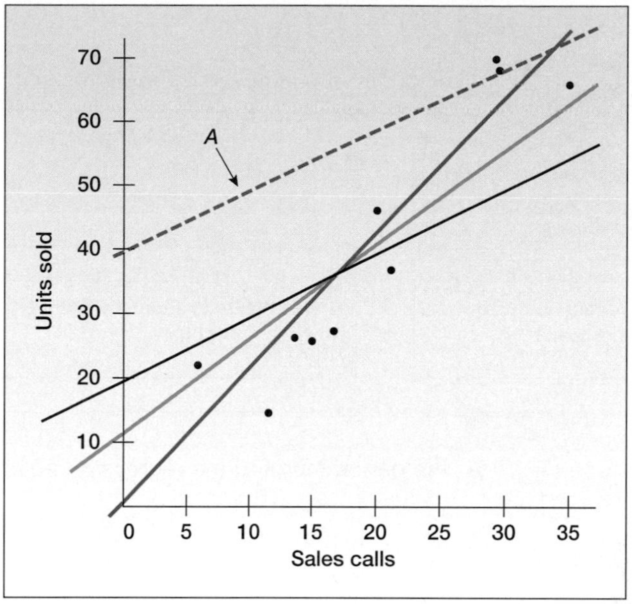

Least Squares Principle

Least squares line gives "best" fit; freehand method is unreliable

Judgment is eliminated by determining the regression line using a mathematical method called the **least squares principle.** This method gives what is commonly referred to as the "best-fitting" straight line. It *minimizes the sum of the squares of the vertical deviations about the line.*

> **Least squares principle** Determining a regression equation by minimizing the sum of the squares of the vertical distances between the actual *Y* values and the predicted values of *Y.*

To illustrate this concept, the same data are plotted in the three charts that follow. The regression line in Chart 12–7 was determined using the least squares method. It is the best-fitting line because the sum of the squares of the vertical deviations about it is at a minimum. The first plot ($X = 3$, $Y = 8$) deviates by 2 from the line, found by $10 - 8$. The deviation squared is 4. The squared deviation for the plot $X = 4$, $Y = 18$ is 16. The squared deviation for the plot $X = 5$, $Y = 16$ is 4. The sum of the squared deviations is 24, found by $4 + 16 + 4$.

Assume that the straight lines in Charts 12–8 and 12–9 were drawn using a straight edge. The sum of the squared vertical deviations in Chart 12–8 is 44. For Chart 12–9 it is 132. Both sums are greater than the one in Chart 12–7 found using the least squares method.

CHART 12–7
The Least Squares Line

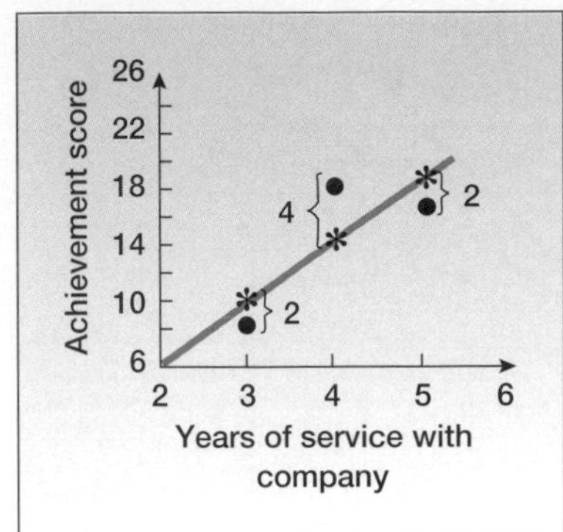

CHART 12–8
Line Drawn Using a Straight Edge

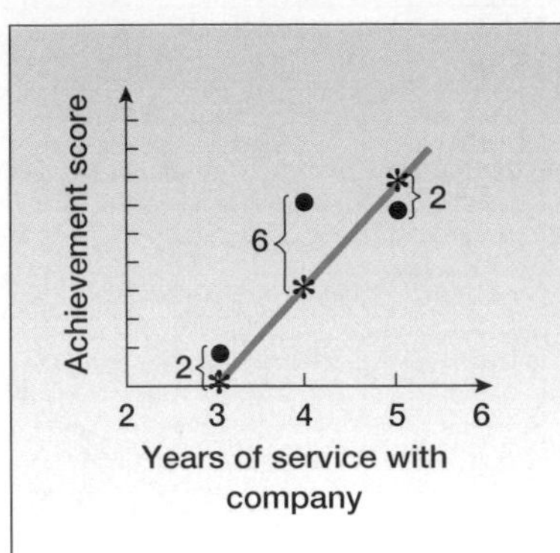

CHART 12–9
Line Drawn Using a Straight Edge

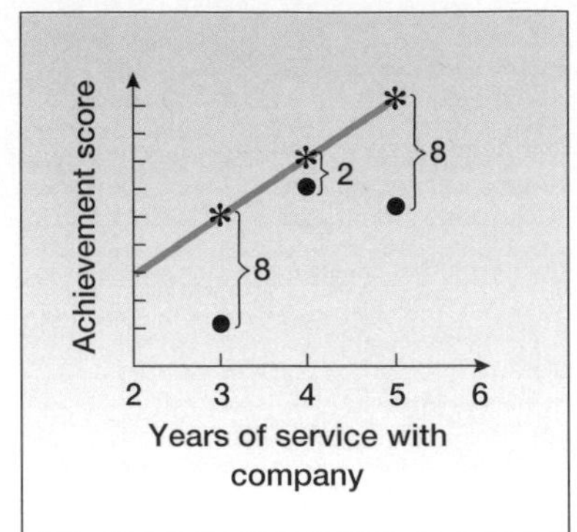

The general form of the regression equation is:

General form of the linear equation

$$Y' = a + bX \tag{12–3}$$

where

Y' read Y prime, is the predicted value of the Y variable for a selected X value.

a is the Y-intercept. It is the estimated value of Y when $X = 0$. Another way to put it is: a is the estimated value of Y where the regression line crosses the Y-axis when X is zero.

b is the slope of the line, or the average change in Y' for each change of one unit (either increase or decrease) in the independent variable X.

X is any value of the independent variable that is selected.

It should be noted that the linear regression equation for the sample of salespeople is just an estimate of the relationship between the two variables in the population. Thus, the values of a and b in the regression equation are usually referred to as the *estimated regression coefficients,* or just the *regression coefficients.*

The formulas for b and a are:

How to solve for b and a

$$b = \frac{n(\Sigma XY) - (\Sigma X)(\Sigma Y)}{n(\Sigma X^2) - (\Sigma X)^2} \tag{12–4}$$

$$a = \frac{\Sigma Y}{n} - b\frac{\Sigma X}{n} \tag{12–5}$$

where:

X is a value of the independent variable.

Y is a value of the dependent variable.

n is the number of items in the sample.

EXAMPLE

Returning to the illustration involving sales calls and units sold for Intrepid, Inc., the sums and the other essential values needed to solve for *a* and *b* are given in Table 12–4.

TABLE 12–4 **Calculations Needed for Determining the Regression Equation**

Sales representative	Sales calls, X	Units sold, Y	X^2	XY	Y^2
Frank Rouses	14	28	196	392	784
Sue Navchek	35	66	1,225	2,310	4,356
Art Seiple	22	38	484	836	1,444
Carma Lopez	29	70	841	2,030	4,900
Todd Bortz	6	22	36	132	484
Sara Jones	15	27	225	405	729
Susan Welch	17	28	289	476	784
Carlos Ramirez	20	47	400	940	2,209
Mike Keil	12	14	144	168	196
Mark Reynolds	29	68	841	1,972	4,624
Total	199	408	4,681	9,661	20,510

What is the regression equation? Interpret it.

Solution

▶ The sums from Table 12–4 and formulas (12–4) and (12–5) are used to show the computations for *a* and *b* in the regression equation.

$$b = \frac{n(\Sigma XY) - (\Sigma X)(\Sigma Y)}{n(\Sigma X^2) - (\Sigma X)^2} = \frac{10(9{,}661) - (199)(408)}{10(4{,}681) - (199)^2} = 2.1387$$

$$a = \frac{\Sigma Y}{n} - b\frac{\Sigma X}{n} = \frac{408}{10} - 2.1387\left(\frac{199}{10}\right) = -1.7601$$

Thus, the regression equation is $Y' = -1.7601 + 2.1387X$. So if a sales representative makes 20 calls in a month, the expected number of units sold is 41.0139, found by $Y' = -1.7601 + 2.1387X = -1.7601 + 2.1387(20)$. The *b* of 2.1387 indicates that for each additional sales call made during the month, sales are expected to increase 2.1387 units. That is, for each sales call made, about two units are sold. The *a* value of -1.7601 indicates that the intercept with the *Y*-axis is below the origin. A literal interpretation is that if no sales calls were made, a negative 1.7601 units would be sold. Note that the value of $X = 0$ is outside the range of values included in the sample and therefore should not be used to estimate the number of units sold. The number of sales calls ranged from 6 to 35.

Drawing the Line of Regression

The least squares equation $Y' = -1.7601 + 2.1387X$ is used to determine the least squares line of regression to be drawn on the scatter diagram. The first sales representative in the sample is Frank Rouses, and he made 14 sales calls. His estimated number of units sold is 28.1817, found by $Y' = -1.7601 + 2.1387X = -1.7601 + 2.1387(14)$. The other points on the regression line can be determined by substituting the particular values of X into the regression equation.

Sales calls, *X*	**Estimated monthly sales, *Y′***	**Equation**
14	28.1817	$Y' = -1.7601 + 2.1387(14)$
35	73.0944	$= -1.7601 + 2.1387(35)$
22	45.2913	$= -1.7601 + 2.1387(22)$
29	60.2622	$= -1.7601 + 2.1387(29)$
6	11.0721	$= -1.7601 + 2.1387(6)$
15	30.3204	$= -1.7601 + 2.1387(15)$
17	34.5978	$= -1.7601 + 2.1387(17)$
20	41.0139	$= -1.7601 + 2.1387(20)$
12	23.9043	$= -1.7601 + 2.1387(12)$
29	60.2622	$= -1.7601 + 2.1387(29)$

The plot $X = 14$, $Y' = 28.1817$ is located by moving to 14 on the X-axis and then going vertically to 28.1817. All the other points are connected to give the straight line. (See Chart 12–10.)

CHART 12–10 **The Line of Regression Drawn in the Scatter Diagram**

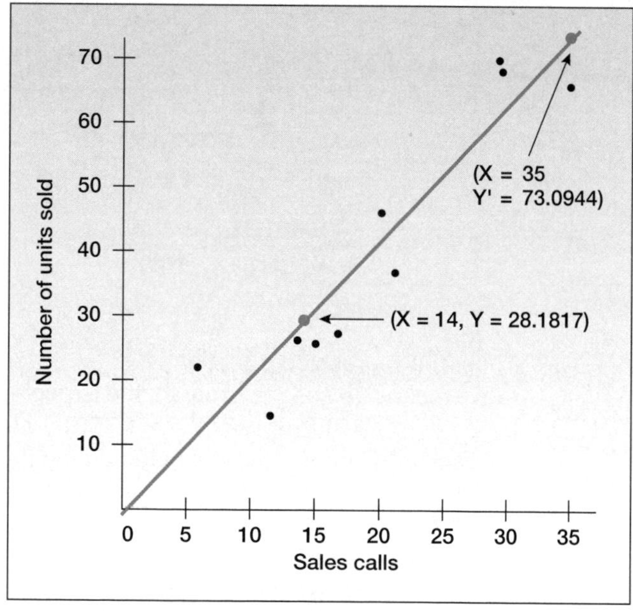

This straight line has some interesting features. As we have discussed, there is no straight line through the data for which the sum of the squared deviations, $\Sigma(Y - Y')^2$, is less. In addition, this line will always pass through the points representing the mean of the X values and the mean of the Y values, that is $\overline{X}$ and $\overline{Y}$. In this example $\overline{X} = 19.9$ and $\overline{Y} = 40.8$.

SELF-REVIEW 12–3

The answers are at the end of the chapter.

Refer to Self-Review 12–1, where an agronomist experimented with different amounts of liquid fertilizer on a sample of equal-size plots. The amounts of fertilizer and the corresponding yields are:

Plot	Amount of fertilizer (tons)	Yield (hundreds of bushels)
A	2	7
B	1	3
C	3	8
D	4	10

Determine the regression equation. Estimate the yield for a plot of land with 3 tons of fertilizer.

EXERCISES

The answers to the odd-numbered exercises are at the end of the book.

Note: It is suggested that you save your values for ΣX, ΣX^2, ΣXY, ΣY, and ΣY^2, as these problems will be referred to later in the chapter.

9. The following sample observations were selected.

X	*Y*
4	4
5	6
3	5
6	7
10	7

a. Determine the regression equation.
b. Determine the value of Y' when X is 7.

10. The following sample observations were selected.

X	*Y*
5	13
3	15
6	7
3	12
4	13
4	11
6	9
8	5

a. Determine the regression equation.
b. Determine the value of Y' when X is 7.

11. The Bradford Electric Illuminating Company is studying the relationship between kilowatt-hours (thousands) and the number of rooms in a private single-family residence. A random sample of 10 homes yielded the following.

Number of rooms	Kilowatt-hours (thousands)	Number of rooms	Kilowatt-hours (thousands)
12	9	8	6
9	7	10	8
14	10	10	10
6	5	5	4
10	8	7	7

a. Determine the regression equation.
b. Determine the number of kilowatt-hours, in thousands, for a six-room house.

12. Mr. James McWhinney, president of Daniel-James Financial Services, believes there is a relationship between the number of client contacts and the dollar amount of sales. To document this assertion, Mr. McWhinney gathered the following sample information. The X column indicates the number of client contacts last month, and the Y column shows the value of sales ($ thousands) last month for each client sampled.

Number of contacts, X	Sales ($ thousands), Y	Number of contacts, X	Sales ($ thousands), Y
14	24	23	30
12	14	48	90
20	28	50	85
16	30	55	120
46	80	50	110

a. Determine the regression equation.
b. Determine the estimated sales if 40 contacts are made.

13. The cover story in a 1994 issue of *Business Week* was entitled "The Best Small Companies." We are interested in the current results of the companies' sales and earnings. A random sample of 12 companies was selected and the sales and earnings, in millions of dollars are reported below.

Company	Sales ($ millions)	Earnings ($ millions)
Papa John's International	$89.2	$ 4.9
Applied Innovation	18.6	4.4
Integracare	18.2	1.3
Wall Data	71.7	8.0
Davidson Associates	58.6	6.6
Chico's Fas	46.8	4.1
Checkmate Electronics	17.5	2.6
Royal Grip	11.9	1.7
M-Wave	19.6	3.5
Serving-N-Slide	51.2	8.2
Daig	28.6	6.0
Cobra Golf	69.2	12.8

Source: *Business Week,* May 23, 1994, p. 101.

Let sales be the independent variable and earnings be the dependent variable.

a. Draw a scatter diagram.
b. Compute the coefficient of correlation.
c. Compute the coefficient of determination.
d. Interpret your findings in parts *b* and *c.*
e. Determine the regression equation.
f. For a small company with $50.0 million in sales, estimate the earnings.

14. We are studying mutual bond funds for the purpose of investing in several funds. For this particular study we want to focus on the assets of a fund and its five-year performance. The question is: Can the five-year rate of return be estimated based on the assets of the fund? Ten mutual funds were selected at random, and their assets and rates of return are shown below.

Fund	Assets ($ millions)	Return (%)
AARP High Quality Bond	$622.2	10.8
Babson Bond L	160.4	11.3
Compass Capital Fixed Income	275.7	11.4
Galaxy Bond Retail	433.2	9.1
Keystone Custodian B-1	437.9	9.2
MFS Bond A	494.5	11.6
Nichols Income	158.3	9.5
T. Raive Price Short-term	681.0	8.2
Thompson Income B	241.3	6.8

Source: *Business Week,* February 21, 1994, pp. 93–103.

a. Draw a scatter diagram.
b. Compute the coefficient of correlation.
c. Calculate the coefficient of determination.
d. Write a brief report of your findings for parts *b* and *c.*
e. Determine the regression equation. Use assets as the independent variable.
f. For a fund with $400.0 million in assets, determine the five-year rate of return (in percent).

THE STANDARD ERROR OF ESTIMATE

Note in the preceding scatter diagram (Chart 12–10) that all of the points do not lie on the regression line. If they all were on the line, and if the number of observations were sufficiently large, there would be no error in estimating the number of units sold. To put it another way, if all the points were on the regression line, units sold could be predicted with 100 percent accuracy. Thus, there would be no error in predicting the Y variable based on an X variable. This is true in the following hypothetical case (see Chart 12–11). Theoretically, if $X = 6$, then an exact Y of 200 could be predicted with 100 percent confidence. Or if $X = 10$, then $Y = 800$. Because there is no difference between the observed values and the predicted values, there is no error in this estimate.

CHART 12–11 **Example of Perfect Prediction: Horsepower of Motor and Cost of Electricity**

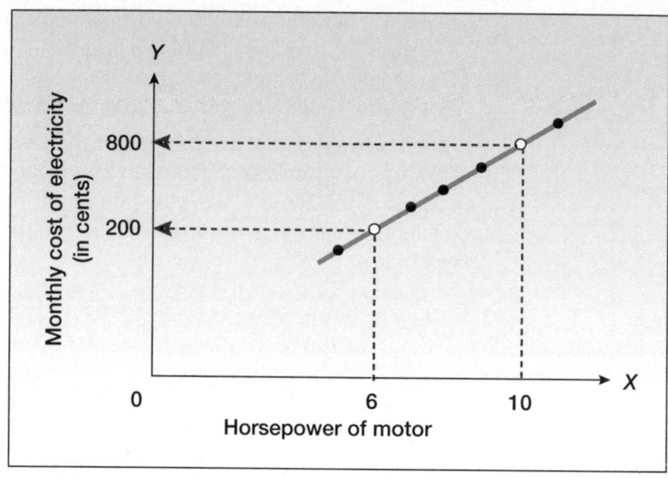

Perfect prediction unrealistic in business

Perfect prediction in problems involving economics and business is practically impossible. For example, the revenue for the year from gasoline sales (Y) based on the number of automobile registrations (X) as of a certain date could no doubt be approximated fairly closely, but the prediction would not be exact to the nearest dollar, or probably even to the nearest thousand dollars. Even predictions of tensile strength of steel wires based on the outside diameters of the wires are not always exact (due to slight differences in the composition of the steel).

What is needed, then, is a measure that would indicate how precise the prediction of Y is based on X or, conversely, how inaccurate the estimate might be. This measure is called the **standard error of estimate.** The standard error of estimate, symbolized by $s_{y \cdot x}$, is the same concept as the standard deviation discussed in Chapter 4. The standard deviation measures the dispersion around the mean. The standard error of estimate measures the dispersion about an average line, the regression line.

Standard error of estimate defined

Standard error of estimate Measures the scatter, or dispersion, of the observed values around the line of regression.

The standard error of estimate is found by the following equation. (Note that the equation is quite similar to the one for the standard deviation of a sample.)

Formula for the standard error

$$s_{y \cdot x} = \sqrt{\frac{\Sigma(Y - Y')^2}{n - 2}} \qquad (12\text{–}6)$$

EXAMPLE

The symbol for the standard error of estimate ($s_{y \cdot x}$) represents the standard deviation of the *Y*s based on the *X*s. Returning to the problem involving the number of sales calls and units sold, the first step is to determine each value of Y' (the point on the straight line) for each *X* value. These Y' points were computed previously in order to plot the straight line on the scatter diagram (Chart 12–10). The next step is to subtract each Y' value from its corresponding *Y* value. These differences are squared and then summed. (See Table 12–5.)

TABLE 12–5 **Computations Needed for the Standard Error of Estimate**

Sales calls, X	Actual units sold, Y	Estimated units sold, Y'	Deviation, $(Y - Y')$	Deviation squared, $(Y - Y')^2$
14	28	28.1817	−0.1817	0.0330
35	66	73.0944	−7.0944	50.3305
22	38	45.2913	−7.2913	53.1631
29	70	60.2622	9.7378	94.8247
6	22	11.0721	10.9279	119.4190
15	27	30.3204	−3.3204	11.0251
17	28	34.5978	−6.5978	43.5310
20	47	41.0139	5.9861	35.8334
12	14	23.9043	−9.9043	98.0952
29	68	60.2622	7.7378	59.8735
			0.0000	566.1285

What is the standard error of estimate?

Solution ► The standard error of estimate is 8.412, determined by applying formula (12–6).

$$s_{y \cdot x} = \sqrt{\frac{\Sigma(Y - Y')^2}{n - 2}}$$

$$= \sqrt{\frac{566.1285}{10 - 2}}$$

$$= 8.412$$

The deviations $(Y - Y')$ are vertical deviations from the regression line. To illustrate, the 10 deviations from Table 12–5 are shown in Chart 12–12. Note in Table 12–5 that the sum of the deviations is equal to zero, indicating that the positive deviations (above the regression line on the scatter diagram) are offset by the negative deviations (below the line).

CHART 12–12 **Vertical Distances between Scatter Points and the Line of Regression**

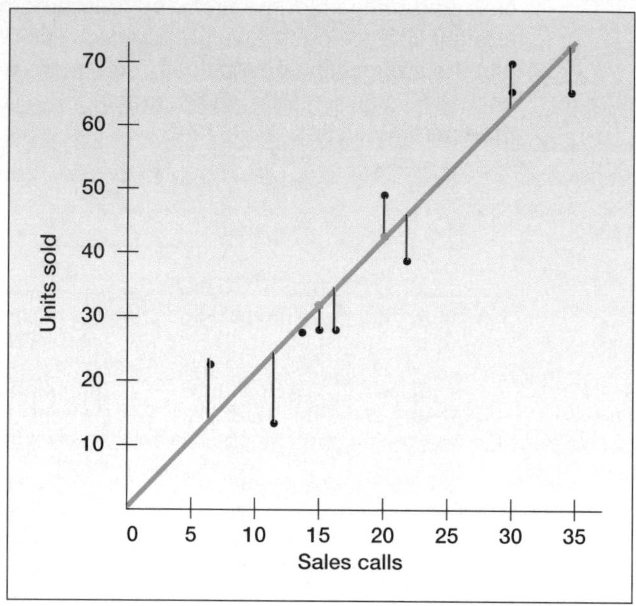

Formula (12–6) for the standard error of estimate was applied to show the similarity in concept and computation between the standard deviation and the standard error of estimate. Suppose a large number of observations are being studied, and the numbers are large. Computing each Y' point on the regression line and then squaring the differences—that is, $(Y - Y')^2$—would be rather tedious. The following formula is algebraically equivalent to formula (12–6) but is much easier to use.

More convenient formula for the standard error

$$s_{y \cdot x} = \sqrt{\frac{\Sigma Y^2 - a(\Sigma Y) - b(\Sigma XY)}{n - 2}} \qquad (12\text{–}7)$$

The squares, sums, and other numbers for the examples concerning number of sales calls and units sold were calculated in Table 12–4. Inserting these values into the formula:

$$s_{y \cdot x} = \sqrt{\frac{20{,}510 - (-1.7601)(408) - 2.1387(9{,}661)}{10 - 2}}$$

$$= 8.412$$

This is the same standard error of estimate as computed previously.

For a better understanding of the application of the standard error of estimate of 8.412 in regression analysis, the underlying assumptions about linear regression and correlation should be stated.

ASSUMPTIONS UNDERLYING LINEAR REGRESSION

Assumptions required to apply linear regression analysis

1. For each value of X, there is a group of Y values, and these Y values are *normally distributed.*
2. The *means* of these normal distributions of Y values all lie on the straight line of regression.
3. The *standard deviations* of these normal distributions are *equal.*
4. The Y values are statistically *independent.* This means that in the selection of a sample, the Y values chosen for a particular X value do not depend on the Y values for any other X value.

Chart 12–13 illustrates these assumptions. Note that these statements are true for each of the three X values: (1) The Y values are normally distributed. (2) The means are all on the line of regression. (3) The standard deviations, as represented by the standard error of estimate $s_{y \cdot x}$, are equal.

Visual presentation of the assumptions

CHART 12–13 Assumptions Underlying Regression Depicted Graphically

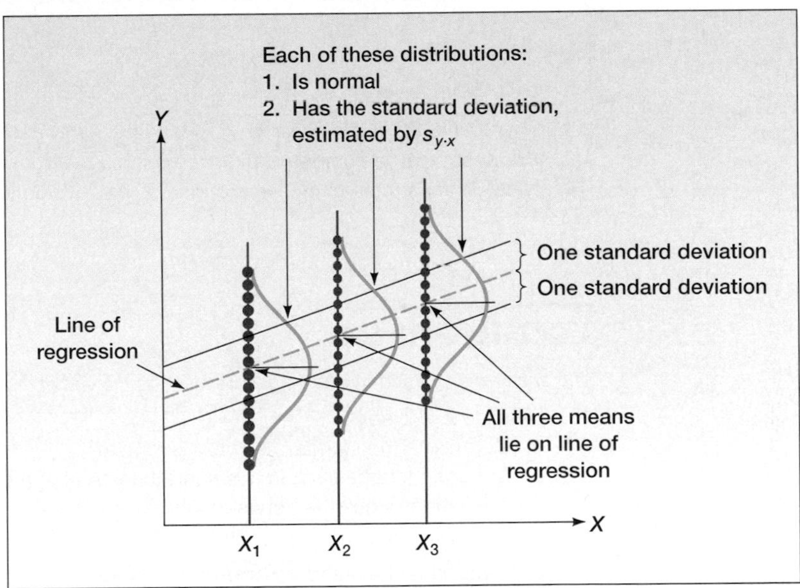

Recall from Chapter 7 that if the values are somewhat normally distributed:

$\overline{X} \pm 1s$ encompasses approximately the middle 68 percent of the values.

$\overline{X} \pm 2s$ encompasses approximately the middle 95.5 percent of the values.

$\overline{X} \pm 3s$ encompasses approximately the middle 99.7 percent of the values.

If the distribution is highly skewed, these relationships will not hold.

The same relationships exist between the average predicted value, Y', and the standard error of estimate, $s_{y \cdot x}$. Again, if the scatter about the regression line is somewhat normally distributed and the sample is large, then:

$Y' \pm 1s_{y \cdot x}$ encompasses the middle 68 percent of the observed values.

$Y' \pm 2s_{y \cdot x}$ encompasses the middle 95.5 percent of the observed values.

$Y' \pm 3s_{y \cdot x}$ encompasses the middle 99.7 percent of the observed values.

We can now relate these assumptions and the standard error of estimate to our sales calls and units sold experiment. The difference between predicted sales, Y', and actual sales would be less than one standard error (± 8.412 units) for 68 percent of the salespeople. Further, 95 percent of the predictions would not vary more than 2 (8.412) or ± 16.824 units. More than 99 percent of weekly sales predictions would be "off" by no more than 3 (8.412) or ± 25.236 units. Hence, $s_{y \cdot x}$ is to a regression line what s is to a set of X values. Just as s measures the spread of Xs around the mean, $s_{y \cdot x}$ measures the spread of points around a regression line.

SELF-REVIEW 12–4

The answers are at the end of the chapter.

Refer to Self-Review 12–3.

1. Determine the standard error of estimate.

2. Suppose a large number of plots were included in the experiment (instead of just four). Ninety-five percent of our predictions of yield would lie between what two values?

EXERCISES

The answers to the odd-numbered exercises are at the end of the book.

15. Refer to Exercise 9.
    a. Determine the standard error of estimate.
    b. Suppose a large sample is selected (instead of just five). About 68 percent of the predictions would be between what two values?
16. Refer to Exercise 10.
    a. Determine the standard error of estimate.
    b. Suppose a large sample is selected (instead of just eight). About 95 percent of the predictions would be between what two values?
17. Refer to Exercise 11.
    a. Determine the standard error of estimate.
    b. Suppose a large sample is selected (instead of just 10). About 95 percent of the predictions regarding kilowatt-hours would occur between what two values?
18. Refer to Exercise 12.
    a. Determine the standard error of estimate.
    b. Suppose a large sample is selected (instead of just 10). About 95 percent of the predictions regarding sales would occur between what two values?

CONFIDENCE INTERVALS AND PREDICTION INTERVALS

The standard error of estimate is a valid measure to use in setting confidence intervals when the sample size is large and the scatter around the regression line approximates the normal distribution. In our example involving the number of sales calls and the number of units sold, the sample size is small; hence, we need a correction factor to account for the size of the sample. In addition, when we move away from the mean of the independent variable, our estimates are subject to more variation, and we also need to correct for this.

We are interested in providing interval estimates of two types. The first, which is called a **confidence interval,** reports the *mean* value for a given X. The second type of estimate is called a **prediction interval,** and it reports the range of values for a *particular* value of X. To explain further, suppose we estimate the salary of executives in the retail industry based on their years of experience. If we want an interval estimate of the salary of *all* retail executives with 20 years of experience, we calculate a confidence interval. If we want an estimate of Curtis Bender, a particular retail executive with 20 years experience, we calculate a prediction interval.

To determine the confidence interval for the mean value of Y for a given X, the formula is:

How to determine the confidence interval for the mean of Y, given X

$$Y' \pm t(s_{y \cdot x}) \sqrt{\frac{1}{n} + \frac{(X - \overline{X})^2}{\Sigma X^2 - \frac{(\Sigma X)^2}{n}}} \quad (12\text{–}8)$$

where, in this problem:

- Y' is the predicted value for any selected X value.
- X is any selected value of X.
- $\overline{X}$ is the mean of the Xs, found by $\Sigma X/n$.
- n is the number of observations.
- $s_{y \cdot x}$ is the standard error of estimate.
- t is the value of t from Appendix F for $n - 2$ degrees of freedom.

It is sufficient to again note that the concept of t was developed by William Gossett in the early 1900s. He noticed that $\overline{X} \pm z(s)$ was not precisely correct for small samples. He observed, for example, for samples of size 120, that 95 percent of the items fell within $\overline{X} \pm 1.98s$ instead of $\overline{X} \pm 1.96s$. This is not too critical, but note what happens as the sample size becomes smaller:

df	*t*
120	1.980
60	2.000
21	2.080
10	2.228
3	3.182

This is logical. The smaller the sample, the larger the possible error. The increase in the *t* value compensates for this possibility.

EXAMPLE

We return to the problem of sales calls and the number of units sold for Intrepid, Inc. Determine a 95 percent confidence interval for all sales representatives that make 25 calls. Determine a 95 percent prediction interval for Sheila Baker, who made 25 sales calls.

Solution

▸ Table 12–6 includes the necessary totals, and formula (12–8) is used to determine the computations for the confidence interval for the mean of *Y* given *X*.

TABLE 12–6 Calculations Needed for Determining the Confidence and Prediction Intervals

Sales representative	Sales calls, *X*	Units sold, *Y*	X^2	*XY*	Y^2
Frank Rouses	14	28	196	392	784
Sue Navchek	35	66	1,225	2,310	4,356
Art Seiple	22	38	484	836	1,444
Carma Lopez	29	70	841	2,030	4,900
Todd Bortz	6	22	36	132	484
Sara Jones	15	27	225	405	729
Susan Welch	17	28	289	476	784
Carlos Ramirez	20	47	400	940	2,209
Mike Keil	12	14	144	168	196
Mark Reynolds	29	68	841	1,972	4,624
Total	199	408	4,681	9,661	20,510

The first step is to determine the estimated number of units sold for a sales representative who made 25 calls. It is 51.7074, found by $Y' = -1.7601 + 2.1387X = -1.7601 + 2.1387(25)$.

The *t* value associated with the 95 percent level of confidence and $n - 2 = 10 - 2 = 8$ degrees of freedom is 2.306. By our computations, $s_{y \cdot x} = 8.412$, $X = 25$, $\Sigma X = 199$, and $\Sigma X^2 = 4{,}681$. In addition, $\bar{X} = \Sigma X/n = 199/10 = 19.9$. Inserting these values in formula (12–8), we can determine the confidence interval.

$$Y' \pm t(s_{y \cdot x})\sqrt{\frac{1}{n} + \frac{(X-\bar{X})^2}{\Sigma X^2 - \frac{(\Sigma X)^2}{n}}} = 51.7074 \pm 2.306(8.412)\sqrt{\frac{1}{10} + \frac{(25-19.9)^2}{4{,}681 - \frac{(199)^2}{10}}}$$

$$= 51.7074 \pm 2.306(8.412)\sqrt{0.13608}$$

$$= 51.7074 \pm 7.1558$$

So the 95 percent confidence interval for the number of units sold by sales representatives who made 25 calls is 51.7074 ± 7.1558, or 44.5516 units up to 58.8632 units.

To determine the prediction interval for a particular value of *Y* for a given value of *X*, formula (12–8) is modified slightly: A 1 is added under the radical. The formula becomes:

Formula for the prediction interval for an individual Y, given X

$$Y' \pm t(s_{y \cdot x}) \sqrt{1 + \frac{1}{n} + \frac{(X - \bar{X})^2}{\Sigma X^2 - \frac{(\Sigma X)^2}{n}}} \tag{12–9}$$

Suppose we want to estimate the sales for Sheila Baker, who made 25 sales calls. The 95 percent prediction interval is determined as follows:

$$Y' \pm t(s_{y \cdot x}) \sqrt{1 + \frac{1}{n} + \frac{(X - \bar{X})^2}{\Sigma X^2 - \frac{(\Sigma X)^2}{n}}} = 51.7074 \pm (2.306)(8.412) \sqrt{1 + \frac{1}{10} + \frac{(25 - 19.9)^2}{4{,}681 - \frac{(199)^2}{10}}}$$

$$= 51.7074 \pm (2.306)(8.412)\sqrt{1.13608}$$

$$= 51.7074 \pm 20.6758$$

$$= 31.0316 \text{ up to } 72.3832$$

We conclude that the probability is .95 that the number of units sold by Ms. Baker is between 31.0316 units and 72.3832 units. This interval is quite large. It is much larger than the interval for all salespeople who make 25 calls. It is logical, however, that there should be more variation in the sales estimate for an individual than for a group. What can we do to make the interval smaller? We can decrease the level of confidence from 95 percent to, say, 90 percent, or a more likely alternative would be to increase the sample size.

Again, there is an important distinction between a confidence interval and a prediction interval. A confidence interval refers to all cases with a given value of X and is computed using formula (12–8). A prediction interval refers to a particular case for a given value of X and is computed using formula (12–9). The prediction interval will have the wider range, as a result of the extra 1 under the radical.

SELF-REVIEW 12–5

The answers are at the end of the chapter.

Sample data for Self-Reviews 12–3 and 12–4 are repeated below.

Plot	Amount of fertilizer (tons), X	Yield (hundreds of bushels), Y
A	2	7
B	1	3
C	3	8
D	4	10

The regression equation was computed to be $Y' = 1.5 + 2.2X$ (in hundreds of bushels). The standard error was computed to be 0.9487 (in hundreds of bushels).

1. Keeping in mind that this is a small sample, determine the .90 confidence interval for a group of plots that received exactly three tons of fertilizer each.
2. Interpret your findings.

EXERCISES

The answers to the odd-numbered exercises are at the end of the book.

19. Refer to Exercise 9.
    a. Determine the .95 confidence interval for the mean predicted value of 7.
    b. Determine the .95 prediction interval for an individual predicted value of 7.
20. Refer to Exercise 10.
    a. Determine the .95 confidence interval for the mean predicted value of 7.
    b. Determine the .95 prediction interval for an individual predicted value of 7.
21. Refer to Exercise 11.
    a. Determine the .95 confidence interval, in thousands of kilowatt-hours, for the mean of all six-room homes.
    b. Determine the .95 prediction interval, in thousands of kilowatt-hours, for a particular six-room home.
22. Refer to Exercise 12.
    a. Determine the .95 confidence interval, in thousands of dollars, for the mean of all sales personnel who make 40 contacts.
    b. Determine the .95 prediction interval, in thousands of dollars, for a particular salesperson who makes 40 contacts.

MORE ON THE COEFFICIENT OF DETERMINATION

Formula (12–1) is a convenient computational formula to determine the coefficient of correlation, r. The coefficient of determination is found by squaring the coefficient of correlation.

To further examine the basic concept of the coefficient of determination, suppose there is interest in the relationship between years on job, X and weekly production, Y. Sample data revealed:

Employee	Years on job, X	Weekly production, Y
Gordon	14	6
James	7	5
Ford	3	3
Salter	15	9
Artes	11	7

The sample data were plotted in a scatter diagram. Since the relationship between X and Y appears to be linear, a straight line was drawn through the plots (see Chart 12–14). The equation is $Y' = a + bX$ or $2 + 0.4X$.

Note in Chart 12–14 that if we were to use that straight line to predict weekly production for an employee, in no case would our prediction be exact. That is, there would be some error in each of our predictions. As an example, for Gordon, who has been with the company 14 years, we would predict weekly production to be 7.6 units; however, he only produces 6 units.

CHART 12–14 Observed Data and Straight Line

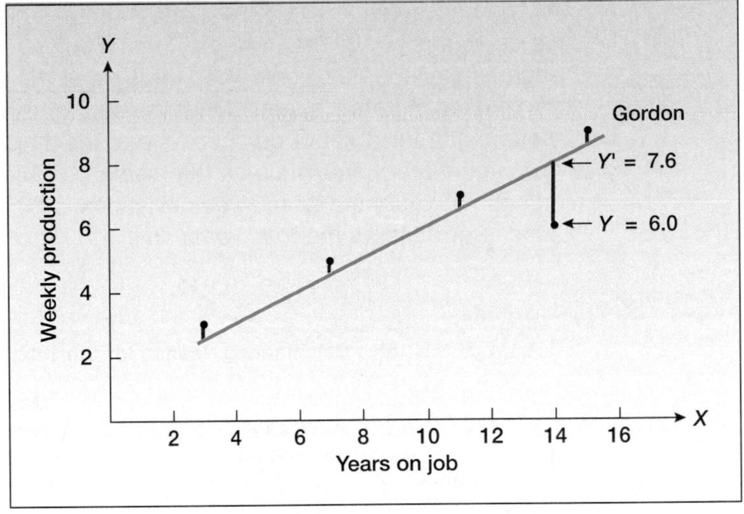

Unexplained variation

To measure the overall error in our prediction, every deviation from the straight line is squared and the squares summed. The predicted point on the straight line is designated Y', read Y prime, and the observed point is designated Y. For Gordon, $(Y - Y')^2 = (6 - 7.6)^2 = (-1.6)^2 = 2.56$. Logically, this variation cannot be explained by the independent variable, so it is referred to as the *unexplained variation.* Specifically, we cannot explain why Gordon's production of 6 units is 1.6 units below his predicted production of 7.6 units, based on the number of years he has been on the job.

The sum of the squared deviations, $\Sigma(Y - Y')^2$, is 4.00. (See Table 12–7.) The term $\Sigma(Y - Y')^2 = 4.00$ is the variation in Y (production) that cannot be predicted from X. It is the "unexplained" variation in Y.

TABLE 12–7 Computations Needed for the Unexplained Variation

	X	Y	Y'	$Y - Y'$	$(Y - Y')^2$
Gordon	14	6	7.6	−1.6	2.56
James	7	5	4.8	0.2	0.04
Ford	3	3	3.2	−0.2	0.04
Salter	15	9	8.0	1.0	1.00
Artes	11	7	6.4	0.6	0.36
Total	50	30		0.0*	4.00

*Must be 0.

Now suppose *only* the Y values (weekly production, in this problem) are known and we want to predict production for every employee. The actual production figures for the employees are 6, 5, 3, 9, and 7 (from Table 12–7). To make these predictions, we could assign the mean weekly production (6 units, found by $\Sigma Y/n = 30/5 = 6$) to each employee. This would keep the sum of the squared prediction errors at a minimum. (Recall from Chapter 3 that the sum of the squared deviations from the arithmetic mean for a set of numbers is smaller than the sum of the squared deviations from any other value, such as the median.) Table 12–8 shows the necessary calculations. The sum of the squared deviations is 20, as shown in Table 12–8. The value 20 is referred to as the *total variation in Y*.

Total variation in Y

TABLE 12–8 Calculations Needed for the Total Variation in Y

Name	Weekly production, Y	Mean weekly production, $\bar{Y}$	$Y - \bar{Y}$	Mean squared, $(Y - \bar{Y})^2$
Gordon	6	6	0	0
James	5	6	−1	1
Ford	3	6	−3	9
Salter	9	6	3	9
Artes	7	6	1	1
Total			0*	20

*Must be 0.

What we did to arrive at the total variation in Y is shown diagrammatically in Chart 12–15.

CHART 12–15 Plots Showing Deviations from the Mean of Y

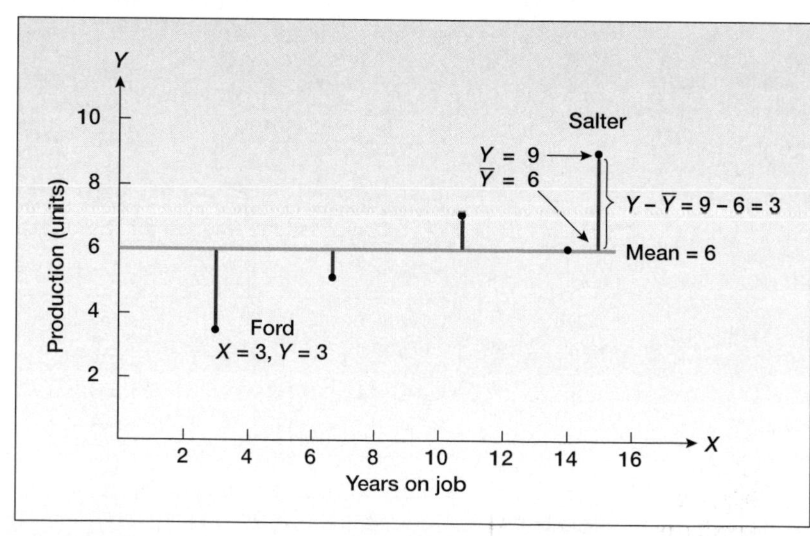

Explained variation

Coefficient of determination

Logically, the total variation in Y can be subdivided into unexplained variation and explained variation. To arrive at the explained variation, since we know the total variation and unexplained variation, we simply subtract: Explained variation = Total variation − Unexplained variation. Dividing the explained variation by the total variation gives the coefficient of determination, r^2, which is a proportion. In terms of a formula:

$$r^2 = \frac{\text{Total variation} - \text{Unexplained variation}}{\text{Total variation}} = \frac{\Sigma(Y-\overline{Y})^2 - \Sigma(Y-Y')^2}{\Sigma(Y-\overline{Y})^2} \quad (12\text{–}10)$$

In this problem:

$$r^2 = \frac{20-4}{20} = \frac{16}{20} = .80$$

Table 12–8

Table 12–7

Explained variation

Total variation

As mentioned, .80 is a proportion. We say that 80 percent of the variation in weekly production, Y, is determined, or accounted for, by its linear relationship with X (years on the job).

As a check, the computational formula (12–1) for the coefficient of correlation could be used. Squaring r gives the coefficient of determination. Exercise 23 offers a check on the preceding problem.

EXERCISES

The answers to the odd-numbered exercises are at the end of the book.

23. Using the preceding problem, involving years on the job and weekly production, verify that the coefficient of determination is in fact .80.

24. The number of shares of Icom, Inc. that turned over during a month, and the price at the end of the month, are listed in the following table. Also, the Y' plots on the straight line going through observed data are given.

Turnover (thousands of shares), X	Actual price, Y	Estimated price, Y'
4	\$2	\$2.7
1	1	0.6
5	4	3.4
3	2	2.0
2	1	1.3

a. Draw a scatter diagram. Plot a straight line through the dots.
b. Compute the coefficient of determination using formula (12–10).
c. As a check, use the computational formula for r.
d. Interpret the coefficient of determination.

THE RELATIONSHIP AMONG THE COEFFICIENT OF CORRELATION, THE COEFFICIENT OF DETERMINATION, AND THE STANDARD ERROR OF ESTIMATE

In an earlier section, we discussed the standard error of estimate, which measures how close the actual values are to the regression line. When the standard error is small, it indicates that the two variables are closely related. In the calculation of the standard error, the key term is $\Sigma(Y - Y')^2$. If the value of this term is "small," then the standard error will also be small.

The correlation coefficient measures the strength of the association between two variables. When the points on the scatter diagram appear close to the straight line, we note that the correlation coefficient tends to be "large." Thus, the standard error of estimate and the coefficient of correlation relate the same information but use a different scale to report the strength of the association. However, both measures involve the term $\Sigma(Y - Y')^2$.

We also noted that the square of the correlation coefficient is called the coefficient of determination. The coefficient of determination measures the percent of the variation in Y that is explained by the variation in X.

A convenient vehicle for showing the relationship between these three measures is an ANOVA table. This table is similar to the analysis of variance table developed in Chapter 11. In that chapter, the variation was divided into two components: that due to the *treatments* and that due to *random error.* The concept is similar in regression analysis. The total variation, $\Sigma(Y - \overline{Y})^2$, is divided into two components: (1) that explained by the *regression* (explained by the independent variable) and (2) the *error,* or unexplained variation. These two categories are identified in the first column of the ANOVA table that follows. The column headed "DF" refers to the degrees of freedom associated with each category. The total number of degrees of freedom is found by $n - 1$. The number of degrees of freedom in the regression is 1, since there is only one independent variable. The number of degrees of freedom associated with the error term is $n - 2$. The term "SS" located in the middle of the ANOVA table refers to the sum of squares—the variation. The terms are computed as follows:

$$\text{Regression} = \quad \text{SSR} = \Sigma(Y' - \overline{Y})^2$$

$$\text{Error variation} = \quad \text{SSE} = \Sigma(Y - Y')^2$$

$$\text{Total variation} = \text{SS total} = \Sigma(Y - \overline{Y})^2$$

The format for the ANOVA table is:

Source	DF	SS	MS
Regression	1	SSR	SSR/1
Error	$n - 2$	SSE	SSE/($n - 2$)
Total	$n - 1$	SS total*	

*SS total = SSR + SSE.

The coefficient of determination, r^2, can be obtained directly from the ANOVA table by:

$$r^2 = \frac{\text{SSR}}{\text{SS total}} = 1 - \frac{\text{SSE}}{\text{SS total}} \qquad (12\text{–}11)$$

The term "SSR/SS total" is the proportion of the variation in Y *explained* by the independent variable, X. Note the effect of the SSE term on r^2. As SSE decreases, r^2 will increase. Conversely, as the standard error decreases, the r^2 term increases.

The standard error of estimate can also be obtained from the ANOVA table using the following equation:

$$s_{y \cdot x} = \sqrt{\frac{\text{SSE}}{n-2}} \qquad (12\text{–}12)$$

The problem involving the number of sales calls and units sold is used to illustrate the computations of the coefficient of determination and the standard error of estimate from an ANOVA table.

EXAMPLE

The data for number of sales calls and units sold for a sample of 10 salespeople from Table 12–1 are repeated here.

Sales representative	Sales calls	Units sold
Frank Rouses	14	28
Sue Navchek	35	66
Art Seiple	22	38
Carma Lopez	29	70
Todd Bortz	6	22
Sara Jones	15	27
Susan Welch	17	28
Carlos Ramirez	20	47
Mike Keil	12	14
Mark Reynolds	29	68

The following ANOVA table is part of the regression output from the MINITAB system. It reports the regression equation, the standard error of estimate, and the coefficient of determination.

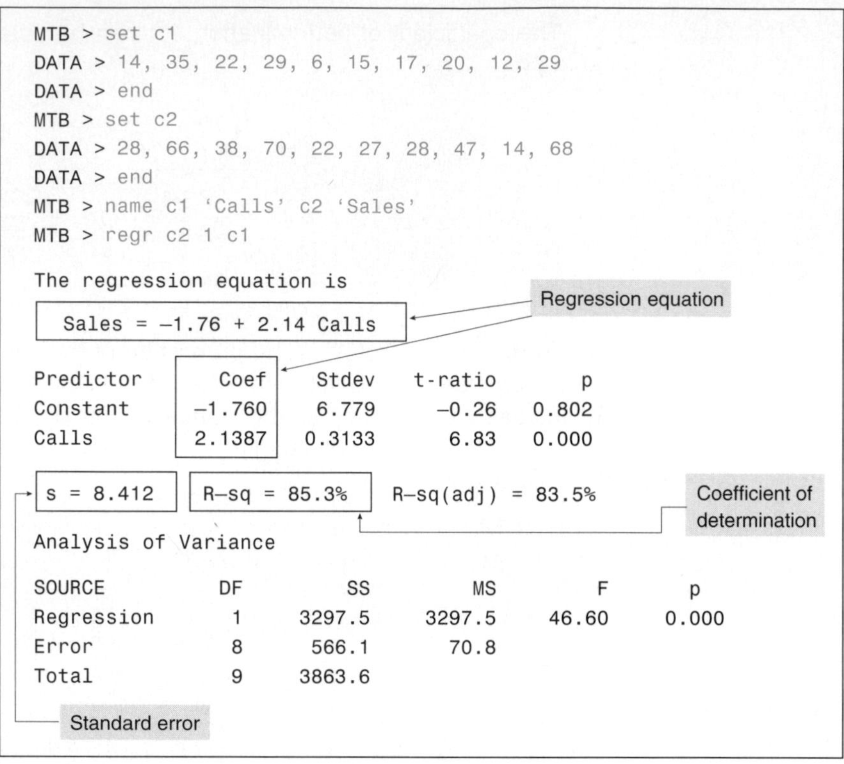

```
MTB > set c1
DATA > 14, 35, 22, 29, 6, 15, 17, 20, 12, 29
DATA > end
MTB > set c2
DATA > 28, 66, 38, 70, 22, 27, 28, 47, 14, 68
DATA > end
MTB > name c1 'Calls' c2 'Sales'
MTB > regr c2 1 c1

The regression equation is
  Sales = -1.76 + 2.14 Calls

Predictor       Coef     Stdev    t-ratio        p
Constant      -1.760     6.779      -0.26    0.802
Calls         2.1387    0.3133       6.83    0.000

s = 8.412     R-sq = 85.3%     R-sq(adj) = 83.5%

Analysis of Variance

SOURCE          DF         SS         MS         F        p
Regression       1     3297.5     3297.5     46.60    0.000
Error            8      566.1       70.8
Total            9     3863.6
```


Locate the standard error of estimate, the coefficient of determination, and the regression equation on the output. Then determine the coefficient of determination and the standard error of estimate from formulas (12–11) and (12–12). What is the coefficient of correlation?

Solution ▶ The coefficient of determination is .853, found by:

$$r^2 = \frac{\text{SSR}}{\text{SS total}} = \frac{3{,}297.5}{3{,}863.6} = .853$$

This is approximately the same value as computed on page 483. Again, we can say that about 85.3 percent of the total variation in the dependent variable (units sold) is explained, or accounted for, by the variation in the independent variable (sales calls). If we had needed the coefficient of correlation, r, we would take the square root of the coefficient of determination: $\sqrt{r^2} = \sqrt{.853} = .924$, indicating a strong relationship between number of sales calls and units sold. (This value is also the same as the one computed earlier in the chapter.)

The standard error of estimate is determined as follows:

$$s_{y \cdot x} = \sqrt{\frac{\text{SSE}}{n-2}} = \sqrt{\frac{566.1}{10-2}} = 8.412$$

It is the same as computed on page 499 of this chapter.

Again, we see how efficient a computer system is in supplying us with essential statistical measures.

CHAPTER OUTLINE

I. Correlation analysis—interval or ratio level of measurement.
   A. The purpose is to find the degree of association between two variables.
   B. There are two measures of association.
      1. The correlation coefficient, *r*, measures the degree of linear association between *X* and *Y*. It can assume any value between −1 and +1. The formula for *r* is:

$$r = \frac{n(\Sigma XY) - (\Sigma X)(\Sigma Y)}{\sqrt{[n(\Sigma X^2) - (\Sigma X)^2][n(\Sigma Y^2) - (\Sigma Y)^2]}} \qquad (12\text{–}1)$$

      2. The coefficient of determination, r^2, is the proportion of the variation in *Y* explained by *X*. It can assume any value between 0 and 1 inclusive.
   C. Testing the significance of *r*: Is the correlation in the population zero? For small samples Student's *t* distribution is the test statistic:

$$t = \frac{r\sqrt{n-2}}{\sqrt{1-r^2}} \qquad (12\text{–}2)$$

II. Regression analysis.
   A. Its purpose is to determine the regression equation to predict the value of one variable (designated by *Y* and called the dependent variable) based on another variable (denoted by *X* and called the independent variable).
   B. The procedure.
      1. Select a sample from the population, and list the paired data (*X* and *Y*) for each observation.
      2. Draw a scatter diagram to give a visual portrayal of the relationship.
      3. Determine the regression equation mathematically, which has the form $Y' = a + bX$, where:

         Y' is the mean predicted value of the *Y* variable for any *X* value.

         a is the *Y*-intercept, or the estimated value of *Y* when $X = 0$.

         b called the slope of the line, is the mean charge in Y' for each change of one unit in *X*.

         X is any value of *X*.

      4. The computations for *a* and *b* are:

$$b = \frac{n(\Sigma XY) - (\Sigma X)(\Sigma Y)}{n(\Sigma X^2) - (\Sigma X)^2} \qquad (12\text{–}4)$$

$$a = \frac{\Sigma Y}{n} - b\left(\frac{\Sigma X}{n}\right) \qquad (12\text{–}5)$$

      5. The standard error of estimate measures the variation around the regression line. Two formulas used to determine the standard error are:

$$s_{y \cdot x} = \sqrt{\frac{\Sigma Y^2 - a(\Sigma Y) - b(\Sigma XY)}{n-2}} \qquad (12\text{–}7)$$

$$s_{y \cdot x} = \sqrt{\frac{\Sigma(Y - Y')^2}{n-2}} \qquad (12\text{–}6)$$

6. The confidence interval for the mean value of Y for a given value of X is found by:

$$Y' \pm t(s_{y \cdot x}) \sqrt{\frac{1}{n} + \frac{(X - \bar{X})^2}{\Sigma X^2 - \frac{(\Sigma X)^2}{n}}}$$

To determine the prediction interval for an individual value of Y for a given value of X:

$$Y' \pm t(s_{y \cdot x}) \sqrt{1 + \frac{1}{n} + \frac{(X - \bar{X})^2}{\Sigma X^2 - \frac{(\Sigma X)^2}{n}}}$$

EXERCISES

The answers to the odd-numbered exercises are at the end of the book.

25. A sample of 30 used cars sold by Northcut Motors in 1992 revealed that the correlation between the selling price and the number of miles driven was −.45. At the .05 significance level, can we conclude that there is a negative association in the population between the two variables?
26. For a sample of 32 large U.S. cities, the correlation between the mean number of square feet per office worker and the mean monthly rental rate in the central business district is −.363. At the .05 significance level, can we conclude that there is a negative association in the population between the two variables?
27. What is the relationship between the amount spent per week on food and the size of the family? Do larger families spend more on food? A sample of 10 families in the Chicago area revealed the following figures for family size and the amount spent on food last week.

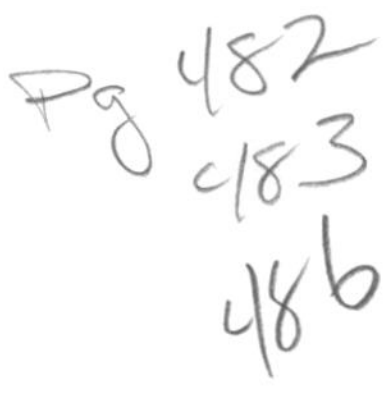

Family size	Amount spent on food	Family size	Amount spent on food
3	$ 99	3	$111
6	104	4	74
5	151	4	91
6	129	5	119
6	142	3	91

a. Compute the coefficient of correlation.
b. Determine the coefficient of determination.
c. Can we conclude that there is a positive association between the amount spent on food and the family size? Use the .05 significance level.

28. A sample of 12 homes sold last week in St. Paul, Minnesota, is selected. Can we conclude that as the size of the home (reported below in thousands of square feet) increases, the selling price (reported in $ thousands) also increases?

Home size (thousands of square feet)	Selling price ($ thousands)	Home size (thousands of square feet)	Selling price ($ thousands)
1.4	100	1.3	110
1.3	110	0.8	85
1.2	105	1.2	105
1.1	120	0.9	75
1.4	80	1.1	70
1.0	105	1.1	95

a. Compute the coefficient of correlation.
b. Determine the coefficient of determination.
c. Can we conclude that there is a positive association between the size of the home and the selling price? Use the .05 significance level.

29. Is there a relationship between the length of a toll road and the cost per mile to drive the toll road? The following information was recently reported.

Toll road	Length (miles)	Cost per mile (cents)
Massachusetts Turnpike	123.0	4.15
Pennsylvania (east-west)	358.9	4.10
Pennsylvania (northeast)	111.1	3.74
New Jersey Turnpike	118.0	3.89
Florida Turnpike	265.0	3.75
New York Thruway (Mainline)	390.0	3.10
New York Thruway (Erie)	67.0	3.13
New York Thruway (Saratoga)	24.0	3.13
Kansas Turnpike	236.0	2.97
Indiana	156.9	2.96
Maine Turnpike	106.0	2.92
Oklahoma (Turner Turnpike)	86.0	2.33
Oklahoma (Will Rogers)	88.5	2.26
Ohio	241.2	2.03

a. Determine the coefficient of correlation.
b. Determine the coefficient of determination.

(Source: "The Tale of the Tolls," *USA Today,* March 22, 1991, p. A3.)

30. The following regression equation was computed from a sample of 20 observations.

$$Y' = 15 - 5X$$

SSE was found to be 100 and SS total 400.
a. Determine the standard error of estimate.
b. Determine the coefficient of determination.
c. Determine the coefficient of correlation. (Caution: Watch the sign!)

31. An ANOVA table is:

SOURCE	DF	SS	MS	F
Regression	1	50		
Error				
Total	24	500		

a. Complete the ANOVA table.
b. How large was the sample?
c. Determine the standard error of estimate.
d. Determine the coefficient of determination.

32. Following is a regression equation.

$$Y' = 17.08 + 0.16X$$

This information is also available: $s_{y \cdot x} = 4.05$, $\Sigma X = 210$, $\Sigma X^2 = 9{,}850$, and $n = 5$.
a. Estimate the value of Y' when $X = 50$.
b. Develop a 95 percent prediction interval for an individual value of Y for $X = 50$.

33. The National Highway Association is studying the relationship between the number of bidders on a highway project and the winning (lowest) bid for the project. Of particular interest is whether the number of bidders increases or decreases the amount of the winning bid.

Project	Number of bidders, *X*	Winning bid ($ millions), *Y*	Project	Number of bidders, *X*	Winning bid ($ millions), *Y*
1	9	5.1	9	6	10.3
2	9	8.0	10	6	8.0
3	3	9.7	11	4	8.8
4	10	7.8	12	7	9.4
5	5	7.7	13	7	8.6
6	10	5.5	14	7	8.1
7	7	8.3	15	6	7.8
8	11	5.5			

a. Determine the regression equation. Interpret the equation. Do more bidders tend to increase or decrease the amount of the winning bid?
b. Estimate the amount of the winning bid if there were seven bidders.
c. A new turnpike entrance is to be constructed on the Ohio Turnpike at the junction of I-75. There are seven bidders on the project. Develop a 95 percent prediction interval for the winning bid.
d. Determine the coefficient of determination. Interpret its value.

34. Mr. William Profit is studying companies going public for the first time. He is particularly interested in the relationship between the size of the offering and the price per share. A sample of 15 companies that recently went public revealed the following information.

Company	Size ($ millions), X	Price per share, Y	Company	Size ($ millions), X	Price per share, Y
1	9.0	10.8	9	160.7	11.3
2	94.4	11.3	10	96.5	10.6
3	27.3	11.2	11	83.0	10.5
4	179.2	11.1	12	23.5	10.3
5	71.9	11.1	13	58.7	10.7
6	97.9	11.2	14	93.8	11.0
7	93.5	11.0	15	34.4	10.8
8	70.0	10.7			

a. Determine the regression equation.
b. Determine the coefficient of determination. Do you think Mr. Profit should be satisfied with using the size of the offering as the independent variable?

35. The Bardi Trucking Co., located in Cleveland, Ohio, makes deliveries in the Great Lakes region, the Southeast, and the Northeast. Jim Bardi, the president, is studying the relationship between the distance a shipment must travel and the length of time, in days, it takes the shipment to arrive at its destination. To investigate, Mr. Bardi selected a random sample of 20 shipments made last month. Shipping distance is the independent variable, and shipping time is the dependent variable. The results are as follows.

Shipment	Distance (miles)	Shipping time (days)
1	656	5
2	853	14
3	646	6
4	783	11
5	610	8
6	841	10
7	785	9
8	639	9
9	762	10
10	762	9
11	862	7
12	679	5
13	835	13
14	607	3
15	665	8
16	647	7
17	685	10
18	720	8
19	652	6
20	828	10

a. Draw a scatter diagram. Based on these data, does it appear that there is a relationship between how many miles a shipment has to go and how long it takes to arrive at its destination?
b. Determine the coefficient of correlation. Can we conclude that there is a positive correlation between distance and time?
c. Determine and interpret the coefficient of determination.
d. Determine the standard error of estimate.

e. Determine the regression equation. How long would you estimate that a shipment going 700 miles will take to arrive at its destination?
f. Develop a 95 percent confidence interval for all shipments going 700 miles.
g. Develop a 95 percent prediction interval for a particular shipment going 700 miles from Cleveland.

36. Mr. Greg Harmon is the business manager for a symphony orchestra located in the metropolitan area. He is preparing to make a presentation to a civic group that has pledged to make a large contribution. As a part of his presentation, he would like to show that there is a relationship between the number of full-time employees and the number of performances. He would also like to be able to estimate the number of performances based on the size of the orchestra. He selected a sample of 19 cities throughout the United States and Canada and determined the number of performances given last year and the number of full-time employees. The sample information is reported below.

City	Performances last year	Full-time employees
1	137	52
2	149	54
3	157	52
4	164	63
5	166	52
6	170	48
7	173	64
8	175	47
9	176	55
10	179	62
11	179	75
12	181	57
13	182	53
14	183	53
15	190	57
16	192	87
17	195	81
18	196	84
19	200	88

a. Determine the correlation between the two variables. Is it reasonable to conclude that there is a positive association between the variables?
b. Determine the regression equation. How many concerts would you estimate for an orchestra that had 40 full-time employees?
c. Develop a 95 percent confidence interval for all orchestras with 40 full-time employees.
d. Develop a 95 percent prediction interval for the Tucson orchestra, which has 40 employees.

37. Each year *Business Week* magazine publishes a special report on executive compensation. Following is the portion of that report that relates to the 35 largest banks and bank holding companies and their chief executive officers.

In the third column is the total sales for each bank, which is reported in millions of dollars. The column headed ROE is the return on equity. This is a financial measure, reported as a percent, that shows the bank's improvement in profitability over the 1991–

1993 period. The final column is the total salary for the chief executive officer, reported in thousands of dollars.

Bank	Executive	Sales ($ millions)	ROE	Salary ($ thousands)
Bank One	J. B. McCoy	$ 7,270.0	16.9	$2,063
Bank of Boston	I. Stepanian	7,396.0	10.6	1,569
Bank of New York	J. C. Bacot	3,822.0	14.1	2,876
BankAmerica	R. M. Rosenberg	15,900.0	12.1	2,200
Bankers Trust New York	C. S. Sanford	7,800.0	24.4	8,866
Barnett Banks	C. E. Rice	3,130.0	15.1	2,210
Boatmen's Bancshares	A. B. Craig	2,107.0	14.9	961
Chase Manhattan	T. G. Labrecque	11,417.0	4.8	2,257
Chemical Banking	J. F. McGillicuddy	12,427.0	14.9	3,350
Citicorp	J. S. Reed	32,196.0	15.9	4,150
Corestates Financial	T. A. Larsen	2,014.0	17.6	1,133
Fifth Third	G. A. Schaefer	954.0	16.4	799
First Bank System	J. F. Grundhofer	2,231.0	13.7	1,315
First Chicago	R. L. Thomas	4,827.0	21.3	2,030
First Fidelity	A. P. Terracciano	2,429.0	15.7	1,213
First Interstate	E. M. Carson	3,898.0	16.0	1,846
First Union	E. E. Crutchfield	5,755.0	15.3	1,650
Firstar	R. L. Fitzsimonds	1,209.0	17.4	927
Fleet Financial	T. Murry	4,678.0	15.3	1,892
Hunington Bankshares	F. G. Wobst	1,542.0	17.9	1,465
MBNA	A. Lerner	1,392.8	28.5	1,817
Mellon Bank	F. V. Cahouet	3,237.0	11.0	1,391
J. P. Morgan	D. Weatherstone	11,941.0	18.2	3,100
National City	E. B. Brandon	2,702.0	15.1	1,049
Nationsbank	H. L. McColl	10,392.0	13.1	2,600
NBD Bancorp	C. T. Fisher III	3,208.0	15.2	2,467
Northern Trust	D. W. Fox	1,259.0	16.5	1,031
Norwest	R. M. Kovacevich	5,277.0	19.4	2,323
PNC Bank	T. H. O'Brien	4,146.0	18.1	2,003
Signet Banking	R. M. Freeman	1,169.0	18.8	1,019
State Street Boston	M. N. Carter	1,532.0	16.3	1,094
Suntrust Banks	J. B. Williams	3,089.0	13.1	756
U.S. Bancorp	R. L. Breezley	1,966.0	14.7	750
Wachovia	J. G. Medlin	2,750.0	16.3	1,243
Wells Fargo	C. E. Reichardt	4,854.0	15.3	2,125

(Source: *Business Week*, April 25, 1994, p. 59.)

a. Determine the correlations between salary and sales and between salary and ROE. Which variable has the stronger correlation with salary? In both cases can we conclude that the relationship is significant and positive? Use the .05 significance level.

b. Determine the coefficients of determination between salary and ROE and between salary and sales.

c. Can we conclude that the executives with the most profitable banks, as measured by ROE, and have the largest sales receive the largest salaries? Write a brief report summarizing your findings.

38. Following is a summary of the total assets, in millions of dollars, for the 26 credit unions located in Toledo, Ohio. Also reported are the capital ratio, a financial measure showing the ratio of total equity to total liabilities, and the profit for each credit union for the year 1993, in thousands of dollars.

Credit union	Assets ($ millions)	Capital ratio	1993 profit ($ thousands)
Toledo Area Catholic	74.139	8.759	1,147
Sun Federal	69.624	7.505	589
Glass City Federal	58.033	8.185	789
OC Federal	49.235	9.207	449
Toledo Telephone Employees	37.639	12.572	414
Erie Shores Federal	30.650	13.537	191
Champion	27.070	13.631	259
Mutual Federal	22.008	8.451	105
UT-MCO Federal	21.288	8.441	232
AP Federal (AP Parts)	21.092	12.635	218
Great Lakes Federal	20.153	7.711	181
Toledo Fire Fighters	19.923	9.075	180
Sohio Toledo Refinery	19.153	10.808	283
Toledo Metro Federal	13.788	10.110	98
Toledo Hospital Employees	11.990	9.116	199
Conrail Toledo	11.887	14.705	206
General Mills Toledo	11.695	9.987	139
Jeep Federal	11.234	11.786	353
Toledo Police Federal	10.734	11.608	189
Toledo St. Vincent Federal	9.631	9.179	109
United Services Federal	8.724	8.517	22
Blade Federal	8.584	10.916	85
North West Federal	8.342	11.496	76
Co-Op Toledo	8.422	10.057	81
Sylvania Education and Municipal Employees	7.291	8.874	130
Local 50 Plumbers and Steamfitters	5.812	8.448	44

(Source: *Toledo Blade,* May 26, 1994, p. 47.)

a. Determine the correlation between the total assets of the credit unions and their 1993 profits. Can we conclude that there is a significant positive correlation between these two variables? Plot the variables in the form of a scatter diagram. Do you see any problems?

b. Determine the correlation between capital ratio and 1993 profits. Can we conclude that there is a significant negative correlation between the two variables?

39. A recent report by the *Business Journal* of Santa Clara County, California, reported the number of local employees and the number of square feet cleaned per night (reported in millions) for 21 janitorial firms in the county. The information is reported below and at the top of the following page.

Company	Employees	Square feet cleaned
Commercial Building Maintenance	800	15.00
Acme Building Maintenance	665	22.00
Pacific Maintenance	500	8.30
American Building Maintenance	380	10.40
Jani-King of California	300	6.00
Service Performance Co.	206	5.00
Centennial Contract Services	196	6.70
United Maintenance Co.	160	5.50
Continental Building Maintenance	160	4.80
Regional Building Maintenance	125	4.50
Tiger Maintenance Co.	92	2.00
California Janitorial Service	81	1.10
Cave Imaging Systems	80	2.80

Company	Employees	Square feet cleaned
Polaros Building Maintenance	71	1.60
Pro Clean Enterprises	65	3.00
California Building Maintenance	63	0.83
Environmental Control Building Maintenance	48	1.00
Valley Building Maintenance Co.	47	1.70
Universal Maintenance	45	1.20
Associated Building Maintenance	45	1.30
Salinas Valley Corp.	42	1.50

a. Determine the regression equation. Let the number of square feet cleaned be the dependent variable. How much additional area does each additional employee clean?

b. Determine the coefficients of determination and correlation. Can you conclude that the correlation between the area cleaned and the number of employees is greater than 0?

COMPUTER DATA EXERCISES

40. Refer to data set 1, which reports information on homes sold in Florida during 1994.
    a. Let selling price be the dependent variable and size of the home the independent variable. Determine the regression equation. Estimate the selling price for a home with an area of 2,200 square feet. Determine the 95 percent confidence interval and the 95 percent prediction interval for the selling price of a home with 2,200 square feet.
    b. Let selling price be the dependent variable and distance from the center of the city the independent variable. Determine the regression equation. Estimate the selling price of a home 20 miles from the center of the city. Determine the 95 percent confidence interval and the 95 percent prediction interval for homes 20 miles from the center of the city.
    c. Can you conclude that the independent variables "distance from the center of the city" and "selling price" are negatively correlated and that the area of the home and the selling price are positively correlated? Use the .05 significance level. Report the *p*-value of the test.
41. Refer to data set 2, which reports information on the 1993 major league baseball season.
    a. Let number of games won be the dependent variable and team salary the independent variable. Can you conclude that there is a positive association between the variables? Determine the regression equation. About how many additional wins will an additional $5 million in salary bring?
    b. Determine the correlation between games won and ERA and games won and team batting average. Which has the stronger correlation? Can we conclude that there is a positive correlation between wins and team batting and a negative correlation between wins and ERA? Use the .05 significance level.
    c. Let number of games won be the dependent variable and attendance the independent variable. Can we conclude that the correlation between these two variables is greater than 0? Use the .05 significance level. What is the *p*-value?
42. Refer to data set 3, which refers to information on the circulation of magazines.
    a. Determine the correlations between the magazine circulation and the cost of (1) the color and (2) the black and white advertisements. Can you conclude that both of the correlations are significant? Use the .05 significance level.
    b. Determine the correlation between the magazine circulation and the median income of subscribers. Can you show that there is a significant negative association? Use the .05 significance level. What is the *p*-value?

CHAPTER 12 EXAMINATION

The answers are at the end of the chapter.

For Questions 1 through 10, fill in the correct answer. Questions 1 through 3 refer to the following chart.

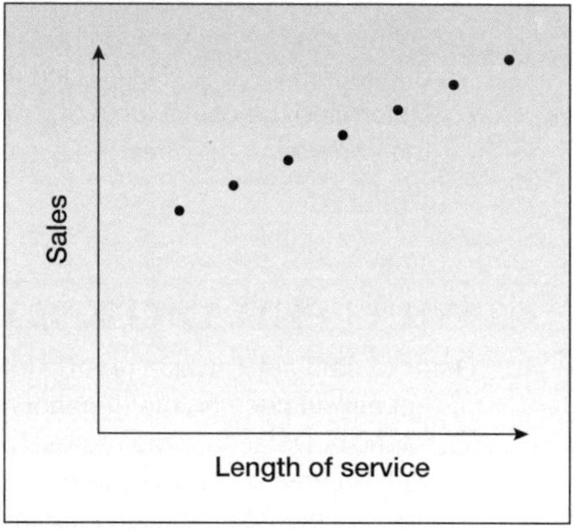

1. This chart is called a ________.
2. The relationship between sales and length of service is ________ (positive or negative).
3. If the coefficient of correlation were computed, it would be about ________.

Questions 4 through 6 are based on the following chart.

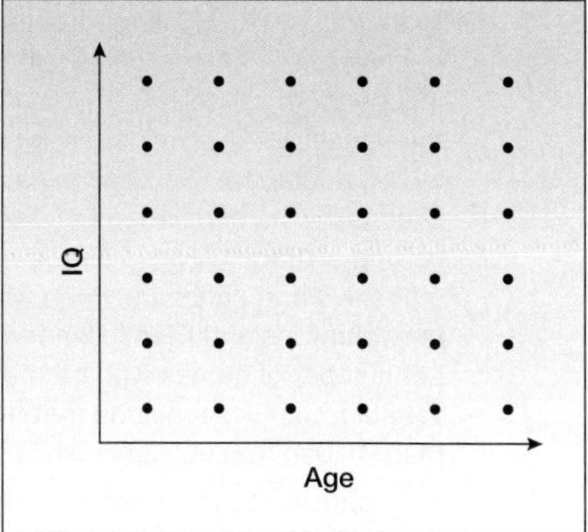

4. If the coefficient of correlation were computed, it would be about ________.
5. The dependent variable is ________.
6. If computed, the coefficient of determination would be about ________.

Questions 7 through 9 are based on the following chart.

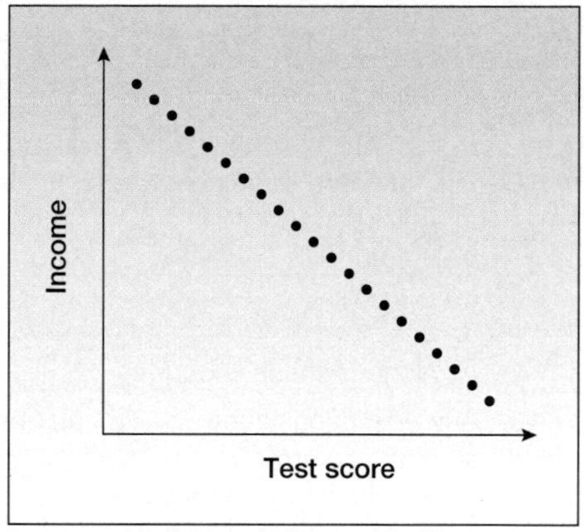

7. In this particular problem, the independent variable is ________.
8. If computed, the coefficient of determination would be about ________.
9. Based on the chart, as test scores increase, income will ________.
10. The square of the coefficient of correlation is called ________.

Questions 11 through 16 are based on the following picture.

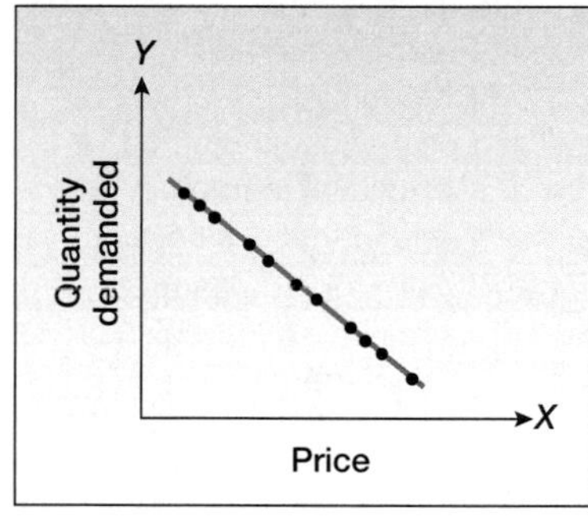

11. The picture is called a:
    a. Dotted-swiss chart.
    b. Bar chart.
    c. Scatter diagram.
    d. Straight-line chart.
    e. None of these is correct.
12. The equation for the line going through the points would take the form of:
    a. $Y' = a + b + c$.
    b. $Y' = a - bX$.
    c. $Y' = X - 1$.
    d. $Y' = a + bX^2$.
    e. None of these is correct.
13. In this particular problem, the researcher is trying to predict:
    a. Quantity demanded based on price.
    b. Price based on quantity demanded.
    c. Both price and quantity demanded.
    d. None of these is correct.

14. If computed, the sign of *b* in the equation would be:
    a. Either positive or negative.
    b. Positive.
    c. Negative.
    d. Infinity.
    e. None of these is correct.
15. The standard error of estimate, if computed, would be:
    a. Infinity.
    b. +1.00.
    c. −1.00.
    d. 0.
    e. None of these is correct.
16. Any predictions based on this picture would:
    a. Have no error.
    b. Be of little or no use.
    c. None of these is correct.
17. The variable used to predict another variable is called the:
    a. Dependent variable.
    b. Independent variable.
    c. Correlation variable.
    d. Student's *t* variable.
    e. None of these is correct.
18. The method used to arrive at the "best-fitting" straight line in regression analysis is referred to as the:
    a. Freehand method.
    b. Determination method.
    c. Least squares method.
    d. Correlation method.
    e. None of these is correct.

Questions 19 and 20 are based on the following chart.

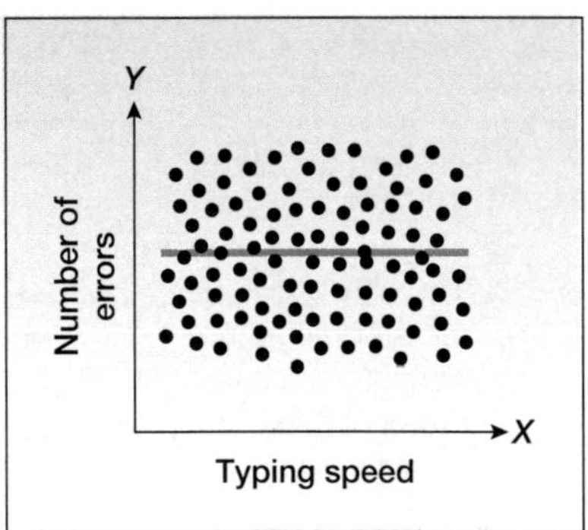

19. In the regression equation for the straight line, the value of *b* would be about:
    a. −1.00.
    b. +1.00.
    c. 0.
    d. None of these is correct.
20. The independent variable is scaled on the:
    a. *Y*-axis.
    b. *X*-axis.

Sales of toothpaste seem to be heavily dependent on the level of advertisement. The annual advertising expenditures for several well-known brands and their annual sales are:

Brand	Annual advertising expenditures ($ millions)	Annual sales ($ millions)
Glint	2	5
Pearl One	4	7
Shine On	3	6
Number 1	1	2

21. *a.* Draw a scatter diagram.
    b. Compute the least squares regression equation.
    c. Based on the regression equation, an advertising expenditure of $1.9 million should produce what amount of sales on the average?
    d. Compute three points, and plot the straight line on the scatter diagram.
22. *a.* Determine the standard error of estimate.
    b. For a group of toothpastes whose annual advertising expenditures are exactly $1.9 million, what is the 95 percent confidence interval for their arithmetic mean annual sales?
    c. Interpret the limits in part *b.*
23. *a.* Compute the coefficient of correlation.
    b. Compute the coefficient of determination.

CHAPTER 12 Answers

Self-Review

12–1 1. Yield is the dependent variable. The amount of fertilizer is the independent variable.

2.

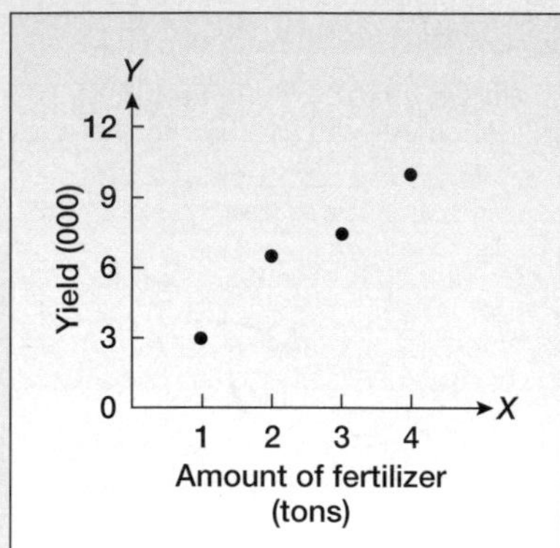

3.

X	Y	XY	X^2	Y^2
2	7	14	4	49
1	3	3	1	9
3	8	24	9	64
4	10	40	16	100
10	28	81	30	222

$r = .96$, found by

$$r = \frac{4(81) - (10)(28)}{\sqrt{[4(30) - (10)^2][4(222) - (28)^2]}}$$

$$= \frac{44}{\sqrt{2{,}080}} = \frac{44}{45.607017} = .9648$$

4. A very strong (almost perfect) correlation between the amount of fertilizer applied and yield is indicated by .9648.

12–2 H_0: $\rho \leq 0$, H_1: $\rho > 0$. H_0 is rejected if $t > 1.714$.

$$t = \frac{.43\sqrt{25 - 2}}{\sqrt{1 - (.43)^2}} = 2.284$$

H_0 is rejected. There is a positive correlation between the percent of the vote received and the amount spent on the campaign.

12–3

X	Y	XY	X^2	Y^2
2	7	14	4	49
1	3	3	1	9
3	8	24	9	64
4	10	40	16	100
10	28	81	30	222

$$b = \frac{4(81) - (10)(28)}{4(30) - (10)^2}$$

$$= \frac{324 - 280}{120 - 100} = 2.2$$

$$a = \frac{28}{4} - 2.2\left(\frac{10}{4}\right)$$

$$= 7 - 5.5 = 1.5$$

The equation is: $Y' = 1.5 + 2.2X$ (in hundreds of bushels).
$Y' = 1.5 + 2.2(3) = 8.1$

12–4 1. 0.9487 (in hundreds of bushels), found by:

$$s_{y \cdot x} = \sqrt{\frac{\Sigma Y^2 - a(\Sigma Y) - b(\Sigma XY)}{n - 2}}$$

$$= \sqrt{\frac{222 - 1.5(28) - 2.2(81)}{4 - 2}}$$

$$= \sqrt{\frac{1.8}{2}}$$

$$= 0.9487 \text{ or } 94.87 \text{ bushels}$$

2. ± 189.74 bushels, found by 2(94.87).

12–5 1. 6.58 and 9.52, since Y' for an X of 3 is 8.1, found by $Y' = 1.5 + 2.2(3) = 8.1$. $\bar{X} = 2.5$. Then $\Sigma X^2 = 30$ and $\Sigma X = 10$.

t from Appendix F for 4 − 2 − 2 degrees of freedom at the .10 level is 2.920.

$$Y' \pm t(s_{y \cdot x})\sqrt{\frac{1}{n} + \frac{(X - \bar{X})^2}{\Sigma X^2 - \frac{(\Sigma X)^2}{n}}}$$

$$= 8.1 \pm 2.920(0.9487)\sqrt{\frac{1}{4} + \frac{(3 - 2.5)^2}{30 - \frac{(10)^2}{4}}}$$

$$= 8.1 \pm 2.920(0.9487)(0.5477)$$

$= 6.58$ and 9.62 (in hundreds of bushels), or 658 and 962 bushels

2. For a group of plots receiving exactly three tons of fertilizer, the probability is .90 that the mean yield is in the interval between 658 and 962 bushels.

Examination

1. Scatter diagram.
2. Positive.
3. 1.00.
4. Zero.
5. IQ.
6. 0
7. Test score.
8. −1.00.
9. Decrease.
10. Coefficient of determination.
11. c.
12. b.
13. a.
14. c.
15. d.
16. a.
17. b.
18. c.
19. c.
20. b.
21. *a.*

b. $Y' = a + bX = 1 + 1.6X$ (in $ millions)

$$b = \frac{4(58) - 10(20)}{4(30) - (10)^2} = \frac{32}{20} = 1.6$$

$$a = \frac{20}{4} - 1.6\left(\frac{10}{4}\right) = 5 - 4 = 1$$

c. $4.04 million, found by $Y' = 1 + 1.6(1.9)$.

d.

X	**Y'**
1	2.6
2	4.2
3	5.8
4	7.4

22. *a.* 0.77 (in $ millions), found by:

$$\sqrt{\frac{114 - 1(20) - 1.6(58)}{4 - 2}} = \sqrt{\frac{1.2}{2}} = 0.77$$

b. $2.16 and $5.92 (in $ millions), found by:

$$4.04 \pm 4.303(0.77)\sqrt{\frac{1}{4} + \frac{(1.9 - 2.5)^2}{5.0}}$$

$$= 4.04 \pm 4.303(0.77)(0.5674504)$$

$$= 4.04 \pm 1.88$$

c. For a group of toothpastes with advertising expenditures of exactly $1.9 million, the probability is .95 that the mean sales amount is in the interval between $2.16 million and $5.92 million.

23. *a.* $r = \dfrac{4(58) - 10(20)}{\sqrt{[4(30) - (10)^2][4(114) - (20)^2]}} = \dfrac{32}{\sqrt{(20)(56)}} = 0.956$

b. $r^2 = (0.956)^2 = 0.914$

Chapter 13

Multiple Regression and Correlation

GOALS

When you have completed this chapter, you will be able to:

1
Describe the relationship between two or more independent variables and a dependent variable using a multiple regression equation.

2
Describe the error in the prediction using the multiple standard error of estimate.

3
Describe the strength of the relationship between the independent variables and the dependent variable using the coefficient of determination.

4
Conduct a global test to determine whether or not the multiple regression model is useful.

5
Evaluate individual regression coefficients.

6
Explain a stepwise multiple regression and correlation computer output.

The district manager of stores is investigating why certain stores perform better than others. She believes the number of competitors, population, and advertising expenses are related to total sales. Describe the strength of the relationship between the independent variables. (See Goal 3 and Exercise 5.)

INTRODUCTION

The previous chapter was concerned with the relationship between two sets of interval- or ratio-scaled measurements. One was designated as the independent variable and the other as the dependent variable. We noted that if the relationship between the two variables is linear, the regression equation $Y' = a + bX$ is used to predict the dependent variable, Y, based on the independent variable, X. Further, the coefficient of correlation is one measure we examined that reveals whether the relationship is strong, moderate, or weak. A coefficient near plus or minus 1.00 indicates a very strong relationship between X and Y. A coefficient near 0 (say, $-.12$ or $+.12$) means that the relationship is quite weak.

Use of only one independent variable to predict the dependent variable ignores the relationship of other variables to the dependent variable. This chapter expands our study of correlation and regression by examining the influence of *two or more* independent variables on the dependent variable. This approach is referred to as **multiple regression and correlation analysis.** We will present multiple regression analysis first by developing and explaining the use of the multiple regression equation and the multiple standard error of estimate. Then the strength of the relationship between the independent variables and the dependent variable will be measured using the multiple coefficient of determination. Finally, several computer applications using MINITAB will be presented and analyzed.

MULTIPLE REGRESSION ANALYSIS

Recall from Chapter 12 that the linear regression equation encompassing one independent variable and one dependent variable has the form $Y' = a + bX$. The multiple regression case merely extends the equation to include additional independent variables. For two independent variables, the general form of the **multiple regression equation** is:

$$Y' = a + b_1X_1 + b_2X_2 \qquad (13\text{–}1)$$

where:

X_1, X_2 are the two independent variables.

a is the Y-intercept, that is, the point of intercept with the Y-axis.

b_1 is the net change in Y for each unit change in X_1, *holding X_2 constant* (unchanged). It is called a **partial regression coefficient,** a **net regression coefficient,** or just a **regression coefficient.**

b is called a regression coefficient

b_2 is the net change in Y for each single unit change in X_2 *holding X_1 constant* (unchanged). It is also referred to as a partial regression coefficient, or just a regression coefficient.

To illustrate the interpretation of a and the two regression coefficients, suppose a vehicle's mileage per gallon of gasoline is directly related to the octane rating of the gasoline being used (X_1) and inversely related to the weight of the automobile (X_2). Assume that the multiple regression equation was computed to be $Y' = 6.3 + 0.2X_1 + (-0.001)X_2$. The a value of 6.3 indicates that the regression plane intercepts the Y-axis at 6.3 when both X_1 and X_2 are zero. Of course, it does not make any sense to own an automobile that has no (zero) weight and to use gasoline with no octane. It is important to keep in mind that a regression equation is not effective outside the range of the sample values.

Negative b indicates inverse relationship

The b_1 of 0.2 indicates that for each increase of 1 in the octane rating of the gasoline, the automobile would travel two tenths of a mile more per gallon, *regardless of the weight of the vehicle.* That is, the vehicle's weight is held constant. The b_2 value of -0.001 reveals that for each increase of one pound in the vehicle's weight, the number of miles traveled per gallon decreases by 0.001, *regardless of the octane of the gasoline being used.*

As an example, an automobile with 92-octane gasoline in the tank and weighing 2,000 pounds would travel an average 22.7 miles per gallon, found by:

$$\begin{aligned} Y' &= a + b_1X_1 + b_2X_2 \\ &= 6.3 + 0.2(92) + (-0.001)2{,}000 \\ &= 22.7 \text{ miles per gallon} \end{aligned}$$

For three independent variables designated X_1, X_2, and X_3, the general multiple regression equation is:

$$Y' = a + b_1X_1 + b_2X_2 + b_3X_3 \qquad (13\text{–}2)$$

General form of the multiple regression equation

This can be extended for any number of independent variables (k), with the general multiple regression equation being:

$$Y' = a + b_1X_1 + b_2X_2 + b_3X_3 + \cdots + b_kX_k \qquad (13\text{–}3)$$

Need computer to solve these

As was demonstrated in Chapter 12, the least squares method minimizes the sum of the squares of the vertical deviations about the straight line. The same applies to multiple regression. To arrive at a, b_1, and b_2 in the multiple regression equation, however, the many calculations are very tedious—even using a hand calculator. As an example, for two independent variables, three equations must be solved simultaneously, namely:

$$\Sigma Y = na + b_1\Sigma X_1 + b_2\Sigma X_2$$

$$\Sigma X_1Y = a\Sigma X_1 + b_1\Sigma X_1^2 + b_2\Sigma X_1X_2$$

$$\Sigma X_2Y = a\Sigma X_2 + b_1\Sigma X_1X_2 + b_2\Sigma X_2^2$$

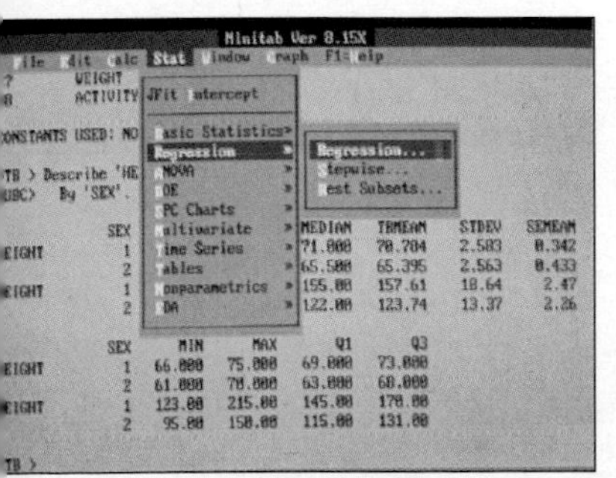

There are many computer software packages available, and the format of their output is fairly standard. MINITAB, SPSS, and SAS are three of the most widely used packages. Before presenting the MINITAB multiple regression package, we will examine the meaning of the intercept term, a, and the partial regression coefficients, b_1 and b_2. To do this, the two-variable sales problem from Chapter 12 will be reintroduced and another independent variable added. Thus, we will have a multiple regression problem involving one dependent variable, Y, and two independent variables, X_1 and X_2.

TABLE 13–1 Units Sold, Number of Calls, and Number of Different Products Sold

Salesperson	Number of units sold, Y	Number of sales calls, X_1	Number of different products sold, X_2
Frank Rouses	28	14	2
Sue Navchek	66	35	5
Art Seiple	38	22	4
Carma Lopez	70	29	4
Todd Bortz	22	6	3
Sara Jones	27	15	3
Susan Welch	28	17	3
Carlos Ramirez	47	20	4
Mike Keil	14	12	2
Mark Reynolds	68	29	5

EXAMPLE

Recall from Chapter 12 that the sales manager at Intrepid, Inc. selected a sample of 10 sales representatives. He found the number of units they sold last month and the number of sales calls they made. Suppose the sales manager now wants to consider the number of different products each representative sold. Table 13–1 above shows the number of units sold, the dependent variable, which is designated as Y. The number of sales calls and the number of products sold, the independent variables, are designated X_1 and X_2.

Determine the regression equation. Estimate the number of units sold for a sales representative who made 20 sales calls and sold five different products.

Solution

The general form of the regression equation is $Y' = a + b_1X_1 + b_2X_2$. For this example, suppose the regression equation was found to be $Y' = -11.452 + 1.467X_1 + 6.588X_2$. The estimated number of units sold for a representative who made 20 calls and sold five different products is 50.828, found by $Y' = -11.452 + 1.467(20) + 6.588(5)$.

To understand how sample data are portrayed in three dimensions, think of the walls and floor of a room. Let a lower corner of the room, where the wall and the floor meet, represent the point where Y and X_1 and X_2 are all equal to 0. The data are

CHART 13–1 Three-Dimensional Representation of Units Sold, Number of Sales Calls, and Products Sold

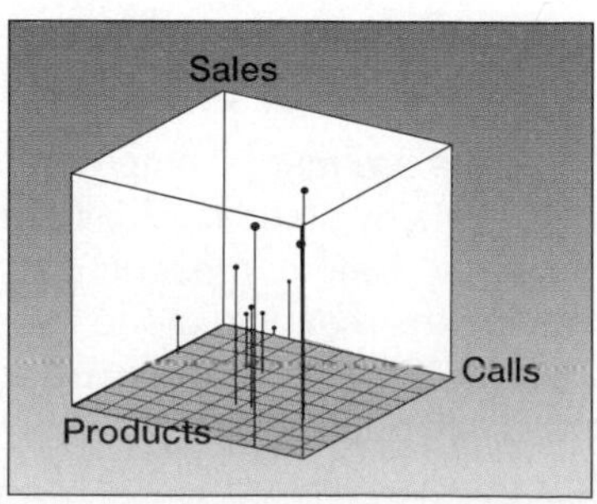

represented by tennis balls suspended at various distances from the walls and the floor. The height of a ball above the floor is the value of Y, the distance the ball is from the right wall is X_1, and its distance from the left wall is X_2. Chart 13–1 is a three-dimensional representation of the sales data in Table 13–1.

How do we view the multiple regression equation? It corresponds to a plane that is slanted to provide the best fit to the sample data. The method of least squares is used to determine the exact position of the plane.

SELF-REVIEW 13–1

The answers are at the end of the chapter.

The quality control engineer at Bethel Steel is interested in estimating the tensile strength of steel wire based on its outside diameter and the amount of molybdenum in the steel. As an experiment, she selected four pieces of wire, measured the outside diameters, and determined the molybdenum content. Then she measured the tensile strength of each piece. The results were:

Piece	Tensile strength (psi), Y	Outside diameter (cm), X_1	Amount of molybdenum (units), X_2
A	11	3	6
B	9	2	5
C	16	4	8
D	12	3	7

Suppose the multiple regression equation is $Y' = -0.5 + 2X_1 + 1X_2$.

1. Based on the equation, what is the predicted tensile strength of a steel wire having an outside diameter of 3.5 cm and 6.4 units of molybdenum?

2. Explain what the value of b_1 in the equation means.

EXERCISES

The answers to the odd-numbered exercises are at the end of the book.

1. The director of marketing at Reeves Wholesale Products is studying the monthly sales of his company's six regions. Three independent variables were selected as predictors of sales: regional population, per-capita income, and regional unemployment rate. The regression equation was computed to be (in dollars):

$$Y' = 64{,}100 + 0.394X_1 + 9.6X_2 - 11{,}600X_3$$

   a. What is the full name of the equation?

   b. Explain what the number 64,100 is.

   c. What is the estimated monthly sales total for region IV? The region has a population of 796,000, per-capita income of $6,940, and an unemployment rate of 6.0 percent.

2. Thompson Machine Works purchased several new, highly sophisticated machines. The production department needed some guidance with respect to qualifications needed by an operator. Is age a factor? Is the length of service as a machine operator important? In order to explore further the factors needed to estimate performance on the new machines, four variables were listed:

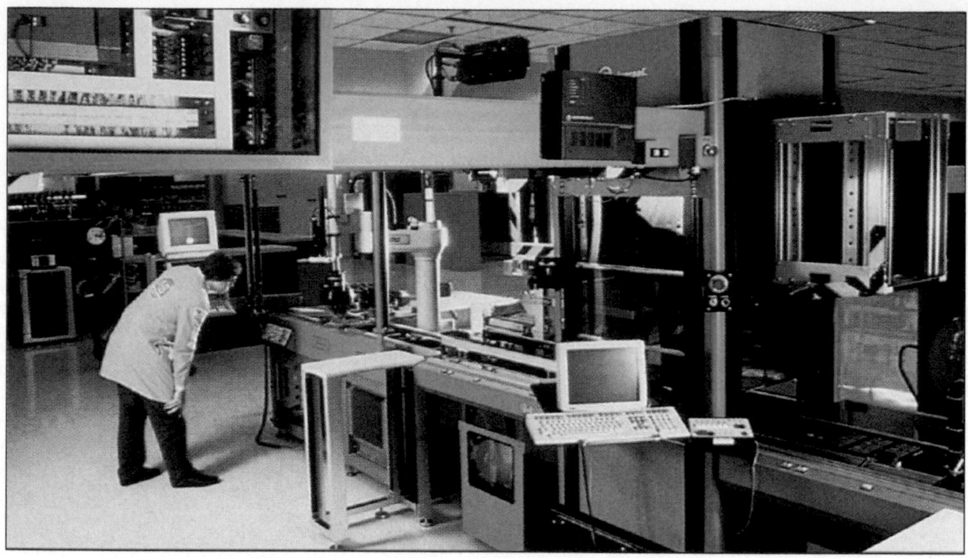

X_1 = Length of time employee was a machinist.

X_2 = Mechanical aptitude test score.

X_3 = Prior on-the-job rating.

X_4 = Age.

Performance on the new machine is designated Y.

Twelve machinists were selected at random. Data were collected for each, and their performances on the new machines were recorded. A few results are:

Name	Performance on new machine, Y	Length of time as a machinist, X_1	Mechanical aptitude score, X_2	Prior on-the-job performance, X_3	Age, X_4
Andy Kosin	112	12	312	121	52
Sue Annis	113	2	380	123	27

Suppose the equation is:

$$Y' = 11.6 + 0.4X_1 + 0.286X_2 + 0.112X_3 + 0.002X_4$$

a. What is the full designation of the equation?
b. How many dependent variables are there? Independent variables?
c. What is the number 0.286 called?
d. As age increases by one year, how much does estimated performance on the new machine increase?
e. Carl Knox applied for a job on a new machine. He has been a machinist for six years, and he scored 280 on the mechanical aptitude test. Carl's prior on-the-job performance rating is 97, and he is 35 years old. Estimate Carl's performance on the new machine.

3. A sample of widowed senior citizens was studied to determine their degree of satisfaction with their present life. A special index, called the index of satisfaction, was used to measure satisfaction. Six factors were studied, namely, age at the time of first marriage (X_1), annual income (X_2), number of children living (X_3), value of all

assets (X_4), status of health in the form of an index (X_5), and the average number of social activities per week—such as bowling and dancing (X_6). Suppose the multiple regression equation is:

$$Y' = -16.24 + 0.017X_1 + 0.0028X_2 + 42X_3 + 0.0012X_4 + 0.19X_5 + 26.8X_6$$

a. What is the estimated index of satisfaction for a person who first married at 18, has an annual income of \$26,500, has three children living, has assets of \$156,000, has an index of health status of 141, and has 2.5 social activities a week on the average?
b. Which would add more to satisfaction, an additional income of \$10,000 a year or two more social activities a week?

4. Cellulon, a manufacturer of a new type of home insulation, wants to develop guidelines for builders and consumers regarding the effects on natural gas consumption (1) of the thickness of the insulation in the attic of a home and (2) of the outdoor temperature. In the laboratory they varied the insulation thickness and temperature. A few of the findings are:

Monthly natural gas consumption (cubic feet), Y	Thickness of insulation (inches), X_1	Outdoor temperature (Fahrenheit), X_2
30.3	6	40
26.9	12	40
22.1	8	49

Based on the sample results, the regression equation is:

$$Y' = 62.65 - 1.86X_1 - 0.52X_2$$

a. How much natural gas can homeowners expect to use per month if (1) they install 6 inches of insulation and (2) the outdoor temperature is 40 degrees F?
b. What effect would installing 7 inches of insulation instead of 6 have on the monthly natural gas consumption (assuming the outdoor temperature remains at 40 degrees F)?
c. Why are the regression coefficients b_1 and b_2 negative? Is this logical?

MULTIPLE STANDARD ERROR OF ESTIMATE

Returning to the example in Table 13–1, we found that a sales representative who made 20 sales calls and sold five different products can be expected to sell 50.828 units. Of course, we would round off 50.828 to whole units (51). In some months a sales representative with these statistics would sell more than 51 units, and in others the representative would sell fewer than 51 units. The error in this estimate is measured by the **multiple standard error of estimate,** denoted $s_{y \cdot 12}$. (The subscripts indicate that two independent variables are being used to estimate the error in Y.)

Recall from Chapter 12 that the standard error of estimate in regression analysis measures the variation about the regression line. Likewise, the standard error of estimate in multiple regression analysis with two independent variables measures the error for values of Y about the regression plane. Formula (13–4) for the multiple standard error of estimate is almost the same as that used for only one independent variable. The formula is:

$$s_{y \cdot 12 \cdots k} = \sqrt{\frac{\Sigma(Y - Y')^2}{n - (k + 1)}} \qquad (13\text{–}4)$$

where n is the number of observations in the sample and k is the number of *independent* variables—two in this problem.

The sales problem is again used to illustrate. The first representative selected was Frank Rouses. He made 14 sales calls and sold two different products. These values are substituted into the regression equation determined earlier, and his sales total is estimated at 22.262, determined by $Y' = -11.452 + 1.467(14) + 6.588(2)$. The values of Y' for the other sales representatives are found similarly and are reported in Table 13–2.

Frank Rouses actually sold 28 units, in contrast to his estimated sales of 22.262 units. The error in the estimate is 5.738 units, found by 28.00 − 22.262. This difference between the actual sales and the estimated sales is called the **residual.** To find the multiple standard error of estimate, first determine the residual for each salesperson. Next square the residual and total the squared residuals. The total is reported in the lower right corner of Table 13–2.

TABLE 13–2 Calculations Needed for the Multiple Standard Error of Estimate

Salesperson	Number of sales calls, X_1	Number of different products sold, X_2	Number of units sold, Y	Y'	$(Y - Y')$	$(Y - Y')^2$
Frank Rouses	14	2	28	22.262	5.738	32.9246
Sue Navchek	35	5	66	72.833	−6.833	46.6899
Art Seiple	22	4	38	47.174	−9.174	84.1623
Carma Lopez	29	4	70	57.443	12.557	157.6783
Todd Bortz	6	3	22	17.114	4.886	23.8730
Sara Jones	15	3	27	30.317	−3.317	11.0025
Susan Welch	17	3	28	33.251	−5.251	27.5730
Carlos Ramirez	20	4	47	44.240	2.760	7.6176
Mike Keil	12	2	14	19.328	−5.328	28.3876
Mark Reynolds	29	5	68	64.031	3.969	15.7530
						435.6618

In this problem $n = 10$ and $k = 2$ (two independent variables). So the multiple standard error of estimate is:

$$s_{y \cdot 12} = \sqrt{\frac{\Sigma(Y - Y')^2}{n - (k + 1)}} = \sqrt{\frac{435.6618}{10 - (2 + 1)}} = 7.889$$

The standard error of estimate computed in Chapter 12 was 8.412. It included only the independent variable regarding the number of sales calls. Adding an independent variable to the number of products sold reduces the standard error to 7.889. Adding a second independent variable has had the effect of making the estimates more precise.

How is the multiple standard error of estimate interpreted? What does 7.889 units mean? If the number of units sold is normally distributed about the multiple regression plane, approximately 68 percent of the values for units sold will fall within 7.889 units of the estimated Y' value. And 95.5 percent of the weekly sales will be within $2s_{y \cdot 12}$, that is, within 2(7.889) of the Y' predicted by the equation. Further, approximately 99.7 percent of the sales will be within $3s_{y \cdot 12}$.

In Chapter 12 we used the standard error of estimate to construct confidence intervals. The procedure for constructing these intervals for the multiple regression case is similar and will not be detailed here. These intervals can be determined using the MINITAB system.

SELF-REVIEW 13–2

The answers are at the end of the chapter.

The multiple regression equation for Exercise 4 was given as $Y' = 62.65 - 1.86X_1 - 0.52X_2$, where X_1 is the amount of insulation installed in the attic and X_2 is the outdoor temperature.

1. For a home installing 8 inches of insulation and for an outdoor temperature of 45 degrees F, what is the estimated natural gas consumption?
2. For the Asmus home, with 8 inches of insulation and an outdoor temperature of 45 degrees F, the actual natural gas consumption was 22.0 cubic feet. What is the difference between the actual consumption and the best estimate of natural gas consumption for the Asmus home? What is this difference called?

ASSUMPTIONS ABOUT MULTIPLE REGRESSION AND CORRELATION

Before beginning our discussion of multiple correlation, we will list the assumptions underlying both multiple regression and multiple correlation. As noted in several previous chapters, we need to identify the assumptions because if they are not fully met, the results might be biased. For instance, in selecting a sample, we assume that all the items in the population have a chance of being selected. If our research involves surveying all those who ski, but we ignore those over 40 because we believe they are "too old," we would be biasing the responses toward the younger skiers. It should be mentioned, however, that in actual practice strict adherence to the following assumptions is not always possible in multiple regression and correlation problems involving the ever-changing business climate. But the statistical techniques discussed in this chapter appear to work well even when one or more of the following assumptions are violated. Even if the values in the multiple regression equation are "off" slightly, our estimates based on the equation will be closer than any that could otherwise be made.

Each of the following assumptions will be discussed in more detail as we progress through the chapter.

1. The independent variables and the dependent variables have a linear, or straight-line, relationship.
2. The dependent variable must be continuous and at least interval-scale.

3. The variation in the difference between the actual and the predicted values must be the same for all fitted values of Y. That is, $(Y - Y')$ must be approximately the same for all values of Y'. When this is the case, differences exhibit **homoscedasticity.** Further, the residuals, computed by $Y - Y'$, should be normally distributed with a mean of 0.

Homoscedasticity

4. Successive observations of the dependent variable must be uncorrelated. Violation of this assumption is called **autocorrelation.** Autocorrelation often happens when data are collected over periods of time.

Autocorrelation

Statistical tests are available to detect homoscedasticity and autocorrelation. For those interested, these tests are covered in more advanced textbooks such as *Applied Linear Regression Models* by Neter, Kutner, Nachtsheim, and Wasserman (3rd ed., 1996, published by Richard D. Irwin, Inc.).

THE ANOVA TABLE

As mentioned previously, the calculations involved in multiple regression are lengthy. Fortunately, many computer software systems are available to perform the calculations. Most of the systems output the information in a fairly standard format. The following output, from the MINITAB statistical software system for the sales data in Table 13–1, is typical. It includes the regression equation and the analysis of variance table. We have already described the meaning of the terms in the regression equation $Y' = -11.452 + 1.467X_1 + 6.588X_2$, as well as the meaning of the multiple standard error of estimate. We will discuss the "Coef," "Stdev," and "t-ratio" columns later. To solve for the regression equation and generate the ANOVA table using MINITAB, type the first 11 lines listed below.

```
MTB > set c1
DATA> 28 66 38 70 22 27 28 47 14 68
DATA> end
MTB > set c2
DATA> 14 35 22 29 6 15 17 20 12 29
DATA> end
MTB > set c3
DATA> 2 5 4 4 3 3 3 4 2 5
DATA> end
MTB > name c1 'Sales' c2 'Calls' c3 'Products'
MTB > regr c1 2 c2 c3

The regression equation is
Sales = - 11.5 + 1.47 Calls + 6.59 Products

Predictor        Coef      Stdev     t-ratio        p
Constant      -11.452      9.231       -1.24    0.255
Calls          1.4671     0.5491        2.67    0.032
Products        6.588      4.550        1.45    0.191

s = 7.889       R-sq = 88.7%       R-sq(adj) = 85.5%

Analysis of Variance

SOURCE        DF         SS         MS         F         p
Regression     2     3427.9     1714.0     27.54     0.000
Error          7      435.7       62.2
Total          9     3863.6
```

Annotations: $s_{y \cdot 12}$ → s = 7.889; Coefficient of determination → R-sq = 88.7%; MSE → 62.2

First let's focus on the analysis of variance table. It is similar to the ANOVA table described in Chapter 10. In that chapter the variation was divided in two components: that due to the *treatments* and that due to random *error.* Here the total is also divided into two components: that explained by the **regression,** that is, the independent variables, and the **error,** or unexplained variation. These two categories are identified in the "SOURCE" column of the analysis of variance table. In the example there are 10 observations, so $n = 10$. The *total* number of degrees of freedom is $n - 1$, or $10 - 1 = 9$. The number of degrees of freedom in the "Regression" row is equal to the number of independent variables. We let k represent the number of independent variables, so $k = 2$. The number of degrees of freedom in the "Error" row is $n - (k + 1) = 10 - (2 + 1) = 7$ degrees of freedom.

The heading "SS" in the middle of the ANOVA table refers to the sum of squares, or the variation.

$$\text{Total variation} = \text{SS total} = \Sigma(Y - \overline{Y})^2 = 3{,}863.6$$

$$\text{Error variation} = \text{SSE} = \Sigma(Y - Y')^2 = 435.7$$

$$\text{Regression variation} = \text{SSR} = \text{SS total} - \text{SSE} = 3{,}863.6 - 435.7 = 3{,}427.9$$

The column headed "MS" (mean square) is determined by dividing the SS term by the df term. Thus, MSR, the mean square regression, is equal to SSR/k, and MSE equals SSE/$[n - (k + 1)]$. The general format of the ANOVA table is:

Source	*df*	SS	MS	*F*
Regression	k	SSR	MSR = SSR/k	MSR/MSE
Error	$n - (k + 1)$	SSE	MSE = SSE/$[n - (k + 1)]$	
Total	$n - 1$	SS total		

The **coefficient of multiple determination,** written as R^2, is the percent of the variation explained by the regression. It is the sum of squares due to the regression divided by the sum of squares total.

$$R^2 = \frac{\text{SSR}}{\text{SS total}} = \frac{3{,}427.9}{3{,}863.6} = .887$$

The multiple standard error of estimate may also be found directly from the ANOVA table.

$$s_{y \cdot 12} = \sqrt{\frac{\text{SSE}}{n - (k + 1)}} = \sqrt{\frac{435.7}{(10 - (2 + 1)}} = 7.889$$

These values, $R^2 = .887$ and $s_{y \cdot 12} = 7.889$, are included in the MINITAB output.

A Case Study

To cite an example of the use of multiple regression and correlation, and to show the universal application of a computer in problem solving, we will expand on an earlier exercise. Suppose a large, nationwide real estate firm wants to develop some guidelines for prospective buyers of small, single-family houses the firm lists. One of the most common questions prospective buyers ask is: If we purchased this home, what would we probably pay for heat during the winter months? The agent considered three variables important in predicting heating costs: (1) average daily minimum outside temperature, (2) number of inches of insulation in the attic, and (3) age of the furnace.

The agent had 20 local offices in various sections of the country gather information on the small houses they had listed. (See Table 13–3.)

TABLE 13–3 Cost of Heating and Other Characteristics about Small Houses

Small home	Heating cost (in dollars), Y	Minimum outside temperature, X_1	Inches of insulation, X_2	Age of furnace, X_3
1	250	35	3	6
2	360	29	4	10
3	165	36	7	3
4	43	60	6	9
5	92	65	5	6
6	200	30	5	5
7	355	10	6	7
8	290	7	10	10
9	230	21	9	11
10	120	55	2	5
11	73	54	12	4
12	205	48	5	1
13	400	20	5	15
14	320	39	4	7
15	72	60	8	6
16	272	20	5	8
17	94	58	7	3
18	190	40	8	11
19	235	27	9	8
20	139	30	7	5

Three independent variables, one dependent variable

There are three independent variables, designated X_1, X_2, and X_3. The dependent variable, the cost of heating, is Y. In order to visualize the relationship between two of the independent variables and the dependent variable (cost), scatter diagrams have been drawn.

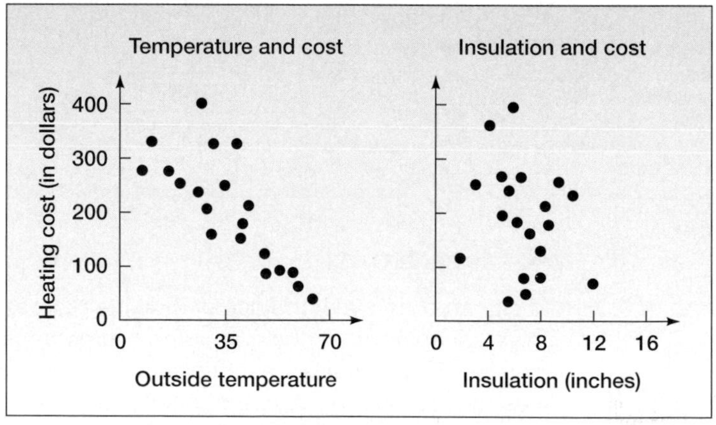

Of the independent variables shown, it does appear that there is a strong correlation between minimum outside temperature and heating cost. The relationship does not appear as strong between cost and insulation.

Correlation matrix

Correlation Matrix As a first step in analyzing the factors involved in the cost of heating a home, we develop a **correlation matrix.** A correlation matrix shows the simple correlation coefficients among all the variables. The output from MINITAB is as follows:

```
MTB > corr c1 c2 c3
            Cost       Temp     Insul
Temp      -0.812
Insul     -0.257     -0.103
Age        0.537     -0.486     0.064
```

Cost is the dependent variable, Y. We are particularly interested in which independent variable has the strongest correlation with cost. As indicated in the output, temperature has the strongest correlation (−.812) with cost. The negative sign indicates that as temperature increases, the cost to heat the home decreases.

Multicollinearity

A second use of the correlation matrix is to check for **multicollinearity.** Multicollinearity occurs when the independent variables are themselves correlated. This distorts the standard error of estimate and may lead to incorrect conclusions regarding which independent variables are statistically significant and which are not. In this example, the correlation between the age of the furnace and outside temperature is −.486. This is not large enough to cause a problem. A common rule of thumb is that correlations among the independent variables from −.70 to .70 do not cause problems. Usually when there is a strong correlation between two independent variables, one of the variables is deleted.

GLOBAL TEST: TESTING WHETHER OR NOT THE MULTIPLE REGRESSION MODEL IS VALID

The overall ability of the independent variables $X_1, X_2, \ldots, X_k$ to explain the behavior of the dependent variable Y can be tested. To put this in question form: Can the dependent variable be estimated without relying on the independent variables? The test used is referred to as the **global test.** Basically, it investigates whether all the independent variables have zero net regression coefficients. To put it another way, could the amount of explained variation, R^2, occur by chance?

Global test

To relate this question to the heating cost problem, we will test whether the independent variables (amount of insulation in the attic, minimum daily temperature, and age of furnace) are capable of effectively estimating home heating costs.

Null hypothesis

Recall that in testing a hypothesis, we first state the null hypothesis and the alternate hypothesis. In the heating cost problem, there are three independent variables. Recall that b_1, b_2, and b_3 are sample net regression coefficients. The corresponding coefficients in the population are given the symbols β_1, β_2, and β_3. We now test whether the net regression coefficients in the population are zero. The null hypothesis is:

$$H_0\text{: } \beta_1 = \beta_1 = \beta_3 = 0$$

Alternate hypothesis

The alternate hypothesis is:

$$H_1\text{: Not all the } \beta\text{s are 0.}$$

If the null hypothesis is true, it implies that the regression coefficients are all zero and, logically, are of no use in estimating the dependent variable (heating cost). Should that be the case, we would have to search for some other independent variables—or take a different approach—to predict home heating costs.

F test applied

To test the null hypothesis that the multiple regression coefficients are all zero, we employ the *F* distribution introduced in Chapter 11. We will use the .05 level of significance. Recall these characteristics of the *F* distribution:

1. It is positively skewed, with the critical value for the .05 level located in the right tail. The critical value is the point that separates the region where H_0 is not rejected from the region of rejection.
2. It is constructed by knowing the number of degrees of freedom in the numerator and the number of degrees of freedom in the denominator.

The degrees of freedom for the numerator and the denominator may be found in the computer summary in the analysis of variance table. That portion of the table is included below. The top number in the column marked "DF" is 3, indicating that there are 3 degrees of freedom in the numerator. The middle number in the "DF" column (16) indicates that there are 16 degrees of freedom in the denominator. The number 16 is found by $n - (k + 1) = 20 - (3 + 1) = 16$. The number 3 corresponds to the number of independent variables.

Analysis of Variance

SOURCE	DF	SS	MS	F	p
Regression	3	171220	57073	21.90	0.000
Error	16	41695	2606		
Total	19	212916			

The value of *F* is computed by dividing the MSR term by MSE.

$$F = \frac{\dfrac{\text{SSR}}{k}}{\dfrac{\text{SSE}}{n-(k+1)}} = \frac{\text{MSR}}{\text{MSE}} = \frac{57{,}073}{2{,}606} = 21.90$$

Diagram showing regions of acceptance and rejection

The critical value of *F* is found in Appendix G. Using the table for the .05 level, move horizontally to 3 degrees of freedom in the numerator, then down to 16 degrees of freedom in the denominator, and read the critical value. It is 3.24. The region where H_0 is not rejected and the region where H_0 is rejected are shown in the diagram at the top of the following page.

Decision rule

Continuing with the global test, the decision rule is: Do not reject the null hypothesis that all the regression coefficients are 0 if the computed value of *F* is less than or equal to 3.24. If computed *F* is greater than 3.24, reject H_0 and accept the alternate hypothesis, H_1.

The decision

The computed value of *F* is 21.90, which is in the rejection region. The null hypothesis that all the multiple regression coefficients are zero is therefore rejected. The *p*-value is 0.000 from the above Analysis of Variance table, so it is unlikely that H_0 is true. The alternate hypothesis is accepted, indicating that not all the regression coefficients are zero. From a practical standpoint, this means that the independent

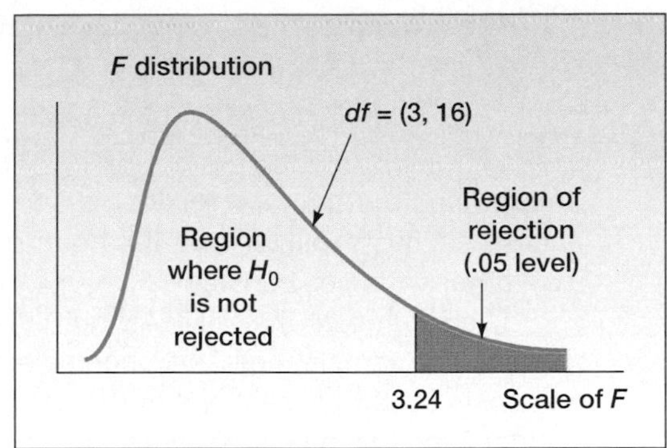

variables (amount of insulation, etc.) do have the ability to explain the variation in the dependent variable (heating cost). We expected this decision. Logically, the outside temperature, the amount of insulation, and so on have a great bearing on heating costs. The global test assures us that they do.

Evaluating Individual Regression Coefficients

In the heating cost problem, we showed that some, but not necessarily all, of the regression coefficients are not equal to zero. The next step is to test the variables *individually* to determine which regression coefficients may be 0 and which are not.

Why is it important to find out if it is possible that any of the βs equal 0? If a β could equal 0, it implies that this particular independent variable is of no value in explaining any variation in the dependent variable. If there are coefficients for which H_0 cannot be rejected, we may want to eliminate them from the regression equation.

We will now conduct three separate tests of hypothesis—for temperature, for insulation, and for the age of the furnace.

For temperature:	For insulation:	For furnace age:
$H_0: \beta_1 = 0$	$H_0: \beta_2 = 0$	$H_0: \beta_3 = 0$
$H_1: \beta_1 \neq 0$	$H_1: \beta_2 \neq 0$	$H_1: \beta_3 \neq 0$

We will test the hypotheses at the .05 level. The way the alternate hypothesis is stated indicates that the test is two-tailed.

The test statistic is the Student *t* distribution with $n - (k + 1)$ degrees of freedom. The number of sample observations is *n*. There are 20 homes in the study, so $n = 20$. The number of independent variables is *k*, which is 3. Thus, there are $n - (k + 1) = 20 - (3 + 1) = 16$ degrees of freedom.

The critical value for *t* is in Appendix F. For a two-tailed test with 16 degrees of freedom and using the .05 significance level, H_0 is rejected if *t* is less than −2.120 or greater than 2.120. The MINITAB system produced the following output.

```
Predictor         Coef       Stdev      t-ratio         p
Constant        427.19       59.60         7.17     0.000
Temp           -4.5827      0.7723        -5.93     0.000
Insul          -14.831       4.754        -3.12     0.007
Age              6.101       4.012         1.52     0.148

s = 51.05     R-sq = 80.4%      R-sq(adj) = 76.7%
```

The column headed "Coef" gives the multiple regression equation:

$$Y' = 427.19 - 4.5827X_1 - 14.831X_2 + 6.101X_3$$

Interpreting the term $-4.5827X_1$ in the equation: For each degree the temperature increases, it is expected that the heating cost will decrease about $4.58, holding the two other variables constant.

The column on the MINITAB output labeled "Stdev" indicates the standard deviation of the sample regression coefficient. Recall that we selected a sample of heating costs in various sections of the country. If we were to select a second sample at random and compute the regression coefficients of that sample, the values would not be exactly the same. If we were to repeat the sampling process many times, however, we could design a sampling distribution of the regression coefficients. The column labeled "Stdev" estimates the variability of these regression coefficients. The sampling distribution of Coef/Stdev follows the t distribution with $n - (k + 1)$ degrees of freedom. Hence, we are able to test the independent variables individually to determine if the net regression coefficients differ from zero. The computed t ratio is -5.93 for temperature and -3.12 for insulation. Both of these t values are in the rejection region to the left of -2.120. Thus, we conclude that the regression coefficients for the temperature and insulation variables are *not* zero. The computed t for age of the

SELF-REVIEW 13–3

The answers are at the end of the chapter.

The multiple regression and correlation data for the preceding heating cost problem were rerun on the computer using only the two significant independent variables—temperature and insulation. (See the following MINITAB output.)

1. What is the new multiple regression equation? (Temperature is X_1 and insulation X_2.)
2. What is the coefficient of multiple determination? Interpret.
3. How can you tell that these two independent variables are of value in predicting heating costs?
4. What is the p-value of insulation? Interpret.

```
The regression equation is
cost = 490 - 5.15 temp - 14.7 insul
Predictor        Coef       Stdev     t-ratio     p-value
Constant       490.29       44.41       11.04       0.000
temp          -5.1499      0.7019       -7.34       0.000
insul         -14.718       4.934       -2.98       0.008

s = 52.98        R-sq = 77.6%       R-sq(adj) = 74.9%

Analysis of Variance
SOURCE          DF         SS        MS         F     p-value
Regression       2     165195     82597     29.42       0.000
Error           17      47721      2807
Total           19     212916
```

furnace is 1.52, so we conclude that β_3 could equal 0. The independent variable "age of the furnace" is not a significant predictor of heating cost.

p-value

In Chapter 10 we described how a *p*-value is used to interpret the strength of the rejection. *p*-values are also reported on this output. The value .007 in the *p*-value column and insulation row is the two-tailed probability of a *t* value less than -3.12 or greater than 3.12, given a true H_0. In summary, we recommend that the independent variable "furnace age" be removed from the study and the variables "temperature" and "insulator" retained.

As noted in Self-Review 13–3 and the accompanying output, the multiple regression problem was run again using MINITAB, but only two variables—"temperature" and "insulation"—were included. These two variables explained 77.6 percent of the variation in heating cost. Using all three variables—temperature, insulation, and furnace age—a total of 80.4 percent of the variation is explained. The additional variable increased R^2 by only 2.8 percent—a rather small increase for the addition of an independent variable.

QUALITATIVE VARIABLES IN REGRESSION

So far the variables used to estimate the cost of heating a home have been *quantitative*; that is, numerical in nature. Frequently, we wish to use **qualitative variables,** which describe a quality rather than a quantity. To use qualitative variables in regression, we employ a scheme of **dummy variables** in which one of the conditions is coded 0 and the other condition 1.

For example, we might be interested in estimating an executive's salary based on years of job experience and whether or not he or she graduated from college. We presume that a graduate will earn a larger salary than someone who did not graduate. "Graduation from college" can take on only one of two conditions—yes or no. Thus, it is considered a qualitative variable.

Is it possible to use a qualitative variable with more than two possible outcomes? Yes, but the coding scheme becomes more complex and will require a series of dummy variables. To explain, suppose a company is studying its sales as they relate to advertising expense by quarter for the last five years. Let sales be the dependent variable and advertising expense be the first independent variable, X_1. To include the qualitative information regarding the quarter, we will need three additional independent variables. For the variable X_2, the five observations referring to the first quarter of each of the five years are coded 1 and the other quarters 0. Similarly, for X_3 the five observations referring to the second quarter are coded 1 and the other quarters 0. For X_4 the five observations referring to the third quarter are coded 1 and the other quarters 0. An observation that does not refer to any of the first three quarters must refer to the fourth quarter, so a distinct independent variable referring to this quarter is not necessary.

Suppose in the heating cost study the independent variable "garage" is added. For those homes without an attached garage, 0 is used; for homes with an attached garage, a 1 is used. We will refer to the "garage" variable as X_4. The data from Table 13–4 are entered into the MINITAB system.

TABLE 13–4 Home Heating Costs, Temperature, Insulation, and Presence of a Garage for a Sample of 20 Homes

Cost, Y	Temperature, X_1	Insulation, X_2	Garage, X_4
$250	35	3	0
360	29	4	1
165	36	7	0
43	60	6	0
92	65	5	0
200	30	5	0
355	10	6	1
290	7	10	1
230	21	9	0
120	55	2	0
73	54	12	0
205	48	5	1
400	20	5	1
320	39	4	1
72	60	8	0
272	20	5	1
94	58	7	0
190	40	8	1
235	27	9	0
139	30	7	0

The output from MINITAB is:

```
MTB > NAME C5 'GARAGE'
MTB > REGR C1 3 C2 C3 C5

The regression equation is
cost = 394 - 3.96 temp - 11.3 insul + 77.4 garage

Predictor        Coef      Stdev     t-ratio     p-value
Constant       393.67      45.00        8.75       0.000
temp          -3.9628     0.6527       -6.07       0.000
insul         -11.334      4.002       -2.83       0.012
garage          77.43      22.78        3.40       0.004

s = 41.62       R-sq = 87.0%       R-sq(adj) = 84.5%

Analysis of Variance

SOURCE        DF         SS        MS         F     p-value
Regression     3     185202     61734     35.64       0.000
Error         16      27713      1732
Total         19     212916
```

What is the effect of the variable "garage"? Should it be included in the analysis? To show the effect of the variable, suppose we have two houses exactly alike next to each other in Buffalo, New York; one has an attached garage, and the other does not. Both homes have 3 inches of insulation, and the mean January temperature in

Buffalo is 20 degrees. For the house without an attached garage, a 0 is substituted for X_4 in the regression equation. The estimated heating cost is $280.90, found by:

$$Y' = 394 - 3.96X_1 - 11.3X_2 + 77.4X_4$$

$$= 394 - 3.96(20) - 11.3(3) + 77.4(0) = 280.90$$

For the house with an attached garage, a 1 is substituted for X_4 in the regression equation. The estimated heating cost is $385.30, found by:

$$Y' = 394 - 3.96X_1 - 11.3X_2 + 77.4X_4$$

$$= 394 - 3.96(20) - 11.3(3) + 77.4(1) = 358.30$$

The difference between the estimated heating costs is $77.40 ($358.30 − $280.90). Hence, we can expect the cost to heat a house with an attached garage to be $77.40 more than the cost for an equivalent house without a garage.

We have shown the difference between the two types of homes to be $77.40, but is the difference significant? We conduct the following test of hypothesis.

$$H_0: \beta_4 = 0$$

$$H_1: \beta_4 \neq 0$$

The information necessary to answer this question can be found in the MINITAB output given on the previous page. The computed t ratio is 3.40. There are three independent variables in the analysis, so there are $n - (k + 1) = 20 - (3 + 1) = 16$ degrees of freedom. The critical value from Appendix F is 2.120. The decision rule, using a two-tailed test and the .05 significance level, is to reject H_0 if the computed t is to the left of −2.120 or to the right of 2.120. Since the computed value of 3.40 is to the right of 2.120, the null hypothesis is rejected. It is concluded that the regression coefficient is not zero. The independent variable "garage" should be included in the analysis.

STEPWISE REGRESSION

The regression equation we developed for the heating cost problem included three independent variables: minimum average temperature, inches of insulation, and whether or not there is an attached garage. To obtain the equation, we first ran a global or "all at once" test to determine if any of the regression coefficients were significant. When we found at least one to be significant, we then tested the coefficients individually to determine which were significant. We dropped those that were not significant and retained the others. We argued that by retaining the significant coefficients, we found the regression equation that used the fewest independent variables possible, making it easy to interpret and explaining as much of the variation in the dependent variable as possible. We are now going to describe a technique called **stepwise regression,** which is more efficient in building the equation.

The stepwise technique

In the stepwise method, a sequence of equations is developed. The first equation contains only one independent variable. However, this independent variable is the one from the set of proposed variables that explains the most variation in the dependent variable. Stated differently, if all the simple correlations between each independent variable and the dependent variable are computed, the stepwise method selects the independent variable with the strongest correlation with the dependent variable.

Next, the stepwise method looks at the remaining independent variables and selects the one that will explain the largest percentage of the variation yet unexplained. This process is continued until all the independent variables with significant net regression coefficients are included in the equation. The advantages to the stepwise method are: (1) Only significant regression coefficients are included in the equation, (2) the steps involved in building the equation are clearly seen, and (3) the step-by-step changes in the standard error of estimate and the coefficient of determination are shown.

The stepwise MINITAB output for the heating problem follows. Note that the final equation includes the same three variables we obtained using the preceding global test. The variables with nonsignificant regression coefficients have been eliminated.

```
MTB > STEP C1 C2 - C5

STEPWISE REGRESSION OF COST ON 4 PREDICTORS, WITHIN N = 20

    STEP          1        2        3
CONSTANT      388.8    300.3    393.7

temp          -4.93    -3.56    -3.96
T-RATIO       -5.89    -4.70    -6.07

garage                    93       77
T-RATIO                 3.56     3.40

insul                           -11.3
T-RATIO                         -2.83

S              63.6     49.5     41.6
R-SQ          65.85    80.46    86.98
```

Reviewing the steps: The regression equation after the first step is:

$$Y' = 388.8 - 4.93X_1$$

The independent variable "temperature" explains 65.85 percent of the variation in heating cost. The standard error of estimate is $63.60.

The next independent variable to enter the equation is the variable for whether or not there is an attached garage. Including the two independent variables "temperature" and "garage," the R-square term is increased from 65.85 percent to 80.46 percent. That is, by adding the second variable, "garage," R^2 increased 14.61 percentage points. This increase is larger than the increase would have been if any other independent variable had been added. The regression equation after step 2 is:

$$Y' = 300.3 - 3.56X_1 + 93.0X_4$$

Usually the regression coefficients will change from one step to the next. In this case the coefficient for temperature has retained its negative sign, but it changed from

-4.93 to -3.56. This change is reflective of the added influence of the independent variable "garage." Why did the stepwise method select the variable for garage instead of the variable for insulation? Again, it is because the increase in R^2 (the coefficient of determination) is larger if garage is used than if insulation were used.

After the third step the regression equation is:

$$Y' = 393.7 - 3.96X_1 - 11.3X_2 + 77.0X_4$$

This is the same equation we obtained using the global test followed by the individual test on each of the regression coefficients. The R^2 value is 86.98 percent, the same as calculated earlier. Thus, with the stepwise method we have developed the same regression equation, and it consists of the same variables. However, the stepwise method offers a more direct route to the optimal equation.

ANALYSIS OF RESIDUALS

In an earlier section we described the basic assumptions required for regression and correlation analysis. These assumptions are:

1. There is a linear (straight-line) relationship between the dependent variable and the independent variables.
2. The dependent variable is interval- or ratio-scale.
3. Successive observations of the dependent variable are not correlated.
4. The differences between the actual values and the estimated values are approximately normally distributed, and they are the same for all estimated values.

Residuals

The last assumption can be verified by plotting the residuals. As discussed earlier, a residual is the difference between the actual value of Y and the predicted value of Y, namely, $(Y - Y')$.

The MINITAB system is useful for investigating if the residuals are normally distributed and also if they have a constant variance around the values of Y'. Table 13–5 presents the data necessary for further analysis of the heating cost problem. Column 1 shows the actual heating costs, originally presented in Table 13–3. Column 2 presents the fitted or estimated value of Y; this is Y'. The value for Y' is found by substituting the actual values of the three independent variables into the regression equation. For example, the first fitted value is 221.08, found by:

$$Y' - 393.67 - 3.96(35) - 11.33(3) + 77.43(0) = 221.08$$

(The difference between 221.08 and the value 220.964 in Table 13–5 is due to rounding in the computer software.) The residual in column 3 is 29.0358, found by 250.00 − 220.964. The residuals for the other 19 observations are computed similarly.

TABLE 13–5 Summary of Actual Costs, Estimated Costs, and Residuals for Heating Cost Problem

Home	Actual cost, Y	Estimated cost, Y'	Residual, $Y - Y'$
1	$250	$220.964	29.0358
2	360	310.839	49.1606
3	165	171.665	−6.6655
4	43	87.891	−44.8911
5	92	79.411	12.5892
6	200	218.110	−18.1105
7	355	363.466	−8.4656
8	290	330.018	−40.0183
9	230	208.440	21.5597
10	120	153.041	−33.0412
11	73	43.664	29.3355
12	205	224.211	−19.2113
13	400	335.171	64.8289
14	320	271.211	48.7891
15	72	65.223	6.7768
16	272	335.171	−63.1711
17	94	84.483	9.5171
18	190	221.912	−31.9123
19	235	184.663	50.3368
20	139	195.443	−56.4426

The fitted values and the residuals can be computed by MINITAB. The following statements are required to place the fitted values in C11 and the residuals of C20 of the MINITAB output. (The information in C10 is not described here but is required to obtain the fitted values from MINITAB.) The ";" at the end of the first line and the "." at the end of the second line are required.

```
MTB>  regr c1 3 c2 c3 c5, c10 c11;
SUBC> residuals c20.
```

The MINITAB system also develops both a step-and-leaf display, introduced in Chapter 2 (see Chart 13–2), and a histogram (see Chart 13–3) for the residuals. Both charts indicate that the distribution of the residuals is somewhat normal, as required in the assumptions. To interpret the histogram in Chart 13–3, note that it is constructed so the residuals are tallied in classes: −50 up to −70, with a midpoint of −60; −30 up to −50, with a midpoint of −40; and so on. Some of the classes are:

Class	Midpoint	Residuals	Count
−50 up to −70	−60	−63.1711, −56.4426	2
−30 up to −50	−40	−44.8911, −40.0183 −33.0142, −31.9123	4
−10 up to −30	−20	−18.1105, −19.2113	2

CHART 13–2 Stem-and-Leaf Display of Residuals

```
MTB > STEM C20
Stem-and-leaf of residual N = 20
Leaf Unit = 10
 1    -0 6
 4    -0 544
 6    -0 33
10    -0 1100
10     0 001
 7     0 222
 4     0 445
 1     0 6
```

CHART 13–3 Histogram of Residuals

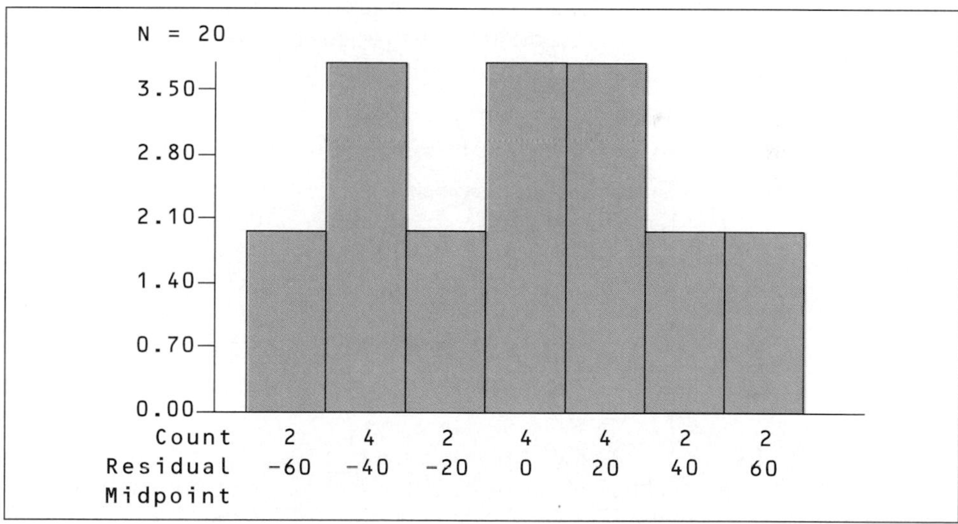

Homoscedasticity

The assumptions for regression analysis also require that the residuals remain constant for all values of Y'. Recall that this condition is called **homoscedasticity.** To check for homoscedasticity, the residuals are plotted against the fitted values of Y (see Chart 13–4). Because there is no more variation around large values of Y' than around small values of Y', we can conclude that this assumption is met.

CHART 13–4 **Fitted Values of *Y'* and Residuals**

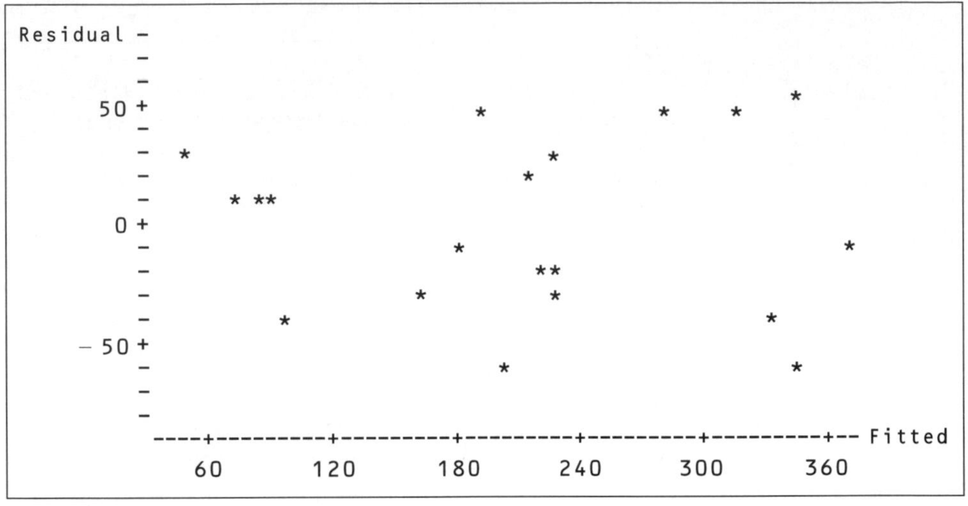

Following are two examples where the homoscedasticity requirement is not met. Note that in the first example, the plot of residuals is funnel-shaped. That is, as the fitted *Y* values increase, so does the variation in the residuals. In the second example, there is a pattern to the residuals. The residuals seem to take the shape of a polynomial, or second-degree equation.

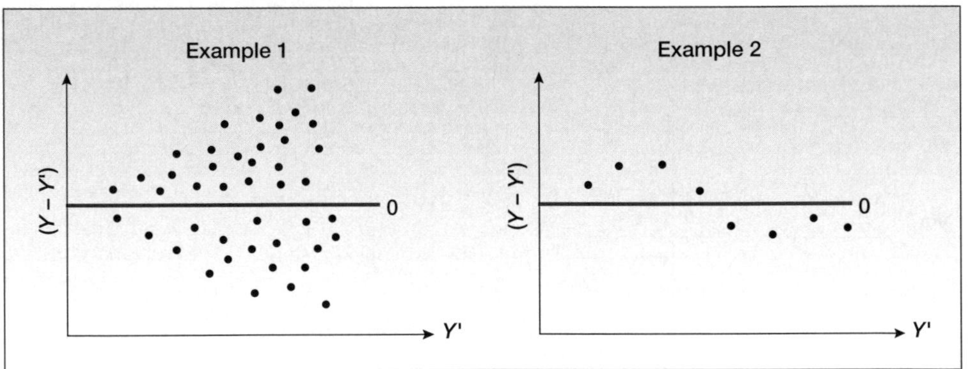

What problems are caused by residuals that fail to show homoscedasticity? The standard deviations of the regression coefficients will be understated (too small), causing potential independent variables to appear to be significant when they may not be. The remedy for this condition is to select other independent variables or to transform some of the variables. For a more detailed discussion of residual analysis, refer to an advanced text, such as *Applied Linear Regression Models* by Neter, Kutner, Nachtsheim, and Wasserman (Irwin, 1996).

CHAPTER OUTLINE

I. Multiple regression and correlation analysis is based on these assumptions.
   A. There is a linear relationship between the independent variables and the dependent variable.
   B. The dependent variable is continuous and of interval scale.
   C. The residual variation is the same for all fitted values of Y, and these residuals are normally distributed.
   D. Successive observations of the dependent variable are uncorrelated.

II. The general form of the sample multiple regression equation is:

$$Y' = a + b_1X_1 + b_2X_2 + \cdots + b_kX_k \quad (13\text{–}3)$$

where Y' is the estimated value, a is the Y-intercept, the bs are the sample regression coefficients, and the Xs represent the values of the various independent variables.
   A. There can be an unlimited number of independent variables.
   B. The least squares criterion is used to develop the equation.
   C. A computer is needed to determine a and the various b values.

III. There are two measures of the effectiveness of the regression equation.
   A. The multiple standard error of estimate is similar to the standard deviation.
      1. It is measured in the same units as the dependent variable.
      2. It is difficult to determine what is a large value and what is a small value of the standard error.
   B. The coefficient of determination may range from 0 to 1.
      1. It shows the fraction of the variation in Y that is explained by the set of independent variables.
      2. It does not reveal the direction of the relationship.

IV. The ANOVA table gives the variation in the dependent variable that is explained by the regression equation, as well as that which is not explained.

V. A correlation matrix is used to show all possible simple correlation coefficients between all the variables.

VI. A global test is used to investigate whether any of the independent variables have significant regression coefficients.
   A. The null hypothesis is: All the regression coefficients are zero.
   B. The alternate hypothesis is: At least one regression coefficient is not zero.
   C. The test statistic is the F distribution with k (the number of independent variables) and $n - (k + 1)$ degrees of freedom, where n is the sample size.

VII. The test for individual variables is used to determine which independent variables have nonzero regression coefficients.
   A. The variables that have zero regression coefficients are usually dropped from the analysis.
   B. The test statistic is the t distribution with $n - (k + 1)$ degrees of freedom.

VIII. Dummy variables are used to represent qualitative variables.

IX. A stepwise regression leads directly to the most efficient regression equation.
   A. Only independent variables with significant regression coefficients are entered into the analysis.
   B. Variables are entered in the order in which they increase the R^2 term the greatest amount.

X. A residual is the difference between the actual value of Y and the predicted value of Y'.
   A. Residuals should be approximately normally distributed. Histograms and stem-and-leaf charts are useful in checking this requirement.
   B. A plot of the residuals and their corresponding Y' values is useful for showing that there are no trends or patterns in the residuals.

EXERCISES

The answers to the odd-numbered exercises are at the end of the book.

5. The district manager of Jasons, a large discount retail chain, is investigating why certain stores in her region are performing better than others. She believes that three factors are related to total sales: the number of competitors in the region, the population in the surrounding area, and the amount spent on advertising. From her district, consisting of several hundred stores, she selects a random sample of 30 stores. For each store she gathered the following information.

   Y = total sales last year (in $ thousands).

   X_1 = number of competitors in the region.

   X_2 = population of the region (in millions).

   X_3 = advertising expense (in $ thousands).

   The sample data were run on the MINITAB software package, with the following results.

```
Analysis of variance

Source        DF        SS          MS
Regression     3     3050.00      762.50
Error         26     2200.00       84.62
Total         29     5250.00

Predictor      Coef      Stdev     t-ratio
Constant      14.00       7.00       2.00
   X1         -1.00       0.70      -1.43
   X2         30.00       5.20       5.77
   X3          0.20       0.08       2.50
```

   a. What is the estimated sales for the Bryne Store, which has four competitors, a regional population of 0.4 (400,000), and advertising expense of 30 ($30,000)?
   b. Compute the R^2 value.
   c. Compute the multiple standard error of estimate.
   d. Conduct a global test of hypothesis to determine if any of the regression coefficients are not equal to zero. Use the .05 level of significance.
   e. Conduct tests of hypotheses to determine which of the independent variables have significant regression coefficients. Which variables would you consider eliminating? Use the .05 significance level.

6. In a multiple regression equation $k = 5$ and $n = 20$, the MSE value is 5.10, and SS total is 519.68. At the .05 significance level, can we conclude that any of the regression coefficients are not equal to 0?

7. A multiple regression equation yields the following partial results.

Source	Sum of squares	*df*
Regression	750	4
Error	500	35

   a. What is the total sample size?
   b. How many independent variables are being considered?
   c. Compute the coefficient of determination.

d. Compute the standard error of estimate.
e. Test the hypothesis that none of the regression coefficients is equal to zero. Let $\alpha = .05$.

8. In a multiple regression equation two independent variables are considered, and the total sample size is 25. The regression coefficients and the standard errors are as follows.

$$b_1 = \quad 2.676 \quad s_{b1} = 0.56$$

$$b_2 = -0.880 \quad s_{b2} = 0.71$$

Conduct a test of hypothesis to determine if either independent variable has a coefficient equal to zero. Would you consider deleting either variable from the regression equation? Use the .05 significance level.

9. The following MINITAB output was obtained.

Analysis of variance

Source	DF	SS	MS
Regression	5	100	20
Error	20	40	2
Total	25	140	

Predictor	Coef	Stdev	t-ratio
Constant	3.00	1.50	2.00
X_1	4.00	3.00	1.33
X_2	3.00	0.20	15.00
X_3	0.20	0.05	4.00
X_4	−2.50	1.00	−2.50
X_5	3.00	4.00	0.75

a. What is the total sample size?
b. Compute the value of R^2.
c. Compute the multiple standard error of estimate.
d. Conduct a global test of hypothesis to determine if any of the regression coefficients are significant. Use the .05 significance level.
e. Test the regression coefficients individually. Would you consider omitting any variable(s)? If so, which one(s)? Use the .05 significance level.

10. Suppose that the sales manager of a large automotive parts distributor wants to estimate as early as April the total annual sales of a region. Based on regional sales, the total sales for the company can also be estimated. If, based on past experience, it is found that the April estimates of annual sales are reasonably accurate, then in future years the April forecast could be used to revise production schedules and maintain the correct inventory at the retail outlets.

Several factors appear to be related to sales, including the number of retail outlets in the region stocking the company's parts, the number of automobiles in the region registered as of April 1, and the total personal income for the first quarter of the year. A total of five independent variables was finally selected as being the most important (according to the sales manager). Then the data were gathered for a recent year. The total annual sales for that year for each region were also recorded. Note in the following table that for region 1 there were 1,739 retail outlets stocking the company's automotive parts, there were 9,270,000 registered automobiles in the region as of April 1, and sales for that year were $37,702,000.

Annual sales ($ millions), Y	Number of retail outlets, X_1	Number of automobiles registered (millions), X_2	Personal income ($ billions), X_3	Average age of automobiles (years), X_4	Number of supervisors, X_5
37.702	1,739	9.27	85.4	3.5	9.0
24.196	1,221	5.86	60.7	5.0	5.0
32.055	1,846	8.81	68.1	4.4	7.0
3.611	120	3.81	20.2	4.0	5.0
17.625	1,096	10.31	33.8	3.5	7.0
45.919	2,290	11.62	95.1	4.1	13.0
29.600	1,687	8.96	69.3	4.1	15.0
8.114	241	6.28	16.3	5.9	11.0
20.116	649	7.77	34.9	5.5	16.0
12.994	1,427	10.92	15.1	4.1	10.0

The MINITAB software system was used to generate the following output.

a. Consider the following correlation matrix. Which variable has the strongest correlation with the dependent variable? The correlations between the independent variables "outlets" and "income" and between "cars" and "outlets" is fairly strong. Could this be a problem? What is this condition called?

```
          sales    outlets      cars    income      age
outlets   0.899
cars      0.605     0.775
income    0.964     0.825     0.409
age      -0.323    -0.489    -0.447    -0.349
bosses    0.286     0.183     0.395     0.155    0.291
```

b. The following regression equation was obtained using the five independent variables. What percent of the variation is explained by the regression equation?

```
The regression equation is
sales = -19.7 - 0.00063 outlets + 1.74 cars + 0.410 income
        + 2.04 age - 0.034 bosses

         Predictor          Coef        Stdev     t-ratio
         Constant        -19.672        5.422       -3.63
         outlets       -0.000629     0.002638       -0.24
         cars             1.7399       0.5530        3.15
         income          0.40994      0.04385        9.35
         age              2.0357       0.8779        2.32
         bosses          -0.0344       0.1880       -0.18

Analysis of Variance

         SOURCE        DF         SS         MS
         Regression     5    1593.81     318.76
         Error          4       9.08       2.27
         Total          9    1602.89
```

c. Conduct a global test of hypothesis to determine if any of the regression coefficients are not zero.

d. Conduct a test of hypothesis on each of the independent variables. Would you consider eliminating "outlets" and "bosses"?

e. The regression has been rerun below with "outlets" and "bosses" eliminated. Compute the coefficient of determination. How much has R^2 changed from the previous analysis?

```
The regression equation is
       sales = −18.9 + 1.61 cars + 0.400 income + 1.96 age

          Predictor            Coef         Stdev    t-ratio
          Constant          −18.924         3.636      −5.20
          Cars               1.6129        0.1979       8.15
          Income            0.40031       0.01569      25.52
          Age                1.9637        0.5846       3.36

Analysis of Variance

          SOURCE        DF          SS          MS
          Regression     3     1593.66      531.22
          Error          6        9.23        1.54
          Total          9     1602.89
```

f. Following is a histogram and a stem-and-leaf chart of the residuals. Does the normality assumption appear reasonable?

```
Histogram of residual N = 10     Stem-and-leaf of residual N = 10
                                 Leaf Unit = 0.10
Midpoint  Count
    −1.5      1  *                1   −1 7
    −1.0      1  *                2   −1 2
    −0.5      2  **               2   −0
     0.0      2  **               5   −0 440
     0.5      2  **               5    0 24
     1.0      1  *                3    0 68
     1.5      1  *                1    1
                                  1    1 7
```

g. Following is a plot of the fitted values of Y (i.e., Y') and the residuals. Do you see any violations of the assumptions?

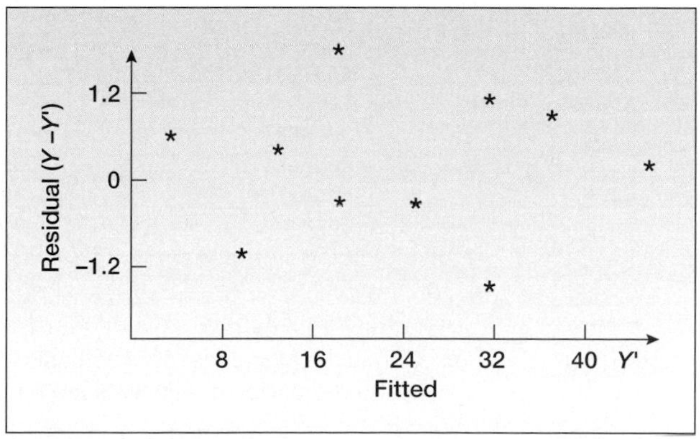

11. The administrator of a new paralegal program at Seagate Technical College wants to estimate the grade point average in the new program. He thought that high school GPA, the verbal score on the Scholastic Aptitude Test (SAT), and the mathematics score on the SAT would be good predictors of paralegal GPA. The data on nine students are:

Student	High school GPA	SAT verbal	SAT math	Paralegal GPA
1	3.25	480	410	3.21
2	1.80	290	270	1.68
3	2.89	420	410	3.58
4	3.81	500	600	3.92
5	3.13	500	490	3.00
6	2.81	430	460	2.82
7	2.20	320	490	1.65
8	2.14	530	480	2.30
9	2.63	469	440	2.33

The MINITAB software system was used to generate the following output.

a. The following correlation matrix was obtained. Which variable has the strongest correlation with the dependent variable? Some of the correlations among the independent variables are strong. Does this appear to be a problem?

```
             legal       gpa      verbal
gpa          0.911
verbal       0.616     0.609
math         0.487     0.636      0.599
```

b. Consider the following output. Compute the coefficient of multiple determination.

```
The regression equation is
legal = −0.411 + 1.20 gpa + 0.00163 verbal −0.00194 math

Predictor          Coef         Stdev      t-ratio
Constant        −0.4111        0.7823        −0.53
gpa              1.2014        0.2955         4.07
verbal         0.001629      0.002147         0.76
math          −0.001939      0.002074        −0.94

Analysis of Variance

SOURCE         DF        SS         MS
Regression      3    4.3595     1.4532
Error           5    0.7036     0.1407
Total           8    5.0631
```

c. Conduct a global test of hypothesis from the preceding output. Does it appear that any of the regression coefficients are not equal to zero?

d. Conduct a test of hypothesis on each independent variable. Would you consider eliminating the variables "verbal" and "math"? Let $\alpha = .05$.

e. The analysis has been rerun without "verbal" and "math." See the following output. Compute the coefficient of determination. How much has R^2 changed from the previous analysis?

```
The regression equation is
legal = −0.454 + 1.16 gpa

  Predictor        Coef       Stdev     t-ratio
  Constant      −0.4542      0.5542       −0.82
  gpa            1.1589      0.1977        5.86

Analysis of Variance

SOURCE        DF       SS          MS
Regression     1     4.2061      4.2061
Error          7     0.8570      0.1224
Total          8     5.0631
```

f. Following are a histogram and a stem-and-leaf diagram of the residuals. Does the normality assumption for the residuals seem reasonable?

```
Histogram of residual N = 9

Midpoint      Count
    −0.4          1 *
    −0.2          3 ***
     0.0          3 ***
     0.2          1 *
     0.4          0
     0.6          1 *
Stem-and-leaf of residual N = 9
Leaf Unit = 0.10

 1       −0 4
 2       −0 2
(3)      −0 110
 4        0 00
 2        0 2
 1        0
 1        0 6
```

g. Following is a plot of the residuals and the Y' values. Do you see any violation of the assumptions?

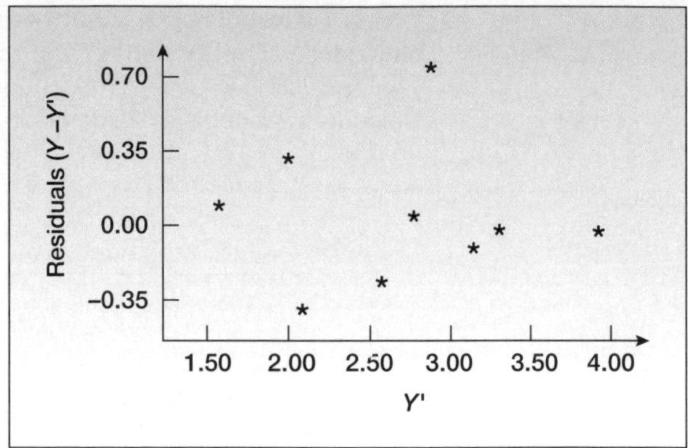

The following problems require the MINITAB system or a similar software package.

12. Mr. Mike Wilde is president of the teachers' union for the Otsego School District. In preparing for the upcoming negotiations, he would like to investigate the salary structure of classroom teachers in the district. He believes there are three factors that affect a teacher's salary: years of experience, a rating of teaching effectiveness given by the principal, and whether or not the teacher has a master's degree. A sample of 20 teachers resulted in the following data.

Salary ($ thousands), Y	Years of experience, X_1	Principal's rating, X_2	Master's degree,* Y_3
21.1	8	35	0
23.6	5	43	0
19.3	2	51	1
33.0	15	60	1
28.6	11	73	0
35.0	14	80	1
32.0	9	76	0
26.8	7	54	1
38.6	22	55	1
21.7	3	90	1
15.7	1	30	0
20.6	5	44	0
41.8	23	84	1
36.7	17	76	0
28.4	12	68	1
23.6	14	25	0
31.8	8	90	1
20.7	4	62	0
22.8	2	80	1
32.8	8	72	0

*1 = yes, 0 = no.

a. Develop a correlation matrix. Which independent variable has the strongest correlation with the dependent variable? Does it appear that there will be any problems with multicollinearity?

b. Determine the regression equation. What salary would you estimate for a teacher with five years' experience, a rating by the principal of 60, and no master's degree?

c. Conduct a global test of hypothesis to determine if any of the net regression coefficients differ from zero.
d. Conduct a test of hypothesis for the individual regression coefficients. Would you consider deleting any of the independent variables?
e. If your conclusion in part *d* was to delete one or more independent variables, run the analysis again without those variables.
f. Determine the residuals for the equation of part *e.* Use a stem-and-leaf chart or a histogram to verify that the distribution of the residuals is approximately normal.
g. Plot the residuals computed in part *f* in a scatter diagram with the residuals on the Y-axis and the Y' values on the X-axis. Does the plot reveal any violations of the assumptions of regression?

13. The district sales manager for a major automobile manufacturer is studying car sales. Specifically, he would like to determine what factors affect the number of cars sold at a dealership. To investigate, he randomly selects 12 dealers. From these dealers he obtains the number of cars sold last month, the minutes of radio advertising purchased last month, the number of full-time salespeople employed in the dealership, and whether the dealer is located in the city or not. The information is as follows:

Cars sold last month, Y	Advertising, X_1	Sales force, X_2	City, X_3
127	18	10	Yes
138	15	15	No
159	22	14	Yes
144	23	12	Yes
139	17	12	No
128	16	12	Yes
161	25	14	Yes
180	26	17	Yes
102	15	7	No
163	24	16	Yes
106	18	10	No
149	25	11	Yes

a. Develop a correlation matrix. Which independent variable has the strongest correlation with the dependent variable? Does it appear that there will be any problems with multicollinearity?
b. Determine the regression equation. How many cars would you expect to be sold by a dealership employing 20 salespeople, purchasing 15 minutes of advertising, and located in a city?
c. Conduct a global test of hypothesis to determine if any of the net regression coefficients differ from zero. Let $\alpha = .05$.
d. Conduct a test of hypothesis for the individual regression coefficients. Would you consider deleting any of the independent variables? Let $\alpha = .05$.
e. If your conclusion in part *d* was to delete one or more independent variables, run the analysis again without those variables.
f. Determine the residuals for the equation of part *e.* Use a stem-and-leaf chart or a histogram to verify that the distribution of the residuals is approximately normal.
g. Plot the residuals computed in part *f* in a scatter diagram with the residuals on the Y-axis and the Y' values on the X-axis. Does the plot reveal any violations of the assumptions of regression?

14. Fran's Convenience Marts are located throughout metropolitan Erie, Pennsylvania. Fran, the owner, would like to expand into other communities in northwestern Pennsylvania and southwestern New York, such as Jamestown, Corry, Meadville, and Warren. As part

of her presentation to the local bank, she would like to better understand the factors that make a particular outlet profitable. She must do all the work herself, so she will not be able to study all her outlets. She selects a random sample of 15 marts and records the average daily sales (Y), the floor space (area), the number of parking spaces, and the median income of families in that ZIP code region for each. The sample information is reported below.

Sampled mart	Daily sales	Store area	Parking spaces	Income ($ thousands)
1	$1,840	532	6	44
2	1,746	478	4	51
3	1,812	530	7	45
4	1,806	508	7	46
5	1,792	514	5	44
6	1,825	556	6	46
7	1,811	541	4	49
8	1,803	513	6	52
9	1,830	532	5	46
10	1,827	537	5	46
11	1,764	499	3	48
12	1,825	510	8	47
13	1,763	490	4	48
14	1,846	516	8	45
15	1,815	482	7	43

a. Determine the regression equation.
b. What is the value of R^2? Comment on the value.
c. Conduct a global hypothesis test to determine if any of the independent variables are different from zero.
d. Conduct individual hypothesis tests to determine if any of the independent variables can be dropped.
e. If variables are dropped, recompute the regression equation and R^2.

15. Mr. Steve Douglas recently graduated from a large university with a degree in finance. He has been hired as a management trainee by a large brokerage firm. As his first project, he is asked to study the gross profit of firms in the chemical industry. What factors affect profitability in that industry? Steve selects a sample of 16 firms and obtains data on the number of employees, number of consecutive common stock dividends paid, the total value of inventory at the start of the current year, and the gross profit for each firm. His findings are:

Company	Gross profit ($ thousands), Y	Number of employees, X_1	Consecutive dividends, X_2	Beginning inventory ($ thousands), X_3
1	2,800	140	12	1,800
2	1,300	65	21	320
3	1,230	130	42	820
4	1,600	115	80	76
5	4,500	390	120	3,600
6	5,700	670	64	8,400
7	3,150	205	43	508
8	640	40	14	870
9	3,400	480	88	5,500
10	6,700	810	98	9,875

Company	Gross profit ($ thousands), Y	Number of employees, X_1	Consecutive dividends, X_2	Beginning inventory ($ thousands), X_3
11	3,700	120	44	6,500
12	6,440	590	110	9,130
13	1,280	440	38	1,200
14	4,160	280	24	890
15	3,870	650	60	1,200
16	980	150	24	1,300

a. Determine the regression equation. The Master Chemical Company employs 220 people, has paid 64 consecutive common stock dividends, and has an inventory valued at $1,500,000 at the start of the year. What is the estimate of the gross profit?

b. Conduct a global test of hypothesis to determine if any of the net regression coefficients differ from zero.

c. Conduct a test of hypothesis for the individual regression coefficients. Would you consider deleting any of the independent variables?

d. If your conclusion in part *c* was to delete one or more independent variables, run the analysis again, deleting those variables.

e. Determine the residuals for the equation of part *d.* Use a stem-and-leaf chart or a histogram to verify that the distribution of the residuals is approximately normal.

f. Plot the residuals computed in part *e* in a scatter diagram with the residuals on the Y-axis and the Y' values on the X-axis. Does the plot reveal any violations of the assumptions of regression?

16. The *Times-Observer* is a daily newspaper in Metro City. Like many city newspapers, the *Times-Observer* is suffering through difficult financial times. The circulation manager is interested in studying other papers in similar cities in the United States and Canada. She is particularly interested in what variables relate to the number of subscriptions to the paper. She is able to obtain the following sample information on 25 newspapers in similar cities. The following notation is used:

Sub = Number of subscriptions (in thousands).

Popul = The metropolitan population (in thousands).

Adv = The advertising budget of the paper (in hundreds of dollars).

Income = The median family income in the metropolitan area (in $ thousands).

Paper	Sub	Popul	Adv	Income
1	37.95	588.9	13.2	35.1
2	37.66	585.3	13.2	34.7
3	37.55	566.3	19.8	34.8
4	38.78	642.9	17.6	35.1
5	37.67	624.2	17.6	34.6
6	38.23	603.9	15.4	34.8
7	36.90	571.9	11.0	34.7
8	38.28	584.3	28.6	35.3
9	38.95	605.0	28.6	35.1
10	39.27	676.3	17.6	35.6
11	38.30	587.4	17.6	34.9
12	38.84	576.4	22.0	35.4
13	38.14	570.8	17.6	35.0
14	38.39	586.5	15.4	35.5
15	37.29	544.0	11.0	34.9
16	39.15	611.1	24.2	35.0

Paper	Sub	Popul	Adv	Income
17	38.29	643.3	17.6	35.3
18	38.09	635.6	19.8	34.8
19	37.83	598.9	15.4	35.1
20	39.37	657.0	22.0	35.3
21	37.81	595.2	15.4	35.1
22	37.42	520.0	19.8	35.1
23	38.83	629.6	22.0	35.3
24	38.33	680.0	24.2	34.7
25	40.24	651.2	33.0	35.8

a. Determine the regression equation.
b. Conduct a global test of hypothesis to determine if any of the net regression coefficients are not equal to zero.
c. Conduct a test for the individual regression coefficients. Would you consider deleting any coefficients?
d. Determine the residuals, and plot them against the fitted values. Do you see any problems?
e. Develop a histogram of the residuals. Do you see any problems with the normality assumption?

17. The *Toledo* (Ohio) *Blade* recently ran an advertisement indicating that they had openings for carriers. "Wake up to opportunities," the advertisement said. "With a *Blade* route, you'll work about an hour a day—in the morning, when you can afford the time." The announcement went on to list the following available carrier routes. Let the average weekly profit be the dependent variable and the number of daily customers and the number of Sunday customers the independent variables.

Route	Average weekly profit	Number of daily customers	Number of Sunday customers
Greenwood	$47.00	66	78
Oswald	70.00	98	117
Neveda	24.00	32	45
Forsythe	30.00	42	51
Idaho	25.00	34	44
Valleywood	44.00	60	76
Oak Hill	26.00	40	40
Burbank	19.50	30	30
Burke Glen	33.20	46	57
Penelope	35.00	48	61

(Source: *Toledo Blade,* May 30, 1994, p. P-1.)

a. Develop a correlation matrix. Do you see any problems with multicollinearity?
b. Determine the regression equation. How much profit would you estimate for a route that had 50 daily customers and 100 Sunday customers?
c. Can we conclude that the two variables account for the variation in weekly profit?
d. How much does an additional Sunday customer add to the profit per week? How much does each daily customer add to weekly profit?
e. The R^2 value is very large. Does this surprise you? Would you consider adding any other independent variables?

18. A mortgage department of a large bank is studying its recent loans. Of particular interest is how such factors as the value of the home (in thousands of dollars), education level of the head of the household, age of the head of the household, current monthly mortgage payment, and sex of the head of the household (male = 1, female = 0) relate to the family income. Are these variables effective predictors of the income of the household? A sample of 25 recent loans is obtained.

Income ($ thousands)	Value ($ thousands)	Years of education	Age	Mortgage	Sex
$40.3	$190	14	53	230	1
39.6	121	15	49	370	1
40.8	161	14	44	397	1
40.3	161	14	39	181	1
40.0	179	14	53	378	0
38.1	99	14	46	304	0
40.4	114	15	42	285	1
40.7	202	14	49	551	0
40.8	184	13	37	370	0
37.1	90	14	43	135	0
39.9	181	14	48	332	1
40.4	143	15	54	217	1
38.0	132	14	44	490	0
39.0	127	14	37	220	0
39.5	153	14	50	270	1
40.6	145	14	50	279	1
40.3	174	15	52	329	1
40.1	177	15	47	274	0
41.7	188	15	49	433	1
40.1	153	15	53	333	1
40.6	150	16	58	148	0
40.4	173	13	42	390	1
40.9	163	14	46	142	1
40.1	150	15	50	343	0
38.5	139	14	45	373	0

a. Determine the regression equation.
b. What is the value of R^2? Comment on the value.
c. Conduct a global hypothesis test to determine if any of the independent variables are different from zero.
d. Conduct individual hypothesis tests to determine if any of the independent variables can be dropped.
e. If variables are dropped, recompute the regression equation and R^2.

19. Mr. Fred G. Hire is the manager of human resources at St. Luke's Medical Center. As a part of his yearly report to the president of the medical center, he is required to present an analysis of the salaried employees. Because there are over 1,000 employees, he does not have the staff to gather information on each salaried employee, so he selects a sample of 30. For each employee he records monthly salary; service at St. Luke's, in months; gender (1 = male, 0 = female); and whether the employee has a technical or clerical job. Those working technical jobs are coded 1 and those who are clerical 0.

Sampled employee	Monthly salary	Length of service	Age	Gender	Job
1	$ 1,769	93	42	1	0
2	1,740	104	33	1	0
3	1,941	104	42	1	1
4	2,367	126	57	1	1
5	2,467	98	30	1	1
6	1,640	99	49	1	1
7	1,756	94	35	1	0
8	1,706	96	46	0	1
9	1,767	124	56	0	0
10	1,200	73	23	0	1
11	1,706	110	67	0	1
12	1,985	90	36	0	1
13	1,555	104	53	0	0
14	1,749	81	29	0	0
15	2,056	106	45	1	0
16	1,729	113	55	0	1
17	2,186	129	46	1	1
18	1,858	97	39	0	1
19	1,819	101	43	1	1
20	1,350	91	35	1	1
21	2,030	100	40	1	0
22	2,550	123	59	1	0
23	1,544	88	30	0	0
24	1,766	117	60	1	1
25	1,937	107	45	1	1
26	1,691	105	32	0	1
27	1,623	86	33	0	0
28	1,791	131	56	0	1
29	2,001	95	30	1	1
30	1,874	98	47	1	0

a. Determine the regression equation using salary as the dependent variable and the other four variables as independent variables.

b. What is the value of R^2? Comment on this value.

c. Conduct a global test of hypothesis to determine if any of the independent variables are different from 0.

d. Conduct an individual test to determine if any of the independent variables can be dropped.

e. Rerun the regression equation, using only the independent variables that are significant. How much more does a man earn per month than a woman? How much does each additional month of service add to the monthly salary? Does it make a difference whether the employee has a technical or a clerical job?

COMPUTER DATA EXERCISES

20. Refer to data set 1, which reports information on homes sold in Florida during 1994.
    a. Use price as the dependent variable, and determine the regression equation with bedrooms, size of the house, whether there is a pool, whether there is an attached garage, distance from the city, and number of bathrooms as independent variables.
    b. Determine the R^2 value.
    c. Conduct a global test of hypothesis on the set of independent variables.
    d. Conduct a test of hypothesis on each of the independent variables. Would you consider deleting any variables?
    e. Rerun the regression equation using the following independent variables: size of the home, distance from the center of the city, whether there is an attached garage, and number of bathrooms.
    f. Plot the residuals against the fitted values using the regression equation developed in part *e.* Does it appear that the requirement of homoscedasticity is met?
    g. Develop a histogram of the residuals using the regression equation from part *e.* Does it appear that the normality assumption is met?

21. Refer to data set 2, which reports information on the 28 major league baseball teams for the 1993 season.
    a. Determine the regression equation using the number of games won as the dependent variable and the following independent variables: team batting average, number of home runs hit by the team, team ERA, number of stolen bases, number of errors committed by the team, and whether or not the team played their home games on a turf field.
    b. Determine the R^2 value.
    c. Conduct a global test of hypothesis on the set of independent variables. What do you recommend?
    d. Conduct a test of hypothesis on each of the independent variables. Would you consider eliminating any of the independent variables?
    e. Rerun the regression equation deleting any of the independent variables suggested in part *d.*
    f. Develop a histogram of the residuals using the regression equation from part *e.* Does it appear that the normality assumption is reasonable?
    g. Plot the residuals against the fitted values using the regression equation developed in part *e.* Does it appear that the requirement of homoscedasticity is met?

22. Refer to data set 3, which reports information on the circulation of 48 magazines.
    a. Determine a correlation matrix using circulation as the dependent variable and percent of male readers, percent of female readers, median age, percent of readers who attended college, cost of color advertising, and cost of black and white advertising as independent variables. Do you see any potential problems?
    b. Use the following independent variables to develop a multiple regression equation with circulation as the dependent variable: median age, percent attending college, and cost of color advertising.
    c. Determine the coefficient of determination.
    d. Conduct a global test of hypothesis on the set of independent variables.
    e. Conduct a test of hypothesis on each of the selected independent variables. Would you consider deleting any of these variables?

CHAPTER 13 EXAMINATION

The answers are at the end of the chapter.

1. What is the general form of a multiple regression equation having three independent variables?

Questions 2 through 7 refer to the following multiple regression output.

Analysis of Variance

Source	DF	SS	MS	F
Regression	3	75		
Error	25	25		
Total				

Predictor	Coef	Stdev	t-ratio
Constant	6.00	3.35	
X_1	0.70	0.50	
X_2	−9.00	4.00	
X_3	5.00	2.00	

2. How many independent variables are there in this analysis?
3. What is the total number of observations, n?
4. Compute the value of R^2.
5. Compute the multiple standard of error of estimate.
6. Conduct the following global test of hypothesis.

$$H_0: \beta_1 = \beta_2 = \beta_3 = 0$$

$$H_1: \text{The } \beta_j\text{s are not all equal to zero.}$$

   a. What is the decision rule for this test? Use the .05 significance level.
   b. What is your decision regarding the null hypothesis?

7. Conduct the three tests of hypotheses stated below. Use the .05 significance level.

$$H_0: \beta_1 = 0 \qquad H_0: \beta_2 = 0 \qquad H_0: \beta_3 = 0$$

$$H_1: \beta_1 \neq 0 \qquad H_1: \beta_2 \neq 0 \qquad H_1: \beta_3 \neq 0$$

   a. What is the decision rule for this test?
   b. Which independent variables have significant regression coefficients, and which do not? Which variable or variables would you consider eliminating?

CHAPTER 13 Answers

Self-Review

13–1

1. 12.9 psi, found by $Y' = -0.5 + 2(3.5) + 1(6.4)$.
2. The b_1 of 2 indicates that the tensile strength of the wire will increase 2 psi for each increase of 1 cm in outside diameter, with the amount of molybdenum held constant. That is, tensile strength will increase 2 psi regardless of the amount of molybdenum in the wire.

13–2

1. 24.37 cubic feet, found by $Y' = 62.65 + (-1.86)8 + (-0.52)45$.
2. 2.37 cubic feet, found by 24.37 − 22.00. Fuel consumption is 2.37 cubic feet less than anticipated. This is called the *residual.*

13–3

1. $Y' = 490 - 5.15X_1 - 14.7X_2$
2. .776. A total of 77.6% of the variation in heating cost is explained by temperature and insulation.
3. The results of the global test indicate that at least one of the regression coefficients is not zero. To arrive at that conclusion, we first stated the null hypothesis as H_0: $\beta_1 = \beta_2 = 0$. The critical value of F is 3.59, and the computed value 29.4, found by 82,597/2,807. Since 29.4 lies in the region of rejection beyond 3.59, we reject H_0.
4. The p-value is .008. The probability of a t-value less than −2.98 or greater than 2.98, with 17 degrees of freedom, is .008.

Examination

1. $Y' = a + b_1X_1 + b_2X_2 + b_3X_3$
2. Three independent variables.
3. $n = 29$
4. $R^2 = 75/100 = .75$
5. $s_{y \cdot 123} = \sqrt{1.00} = 1.00$
6. *a.* H_0 is rejected if $F > 2.99$.

   b. $F = \dfrac{75/3}{25/25} = 25.00$

   H_0 is rejected. At least one regression coefficient is not zero.
7. *a.* H_0 is rejected if $t < -2.060$ or $t > 2.060$.

   $t = \dfrac{0.70}{0.50} = 1.40$ for β_1

   $t = \dfrac{-9.00}{4.00} = -2.25$ for β_2

   $t = \dfrac{5.00}{2.00} = 2.50$ for β_3

   b. Drop X_1, and keep X_2 and X_3.

SECTION 5 A REVIEW OF CHAPTERS 12 AND 13

Simple regression and correlation examines the relationship between two variables

This section is a review of the major concepts and terms introduced in Chapters 12 and 13. Chapter 12 noted that the strength of the relationship between the independent variable and the dependent variable can be measured by the *coefficient of correlation.* Developed by Karl Pearson, *Pearson's r* can assume any value between −1.00 and +1.00 inclusive. Coefficients of −1.00 and + 1.00 indicate perfect relationship, and 0 indicates no relationship. A value near 0, such as −.14 or .14, indicates a weak relationship. A value near −1 or + 1, such as −.90 or + .90, indicates a strong relationship. Squaring r gives the *coefficient of determination,* also called r^2. It indicates the proportion of the total variation in the dependent variable explained by the independent variable.

Multiple regression and correlation concerned with relationship between two or more independent variables and the dependent variable

Likewise, the strength of the relationship between a group of many independent variables and a dependent variable is measured by the *coefficient of multiple determination,* R^2. It measures the proportion of the variation in Y explained by the two or more independent variables.

The linear relationship in the simple case involving one independent variable and one dependent variable is described by the equation $Y' = a + bX$. For three independent variables, X_1, X_2, and X_3, the sample multiple regression equation is

$$Y' = a + b_1X_1 + b_2X_2 + b_3X_3$$

Computer invaluable in multiple regression and correlation

Solving for $b_1, b_2, b_3 \ldots, b_k$ would involve hours of tedious calculations. Fortunately, this type of problem can be quickly solved using one of the many statistical packages available for the computer. Commonly used are MINITAB and SPSS. One program uses a stepwise procedure. The independent variable most highly correlated with the dependent variable is brought in first, and only independent variables with nonzero net regression coefficients are used in the analysis. Various measures, such as the coefficient of determination and the multiple standard error of estimate, are reported in the output of most computer software programs.

GLOSSARY

Chapter 12

Coefficient of correlation A measure of the strength of association between two variables. It is computed by:

$$r = \frac{n(\Sigma XY) - (\Sigma X)(\Sigma Y)}{\sqrt{[n(\Sigma X^2) - (\Sigma X)^2][n(\Sigma Y^2) - (\Sigma Y)^2]}} \qquad (12\text{–}1)$$

Coefficient of determination The proportion of the total variation in the dependent variable that is explained by the independent variable. It can assume any value between 0 and +1.00 inclusive. A coefficient of .82 indicates that 82 percent of the variation in Y is accounted for by X. This coefficient is computed by squaring the coefficient of correlation, r.

Correlation analysis A group of statistical techniques used to measure the strength of the relationship between two variables.

Least squares method A technique used to arrive at the regression equation by minimizing the sum of the squares of the vertical distances between the actual Y values and the predicted Y values.

Linear regression equation A mathematical equation that defines the relationship between two variables. It has the form $Y' = a + bX$. It is used to predict Y based on a selected X value.

Scatter diagram A chart that visually depicts the relationship between two variables.

Standard error of estimate Measures the dispersion of the actual Y values about the linear regression line. It tells us how far off our prediction might be.

Test for significance of *r* A formula to answer the question: Is the correlation in the population from which the sample was selected zero? The test statistic is t, and the number of degrees of freedom is $n - 2$.

$$t = \frac{r\sqrt{n-2}}{\sqrt{1-r^2}} \qquad (12\text{–}2)$$

Chapter 13

Autocorrelation Correlation of successive residuals. This condition frequently occurs when time is involved in the analysis.

Correlation matrix A listing of all possible simple coefficients of correlation. A correlation matrix includes the correlations between each of the independent variables and the dependent variable, as well as those among all the independent variables.

Homoscedasticity The standard error of estimate is the same for all fitted values of the dependent variable.

Multicollinearity A condition that occurs in multiple regression analysis if the independent variables are themselves correlated.

Multiple regression equation The relationship in the form of a mathematical equation between many independent variables and a dependent variable. The general form is $Y' = a + b_1X_1 + b_2X_2 + b_3X_3 + \cdots + b_kX_k$. It is used to estimate Y given selected X values.

Qualitative variables A nominal-scale variable that can assume only one of two possible outcomes. For example, a person is considered either employed or unemployed.

Residual The difference between the actual value of the dependent variable and the estimated value of the dependent variable.

Stepwise regression A method for determining the order in which independent variables enter a multiple regression equation. Independent variables enter the regression equation in the order in which they will increase R^2 by the largest amount. Only independent variables whose regression coefficients are significantly different from zero are entered into the equation.

EXERCISES

The answers to the odd-numbered exercises are at the end of the book.

Part I—Fill in the Blanks and Discussion

1. The strength of the relationship between a set of independent variables X and a dependent variable Y is measured by the ________.
2. A coefficient of correlation was computed to be $-.90$. Comment.
3. Pearson's r for a problem involving 60 pairs of data was computed to be .40. Comment. Is the correlation in the population zero? Give evidence.
4. The coefficient of determination was computed to be .38 in a problem involving one independent and one dependent variable. What does this mean?
5. Explain the function of the "stepwise" procedure followed in MINITAB.

Exercises 6 through 10 are based on the following table. The accounting division for a large chain of department stores is trying to predict the net profit for each of the chain's many stores based on the number of employees in the store, overhead cost, and so on. A few statistics from some of the stores are:

Store	Net profit ($ thousands)	Number of employees	Overhead cost ($ thousands)	Average markup rate (percent)	Loss from theft ($ thousands)
1	$846	143	$79	69	$52
2	513	110	64	50	45

6. The dependent variable is ________.
7. The general equation for this problem is ________.
8. The multiple regression equation was computed to be $Y' = 67 + 8X_1 - 10X_2 + 0.004X_3 - 3X_4$. What is predicted sales for a store with 112 employees, an overhead cost of $65,000, a markup rate of 50 percent, and a loss from theft of $50,000?
9. Suppose R^2 was computed to be .86. Explain.
10. Suppose that the multiple standard error of estimate was computed to be 3 (in $ thousands). Explain what this means in this problem.

Part II—Problems

11. Quick-print firms in a large downtown business area spend most of their advertising dollars on advertisements on bus benches. A research project involves predicting monthly sales based on the annual amount spent on placing ads on bus benches. A sample of quick-print firms revealed these advertising expenses and sales:

Firm	Annual amount spent on bus bench advertisements ($ thousands)	Monthly sales ($ thousands)
A	2	10
B	4	40
C	5	30
D	7	50
E	3	20

a. Draw a scatter diagram.
b. Determine the coefficient of correlation.
c. What is the coefficient of determination?
d. Compute the regression equation.
e. Estimate the monthly sales of a quick-print firm that spends $4,500 on bus bench advertisements.
f. Summarize your findings.

12. The following ANOVA output is given.

Source	Sum of Squares	DF	MS
Regression	1050.8	4	262.70
Error	83.8	20	4.19
Total	1134.6	24	

Predictor	Coef	St.Dev.	t-ratio
Constant	70.06	2.13	32.89
X_1	0.42	0.17	2.47
X_2	0.27	0.21	1.29
X_3	0.75	0.30	2.50
X_4	0.42	0.07	6.00

a. Compute the coefficient of determination.
b. Compute the multiple standard error of estimate.
c. Conduct a test of hypothesis to determine if any of the net regression coefficients are different from zero.
d. Conduct a test of hypothesis on the individual regression coefficients. Can any of the variables be deleted?

CASE

Refer to the Century National Bank data. Using checking account balance as the dependent variable and using the number of ATM transactions, the number of other services used, whether or not the individual has a debit card, and whether or not interest is paid on the particular account as independent variables, write a report indicating which of the variables seem related to the account balance and how well they explain the variation in account balances. Should all of the independent variables proposed be used in the analysis, or can some be dropped?

Chapter 14

Nonparametric Methods: Chi-Square Applications

GOALS

When you have completed this chapter, you will be able to:

1
List the characteristics of the chi-square distribution.

2
Conduct a test of hypothesis involving the difference between a set of observed frequencies and a corresponding set of expected frequencies for cases where the expected frequencies in each category are equal and cases where they are not equal.

3
Conduct a test for normality.

4
Conduct a test of hypothesis to determine whether two criteria of classification are related.

Managers from various levels of management were interviewed on environmental issues. Their responses were tallied into three categories—no concern, some concern, and great concern. Using the .01 level, determine if there is any difference in response with respect to their level of management. (See Goal 4 and Chapter Exam Exercise 2.)

INTRODUCTION

Chapters 8 through 11 dealt with data that were at least interval-scale, such as weights, incomes, and ages. We conducted a number of tests of hypotheses about a population mean and two or more population means. For these tests it was assumed that the population was normal. Can tests of hypotheses be made if the data are not interval-scale, but are nominal- or ordinal-scale, and if no assumptions are made about the shape of the parent population?

To answer this question, there are tests for nominal and ordinal levels of measurement, and no assumptions need be made about the shape of the population. Recall from Chapter 1 that *nominal*-level data are the "lowest" type of data. This type of data can only be classified into categories, such as Republican, Democrat, and "all others," or male and female. *Ordinal* level of measurement assumes that one category is ranked higher than the next one. As an example, a sample of joggers are asked by Marketing Research Associates to rate a newly developed shoe as either outstanding, good, fair, or unsatisfactory. It is implied that a ranking of outstanding is higher than good, good is higher than fair, and so on.

Tests of hypotheses concerned with nominal or ordinal levels of measurement are called **nonparametric tests** or **distribution-free tests.** The latter name implies that these tests are free of assumptions regarding the distribution of the parent population. These distribution-free tests are relatively easy to apply, and the computations are generally easy to perform.

GOODNESS-OF-FIT TEST: EQUAL EXPECTED FREQUENCIES

The **goodness-of-fit test** is one of the most commonly used nonparametric tests. Developed by Karl Pearson in the early 1900s, it is appropriate for both nominal and ordinal levels of data. It can also be used for interval- and ratio-level data. The first test of significance involves *equal expected frequencies.*

As the full name implies, the purpose of the goodness-of-fit test is to determine how well an *observed* set of data fits an *expected* set of data. An illustration can best describe the hypothesis-testing situation.

EXAMPLE

Ms. Jan Kilpatrick is the marketing manager for a manufacturer of sports cards. She plans to begin a series of cards with the pictures and playing statistics of former major league baseball players. One problem is the selection of the former players. At the baseball card show at the Southwyck Mall last weekend, she set up a booth and offered cards of the following six Hall of Fame former major league baseball players: Dizzy Dean, Bob Feller, Phil Rizzuto, Warren Spahn, Mickey Mantle, and Willie Mays. At the end of the first day she sold a total of 120 cards. The number of cards sold for each old-time player is shown in Table 14–1. Can she conclude that the sales of cards are the same for the six players, or should she conclude that the sales are not the same?

TABLE 14–1 **Number of Cards Sold for Each Player**

Player	Number of cards sold
Dizzy Dean	13
Bob Feller	33
Phil Rizzuto	14
Warren Spahn	7
Mickey Mantle	36
Willie Mays	17
Total	120

If there is no significant difference between the observed frequencies and the expected frequencies, we would expect that the observed frequencies (f_0) would be equal—or nearly equal. That is, we would expect to sell as many cards for Phil Rizzuto as for Dizzy Dean. Thus, any discrepancy in the set of observed and expected frequencies could be attributed to sampling (chance).

Because there are 120 cards in the sample, we expect that 20 cards will fall in each of the six categories. These categories are called **cells.** An examination of the set of observed frequencies in Table 14–2 indicates that the card for Warren Spahn is sold rather infrequently, whereas the cards for Mickey Mantle and Bob Feller are sold more often. Is the difference in sales due to chance, or can we conclude that there is a preference for the cards of certain players?

TABLE 14–2 Observed and Expected Frequencies for the 120 Cards Sold

Former baseball player	Number of cards sold, f_0	Expected number sold, f_e
Dizzy Dean	13	20
Bob Feller	33	20
Phil Rizzuto	14	20
Warren Spahn	7	20
Mickey Mantle	36	20
Willie Mays	17	20
Total	120	120

Solution ▶ The same systematic five-step hypothesis-testing procedure followed in Chapters 8 through 11 will be used.

State H_0 and H_1

Step 1 The null hypothesis and the alternate hypothesis are stated. The null hypothesis, H_0, is that there is no difference between the set of observed frequencies and the set of expected frequencies; that is, any differences between the two sets of frequencies can be attributed to sampling (chance). The alternate hypothesis, H_1, is that there is a difference between the observed and expected sets of frequencies. If H_0 is rejected and H_1 is accepted, it means that sales are not equally distributed among the six categories (cells).

Alpha is .05

Step 2 A level of significance is chosen. We selected the .05 level, which is the same as the Type I error probability. Thus, the probability is .05 that a true null hypothesis will be rejected.

The test statistic

Step 3 The test statistic is selected. It is the chi-square distribution, designated as χ^2:

$$\chi^2 = \sum\left[\frac{(f_0 - f_e)^2}{f_e}\right] \tag{14–1}$$

with $k - 1$ degrees of freedom, where k is the number of categories, and

f_0 is an observed frequency in a particular category.

f_e is an expected frequency in a particular category.

We will examine the characteristics of the chi-square distribution in more detail shortly.

The decision rule

The critical value

Step 4 The *decision rule* is formulated. Recall that the decision rule in hypothesis testing requires finding a number that separates the region where we do not reject H_0 from the region of rejection. This number is called the *critical value.* As we will soon see, the chi-square distribution is really a family of distributions. Each distribution has a different shape, depending on the number of degrees of freedom. The number in this type of problem is found by $k - 1$, where k stands for the number of categories. In this particular problem there are six. Since there are six categories, there are $k - 1 = 6 - 1 = 5$ degrees of freedom. As noted, a category is called a *cell,* so there are six cells. The critical value for 5 degrees of freedom and the .05 level of significance is found in Appendix I. A portion of that table is shown in Table 14–3. The critical value is 11.070, found by locating 5 degrees of freedom in the left margin and then moving horizontally (to the right) and reading the critical value in the .05 column.

TABLE 14–3 **A Portion of the Chi-Square Table**

Degrees of freedom, *df*	Right-tail area .10	.05	.02	.01
1	2.706	3.841	5.412	6.635
2	4.605	5.991	7.824	9.210
3	6.251	7.815	9.837	11.345
4	7.779	9.488	11.668	13.277
5	9.236	11.070	13.388	15.086

The decision rule, therefore, is: Do not reject the null hypothesis if the computed value of chi-square is equal to or less than 11.070. If it is greater than 11.070, reject H_0 and accept the alternate hypothesis, H_1. Chart 14–1 shows the two regions.

CHART 14–1 **Chi-Square Probability Distribution for 5 Degrees of Freedom, Showing the Region of Rejection, .05 Level of Significance**

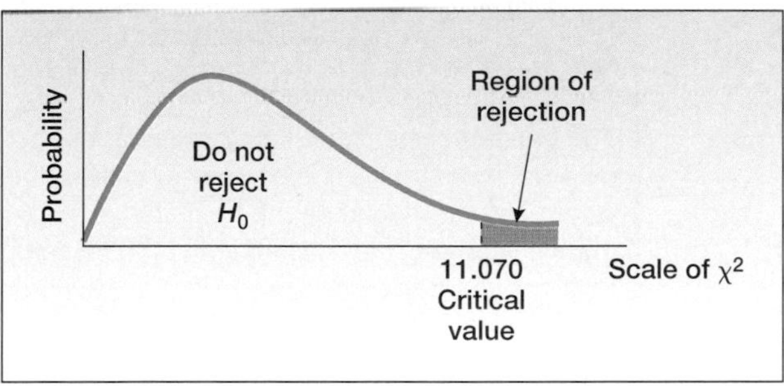

In essence, the decision rule indicates that if there are large differences between the observed and expected frequencies, resulting in a computed χ^2 of more than 11.070, the null hypothesis should be rejected. However, if the differences between f_0 and f_e are small, the computed χ^2 value will be 11.070 or less, and the null hypothesis should not be rejected. The reasoning is that such small differences between the observed and expected frequencies are probably due to chance.

Step 5 A sample is selected, the value of chi-square computed, and a decision made to reject or not reject the null hypothesis. Of the 120 cards sold in the sample, we counted the number of times Bob Feller, Willie Mays, and each of the others were sold. The counts were reported in Table 14–1. The calculations for chi-square follow. Note again that the expected frequencies are the same for each cell.

Calculations needed for χ^2

Referring to the following computations, the steps required to determine chi-square are:

Column 1: The difference between each paired f_0 and f_e is calculated. (*Note:* The sum of the differences must equal zero.)

Column 2: The differences are squared.

Column 3: Each squared difference is divided by the appropriate frequency expected, f_e. These quotients are then summed. The sum (34.40) is the computed value of chi-square.

Baseball player	f_0	f_e	(1) $f_0 - f_e$	(2) $(f_0 - f_e)^2$	(3) $\frac{(f_0 - f_e)^2}{f_e}$
Dizzy Dean	13	20	−7	49	49/20 = 2.45
Bob Feller	33	20	13	169	169/20 = 8.45
Phil Rizzuto	14	20	−6	36	36/20 = 1.80
Warren Spahn	7	20	−13	169	169/20 = 8.45
Mickey Mantle	36	20	16	256	256/20 = 12.80
Willie Mays	17	20	−3	9	9/20 = 0.45
			0 (must be)		34.40 (χ^2)

The decision

The computed χ^2 of 34.40 is in the rejection region, beyond the critical value of 11.070. The decision, therefore, is to reject H_0 at the .05 level and to accept H_1, which states that the difference between the observed and the expected frequencies is not

SELF-REVIEW 14–1

The answers are at the end of the chapter.

The personnel manager is concerned about absenteeism. She decides to sample the records to determine if absenteeism is distributed evenly throughout the six-day work-week. The null hypothesis to be tested is: Absenteeism is distributed evenly throughout the week. The .01 level is to be used. The sample results are:

	Number absent
Monday	12
Tuesday	9
Wednesday	11
Thursday	10
Friday	9
Saturday	9

1. What kind of frequencies are the numbers 12, 9, 11, 10, 9, and 9 called?
2. How many categories (cells) are there?
3. What is the *expected* frequency for each day?
4. How many degrees of freedom are there?
5. What is the chi-square critical value at the 1 percent level?
6. Using the chi-square test of significance, compute χ^2.
7. Is the null hypothesis rejected?
8. Specifically, what does this indicate to the personnel manager?

due to chance. Rather, the differences between f_0 and f_e are large enough to be considered significant. The chance of these differences being due to sampling is very small. So we conclude that it is unlikely that card sales are the same among the six players.

Both the example-solution and self-review involved *equal* expected frequencies. Before considering problems with *unequal* expected frequencies, we will look briefly at the characteristics of the chi-square distribution.

Characteristics of the Chi-Square Distribution

χ^2 is always positive

1. The computed value of chi-square is *always positive* because the difference between f_0 and f_e is squared, that is, $(f_0 - f_e)^2$.

Shape of chi-square distribution depends on number of cells

2. There is a family of chi-square distributions. There is a chi-square distribution for 1 degree of freedom, another for 2 degrees of freedom, another for 3 degrees of freedom, and so on. In this type of problem the number of degrees of freedom is determined by $k - 1$, where k is the number of categories. Therefore, the shape of the chi-square distribution does *not* depend on the size of the sample. For example, if 200 employees of an airline were classified into one of three categories—flight personnel, ground support, and administrative personnel—there would be $k - 1 = 3 - 1 = 2$ degrees of freedom.

Chi-square distribution is positively skewed

3. The chi-square distribution is *positively skewed.* However, as the number of degrees of freedom increases, the distribution begins to approximate the normal distribution. Chart 14–2 shows the distributions for selected degrees of freedom. Notice that for 10 degrees of freedom, the curve is approaching a normal curve.

CHART 14–2 **Chi-Square Distributions for Selected Degrees of Freedom**

Shape of χ^2 distribution approaches normal curve as *df* becomes larger

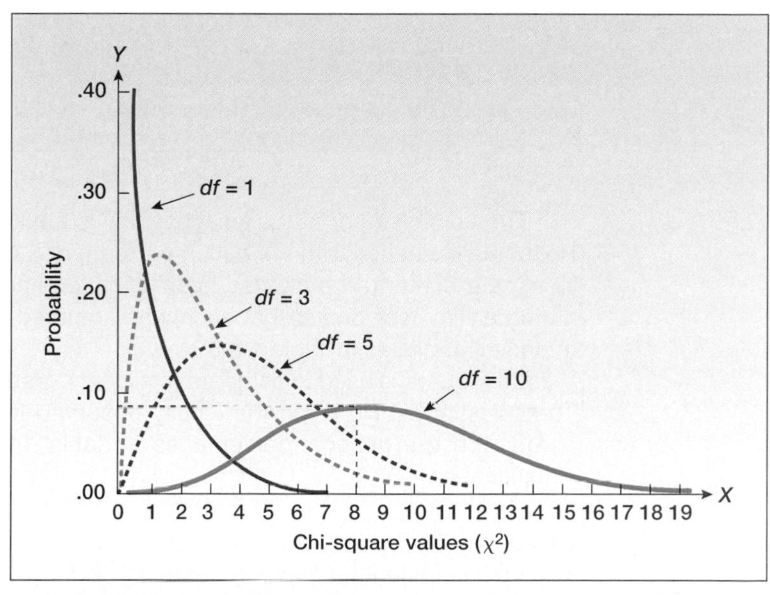

GOODNESS-OF-FIT TEST: UNEQUAL EXPECTED FREQUENCIES

Expected frequencies not equal in this problem

The expected frequencies (f_e) in the previous problem involving baseball cards were all equal (20). Theoretically it was expected that a picture of Dizzy Dean would appear 20 times at random, the picture of Willie Mays would appear 20 times out of 120 trials, and so on. The chi-square test can also be used if the expected frequencies are not equal.

The following example illustrates the case of unequal frequencies and also gives a practical use of chi-square—namely, to find out if a local experience differs from the national experience.

EXAMPLE

A national study of hospital admissions during a two-year period revealed these statistics concerning senior citizens who resided in care centers and who were hospitalized anytime during the period: Forty percent were admitted only once in the two-year period. Twenty percent were admitted twice. Fourteen percent were admitted three times, and so on. The complete percentage distribution is given in Table 14–4.

TABLE 14–4 National Study: Admission of Senior Citizens to Hospitals

Number of admissions in a two-year period	Percent of total
1	40
2	20
3	14
4	10
5	8
6	6
7	2
	100

TABLE 14–5 Local Study: Number of Admissions to the Bartow County Hospital during a Two-Year Period

Number of admissions	Number of senior citizens, f_0
1	165
2	79
3	50
4	44
5	32
6	20
7	10
	400

The administrator of the local hospital is anxious to compare her Bartow County Hospital experience with the national experience. She selected 400 senior citizens in local care centers who needed hospitalization and determined the number of times during a two-year period that each was admitted to her hospital. The observed frequencies are listed in Table 14–5.

Chi-square is used to compare this local experience with the national experience. The question is: How can the locally observed frequencies in Table 14–5 be compared with the national percentages in Table 14–4? We will use the .05 level of significance.

Solution ► Obviously, the *number* of observed frequencies resulting from the study of local senior citizens cannot be compared directly with the *percentages* given for the nation's hospitals. However, the percentages for the nation in Table 14–4 can be converted to

Determining expected frequencies

expected frequencies, f_e. Table 14–4 shows that 40 percent of the senior citizens who required hospitalization went only once in a two-year period. Thus, if there is *no* difference between the experience at Bartow County Hospital and the national experience, then 40 percent of the 400 sampled by the hospital administrator (160 senior citizens) would have been admitted just once in the period. Further, 20 percent of the 400 sampled (80 people) would have been admitted twice, and so on. The observed local frequencies and the expected local frequencies based on the percents resulting from the national study are given in Table 14–6.

TABLE 14–6 Observed and Expected Frequencies for Bartow County Hospital

Expected frequencies unequal

Number of times admitted	Observed number of admissions, f_0	Expected number of admissions, f_e	
1	165	160	← 40% × 400
2	79	80	← 20% × 400
3	50	56	← 14% × 400
4	44	40	← 10% × 400
5	32	32	← 8% × 400
6	20	24	← 6% × 400
7	10	8	← 2% × 400
	400	400	

Must be equal

The null and alternate hypotheses are:

H_0: No difference between local and national experience

H_0: There is no difference between the local experience and the national experience.

H_1: There is a difference between the local experience and the national experience.

To find the decision rule we use Appendix I. There are seven admitting categories, so the degree of freedom is $df = k - 1 = 7 - 1 = 6$. The critical value is 12.592, therefore the decision rule is to reject H_0 if $\chi^2 > 12.592$. The decision rule is portrayed graphically in Chart 14–3.

CHART 14–3 Decision Criteria for the Bartow County Hospital Research Study

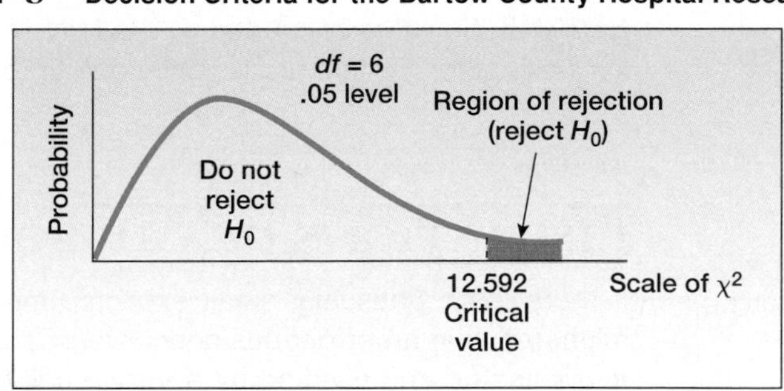

Now to compute chi-square:

Number of times admitted	f_0	f_e	$f_0 - f_e$	$(f_0 - f_e)^2$	$\frac{(f_0 - f_e)^2}{f_e}$
1	165	160	+5	25	0.156
2	79	80	−1	1	0.013
3	50	56	−6	36	0.643
4	44	40	+4	16	0.400
5	32	32	0	0	0.000
6	20	24	−4	16	0.667
7	10	8	+2	4	0.500
			0		$\chi^2 = 2.379$

No difference between local and national experience

The computed value of chi-square (2.379) lies to the left of 12.592 and is therefore in the region where we cannot reject H_0. The null hypothesis, that there is no difference between the local experience at Bartow County Hospital and the national experience, is therefore not rejected. The hospital administrator would conclude that the local situation with respect to the hospitalization of senior citizens in care centers is like that in other parts of the country.

The MINITAB system can be used to compute the value of chi-square. The first step is to enter the observed set of frequencies into the system. Next, the expected frequencies are input. The value of chi-square is then computed using the LET command. The final step is to print the value of chi-square, which is called K1.

```
MTB > set c1
DATA > 165, 79, 50, 44, 32, 20, 10
DATA > end
MTB > set c2
DATA > 160, 80, 56, 40, 32, 24, 8
DATA > end
MTB > name c1 'observed' c2 'expected'
MTB > let k1=sum((c1-c2)**2 / c2)
MTB > print k1

K1        2.37827
```

Note that the value computed by the MINITAB system is the same as computed earlier (except for a slight discrepancy due to rounding).

LIMITATIONS OF CHI-SQUARE

Be careful in applying χ^2 to some problems

If there is an unusually small expected frequency in a cell, chi-square (if applied) might result in an erroneous conclusion. This can happen because f_e appears in the denominator, and dividing by a very small number makes the quotient quite large! Two generally accepted rules regarding small cell frequencies are:

1. If there are only two cells, the *expected* frequency in each cell should be 5 or more. The computation of chi-square would be permissible in the following problem, involving a minimum f_e of 6.

Individual	f_0	f_e
Literate	643	642
Illiterate	7	6

2. For more than two cells, χ^2 should not be applied if more than 20 percent of the f_e cells have expected frequencies less than 5. According to this rule, it would be permissible to compute χ^2 for the management data in the left-hand table below. Only one out of six cells, or 17 percent, contains a frequency less than 5.

Level of management	**Number** f_0	f_e
Foreman	18	16
Supervisor	39	37
Manager	8	13
Middle management	6	4
Assistant vice president	82	78
Vice president	10	15
	163	163

Level of management	**Number** f_0	f_e
Foreman	30	32
Supervisor	110	113
Manager	86	87
Middle management	23	24
Assistant vice president	5	2
Vice president	5	4
Senior vice president	4	1

Chi-square should not be used for the management data in the right-hand table because three of the seven expected frequencies, or 43 percent, are less than 5.

Using this example to develop the reasoning behind the rule, note that most of the paired observed and expected frequencies in the right-hand table are almost equal. The largest difference is just 3. One might conclude, therefore, that there is no significant difference between the observed set and the expected set of frequencies. However, actually computing chi-square and evaluating it against the appropriate critical value will refute that conclusion. Instead, it would be concluded that there is a difference between the frequencies observed in the sample and the expected frequencies. This conclusion, however, does not seem logical. Verify this by solving the self-review that follows.

SELF-REVIEW 14–2

The answers are at the end of the chapter.

Using the management data shown in the preceding right-hand table, test the null hypothesis at the .05 level that there is no significant difference between the observed set and the expected set of frequencies.

The dilemma can be resolved if the data are such that some of the categories can be combined. This seems to be the case in the management problem above. The three vice-presidential levels were combined into one category in order to satisfy the 20 percent rule.

Level of management	Number in sample, f_0	Expected number, f_e
Foreman	30	32
Supervisor	110	113
Manager	86	87
Middle management	23	24
Vice president	14	7

The computed value of chi-square for the revised set of frequencies is 7.26. This is less than the critical value of 9.488 for the .05 level. The null hypothesis is therefore not rejected at the .05 level of significance. This indicates that there is no difference between the observed sample results and the expected results. The small differences between the observed and expected observations can be attributed to sampling. This is, of course, a more logical conclusion.

SELF-REVIEW 14–3

The answers are at the end of the chapter.

Refer to the preceding discussion.

1. Verify that computed chi-square is in fact 7.26.
2. Using the same level of significance (.05), what is the decision rule? (*Caution:* The data have been reorganized.)
3. Do you agree that the null hypothesis should not be rejected at the .05 level?

EXERCISES

The answers to the odd-numbered exercises are at the end of the book.

1. The null and alternate hypotheses are:

   H_0: The cell categories are equal.

   H_1: The cell categories are not equal.

   We took a sample of 60, with the following results.

Category	f_0
A	10
B	20
C	30

   a. Use the .05 significance level, and state the decision rule.
   b. Compute the value of chi-square.
   c. What is your decision regarding H_0?

2. The following hypotheses are given:

   H_0: Forty percent of the observations are in category A, 40 percent are in B, and 20 percent are in C.

   H_1: The observations are not as described in H_0.

   We took a sample of 60, with the following results.

Category	f_o
A	30
B	20
C	10

a. State the decision rule using the .01 significance level.
b. Compute the value of chi-square.
c. What is your decision regarding H_0?

3. The chief of security of a large shopping mall was directed to study the problem of missing goods. He selected a sample of 100 boxes that had been tampered with and ascertained that for 60 of the boxes, the missing pants, shoes, and so on were attributed to shoplifting. For 30 other boxes employees had stolen the goods, and for the remaining 10 boxes he blamed poor inventory control.

   In his report to the mall management, can he say that shoplifting is *twice* as likely to be the cause of the loss as compared with employee theft or poor inventory control? Use the .02 level.

4. The director of human resources collected the following data on absenteeism by day of the week. At the .05 significance level, can she conclude that there is a difference in the absence rate by day of the week?

Day	Frequency
Monday	124
Tuesday	74
Wednesday	104
Thursday	98
Friday	120

5. A group of department store buyers viewed a new line of dresses and gave their opinions of them. The results were:

Opinion	Number of buyers
Outstanding	47
Excellent	45
Very good	40
Good	39
Fair	35
Undesirable	34

Source: Unpublished study, Office of Institutional Research, University of Toledo.

   Because the largest number (47) indicated the new line is outstanding, the head designer thinks that this is a mandate to go into mass production of the dresses. The head sweeper (who somehow became involved in this) believes that there is not a clear mandate and claims that the opinions are evenly distributed among the six categories. He further says that the slight differences among the various counts are probably due to chance. Test the null hypothesis that there is no significant difference among the opinions of the buyers. Test at the .01 level of risk. Follow a formal approach; that is, state the null hypothesis, the alternate hypothesis, and so on.

6. The safety director of Honda USA took samples at random from the file of minor accidents and classified them according to the time the accident took place.

Time	Number of accidents
8 up to 9 A.M.	6
9 up to 10 A.M.	6
10 up to 11 A.M.	20
11 up to 12 P.M.	8
1 up to 2 P.M.	7
2 up to 3 P.M.	8
3 up to 4 P.M.	19
4 up to 5 P.M.	6

Using the goodness-of-fit test and the .01 level of significance, determine whether or not the accidents are evenly distributed throughout the day. Write a brief explanation of your conclusion.

7. Column 1 of the following table gives the number of students enrolled, by college, at Midwestern University during the fall quarter.

College	(1) Number enrolled	(2) Number responding
Arts and sciences	4,700	90
Business administration	2,450	45
Education	3,250	60
Engineering	1,300	30
Law	850	15
Pharmacy	1,250	15
University college	3,400	45

The editor of the student newspaper selected names at random from each college and mailed the students questionnaires dealing with campus activities, fees, the sports program, and so on. The numbers responding, by college, are in column 2. Using the .05 level, determine whether or not the sample response is representative of the student population.

8. A national study was conducted with respect to the major leisure indoor activity of males. The percent of the total for each activity is shown in the center column of the following table. The results of a similar study of a sample of males older than 60 living in the Rocky Mountain area are given in the right column.

Major indoor activity	National results (percent of total)	Rocky Mountain study (number)
Photography	22	337
Stamp and coin collecting	19	293
Needlework, crocheting, and sewing	6	82
Greenhouse and indoor gardening	9	128
Metalworking and woodworking	12	182
Gourmet cooking	4	54
Painting and sculpture	7	99
Chess, checkers, and all others	21	325

Test at the .05 level that there is no difference between the national results and those of males older than 60 in the Rocky Mountain area.

9. Did you ever purchase a bag of M&M Peanut candies and wonder about the distribution of the colors? A recent article in the *Lansing State Journal* reported that 30 percent of

the candies are brown, 20 percent yellow, 20 percent red, 20 percent green, and 10 orange. A one-pound bag of M&M peanut candies was purchased at the Anderson's in Maumee, Ohio. A total of 188 candies were in the bag, with 67 brown, 22 yellow, 51 red, 24 green, and 24 orange. At the .05 significance level, can we conclude that this agrees with the expected distribution?

USING THE GOODNESS-OF-FIT TEST TO TEST FOR NORMALITY

We can also use the goodness-of-fit test to determine whether a set of observed frequencies matches a set of expected frequencies that conforms to a normal distribution. To put it another way, do the observed values in a frequency distribution coincide with the theoretical expected values based on a normal distribution? Recall that in Chapters 10 and 11 we assumed that the sampled populations were normally distributed. This test offers a means to validate that assumption.

EXAMPLE

Chapter 2 introduced the research problem in which Dr. Beth McPherson, president of Duval University, collected data on the annual salaries of full professors at 160 colleges. The frequency distribution for these annual salaries is repeated below.

TABLE 14–7 **Average Annual Salaries of Professors at 160 Colleges**

Salary ($ thousands)	Number of colleges
$20 up to $ 30	4
30 up to 40	20
40 up to 50	41
50 up to 60	44
60 up to 70	29
70 up to 80	16
80 up to 90	2
90 up to 100	4
Total	160

Do the observed frequencies coincide with the theoretical expected frequencies based on the normal probability distribution?

Solution

Step 1 Using the MINITAB system and the raw data in Table 2–1, the mean salary was computed to be $54.03 (in thousands) and the standard deviation $13.76 (in thousands).

Step 2 The mean and the standard deviation are inserted into formula 7–1 (the formula for finding z). X in the formula is the lower or the upper class limit. To illustrate the computation of the z values, we selected the "70 up to 80" class.

$$z = \frac{X - \mu}{\sigma}$$

where X is the particular salary class limit, such as $70 (thousand), μ is the mean (54.03), and σ is the standard deviation (13.76).

The z value for 70, the lower limit of the "70 up to 80" class, is 1.16.

$$z = \frac{X - \mu}{\sigma} = \frac{70 - 54.03}{13.76} = 1.16$$

This indicates that 70 is 1.16 standard deviations from the mean of 54.03.

For the upper limit of the "70 up to 80" class, $z = 1.89$, found by

$$z = \frac{X - \mu}{\sigma} = \frac{80 - 54.03}{13.76} = 1.89$$

Thus, 80 is 1.89 standard deviations from the mean of 54.03.

To determine the area in the standard normal distribution from 0 to 1.16, refer to Appendix D or the standard normal distribution on the back inside cover of this book. Go down the left margin to 1.1 and then horizontally to 0.06, and read the area. It is .3770. This is also the area under the curve between the mean of 54.03 and 70.00.

Next, the area between 54.03 (the mean) and 80 is .4706. To find the area under the curve between 1.16 and 1.89, we subtract .4706 − .3770 = .0936. Thus we expect .0936 or 9.36 percent of the salaries to be between 1.16 and 1.89 standard deviations from the mean. Thus, the expected number of salaries between \$70 and \$80 (thousand) is 14.976, found by 160(.0936). This information is summarized in the following graph.

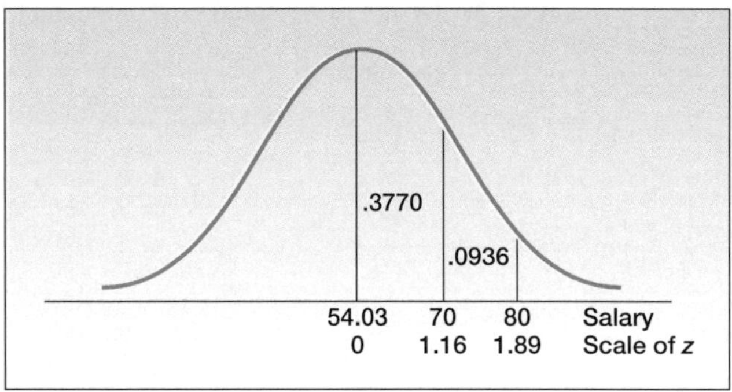

The expected frequencies for all the other categories are listed in Table 14–8.

SELF-REVIEW 14–4

The answers are at the end of the chapter.

Refer to the problem of salaries of full professors. What is the expected number of salaries between \$60 and \$70 (thousand)?

Before continuing, we should emphasize one of the limitations of tests using chi-square as the test statistic. The second limitation on page 585 indicates that if more than 20 percent of the cells have *expected frequencies* of less than 5, some of the categories should be combined. In Table 14–7 there are three cases where the *observed frequencies* are less than 5. To avoid the possibility that there will be too many cells with expected frequencies less than 5, the two largest categories are combined in Table 14–8. So the groups "80 up to 90" and "90 up to 100" are combined into a single group of "80 or more." The details for determining the expected frequency (f_e) for each of the categories are shown in Table 14–8.

TABLE 14–8 Salaries, *z* Values, Areas under the Normal Curve, and f_e

Salary ($ thousands)	*z* value	Area	Expected frequency, f_e
Under $30	Under −1.75	.0401	6.416 ← .0401 × 160
30 to 40	−1.75 to −1.02	.1138	18.208 ← .1138 × 160
40 to 50	−1.02 to −0.29	.2320	37.120 ← .2320 × 160
50 to 60	−0.29 to 0.43	.2805	44.880 ← .2805 × 160
60 to 70	0.43 to 1.16	.2106	33.696 ← .2106 × 160
70 to 80	1.16 to 1.89	.0936	14.976 ← .0936 × 160
80 and over	Over 1.89	.0294	4.704 ← .0294 × 160
		1.0000	160

Now to compute the value of chi-square. (See Table 14–9.) Column 2 shows the observed frequency and column 3 the expected frequency for each of the salary categories. Columns 4, 5, and 6 show the computations for finding the chi-square value. Computed chi-square is 2.590.

TABLE 14–9 Calculations for Chi-Square

(1) Salary ($ thousands)	(2) f_0	(3) f_e	(4) $f_0 - f_e$	(5) $(f_0 - f_e)^2$	(6) $\frac{(f_0 - f_e)^2}{f_e}$
Under $30	4	6.416	−2.416	5.837	0.910
30 to 40	20	18.208	1.792	3.211	0.176
40 to 50	41	37.120	3.880	15.054	0.406
50 to 60	44	44.880	−0.880	0.774	0.017
60 to 70	29	33.696	−4.696	22.052	0.654
70 to 80	16	14.976	1.024	1.049	0.070
80 and over	6	4.704	1.296	1.680	0.357
	160	160			2.590

Must be equal (columns 2 and 3 totals); χ^2 (column 6 total)

As usual, the null and the alternate hypotheses are stated.

H_0: The population is normally distributed.

H_1: The population is not normally distributed.

To find the critical value of chi-square, we need to know the degrees of freedom. In this case there are 7 categories (see Table 14–9), so the degrees of freedom is $7 - 1 = 6$. In addition, the values of $54.03, the mean salary, and $13.76, the standard deviation of the salaries of full professors, were computed from a sample of all the professors. When we estimate population parameters from sample data, we lose a degree of freedom for each estimate. So we lose two more degrees of freedom for estimating the population mean and the population standard deviation. Thus, the number of degrees of freedom in this problem is 4, found by $k - 1 - 2 = 7 - 1 - 2 = 4$.

From Appendix I, using the .05 significance level, the critical value of χ^2 is 9.488. H_0 is rejected if the computed value of chi-square is greater than 9.488. In this case we computed χ^2 to be 2.590, so the null hypothesis is not rejected. We conclude that the distribution of full professors' salaries follows the normal distribution.

To expand on the calculation of the number of degrees of freedom, suppose we knew the mean and standard deviation of a population but wished to find out if some sample information conformed to the normal distribution. In this case the degrees of freedom is *k*, the number of categories minus 1. On the other hand, suppose we have sample data grouped into a frequency distribution, but we do not know the population mean or the population standard deviation. We wish to test whether the sample data are normally distributed. Because we are estimating the population mean and the population standard deviation from the sample data, the number of degrees of freedom is $k - 2 - 1$. In general, when we use sample statistics to estimate population parameters, the number of degrees of freedom is found by $k - p - 1$, where p represents the number of population parameters being estimated from the sample data.

EXERCISES

The answers to the odd-numbered exercises are at the end of the book.

10. The manufacturer of a computer terminal reports in its advertising material that the mean life of the terminal, under normal use, is 6 years with a standard deviation of 1.4 years. A sample of 90 units sold 10 years ago revealed the following distribution of the lengths of life. At the .05 significance level, can the manufacturer conclude that the terminal lives are normally distributed?

Length of life (years)	Frequency
Up to 4	7
4 up to 5	14
5 up to 6	25
6 up to 7	22
7 up to 8	16
8 or more	6

11. The commissions for sales of new cars are reported to average $1,500 per month with a standard deviation of $300. A sample of 500 sales representatives in the Northwest revealed the following distribution of commissions. At the .01 significance level, can we conclude that the population is normally distributed with a mean of $1,500 and a standard deviation of $300?

Commission ($)	Frequency
Less than $900	9
900 up to 1,200	63
1,200 up to 1,500	165
1,500 up to 1,800	180
1,800 up to 2,100	71
2,100 or more	12
Total	500

CONTINGENCY TABLE ANALYSIS

The goodness-of-fit tests applied in the previous sections were concerned with only a single variable and a single trait. The chi-square test can also be used for a research project involving *two* traits. As examples:

- Does a male released from federal prison make a better adjustment to civilian life if he returns to his hometown or if he goes elsewhere to live? The two traits are adjustment to civilian life and place of residence. Note that both traits are measured on the nominal scale.
- Is there any relationship between the grade point average students earn in college and their income 10 years after graduation? The two traits measured for each individual are grade point average and income.

EXAMPLE

Suppose the Federal Correction Agency wants to investigate the first question cited above: Does a male released from federal prison make better adjustment to civilian life if he returns to his hometown or if he goes elsewhere to live? To put it another way, is there a relationship between adjustment to civilian life and place of residence after release from prison?

Solution

▸ As before, the first step in hypothesis testing is to state the null and alternate hypotheses.

H_0: There is no relationship between adjustment to civilian life and where the individual lives after being released from prison.

H_1: There is a relationship between adjustment to civilian life and where the individual lives after being released from prison.

The .01 level of significance will be used to test the hypothesis. Recall that this is the probability of a Type I error (i.e., the probability is .01 that a true null hypothesis is rejected).

The agency's psychologists interviewed 200 randomly selected former prisoners. Using a series of questions, the psychologists classified the adjustment of each individual to civilian life as outstanding, good, fair, or unsatisfactory. The classifications for the 200 former prisoners were tallied as follows. Joseph Camden, for example, returned to his hometown and has shown outstanding adjustment to civilian life. His case is one of the 27 tallies in the upper left box.

Residence after release from prison	Adjustment to civilian life			
	Outstanding	**Good**	**Fair**	**Unsatisfactory**
Hometown	卌 卌 卌 卌 卌 II	卌 卌 卌 卌 卌 卌 卌	卌 卌 卌 卌 卌 卌 III	卌 卌 卌 卌 卌
Not hometown	卌 卌 III	卌 卌 卌	卌 卌 卌 卌 卌 II	卌 卌 卌 卌 卌

Contingency table consists of count data

The tallies in each box, or *cell,* were counted. The counts are given in the following **contingency table.** (See Table 14–10.) In this case, the Federal Correction Agency wondered whether or not adjustment to civilian life is *contingent on* where the prisoner goes after release from prison.

TABLE 14–10 **Adjustment to Civilian Life and Place of Residence**

Residence after release from prison	Adjustment to civilian life				
	Outstanding	**Good**	**Fair**	**Unsatisfactory**	**Total**
Hometown	27	35	33	25	120
Not hometown	13	15	27	25	80
Total	40	50	60	50	200

Contingency table has rows and columns

Once we know how many rows (2) and how many columns (4) there are in the contingency table, the critical value and the decision rule can be determined. For a chi-square test of significance where two traits are classified in a contingency table the degrees of freedom are found by:

df found by $(r-1)(c-1)$

$$\begin{aligned} df &= (\text{number of rows} - 1)(\text{number of columns} - 1) \\ &= (r-1)(c-1) \end{aligned}$$

In this problem:

$$\begin{aligned} df &= (r-1)(c-1) \\ &= (2-1)(4-1) \\ &= 3 \end{aligned}$$

The decision rule

To find the critical value for 3 degrees of freedom and the .01 level (selected earlier), refer to Appendix I. It is 11.345. The decision rule is therefore: Do not reject the null hypothesis if the computed value of χ^2 is equal to or less than 11.345; reject H_0 and accept H_1 if it is greater than 11.345. The decision rule is portrayed graphically in Chart 14–4.

CHART 14–4 Chi-Square Distribution for 3 Degrees of Freedom

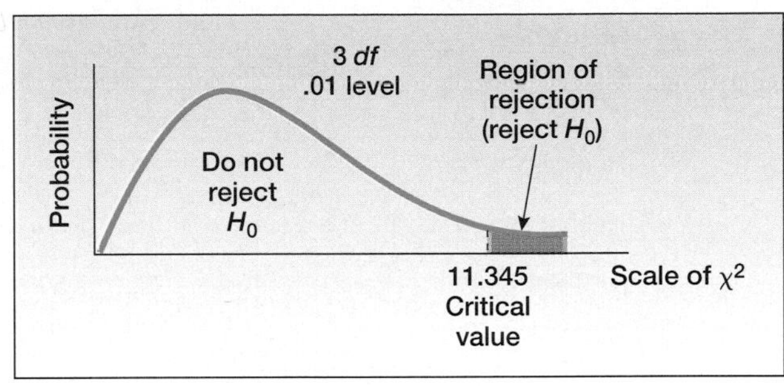

Now to find the computed value of χ^2. The observed frequencies, f_0, are shown in Table 14–10. How are the corresponding expected frequencies, f_e, determined? Note in the "Total" column of Table 14–10 that 120 of the 200 former prisoners (60 percent) returned to their hometowns. *If there were no relationship whatsoever* between adjustment and residency after release from prison, we would expect 60 percent of the 40 ex-prisoners who made outstanding adjustment to civilian life to reside in their hometowns. Thus, the expected frequency f_e for the upper left cell is $.60 \times 40$, or 24. Likewise, if there were no relationship between adjustment and present residence, we would expect 60 percent of the 50 ex-prisoners (30) who had "good" adjustment to civilian life to reside in their hometowns.

Further, notice that 80 of the 200 ex-prisoners studied (40 percent) did not return to their hometowns to live. Thus, of the 60 considered by the psychologists to have made "fair" adjustment to civilian life, $.40 \times 60$, or 24, would be expected not to return to their hometowns.

Convenient formula for determining expected frequency

The expected frequency for any cell can be determined by

$$\text{Expected frequency for a cell} = \frac{(\text{Row total})(\text{Column total})}{\text{Grand total}} \qquad (14\text{–}2)$$

Using this formula, the expected frequency for the upper left cell in Table 14–10 is:

$$\begin{aligned} \text{Expected frequency} &= \frac{(\text{Row total})(\text{Column total})}{\text{Grand total}} \\ &= \frac{(120)(40)}{200} \\ &= 24 \end{aligned}$$

The observed frequencies, f_0, and the expected frequencies, f_e, for all of the cells in the contingency table are listed in Table 14–11.

TABLE 14–11 Observed Frequencies and Expected Frequencies

Residence after release from prison	Adjustment to civilian life								Total	
	Outstanding		Good		Fair		Unsatisfactory			
	f_0	f_e	f_0	f_e	f_0	f_e	f_0	f_e	f_0	f_e
Hometown	27	24	35	30	33	36	25	30	120	120
Not hometown	13	16	15	20	27	24	25	20	80	80
Total	40	40	50	50	60	60	50	50	200	200

Must be equal (Outstanding totals 40 and 40)

$\frac{(80)(50)}{200}$ (Not hometown, Good, f_e = 20)

Must be equal (Total 200 and 200)

Recall that the computed value of chi-square using formula (14–1) is found by:

$$\chi^2 = \sum\left[\frac{(f_0 - f_e)^2}{f_e}\right]$$

Computed $\chi^2 = 5.729$

Starting with the upper left cell:

$$\chi^2 = \frac{(27-24)^2}{24} + \frac{(35-30)^2}{30} + \frac{(33-36)^2}{36} + \frac{(25-30)^2}{30} + \frac{(13-16)^2}{16} + \frac{(15-20)^2}{20} + \frac{(27-24)^2}{24} + \frac{(25-20)^2}{20}$$

$$= 0.375 + 0.833 + 0.250 + 0.833 + 0.563 + 1.250 + 0.375 + 1.250$$

$$= 5.729$$

Conclusion: No relationship between adjustment and residence

Since the computed value of chi-square (5.729) lies in the region to the left of 11.345, the null hypothesis is not rejected at the .01 level. We conclude that there is no relationship between adjustment to civilian life and where the prisoner resides after being released from prison. For the Federal Correction Agency's advisement program, adjustment to civilian life is not related to where the ex-prisoner lives.

The MINITAB output for this problem follows. The READ command was used to input the data instead of the usual SET command. The command used to compute chi-square is CHISQUARE.

```
MTB > read c1 c2 c3 c4
DATA > 27, 35, 33, 25
DATA > 13, 15, 27, 25
DATA > end
MTB > chisquare c1-c4
MTB > name c1 'outstand' c2 'good' c3 'fair' c4 'poor'
MTB > chisquare c1-c4

Expected counts are printed below observed counts

          outstand      good      fair      poor          Total
    1          27        35        33        25             120
             24.0      30.0      36.0      30.0

    2          13        15        27        25              80
             16.0      20.0      24.0      20.0

Total          40        50        60        50             200

ChiSq=       0.37+     0.83+     0.25+     0.83+
             0.56+     1.25+     0.37+     1.25=5.73 <- χ²

df=3
```

Observe that the computed value of chi-square (5.73) is the same as that found earlier.

SELF-REVIEW 14–5

The answers are at the end of the chapter.

A sociologist was researching this question: Is there any relationship between the level of education and social activities of an individual? She decided on three levels of education: attended or completed college, attended or completed high school, and attended or completed grade school or less. Each individual kept a record of his or her social activities, such as bowling with a group, dancing, and church functions. The sociologist divided them into above-average frequency, average frequency, and below-average frequency.

	Social activity		
Education	**Above average**	**Average**	**Below average**
College	20	10	10
High school	30	50	80
Grade school	10	60	130

1. What is the table called?
2. State the null hypothesis. It is to be tested at the .05 level.
3. Should the null hypothesis be rejected? Cite figures to substantiate your decision.
4. What specifically does this indicate in this problem?

EXERCISES

The answers to the odd-numbered exercises are at the end of the book.

12. A survey of industrial salespeople who are either self-employed or work for small, medium-size, or large firms revealed the following with respect to incomes:

    Of those who earn less than $20,000 a year, 9 are self-employed, and 12 are employed by small firms, 40 by medium-size firms, and 89 by large firms.

    Of those who earn $20,00–$39,999, 11 are self-employed, and 10 are employed by small firms, 45 by medium-sized firms, and 104 by large firms.

    Of those who earn $40,000 or more, 10 are self-employed, and 13 are employed by small firms, 50 by medium-size firms, and 107 by large firms.

    Examine the hypothesis that there is no relationship between the income level of the industrial salespeople and their employment status (self-employed or employed by small, medium-size, or large firms). Test at the .05 level.

13. The survey mentioned in Exercise 12 included questions on the age of the respondent and the degree of pressure the industrial salesperson felt in connection with the job. Ages and amounts of job pressure were cross-classified in the following table.

	Degree of pressure (number of salespeople)		
Age (years)	**Low**	**Medium**	**High**
Less than 25	20	18	22
25 up to 40	50	46	44
40 up to 60	58	63	59
60 and over	34	43	43

    Examine whether there is any relationship between age and the degree of job pressure. Use the .01 level.

14. The marketing director for a metropolitan daily newspaper is studying the relationship between the type of community the reader lives in and the portion of the paper he or she reads first. For a sample of readers the following information was collected.

	National news	Sports	Comics
Urban	170	124	90
Rural	120	112	100
Farm	130	90	88

At the .05 significance level, can we conclude that there is a relationship between the type of community where the person resides and the portion of the paper read first?

15. Four different brands of light bulbs are being considered for use in a large manufacturing plant. The director of purchasing asked for samples of 100 from each manufacturer. The numbers of acceptable and unacceptable bulbs from each manufacturer are shown below. At the .05 significance level, is there a difference in the quality of the bulbs?

	Manufacturer			
	A	B	C	D
Acceptable	12	8	5	11
Unacceptable	88	92	95	89
Total	100	100	100	100

CHAPTER OUTLINE

I. Goodness-of-fit test.
   A. A goodness-of-fit test is applied to find out if a set of observed frequencies fits a set of matching expected frequencies. It can be used for all levels of data—nominal, ordinal, interval, and ratio. No assumptions about the shape of the parent population are required.
   B. The procedure is:
      1. State H_0 and H_1.
      2. Selected a level of risk—usually .10, .05, or .01.
      3. The formula for chi-square is:

$$\chi^2 = \sum \left[\frac{(f_0 - f_e)^2}{f_e} \right] \qquad (14\text{–}1)$$

      with $k - 1$ degrees of freedom, where k is the number of categories.
      4. The decision rule is based on $k - 1$ degrees of freedom and the level of significance selected.
      5. A sample from the population is chosen, χ^2 is computed, and its magnitude is compared with the critical value in order to reach a decision regarding H_0.

II. Testing for normality.
   A. Purpose: To test whether the observed frequencies in a frequency distribution match the theoretical normal distribution.
   B. Procedure: Determine the area between the lower class limit and the upper class limit. Then multiply that area by the total number of frequencies to give f_e. Use f_0 and f_e to compute χ^2. Finally, make a decision regarding H_0.

III. Contingency table analysis.
   A. It is used to test whether or not two traits are related. Two traits an individual possesses might be political affiliation and view of current policy aimed at reducing the federal deficit.
   B. The procedure is:
      1. Cross-classify the two traits in a contingency table.
      2. Determine the expected frequency, f_e, for a particular cell:

$$\text{Expected frequency} = \frac{(\text{Row total})(\text{Column total})}{\text{Grand total}} \qquad (14\text{–}2)$$

      3. Find the degrees of freedom for the contingency table by: (rows − 1)(columns − 1).
      4. Compute chi-square, and arrive at a decision.

IV. Characteristics of the chi-square distribution:
   A. The value of chi-square is always positive.
   B. There is a family of chi-square distributions. The shape of the distribution changes for each number of degrees of freedom.
   C. The distributions of the chi-square statistic are positively skewed, but as the number of degrees of freedom increases, the distributions approach normality.

EXERCISES

The answers to the odd-numbered exercises are at the end of the book.

16. A sample of the employees of Carter Industries regarding acceptance of a new pension plan revealed the following:

	Opinion regarding new pension plan				
Age	**Superior**	**Very good**	**Good**	**Fair**	**Unsatisfactory**
20 up to 30	19	27	25	52	81
30 up to 40	10	17	15	29	41
40 up to 50	51	40	31	21	27
50 and over	142	81	16	9	8

Is there a relationship between age and an employee's opinion of the new plan? Test at the .05 level. Use the five-step hypothesis-testing procedure.

17. A sample of unpaid balances on Southwestern charge accounts as of September 1 was organized into the following frequency distribution.

Size of unpaid balance	Number of accounts
Less than $20	13
$20 to under $40	10
$40 to under $60	15
$60 to under $80	14
$80 to under $100	9
$100 to under $150	12
$150 and over	11

The hypothesis that the unpaid balances are evenly distributed among the seven categories is to be tested at the .01 level of risk.
a. State the null and alternate hypotheses.
b. Show the decision rule graphically.
c. Arrive at a decision.

18. Suppose that there is interest in testing if there is any relationship between the scholastic achievement (final grade point average in college) of a business administration graduate and his or her level of income. The null hypothesis is: There is no relationship between scholastic achievement and level of income. H_1 states that there is a relationship. For this test, the .05 level of significance was selected.

    It was decided to classify the scholastic achievement levels of the business administration graduates into three groups: above average, average, and below average, represented by final grade point scores of 3.0–4.0, 2.5–2.9999, and 2.0–2.4999, respectively (2.0 is needed for graduation, and 4.0 indicates that an alumnus had all A grades when in college).

    The incomes of the 751 respondents were classified into four levels: low, lower middle, upper middle, and high. The responses of the 751 graduates were tallied into a table.

Scholastic achievement	Income level				
	Low	**Lower middle**	**Upper middle**	**High**	**Total**
Above average	22	31	31	8	92
Average	67	80	73	17	237
Below average	124	161	122	15	422

Source: Robert D. Mason, *Alumni Study* (Toledo, Ohio: University of Toledo, College of Business Administration).

Is there a relationship between scholastic achievement and level of income? Use the five-step hypothesis-testing procedure.

COMPUTER DATA EXERCISES

19. Refer to data set 1, which reports information on homes sold in Florida during 1994.
    a. Develop a contingency table that shows whether or not a home has a pool according to the township in which the home is located. Is there any association between the variables pool and township? Use the .05 significance level.
    b. Develop a contingency table that shows whether or not a home has an attached garage according to the township in which the home is located. Is there any association between the variables attached garage and township? Use the .05 significance level.
    c. Develop a frequency distribution for the number of bedrooms in a home. Is it reasonable to conclude that this distribution is normal? Use the .01 significance level.
20. Refer to data set 2, which reports information on the 28 major league baseball teams for the 1993 season. Set up a variable that divides the teams into two groups: those that had a winning season and those that did not. That is, create a variable to count the cases where the variable "win" is less than 81 and those where it is 81 or more. We'll call this variable "Winning." Next create a new variable for attendance, where there are two categories: less than 2.5 million, and 2.5 million or more. Is there an association between winning and team attendance? Use the .05 significance level.

CHAPTER 14 EXAMINATION

The answers are at the end of the chapter.

1. In recent years, 55 percent of the American-made automobiles sold in the United States were manufactured by General Motors, 25 percent by Ford, 15 percent by Chrysler, and 5 percent by all others (Honda USA, etc.). A sample of the sales of American-made

automobiles conducted last week revealed that 174 were manufactured by Chrysler, 275 by Ford, 330 by GM, and 21 by all others. Test the hypothesis at the .05 level that there has been no change in the sales pattern.

2. Two hundred people selected at random from various levels of management were interviewed regarding their concern about environmental issues. The response of each person was tallied into one of three categories: no concern, some concern, and great concern. The results were:

Level of management	No concern	Some concern	Great concern
Top management	15	13	12
Middle management	20	19	21
Supervisor	7	7	6
Group leader	28	21	31

Using the .01 level, determine if there is any difference in the responses with respect to the level of management.

CHAPTER 14 Answers

Self-Review

14–1
1. Observed frequencies.
2. Six (six days of the week).
3. 10. Total observed frequencies ÷ 6 = 60/6 = 10.
4. 5; $k - 1 = 6 - 1 = 5$.
5. 15.086 (from the chi-square table in Appendix I).
6. Computed:

$$\chi^2 = \sum\left[\frac{(f_0 - f_e)^2}{f_e}\right] = \frac{(12-10)^2}{10} + \frac{(9-10)^2}{10} + \frac{(11-10)^2}{10} + \frac{(10-10)^2}{10} + \frac{(9-10)^2}{10} + \frac{(9-10)^2}{10} = 0.8$$

7. No. We do not reject H_0.
8. Absenteeism is distributed evenly throughout the week. The observed differences are due to sampling variation.

14–2 χ^2 was computed to be 14.01, found by:

f_0	f_e	$f_0 - f_e$	$(f_0 - f_e)^2$	$\frac{(f_0 - f_e)^2}{f_e}$
30	32	−2	4	4/32 = 0.13
110	113	−3	9	9/113 = 0.08
86	87	−1	1	1/87 = 0.01
23	24	−1	1	1/24 = 0.04
5	2	3	9	9/2 = 4.50
5	4	1	1	1/4 = 0.25
4	1	3	9	9/1 = 9.00
		0		14.01

The critical value of χ^2 for $k - 1 = 7 - 1 = 6$ degrees of freedom and the .05 level is 12.592. The computed χ^2 (14.01) is greater than this critical value, so the null hypothesis is rejected. There is a difference between the set of observed frequencies and the set of expected frequencies.

14–3
1. $\chi^2 = 7.26$, found by:

f_0	f_e	$f_0 - f_e$	$(f_0 - f_e)^2$	$\frac{(f_0 - f_e)^2}{f_e}$
30	32	−2	4	0.13
110	113	−3	9	0.08
86	87	−1	1	0.01
23	24	−1	1	0.04
14	7	7	49	7.00
		0		7.26

2. The critical value of χ^2 for $k - 1 = 5 - 1 = 4$ degrees of freedom and the .05 level is 9.488. The computed value of 7.26 is less than 9.488, so the null hypothesis of no difference between the sample results and the expected results is not rejected at the .05 level of significance.
3. Yes.

14–4 33.696, found by $z = (60 - 54.03)/13.76 = 0.43$ and $z = (70 - 54.03)/13.76 = 1.16$. Then $.3770 - .1664 = .2106$ and $.2106 \times 160 = 33.696$.

14–5
1. Contingency table.
2. There is no relationship between the level of education and the frequency of social activity.
3. Computing chi-square:

Above average		Average		Below average			
f_0	f_e	f_0	f_e	f_0	f_e	Total	Percent
20	6	10	12	10	22	40	10
30	24	50	48	80	88	160	40
10	30	60	60	130	110	200	50
60	60	120	120	220	220	400	100

$$\chi^2 = \frac{(20-6)^2}{6} + \frac{(10-12)^2}{12} + \cdots + \frac{(130-110)^2}{110}$$
$$= 32.67 + 0.33 + \cdots + 3.64$$
$$= 58.83$$

The computed value of chi-square is 58.83. Because it is greater than the critical value of 9.488, the null hypothesis is rejected at the .05 level.

4. There is a relationship between the level of education and the frequency of social activity.

Examination

1. H_0: There has been no change in the pattern of sales.

   H_1: There has been a change.

   The computed value of chi-square (88.950) is in the region of rejection (to the right of 7.815).

	f_0	f_e	$f_0 - f_e$	$\frac{(f_0 - f_e)^2}{f_e}$
GM	330	440	−110	27.500
Ford	275	200	75	28.125
Chrysler	174	120	54	24.300
All others	21	40	−19	9.025
	800	800	0	88.950

2. As indicated by the following computations, the computed value of chi-square is about 1.550, which is less than the critical value of 16.812. Thus, the null hypothesis, which states that there is no significant difference in the responses with regard to the level of management, is not rejected. To put it another way, there is no relationship between the degree of concern about environmental issues and the level of management. The critical value of 16.812 was determined by referring to Appendix I for (rows − 1)(columns − 1) = (4 − 1) × (3 − 1) = 6 degrees of freedom.

Level of management	No concern		Some concern		Very concerned		Total	
	f_0	f_e	f_0	f_e	f_0	f_e	Number	Percent
Top management	15	(14)	13	(12)	12	(14)	40	20
Middle management	20	(21)	19	(18)	21	(21)	60	30
Supervisor	7	(7)	7	(6)	6	(7)	20	10
Group leader	28	(28)	21	(24)	31	(28)	80	40
	70	(70)	60	(60)	70	(70)	200	100

$$\chi^2 = \frac{(15-14)^2}{14} + \frac{(13-12)^2}{12} + \frac{(12-14)^2}{14} + \frac{(20-21)^2}{21} + \cdots = 1.550$$

Chapter 15

Nonparametric Methods: Analysis of Ranked Data

GOALS

When you have completed this chapter, you will be able to:

1
Conduct a sign test and explain its applications using both the large- and small-sample methods.

2
Conduct a test of hypothesis about the population median.

3
Describe and apply the Wilcoxon matched-pairs signed-rank test.

4
Describe and apply the Wilcoxon rank-sum test.

5
Describe and apply the Kruskal-Wallis one-way analysis of variance test.

6
Determine the coefficient of rank correlation and explain its use.

A department store chain wants to handle just one brand of compact disc player. Conduct a test of hypothesis on two brands of CD players to determine if there is a difference in preference between the two brands. (See Goal 1 and Exercise 31.)

INTRODUCTION

Chapter 14 introduced nonparametric, or distribution-free, tests of hypotheses. We stressed that the goodness-of-fit test is especially useful for *nominal* level of measurement. (Recall from Chapter 1 that nominal level of measurement implies that the data can only be classified into categories, and there is no particular order to the categories.) The purpose of these tests is to determine whether or not an observed set of frequencies, f_0, is significantly different from a corresponding set of expected frequencies, f_e. Likewise, if we are interested in the relationship between two characteristics—such as the age of an individual and his or her music preference—we would tally the data into a contingency table and use the chi-square distribution as the test statistic. For both these types of problems, no assumptions need to be made about the shape of the parent population. We do not have to assume, for example, that the population of interest is normally distributed, as was done with tests of hypotheses in Chapters 8 through 11.

This chapter is a continuation of tests of hypotheses designed especially for nonparametric data. However, instead of being applicable to nominal-level data, these tests require that the responses be at least *ordinal-level.* That is, the responses can be ranked from low to high. An example of ranking is the executive title. Executives are ranked assistant vice president, vice president, senior vice president, and president. A vice president is ranked higher than an assistant vice president, a senior vice president is ranked higher than a vice president, and so on.

Five distribution-free tests requiring ranking will be considered in this chapter: the sign test, the median test, the Wilcoxon matched-pairs signed-rank test, the Wilcoxon rank-sum test, and the Kruskal-Wallis analysis of variance by ranks. In addition, the Spearman coefficient of rank correlation is described.

THE SIGN TEST

Sign test

The **sign test** is one of the simplest nonparametric tests. As the name suggests, it is based on the sign of a difference—a plus sign for a positive difference and a minus sign for a negative difference. If, for example, sales increased from $34,698 million in October to $51,276 million in November, we record the $16,578 difference as a plus sign. If production dropped from 98,000 computers in the first quarter to 51,000 in the second quarter, a minus sign is recorded. For a sign test, we are not concerned with the magnitude of the difference.

The sign test has many applications. One is for "before/after" experiments. To illustrate, suppose an evaluation is to be made on a new tune-up program for automobiles. The number of miles traveled per gallon of gasoline is recorded before the tune-up and again after the tune-up. If the tune-up is not effective, that is, had no effect on performance, theoretically about half of the automobiles tested would show an increase in miles per gallon and the other half a decrease. A "+" sign is assigned to an increase, a "−" sign to a decrease.

A product-preference experiment illustrates another use of the sign test. Taster's Choice markets two kinds of coffee in a 4-ounce jar: decaffeinated and regular. Their market research department wants to determine whether coffee drinkers prefer decaffeinated or regular coffee. Coffee drinkers are given two small, unmarked cups of coffee, and each is asked his or her preference. Preference for decaffeinated could be coded "+" and preference for regular "−." In a sense the data are ordinal-level because the coffee drinker gives his/her preferred coffee the higher rank; the other kind is ranked below it. Here again, if the population of consumers do not have a preference, we would expect half of the sample of coffee drinkers to prefer decaffeinated and the other half regular coffee.

We can best show the application of the sign test by an example. We will use a "before/after" experiment.

EXAMPLE

Top management at Samuelson Chemicals recommended that an in-plant computer training program be instituted for managers, with the objective of improving their knowledge of computer usage in accounting, procurement, production, and so on. Some managers thought it would be a worthwhile program; others resisted it, saying it would be of no value. Despite these objections, it was announced that the computer sessions would commence the first of the month.

A sample of 15 managers was selected at random. The general level of competence of each manager with respect to the computer was determined by a panel of experts before the program started. Their competence and understanding were rated as being either outstanding, excellent, good, fair, or poor. (See Table 15–1.) After the three-month training program, the same panel of computer experts rated each manager again. The two ratings (before and after) are shown along with the sign of the difference. A "+" sign indicates improvement, and a "−" sign indicates that the manager's competence on the computer had declined after the training program.

TABLE 15–1 **Competence before and after the Computer Training Program**

	Name	Before	After	Sign of difference
	T. J. Bowers	Good	Outstanding	+
	Sue Jenkins	Fair	Excellent	+
	James Brown	Excellent	Good	−
	Tad Jackson	Poor	Good	+
Dropped from analysis	~~Andy Love~~	~~Excellent~~	~~Excellent~~	~~0~~
	Sarah Truett	Good	Outstanding	+
	John Sinshi	Poor	Fair	+
	Jean Unger	Excellent	Outstanding	+
	Coy Farmer	Good	Poor	−
	Troy Archer	Poor	Good	+
	V. A. Jones	Good	Outstanding	+
	Coley Casper	Fair	Excellent	+
	Candy Fry	Good	Fair	−
	Arthur Seiple	Good	Outstanding	+
	Sandy Gumpp	Poor	Good	+

We are interested in finding out whether the in-plant computer training program was effective in increasing the competence of the managers on the computer. That is, are the managers more competent after the training program than before?

Solution

▸ **Step 1** As is the usual procedure, the null and alternate hypotheses are stated. These are the hypotheses to be tested:

Hypothesis	Meaning
H_0: $p \leq .50$	There is no change in competence as a result of the in-plant computer training program.
H_1: $p > .50$	The computer competence of the managers has increased.

If we *do not reject* the null hypothesis, it will indicate that the skeptics are correct: the training program has produced no change in the level of computer competence, or competence actually decreased. If we *reject* the null hypothesis, it will mean that the computer competence of the managers has increased as a result of the training program.

The binomial distribution discussed in Chapter 6 is used as the test statistic. It is appropriate because the sign test meets all the binomial assumptions, namely:

1. There are only two outcomes: a "success" and a "failure." A manager either increased his or her computer competence (a success) or did not.
2. For each trial the probability of a success is assumed to be .50. Thus, the probability of a success is the same for all trials (managers in this case).
3. The total number of trials is fixed (15 in this experiment).
4. Each trial is independent. This means, for example, that Arthur Seiple's performance in the three-month course is unrelated to Sandy Gumpp's performance.

Step 2 Select a level of significance. We chose the .10 level.

Step 3 Decide on the test statistic. It is *the number of plus signs* resulting from the experiment (11 in this case).

Step 4 Formulate a decision rule. Fifteen managers were enrolled in the computer course, but Andy Love showed no increase or decrease in competence. (See Table 15–1.) He was therefore eliminated from the test, so $n = 14$. From the binomial probability distribution in Appendix A, for an n of 14 and a probability of .50, we copied the binomial probability distribution in Table 15–2. The number of successes is in column 1, the probability of success in column 2, and the cumulative probabilities in column 3. To arrive at the cumulative probabilities, we *add up* the probabilities of success in column 2 from the bottom. For illustration, to get the cumulative probability of 11 or more successes, we add $.000 + .001 + .006 + .022 = .029$.

This is a one-tailed test because the alternate hypothesis gives a direction. The inequality ($>$) points to the right. Thus, the region of rejection is in the upper tail. If the inequality sign pointed toward the left tail ($<$), the region of rejection would be in the lower tail. If that were the case, we would add the probabilities in column 2 *down* to get the cumulative probabilities in column 3.

Recall that the .10 level of significance was selected. To arrive at the decision rule for this problem, we go to the cumulative probabilities in (Table 15–2) column 3. We read up from the bottom until we come to the *cumulative probability nearest to but not exceeding the level of significance (.10).* That cumulative probability is .090. The number of successes (plus signs) corresponding to .090 in column 1 is 10. Therefore, the decision rule is: If the number of pluses in the sample is 10 or more, the null hypothesis is rejected and the alternate hypothesis accepted.

TABLE 15–2 Binomial Probability Distribution for $n = 14$, $p = .50$

(1) Number of successes	(2) Probability of success		(3) Cumulative probability	
0	.000		1.000*	
1	.001		.999	
2	.006		.998	
3	.022		.992	
4	.061		.970	
5	.122		.909	
6	.183		.787	
7	.209		.604	
8	.183		.395	
9	.122	↑	.212	
10	.061		.090	
11	.022		.029 ←	.000 + .001 +
12	.006		.007	.006 + .022
13	.001	Add	.001	
14	.000	up	.000	

*Slight discrepancy due to rounding.

To repeat: We add the probabilities up from the bottom because the direction of the inequality (>) is toward the right, indicating that the region of rejection is in the upper tail. If the number of plus signs in the sample is 10 or more, we reject the null hypothesis; otherwise, we do not reject H_0. The region of rejection is portrayed in Chart 15–1.

CHART 15–1 Region of Rejection, $n = 14$, $p = .50$

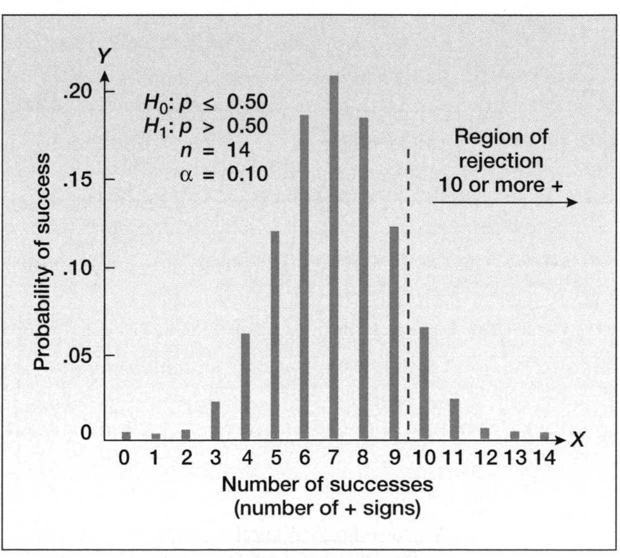

What procedure is followed for a two-tailed test? We combine (add) the probabilities of success in the two tails until we come as close to α as possible without exceeding it. In this example α is .10. The probability of 3 or fewer successes is .029, found by .000 + .001 + .006 + .022. The probability of 11 or more successes is also .029. Adding the two probabilities gives .058. This is the closest we can come to .10 without exceeding it. (Had we included the probabilities of 4 and 10 successes, the total would be .180, which exceeds .10.) Hence, the decision rule for a two-tailed test would be to reject the null hypothesis if there are 3 or fewer plus signs, or 11 or more plus signs.

Step 5 Eleven out of the 14 managers in the computer course increased their computer competency. The number 11 is in the rejection region, which starts at 10, so H_0 is rejected. The three-month computer course was effective in that it increased the computer competency of the managers.

It should be noted again that if the alternate hypothesis does not give a direction—for example, $H_0 : p = .50$ and $H_1 : p \neq .50$—the test of hypothesis is *two-tailed.* In such cases there will be two rejection regions—one in the lower tail and one in the upper tail. If $\alpha = .10$ and the test is two-tailed, the area in each tail is .05 ($\alpha/2 = .10/2 = .05$). Self-Review 15–1 illustrates this.

SELF-REVIEW 15–1

The answers are at the end of the chapter.

Recall the Taster's Choice example described on page 606, involving a consumer test to determine the preference for decaffeinated versus regular coffee. The null and alternate hypotheses are:

$$H_0: p = .50 \qquad n = 12$$

$$H_1: p \neq .50 \qquad \alpha = .10$$

1. Is this a one-tailed or a two-tailed test of hypothesis?
2. Show the decision rule in a chart.
3. Letting consumer preference for decaffeinated coffee be a "+" and preference for regular coffee a "−," it was found that two consumers preferred decaffeinated. What is your decision? Explain.

EXERCISES

The answers to the odd-numbered exercises are at the end of the book.

1. The following hypothesis-testing situation is given.

$$H_0: p \leq .50$$

$$H_1: p > .50$$

The significance level is .10, and the sample size is 12.

a. What is the decision rule?

b. There were nine successes. What is your decision regarding the null hypothesis? Explain.

2. The following hypothesis-testing situation is given.

$$H_0: p = .50$$

$$H_1: p \neq .50$$

The significance level is .05, and the sample size is 9.

a. What is the decision rule?

b. There were five successes. What is your decision regarding the null hypothesis?

3. Calorie Watchers has low-calorie breakfasts, lunches, and dinners. If you join the club, you receive two packaged meals a day. CW claims that you can eat anything you want for the third meal and still lose at least five pounds the first month. Members of the club are weighed before commencing the program and again at the end of the first month. The experiences of a random sample of 11 enrollees are:

Name	Weight change	Name	Weight change
Foster	Lost	Hercher	Lost
Taoka	Lost	Camder	Lost
Lange	Gained	Hinckle	Lost
Rousos	Lost	Hinkley	Lost
Stephens	No change	Justin	Lost
Cantrell	Lost		

We are interested in finding out whether there has been a weight loss as a result of the Calorie Watchers program.

a. State H_0 and H_1.

b. Using the .05 level of significance, what is the decision rule?

c. What is your conclusion about the Calorie Watchers program?

4. Many new stockbrokers resist giving presentations to bankers and certain other groups. Sensing this lack of self-confidence, management arranged to have a confidence-building seminar for a sample of new stockbrokers and enlisted Career Boosters for a three-week course. Before the first session, Career Boosters measured the level of confidence of each participant. It was measured again after the three-week seminar. The "before" and "after" levels of self-confidence for the 14 in the course are shown below. Self-confidence was classified as being either negative, low, high, or very high.

Stockbroker	Before seminar	After seminar
J. M. Martin	Negative	Low
T. D. Jagger	Negative	Negative
A. D. Hammer	Low	High
T. A. Jones, Jr.	Very high	Low
J. J. Cornwall	Low	High
D. A. Skeen	Low	High
C. B. Simmer	Negative	High
F. M. Orphey	Low	Very high
C. C. Ford	Low	High
A. R. Utz	Negative	Low
M. R. Murphy	Low	High
P. A. Arms	Negative	Low
B. K. Pierre	Low	High
N. S. Walker	Low	Very high

The purpose of this study is to find out if Career Boosters was effective in raising the self-confidence of the new stockbrokers. That is, was the level of self-confidence higher after the seminar than before it? Use the .05 significance level.

a. State the null and alternate hypotheses.
b. Using the .05 level of significance, state the decision rule—either in words or in chart form.
c. Draw conclusions about the seminar offered by Career Boosters.

Using the Normal Approximation

If the total number of usable pairs in the sample is larger than 20, the sample is considered "large." Some researchers consider a sample of 11 or more large, but we will use a limit of 20.

Instead of applying the binomial distribution to problems involving large samples and the sign test, we use the normal probability distribution. Both np and $n(1-p)$ must be greater than 5 for the test to be applied.

The mean of a normal distribution is

$$\mu = .50n$$

The standard deviation is

$$\sigma = .50\sqrt{n}$$

The test statistic z is

$$z = \frac{(X \pm .50) - \mu}{\sigma} \qquad (15\text{–}1)$$

If the number of pluses or minuses *is more than n/2,* we use the following form as the test statistic:

$$z = \frac{(X - .50) - \mu}{\sigma} = \frac{(X - .50) - .50n}{.50\sqrt{n}} \qquad (15\text{–}2)$$

If the number of pluses or minuses is *less than n/2,* the test statistic z is:

$$z = \frac{(X + .50) - \mu}{\sigma} = \frac{(X + .50) - .50n}{.50\sqrt{n}} \qquad (15\text{–}3)$$

In the preceding formulas, X is the number of plus (or minus) signs. The value $+.50$ or $-.50$ is the *continuity correction factor,* discussed in Chapter 7. Briefly, it is applied when a continuous distribution such as the normal distribution (which we are using) is used to approximate a discrete distribution (the binomial).

EXAMPLE

The market research department of Cola, Inc. has been given the assignment of testing a new soft drink. Two versions of the drink are considered—a rather sweet drink and a somewhat bitter one. A preference test is to be conducted consisting of a sample of 64 consumers. Each will taste both the sweet cola (labeled A) and the bitter one (labeled B) and indicate a preference. How will the test of hypothesis be conducted, and what cola, if any, should be marketed?

Solution ▸ **Step 1** State the null and alternate hypotheses.

H_0: $p = .50$ There is no preference.

H_1: $p \neq .50$ There is a preference.

Step 2 Select a level of significance. It is the .05 level.

Step 3 The test statistic is selected. It is z, given in formula (15–1).

$$z = \frac{(X \pm .50) - \mu}{\sigma}$$

where $\mu = .50n$ and $\sigma = .50\sqrt{n}$.

Step 4 Formulate the decision rule. Referring to Appendix D, Areas under the Normal Curve, for a two-tailed test (because H_1, states that $p \neq .50$), and the .05 significance level, the critical values are +1.96 and −1.96. Recall from Chapter 9 that for a two-tailed test we split the rejection region in half and place one half in each tail. That is, $\alpha/2 = .05/2 = .025$. Continuing, $.5000 - .025 = .4750$. Searching for .4750 in the body of the table and reading the z value in the left margin gives 1.96, the critical value. Therefore, do not reject H_0 if the computed z value is between +1.96 and −1.96. Otherwise, reject H_0 and accept H_1.

Step 5 Compute z, and then compare the computed value with the critical value of −1.96 or 1.96. Arrive at a decision regarding H_0.

Preference for cola A was given a "+" sign and preference for B a "−" sign. Out of the 64 in the sample, 46 preferred the sweet cola, A. Therefore, there are 46 pluses. Since 46 is *more than* $n/2 = 64/2 = 32$, we use formula (15–2) for z:

$$z = \frac{(X - .50) - .50n}{.50\sqrt{n}}$$

$$= \frac{(46 - .50) - .50(64)}{.50\sqrt{64}} = 3.375$$

The computed z of 3.375 is in the region beyond 1.96. Therefore, the null hypothesis of no difference is rejected at the .05 level. We conclude that there is a difference in consumer preference. That is, we conclude that consumers prefer one cola over the other.

SELF-REVIEW 15–2

The answers are at the end of the chapter.

The following information is given.

H_0: $p \leq .50$ H_1: $p > .50$ .05 level $n = 100$

For a "before/after" test, a "+" indicates that an athlete gained weight after taking extremely large doses of selected vitamins. A "−" indicates a loss in weight. Eighty athletes gained weight. Can we say that the vitamins were effective in adding weight to the athletes? Explain your procedure and your decision.

EXERCISES

The answers to the odd-numbered exercises are at the end of the book.

5. A sample of 45 overweight men participated in an exercise program. A total of 32 showed a loss of weight at the completion of the program. At the .05 significance level, can we conclude that the program is effective?
   a. State the null hypothesis and the alternate hypothesis.
   b. State the decision rule.
   c. Compute the value of the test statistic.
   d. What is your decision regarding the null hypothesis?
6. A sample of 60 college students was given a special training program designed to improve their study and time management skills. One month after completing the course the students were contacted and asked if the skills learned in the program were effective. A total of 42 responded yes. At the .05 significance level, can we conclude that the program is effective?
   a. State the null hypothesis and the alternate hypothesis.
   b. State the decision rule.
   c. Compute the value of the test statistic.
   d. What is your decision regarding the null hypothesis?
7. Pierre's Restaurant announced that on Thursday night the menu would consist of unusual gourmet items, such as squid, rabbit, snails from Scotland, and dandelion greens. As part of a larger survey, a sample of 81 regular customers was asked if they preferred the regular menu or the gourmet menu. Forty-three preferred the gourmet menu. Using the sign test and the .02 level, test whether his customers like the gourmet menu better than the regular menu. Justify your conclusion.
8. Assembly workers at Computer Associates assemble just one or two subassemblies and insert them in a frame. The executives at CA think that the employees would have more pride in their work if they assembled all of the subassemblies and tested the complete computer. The null hypothesis is that the employees have no preference. A sample of 25 employees was selected to experiment with the idea. After a training program, each was asked his or her preference. Twenty liked assembling the entire unit and testing it. At the .05 level, use the sign test to arrive at a decision regarding employee preference. Explain the steps you used to arrive at your decision.

Testing a Hypothesis about a Median

Most of the tests of hypothesis we have conducted so far involved the population mean or a proportion. The sign test is one of the few tests that can be used to test the value of a median. Recall from Chapter 3 that the median is the value above which half of the observations lie and below which the other half lie. For hourly wages of \$7, \$9, \$11, and \$18, the median is \$10. Half of the wages are above \$10 an hour and the other half below \$10.

To conduct a test of hypothesis, a value above the median is assigned a plus sign, and a value below the median is assigned a minus sign. If a value is the same as the median, it is dropped from further analysis. The procedure is identical to that followed in the small-sample and large-sample cases just discussed.

EXAMPLE

The district manager of Superior Grocers hypothesized that the median grocery bill of the customers in his region is \$23.00. He wants to investigate his hypothesis. The null hypothesis to be tested is H_0: Median $=$ \$23.00. If the population median is

$23.00, half of the bills will be less than $23.00, and the other half will be more than $23.00. Suppose, however, that the manager randomly selected 102 grocery bills and found that 50 were over the median and 52 were under the median of $23.00. Is that sufficient evidence to reject the null hypothesis that the median is $23.00, or could this slight imbalance be due to sampling error? What if the sample survey revealed that 55 grocery bills were greater than the median and 47 were less than the median? Should we reject H_0?

When the district manager did randomly select 102 grocery bills, he found that 60 of them were above his hypothesized median of $23.00, 40 were below $23.00, and 2 were exactly $23.00. Based on these sample results, should we conclude that the median bill is not $23.00? That is, is this imbalance (60 above, 40 below the median) so great that we need to reject H_0 and accept H_1, which states that the median is not equal to $23.00? We will use the .10 significance level.

Solution ► The null and alternate hypothese are:

$$H_0\text{: Median} = \$23.00$$

$$H_1\text{: Median} \neq \$23.00$$

This is a two-tailed test because the alternate hypothesis does not state a direction (either less than or more than $23.00).

The critical values are ± 1.645, found by $\alpha/2 = .10/2 = .05$. Then $.5000 - .05 = .4500$. Find .4500 in Appendix D, and read the critical value of z. It is 1.645.

As noted previously, the district manager selected 102 grocery bills. Since 2 were exactly $23.00 (the hypothesized median), they are omitted. Thus, $102 - 2 = 100$, which is n. Substituting 100 for n and solving for the mean, μ, and the standard deviation, σ:

$$\mu = .50n = .50(100) = 50$$

$$\sigma = .50\sqrt{n} = .50\sqrt{100} = 5$$

We use formula (15–2) for z because 60 is greater than $n/2$ $(100/2 = 50)$.

$$z = \frac{(X - .50) - .50n}{.50\sqrt{n}} = \frac{(60 - .50) - .50(100)}{.50\sqrt{100}} = 1.90$$

Since 1.90 is in the area beyond 1.645, the null hypothesis is rejected at the .10 significance level. The median grocery bill is not $23.00.

A MINITAB Solution Arranging the values from low to high and then determining whether each value is above, below, or equal to the hypothesized median is rather tedious—especially if the sample size is quite large. Instead, MINITAB can quickly tell us how many observations are above, below, or equal to the hypothesized median.

Suppose a local store manager wanted to check the district manager's hypothesis that the median bill is $23.00. She selected a sample of 64 grocery bills and entered them in her MINITAB software package, with the following results:

```
MTB > set c1
DATA> 27.5, 103, 41.62, 214.25, 16.26, 91.3, 18.52, 89.18, 19.31, 106.01, 8.5
DATA> 4.8, 87.52, 26.4, 41.61, 1.87, 52.91, 56.4, 52.9, 86.14, 71.16, 36.18, 291.67
DATA> 23, 11.12, 12.91, 28, 15, 3.96, 3.8, 29.81, 9.26, 7.14, 23, 62.14, 39.03, 47.16
DATA> 103.62, 99.91, 15.14, 71, 46.18, 11.9, 41.6, 37.42, 88.18, 91.65, 18.19, 46.8
DATA> 14.22, 19.67, 39.05, 5.6, 49.09, 103.2, 97.62, 77.8, 39.16, 46, 21, 32.18, 61.03
DATA> 77.16, 27.14
DATA> end
MTB > name c1 'Amount'
MTB > stest median=23 data in c1

SIGN TEST OF MEDIAN = 23.00 VERSUS N.E. 23.00

              N     BELOW     EQUAL     ABOVE     P-VALUE     MEDIAN
Amount       64        20         2        42      0.0077      39.10
```

Assist the local grocery store manager by doing Self-Review 15–3.

SELF-REVIEW 15–3

The answers are at the end of the chapter.

Referring to the preceding MINITAB output:

1. What is the null hypothesis? Assuming that the local manager is going to conduct a two-tailed test, what is the alternate hypothesis?
2. How many bills were below the hypothesized median of $23.00? Above it? Equal to it?
3. What is n?
4. Using the .10 level of significance, what is the critical value of z?
5. What is the computed value of z?
6. What action should the local manager take regarding the null hypothesis? Explain your decision.
7. What is the actual median grocery bill based on her sample results?
8. Based on the sample results, isn't the actual median bill close enough to the hypothesized median to say that the difference could be due to sampling?

EXERCISES

The answers to the odd-numbered exercises are at the end of the book.

9. It is claimed that the median annual income of computer programmers with at least five years of experience is $40,000. The claim is being challenged by the programmers, who say the median annual income is greater than $40,000. To resolve the controversy, a random sample of 205 programmers was selected. It was found that 170 had incomes above $40,000, 5 earned exactly $40,000, and the remaining number had incomes under $40,000.
   a. State the null and alternate hypotheses.
   b. Using the .05 level, state the decision rule in words.
   c. Do the necessary computations, and write out your conclusions.
10. Central Airlines claims that the median price of a round-trip ticket to Jackson Hole, Wyoming, is $503. This claim is being challenged by the Association of Travel Agents. To resolve the issue, a random sample of 400 round-trip tickets was selected. Of these, 160 tickets were below $503. None of the tickets were exactly $503. Let $\alpha = .05$.

a. Decide on the null and alternate hypotheses, level of significance, and so on.
b. Reach a decision regarding the controversy.

WILCOXON MATCHED-PAIR SIGNED-RANK TEST OF DIFFERENCES

Wilcoxon test replaces paired *t* test when assumptions for *t* cannot be met

The paired *t* test described in Chapter 10 is used when the differences between two sets of *paired observations* approximate a normal distribution. If this assumption cannot be met, a nonparametric test developed by Frank Wilcoxon (1945) should be applied. It is known as the **Wilcoxon matched-pair signed-rank test of differences.** We will refer to it as the Wilcoxon signed-rank test. It requires that the data be at least ordinal-scale and that the two samples be related (paired).

EXAMPLE

Suppose that a radical new experimental word processor has been developed by the engineering section of Computer Technologies. A vice president is somewhat skeptical, however, that even after a period of transition the number of words per minute a data entry clerk can achieve will differ significantly from that achieved using the current model. Plans are to randomly select a group of data entry clerks and check their performance on the current model. Then each will be provided with the newly developed word processor, and after a few weeks their performance will be again recorded. Thus, for each operator there will be a matched pair of data. For this type of experiment, it is said that each person is *acting as his/her own control.* How can the Wilcoxon matched-pair signed-rank test be used to test for the difference in performance between the old and new models by data entry clerks?

Solution ▶ As usual, the first step is to state the null and alternate hypotheses.

Null and alternate hypotheses stated

H_0: There is no difference between the peformance using the current model and that using the new model.

H_1: There is a difference in the two typing speeds.

Since no direction is specified (such as "the speed attained on the new data processor is greater than that on the old model"), a two-tailed test will be applied.

Level of significance

The null hypothesis is to be tested at the .01 level. To test the hypothesis, 29 operators selected at random were first given a test on the current model. Then each operator was assigned to one of the experimental word processors. After a period of training, the operators were given another test. Table 15–3 shows the results and the differences.

The steps necessary to ultimately reject or not reject the null hypothesis are:

1. Compute the difference between the number of words per minute typed on the current model and the number typed on the experimental model for each of the 29 operators. The differences are shown in column 4 of Table 15–3.
2. Only the positive and negative changes are considered further. That is, if the difference between the words per minute typed on the current model and the words per minute typed on the newly developed processor is zero, those data will be ignored (because there is only interest in ranking actual differences). Seven of the 29 operators showed no change in typing speed. Therefore, $N = 22$, found by $29 - 7$.

TABLE 15–3 Number of Words per Minute Typed on Current Word Processor and on a Newly Developed Model (29 typists)

(1) Operator number	(2) Speed on current word processor	(3) Speed on experimental word processor	(4) Difference (3) − (2)	(5) Rank	(6) Signed rank −	(6) Signed rank +
1	43	49	6	13.5		13.5
2	91	92	1	2.5		2.5
3	33	32	−1	2.5	2.5	
4	54	54	—			
5	45	65	20	18		18
6	55	90	35	21		21
7	65	64	−1	2.5	2.5	
8	90	85	−5	11.5	11.5	
9	53	56	3	8		8
10	70	70	—			
11	76	74	−2	5.5	5.5	
12	87	87	—			
13	32	64	32	20		20
14	99	104	5	11.5		11.5
15	87	87	—			
16	80	77	−3	8	8	
17	88	88	—			
18	23	32	9	15		15
19	75	90	15	16.5		16.5
20	54	51	−3	8	8	
21	43	49	6	13.5		13.5
22	23	90	67	22		22
23	56	78	22	19		19
24	56	57	1	2.5		2.5
25	70	70	—			
26	76	78	2	5.5		5.5
27	45	60	15	16.5		16.5
28	76	80	4	10		10
29	54	54	—			
					38.0	215.0

Calculate difference between each pair of values

3. Next rank the absolute differences listed in column 4 of Table 15–3. That is, ignore the fact that some of the differences are positive and some are negative. The 22 ranked differences are shown in column 5 of Table 15–3. To explain how these ranks were determined, note that there were four operators (numbers 2, 3, 7, and 24) who had a difference of one word per minute. These four operators are therefore each assigned a rank of 2.5, found by averaging the ranks of 1, 2, 3, and 4. We ignore the fact that operator 2 had a difference of +1 word per minute and operator 3 had a difference of −1 word per minute.
4. Each assigned rank in column 5 is then given the same sign as the original difference, and the results reported in column 6. For example, operator 2 had a difference of +1 word per minute and so in column 6 is assigned a rank of +2.5. Operator 8 had a decrease of 5 words per minute and was assigned a rank of 11.5. This operator is assigned a rank of −11.5 in column 6.

5. Next the negative ranks and the positive ranks in column 6 are summed. The sum of the negative ranks is 38, and the sum of the positive ranks is 215. The smaller of the two rank sums is 38. The smaller of the rank sums is referred to as *T*, and this is used as the test statistic.

Again the sum of the negative ranks is 38, and the sum of the positive ranks is 215. If any improvement in proficiency were exactly offset by a loss in proficiency, each of the two rank sums would have been about 126.5, found by 253/2.

Decision rule

The Wilcoxon critical value in Appendix J for $N = 22$ at the .01 level of significance and a two-tailed test is 48. This indicates that a computed T value greater than 48 up to (and including) 126.5 could result by chance; that is, a computed T value greater than 48 but equal to or less than 126.5 would indicate that the sum of the positive and negative ranks do *not* depart significantly from zero.

The decision rule is shown schematically as follows:

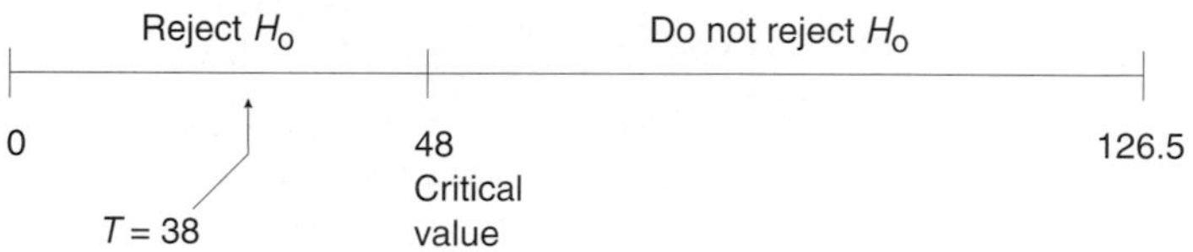

Decision regarding H_0

Since the computed T value of 38 is less than the critical T value of 48, the null hypothesis is *rejected* at the .01 level. H_1 is accepted. We conclude that there is a difference in the typing speeds between the two models.

SELF-REVIEW 15–4

The answers are at the end of the chapter.

A record of the production for each machine operator was kept over a period of time. Certain changes in the production procedure were suggested, and 11 operators were picked as an experimental test group to determine whether or not the new procedures were worthwhile. Their production rates before and after the new procedures were established are as follows:

Operator	Production before	Production after
S. M.	17	18
D. J.	21	23
M. D.	25	22
B. B.	15	25
M. F.	10	28
A. A.	16	16
U. Z.	10	22
Y. U.	20	19
U. T.	17	20
Y. H.	24	30
Y. Y.	23	26

1. How many usable pairs are there? That is, what is N?
2. Using the Wilcoxon signed-rank test, determine whether or not the new procedures actually increased production. Use the .05 level and a one-tailed test.

EXERCISES

The answers to the odd-numbered exercises are at the end of the book.

11. A random sample of seven young urban professional couples (yuppies) that own their homes is selected. The size of their home is compared with that of their parents, in terms of square feet. At the .05 significance level, can we conclude that the yuppies live in larger homes?

Couple name	Professional	Parent
Gordon	1,725	1,175
Sharkey	1,310	1,120
Uselding	1,670	1,420
Bell	1,520	1,640
Kulhman	1,290	1,360
Welch	1,880	1,750
Anderson	1,530	1,440

12. One of the major car manufacturers is studying the effect of regular versus high-octane gasoline in its economy cars. Ten executives are selected and asked to maintain records on the number of miles traveled per gallon of gas. The results are:

	Miles per gallon	
Executive	Regular	High-octane
Bowers	25	28
Demars	33	31
Grasser	31	35
DeToto	45	44
Kleg	42	47
Rau	38	40
Greolke	29	29
Burns	42	37
Snow	41	44
Lawless	30	44

At the .05 significance level, is there a difference in the number of miles traveled per gallon between regular and high-octane gasoline?

13. A new assembly-line procedure has been suggested by Mr. Mump. In order to test whether or not the new procedure is superior to the old procedure, a sample group of 15 men was selected at random. First their production under the old system was determined. Then the new Mump procedure was introduced. After an appropriate break-in period, their production was measured again. The results were:

	Production	
Employee	Old system	Mump method
A	60	64
B	40	52
C	59	58
D	30	37
E	70	71
F	78	83
G	43	46
H	40	52

Employee	Production: Old system	Production: Mump method
I	87	84
J	80	80
K	56	57
L	21	21
M	99	108
N	50	56
O	56	62

At the .05 significance level can we conclude that the production is greater using the Mump method?

a. State the null and alternate hypotheses.

b. State the decision rule.

c. Arrive at a decision regarding the null hypothesis.

14. It has been suggested that the daily production of a subassembly would be increased if better portable lighting were installed and background music and free coffee and doughnuts were provided during the day. Management agreed to try the scheme for a limited time. The numbers of subassemblies produced per week by a small test group of employees are as follows.

Employee	Past production record	Production after installing lighting, music, etc.
JD	23	33
SB	26	26
MD	24	30
RCF	17	25
MF	20	19
UHH	24	22
IB	30	29
WWJ	21	25
OP	25	22
CD	21	23
PA	16	17
RRT	20	15
AT	17	9
QQ	23	30

Using the Wilcoxon signed-rank test, determine whether or not the suggested changes are worthwhile—that is, whether or not they increased production.

a. State the null hypothesis.

b. You decide on the alternate hypothesis.

c. You decide on the level of significance.

d. State the decision rule.

e. Compute T, and arrive at a decision.

THE WILCOXON RANK-SUM TEST

One test specifically designed to determine whether two independent samples came from the same or equal populations is the **Wilcoxon rank-sum test.** This test is an alternative to the two-sample t test described in Chapter 10. Recall that the t test requires that the two populations be normally distributed and have equal population variances. These conditions are not required for the Wilcoxon rank-sum test.

Test using independent samples

The Wilcoxon rank-sum test is based on the sum of the ranks. The data are ranked as if the observations were part of a single sample. If the null hypothesis is true, then the ranks will be about evenly distributed between the two samples, and the sum of the ranks for the two samples will be about the same. That is, the low, medium, and high ranks should be about equally divided between the two samples. If the alternate hypothesis is true, one of the samples will have more of the lower ranks and thus a smaller rank total. The other sample will have more of the higher ranks and therefore a larger total. If each of the samples contains at *least eight observations,* the standard normal distribution is used as the test statistic. The formula is:

$$z = \frac{W - \dfrac{n_1(n_1 + n_2 + 1)}{2}}{\sqrt{\dfrac{n_1 n_2(n_1 + n_2 + 1)}{12}}} \qquad (15\text{–}4)$$

where:

n_1 is the number of observations from the first population.

n_2 is the number of observations from the second population.

W is the sum of the ranks from the first population.

EXAMPLE

Mr. Dan Thompson, the president of CEO Airlines, has noted an increase in the number of no-shows for flights out of Atlanta. He is particularly interested in determining whether there are more no-shows for flights that originate in Atlanta compared with flights leaving Chicago. A sample of nine flights from Atlanta and eight from Chicago is obtained. The results are reported in Table 15–4. At the .05 significance level, can we conclude that there are more no-shows for the flights originating in Atlanta?

TABLE 15–4 **Number of No-Shows for Scheduled Flights**

Atlanta	Chicago
11	13
15	14
10	10
18	8
11	16
20	9
24	17
22	21
25	

Solution ► If we were to assume that the populations of no-shows were normally distributed and had equal variances, the two-sample *t* test, discussed in Chapter 10, would be appropriate. In this case Mr. Thompson believes that these two conditions cannot be met. Therefore, a nonparametric test, the Wilcoxon rank-sum test, is appropriate.

If the number of no-shows is the same for Atlanta and Chicago, then we expect the totals of the two ranks to be about the same. If the number of no-shows is not the same, we expect the two sums of ranks to be quite different.

Mr. Thompson believes that there are more no-shows for Atlanta flights. Thus, a one-tailed test is appropriate, with the rejection region located in the upper tail. The null and alternate hypotheses are:

H_0: The distribution of no-shows is the same for Atlanta and Chicago.

H_1: The distribution of no-shows is larger for Atlanta than for Chicago.

The test statistic follows the standard normal distribution. At the .05 significance level, we find from Appendix D that the critical value of z is 1.645. So the null hypothesis is rejected if the computed value of z is greater than 1.645.

The alternate hypothesis is that there are more no-shows in Atlanta, which means that distribution is larger and is located to the right of the Chicago distribution. The value of W is calculated for the Atlanta group and is found to be 96.5, which is the sum of the ranks for the no-shows for the Atlanta flights. (See Table 15–5.) The details of rank assignment are shown in Table 15–5. We rank the observations from *both* samples as if they were a single group. The Chicago flight with only 8 no-shows had the fewest, so it is assigned a rank of 1. The Chicago flight with 9 no-shows is ranked 2, and so on. The Atlanta flight with 25 no-shows is the highest, so it is assigned the largest rank, 17. There are also two instances of tied ranks. There is an Atlanta and a Chicago flight that each had 10 no-shows and two Atlanta flights with 11 no-shows. How do we resolve these ties? The solution is to average the ranks involved and assign the average rank to both flights. In the case involving 10 no-shows the ranks involved are 3 and 4. The mean of these ranks is 3.5, so a rank of 3.5 is assigned to both the Atlanta and the Chicago flights with 10 no-shows.

TABLE 15–5 Ranked Numbers of No-Shows for Scheduled Flights

Atlanta		Chicago	
No-shows	Rank	No-shows	Rank
11	5.5	13	7
15	9	14	8
10	3.5	10	3.5
18	12	8	1
11	5.5	16	10
20	13	9	2
24	16	17	11
22	15	21	14
25	17		
	96.5		56.5

Note from Table 15–5 that there are nine flights originating in Atlanta and eight in Chicago, so $n_1 = 9$ and $n_2 = 8$. Computing z from formula (15–4) gives:

$$z = \frac{W - \frac{n_1(n_1 + n_2 + 1)}{2}}{\sqrt{\frac{n_1 n_2(n_1 + n_2 + 1)}{12}}} = \frac{96.5 - \frac{9(9 + 8 + 1)}{2}}{\sqrt{\frac{9(8)(9 + 8 + 1)}{12}}} = 1.49$$

Because the computed z value (1.49) is less than 1.645, the null hypothesis is not rejected. The evidence does not show a difference in the distributions of no-shows. That is, it appears that the number of no-shows is the same in Atlanta as in Chicago. The p-value is .0681, found by determining the area to the right of 1.49 (.5000 − .4319).

In using the Wilcoxon rank-sum test, you may number the two populations in either order. However, once you have made a choice, *W must be* the sum of the ranks identified as population 1. If, in the no-show example, the population of Chicago was identified as number 1, the direction of the alternate hypothesis would be changed, but the *absolute value of z* remains the same.

H_0: The distribution of no-shows is the same for Chicago and Atlanta.

H_1: The distribution of no-shows is smaller for Chicago than for Atlanta.

The computed value of z is −1.49, found by:

$$z = \frac{W - \frac{n_1(n_1 + n_2 + 1)}{2}}{\sqrt{\frac{n_1 n_2(n_1 + n_2 + 1)}{12}}} = \frac{56.5 - \frac{8(8 + 9 + 1)}{2}}{\sqrt{\frac{8(9)(8 + 9 + 1)}{12}}} = -1.49$$

SELF-REVIEW 15–5

The answers are at the end of the chapter.

The research director for a golf ball manufacturer wants to know if there is a difference in the distribution of the distances traveled by two of the company's golf balls. Eight of their Dino brand and eight of their Maxi brand balls were hit by an automatic driver. The distances (in yards) were as follows:

Dino: 252, 263, 279, 273, 271, 265, 257, 280
Maxi: 262, 242, 256, 260, 258, 243, 239, 265

Assume that the distributions are not normally distributed. At the .05 significance level, is there a difference between the two distributions?

EXERCISES

15. The following observations were selected from populations that were not normally distributed. Use the .05 significance level, a two-tailed test, and the Wilcoxon rank-sum test to determine if there is a difference between the two populations.

Population A: 38, 45, 56, 57, 61, 69, 70, 79
Population B: 26, 31, 35, 42, 51, 52, 57, 62

16. The following observations were selected from populations that are not normally distributed. Use the .05 significance level, a two-tailed test, and the Wilcoxon rank-sum test to determine if there is a difference between the two populations.

Population A:	12, 14, 15, 19, 23, 29, 33, 40, 51
Population B:	13, 16, 19, 21, 22, 33, 35, 43

17. Two groups of professional musicians—rock and country-western—are being studied. One facet of the study involves the ages of those in the two groups. Assume that the populations of ages are not normally distributed. A sample of 10 rock and 12 country-western musicians revealed the following ages, in years.

Rock:	28, 16, 42, 29, 31, 22, 50, 42, 23, 25
Country-western:	26, 42, 65, 38, 29, 32, 59, 42, 27, 41, 46, 18

At the .05 significance level, can we conclude that the country-western singers are older?

18. One group was taught an assembly procedure using a standard sequence of steps and another group was taught a new experimental technique. The time to complete the assembly, in seconds, for a sample of workers is shown below.

Current method:	41, 36, 42, 39, 36, 48, 49, 38
Experimental:	21, 27, 36, 20, 19, 21, 39, 24, 22

At the .05 significance level, can we conclude that the experimental method is faster? Assume that the distribution of assembly times is not normal.

KRUSKAL-WALLIS TEST: ANALYSIS OF VARIANCE BY RANKS

Kruskal-Wallis test less restrictive than ANOVA

The analysis of variance (ANOVA) procedure discussed in Chapter 11 was concerned with whether three or more population means are equal. The data were interval- or ratio-level, and it was assumed the populations were normally distributed and the standard deviations of those populations were equal. What if the data are ordinal-scale and/or the populations are not normal? Fortunately, W. H. Kruskal and W. A. Wallis reported a nonparametric test of significance in 1952 requiring only ordinal-level (ranked) data. No assumptions about the shape of the populations are required by that test. The test is referred to as the **Kruskal-Wallis one-way analysis of variance by ranks.**

For the Kruskal-Wallis test to be applied, the samples selected from the populations must be *independent.* For example, if samples from three groups—executives, staff, and supervisors—are to be selected and interviewed, the responses of one group (say, the executives) must in no way influence the responses of the others.

Kruskal-Wallis: All sample values combined, then ranked

For the Kruskal-Wallis test, (1) all the sample values are combined, (2) the combined values are ordered from low to high, and (3) the ordered values are *replaced by ranks, starting with 1 for the smallest value.* An example will clarify the procedure.

EXAMPLE

A management seminar consisting of a large number of executives from manufacturing, finance, and trade is to be conducted. Before scheduling the seminar sessions, the seminar leader is interested in finding out whether the three groups are equally

knowledgeable about management principles. Plans are to take samples of the executives in manufacturing, in finance, and in trade and to administer a test to each executive. If there is no difference in the scores for the three distributions, the seminar leader will conduct just one session. However, if there is a difference in the scores, separate sessions will be given.

We will use the Kruskal-Wallis test instead of ANOVA because the seminar leader is unwilling to assume that (1) the populations of management scores are normally distributed or (2) the population variances are the same.

Solution ▶ The usual first step in hypothesis testing is to state the null and the alternate hypotheses.

H_0 and H_1 same as for ANOVA

H_0: The distributions of the management scores for the populations of executives in manufacturing, finance, and trade are equal.

H_1: The distributions are not all equal.

The seminar leader selected the .05 level of risk.

The test statistic used for the Kruskal-Wallis test is designated *H.* Its formula is:

Formula for the *H* statistic

$$H = \frac{12}{N(N+1)}\left[\frac{(\Sigma R_1)^2}{n_1} + \frac{(\Sigma R_2)^2}{n_2} + \cdots + \frac{(\Sigma R_k)^2}{n_k}\right] - 3(N+1) \qquad (15\text{–}5)$$

with $k - 1$ degrees of freedom (k is the number of populations), where

$\Sigma R_1, \Sigma R_2, \ldots, \Sigma R_k$ are the sums of the ranks of samples 1, 2, . . . , k.

$n_1, n_2, \ldots, n_k$ are the sizes of samples 1, 2, . . . , k.

N is the combined number of observations for all samples.

Chi-square used if every sample is at least 5

The distribution of the sample *H* statistic is very close to the chi-square distribution with $k - 1$ degrees of freedom *if every sample size is at least 5.* Therefore, we will use chi-square in formulating the decision rule. In this problem there are three populations—a population of executives in manufacturing, another for executives in finance, and a third population of trade executives. So there are $k - 1$, or $3 - 1 = 2$ degrees of freedom. Refer to the chi-square table of critical values in Appendix I. The critical value for 2 degrees of freedom and the .05 level of risk is 5.991. Do not reject H_0 if the computed value of the test statistic H is less than or equal to 5.991. Reject H_0 if the computed value of H is greater than 5.991, and accept H_1.

The next step is to select samples from the three populations. A sample of seven manufacturing, eight finance, and six trade executives was selected. Their scores on the test are recorded in Table 15–6.

Lowest score is 14, ranked 1

TABLE 15–6 Management Test Scores for the Manufacturing, Finance, and Trade Executives

Manufacturing executives		Finance executives	Trade executives
51	lowest →	14	89
32		31	20
17	← second lowest	68	60
69		87	72
86		20 (tie with Trade 20)	56
62		28	22
96		77	
		97	

Tie for third rank resolved by giving each score a rank of 3.5

Considering the scores as a single population, the score of 14 for the first finance executive is the lowest so it is ranked 1. The score of 17 for the third manufacturing executive is the second lowest so it is ranked 2. There are two scores of 20. To resolve the tie, each score is given the rank 3.5, found by $(3 + 4)/2$. The next score, 22, is ranked 5. This process is continued until all the scores are ranked. The scores, the ranks, and the sum of the ranks for each of three samples are given in Table 15–7.

TABLE 15–7 Scores, Ranks, and Sum of Ranks of Management Test Scores

Manufacturing executives		Finance executives		Trade executives	
Score	Rank	Score	Rank	Score	Rank
51	9	14	1	89	19
32	8	31	7	20	3.5
17	2	68	13	60	11
69	14	87	18	72	15
86	17	20	3.5	56	10
62	12	28	6	22	5
96	20	77	16		
		97	21		
$\Sigma R_1 = 82$		$\Sigma R_2 = 85.5$		$\Sigma R_3 = 63.5$	
$n_1 = 7$		$n_2 = 8$		$n_3 = 6$	

Computed $H = 0.14$

Solving for H:

$$H = \frac{12}{N(N+1)}\left[\frac{(\Sigma R_1)^2}{n_1} + \frac{(\Sigma R_2)^2}{n_2} + \frac{(\Sigma R_3)^2}{n_3}\right] - 3(N+1)$$

$$= \frac{12}{21(21+1)}\left[\frac{(82)^2}{7} + \frac{(85.5)^2}{8} + \frac{(63.5)^2}{6}\right] - 3(21+1)$$

$$= \frac{12(2{,}546.394)}{462} - 66$$

$$= 0.14$$

Decision: distributions are equal

Because the computed value of H (0.14) is less than the critical value of 5.991, the null hypothesis is not rejected. There is no difference among the executives from manufacturing, finance, and trade with respect to their knowledge of management principles. From a practical standpoint, the seminar leader should consider offering only one seminar session including executives from all three areas.

The Kruskal-Wallis test is available on the MINITAB system. The data for all three groups of executives are entered in column C1 and the code identifying the executives group in C2. The level "1" refers to manufacturing, "2" to finance, and "3" to trade executives. Note in the following output that the value of H (0.14) is the same as computed before.

```
MTB > set c1
DATA> 51,32,17,69,86,62,96,14,31,68,87,20,28,77,97,89,20,60,72,56,22
DATA> end
MTB > set c2
DATA> 1,1,1,1,1,1,1,2,2,2,2,2,2,2,2,3,3,3,3,3,3
DATA> end
MTB > kruskal c1 c2

LEVEL      NOBS     MEDIAN      AVE. RANK     Z VALUE
    1         7      62.00           11.7        0.37
    2         8      49.50           10.7       -0.18
    3         6      58.00           10.6       -0.19
OVERALL      21                      11.0

H = 0.14  d.f. = 2  p = 0.932
H = 0.14  d.f. = 2  p = 0.932 (adj. for ties)
```

Recall from Chapter 11 that for the analysis of variance technique to apply, it is assumed that: (1) the three or more populations of interest are normally distributed, (2) these populations have equal standard deviations, and (3) the samples selected from the populations are random and independent—that is, they are not related. If these assumptions are met, we use the F distribution as the test statistic. If these three assumptions cannot be met, the distribution-free test by Kruskal and Wallis is applied.

To show the similarity between the two approaches we will solve a problem using the analysis of variance (ANOVA) and then solve the same problem using Kruskal-Wallis.

EXAMPLE

Micom Electronic uses a performance rating system in which all employees rate their manager's performance as being excellent, good, fair, or poor.

The research department plans to conduct an in-depth study of the rating system and make recommendations on how to improve it. One of the questions to be explored is: Does the salary increase awarded an employee affect his or her end-of-year rating? Logically, one might expect that employees who received a substantial salary increase would rate the manager "excellent." It would also seem that those who rated the performance of the manager "poor" would probably have the lowest salary increases.

A random sample of 42 employees was chosen. Six employees rated their manager's performance excellent, 19 rated it good, and so on. The weekly salary increases for the 42 in the sample are given in the following table. The number in the upper left corner of the table, for example, indicates that the employee received a raise of $85 a week and rated the performance of his or her manager as excellent.

Ratings of 42 employees and their weekly salary increases

Excellent	Good		Fair	Poor
$85	$80	$78	$73	$81
77	70	75	71	85
74	78	73	70	76
77	72	80	79	81
70	74	82	73	79
74	77	73	76	70
	79	74	76	79
	78	76	68	
	82	91	80	
		78	78	

Solution ▶ The question to be explored is whether the distributions of salary increases are the same for the four ratings. Assuming that the assumptions underlying the ANOVA test are met, we can conduct a test regarding the population means. The null and alternate hypotheses are:

H_0: $\mu_1 = \mu_2 = \mu_3 = \mu_4$

H_1: The treatment means are not the same.

Using the .01 significance level, with $k - 1 = 4 - 1 = 3$ degrees of freedom in the numerator and $N - k = 42 - 4 = 38$ degrees of freedom in the denominator, the decision rule is to reject H_0 if the computed value of F is greater than 4.31. From the following MINITAB output we see that the computed value of F is 1.44 and the p-value is .246. Hence, the null hypothesis is not rejected. We conclude that the mean salary increase is the same for the four groups of employees. We cannot conclude, for example, that the mean weekly increase in salary is larger for the employees who rated their manager as excellent compared with those who rated their manager as poor. The p-value of .246 indicates the likelihood of finding an F value of 1.44 or larger when H_0 is true.

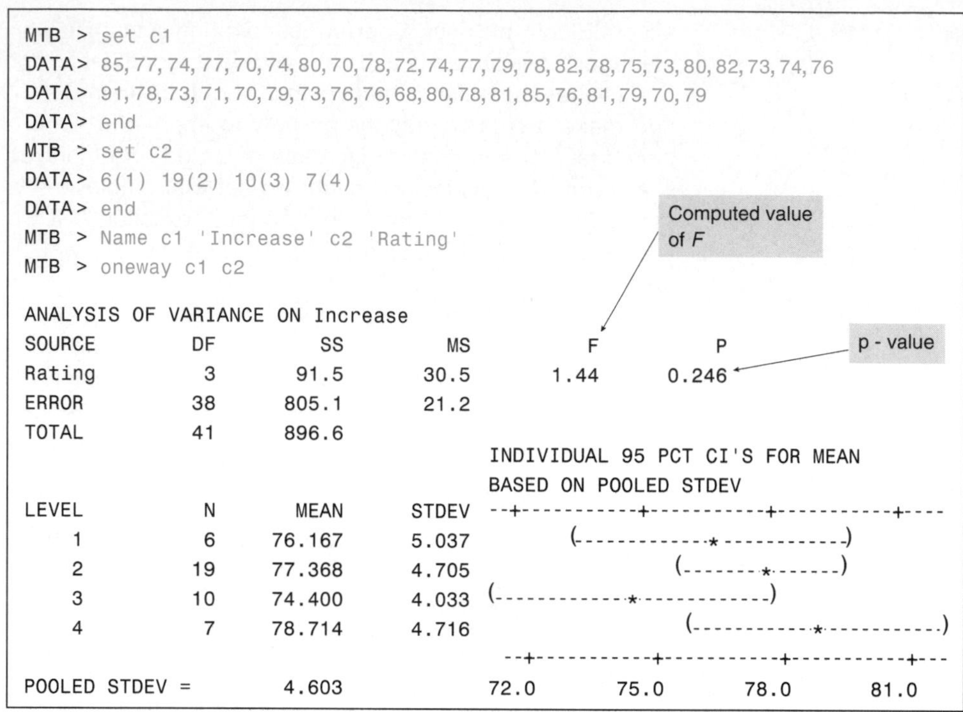

```
MTB > set c1
DATA> 85,77,74,77,70,74,80,70,78,72,74,77,79,78,82,78,75,73,80,82,73,74,76
DATA> 91,78,73,71,70,79,73,76,76,68,80,78,81,85,76,81,79,70,79
DATA> end
MTB > set c2
DATA> 6(1) 19(2) 10(3) 7(4)
DATA> end
MTB > Name c1 'Increase' c2 'Rating'
MTB > oneway c1 c2

ANALYSIS OF VARIANCE ON Increase
SOURCE     DF        SS        MS        F        P
Rating      3      91.5      30.5     1.44    0.246
ERROR      38     805.1      21.2
TOTAL      41     896.6
                                   INDIVIDUAL 95 PCT CI'S FOR MEAN
                                   BASED ON POOLED STDEV
LEVEL       N      MEAN     STDEV  --+-----------+-----------+-----------+----
    1       6    76.167     5.037        (------------*------------)
    2      19    77.368     4.705                (-------*-------)
    3      10    74.400     4.033  (------------*------------)
    4       7    78.714     4.716                 (------------*-----------)
                                   --+-----------+-----------+-----------+---
POOLED STDEV =    4.603             72.0        75.0        78.0        81.0
```


Suppose, however, that the populations of salary increases are not normally distributed. Under these circumstances the ANOVA test is not appropriate, and the nonparametric Kruskal-Wallis test is applied. For the .01 level of significance, the decision rule is portrayed in the following diagram (the critical value of 11.345 is found in Appendix I for the .01 level and $k - 1$ degrees of freedom, where k is the number of populations; $k - 1 = 4 - 1 = 3$ degrees of freedom).

Decision rule portrayed graphically

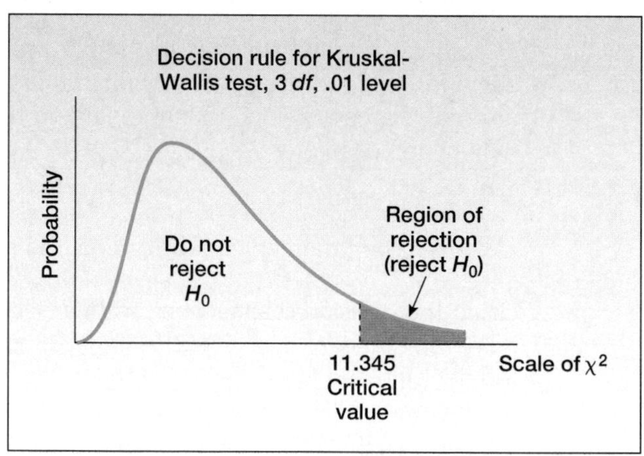

The null hypothesis and the alternate hypothesis are:

H_0: The distributions of salary increases are the same.

H_1: The distributions of salary increases are not the same.

Recall from our earlier discussions that the Kruskal-Wallis test uses the chi-square distribution as the test statistic, and the computed value is referred to as *H*. The computed value of the test statistic is 4.70 (see the following MINITAB output), which is less than the critical value of 11.345. The null hypothesis is not rejected. We have failed to show a difference in the distributions of the salary increases. We cannot conclude, for example, that the distribution of salary increases is to the right, or larger, for those who rated their manager as excellent compared with those who rated their manager as poor. The job performance ratings are unrelated to the magnitude of the salary increases of the employees.

As indicated in the MINITAB output, the *p*-value for this test is .196. This is the probability of finding a value of the test statistic this large or larger when H_0 is true. Recall that the *p*-value for the ANOVA test was .246, a difference of only .050. We conclude the results are similar for the ANOVA and the Kruskal-Wallis tests.

```
MTB  > kruskal c1 c2
LEVEL          NOBS       MEDIAN      AVE. RANK        Z VALUE
    1             6        75.50           19.2          -0.50
    2            19        78.00           22.9           0.66
    3            10        74.50           15.7          -1.71
    4             7        79.00           28.1           1.55
OVERALL          42                        21.5
H = 4.70       d.f. = 3     p = 0.196
H = 4.73       d.f. = 3     p = 0.194 (adj. for ties)
```

Computed value of *H*

SELF-REVIEW 15–6

The answers are at the end of the chapter.

The regional bank manager of Statewide Financial is interested in the turnover rate of personal checking accounts in four of the large branch banks. He is wondering whether or not there is a difference in the turnover rates among the four branch banks. (Turnover rate is the speed at which the money in an account is deposited and withdrawn. An extremely active account may have a rate of 300; if only one or two checks were written, the rate could be about 30.) The turnover rates of the samples selected from the four branch banks are:

Englewood branch	West Side branch	Great Northern branch	Sylvania branch
208	91	302	99
307	62	103	116
199	86	319	189
142	91	340	103
91	80	180	100
296			131

Using the .01 level and the Kruskal-Wallis test, determine if there is a difference in the turnover rates of the personal checking accounts among the four branches.

EXERCISES

The answers to the odd-numbered exercises are at the end of the book.

19. Under what conditions should the Kruskal-Wallis test be used instead of analysis of variance?
20. Under what conditions should the Kruskal-Wallis test be used instead of the Wilcoxon rank-sum test?
21. The following sample data were obtained from three populations that were not normal.

Sample 1	Sample 2	Sample 3
50	48	39
54	49	41
59	49	44
59	52	47
65	56	51
	57	

a. State the null hypothesis.
b. Using the .05 level of risk, state the decision rule.
c. Compute the value of the test statistic.
d. What is your decision on the null hypothesis?

22. The following sample data were obtained from three populations where the variances were not equal.

Sample 1	Sample 2	Sample 3
21	15	38
29	17	40
35	22	44
45	27	51
56	31	53
71		

a. State the null hypothesis.
b. Using the .01 level of risk, state the decision rule.
c. Compute the value of the test statistic.
d. What is your decision on the null hypothesis?

23. An outboard motor manufacturer has developed an epoxy painting process for corrosion protection on exhaust components. The engineers want to determine if the distributions of the lengths of life for the paint are equal for three different conditions—salt water, fresh water without weeds, and fresh water with a heavy concentration of weeds. Accelerated-life tests were conducted in the laboratory, and the number of hours the paint lasted before peeling was recorded.

Salt water	Fresh water	Fresh water with weeds
167.3	160.6	182.7
189.6	177.6	165.4
177.2	185.3	172.9
169.4	168.6	169.2
180.3	176.6	174.7

Use the Kruskal-Wallis test and the .01 level to determine whether the lasting quality of the paint is the same for the three water conditions.

24. The National Turkey Association wants to experiment with three different food mixtures for very young turkeys. Since no experience exists regarding the three food mixtures, no assumptions can be made about the shape of the distribution weights. The Kruskal-Wallis test must be used to test if the turkeys are equal in weight after eating the food for a specified length of time. Five young turkeys were given food A, six were given food B, and five were given food C. Test at the .05 level whether the mean weights of the turkeys who ate food A, food B, and food C are equal.

Weight (in pounds)		
Food mixture A	**Food mixture B**	**Food mixture C**
11.2	12.6	11.3
12.1	10.8	11.9
10.9	11.3	12.4
11.3	11.0	10.6
12.0	12.0	12.0
	10.7	

RANK-ORDER CORRELATION

In Chapter 12 we discussed *r*, the coefficient of correlation, which measures the association between two interval- or ratio-scaled variables. For example, the coefficient of correlation reports the association between the salary of executives and their years of experience, or the association between the number of miles a shipment had to travel and the number of days it took to arrive at its destination.

Charles Spearman, a British statistician, introduced a measure of correlation for ordinal-level data. This measure allows us to study the relationship between sets of ranked data. For example, two staff members in the Office of Research at the University of the Valley are asked to rank 10 faculty research proposals. We want to study the association between the ratings of the two staff members. That is, do the two staff members rate the same proposals as the most worthy and the least worthy

of funding? Spearman's coefficient of rank correlation, denoted r_s, provides a measure of the association.

The coefficient of rank correlation is computed using the following formula.

$$r_s = 1 - \frac{6\Sigma d^2}{n(n^2 - 1)} \tag{15–6}$$

where:

d is the difference between the ranks for each pair.

n is the number of paired observations.

Like the coefficient of correlation, the coefficient of rank correlation can assume any value from −1.00 up to 1.00. A value of −1.00 indicates perfect negative correlation and a value of 1.00 perfect positive correlation among the ranks. A rank correlation of 0 indicates that there is no association among the ranks. A rank correlation of −.84 and .84 both indicate a strong association, but the former indicates an inverse relationship between the ranks and the latter a direct relationship.

EXAMPLE

This problem involves a composite rating given by executives to each college graduate joining a plastic manufacturing firm. The executive rating is an expression of the future potential of the college graduate. (The ratings represent, of course, the ordinal level of measurement.) The recent college graduate then enters an in-plant training program and is given another composite rating (based on tests, opinions of group leaders, training officers, and so on). The executive ratings and the in-plant training ratings are given in Table 15–8.

TABLE 15–8 **Executive Ratings and In-Plant Training Ratings for a Selected Group of College Graduates**

Graduate	Executive rating, *X*	Training rating, *Y*
A	8	4
B	10	4
C	9	4
D	4	3
E	12	6
F	11	9
G	11	9
H	7	6
I	8	6
J	13	9
K	10	5
L	12	9

The problem is to determine the relationship between the ratings college graduates received from the executives before they entered the in-plant training program (X) and the ratings they received in the training program (Y). That is, what is the coefficient of rank correlation?

Solution ▶ It was decided to rank the variables from low (1) to high. The lowest rating given by the executives was a 4 to graduate D, so it was ranked 1. The next lowest was a 7 to graduate H, so it was ranked 2. There were two graduates rated 8. The tie is resolved by giving each a rank of 3.5, which is the average of ranks 3 and 4. The same procedure is followed when there are more than two ratings tied. For example, note that the lowest training rating is 3, and it is given a rank of 1. Then there are three ratings of 4. The average of the three tied ranks is 3.00, found by (2 + 3 + 4)/3. This is illustrated along with the necessary calculations for r_s in Table 15–9.

TABLE 15–9 Calculations Needed for r_s

Graduate	Executive rating, X	Training rating, Y	Rank: Executive	Rank: Training	Difference between ranks, d	Difference squared, d^2
A	8	4	3.5	3.0	0.5	0.25
B	10	4	6.5	3.0	3.5	12.25
C	9	4	5.0	3.0	2.0	4.00
D	4	3	1.0	1.0	0	0
E	12	6	10.5	7.0	3.5	12.25
F	11	9	8.5	10.5	−2.0	4.00
G	11	9	8.5	10.5	−2.0	4.00
H	7	6	2.0	7.0	−5.0	25.00
I	8	6	3.5	7.0	−3.5	12.25
J	13	9	12.0	10.5	1.5	2.25
K	10	5	6.5	5.0	1.5	2.25
L	12	9	10.5	10.5	0	0
					0.0*	78.50

*Sum of deviations must equal 0.

A value of .726 indicates a rather strong relationship between the paired data

r_s is computed to be .726, found by:

$$r_s = 1 - \frac{6\Sigma d^2}{n(n^2 - 1)} = 1 - \frac{6(78.50)}{12(143)} = .726$$

This problem may also be solved on the MINITAB system. The first step is to enter the data in the usual fashion. Next the ranks for each column of data are determined, and then the correlation of the ranks is determined. (Note there is a small difference between the two answers. This is due to using different forms of the equation and rounding.)

```
MTB > set c1
DATA> 8,10,9,4,12,11,11,7,8,13,10,12
DATA> end
MTB > set c2
DATA> 4,4,4,3,6,9,9,6,6,9,5,9
DATA> end
MTB > rank c1, put in c10
MTB > rank c2, put in c11
MTB > name c1 'Exec' c2 'Train' c10 'Rank-ex' c11 'Rank-tr'
MTB > corr c10 c11

Correlation of Rank-ex and Rank-tr = 0.715
```

Testing the Significance of r_s

Testing whether correlation in the population is zero

In an earlier chapter we tested the significance of Pearson's *r*. For ranked data using a small sample, the question also arises whether the correlation in the population is actually zero. For instance, there were only 12 graduates sampled in the preceding example. In the solution to the example, the rank correlation coefficient of .726 indicates a rather strong relationship between the two sets of ranks. Is it possible that the correlation of .726 is due to chance and that the correlation in the population is really 0? We will now conduct a test of significance to answer that question.

"Large" samples—10 or more

For a sample of 10 or more, the significance of r_s is determined by computing *t* using the following formula. The sampling distribution of r_s follows the *t* distribution with $n - 2$ degrees of freedom.

$$t = r_s \sqrt{\frac{n-2}{1-r_s^2}} \quad (15\text{–}7)$$

The null and the alternate hypotheses are:

H_0: The rank correlation in the population is zero.

H_1: The rank correlation in the population is greater than zero.

The decision rule is to reject H_0 if the computed value of *t* is greater than 1.812 (from Appendix F, .05 significance level, one-tailed test, and 10 degrees of freedom, found by $n - 2 = 12 - 2 = 10$).

SELF-REVIEW 15–7

The answers are at the end of the chapter.

A small sample of individuals revealed the following scores on an eye perception test (*X*) and a mechanical aptitude test (*Y*):

Subject	Eye perception	Mechanical aptitude
001	805	23
002	777	62
003	820	60
004	682	40
005	777	70
006	810	28
007	805	30
008	840	42
009	777	55
010	820	51

a. Compute the coefficient of rank correlation.

b. At the .05 significance level, can we conclude that the correlation in the population is different from 0?

The computed value of t is 3.338:

$$t = r_s \sqrt{\frac{n-2}{1-r_s^2}} = .726 \sqrt{\frac{12-2}{1-(.726)^2}} = 3.338$$

H_0 is rejected because the computed t of 3.338 is greater than 1.812. H_1 is accepted. There is positive correlation between the ranks given by the executives and the ranks assigned during training.

EXERCISES

The answers to the odd-numbered exercises are at the end of the book.

25. The ABC network television research staff wants to pretest a questionnaire to be mailed to several thousand viewers. One question involves the ranking of male and female senior citizens with respect to the popularity of certain prime-time programs. The composite rankings of a small group of senior citizens are:

Program	Ranking by males	Ranking by females
"Monday Night Football"	1	5
"Robin Crest"	4	1
"Simon and Sandor"	3	2
Evening News	2	4
"Our Hero"	5	3

   a. Draw a scatter diagram. Let the rankings by males be X.
   b. Compute Spearman's rank-order correlation coefficient. Interpret.

26. Far West University offers both day and evening classes in business administration. An extensive survey is to be conducted. One question involves sophomore students and how they perceive the prestige associated with certain careers, such as accounting. Each student was asked to rank the careers from 1 to 8, with 1 having the most prestige and 8 the least prestige. The composite results were:

Career	Ranking by day students	Ranking by evening students
Accountant	6	3
Computer programmer	7	2
Branch bank manager	2	6
Hospital administrator	5	4
Statistician	1	7
Marketing researcher	4	8
Stock analyst	3	5
Production manager	8	1

Find the coefficient of rank correlation.

27. New representatives for the John Ford Metal and Wheel Company attend a brief training program before being assigned to a regional office. At the end of such a program, each representative was ranked with respect to future sales potential. At the end of the first sales year, their rankings were paired with their annual sales:

Representative	Annual sales ($ thousands)	Ranking in training program
Kitchen	319	3
Bond	150	9
Gross	175	6
Arbuckle	460	1
Greene	348	4
Arden	300	10
Crane	280	5
Arthur	200	2
Keene	190	7
Knopf	300	8

a. Compute and interpret Spearman's rank correlation coefficient.
b. At the .05 significance level, can we conclude that there is a positive association among the ranks?

28. The University of Winston has five scholarships available for the women's basketball team. The coach provided two scouts with the names of 10 high school players with potential. Each scout attended at least three games and then ranked the players with respect to potential.

Player	Rank, by scout	
	Jean Cann	John Cannelli
Cora Jean Seiple	7	5
Bette Jones	2	4
Jeannie Black	10	10
Norma Tidwell	1	3
Kathy Marchal	6	6
Candy Jenkins	3	1
Rita Rosinski	5	7
Anita Lockes	4	2
Brenda Towne	8	9
Denise Ober	9	8

a. Determine Spearman's rank correlation coefficient.
b. At the .05 significance level, can we conclude that there is a positive association between the ranks?

CHAPTER OUTLINE

I. Sign test.
   A. No assumptions need be made about the shape of the two populations.
   B. It is especially useful for "before/after" experiments, product-preference tests, and testing a hypothesis about the median.
   C. For small samples find the number of + or − signs and refer to the binomial distribution for the critical value.
   D. For large samples (more than 20) use the standard normal distribution and the following formula.

$$z = \frac{(X \pm .50) - .50n}{.50\sqrt{n}} \qquad (15\text{–}2)(15\text{–}3)$$

II. The median test is used to test a hypothesis about a population median.
   A. The normal approximation to the binomial distribution is used.
   B. The z distribution is used as the test statistic.
   C. The value of z is computed from the following formula, where X is the number of observations above or below the median.

$$z = \frac{(X \pm .50) - \mu}{\sigma} \qquad (15\text{–}1)$$

III. Wilcoxon matched-pair signed-rank test.
   A. Data must be at least ordinal-scaled, and the two samples must be related. One way to accomplish this is to have each person act as his or her own control, meaning that the same person (or item) is in both sample 1 and sample 2.
   B. It is used extensively in "before/after" situations.
   C. Procedure.
      1. Rank absolute differences between old method and new method.
      2. Recognize ties, and give ranks appropriate signs.
      3. Sum negative ranks and positive ranks.
      4. Disregarding signs, the smaller of the two sums is the computed T value.
      5. Refer to Appendix J for the critical value, and make a decision regarding H_0.

IV. The Wilcoxon rank-sum test is used to test whether two independent samples came from the same or equal populations.
   A. No assumption about the shape of the population is required.
   B. To apply the test, the data must be capable of being ranked.
   C. Each sample must contain at least eight observations.
   D. To determine the value of the test statistic W, all data values are ranked from low to high as if they were from a single population.
   E. The sum of ranks for each of the two samples is determined.
   F. The smaller of the two sums W is used to compute z from:

$$z = \frac{W - \dfrac{n_1(n_1 + n_2 + 1)}{2}}{\sqrt{\dfrac{n_1 n_2(n_1 + n_2 + 1)}{12}}} \qquad (15\text{–}4)$$

V. Kruskal-Wallis one-way analysis of variance by ranks.
   A. No assumptions about the shape of the populations are required. To apply the test, the data must be capable of being ranked, and samples must be independent.
   B. It is used to test if three or more populations are identical.
   C. Combine all the values, and rank them starting with the lowest value, which is given the rank of 1. Sum the ranks for each sample, and insert them in the following formula:

$$H = \frac{12}{N(N+1)}\left[\frac{(\Sigma R_1)^2}{n_1} + \frac{(\Sigma R_2)^2}{n_2} + \cdots + \frac{(\Sigma R_k)^2}{n_k}\right] - 3(N+1) \qquad (15\text{–}5)$$

VI. Spearman's coefficient of rank correlation.
   A. The rank-order correlation coefficient is used to explain the degree of relationship between two sets of data that are at least ordinal-level. The formula is:

$$r_s = 1 - \frac{6\Sigma d^2}{n(n^2 - 1)} \qquad (15\text{–}6)$$

   r_s can assume any value between -1 and $+1$ inclusive. A -1 or $+1$ indicates perfect correlation between the ranks.
   B. Testing the significance of r_s.
      1. State null and alternate hypotheses.

H_0: Rank correlation in population is 0.

H_1: Rank correlation in population is not 0.

2. If n is greater than 10, use Student's t and Appendix F to locate the critical value or values.
3. The value of t is computed from the following formula.

$$t = r_s \sqrt{\frac{n-2}{1-r_s^2}} \tag{15–7}$$

EXERCISES

The answers to the odd-numbered exercises are at the end of the book.

29. Suppose NBC-TV is considering two western series for the forthcoming season. One is "Loner," the other "Cattleman." Only one will be aired. To assess whether there is a preference, 20 critics selected at random were shown a preview of an episode of each program. The null hypothesis to be tested is: There is no difference in preference for one show over the other. The alternate hypothesis is: There is a preference for one show over the other. The hypothesis is to be tested at the .10 level.
    a. Will a one-tailed or two-tailed sign test be used?
    b. When the preferences were tallied, a "+" sign was recorded if the critic preferred "Loner," and "−" sign was recorded if the preference was for "Cattleman." A count of the pluses revealed that 12 critics preferred "Loner," 7 liked "Cattleman," and 1 was undecided. State the decision rule in words. Picture it in a chart.
    c. What conclusion would you forward to NBC-TV? Explain.
30. Suppose Merrill Lynch wants to award a substantial contract for fine-line pens to be used nationally in their offices. Two suppliers, Bic and Pilot, have submitted the lowest bids. To determine the preference of office employees, brokers, and others, a personal preference test is to be conducted using a randomly selected sample of 20 employees. The .05 level of significance is to be used.
    a. If the alternate hypothesis states that Bic is preferred over Pilot, is the sign test to be conducted as a one-tailed test or a two-tailed test? Explain.
    b. As each of the sample members told the researchers his or her preference, a "+" was recorded if it was Bic and a "−" if it was the Pilot fine-line pen. A count of the pluses revealed that 12 employees preferred Bic, 5 preferred Pilot, and 3 were undecided. What is n?
    c. What is the decision rule in words? Show it in a chart.
    d. What conclusion did you reach regarding pen preference? Explain.
31. Cornwall and Hudson, a large department store chain, wants to handle just one brand of high-quality compact disc player. The list has been narrowed to two brands: Sony and Pioneer. To help make a decision, a panel of 16 audio experts met. A passage using Sony components (labeled A) was played. Then the same passage was played using Pioneer components (labeled B). A "+" in the following table indicates an individual's preference for the Sony components, a "−" indicates preference for Pioneer, and a 0 signifies no preference.

Expert

1	2	3	4	5	6	7	8	9	10	11	12	13	14	15	16
+	−	+	−	+	+	−	0	−	+	−	+	+	−	+	−

Conduct a test of hypothesis at the .10 significance level to determine if there is a difference in preference between the two brands.

32. The South Carolina Real Estate Association claims that the median rental for three-bedroom condominiums in the metropolitan area is \$1,200 a month. To check this, a random sample of 149 units was selected. Of the 149, 5 rented for exactly \$1,200 a month, and 75 rented for more than \$1,200. At the .05 level, test the statement that the median rental is \$1,200.
    a. State H_0 and H_1.
    b. Give the decision rule.
    c. Do the necessary calculations, and arrive at a decision.
33. The Citrus Council wants to find out if consumers prefer plain orange juice or juice with some orange pulp in it. A random sample of 212 consumers was selected. Each member of the sample tasted a small, unlabeled cup of one kind and then tasted the other kind. Twelve consumers said they had no preference, 40 preferred plain juice, and the remainder liked the juice with pulp better. Test at the .05 level that the preferences for plain juice and for orange juice with pulp are equal.
34. A research project involving community responsibility is to be conducted. The objective is to find out if women are more community-conscious before marriage or after five years of marriage. A test to measure community consciousness was administered to a sample of women before marriage, and the same test was given to them five years after marriage. The test scores are:

Name	Before marriage	After marriage
Beth	110	114
Jean	157	159
Sue	121	120
Cathy	96	103
Mary	130	139
Carol	186	196
Lisa	116	116
Sandy	160	140
Petra	149	142

Test at the .05 level. H_0 is: There is no difference in community consciousness before and after marriage. H_1 is: There is a difference.

35. Is there a difference in the annual divorce rates in predominantly rural counties among three geographic regions, namely, the Southwest, the Southeast, and the Northwest? Test at the .05 level. Annual divorce rates per 1,000 population for randomly selected counties are:

    Southwest: 5.9, 6.2, 7.9, 8.6, 4.6

    Southeast: 5.0, 6.4, 7.3, 6.2, 8.1, 5.1

    Far west: 6.7, 6.2, 4.9, 8.0, 5.5

36. The idle times during the eight-hour day shift and the night shift are to be compared. A time study revealed the following numbers of minutes of idle time for eight-hour periods.

    Day shift: 92, 103, 116, 81, 89

    Night shift: 96, 114, 80, 82, 88, 91

    Is there a difference in the idle time between the two shifts? Test at the .05 level.

37. The mobility of executives in stock exchanges, in service, in heavy construction, and in air transportation is to be researched. Samples from each of these industries were selected, and the number of times an executive moved during a 10-year period was converted to an index. An index of 0 would indicate no movement, whereas 100 would

indicate almost constant movement from one location to another or one firm to another. The indexes for the four groups are:

Stock exchange	Service	Heavy construction	Air transportation
4	3	62	30
17	12	40	38
8	40	81	46
20	17	96	40
16	31	76	21
	19		

We cannot assume that the indexes are normally distributed. Thus, we must use a nonparametric test. Using the .05 level, determine whether the four populations of mobility indexes are identical.

38. A series of questions on sports and world events was asked of a randomly selected group of male senior citizens. The results were translated into a "knowledge" score. The scores were:

Citizen	Sports	World events
Mr. J. C. McCarthy	47	49
Mr. A. N. Baker	12	10
Mr. B. B. Beebe	62	76
Mr. L. D. Gaucet	81	92
Mr. C. A. Jones	90	86
Mr. J. N. Narko	35	42
Mr. A. F. Nissen	61	61
Mr. L. M. Zaugg	87	75
Mr. J. B. Simon	59	86
Mr. J. Goulden	40	61
Mr. A. A. Davis	87	18
Mr. A. M. Carbo	16	75
Mr. A. O. Smithy	50	51
Mr. J. J. Pascal	60	61

a. Determine the degree of association between how the senior citizens ranked with respect to knowledge of sports and how they ranked on world events.

b. At the .05 significance level, is the rank correlation in the population greater than zero?

39. Early in the basketball season, 12 teams appeared to be outstanding. A panel of sports writers and a panel of college basketball coaches were asked to rank the 12 teams. Their composite rankings were as follows.

Team	Coaches	Sports writers
Duke	1	1
UNLV	2	5
Indiana	3	4
North Carolina	4	6
Louisville	5	3
Ohio State	6	2
Syracuse	7	10
Georgetown	8	11
Villanova	9	7
LSU	10	12
St. Johns	11	8
Michigan	12	9

Determine the correlation between the rankings of the coaches and the sports writers. At the .05 significance level, can we conclude that it is different from zero?

40. Professor Bert Forman believes that the students who complete his examinations in the shortest time receive the highest grades and those that take the longest to complete them receive the lowest grades. To verify his suspicion, he assigns a rank to the order of finish and then grades the examinations. The results are shown below.

Student	Order of completion	Score (50 possible)
Gromney	1	48
Bates	2	48
MacDonald	3	43
White	4	49
Harris	5	50
Cribb	6	47
Smythe	7	39
Arquette	8	30
Govito	9	37
Gankowski	10	35
Bonfigilo	11	36
Hineman	12	33

Convert the test scores to a rank and then find the coefficient of rank correlation. At the .05 significance level, can Professor Forman conclude that there is a positive association between the order of finish and the test scores?

41. The following table lists figures on the starting position, number of laps completed, and finish position for drivers in the 1994 Indianapolis 500 race.
    a. What is the relationship (correlation) between the starting position rank and the driver's rank at the finish of the race? Can we conclude, at the .05 significance level, that there is a positive association?
    b. What is the correlation between the rank of the number of laps completed and the starting position? Can we conclude, at the .05 significance level, that there is a positive association?

Driver	Starting position	Laps	Finish
Al Unser, Jr.	1	200	1
Jacques Villeneuve	4	200	2
Bobby Rahal	28	199	3
Jimmy Vasser	16	199	4
Robby Gordon	19	199	5
Michael Andretti	5	198	6
Teo Fabi	24	198	7
Eddie Cheever	11	197	8
Bryan Herta	22	197	9
John Andretti	10	196	10
Mauricio Gugelmin	29	196	11
Brian Till	21	194	12
Stan Fox	13	193	13
Hiro Matsushita	18	193	14
Stefan Johansson	27	192	15
Scott Sharp	17	186	16
Emerson Fittipaldi	3	184	17
Arie Luyendyk	8	179	18
Lyn St. James	6	170	19
Scott Brayton	23	116	20

Driver	Starting position	Laps	Finish
Raul Boesel	2	100	21
Nigel Mansell	7	92	22
Paul Tracy	25	92	23
Hideshi Matsuda	14	90	24
John Paul, Jr.	30	89	25
Dennis Vitolo	15	89	26
Marco Greco	32	53	27
Adrian Fernandez	26	30	28
Dominic Dobson	12	29	29
Scott Goodyear	33	29	30
Mike Groff	31	28	31
Mario Andretti	9	23	32
Roberto Guerrero	20	21	33

Source: *Toledo Blade,* May 30, 1994, p. 33.

COMPUTER DATA EXERCISES

42. Refer to data set 1, which reports information on homes sold in Florida during 1994. Use the .05 significance level.
    a. Use an appropriate nonparametric method to determine if there is a difference in the price of the homes among the various townships.
    b. Combine the homes with six or more bedrooms, and determine if there is a difference in the prices of the homes by the number of bedrooms. Assume that the prices of homes are not normally distributed.
    c. Use nonparametric methods to determine if the distribution of the distances from the center of the city is different between homes that have a pool and those that do not have a pool.
43. Refer to data set 2, which reports information on the 1993 major league baseball season.
    a. Assume that the distributions of team salaries for the American and the National Leagues do not follow the normal distribution. Conduct a nonparametric test to find out if there is a difference in the two distributions. Estimate the *p*-value. Assume that the distributions are normally distributed, and conduct an appropriate test. Is there a major difference in the *p*-values? What can you conclude?
    b. Rank the teams by the number of wins and the total salary paid the players. Determine the coefficient of rank correlation. At the .05 significance level, can we conclude that there is a positive correlation between the ranks of the two variables? Determine the coefficient of correlation for the same two variables and compare the results. Do you think it is reasonable to use the coefficient of correlation?

CHAPTER 15 EXAMINATION

The answers are at the end of the chapter.

For Questions 1–11, record the letter in front of the correct answer.

1. If the assumptions for the paired *t* test (Chapter 11) cannot be met, the nonparametric alternative is:
    a. The Wilcoxon rank-sum test.
    b. The Kruskal-Wallis test.

   c. The Wilcoxon matched-pair signed-rank test.
   d. Spearman's coefficient of rank correlation.

2. The nonparametric tests presented in this chapter require that the populations of interest be normally distributed and that the observations be at least interval-scale.
   a. True.
   b. False.

3. The Wilcoxon rank-sum test requires that the observations be paired. (An example of paired data would be the score an applicant had before attending the police academy and the score at the end of the course.)
   a. True.
   b. False.

4. Which one of the nonparametric tests presented in this chapter requires at least five samples from each population and at least the ordinal level of measurement?
   a. The median test.
   b. Kruskal-Wallis test.
   c. Wilcoxon test.
   d. The sign test.

5. Which of the following is not a distribution-free test?
   a. The median test.
   b. The Student *t* test.
   c. Kruskal-Wallis test.
   d. Wilcoxon test.
   e. None of these is correct.

6. The region of rejection for the Kruskal-Wallis test:
   a. Is in the upper tail only.
   b. Is in the lower tail only.
   c. Can be in the upper or lower tail.
   d. Is identified in none of these statements.

7. If the null hypothesis for the Kruskal-Wallis test is rejected, it indicates:
   a. There is no difference between the two groups.
   b. There is no difference between the set of "before" observations and the set of "after" observations.
   c. The distributions are not equal.
   d. None of these.

8. The test statistic for the large-sample sign test is:
   a. z.
   b. t.
   c. H.
   d. χ^2.
   e. None of these.

9. For the Kruskal-Wallis test, the rankings are determined by combining all the groups and ranking all the values starting with 1.
   a. True.
   b. False.

10. For the Wilcoxon signed-rank test:
   a. There must be an expected set of frequencies, f_e, and an observed set of frequencies, f_0.
   b. Paired data are required.
   c. There must be three or more populations.
   d. The data must be at least interval-scaled.
   e. None of these is correct.

11. The sign test is an appropriate nonparametric test for "before/after" experiments and consumer preference tests.
    a. True.
    b. False.
12. The hourly production of a sample of employees before attending a special course and after completing the course are:

	Production	
Employee	Before course	After course
Frank Unati	21	26
Sue Marker	29	28
Arthur Noble	20	20
Jean Sobecki	39	47
Agnes Locker	25	30
George Taoka	44	48
Dan Obet	18	27
Mirmie Gladen	33	36
Yando Larkin	31	34
Nastir Ufasse	45	48
Gladys Rollins	36	41

    Test at the .05 level that the special course significantly increased production.
13. The murder rates in large cities, small cities, and rural areas are to be compared. Samples were selected from the three areas. The rates given are per 10,000 population.

Large cities	Small cities	Rural areas
6.7	7.8	12.6
5.2	7.1	8.4
11.2	12.2	8.2
8.6	9.6	4.9
5.5	5.2	11.7
	6.8	7.1

    Assuming that the rates are not normally distributed, apply a nonparametric test. Use the .01 level to find out if there is a difference among the distributions of the murder rates for the three groups.
14. We want to test whether there has been a decrease in the median age of international flight travelers. The null hypothesis is H_0: Median = 37.0 years. A sample of 410 travelers revealed that 208 were younger than 37 years, 10 were exactly 37, and the remainder were over 37 years. Using the .10 level, has the median age of international travelers decreased?

15. The football coaches rate the performance of the players on a scale of 0 to 100 both during the weekly practice and during the game on Saturday. A sample of the players who played in the big game against Carson College revealed these ratings:

	Rating	
Player	**In practice**	**During game**
Art	80	80
Bob	20	10
Jim	100	90
Abe	65	50
Arch	50	35
John	40	30
Dean	90	95
Jimmie	60	35
Doug	80	85
Mike	70	70
Steve	55	94
Mark	70	40

a. Determine the degree of relationship between how the players ranked in performance during the practice and how they ranked during the game by computing the rank-order correlation coefficient.

b. Test the significance of the coefficient of rank correlation. Use $\alpha = .01$.

CHAPTER 15 Answers

Self-Review

15–1 1. Two-tailed because H_1 does not state a direction.

2.

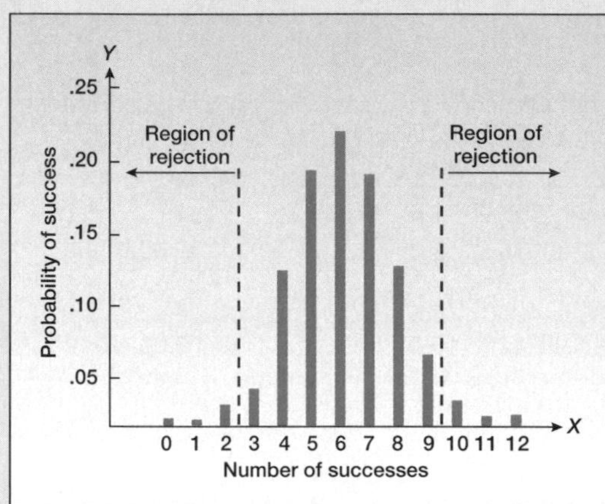

Adding down, .000 + .003 + .016 = .019. This is the largest cumulative probability up to but not exceeding .050, which is half the level of significance.

3. Reject H_0; accept H_1. There is a preference.

15–2 Since 80 is more than $n/2 = 100/2 = 50$, we use:

$$z = \frac{(80 - .50) - .50(100)}{.50\sqrt{100}} = \frac{29.5}{5} = 5.9$$

Since 5.9 lies in the tail beyond 1.645 (Appendix D), H_0 is rejected. The vitamins were effective.

15–3 1. H_0: The median is 23.
H_1: The median is not 23.

2. Twenty bills were below $23.00, 42 were above $23.00, and 2 were exactly equal to $23.00.
3. $n = 62$
4. Reject H_0 if $z < -1.645$ or $z > 1.645$.
5. 2.67, found by $[(42 - .50) - .50(62)]/.50\sqrt{62}$.
6. Reject H_0 because computed z of 2.67 is in the rejection region beyond 1.645.
7. The sample median is $39.10.
8. No. The median is *not* $23.00. The difference between $23.00 and $39.10 is not due to chance.

15–4 1. $N = 10$

2.

Before	After	Difference	Absolute difference	Rank of absolute difference	Negative rank	Positive ranks
17	18	−1	1	1.5	1.5	
21	23	−2	2	3.0	3.0	
25	22	3	3	5.0		5.0
15	25	−10	10	8.0	8.0	
10	28	−18	18	10.0	10.0	
16	16	—	—	—	—	—
10	22	−12	12	9.0	9.0	
20	19	1	1	1.5		1.5
17	20	−3	3	5.0	5.0	
24	30	−6	6	7.0	7.0	
23	26	−3	3	5.0	5.0	
					48.5	6.5

H_0: Production is the same.
H_1: Production is not the same.
The sum of the positive signed ranks is 6.5; the negative sum is 48.5. From Appendix J, one-tailed test, $N = 10$, the critical value is 10. Since 6.5 is less than 10, reject the null hypothesis and accept the alternate. New procedures did increase production.

15–5 H_0: There is no difference in the distances traveled by Dino and by Maxi.
H_1: There is a difference in the distances traveled by Dino and by Maxi.
Do not reject H_0 if the computed z is between 1.96 and −1.96 (from Appendix D); otherwise, reject H_0 and accept H_1. $n_1 = 8$, the number of observations in the first sample.

Dino Distance	Dino Rank	Maxi Distance	Maxi Rank
252	4	262	9
263	10	242	2
279	15	256	5
273	14	260	8
271	13	258	7
265	11.5	243	3
257	6	239	1
280	16	265	11.5
Total	89.5		46.5

$W = 89.5$

$$z = \frac{89.5 - \dfrac{8(8+8+1)}{2}}{\sqrt{\dfrac{(8)(8)(8+8+1)}{12}}}$$

$$= \frac{21.5}{9.52} = 2.26$$

Reject H_0; accept H_1. There is a difference in the distances traveled by the two golf balls.

15–6

Ranks

Englewood	West Side	Great Northern	Sylvania
17	5	19	7
20	1	9.5	11
16	3	21	15
13	5	22	9.5
5	2	14	8
18			12

$\Sigma R_1 = 89$ $\Sigma R_2 = 16$ $\Sigma R_3 = 85.5$ $\Sigma R_4 = 62.5$

$n_1 = 6$ $n_2 = 5$ $n_3 = 5$ $n_4 = 6$

H_0: The distributions are the same.

H_1: The distributions are not the same.

$$H = \frac{12}{22(22+1)}\left[\frac{(89)^2}{6} + \frac{(16)^2}{5} + \frac{(85.5)^2}{5} + \frac{(62.5)^2}{6}\right]$$

$$- 3(22+1)$$

$$= 0.0237154(3484.459) - 69$$

$$= 13.635$$

The critical value of chi-square for $k - 1 = 4 - 1 = 3$ degrees of freedom is 11.345. Since the computed value of 13.635 is greater than 11.345, the null hypothesis is rejected. We conclude that the distributions are not the same.

15–7

a.

$$r_s = 1 - \frac{6(193)}{10(99)} = -.170$$

X	Y	Rank X	Rank Y	d	d^2
805	23	5.5	1	4.5	20.25
777	62	3.0	9	−6.0	36.00
820	60	8.5	8	0.5	0.25
682	40	1.0	4	−3.0	9.00
777	70	3.0	10	−7.0	49.00
810	28	7.0	2	5.0	25.00
805	30	5.5	3	2.5	6.25
840	42	10.0	5	5.0	25.00
777	55	3.0	7	−4.0	16.00
820	51	8.5	6	2.5	6.25
				0	193.00

b. H_0: $\rho = 0$; H_1: $\rho \neq 0$. Reject H_0 if $t < -2.306$ or $t > 2.306$.

$$t = -0.170\sqrt{\frac{10-2}{1-(-0.170)^2}} = -0.488$$

H_0 is not rejected. We have not shown a relationship between the two tests.

Examination

1. *c.*
2. *b.* False. Only ordinal scale needed. No assumptions about normality required.
3. *b.* False. Samples must be independent.
4. *b.*
5. *b.*
6. *a.*
7. *c.*
8. *a.*
9. *a.*
10. *b.*
11. *a.*
12. H_0: There is no difference in production before the course and after the course.

    H_1: The course significantly increased production (a one-tailed test).

Before course	After course	Difference	Absolute differences ranked	Assigned ranks correctly signed
21	26	−5	1	+1
29	28	+1	3	−3
20	20	0	3	−3
39	47	−8	3	−3
25	30	−5	4	−5
44	48	−4	5	−7
18	27	−9	5	−7
33	36	−3	5	−7
31	34	−3	8	−9
45	48	−3	9	−10
36	41	−5		

Sum of negative ranks = −54, sum of positive ranks = +1. Computed T value = +1. Critical value at .05 level = 10, where $N = 10$. Reject H_0. The course has significantly increased production.

13. H_0: There is no difference in the distributions of the murder rates for the three groups.

    H_1: There is a difference in the distributions of the murder rates.

Large cities		Small cities		Rural areas	
Rates	Rank	Rates	Rank	Rates	Rank
6.7	5	7.8	9.0	12.6	17.0
5.2	2.5	7.1	7.5	8.4	11.0
11.2	14.0	12.2	16.0	8.2	10.0
8.6	12.0	9.6	13.0	4.9	1.0
5.5	4.0	5.2	2.5	11.7	15.0
$\Sigma R_1 = 37.5$		6.8	6.0	7.1	7.5
		$\Sigma R_2 = 54.0$		$\Sigma R_3 = 61.5$	
$n_1 = 5$		$n_2 = 6$		$n_3 = 6$	

$$H = \frac{12}{17(17+1)}\left[\frac{(37.5)^2}{5} + \frac{(54)^2}{6} + \frac{(61.5)^2}{6}\right] - 3(17+1)$$

$$= \frac{12}{306}[281.25 + 486 + 630.375] - 54 = 0.81$$

$N = 17$; critical value of chi-square at .01 level and 2 degrees of freedom is 9.210. Computed value of H is 0.81. Since 0.81 is less than 9.210, the null hypothesis is not rejected.

14. H_0: Median ≤ 37; H_1: Median > 37. Critical value of z is 1.28 (one-tailed test; search Appendix D for .5000 − .10 = .4000). Since 208 is greater than $n/2 = 400/2 = 200$, use

$$z = \frac{(208 - .50) - .50(400)}{.50\sqrt{400}} = \frac{7.50}{10} = 0.75$$

Since 0.75 is in the area of the standard normal curve between 0 and 1.28, we do not reject H_0. Median age hasn't changed. It is still 37.

15. *a.*

Player	Practice score	Game score	Practice rank	Game rank	d
Art	80	80	3.5	5	−1.5
Bob	20	10	12	12	0
Jim	100	90	1	3	−2
Abe	65	50	7	7	0
Arch	50	35	10	9.5	.5
John	40	30	11	11	0
Dean	90	95	2	1	1
Jimmie	60	35	8	9.5	−1.5
Doug	80	85	3.5	4	−.5
Mike	70	70	5.5	6	−.5
Steve	55	94	9	2	7
Mark	70	40	5.5	8	−2.5

$$r_s = 1 - \frac{6(65.5)}{12(12^2 - 1)} = .771$$

b. H_0: There is no rank correlation; H_1: There is rank correlation. H_0 is rejected if $t < -2.228$ or $t > 2.228$.

$$t = .771\sqrt{\frac{12 - 2}{1 - (.771)^2}} = 3.828$$

H_0 is rejected. There is rank correlation.

SECTION 6 A REVIEW OF CHAPTERS 14 AND 15

Goodness-of-fit test and contingency table analysis applicable to nominal-level data

This section is a review of the major concepts and terms introduced in Chapters 14 and 15. Chapter 14 began the study of *nonparametric,* or *distribution-free,* tests by discussing the *chi-square goodness-of-fit test.* This test is applied to a set of observed frequencies, f_0, and a corresponding set of frequencies, f_e, to test how well the sets fit. This test involves only one characteristic possessed by an individual, such as education. If we are interested in two characteristics, such as a relationship between education level and income, the data are cross-classified into a contingency table, and the chi-square test is applied. For these two tests, no assumption about the shape of the population is needed; they require only that the data be nominal-level. The chi-square goodness-of-fit test is also used to determine if a set of observed frequencies is normally distributed.

Five tests for ordinal-level data

Chapter 15 presented five nonparametric tests of hypothesis and the coefficient of rank correlation, all of which require the ordinal level of measurement. That is, the data must be ranked from low to high. The tests discussed were the *sign test,* the median test, the *Wilcoxon rank-sum test,* the *Kruskal-Wallis analysis of variance test,* and the *Wilcoxon signed-rank test.*

GLOSSARY

Chapter 14

Chi-square distribution A distribution with these characteristics: (1) Its value can only be positive. (2) There is a family of chi-square distributions, a different one for each different degree of freedom. (3) The distributions are positively skewed, but as the number of degrees of freedom increases, the distribution approaches the normal distribution.

Chi-square goodness-of-fit test A test with the objective of determining how well an observed set of frequencies fits an expected set of frequencies. It is concerned with one nominal scale variable, such as the color of a car.

Contingency table If two characteristics, such as education and income, are cross-classified into a table, the result is called a contingency table. The chi-square test statistic is applied to find out if the two characteristics are related.

Nominal level of measurement The "lowest" level of measurement. Such data can only be classified into categories, and there is no particular order for the categories. For example, it makes no difference whether the categories "male" and "female" are listed in that order, or female first and male second. The categories are mutually exclusive—meaning, in this illustration, that a person cannot be a male and a female at the same time.

Nonparametric or distribution-free tests Hypothesis tests involving nominal- and ordinal-level data. No assumptions need be made about the shape of the parent population; that is, we do not have to assume that the population is normally distributed.

Chapter 15

Kruskal-Wallis one-way analysis of variance by ranks A test used when the assumptions for the parametric analysis of variance (ANOVA) cannot be met. Its purpose is to test whether or not three or more populations are equal. Again, the data must be at least ordinal-scaled.

Sign test A test used for dependent samples. The calculations for both the small-sample and the large-sample cases are minimal. The sign test is used to find out if there is a brand preference for two products and to determine whether performance after an experiment is greater than before the experiment. Also, the sign test is used to test a hypothesis about the median.

Spearman's coefficient of rank correlation A measure of the association between the ranks of two variables. It can range from −1.00 to 1.00. A value of −1.00 indicates a perfect negative association among the ranks and a value of 1.00 a perfect positive association among the ranks. A value of 0 indicates no association among the ranks.

Wilcoxon matched-pair signed-rank test Another nonparametric test requiring at least ordinal-level data. Its purpose is to find out if there is any difference between two sets of paired (related) observations. It is used if the assumptions required for the paired *t* test cannot be met.

Wilcoxon rank-sum test A nonparametric test requiring independent samples. The data must be at least ordinal-level. That is, the data must be capable of being ranked. The test is used when the assumptions for the parametric Student *t* test cannot be met. The objective of the test is to find out if two independent samples can be considered as coming from the same population.

EXERCISES

The answers to the odd-numbered exercises are at the end of the book.

1. For a chi-square test, what do f_0 and f_e stand for?
2. The following is an example of what?

Political affiliation	Amount contributed to campaign		
	$1–$99	**$100–$999**	**$1,000 and more**
Republican	42	87	342
Democrat	596	302	116
Socialist	42	49	36
All others	19	17	11

3. Refer to Exercise 2. What test statistic would be used to find out if there is any relationship between political affiliation and the amount contributed?
4. Refer to Exercise 2. How many degrees of freedom are there?
5. Refer to Exercise 2. Suppose the computed value of χ^2 is 11.248, and the .05 level is being used. Should the null hypothesis be rejected?
6. For a goodness-of-fit test, the computed value of chi-square is 8.403, and the critical value is 5.991. The .05 level is being used. Is the null hypothesis rejected?

7. Refer to Exercise 6. What is the null hypothesis?
8. What level of measurement is required for the parametric tests of hypotheses discussed in Chapters 10 and 11?
9. What level of measurement is required for the goodness-of-fit test?
10. What level of measurement is required for the Wilcoxon rank-sum test?
11. What is the purpose of the Wilcoxon rank-sum test?
12. What assumptions are made about the shape of the populations in using the Kruskal-Wallis test?
13. What is the objective of the Kruskal-Wallis test?
14. What is the objective of the Wilcoxon signed-rank test?
15. Of the following nonparametric tests (sign test, Wilcoxon rank-sum, Kruskal-Wallis, and Wilcoxon signed-rank), which one deals with three or more samples?
16. Refer to Exercise 15. Which test deals with paired data?
17. Refer to Exercise 15. Can these tests be applied to interval- and ratio-level data?
18. For a Wilcoxon rank-sum test, the alternate hypothesis is: The women have better eye perception than the men. Would a one-tailed or a two-tailed test be applied?
19. The chi-square distribution for 5 degrees of freedom is approximately normally distributed. Is that statement true?
20. How are the degrees of freedom for a goodness-of-fit test determined?
21. Describe the steps followed, using a simple example, to test a hypothesis involving the median.

Chapter 16 Statistical Quality Control

GOALS

When you have completed this chapter, you will be able to:

1
Discuss the impact that Drs. Walter A. Shewhart and W. Edwards Deming had on quality control in the United States and Japan.

2
Define several terms unique to quality control, including *chance causes, assignable causes, in control,* and *out of control.*

3
Construct two charts for variables—a mean chart and a range chart.

4
Construct two charts for attributes—a percent defective chart and a chart for the number of defects per unit.

5
Discuss what is meant by acceptance sampling.

6
Construct an operating characteristic curve for various sampling plans.

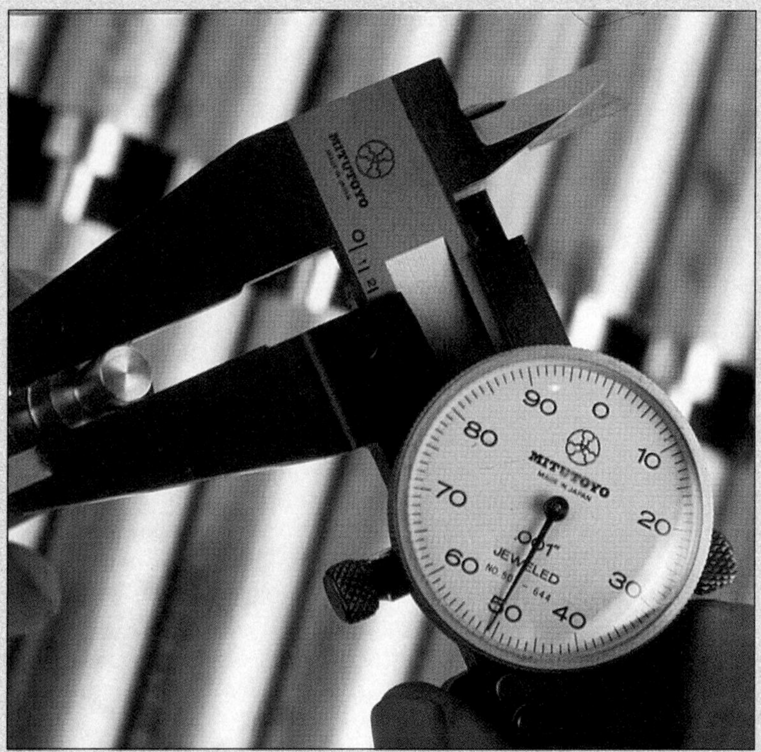

The quality-control inspector checks four pieces and records the diameters. Compute the overall mean, determine the control limits, and show the limits and the mean on a mean chart. (See Goal 3 and Self-Review 16–1.)

INTRODUCTION

Prior to the early 1900s American industry was largely characterized by small shops making such relatively simple products as buggies, furniture, plows, and stoves. In these shops the individual worker was generally a crafter who was completely responsible for the "quality" of the work and could ensure it through personal selection of material, skillful manufacture, and selective fitting and adjustment.

With the spread of the Industrial Revolution in the early 1900s, factories sprang up. People with limited training were formed into long assembly lines. Products became more complex. The individual worker no longer had complete control over the quality of the product. A semiprofessional staff was developed (the inspection department) and became responsible for the quality. This responsibility was fulfilled by a 100 percent evaluation of all characteristics deemed important, with corrective action on discrepancies handled by the production department supervisors. During this period, quality was obtained by "inspecting it into the product."

During the 1920s, the concepts of statistical quality control were developed, primarily through the work of Dr. Walter A. Shewhart of the Bell Telephone Laboratories. Shewhart introduced the concept of "controlling" the quality rather than inspecting it into the part. For the purpose of controlling quality, the Shewhart control chart technique was developed for in-process manufacturing operations. In addition, he introduced the concept of statistical sampling inspection to estimate whether manufactured lots were good or bad, replacing the old method of inspecting every part.

Statistical quality control, with its emphasis on in-process control of the quality, came into its own during World War II. The need for mass-produced, intricate bomb sights, accurate radar, and other electronic equipment at the lowest cost possible accelerated the use of control charts and statistical sampling. These statistical techniques have been retained, refined, and augmented since the war.

Meanwhile, Japanese production was virtually destroyed during World War II. Rather than retool and continue to produce inferior products, the Japanese enlisted the aid of the late W. Edwards Deming of the U.S. Department of Agriculture to guide them in developing an overall plan. In a series of seminars with the Japanese he stressed a philosophy of production that is known today as **Deming's fourteen points.** He emphasized that quality originates from *improving the process,* not from "inspecting out" the unsatisfactory results of poor production.

Deming stated that quality is determined by the customers. The manufacturer must be able, through market research, to anticipate the future needs of its customers. Top management, he claimed, is responsible for long-term improvement. Another of his points, one that the Japanese strongly endorsed, is that every member of the firm must contribute to this improvement. To achieve this, ongoing education and training of all employees is imperative. Also, Deming said that suppliers must continually upgrade the quality of their products.

Deming had some ideas that were counter (and still are) to management philosophies in the United States. For example, many firms believe that there should be production quotas; that is, an employee should be expected to produce at least 352 automobile transmissions during a one-week period. Also, Deming was against the merit rating awarded to an employee. He claimed that these two practices, which are common in the United States, were counterproductive and should be eliminated. In his fourteen points, he noted that American managers are mainly interested in good news, not bad news. Good news, he points out, usually does not reveal opportunities

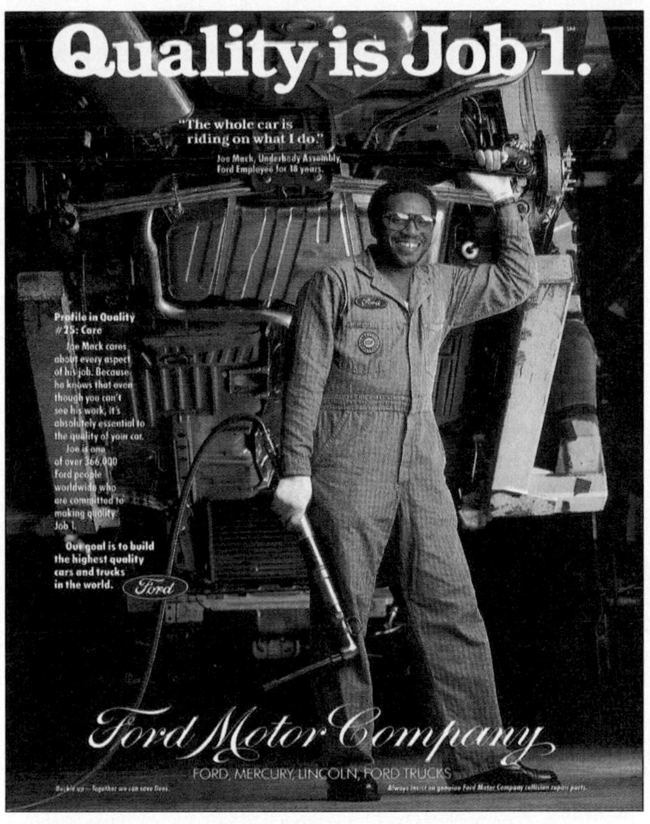

for improvement. On the other hand, bad news opens the door to new products and allows for company improvement.[1]

It should be mentioned that in his fourteen points Dr. Deming did not ignore statistical quality control, which is often abbreviated as SQC, TQC, or just QC. The objective of statistical quality control is to monitor production through the many stages of manufacturing. In our manufacturing processes and to monitor the quality of many services, we use statistical quality control tools such as X-bar charts, range charts, and percent defective charts. Control charts allow us to identify when a production process or a service becomes "out of control," that is, when the point is reached where an excessive number of defective units are being produced. In this chapter we will address such questions as:

- Are an excessively large number of cola bottles being overfilled?
- Is the 5 percent defective rate for the last hour of production too high?
- Are the six defects counted on the door of a Ford Taurus too many?

Interest in quality has accelerated dramatically in the United States during the past 10 years. We need only to turn on the television and watch the commercials sponsored by GM, Ford, and Chrysler to verify that there is tremendous emphasis on quality control on the assembly line. It is now the "in" topic in all facets of business.

[1]An excellent book on W. Edwards Deming, his philosophy, and his contribution to quality control is Andrea Gabor's *The Man Who Discovered Quality* (New York: Penguin Books, 1992).

Quoting from just a few recently published articles in business magazines such as *Business Week,* speeches, and books written on the subject: "Quality is entering a new dimension." "Quality: the way to export success." "Quality starts with design." "Futuristic agile factories must be based on work performed with quality foremost." "Quality first." "Lumbering corporate hierarchies must be streamlined in order to focus on teamwork, quality, and speed." To emphasize the need for better quality, V. Daniel Hunt, president of Technology Research Corporation, stated in his book *Quality in America* that in America, 20 to 25 percent of production costs are currently spent finding and correcting mistakes. And, he added, the additional cost incurred in repairing or replacing faulty products in the field drives the total cost of poor quality to nearly 30 percent. In Japan, he said, it is about 3 percent.[2]

What is quality? There is no commonly agreed upon definition of quality. To cite a few diverse definitions: From Westinghouse, "Total quality is performance leadership in meeting customer requirements by doing the right things right the first time." From AT&T, "Quality is meeting customer expectations." "Quality is achieving or reaching the highest standard as against being satisfied with the sloppy or fraudulent," said Barbara W. Tuchman.

In this chapter we will be concerned with only two statistical techniques used in total quality control: **control charts** and **acceptance sampling.**

THE CONTROL CHART

Variation is a basic law of nature. The amount of rainfall each year will vary, as will the weight of a McDonald's Quarter Pounder and the parts produced by a manufacturing process.

On the production line, a most important concept is that *there is no such thing as two identical parts.* The difference from one part to the next is minute (perhaps one millionth of an inch), but the parts are different. One automobile engine block is different from the next one, and any one valve is different from the next one produced. Even the tensile strength of a roll of steel wire varies throughout the length of the wire. This variation is recognized in the tolerances and limits specified on blueprints. For example, a roll of steel wire may be acceptable if it tests between, say, 14,000 and 14,500 psi tensile strength.

To illustrate the pattern of variation inherent in quantitative data, 100 measurements of coiled wire (readings in hundredths of an inch) are summarized in Chart 16–1. Note that the readings tend to cluster about the arithmetic mean of 350 (which is actually 0.0350). Some of the readings are more and some are less. Practically all of the readings are between 344 (0.0344) and 358 (0.0358). If all the coils were measured, it is possible that some would be less than 0.0340 and some would be more than 0.0360.

Machined parts cluster about the average

Machined parts follow somewhat this inherent pattern. Suppose a gang drill drilling holes in bushings is set for 2.9870 inches diameter. A sample of bushings from this machine might reveal the results shown in Table 16–1.

[2]V. Daniel Hunt, *Quality in America* (Homewood, Ill.; Business One Irwin, 1992), p. 9.

CHART 16–1 Measurements of Wire Diameter

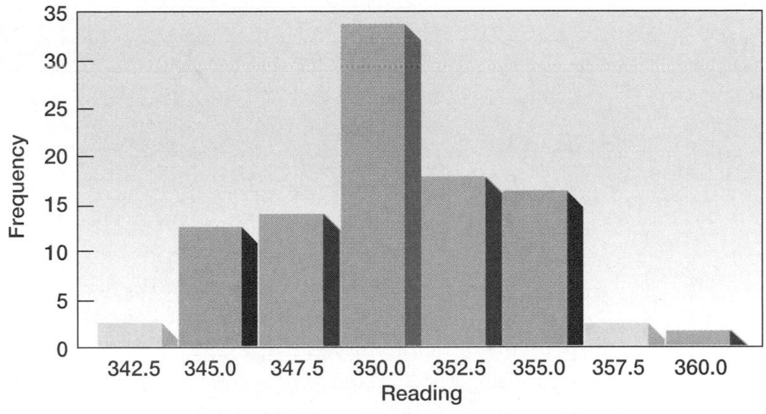

TABLE 16–1 Variations in the Inside Diameters of Bushings

Inside diameter							Number of bushings
2.9873	○						1
2.9872	○	○					2
2.9871	○	○	○	○			4
2.9870	○	○	○	○	○	○	6
2.9869	○	○	○	○			4
2.9868	○	○					2
2.9867	○						1

The inside diameters of the bushings can be considered to be approximately normally distributed. The normal distribution has the familiar form of a bell-shaped curve, and its characteristics are generally described by measures of central tendency, discussed in Chapter 3, and measures of dispersion and areas under the curve from Chapters 4 and 7.

The measure of central tendency most commonly used in quality control is the arithmetic mean. The range and the standard deviation are the two most often used measures of dispersion. The relationship between the mean (μ) and the standard deviation (σ) is portrayed graphically in Chart 16–2.

CHART 16–2 **Areas under the Normal Curve within $\mu \pm \sigma$, $\mu \pm 2\sigma$, and $\mu \pm 3\sigma$**

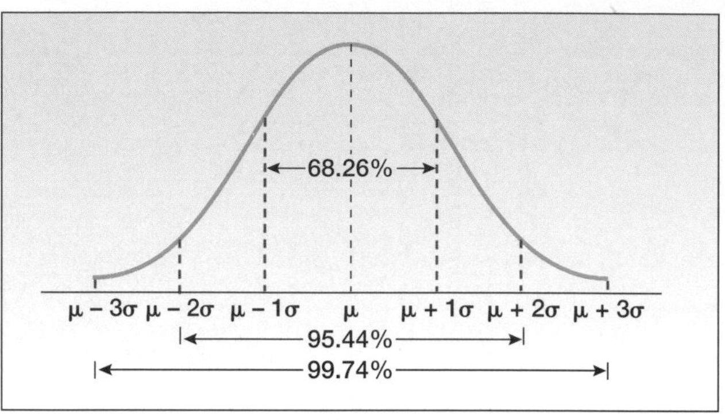

To understand why control charts are a basic tool in quality control, the following two questions must be answered:

1. What causes the basic pattern of variation in a manufacturing process?
2. What is the purpose of control charts?

CAUSES OF VARIATION

Variation may be due to chance

There are two general causes of variation in a manufacturing process: **chance** and **assignable variation.** Chance variations are usually large in number and random in nature, and they cannot be eliminated unless, for example, there is a major change in equipment or material. Internal machine friction, slight variations in materials or process conditions (such as the temperature of a mold being used to make glass bottles), atmospheric conditions (such as temperature, humidity, and the dust content of the air), and vibrations transmitted to a machine from a passing forklift are a few examples of sources of chance variation.

Variation may be assignable

Assignable variation is usually nonrandom in nature and can be eliminated or reduced. If the hole drilled in a piece of steel is much too large due to a dull drill, the drill may be sharpened or a new drill inserted. An operator who continually sets up the machine incorrectly can be replaced. If the roll of steel to be used in the process does not have the correct tensile strength, it can be rejected.

Why be concerned with the causes of variation?

1. Variation can (and will) change the shape, dispersion, and central tendency of the distribution of the product characteristic being measured.
2. Assignable variation is usually correctable, whereas chance variation usually cannot be corrected or stabilized economically.

To illustrate the effect of variation, the frequency distribution of the inside diameters of the bushings noted previously (Table 16–1) has been smoothed out to approximate a normal distribution curve and plotted in Chart 16–3A. Assuming that the upper and lower blueprint specifications match the inherent pattern of variation, 99.74 percent of the bushings would be acceptable. This indicates that 997 bushings out of 1,000 would be expected to fall between the specified tolerances.

CHART 16–3 **The Usual Pattern of Variation and the Effects of Upward and Downward Shifts in the Arithmetic Mean Inside Diameter**

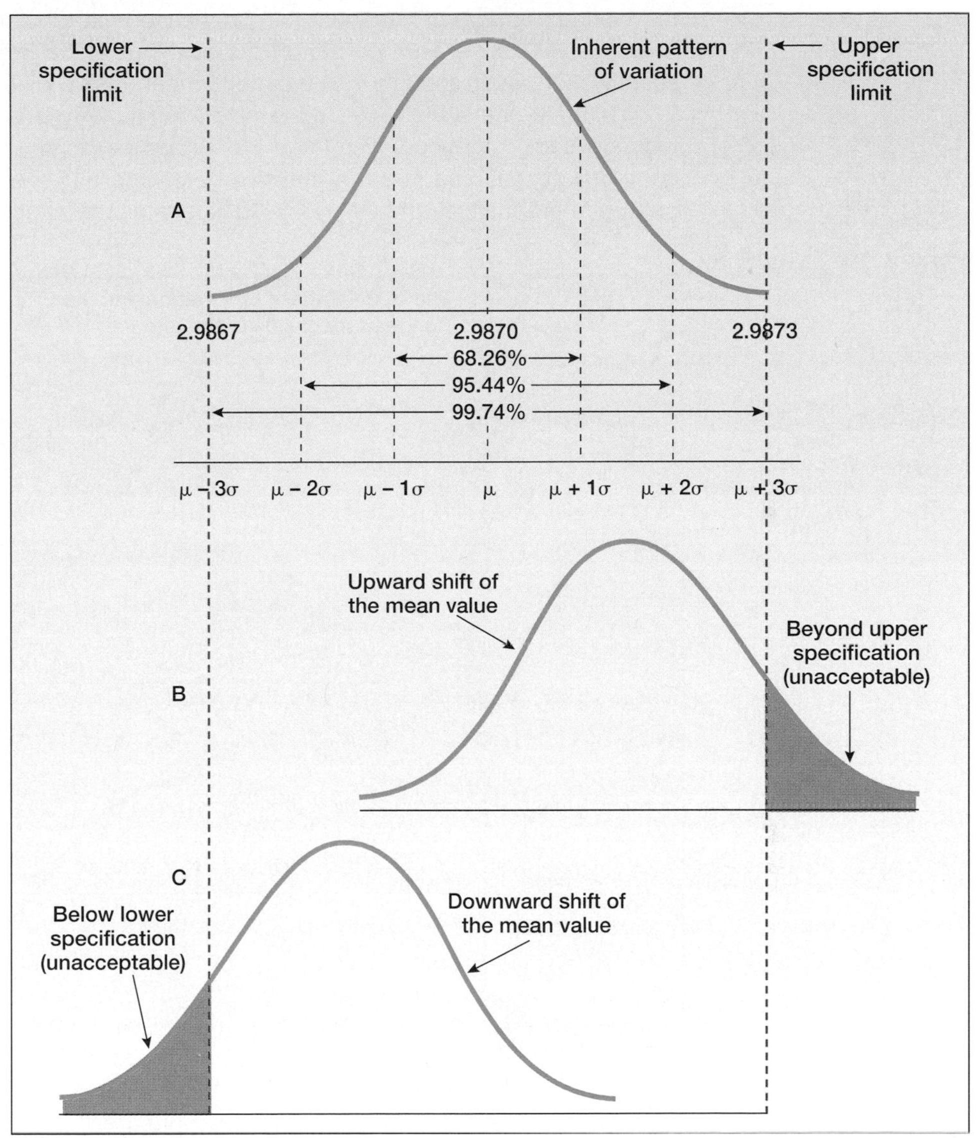

Larger mean inside diameter

Chart 16–3B shows graphically the effect of an upward shift in the mean inside diameter; that is, the mean inside diameter of the bushings has become much larger. This may be due to excessive vibration of the drill as it bites through the steel. Chart 16–3C shows the effect of a downward shift in the arithmetic mean diameter. The mean inside diameter has become much smaller, perhaps due to excessive drill wear. In both cases a large proportion of the output would be unacceptable.

Smaller mean inside diameter

In summary, if specifications have been established on the basis of the inherent pattern, then a shift in the arithmetic mean value results in defective parts. Chart 16–3A represents the pattern of *chance* variation. The areas above and below the upper and lower specifications in Chart 16–3B and C represent *assignable* causes of variation.

Again, assuming that the upper and lower specifications of the bushings match the inherent pattern of variation, then any change in the range of the distribution of bushings will cause a proportion of the bushings to be beyond the upper or lower specification, even though the arithmetic mean inside diameter stays the same, at 2.9870. A change in the range indicates that some very small and/or very large bushings are being produced. The large inside diameters may be caused by one of the gang drills expanding due to excessive heat. Chart 16–4A shows the usual normal pattern of production, and Chart 16–4B illustrates the effect of an increased range.

CHART 16–4 **The Usual Pattern of Variation and the Effects of an Increase in the Range of the Inside Diameters**

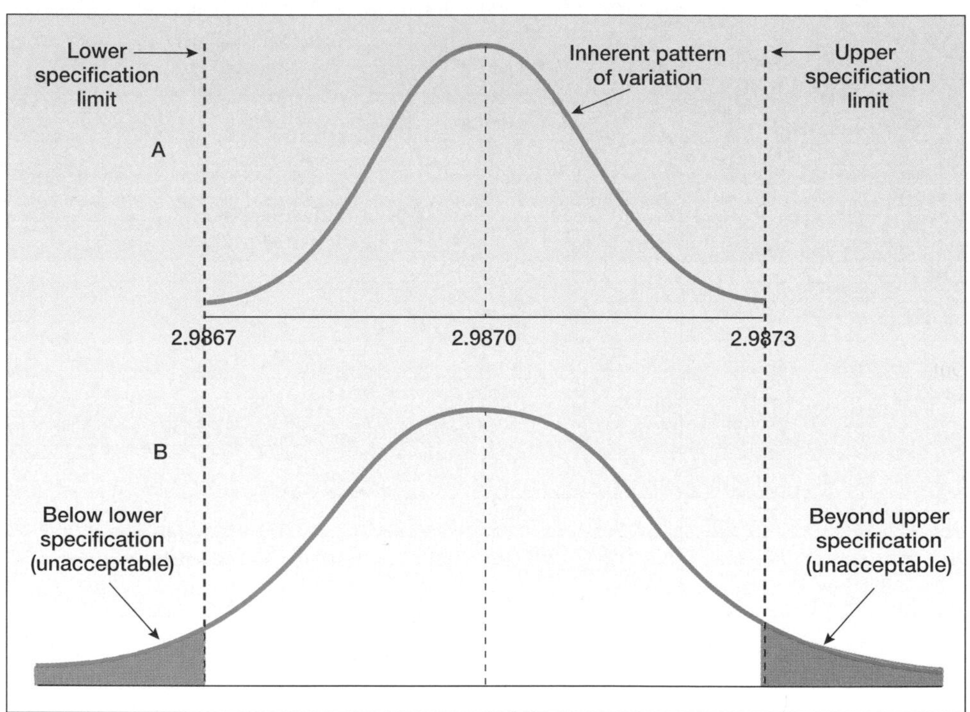

In summary, if specifications have been established on the basis of the inherent pattern, then an increase in the range results in defective parts. Chart 16–4A shows the pattern of chance variation. The areas above and below the upper and lower specifications in Chart 16–4B represent assignable causes of variation.

PURPOSE AND TYPES OF QUALITY-CONTROL CHARTS

Purpose of QC charts

What is the purpose of a statistical quality-control chart? Fundamentally, it is to identify when assignable causes of variation or changes in process level have entered the production system. It is important to know when these changes have occurred so that the cause may be identified and corrected before a large number of defective items are produced.

Statistical quality-control charts may be compared to a football scoreboard. By looking at the scoreboard, the fans, coaches, and players can tell which team is ahead. The scoreboard can do nothing to win or lose the game; it is merely a signal to the losing coach to try to do something about the situation. Changing the quarterback, for example, might turn the tide. Quality-control charts are similar in function. These charts indicate to the workers, group leaders, quality-control engineers, and management whether the production of a part or parts is **in control** or **out of control.** If production is out of control, the quality-control chart cannot correct the situation; it is just a piece of paper with figures and dots on it. Instead, the person responsible will adjust the machine manufacturing the part or do whatever is necessary to return production to "in control" status. "In control" means satisfactory production; "out of control" indicates unsatisfactory production. Unsatisfactory production might mean that the part being produced is too heavy, too light, too large, too small, or that it has other manifestations of poor, unacceptable production.

Control charts have been developed for both variables and attributes. A **variable chart** deals with and portrays graphically actual measurements, such as the outside diameter of a piston ring or the net weight of a can of tomato juice. An **attribute chart** is based on a product being classified as either acceptable or unacceptable. An electric light bulb coming off the production line is either acceptable (it lights) or unacceptable (it does not light).

Charts for Variables

Outside diameter, length, and weight are variables.

As has been pointed out previously, parts vary in length, inside diameter, outside diameter, tensile strength, and so on. One group of statistical quality-control charts is used for these variables. Two charts will be studied—*X bar charts* (alternatively called *mean charts*) and *range charts.*

Statistical quality-control charts utilize the theoretical concepts with respect to sampling developed in the foregoing chapters. Suppose that a small sample of five pieces is selected from the population, and the arithmetic mean is computed. Many additional samples of five pieces are then selected and the means computed. The means of these samples could be designated $\overline{X}_1$, $\overline{X}_2$, $\overline{X}_3$, and so on. The mean of these sample means is denoted by $\overline{\overline{X}}$. We use k for the number of sample means.

$$\overline{\overline{X}} = \frac{\text{Sum of the means of the subgroups (samples)}}{\text{Number of sample means}} = \frac{\Sigma\overline{X}}{k} \tag{16–1}$$

The standard error of the distribution of the individual sample (subgroup) means is designated $\sigma_{\bar{x}}$ and found by:

$$\sigma_{\bar{x}} = \frac{\sigma}{\sqrt{n}}$$

If all the sample means were plotted in a frequency distribution, the plot would approximate the bell-shaped curve in Chart 16–5. The plot distribution of sample means superimposed on the distribution of the actual measurements might appear as shown in the chart.

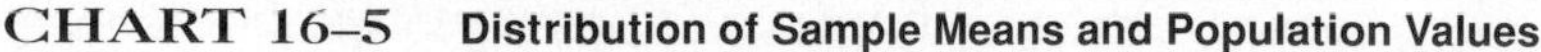

CHART 16–5 **Distribution of Sample Means and Population Values**

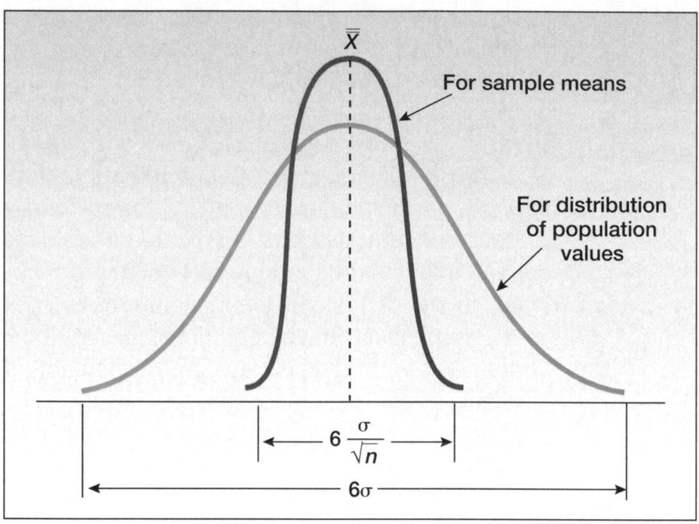

The arithmetic mean of a population is equal to the mean of all the means of the random samples selected from that population. Also, the total dispersion in the population is greater than that of the distribution of sample means by the factor $\sqrt{n}$. It also should be noted that even if the population is only approximately normal, inferences regarding the distribution of sample means can be made based on the normal distribution. They are:

68.26 percent of the sample means will be within plus or minus 1 standard error of the population mean.

95.44 percent of the sample means will be within plus or minus 2 standard errors of the population mean.

99.74 percent of the sample means will be within plus or minus 3 standard errors of the population mean.

These relationships allow limits to be set up around the sample means to show how much variation can be expected for subgroup samples of a given size. These expected limits are called the **upper control limits,** usually abbreviated **UCL,** and the **lower control limits,** usually abbreviated **LCL.**

Mean Chart One of the most common charts designed for variables is called a **mean chart.** Its purpose is to portray the fluctuation in the sample means.

EXAMPLE

Suppose a new bottle-making machine has just been installed. The machine is set to produce 41-ounce bottles, but variation in the weights of these bottles is expected. This expected variation is due to a number of factors, namely, the temperature of the glass, the temperature of the molds, and the composition of the glass mixture. The quality control design calls for taking a sample of five bottles every hour, weighing them, and computing the arithmetic mean weight.

How is a mean chart constructed?

Solution ▶

UCL is upper control limit

LCL is lower control limit

A mean chart has two limits, an upper control limit (UCL), and a lower control limit (LCL). The meaning of these two limits will be discussed shortly. We will first construct a mean chart and plot the sample data on the chart.

The upper control limit (UCL) and the lower control limit (LCL) may be computed by:

$$\text{UCL} = \overline{\overline{X}} + 3\frac{s}{\sqrt{n}} \qquad \text{LCL} = \overline{\overline{X}} - 3\frac{s}{\sqrt{n}}$$

where s is an estimate of the standard deviation of the population, σ. Notice that in the calculation of the upper and lower control limits, the number 3 represents the 99.74 percent confidence limits. However, it should be pointed out that although the 99.74 percent confidence level is commonly used, other confidence levels (90 percent, 95 percent, etc.) can be used, depending on the risk one is willing to assume of being out of control. This will become clearer as we progress through the chapter. The calculations for UCL and LCL have been simplified by using:[3]

$$\text{UCL} = \overline{\overline{X}} + A_2\overline{R} \qquad \text{LCL} = \overline{\overline{X}} - A_2\overline{R} \tag{16–2}$$

where:

A_2 is a factor used in the computation of the upper and lower control limits based on the range, $\overline{R}$. The factors for various sample sizes can be found in Appendix B. (*Note:* n in the table refers to the number in the sample.) A partial table is shown below. To find the factor, first locate the sample size, n (5 in this example) in the left margin. Then move horizontally to the A_2 column and read the factor. It is 0.577.

Factors for control charts

Number of items in sample	Chart for averages	Chart for ranges		
	Factors for control limits	Factors for central line	Factors for control limits	
n	A_2	d_2	D_3	D_4
2	1.880	1.128	0	3.267
3	1.023	1.693	0	2.575
4	.729	2.059	0	2.282
5	.577	2.326	0	2.115
6	.483	2.534	0	2.004

$\overline{\overline{X}}$ is the mean of the sample means.

$\overline{\overline{X}}$ is the mean of the sample means, computed by $\Sigma\overline{X}/k$, where k is the number of samples selected. In this problem a sample will be taken every hour for four hours, so $k = 4$.

[3]For this conversion, see Acheson J. Duncan, *Quality Control and Industrial Statistics,* 5th ed. (Homewood, Ill.: Richard D. Irwin, 1986), pp. 479–87.

$\overline{R}$ is the mean of the ranges

$\overline{R}$ is the mean of the sample ranges, computed by $\Sigma R/k$. (Recall that a sample range is the difference between the largest and smallest values in the sample.)

The quality-control inspector recorded the weight of each of the five bottles she selected. The data for the samples, taken at 8, 9, 10, and 11 A.M., are given in Table 16–2.

TABLE 16–2 Weights of Five Bottles Selected at Random, 8–11 A.M. (in ounces)

Time	Bottle 1	2	3	4	5	Arithmetic mean, $\overline{X}$	Range, R
8 A.M.	41	43	42	41	43	42	2
9 A.M.	39	40	40	39	42	40	3
10 A.M.	41	44	43	46	41	43	5
11 A.M.	38	39	40	39	39	39	2
Total						164	12

The centerline ($\overline{\overline{X}}$) for the mean chart is 41, found by 164/4. The mean of the range ($\overline{R}$) is 3, found by 12/4. Thus, the upper control limit (UCL) of the X bar chart, found by using formula (16–2), is:

$$\overline{\overline{X}} + A_2\overline{R} = 41 + 0.577(3)$$
$$= 42.731$$

The lower control limit (LCL) of the X bar chart is:

$$\overline{\overline{X}} - A_2\overline{R} = 41 - 0.577(3)$$
$$= 39.269$$

$\overline{\overline{X}}$, UCL, LCL, and the means of the samples are portrayed in Chart 16–6.

CHART 16–6 Mean Chart for the Weights of Bottles

The 10 A.M. and 11 A.M. checks are "out of control"

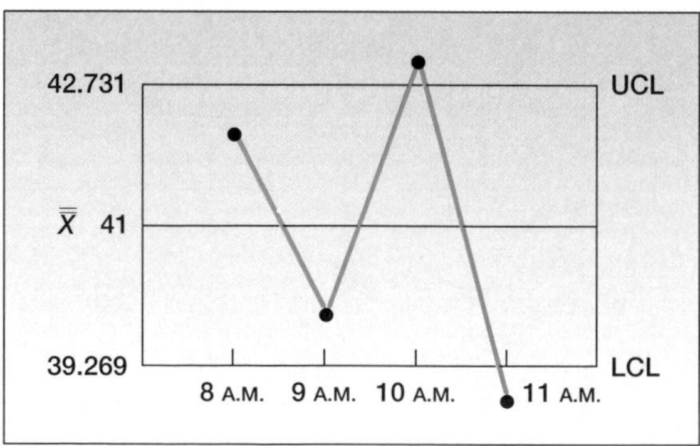

There is considerable variation in the process mean. In fact, both the 10 A.M. and the 11 A.M. samples indicate that the process is out of control. It is the responsibility

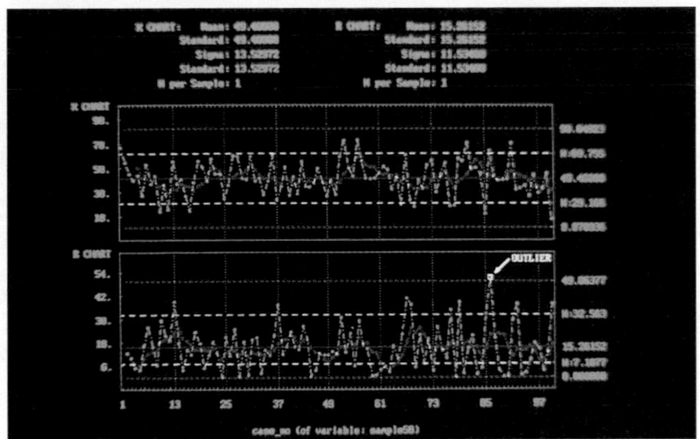

Computer software such as CSS: STATISTICA by Statsoft, Inc., is an important tool in the improvement of quality.

of the QC inspector to inform the production department so that an adjustment can be made as soon as possible.

To summarize, based on just the first four hours of experience with this new bottling machine: (1) If a sample of five bottles is picked at random and weighed, the arithmetic mean weight will fall between 39.269 and 42.731 ounces about 99.74 percent of the time. (2) If many samples of five bottles are taken and the arithmetic means computed, the mean of 41 ounces will appear more than any other. This figure (41 ounces) is the grand mean of the subgroup means. UCL and LCL represent $\overline{\overline{X}} \pm 3s/\sqrt{n}$.

Generally, quality-control charts should be developed after the process has stabilized. One rule of thumb is to design a chart after at least 25 samples have been selected. In this example, the mean chart was drawn after only four samples were chosen.

SELF-REVIEW 16–1

The answers are at the end of the chapter.

Every half hour the quality-control inspector checks four pieces and records the outside diameters of each of the four pieces. The results are shown in the following table.

	Sample piece			
Time	**1**	**2**	**3**	**4**
9:00 A.M.	1	4	5	2
9:30 A.M.	2	3	2	1
10:00 A.M.	1	7	3	5

Compute the overall mean, determine the control limits, and show the limits and the mean on a mean chart. Then plot the sample means.

Range Chart Another control chart for variables is referred to as a **range chart.** Logically it shows the variation in the sample ranges. If the dots representing the ranges fall between the upper and lower limits, it is concluded that production is in control. According to chance, 997 times out of 1,000 the range of the sample will fall between the two limits. If a range should fall above or below the limits, it is concluded that some *assignable* cause affected the production, resulting in some individual pieces being too large, too small, too heavy, or too light, depending on what is being measured. UCL and LCL represent $\bar{R} \pm 3\sigma_R$. The upper and lower control limits for the range chart can be quickly determined by:

How to compute UCL and LCL of range chart

$$\boxed{UCL = D_4\bar{R} \quad LCL = D_3\bar{R}} \tag{16–3}$$

where D_3 and D_4 are factors from Appendix B (also given in the partial table on page 665).

EXAMPLE

The weights of the samples of five bottles from Table 16–2 are repeated below.

	Weight (ounces)				
Time	**1**	**2**	**3**	**4**	**5**
8 A.M.	41	43	42	41	43
9 A.M.	39	40	40	39	42
10 A.M.	41	44	43	46	41
11 A.M.	38	39	40	39	39

How is a range chart for these weights constructed?

Solution

The first step is to find the mean range, $\bar{R}$. The range of the 8 A.M. sample is 2, found by 43 − 41. The range of the 9 A.M. sample is 3, found by 42 − 39. The ranges for the 10 A.M. and 11 A.M. samples are 5 and 2, respectively. The mean range, $\bar{R}$, is 3, found by $(2 + 3 + 5 + 2)/4 = 12/4 = 3$.

Locating D_3 and D_4

Referring to Appendix B for D_3 and D_4 and a sample size of 5, we get $D_4 = 2.115$ and $D_3 = 0$. Determining the upper and lower control limits for the range chart:

$$UCL = D_4\bar{R} \qquad LCL = D_3\bar{R}$$
$$= 2.115(3) \qquad = (0)(3)$$
$$= 6.345 \qquad = 0$$

Construction of the range chart and plotting of the 8–11 A.M. ranges is shown in Chart 16–7.

CHART 16–7 Range Chart for the Weights of Bottles

Ranges of weights of bottles are "in control"

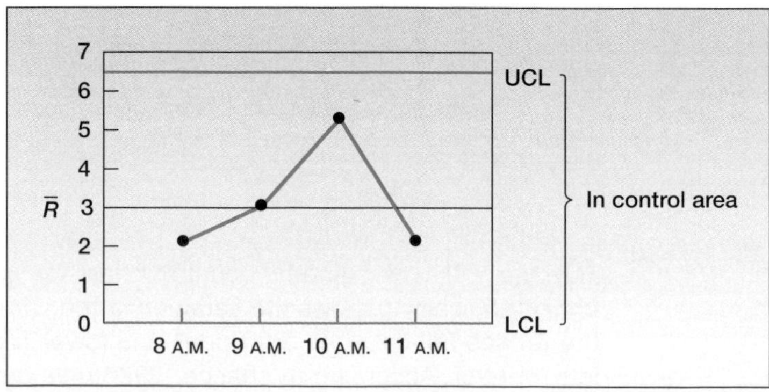

The lower control limit of 0 for the range chart is really not needed. No doubt management would be very pleased if there were no variation in the bottle weights.

Note that all the ranges lie in the "in control" area, indicating that the fluctuations in the weights of the bottles are as expected. That is, there are no unusual fluctuations in the weights. No adjustment to the process is needed.

SELF-REVIEW 16–2

The answers are at the end of the chapter.

1. Using the data from Self-Review 16–1 (repeated here), construct a range chart showing the control limits. Plot the ranges.
2. Is the process in control?

	Sample piece			
Time	**1**	**2**	**3**	**4**
9:00 A.M.	1	4	5	2
9:30 A.M.	2	3	2	1
10:00 A.M.	1	7	3	5

The MINITAB system has a procedure for computing the control limits for the mean and the range. The necessary steps and the output are as follows. There are some slight differences in the limits, which are due to rounding.

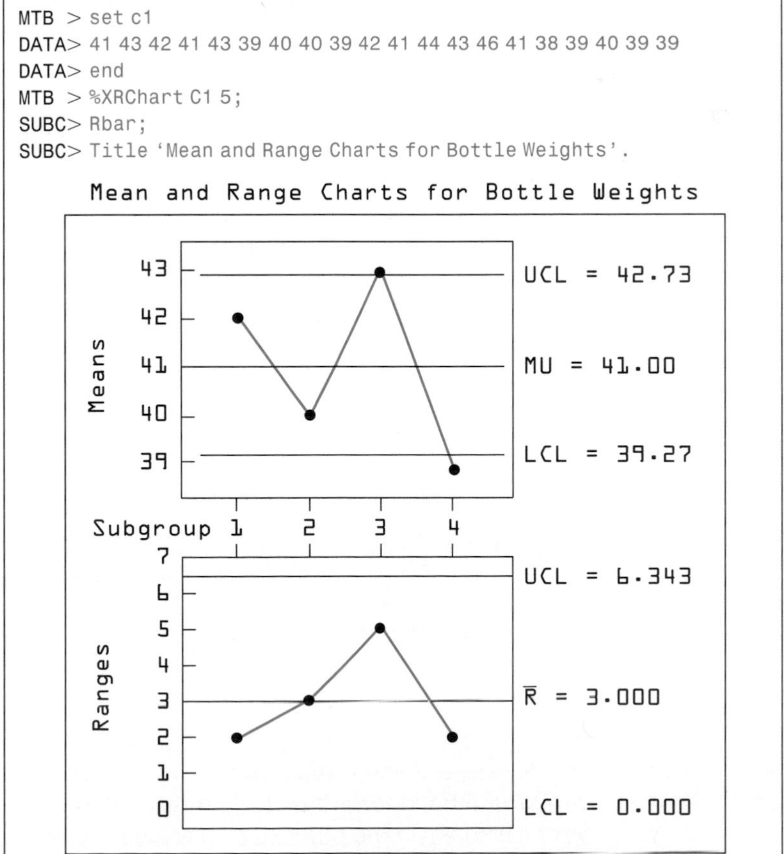

Some In-Control and Out-of-Control Situations

Following are three illustrations of in-control and out-of-control production processes.

Everything OK

1. The mean chart and the range chart together indicate that the process is in control. Note that the sample means and sample ranges are clustered close to the centerlines. Some are above and some below the centerlines, indicating that the process is quite stable. That is, there is no visible tendency for the means and ranges to move toward the "out of control" areas.

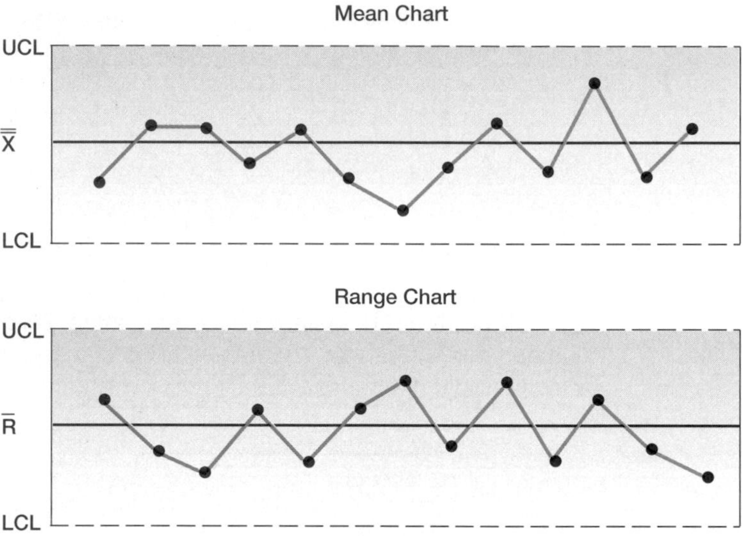

Considerable variation in ranges

2. The sample means are in control, but the ranges of the last two samples are out of control. This indicates there is considerable variation from piece to piece. Some pieces are large; others are small. An adjustment in the process is necessary.

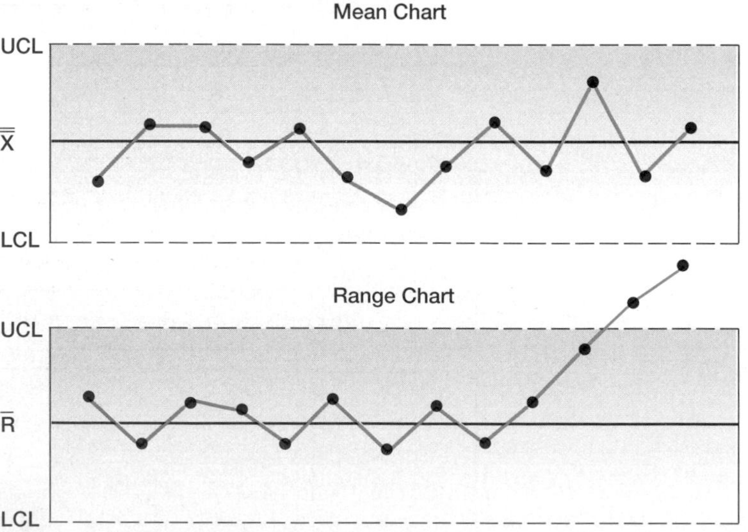

Mean measurement mean getting larger and larger

3. The arithmetic mean weight was in control for the first samples, but there was an upward trend toward UCL. The mean weights of the last two were out of control. An adjustment in the process is indicated.

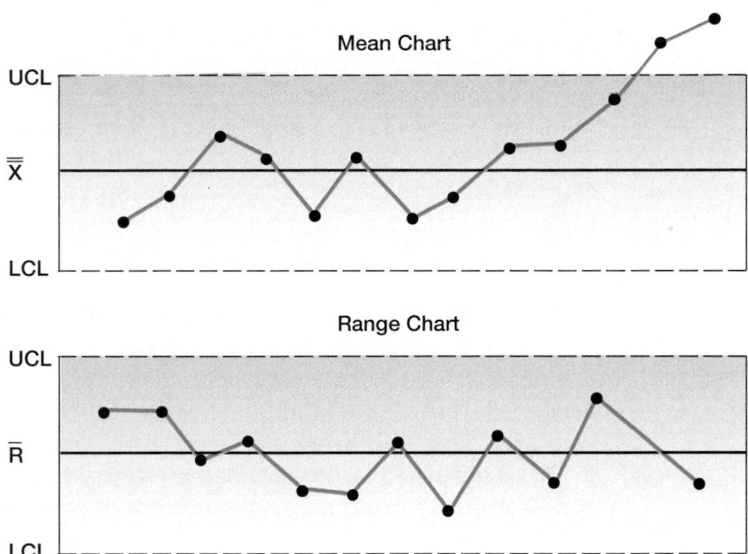

The above chart for the mean is an example in which the control chart offers some additional information. Note the direction of the last five observations of the mean. They are all above $\overline{\overline{X}}$ and increasing, and, in fact, the last two observations are out of control. The fact that the sample means were increasing for seven consecutive observations is an indication that the process is out of control.

EXERCISES

The answers to the odd-numbered exercises are at the end of the book.

1. Describe the difference between assignable variation and chance variation.
2. Describe the difference between a variable control chart and an attribute control chart.
3. Samples of size $n = 4$ are selected hourly from a production line.
   a. What is the value of the A_2 factor used to determine the upper and lower control limits for the mean?
   b. What are the values of the D_3 and D_4 factors used to determine the upper and lower control limits for the range?
4. Samples of size 5 are selected from a manufacturing process. The mean of the sample ranges is 0.25. What is the estimated standard deviation of the population?
5. A new industrial oven has just been installed. In order to develop experience regarding the temperature of the oven, the inspector reads the temperature in the oven at four different places every half hour. The first reading, taken at 8 A.M., was 2,040 degrees Fahrenheit. (Only the last two digits are given in the following table to facilitate computations.)

	Reading			
Time	**1**	**2**	**3**	**4**
8:00 A.M.	40	50	55	39
8:30 A.M.	44	42	38	38
9:00 A.M.	41	45	47	43
9:30 A.M.	39	39	41	41
10:00 A.M.	37	42	46	41
10:30 A.M.	39	40	39	40

a. Based on this initial experience, set up a mean chart. Mark the upper and lower control limits and the grand mean. Then plot the 8:00–10:30 experience.
b. Interpret the chart.

6. *a.* Design a range chart for the data from Exercise 5, and plot it immediately below the mean chart. Indicate the upper and lower control limits and mean range.
b. Interpret the chart.

Charts for Attributes

Attribute charts—used mainly to show percent or number defective

A weld either has a crack in it or it doesn't; a relay works or it doesn't; a radiator leaks or it doesn't; the lock on a car door works or it doesn't; a tire fits on the rim or it doesn't. These are examples of *attributes.* If a part leaks, doesn't fit, won't lock, or doesn't work, it is said to be defective. Go/no-go gauges are one type of inspection tool for attributes; X-ray is another. Two types of quality-control charts for attributes will be examined. A **percent defective chart** shows the percent of production that is defective. A **$\bar{c}$ chart** shows the number of defects per unit.

Percent Defective Chart A percent defective chart is also known as a *p chart* or $\bar{p}$ *chart;* the latter is pronounced "*p* bar chart." The percent defective chart shows graphically the proportion of the production that is not acceptable.

EXAMPLE

Percent defective

A new shearing machine is set to cut off a piece of steel from a long bar. For various reasons, the machine at times cuts off a piece that is too long or too short. These unacceptable pieces are automatically dropped in a box, and the operator of the shearing machine must count these defectives after every 100 pieces are sheared off. The record after the first day of operation is:

Number sheared off	Number defective	Proportion defective
100	5	.05
100	6	.06
100	7	.07
100	4	.04
100	8	.08
		.30

How is a percent defective chart constructed?

Solution ▶

Mean percent defective = 6 percent

The mean proportion defective ($\bar{p}$) is found by:

$$\bar{p} = \frac{\text{Sum of the percent defectives}}{\text{Number of samples}} \qquad (16\text{–}4)$$

In this example:

$$\bar{p} = \frac{.30}{5}$$

$$= .06$$

The upper control limit and the lower control limit are computed as the mean percent defective plus and minus three times the standard error of the percents.

$$\text{UCL and LCL} = \bar{p} \pm 3\sqrt{\frac{\bar{p}(1-\bar{p})}{n}} \tag{16–5}$$

For this example:

UCL = 13.12 percent, LCL = 0

$$\begin{aligned}\text{UCL and LCL} &= \bar{p} \pm 3\sqrt{\frac{\bar{p}(1-\bar{p})}{n}}\\ &= .06 \pm 3\sqrt{\frac{(.06)(.94)}{100}}\\ &= .06 \pm .0712\\ &= .1312 \text{ and } -.0112\end{aligned}$$

The upper control limit is .1312, and the lower control limit is 0, since there cannot be less than 0 percent defective.

Note in Chart 16–8 that the average percent defective ($\bar{p}$) of .06 along with UCL and LCL are shown. To complete the chart, the percent defective for each sample is plotted—namely, .05, .06, .07, .04, and .08, respectively.

CHART 16–8 **Percent Defective Chart for Shearing Machine**

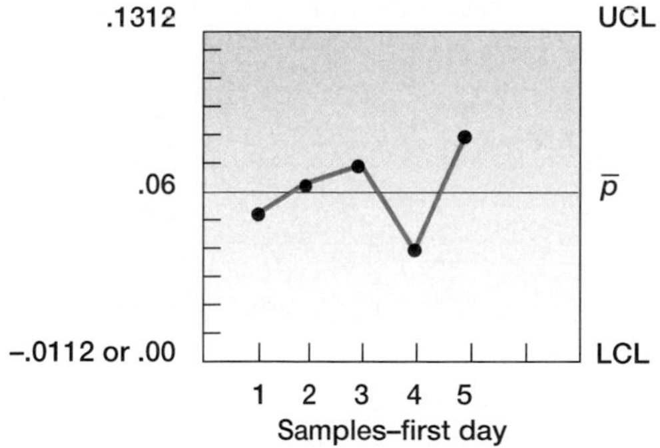

Several observations can be made after the first day of operation: (1) The arithmetic mean percent defective is 6 percent. (2) About 99.7 percent of the time there will be between 0 percent and 13.1 percent defective pieces. (3) Only in 3 out of 1,000 samples of size 100 (1,000 − 997) will the percent defective either exceed 13.1 percent or, theoretically, be below 0 percent. (4) The first few samples revealed that the process is in control. No adjustments are warranted.

Management might or might not be satisfied with an average of 6 percent scrap or scrap as high as 13.1 percent. The chart cannot make a decision; that is management's responsibility. The $\bar{p}$ chart merely sets limits based on actual experience.

MINITAB has a system for generating a percent defective chart. Using the data from the previous example:

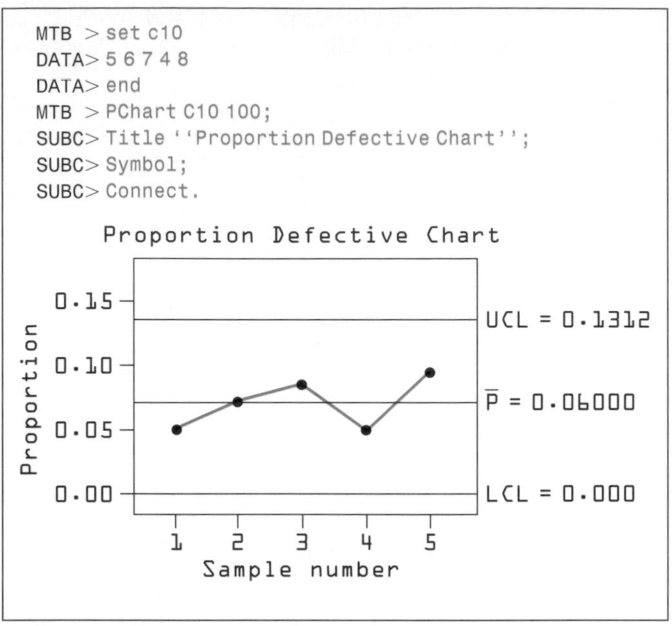

SELF-REVIEW 16–3

The answers are at the end of the chapter.

Samples of 200 parts were taken every day. The numbers of defectives were counted. Set up a percent defective chart, and plot the sample percents.

Day	Number checked	Number defective
1	200	4
2	200	3
3	200	5
4	200	4

EXERCISES

The answers to the odd-numbered exercises are at the end of the book.

7. The number of defectives in each of 10 samples of $n = 50$ is given below.

Sample	Number defective	Sample	Number defective
1	2	6	2
2	1	7	2
3	0	8	4
4	2	9	3
5	3	10	5

a. Design a percent defective chart. Indicate the upper and lower control limits.

b. The 11th sample of $n = 50$ contained 10 defects. Does this indicate the process is out of control?

8. A new high-speed machine appears to be producing a large percentage of defective bolts. A frequent check of its output on Tuesday resulted in the following:

Sample number	Sample size	Number of defects	Sample number	Sample size	Number of defects
1	50	4	11	50	2
2	50	0	12	50	3
3	50	3	13	50	6
4	50	5	14	50	4
5	50	6	15	50	5
6	50	4	16	50	7
7	50	1	17	50	6
8	50	6	18	50	5
9	50	7	19	50	10
10	50	8	20	50	2

a. Design a percent defective chart. Indicate the upper and lower control limits and $\bar{p}$ on the chart. Plot Tuesday's experience.
b. Interpret the chart.

$\bar{c}$ bar chart for number of defects per unit

$\bar{c}$ Bar Chart The **$\bar{c}$ chart** is alternatively called a ***c*** **bar chart.** It portrays the *number of defects per unit.* A glass bottle might be considered defective if there are "stones" or imperfections 1/32 inch in size or more. If eight stones are found in a bottle picked at random from the assembly line, then the number of defects per unit is eight. In an automotive assembly plant, the number of defects per car door are counted. The defects might be two open seams, three slivers of steel that might scratch the new owner, one wavy section, and three small areas not completely painted. Thus, on this one car door there would be nine defects.

The purpose of a $\bar{c}$ chart, therefore, is to show how many defects appear in a unit of production. $\bar{c}$ charts on subassemblies and the final assembly show management weak areas in the construction process. Remedial action can be taken, including shift of personnel or closer supervision of certain subassemblies.

EXAMPLE

A high-fidelity tuner is subjected to a final inspection. It is plugged in and tested by tuning to a local radio station. The tuners that work are packed and shipped. The others must be repaired before being released for sale. Possible defects might lie in the soldering or in the omission of parts. The quality-control inspector checks these defective tuners and counts the number of defects per tuner. Checks on 10 new-model tuners revealed the following number of defects per tuner: 8, 5, 6, 4, 3, 8, 8, 10, 9, and 9.

How is a *c* bar chart constructed?

Solution ▶ The formula for the upper and lower control limits of a *c* bar chart is:

Formula for UCL and LCL for $\bar{c}$ chart

$$\text{UCL and LCL} = \bar{c} \pm 3\sqrt{\bar{c}} \qquad (16\text{–}6)$$

The total number of defects in the 10 new-model tuners is 70, found by $8 + 5 + 6 + 4 + 3 + 8 + 8 + 10 + 9 + 9$. The arithmetic mean number of defects per tuner ($\bar{c}$) is:

$$\bar{c} = \frac{\text{Sum of the defects}}{\text{Total number of tuners}} = \frac{70}{10} = 7$$

The upper control limit and the lower control limit are:

$$\text{UCL and LCL} = \bar{c} \pm 3\sqrt{\bar{c}} = 7 \pm 3\sqrt{7} = 7 \pm 7.94$$

$$\text{UCL} = 14.94$$

$$\text{LCL} = 0 \text{ (since the number of defects per unit cannot be less than 0)}$$

Again, a lower control limit for a $\bar{c}$ chart is of no value. No doubt the assembly line workers, and management, would be very pleased if a tuner had no defects!

Production "in control"

The number of defects per tuner is plotted in Chart 16–9.

CHART 16–9 ***c* Bar Chart for High-Fidelity Tuner**

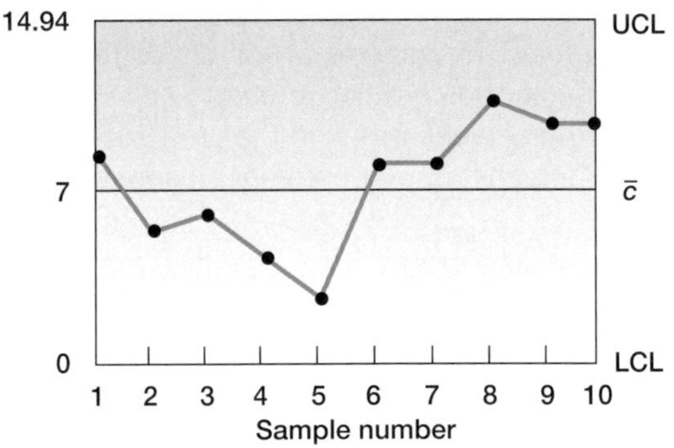

Interpreting the results, the mean number of defects per unit is 7. In the long run, about 997 out of 1,000 tuners would have between 0 and 15 defects. UCL and LCL represent $\bar{c} \pm 3\sigma_c$.

The $\bar{c}$ chart would no doubt be revised after more samples were taken. It is reasoned that during the production of the first units of a new model, the machine operators and group leaders are somewhat unfamiliar with the process. Days or weeks are usually necessary before the process is stabilized.

Following is the MINITAB *c* bar chart for the high-fidelity tuner example.

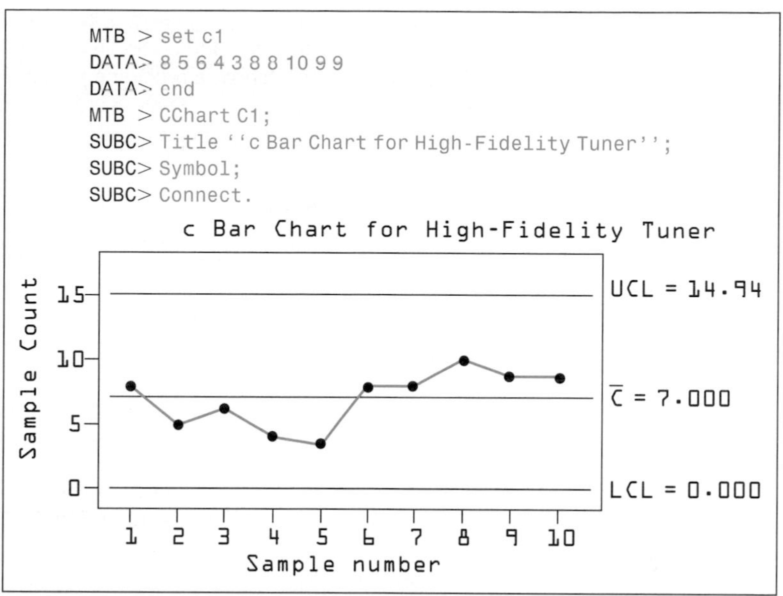

SELF-REVIEW 16–4

The answers are at the end of the chapter.

A subassembly is thoroughly inspected, and the number of defects is recorded. A new group of assemblers began work Monday morning. The numbers of defects per subassembly for the first 10 they produced were: 3, 2, 0, 5, 4, 6, 0, 7, 7, and 6.

1. Set up a control chart for the average number of defects per subassembly, and plot the number of defects per subassembly.

2. Does it appear that the process is in control?

EXERCISES

The answers to the odd-numbered exercises are at the end of the book.

9. The number of defects per unit in each of 10 samples is given below.

Unit	Number of defects	Unit	Number of defects
1	2	6	2
2	1	7	2
3	0	8	4
4	2	9	3
5	3	10	5

   a. Design a *c* bar chart. Indicate the upper and lower control limits.

   b. The 11th unit sampled contained 6 defects. Does this indicate the process is out of control?

10. The manufacturer of a newly designed metal storage cabinet ships the cabinet unassembled, and the purchaser assembles it. An increasing number of complaints have

been received regarding missing parts, sharp edges, hinges that did not align properly, imperfections in the enamel, and so on. In order to eliminate these complaints as far as possible, starting with Monday's production, each cabinet was fully assembled at the factory and the defects corrected before it was disassembled for shipment. A record of the number of defects per cabinet for the first 12 cabinets checked follows.

Cabinet designation	Number of defects	Cabinet designation	Number of defects
OA1	7	OA7	9
OA2	6	OA8	3
OA3	8	OA9	4
OA4	10	OA10	6
OA5	8	OA11	5
OA6	4	OA12	2

a. Design a chart to show the number of defects per unit. Show the upper and lower control limits and other essential data. Plot the experience for the first 12 cabinets inspected.

b. Interpret the chart.

ACCEPTANCE SAMPLING

The previous section was concerned with maintaining the *quality of the product as it is being produced.* In many business situations we are also concerned with the *quality of the incoming finished product.* What do the following cases have in common?

- Sims Software, Inc. purchased diskettes from Diskettes International. The normal purchase order is for 100,000 diskettes, packaged in lots of 1,000. Todd Sims, president, does not expect each diskette to be perfect. In fact, he has agreed to accept lots of 1,000 with up to 10 percent defective. He would like to develop a plan to inspect incoming lots, to ensure that the quality standard is met. The purpose of the inspection procedure is to separate the acceptable from the unacceptable lots.
- Zenith Electric purchases magnetron tubes from Bono Electronics for use in their new microwave oven. The tubes are shipped to Zenith in lots of 10,000. Zenith allows the incoming lots to contain up to 5 percent defective tubes. They would like to develop a sampling plan to determine which lots meet the criterion and which do not.
- General Motors purchases windshields from many suppliers. GM insists that the windshields be in lots of 1,000. They are willing to accept 50 or fewer defects in each lot, that is, 5 percent defective. They would like to develop a sampling procedure to verify that incoming shipments meet the criterion.

The common thread in these cases is a need to verify that incoming product meet the stipulated requirements. The situation can be likened to a screen door, which allows the warm summer air to enter the room while keeping the bugs out. Acceptance sampling lets the lots of acceptable quality into the manufacturing area and screens out lots that are not acceptable.

Of course, the situation in modern business is more complex. The buyer wants protection against accepting lots that are below the quality standard. The best protection against inferior quality is 100 percent inspection. Unfortunately, the cost of 100 percent inspection is often prohibitive. Another problem with checking each item is that the test may be destructive. If all light bulbs were tested until burning out before they were shipped, there would be none left to sell. Also, 100 percent inspection may not lead to the identification of all defects due to boredom and the consequent loss of perception on the part of the inspectors. Thus, complete inspection is rarely employed in practical situations.

100 percent inspection not feasible

The usual procedure is to screen the quality of incoming parts by use of a statistical sampling plan. According to this plan a sample of n units is randomly selected from the lots of N units (the population). This is called **acceptance sampling.** The inspection will determine the number of defects in the sample. This number is compared with a predetermined number called the **critical number** or the **acceptance number.** The acceptance number is usually designated c. If the number of defects in the sample of size n is less than or equal to c, the lot is accepted. If the number of defects exceeds c, the lot is rejected and returned to the supplier, or perhaps submitted to 100 percent inspection.

Acceptance sampling

Acceptance number

Acceptance sampling is a decision-making process. There are two possible decisions: accept or reject the lot. In addition, there are two situations under which the decision is made: the lot is good or the lot is bad. These are the states of nature. If the lot is good and the sample inspection reveals the lot to be good, or if the lot is bad and the sample inspection indicates it is bad, then a correct decision is made. However, there are two other possibilities. The lot may actually contain more defects than it should, but it is accepted. This is called **consumer's risk.** Similarly, the lot may be within the agreed-upon limits, but it is rejected during the sample inspection. This is called the **producer's risk.** The following summary table for acceptance decisions shows these possibilities.

Consumer's risk

Producer's risk

	States of nature	
Decision	**Good lot**	**Bad lot**
Accept lot	Correct	Beta error
Reject lot	Alpha error	Correct

To evaluate a sampling plan and determine that it is fair to both the producer and the consumer, the usual procedure is to develop an **operating characteristic curve,** or an **OC curve,** as it is usually called. An OC curve reports the percent defective along the horizontal axis and the probability of accepting that percent defective along the vertical axis. A smooth curve is usually drawn connecting all the possible levels of quality. The binomial distribution is used to develop the probabilities for an OC curve.

OC curve

EXAMPLE

Sims Software, as mentioned earlier, purchases diskettes from Diskettes International. The diskettes are packaged in lots of 1,000 each. Todd Sims, president of Sims Software, has agreed to accept lots with 10 percent or fewer defective diskettes. Todd has directed his inspection department to select a sample of 20 diskettes and examine them carefully. He will accept the lot if it has two or fewer defectives in the sample. Develop an OC curve for this inspection plan. What is the probability of accepting a lot that is 10 percent defective?

Solution ▶ This type of sampling is called **attribute sampling** because the sampled item, a diskette in this case, is classified as acceptable or unacceptable. No "reading" or "measurement" is obtained on the diskette. Let's structure the problem in terms of the states of nature. Let p represent the actual proportion defective in the population.

Attribute sampling

The lot is good if $p \leq .10$.

The lot is bad if $p > .10$.

Decision rule

Let X be the number of defects in the sample. The decision rule is:

Reject the lot if $X \geq 3$.

Accept the lot if $X \leq 2$.

Here the acceptable lot is one with 10 percent or fewer defective diskettes. If the lot is acceptable when it has exactly 10 percent defectives, it would be even more acceptable if it contained fewer than 10 percent defective. Hence, it is the usual practice to work with the upper limit of the percent of defectives.

The binomial distribution is used to compute the various values on the OC curve. Recall that for us to use the binomial, there are four requirements.

1. There are only two possible outcomes. Here the diskette is either acceptable or unacceptable.
2. There is a fixed number of trials. In this instance the number of trials is the sample size of 20.
3. There is a constant probability of success. A success is the probability of finding a defective part. It is assumed to be .10.
4. The trials are independent. The probability of obtaining a defective diskette on the third one selected is not related to the likelihood of finding a defect on the fourth diskette selected.

Appendix A gives the various binomial probabilities. We need to convert the acceptance sampling nomenclature to that used in Chapter 6 for discrete probability distributions. Let $p = .10$, the probability of a success, and $n = 20$, the number of trials. c is the number of defects allowed—two in this case. We will now determine the probability of accepting an incoming lot that is 10 percent defective using a sample size of 20 and allowing zero, one, or two defects. First, locate within Appendix A the case where $n = 20$ and $p = .10$. Find the row where r, the number of defects, is 0. The probability is .122. Next find the probability of one defect, that is, where $r = 1$. It is .270. Similarly, the probability of $r = 2$ is .285. To find the probability of two or fewer defects, we need to add these three probabilities. The total is .677. Hence, the probability of accepting a lot that is 10 percent defective, that is, containing two or fewer defects in a sample of 20, is .677. The probability of rejecting this lot is .323, found by $1 - .677$. This result is usually written in shorthand notation as follows (the bar, |, means "given that"):

$$P(X \leq 2 \mid p = .10 \text{ and } n = 20) = .677$$

The OC curve in Chart 16–10 shows various values of p and the corresponding probabilities of accepting a lot of that quality. Management of Sims Software will be able to quickly evaluate the probabilities of various quality levels.

CHART 16–10 **OC Curve for Sampling Plan (n = 20, c = 2)**

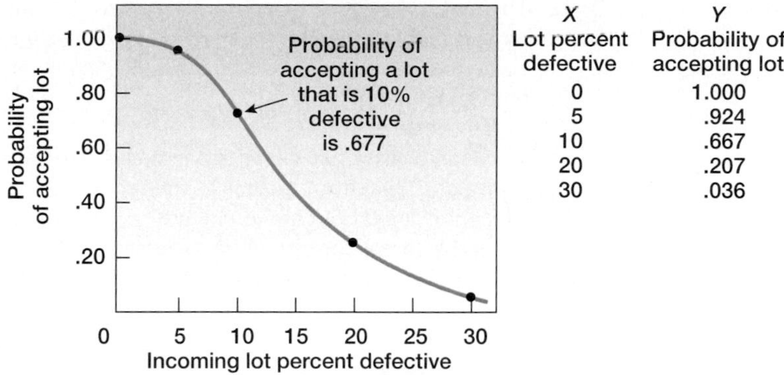

X Lot percent defective	Y Probability of accepting lot
0	1.000
5	.924
10	.667
20	.207
30	.036

SELF-REVIEW 16–5

The answers are at the end of the chapter.

Compute the probability of accepting a lot of diskettes that is actually 30 percent defective, using the sampling plan for Sims Software.

EXERCISES

The answers to the odd-numbered exercises are at the end of the book.

11. Determine the probability of accepting lots that are 10 percent, 20 percent, 30 percent, and 40 percent defective using a sample of size 12 and an acceptance number of 2.
12. Determine the probability of accepting lots that are 10 percent, 20 percent, 30 percent, and 40 percent defective using a sample of size 14 and an acceptance number of 3.
13. Warren Electric manufactures fuses for many customers. To ensure the quality of the outgoing product, they test 10 fuses each hour. If no more than one fuse is defective, they package the fuses and prepare them for shipment. Develop an OC curve for this sampling plan. Compute the probabilities of accepting lots that are 10 percent, 20 percent, 30 percent, and 40 percent defective. Draw the OC curve for this sampling plan using the four quality levels.
14. Grills Radio Products purchases transistors from Mira Electronics. According to his sampling plan, Art Grills, owner of Grills Radio, will accept a shipment of transistors if three or fewer are defective in a sample of 25. Develop an OC curve for these percents defective: 10 percent, 20 percent, 30 percent, and 40 percent.

CHAPTER OUTLINE

I. The objective of statistical quality control is to control the quality of a manufacturing or service operation using sampling techniques.

II. Control chart.

   A. There are two causes of variation in production.

1. Chance causes: Few in number, random in nature, cannot be entirely eliminated.
2. Assignable causes: Few in number, nonrandom, can be reduced or eliminated.

B. The purpose of quality-control charts is to determine and portray graphically just when an assignable cause enters the production system so that it can be identified and corrected. This is accomplished by selecting a very small random sample from current production periodically.

C. Types of charts.

1. Mean charts, also called X bar charts, are designed to control variables, such as weights, lengths, and tensile strengths. The upper control limit (UCL) and lower control limit (LCL) are found by $\overline{\overline{X}} \pm A_2\overline{R}$ [formula (16–2)], where $\overline{\overline{X}}$ is the mean of the sample means, A_2 is a factor from Appendix B, and $\overline{R}$ is the mean of the sample ranges. The chart on the left indicates that production is "in control." The one on the right is an "out-of-control" situation, with the outside diameter of the part in question much too large and unacceptable at the last two checks.

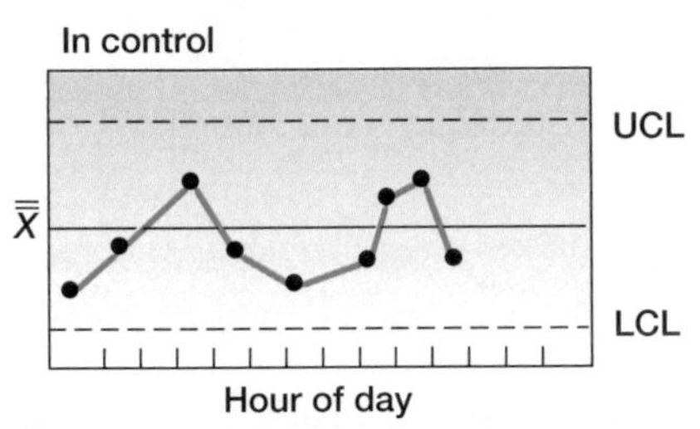

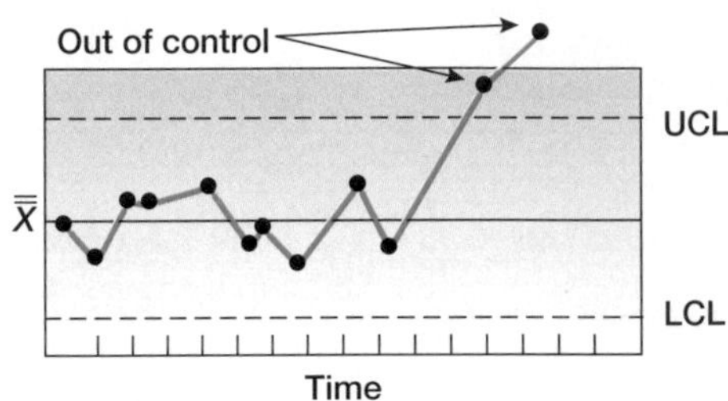

2. A range chart is another chart for variables. It shows whether the overall range of measurement is in or out of control. UCL and LCL are found by $D_4\overline{R}$ and $D_3\overline{R}$, respectively. The factors D_4 and D_3 are given in Appendix B, $\overline{R}$ is the mean of the sample ranges.
3. The percent defective chart is a chart for an attribute. An example of an attribute is: Ball bearing is either good or defective. UCL and LCL are found by:

$$\bar{p} \pm 3\sqrt{\frac{\bar{p}(1-\bar{p})}{n}} \qquad (16\text{–}5)$$

where $\bar{p}$ is the mean proportion defective based on samples taken from the production line.

4. The $\bar{c}$ chart is another attribute chart designed to control the number of defects per unit. UCL and LCL are found by:

$$\bar{c} \pm 3\sqrt{\bar{c}} \qquad (16\text{–}6)$$

where $\bar{c}$ is the mean number of defects per unit.

III. Acceptance sampling is a method of determining whether an incoming lot of a product meets specified standards.

A. It is based on random sampling techniques.
B. A random sample of n units is obtained from the entire lot.
C. c is the maximum number of defective units that may be found in the sample for the lot to still be considered acceptable.
D. An OC, or operating characteristic, curve is developed using the binomial probability distribution, in order to determine the probabilities of accepting lots of various quality levels.

EXERCISES

The answers to the odd-numbered exercises are at the end of the book.

15. McBurger fast food restaurants fill their soft drinks with an automatic machine that works based on the weight of the soft drink. When the process is in control, the machine fills

each cup so that the grand mean is 10.0 ounces and the mean range is 0.25 ounce for samples of size 5.

a. Determine the upper and lower control limits for the process.

b. The manager of the I-280 store tested five soft drinks served during the last hour and found that the mean was 10.16 ounces and the range was 0.35 ounce. Is the process in control? Should action be taken?

16. The Clean City Police Department maintains records on crimes per 1,000 residents in its various precincts. The mean is 4.00 crimes per 1,000 residents.
    a. Determine control chart limits for the number of crimes per precinct.
    b. Last month there were 11.3 crimes committed per 1,000 residents in Willoughby Hills. Does crime seem to be out of control in Willoughby Hills?

17. The Early Morning delivery service guarantees delivery of its packages by 10:30 A.M. Of course, all packages do not meet this standard. For a sample of 200 packages delivered each of the last 15 working days, the following numbers were delivered after 10:30: 9, 14, 2, 13, 9, 5, 9, 3, 4, 3, 4, 3, 3, 8, 4.
    a. Determine the mean proportion of packages delivered after 10:30 A.M.
    b. Determine the upper and lower control limits for the proportion of packages delivered after 10:30 A.M.
    c. If 10 packages out of 200 were delivered after 10:30 A.M. today, does this exceed the usual standard?

18. Eric's Cookie House sells chocolate chip cookies in shopping malls. Of concern is the number of chocolate chips in each cookie. Eric, the owner and president, would like to establish a control chart for the number of chocolate chips per cookie. He selected a sample of 10 cookies from today's production and counted the number of chocolate chips in each of the sampled cookies. The results are: 15, 18, 15, 4, 14, 18, 9, 17, 12, 15. What are the appropriate control limits?

19. A mean chart and a range chart are to be designed. Every hour a quality-control technician measures the thickness of the part and records the measurements. She also computes the mean thickness of the four parts and determines the range. After 30 hours had elapsed, the sum of the 30 means was computed to be 1,356 inches and the sum of the ranges 375 inches. Assume that the process is in control.
    a. Determine the centerline, the upper control limit, and the lower control limit for the X bar chart.
    b. Determine the centerline, the upper control limit, and the lower control limit for the range chart.

20. A glass manufacturer installed a new furnace and automatic equipment to make clear glass bowls. One of the problems associated with glassmaking is the appearance of unwanted stones. (Stones are small bubbles in the glass, which are considered imperfections if over a specified diameter.)

    To monitor the number of stones per bowl, a quality-control inspector selected 15 bowls at random and counted the number of stones over 1.5 millimeters in diameter in each bowl. The number of stones per bowl were 14, 15, 10, 10, 14, 13, 12, 10, 11, 12, 9, 12, 12, 8, and 21.
    a. Construct a chart specifically designed to monitor the number of defects per unit. Show essential figures on the chart.
    b. Plot the number of imperfections for the 15 bowls selected at random.
    c. Interpret your chart.

21. An automatic machine produces 5.0 millimeter bolts at a high rate of speed. A quality-control program has been started to control the number of defectives. The quality-control inspector selects 50 bolts at random and determines how many are defective. The numbers defective for the first 10 samples follow.

Sample number	Size of sample	Number of defects
1	50	3
2	50	5
3	50	0
4	50	4
5	50	1
6	50	2
7	50	6
8	50	5
9	50	7
10	50	7

a. Design a percent defective chart. Insert $\bar{p}$, LCL, and the percents defective on the chart.
b. Plot the number of defects for the first 10 samples on the chart.
c. Interpret the chart.

22. A new machine has just been installed to cut and rough-shape large slugs. The slugs are then transferred to a precision grinder. One critical measurement is the outside diameter. The quality-control inspector was instructed to select five slugs at random every half hour from the output of the new machine, measure the outside diameter, and record the results. The measurements (in millimeters) for the period from 8:00 A.M. to 10:30 A.M. follow.

	Outside diameter (millimeters)				
Time	1	2	3	4	5
8:00 A.M.	87.1	87.3	87.9	87.0	87.0
8:30 A.M.	86.9	88.5	87.6	87.5	87.4
9:00 A.M.	87.5	88.4	86.9	87.6	88.2
9:30 A.M.	86.0	88.0	87.2	87.6	87.1
10:00 A.M.	87.1	87.1	87.1	87.1	87.1
10:30 A.M.	88.0	86.2	87.4	87.3	87.8

a. Design a mean chart. Insert the control limits and other essential figures on the chart.
b. Plot the means on the chart.
c. Immediately below the mean chart, draw a range chart. Plot the ranges on the chart.
d. Interpret the two charts.

23. The numbers of near misses recorded for the last 20 months at the Lima International Airport are shown below. Develop an appropriate control chart. What would you conclude from a general upward trend, even though the upper control limit was not reached?

Month	Near misses	Month	Near misses
1	3	11	5
2	2	12	2
3	1	13	3
4	4	14	1
5	5	15	1
6	0	16	3
7	1	17	3
8	3	18	2
9	0	19	3
10	2	20	3

24. At the beginning of each football season Team Sports, the local sporting goods store, purchases 5,000 footballs. A sample of 25 balls is selected, and they are inflated, tested, and then deflated. If more than two balls are found defective, the lot of 5,000 is returned to the manufacturer. Develop an OC curve for this sampling plan.
    a. What are the probabilities of accepting lots that are 10 percent, 20 percent, and 30 percent defective?
    b. Estimate the probability of accepting a lot that is 15 percent defective.
    c. John Brennen, owner of Team Sports, would like the probability of accepting a lot that is 5 percent defective to be more than 90 percent. Does this appear to be the case with this sampling plan?
25. Marchal Screen Door Manufacturing Company purchases door latches from a number of vendors. The purchasing department is responsible for inspecting the incoming latches. Marchal purchases 10,000 door latches per month and inspects 20 latches selected at random. Develop an OC curve for the sampling plan if three latches can be defective and the incoming lot is still accepted.

CHAPTER 16 EXAMINATION

The answers are at the end of the chapter.

For Questions 1 through 3 fill in the blank with the correct answer.

1. Percent defective and *c* bar charts are examples of ________ (attribute or variable) control charts.
2. In a percent defective chart the underlying distribution is the ________ .
3. A *c* bar chart is based on the number of ________ .

Questions 4 through 10 are based on Charts A, B, and C.

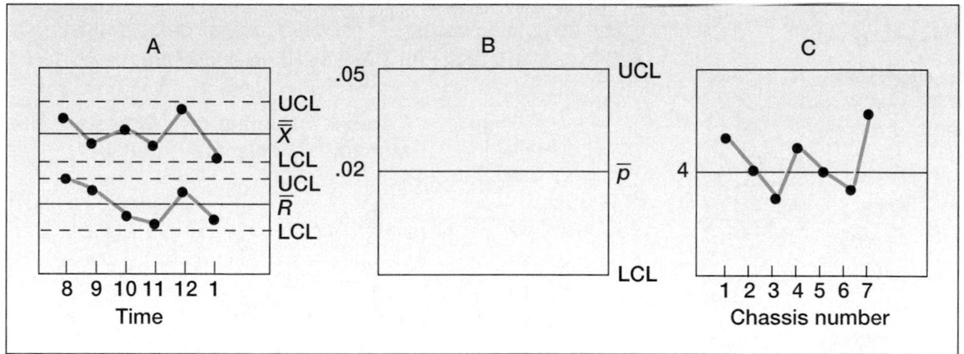

4. Chart A combines which two charts?
5. For Chart A, is the process in control or out of control?
6. What will Chart B be called when its construction is completed?
7. Referring again to Chart B, what is the lower control limit?
8. Referring to Chart C, based on past experience, how many defects are there per chassis on the average?
9. What is Chart C called?
10. What are the upper and lower control limits of Chart C?
11. The quality-control inspector checks five pieces of the output of a shearing machine every hour. She measures and records each piece to the nearest hundredth of an inch. The record for the first four hours is:

Time	1	2	3	4	5
8 A.M.	6.04	6.01	6.05	6.02	6.06
9 A.M.	6.01	6.02	6.03	6.02	6.02
10 A.M.	6.01	6.05	6.07	6.03	6.04
11 A.M.	6.02	6.04	6.04	6.03	6.02

a. Design an *X* bar chart, and plot the essential data for the four hours.
b. Design a range chart, and plot the essential data for the four hours.

12. The quality-control inspector from the previous problem goes to another operation, where she checks 200 pieces. The piece is either good or defective. The record for nine hours is:

Time	Number of pieces checked	Number of defects
8 A.M.	200	0
9 A.M.	200	3
10 A.M.	200	4
11 A.M.	200	0
12 P.M.	200	5
1 P.M.	200	2
2 P.M.	200	0
3 P.M.	200	1
4 P.M.	200	3

a. Design a percent defective chart, and plot the essential data.
b. Interpret the chart.

13. A new assembly operation has just been started. A small group of assembly-line employees inserts parts, solders, and performs other tasks to produce a radio chassis. The completed chassis is checked, and all defects must be repaired. The numbers of defects per chassis for the first 10 produced are:

Chassis number	Number of defects	Chassis number	Number of defects
1	0	6	0
2	1	7	1
3	0	8	1
4	2	9	2
5	3	10	4

a. Design a $\bar{c}$ chart, and plot the essential data.
b. Interpret the chart.

14. Seiko purchases watch stems for their watches in lots of 10,000. Seiko's sampling plan calls for checking 20 stems, and if 3 or fewer stems are defective, the lot is accepted.
a. Based on their sampling plan, what is the probability that a lot of 40 percent defective will be accepted?
b. Design an OC curve for incoming lots that have zero, 10 percent, 20 percent, 30 percent, and 40 percent defective stems.

CHAPTER 16 Answers

Self-Review

16–1

Sample piece						
1	2	3	4	Total	Average	Range
1	4	5	2	12	3	4
2	3	2	1	8	2	2
1	7	3	5	16	4	6
					9	12

$$\bar{\bar{X}} = \frac{9}{3} = 3$$

$$\bar{R} = \frac{12}{3} = 4$$

$$\text{UCL and LCL} = \bar{\bar{X}} \pm A_2\bar{R}$$

$$= 3 \pm 0.729(4)$$

$$\text{UCL} = 5.916$$

$$\text{LCL} = 0.084$$

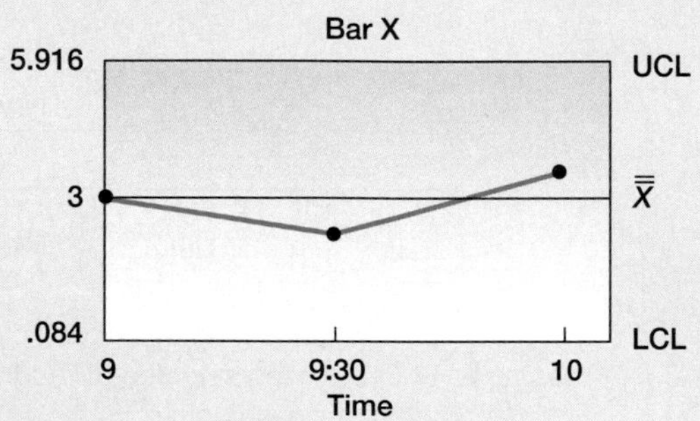

16–2 1.

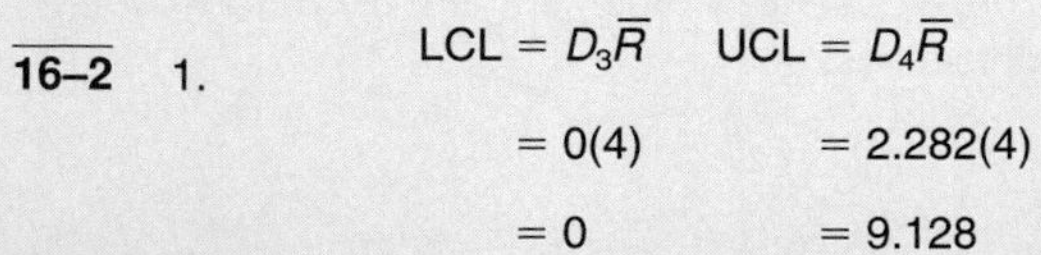

$$\text{LCL} = D_3\bar{R} \qquad \text{UCL} = D_4\bar{R}$$

$$= 0(4) \qquad = 2.282(4)$$

$$= 0 \qquad = 9.128$$

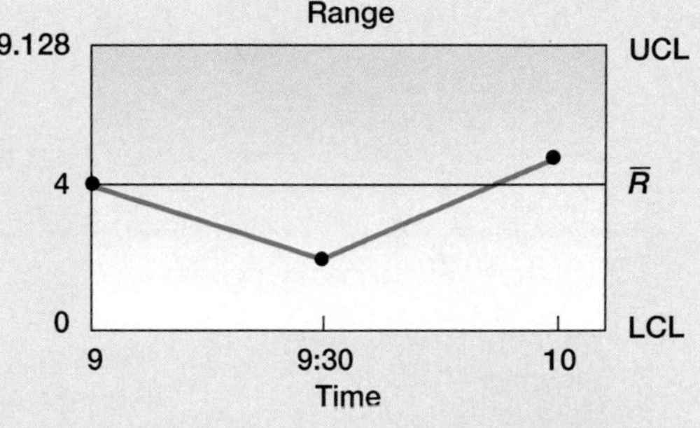

2. Yes. Both the mean chart (Self-Review 16–1) and the range chart indicate that the process is in control.

16–3

Day	Number checked	Number defective	Percent defective
1	200	4	.020
2	200	3	.015
3	200	5	.025
4	200	4	.020
			.080

$$\bar{p} = \frac{.08}{4} = .02$$

$$\text{UCL and LCL} = .02 \pm 3\sqrt{\frac{.02(.98)}{200}}$$

$$= .02 \pm .0297$$

$$= .0497 \text{ and } 0$$

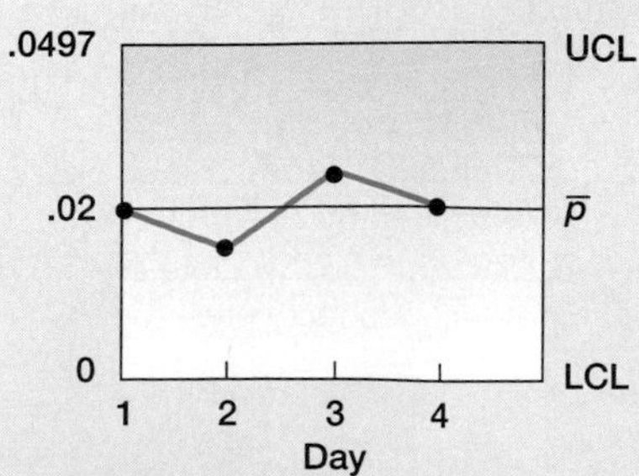

16–4 1. $\bar{c} = 40/10 = 4.0$

$$\text{UCL and LCL} = \bar{c} \pm 3\sqrt{\bar{c}} = 4 \pm 3\sqrt{4}$$
$$= 10, -2 \text{ (or 0)}$$

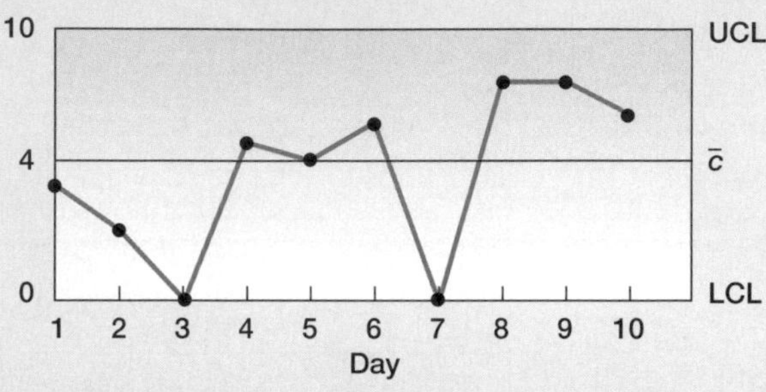

16–5 Using Appendix A

$$P(x \leq 2 \mid p = .30 \text{ and } n = 20) = .036$$

Chapter Examination

1. Attribute.
2. Binomial.
3. Defects per unit.
4. A mean chart and a range chart.
5. In control.
6. A percent defective chart.
7. Zero.
8. 4.
9. A chart for the number of defects per unit, called a *c* bar chart.
10. 10 and 0, found by $4 \pm 3\sqrt{4}$.
11. *a.* UCL and LCL are 6.0531375 inches and 6.0098625 inches, respectively, found by $\bar{\bar{X}} \pm A_2\bar{R} = 6.0315 \pm 0.577(0.0375)$. Plots are 6.036, 6.020, 6.04, and 6.03, respectively.

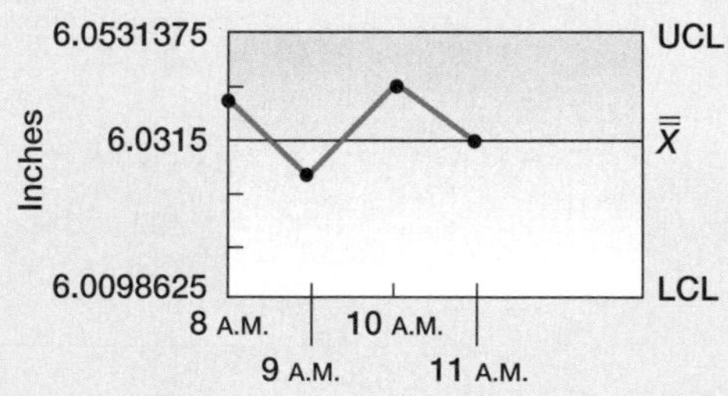

b. UCL and LCL for the range chart are 0.0793125 and 0, found by $D_4\bar{R} = (2.115)(0.0375)$ and $D_3\bar{R} = (0)(0.0375)$. Plots are 0.05, 0.02, 0.06, and 0.02, respectively.

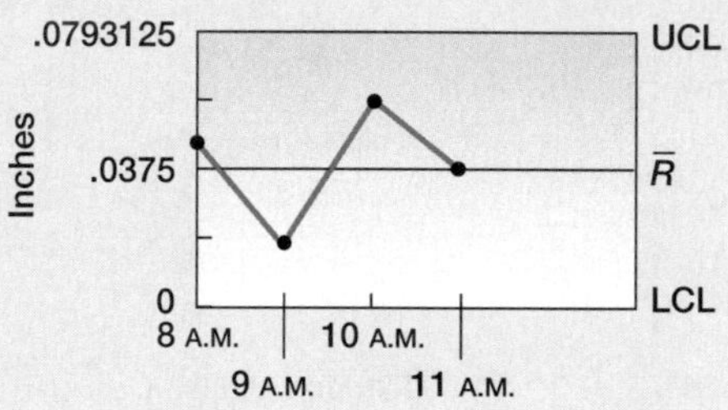

12. *a.* UCL and LCL are 3.1108 and 0 percent, found by:

$$.01 \pm 3\sqrt{\frac{(.01)(.99)}{200}}$$

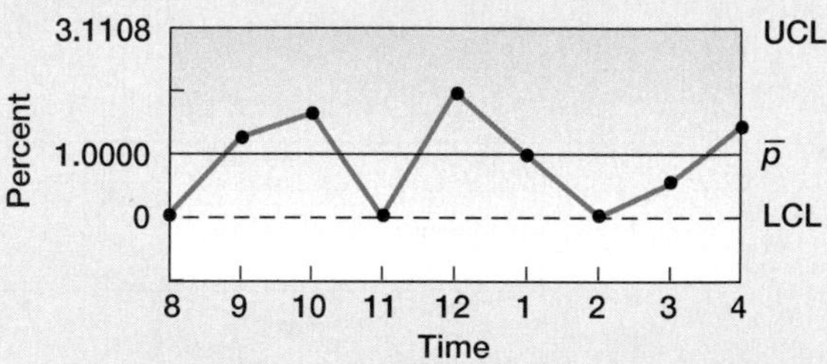

b. If production continues, as evidenced by the nine samples of 200 pieces selected at random, then the average percent defective will be 1.0 percent. More than 99 percent of the samples of 200 will contain between 0 percent and 3.1108 percent defectives.

13. *a.* UCL and LCL for the $\bar{c}$ chart are 4.949648 and 0, found by $\bar{c} \pm 3\sqrt{\bar{c}} = 1.4 \pm 3(1.83216)$.

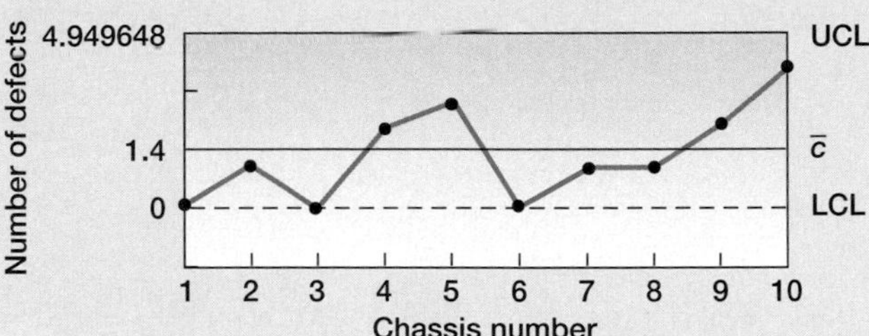

b. If the assembly process continues as evidenced by the first 10 produced, more than 99 percent of the chassis will have between 0 and 4.949648 defects. The mean will be 1.4 defects per chassis.

14. *a.* .015, found by .012 + .003.

b.

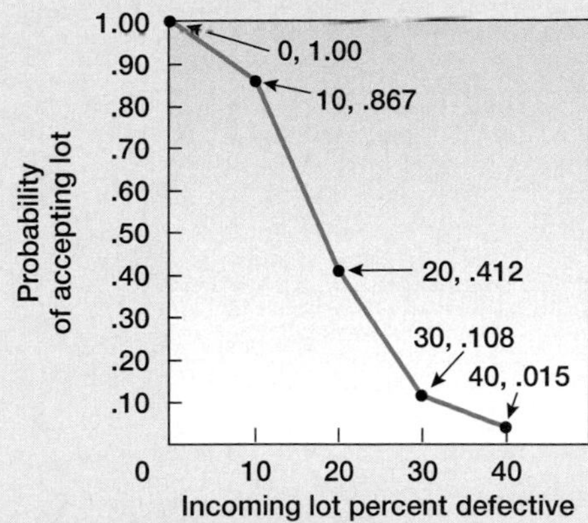

Chapter 17 Index Numbers

GOALS

When you have completed this chapter, you will be able to:

1
Indicate why millions of dollars are spent yearly constructing and publishing indexes.

2
Construct unweighted and weighted indexes.

3
Construct a price, quantity, value, and special-purpose index.

4
Explain how the Consumer Price Index is constructed and used.

5
Cite the special applications of the Consumer Price Index in determining real income, deflating sales, and determining the purchasing power of the dollar.

An index of clothing and shoe prices for 1995 needs to be prepared. Given the prices and quantities consumed in 1982, what is the weighted index of price for 1995? (See Goal 2 and Self-Review 17–3.)

INTRODUCTION

In this chapter we will examine a useful descriptive tool called an **index.** No doubt you are familiar with indexes such as the **Consumer Price Index,** which is released monthly. There are many other indexes, such as the Dow Jones Industrial Average and Standard & Poor's 500 Stock Average. Indexes are published on a regular basis by the federal government and by business publications such as *Business Week* and *Forbes.*

Of what importance is an index? Why is the Consumer Price Index so important and so widely reported? As the name implies, it measures the change in the price of a large group of items consumers purchase. The Federal Reserve Board, consumer groups, unions, management, senior citizens organizations, and others in business and economics are very concerned about changes in prices. The Consumer Price Index and the **Producer Price Index** (formerly the **Wholesale Price Index**), which measures price fluctuations at all stages of production, are closely watched by these groups. To combat sharp price increases, the Federal Reserve often raises the interest rate to "cool down" the economy. Likewise, the Dow Jones Industrial Average, which is published daily, describes the overall change in common stock prices of 30 large companies during the day.

According to a recent newspaper article, "IBM and other companies whose second-quarter profits beat the predictions of Wall Street prognosticators were rewarded Thursday by investors who sent their stocks up strongly. Thanks to IBM, the Dow Jones industrial average gained 5.18 points to close at 3,732.45. Broader market averages, such as the Standard & Poor's 500, were also up slightly."[1]

A few stock market indexes that appear daily in the financial section of most newspapers are:[2]

[1]Sarasota (Florida) *Herald Tribune,* July 22, 1994, p. D2.

[2]Sarasota (Florida) *Herald Tribune,* July 24, 1994, p. D3.

INDEX SUMMARY

Dow Jones Industrials	3735.04	− 18.77
S&P 500	453.11	− 1.05
NYSE Composite	250.24	− 0.82
Amex Index	433.45	+ 1.90
NASD Composite	716.68	− 4.68
NMS Composite	318.09	− 1.24
Value Line Geometric	280.03	− 1.22
Value Line Arithmetic	446.42	− 1.44

Wilshire 5000 was $4,481.767 billion, off $17.615 billion.

STANDARD & POORS

	High	Low	Close	Chg.
Indust	530.44	526.43	528.49	− 0.48
Transpt	388.84	384.45	386.13	− 1.52
Utilities	155.85	155.28	155.44	− 0.41
Financi	45.32	44.51	44.60	− 0.49
MidCap 400	170.19	168.51	168.74	− 1.40
500 Stocks	455.22	451.60	453.11	− 1.05
100 Stocks	421.81	418.88	420.65	− 1.04

	Close	Chg.	Yr. Ago
Value Line			
Geometric	280.03	− 1.22	276.63
Arithmetic	446.42	− 1.44	416.35
Russell 2,000	243.33	− 2.29	234.31

Of interest to economists, governments, industry, retailers, and other businesses is the **Index of Consumer Sentiment.** It records the confidence Americans have in the economy. As an example:[3]

NEW YORK

Confidence weakens

Consumer confidence in the economy weakened slightly in July as Americans turned more pessimistic about future business conditions and job opportunities, the Conference Board reported Tuesday.

Still, consumer confidence remains close to the highest levels in four years and reflects a continuation of the steady, moderate growth that has characterized the U.S. economy in recent months, the research group said.

Its index of consumer sentiment eased to 91.6 this month from 92.5 in June. The index, calculated on a 1985 base of 100, is derived from responses to a questionnaire sent to 5,000 households nationwide.

Other nations are equally concerned with price rises. As an illustration, a headline in the *South China Morning Post* was "Price Rises Hit Inflation Battle Plan."[4] A passage from the accompanying article emphasizes the concern for the high inflation rate in Hong Kong.

> The Government's fight against inflation is continuing to spin off course with the latest monthly figures showing a mild acceleration in price rises. Strong increases in the cost of fresh food, services and housing all pushed the main indicator of retail inflation, the Consumer Price Index (A) which covers low income families, up by 12.7 percent in August. Drought and flooding in China is blamed for the extra cost of foodstuffs. However, in terms of CPI (A) alcoholic drinks and tobacco recorded the single largest year-on-year increase at 42.1 percent.
>
> Consumer Price Index (B), which covers households with slightly higher incomes, rose by 12.0 percent during August. The Hang Seng Consumer Price Index, which covers high income households, rose by 10.9 percent.

[3]Sarasota (Florida) *Herald Tribune,* July 27, 1994, p. D2.

[4]*South China Morning Post,* September 27, 1991, p. 1.

What is an index number?

What is an index?

> **Index number** A number that measures the relative change in price, quantity, value, or some other item of interest from one time period to another.

SIMPLE INDEX NUMBERS

If an index number is used to measure the relative change in just one variable—such as hourly wages in manufacturing—we refer to it as a **simple index number.** It is merely the ratio of two values of the variable converted to a percentage.

The following four examples involve simple index numbers.

EXAMPLE

As noted in the above definition, the main use of an index number in business is to show the percent change in one or more items from one time period to another. To illustrate, the average hourly wage in manufacturing in 1980 was \$7.27, according to the Bureau of Labor Statistics. In March 1994 it was \$12.01. What is the index of hourly earnings in manufacturing for March 1994 based on 1980?

Solution

Wages increased

▶ It is 165.2, found by:

$$\frac{\text{Hourly earnings in March 1994}}{\text{Hourly earnings in 1980}} \times 100 = \frac{\$12.01}{\$7.27} \times 100 = 165.2$$

Thus, hourly earnings in manufacturing in 1994 compared with 1980 were 165.2 percent; that is, they increased 65.2 percent during that period, found by 165.2 − 100.

EXAMPLE

The Bureau of the Census reported that the farm population dropped from 30,529,000 in 1930 to an estimated 5,100,000 in 1994. What is the index of farm population for 1994 based on 1930?

Solution

▶ The index is 16.7, found by

$$\frac{\text{1994 population}}{\text{1930 population}} \times 100 = \frac{5{,}100{,}000}{30{,}529{,}000} \times 100 = 16.7$$

This indicates that the farm population in 1994 compared with 1930 was 16.7 percent, or it decreased 83.3 percent during the period, found by 100.0 − 16.7.

EXAMPLE

An example can also be used to compare one thing with another: The population of the Canadian province of British Columbia is estimated to be 3,044,200; for Ontario, 9,546,200. What is the population of British Columbia compared with that of Ontario?

Solution

▶ The index of population for British Columbia is 31.9, found by:

$$\frac{\text{Population of British Columbia}}{\text{Population of Ontario}} \times 100 = \frac{3{,}044{,}200}{9{,}546{,}200} \times 100 = 31.9$$

This indicates that the population of British Columbia is 31.9 percent (about one third) of the population of Ontario, or the population of British Columbia is 68.1 percent less than the population of Ontario (100.0 − 31.9 = 68.1).

EXAMPLE

The number of passengers arriving and departing at Chicago's O'Hare International Airport, the largest in the United States, is 65,091,168 a year; for the eighth largest, JFK in New York, the number is 26,796,036.[5] What is the arrival and departure rate for O'Hare compared with that of JFK, expressed as an index?

Solution

▶ The index for O'Hare is 242.9, found by:

$$\frac{\text{Arrive/depart O'Hare}}{\text{Arrive/depart JFK}} \times 100 = \frac{65{,}091{,}168}{26{,}796{,}036}(100) = 242.9$$

This indicates that the number of arrivals and departures from Chicago's O'Hare is 242.9 percent of that of New York's JFK; that is, O'Hare's arrival and departure rate is 142.9 percent greater than that for JFK.

Note from the previous discussion that:

1. The index of hourly earnings in manufacturing (165.2) and the index of farm population (16.7) are actually percents. The percent sign, however, is usually omitted.

Base period

2. Each index number has a **base.** Until recently the **base period** for most indexes compiled and published by the federal government was 1967, written "1967 = 100." However, this has changed, and indexes now have various base periods. As examples, the Consumer Price Index now has a 1982–84 base period. The U.S. import and export price indexes have 1977 as the base period. The Producer Price Index uses 1982 = 100, and the parity ratio, which is an index—the ratio of prices received by farmers to prices paid by the farmers—still has 1910–14 as the base period.

SELF-REVIEW 17–1

The answers are at the end of the chapter.

1. The average hourly earnings in mining in March 1994 were $14.85. In 1979 they were $8.49. Express the average hourly earnings in 1994 as an index using the 1979 average as the base (denominator). Interpret.
2. The annual sales of a few selected industrial corporations are:

Rank	Company	Sales ($ millions)
1	GM	101,781.9
2	Exxon	76,416.0
3	Ford	71,643.4
4	IBM	54,217.0
10	Chrysler	26,257.7

   a. Express the annual sales of General Motors as an index using the sales of International Business Machines as the base (denominator). Interpret.
   b. Express the annual sales of Chrysler as an index using the sales of IBM as the base. Interpret.

[5] *Universal Almanac,* 1995, p. 287.

Base number for most indexes is 100.0

3. The **base number** of most indexes is 100.0. Thus, when we computed the index of hourly earnings in manufacturing for 1994 based on 1980, we divided $12.01 by $7.27 and then multiplied the quotient of 1.652 by 100. This gave us the index of 165.2, which is easy to interpret: the average hourly earnings in manufacturing increased 65.2 percent from 1980 to 1994. There is no reason, however, why 10, 50, 1,000, or any other number cannot be used as the base number. In fact, the New York Stock Exchange index has December 31, 1965 = 50. Standard & Poor's Corporation Index uses 1941–43 as the base period and 10 as the base, written 1941–43 = 10. And the American Stock Exchange uses August 31, 1973 = 50.

4. Most business and economic indexes are carried either to the nearest whole percent, such as 312 or 96, or to the nearest tenth of a percent, such as 97.5 or 178.6.

WHY CONVERT DATA TO INDEXES?

Indexes allow us to express a change in price, quantity, or value as a percent

Compiling index numbers is not a recent innovation. An Italian, G. R. Carli, has been credited with originating the first index numbers in 1764. They were incorporated in a report he made regarding price fluctuations in Europe from 1500 to 1750. No systematic approach to collecting and reporting data in index form was evident in the United States until about 1900. The cost-of-living index (now called the Consumer Price Index) was introduced in 1913, and a long list of indexes have been compiled since then.

Why convert data to indexes? An index is a convenient way of expressing a change in a heterogeneous group of items. The Consumer Price Index (CPI), for example, encompasses about 400 items—including golf balls, lawn mowers, hamburgers, funeral services, and dentists' fees. Prices are expressed in dollars per pound, box, yard, and many other different units. Only by converting the prices of these many diverse goods and services to one index number every month can the federal government and others concerned with inflation keep informed of the overall movement of consumer prices.

Converting data to indexes also makes it easier to assess the trend in a series composed of exceptionally large numbers. For example, suppose retail sales for the first six months of 1995 were $185,679,432,621.87 and 1982 six-month sales were $185,500,000,000.00. The increase of $179,432,621.87 appears significant. Yet if the 1995 sales total were expressed as an index based on 1982 sales, the increase would be less than one tenth of 1 percent!

$$\frac{\text{Retail sales in 1995}}{\text{Retail sales in 1982}} = \frac{\$185{,}679{,}432{,}621.87}{\$185{,}500{,}000{,}000.00} \times 100 = 100.09$$

TYPES OF INDEX NUMBERS

An index can be classified as a **price index,** a **quantity index,** a **value index,** or a **special-purpose index.** A few examples of the four types of indexes published on a regular basis follow.

Price Indexes

Some important indexes

Consumer Price Index. Actually, there are two consumer price indexes, one for all urban consumers and the other for urban wage earners and clerical workers.

Also, there are separate indexes to show the changes in the price of food, transportation, and so on (1982–84 = 100).

Producer Price Index. This measures the average change in prices received in the primary markets of the United States by producers of commodities in all stages of processing (1982 = 100).

U.S. import and export prices indexes. These are published in the *Monthly Labor Review* (1990 = 100).

Quantity Indexes

Federal Reserve Board indexes of quantity output. In addition, there are output indexes by market grouping and industry grouping. They are published monthly in the *Survey of Current Business.*

Value Indexes

Value-of-construction contracts awarded in 50 states.

McCann-Erickson Advertising Index. Subdivided into network TV, spot TV, magazine, and newspaper, this index is reported monthly in the *Survey of Current Business.*

Special-Purpose Indexes

There are several indexes that reflect the overall economic activity in the United States. The federal government puts out an index of leading economic indicators (1987 = 100). It includes such diverse economic indicators as stock prices, new orders for plant and equipment, and building permits issued. Another such index, the Forbes index, combines production, department store sales, and several other business indicators. *Business Week* has what it calls a "leading index." It consists of such business and economic indicators as stock prices, bond yields, material prices, number of business failures, and real estate loans.

CONSTRUCTION OF INDEX NUMBERS

We already discussed the construction of a simple price index. The price in a selected year (such as 1995) is divided by the price in the base year.

The base-period price is designated as p_0, and a price other than the base period is often referred to as the *given period* or *selected period* and designated p_t. To calculate the simple price index P for any given period:

$$P = \frac{p_t}{p_0}(100) \qquad (17\text{–}1)$$

Suppose that the price of a standard lot at the Shady Rest Cemetery in 1982 was \$450. The price rose to \$795 in 1995. What is the price index for 1995 using 1982 as the base period? It is 176.7, found by:

$$P = \frac{p_t}{p_0}(100) = \frac{\$795}{\$450}(100) = 176.7$$

Interpreting this result, the price of a cemetery lot increased 76.7 percent from 1982 to 1995.

The base period need not be a single year. Note in Table 17–1 that if we use 1970–71 = 100, the base price for the stapler would be $21 [found by determining the mean price of 1970 and 1971, ($20 + $22)/2 = $21]. The prices $20, $22, and $23 would be averaged if 1970–72 had been selected as the base. The mean price would be $21.67. The indexes constructed using the three different base periods are presented in Table 17–1. (Note that when 1970–72 = 100, the index numbers for 1970, 1971, and 1972 average 100.0, as we would expect.) Logically, the index numbers for 1995 using the three different bases are not the same.

Table 17–1 Prices of a Benson Automatic Stapler, Model 3, Converted to Indexes Using Three Different Base Periods

Year	Price of stapler	Price index (1970 = 100)	Price index (1970–71 = 100)	Price index (1970–72 = 100)
1965	$18	90.0	$\frac{18}{21} \times 100 = 85.7$	$\frac{18}{21.67} \times 100 = 83.1$
1970	20	100.0	$\frac{20}{21} \times 100 = 95.2$	$\frac{20}{21.67} \times 100 = 92.3$
1971	22	110.0	$\frac{22}{21} \times 100 = 104.8$	$\frac{22}{21.67} \times 100 = 101.5$
1972	23	115.0	$\frac{23}{21} \times 100 = 109.5$	$\frac{23}{21.67} \times 100 = 106.1$
1995	38	190.0	$\frac{38}{21} \times 100 = 181.0$	$\frac{38}{21.67} \times 100 = 175.4$

SELF-REVIEW 17–2

The answers are at the end of the chapter.

The average hourly earnings in retail trade for selected periods are:

Year	Average hourly earnings
1968	$2.16
1969	2.30
1970	2.44
1994 (Apr.)	7.45

Source: U.S. Department of Labor, *Monthly Labor Review,* June 1988, p. 85; and June 1994, p. 79.

1. Using 1968 as the base period, determine an index number for April 1994 that might aptly be called the index of average hourly earnings in retail trade. Interpret.
2. Using the average of 1968 and 1969 (that is, 1968–69 = 100), determine the index for March 1994.
3. What is the index for 1968 using 1970 = 100? Interpret.

A slightly more complex problem is to determine a price index for several foods for 1995, using 1977 = 100. Assume for the illustration below that the typical family eats only three food items: milk, bread, and avocados. Using the foregoing procedure for calculating simple indexes, we find that the index of food prices for 1995 (see Table 17–2) would be 122.9 (1977 is the base period). The index for 1995 was computed by dividing the total of the prices for 1995 by the total of the 1977 prices.

TABLE 17–2 Computation of an Index of Food Prices for 1995

Item	1977 price, p_0	1995 price, p_t
Milk (quart)	$0.64	$0.61
Bread (small loaf)	0.65	0.59
Avocado (each)	0.50	1.00
Total	$1.79	$2.20

The index of price, using formula (17–1) and adjusting it to include all three items, is:

$$P = \frac{\Sigma p_t}{\Sigma p_0}(100) = \frac{\$2.20}{\$1.79}(100) = 122.9$$

The price index of 122.9, however, seems illogical because the two major food items *declined* in price from 1977 to 1995; only the price of avocados increased. Avocados are eaten only infrequently by most consumers. It seems, therefore, that the prices of bread and milk should be given more weight (importance) than the price of avocados.

Also, the simple method of computing an index illustrated in the preceding problem does not meet the *units test.* This means that if the items were quoted in different units, the answer would be different from 122.9. For example, if the price of milk were quoted in gallons instead of quarts, and if avocados were quoted by the box instead of singly, the price index would probably not be 122.9. Because of these inadequacies, the simple method is seldom used in actual practice for this type of problem. Instead the weighted method, described in the following section, is applied.

Weighted Indexes

Two methods of computing a **weighted price index** are the **Laspeyres** method and the **Paasche** method. They differ only with respect to the period used for weighting. The Laspeyres method uses *base-period weights*; that is, the original prices and quantities of the items bought are used to find the percent change over a period of time in either price or quantity consumed, depending on the problem. The Paasche method uses *current-year weights* for the denominator of the weighted index.

Laspeyres' Price Index Etienne Laspeyres developed a method in the latter part of the 18th century to determine a weighted index using base-period weights. Applying his method, a weighted price index is computed by:

$$P = \frac{\Sigma p_t q_0}{\Sigma p_0 q_0}(100) \qquad (17\text{–}2)$$

where:

P is the price index.
p_t is the current price.
p_0 is the price in the base period.
q_0 is the quantity consumed in the base period.

EXAMPLE

Laspeyres method uses base-period weights

The prices of three foods for 1977 and 1995 and the quantities consumed by a typical consumer in 1977 are:

Item	1977 price, p_0	1977 amount consumed, q_0	1995 price, p_t
Milk (quart)	\$0.64	100	\$0.61
Bread (small loaf)	0.65	1,000	0.59
Avocado (each)	0.50	1	1.00

What is the weighted index of price for 1995 using 1977 = 100?

Solution ▸ The total amount spent for food by the typical consumer in the base period, 1977, is determined first. The total amount spent on the three food items was \$714.50 (see Table 17–3). In measuring the effect of price, *it is assumed that the amount of food consumed did not change between the base period (1977)* and 1995. Thus, to find how much the typical consumer spent on food in 1995, the 1995 prices are multiplied by the corresponding quantities consumed in the original year of 1977. The total is \$652.00.

TABLE 17–3 **Computation of a Weighted Price Index for 1995 Using the Laspeyres Method (1977 = 100)**

Item	1977 price, p_0	1977 amount consumed, q_0	p_0q_0	1995 price, p_t	p_tq_0
Milk (quart)	\$0.64	100	\$ 64.00	\$0.61	\$ 61.00
Bread (small loaf)	0.65	1,000	650.00	0.59	590.00
Avocado (each)	0.50	1	0.50	1.00	1.00
			\$714.50		\$652.00

The weighted index of price for 1995 is 91.3, found by:

$$P = \frac{\Sigma p_t q_0}{\Sigma p_0 q_0}(100) = \frac{\$652.00}{\$714.50}(100) = 91.3$$

Index of 91.3 means overall price declined 8.7 percent from 1977 to 1995

Based on this analysis, the average price of food *declined* about 8.7 percent from 1977 to 1995. The weighted method results in a more logical answer (91.3) than the simple index (122.9), which indicated an *increase* of about 23 percent in the price of food.

Both prices weighted by amount consumed in base period (1977)

Note that the weighted method, alternatively called the *weighted aggregative method,* uses the amounts consumed in the *base period* (q_0) as weights. It assumes that the eating habits of the typical consumer did not change from 1977 to 1995. Thus, *only price* fluctuated, causing a decrease in the index from 100 in the base period to 91.3 in 1995.

SELF-REVIEW 17–3

The answers are at the end of the chapter.

An index of clothing prices for 1995 based on 1982 is to be constructed. The prices for 1982 and 1995 and the quantity consumed in 1982 are shown below.

Item	1982 price	1982 amount sold	1995 price
Dress (each)	$35	500	$65
Shoes (pair)	40	1,200	90

1. Assuming that the number sold remained constant—that is, the same number were sold in 1995 as in 1982—what is the weighted index of price for 1995 using 1982 as the base?
2. Interpret.

EXERCISES

The answers to the odd-numbered exercises are at the end of the book.

1. Suppose the average purchase prices and loan amounts on conventional mortgages on new homes for selected years are:

Year	Purchase price	Amount of loan
1981	$ 90,400	$65,300
1982	94,600	69,800
1983	92,800	69,500
1994	115,500	87,200

   a. Using 1981 as the base period, what is the index of the purchase price of a new home for 1994? Interpret.

   b. Using 1981–82 = 100, what is the index of the amount of the loan on conventional mortgages for 1994? Interpret.

2. The hourly earnings in selected durable-goods manufacturing groups for December 1979 and April 1994 are:

Manufacturing group	Hourly earnings December 1979	April 1994
Lumber and wood products	$6.24	$ 9.75
Furniture and fixtures	5.26	9.47
Stone, clay, and glass	7.11	11.99
Instruments and related products	6.50	12.46

Source: U.S. Department of Labor, *Monthly Labor Review,* February 1981, Table 17; and June 1994, p. 79.

a. Convert the hourly earnings for April 1994 to indexes for each of the four groups, using December 1979 = 100.
b. Interpret your findings.

3. Fruit prices and the amounts of fruit consumed for 1983 and 1995 are:

Fruit	Price 1983	Amount consumed 1983	Price 1995
Bananas (pound)	$0.23	100	$0.35
Grapefruit (each)	0.29	50	0.27
Apples (pound)	0.35	85	0.35
Strawberries (basket)	1.02	8	1.69
Oranges (bag)	0.89	6	0.99

a. Assuming that the amounts of fruit consumed did not change between 1983 and 1995, determine the weighted index of price using the Laspeyres method for 1995 (1983 = 100).
b. Interpret your findings.

4. The prices and numbers of various items produced by a small machine and stamping plant for January 1982 and the prices of these items for January 1995 are:

Item	January 1982		January 1995 price
	Price	Number produced	
Washer	$0.07	17,000	$0.10
Cotter pin	0.04	125,000	0.03
Stove bolt	0.15	40,000	0.15
Hex nut	0.08	62,000	0.05

a. Assuming that the numbers produced did not change between January 1982 and January 1995, determine the weighted index of price for January 1995 using the Laspeyres method and January 1982 as the base period.
b. Interpret your findings.

Laspeyres' Quantity Index The Laspeyres method of weighting is also used to compute a *weighted quantity index.* The procedure is similar to the method of constructing a weighted price index, except that the original *base-year prices* are used as weights instead of base-year quantities. The formula for a weighted quantity index, designated Q, is:

$$Q = \frac{\Sigma p_0 q_t}{\Sigma p_0 q_0}(100) \qquad (17\text{–}3)$$

where:

Q is the weighted quantity index.
p_0 is the original price in the base period.
q_0 is the original quantity consumed in the base period.
q_t is the current quantity consumed.

EXAMPLE

The prices of selected commodities for 1983 and the quantities mined in 1983 and 1994 follow.

Commodity	1983 price, p_0	1983 quantity mined, q_0	1994 quantity mined, q_t
Oil (barrels)	$ 2	100	110
Coal (ton)	20	10	9
Sulfur (tank car)	15	90	80
Granite (block)	60	5	5

What is the index of quantity mined in 1994 using 1983 as the base period?

Solution ▶ One might be tempted to add the quantities in 1994 and divide this total by the total of the 1983 quantities. Of course, it is impossible to add barrels, tons, tank cars, and blocks. The quantities, therefore, have to be converted to a common denominator using 1983 prices.

Quantity mined dropped 7.3 percent from 1983 to 1994

In computing the quantity index it is assumed that 1983 prices still prevailed in 1994—that is, the price of each commodity is held constant. Thus, any change in the quantity index is *due only to the quantity mined.* In this problem the quantity of minerals mined declined 7.3 percent from 1983 to 1994. See Table 17–4 for computations. Using formula (17–3):

$$Q = \frac{\Sigma p_0 q_t}{\Sigma p_0 q_0}(100) = \frac{\$1,900}{\$2,050}(100) = 92.7$$

Quantities mined in 1983 and 1994, weighted by price in base period (1983)

TABLE 17–4 Computation of Weighted Index of the Quantity of Minerals Mined for 1994 Using the Laspeyres Method (1983 = 100)

Commodity	1983 price p_0	1983 quantity mined, q_0	p_0q_0	1994 quantity mined, q_t	p_0q_t
Oil (barrels)	$ 2	100	$ 200	110	$ 220
Coal (ton)	20	10	200	9	180
Sulfur (tank car)	15	90	1,350	80	1,200
Granite (block)	60	5	300	5	300
			$2,050		$1,900

SELF-REVIEW 17–4

The answers are at the end of the chapter.

The wholesale price and the numbers produced for selected agricultural items are:

Item	Price 1975	Price 1994	Production 1975	Production 1994
Wheat (bushel)	$ 2.00	$ 4.00	100	700
Egg (dozen)	0.30	0.20	1,000	800
Pork (cwt.)	60.00	70.00	50	110

1. Using the Laspeyres method, compute an index of the quantity of agricultural production for 1994 (1975 = 100).
2. Interpret the index.

Paasche method uses present-year weights

Paasche Price Index Several years after Laspeyres introduced the concept of using base-period figures as weights, Paasche suggested a similar procedure—except that present-year weights were substituted for the original base-period weights. The Paasche formula for a weighted price index using present-year figures as weights is:

$$P = \frac{\sum p_t q_t}{\sum p_0 q_t}(100) \qquad (17\text{–}4)$$

The calculations needed for the weighted price index using the Paasche formula are illustrated in Table 17–5. The data are the same as used in Table 17–3, but the quantities consumed in 1995 have been added. Using formula (17–4):

$$P = \frac{\sum p_t q_t}{\sum p_0 q_t}(100) = \frac{\$655}{\$714}(100) = 91.7$$

TABLE 17–5 **Computation of a Weighted Price Index for 1995 Using the Paasche Formula (1977 = 100)**

Commodity	1977 price, p_0	1995 price, p_t	1995 quantity consumed, q_t	p_0q_t	p_tq_t
Milk (quart)	$0.64	$0.61	200	$128	$122
Bread (small loaf)	0.65	0.59	900	585	531
Avocado (each)	0.50	1.00	2	1	2
				$714	$655

The interpretation of the index of price (91.7) using the Paasche method is as follows: A market basket of food selected in 1995 costs 8.3 percent less than the same food cost at 1977 prices, found by 100.0 − 91.7.

Advantages and disadvantages of Paasche method

The Paasche method has the advantage of using current consumption figures as weights; that is, the consumption pattern is always up to date. However, the method poses a practical problem. The index must be revised every year using new present-year weights. If the Paasche method were used to compute the producer price indexes, for example, the consumption of approximately 2,800 wholesale items would have to be determined every year in order to weight the present-year prices. The Laspeyres method of using base-period weights, therefore, is the most commonly used (with some modification).

VALUE INDEX

Value index measures percent change in value

A **value index,** such as the index of department store sales, needs the original base-year prices, the original base-year quantities, the present-year prices, and the present-year quantities for its construction. Its formula is:

$$V = \frac{\sum p_t q_t}{\sum p_0 q_0}(100) \qquad (17\text{–}5)$$

EXAMPLE

Suppose the prices and quantities sold at the Waleska Department Store for various items of apparel for May 1982 and May 1995 are:

Item	1982 price, p_0	1982 quantity sold (thousands), q_0	1995 price, p_t	1995 quantity sold (thousands), q_t
Ties (each)	$ 1	1,000	$ 2	900
Suits (each)	30	100	40	120
Shoes (pair)	10	500	8	500

What is the index of value for May 1995 using May 1982 as the base period?

Solution ▶ Total sales in May 1995 were $10,600,000, and the comparable figure for 1982 is $9,000,000. (See Table 17–6.) Thus, the index of value for May 1995 using 1982 = 100 is 117.8. The value of apparel sales in 1995 was 117.8 percent of the 1982 sales. To put it another way, apparel sales increased 17.8 percent from May 1982 to May 1995.

$$V = \frac{\Sigma p_t q_t}{\Sigma p_0 q_0}(100) = \frac{\$10{,}600{,}000}{\$9{,}000{,}000}(100) = 117.8$$

TABLE 17–6 **Construction of a Value Index for 1995 (1982 = 100)**

Item	1982 price, p_0	1982 quantity sold (thousands), q_0	p_0q_0 ($ thousands)	1995 price, p_t	1995 quantity sold (thousands), q_t	p_tq_t ($ thousands)
Ties (each)	$ 1	1,000	$1,000	$ 2	900	$ 1,800
Suits (each)	30	100	3,000	40	120	4,800
Shoes (pair)	10	500	5,000	8	500	4,000
			$9,000			$10,600

SELF-REVIEW 17–5

The answers are at the end of the chapter.

The number of items produced by Houghton Products for 1983 and 1994 and the wholesale prices for the two periods are:

Item produced	Price 1983	Price 1994	Number produced 1983	Number produced 1994
Shear pins (box)	$ 3	$4	10,000	9,000
Cutting compound (pound)	1	5	600	200
Tie rods (each)	10	8	3,000	5,000

1. Find the index of the value of production for 1994 using 1983 as the base period.
2. Interpret the index.

EXERCISES

The answers to the odd-numbered exercises are at the end of the book.

5. The prices and production of grains for August 1977 and August 1995 are:

Grain	1977 price	1977 quantity produced (millions of bushels)	1995 price	1995 quantity produced (millions of bushels)
Oats	$1.52	200	$1.87	214
Wheat	2.10	565	2.05	489
Corn	1.48	291	1.48	203
Barley	3.05	87	3.29	106

   a. Using 1977 as the base period and the Laspeyres method, determine the weighted index of the quantity of grains produced for August 1995. Interpret.
   b. Using 1977 as the base period, find the index of the value of grains produced for August 1995. Interpret.

6. The Johnson Wholesale Company manufactures a variety of products. The prices and quantities produced for April 1974 and April 1995 are:

Product	1974 price	1995 price	1974 quantity produced	1995 quantity produced
Small motor (each)	$23.60	$28.80	1,760	4,259
Scrubbing compound (gallon)	2.96	3.08	86,450	62,949
Nails (pound)	0.40	0.48	9,460	22,370

   a. Using 1974 as the base period and the Laspeyres method, determine the weighted index of the quantity produced for April 1995. Interpret.
   b. Using 1974 as the base period, find the index of the value of goods produced for April 1995.

SPECIAL-PURPOSE INDEX

Special-purpose indexes usually employ a combination of business and economic indicators, such as sales, employment, and stock prices. As mentioned, the federal government compiles and publishes an index of leading economic indicators. So do *Forbes* and *Business Week.* The Forbes Index is a measure of U.S. economic activity composed of eight equally weighted elements: total industrial production, new claims for unemployment compensation, the cost of services relative to all consumer prices, the level of new orders for durable goods compared with manufacturers' inventories, total retail sales, new housing starts, personal income, and total consumer installment credit. To measure these eight elements, *Forbes* monitors 10 series of U.S. government data, including the Consumer Price Index and consumer installment credit released by the Federal Reserve Board.

One of the uses of an index of leading economic indicators is to predict possible changes in the direction of our economy. If the index declines steadily for three or four time periods, it may lead many economists to forecast that a recession is imminent. History, however, indicates that these forecasts are not infallible. For example, in the 20-year period from 1950 to 1970, the forecast based on the trend of the leading indexes was incorrect three times. However, most economists consider the federal index of leading economic indicators and others as rough guides to the future trend of our economy.

Most special-purpose indexes designed to monitor economy

The data needed for the construction of a special-purpose index designed to measure general business activity is shown in Table 17–7. Note that weights, based on the judgments of the statistician, are assigned to each series, and the series are in different units—dollars, freight car loadings, and so on. This weighting is somewhat different from the *Forbes* weighting, which applies equal weights to the elements.

TABLE 17–7 Data for the Computation of the Index of General Business Activity

Year	Department store sales ($ billions)	Index of employment (1986 = 100)	Freight car loadings (millions)	Exports (thousands of tons)
1986	20	100	50	500
1993	41	110	30	900
1995 (June)	44	125	18	700
Weight	(.40)	(.30)	(.10)	(.20)

To compute the index of general business activity for June 1995 using 1986 = 100, each 1995 figure is first expressed as a percentage using the base-period figure as the denominator. For illustration, department store sales for 1995 are converted to a percentage by ($44/$20) × 100 = 220. The percentages are then adjusted by the appropriate weights. For the department store, 220 × .40 = 88.0. (See the calculations below.)

Business activity up 57.1 percent from 1986 to 1995

The index of general business activity for June 1995 is 157.1. Interpreting, business activity increased 57.1 percent from the base period (arbitrarily selected as 1986) to June 1995.

$$\text{Department store sales:} \quad \left(\frac{\$44}{\$20}\right) 100 \times .40 = 88.0$$

$$\text{Employment} \quad \left(\frac{125}{100}\right) 100 \times .30 = 37.5$$

$$\text{Freight car loadings:} \quad \left(\frac{18}{50}\right) 100 \times .10 = 3.6$$

$$\text{Exports:} \quad \left(\frac{700}{500}\right) 100 \times .20 = \underline{28.0}$$

$$157.1$$

SELF-REVIEW 17–6

The answers are at the end of the chapter.

As chief statistician for the county, you want to compute and publish every year a special-purpose index, which you plan to call the *Index of County Business Activity.* Three series seem to hold promise as the basis for the index, namely, the price of cotton, the number of new automobiles sold, and the rate of money turnover for the county (published by a local bank). Arbitrarily you decide that money turnover during the month should have a weight of 60 percent, the number of new automobiles sold 30 percent, and the price of cotton 10 percent.

1. Construct the *Index of County Business Activity* for 1981 (the base period) and June 1995.

Year	Price of cotton (per pound)	Number of automobiles sold	Rate of money turnover (an index)
1981	$0.20	100,000	80
1995 (June)	0.50	80,000	120

2. Interpret the indexes.

EXERCISES

The answers to the odd-numbered exercises are at the end of the book.

7. The index of leading economic indicators compiled and published by the U.S. National Bureau of Economic Research is composed of 12 time series, such as the average work hours of production in manufacturing, manufacturers' new orders, and money supply. This index and similar indexes are designed to move up or down before the economy begins to move the same way. Thus, an economist has statistical evidence to forecast future trends.

   You want to construct a leading indicator for Erie County in upstate New York. The index is to be based on 1989 data. Because of the time and work involved, you decide to use only four time series. As an experiment, you select these four series: unemployment in the county, a composite index of county stock prices, county price index, and retail sales. Here are the figures for April 1989 and April 1994:

	1989	1994
Unemployment rate (percent)	5.3	6.8
Composite county stocks	265.88	362.26
County Price Index (1982 = 100)	109.6	125.0
Retail sales ($ millions)	529,917.0	622,864.0

   The weights you arbitrarily assigned are: unemployment rate 20 percent, stock prices 40 percent, County Price Index 25 percent, and retail 15 percent.

   a. Using 1989 as the base period, construct a leading economic indicator for April 1994.
   b. Interpret your leading index.

8. You are employed by the state bureau of economic development. There is a demand for a leading economic index to review past economic activity and to forecast future economic trends in the state. You decide that several key factors should be included in the index:

number of new businesses started during the year, number of business failures, state income tax receipts, college enrollment, and the state sales tax receipts. The data for 1987 and the present year are:

	1987	Present year
New businesses	1,088	1,162
Business failures	627	520
State income tax receipts ($ millions)	191.7	162.6
College student enrollment	242,119	290,841
State sales tax ($ millions)	41.6	39.9

a. Decide on the weights to be applied to each item going into the leading index.
b. Compute the leading economic indicator for the present year.
c. Interpret the indexes for 1987 and the present year.

CONSUMER PRICE INDEX

There are two consumer price indexes

Frequent mention has been made of the Consumer Price Index (CPI) in the preceding pages. It measures the change in price of a fixed market basket of goods and services from one period to another. In January 1978 the Bureau of Labor Statistics began publishing CPIs for two groups of the population. One index, for all urban consumers, covers about 80 percent of the total population. The other index is for urban wage earners and clerical workers and covers about 32 percent of the population.

In brief, the CPI serves several major functions. It allows consumers to determine the degree to which their purchasing power is being eroded by price increases. In that respect, it is a yardstick for revising wages, pensions, and other income payments to keep pace with changes in price. Equally important, it is an economic indicator of the rate of inflation in the United States.

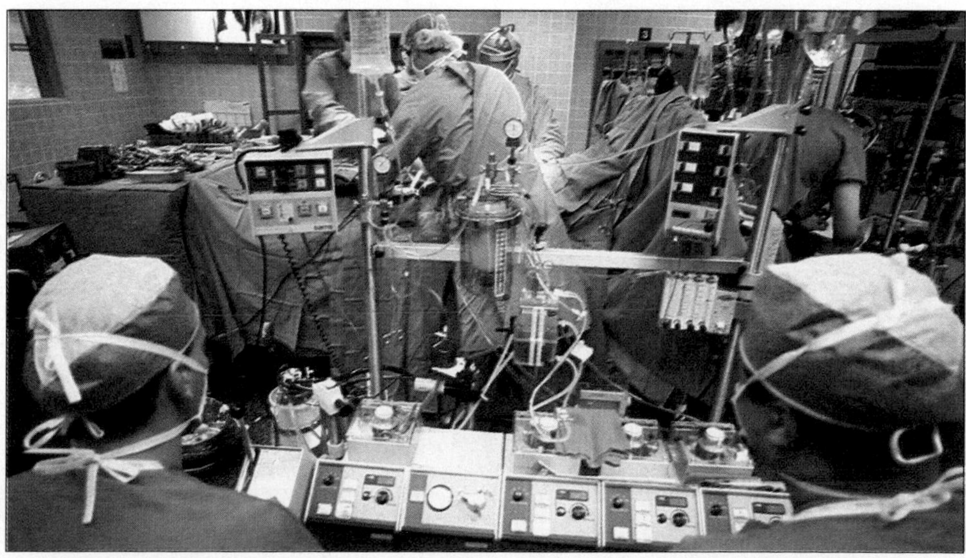

The index includes about 400 items, and about 250 part-time and full-time agents collect price data monthly. Prices are collected from more than 21,000 retail establishments and 60,000 housing units in 91 urban areas across the country. The prices of baby cribs, bread, beer, cigars, gasoline, haircuts, mortgage interest rates, physicians' fees, taxes, and operating-room charges are just a few of the items included in what is often termed a typical "market basket" of goods and services that you purchase.

The CPI originated in 1913 and has been published regularly since 1921. The standard reference period (the base period) has been updated periodically. The base periods prior to the present (1982–84) base were 1967, 1957–59, 1947–49, 1935–39, and 1925–29. The need for this rather frequent rebasing is somewhat obvious. Consumption patterns have changed drastically. The automobile replaced the horse as a mode of transportation. In the 1910s and 1920s a relatively small proportion of the income of wage earners and clerical workers was spent on higher education. Now the typical family spends a sizable amount on the higher education of its children, and the CPI reflects any changes in costs of tuition, books, and home computers.[6]

In addition to changing the base period periodically, the Bureau of Labor Statistics conducts an extensive consumer expenditure survey from time to time to determine the items to be included in the CPI and the relative weights to be put on stereo cassettes, bananas, gasoline, rent, and so on.

The CPI is not just one index. There are consumer price indexes for New York City, Chicago, and a number of other large cities. There are also price indexes for food, apparel, medical care, and other items. A few of them are shown below as of January 1994 (1982–84 = 100).

Items	CPI
All items	144.5
Food and beverages	141.6
Apparel and upkeep	133.7
Transportation	130.4
Medical care	201.4
Entertainment	145.8
Housing	141.2

Source: *Statistical Abstract of the United States,* U.S. Department of Commerce, September 1994, p. 489.

A perusal of this listing shows that the weighted price of all items combined increased 44.3 percent since 1982–84; medical care increased the most (101.4 percent), and transportation went up the least (30.4 percent) during the 11-year period.

Special Uses of the Consumer Price Index

In addition to measuring changes in the prices of goods and services, both consumer price indexes have a number of other applications. The CPI is used to determine real disposable personal income, to deflate sales or other series, to find the purchasing power of the dollar, and to establish cost-of-living increases. We first discuss the use of the CPI in determining **real income.**

[6]For a discussion of the general method for computing the CPI, see *BLS Handbook of Methods,* Bulletin 2285 (Bureau of Labor Statistics, 1988). An overview of the recently introduced revised CPI, reflecting 1982–84 expenditure patterns, is contained in *The Consumer Price Index: 1987 Revision,* Report 736 (Bureau of Labor Statistics, 1987).

Real income

Real Income As an example of the meaning and computation of *real income,* assume for the sake of simplicity that the Consumer Price Index is presently 200 with 1982–84 = 100. Also, assume that Ms. Watts earned $20,000 in the base period of 1982, 1983, and 1984. She has a current income of $40,000. Note that although her *money income* has doubled since the base period of 1982–84, the prices she paid for food, gasoline, clothing, and other items has also doubled. Thus, Ms. Watts' standard of living has remained the same from the base period to the present time. Price increases have exactly offset an increase in income, so her present buying power (real income) is still $20,000. (See Table 17–8 for computations.)

Money income

In general:

Formula for real income

$$\text{Real income} = \frac{\text{Money income}}{\text{CPI}} \times 100 \quad (17\text{–}6)$$

TABLE 17–8 **Computation of Real Income for 1982–84 and Present Year**

Year	Money income	Consumer Price Index (1982–84 = 100)	Real income	Computation of real income
1982–84	$20,000	100	$20,000	$\frac{\$20,000}{100}(100)$
Present year	40,000	200	20,000	$\frac{\$40,000}{200}(100)$

Deflated income and real income are the same

The concept of real income is sometimes called *deflated income,* and the CPI is called the *deflator.* Also, a popular term for deflated income is *income expressed in constant dollars.* Thus, in Table 17–8, in order to determine whether or not Ms. Watts' standard of living changed, her money income was converted to constant dollars. It was found that her purchasing power, expressed in 1982–84 dollars (constant dollars), remained at $20,000.

SELF-REVIEW 17–7

The answers are at the end of the chapter.

The take-home pay of Jon Greene and the CPI for 1986 and 1994 are:

Year	Take-home pay	CPI (1982–84 = 100)
1986	$25,000	109.60
1994	41,200	140.00

1. What was Jon's real income in 1986?
2. What was his real income in 1994?
3. Interpret your findings.

Deflated sales important for showing the trend in "real" sales

Deflating Sales A price index can also be used to "deflate" sales or similar money series. Deflated sales are determined by

$$\text{Deflated sales} = \frac{\text{Actual sales}}{\text{An appropriate index}}(100) \qquad (17\text{–}7)$$

EXAMPLE

The sales of Eugene Enterprises, a small manufacturer, increased from $1,482,000 in 1982 (the base period) to $1,502,000 in 1994. Eugene Enterprises knows that the price of raw materials used in production has also risen since 1982, so EE wants to deflate the 1994 sales to account for the rise in raw material prices. What are the deflated sales for 1994? That is, what are the 1994 sales expressed in constant 1982 dollars?

Solution ▶

"Sales in constant dollars" same as deflated sale

The Producer Price Index (PPI) is an index released every month and published in the *Monthly Labor Review.* The prices included in the PPI reflect the prices charged the manufacturer for the metals, rubber, and other items purchased. So the PPI seems an appropriate index to use to deflate the manufacturer's sales. The manufacturer's sales are listed in the second column of Table 17–9 and the PPI is in the third column. The next column shows sales divided by the Producer Price Index, and the deflated sales are in the extreme right column.

TABLE 17–9 **Computations for Deflating Sales**

Year	Sales	PPI* (1982 = 100)	Computation of deflated sales	Sales in constant 1982 dollars
1982	$1,482,000	100.0	$\frac{\$1,482,000}{100.0} \times 100 =$	$1,482,000
1990	1,491,000	119.2	$\frac{\$1,491,000}{119.2} \times 100 =$	$1,250,839
1994 (Nov.)	1,502,000	126.1	$\frac{\$1,502,000}{126.1} \times 100 =$	$1,191,118

*Source: U.S. Department of Labor, *Monthly Labor Review,* Jan. 1995, p. 107

The conclusion is that although the actual dollar sales of Eugene Enterprises increased from 1982 to 1994, sales deflated for the rise in prices the company paid for raw materials actually declined (from about $1,482,000 down to about $1,191,118). This is so because the prices Eugene paid for raw materials increased at a more rapid rate than did sales.

What has happened to the purchasing power of your dollar?

Purchasing Power of the Dollar The Consumer Price Index is also used to determine the *purchasing power of the dollar.*

$$\text{Purchasing power of dollar} = \frac{\$1}{\text{CPI}} \times 100 \qquad (17\text{–}8)$$

EXAMPLE

Suppose the Consumer Price Index this month is 200.0 (1982–84 = 100). What is the purchasing power of the dollar?

Solution

▶ Using formula (17–8), it is 50 cents, found by:

$$\text{Purchasing power of dollar} = \frac{\$1}{200.0}(100) = \$0.50$$

The CPI of 200.0 indicates that prices have doubled from the years 1982–84 to this month. Thus, the purchasing power of a dollar has been cut in half. That is, a 1982–84 dollar is worth only 50 cents this month. To put it another way, if you lost $1,000 in the period 1982–84 and just found it, the $1,000 could only buy half of what it could have bought in the years 1982, 1983, and 1984.

The Bureau of Labor Statistics still cites the CPI on the previous base period (1967) for those who still need to use it on that base. Table 17–10 shows the computation of the purchasing power of the dollar for a few actual periods using 1967 = 100. Note that the purchasing power of the dollar for November 1994 was 22.3 cents. Theoretically, if $1,000 could purchase 1,000 porterhouse steaks at $1 each in 1967, by November 1994 the same $1,000 could buy only 223 steaks.

TABLE 17–10 Computing the Purchasing Power of the Dollar

Year	Consumer Price Index* (1967 = 100)	Computations: $\frac{\$1}{CPI}(100)$	Purchasing power of the dollar (1967 = $1)
1967	100.0	$\frac{\$1}{100.0}(100) =$	$1.000
1989	371.3	$\frac{\$1}{371.3}(100) =$	0.269
1990	391.4	$\frac{\$1}{391.4}(100) =$	0.255
1994 (Nov.)	448.6	$\frac{\$1}{448.6}(100) =$	0.223

*Source: U.S. Department of Labor, *Monthly Labor Review,* January 1995, p. 102.

SELF-REVIEW 17–8

The answers are at the end of the chapter.

Suppose the Consumer Price Index for the latest month is 145.6 (1982–84 = 100).

a. What is the purchasing power of the dollar? Interpret.

b. Why is the purchasing power in Table 17–10 different from the one in part *a*?

CPI used to adjust wages, pensions, and so on

Cost-of-Living Adjustments The Consumer Price Index is also the basis for so-called cost-of-living adjustments in many management-union contracts. The specific clause in the contract is often referred to as the "escalator clause." About 31 million Social Security beneficiaries, 2.5 million retired military and federal civil service employees and survivors, and 600,000 postal workers have their incomes or pensions pegged to the Consumer Price Index.

The CPI is also used to adjust alimony and child support payments; attorneys' fees; workers' compensation payments; rentals on apartments, homes, and office buildings; welfare payments; and so on. In brief, say a retiree receives a pension of $500 a month and the Consumer Price Index increases 5 points. Suppose for each point (percent) that the CPI increases the pension benefits increase 1.0 percent, so the monthly increase in benefits will be $25, found by $500 (5 points)(.01). Now the retiree will receive $525 per month.

SHIFTING THE BASE

If two or more series have the same base period, they can be compared directly. As an example, suppose we are interested in the trend in the prices of food and beverages, housing, medical care, and so on since the base period, 1982–84. Note in Table 17–11 that all of the consumer price indexes use the same base. Thus, it can be said that the price of all consumer items combined increased 49.7 percent from the base period (1982–84) to November 1994. Likewise, housing prices increased 45.5 percent, medical care 114.7 percent, and so on.

TABLE 17–11 **Trend in Consumer Prices to 1995 (1982–84 = 100)**

Year	All items	Food and beverages	Housing	Apparel and upkeep	Medical care
1982–84	100.0	100.0	100.0	100.0	100.0
1986	109.6	109.1	110.9	105.9	122.0
1987	113.6	113.5	114.2	110.6	130.1
1994 (Nov.)	149.7	145.9	145.5	134.2	214.7

Source: U.S. Department of Labor, *Monthly Labor Review,* November 1994, p. 102.

A problem arises, however, when two or more series being compared do not have the same base period.

EXAMPLE

We want to compare the price changes on the New York Stock Exchange and the American Stock Exchange since 1985. The two price indexes are as follows.

Index	Year 1985	1986	1987	1993
New York Stock Exchange (Dec. 31, 1965 = 50)	108.09	136.00	161.70	244.72
American Stock Exchange (Aug. 31, 1973 = 50)	229.10	264.38	316.61	418.54

Source: *Federal Reserve Bulletin,* July 1988, p. A25; and p. A24; and June 1993, PA27

Solution ▶

Price indexes are on different base years and cannot be compared directly

Note again that the two price indexes have different base periods—the New York base period is 1965, and the American base is 1973. Thus, a direct comparison of 418.54 and 244.72 is meaningless. We want to compare the movement of price since 1985, so the logical thing to do is to let the base period be 1985 for both series. For the New York price series 108.09 becomes the base, and for the American series the base is 229.10.

The calculations for the 1993 American Stock Exchange price index using 1985 = 100 are:

$$\frac{418.54}{229.10} \times 100 = 182.7$$

The complete set of indexes using 1985 = 100 is:

	Year			
Index	**1985**	**1986**	**1987**	**1993**
New York Stock Exchange	100.0	125.8	149.6	226.4
American Stock Exchange	100.0	115.4	138.2	182.7

We can now conclude that common stock prices on both the New York Stock Exchange and the American Stock Exchange since 1985 have risen, with the rise on the New York Stock Exchange being significantly greater (126.4 percent compared with 82.7 percent on the American exchange).

SELF-REVIEW 17–9

The answers are at the end of the chapter.

1. In the preceding example, verify that the New York Stock Exchange price index for 1993, using 1985 as the base period, is 226.4.
2. The changes in industrial production and in the prices manufacturers have paid for raw materials since 1982 are to be compared. Unfortunately, the index of industrial production, which measures changes in production, and the Producer Price Index, which measures the change in the prices of raw materials, have different base periods. The production index has a 1977 base period, and the Producer Price Index uses 1982 as the base period.

Year	Industrial production index (1977 = 100)	Producer Price Index (1982 = 100)
1982	115.3	100.0
1987	129.8	105.4
1994	142.8	119.2

Sources: *Survey of Current Business,* August 1988, p. A47; U.S. Department of Labor, *Monthly Labor Review,* May 1994, p. 88.

   a. Shift the base to make the two series comparable.
   b. Interpret.

EXERCISES

The answers to the odd-numbered exercises are at the end of the book.

9. In 1994 the average salary for experienced bedside nurses was $32,000. The Consumer Price Index for November 1994 is 149.7 (1982–84 = 100). A nurse's average annual money income for the 1982–84 period was $19,800. What was the real income of a bedside nurse in 1994? What was a nurse's real income in the 1982–84 period? Compare

the two real incomes; that is, indicate what happened to a nurse's purchasing power between the two periods.

10. Lee Iacocca was the head of Chrysler from 1980 to 1990. The Sarasota (Florida) *Herald Tribune* cited his compensation during that period in the form of a bar chart.

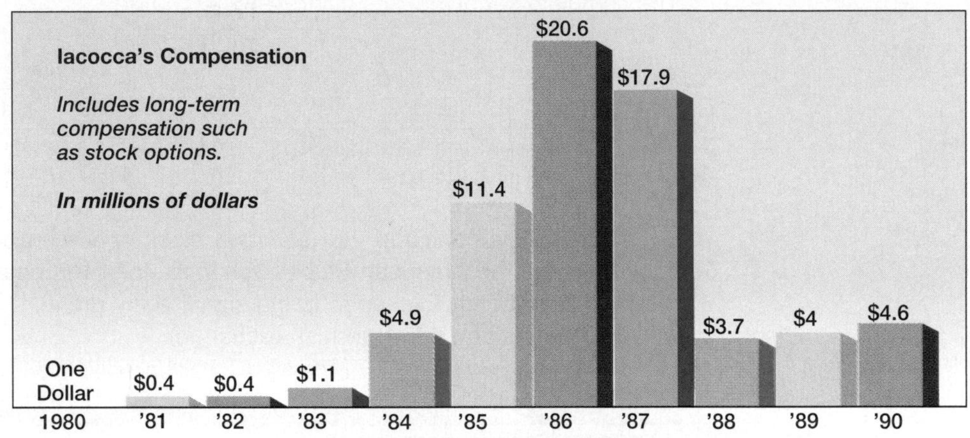

Sources: The Chrysler Corporation and the Sarasota (Florida) *Herald Tribune,* April 13, 1991, p. D1.

The Consumer Price Index figures for selected years are:

Year	CPI	Year	CPI
1980	82.4	1987	113.6
1982–84	100.0	1988	118.3
1985	107.6	1989	124.0
1986	109.6	1990	130.7

Source: Bureau of Labor Statistics, U.S. Labor Department.

a. During the period 1982–84, what was Iacocca's real income? What was his real income in 1990 based on the 1982–84 period? Compare the two real incomes for Iacocca, and explain the difference.

b. Using 1985 as the base period, compare his real income for 1985 with that for 1990.

c. Explain the CPI for 1980.

11. The Consumer Price Index values for 1989, 1990, and 1994 and the average weekly earnings for selected industries are:

Year	CPI (1982–84 = 100)	Mining	Apparel	Printing and publishing	Retail trade
1989	124.0	$569.75	$234.34	$412.35	$188.72
1990	130.7	600.60	239.88	426.38	195.26
1994 (June)	146.8	680.60	295.10	490.20	210.30

Source: U.S. Department of Labor, *Monthly Labor Review,* September 1994, p. 81.

Compare and interpret the trends in real weekly income for these selected industries.

CHAPTER OUTLINE

I. Index numbers.
   A. The purpose of an index is to show the change in either price, quantity, or value from one period to another.
   B. Characteristics.
      1. An index number, such as 185.0, is a percent, but the percent sign is usually omitted.
      2. An index number has a base period. The base period for the CPI currently is 1982–84; for the composite index of leading indicators it is 1987. Other base periods are 1982, 1984, and 1965.
      3. The base number of most indexes is 100. Thus, a price index of 185.0 for last month, using 1982 = 100, means that prices increased 85 percent from 1982 to last month.
      4. Most indexes are carried to the nearest whole percent, such as 164 or 96, or to the nearest tenth of a percent, such as 185.6 or 83.2.
   C. The reasons for computing indexes.
      1. Indexes facilitate a comparison of unlike series.
      2. An index is a convenient way to express the change in the total of a heterogeneous group of items.
      3. A percent change is sometimes easier to comprehend than actual numbers, especially when the numbers are extremely large.
   D. Types of index numbers.
      1. Price: Its purpose is to measure the change in prices from a selected base period to another period, such as this year.
      2. Quantity: Portrays the change in quantity consumed from the base period to another period.
      3. Value: Shows the change in the value of one or more items from say, 1977 to 1995. The value for 1995, found by Price × Quantity, is divided by the value in 1977 to give a value index for 1995.
      4. A special-purpose index combines and weights a heterogeneous group of series, such as employment, prices, production, and bank debits, to arrive at an overall index showing the change in business activity from the base period to the present.

II. Construction of index numbers.
   A. Simple index numbers.
      1. The formula for simple (unweighted) price and quantity indexes are similar:

$$P = \frac{p_t}{p_0}(100) \qquad (17\text{–}1)$$

where

p_t is the price of an item in the present time period.

p_0 is the price in the base period.

      2. A simple index is used to show the change in a single price or a single commodity from one period to another.
      3. To determine the change in the quantity of a market basket of items, such as food items, it is impossible to add quarts of milk, pounds of coffee, and heads of lettuce.
   B. Weighted index numbers.
      1. Formulas.
         a. Price:

Laspeyres method:

$$P = \frac{\Sigma p_t q_0}{\Sigma p_0 q_0}(100) \qquad (17\text{–}2)$$

Paasche method: $$P = \frac{\Sigma p_t q_t}{\Sigma p_0 q_t}(100) \qquad (17\text{–}4)$$

b. Quantity:

Laspeyres method: $$Q = \frac{\Sigma p_0 q_t}{\Sigma p_0 q_0}(100) \qquad (17\text{–}3)$$

c. Value:

$$V = \frac{\Sigma p_t q_t}{\Sigma p_0 q_0}(100) \qquad (17\text{–}5)$$

2. Using the weighted aggregative method, (1) a price index reflects the change in the price paid *only* (because the quantity consumed is held constant), and (2) a quantity index reflects the change in the quantity consumed *only* (because price is held constant).

III. Consumer Price Index.
   A. Starting in 1978 two consumer price indexes were published. One was designed for urban wage earners and clerical workers. It covers about one third of the population. Another was designed for all urban households. It covers about 80 percent of the population.
   B. The uses of the CPI.
      1. It allows consumers to determine the effect of price increases on their purchasing power.
      2. It is a yardstick for revising wages, pensions, alimony payments, and so on.
      3. It is an economic indicator of the rate of inflation in the United States.
   C. Other uses of the Consumer Price Index.
      1. Computing real income:

$$\text{Real income} = \frac{\text{Money income}}{\text{CPI}}(100) \qquad (17\text{–}6)$$

      2. Deflating sales:

$$\text{Deflated sales} = \frac{\text{Actual sales}}{\text{An appropriate index}}(100) \qquad (17\text{–}7)$$

      3. Determining the purchasing power of the dollar compared with its value for the base period:

$$\text{Purchasing power of dollar} = \frac{\$1}{\text{CPI}}(100) \qquad (17\text{–}8)$$

      4. Millions of employees in automobile, steel, and other industries have their wages adjusted upward when the CPI increases. The specifics are in the management-union contracts. Likewise, persons receiving social security payments have their pensions increased when the CPI goes up.
   D. Shifting the base.
      1. It is necessary when two or more series of index numbers to be compared do not have the same base period.
      2. First select a common base period for all series. Then use the respective base numbers as the denominators, and convert each series to the new base period.

EXERCISES

The answers to the odd-numbered exercises are at the end of the book.

12. Figures for the domestic sales to customers, the international sales, and the cost of products sold for Johnson & Johnson from 1983 to 1993 are (in millions of dollars):

Year	Domestic sales ($ millions)	International sales ($ millions)	Cost of products sold ($ millions)
1983	$3,611	$2,362	$2,469
1984	3,736	2,389	2,485
1985	3,990	2,431	2,592
1986	3,972	3,031	2,632
1987	4,167	3,845	2,958
1988	4,576	4,424	3,292
1989	4,881	4,876	3,480
1990	5,427	5,805	3,937
1991	6,248	6,199	4,204
1992	6,903	6,850	4,678
1993	7,203	6,935	4,791

Source: Johnson & Johnson, *Annual Report*, 1993, p. 42.

a. Using 1983 as the base period, compute a simple index for domestic sales for each of the years from 1983 to 1993.

b. Using the indexes just computed, interpret the trend of domestic sales.

13. Refer to Exercise 12.

    a. Convert the international sales and the cost of products sold for 1985 and 1993 into indexes using 1983–84 as the base period.

    b. Using the indexes computed in part *a,* interpret the trend in international sales and the cost of products sold.

14. The numbers of employees for Johnson & Johnson (in thousands) for selected years are:

Year	Number of employees
1983	77.4
1984	74.2
1985	74.9
1990	82.2
1993	81.6

Source: Johnson & Johnson, *Annual Report,* 1993, p. 42.

Using 1983–85 = 100, determine the index of employment for 1993. Interpret the index.

15. The average weekly earnings of production or nonsupervisory workers on nonagricultural payrolls for selected industries follow. Use 1979 = 100.

Year	Construction	Finance, insurance, and real estate	Wholesale trade	Transportation and public utilities
1979	$342.99	$190.77	$247.93	$325.56
1983	442.97	263.90	329.18	420.81
1987 (Jan.)	477.28	317.11	367.10	469.59
1991	512.45	369.81	481.82	503.26
1994 (Jan.)	571.34	422.32	464.64	557.79

Source: U.S. Department of Labor, *Monthly Labor Review,* June 1988, pp. 86, 88; May 1991, p. 71; and January 1994, p. 89.

a. Compare, using index numbers, the percent change in the average weekly wages of construction workers and of those working in finance, insurance, and real estate.

b. Compare, using index numbers, the percent change in the average weekly wages of those in wholesale trade and of those working in transportation and public utilities from 1979 to 1994.

16. The Consumer Price Index and the average hourly earnings in selected industries are:

Year	CPI (all items) (1982–84 = 100)	Hourly earnings: Services	Retail trade	Manufacturing
1982–84	100.0	$ 7.27	$5.69	$ 8.84
1986	109.6	8.16	6.03	9.73
1987	113.6	8.47	6.12	9.73
1994 (Nov.)	149.7	11.16	7.55	12.17

Source: U.S. Department of Labor, *Monthly Labor Review,* June 1988, pp. 86, 88, 94 and Jan. 1995, p. 87.

What happened to the real hourly earnings of a "typical" employee in each of the three selected industries between the 1982–84 period and November 1994? Explain.

17. Refer to Exercise 16. What happened to the purchasing power of the dollar between the years 1982, 1983, and 1984 and the month of November 1994? Explain.

18. Refer to Exercise 16. Jose Gomez's monthly income in 1986 was $2,040. By November 1994 it had risen to $2,090. Explain what happened to his real monthly income.

19. A special-purpose index is to be designed to monitor the overall economy of the Southwest. Four key series were selected. After considerable deliberation it was decided to weight retail sales 20 percent, total bank deposits 10 percent, industrial production in the area 40 percent, and nonagricultural employment 30 percent. The data for 1983, 1986, and 1994 are:

Year	Retail sales ($ millions)	Bank deposits ($ billions)	Industrial production (1977 = 100)	Employment
1983	1,159.0	87	110.6	1,214,000
1986	1,467.0	85	111.1	1,316,000
1994	1,971.0	91	114.7	1,501,000

a. Construct a special-purpose index for 1994 using 1983 as the base period.

b. Interpret.

20. We are making a historical study of certain facets of the American economy from 1950 to 1980. Data on prices, the labor force, productivity, and the GNP were collected. Note in the following table that the CPI is on a 1967 base, employment is in millions of persons, and so on. A direct comparison, therefore, is not feasible.

a. Make whatever calculations are necessary to compare the trend in the four series from 1950 to 1980.

b. Interpret.

Year	Consumer Price Index (1967 = 100)	Total labor force (millions)	Index of productivity in manufacturing (1967 = 100)	Gross national product ($ billions)
1950	72.1	64	64.9	286.2
1967	100.0	81	100.0	789.6
1971	121.3	87	110.3	1,063.4
1975	161.2	95	114.9	1,516.3
1980	246.8	107	146.6	2,626.0

Sources: U.S. Department of Labor, *Monthly Labor Review,* April 1977, pp. 91, 103, 109; *National Income and Products Accounts of the United States; Survey of Current Business,* March 1981, p. S–1.

21. Prices of selected foods for 1977 and 1995 are given in the following table.

	1977		1995	
Item	Price	Amount produced	Price	Amount produced
Cabbage (pound)	$0.06	2,000	$0.05	1,500
Carrots (bunch)	0.10	200	0.12	200
Peas (quart)	0.20	400	0.18	500
Endive (bunch)	0.15	100	0.15	200

a. Using the Laspeyres formula, calculate a weighted index of price for 1995 (1977 = 100). Interpret.
b. Using the Paasche formula, calculate a weighted index of price for 1995. Interpret.
c. Explain the difference between the price index for 1995 using the Laspeyres method and the Paasche method.
d. Using the Laspeyres formula, determine a weighted index of quantity for 1995 (1977 = 100). Interpret.
e. Calculate an index of value for 1995 (1977 = 100). Interpret.

22. The prices of selected items for 1980 and 1995 follow. Production figures for those two periods are also given.

Items	1980 price	1995 price	1980 production	1995 production
Aluminum (cents per lb.)	$ 0.287	$ 0.76	1,000	1,200
Natural gas (1,000 cu. ft.)	0.17	2.50	5,000	4,000
Petroleum, crude (barrel)	3.18	26.00	60,000	60,000
Platinum (troy ounce)	133.00	490.00	500	600

a. Using 1980 as the base period, determine the weighted index of price for 1995 using the Laspeyres method. Interpret.
b. Using 1980 as the base period, determine the weighted index of the quantity produced for 1995 using the Laspeyres method. Interpret.

23. Refer to Exercise 24.
    a. Using the Paasche method and 1980 as the base period, determine a weighted index of price for 1995.
    b. Determine a value index for 1995 using 1980 as the base period. Interpret.
24. Discuss the main features of the two consumer price indexes that are compiled and published, including what they measure, the base period, and so on.
25. Discuss the escalator clause (also called the cost-of-living clause) found in many management-union contracts.
26. If a management-union contract is available, cite any provisions that pertain to changes in wages resulting from changes in the Consumer Price Index.

CHAPTER 17 EXAMINATION

The answers are at the end of the chapter.

1. The prices of aluminum scrap for three years are:

Year	Price of aluminum scrap (per ton)
1977	$40.00
1982	50.00
1994	80.65

   a. Using 1982 as the base period, determine price indexes for 1977 and for 1994.
   b. Interpret.

Questions 2–5 are based on the following prices and quantities consumed for 1983 and 1995.

	1983		1995	
Item	Price (bushel)	Amount consumed (millions of bushels)	Price (bushel)	Amount consumed (millions of bushels)
Corn	$2	10	$4	12
Wheat	3	6	1	8
Oats	7	2	5	9

2. Using the Laspeyres formula and 1983 as the base period, determine a weighted price index for 1995.
3. Using the Laspeyres formula and 1983 as the base period, determine a weighted quantity index for 1995.
4. Compute a value index for 1995 using 1983 = 100.
5. *a.* Using the Paasche formula and 1983 as the base period, determine a weighted price index for 1995.
   b. Why is this price index different from the one found in Question 2? Which one is more commonly used?

Questions 6 and 7 are based on the following.

Year	Consumer Price Index (1982–84 = 100)	Mr. Martin's monthly take-home pay
1982–84	100.0	$ 600
1986	109.6	700
1994 (Mar.)	135.0	2,000

6. What is the purchasing power of the dollar for March 1994 based on the period 1982–84?
7. *a.* Determine Mr. Martin's "real" monthly income for each of the three time periods.
   b. Interpret.
8. Suppose that the Producer Price Index and the sales of Hoskin's Wholesale Distributors for 1983 and 1994 are:

Year	Producer Price Index	Sales
1983	120.0	$2,400,000
1994	265.9	3,500,000

   a. What are Hoskin's real sales (also called deflated sales) for the two years?
   b. Interpret.
9. The management of Ingalls Super Discount stores, with several stores in the Oklahoma City area, wants to construct an index of economic activity for the metropolitan area. Management contends that if the index reveals that the economy is slowing down, inventory should be kept at a low level.

   Three series seem to hold promise as predictors of economic activity—area retail sales, bank deposits, and employment. All of these data can be secured monthly from the U.S. government. Retail sales is to be weighted 40 percent, bank deposits 35 percent, and employment 25 percent. Seasonally adjusted data for the first three months of the year are:

Month	Retail sales ($ millions)	Bank deposits ($ billions)	Employment (thousands)
January	8.0	20	300
February	6.8	23	303
March	6.4	21	297

   a. Construct an index of economic activity for each of the three months using January as the base period.
   b. Send a recommendation to management.

CHAPTER 17 Answers

Self-Review

17–1 1. 174.9, found by ($14.85/$8.49)100. Hourly earnings increased 74.9 percent from 1979 to March 1994.

2. *a.* 187.7, found by ($101,781.9/$54,217.0) × 100. Sales of GM are 87.7 percent greater than sales of IBM.

b. 48.4, found by ($26,257.7/$54,217.0)100. Sales of Chrysler are 51.6 percent below IBM sales.

17–2 1. 344.9 found by ($7.45/$2.16)100. Earnings increased 244.9 percent in the period.

2. 344.1 found by ($7.45/$2.23)100.

3. 88.5, found by ($2.16/$2.44)100. Earnings in 1968 were 11.5 percent less than in 1970, found by 100.0 − 88.5.

17–3 1. 214.5, found by P = ($140,500/$65,500)100.

p_0	q_0	p_0q_0	p_t	p_tq_0
$35	500	$17,500	$65	$ 32,500
40	1,200	48,000	90	108,000
		$65,500		$140,500

2. The price of clothing in 1995 was 214.5 percent of the price in 1982. Or the price of clothing increased 114.5 percent from 1982 to 1995.

17–4 1. 235.4, found by Q = ($8,240/$3,500)100.

p_0q_0	p_0q_t
$ 200	$1,400
300	240
3,000	6,600
$3,500	$8,240

2. Quantity produced between 1975 and 1994 increased 135.4 percent.

17–5 1. 127.1, found by V = ($77,000/$60,600)100.

p_0q_0	p_tq_t
$30,000	$36,000
600	1,000
30,000	40,000
$60,600	$77,000

2. Value of sales up 27.1 percent from 1983 to 1994.

17–6 1. 1981 = 100
1995 = 139, found by:

	Weight
($0.50/$0.20)(100) × .10 =	25
(80,000/100,000)(100) × .30 =	24
(120/80)(100) × .60 =	90
	139

2. Business activity in 1995 was 139 percent of the activity in 1981. Or business activity in 1995 was 39 percent higher than in 1981.

17–7 1. $22,810.22, found by ($25,000/109.6)100.

2. $29,428.57, found by ($41,200/140.0)100

3. Jon's real income increased from about $22,810 in 1986 to $29,429 in 1994. This indicates that his take-home pay increased at a faster rate than the price he paid for food, transportation, etc.

17–8 *a.* 68.7 cents, found by:

$$\frac{\$1}{145.6} \times 100$$

b. The base periods are different.

17–9 1. (244.72/108.09)100 = 226.4

2. *a.* Using 1982 as the base period for both series:

	Industrial production index	Producer Price Index
1982	100.0	100.0
1987	112.6	105.4
1994	123.9*	119.2

*(142.8/115.3)100 = 123.9

b. From the base period of 1982 to 1994, industrial production increased at a faster rate (23.9 percent) than prices (19.2 percent).

Examination

1. *a.* For 1977, 80.0; for 1994, 161.3, found by (80.65/50.00)100.
   b. In 1977 the price of aluminum scrap was 80 percent of the 1982 price, or it was 20 percent below the 1982 price. In 1994 the price was 61.3 percent above the 1982 price, or the price of aluminum scrap increased 61.3 percent from 1982 to 1994.

Questions 2–5 are based on the following sums:

	p_0q_0	p_tq_0	p_0q_t	p_tq_t
Corn	$20	$40	$24	$ 48
Wheat	18	6	24	8
Oats	14	10	63	45
	$52	$56	$111	$101

2. 107.7, found by ($56/$52)100.
3. 213.5, found by ($111/$52)100.
4. 194.2, found by ($101/$52)100.
5. *a.* 91.0, found by ($101/$111)100.
   b. The difference is explained by the two different weighting systems. The Laspeyres system is used more frequently.
6. $0.741, found by ($1/135.0)100.
7. *a.*

Year	Real income	Calculations
1982–84	$ 600	($600/100.0)100
1986	639	($700/109.6)100
1994 (Mar.)	1,481	($2,000/135.0)100

   b. Mr. Martin's purchasing power increased almost 2½ times from the period 1982–84 to 1994. His real income increased from $600 a month to $1,481.
8. *a.* 1983 deflated sales were $2,000,000, found by ($2,400,000/120.0)100. For 1994 real sales are $1,316,284, found by ($3,500,000/265.9)100.
   b. Real sales dropped from $2,000,000 in 1983 to $1,316,284 in 1994, caused by a sharp increase in the price of raw materials.
9. *a.* The three indexes of economic activity are: January, 100.0; February 99.5; March, 93.5. The calculations for February are:

Retail sales	(6.8/8.0)100 = 85. Then 85 × .40 =	34.00
Bank deposits	(23/20)100 = 115. Then 115 × .35 =	40.25
Employment	(303/300)100 = 101. Then 101 × .25 =	25.25
		99.50

   b. The overall economic level declined 6.5 percent during the first three months (found by 100.0 − 93.5). Management might be advised to carefully regulate the size of the inventories at their stores.

Chapter 18 Time Series and Forecasting

GOALS

When you have completed this chapter, you will be able to:

1
Explain the meaning of each of the components of a time series.

2
Determine the linear trend equation.

3
Compute a moving average.

4
Compute the trend equation for a nonlinear trend.

5
Use the linear and nonlinear trend equations to arrive at estimates for future time periods.

6
Determine a set of seasonal indexes by applying the ratio-to-moving-average method.

7
Deseasonalize data using seasonal indexes.

8
Determine a seasonally adjusted forecast.

Given expenditures for telephone use for 1980 through 1994, determine the least squares equation and estimate expenditures for 1997. (See Goal 2 and 5 and Exercise 2.)

INTRODUCTION

What is a time series?

The emphasis in this chapter is on time series analysis and forecasting. A **time series** is a collection of data recorded over a period of time—usually weekly, monthly, quarterly, or yearly. Two examples of time series are (1) a department store's sales by quarter since its opening in 1962 and (2) the annual production of sulfuric acid since 1970.

An analysis of past history—a time series—can be used by management to make current decisions and for long-term forecasting and planning. Long-term forecasts usually extend more than 1 year into the future; 5-, 10-, 15-, and 20-year projections are common. Long-range predictions are considered essential in order to allow sufficient time for the procurement, manufacturing, sales, finance, and other departments of a company to develop plans for possible new plants, financing, development of new products, and new methods of assembling.

Forecasting the level of sales, both short-term and long-term, is practically dictated by the very nature of business organizations in the United States. Competition for the consumer's dollar, stress on earning a profit for the stockholders, a desire to procure a larger and larger share of the market, and the ambitions of executives are some of the prime motivating forces in business. Thus, a forecast (a statement of the goals of management) is considered necessary in order to have the raw materials, production facilities, and staff available to meet the projected demand.

This chapter deals with the use of past data to forecast future events. First we look at the components of a time series, then we examine some of the techniques used in analyzing past data, and finally we project future events.

COMPONENTS OF A TIME SERIES

There are four components to a time series: the trend, the cyclical variation, the seasonal variation, and the irregular variation.

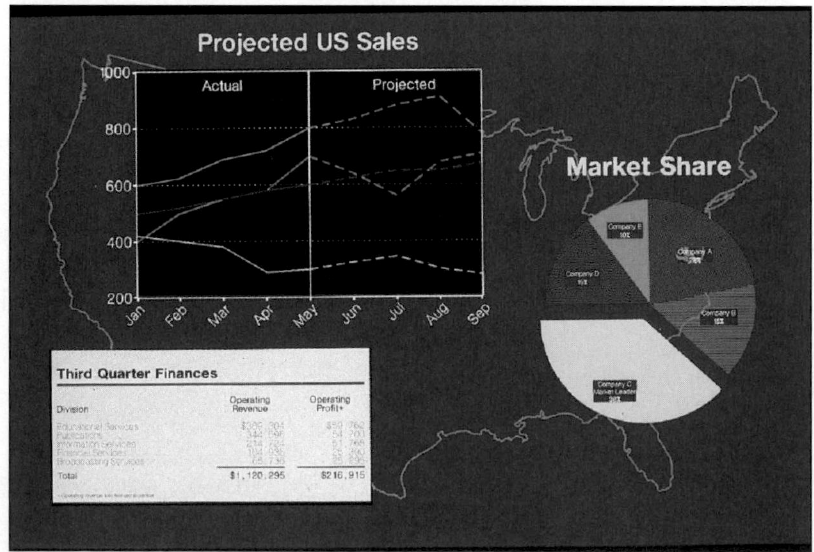

Many computer programs such as SPSS have become popular in visually depicting time series data.

Secular Trend

Secular or long-term trend

The **secular trend** is the smooth long-term direction of the time series. Long-term trends of sales, employment, stock prices, and other business and economic series follow various patterns. Some move steadily upward, others decline, and others stay the same over a period of time. A few of these are depicted graphically in the following charts.

- Chart 18–1 shows the sales of antibiotics to drugstores and hospitals from 1988 to 1993. Note that there has been an upward trend during the period. Sales increased from $3.7 billion in 1988 to $5.6 billion in 1993.

CHART 18–1 **Antibiotics Sales to Drugstores and Hospitals, 1988 to 1993**

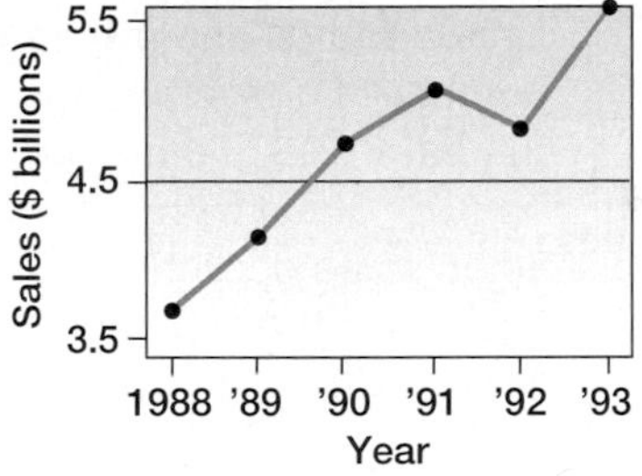

Source: *Newsweek,* March 28, 1994, p. 50.

- Charts 18–2 and 18–3 show information contained in the 1993 Monsanto annual report. Chart 18–2 depicts an upward trend. The high stock prices for the year increased from $46.25 per share in 1988 to $75 in 1993, and on August 17, 1994, it was at $82.25. Chart 18–3, which shows the number of employees, depicts a downward trend. The number of employees declined from over 45,000 in 1988 to 30,000 in 1993.

CHART 18–2 **Stock Price High for Monsanto Corporation, 1988 to 1994**

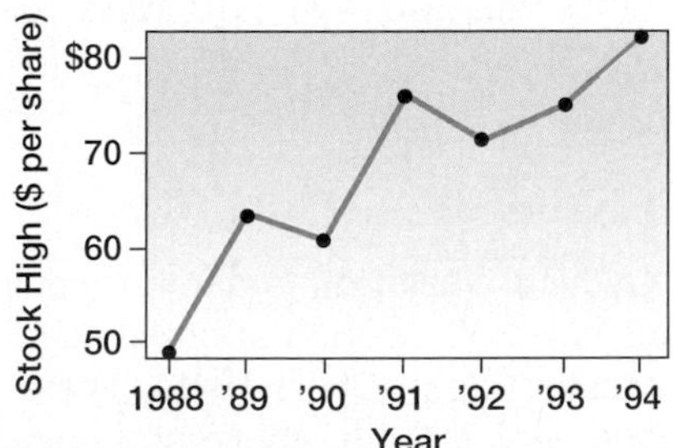

Source: Monsanto Corporation, *Annual Report,* 1993, p. 52.

CHART 18–3 **Number of Employees for Monsanto Corporation, 1988 to 1993**

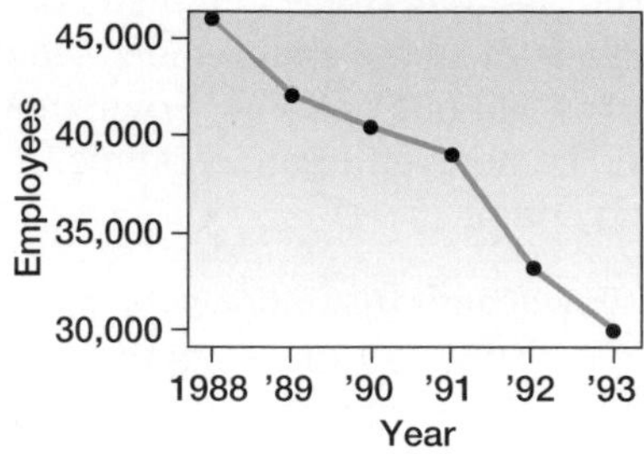

Source: Monsanto Corporation, *Annual Report,* 1993, p. 52.

- Chart 18–4 portrays the trend of smoking from 1960 until 1993 both in the United States and overseas. Note that from 1960 to the early 1980s the number of cigarettes sold was increasing in the United States. However, since the early 1980s there has been a dramatic change in the general trend. Sales have declined by nearly 150 billion during the last decade. During the period when sales declined in the United States, the sales overseas increased. Does it look like the tobacco companies have replaced the lost sales in the United States with sales overseas?

CHART 18–4 **Sales of Cigarettes, 1960 to 1993**

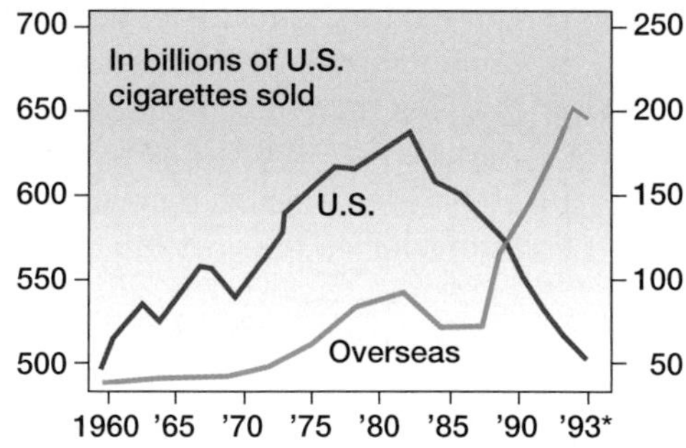

Source: *Newsweek,* March 21, 1994, p. 53.

Cyclical Variation

Cyclical variation: Prosperity, recession, depression, expansion

Cyclical variation is another component of a time series. A typical business cycle consists of a period of prosperity followed by periods of recession, depression, and recovery (see Chart 18–5). There are sizable fluctuations, representing more than one year in time, above and below the secular trend. In a recession, for example, employment, production, the Dow Jones Industrial Average, and many other business and economic series are below their long-term trend lines. Conversely, in periods of prosperity, they are above their long-term trend lines.

CHART 18–5 **A Typical Business Cycle**

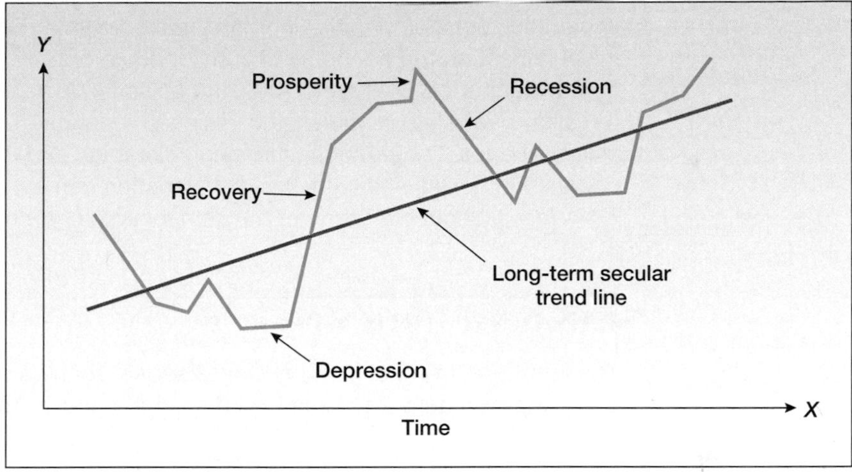

Seasonal Variation

Seasonal variation: A short-term pattern repeated yearly

Another component of a time series is **seasonal variation.** Many sales, production, and other series fluctuate with the seasons. The unit of time may be either quarterly, monthly, weekly, or even daily.

Practically all business and economic series have recurring seasonal patterns. A few exceptions are found in certain electronic and aircraft firms under contract to the federal government to supply aerospace and military parts. Sales of men's and boys' clothing, for example, have extremely high sales prior to Christmas and relatively low sales after Christmas and in the summer. Department store sales have a similar pattern, as shown in Chart 18–6.

CHART 18–6 **Sales of Department Stores, by Month, 1991–94**

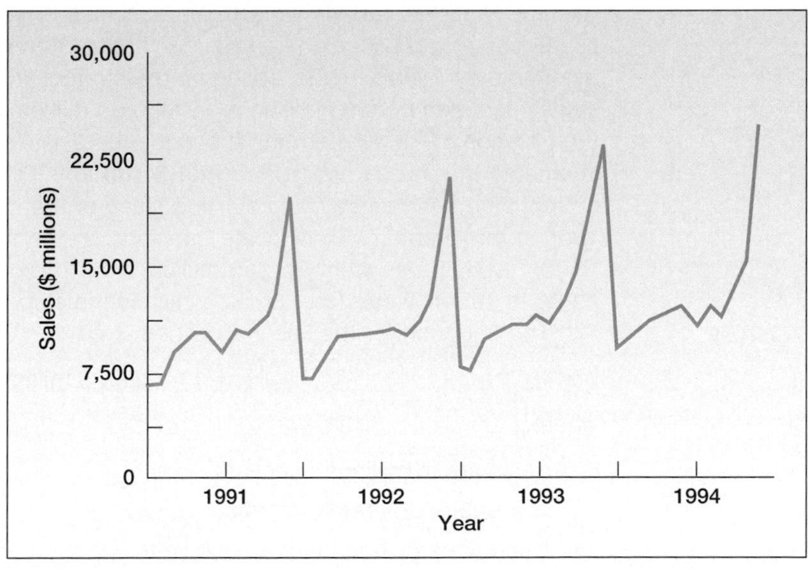

Irregular Variation

Many analysts prefer to subdivide the **irregular variation** into *episodic* and *residual* variations. Episodic fluctuations are unpredictable, but they can be identified. The initial impact on the economy of a major strike or a war can be identified, but a strike or war cannot be predicted. After the episodic fluctuations have been removed, the remaining variation is called the residual variation. The residual fluctuations, often called chance fluctuations, are unpredictable, and they cannot be identified. Of course, neither episodic nor residual variation can be projected into the future.

We will begin our study of the components of a time series with linear trend.

LINEAR TREND

The long-term trend of many business series, such as sales, exports, and production, often approximates a straight line. If so, the equation to describe this growth is:

$$Y' = a + bt \tag{18–1}$$

where:

- Y' read Y prime, is the projected value of the Y variable for a selected value of t.
- a is the Y-intercept. It is the estimate value of Y when $t = 0$. Another way to put it is: a is the estimated value of Y where the straight line crosses the Y-axis when t is zero.
- b is the slope of the line, or the average change in Y' for each change of one unit (either increase or decrease) in t.
- t is any value of time that is selected.

Slope of trend line is b

To illustrate further the meaning of Y', a, b, and t in a time series problem, a straight line has been drawn in Chart 18–7 to represent the typical trend of sales. Assume that this company started in business in 1986. This beginning year (1986) has been arbitrarily designated as year 1. Note that sales increased $2 million on the average every year; that is, based on the straight line drawn through the sales data, sales increased from $3 million in 1986 to $5 million in 1987, to $7 million in 1988, to $9 million in 1989, and so on. The slope, or b, is therefore 2. Note too that the line intercepts the Y-axis (when $t = 0$) at $1 million. This point (1) is a. Another way of determining b is to locate the starting place of the straight line in year (1). It is 3 for 1986 in this problem. Then locate the value on the straight line for the last year. It is 19 for 1994. Sales went up $19 million − $3 million, or $16 million, in eight years (1986 to 1994). Thus, $16 \div 8 = 2$, which is the slope of the line, or b.

The equation for the line in Chart 18–7 is:

$$Y' = 1 + 2t \text{ (in \$ millions)}$$

where:

Sales are in millions of dollars.

The origin, or year 0, is 1985.

t increases by one unit for each year.

CHART 18–7 **A Straight Line Fitted to Sales Data**

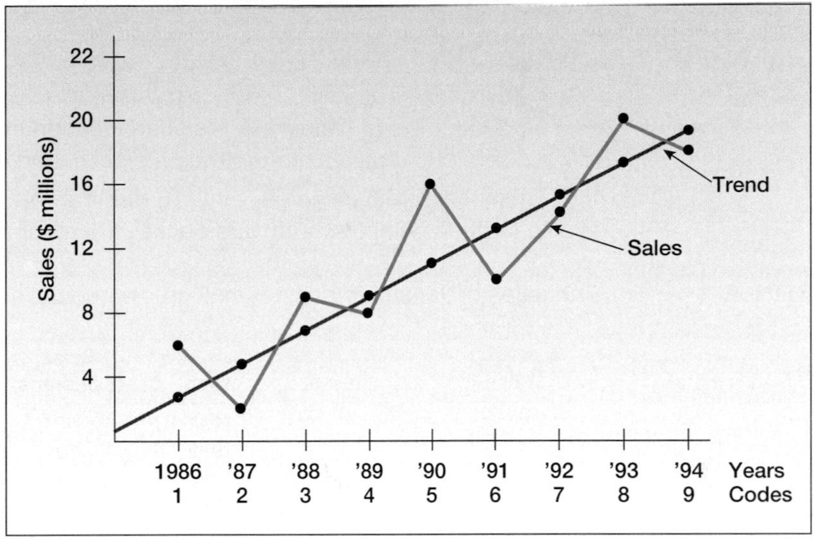

In Chapter 12 we drew a straight line through points on a scatter diagram to approximate the regression line. We stressed, however, that this method for determining the regression equation has a serious drawback—namely, the position of the line depends on the judgment of the individual who drew the line. Three people would probably draw three different lines through the scatter plots. Likewise, the line we drew through the sales data in Chart 18–7 might not be the "best-fitting" line.

Such lines usually inaccurate

Because of the subjective judgment involved, this method should be used only when a quick approximation of the straight-line equation is needed, or to check the reasonableness of the least squares line, which is discussed next.

LEAST SQUARES METHOD

We could solve these two equations simultaneously

The **least squares method** of computing the equation for a straight line through the data of interest gives the "best-fitting" line. Two equations may be solved simultaneously to arrive at the least squares trend equation. They are:

$$\Sigma Y = na + b\Sigma t$$
$$\Sigma tY = a\Sigma t + b\Sigma t^2 \qquad (18\text{–}2)$$

You may recognize these as the normal equations discussed in Chapter 12, with t replacing X in the equations. As we described in Chapter 12, using the normal equations to determine a and b can be tedious. A better approach is to use the following computational equations.

$$b = \frac{\Sigma tY - (\Sigma Y)(\Sigma t)/n}{\Sigma t^2 - (\Sigma t)^2/n} \tag{18–3}$$

$$a = \frac{\Sigma Y}{n} - b\left(\frac{\Sigma t}{n}\right) \tag{18–4}$$

If the number of years is large—say, 15 or more—and the magnitude of the numbers is also large, a computer software package is recommended.

EXAMPLE

The sales of Jensen Foods, a small grocery chain, since 1991 are:

Year	Sales ($ millions)
1991	7
1992	10
1993	9
1994	11
1995	13

Determine the least squares trend line equation.

Solution ▸ To simplify the calculations, the years are replaced by *coded* values. That is, we let 1991 be 1, 1992 be 2, and so forth. This reduces the size of the values of Σt, Σt^2, and ΣtY. (See Table 18–1.) This is often referred to as the **coded method.**

TABLE 18–1 Computations Needed for Determining the Trend Equation

Year	Sales ($ millions), Y	t	tY	t^2
1991	7	1	7	1
1992	10	2	20	4
1993	9	3	27	9
1994	11	4	44	16
1995	13	5	65	25
	50	15	163	55

Determining a and b using formulas (18–3) and (18–4):

$$b = \frac{\Sigma tY - (\Sigma Y)(\Sigma t)/n}{\Sigma t^2 - (\Sigma t)^2/n} = \frac{163 - 50(15)/5}{55 - (15)^2/5} = 1.30$$

$$a = \frac{\Sigma Y}{n} - b\left(\frac{\Sigma t}{n}\right) = \frac{50}{5} - 1.30\left(\frac{15}{5}\right) = 6.1$$

The trend equation is therefore $Y' = 6.1 + 1.30t$, where:

Sales are in millions of dollars.

The origin, or year 0, is in the middle of 1990 (i.e., July 1, 1990), and t increases by one unit for each year.

How do we interpret the equation? The value of 1.30 indicates that sales increased at a rate of \$1.3 million per year. The value 6.1 is the estimated sales when $t = 0$. That is, the estimated sales amount for 1990 (the zero year) is \$6.1 million.

Plotting the Straight Line

The least squares equation can be used to find the points on the straight line going through the middle of the data. The sales data from Table 18–1 are repeated in Table 18–2 to show the procedure. The equation determined earlier is $Y' = 6.1 + 1.30t$. To get the coordinates of the point on the straight line for 1994, for example, insert the t value of 4 in the equation. Then $Y' = 6.10 + 1.30(4) = 11.3$.

TABLE 18–2 **Calculations Needed for Determining the Points on the Straight Line Using the Coded Method**

Year	Sales (\$ millions), *Y*	*t*	*Y'*		Found by
1991	\$ 7	1	7.4	⟵	6.10 + 1.30(1)
1992	10	2	8.7	⟵	6.10 + 1.30(2)
1993	9	3	10.0	⟵	6.10 + 1.30(3)
1994	11	4	11.3	⟵	6.10 + 1.30(4)
1995	13	5	12.6	⟵	6.10 + 1.30(5)

The actual sales and the trend in sales as represented by the straight line are shown in Chart 18–8. The first point on the straight line has the coordinates $t = 1$, $Y' = 7.4$. Another point is $t = 3$, $Y' = 10$.

CHART 18–8 **Actual Sales and Straight-Line Trend**

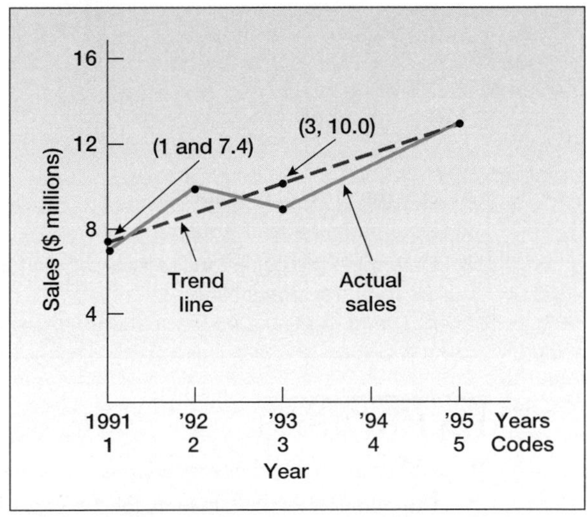

Estimation

If the sales, production, or other data over a period of time tend to approximate a straight-line trend, the equation developed by the least squares method can be used to estimate sales for some future period.

EXAMPLE

Refer to the sales data in Table 18–1. The year 1991 is coded 1, and 1992 is coded 2. What is the sales forecast for 1998?

Solution ▸

Estimating sales for 1997

The year 1993 is coded 3, 1994 is logically coded 4, 1995 is coded 5, 1996 is coded 6, 1997 is coded 7, and 1998 is coded 8. So in 1998, $t = 8$. Substituting the period 8 in the straight-line equation [formula (18–1)]:

$$Y' = a + bt = 6.1 + 1.30(8) = 16.5$$

Thus, based on past sales, the sales estimate for 1998 is $16.5 million.

In this time series problem, there were five years of sales data. Based on those five sales figures, we estimated sales for 1998. Many researchers suggest that we do not project sales, production, and other business and economic series more than $n/2$ time periods into the future. If, for example, there are 10 years of past data, we would make estimates only up to 5 years into the future ($n/2 = 10/2 = 5$). Others suggest that the forecast may be for no longer than 2 years, especially in rapidly changing economic times.

SELF-REVIEW 18–1

The answers are at the end of the chapter.

Annual production of king-size rockers by Wood Products, Inc. since 1988 follows:

Year	Production (thousands)
1988	4
1989	8
1990	5
1991	8
1992	11
1993	9
1994	11
1995	14

1. Plot the production data.
2. Determine the least squares equation.
3. Determine the points on the straight line for 1988 and 1994. Connect the two points to arrive at the straight line.
4. Based on the equation for the straight line, what is the estimated production for 1998?

EXERCISES

The answers to the odd-numbered exercises are at the end of the book.

1. The numbers of bank failures for the years 1990 to 1994 are given below. Determine the least squares equation, and estimate the number of failures in 1997.

Year	Code	Number of failures
1990	1	79
1991	2	120
1992	3	138
1993	4	184
1994	5	200

2. The personal consumption expenditures for telephone and telegraph, in billions of dollars, in the United States for the years 1989 to 1994 are given below. Determine the least squares equation, and estimate the expenditure for 1997.

Year	Code	Expenditures ($ billions)
1989	1	37.9
1990	2	39.8
1991	3	40.4
1992	4	42.7
1993	5	44.1
1994	6	47.1

3. The following table gives the annual amount of scrap produced by Machine Products, Inc.

Year	Code	Scrap (tons)
1991	1	2.0
1992	2	4.0
1993	3	3.0
1994	4	5.0
1995	5	6.0

Determine the least squares trend equation. Estimate the amount of scrap for the year 1997.

4. The amounts spent in vending machines in the United States, in billions of dollars, for the years 1991 through 1995 are given below. Determine the least squares equation, and estimate vending sales for 1997.

Year	Code	Vending machine sales ($ billions)
1991	1	17.5
1992	2	19.0
1993	3	21.0
1994	4	22.7
1995	5	24.5

THE MOVING-AVERAGE METHOD

Moving-average method smooths out fluctuations

The **moving-average method** is not only useful in smoothing out a time series; it is the basic method used in measuring the seasonal fluctuation, described later in the chapter. In contrast to the least squares method, which expresses the trend in terms of a mathematical equation ($Y' = a + bt$), the moving-average method merely smooths out the fluctuations in the data. This is accomplished by "moving" the arithmetic mean values through the time series.

To apply the moving-average method to a time series, the data should follow a fairly linear trend and have a definite rhythmic pattern of fluctuations (repeating, say, every three years). The data in the following example have three components—trend, cycle, and irregular, abbreviated *T, C,* and *I.* There is no seasonal variation because the data are recorded annually. What the moving-average method does, in effect, is average out *C* and *I.* The residual is trend.

If the duration of the cycles is constant, and if the amplitudes of the cycles are equal, the cyclical and irregular fluctuations can be removed entirely using the moving-average method. The result is a straight line. For example, in the following time series the cycle repeats itself every seven years, and the amplitude of each cycle is 4; that is, there are exactly four units from the trough (lowest time period) to the peak. The seven-year moving average, therefore, averages out the cyclical and irregular fluctuations perfectly, and the residual is a straight-line trend.

Compute mean of first seven years.

The first step in computing the seven-year moving average is to determine the seven-year moving totals. The total sales for the first seven years (1970–76 inclusive) are $22 million, found by 1 + 2 + 3 + 4 + 5 + 4 + 3. (See Table 18–3.) The total of $22 million is divided by 7 to determine the arithmetic mean sales per year. The seven-year total (22) and the seven-year mean (3.134) are positioned opposite the middle year of 1973, as shown in Table 18–3. Then the total sales for the next seven years (1971–77 inclusive) are determined. [A convenient way of doing this is to subtract the sales for 1970 ($1 million) from the first seven-year total ($22 million) and add the sales for 1977 ($2 million), to give the new total of $23 million.] The mean of this total, $3.286 million, is positioned opposite the middle year, 1974.

TABLE 18–3 The Computations for the Seven-Year Moving Average

Year	Sales ($ millions)	Seven-year moving total	Seven-year moving average
1970	$1		
1971	2		
1972	3		
1973	4	22	3.143
1974	5	23	3.286
1975	4	24	3.429
1976	3	25	3.571
1977	2	26	3.714
1978	3	27	3.857
1979	4	28	4.000
1980	5	29	4.143
1981	6	30	4.286
1982	5	31	4.429
1983	4	32	4.571
1984	3	33	4.714
1985	4	34	4.857
1986	5	35	5.000
1987	6	36	5.143
1988	7	37	5.286
1989	6	38	5.429
1990	5	39	5.571
1991	4	40	5.714
1992	5	41	5.857
1993	6		
1994	7		
1995	8		

This procedure is repeated until all possible seven-year totals and their means are found. (Note that there are no totals for the first three years and the last three years.) See Table 18–3 and Chart 18–9.

CHART 18–9 **Sales and Seven-Year Moving Average**

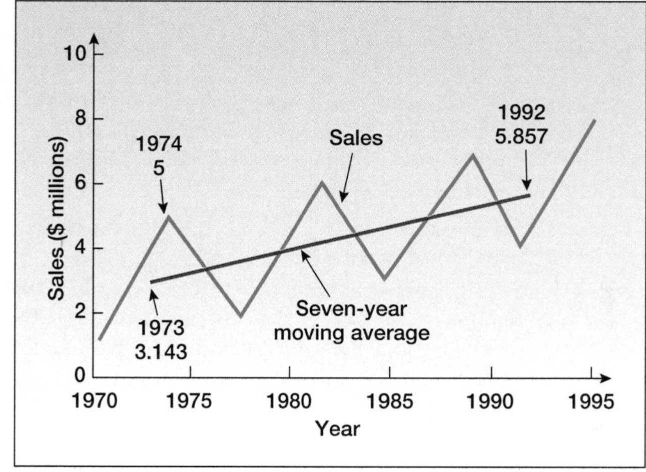

A three-year and a five-year moving average are shown in Table 18–4 and depicted in Chart 18–10.

TABLE 18–4 **A Three-Year Moving Average and a Five-Year Moving Average**

Year	Production, *Y*	Three-year moving total	Three-year moving average	Five-year moving total	Five-year moving average
1976	5				
1977	6	19	6.3		
1978	8	24	8.0	34	6.8
1979	10	23	7.7	32	6.4
1980	5	18	6.0	33	6.6
1981	3	15	5.0	35	7.0
1982	7	20	6.7	37	7.4
1983	10	29	9.7	43	8.6
1984	12	33	11.0	49	9.8
1985	11	32	10.7	55	11.0
1986	9	33	11.0	60	12.0
1987	13	37	12.3	66	13.2
1988	15	46	15.3	70	14.0
1989	18	48	16.0	72	14.4
1990	15	44	14.7	73	14.6
1991	11	40	13.3	75	15.0
1992	14	42	14.0	79	15.8
1993	17	53	17.7		
1994	22				

CHART 18–10 **A Three-Year Moving Average and a Five-Year Moving Average**

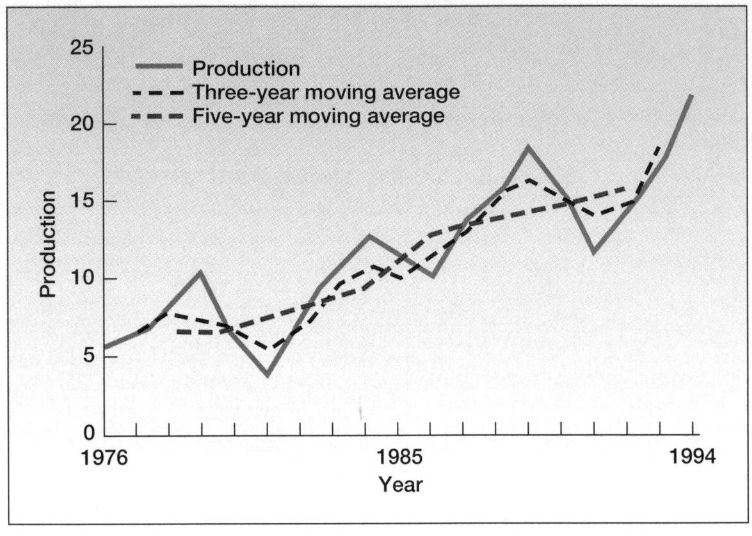

Three-year moving average-using MINITAB

```
MTB>  set c1
DATA> 5, 6, * * *, 17, 22
DATA> end
MTB>  lag 1 c1 c2
MTB>  lag 2 c1 c3
MTB>  let c4= (c1+c2+c3)/3
MTB>  name c1 'Prod' c2 'lag-1' c3 'lag-2' c4 'Mov-avg'
MTB>  print c1 c2 c3 c4
```

ROW	Prod	lag-1	lag-2	Mov-avg
1	5	*	*	*
2	6	5	*	*
3	8	6	5	6.3333
4	10	8	6	8.0000
5	5	10	8	7.6667
6	3	5	10	6.0000
7	7	3	5	5.0000
8	10	7	3	6.6667
9	12	10	7	9.6667
10	11	12	10	11.0000
11	9	11	12	10.6667
12	13	9	11	11.0000
13	15	13	9	12.3333
14	18	15	13	15.3333
15	15	18	15	16.0000
16	11	15	18	14.6667
17	14	11	15	13.3333
18	17	14	11	14.0000
19	22	17	14	17.6667

Moving-average method does not result in straight line

Sales, production, and other economic and business series usually do not have (1) periods of oscillation that are of equal length or (2) oscillations that have identical amplitudes. Thus, in actual practice, the application of the moving-average method to data does not result precisely in a straight line. For example, the production series in Table 18–4 repeats about every five years, but the amplitude of the data varies from one oscillation to another. The trend appears to be upward and somewhat linear. Both moving averages—the three-year and the five-year—seem to adequately describe the trend in production since 1976.

Three-year and five-year moving averages

The MINITAB system can be used to compute the moving average. The production data in Table 18–4 are used to show the MINITAB procedure for a three-year moving average. The first step is to lag each of the production values one period. The data in column C2 are the yearly production figures from column C1 lagged one year. Column C3 is the yearly production lagged two years. Next, the three columns are averaged, creating the moving average. Note that the moving averages are the same as the ones in Table 18–4 (except for rounding).

Determining a moving average for an even-numbered period, such as four years

Four-year, six-year, and other even-numbered-year moving averages present one minor problem regarding the centering of the moving totals and moving averages. Note in Table 18–5 that there is no center time period, so the moving totals are positioned *between* two time periods. The total for the first four years ($42) is positioned between 1988 and 1989. The total for the next four years is $43. The averages of the first four years and the second four years ($10.50 and $10.75, respectively) are averaged, and the resulting figure is centered on 1989. This procedure is repeated until all possible four-year averages are computed.

TABLE 18–5 A Four-Year Moving Average

Year	Sales, Y	Four-year moving total	Four-year moving average	Centered four-year moving average
1987	$ 8			
1988	11			
		$42 (8 + 11 + 9 + 14)	$10.50 ($42 ÷ 4)	
1989	9			10.625
		43 (11 + 9 + 14 + 9)	10.75 ($43 ÷ 4)	
1990	14			10.625
		42	10.50	
1991	9			10.625
		43	10.75	
1992	10			10.000
		37	9.25	
1993	10			9.625
		40	10.00	
1994	8			
1995	12			

To summarize the technique of using moving averages, its purpose is to help identify the long-term trend in a time series (because it smooths out short-term fluctuations). It is used to reveal any cyclical and seasonal fluctuations.

SELF-REVIEW 18–2

The answers are at the end of the chapter.

1. Complete a three-year moving average for the following production series.
2. Plot both the original data and the moving average.

Year	Number produced (thousands)
1990	2
1991	6
1992	4
1993	5
1994	3
1995	10

NONLINEAR TRENDS

The emphasis in the previous discussion was on a time series whose growth or decline approximated a straight line. A straight-line trend equation is used to represent the time series when it is believed that the data are increasing (or decreasing) by *equal amounts,* on the average, from one period to another.

A straight line will not be the "best" fit for these data

Data that increase (or decrease) by *increasing amounts* over a period of time appear *curvilinear* when plotted on paper having an arithmetic scale. To put it another way, data that increase (or decrease) by *equal percents or proportions* over a period of time appear curvilinear on arithmetic paper. (See Chart 18–11.)

The trend equation for a time series that does approximate a curvilinear trend, such as the one portrayed in Chart 18–11, can be computed by using the logarithms of the data and the least squares method.

Formula for logarithmic trend equation

The general equation for the logarithmic trend equation is:

$$\log Y' = \log a + \log b(t) \tag{18–5}$$

CHART 18–11 Imports from 1983 to 1995 on an Arithmetic Scale

Year	Imports
1983	3.0
1984	4.2
1985	5.7
1986	8.3
1987	11.5
1988	16.0
1989	22.4
1990	31.0
1991	44.6
1992	60.1
1993	84.3
1994	118.6
1995	163.9

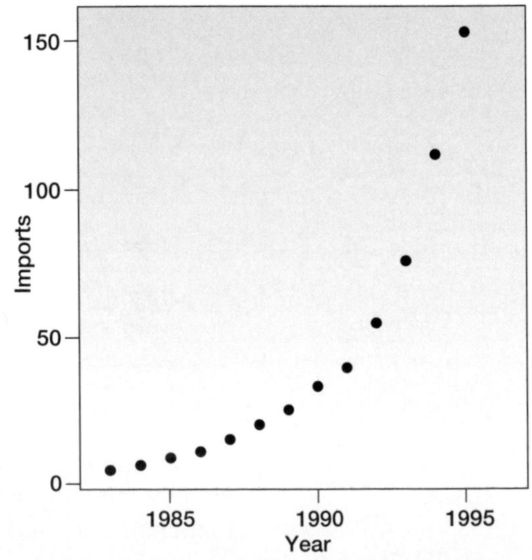

The logarithmic equation can be determined for the import data given in Chart 18–11 using the MINITAB system. The first step is to enter the years and the codes for the years. The import data are entered next. The LET command is used to determine the log to the base 10 for each import value. Finally, the regression procedure is used, with the logarithm of the imports as the dependent variable and the coded years as the independent variable. The output is as follows.

```
MTB> set c1
DATA> 1983:1995
DATA> end
MTB> set c2
DATA> 1:13
DATA> end
MTB> set c3
DATA> 3 4.2 5.7 8.3 11.5 16 22.4 31 44.6 60.1 84.3 118.6 163.9
DATA> end
MTB> let c4=logten(c3)
MTB> name c1 'Year' c2 'Code' c3 'Imports' c4 'Logs'
MTB> print c1 c2 c3 c4

Row    Year    Code    Imports      Logs

  1    1983       1        3.0   0.47712
  2    1984       2        4.2   0.62325
  3    1985       3        5.7   0.75587
  4    1986       4        8.3   0.91908
  5    1987       5       11.5   1.06070
  6    1988       6       16.0   1.20412
  7    1989       7       22.4   1.35025
  8    1990       8       31.0   1.49136
  9    1991       9       44.6   1.64933
 10    1992      10       60.1   1.77887
 11    1993      11       84.3   1.92583
 12    1994      12      118.6   2.07408
 13    1995      13      163.9   2.21458

MTB> regress c4 1 c2

Regression Analysis

The regression equation is
Logs = 0.333 + 0.145 Code

Predictor        Coef       Stdev     t-ratio        p
Constant     0.332549    0.003381       98.36    0.000
Code         0.145069    0.000426      340.56    0.000
```

The regression (trend) equation is:

$$
\begin{aligned}
\log Y' &= \log a + \log b(t) \\
&= 0.333 + 0.145t
\end{aligned}
$$

or, more precisely,

$$\log Y' = 0.332549 + 0.145069t$$

What we now have is the trend equation in terms of percent change. That is, the value 0.145 represents a percent change in Y' for each unit change in t. This value is similar in concept and computation to the geometric mean, discussed in Chapter 3, which gives the percent change in Y (sales, production, and so on) from one time period to another.

The log of b is 0.145, and its antilog is about 1.3964. Subtracting 1 from this value, as we did in Chapter 3, indicates that the imports increased at a rate of about 39.64 percent per year from 1983 to 1995.

The logarithmic straight line is also used to make estimates. Suppose we wanted to estimate imports for the year 2000. The first step is to determine the code for the year 2000, which is 18. How did we get the value of 18? The year 1995 has a code of 13 and the year 2000 is five years later, so 13 + 5 = 18. The log of imports for 2000 is

$$Y' = 0.332549 + 0.145069t$$

$$= 0.332549 + 0.145069(18) = 2.943791$$

To obtain the estimated imports for the year 2000, we need to take the antilog of 2.943791, which is 878.6. This is our estimate of imports for 2000. Recall that the original data are in thousands of dollars, so the actual value is $878,600.

SELF-REVIEW 18–3

The answers are at the end of the chapter.

Sales at Tomlin Manufacturing since 1988 are:

Year	Sales ($ millions)
1991	2.13
1992	18.10
1993	39.80
1994	81.40
1995	112.00

1. Determine the logarithmic straight-line equations for the sales data.
2. Sales increased by what percent annually?
3. What is the projected sales amount for 1996?

EXERCISES

The answers to the odd-numbered exercises are at the end of the book.

5. Sally's Software, Inc. is a rapidly growing supplier of computer software to the Sarasota area. Sales for the last five years are given below.

Year	Sales ($ millions)
1990	1.1
1991	1.5
1992	2.0
1993	2.4
1994	3.1

a. Determine the logarithmic straight-line equation.
b. By what percent did sales increase, on the average, during the period?
c. Estimate sales for the year 1997.

6. It appears that the imports of carbon black have been increasing by about 10 percent annually.

Year	Imports of carbon black (thousands of tons)
1987	92.0
1988	101.0
1989	112.0
1990	124.0
1991	135.0
1992	149.0
1993	163.0
1994	180.0

a. Determine the logarithmic straight-line equation.
b. By what percent did imports increase, on the average, during the period?
c. Estimate imports for the year 1997.

SEASONAL VARIATION

We mentioned that *seasonal variation* is another of the components of a time series. Business series, such as automobile sales, shipments of soft-drink bottles, and residential construction, have periods of above-average and below-average activity during the year.

In the area of production, one of the reasons for analyzing seasonal fluctuations is to have a sufficient supply of raw materials on hand to meet the varying seasonal demand. The glass container division of a large glass company, for example, manufactures nonreturnable beer bottles, returnable beer bottles, iodine bottles, aspirin bottles, bottles for rubber cement, and so on. The production scheduling department must know how many bottles to produce and when to produce each kind. A run of too many bottles of one kind may cause a serious storage problem. Production cannot be based entirely on orders on hand because many orders are telephoned in for immediate shipment. Since the demand for many of the bottles varies according to the season, a forecast a year or two in advance, by month, is essential to good scheduling.

An analysis of seasonal fluctuations over a period of years can also be of help in evaluating current sales. The typical sales of department stores in the United States, excluding mail-order sales, are expressed as indexes in Table 18–6. Each index represents the average sales for a period of several years. The actual sales for some months were above average (which is represented by an index of 100.0 or more), and the sales for other months were below average. The index of 126.8 for December indicates that, typically, sales for December are 26.8 percent above an average month; the index of 86.0 for July indicates that department store sales for July are typically 14 percent below an average month.

TABLE 18–6 Typical Seasonal Indexes for U.S. Department Store Sales, Excluding Mail-Order Sales

January	87.0	July	86.0
February	83.2	August	99.7
March	100.5	September	101.4
April	106.5	October	105.8
May	101.6	November	111.9
June	89.6	December	126.8

Source: Computed from data in the *Survey of Current Business.*

Suppose that an enterprising store manager, in an effort to stimulate sales during December, introduced a number of unique promotions, including bands of carolers strolling through the store singing holiday songs, large mechanical exhibits, and clerks dressed in Santa Claus costumes. When the index of sales was computed for that December, it was 150.0. Compared with the typical sales of 126.8, it was concluded that the promotional program was a huge success.

Determining a Seasonal Index

Objective: To determine a set of "typical" seasonal indexes

A typical set of monthly indexes consists of 12 indexes that are representative of the data for a 12-month period. Logically, there are four typical seasonal indexes for data reported quarterly. Each index is a percent, with the average for the year equal to 100.0; that is, each monthly index indicates the level of sales, production, or other variable in relation to the annual average of 100.0. A typical index of 96.0 for January indicates that sales (or whatever the variable is) are usually 4 percent below the average for the year. An index of 107.2 for October means that the variable is typically 7.2 percent above the annual average.

Several methods have been developed to measure the typical seasonal fluctuation in a time series. The method most commonly used to compute the typical seasonal pattern is called the **ratio-to-moving-average method.** It eliminates the trend, cyclical, and irregular components from the original data (Y). In the following discussion, T refers to trend, C to cyclical, S to seasonal, and I to irregular variation. The numbers that result are called the *typical seasonal index.*

Ratio-to-moving-average method

We will discuss in detail the steps followed in arriving at typical seasonal indexes using the ratio-to-moving-average method. As before, simple figures are used to illustrate.

The data of interest might be monthly or quarterly. To illustrate, we have chosen the quarterly sales of Toys International. First we will show the steps needed to arrive at a set of typical quarterly indexes. Then we will apply a procedure by Hall from *Computerized Business Statistics,* a statistical software package published by Richard D. Irwin, Inc.

EXAMPLE

Table 18–7 shows the quarterly sales for Toys International for the years 1990 to 1995. The sales are reported in millions of dollars. Determine a quarterly seasonal index using the ratio-to-moving-average method.

TABLE 18–7 Quarterly Sales of Toys International ($ millions)

Year	Winter	Spring	Summer	Fall
1990	6.7	4.6	10.0	12.7
1991	6.5	4.6	9.8	13.6
1992	6.9	5.0	10.4	14.1
1993	7.0	5.5	10.8	15.0
1994	7.1	5.7	11.1	14.5
1995	8.0	6.2	11.4	14.9

Solution ► Chart 18–12 depicts the quarterly sales for Toys International over the six-year period. Notice the seasonal nature of the sales. For each year the fourth-quarter sales are the largest and the second-quarter sales are the smallest. Also, there is a moderate increase in the sales from one year to the next. To observe this feature, look only at the six fourth-quarter sales values. Over the six-year period the sales in the fourth quarter increased. If you connect these points in your mind as we did in Chart 18–12, you can visualize fourth-quarter sales increasing for 1996.

CHART 18–12 Quarterly Sales ($ millions) of Toys International

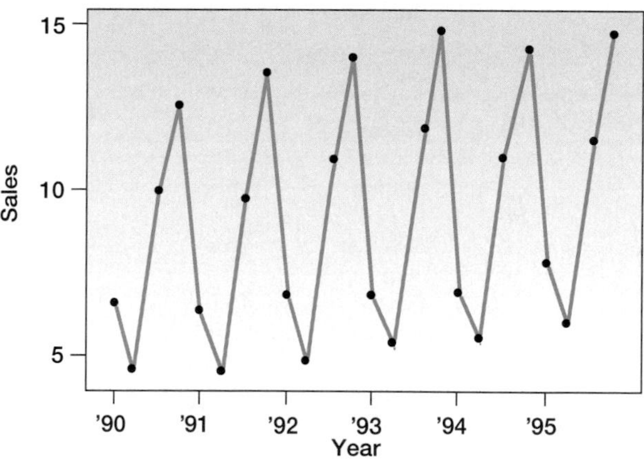

There are six steps to determine the quarterly seasonal indexes.

Step 1 For the following discussion, refer to Table 18–8. The first step is to determine the four-quarter moving total for 1990. Starting with the winter quarter of 1990, we add $6.7, $4.6, $10.0, and $12.7. The total is $34.0 (million). The four-quarter total is "moved along" by adding the spring, summer, and fall sales of 1990 to the winter sales of 1991. The total is $33.8 (million), found by 4.6 + 10.0 + 12.7 + 6.5. This procedure is continued for the quarterly sales for each of the six years. Column 2 of Table 18–8 shows all of the moving totals. Note that the moving total 34.0 is positioned between the spring and summer sales of 1990. The next moving total, 33.8, is positioned between sales for summer and fall of 1990, and so on. Check the totals frequently to avoid arithmetic errors.

TABLE 18–8 Computations Needed for the Specific Seasonal Indexes

Year	Quarter	(1) Sales ($ millions)	(2) Four-quarter moving total	(3) Four-quarter moving average	(4) Centered moving average	(5) Specific seasonal
1990	Winter	6.7				
	Spring	4.6				
			34.0	8.500		
	Summer	10.0			8.4750	1.1799
			33.8	8.450		
	Fall	12.7			8.4500	1.5030
			33.8	8.450		
1991	Winter	6.5			8.4250	0.7715
			33.6	8.400		
	Spring	4.6			8.5125	0.5404
			34.5	8.625		
	Summer	9.8			8.6750	1.1297
			34.9	8.725		
	Fall	13.6			8.7750	1.5499
			35.3	8.825		
1992	Winter	6.9			8.9000	0.7753
			35.9	8.975		
	Spring	5.0			9.0375	0.5533
			36.4	9.100		
	Summer	10.4			9.1125	1.1413
			36.5	9.125		
	Fall	14.1			9.1875	1.5347
			37.0	9.250		
1993	Winter	7.0			9.3000	0.7527
			37.4	9.350		
	Spring	5.5			9.4625	0.5812
			38.3	9.575		
	Summer	10.8			9.5875	1.1265
			38.4	9.600		
	Fall	15.0			9.6250	1.5584
			38.6	9.650		
1994	Winter	7.1			9.6875	0.7329
			38.9	9.725		
	Spring	5.7			9.6625	0.5899
			38.4	9.600		
	Summer	11.1			9.7125	1.1429
			39.3	9.825		
	Fall	14.5			9.8875	1.4665
			39.8	9.950		
1995	Winter	8.0			9.9875	0.8010
			40.1	10.025		
	Spring	6.2			10.0750	0.6154
			40.5	10.125		
	Summer	11.4				
	Fall	14.9				

Step 2 Each quarterly moving total in column 2 is divided by 4 to give the four-quarter moving average. (See column 3.) All the moving averages are still positioned between the quarters. For example, the first moving average (8.500) is positioned between spring and summer of 1990.

Step 3 The moving averages are then centered. The first centered moving average is found by (8.500 + 8.450)/2 = 8.4750. The second moving average is found by (8.450 + 8.450)/2 = 8.450. The others are found similarly. Note in column 4 that a centered moving average is positioned on a particular quarter.

Step 4 The **specific seasonal** for each quarter is then computed by dividing the sales in column 1 by the centered moving average in column 4. The specific seasonal reports the ratio of the original time series value to the moving average. To explain further, if the time series is represented by *TSCI* and the moving average by *TCI*, then algebraically if we compute *TSCI/TCI*, the result is the seasonal component. The specific seasonal for the summer quarter of 1990 is 1.1799, found by 10.0/8.4750.

Step 5 The specific seasonals are organized in a table. (See Table 18–9.) This table will help us locate the specific seasonals for the corresponding quarters. The values 1.1799, 1.1297, 1.1413, 1.1265, and 1.1429 all represent estimates of the typical seasonal index for the summer quarter. A reasonable method to find a typical seasonal index is to average these values. So we find the typical index for the summer quarter by: (1.1799 + 1.1297 + 1.1413 + 1.1265 + 1.1429)/5 = 1.1441. We used the arithmetic mean, but the median or a modified mean can also be used.

Step 6 The four quarterly means (0.7667, 0.5760, 1.1441, and 1.5225) should theoretically total 4.00 because the average is set at 1.0. The total of the four quarterly means may not exactly equal 4.00 due to rounding. In this problem the total of the means is 4.0093. A *correction factor* is therefore applied to each of the four means to force them to total 4.00.

$$\text{Correction factor} = \frac{4.00}{\text{Total of four means}} \tag{18–6}$$

In this problem,

$$\text{Correction factor} = \frac{4.00}{4.0093} = 0.99768$$

To adjust the winter quarterly index, (0.7667)(0.99768) = 0.7649. Each of the means is adjusted downward so that the total of the four quarterly means is 4.00. Usually indexes are reported as percentages, so each value in the last row of Table 18–9 has been multiplied by 100. So the index for the winter quarter is 76.49 and for the fall it is 151.90. How are these values interpreted? Sales for the fall quarter are 51.90 percent above the typical quarter, and for winter they are 23.51 below the typical quarter (100.00 − 76.49). These findings should not surprise you. The period prior to Christmas (the fall quarter) is when toy sales are brisk. After Christmas (the winter quarter) sales of the toys decline drastically.

Now to briefly summarize the reasoning underlying the preceding calculations. The original data in column 1 of Table 18–8 contain trend (*T*), cycle (*C*), seasonal (*S*), and irregular (*I*) components. The ultimate objective is to remove seasonal (*S*) from the original sales valuation.

Columns 2 and 3 in Table 18–8 were concerned with deriving the centered moving average given in column 4. Basically, we "averaged out" the seasonal and irregular fluctuations from the original data in column 1. Thus, in column 4 we have only trend and cycle (*TC*).

TABLE 18–9 Calculations Needed for the Typical Quarterly Indexes

Year	Winter	Spring	Summer	Fall	
1990			1.1799	1.5030	
1991	0.7715	0.5404	1.1297	1.5499	
1992	0.7753	0.5533	1.1413	1.5347	
1993	0.7527	0.5812	1.1265	1.5584	
1994	0.7329	0.5899	1.1429	1.4665	
1995	0.8010	0.6154			
Total	3.8334	2.8802	5.7203	7.6125	
Mean	0.7667	0.5760	1.1441	1.5225	4.0093
Typical index	76.49	57.47	114.14	151.90	4.0000

Next we divided the sales data in column 1 (*TCSI*) by the centered four-month moving average in column 4 (*TC*) to arrive at the specific seasonals in column 5 (*SI*). In terms of letters, *TCSI/TC* = *SI*. We multiplied *SI* by 100.0 in order to express the typical seasonal in index form.

Finally, we took the mean of all the winter typical indexes, all the spring indexes, and so on. This averaging eliminates most of the irregular fluctuations from the seasonals, and the resulting four indexes indicate the typical seasonal sales pattern.

A Computer Solution As noted previously, a statistical software package called *Computerized Business Statistics,* developed by Hall, has a routine for computing seasonal indexes. The following is the output obtained for the previous example. Much of the same information on the trend and seasonal-irregular components is shown. The final answers differ slightly, due to rounding, from those in Table 18–9. Use of a package such as Hall will greatly reduce computational time and the possibility of an error in arithmetic. The seasonal values obtained from the Hall software package will be used in the analyses later in the chapter.

SELF-REVIEW 18–4

The answers are at the end of the chapter.

Teton Village, Wyoming, near Grand Teton Park and Yellowstone Park, contains shops, restaurants, and motels. They have two peak seasons—winter, for skiing on the 10,000–foot slopes, and summer, for tourists visiting the parks. The specific seasonals with respect to the total sales volume for recent years are:

	Quarter			
Year	**Winter**	**Spring**	**Summer**	**Fall**
1990	117.0	80.7	129.6	76.1
1991	118.6	82.5	121.4	77.0
1992	114.0	84.3	119.9	75.0
1993	120.7	79.6	130.7	69.6
1994	125.2	80.2	127.6	72.0

1. Develop the typical seasonal sales pattern for Teton Village using the ratio-to-moving-average method.
2. Explain the typical index for the winter season.

CBS-Time Series and Forecasting 08–18–1994 -17:20:21

Information Entered

Model: Seasonal Indices
Number of Periods: 24

Period	Quarter	Value	Period	Quarter	Value
1	1	6.7		2	5.5
	2	4.6		3	10.8
	3	10		4	15
	4	12.7	5	1	7.1
2	1	6.5		2	5.7
	2	4.6		3	11.1
	3	9.8		4	14.5
	4	13.6	6	1	8
3	1	6.9		2	6.2
	2	5		3	11.4
	3	10.4		4	14.9
	4	14.1			
4	1	7			

Results

Model: Seasonal Indices
Number of Periods: 24

Classical Seasonal Indices

Period	Quarter	Value	Trend	S–I
1	1	6.7000	–	–
	2	4.6000	–	–
	3	10	8.4750	1.1799
	4	12.7000	8.4500	1.5030
2	1	6.5000	8.4250	0.7715
	2	4.6000	8.5125	0.5404
	3	9.8000	8.6750	1.1297
	4	13.6000	8.7750	1.5499
3	1	6.9000	8.9000	0.7753
	2	5	9.0375	0.5533
	3	10.4000	9.1125	1.1413
	4	14.1000	9.1875	1.5347
4	1	7	9.3000	0.7527
	2	5.5000	9.4625	0.5812
	3	10.8000	9.5875	1.1265
	4	15	9.6250	1.5584
5	1	7.1000	9.6875	0.7329
	2	5.7000	9.6625	0.5899
	3	11.1000	9.7125	1.1429
	4	14.5000	9.8875	1.4665
6	1	8	9.9875	0.8010
	2	6.2000	10.0750	0.6154
	3	11.4000	–	–
	4	14.9000	–	–

Seasonal Index by Quarter

Quarter	Average SI Component	Seasonal Index
1	0.7667	0.7667
2	0.5760	0.5760
3	1.1440	1.1440
4	1.5225	1.5225

← Multiply by 100 to obtain index

EXERCISES

The answers to the odd-numbered exercises are at the end of the book.

7. Victor Anderson, the owner of Anderson Belts, Inc., is studying absenteeism among his employees. His work force is very small, consisting of only five employees. For the last three years he recorded the following number of employee absences, in days, for each quarter.

	Quarter			
Year	**I**	**II**	**III**	**IV**
1992	4	10	7	3
1993	5	12	9	4
1994	6	16	12	4

Determine a typical seasonal index for each of the four quarters.

8. The Appliance Center sells a variety of electronic equipment and home appliances. For the last four years the following quarterly sales (in $ millions) were reported.

	Quarter			
Year	**I**	**II**	**III**	**IV**
1991	5.3	4.1	6.8	6.7
1992	4.8	3.8	5.6	6.8
1993	4.3	3.8	5.7	6.0
1994	5.6	4.6	6.4	5.9

Determine a typical seasonal index for each of the four quarters.

Deseasonalizing Data

A set of typical indexes is very useful in adjusting a sales series, for example, for seasonal fluctuations. The resulting sales series is called **deseasonalized sales** or **seasonally adjusted sales.** The reason for deseasonalizing the sales series is to remove the seasonal fluctuations so that the trend and cycle can be studied. To illustrate the procedure, the quarterly sales totals of Toys International from Table 18–7 are repeated in column 1 of Table 18–10.

To remove the effect of seasonal variation, the sales amount for each quarter (which contains trend, cyclical, irregular, and seasonal effects) is divided by the seasonal index for that quarter, that is, *TSCI/TCI.* For example, the actual sales for the first quarter of 1990 were $6.7 million. The seasonal index for the winter quarter is 76.67, using the Hall results on page 751. The index of 76.67 indicates that sales for the first quarter are typically 23.33 percent below the average for a typical quarter. By dividing the actual sales of $6.7 million by 76.67 and multiplying the result by 100, we find the *deseasonalized* sales value for the first quarter of 1990. It is $8,738,750, found by ($6,700,000/76.67)100. We continue this process for the other quarters in column 3 of Table 18–10, with the results reported in millions of dollars. Because the seasonal component has been removed (divided out) from the quarterly sales, the deseasonalized sales figure contains only the trend (T), cyclical (C), and irregular (I) components. Scanning the deseasonalized sales in column 3 of Table 18–10, we see that the sales of toys showed a moderate increase over the six-year period. Chart

18–13 show both the actual sales and the deseasonalized sales. It is clear that removing the seasonal factor allows us to focus on the overall long-term trend of sales. We will also be able to determine the regression equation of the trend data and use it to forecast future sales.

TABLE 18–10 **Actual and Deseasonalized Sales for Toys International**

Year	Quarter	(1) Sales	(2) Seasonal index	(3) Deseasonalized sales
1990	Winter	6.7	0.7667	8.7387
	Spring	4.6	0.5760	7.9861
	Summer	10.0	1.1440	8.7413
	Fall	12.7	1.5225	8.3415
1991	Winter	6.5	0.7667	8.4779
	Spring	4.6	0.5760	7.9861
	Summer	9.8	1.1440	8.5664
	Fall	13.6	1.5225	8.9327
1992	Winter	6.9	0.7667	8.9996
	Spring	5.0	0.5760	8.6806
	Summer	10.4	1.1440	9.0909
	Fall	14.1	1.5225	9.2611
1993	Winter	7.0	0.7667	9.1300
	Spring	5.5	0.5760	9.5486
	Summer	10.8	1.1440	9.4406
	Fall	15.0	1.5225	9.8522
1994	Winter	7.1	0.7667	9.2605
	Spring	5.7	0.5760	9.8958
	Summer	11.1	1.1440	9.7028
	Fall	14.5	1.5225	9.5238
1995	Winter	8.0	0.7667	10.4343
	Spring	6.2	0.5760	10.7639
	Summer	11.4	1.1440	9.9650
	Fall	14.9	1.5225	9.7865

CHART 18–13 **Actual Sales and Deseasonalized Sales for Toys International, 1990 to 1995**

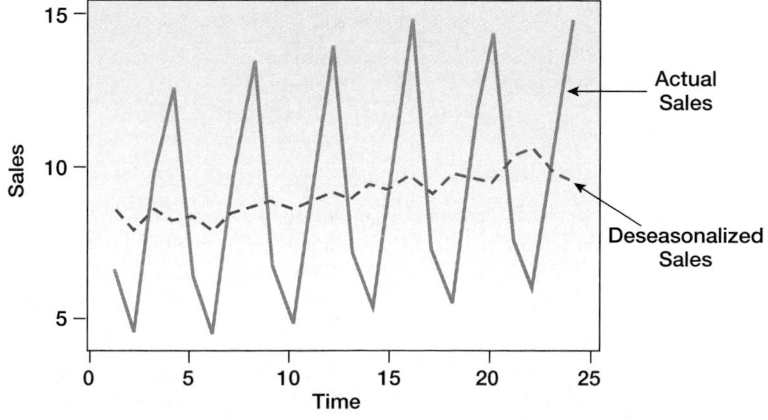

Using Deseasonalized Data to Forecast The procedure for identifying trend and the seasonal adjustments can be combined to yield seasonally adjusted forecasts. To identify the trend, we determine the least squares trend equation on the historical data. Then we project this trend into future periods, and finally we adjust these trend values to account for the seasonal factors. The following example will help to clarify.

EXAMPLE

Toys International would like to forecast their sales for each quarter of 1996. Use the information in Table 18–10 to determine the forecast.

Solution

▶ The first step is to use the deseasonalized data in column 3 of Table 18–10 to determine the least squares trend equation. The deseasonalized trend equation is:

$$Y' = a + bt$$

where:

- Y' is the estimated trend for Toys International sales for period t.
- a is the intercept of the trend line at time 0.
- b is the slope of the trend line.

The winter quarter of 1990 is the period $t = 1$, and $t = 24$ corresponds to the fall quarter of 1995. (See column 1 in Table 18–11.) The sums needed to compute a and b are also shown in Table 18–11.

TABLE 18–11 **Deseasonalized Sales for Toys International: Data Needed for Determining Trend Line**

Year	Quarter	(1) t	(2) Y	(3) tY	(4) t^2
1990	Winter	1	8.7387	8.7387	1
	Spring	2	7.9861	15.9722	4
	Summer	3	8.7413	26.2239	9
	Fall	4	8.3415	33.3660	16
1991	Winter	5	8.4779	42.3895	25
	Spring	6	7.9861	47.9166	36
	Summer	7	8.5664	59.9648	49
	Fall	8	8.9327	71.4616	64
1992	Winter	9	8.9996	80.9964	81
	Spring	10	8.6806	86.8060	100
	Summer	11	9.0909	99.9999	121
	Fall	12	9.2611	111.1332	144
1993	Winter	13	9.1300	118.6900	169
	Spring	14	9.5486	133.6804	196
	Summer	15	9.4406	141.6090	225
	Fall	16	9.8522	157.6352	256
1994	Winter	17	9.2605	157.4285	289
	Spring	18	9.8958	178.1244	324
	Summer	19	9.7028	184.3532	361
	Fall	20	9.5238	190.4760	400
1995	Winter	21	10.4343	219.1203	441
	Spring	22	10.7639	236.8058	484
	Summer	23	9.9650	229.1950	529
	Fall	24	9.7865	234.8760	576
Total		300	221.1069	2,866.9626	4,900

$$b = \frac{\Sigma tY - (\Sigma Y)(\Sigma t)/n}{\Sigma t^2 - (\Sigma t)^2/n} = \frac{2{,}866.9626 - (221.1069)(300)/24}{4{,}900 - (300)^2/24}$$

$$= 0.0897$$

$$a = \frac{\Sigma Y}{n} - b\left(\frac{\Sigma t}{n}\right) = \frac{221.1069}{24} - 0.0897\left(\frac{300}{24}\right) = 8.0915$$

The trend equation is:

$$Y' = 8.0915 + 0.0897t$$

The slope of the trend line is 0.0897. This shows that over the 24 quarters the deseasonalized sales increased at a rate of 0.0897 ($ millions) per quarter, or $89,700 per quarter. The value of 8.0915 is the intercept of the trend line on the Y-axis (i.e., for $t = 0$).

Of course, we can use the MINITAB system to find the regression equation. This will reduce the possibility of an error in arithmetic. We can use the value of R^2 to give us an indication of the fit of the data. Because this is *not* sample information, technically we should not use R^2 as a basis for judging the regression equation; however, it will serve to quickly evaluate the fit of the deseasonalized data. In this instance the R^2 value is 78.5 percent, which indicates that time does an effective job of explaining the variation in the deseasonalized data.

```
MTB > Regress 'Deseason' 1 'Time';
SUBC> Constant.
Regression Analysis

The regression equation is
Deseason = 8.09 + 0.0897 Time

Predictor       Coef        Stdev       t-ratio      p
Constant      8.0919       0.1429        56.64     0.000
Time          0.089675     0.009998       8.97     0.000

s = 0.3391   R-sq = 78.5%   R-sq(adj) = 77.5%

Analysis of Variance

SOURCE        DF       SS         MS         F          p
Regression     1     9.2479     9.2479     80.45      0.000
Error         22     2.5291     0.1150
Total         23    11.7770
```

If we assume that the past 24 periods are a good indicator of future sales, we can use the trend equation to estimate future sales. For example, for the winter quarter of 1996, the value of t is 25. The estimated sales total for that period is $10,334,000, found by

$$Y' = 8.0915 + 0.0897(25) = 10.334$$

Using the trend equation, we can forecast sales at Toys International for the four quarters of 1996. These estimates are shown in Table 18–12.

TABLE 18–12 Quarterly Forecast for Toys International for 1996

Quarter	t	Estimated sales	Seasonal index	Quarterly forecast
Winter	25	10.3340	0.7667	7.923
Spring	26	10.4237	0.5760	6.004
Summer	27	10.5134	1.1440	12.027
Fall	28	10.6031	1.5225	16.143

Now that we have the forecasts for the four quarters of 1996, we can seasonally adjust them. The index for the winter quarter is 0.7667 (see the Hall computer solution earlier in the chapter), so we can estimate the sales in this quarter by $10.3340(0.7667) = 7.923$. The estimates for the four quarters of 1996 are shown in the last column of Table 18–12. Notice how the seasonal adjustments drastically increase the sales estimates for the last two quarters of the year.

SELF-REVIEW 18–5

The answers are at the end of the chapter.

The Westberg Electric Company sells electric motors to customers in the Jamestown, New York, area. The monthly trend equation, based on five years of monthly data, is

$$Y' = 4.40 + 0.50t$$

The seasonal factor for the month of January is 120, and it is 95 for February. Determine the seasonally adjusted forecast for January and February of the sixth year.

EXERCISES

The answers to the odd-numbered exercises are at the end of the book.

9. The planning department of Padget and Kure Shoes, the manufacturer of an exclusive brand of women's shoes, developed the following trend equation, in millions of pairs, based on five years of quarterly data.

$$Y' = 3.30 + 1.75t$$

The following table gives the seasonal factors for each quarter.

	Quarter			
	I	II	III	IV
Index	110.0	120.0	80.0	90.0

Determine the seasonally adjusted forecast for each of the four quarters of the sixth year.

10. Team Sports, Inc. sells sporting goods to high schools and colleges via a nationally distributed catalog. Management at Team Sports estimates they will sell 2,000 Wilson Model A2000 catcher's mitts next year. The deseasonalized sales are projected to be the same for each of the four quarters next year. The seasonal factor for the second quarter is 145. Determine the seasonally adjusted sales for the second quarter of next year.
11. Refer to Exercise 7, regarding the absences at Anderson Belts, Inc. Use the seasonal indexes you computed to determine the deseasonalized absences. Determine the trend equation based on the quarterly data for the three years. Forecast the seasonally adjusted absences for 1995.

12. Refer to Exercise 8, regarding sales at the Appliance Center. Use the seasonal indexes you computed to determine the deseasonalized sales. Determine the trend equation based on the quarterly data for the four years. Forecast the seasonally adjusted sales for 1995.

CHAPTER OUTLINE

I. A time series is a collection of data over a period of time.
   A. The trend is the long-run direction of the time series.
   B. The cyclical component is the fluctuation above and below the long-term trend line.
   C. The seasonal variation is the pattern in a time series within a year. These patterns tend to repeat themselves from year to year for most businesses.
   D. The irregular variation is divided into two components.
      1. The episodic variations are unpredictable, but they can usually be identified. A flood is an example.
      2. The residual variations are random in nature.

II. The long-run trend equation is $Y' = a + bt$, where a is the Y-intercept, b is the slope of the line, and t is the time.
   A. The trend equation is determined using the least squares principle.
   B. If the trend is not linear, but rather the increases tend to be a constant percent, the Y values are converted to logarithms, and a least squares equation is determined using the logs.

III. A moving average is used to smooth the trend in a time series.

IV. A seasonal factor can be estimated using the ratio-to-moving-average method.
   A. The six-step procedure yields a seasonal index for each period.
      1. Seasonal factors are usually computed on a monthly or a quarterly basis.
      2. The seasonal factor is used to adjust forecasts, taking into account the effects of the season.

EXERCISES

The answers to the odd-numbered exercises are at the end of the book.

13. Refer to the following diagram.
   a. Estimate the linear equation for the following production series by drawing a straight line through the data.
   b. What is the average annual decrease in production?
   c. Based on the trend equation, what is the forecast for the year 2000?

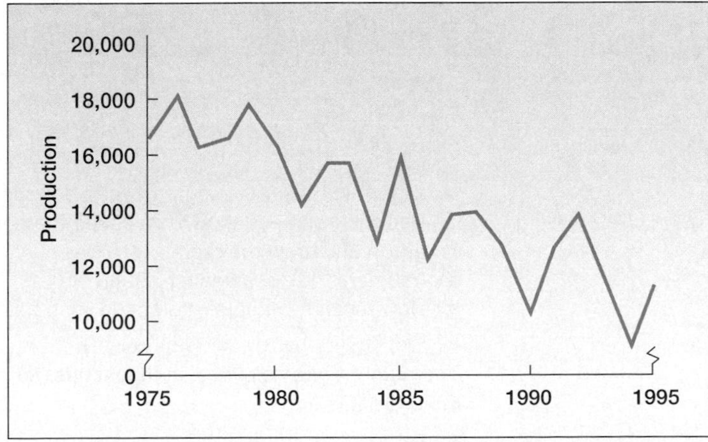

14. *a.* Estimate the trend equation for the following personal income series.
    b. What is the average annual increase in personal income?

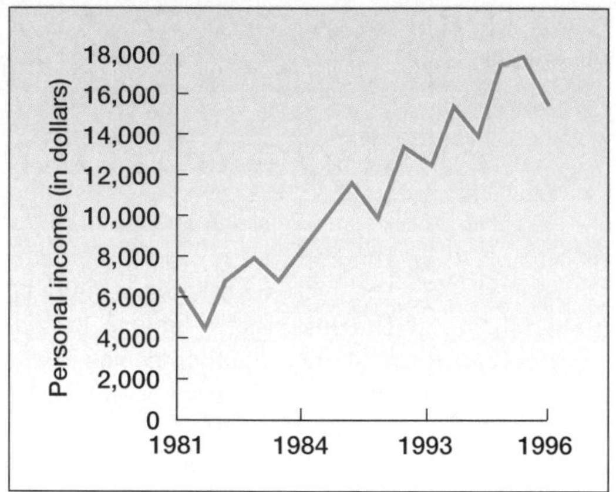

15. The asset turnovers, excluding cash and short-term investments, for the RNC Company from 1983 to 1993 are:

1983	1984	1985	1986	1987	1988	1989	1990	1991	1992	1993
1.11	1.28	1.17	1.10	1.06	1.14	1.24	1.33	1.38	1.50	1.65

a. Plot the data.
b. Determine the least squares trend equation.
c. Calculate the points on the trend line for 1986 and 1991, and plot the line on the graph.
d. Estimate the asset turnover for 1998.
e. How much did the asset turnover increase per year, on the average, from 1983 to 1993?

16. The sales, in billions of dollars, for the Monsanto Corporation based on their annual reports for 1988 to 1993 are:

Year	Sales
1988	7.45
1989	7.83
1990	8.07
1991	7.94
1992	7.76
1993	7.90

a. Plot the data.
b. Determine the least squares trend equation.
c. Use the trend equation to calculate the points for 1990 and 1992. Plot them on the graph and draw the regression line.
d. Estimate the net sales for 1996.
e. How much have sales increased (or decreased) per year on the average during the period?

17. The number of employees, in thousands, for the Monsanto Corporation for the years 1988 to 1993 are:

Year	Sales
1988	45.6
1989	42.2
1990	41.1
1991	39.3
1992	34.0
1993	30.0

a. Plot the data.
b. Determine the least squares trend equation.
c. Use the trend equation to calculate the points for 1990 and 1992. Plot them on the graph and draw the regression line.
d. Estimate the number of employees in 1996.
e. By how much has the number of employees increased (or decreased) per year on the average during the period?

18. Since 1988 the annual value of merchandise trade from Canada to the United States, in billions of Canadian dollars, is:

Year	Merchandise value
1988	121.9
1989	123.8
1990	129.6
1991	127.6
1992	142.2
1993	168.2

a. Plot the data.
b. Determine the least squares trend equation.
c. Calculate the points for the years 1990 and 1992 based on the trend equation. Plot them on the graph and draw the regression line.
d. Estimate the trade in 1996.
e. How much has the trade increased (or decreased) per year on the average during the period?

19. If plotted on arithmetic paper, the following sales series would appear curvilinear. This indicates that sales are increasing at a somewhat constant annual rate (percent). To fit the sales, therefore, a logarithmic straight-line equation should be used.

Year	Sales ($ millions)	Year	Sales ($ millions)
1985	8.0	1990	29.3
1986	10.4	1991	39.4
1987	13.5	1992	50.5
1988	17.6	1993	65.0
1989	22.8	1994	84.1
		1995	109.0

a. Determine the logarithmic straight-line equation.
b. Determine the coordinates of the points on the logarithmic straight line for 1988 and 1993.
c. By what percent did sales increase per year, on the average, during the period from 1985 to 1995?
d. Based on the equation, what are the estimated sales for 1996?

20. Reported below are the amounts spent on advertising ($ billions) from 1987 to 1993.

Year	Amount
1987	88.1
1988	94.7
1989	102.1
1990	109.8
1991	118.1
1992	125.6
1993	132.6

a. Determine the logarithmic straight-line equation.
b. Estimate the advertising expenses for 1996.
c. By what percent did advertising expense increase during the period?

21. The numbers of households (in millions) in the United States with videocassette recorders (VCRs) for each year from 1980 to 1992 are shown below.

Year	Number	Year	Number
1980	0.8	1986	30.9
1981	1.4	1987	42.6
1982	3.0	1988	51.4
1983	4.6	1989	58.4
1984	8.9	1990	63.2
1985	17.6	1991	67.1
		1992	72.3

a. Determine the logarithmic straight-line equation.
b. Estimate the number of households with VCRs in 1997.
c. By what percent did the number of households with VCRs increase during the period?

22. The production of the Reliable Manufacturing Company for 1991 and part of 1992 follows.

Month	1991 production (thousands)	1992 production (thousands)
January	6	7
February	7	9
March	12	14
April	8	9
May	4	5
June	3	4
July	3	4
August	5	
September	14	
October	6	
November	7	
December	6	

a. Using the ratio-to-moving-average method, determine the specific seasonals for July, August, and September 1991.
b. Assume that the specific seasonal indexes in the following table are correct. Insert in the table the specific seasonals you computed in part *a* for July, August, and September 1991, and determine the 12 typical seasonal indexes.

Year	Jan.	Feb.	Mar.	Apr.	May	June	July	Aug.	Sept.	Oct.	Nov.	Dec.
1991							?	?	?	92.1	106.5	92.9
1992	88.9	102.9	178.9	118.2	60.1	43.1	44.0	74.0	200.9	90.0	101.9	90.9
1993	87.6	103.7	170.2	125.9	59.4	48.6	44.2	77.2	196.5	89.6	113.2	80.6
1994	79.8	105.6	165.8	124.7	62.1	41.7	48.2	72.1	203.6	80.2	103.0	94.2
1995	89.0	112.1	182.9	115.1	57.6	56.9						

c. Interpret the typical seasonal index.

23. The sales of Andre's Boutique for 1990 and part of 1991 are:

Month	1990 sales (thousands)	1991 sales (thousands)
January	78	65
February	72	60
March	80	72
April	110	97
May	92	86
June	86	72
July	81	65
August	85	61
September	90	75
October	98	
November	115	
December	130	

a. Using the ratio-to-moving-average method, determine the specific seasonals for July, August, September, and October 1990.

b. Assume that the specific seasonals in the following table are correct. Insert in the table the specific seasonals you computed in part *a* for July, August, September, and October 1990, and determine the 12 typical seasonal indexes.

Year	Jan.	Feb.	Mar.	Apr.	May	June	July	Aug.	Sept.	Oct.	Nov.	Dec.
1990							?	?	?	?	123.6	150.9
1991	83.9	77.6	86.1	118.7	99.7	92.0	87.0	91.4	97.3	105.4	124.9	140.1
1992	86.7	72.9	86.2	121.3	96.6	92.0	85.5	93.6	98.2	103.2	126.1	141.7
1993	85.6	65.8	89.2	125.6	99.6	94.4	88.9	90.2	100.2	102.7	121.6	139.6
1994	77.3	81.2	85.8	115.7	100.3	89.7						

c. Interpret the typical seasonal index.

24. The quarterly production of pine lumber, in millions of board feet, by Northwest Lumber since 1990 is:

	Quarter			
Year	Winter	Spring	Summer	Fall
1990	7.8	10.2	14.7	9.3
1991	6.9	11.6	17.5	9.3
1992	8.9	9.7	15.3	10.1
1993	10.7	12.4	16.8	10.7
1994	9.2	13.6	17.1	10.3

a. Determine the typical seasonal pattern for the production data using the ratio-to-moving-average method.
b. Interpret the pattern.
c. Deseasonalize the data, and determine the trend equation.
d. Project the seasonally adjusted production for the four quarters of 1995.

25. Work Gloves Corp. is reviewing its quarterly sales of Toughie, the most durable glove they produce. The numbers of pairs produced (in thousands) by quarter are:

	Quarter			
Year	**I Jan.–Mar.**	**II Apr.–June**	**III July–Sept.**	**IV Oct.–Dec.**
1989	142	312	488	208
1990	146	318	512	212
1991	160	330	602	187
1992	158	338	572	176
1993	162	380	563	200
1994	162	362	587	205

a. Using the ratio-to-moving-average method, determine the four typical quarterly indexes.
b. Interpret the typical seasonal pattern.

26. Sales of aluminum, by quarter, since 1988 are shown below (in $ millions).

	Quarter			
Year	**I**	**II**	**III**	**IV**
1988	210	180	60	246
1989	214	216	82	230
1990	246	228	91	280
1991	258	250	113	298
1992	279	267	116	304
1993	302	290	114	310
1994	321	291	120	320

a. Determine the typical seasonal patterns for sales using the ratio-to-moving-average method.
b. Deseasonalize the data, and determine the trend equation.
c. Project the sales for 1995, and then seasonally adjust each quarter.

27. The inventory turnover rates for Bassett Wholesale Enterprises, by quarter, are:

	Quarter			
Year	**I**	**II**	**III**	**IV**
1990	4.4	6.1	11.7	7.2
1991	4.1	6.6	11.1	8.6
1992	3.9	6.8	12.0	9.7
1993	5.0	7.1	12.7	9.0
1994	4.3	5.2	10.8	7.6

a. Arrive at the four typical quarterly turnover rates for the Bassett Company using the ratio-to-moving-average method.
b. Deseasonalize the data, and determine the trend equation.
c. Project the turnover rates for 1995, and seasonally adjust each quarter of 1995.

28. The following is the enrollment at the University of Toledo from 1967 until 1994. Develop both a linear and a logarithmetic trend equation. Estimate the enrollment for 1995 using

both equations. Which trend equation would you recommend? Why? Plot the data and comment on your forecast.

Year	Enrollment	Year	Enrollment
1967	12,755	1981	21,117
1968	13,501	1982	21,386
1969	14,489	1983	21,589
1970	15,158	1984	21,039
1971	14,903	1985	21,238
1972	14,669	1986	21,176
1973	14,343	1987	21,740
1974	15,730	1988	22,806
1975	17,109	1989	23,928
1976	17,204	1990	24,781
1977	17,498	1991	24,969
1978	17,257	1992	24,541
1979	18,246	1993	24,188
1980	20,270	1994	23,123

29. Ray Anderson, owner of the Anderson Ski Lodge in upstate New York, is interested in forecasting the number of visitors for the upcoming year. The following data are available, by quarter since 1988. Develop a seasonal index for each quarter. How many visitors would you expect for each quarter of 1995, if Ray projects that there will be a 10 percent increase from the total number of visitors in 1994? Determine the trend equation, project the number of visitors for 1995, and seasonally adjust the forecast. Which forecast would you choose?

Year	Quarter	Visitors	Year	Quarter	Visitors
1988	I	86	1992	I	188
	II	62		II	172
	III	28		III	128
	IV	94		IV	198
1989	I	106	1993	I	208
	II	82		II	202
	III	48		III	154
	IV	114		IV	220
1990	I	140	1994	I	246
	II	120		II	240
	III	82		III	190
	IV	154		IV	252
1991	I	162			
	II	140			
	III	100			
	IV	174			

30. The enrollment in the College of Business at Midwestern University by quarter since 1990 is:

	Quarter			
Year	Winter	Spring	Summer	Fall
1990	2,033	1,871	714	2,318
1991	2,174	2,069	840	2,413
1992	2,370	2,254	927	2,704
1993	2,625	2,478	1,136	3,001
1994	2,803	2,668	—	—

Using the ratio-to-moving-average method:

a. Determine the four quarterly indexes.

b. Interpret the quarterly pattern of enrollment. Does the seasonal variation surprise you?

c. Compute the trend equation, and forecast the 1995 enrollment by quarter.

CHAPTER 18 EXAMINATION

The answers are at the end of the chapter.

1. The numbers of computers sold by P. C. Modem Computers, Inc. by year for the last four years are:

Year	Sales (hundreds)
1992	10.1
1993	17.5
1994	25.0
1995	31.3

Determine the least squares equation, and estimate sales for 1997 and 1998. Code 1992 as 1.

2. Following are the quarterly sales for a time series.

Year	Quarter	Sales
1994	I	26
	II	14
	III	6
	IV	10
1995	I	34
	II	20

a. Determine the trend and cyclical components for the third and fourth quarters of 1994.

b. Determine the seasonal and irregular components for the third and fourth quarters of 1994.

3. The trend equation describing the monthly sales, in thousands of units, for a large manufacturer of snow blowers is

$$Y' = 2.50 + 4.56t$$

a. The equation was developed using five years of monthly data. Determine the projected number of snow blowers sold in April of the sixth year. Code the first quarter as 1.

b. The seasonal index for the month of April is 75.0. Determine the seasonally adjusted sales forecast for April of the sixth year.

CHAPTER 18 Answers

Self-Review

18–1 1.

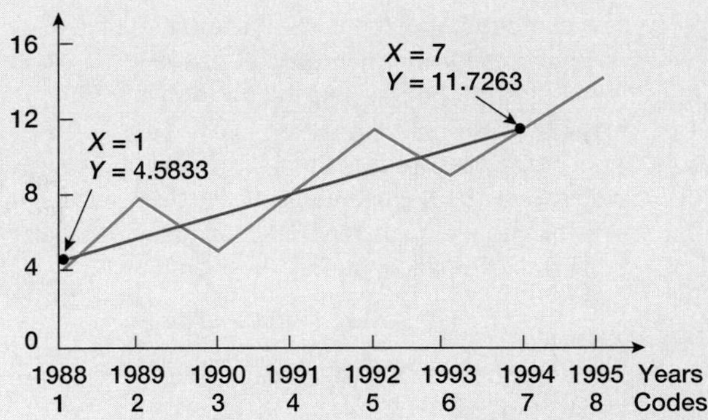

2. $Y' = a + bt = 3.3928 + 1.1905t$ (in thousands)

$$b = \frac{365 - 36(70)/8}{204 - (36)^2/8} = \frac{50}{42} = 1.1905$$

$$a = \frac{70}{8} - 1.1905\left(\frac{36}{8}\right) = 3.3928$$

3. For 1988:

$$Y' = 3.3928 + 1.1905(1) = 4.5833$$

for 1994:

$$Y' = 3.3928 + 1.1905(7) = 11.7263$$

4. For 1998, $t = 11$, so

$$Y' = 3.3928 + 1.1905(11) = 16.488$$

or 16,488 king-size rockers.

18–2 1.

Year	Production (thousands)	Three-year moving total	Three-year moving average
1990	2	—	—
1991	6	12	4
1992	4	15	5
1993	5	12	4
1994	3	18	6
1995	10	—	—

2.

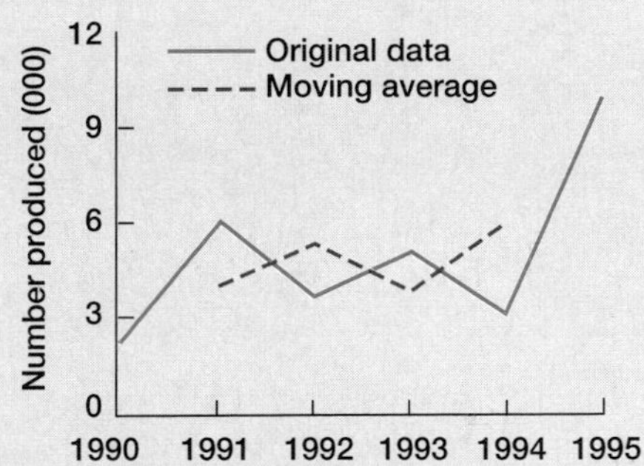

18–3 1.

Year	Y	log Y	t	t log Y	t^2
1991	2.13	0.3284	1	0.3284	1
1992	18.10	1.2577	2	2.5154	4
1993	39.80	1.5999	3	4.7997	9
1994	81.40	1.9106	4	7.6424	16
1995	112.00	2.0492	5	10.2460	25
		7.1458	15	25.5319	55

$$b = \frac{25.5319 - (7.1458)(15)/5}{55 - (15)^2/5} = \frac{4.0945}{10} = 0.40945$$

$$a = \frac{7.1458}{5} - 0.40945\left(\frac{15}{5}\right) = 0.20081$$

2. About 156.7 percent. The antilog of 0.40945 is 2.567, and subtracting 1 yields 1.567.
3. About 454.5, found by $Y' = 0.20081 + .40945(6) = 2.65751$. The antilog of 2.65751 is 454.5.

18–4 1. The following values are from the Hall package. Due to rounding, your figures might be slightly different.

	Winter	Spring	Summer	Fall
Mean	119.35	81.66	125.31	74.24
Typical seasonal	119.35	81.66	125.31	74.24

No correction is needed.

2. Total sales at Teton Village for the winter season are typically 19.35 percent above the annual average.

18–5 The forecast value for January of the sixth year is 34.9, found by

$$Y' = 4.40 + 0.50(61) = 34.9$$

Seasonally adjusting the forecast, 34.9(120)/100 = 41.88. For February, $Y' = 4.40 + 0.50(62) = 35.4$. Then (35.4)95/100 = 33.63.

Examination

1.

Year	t	Sales	tY	t^2
1992	1	10.1	10.1	1
1993	2	17.5	35.0	4
1994	3	25.0	75.0	9
1995	4	31.3	125.2	16
	10	83.9	245.3	30

$$b = \frac{245.30 - 10(83.9)/4}{30 - (10)^2/4} = \frac{35.55}{5} = 7.11$$

$$a = \frac{83.9}{4} - 7.11\left(\frac{10}{4}\right) = 3.20$$

The estimates for 1997 and 1998 in hundreds, respectively, are:

$$Y' = 3.20 + 7.11(6) = 45.86$$

$$Y' = 3.20 + 7.11(7) = 52.97$$

2.

Year	Quarter	Sales	Total	Moving average	Centered average
1994	I	26			
	II	14			
			56	14.0	
	III	6			15.00
			64	16.0	
	IV	10			16.75
			70	17.5	
1995	I	34			
	II	20			

a. The trend and cyclical components for the third and fourth quarters of 1994 are 15.00 and 16.75.

b. The contribution of the seasonal and irregular components for the third quarter of 1994 is 0.40, found by 6/15. For the fourth quarter it is 0.597, found by 10/16.75.

3. *a.* April of the sixth year is the 64th month of the study, found by 5 years times 12 months, plus 4 months into the sixth year. The estimated number of snow blowers sold during that month is

$$Y' = 2.50 + 4.56(64) = 294.34$$

b. The seasonally adjusted forecast is 220.755, found by 291.84(75.0)/100.

Chapter 19 An Introduction to Decision Making under Uncertainty

GOALS

When you have completed this chapter, you will be able to:

1
Define the terms *state of nature, event, act,* and *payoff.*

2
Organize data into a payoff table.

3
Determine the expected payoff of an act.

4
Compute opportunity loss and expected opportunity loss.

5
Assess the value of perfect information.

Given the opportunity loss data, verify that the opportunity loss for an electronics stock given a market rise is $500 (See Goal 4 and Self-Review 19–2.)

INTRODUCTION

A new branch of statistics, called **statistical decision theory,** has developed rapidly since the early 1950s. The term **Bayesian statistics** is also used to indicate this branch of statistics. It is given this name in honor of Reverend Thomas Bayes for his work in the 1700s. As the name implies, the major focus of statistical decision theory is on the process of making decisions. In contrast, classical statistics focuses on estimating a parameter, such as the population mean, constructing confidence intervals, or hypothesis testing.

Statistical decision theory is concerned with determining which decision, from a set of possible decisions, is optimal for a particular set of conditions. Consider the following examples of statistical decision theory problems.

- Ford Motor Company must decide whether to purchase assembled door locks for the new model Ford Escort or to manufacture and assemble the parts at their Sandusky, Ohio, plant. If sales of the Escort continue to increase, it will be more profitable to manufacture and assemble the parts. If sales level off or decline, it will be more profitable to purchase the door locks assembled. Which decision should be made?
- Haggar slacks has just developed new wool slacks that are very popular in the cold-weather regions of the country. Haggar would like to purchase commercial television time during the upcoming Super Bowl. If both teams that play in the Super Bowl are from warm parts of the country, Haggar estimates that only a small proportion of the viewers will be interested in the wool slacks. However, a match-up between the Cleveland Browns and the Chicago Bears, who come from cold climates, would reach a large proportion of viewers who wear wool slacks. What decision should Haggar make?
- General Electric is considering three options regarding the prices of refrigerators for next year. GE could (1) raise the prices 5 percent, (2) raise the prices 2.5 percent, or (3) leave the prices as they are. The final decision will be based on sales estimates and on GE's knowledge of what other refrigerator manufacturers might do.

In each of these cases note that the decision is characterized by several courses of action and several factors not under the control of the decision maker. For example, Haggar has no control over which teams reach the Super Bowl. These cases characterize the nature of decision making. Possible decision alternatives can be listed, possible future events determined, and even probabilities established, but *the decisions are made in the face of uncertainty.*

ELEMENTS OF A DECISION

There are three components to any decision-making situation: (1) the choices available, or alternatives; (2) the states of nature, which are not under the control of the decision maker; and (3) the payoffs. These concepts will be explained in the following paragraphs.

Acts or alternatives

The **alternatives,** or **acts,** are the choices available to the decision maker. Ford can decide to manufacture and assemble the door locks in Sandusky, or they can decide to purchase them. To simplify our presentation, we are going to assume that the decision maker can select from a rather small number of outcomes. However, with the help of computers, the decision alternatives can be expanded to a large number of possibilities.

States of nature

The **states of nature** are the uncontrollable future events. The state of nature that actually happens is outside the control of the decision maker. Ford does not know whether demand will remain high for the Escort. Haggar cannot determine whether warm-weather or cold-weather teams will play in the Super Bowl.

Payoff

A **payoff** is needed for each combination of decision alternative and state of nature. Ford may estimate that if they assemble door locks at their Sandusky Plant and the demand for Escorts is low, the payoff will be $40,000. Conversely, if they purchase the door locks assembled and the demand is high, the payoff is estimated to be $22,000.

The main elements of the decision problem under conditions of uncertainty are identified schematically:

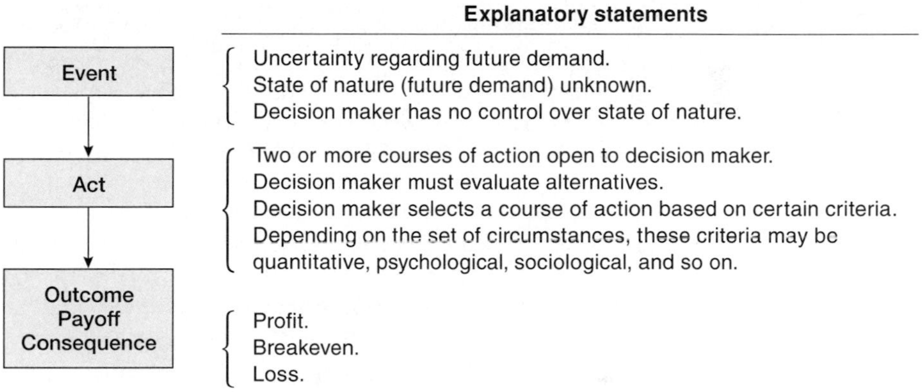

	Explanatory statements
Event	Uncertainty regarding future demand. State of nature (future demand) unknown. Decision maker has no control over state of nature.
↓ Act	Two or more courses of action open to decision maker. Decision maker must evaluate alternatives. Decision maker selects a course of action based on certain criteria. Depending on the set of circumstances, these criteria may be quantitative, psychological, sociological, and so on.
↓ Outcome Payoff Consequence	Profit. Breakeven. Loss.

In many cases we can make better decisions if we establish probabilities for the various states of nature. These probabilities may be based on historical data or subjective estimates. Ford may estimate the probability of continued high demand as .70. GE may estimate the probability to be .25 that Sears and other manufacturers will raise the prices of their refrigerators.

A CASE INVOLVING DECISION MAKING UNDER CONDITIONS OF UNCERTAINTY

At the outset it should be emphasized that this case description includes only the fundamental concepts found in a decision-making problem. The purpose of examining the case is to explain the logical procedure that might be followed. In many problems there are other variables to consider.

The first step is to set up a payoff table.

Payoff Table

Payoff table

Bob Hill, a small investor, has $1,100 to invest. He has studied the performance of several common stocks and narrowed his choice to three, namely, Kayser Chemicals, Rim Homes, and Texas Electronics. He estimated that if his $1,100 were invested in Kayser Chemicals and a strong bull market developed by the end of the year (that is,

stock prices increased drastically), the value of his Kayser stock would more than double, to $2,400. However, if there were a bear market (i.e., stock prices declined), the value of his Kayser stock could conceivably drop to $1,000 by the end of the year. His predictions regarding the value of his $1,100 investment for the three stocks for a bull market and for a bear market are shown in Table 19–1. This table is a **payoff table.**

TABLE 19–1 **Payoff Table for Three Common Stocks under Two Market Conditions**

Purchase	Bull market, S_1	Bear market, S_2
Kayser Chemicals (A_1)	$2,400	$1,000
Rim Homes (A_2)	2,200	1,100
Texas Electronics (A_3)	1,900	1,150

Decision alternatives

The various choices are called the **decision alternatives** or the **acts.** There are three in this problem. Let A_1 be the purchase of Kayser Chemicals, A_2 the purchase of Rim Homes, and A_3 the purchase of Texas Electronics. Whether the market turns out to be bear or bull is not under the control of Bob Hill. These uncontrolled future events are the states of nature. Let the bull market be represented by S_1 and the bear market by S_2.

Expected Payoff

If the payoff table were the only information available, the investor might take a conservative action and buy Texas Electronics in order to be assured of at least $1,150 at the end of the year (a slight profit). A speculative venture, however, might be to buy Kayser Chemicals, with the possibility of more than doubling the $1,100 investment.

Any decision regarding the purchase of one of the three common stocks made solely on the information in the payoff table would ignore the valuable historical records kept by Moody's, Value Line, and other investment services relative to stock price movements over a long period. A study of these records, for example, revealed that during the past 10 years stock market prices increased six times and declined only four times. Thus, it can be said that the probability of a market rise is .60 and the probability of a market decline is .40.

Expected payoff

Assuming that these historical frequencies are somewhat typical, we see that the payoff table and the probability estimates (.60 and .40) can be combined to arrive at the **expected payoff** of buying each of the three stocks. Expected payoff is also called **expected monetary value,** shortened to EMV. The calculations needed to arrive at the expected payoff for the act of purchasing Kayser Chemical are shown in Table 19–2.

Computing expected profit

TABLE 19–2 **Expected Payoff for the Act of Buying Kayser Chemicals, EMV(A_1)**

State of nature	Payoff	Probability of state of nature	Expected value
Market rise, S_1	$2,400	.60	$1,440
Market decline, S_2	1,000	.40	400
			$1,840

To explain one expected monetary value calculation, note that if the investor had purchased Kayser Chemicals and the market prices declined, the value of the stock would be only $1,000 at the end of the year (from Table 19–1). Past experience, however, revealed that this event (a market decline) occurred only 40 percent of the time. In the long run, therefore, a market decline would contribute $400 to the total expected payoff from the stock, found by $1,000 × .40. Adding the $400 to the $1,400 expected under rising market conditions gives $1,840, the total payoff in the long run.

These calculations are summarized as follows.

$$\text{EMV}(A_i) = \Sigma[P(S_j) \cdot V(A_i, S_j)] \tag{19–1}$$

where:

- $\text{EMV}(A_i)$ refers to the expected monetary value of the various decision alternatives. There may be many decisions possible. We will let 1 stand for the first decision, 2 for the second, and so on. The lowercase letter i represents the entire set of decisions.
- $P(S_j)$ refers to the probability of the various states of nature. There can be an unlimited number, so we will let j represent the various possible outcomes.
- $V(A_i, S_j)$ refers to the value of the various payoffs. Note that each payoff is the result of a combination of a decision alternative and a state of nature.

$\text{EMV}(A_1)$, the expected monetary value for the decision alternative of purchasing Kayser Chemical Stock, is computed by:

$$\begin{aligned}\text{EMV}(A_1) &= P(S_1) \cdot V(A_1, S_1) + P(S_2) \cdot V(A_1, S_2) \\ &= .60(\$2{,}400) + .40(\$1{,}000) = \$1{,}840\end{aligned}$$

Purchasing Kayser Chemicals stock is only one possible choice. The expected payoffs in the long run for the acts of buying Kayser Chemicals, Rim Homes, and Texas Electronics are given in Table 19–3.

TABLE 19–3 Expected Payoffs for Three Stocks

Purchase	Expected payoff
Kayser Chemicals	$1,840
Rim Homes	1,760
Texas Electronics	1,600

Kayser Chemicals—highest expected payoff

An analysis of the expected payoffs in Table 19–3 indicates that purchasing Kayser Chemicals would yield the greatest expected profit. This outcome is based upon (1) the investor's estimated future value of the stocks and (2) historical experience with respect to the rise and decline of stock prices. It should be emphasized that although the purchase of Kayser stock represents the best action under the expected-value criterion, the investor might decide to buy Texas Electronics stock in order to minimize the risk of losing some of the $1,100 investment.

SELF-REVIEW 19–1

The answers are at the end of the chapter.

Verify the conclusion, shown in Table 19–3, that the expected payoff for the act of purchasing Rim Homes stock is $1,760.

EXERCISES

The answers to the odd-numbered exercises are at the end of the book.

1. The following payoff table was developed. Let $P(S_1) = .30$, $P(S_2) = .50$, and $P(S_3) = .20$. Compute the expected monetary value for each of the alternatives. What decision would you recommend?

	State of nature		
Alternative	S_1	S_2	S_3
A_1	$50	$70	$100
A_2	90	40	80
A_3	70	60	90

2. The Wilhelms Cola Company plans to market a new pineapple-flavored cola this summer. The decision is whether to package the cola in returnable or in no-return bottles. Currently, the state legislature is considering the elimination of no-return bottles. Tybo Wilhelms, president of Wilhelms Cola Company, has discussed the problem with his state representative and estimated the probability to be .70 that no-return bottles will be eliminated. The following table shows the estimated monthly profits (in thousands of dollars) if the pineapple cola is bottled in returnable versus no-return bottles. Of course, if the law is passed and the decision is to bottle the cola in no-return bottles, all profits would be from out-of-state sales. Compute the expected profit for both bottling decisions. Which decision do you recommend?

Alternative	**Law is passed ($000)** ($S_1$)	**Law is not passed ($000)** ($S_2$)
Returnable bottle	80	40
No-return bottle	25	60

Opportunity Loss

Opportunity loss or regret

Another way of arriving at a decision regarding which common stock to purchase is to determine the profit that might be lost because the exact state of nature (the market behavior) was not known at the time the investor bought the stock. This potential loss is called **opportunity loss** or **regret.** To illustrate, suppose the investor had purchased the common stock of Rim Homes, and a bull market developed. Further, suppose the value of his Rim Homes stock increased from $1,100 to $2,200, as anticipated. But had the investor bought Kayser Chemicals stock and market values increased, the value of his Kayser stock would be $2,400 (from Table 19–1). Thus, the investor missed making an extra profit of $200 by buying Rim Homes instead of Kayser Chemicals. To put it another way, the $200 represents the opportunity loss for not knowing the correct state of nature. If market prices did increase, the investor would have *regretted* buying Rim Homes. However, had the investor bought Kayser Chemicals and market prices increased, he would have had no regret, that is, no opportunity loss.

The opportunity losses corresponding to this example are given in Table 19–4. Each amount is the outcome (opportunity loss) of a particular combination of acts and a state of nature, that is, stock purchase and market reaction.

It is apparent that the stock of Kayser Chemicals would be a good investment choice in a rising (bull) market, Texas Electronics would be the best buy in a declining (bear) market, and Rim Homes is somewhat of a compromise.

TABLE 19–4 **Opportunity Losses for Various Combinations of Stock Purchase and Market Movement**

	Opportunity loss	
Purchase	**Market rise**	**Market decline**
Kayser Chemicals	$ 0	$150
Rim Homes	200	50
Texas Electronics	500	0

SELF-REVIEW 19–2

The answers are at the end of the chapter.

Refer to Table 19–4. Verify that:

1. The opportunity loss for Rim Homes given a market decline is $50.
2. The opportunity loss for Texas Electronics given a market rise is $500.

EXERCISES

The answers to the odd-numbered exercises are at the end of the book.

3. Refer to Exercise 1. Develop an opportunity loss table. Determine the opportunity loss for each decision.
4. Refer to Exercise 2, involving the Wilhelms Cola Company. Develop an opportunity loss table, and determine the opportunity loss for each decision.

Expected Opportunity Loss

The opportunity losses in Table 19–4 again ignore the historical experience of market movements. Recall that the probability of a market rise is .60 and that of a market decline .40. These probabilities and the opportunity losses are combined to determine the *expected opportunity loss.* The essential calculations are shown in Table 19–5 for the decision to purchase Rim Homes. The expected opportunity loss is $140.

Expected opportunity loss

Interpreting, the expected opportunity loss of $140 means that, in the long run, the investor would lose the opportunity to make an additional profit of $140 if he decided to buy Rim Homes stock. This expected loss would be incurred because the investor was unable to accurately predict the trend of the stock market. In a bull market, he could earn an additional $200 by purchasing the common stock of Kayser Chemicals, but in a bear market an investor could earn an additional $50 by buying Texas Electronics stock. When weighted by the probability of the event, the opportunity loss is $140.

Computing expected opportunity loss

TABLE 19–5 Expected Opportunity Loss for the Act of Buying Rim Homes Stock

State of nature	Opportunity loss	Probability of state of nature	Expected opportunity loss
Market rise, S_1	$200	.60	$120
Market decline, S_2	50	.40	20
			$140

These calculations are summarized as follows:

$$\text{EOL}(A_i) = P(S_j) \cdot R(A_i, S_j) \tag{19–2}$$

where:

- $\text{EOL}(A_i)$ refers to the expected opportunity loss for a particular decision alternative.
- $P(S_j)$ refers to the probability associated with the various states of nature.
- $R(A_i, S_j)$ refers to the regret or loss for a particular combination of a state of nature and a decision alternative.

$\text{EOL}(A_2)$, the regret or opportunity loss for selecting Rim Homes, is computed as follows:

$$\text{EOL}(A_2) = P(S_1) \cdot R(A_2, S_1) + P(S_2) \cdot R(A_2, S_2)$$
$$= .60(\$200) + .40(\$50) = \$140$$

The expected opportunity losses for the three decision alternatives are given in Table 19–6. The lowest expected opportunity loss is $60, meaning that the investor would experience the least regret in the long run if he purchased Kayser Chemicals.

Least regret buying Kayser Chemicals

TABLE 19–6 Expected Opportunity Losses for the Three Stocks

Purchase	Expected opportunity loss
Kayser Chemicals	$ 60
Rim Homes	140
Texas Electronics	300

Incidentally, note that the decision to purchase Kayser Chemicals stock, based on the fact that it offers the lowest expected opportunity loss, reinforces the decision made previously, that Kayser stock would ultimately result in the highest payoff ($1,840). These two approaches (lowest expected opportunity loss and highest expected payoff) will always lead to the same decision concerning which course of action to follow.

SELF-REVIEW 19–3

The answers are at the end of the chapter.

Referring to Table 19–6, verify that the expected opportunity loss for the act of purchasing Texas Electronics is $300.

EXERCISES

The answers to the odd-numbered exercises are at the end of the book.

5. Refer to Exercises 1 and 3. Compute the expected opportunity losses.
6. Refer to Exercises 2 and 4. Compute the expected opportunity losses.

MAXIMIN, MAXIMAX, AND MINIMAX REGRET STRATEGIES

Maximin strategy

Several financial advisors consider the purchase of Kayser Chemicals stock too risky. They note that the payoff might not be $1,840, but only $1,000 (from Table 19–1). Arguing that the stock market is too unpredictable, they urge the investor to take a more conservative position and buy Texas Electronics. This is called a **maximin strategy:** it maximizes the minimum gain. Based on the payoff table (Table 19–1), they reason that the investor would be assured of at least a $1,150 return, that is, a small profit. Those who subscribe to this somewhat pessimistic strategy are sometimes called **maximiners.**

Maximax strategy

At the other extreme are the optimistic *maximaxers.* If their **maximax strategy** were followed, the investor would purchase Kayser Chemicals stock. These extreme optimists stress that there is a possibility of selling the stock in the future for $2,400 instead of only $1,150, as advocated by the maximiners.

Minimax strategy

Another possible strategy is the **minimax regret strategy.** Financial advisors advocating this would scan the opportunity losses in Table 19–4 and select the stock that minimizes the maximum regret. In this example it would be Kayser Chemicals stock, with a maximum opportunity loss of $150.

VALUE OF PERFECT INFORMATION

How much is "perfect" information worth?

Before deciding on a stock and purchasing it, the investor might want to consider ways of predicting the movement of the stock market in the near future. If he knew precisely what the market would do, he could maximize profit by always purchasing the correct stock. The question is: What is this advance information worth? The dollar value of this information is called the **expected value of perfect information,** written EVPI. In this problem, it would mean that Bob Hill knew beforehand whether the stock market would rise or decline in the near future.

An acquaintance who is an analyst with a large brokerage firm said that he would be willing to supply Bob with information that he might find quite valuable in predicting market rises and declines. Of course, there would be a fee, as yet undetermined, for this information, regardless of whether or not the investor used it. What is the maximum amount that Bob should pay for this special service? $10? $100? $500?

The value of the information from the analyst is in essence the expected value of perfect information, because the investor would then be assured of buying the most profitable stock. The value of perfect information is defined as the *difference between the maximum payoff under conditions of certainty and the maximum payoff under uncertainty.* In this problem it is the difference between the maximum value of the stock at the end of the year under conditions of certainty and the value associated with the optimum decision using the expected-value criterion.

From a practical standpoint, the maximum expected value under conditions of certainty means that the investor would buy Kayser Chemicals if a market rise were predicted and Texas Electronics if a market decline were imminent. The expected payoff in the long run under conditions of certainty is $1,900. (See Table 19–7.)

TABLE 19–7 Calculations for the Expected Payoff under Conditions of Certainty

State of nature	Payoff	Probability of state of nature	Expected payoff
Market rise, S_1	$2,400	.60	$1,440
Market decline, S_2	1,150	.40	460
			$1,900

Recall that if the actual behavior of the stock market were unknown (conditions of uncertainty), the stock to buy would be Kayser Chemicals; its expected value at the end of the period was computed to be $1,840 (from Table 19–3). The value of perfect information is therefore $60, found by:

$1,900	Expected value of stock purchaser under conditions of certainty
−1,840	Expected value of purchase (Kayser) under conditions of uncertainty
$ 60	Expected value of perfect information

In general, the expected value of perfect information is computed as follows:

$$\text{EVPI} = \text{Expected value under conditions of certainty} - \text{Optimal decision under conditions of uncertainty} \qquad (19\text{–}3)$$

Perfect information worth $60

It would be worth up to $60 for the information the stock analyst might supply. In essence, the analyst would be "guaranteeing" a selling price in the long run of $1,900, and if the analyst asked $40 for the information, the investor would be assured of a $1,860 payoff, found by $1,900 − $40. Thus, it would be worthwhile for the investor to agree to this fee ($40) because the expected outcome ($1,860) would be greater than the expected value under conditions of uncertainty ($1,840). However, if his acquaintance wanted a fee of $100 for the service, the investor would realize only $1,800 in the long run, found by $1,900 − $100. Logically, the service would not be worth $100 because the investor could expect $1,840 in the long run without agreeing to this financial arrangement.

It should be noted that the expected value of perfect information ($60) is the same as the minimum of the expected regrets (Table 19–6).

The calculations in the preceding investment problem were mainly kept at a minimum to emphasize the new terms and the decision-making procedures. When the number of decision alternatives and the number of states of nature become large, a computer package is recommended. The output for the investment problem using *Computerized Business Statistics,* developed by Hall and described in the previous chapter, is used as an example. The required inputs are: the decision alternatives, the states of nature and the corresponding probabilities, and the payoffs.

```
CBS-Decision Analysis                                        09-08-1994-14:45:10

                                 Information Entered

                        Decision Making under Risk - Maximization

Number of Decision Alternatives:         3
Number of States of Nature:              2

   State Probabilities

1 =   0.6
2 =   0.4

      Kayse   Rim    Texas

1 =   2400    2200   1900
2 =   1000    1100   1150

                                       Results

                                Decision Alternatives

Criteria            Kayse          Rim          Texas

  EMV                1840          1760          1600
  EOL                  60           140           300
  EPPI               1900          1900          1900

                          Optimal Decision: Kayse (# 1)
```

Note that the results for EMV are the same as in Table 19–3, the EOL figures are the same as in Table 19–6, and EPPI (EVPI) is the same as in Table 19–7.

SENSITIVITY ANALYSIS

Expected payoffs are not highly sensitive

Recall that in the foregoing stock selection problem, the set of probabilities applied to the payoff values was derived from historical experience with similar market conditions. Objections may be voiced, however, that future market behavior may be different from past experiences. Despite these differences, *the expected payoffs are not highly sensitive to any changes within a plausible range.* As an example, suppose the investor's brother believes that instead of a 60 percent chance of a market rise and a 40 percent chance of a decline, the reverse is true—that is, there is a .40 probability that the stock market will rise and a .60 probability of a decline. Further, the investor's cousin thinks the probability of a market rise is .50 and that of a decline is .50. A comparison of the original expected payoffs (left column), the expected payoffs for the set of probabilities suggested by the investor's brother (center column), and those cited by the cousin (right column) is shown in Table 19–8. The decision is the same in all three cases—purchase Kayser Chemicals.

TABLE 19–8 Expected Payoffs for Three Sets of Probabilities

	Expected payoffs		
Purchase	**Historical experience* (probability of .60 rise, .40 decline)**	**Brother's estimate (probability of .40 rise, .60 decline)**	**Cousin's estimate (probability of .50 rise, .50 decline)**
Kayser Chemicals	$1,840	$1,560	$1,700
Rim Homes	1,760	1,540	1,650
Texas Electronics	1,600	1,450	1,525

*From Table 19–3.

SELF-REVIEW 19–4

The answers are at the end of the chapter.

Referring to Table 19–8, verify that:

1. The expected payoff for Texas Electronics for the brother's set of probabilities is $1,450.
2. The expected payoff for Kayser Chemicals for the cousin's set of probabilities is $1,700.

A comparison of the three sets of expected payoffs in Table 19–8 reveals that the best alternative would still be to purchase Kayser Chemicals. As might be expected, there are some differences in the expected future values for each of the three stocks.

If there are any drastic changes in the assigned probabilities, the expected values and the optimal decision may in fact change. As an example, suppose the prognostication for a market rise was .20 and for a market decline .80. The expected payoffs would be as shown in Table 19–9. In the long run, the best alternative would be to buy Rim Homes stock.

TABLE 19–9 Expected Values for Purchasing the Three Stocks

Purchase	**Expected payoff**
Kayser Chemicals	$1,280
Rim Homes	1,320
Texas Electronics	1,300

SELF-REVIEW 19–5

The answers are at the end of the chapter.

Is there any choice of probabilities for which the best alternative would be to purchase Texas Electronics stock? (*Hint:* This can be arrived at algebraically or using a trial-and-error method. Try a somewhat extreme probability for a market rise.)

EXERCISES

The answers to the odd-numbered exercises are at the end of the book.

7. Refer to Exercises 1, 3, and 5. Compute the expected value of perfect information.
8. Refer to Exercises 2, 4, and 6. Compute the expected value of perfect information.
9. Refer to Exercise 1. Revise the probabilities as follows: $P(S_1) = .50$, $P(S_2) = .20$, and $P(S_3) = .30$. Does this change the decision?
10. Refer to Exercise 2. Reverse the probabilities; that is, let $P(S_1) = .30$ and $P(S_2) = .70$. Does this alter your decision?

DECISION TREES

Decision tree; A picture of all possible outcomes

An analytic tool introduced in Chapter 5 that is very useful for studying a decision situation is a *decision tree.* Basically, it is a picture of all the possible courses of action and the consequent possible outcomes. A box is used to indicate the point at which a decision must be made, and the branches going out from the box indicate the alternatives under consideration. Referring to Chart 19–1, on the left is the box with three branches radiating from it, representing the acts of purchasing Kayser Chemicals, Rim Homes, and Texas Electronics.

Decision tree shows Kayser Chemicals best buy

CHART 19–1 Decision Tree for the Investor's Decision

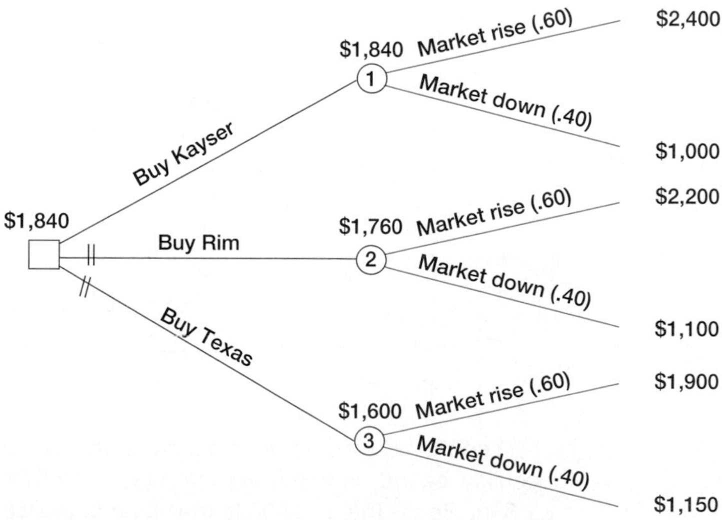

The three nodes or circles, numbered 1, 2, and 3, represent the expected payoff of each of the three stocks. The branches going out to the right of the nodes show the chance events (market rise or decline) and their corresponding probabilities in parentheses. The numbers at the extreme ends of the branches are the estimated future values of stopping the decision process at those points. This is sometimes called the *conditional payoff* to denote that the payoff depends on a particular choice of action and a particular chance outcome. Thus, if the investor purchased Rim Homes stock and the market rose, the estimated value of the stock would be $2,200.

After the decision tree has been constructed, the optimal decision strategy can be found by what is termed *backward induction.* For example, suppose the investor is considering the act of purchasing Texas Electronics. Starting at the lower right in Chart 19–1 with the anticipated payoff given a market rise ($1,900) versus a market decline ($1,150) and going backward (moving left), the appropriate probabilities are applied to give the expected payoff of $1,600 [found by .60($1,900) + .40($1,150)]. The investor would mark the expected value of $1,600 above circled node 3 as shown in Chart 19–1. Similarly, the investor would determine the expected values for Rim Homes and Kayser Chemicals.

Assuming that the investor wants to maximize the expected future value of his stock purchase, $1,840 would be preferred over $1,760 or $1,600. Continuing to the left toward the box, the investor would draw a double bar across branches representing the two alternatives he rejected (numbers 2 and 3, representing Rim Homes and Texas Electronics). The unmarked branch that leads to the box is clearly the best action to follow, namely, buy Kayser Chemicals stock.

The expected value under *conditions of certainty* can also be portrayed via a decision tree analysis (see Chart 19–2). Recall that under conditions of certainty the investor would know *before the stock is purchased* whether the stock market will rise or decline in the near future. Hence, he would purchase Kayser Chemicals in a rising market and Texas Electronics in a falling market, and in the long run the expected payoff would be $1,900. Again, backward induction would be used to arrive at the expected payoff of $1,900.

CHART 19–2 Decision Tree Given Perfect Information

If perfect information is available: Buy Kayser in rising market; buy Texas in declining market

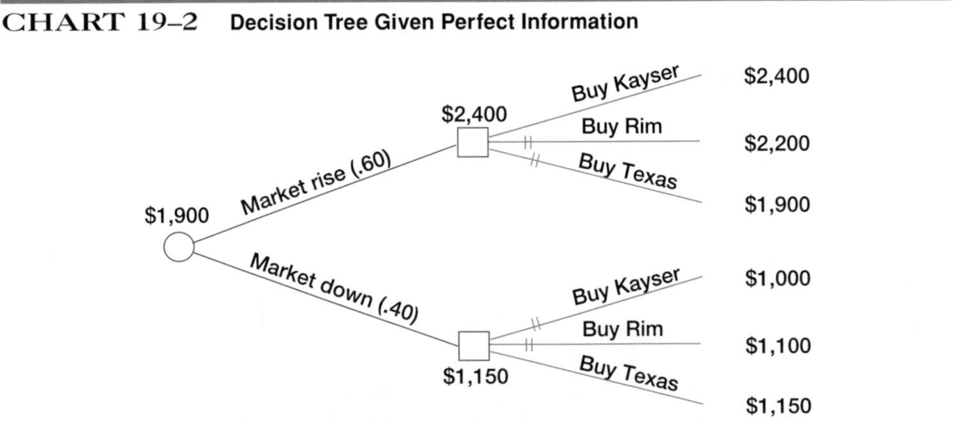

The monetary difference based on the perfect information in Chart 19–2 and the decision based on imperfect information in Chart 19–1 is $60, found by $1,900 − $1,840. Recall that the $60 is the value of perfect information.

Decision tree analysis merely provides an alternative way to perform the same calculations presented earlier in the chapter. Some managers find that these graphic sketches help them in following the decision path.

CHAPTER OUTLINE

I. Statistical decision theory is concerned with making decisions from a set of possible alternatives.
   A. The various courses of action are called the acts or alternatives.
   B. The uncontrollable future events are called the states of nature. Probabilities are usually assigned to the various states of nature.
   C. The combination of a particular decision alternative and state of nature is called the payoff.
   D. All possible combinations of decision alternatives and states of nature result in a payoff table.

II. There are several criteria for selecting the optimal decision.
   A. In the expected monetary value (EMV) criterion, the expected value for each decision alternative is computed, and the optimal (largest if profits, smallest if cost) is selected.
   B. An opportunity loss table can be developed.
      1. An opportunity loss table is constructed by taking the difference between the optimal decision for each state of nature and the other decision alternatives.
      2. The difference between the optimal decision and any other decision is the opportunity loss or regret due to making a decision other than the optimum.
      3. The expected opportunity loss (EOL) is similar to the expected monetary value. The opportunity loss is combined with the probabilities of the various states of nature for each decision alternative to determine the expected opportunity loss.
   C. The strategy of maximizing the minimum gain is referred to as maximin.
   D. The strategy of maximizing the maximum gain is called maximax.
   E. The strategy that minimizes the maximum regret is designated minimax.

III. The expected value of perfect information (EVPI) is the difference between the expected payoff if the state of nature is known and the optimal decision under conditions of uncertainty.

IV. Sensitivity analysis examines the effects of various probabilities for the states of nature on the expected values.

V. Decision trees are useful for structuring the various alternatives. They present a picture of the various courses of action and the possible states of nature.

EXERCISES

The answers to the odd-numbered exercises are at the end of the book.

11. The Twenge Manufacturing Company is considering the introduction of two new products. The company can add both to the current line, neither, or just one of the two. The success of these products depends on the general economy and on the consumer's reaction to the products. These reactions can be summarized as "good," $P(S_1) = .30$; "fair," $P(S_2) = .50$; or "poor," $P(S_3) = .20$. The company's revenues, in thousands of dollars, are estimated in the following payoff table.

	State of nature		
Decision	S_1	S_2	S_3
Neither	0	0	0
Product 1 only	125	65	30
Product 2 only	105	60	30
Both	220	110	40

a. Compute the expected monetary value for each decision.
b. What decision would you recommend?
c. Develop an opportunity loss table.
d. Compute the expected opportunity loss for each decision.
e. Compute the expected value of perfect information.

12. A financial executive lives in Boston but frequently must travel to New York. She can go to New York by car, train, or plane. The cost for a plane ticket from Boston to New York is $100, and it is estimated that the trip takes 30 minutes in good weather and 45 minutes in bad weather. The cost for a train ticket is $50, and the trip takes an hour in good weather and two hours in bad weather. The cost to drive her own car from Boston to New York is $20, and this trip takes three hours in good weather and four in bad weather. The executive places a cost of $30 per hour on her time. The weather forecast is for a 60 percent chance of bad weather tomorrow.

    What decision would you recommend? (*Hint:* Set up a payoff table, and remember that you want to minimize costs.) What is the expected value of perfect information?

13. The Thomas Manufacturing Company has $100,000 available to invest. Doctor Thomas, the president and CEO of the company, would like to either expand his production, invest the money in stocks, or purchase a certificate of deposit from the bank. Of course, the unknown is whether the economy will continue at a high level or there will be a recession. He estimates the likelihood of a recession at .20. Whether there is a recession or not, the certificate of deposit will result in a gain of 6 percent. If there is a recession, he predicts 10 percent loss if he expands his production and a 5 percent loss if he invests in stocks. If there is not a recession, an expansion of production will result in a 15 percent gain, and stock investment will produce a 12 percent gain.
    a. What decision should he make if he uses the maximin strategy?
    b. What decision should Doctor Thomas make if the maximax strategy is used?
    c. What decision would be made if he uses the expected-monetary-value criterion?
    d. What is the expected value of perfect information?

14. The quality-assurance department at Malcomb Products must either inspect each part in a lot or not inspect any of the parts. That is, there are two decision alternatives: inspect all the parts or inspect none of the parts. The proportion of parts defective in the lot, S_i, is known from historical data to assume the following probability distribution.

State of nature, S_i	Probability, $P(S_i)$
.02	.70
.04	.20
.06	.10

For the decision not to inspect any parts, the cost of quality is

$$C = NS_iK$$

For inspecting all the items in the lot, it is

$$C = Nk$$

where:

N = 20 (lot size)

K = $18.00 (the cost of finding a defect)

k = $0.50 (the cost of sampling one item)

a. Develop a payoff table.
b. What decision should be made if the expected-value criterion is used?
c. What is the expected value of perfect information?

15. Dude Ranches Incorporated was founded on the idea that many families in the eastern and southern areas of the United States do not have a sufficient amount of vacation time to drive to the dude ranches in the Southwest and Rocky Mountain areas for their vacations. Various surveys indicated, however, that there was a considerable interest in this type of family vacation, which includes horseback riding, cattle drives, swimming, fishing, and the like. Dude Ranches Incorporated bought a large farm near several eastern cities and constructed a lake, a swimming pool, and other facilities. However, to build a number of family cottages on the ranch would have required a considerable amount of investment. Further, they reasoned that most of this investment would be lost should the ranch-farm complex be a financial failure. Instead, they decided to enter into an agreement with the Mobile Homes Manufacturing Company to supply a very attractive authentic ranch-type mobile home. Mobile Homes agreed to deliver a mobile home on Saturday for $300 a week. Mobile Homes must know early Saturday morning how many mobile homes Dude Ranches Incorporated wants for the forthcoming week. They have other customers to supply and can only deliver the homes on Saturday. This presents a problem. Dude Ranches will have some reservations by Saturday, but indications are that many families do not make them. Instead, they prefer to examine the facilities before making a decision. An analysis of the various costs involved indicated that $350 a week should be charged for a ranch home, including all privileges. The basic problem is how many mobile ranch homes to order from Mobile Homes each week. Should Dude Ranches Incorporated order 10 (considered the minimum), 11, 12, 13, or 14 (considered the maximum)?

    Any decision made solely on the information in the payoff table would ignore, however, the valuable experience that Dude Ranches Incorporated has acquired in the past four years (about 200 weeks) actually operating a dude ranch in the Southwest. Their records showed that they always had nine advance reservations. Also, they never had a demand for 15 or more cottages. The occupancy of 10, 11, 12, 13, or 14 ranch cottages, in part, represented families who drove in and inspected the facilities before renting. A frequency distribution showing the number of weeks in which 10, 11, . . . , 14 ranch cottages were rented during the 200-week period is found in the following table.

Number of cottages rented	Number of weeks
10	26
11	50
12	60
13	44
14	20
	200

a. Construct a payoff table.
b. Determine the expected payoffs, and arrive at a decision.
c. Set up an opportunity loss table.
d. Compute the expected opportunity losses, and arrive at a decision.
e. Determine the value of perfect information.

16. The proprietor of the newly built Ski and Swim Lodge has been considering the purchase or lease of several snowmobiles for the use of guests. The owner found that other financial obligations made it impossible to purchase the machines. Snowmobiles Incorporated (SI) will lease a machine for $20 a week, including any needed

maintenance. According to SI, the usual rental charge to the guests of the lodge is $25 a week. Gasoline and oil are extra. Snowmobiles Incorporated only leases a machine for the full season. The proprietor of Ski and Swim, knowing that leasing an excessive number of snowmobiles might cause a net loss for the lodge, investigated the records of other resort owners. The combined experience at several other lodges was found to be:

Number of snowmobiles demanded by guests	Number of weeks
7	10
8	25
9	45
10	20

a. Design a payoff table.
b. Compute the expected profits for leasing 7, 8, 9, and 10 snowmobiles based on the cost of leasing of $20, the rental charge of $25, and the experience of other lodges.
c. Which alternative is the most profitable?
d. Design an opportunity loss table.
e. Find the expected opportunity losses for leasing 7, 8, 9, and 10 snowmobiles.
f. Which act would give the least expected opportunity loss?
g. Determine the value of perfect information.
h. Suggest a course of action to the proprietor of the Ski and Swim Lodge, and include in your explanation the various figures, such as expected profit.

17. A furniture store has had numerous inquiries regarding the availability of furniture and equipment that could be rented for large outdoor summer parties. This includes such items as folding chairs and tables, a deluxe grill, propane gas, and lights. No rental equipment of this nature is available locally, and the management of the furniture store is considering forming a subsidiary to handle rentals.

    An investigation revealed that most people interested in renting wanted a complete group of party essentials (about 12 chairs, four tables, a deluxe grill, a bottle of propane gas, tongs, etc.). Management decided not to buy a large number of complete sets because of the financial risk involved. That is, if the demand for the rental groups was not as large as anticipated, a large financial loss might be incurred. Further, outright purchase would mean that the equipment would have to be stored during the off-season.

It was then discovered that a firm in Boston leased a complete party set for $560 for the summer season. This amounts to about $5 a day. In the promotional literature from the Boston firm, a rental fee of $15 was suggested. For each set rented, a profit of $10 would thus be earned. It was then decided to lease from the Boston firm, at least for the first season.

The Boston firm suggested that, based on the combined experience of similar rental firms in other cities, either 41, 42, 43, 44, 45, or 46 complete sets be leased for the season. Based on this suggestion, management must now decide on the most profitable number of complete sets to lease for the season.

The leasing firm in Boston also made available some additional information gathered from several rental firms similar to the newly formed subsidiary. Note in the following table (which is based on the experience of the other rental firms) that for 360 days of the total of 6,000 days' experience—or about 6 percent of the days—these rental firms rented out 41 complete party sets. On 10 percent of the days during a typical summer, they rented 42 complete sets, and so on.

Number of sets rented	**Number of days out of the total (6,000 days)**
40	0
41	360
42	600
43	840
44	2,400
45	1,500
46	300
47	0

a. Construct a payoff table. (As a check figure, for the act of having 41 complete sets available and the event of renting 41, the payoff is $410.)

b. The expected daily profit for leasing 43 complete sets from the Boston firm is $426.70; for 45 sets, $431.70; and for 46 sets, $427.45. Organize these expected daily profits into a table, and complete the table by finding the expected daily profit for leasing 41, 42, and 44 sets from the Boston firm.

c. Based on the expected daily profit, what is the most profitable action to take?

d. The expected opportunity loss for leasing 43 party sets from the Boston firm is $11.60; for 45 sets, $6.60; for 46 sets, $10.85. Organize these into an expected opportunity loss table, and complete the table by computing the expected opportunity loss for 41, 42, and 44.

e. Based on the expected opportunity loss table, what is the most profitable course of action to take? Does this agree with your decision for part *c*?

f. Determine the value of perfect information. Explain what it indicates in this problem.

18. Tim Waltzer owns and operates Waltzer's Wrecks, a discount car rental agency near the Cleveland Hopkins International Airport. He rents a wreck for $20 a day. He has an arrangement with Landrum Leasing to purchase used cars at $6,000 each. His cars receive only needed maintenance and, as a result, are worth only $2,000 at the end of the first year of operation. Tim has decided to sell all his wrecks every year and purchase a complete set of used cars from Landrum Leasing.

His clerk-accountant provided him with a probability distribution with respect to the number of cars rented per day.

	Average number of cars rented per day			
	20	**21**	**22**	**23**
Probability	.10	.20	.50	.20

Tim is an avid golfer and tennis player. He is either on the golf course on weekends or playing tennis indoors. Thus, his car rental agency is only open weekdays. Also, he closes for two weeks during the summer and goes on a golfing tour.

The clerk-accountant estimated that it cost $1.50 per car rental for minimal maintenance and cleaning.

a. How many cars should he purchase every year to maximize profit?

b. What is the expected value of perfect information?

CHAPTER 19 EXAMINATION

The answers are at the end of the chapter.

For Questions 1 through 10, fill in the blank.

1. The choices available to the decision maker are called the ____________.
2. The future events that cannot be controlled are called the ____________.
3. The combination of a particular state of nature and a particular decision alternative is called the ____________.
4. All possible combinations of states of nature and decision alternatives is called a ____________.
5. The difference between the expected payoff when the state of nature is known and the optimal decision under conditions of uncertainty is called the ____________.
6. The EVPI and the expected opportunity loss are always ____________.
7. The strategy of maximizing the minimum gain is called ____________.
8. The EMV is computed by multiplying the payoff for a particular decision alternative and the probability of the ____________.
9. The difference between the optimal decision and any other decision is the ____________.
10. The strategy of maximizing the maximum gain is called ____________.
11. A manufacturer has $100,000 available to make either lightweight or heavy jackets for winter wear. A decision must be made in the summer in order to have the jackets available for early fall shipments. Of course, the manufacturer is unable to predict whether the winter will be mild or severe. If lightweight jackets are manufactured and the winter is mild, the payoff will be $120,000; but if weather is severe, the payoff will only be $105,000 (because consumers will purchase heavy jackets from competitors). If heavy jackets are produced, the payoffs for mild and severe winters are $110,000 and $125,000, respectively. Past records showed that 70 percent of the winters were mild and 30 percent were severe.
    a. Construct a payoff table.
    b. Determine the two expected payoffs, and arrive at a decision.
    c. Construct an opportunity loss table, and determine the expected opportunity losses.
    d. Compute the value of perfect information.
    e. Design a decision tree for this problem.

CHAPTER 19 Answers

Self-Review

19–1

Event	Payoff	Probability of event	Expected value
Market rise	$2,200	.60	$1,320
Market decline	1,100	.40	440
			$1,760

19–2

1. Suppose the investor purchased Rim Homes stock, and the value of the stock in a bear market dropped to $1,100 as anticipated (Table 19–1). Instead, had the investor purchased Texas Electronics and the market declined, the value of the Texas Electronics stock would be $1,150. The difference of $50, found by $1,150 − $1,100, represents the investor's regret for buying Rim Homes stock.
2. Suppose the investor purchased Texas Electronics stock, and then a bull market developed. The stock rose to $1,900, as anticipated (Table 19–1). However, had the investor bought Kayser Chemicals stock and the market value increased to $2,400 as anticipated, the difference of $500 represents the extra profit the investor could have made by purchasing Kayser Chemicals stock.

19–3

Event	Payoff	Probability of event	Expected opportunity loss
Market rise	$500	.60	$300
Market decline	0	.40	0
			$300

19–4

1.

Event	Payoff	Probability of event	Expected value
Market rise	$1,900	.40	$ 760
Market decline	1,150	.60	690
			$1,450

2.

Event	Payoff	Probability of event	Expected value
Market rise	$2,400	.50	$1,200
Market decline	1,000	.50	500
			$1,700

19–5 For probabilities of a market rise (or decline) down to .333, Kayser Chemicals stock would provide the largest expected profit in the long run. For probabilities .333 to .143, Rim Homes would be the best buy. For .143 and below, Texas Electronics would give largest expected profit. Algebraic solutions:

Kayser: $2{,}400p + (1 - p)1{,}000$
Rim: $2{,}200p + (1 - p)1{,}100$

$$1{,}400p + 1{,}000 = 1{,}100p + 1{,}100$$
$$p = .333$$

Rim: $2{,}200p + (1 - p)1{,}100$
Texas: $1{,}900p + (1 - p)1{,}150$

$$1{,}100p + 1{,}100 = 750p + 1{,}150$$
$$p = .143$$

Examination

1. Alternatives.
2. States of nature.
3. Payoff.
4. Payoff table.
5. Expected value of perfect information (EVPI).
6. The same.
7. Maximin.
8. State of nature.

9. Opportunity loss.
10. Maximax.
11. *a.*

Manufacture	Payoff	
	Mild winter	Severe winter
Lightweight jacket	$120,000	$105,000
Heavy jacket	110,000	125,000

b.

$$\text{EMV}(A_1) = .70(\$120{,}000) + .30(\$105{,}000) = \$115{,}500$$

$$\text{EMV}(A_2) = .70(\$110{,}000) + .30(\$125{,}000) = \$114{,}500$$

Expected payoffs: lightweight, $115,500; heavy, $114,500. Decision: Manufacture lightweight jackets because payoff is greater.

c.

Manufacture	Opportunity loss	
	Mild winter	Severe winter
Lightweight jacket	$ 0	$20,000
Heavy jacket	10,000	0

$$\text{EOL}(A_1) = .70(0) + .30(\$20{,}000) = \$6{,}000$$

$$\text{EOL}(A_2) = .70(\$10{,}000) + .30(0) = \$7{,}000$$

The expected opportunity loss for lightweight jackets is $6,000; for heavy jackets it is $7,000. Decision: Manufacture lightweight jackets.

d. The value of perfect information is $6,000, found by:

$121,500	Expected payoff under conditions of certainty.
−115,500	Expected payoff under conditions of uncertainty.
$6,000	Value of perfect information.

Note: This is the same as the minimum expected opportunity loss.

e. The decision tree is:

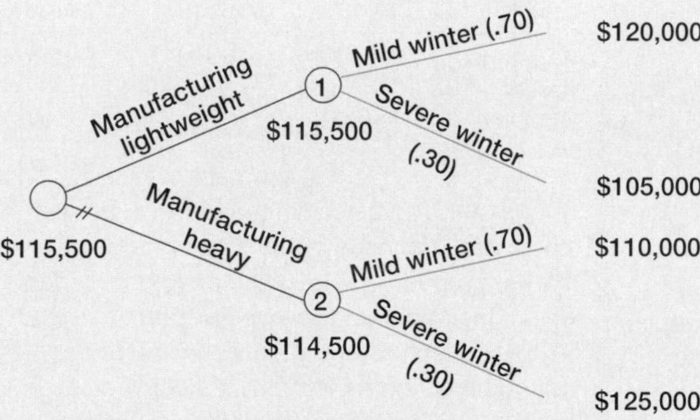

Appendixes

TABLES AND DATA SETS

APPENDIX A

BINOMIAL PROBABILITY DISTRIBUTION

$n = 1$
Probability

r	0.05	0.10	0.20	0.30	0.40	0.50	0.60	0.70	0.80	0.90	0.95
0	0.950	0.900	0.800	0.700	0.600	0.500	0.400	0.300	0.200	0.100	0.050
1	0.050	0.100	0.200	0.300	0.400	0.500	0.600	0.700	0.800	0.900	0.950

$n = 2$
Probability

r	0.05	0.10	0.20	0.30	0.40	0.50	0.60	0.70	0.80	0.90	0.95
0	0.903	0.810	0.640	0.490	0.360	0.250	0.160	0.090	0.040	0.010	0.003
1	0.095	0.180	0.320	0.420	0.480	0.500	0.480	0.420	0.320	0.180	0.095
2	0.003	0.010	0.040	0.090	0.160	0.250	0.360	0.490	0.640	0.810	0.903

$n = 3$
Probability

r	0.05	0.10	0.20	0.30	0.40	0.50	0.60	0.70	0.80	0.90	0.95
0	0.857	0.729	0.512	0.343	0.216	0.125	0.064	0.027	0.008	0.001	0.000
1	0.135	0.243	0.384	0.441	0.432	0.375	0.288	0.189	0.096	0.027	0.007
2	0.007	0.027	0.096	0.189	0.288	0.375	0.432	0.441	0.384	0.243	0.135
3	0.000	0.001	0.008	0.027	0.064	0.125	0.216	0.343	0.512	0.729	0.857

$n = 4$
Probability

r	0.05	0.10	0.20	0.30	0.40	0.50	0.60	0.70	0.80	0.90	0.95
0	0.815	0.656	0.410	0.240	0.130	0.063	0.026	0.008	0.002	0.000	0.000
1	0.171	0.292	0.410	0.412	0.346	0.250	0.154	0.076	0.026	0.004	0.000
2	0.014	0.049	0.154	0.265	0.346	0.375	0.346	0.265	0.154	0.049	0.014
3	0.000	0.004	0.026	0.076	0.154	0.250	0.346	0.412	0.410	0.292	0.171
4	0.000	0.000	0.002	0.008	0.026	0.063	0.130	0.240	0.410	0.656	0.815

$n = 5$
Probability

r	0.05	0.10	0.20	0.30	0.40	0.50	0.60	0.70	0.80	0.90	0.95
0	0.774	0.590	0.328	0.168	0.078	0.031	0.010	0.002	0.000	0.000	0.000
1	0.204	0.328	0.410	0.360	0.259	0.156	0.077	0.028	0.006	0.000	0.000
2	0.021	0.073	0.205	0.309	0.346	0.313	0.230	0.132	0.051	0.008	0.001
3	0.001	0.008	0.051	0.132	0.230	0.313	0.346	0.309	0.205	0.073	0.021
4	0.000	0.000	0.006	0.028	0.077	0.156	0.259	0.360	0.410	0.328	0.204
5	0.000	0.000	0.000	0.002	0.010	0.031	0.078	0.168	0.328	0.590	0.774

APPENDIX A

BINOMIAL PROBABILITY DISTRIBUTION (*continued*)

$n = 6$

Probability

r	0.05	0.10	0.20	0.30	0.40	0.50	0.60	0.70	0.80	0.90	0.95
0	0.735	0.531	0.262	0.118	0.047	0.016	0.004	0.001	0.000	0.000	0.000
1	0.232	0.354	0.393	0.303	0.187	0.094	0.037	0.010	0.002	0.000	0.000
2	0.031	0.098	0.246	0.324	0.311	0.234	0.138	0.060	0.015	0.001	0.000
3	0.002	0.015	0.082	0.185	0.276	0.313	0.276	0.185	0.082	0.015	0.002
4	0.000	0.001	0.015	0.060	0.138	0.234	0.311	0.324	0.246	0.098	0.031
5	0.000	0.000	0.002	0.010	0.037	0.094	0.187	0.303	0.393	0.354	0.232
6	0.000	0.000	0.000	0.001	0.004	0.016	0.047	0.118	0.262	0.531	0.735

$n = 7$

Probability

r	0.05	0.10	0.20	0.30	0.40	0.50	0.60	0.70	0.80	0.90	0.95
0	0.698	0.478	0.210	0.082	0.028	0.008	0.002	0.000	0.000	0.000	0.000
1	0.257	0.372	0.367	0.247	0.131	0.055	0.017	0.004	0.000	0.000	0.000
2	0.041	0.124	0.275	0.318	0.261	0.164	0.077	0.025	0.004	0.000	0.000
3	0.004	0.023	0.115	0.227	0.290	0.273	0.194	0.097	0.029	0.003	0.000
4	0.000	0.003	0.029	0.097	0.194	0.273	0.290	0.227	0.115	0.023	0.004
5	0.000	0.000	0.004	0.025	0.077	0.164	0.261	0.318	0.275	0.124	0.041
6	0.000	0.000	0.000	0.004	0.017	0.055	0.131	0.247	0.367	0.372	0.257
7	0.000	0.000	0.000	0.000	0.002	0.008	0.028	0.082	0.210	0.478	0.698

$n = 8$

Probability

r	0.05	0.10	0.20	0.30	0.40	0.50	0.60	0.70	0.80	0.90	0.95
0	0.663	0.430	0.168	0.058	0.017	0.004	0.001	0.000	0.000	0.000	0.000
1	0.279	0.383	0.336	0.198	0.090	0.031	0.008	0.001	0.000	0.000	0.000
2	0.051	0.149	0.294	0.296	0.209	0.109	0.041	0.010	0.001	0.000	0.000
3	0.005	0.033	0.147	0.254	0.279	0.219	0.124	0.047	0.009	0.000	0.000
4	0.000	0.005	0.046	0.136	0.232	0.273	0.232	0.136	0.046	0.005	0.000
5	0.000	0.000	0.009	0.047	0.124	0.219	0.279	0.254	0.147	0.033	0.005
6	0.000	0.000	0.001	0.010	0.041	0.109	0.209	0.296	0.294	0.149	0.051
7	0.000	0.000	0.000	0.001	0.008	0.031	0.090	0.198	0.336	0.383	0.279
8	0.000	0.000	0.000	0.000	0.001	0.004	0.017	0.058	0.168	0.430	0.663

$n = 9$

Probability

r	0.05	0.10	0.20	0.30	0.40	0.50	0.60	0.70	0.80	0.90	0.95
0	0.630	0.387	0.134	0.040	0.010	0.002	0.000	0.000	0.000	0.000	0.000
1	0.299	0.387	0.302	0.156	0.060	0.018	0.004	0.000	0.000	0.000	0.000
2	0.063	0.172	0.302	0.267	0.161	0.070	0.021	0.004	0.000	0.000	0.000
3	0.008	0.045	0.176	0.267	0.251	0.164	0.074	0.021	0.003	0.000	0.000
4	0.001	0.007	0.066	0.172	0.251	0.246	0.167	0.074	0.017	0.001	0.000
5	0.000	0.001	0.017	0.074	0.167	0.246	0.251	0.172	0.066	0.007	0.001
6	0.000	0.000	0.003	0.021	0.074	0.164	0.251	0.267	0.176	0.045	0.008
7	0.000	0.000	0.000	0.004	0.021	0.070	0.161	0.267	0.302	0.172	0.063
8	0.000	0.000	0.000	0.000	0.004	0.018	0.060	0.156	0.302	0.387	0.299
9	0.000	0.000	0.000	0.000	0.000	0.002	0.010	0.040	0.134	0.387	0.630

APPENDIX A

BINOMIAL PROBABILITY DISTRIBUTION (*continued*)

$n = 10$
Probability

r	0.05	0.10	0.20	0.30	0.40	0.50	0.60	0.70	0.80	0.90	0.95
0	0.599	0.349	0.107	0.028	0.006	0.001	0.000	0.000	0.000	0.000	0.000
1	0.315	0.387	0.268	0.121	0.040	0.010	0.002	0.000	0.000	0.000	0.000
2	0.075	0.194	0.302	0.233	0.121	0.044	0.011	0.001	0.000	0.000	0.000
3	0.010	0.057	0.201	0.267	0.215	0.117	0.042	0.009	0.001	0.000	0.000
4	0.001	0.011	0.088	0.200	0.251	0.205	0.111	0.037	0.006	0.000	0.000
5	0.000	0.001	0.026	0.103	0.201	0.246	0.201	0.103	0.026	0.001	0.000
6	0.000	0.000	0.006	0.037	0.111	0.205	0.251	0.200	0.088	0.011	0.001
7	0.000	0.000	0.001	0.009	0.042	0.117	0.215	0.267	0.201	0.057	0.010
8	0.000	0.000	0.000	0.001	0.011	0.044	0.121	0.233	0.302	0.194	0.075
9	0.000	0.000	0.000	0.000	0.002	0.010	0.040	0.121	0.268	0.387	0.315
10	0.000	0.000	0.000	0.000	0.000	0.001	0.006	0.028	0.107	0.349	0.599

$n = 11$
Probability

r	0.05	0.10	0.20	0.30	0.40	0.50	0.60	0.70	0.80	0.90	0.95
0	0.569	0.314	0.086	0.020	0.004	0.000	0.000	0.000	0.000	0.000	0.000
1	0.329	0.384	0.236	0.093	0.027	0.005	0.001	0.000	0.000	0.000	0.000
2	0.087	0.213	0.295	0.200	0.089	0.027	0.005	0.001	0.000	0.000	0.000
3	0.014	0.071	0.221	0.257	0.177	0.081	0.023	0.004	0.000	0.000	0.000
4	0.001	0.016	0.111	0.220	0.236	0.161	0.070	0.017	0.002	0.000	0.000
5	0.000	0.002	0.039	0.132	0.221	0.226	0.147	0.057	0.010	0.000	0.000
6	0.000	0.000	0.010	0.057	0.147	0.226	0.221	0.132	0.039	0.002	0.000
7	0.000	0.000	0.002	0.017	0.070	0.161	0.236	0.220	0.111	0.016	0.001
8	0.000	0.000	0.000	0.004	0.023	0.081	0.177	0.257	0.221	0.071	0.014
9	0.000	0.000	0.000	0.001	0.005	0.027	0.089	0.200	0.295	0.213	0.087
10	0.000	0.000	0.000	0.000	0.001	0.005	0.027	0.093	0.236	0.384	0.329
11	0.000	0.000	0.000	0.000	0.000	0.000	0.004	0.020	0.086	0.314	0.569

$n = 12$
Probability

r	0.05	0.10	0.20	0.30	0.40	0.50	0.60	0.70	0.80	0.90	0.95
0	0.540	0.282	0.069	0.014	0.002	0.000	0.000	0.000	0.000	0.000	0.000
1	0.341	0.377	0.206	0.071	0.017	0.003	0.000	0.000	0.000	0.000	0.000
2	0.099	0.230	0.283	0.168	0.064	0.016	0.002	0.000	0.000	0.000	0.000
3	0.017	0.085	0.236	0.240	0.142	0.054	0.012	0.001	0.000	0.000	0.000
4	0.002	0.021	0.133	0.231	0.213	0.121	0.042	0.008	0.001	0.000	0.000
5	0.000	0.004	0.053	0.158	0.227	0.193	0.101	0.029	0.003	0.000	0.000
6	0.000	0.000	0.016	0.079	0.177	0.226	0.177	0.079	0.016	0.000	0.000
7	0.000	0.000	0.003	0.029	0.101	0.193	0.227	0.158	0.053	0.004	0.000
8	0.000	0.000	0.001	0.008	0.042	0.121	0.213	0.231	0.133	0.021	0.002
9	0.000	0.000	0.000	0.001	0.012	0.054	0.142	0.240	0.236	0.085	0.017
10	0.000	0.000	0.000	0.000	0.002	0.016	0.064	0.168	0.283	0.230	0.099
11	0.000	0.000	0.000	0.000	0.000	0.003	0.017	0.071	0.206	0.377	0.341
12	0.000	0.000	0.000	0.000	0.000	0.000	0.002	0.014	0.069	0.282	0.540

APPENDIX A

BINOMIAL PROBABILITY DISTRIBUTION (*continued*)

$n = 13$
Probability

r	0.05	0.10	0.20	0.30	0.40	0.50	0.60	0.70	0.80	0.90	0.95
0	0.513	0.254	0.055	0.010	0.001	0.000	0.000	0.000	0.000	0.000	0.000
1	0.351	0.367	0.179	0.054	0.011	0.002	0.000	0.000	0.000	0.000	0.000
2	0.111	0.245	0.268	0.139	0.045	0.010	0.001	0.000	0.000	0.000	0.000
3	0.021	0.100	0.246	0.218	0.111	0.035	0.006	0.001	0.000	0.000	0.000
4	0.003	0.028	0.154	0.234	0.184	0.087	0.024	0.003	0.000	0.000	0.000
5	0.000	0.006	0.069	0.180	0.221	0.157	0.066	0.014	0.001	0.000	0.000
6	0.000	0.001	0.023	0.103	0.197	0.209	0.131	0.044	0.006	0.000	0.000
7	0.000	0.000	0.006	0.044	0.131	0.209	0.197	0.103	0.023	0.001	0.000
8	0.000	0.000	0.001	0.014	0.066	0.157	0.221	0.180	0.069	0.006	0.000
9	0.000	0.000	0.000	0.003	0.024	0.087	0.184	0.234	0.154	0.028	0.003
10	0.000	0.000	0.000	0.001	0.006	0.035	0.111	0.218	0.246	0.100	0.021
11	0.000	0.000	0.000	0.000	0.001	0.010	0.045	0.139	0.268	0.245	0.111
12	0.000	0.000	0.000	0.000	0.000	0.002	0.011	0.054	0.179	0.367	0.351
13	0.000	0.000	0.000	0.000	0.000	0.000	0.001	0.010	0.055	0.254	0.513

$n = 14$
Probability

r	0.05	0.10	0.20	0.30	0.40	0.50	0.60	0.70	0.80	0.90	0.95
0	0.488	0.229	0.044	0.007	0.001	0.000	0.000	0.000	0.000	0.000	0.000
1	0.359	0.356	0.154	0.041	0.007	0.001	0.000	0.000	0.000	0.000	0.000
2	0.123	0.257	0.250	0.113	0.032	0.006	0.001	0.000	0.000	0.000	0.000
3	0.026	0.114	0.250	0.194	0.085	0.022	0.003	0.000	0.000	0.000	0.000
4	0.004	0.035	0.172	0.229	0.155	0.061	0.014	0.001	0.000	0.000	0.000
5	0.000	0.008	0.086	0.196	0.207	0.122	0.041	0.007	0.000	0.000	0.000
6	0.000	0.001	0.032	0.126	0.207	0.183	0.092	0.023	0.002	0.000	0.000
7	0.000	0.000	0.009	0.062	0.157	0.209	0.157	0.062	0.009	0.000	0.000
8	0.000	0.000	0.002	0.023	0.092	0.183	0.207	0.126	0.032	0.001	0.000
9	0.000	0.000	0.000	0.007	0.041	0.122	0.207	0.196	0.086	0.008	0.000
10	0.000	0.000	0.000	0.001	0.014	0.061	0.155	0.229	0.172	0.035	0.004
11	0.000	0.000	0.000	0.000	0.003	0.022	0.085	0.194	0.250	0.114	0.026
12	0.000	0.000	0.000	0.000	0.001	0.006	0.032	0.113	0.250	0.257	0.123
13	0.000	0.000	0.000	0.000	0.000	0.001	0.007	0.041	0.154	0.356	0.359
14	0.000	0.000	0.000	0.000	0.000	0.000	0.001	0.007	0.044	0.229	0.488

APPENDIX A

BINOMIAL PROBABILITY DISTRIBUTION (*continued*)

$n = 15$

Probability

r	0.05	0.10	0.20	0.30	0.40	0.50	0.60	0.70	0.80	0.90	0.95
0	0.463	0.206	0.035	0.005	0.000	0.000	0.000	0.000	0.000	0.000	0.000
1	0.366	0.343	0.132	0.031	0.005	0.000	0.000	0.000	0.000	0.000	0.000
2	0.135	0.267	0.231	0.092	0.022	0.003	0.000	0.000	0.000	0.000	0.000
3	0.031	0.129	0.250	0.170	0.063	0.014	0.002	0.000	0.000	0.000	0.000
4	0.005	0.043	0.188	0.219	0.127	0.042	0.007	0.001	0.000	0.000	0.000
5	0.001	0.010	0.103	0.206	0.186	0.092	0.024	0.003	0.000	0.000	0.000
6	0.000	0.002	0.043	0.147	0.207	0.153	0.061	0.012	0.001	0.000	0.000
7	0.000	0.000	0.014	0.081	0.177	0.196	0.118	0.035	0.003	0.000	0.000
8	0.000	0.000	0.003	0.035	0.118	0.196	0.177	0.081	0.014	0.000	0.000
9	0.000	0.000	0.001	0.012	0.061	0.153	0.207	0.147	0.043	0.002	0.000
10	0.000	0.000	0.000	0.003	0.024	0.092	0.186	0.206	0.103	0.010	0.001
11	0.000	0.000	0.000	0.001	0.007	0.042	0.127	0.219	0.188	0.043	0.005
12	0.000	0.000	0.000	0.000	0.002	0.014	0.063	0.170	0.250	0.129	0.031
13	0.000	0.000	0.000	0.000	0.000	0.003	0.022	0.092	0.231	0.267	0.135
14	0.000	0.000	0.000	0.000	0.000	0.000	0.005	0.031	0.132	0.343	0.366
15	0.000	0.000	0.000	0.000	0.000	0.000	0.000	0.005	0.035	0.206	0.463

$n = 16$

Probability

r	0.05	0.10	0.20	0.30	0.40	0.50	0.60	0.70	0.80	0.90	0.95
0	0.440	0.185	0.028	0.003	0.000	0.000	0.000	0.000	0.000	0.000	0.000
1	0.371	0.329	0.113	0.023	0.003	0.000	0.000	0.000	0.000	0.000	0.000
2	0.146	0.275	0.211	0.073	0.015	0.002	0.000	0.000	0.000	0.000	0.000
3	0.036	0.142	0.246	0.146	0.047	0.009	0.001	0.000	0.000	0.000	0.000
4	0.006	0.051	0.200	0.204	0.101	0.028	0.004	0.000	0.000	0.000	0.000
5	0.001	0.014	0.120	0.210	0.162	0.067	0.014	0.001	0.000	0.000	0.000
6	0.000	0.003	0.055	0.165	0.198	0.122	0.039	0.006	0.000	0.000	0.000
7	0.000	0.000	0.020	0.101	0.189	0.175	0.084	0.019	0.001	0.000	0.000
8	0.000	0.000	0.006	0.049	0.142	0.196	0.142	0.049	0.006	0.000	0.000
9	0.000	0.000	0.001	0.019	0.084	0.175	0.189	0.101	0.020	0.000	0.000
10	0.000	0.000	0.000	0.006	0.039	0.122	0.198	0.165	0.055	0.003	0.000
11	0.000	0.000	0.000	0.001	0.014	0.067	0.162	0.210	0.120	0.014	0.001
12	0.000	0.000	0.000	0.000	0.004	0.028	0.101	0.204	0.200	0.051	0.006
13	0.000	0.000	0.000	0.000	0.001	0.009	0.047	0.146	0.246	0.142	0.036
14	0.000	0.000	0.000	0.000	0.000	0.002	0.015	0.073	0.211	0.275	0.146
15	0.000	0.000	0.000	0.000	0.000	0.000	0.003	0.023	0.113	0.329	0.371
16	0.000	0.000	0.000	0.000	0.000	0.000	0.000	0.003	0.028	0.185	0.440

APPENDIX A

BINOMIAL PROBABILITY DISTRIBUTION (*continued*)

$n = 17$
Probability

r	0.05	0.10	0.20	0.30	0.40	0.50	0.60	0.70	0.80	0.90	0.95
0	0.418	0.167	0.023	0.002	0.000	0.000	0.000	0.000	0.000	0.000	0.000
1	0.374	0.315	0.096	0.017	0.002	0.000	0.000	0.000	0.000	0.000	0.000
2	0.158	0.280	0.191	0.058	0.010	0.001	0.000	0.000	0.000	0.000	0.000
3	0.041	0.156	0.239	0.125	0.034	0.005	0.000	0.000	0.000	0.000	0.000
4	0.008	0.060	0.209	0.187	0.080	0.018	0.002	0.000	0.000	0.000	0.000
5	0.001	0.017	0.136	0.208	0.138	0.047	0.008	0.001	0.000	0.000	0.000
6	0.000	0.004	0.068	0.178	0.184	0.094	0.024	0.003	0.000	0.000	0.000
7	0.000	0.001	0.027	0.120	0.193	0.148	0.057	0.009	0.000	0.000	0.000
8	0.000	0.000	0.008	0.064	0.161	0.185	0.107	0.028	0.002	0.000	0.000
9	0.000	0.000	0.002	0.028	0.107	0.185	0.161	0.064	0.008	0.000	0.000
10	0.000	0.000	0.000	0.009	0.057	0.148	0.193	0.120	0.027	0.001	0.000
11	0.000	0.000	0.000	0.003	0.024	0.094	0.184	0.178	0.068	0.004	0.000
12	0.000	0.000	0.000	0.001	0.008	0.047	0.138	0.208	0.136	0.017	0.001
13	0.000	0.000	0.000	0.000	0.002	0.018	0.080	0.187	0.209	0.060	0.008
14	0.000	0.000	0.000	0.000	0.000	0.005	0.034	0.125	0.239	0.156	0.041
15	0.000	0.000	0.000	0.000	0.000	0.001	0.010	0.058	0.191	0.280	0.158
16	0.000	0.000	0.000	0.000	0.000	0.000	0.002	0.017	0.096	0.315	0.374
17	0.000	0.000	0.000	0.000	0.000	0.000	0.000	0.002	0.023	0.167	0.418

$n = 18$
Probability

r	0.05	0.10	0.20	0.30	0.40	0.50	0.60	0.70	0.80	0.90	0.95
0	0.397	0.150	0.018	0.002	0.000	0.000	0.000	0.000	0.000	0.000	0.000
1	0.376	0.300	0.081	0.013	0.001	0.000	0.000	0.000	0.000	0.000	0.000
2	0.168	0.284	0.172	0.046	0.007	0.001	0.000	0.000	0.000	0.000	0.000
3	0.047	0.168	0.230	0.105	0.025	0.003	0.000	0.000	0.000	0.000	0.000
4	0.009	0.070	0.215	0.168	0.061	0.012	0.001	0.000	0.000	0.000	0.000
5	0.001	0.022	0.151	0.202	0.115	0.033	0.004	0.000	0.000	0.000	0.000
6	0.000	0.005	0.082	0.187	0.166	0.071	0.015	0.001	0.000	0.000	0.000
7	0.000	0.001	0.035	0.138	0.189	0.121	0.037	0.005	0.000	0.000	0.000
8	0.000	0.000	0.012	0.081	0.173	0.167	0.077	0.015	0.001	0.000	0.000
9	0.000	0.000	0.003	0.039	0.128	0.185	0.128	0.039	0.003	0.000	0.000
10	0.000	0.000	0.001	0.015	0.077	0.167	0.173	0.081	0.012	0.000	0.000
11	0.000	0.000	0.000	0.005	0.037	0.121	0.189	0.138	0.035	0.001	0.000
12	0.000	0.000	0.000	0.001	0.015	0.071	0.166	0.187	0.082	0.005	0.000
13	0.000	0.000	0.000	0.000	0.004	0.033	0.115	0.202	0.151	0.022	0.001
14	0.000	0.000	0.000	0.000	0.001	0.012	0.061	0.168	0.215	0.070	0.009
15	0.000	0.000	0.000	0.000	0.000	0.003	0.025	0.105	0.230	0.168	0.047
16	0.000	0.000	0.000	0.000	0.000	0.001	0.007	0.046	0.172	0.284	0.168
17	0.000	0.000	0.000	0.000	0.000	0.000	0.001	0.013	0.081	0.300	0.376
18	0.000	0.000	0.000	0.000	0.000	0.000	0.000	0.002	0.018	0.150	0.397

APPENDIX A

BINOMIAL PROBABILITY DISTRIBUTION (*continued*)

$n = 19$

Probability

r	0.05	0.10	0.20	0.30	0.40	0.50	0.60	0.70	0.80	0.90	0.95
0	0.377	0.135	0.014	0.001	0.000	0.000	0.000	0.000	0.000	0.000	0.000
1	0.377	0.285	0.068	0.009	0.001	0.000	0.000	0.000	0.000	0.000	0.000
2	0.179	0.285	0.154	0.036	0.005	0.000	0.000	0.000	0.000	0.000	0.000
3	0.053	0.180	0.218	0.087	0.017	0.002	0.000	0.000	0.000	0.000	0.000
4	0.011	0.080	0.218	0.149	0.047	0.007	0.001	0.000	0.000	0.000	0.000
5	0.002	0.027	0.164	0.192	0.093	0.022	0.002	0.000	0.000	0.000	0.000
6	0.000	0.007	0.095	0.192	0.145	0.052	0.008	0.001	0.000	0.000	0.000
7	0.000	0.001	0.044	0.153	0.180	0.096	0.024	0.002	0.000	0.000	0.000
8	0.000	0.000	0.017	0.098	0.180	0.144	0.053	0.008	0.000	0.000	0.000
9	0.000	0.000	0.005	0.051	0.146	0.176	0.098	0.022	0.001	0.000	0.000
10	0.000	0.000	0.001	0.022	0.098	0.176	0.146	0.051	0.005	0.000	0.000
11	0.000	0.000	0.000	0.008	0.053	0.144	0.180	0.098	0.017	0.000	0.000
12	0.000	0.000	0.000	0.002	0.024	0.096	0.180	0.153	0.044	0.001	0.000
13	0.000	0.000	0.000	0.001	0.008	0.052	0.145	0.192	0.095	0.007	0.000
14	0.000	0.000	0.000	0.000	0.002	0.022	0.093	0.192	0.164	0.027	0.002
15	0.000	0.000	0.000	0.000	0.001	0.007	0.047	0.149	0.218	0.080	0.011
16	0.000	0.000	0.000	0.000	0.000	0.002	0.017	0.087	0.218	0.180	0.053
17	0.000	0.000	0.000	0.000	0.000	0.000	0.005	0.036	0.154	0.285	0.179
18	0.000	0.000	0.000	0.000	0.000	0.000	0.001	0.009	0.068	0.285	0.377
19	0.000	0.000	0.000	0.000	0.000	0.000	0.000	0.001	0.014	0.135	0.377

$n = 20$

Probability

r	0.05	0.10	0.20	0.30	0.40	0.50	0.60	0.70	0.80	0.90	0.95
0	0.358	0.122	0.012	0.001	0.000	0.000	0.000	0.000	0.000	0.000	0.000
1	0.377	0.270	0.058	0.007	0.000	0.000	0.000	0.000	0.000	0.000	0.000
2	0.189	0.285	0.137	0.028	0.003	0.000	0.000	0.000	0.000	0.000	0.000
3	0.060	0.190	0.205	0.072	0.012	0.001	0.000	0.000	0.000	0.000	0.000
4	0.013	0.090	0.218	0.130	0.035	0.005	0.000	0.000	0.000	0.000	0.000
5	0.002	0.032	0.175	0.179	0.075	0.015	0.001	0.000	0.000	0.000	0.000
6	0.000	0.009	0.109	0.192	0.124	0.037	0.005	0.000	0.000	0.000	0.000
7	0.000	0.002	0.055	0.164	0.166	0.074	0.015	0.001	0.000	0.000	0.000
8	0.000	0.000	0.022	0.114	0.180	0.120	0.035	0.004	0.000	0.000	0.000
9	0.000	0.000	0.007	0.065	0.160	0.160	0.071	0.012	0.000	0.000	0.000
10	0.000	0.000	0.002	0.031	0.117	0.176	0.117	0.031	0.002	0.000	0.000
11	0.000	0.000	0.000	0.012	0.071	0.160	0.160	0.065	0.007	0.000	0.000
12	0.000	0.000	0.000	0.004	0.035	0.120	0.180	0.114	0.022	0.000	0.000
13	0.000	0.000	0.000	0.001	0.015	0.074	0.166	0.164	0.055	0.002	0.000
14	0.000	0.000	0.000	0.000	0.005	0.037	0.124	0.192	0.109	0.009	0.000
15	0.000	0.000	0.000	0.000	0.001	0.015	0.075	0.179	0.175	0.032	0.002
16	0.000	0.000	0.000	0.000	0.000	0.005	0.035	0.130	0.218	0.090	0.013
17	0.000	0.000	0.000	0.000	0.000	0.001	0.012	0.072	0.205	0.190	0.060
18	0.000	0.000	0.000	0.000	0.000	0.000	0.003	0.028	0.137	0.285	0.189
19	0.000	0.000	0.000	0.000	0.000	0.000	0.000	0.007	0.058	0.270	0.377
20	0.000	0.000	0.000	0.000	0.000	0.000	0.000	0.001	0.012	0.122	0.358

APPENDIX A

BINOMIAL PROBABILITY DISTRIBUTION (*concluded*)

$n = 25$

Probability

r	0.05	0.10	0.20	0.30	0.40	0.50	0.60	0.70	0.80	0.90	0.95
0	0.277	0.072	0.004	0.000	0.000	0.000	0.000	0.000	0.000	0.000	0.000
1	0.365	0.199	0.024	0.001	0.000	0.000	0.000	0.000	0.000	0.000	0.000
2	0.231	0.266	0.071	0.007	0.000	0.000	0.000	0.000	0.000	0.000	0.000
3	0.093	0.226	0.136	0.024	0.002	0.000	0.000	0.000	0.000	0.000	0.000
4	0.027	0.138	0.187	0.057	0.007	0.000	0.000	0.000	0.000	0.000	0.000
5	0.006	0.065	0.196	0.103	0.020	0.002	0.000	0.000	0.000	0.000	0.000
6	0.001	0.024	0.163	0.147	0.044	0.005	0.000	0.000	0.000	0.000	0.000
7	0.000	0.007	0.111	0.171	0.080	0.014	0.001	0.000	0.000	0.000	0.000
8	0.000	0.002	0.062	0.165	0.120	0.032	0.003	0.000	0.000	0.000	0.000
9	0.000	0.000	0.029	0.134	0.151	0.061	0.009	0.000	0.000	0.000	0.000
10	0.000	0.000	0.012	0.092	0.161	0.097	0.021	0.001	0.000	0.000	0.000
11	0.000	0.000	0.004	0.054	0.147	0.133	0.043	0.004	0.000	0.000	0.000
12	0.000	0.000	0.001	0.027	0.114	0.155	0.076	0.011	0.000	0.000	0.000
13	0.000	0.000	0.000	0.011	0.076	0.155	0.114	0.027	0.001	0.000	0.000
14	0.000	0.000	0.000	0.004	0.043	0.133	0.147	0.054	0.004	0.000	0.000
15	0.000	0.000	0.000	0.001	0.021	0.097	0.161	0.092	0.012	0.000	0.000
16	0.000	0.000	0.000	0.000	0.009	0.061	0.151	0.134	0.029	0.000	0.000
17	0.000	0.000	0.000	0.000	0.003	0.032	0.120	0.165	0.062	0.002	0.000
18	0.000	0.000	0.000	0.000	0.001	0.014	0.080	0.171	0.111	0.007	0.000
19	0.000	0.000	0.000	0.000	0.000	0.005	0.044	0.147	0.163	0.024	0.001
20	0.000	0.000	0.000	0.000	0.000	0.002	0.020	0.103	0.196	0.065	0.006
21	0.000	0.000	0.000	0.000	0.000	0.000	0.007	0.057	0.187	0.138	0.027
22	0.000	0.000	0.000	0.000	0.000	0.000	0.002	0.024	0.136	0.226	0.093
23	0.000	0.000	0.000	0.000	0.000	0.000	0.000	0.007	0.071	0.266	0.231
24	0.000	0.000	0.000	0.000	0.000	0.000	0.000	0.001	0.024	0.199	0.365
25	0.000	0.000	0.000	0.000	0.000	0.000	0.000	0.000	0.004	0.072	0.277

APPENDIX B

FACTORS FOR CONTROL CHARTS

Number of items in sample,	Chart for averages	Chart for ranges		
	Factors for control limits	Factors for central line	Factors for control limits	
n	A_2	d_2	D_3	D_4
2	1.880	1.128	0	3.267
3	1.023	1.693	0	2.575
4	.729	2.059	0	2.282
5	.577	2.326	0	2.115
6	.483	2.534	0	2.004
7	.419	2.704	.076	1.924
8	.373	2.847	.136	1.864
9	.337	2.970	.184	1.816
10	.308	3.078	.223	1.777
11	.285	3.173	.256	1.744
12	.266	3.258	.284	1.716
13	.249	3.336	.308	1.692
14	.235	3.407	.329	1.671
15	.223	3.472	.348	1.652

Source: Adapted from American Society for Testing and Materials, *Manual on Quality Control of Materials,* 1951, Table B2, p. 115. For a more detailed table and explanation, see Acheson J. Duncan, *Quality Control and Industrial Statistics,* 3d ed. (Homewood, Ill.: Richard D. Irwin, 1974), Table M, p. 927.

APPENDIX C

POISSON DISTRIBUTION: PROBABILITY OF EXACTLY *X* OCCURRENCES

	μ								
X	**0.1**	**0.2**	**0.3**	**0.4**	**0.5**	**0.6**	**0.7**	**0.8**	**0.9**
0	0.9048	0.8187	0.7408	0.6703	0.6065	0.5488	0.4966	0.4493	0.4066
1	0.0905	0.1637	0.2222	0.2681	0.3033	0.3293	0.3476	0.3595	0.3659
2	0.0045	0.0164	0.0333	0.0536	0.0758	0.0988	0.1217	0.1438	0.1647
3	0.0002	0.0011	0.0033	0.0072	0.0126	0.0198	0.0284	0.0383	0.0494
4	0.0000	0.0001	0.0003	0.0007	0.0016	0.0030	0.0050	0.0077	0.0111
5	0.0000	0.0000	0.0000	0.0001	0.0002	0.0004	0.0007	0.0012	0.0020
6	0.0000	0.0000	0.0000	0.0000	0.0000	0.0000	0.0001	0.0002	0.0003
7	0.0000	0.0000	0.0000	0.0000	0.0000	0.0000	0.0000	0.0000	0.0000

	μ								
X	**1.0**	**2.0**	**3.0**	**4.0**	**5.0**	**6.0**	**7.0**	**8.0**	**9.0**
0	0.3679	0.1353	0.0498	0.0183	0.0067	0.0025	0.0009	0.0003	0.0001
1	0.3679	0.2707	0.1494	0.0733	0.0337	0.0149	0.0064	0.0027	0.0011
2	0.1839	0.2707	0.2240	0.1465	0.0842	0.0446	0.0223	0.0107	0.0050
3	0.0613	0.1804	0.2240	0.1954	0.1404	0.0892	0.0521	0.0286	0.0150
4	0.0153	0.0902	0.1680	0.1954	0.1755	0.1339	0.0912	0.0573	0.0337
5	0.0031	0.0361	0.1008	0.1563	0.1755	0.1606	0.1277	0.0916	0.0607
6	0.0005	0.0120	0.0504	0.1042	0.1462	0.1606	0.1490	0.1221	0.0911
7	0.0001	0.0034	0.0216	0.0595	0.1044	0.1377	0.1490	0.1396	0.1171
8	0.0000	0.0009	0.0081	0.0298	0.0653	0.1033	0.1304	0.1396	0.1318
9	0.0000	0.0002	0.0027	0.0132	0.0363	0.0688	0.1014	0.1241	0.1318
10	0.0000	0.0000	0.0008	0.0053	0.0181	0.0413	0.0710	0.0993	0.1186
11	0.0000	0.0000	0.0002	0.0019	0.0082	0.0225	0.0452	0.0722	0.0970
12	0.0000	0.0000	0.0001	0.0006	0.0034	0.0113	0.0263	0.0481	0.0728
13	0.0000	0.0000	0.0000	0.0002	0.0013	0.0052	0.0142	0.0296	0.0504
14	0.0000	0.0000	0.0000	0.0001	0.0005	0.0022	0.0071	0.0169	0.0324
15	0.0000	0.0000	0.0000	0.0000	0.0002	0.0009	0.0033	0.0090	0.0194
16	0.0000	0.0000	0.0000	0.0000	0.0000	0.0003	0.0014	0.0045	0.0109
17	0.0000	0.0000	0.0000	0.0000	0.0000	0.0001	0.0006	0.0021	0.0058
18	0.0000	0.0000	0.0000	0.0000	0.0000	0.0000	0.0002	0.0009	0.0029
19	0.0000	0.0000	0.0000	0.0000	0.0000	0.0000	0.0001	0.0004	0.0014
20	0.0000	0.0000	0.0000	0.0000	0.0000	0.0000	0.0000	0.0002	0.0006
21	0.0000	0.0000	0.0000	0.0000	0.0000	0.0000	0.0000	0.0001	0.0003
22	0.0000	0.0000	0.0000	0.0000	0.0000	0.0000	0.0000	0.0000	0.0001

APPENDIX D

AREAS UNDER THE NORMAL CURVE

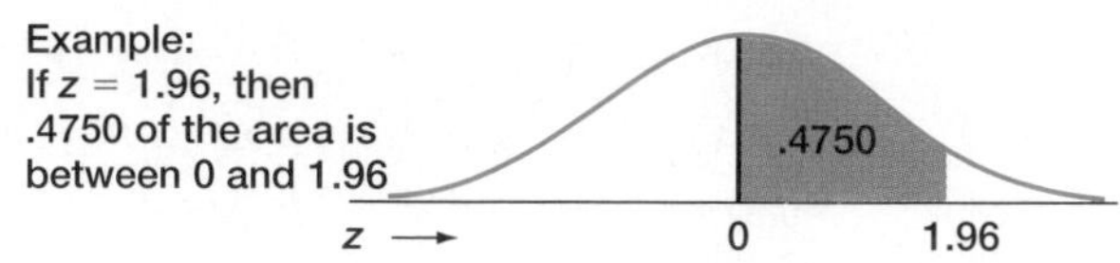

z	0.00	0.01	0.02	0.03	0.04	0.05	0.06	0.07	0.08	0.09
0.0	0.0000	0.0040	0.0080	0.0120	0.0160	0.0199	0.0239	0.0279	0.0319	0.0359
0.1	0.0398	0.0438	0.0478	0.0517	0.0557	0.0596	0.0636	0.0675	0.0714	0.0753
0.2	0.0793	0.0832	0.0871	0.0910	0.0948	0.0987	0.1026	0.1064	0.1103	0.1141
0.3	0.1179	0.1217	0.1255	0.1293	0.1331	0.1368	0.1406	0.1443	0.1480	0.1517
0.4	0.1554	0.1591	0.1628	0.1664	0.1700	0.1736	0.1772	0.1808	0.1844	0.1879
0.5	0.1915	0.1950	0.1985	0.2019	0.2054	0.2088	0.2123	0.2157	0.2190	0.2224
0.6	0.2257	0.2291	0.2324	0.2357	0.2389	0.2422	0.2454	0.2486	0.2517	0.2549
0.7	0.2580	0.2611	0.2642	0.2673	0.2704	0.2734	0.2764	0.2794	0.2823	0.2852
0.8	0.2881	0.2910	0.2939	0.2967	0.2995	0.3023	0.3051	0.3078	0.3106	0.3133
0.9	0.3159	0.3186	0.3212	0.3238	0.3264	0.3289	0.3315	0.3340	0.3365	0.3389
1.0	0.3413	0.3438	0.3461	0.3485	0.3508	0.3531	0.3554	0.3577	0.3599	0.3621
1.1	0.3643	0.3665	0.3686	0.3708	0.3729	0.3749	0.3770	0.3790	0.3810	0.3830
1.2	0.3849	0.3869	0.3888	0.3907	0.3925	0.3944	0.3962	0.3980	0.3997	0.4015
1.3	0.4032	0.4049	0.4066	0.4082	0.4099	0.4115	0.4131	0.4147	0.4162	0.4177
1.4	0.4192	0.4207	0.4222	0.4236	0.4251	0.4265	0.4279	0.4292	0.4306	0.4319
1.5	0.4332	0.4345	0.4357	0.4370	0.4382	0.4394	0.4406	0.4418	0.4429	0.4441
1.6	0.4452	0.4463	0.4474	0.4484	0.4495	0.4505	0.4515	0.4525	0.4535	0.4545
1.7	0.4554	0.4564	0.4573	0.4582	0.4591	0.4599	0.4608	0.4616	0.4625	0.4633
1.8	0.4641	0.4649	0.4656	0.4664	0.4671	0.4678	0.4686	0.4693	0.4699	0.4706
1.9	0.4713	0.4719	0.4726	0.4732	0.4738	0.4744	0.4750	0.4756	0.4761	0.4767
2.0	0.4772	0.4778	0.4783	0.4788	0.4793	0.4798	0.4803	0.4808	0.4812	0.4817
2.1	0.4821	0.4826	0.4830	0.4834	0.4838	0.4842	0.4846	0.4850	0.4854	0.4857
2.2	0.4861	0.4864	0.4868	0.4871	0.4875	0.4878	0.4881	0.4884	0.4887	0.4890
2.3	0.4893	0.4896	0.4898	0.4901	0.4904	0.4906	0.4909	0.4911	0.4913	0.4916
2.4	0.4918	0.4920	0.4922	0.4925	0.4927	0.4929	0.4931	0.4932	0.4934	0.4936
2.5	0.4938	0.4940	0.4941	0.4943	0.4945	0.4946	0.4948	0.4949	0.4951	0.4952
2.6	0.4953	0.4955	0.4956	0.4957	0.4959	0.4960	0.4961	0.4962	0.4963	0.4964
2.7	0.4965	0.4966	0.4967	0.4968	0.4969	0.4970	0.4971	0.4972	0.4973	0.4974
2.8	0.4974	0.4975	0.4976	0.4977	0.4977	0.4978	0.4979	0.4979	0.4980	0.4981
2.9	0.4981	0.4982	0.4982	0.4983	0.4984	0.4984	0.4985	0.4985	0.4986	0.4986
3.0	0.4987	0.4987	0.4987	0.4988	0.4988	0.4989	0.4989	0.4989	0.4990	0.4990

APPENDIX E

TABLE OF RANDOM NUMBERS

02711	08182	75997	79866	58095	83319	80295	79741	74599	84379
94873	90935	31684	63952	09865	14491	99518	93394	34691	14985
54921	78680	06635	98689	17306	25170	65928	87709	30533	89736
77640	97636	37397	93379	56454	59818	45827	74164	71666	46977
61545	00835	93251	87203	36759	49197	85967	01704	19634	21898
17147	19519	22497	16857	42426	84822	92598	49186	88247	39967
13748	04742	92460	85801	53444	65626	58710	55406	17173	69776
87455	14813	50373	28037	91182	32786	65261	11173	34376	36408
08999	57409	91185	10200	61411	23392	47797	56377	71635	08601
78804	81333	53809	32471	46034	36306	22498	19239	85428	55721
82173	26921	28472	98958	07960	66124	89731	95069	18625	92405
97594	25168	89178	68190	05043	17407	48201	83917	11413	72920
73881	67176	93504	42636	38233	16154	96451	57925	29667	30859
46071	22912	90326	42453	88108	72064	58601	32357	90610	32921
44492	19686	12495	93135	95185	77799	52441	88272	22024	80631
31864	72170	37722	55794	14636	05148	54505	50113	21119	25228
51574	90692	43339	65689	76539	27909	05467	21727	51141	72949
35350	76132	92925	92124	92634	35681	43690	89136	35599	84138
46943	36502	01172	46045	46991	33804	80006	35542	61056	75666
22665	87226	33304	57975	03985	21566	65796	72915	81466	89205
39437	97957	11838	10433	21564	51570	73558	27495	34533	57808
77082	47784	40098	97962	89845	28392	78187	06112	08169	11261
24544	25649	43370	28007	06779	72402	62632	53956	24709	06978
27503	15558	37738	24849	70722	71859	83736	06016	94397	12529
24590	24545	06435	52758	45685	90151	46516	49644	92686	84870
48155	86226	40359	28723	15364	69125	12609	57171	86857	31702
20226	53752	90648	24362	83314	00014	19207	69413	97016	86290
70178	73444	38790	53626	93780	18629	68766	24371	74639	30782
10169	41465	51935	05711	09799	79077	88159	33437	68519	03040
81084	03701	28598	70013	63794	53169	97054	60303	23259	96196
69202	20777	21727	81511	51887	16175	53746	46516	70339	62727
80561	95787	89426	93325	86412	57479	54194	52153	19197	81877
08199	26703	95128	48599	09333	12584	24374	31232	61782	44032
98883	28220	39358	53720	80161	83371	15181	11131	12219	55920
84568	69286	76054	21615	80883	36797	82845	39139	90900	18172
04269	35173	95745	53893	86022	77722	52498	84193	22448	22571
10538	13124	36099	13140	37706	44562	57179	44693	67877	01549
77843	24955	25900	63843	95029	93859	93634	20205	66294	41218
12034	94636	49455	76362	83532	31062	69903	91186	65768	55949
10524	72829	47641	93315	80875	28090	97728	52560	34937	79548
68935	76632	46984	61772	92786	22651	07086	89754	44143	97687
89450	65665	29190	43709	11172	34481	95977	47535	25658	73898
90696	20451	24211	97310	60446	73530	62865	96574	13829	72226
49006	32047	93086	00112	20470	17136	28255	86328	07293	38809
74591	87025	52368	59416	34417	70557	86746	55809	53628	12000
06315	17012	77103	00968	07235	10728	42189	33292	51487	64443
62386	09184	62092	46617	99419	64230	95034	85481	07857	42510
86848	82122	04028	36959	87827	12813	08627	80699	13345	51695
65643	69480	46598	04501	40403	91408	32343	48130	49303	90689
11084	46534	78957	77353	39578	77868	22970	84349	09184	70603

APPENDIX F

STUDENT *t* DISTRIBUTION

	Level of significance for one-tailed test					
df	.10	.05	.025	.01	.005	.0005
	Level of significance for two-tailed test					
	.20	.10	.05	.02	.01	.001
1	3.078	6.314	12.706	31.821	63.657	636.619
2	1.886	2.920	4.303	6.965	9.925	31.599
3	1.638	2.353	3.182	4.541	5.841	12.924
4	1.533	2.132	2.776	3.747	4.604	8.610
5	1.476	2.015	2.571	3.365	4.032	6.869
6	1.440	1.943	2.447	3.143	3.707	5.959
7	1.415	1.895	2.365	2.998	3.499	5.408
8	1.397	1.860	2.306	2.896	3.355	5.041
9	1.383	1.833	2.262	2.821	3.250	4.781
10	1.372	1.812	2.228	2.764	3.169	4.587
11	1.363	1.796	2.201	2.718	3.106	4.437
12	1.356	1.782	2.179	2.681	3.055	4.318
13	1.350	1.771	2.160	2.650	3.012	4.221
14	1.345	1.761	2.145	2.624	2.977	4.140
15	1.341	1.753	2.131	2.602	2.947	4.073
16	1.337	1.746	2.120	2.583	2.921	4.015
17	1.333	1.740	2.110	2.567	2.898	3.965
18	1.330	1.734	2.101	2.552	2.878	3.922
19	1.328	1.729	2.093	2.539	2.861	3.883
20	1.325	1.725	2.086	2.528	2.845	3.850
21	1.323	1.721	2.080	2.518	2.831	3.819
22	1.321	1.717	2.074	2.508	2.819	3.792
23	1.319	1.714	2.069	2.500	2.807	3.768
24	1.318	1.711	2.064	2.492	2.797	3.745
25	1.316	1.708	2.060	2.485	2.787	3.725
26	1.315	1.706	2.056	2.479	2.779	3.707
27	1.314	1.703	2.052	2.473	2.771	3.690
28	1.313	1.701	2.048	2.467	2.763	3.674
29	1.311	1.699	2.045	2.462	2.756	3.659
30	1.310	1.697	2.042	2.457	2.750	3.646
40	1.303	1.684	2.021	2.423	2.704	3.551
60	1.296	1.671	2.000	2.390	2.660	3.460
120	1.289	1.658	1.980	2.358	2.617	3.373
∞	1.282	1.645	1.960	2.326	2.576	3.291

APPENDIX G

CRITICAL VALUES OF THE *F* DISTRIBUTION AT A 5 PERCENT LEVEL OF SIGNIFICANCE, $\alpha = .05$

Degrees of freedom for the numerator (columns); Degrees of freedom for the denominator (rows)

	1	2	3	4	5	6	7	8	9	10	12	15	20	24	30	40	60	120	∞
1	161	200	216	225	230	234	237	239	241	242	244	246	248	249	250	251	252	253	254
2	18.5	19.0	19.2	19.2	19.3	19.3	19.4	19.4	19.4	19.4	19.4	19.4	19.4	19.5	19.5	19.5	19.5	19.5	19.5
3	10.1	9.55	9.28	9.12	9.01	8.94	8.89	8.85	8.81	8.79	8.74	8.70	8.66	8.64	8.62	8.59	8.57	8.55	8.53
4	7.71	6.94	6.59	6.39	6.26	6.16	6.09	6.04	6.00	5.96	5.91	5.86	5.80	5.77	5.75	5.72	5.69	5.66	5.63
5	6.61	5.79	5.41	5.19	5.05	4.95	4.88	4.82	4.77	4.74	4.68	4.62	4.56	4.53	4.50	4.46	4.43	4.40	4.37
6	5.99	5.14	4.76	4.53	4.39	4.28	4.21	4.15	4.10	4.06	4.00	3.94	3.87	3.84	3.81	3.77	3.74	3.70	3.67
7	5.59	4.74	4.35	4.12	3.97	3.87	3.79	3.73	3.68	3.64	3.57	3.51	3.44	3.41	3.38	3.34	3.30	3.27	3.23
8	5.32	4.46	4.07	3.84	3.69	3.58	3.50	3.44	3.39	3.35	3.28	3.22	3.15	3.12	3.08	3.04	3.01	2.97	2.93
9	5.12	4.26	3.86	3.63	3.48	3.37	3.29	3.23	3.18	3.14	3.07	3.01	2.94	2.90	2.86	2.83	2.79	2.75	2.71
10	4.96	4.10	3.71	3.48	3.33	3.22	3.14	3.07	3.02	2.98	2.91	2.85	2.77	2.74	2.70	2.66	2.62	2.58	2.54
11	4.84	3.98	3.59	3.36	3.20	3.09	3.01	2.95	2.90	2.85	2.79	2.72	2.65	2.61	2.57	2.53	2.49	2.45	2.40
12	4.75	3.89	3.49	3.26	3.11	3.00	2.91	2.85	2.80	2.75	2.69	2.62	2.54	2.51	2.47	2.43	2.38	2.34	2.30
13	4.67	3.81	3.41	3.18	3.03	2.92	2.83	2.77	2.71	2.67	2.60	2.53	2.46	2.42	2.38	2.34	2.30	2.25	2.21
14	4.60	3.74	3.34	3.11	2.96	2.85	2.76	2.70	2.65	2.60	2.53	2.46	2.39	2.35	2.31	2.27	2.22	2.18	2.13
15	4.54	3.68	3.29	3.06	2.90	2.79	2.71	2.64	2.59	2.54	2.48	2.40	2.33	2.29	2.25	2.20	2.16	2.11	2.07
16	4.49	3.63	3.24	3.01	2.85	2.74	2.66	2.59	2.54	2.49	2.42	2.35	2.28	2.24	2.19	2.15	2.11	2.06	2.01
17	4.45	3.59	3.20	2.96	2.81	2.70	2.61	2.55	2.49	2.45	2.38	2.31	2.23	2.19	2.15	2.10	2.06	2.01	1.96
18	4.41	3.55	3.16	2.93	2.77	2.66	2.58	2.51	2.46	2.41	2.34	2.27	2.19	2.15	2.11	2.06	2.02	1.97	1.92
19	4.38	3.52	3.13	2.90	2.74	2.63	2.54	2.48	2.42	2.38	2.31	2.23	2.16	2.11	2.07	2.03	1.98	1.93	1.88
20	4.35	3.49	3.10	2.87	2.71	2.60	2.51	2.45	2.39	2.35	2.28	2.20	2.12	2.08	2.04	1.99	1.95	1.90	1.84
21	4.32	3.47	3.07	2.84	2.68	2.57	2.49	2.42	2.37	2.32	2.25	2.18	2.10	2.05	2.01	1.96	1.92	1.87	1.81
22	4.30	3.44	3.05	2.82	2.66	2.55	2.46	2.40	2.34	2.30	2.23	2.15	2.07	2.03	1.98	1.94	1.89	1.84	1.78
23	4.28	3.42	3.03	2.80	2.64	2.53	2.44	2.37	2.32	2.27	2.20	2.13	2.05	2.01	1.96	1.91	1.86	1.81	1.76
24	4.26	3.40	3.01	2.78	2.62	2.51	2.42	2.36	2.30	2.25	2.18	2.11	2.03	1.98	1.94	1.89	1.84	1.79	1.73
25	4.24	3.39	2.99	2.76	2.60	2.49	2.40	2.34	2.28	2.24	2.16	2.09	2.01	1.96	1.92	1.87	1.82	1.77	1.71
30	4.17	3.32	2.92	2.69	2.53	2.42	2.33	2.27	2.21	2.16	2.09	2.01	1.93	1.89	1.84	1.79	1.74	1.68	1.62
40	4.08	3.23	2.84	2.61	2.45	2.34	2.25	2.18	2.12	2.08	2.00	1.92	1.84	1.79	1.74	1.69	1.64	1.58	1.51
60	4.00	3.15	2.76	2.53	2.37	2.25	2.17	2.10	2.04	1.99	1.92	1.84	1.75	1.70	1.65	1.59	1.53	1.47	1.39
120	3.92	3.07	2.68	2.45	2.29	2.18	2.09	2.02	1.96	1.91	1.83	1.75	1.66	1.61	1.55	1.50	1.43	1.35	1.25
∞	3.84	3.00	2.60	2.37	2.21	2.10	2.01	1.94	1.88	1.83	1.75	1.67	1.57	1.52	1.46	1.39	1.32	1.22	1.00

CRITICAL VALUES OF THE *F* DISTRIBUTION AT A 1 PERCENT LEVEL OF SIGNIFICANCE, $\alpha = .01$ (*concluded*)

Degrees of freedom for the numerator (columns); Degrees of freedom for the denominator (rows)

	1	2	3	4	5	6	7	8	9	10	12	15	20	24	30	40	60	120	∞
1	4052	5000	5403	5625	5764	5859	5928	5981	6022	6056	6106	6157	6209	6235	6261	6287	6313	6339	6366
2	98.5	99.0	99.2	99.2	99.3	99.3	99.4	99.4	99.4	99.4	99.4	99.4	99.4	99.5	99.5	99.5	99.5	99.5	99.5
3	34.1	30.8	29.5	28.7	28.2	27.9	27.7	27.5	27.3	27.2	27.1	26.9	26.7	26.6	26.5	26.4	26.3	26.2	26.1
4	21.2	18.0	16.7	16.0	15.5	15.2	15.0	14.8	14.7	14.5	14.4	14.2	14.0	13.9	13.8	13.7	13.7	13.6	13.5
5	16.3	13.3	12.1	11.4	11.0	10.7	10.5	10.3	10.2	10.1	9.89	9.72	9.55	9.47	9.38	9.29	9.20	9.11	9.02
6	13.7	10.9	9.78	9.15	8.75	8.47	8.26	8.10	7.98	7.87	7.72	7.56	7.40	7.31	7.23	7.14	7.06	6.97	6.88
7	12.2	9.55	8.45	7.85	7.46	7.19	6.99	6.84	6.72	6.62	6.47	6.31	6.16	6.07	5.99	5.91	5.82	5.74	5.65
8	11.3	8.65	7.59	7.01	6.63	6.37	6.18	6.03	5.91	5.81	5.67	5.52	5.36	5.28	5.20	5.12	5.03	4.95	4.86
9	10.6	8.02	6.99	6.42	6.06	5.80	5.61	5.47	5.35	5.26	5.11	4.96	4.81	4.73	4.65	4.57	4.48	4.40	4.31
10	10.0	7.56	6.55	5.99	5.64	5.39	5.20	5.06	4.94	4.85	4.71	4.56	4.41	4.33	4.25	4.17	4.08	4.00	3.91
11	9.65	7.21	6.22	5.67	5.32	5.07	4.89	4.74	4.63	4.54	4.40	4.25	4.10	4.02	3.94	3.86	3.78	3.69	3.60
12	9.33	6.93	5.95	5.41	5.06	4.82	4.64	4.50	4.39	4.30	4.16	4.01	3.86	3.78	3.70	3.62	3.54	3.45	3.36
13	9.07	6.70	5.74	5.21	4.86	4.62	4.44	4.30	4.19	4.10	3.96	3.82	3.66	3.59	3.51	3.43	3.34	3.25	3.17
14	8.86	6.51	5.56	5.04	4.69	4.46	4.28	4.14	4.03	3.94	3.80	3.66	3.51	3.43	3.35	3.27	3.18	3.09	3.00
15	8.68	6.36	5.42	4.89	4.56	4.32	4.14	4.00	3.89	3.80	3.67	3.52	3.37	3.29	3.21	3.13	3.05	2.96	2.87
16	8.53	6.23	5.29	4.77	4.44	4.20	4.03	3.89	3.78	3.69	3.55	3.41	3.26	3.18	3.10	3.02	2.93	2.84	2.75
17	8.40	6.11	5.18	4.67	4.34	4.10	3.93	3.79	3.68	3.59	3.46	3.31	3.16	3.08	3.00	2.92	2.83	2.75	2.65
18	8.29	6.01	5.09	4.58	4.25	4.01	3.84	3.71	3.60	3.51	3.37	3.23	3.08	3.00	2.92	2.84	2.75	2.66	2.57
19	8.18	5.93	5.01	4.50	4.17	3.94	3.77	3.63	3.52	3.43	3.30	3.15	3.00	2.92	2.84	2.76	2.67	2.58	2.49
20	8.10	5.85	4.94	4.43	4.10	3.87	3.70	3.56	3.46	3.37	3.23	3.09	2.94	2.86	2.78	2.69	2.61	2.52	2.42
21	8.02	5.78	4.87	4.37	4.04	3.81	3.64	3.51	3.40	3.31	3.17	3.03	2.88	2.80	2.72	2.64	2.55	2.46	2.36
22	7.95	5.72	4.82	4.31	3.99	3.76	3.59	3.45	3.35	3.26	3.12	2.98	2.83	2.75	2.67	2.58	2.50	2.40	2.31
23	7.88	5.66	4.76	4.26	3.94	3.71	3.54	3.41	3.30	3.21	3.07	2.93	2.78	2.70	2.62	2.54	2.45	2.35	2.26
24	7.82	5.61	4.72	4.22	3.90	3.67	3.50	3.36	3.26	3.17	3.03	2.89	2.74	2.66	2.58	2.49	2.40	2.31	2.21
25	7.77	5.57	4.68	4.18	3.85	3.63	3.46	3.32	3.22	3.13	2.99	2.85	2.70	2.62	2.54	2.45	2.36	2.27	2.17
30	7.56	5.39	4.51	4.02	3.70	3.47	3.30	3.17	3.07	2.98	2.84	2.70	2.55	2.47	2.39	2.30	2.21	2.11	2.01
40	7.31	5.18	4.31	3.83	3.51	3.29	3.12	2.99	2.89	2.80	2.66	2.52	2.37	2.29	2.20	2.11	2.02	1.92	1.81
60	7.08	4.98	4.13	3.65	3.34	3.12	2.95	2.82	2.72	2.63	2.50	2.35	2.20	2.12	2.03	1.94	1.84	1.73	1.60
120	6.85	4.79	3.95	3.48	3.17	2.96	2.79	2.66	2.56	2.47	2.34	2.19	2.03	1.95	1.86	1.76	1.66	1.53	1.38
∞	6.63	4.61	3.78	3.32	3.02	2.80	2.64	2.51	2.41	2.32	2.18	2.04	1.88	1.79	1.70	1.59	1.47	1.32	1.00

APPENDIX H

CRITICAL VALUES OF THE SPEARMAN RANK CORRELATION COEFFICIENT

N	Significance level (one-tailed test)	
	.05	**.01**
4	1.000	
5	.900	1.000
6	.829	.943
7	.714	.893
8	.643	.833
9	.600	.783
10	.564	.746
12	.506	.712
14	.456	.645
16	.425	.601
18	.399	.564
20	.377	.534
22	.359	.508
24	.343	.485
26	.329	.465
28	.317	.448
30	.306	.432

Sources: Adapted from E. G. Olds, "Distributions of Sums of Squares of Rank Differences for Small Numbers of Individuals," *Annals of Mathematical Statistics* 9 (1938), pp. 133–48; and from E. G. Olds, "The 5 Percent Significance Levels for Sums of Squares of Rank Differences and a Correction," *Annals of Mathematical Statistics* 30 (1949), pp. 117–18, with the kind permission of the author and publisher.

APPENDIX I

CRITICAL VALUES OF CHI-SQUARE

This table contains the values of χ^2 that correspond to a specific right-tail area and specific numbers of degrees of freedom *df*.

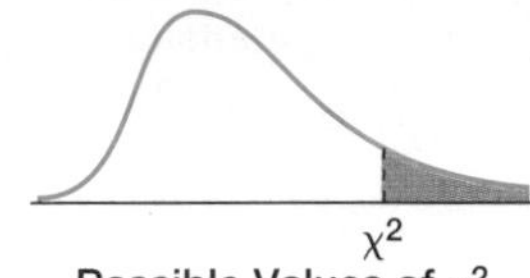

Possible Values of χ^2

Degrees of freedom	Right-tail area			
	.10	.05	.02	.01
df				
1	2.706	3.841	5.412	6.635
2	4.605	5.991	7.824	9.210
3	6.251	7.815	9.837	11.345
4	7.779	9.488	11.668	13.277
5	9.236	11.070	13.388	15.086
6	10.645	12.592	15.033	16.812
7	12.017	14.067	16.622	18.475
8	13.362	15.507	18.168	20.090
9	14.684	16.919	19.679	21.666
10	15.987	18.307	21.161	23.209
11	17.275	19.675	22.618	24.725
12	18.549	21.026	24.054	26.217
13	19.812	22.362	25.472	27.688
14	21.064	23.685	26.873	29.141
15	22.307	24.996	28.259	30.578
16	23.542	26.296	29.633	32.000
17	24.769	27.587	30.995	33.409
18	25.989	28.869	32.346	34.805
19	27.204	30.144	33.687	36.191
20	28.412	31.410	35.020	37.566
21	29.615	32.671	36.343	38.932
22	30.813	33.924	37.659	40.289
23	32.007	35.172	38.968	41.638
24	33.196	36.415	40.270	42.980
25	34.382	37.652	41.566	44.314
26	35.563	38.885	42.856	45.642
27	36.741	40.113	44.140	46.963
28	37.916	41.337	45.419	48.278
29	39.087	42.557	46.693	49.588
30	40.256	43.773	47.962	50.892

APPENDIX J

WILCOXON *T* VALUES

Critical values of *T*, the Wilcoxon signed rank statistic, where *T* is the largest integer such that $P(T \leq t/N) \leq \alpha$, the cumulative one-tail probability.

N	2 α / α	.15 / .075	.10 / .050	.05 / .025	.04 / .020	.03 / .015	.02 / .010	.01 / .005
4		0						
5		1	0					
6		2	2	0	0			
7		4	3	2	1	0	0	
8		7	5	3	3	2	1	0
9		9	8	5	5	4	3	1
10		12	10	8	7	6	5	3
11		16	13	10	9	8	7	5
12		19	17	13	12	11	9	7
13		24	21	17	16	14	12	9
14		28	25	21	19	18	15	12
15		33	30	25	23	21	19	15
16		39	35	29	28	26	23	19
17		45	41	34	33	30	27	23
18		51	47	40	38	35	32	27
19		58	53	46	43	41	37	32
20		65	60	52	50	47	43	37
21		73	67	58	56	53	49	42
22		81	75	65	63	59	55	48
23		89	83	73	70	66	62	54
24		98	91	81	78	74	69	61
25		108	100	89	86	82	76	68
26		118	110	98	94	90	84	75
27		128	119	107	103	99	92	83
28		138	130	116	112	108	101	91
29		150	140	126	122	117	110	100
30		161	151	137	132	127	120	109
31		173	163	147	143	137	130	118
32		186	175	159	154	148	140	128
33		199	187	170	165	159	151	138
34		212	200	182	177	171	162	148
35		226	213	195	189	182	173	159
40		302	286	264	257	249	238	220
50		487	466	434	425	413	397	373
60		718	690	648	636	620	600	567
70		995	960	907	891	872	846	805
80		1318	1276	1211	1192	1168	1136	1086
90		1688	1638	1560	1537	1509	1471	1410
100		2105	2045	1955	1928	1894	1850	1779

Source: Abridged from Robert L. McCormack, "Extended Tables of the Wilcoxon Matched-Pair Signed Rank Statistic," *Journal of the American Statistical Association,* September 1965, pp. 866–67.

APPENDIX K

DATA SET 1—REAL ESTATE

x_1 = Selling price in \$000
x_2 = Number of bedrooms
x_3 = Size of the house in square feet
x_4 = Pool (1 = yes, 0 = no)
x_5 = Distance in miles from center of city
x_6 = Township
x_7 = Garage (1 = yes, 0 = no)
x_8 = Number of bathrooms

x_1	x_2	x_3	x_4	x_5	x_6	x_7	x_8
194.9	4	2349	0	17	5	1	2.0
135.1	4	2102	1	19	4	0	2.0
179.3	3	2271	1	12	3	0	2.0
158.2	2	2188	1	16	2	0	2.5
103.6	2	2148	1	28	1	0	1.5
181.8	2	2117	0	12	1	1	2.0
242.4	6	2484	1	15	3	1	2.0
201.3	2	2130	1	9	2	1	2.5
163.8	3	2254	0	18	1	0	1.5
197.5	4	2385	1	13	4	1	2.0
216.6	4	2108	1	14	3	1	2.0
154.8	2	1715	1	8	4	1	1.5
200.6	6	2495	1	7	4	1	2.0
182.3	4	2073	1	18	3	1	2.0
144.0	2	2283	1	11	3	0	2.0
208.4	3	2119	1	16	2	1	2.0
127.9	4	2189	0	16	3	0	2.0
153.7	5	2316	0	21	4	0	2.5
147.3	3	2220	0	10	4	1	2.0
155.0	6	1901	0	15	4	1	2.0
186.9	4	2624	1	8	4	1	2.0
142.9	4	1938	0	14	2	1	2.5
155.0	5	2101	1	20	5	0	1.5
255.8	8	2644	1	9	4	1	2.0
241.7	6	2141	1	11	5	1	3.0
128.2	2	2198	0	21	5	1	1.5
138.5	2	1912	1	26	4	0	2.0
190.5	2	2117	1	9	4	1	2.0
172.6	3	2162	1	14	3	1	1.5
133.6	2	2041	1	11	5	0	2.0
173.3	2	1712	1	19	3	1	2.0
153.4	2	1974	1	11	5	1	2.0
183.5	5	2438	1	16	2	1	2.0
123.1	3	2019	0	16	2	1	2.0
131.2	2	1919	1	10	5	1	2.0
135.3	4	2023	0	14	4	0	2.5
160.0	4	2310	1	19	2	0	2.0
231.2	6	2639	1	7	5	1	2.5

x_1	x_2	x_3	x_4	x_5	x_6	x_7	x_8
148.0	3	2069	1	19	3	1	2.0
202.4	5	2182	1	16	2	1	3.0
152.6	3	2090	0	9	3	0	1.5
172.0	3	1928	0	16	1	1	1.5
146.9	4	2056	0	19	1	1	1.5
151.9	3	2012	0	20	4	0	2.0
130.1	4	2262	0	24	4	1	2.0
228.0	3	2431	0	21	2	1	3.0
199.4	5	2217	1	8	5	1	3.0
166.5	3	2157	1	17	1	1	2.5
127.1	3	2014	0	16	4	0	2.0
160.6	3	2221	1	15	1	1	2.0
142.7	6	2236	0	14	1	0	2.0
175.1	5	2189	1	20	3	1	2.0
127.7	3	2218	1	23	3	0	2.0
186.2	3	1937	1	12	2	1	2.0
182.2	6	2296	1	7	3	1	3.0
109.2	6	1749	0	12	1	0	2.0
130.4	4	2230	1	15	1	1	2.0
169.2	3	2263	1	17	5	1	1.5
123.3	3	1593	0	19	3	0	2.5
140.3	4	2221	1	24	1	1	2.0
231.2	7	2403	1	13	3	1	3.0
214.7	6	2036	1	21	3	1	3.0
199.9	5	2170	0	11	4	1	2.5
114.3	2	2007	1	13	2	0	2.0
164.5	2	2054	1	9	5	1	2.0
155.3	5	2247	0	13	2	1	2.0
141.4	3	2190	0	18	3	1	2.0
188.4	4	2495	0	15	3	1	2.0
153.7	3	2080	0	10	2	0	2.0
155.3	4	2210	0	19	2	1	2.0
217.8	2	2133	1	13	2	1	2.5
130.6	2	2037	0	17	3	0	2.0
218.0	7	2448	1	8	4	1	2.0
165.9	3	1900	0	6	1	1	2.0
92.6	2	1871	1	18	4	0	1.5

APPENDIX L

DATA SET 2—1993 MAJOR LEAGUE BASEBALL

x_1 = Team
x_2 = Team attendance, in millions
x_3 = Team salary, in millions of dollars
x_4 = Wins
x_5 = Team batting average
x_6 = Number of team home runs
x_7 = Team stolen bases
x_8 = Team errors
x_9 = Team earned run average
x_{10} = Home surface (1 = artificial, 0 = natural grass)
x_{11} = League (1 = National, 0 = American)

	x_1	x_2	x_3	x_4	x_5	x_6	x_7	x_8	x_9	x_{10}	x_{11}
1	Baltimore	3.645	26.914	85	0.267	157	73	100	4.31	0	0
2	Boston	2.422	36.609	80	0.264	114	73	122	3.77	0	0
3	California	2.057	27.230	71	0.260	114	169	120	4.34	0	0
4	Chicago White Sox	2.581	34.568	94	0.265	162	106	112	3.70	0	0
5	Cleveland	2.178	15.718	76	0.275	141	159	148	4.58	0	0
6	Detroit	1.971	36.548	85	0.275	178	104	132	4.65	0	0
7	Kansas City	1.936	39.803	84	0.263	125	100	97	4.04	1	0
8	Milwaukee	1.688	22.949	69	0.258	125	138	131	4.45	0	0
9	Minnesota	2.049	27.285	71	0.264	121	83	100	4.71	1	0
10	New York Yankees	2.417	40.405	88	0.279	118	39	105	4.35	0	0
11	Oakland	2.035	35.565	68	0.254	158	131	111	4.90	0	0
12	Seattle	2.053	31.461	82	0.260	161	91	90	4.20	1	0
13	Texas	2.245	35.605	86	0.267	181	113	132	4.28	0	0
14	Toronto	4.058	45.748	95	0.279	159	170	107	4.21	1	0
15	Atlanta	3.885	38.131	104	0.262	169	125	108	3.14	0	1
16	Chicago Cubs	2.654	38.303	84	0.270	161	100	115	4.18	0	1
17	Cincinnati	2.453	42.851	73	0.264	137	142	121	4.51	1	1
18	Colorado	4.483	8.829	67	0.273	142	146	167	5.41	0	1
19	Florida	3.065	18.197	64	0.248	94	117	125	4.13	0	1
20	Houston	2.085	28.855	85	0.267	138	103	126	3.49	1	1
21	Los Angeles	3.163	37.833	81	0.261	130	126	133	3.50	0	1
22	Montreal	1.641	14.881	94	0.257	122	228	159	3.55	1	1
23	New York Mets	1.873	38.350	59	0.248	158	79	156	4.05	0	1
24	Philadelphia	3.138	26.812	97	0.274	156	91	141	3.95	1	1
25	Pittsburgh	1.651	24.241	75	0.267	110	92	105	4.77	1	1
26	St. Louis	2.841	22.615	87	0.272	118	153	159	4.09	1	1
27	San Diego	1.375	25.557	61	0.252	153	92	160	4.23	0	1
28	San Francisco	2.606	34.568	103	0.276	168	120	101	3.61	0	1

APPENDIX M

DATA SET 3—MAGAZINE CIRCULATION

x_1 = Name of magazine
x_2 = Circulation (000)
x_3 = Percent male readership
x_4 = Percent female readership
x_5 = Number of other magazines read by men
x_6 = Number of other magazines read by women
x_7 = Percent in-home readers
x_8 = Median age of subscribers
x_9 = Median income of subscribers
x_{10} = Percent of subscribers who are college graduates
x_{11} = Black and white advertising cost per page
x_{12} = Color advertising cost per page

	x_1	x_2	x_3	x_4	x_5	x_6	x_7	x_8	x_9	x_{10}	x_{11}	x_{12}
1	Better Homes and Gardens	8000	22	78	1.21	3.23	62	41	23241	36	61030	73820
2	Business Week	845	72	28	4.85	2.10	37	39	30884	68	23120	35140
3	Car and Driver	725	88	12	4.84	0.53	41	31	25982	45	15450	23795
4	Cosmopolitan	2250	17	83	1.19	4.26	56	28	22785	46	21535	28980
5	Ebony	1250	42	58	2.60	3.48	62	33	16505	29	16200	21886
6	Family Circle	7450	13	87	0.75	3.51	72	42	21785	34	53780	62750
7	Field and Stream	2000	79	21	5.38	1.79	49	34	24337	29	22240	33760
8	Forbes	700	74	26	2.53	1.29	40	42	36783	74	16520	25090
9	Fortune	670	71	29	4.01	1.96	29	40	35204	72	10760	30040
10	Glamour	1800	6	94	0.49	4.52	49	27	21828	44	17250	24340
11	Golf Digest	1025	82	18	2.47	0.99	59	43	32949	54	17750	26625
12	Good Housekeeping	5000	13	87	1.25	4.89	62	39	21980	35	46235	58020
13	Harper's Bazaar	650	8	92	1.71	2.57	36	35	25358	55	11200	16200
14	Hot Rod	850	78	22	6.12	1.33	49	27	23056	24	12750	20400
15	House & Garden	1000	19	81	2.78	7.72	47	41	23726	39	17290	25430
16	House Beautiful	800	16	84	1.94	8.44	45	40	24198	42	13525	19775
17	Ladies Home Journal	5000	12	88	0.62	3.55	62	39	21583	36	39000	48000
18	Mademoiselle	1000	9	91	0.53	4.04	48	29	23660	50	11130	16280
19	McCalls	6200	12	88	0.55	3.19	62	40	20690	32	48670	59830
20	Mechanix Illustrated	1600	81	19	3.84	0.89	51	38	22568	38	17500	24815
21	Money	1000	58	42	4.01	2.45	46	37	31587	58	16450	25740
22	Motor Trend	750	84	16	5.18	0.83	42	33	23878	40	13690	21905
23	Ms.	450	16	84	0.65	4.26	51	30	24107	56	6500	7845
24	National Enquirer	4637	40	60	1.57	2.90	68	36	19969	24	21000	26500
25	National Geographic	8400	55	45	1.86	1.65	64	42	26294	51	73520	95575
26	National Lampoon	580	72	27	6.78	1.47	39	25	22888	49	6700	9900
27	Newsweek	2950	62	38	4.12	3.17	45	36	26719	53	40930	63850
28	Outdoor Life	1500	82	18	4.17	1.40	51	35	23596	29	16520	28475
29	Parents Magazine	1650	22	78	1.08	4.13	43	29	20779	37	22240	36960
30	People	2350	40	60	4.19	6.50	48	32	23971	40	43775	56425
31	Playboy	5000	78	22	3.25	0.97	59	31	24051	43	39780	55710
32	Playgirl	650	36	64	2.13	4.26	53	30	19329	36	5415	7220
33	Popular Mechanics	1600	81	19	5.81	1.65	50	38	25474	36	18966	26932
34	Popular Science	1800	80	20	3.97	1.15	49	37	26542	44	18910	26820
35	Reader's Digest	17900	44	56	1.38	1.75	75	46	21802	34	81399	97700
36	Redbook	3800	11	89	0.66	3.26	61	35	22794	35	32270	42675
37	Road & Track	630	89	11	6.06	0.65	61	30	28093	35	11945	18775

APPENDIX M

DATA SET 3—MAGAZINE CIRCULATION (*concluded*)

	x_1	x_2	x_3	x_4	x_5	x_6	x_7	x_8	x_9	x_{10}	x_{11}	x_{12}
38	Rolling Stone	700	66	34	4.65	2.61	48	25	24074	47	11915	17770
39	Scientific American	720	68	32	4.01	1.91	40	35	29531	78	16000	24000
40	Seventeen	1500	9	91	0.84	3.98	51	29	21251	33	13325	19250
41	Sports Illustrated	2250	80	20	5.25	1.66	53	32	26275	46	34720	54165
42	The Star	3400	35	65	1.02	1.99	72	35	19156	20	17400	21350
43	Time	4400	56	44	2.92	2.29	52	36	26908	53	55045	85870
44	True Story	1400	18	82	0.77	3.98	69	39	14325	10	10330	13435
45	TV Guide	17345	45	55	1.24	1.47	87	35	20461	31	65000	77400
46	U.S. News and World Report	2050	63	37	3.25	1.75	45	42	26998	57	26935	42510
47	Vogue	950	11	89	0.88	5.75	40	31	23452	48	12500	18000
48	Woman's Day	7125	8	92	0.66	5.29	46	39	21910	47	51740	60435

APPENDIX N

BANKING DATA SET—CASE

x_1 = Account balance in $
x_2 = Number of ATM transactions in the month
x_3 = Number of other bank services used
x_4 = Has a debit card (1 = yes, 0 = no)
x_5 = Receives interest on the account
x_6 = City where banking is done*

	x_1	x_2	x_3	x_4	x_5	x_6		x_1	x_2	x_3	x_4	x_5	x_6
1	1756	13	4	0	1	2	31	1958	6	2	1	0	2
2	748	9	2	1	0	1	32	634	2	7	1	0	4
3	1501	10	1	0	0	1	33	580	4	1	0	0	1
4	1831	10	4	0	1	3	34	1320	4	5	1	0	1
5	1622	14	6	0	1	4	35	1675	6	7	1	0	2
6	1886	17	3	0	1	1	36	789	8	4	0	0	4
7	740	6	3	0	0	3	37	1735	12	7	0	1	3
8	1593	10	8	1	0	1	38	1784	11	5	0	0	1
9	1169	6	4	0	0	4	39	1326	16	8	0	0	3
10	2125	18	6	0	0	2	40	2051	14	4	1	0	4
11	1554	12	6	1	0	3	41	1044	7	5	1	0	1
12	1474	12	7	1	0	1	42	1885	10	6	1	1	2
13	1913	6	5	0	0	1	43	1790	11	4	0	1	3
14	1218	10	3	1	0	1	44	765	4	3	0	0	4
15	1006	12	4	0	0	1	45	1645	6	9	0	1	4
16	2215	20	3	1	0	4	46	32	2	0	0	0	3
17	137	7	2	0	0	3	47	1266	11	7	0	0	4
18	167	5	4	0	0	4	48	890	7	1	0	1	1
19	343	7	2	0	0	1	49	2204	14	5	0	0	2
20	2557	20	7	1	0	4	50	2409	16	8	0	0	2
21	2276	15	4	1	0	3	51	1338	14	4	1	0	2
22	1494	11	2	0	1	1	52	2076	12	5	1	0	2
23	2144	17	3	0	0	3	53	1708	13	3	1	0	1
24	1995	10	7	0	0	2	54	2138	18	5	0	1	4
25	1053	8	4	1	0	3	55	2375	12	4	0	0	2
26	1526	8	4	0	1	2	56	1455	9	5	1	1	3
27	1120	8	6	1	0	3	57	1487	8	4	1	0	4
28	1838	7	5	1	1	3	58	1125	6	4	1	0	2
29	1746	11	2	0	0	2	59	1989	12	3	0	1	2
30	1616	10	4	1	1	2	60	2156	14	5	1	0	2

*Cincinnati = 1.
Atlanta = 2.
Louisville = 3.
Erie, Pennsylvania = 4.

ANSWERS

TO ODD-NUMBERED CHAPTER EXERCISES

CHAPTER 1

What Is Statistics?

1. The collection of facts and figures is often referred to in everyday usage as statistics. Examples are: Greg Norman shot 68 to take the lead of the USF&G Classic in New Orleans; the yearly low of IBM common stock is 104½, and the high is 130⅞.

   Here we define statistics as the science of collecting, organizing, analyzing, and interpreting numerical data in order to make more informed decisions. For example, to make a decision regarding a newly developed breakfast cereal, the Kellogg Company might have a sample of 270 persons selected at random try it and give their reactions. A sample of 10 pieces of steel wire randomly selected might be tested for tensile strength in order to make a decision about all the wire produced during the day.
3. We could use these random sample results to infer something about all the executives. In this case, it would be estimated that about 30 percent of all executives have some degree of hypertension, found by (60/200)(100). This is just one illustration of the extensive use of sampling to infer something about a population.
5. In order to suggest several sites to management, you would probably first collect data on the population in the metropolitan areas of Orlando, Birmingham, Atlanta, and other cities in the Southeast. Data on the availability and the prices of land, utilities, and so on need to be collected and analyzed. After a location has been decided on, an in-depth survey of, say, 2,000 persons should be conducted to determine whether the park should be constructed to appeal to all ages, just children, or just adults.
7. *a.* Sample. The 112 stocks are just a portion of the total number of stocks listed on the New York Stock Exchange.
   b. Nominal. The data resulted from counts, and the order of the three movements is immaterial.
   c. Yes. A stock cannot increase, decrease, and stay the same at the same time.
   d. A statistic.
9. Customer satisfaction in the economy in June 1995 (50.6) fell below the lowest level since 1986.

CHAPTER 2

Summarizing Data: Frequency Distributions and Graphic Presentation

1. Raw data are an unorganized set of data.
3. "Mutually exclusive" means that the classes are so formulated that a particular value can occur in only one class. As a result, there is no overlapping of classes.
5. *a.* Using the formula $2^k \geq n$, we suggest 4 classes (although a minimum of 5 classes is usually preferred).
   b. Using formula (2–1), the suggested class interval would be 1.5, found by (31 − 25)/4. For ease of computations, 2.0 would be better.
   c. 24
   d.

	f	Relative frequency
24 up to 26	2	.125
26 up to 28	8	.500
28 up to 30	4	.250
30 up to 32	2	.125
Total	16	1.000

   e. The largest concentration of scores is in the 26 up to 28 class (8). Very few scores are over 30 or under 26.
7. *a.*

	f
0 up to 3	9
3 up to 6	21
6 up to 9	13
9 up to 12	4
12 up to 15	3
15 up to 18	1
Total	51

   b. The largest group of shoppers (21) shop at Food Queen 3, 4, or 5 times during a two-week period. Some customers visit the store only 1 time during the two weeks, but others shop as many as

15 times.

c.

Number of Shoppers	Relative frequency
0 up to 3	.1765
3 up to 6	.4118
6 up to 9	.2549
9 up to 12	.0784
12 up to 15	.0588
15 up to 18	.0196
Total	1.0000

9. The five values are 621, 623, 623, 627, and 629.

11.

Stem	Leaves
0	5
1	28
2	
3	0024789
4	12366
5	2

13. *a.* 50
b. 2
c. Using lower limits on the *X*-axis:

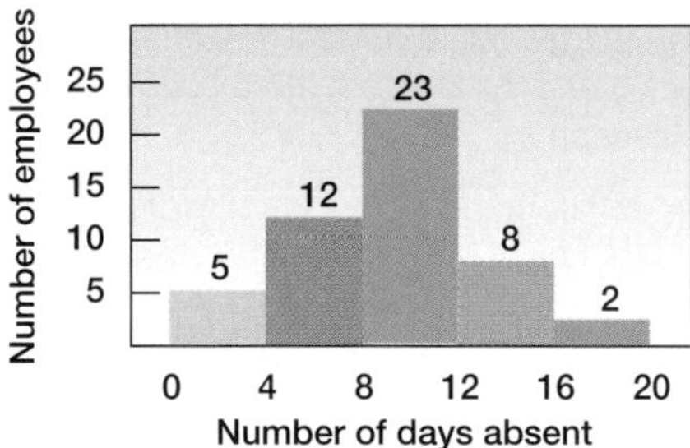

d. $X = 2$, $Y = 5$.
e.

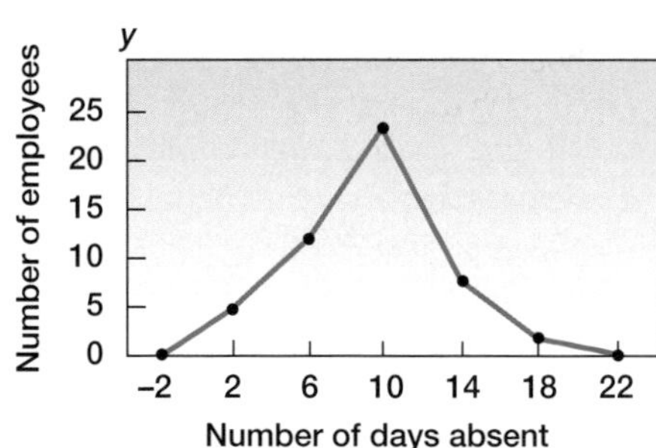

f. Out of 50 employees about half (23) are absent 8 up to 12 days. About 10 percent are absent fewer than 4 days, and 2 out of 50 are absent 16 or more days.

15. *a.*

Time, in minutes	Relative frequencies: Carter method	Manelli method
5 up to 8	.060	.080
8 up to 11	.213	.220
11 up to 14	.530	.500
14 up to 17	.143	.140
17 up to 20	.054	.060
Total	1.000	1.000

b.

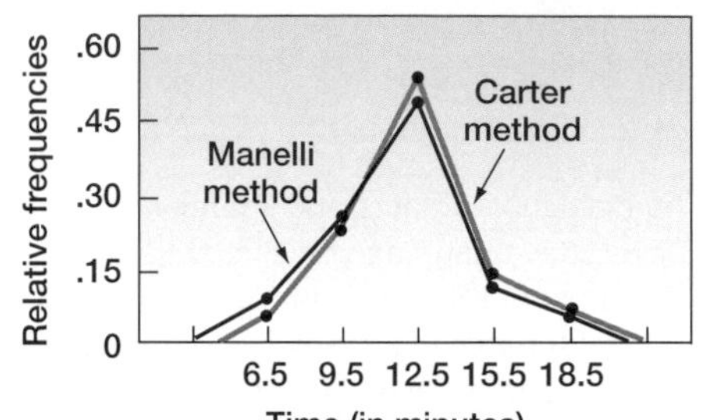

c. The distributions of times are almost identical.

17. *a.* 13
b.

Lead time	Frequency	Cumulative frequency
0 up to 5	6	6
5 up to 10	7	13
10 up to 15	24	37
15 up to 20	11	48
20 up to 25	9	57
25 up to 30	3	60

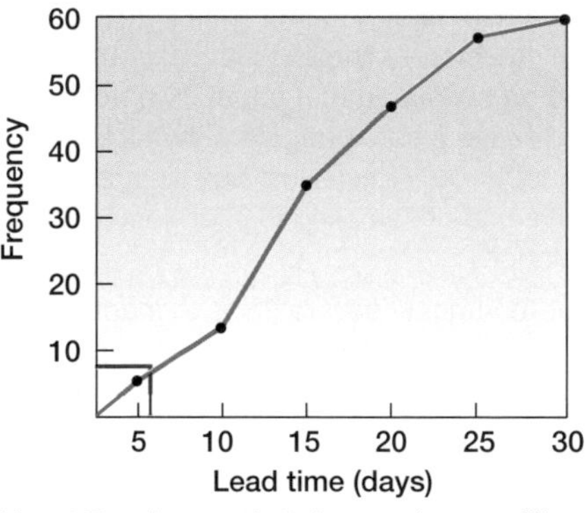

c. About 7 orders took 6 days or less to fill.

19. *a.* 5, 17.
b.

Days absent	*f*	CF
0 up to 4	5	5
4 up to 8	12	17
8 up to 12	23	40
12 up to 16	8	48
16 up to 20	2	50

c.

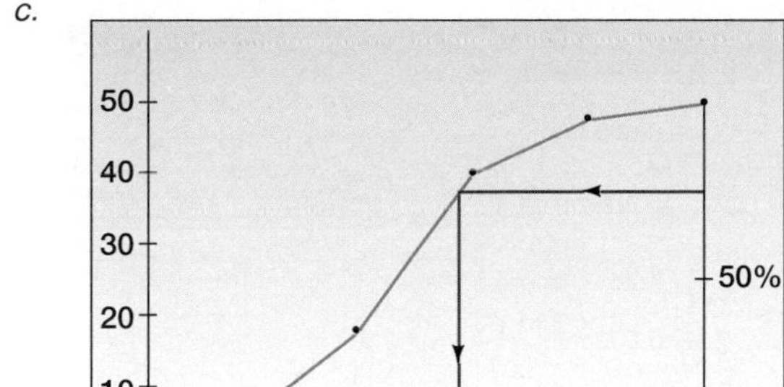

d. About 11.5 days.

21.

3,500
3,000
2,500
2,000
1,500
1,000
500
0
Debt
1984 1989 1994
Year

23. *a.*

Chevron (8,913, 21.9%)
Atlantic Ric (4,757, 11.7%)
Americada He (1,645, 4.0%)
Diamond Sham (627, 1.5%)
Quaker State (191.9, 0.5%)
Exxon (24,612, 60.4%)

b. The fourth-quarter sales for Exxon were the largest. They represented more than 60 percent of the sales for the six companies. Diamond Shamrock sales were 1.5 percent of the total, and Quaker State even less.

25. *a.* \$36.60, found by (\$265−\$82)/5.

b. \$40.

c.

\$ 80 up to \$120	8
120 up to 160	19
160 up to 200	10
200 up to 240	6
240 up to 280	1
Total	44

d. The purchases ranged from a low of about \$80 to a high of about \$280. The concentration is in the "\$120 up to \$160" class.

27. *a.* The class found by (266−133)/7 = 19. We selected 20.

Shareholders (thousands)	Number of companies	Less-than CF
130 up to 150	4	4
150 up to 170	9	13
170 up to 190	4	17
190 up to 210	6	23
210 up to 230	3	26
230 up to 250	2	28
250 up to 270	4	32
Total	32	

b.

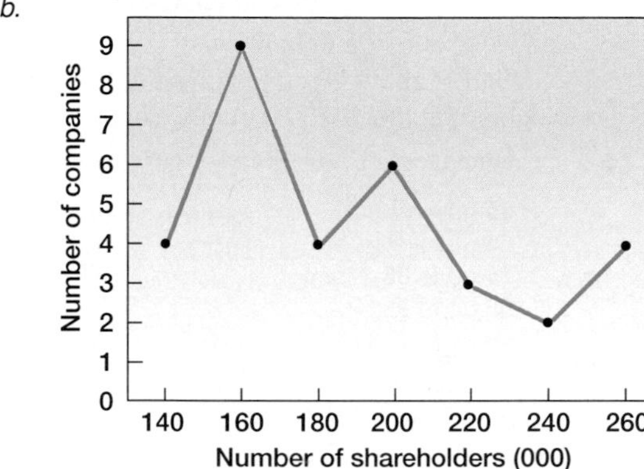

c.

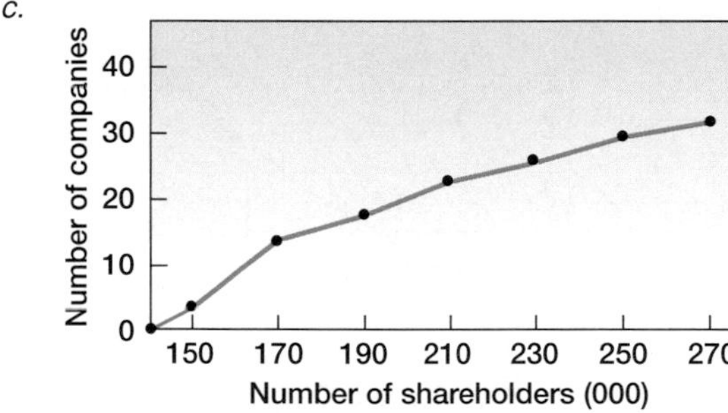

d. About 220 thousand, found by 3/4 of 32 = 24. The 24th company has about 220 thousand shareholders, found by drawing a line to the curve from 24 and down to the *X*-axis.

e. The largest number of companies (9) have 150 up to 170 thousand stockholders. The smallest number is about 130 thousand, and the largest 270 thousand stockholders.

29. *a.*

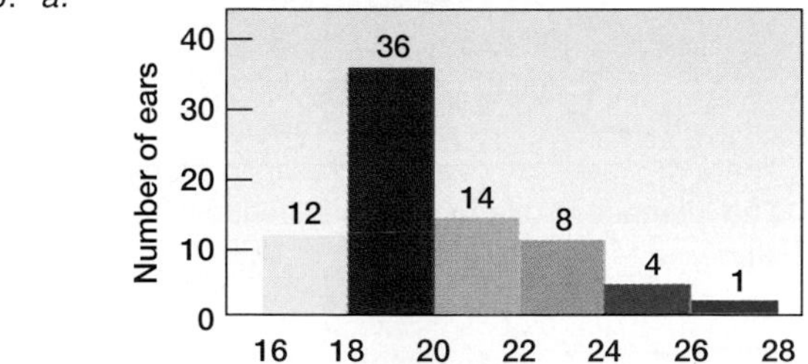

b.

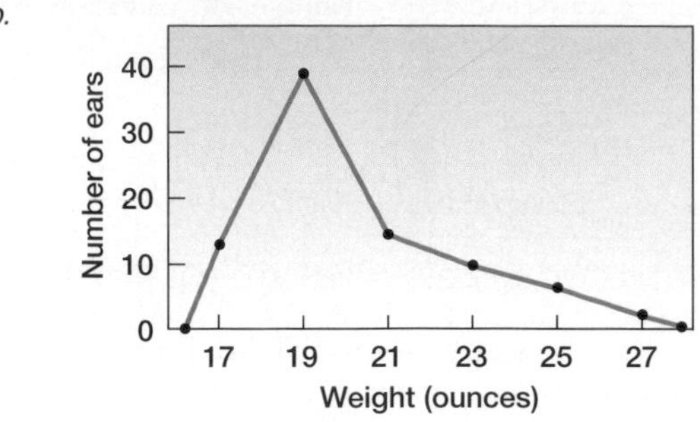

c. The weights range from a low of about 16 ounces to a high of about 28 ounces. The concentration of weights is in the 18 to 20 ounce class.

31. *a.*

Games won	Frequency	CF
55 up to 65	3	3
65 up to 75	6	9
75 up to 85	7	16
85 up to 95	8	24
95 up to 105	4	28
	28	

b. About 80 which is the mode.

c. About 82 wins.

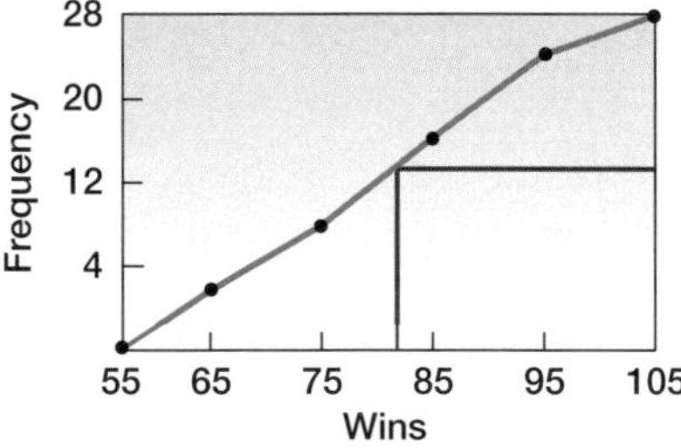

33.

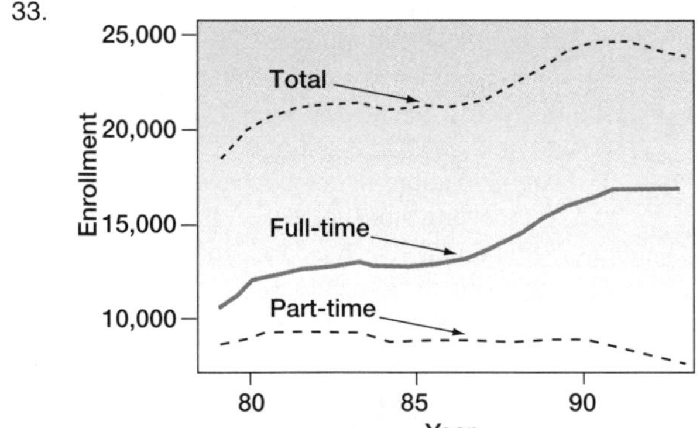

There has been an overall increase in enrollment. The increase is due mostly to increases in full-time students.

35.

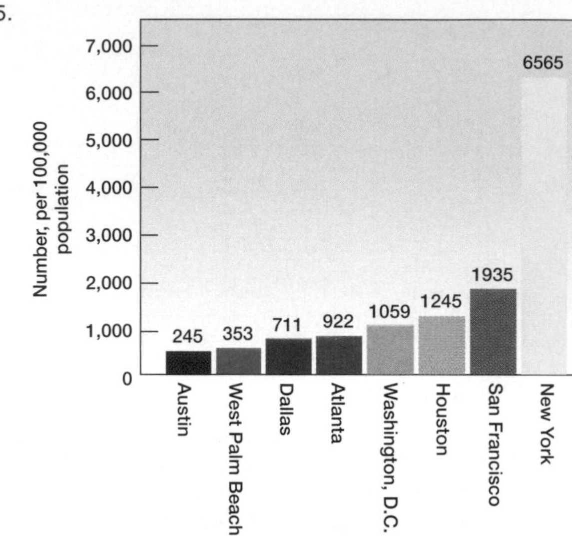

37. *a.* A class interval of 10 ($10,000,000) is selected.

Salary ($ millions)	*f*	CF
0 up to 10	1	1
10 up to 20	3	4
20 up to 30	9	13
30 up to 40	12	25
40 up to 50	3	28
	28	

b. A typical team salary is about $30,000,000. Twenty-one of the 28 teams pay their players between $20,000,000 and $40,000,000 per season.

c.

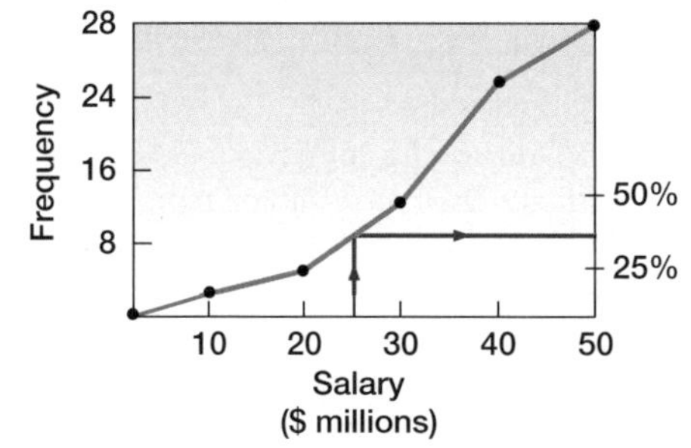

About one third of the teams have total player salaries less than $25,000,000. About 40 percent of the teams pay less than $28,000,000.

d. The distribution has somewhat of a negative skew. Some of the teams (Colorado, Montreal, Cleveland, and Florida) are somewhat low in total salary.

e.

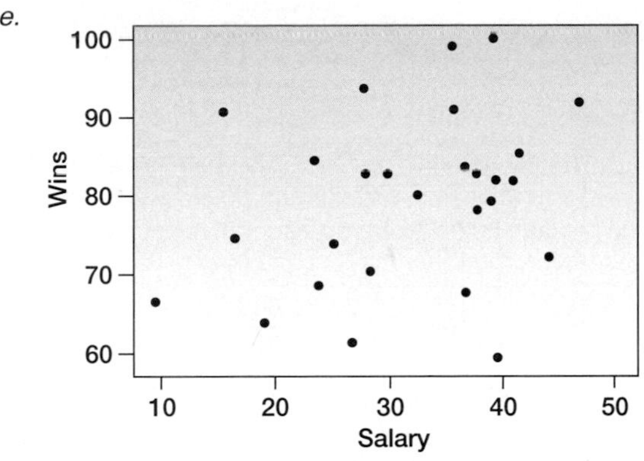

The teams that spend larger amounts on salary do appear to win more games. However, the relationship is not as strong as might be expected. For example, Montreal spent less than $20,000,000 on salary yet won 96 games. On the other hand, the New York Mets won only 59 games and spent $38,350,000 on salaries.

CHAPTER 3
Describing Data—Measures of Central Tendency

1. A sample mean is found by

$$\overline{X} = \frac{\text{Sum of all the values in a sample}}{\text{Number of values in the sample}}$$

Thus, it is a measurable characteristic of a sample. A population mean is found by

$$\mu = \frac{\text{Sum of all the values in a particular population}}{\text{Number of values in the population}}$$

Thus, it is a measurable characteristic of the population of interest. Note that the steps for computing the sample mean and the population mean are the same. Only the symbols are different.

3. *a.* Mean = 7.0, found by 28/4.
   b. $(5 - 7) + (9 - 7) + (4 - 7) + (10 - 7) = 0$
5. 14.58, found by 43.74/3.
7. *a.* 15.4, found by 154/10.
   b. Population, since it includes all the salespeople at Midtown Ford.
9. *a.* $54.55, found by $1,091/20.
   b. A sample statistic—assuming that the power company serves more than 20 customers.
11. *a.*

$$\mu = \frac{369{,}659}{8} = 46{,}207.375$$

b.

$$\mu = \frac{13{,}940}{8} = 1{,}742.50$$

13. $0.775, found by ($10 + $37.50 + $30)/100.
15. $11.50, found by ($400 + $500 + $1,400)/200 = $2,300/200.
17. *a.* When we need to average percents, indexes, and relatives, the geometric mean gives a more representative figure. Also, it is preferred when we need an average rate (percent) of increase from one period of time to another.
    b. Never larger. Geometric mean is always equal to or smaller than the arithmetic mean.
19. 5.4132, found by the product of the six values, which is 737,280. The log of this value divided by 8 is 0.733454057. The antilog of this value is 5.4132.
21. $GM = \sqrt[3]{(80.125)(75.375)(98.375)} = \$84.067$
23.

Class	f	x	fX	CF
0 up to 5	2	2.5	5.00	2
5 up to 10	7	7.5	52.50	9
10 up to 15	12	12.5	150.00	21
15 up to 20	6	17.5	105.00	27
20 up to 25	3	22.5	67.50	30
	30		380.00	

$$\overline{X} = \frac{380}{30} = 12.67$$

25.

Selling price	f	x	fX
70 up to 80	3	75	225
80 up to 90	7	85	595
90 up to 100	18	95	1,710
100 up to 110	20	105	2,100
110 up to 120	12	115	1,380
	60		6,010

$$\overline{X} = \frac{\$6{,}010}{60} = \$100.17$$

27.

$$\text{Median} = 10 + \frac{15 - 9}{12}(5) = 12.5$$

Mode is 12.5. Half of the observations are less than 12.5.

29.

Age	f	CF
18 up to 21	4	4
21 up to 24	8	12
24 up to 27	11	23
27 up to 30	20	43
30 up to 33	7	50
	50	

a.

$$\text{Median} = 27 + \frac{25 - 23}{20}(3) = 27.3 \text{ years}$$

b. Mode is 28.5 years.

31.

Age	Male f	Male CF	Female f	Female CF
10 up to 20	635	635	259	259
20 up to 30	39,959	40,594	6,454	6,713
30 up to 40	99,956	140,550	12,128	18,841
40 up to 50	51,837	192,387	4,398	23,239
50 up to 60	16,367	208,754	1,466	24,705
60 or older	6,227	214,981	1,221	25,926
	214,981			

a.
$$\text{Median} = 30 + \frac{107{,}490.5 - 40{,}594}{99{,}956}(10) =$$
$$30 + 6.69 = 36.69$$

b. The mode is 35 years.

33. *a.* 1,200 tons (same as mean). Half of values above the median, half below it.
b. 1,200 tons (same as the mean and median) values. It is the value that occurs most frequently.

35. *a.* 12.6 inches, found by [2(12.9)+12]/3.
b.

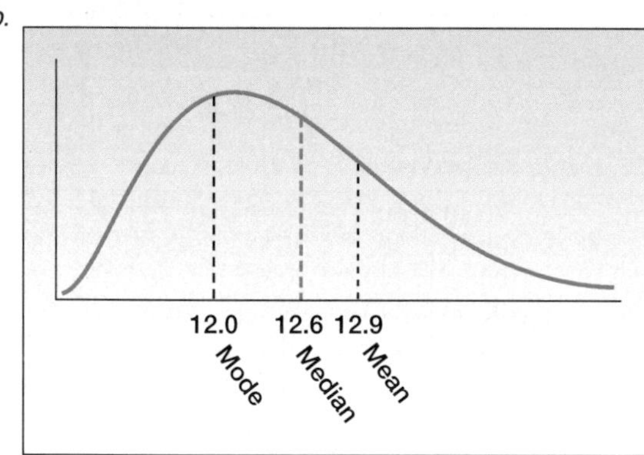

37. *a.*

Fuel economy (mpg)	f	CF
9 up to 12	3	3
12 up to 15	4	7
15 up to 18	16	23
18 up to 21	16	39
21 up to 24	8	47
24 up to 27	4	51
27 up to 30	1	52
	52	

b.
$$\text{Median} = 18 + \frac{26 - 23}{16}(3) = 18.5625$$

c. Mode is 19.5.
d. This is a fairly symmetrical distribution. Using the MINITAB system and the actual data, the mean is 18.308 and the median is 18.00.

39. *a.* Mean = 21.71, median = 22.00
b.
$$(23 - 21.71) + (19 - 21.71) + \cdots + (22 - 21.71) = 0$$

41.
$$\bar{X} = \frac{2{,}116}{30} = 70.5333$$

43.
$$\bar{X} = \frac{15{,}721}{29} = 542.1$$

The mean salary is $542,100. The median is 400. The distribution is skewed in the positive direction, so the median is the most representative salary.

45.
$$GM = \sqrt[21]{\frac{6{,}286{,}800}{5{,}164{,}900}} - 1 = 1.0094$$

About 0.94 percent.

47.
$$GM = \sqrt[10]{\frac{33{,}598}{25{,}000}} - 1 = 1.0300 - 1 =$$
0.03, or 3.0 percent
$$GM = \sqrt[10]{\frac{44{,}771}{25{,}000}} - 1 = 1.0599995 - 1 =$$
0.06, or 6.0 percent

49. $\bar{X} = 60.14$ percent
$GM = 55.209$ percent

51. 227.4667 pounds, found by [7(240) + 4(212) + 3(190) + 1(314)]/15

53. *a.* No. The result of 3,333 pounds assumes that there are an equal number of containers weighing 1,000, 3,000, and 6,000 pounds, respectively. This is not the case.
b. 2,500 pounds, found by [(60 × 1,000) + (40 × 3,000) + (20 × 6,000)]/120. Each of the three sizes of containers is weighted by the number of containers.

55.

Age	f	CF
Under 15	10.1	10.1
15 up to 20	239.7	249.8
20 up to 25	168.6	418.4
25 up to 30	62.4	480.8
30 up to 35	23.7	504.5
35 up to 40	8.8	513.3
40 years or older	2.3	515.6

$$\text{Median} = 20.0 + \frac{\frac{515.6}{2} - 249.8}{168.6}(5) = 20.237$$

Half of the unmarried mothers are less than 20.237 years old.

57. *a.*
$$\text{Median} = \$30{,}000 + \frac{(50.0 - 49.8)}{24.1}(\$10{,}000)$$
$$= \$30{,}083$$

b. The modal income is $25,000.

59. *a.* 46.34 years, found by

$$45.0 + \frac{\frac{1,829}{2} - 854}{450}(10)$$

Half of the divorced males are younger than 46.34 years; the other half are older than 46.34 years.

b. 43.79 years, found by:

$$35.0 + \frac{\frac{2,827}{2} - 837}{656}(10)$$

Half of the divorced females are younger than 43.79 years, the other half older than 43.79 years.

c. Males: 50. Females: distribution bimodal (two modes), 40 and 50.

61. *a.* $3,330, found by [3($3,220) − $3,000]/2.
b. Mean. It is being pulled up by extreme values.
c. $3,000.
d. Positively skewed. The median and the mean are greater than the mode.

63. $$GM = \sqrt[80]{\frac{17,000,000}{22,000}} - 1.0 = 1.08668 - 1.0 = .08668$$

or about 8.668 percent per year.

65. *a.* $$GM = \sqrt[6]{\frac{126,900}{88,300}} - 1.0 = 1.0623 - 1.00 = 0.0623$$

or about 6.23 percent per year.

b. $$GM = \sqrt[6]{\frac{8,910}{6,240}} - 1 = 1.06116 - 1.00 =$$

0.06116 or 6.1 percent

67. *a.* $\overline{X}$ = $166,670 median = $160,000.
b. 3.0 is the median, 3.72 is the mean.
c. 2.0 baths is the median, and 2.0867 is the mean and mode is 2.
d. $\overline{X}$ = 14.893 miles, and the median is 15.0 miles.

69. *a.* The median circulation is 1,600,000, and the mean is 3,048,000. The distribution is skewed to the right. The mean is being pulled to the right by the circulation of *TV Guide, Reader's Digest,* and others.

b.

Circulation	*f*	CF
0 up to 1,000	15	15
1,000 up to 2,000	13	28
2,000 up to 3,000	6	34
3,000 up to 4,000	2	36
4,000 up to 5,000	2	38
5,000 up to 6,000	3	41
6,000 or more	7	48

$$\text{Median} = 1,000 + \frac{(24 - 15)}{13}(1,000) =$$

1,692 or $1,692,000

So the estimated median is close to the actual median of $1,600,000. The mean cannot be computed from the frequency distribution because of the open-ended class.

CHAPTER 4
Measures of Dispersion and Skewness

1. *a.* 7, found by 10 − 3.
b. 6, found by 30/5.
c. 2.4, found by 12/5.
d. The difference between the highest number sold (10) and the smallest number sold (3) is 7.

3. *a.* 30, found by 54 − 24.
b. 38, found by 380/10.
c. 7.2 found by 72/10.
d. On the average, the number of minutes required to install a door deviates 7.2 minutes from the mean of 38 minutes.

5. *a.* 15, found by 41 − 26.
b. 33.9, found by 339 ÷ 10.
c. 4.12, found by 41.2 ÷ 10. The ratings deviate 4.12 from the mean of 33.9 on the average.
d. Since $8 < 15$ and $1.9 < 4.12$, we conclude that there is more dispersion in the first group.

7. *a.* 4.4, found by 22/5 using formula (4–3).
b. 4.4, found by 29.4 − 25 using formula (4–4).

9. *a.* $2.77, found by $13.85/5.
b. 1.2586, found by 6.2928/5.

11. *a.* Range: 7.3, found by 11.6 − 4.3.
Arithmetic mean: 6.94, found by 34.7/5.
Variance: 6.5944, found by 32.972/5.
Standard deviation: 2.568, found by $\sqrt{6.5944}$.
b. Dennis has a higher mean return ($11.76 > 6.94$). However, Dennis has greater spread in their returns on equity ($16.89 > 6.59$).

13. *a.* 2.3452, found by $\sqrt{22/4}$.
b. 5.5, found by (102 − 400/5)/4.

15. *a.* 82.667, found by 744/9.
b. 82.667.
c. 9.09, found by $\sqrt{82.667}$.

17. *a.* 7, found by 127 − 120.
b. 124 grams, found by 1,240/10.
c. 4.667, found by 42/(10 − 1).
d. 2.1602 grams, found by $\sqrt{4.667}$.

19. *a.* 25, found by 25 − 0.

b. 5.331, found by

$$\sqrt{\frac{5{,}637.50 - (380)^2/30}{30 - 1}}$$

21. *a.* 12 minutes, found by 14 − 2.
b. 2.5959 minutes, found by:

$$\sqrt{\frac{2{,}594 - \frac{(312)^2}{42}}{42 - 1}}$$

c. 6.7387, found by $(2.5959)^2$.

23. About 69 percent, found by

$$1 - \frac{1}{(1.8)^2}$$

25. *a.* About 95 percent.
b. 47.5 percent, 2.5 percent.

27. *a.* 8.929, found by

$$5.00 + \frac{30/4 - 2}{7}(5)$$

b. 16.25
c. 7.321, found by 16.25 − 8.929
d. 5.714
e. 20.00, found by

$$20.00 + \frac{\frac{(90)(30)}{100} - 27}{3}(5)$$

29. *a.* 5.625 minutes, found by

$$4 + \frac{10.5 - 4}{8}(2)$$

b. 9.222, found by

$$8 + \frac{31.5 - 26.0}{9}(2)$$

c. 3.597, found by 9.222 − 5.625.
d. 3.597/2 = 1.7985

31. The box plot is as follows.

```
                    -----------------
--------------------I       +       I-----------
                    -----------------
--+---------+---------+---------+---------+---------+----
100       150       200       250       300       350
```

The median is \$253, the smallest value is \$116, and the largest is \$353. About 25 percent of the semiprivate rooms cost less than \$214 and 25 percent more than \$304. The distribution is negatively skewed.

33. Domestic 21.28 percent, found by (10/47)100. Overseas 19.23 percent.

There is slightly less relative dispersion in the weights of luggage for domestic passengers.

35. The relative dispersion in stocks under \$10 is 28.95 percent. For stocks over \$60, it is 5.71 percent. Less relative dispersion in stocks over \$60.

37. 0.95, found by

$$\frac{3(542 - 400)}{448.5} = 0.95$$

Positively skewed.

39. *a.* Negatively skewed.
b. −1.8, found by

$$\frac{3(2.1 - 2.4)}{0.5}$$

41. For a sample, $n-1$ is substituted for N in the denominator of the formula for the sample variance. This substitution prevents the underestimation of the population variance.

43. The distribution with the *CV* of 30 percent has more relative dispersion than the distribution with a 20 percent *CV*.

45. *a.* 55, found by 72 − 17.
b. 14.4, found by 144/10, where $\overline{X} = 43.2$.
c. 17.6245.

47. *a.* Population.
b. 183.4734 thousand volumes
c. 94.92 percent

49. *a.* 30, found by 110 − 80.

b. $$s = \sqrt{\frac{1{,}029{,}937.5 - \frac{(10{,}620)^2}{110}}{109}} = 6.514$$

c. $$Q_1 = 90 + \frac{27.5 - 18.0}{23}(5) = 92.065$$

$$Q_3 = 100 + \frac{82.5 - 76.0}{24}(5) = 101.354$$

Interquartile range = 101.354 − 92.065 = 9.289

d. $$P_{10} = \$85 + \frac{11 - 6}{12}(\$5) = \$87.083$$

$$P_{90} = \$100 + \frac{99 - 76}{24}(\$5) = \$104.792$$

Range = \$104.792 − \$87.083 = \$17.709

About 80 percent of the observations are between \$87.083 and \$104.792.

51. *a.* $$\overline{X} = \frac{2{,}293}{80} = 28.6625$$

$$\text{Median} = 26 + \frac{40 - 26}{20}(3) = 28.1$$

b. $$s = \sqrt{\frac{68{,}342 - \frac{(2{,}293)^2}{80}}{79}} = 5.7576$$

c. $$CV = \frac{5.7576}{28.6625}(100) = 20.1$$

d. $$Sk = \frac{3(28.6625 - 28.1000)}{5.7576} = 0.293$$

Slight positive skew.

53. *a*
55. *b*
57. *a.* $$Q_1 = 15 + \frac{25 - 4.7}{27.8}(5) = 18.651$$

$$Q_3 = 20 + \frac{75 - 32.5}{51.6}(5) = 24.118$$

b. $QD = (24.118 - 18.651)/2 = 2.7335$

59. $Q_1 = 44.25$, $Q_3 = 68.5$, and the median is 55.50. The distribution is approximately symmetric. The box plot is as follows.

```
                    --------------------
--------------------I       +          I-----------------
                    --------------------
--+---------+---------+---------+---------+---------+----
 24        36        48        60        72        84
                                                  Miles
```

The above results were found using MINITAB.

61. *a.* 55.56 percent. Both 21 and 27 are 1.5 standard deviations from the mean.
   b. $CV = 8.33$ percent, found by $(0.02/0.24)100$.
   c. $Sk = -2.25$, found by $3(24 - 25.5)/2$. The distribution is negatively skewed.

63. *a.* From MINITAB (answers in $000):

	N	MEAN	MEDIAN	TRMEAN	STDEV	SEMEAN
Price	75	166.67	160.00	165.82	35.68	4.12
	MIN	MAX	Q1	Q3		
Price	92.60	255.80	140.30	190.50		

$s = 35.68$

$CV = 21.41$ percent found by $(35.68/166.67)100$.

$Sk = 0.5608$, found by $3(166.67 - 160.0)/35.68$.

Positive skewness because mean exceeds median. Observations are spread out 21.41 percent from the mean.

   b. From MINITAB $\overline{X} = 14.893$, median = 15.0, and $s = 4.892$.

$CV = (4.892/14.893)(100) = 32.85$

$sk = 3(14.893 - 15.0)/4.892 = -0.066$

Very little negative skewness.

65. From MINITAB the mean is 3,048, the median 1,600, and the standard deviation 3,756. (These values are in millions.) The largest circulation is 17,900 and the smallest is 450, so the range is 17,450. The distribution is positively skewed, with the coefficient of skewness 1.16.

CHAPTER 5
A Survey of Probability Concepts

1. An experiment is the observation of some activity or the act of taking some measurement, whereas an event is a collection of several outcomes from the experiment.
3. *a.* A probability may range from 0 to 1.00 inclusive.
   b. It cannot be greater than 1.
   c. It cannot be less than 0.
   d. A probability between .80 and 1.00 indicates the event is likely to occur.
5. *a.* The experiment is asking the 500 citizens whether they favor or oppose widening Indiana Avenue to three lanes.
   b. Possible outcomes include 321 favor the widening, 387 favor the widening, 444 favor the widening, and so on.
   c. Answers will vary, but two possibilities are: a majority favor the widening, which would be 251 or more, and more than 300 favor the widening.
7. *a.* Relative frequency.
   b. Classical.
   c. Classical.
   d. Subjective, because this is someone's opinion.
9. *a.* 13/52 = .25
   b. 1/52 = .019
   c. Classical.
11. *a.* The survey of 40 people about abortion.
   b. 26 or more respond yes, for example.
   c. 10/40 = .25
   d. Relative frequency.
   e. The events are not equally likely but they are mutually exclusive.
13. $$\begin{aligned} P(\text{A or } B) &= P(A) + P(B) \\ &= .30 + .20 \\ &= .50 \\ P(\text{neither}) &= 1 - .50 = .50 \end{aligned}$$
15. *a.* 102/200 = .51
   b. .49, found by 61/200 + 37/200 = .305 + .185. Special rule of addition.
17. $$\begin{aligned} P(A \text{ or } B) &= P(A) + P(B) - P(A \text{ and } B) \\ &= .20 + .30 - .15 \\ &= .35 \end{aligned}$$

19. When two events are mutually exclusive, it means that if one occurs the other event cannot occur. Therefore, the probability of their joint occurrence is zero.
21. *a.* .65, found by .35 + .40 − .10.
    b. A joint probability.
    c. No, an executive might read more than one magazine.
23. *a.* A joint probability is the occurrence of two events at the same time.
    b. A conditional probability is the probability of one event occurring, given that another event has already occurred.
25. *a.* Venn diagram.
    b. Sample space.
    c. No. There is an overlapping of events *D* and *H*.
    d. $P(D \text{ or } H) = P(D) + P(H) - P(D \text{ and } H)$
27.
$$\begin{aligned} P(X_1 \text{ and } Y_2) &= P(X_1) \times P(Y_2|X_1) \\ &= .75 \times .40 \\ &= .30 \end{aligned}$$
29. *a.* 6/380 or .01579, found by 3/20 × 2/19.
    b. 272/380 or .7158, found by 17/20 × 16/19.
31. .4286, found by:
$$\begin{aligned} P(A_1|B_1) &= \frac{P(A_1) \times P(B_1|A_1)}{P(A_1) \times P(B_1|A_1) + P(A_2) \times P(B_1|A_2)} \\ &= \frac{.60 \times .05}{(.60 \times .05) + (.40 \times .10)} \end{aligned}$$
33. .5645, found by:
$$\begin{aligned} P(\text{night}|\text{win}) &= \frac{P(\text{night})\,P(\text{win}|\text{night})}{P(\text{night})\,P(\text{win}|\text{night}) + P(\text{day})\,P(\text{win}|\text{day})} \\ &= \frac{(.70)(.50)}{[(.70)(.50)] + [(.30)(.90)]} \end{aligned}$$
35. .1053, found by:
$$\begin{aligned} P(\text{cash})|{>}\$50) &= \frac{P(\text{cash})\,P({>}\$50|\text{cash})}{P(\text{cash})\,P({>}\$50|\text{cash}) + P(\text{check})\,P({>}\$50|\text{check}) + P(\text{charge})\,P({>}\$50|\text{charge})} \\ &= \frac{(.30)(.20)}{[(.30)(.20)] + [(.30)(.90)] + [(.40)(.60)]} \end{aligned}$$
37. *a.* A permutation is the number of arrangements of *r* objects selected from *n* possible objects. Order is important.
    b. A combination is the number of ways to select *r* objects from a group of *n* objects without regard to order.
39. *a.* 6,840
    b. 504
    c. 21
41. 10,000, found by $(10)^4$.
43. 3003, found by ${}_{15}C_{10} = (15 \times 14 \times 13 \times 12 \times 11)/(5 \times 4 \times 3 \times 2)$.
45. *a.* Asking teenagers their reactions to a newly developed soft drink.
    b. More than half of the respondents like it.
47. Subjective.
49. 3/6 or 1/2, found by 1/6 + 1/6 + 1/6. Classical.
51. *a.* The likelihood an event will occur, assuming that another event has already occurred.
    b. The collection of one or more outcomes of an experiment.
    c. A measure of the likelihood that two or more events will happen concurrently.
53. *a.* .8145, found by $(.95)^4$, or (.95)(.95)(.95)(.95).
    b. Special rule of multiplication.
    c. $P(A \text{ and } B \text{ and } C \text{ and } D) = P(A) \times P(B) \times P(C) \times P(D)$
55. *a.* .08, found by .80 × .10.
    b.

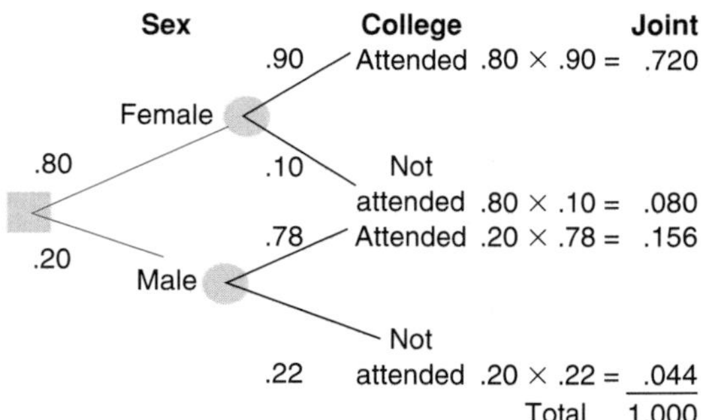

    c. Yes, because all the possible outcomes are shown on the tree diagram.
57. .99, found by 57/100 + 40/100 + 2/100.
59. All hit = .4096, found by $(.80)^4$. None hit = .0016, found by $(.20)^4$.
61. *a.* .3818, found by (9/12)(8/11)(7/10).
    b. .6182, found by 1 − .3818.
63. *a.* .5467, found by 82/150.
    b. .76, found by (39/150) + (75/150).
    c. .6267, found by 82/150 + 39/150 − 27/150. General rule.
    d. .3293, found by 27/82.
    e. .2972, found by (82/150)(81/149).

65. .0294, found by:

$$P(\text{poor}|\text{profit}) = \frac{P(\text{poor})\,P(\text{profit}|\text{poor})}{P(\text{poor})\,P(\text{profit}|\text{poor}) + P(\text{good})\,P(\text{profit}|\text{good}) + P(\text{fair})\,P(\text{profit}|\text{fair})}$$

$$= \frac{(.10)(.20)}{(.10)(.20) + (.60)(.80) + (.30)(.60)}$$

67. *a.* P (pizza or soft drink)

$$= P(\text{pizza})\,P(\text{no drink}) + P(\text{no pizza})\,P(\text{drink})$$

$$= \left(\frac{1}{50}\right)\left(\frac{9}{10}\right) + \left(\frac{49}{50}\right)\left(\frac{1}{10}\right) = .116$$

b. $$P(\text{no prize}) = \left(\frac{9}{10}\right)\left(\frac{49}{50}\right) = .882$$

c. $$P(\text{no prize on 3 visits}) = (.882)^3 = .686$$

d. $P(\text{at least one prize}) = 1 - P(\text{no prize}) = 1 - .686 = .314$

69. 24, found by

$$\frac{4!}{(4-4)!}$$

71. .4545, found by:

$$\frac{(.50)(.625)}{(.50)(.625) + (.50)(.75)} = \frac{.3125}{.6875}$$

73. Yes. 256 is found by 2^8.

75. 2,520, found by

$$_7P_5 = \frac{7!}{(7-5)!}$$

77. .9744, found by $1 - (.40)^4$.

79. *a.* .185, found by (.15)(.95) + (.05)(.85).
    b. .0075, found by (.15)(.05).

81. *a.* $P(\text{F and } {>}60) = .25$, found by solving with the general rule of addition.

$$1 = P(\text{F}) + P({>}60) + P(\text{F and } {>}60)$$
$$1 = .75 + .50 + P(\text{F and } {>}60)$$
$$P(\text{F and } {>}60) = 1.25 - 1.00 = .25$$

b. 0
c. .3333, found by 1/3.

83. *a.* .3041, found by 19,001/62,488.
    b. .7042, found by (5,830/62,488) + (43,487/62,488) − (5,311/62,488).
    c. .3353, found by:

$$\frac{4{,}344 + 2{,}596 + 1{,}719}{12{,}590 + 8{,}038 + 5{,}193}$$

d. First-time

$$\frac{8246 + 5442 + 3474}{43{,}487} = .3946$$

Repeat

$$\frac{4344 + 2596 + 1719}{19{,}001} = .4557$$

A repeat offender is more likely to be over 30.

e. .4843, found by (43,487/62,488)(43,486/62,487).

85. For the system to operate, both components in the series must work. The probability they both work is .81, found by $P(A) \cdot P(B) = (.90)(.90)$.

87. 1/3,628,800

89. *a.* Using MINITAB:

ROWS: Pool 0 = no pool, 1 = pool COLUMNS: Twnship

	1	2	3	4	5	ALL
0	7	6	6	8	2	29
1	5	9	13	10	9	46
ALL	12	15	19	18	11	75

(1) .7067, found by 12/75 + 46/75 − 5/75.
(2) .6842, found by 13/19.
(3) .1733, found by 13/75.

b. From MINITAB:

ROWS: Twnship
COLUMNS: Garage
0 = no garage, 1 = garage

	0	1	ALL
1	4	8	12
2	4	11	15
3	7	12	19
4	7	11	18
5	2	9	11
ALL	24	51	75

(1) .68, found by 51/75.
(2) .1818, found by 2/11.
(3) .16, found by 12/75.
(4) .4667, found by 24/75 + 15/75 − 4/75.

91. Using MINITAB:

	Circulation		
Male	<3000	≥3000	
≤50	14	11	25
>50	20	3	23
	34	14	48

a. $\frac{23}{48} = .4792$

b. $\frac{3}{48} = .0625$

c. $\frac{23}{48} + \frac{14}{48} - \frac{3}{48} = \frac{34}{48} = .7083$

d. $\frac{3}{14} = .2143$

CHAPTER 6
Discrete Probability Distributions

1. A discrete distribution can assume only certain values and is usually found by a counting process. A continuous distribution can assume an infinite number of values within a given range. Continuous distributions are usually determined by some type of measurement.

3. Mean = 1.3, variance = 0.81, found by:

$$\mu = \Sigma XP(X) = 0(.20) + 1(.40) + 2(.30) + 3(.10) = 1.3$$
$$\sigma^2 = \Sigma(X-\mu)^2P(X) = (0-1.3)^2(.2) + (1-1.3)^2(.4) + (2-1.3)^2(.3) + (3-1.3)^2(.10) = 0.81$$

5. Mean = 1.1, variance = 0.89, standard deviation = 0.943, found by:

$$\mu = 0(.3) + 1(.4) + 2(.2) + 3(.1) = 1.1$$
$$\sigma^2 = (0-1.1)^2(.3) + (1-1.1)^2(.4) + (2-1.1)^2(.2) + (3-1.1)^2(.1) = .89$$
$$\sigma = 0.943$$

7. The characteristics are:
   (1) There are only two possible outcomes. That is, an outcome can be classified into one of two mutually exclusive categories.
   (2) The data collected are the result of counts.
   (3) The probability of success remains the same from one trial to another.
   (4) Each trial is independent of another trial.

9. *a.* $P(2) = \frac{4!}{2!(4-2)!}(.25)^2(.75)^{4-2} = .2109$

   b. $P(3) = \frac{4!}{3!(4-3)!}(.25)^3(.75)^{4-3} = .0469$

11. *a.*

r	$P(r)$
0	.064
1	.288
2	.432
3	.216

   b.
$$\mu = np = 3(.6) = 1.8$$
$$\sigma^2 = np(1-p) = 3(.6)(.4) = 0.72$$
$$\sigma = \sqrt{0.72} = 0.8485$$

13. *a.* Number of production employees absent.
   b. Discrete because the number absent can only assume certain values, such as 1, 2, 3, and so on. There cannot be a fractional number of employees absent on a particular day.
   c. .349, found by referring to Appendix A, an n of 10, an r of 0, and a p of .10.
   d.

r	$P(r)$	r	$P(r)$
0	.349	6	.000
1	.387	7	.000
2	.194	8	.000
3	.057	9	.000
4	.011	10	.000
5	.001		

   e. $\mu = 1.00$, found by $np = (10)(.10)$
   $\sigma^2 = 0.90$, found by $np(1-p) = (10)(.10)(.90)$.
   $\sigma = 0.949$, found by $\sqrt{0.90}$.

   f.

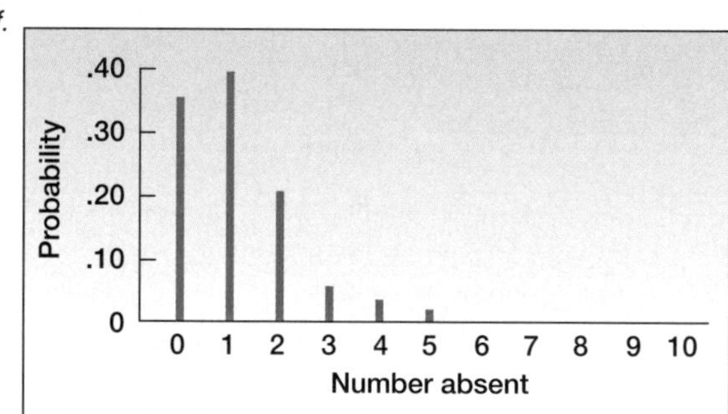

   g. (1) The outcomes can be classified only as "absent" or "not absent"; (2) the number absent is the result of counts; (3) the probability of .10 remains the same; and (4) the daily numbers of absences are independent.

15. *a.* .296, found by using Appendix A with n of 8, p of .30, and r of 2.

   b. $P(r \leq 2) = .058 + .198 + .296 = .552$

c. .448, found by $P(r \geq 3) = 1 - P(r \leq 2) = 1 - .552$.

17. *a.* .387, found from Appendix A with n of 9, p of .90, and r of 9.
b. $P(r < 5) = .001$
c. .992, found by $1 - .008$, which is probability that more than 5 have a color TV.
d. .947, found by $1 - .053$, which is the probability that 6 or less have a color TV.

19. $$P(2) = \frac{[{}_6C_2][{}_4C_1]}{{}_{10}C_3} = \frac{15(4)}{120} = .50$$

21. .4667, found by

$$\frac{\dfrac{7!}{2!5!} \times \dfrac{3!}{0!3!}}{\dfrac{10!}{2!8!}} = \frac{21}{45}$$

23. .4196, found by:

$$\frac{\dfrac{9!}{6!3!} \times \dfrac{6!}{4!2!}}{\dfrac{15!}{5!10!}} = \frac{1,260}{3,003}$$

25. *a.* .6703, found from Appendix C with $\mu = 0.4$ and $x = 0$.
b. .3297, found from Appendix C with $\mu = 0.4$ and $x > 0$.

27. *a.* .0613, where $n = 40$, $p = .025$, and $\mu = 1$. See Appendix C.
b. .0803, found by .0613 + .0153 + .0031 + .0005 + .0001, from Appendix C.

29. .7148, where $\mu = np = .005(1,200) = 6$. Adding, .1606 + .1606 + .1377 + . . . + .0001 = .7148.

31. The characteristics are:
(1) There are only two possible outcomes.
(2) The trials are not independent, so the probability of a success is not the same on each trial.
(3) The distribution results from a count of the number of successes in a fixed number of trials.

33. When n is large and p is small, the Poisson and binomial distributions will yield approximately the same results.

35. Mean = 2.0 units, found by 0 + .20 + .60 + 1.20. Standard deviation = 1.00, found by $\Sigma(X - \mu)^2 \times P(X) = .40 + .20 + 0 + .40 = 1$. The standard deviation is $\sqrt{1.0} = 1$.

37. Mean = 1.30 accidents, found by .00 + .20 + .40 + .30 + .40.
Variance = 1.81, found by $\Sigma(X - \mu)^2P(X) = .676 + .018 + .098 + .289 + .729$.
Standard deviation = $\sqrt{1.81} = 1.3454$ accidents.

39. *a.* .001
b. .001

41. .4286, found by:

$$\frac{6!}{2!4!} \times \frac{4!}{2!2!} \times \frac{4!6!}{10!}$$

43. *a.* $$P(x = 1) = \frac{{}_7C_2\,{}_3C_1}{{}_{10}C_3} = \frac{\left[\dfrac{7!}{2!5!}\right]\left[\dfrac{3!}{2!1!}\right]}{\left[\dfrac{10!}{3!7!}\right]} = .525$$

b. $$P(x = 0) = \frac{{}_7C_3\,{}_3C_0}{{}_{10}C_3} = \frac{35}{120} = 0.292$$

$$P(x \geq 1) = 1 - [P(x = 0)] = [1 - .292] = .708$$

45. $$P(x = 0) = \frac{{}_8C_4\,{}_4C_0}{{}_{12}C_4} = \frac{70}{495} = .141$$

47. *a.* .0498
b. .7746, found by $(1 - .0498)^5$.

49. $\mu = 4.0$ from Appendix C.
a. .0183
b. .1954
c. .6289
d. .5665

51. For the NASA estimate $\mu = np = 25(1/60,000) = 0.0004$. Using MINITAB, the probability of at least one disaster is .9996. The probability of a disaster is .0004, found by $1 - .9996$.

```
MTB > pdf;
SUBC> poisson mu = .0004.
POISSON WITH MEAN = 0.0000
K       P(X = K)
0         0.9996
1         0.0004
2         0.0000
```

Using the Air Force estimates, $\mu = 25(1/35) = 0.7143$. The probability of at least one disaster is .4895, so the probability of a disaster is .5105, found by $1 - .4895$.

```
MTB > pdf;
SUBC> poisson mu = .7143.
POISSON WITH MEAN = 0.714
K       P(X = K)
0         0.4895
1         0.3497
2         0.1249
3         0.0297
4         0.0053
5         0.0008
6         0.0001
7         0.0000
```

Thus, the probability of at least one disaster for NASA (.0004) is considerably less than for the Air Force (.5105).

53. $$\mu = np = 155\left(\frac{1}{3,709}\right) = 0.042$$

Using MINITAB:

```
X   PROBABILITY
0      0.9589
1      0.0403
2      0.0008
3      0.0000
```

So $P(x = 4|\mu = 0.042)$ is .0000.

55. $$P(x = 2) = \frac{{}_{18}C_3\ {}_{10}C_2}{{}_{28}C_5} = \frac{(816)(45)}{98,280} = .3736$$

CHAPTER 7
The Normal Probability Distribution

1. The actual shape of a normal distribution depends on its mean and standard deviation. Thus, there is a normal distribution, and an accompanying normal curve, for a mean of 7 and a standard deviation of 2. There is another normal curve for a mean of $25,000 and a standard deviation of $1,742, and so on.
3. *a.* 490 and 510, found by $500 \pm 1(10)$.
   b. 480 and 520, found by $500 \pm 2(10)$.
   c. 470 and 530, found by $500 \pm 3(10)$.
5. *a.* 1.25, found by:
   $$z = \frac{X - \mu}{\sigma} = \frac{25 - 20}{4.0} = 1.25$$
   b. .3944, found in Appendix D.
   c. .3085, found by:
   $$z = \frac{18 - 20}{4.0} = -0.5$$
   Find .1915 in Appendix D for $z = -0.5$; then $.5000 - .1915 = .3085$.
7. *a.* .3413, found by:
   $$z = \frac{\$20 - \$16.50}{\$3.50} = 1.00$$
   Then find .3413 in Appendix D for $z = 1$.
   b. .1587, found by $.5000 - .3413 = .1587$.
   c. .3336, found by:
   $$z = \frac{\$15.00 - \$16.50}{\$3.50} = -0.43$$
   Find .1664 in Appendix D for $z = -0.43$; then $.5000 - .1664 = .3336$.
9. *a.* .8276. First find $z = -1.5$ found by $[(44 - 50)/4]$ and $z = 1.25$ $[(55 - 50)/4)]$. The area between -1.5 and 0 is .4332, and the area between 0 and 1.25 is .3944, both from Appendix D. Then adding the two areas, we find that $.4332 + .3944 = .8276$.
   b. .1056, found by $.5000 - .3944$, where $z = 1.25$.
   c. .2029. Recall that the area for $z = 1.25$ is .3944. And the area for $z = 0.5$ found by $[(52 - 50)/4]$ is .1915. Then $.3944 - .1915 = .2029$.
   d. $X = 56.58$, found by adding .5000 (the area left of the mean) to the area corresponding to the z value that forces 45 percent of the data to fall inside the curve. That z value is 1.645. $.5000 + .4500 = .9500$. Solving for X: $1.645 = (X - 50)/4$, so $X = 56.58$.
11. *a.* .1525, found by $.4938 - .3413$, which are the areas associated with z values of 2.5 and 1, respectively.
   b. .0062, found by $.5000 - .4938$.
   c. .9710, found by recalling that the area for the z value of 2.5 is .4938. Then find the area for $z = -2.00$, found by $[(6.8 - 7.0)/0.1]$. Then add the areas for $z = 2.5$ and $z = -2$. Thus, $.4938 + .4772 = .9710$.
   d. 7.233. Find the z value where .4900 of area is between 0 and z. That value is $z = 2.33$. Then solve for X; $2.33 = (X - 7)/0.1$, so $X = 7.233$.
13. *a.* .0764, found by $z = (20 - 15)/3.5 = 1.43$. Then $.5000 - .4236 = .0764$.
   b. .9236, found by $.5000 + .4236$, where $z = 1.43$.
   c. .1185, found by $z = (12 - 15)/3.5 = -0.86$. The area under the curve is .3051. Then $z = (10 - 15/3.5) = -1.43$. The area is .4236. Finally, $.4236 - .3051 = .1185$.
   d. 16.84 minutes, found by solving for X where $z = 0.525$. This point forces .20 of the area to fall under the curve between 0 and z. First multiplying 0.525×3.5 and then adding 15, we find $X = 16.84$.

15. *a.*
$$\mu = np = 50(.25) = 12.5$$
$$\sigma^2 = np(1 - p) = 12.5(1 - .25) = 9.375$$
$$\sigma = \sqrt{9.375} = 3.0619$$

b. .2578, found by (14.5 − 12.5)/3.0619 = 0.65. The area is .2422. Then .5000 − .2422 = .2578.

c. .2578, found by (10.5 − 12.5)/3.06 = −0.65. The area is .2422. Then .5000 − .2422 = .2578.

17. *a.* .0655, found by (9.5 − 6)/2.32 = 1.51. The area is .4345. Then .5000 − .4345 = .0655.

b. .1401, found by (8.5 − 6)/2.32 = 1.08. The area is .3599. Then .5000 − .3599 = .1401.

c. .0746, found by .4345 − .3599 = .0746. This is the probability of getting exactly nine errors.

19. *a.* Yes. (1) There are two mutually exclusive outcomes: overweight and not overweight. (2) It is the result of counting the number of successes (overweight members). (3) Each trial is independent. (4) The probability of .30 remains the same for each trial.

b. .0084, found by $\mu = np = 500(.30) = 150$. Variance = $np(1 - p) = 105$. Standard deviation = 10.24695, found by $\sqrt{105}$.

$$z = \frac{X - \mu}{\sigma} = \frac{174.5 - 150}{10.24695} = 2.39$$

Area under the curve for 2.39 is .4916. Then .5000 − .4916 = .0084.

c. .8461, found by:

$$z = \frac{139.5 - 150}{10.24695} = -1.02$$

The area between 139.5 and 150 is .3461. Adding, .3461 + .5000 = .8461.

21. *a.* 46.41 percent, found by (20.27 − 20.00)/0.15 = 1.8.

b. 3.59 percent, found by .5000 − .4641.

c. 81.85 percent, found by .3413 + .4772.

d. 27.43 percent, found by .5000 − .2257.

23. *a.* −0.4 for net sales, found by (170 − 180)/25. And 2.92 for employees, found by (1,850 − 1,500)/120.

b. Net sales are −0.4 standard deviations below the mean. Employees are 2.92 standard deviations above the mean.

c. 65.54 percent of the aluminum fabricators have greater net sales compared with Clarion, found by .1554 + .5000. Only 0.18 percent have more employees than Clarion, found by .5000 − .4982.

25. *a.* 15.87 percent, found by (15 − 20)/5 = −1.0. The area for −1.0 is .3413. Then .5000 − .3413 = .1587.

b. .5403. First, the area between 18 and 20 is .1554. The area between 20 and 26 is .3849. Adding, .1554 + .3849 = .5403.

c. About 1 person, found by $z = (7 - 20)/5 = -2.6$, for which the area is .4953. Then .5000 − .4953 = .0047. Finally, 200(.0047) = 0.94, which is about 1 person.

27. *a.* (860 − 1,000)/50 = −2.8. The area below 860 is .0026, found by .5000 − .4974, or 0.26 percent.

b. (1,055 − 1,000)/50 = 1.1. The area between 1,000 and 1,055 is .3643. The area between 1,000 and 1,100 is .4772. Subtracting, .4772 − .3643 gives .1129, or 11.29 percent.

29. About 4,099 units (rounded to the nearest unit), found by solving for X:

$$1.645 = (X - 4{,}000)/60$$

31. *a.* Only 2.28 percent earn more than John: ($30,400 − $28,000)/$1,200 = 2.00. Then .5000 − .4772 = .0228.

b. Of the other supervisors, 97.72 percent have more service. (10 − 20)/5 = −2.00. Then .4772 + .5000 = .9772.

33. *a.* 15.39 percent, found by (8 − 10.3)/2.25 = −1.02. Then .5000 − .3461 = .1539.

b. 17.31 percent, found by:

$$z = (12 - 10.3)/2.25 = 0.76. \text{ Area is } .2764.$$
$$z = (14 - 10.3)/2.25 = 1.64. \text{ Area is } .4495.$$

The area between 12 and 14 is .1731, found by .4495 − .2764.

c. Yes, but it is rather remote. Reasoning: On 99.73 percent of the days, returns are between 3.55 and 17.05, found by 10.3 ± 3(2.25). Thus, the chance of less than 3.55 returns is rather remote.

35. *a.* .9678, found by:

$$\mu = np = 60(.64) = 38.4$$
$$\sigma^2 = np(1 - p) = 60(.64)(.36) = 13.824$$
$$\sigma = \sqrt{13.824} = 3.72$$

Then (31.5 − 38.4)/3.72 = −1.85, for which the area is .4678. Then .5000 + .4678 = .9678.

b. .0853, found by (43.5 − 38.4)/3.72 = 1.37, for which the area is .4147. Then .5000 − .4147 = .0853.

c. .8083, found by (32.5 − 38.4)/3.72 = −1.59. The area is .4441. And (42.5 − 38.4)/3.72 = 1.10, for which the area is .3643. Adding, the total is .8084.

d. .0348, by finding area for less than 44.0 where $z(44.5 - 38.4)/3.72 = 1.64$. The area is .4495. And recall the area for 43 or less was .4147. Then .4495 − .4147 = .0348.

37. *a.* .8106, where $\mu = 10$, variance = 8, standard deviation = 2.8284. $z = (7.5 - 10)/2.8284 = -0.88$. The area is = .3106. Then .5000 + .3106 = .8106.
    b. .1087, found by: $z = (8.5 - 10)/2.8284 = -0.53$. Then .3106 − .2019 = .1087.
    c. .2981, found by .5000 − .2019.
39. .0968, found by:

$$\mu = np = 50(.40) = 20$$
$$\sigma^2 = np(1 - p) = 50(.40)(.60) = 12$$
$$\sigma = \sqrt{12} = 3.4641$$

$z = (24.5 - 20)/3.4641 = 1.30$. The area is .4032. Then, for 25 or more, .5000 − .4032 = .0968.

41. *a.* 36.775 minutes, found by solving for μ:

$$1.645 = (45 - \mu)/5 = 36.775$$

b. 28.55 minutes, found by solving for μ:

$$1.645 = (45 - \mu)/10 = 28.55$$

c. 55.96 percent, found by (30 − 28.55)/10 = .15. The area is .0596. Then .5000 + .0596 = .5596.

43. *a.* .6687, found by: $z = (2.00 - 2.80)/0.40 = -2.00$; $p = .4772$. And $(3.00 - 2.80)/0.40 = .50$; $p = .1915$. Then .4772 + .1915 = .6687.
    b. .0228, found by: $(2.00 - 2.80)/0.40 = -2.00$; $p = .5000 - .4772 = .0228$.
    c. 122, found by: $z = (3.70 - 2.80)/.040 = 2.25$; $p = .5000 - .4878 = .0122$. Then $10{,}000 \times .0122 = 122$.
    d. 3.312, found by $1.28 = (X - 2.8)/0.40$, so $X = 3.312$
45. *a.* 21.19 percent, found by $z = (9.00 - 9.20)/0.25 = -0.80$; $p = .5000 - .2881 = .2119$.
    b. Increase the mean: $\sigma = (9.00 - 9.25)/0.25 = 1.00$; $p = .5000 - .3413 = .1587$.
    Reduce the standard deviation; $\sigma = (9.00 - 9.20)/.15 = 1.33$; $p = .5000 - .4082 = .0918$. Reducing the standard deviation is better because a smaller percent of the hams will be below the limit.

47. *a.*

$$z = \frac{60 - 52}{5} = 1.60$$

The probability associated with a value greater than 1.60 is .5000 − .4452 = .0548. About 5.48 percent of those leasing go over the mileage.

b. .5000 − .2500 = .2500, so $z = 0.675$.

$$0.675 = \frac{X - 52}{5}$$
$$X = 55.375$$

Set the limit at 55,375 miles.

c.

$$z = \frac{45 - 52}{5} = -1.4$$

Then .5000 − .4192 = .0808.
About 8 percent of the cars are low-mileage.

49. $$\frac{470 - \mu}{\sigma} = 0.25 \quad \text{and} \quad \frac{500 - \mu}{\sigma} = 1.28$$

so $470 - \mu = 0.25\sigma$ and $500 - \mu = 1.28\sigma$.

$$500 = 1.28\sigma + \mu$$
$$470 = 0.25\sigma + \mu$$
$$30 = 1.03\sigma$$
$$\sigma = 29.126$$

$$500 = 1.28(29.126) + \mu$$
$$\mu = 462.719$$

So the distribution of novels has a mean of 462,719 and a standard deviation of 29,126.

51. $$\mu = 150(.15) = 22.5 \qquad z = \frac{30.5 - 22.5}{4.3732} = 1.83$$
$$\sigma = \sqrt{150(.15)(.85)} = 4.3732$$

$$P(z > 1.83) = .5000 - .4664 = .0336$$

53. *a.*

$$z = \frac{4.00 - 2.509}{0.781} = 1.91$$
$$P(z > 1.91) = .5000 - .4719 = .0281$$

.0281(28) = 0.79, or about one team. There were actually two teams with attendance over 4,000,000, Colorado and Toronto, so the estimate is pretty good.

b.

$$z = \frac{160 - 141.79}{23.04} = 0.79$$
$$P(z > 0.79) = .5000 - .2852 = .2148$$
$$(.2148)(28) = 6.0$$

There were actually seven teams that hit 160 or more home runs, so the estimate is close.

CHAPTER 8
Sampling Methods and Sampling Distributions

1. *a.* 303 Louisiana, 5155 S. Main, 3501 Monroe, 2652 W. Central.
   b. Answers will vary.
3. 630 Dixie, 835 S. McCord, 4624 Woodville.
5. Answers will vary.
7. *a.* 6, found by the combination $_4C_2$:

$$_4C_2 = \frac{4!}{2!(4 \times 2)!} = \frac{4 \times 3 \times 2 \times 1}{(2 \times 1)(2 \times 1)} = 6$$

b.

Sample	Values	Sum	Mean
1	12, 12	24	12
2	12, 14	26	13
3	12, 16	28	14
4	12, 14	26	13
5	12, 16	28	14
6	14, 16	30	15

c.

$$\mu_{\bar{x}} = (12 + 13 + 14 + 13 + 14 + 15)/6 = 13.5$$

$$\mu = (12 + 12 + 14 + 16)/4 = 13.5$$

They are equal.

d. The dispersion of the population is greater than that of the sample means. The sample means vary from 12 to 15, whereas the population values vary from 12 to 16.

9. *a.* 6, found by 4!/2!2!.

b.

Test scores	Mean
90, 86	88
90, 70	80
90, 80	85
86, 70	78
86, 80	83
70, 80	75

c.

$$\mu_{\bar{x}} = \frac{88 + 80 + 85 + 78 + 83 + 75}{6} = 81.5$$

$$\mu = \frac{90 + 86 + 70 + 80}{4} = 81.5$$

They are equal.

d.

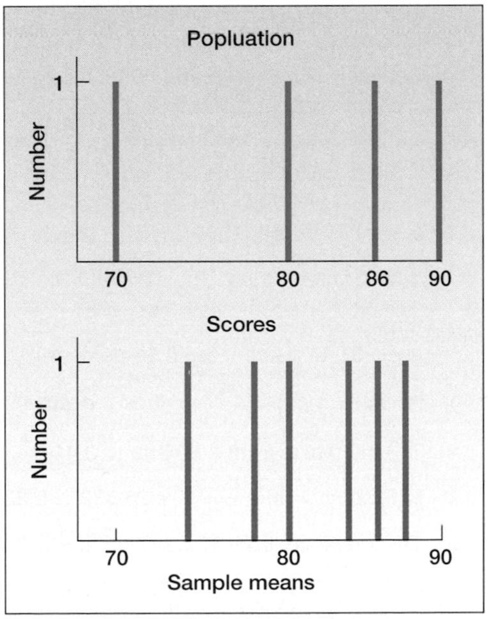

Popluation

Number

1

70 80 86 90

Scores

Number

1

70 80 90

Sample means

e. More dispersion in the population than in sample means. So your grade would average the same over the long run, but there would be more dispersion.

11. Between 51.314 and 58.686, found by $55 \pm 2.58(10/\sqrt{49})$.

13. *a.* 1.581, found by $\sigma_{\bar{x}} = \sigma/\sqrt{n} = 5/\sqrt{10} = 1.581$.
    b. The population is normally distributed and the population variance is known.
    c. 16.901 and 23.099, found by 20 ± 3.099.

15. *a.* \$20. It is our best estimate of the population mean.
    b. Between \$18.60 and \$21.40, found by $\$20 \pm 1.96(\$5/\sqrt{49})$. About 95 percent of the intervals similarly constructed will include the population mean.

17. *a.* 8.60 gallons.
    b. Between 7.83 and 9.37, found by $8.60 \pm 2.58(2.30/\sqrt{60})$.
    c. If 100 such intervals were determined, the population mean would lie in about 99 intervals.

19. *a.* .80, found by 80/100.
    b. .7216 and .8784, found by:

$$.80 \pm 1.96\sqrt{[(.80)(.20)/100]}$$

21. *a.* .625, found by 250/400.
    b. .578 and .672, found by:

$$.625 \pm 1.96\sqrt{[(.625)(.375)/400]}$$

23. Between 33.465 and 36.535, found by:

$$35 \pm 1.96(5/\sqrt{36})\sqrt{\frac{300 - 36}{300 - 1}}$$

25. 1.689 up to 2.031, found by:

$$1.86 \pm 2.58(0.50/\sqrt{50})\sqrt{\frac{400 - 50}{400 - 1}}$$

27. 97, found by $n = [(1.96 \cdot 10)/2]^2 = 96.04$.

29. 554, found by $n = [(1.96 \cdot 3)/0.25]^2 = 553.19$.

31. 196, found by:

$$n = .15(.85)[1.96/.05]^2 = 195.9216$$

33. *a.* 577, found by:

$$n = .60(.40)[1.96/.04]^2 = 576.24$$

    b. 601, found by:

$$n = .50(.50)[1.96/.04]^2 = 600.25$$

35. *a.* It is usually not feasible to study the entire population. Thus, if we want to infer something about a characteristic of a population, a part of the population—called a sample—is needed.

b. Contacting all the voters or all consumers would be too time-consuming and too costly. It is impossible to tag all the whales in the ocean for study. Checking all products for strength is destructive, and none would be available for sale.

37. A nonprobability sample, such as a panel sample, may not give results that are representative of the population because every item or person does not have a chance of being selected for the sample.

39. The metropolitan area could be subdivided into precincts. Four precincts could be selected for study. Suppose there are 74 mobile home parks in the area. Eight could be selected, and the persons conducting the survey would concentrate on the residents of those eight parks.

41. *a.* Jeanne Fiorito, Douglas Smucker, Jeanine S. Huttner, Harry Mayhew, Mark Steinmetz, and Paul Langenkamp.
    b. One randomly selected group of numbers is 05, 06, 74, 64, 66, 55, 27, 22. The members of the sample are Janet Arrowsmith, David DeFrance, Mark Zilkoski, and Larry Johnson.

43. Answers will vary.

45. *a.* 10, found by 5!/3!2!.
    b.

Number correct	Mean	Number correct	Mean
4, 3	3.5	3, 3	3.0
4, 5	4.5	3, 2	2.5
4, 3	3.5	5, 3	4.0
4, 2	3.0	5, 2	3.5
3, 5	4.0	3, 2	2.5

c.

Sample mean	Frequency	Probability
2.5	2	.20
3.0	2	.20
3.5	3	.30
4.0	2	.20
4.5	1	.10
	10	1.00

d. $\mu_{\bar{x}} = (3.5 + 4.5 + \cdots + 2.5)/10 = 3.4$
$\mu = (4 + 3 + 5 + 3 + 2)/5 = 3.4$
The two means are equal.

e. The population values are uniform in shape. The distribution of sample means tends toward normality.

47. A simple random sample would be appropriate, but this means that each 10-foot length would have to be numbered 1, 2, 3, . . . , 720. A faster method would be to (1) select a pipe from the first, say, 20 pipes produced, and (2) select every 20th pipe produced thereafter and measure its inside diameter. Thus, the sample would include about 36 PVC pipes.

49. 6.14 years to 6.86 years, found by $6.5 \pm 1.96(1.7/\sqrt{85})$.

51. 369, found by $n = .60(1 - .60)[1.96/.05]^2 = 368.79$.

53. 133, found by $[(1.645 \times 14)/2]^2$.

55. *a.* 3.01 pounds.
    b. 3.0002 and 3.0198 pounds, found by $3.01 \pm 1.96(0.03/\sqrt{36})$.
    c. About 95 percent of similarly constructed intervals would include the population mean.

57. .345 and .695, found by:

$$.52 \pm 2.58\sqrt{\frac{.52(.48)}{50}}\sqrt{\frac{(650 - 50)}{(650 - 1)}}$$

59. .633 and .687, found by

$$.66 \pm 1.96\sqrt{\frac{.66(.34)}{1{,}200}}$$

61. $26.0 \pm (1.96)\dfrac{6.2}{\sqrt{50}} = 26.0 \pm 1.72$
Interval is from 24.28 up to 27.72.

63. *a.* 708.13, rounded up to 709, found by:

$$.21(1 - .21)[1.96/.03]^2$$

b. 1,068, found by:

$$.50(.50)[1.96/.03]^2$$

65. *a.* Between \$158.59 and \$174.76, found by:

$$\$166.67 \pm 1.96\left(\frac{\$35.68}{\sqrt{75}}\right)$$

b. Between 13.78 miles and 16.00 miles, found by:

$$14.8933 \pm 1.96\left(\frac{4.892}{\sqrt{75}}\right)$$

c. $\bar{p} = 51/75 = .68$. Then

$$.68 \pm 1.96\sqrt{\frac{(.68)(.32)}{75}}$$

gives 57.44 percent to 78.56 percent.

67. *a.* $2.904 \pm (1.96)\dfrac{1.804}{\sqrt{48}} = 2.904 \pm 0.510.$
The interval is from 2.394 up to 3.414.
    b. $\$26{,}622 \pm 1.96\dfrac{\$18{,}858}{\sqrt{48}} = 26{,}622 \pm 5{,}335.$
The interval is from \$21,287 up to \$31,957.
    c. $42.75 \pm 1.96\dfrac{13.74}{\sqrt{48}} = 42.75 \pm 3.89.$
The interval is from 38.86 up to 46.64.

CHAPTER 9
Tests of Hypotheses: Large Samples

1. *a.* Two-tailed.
   b. Reject H_0 and accept H_1 where z does not fall in the region from −1.96 to 1.96.
   c. −1.2, found by:
   $$z = \frac{\overline{X} - \mu}{(\sigma/\sqrt{n})} = \frac{49 - 50}{(5/\sqrt{36})} = -1.2$$
   d. Fail to reject H_0.
   e. $p = .2302$, found by 2(.5000 − .3849).
3. *a.* H_0: $\mu = 60{,}000$
   H_1: $\mu \neq 60{,}000$
   b. Reject H_0 if $z < -1.96$ or $z > 1.96$.
   c. −0.69. found by:
   $$z = \frac{59{,}500 - 60{,}000}{(5{,}000/\sqrt{48})} = -0.69$$
   d. Fail to reject H_0 at the .05 significance level. Crosset's experience is not different from that claimed by the manufacturer. The *p*-value is .4902, found by 2(.5000 − .2549).
5. *a.* One-tailed.
   b. Reject H_0 and accept H_1 where $z > 1.645$.
   c. 1.2, found by:
   $$z = \frac{\overline{X} - \mu}{(s/\sqrt{n})} = \frac{21 - 20}{(5/\sqrt{36})} = 1.2$$
   d. Fail to reject H_0 at the .05 significance level.
   e. $p = .1151$, found by .5000 − .3849.
7. *a.* H_0: $\mu \geq 6.8$
   H_1: $\mu < 6.8$
   b. Reject H_0 if $z < -1.645$.
   c. −7.2, found by:
   $$z = \frac{6.2 - 6.8}{0.5/\sqrt{36}} = -7.2$$
   d. Reject H_0 and conclude that the mean number of videos watched by college students is less than 6.8 at the .05 significance level.
9. *a.* Two-tailed test.
   b. Reject H_0 if $z < -2.055$ or $z > 2.055$.
   c. 2.59, found by:
   $$z = \frac{\overline{X}_1 - \overline{X}_2}{\sqrt{\frac{s_1^2}{n_1} + \frac{s_2^2}{n_2}}} = \frac{102 - 99}{\sqrt{\frac{5^2}{40} + \frac{6^2}{50}}} = 2.59$$
   d. Reject H_0 and accept H_1.
   e. $p = .0096$, found by 2(.5000 − .4952).
11. **Step 1** H_0: $\mu_1 \geq \mu_2$
    H_1: $\mu_1 < \mu_2$
    Step 2 The .05 significance level was chosen.
    Step 3 Reject H_0 and accept H_1 if $z < -1.645$.
    Step 4 −0.94, found by:
    $$z = \frac{7.6 - 8.1}{\sqrt{\frac{(2.3)^2}{40} + \frac{(2.9)^2}{55}}} = -0.94$$
    Step 5 Fail to reject H_0. No difference in lengths of time owners occupied their homes.
    $p = .1736$, found by .5000 − .3264.
13. *a.* Two-tailed test. Because we are trying to show that a difference exists between the two means.
    b. Reject H_0 if $z < -2.58$ or $z > 2.58$.
    c. −2.66, found by:
    $$z = \frac{31.4 - 34.9}{\sqrt{\frac{(5.1)^2}{32} + \frac{(6.7)^2}{49}}} = -2.66$$
    Reject H_0 at the .01 level. There is a difference in the mean turnover rate. $p = .0078$, found by 2(.5000 − .4961).
15. *a.* H_0 is rejected if $z < -1.96$ or $z > 1.96$.
    b. $$z = \frac{.30 - .40}{\sqrt{\frac{.40(.60)}{120}}} = \frac{-.1000}{.0490} = -2.236$$
    c. H_0 is rejected.
17. *a.* H_0: $p \leq .33$, H_1: $p > .33$
    b. H_0 is rejected if $z > 2.05$.
    c. $$z = \frac{.40 - .3333}{\sqrt{\frac{.3333(.6667)}{200}}} - \frac{.0667}{.0333} = 2.001$$
    d. H_0 is not rejected. The proportion of students with jobs is not larger at your school.
19. *a.* H_0: $p \geq .50$, H_1: $p < .50$
    b. H_0 is rejected if $z < -1.645$.
    c. $$z = \frac{.48 - .50}{\sqrt{\frac{.50(.50)}{100}}} = \frac{-.02}{.05} = -0.40$$
    d. H_0 is not rejected. The proportion of students changing majors has not changed.
21. *a.* H_0 is rejected if $z < -1.96$ or $z > 1.96$
    b. $$\bar{p}_c = \frac{170 + 110}{200 + 150} = .80$$
    c. $$z = \frac{.85 - .7333}{\sqrt{\frac{.80(.20)}{200} + \frac{.80(.20)}{150}}} = 2.701$$
    d. H_0 is rejected.

23. H_0: $p_1 \geq p_2$, H_1: $p_1 < p_2$
H_0 is rejected if $z < -1.645$.

$$\bar{p}_c = \frac{2{,}010 + 1{,}530}{3{,}000 + 3{,}000} = .59$$

$$z = \frac{.51 - .67}{\sqrt{\frac{.59(.41)}{3{,}000} + \frac{.59(.41)}{3{,}000}}} = -12.60$$

H_0 is rejected. The proportion of women who think men are thoughtful has declined.

25. H_0: $p_s = p_m$, H_1: $p_s \neq p_m$
H_0 is rejected if $z < -1.96$ or $z > 1.96$.

$$\bar{p}_c = \frac{120 + 150}{400 + 600} = .27$$

$$z = \frac{.30 - .25}{\sqrt{\frac{.27(.73)}{400} + \frac{.27(.73)}{600}}} = 1.745$$

H_0 is not rejected. There is no difference in the proportion of married and single drivers who have accidents.

27. $z = (9{,}922 - 9{,}940)/(400/\sqrt{100}) = -0.45$. Then the area of .1736 + .5000 = .6736, which is the probability of a Type II error.

29.
$$H_0: \mu \leq 16$$
$$H_1: \mu > 16$$

Reject H_0 if $z > 1.645$.
Computed $z = 11.78$, found by:

$$z = \frac{16.05 - 16.0}{(0.03/\sqrt{50})} = 11.78$$

Reject H_0. The cans are being overfilled. *p*-value is very close to .0000.

31.
$$H_0: \mu \leq 90$$
$$H_1: \mu > 90$$

Reject H_0 if $z > 1.28$.
Computed $z = 1.82$:

$$z = \frac{94 - 90}{(22/\sqrt{100})} = 1.82$$

Reject H_0. At the .10 level we can conclude that the farm selling time has increased.

33. H_0: $\mu \geq 40$, H_1: $\mu < 40$. Reject H_0 if $z < -1.645$.

$$z = \frac{37.8 - 40.0}{12.2/\sqrt{60}} = -1.397$$

H_0 is not rejected. *p*-value = .5000 − .4192 = .0808. We cannot conclude that the mean leisure time is less than 40 hours per week.

35. *a.* H_0: $\mu \geq 50$, H_1: $\mu < 50$. Reject H_0 if $z > 2.33$.

$$\bar{X} = 48.18, s = 2.886$$

$$z = \frac{48.18 - 50.00}{3.00/\sqrt{10}} = -1.92$$

H_0 is not rejected. The mean weight is not less than 50 pounds.

b. Mr. Rutter can use the *z* distribution as the test statistic because the population standard deviation ($\sigma = 3$) is known. Also, the population is normal.

c. *p*-value = .5000 − .4726 = 0.0274

37. H_0: $\mu_1 = \mu_2$
H_1: $\mu_1 \neq \mu_2$
Reject H_0 if $z < -2.05$ or $z > 2.05$.
Computed $z = -1.60$, found by:

$$z = \frac{114.6 - 117.9}{\sqrt{\frac{(9.1)^2}{40} + \frac{(10.4)^2}{50}}} = -1.60$$

Fail to reject H_0. There is no difference in the test scores. The *p*-value is .1096, found by 2(.5000 − .4452).

39. H_0: $\mu_1 \geq \mu_2$
H_1: $\mu_1 < \mu_2$
Reject H_0 if *z* is < -1.645.
Computed $z = -0.14$, found by:

$$z = \frac{\$41{,}290 - \$41{,}330}{\sqrt{\frac{(\$1{,}060)^2}{45} + \frac{(\$1{,}900)^2}{60}}} = -0.14$$

Fail to reject H_0. There is no difference in the starting salaries.

41. H_0: $\mu_1 = \mu_2$, H_1: $\mu_1 \neq \mu_2$. Reject H_0 if $z < -1.96$ or $z > 1.96$.

$$z = \frac{4.77 - 5.02}{\sqrt{\frac{(1.05)^2}{40} + \frac{(1.23)^2}{50}}} = \frac{-0.25}{0.24} = -1.04$$

H_0 is not rejected. There is no difference in the mean number of service calls. *p*-value = 2(.5000 − .3508) = .2984.

43. H_0: $\mu_1 \leq \mu_2$, H_1: $\mu_1 > \mu_2$. Reject H_0 if $z > 2.05$.

$$z = \frac{11.00 - 7.67}{\sqrt{\frac{(3.88)^2}{30} + \frac{(4.42)^2}{40}}} = 3.35$$

H_0 is rejected. Those with smaller boats use their boats more often. The actual *p*-value is less than .0001.

45. H_0: $p \leq .60$, H_1: $p > .60$
H_0 is rejected if $z > 2.33$.

$$z = \frac{.70 - .60}{\sqrt{\frac{.60(.40)}{200}}} = \frac{.10}{.0346} = 2.887$$

H_0 is rejected. Ms. Dennis is correct. More than 60 percent of the accounts are more than 3 months old.

47. H_0: $p \leq .44$, H_1: $p > .44$
H_0 is rejected if $z > 1.645$.

$$z = \frac{.480 - .44}{\sqrt{\frac{.44(.56)}{1{,}000}}} = \frac{.04}{.0157} = 2.548$$

H_0 is rejected. We conclude that there has been an increase in the proportion of people wanting to go to Europe.

49. H_0: $p \leq .20$, H_1: $p > 20$. Reject H_0 if $z > 2.33$.

$$z = \frac{\frac{56}{200} - .20}{\sqrt{\frac{.20(.80)}{200}}} = 2.83$$

H_0 is rejected. More than 20 percent of the owners move during a particular year. p-value = .5000 − .4977 = .0023.

51. H_0: $p_a = p_f$, H_1: $p_a \neq p_f$
H_0 is rejected if $z < -1.96$ or $z > 1.96$.

$$\bar{p}_c = \frac{198 + 117}{1{,}000 + 500} = .21$$

$$z = \frac{.198 - .234}{\sqrt{\frac{.21(.79)}{1{,}000} + \frac{.21(.79)}{500}}} = -1.614$$

H_0 is not rejected. There is no difference in the proportion of American-born citizens and foreign-born citizens who favor resumption of diplomatic relations with Cuba.

53. *a.* Reject H_0 if $z > 1.645$. Computed $z = 1.28$, found by:

$$z = \frac{24{,}421 - 24{,}000}{(1{,}944/\sqrt{35})} = 1.28$$

Fail to reject H_0.

b. 24,541, found by:

$$1.645 = \frac{\bar{X}_c - 24{,}000}{(1{,}944/\sqrt{35})}$$

$$\bar{X}_c = 24{,}540.54$$

c. $z = (24{,}540.54 - 25{,}000)/(1{,}944/\sqrt{35}) = -1.40$
.5000 − .4192 = .0808

55. *a.* H_0: $\mu \leq 0.75$, H_1: $\mu > 0.75$. Critical value is 1.645.

$$z = \frac{0.80 - 0.75}{\frac{0.1}{\sqrt{45}}} = 3.35$$

Reject H_0. The shoppers are now spending more than an average of 0.75 hours in the mall.

b. $\bar{X}_c = 0.7745$, found by

$$1.645 = \frac{\bar{X}_c - 0.75}{\frac{0.1}{\sqrt{45}}}$$

$z = .302$, found by:

$$\frac{0.7745 - 0.77}{0.1/\sqrt{45}}$$

Area = .1179. Then .5000 + .1179 = .6179.

c. Increase level of significance to, say, 0.10.

57. *a.* H_0: $\mu \geq 180$, H_1: $\mu < 180$. H_0 is rejected if $z < -1.645$.

$$z = \frac{166.67 - 180.0}{(35.68/\sqrt{75})} = -3.235$$

H_0 is rejected. The mean selling price is less than $180,000. The p-value is .0000.

b. H_0: $\mu \leq 2{,}000$, H_1: $\mu > 2{,}000$. H_0 is rejected if $z > 1.645$.

$$z = \frac{2{,}154.8 - 2{,}000}{(207.4/\sqrt{75})} = 6.464$$

H_0 is rejected. The mean size is greater than 2,000 square feet.

c. H_0: $p \leq 0.5$, H_1: $p > 0.5$. Reject H_0 if $z > 1.645$.

$$z = \frac{.6133 - .50}{\sqrt{\frac{.50(.50)}{75}}} = \frac{.1133}{.0577} = 1.962$$

H_0 is rejected. More than half of the homes have a pool.

d. H_0: $p \leq 0.5$, H_1: $p > 0.5$. Reject H_0 if $z > 1.645$.

$$\bar{p} = \frac{51}{75} = .68$$

$$z = \frac{.68 - .50}{\sqrt{\frac{(.50)(.50)}{75}}} = \frac{.18}{.0577} = 3.118$$

H_0 is rejected. More than half of the homes have a garage.

59. *a.* H_0: $\mu \leq 2.5$, H_1: $\mu > 2.5$. Reject H_0 if $z > 1.645$.

$$z = \frac{2.75 - 2.50}{1.859/\sqrt{48}} = 0.93$$

H_0 is not rejected. The mean number of magazines read is not greater than 2.5 for men.

b. H_0: $\mu \geq 40$, H_1: $\mu < 40$. Reject H_0 if $z < -1.645$.

$$z = \frac{35.167 - 40.00}{5.200/\sqrt{48}} = -6.44$$

H_0 is rejected. The mean age of readers is less than 40 years.

CHAPTER 10
Tests of Hypotheses: Small Samples

1. *a.* Reject H_0 where $t > 1.833$.

b.
$$t = \frac{\overline{X} - \mu}{(s/\sqrt{n})} = \frac{12 - 10}{(3/\sqrt{10})} = 2.108$$

c. Reject H_0. The mean is greater than 10.

3. H_0: $\mu \leq 40$
H_1: $\mu > 40$
Reject H_0 if $t > 1.703$.

$$t = \frac{42 - 40}{(2.1/\sqrt{28})} = 5.04$$

Reject H_0 and conclude that the mean number of calls is greater than 40 per week.

5. H_0: $\mu \leq 22{,}100$
H_1: $\mu > 22{,}100$
Reject H_0 if $t > 1.740$.

$$t = \frac{23{,}400 - 22{,}100}{(1{,}500/\sqrt{18})} = 3.68$$

Reject H_0. The mean life of the spark plugs is greater than 22,100 miles.

7. *a.* Reject H_0 if $t < -3.747$.

b. $\overline{X} = 17$, $s = \sqrt{(1{,}495 - (85)^2/5)/(5 - 1)}$
$= 3.536$

$$t = \frac{17 - 20}{3.536/\sqrt{5}} = -1.90$$

c. Do not reject H_0. We cannot conclude that the population mean is less than 20.

d. Between .05 and .10, about .065

9. H_0: $\mu \leq 4.35$
H_1: $\mu > 4.35$
Reject H_0 if $t > 2.821$.

$$t = \frac{4.368 - 4.35}{(0.0339/\sqrt{10})} = 1.68$$

Do not reject H_0. The additive did not increase the mean weight of the chickens. The *p*-value is between .10 and .05.

11. *a.* H_0: $\mu \leq 4.0$
H_1: $\mu > 4.0$
Reject H_0 if $t > 1.796$.

$$t = \frac{4.50 - 4.0}{(2.68/\sqrt{12})} = 0.65$$

Do not reject H_0. Mean number of fish caught has not been shown to be greater than 4.0. The *p*-value is greater than .10.

13. *a.* Reject H_0 if $t < -2.120$ or $t > 2.120$.

b.
$$s_p^2 = \frac{(10 - 1)4^2 + (8 - 1)5^2}{10 + 8 - 2}$$
$$= 19.9375$$

c.
$$t = \frac{23 - 26}{\sqrt{19.9375(1/10 + 1/8)}} = -1.416$$

d. Do not reject H_0.

e. The *p*-value is greater than .10.

15. H_0: $\mu_1 \geq \mu_2$
H_1: $\mu_1 < \mu_2$
Reject H_0 if $t < -2.624$.

$$s_1^2 = \frac{55{,}476 - (702)^2/9}{9 - 1} = 90 \qquad s_2^2 = \frac{43{,}971 - (553)^2/7}{7 - 1} = 47.33$$

$$s_p^2 = \frac{(9 - 1)(90) + (7 - 1)(47.33)}{9 + 7 - 2} = 71.71$$

$$t = \frac{78 - 79}{\sqrt{71.71(1/9 + 1/7)}} = -0.234$$

Do not reject H_0. There is no difference in the mean grades.

17. H_0: $\mu_1 \leq \mu_2$
H_1: $\mu_1 > \mu_2$
Reject H_0 if $t > 1.301$ (estimated).

$$t = \frac{89 - 87}{\sqrt{26.667(1/22 + 1/25)}} = 1.325$$

Reject H_0. The mean pollen count in the valley is greater than in the mountains. The *p*-value is less than .10.

19. *a.* Reject H_0 if $t > 2.353$.

b. $\bar{d} = 3.000$
$s_d = 0.816$

c.
$$t = \frac{\bar{d}}{s_d/\sqrt{n}} = \frac{3}{0.816/\sqrt{4}} = 7.353$$

d. Reject H_0. The review session was effective.

e. The *p*-value is less than .005. Very little chance that H_0 is true.

21. H_0: $\mu_d \leq 0$
H_1: $\mu_d > 0$
Reject H_0 if $t > 2.764$.
$\bar{d} = 7.3636$, $s_d = 8.3699$.

$$t = \frac{7.3636}{(8.3699/\sqrt{11})} = 2.92$$

Reject H_0. The weights have increased.

23. H_0: $\mu_d \leq 0$
H_1: $\mu_d > 0$
Reject H_0 if $t > 2.821$.
$\bar{d} = 0.10$, $s_d = 4.28$.

$$t = \frac{0.10}{4.28/\sqrt{10}} = 0.07$$

Fail to reject H_0. There has been no reduction.

25. H_0: $\mu \geq 87$
H_1: $\mu < 87$
Reject H_0 if $t < -1.895$.

$$s = \sqrt{\frac{55{,}244 - (664)^2/8}{8 - 1}} = 4.3425$$

$$\bar{X} = \frac{664}{8} = 83.0$$

$$t = \frac{83 - 87}{4.3425/\sqrt{8}} = -2.61$$

Reject H_0. The mileage is less than advertised.

27. H_0: $\mu \leq 9$
H_1: $\mu > 9$
Reject H_0 if $t > 2.998$.
$\bar{X} = 9.488$, $s = 0.467$.

$$t = \frac{9.488 - 9.00}{0.467/\sqrt{8}} = 2.95$$

Do not reject H_0. The mean prime rate for small banks is 9.0 percent. The *p*-value is less than .025.

29. H_0: $\mu \leq 25$, H_1: $\mu > 25$. Reject H_0 if $t > 2.624$.

$$\bar{X} = 26.07, s = 1.5337$$

$$t = \frac{26.07 - 25.00}{1.5337/\sqrt{15}} = 2.702$$

Reject H_0. The mean number of patients per day is more than 25. The *p*-value is less than .01.

31. H_0: $\mu \geq 3.5$, H_1 $\mu < 3.5$. $df = 16$, critical value = -1.746.

$$t = \frac{2.9553 - 3.5}{.5596/\sqrt{17}} = -4.013$$

Reject H_0. Games last less than 3.5 hours on the average.

33. H_0: $\mu_e \leq \mu_b$, H_1: $\mu_e > \mu_b$. Reject H_0 if $t > 1.701$. ("e" refers to the end of the month and "b" to the beginning of the month)

$$s_p^2 = \frac{(20 - 1)(5.84)^2 + (10 - 1)(5.67)^2}{20 + 10 - 2} = 33.4767$$

$$t = \frac{24.80 - 20.25}{\sqrt{33.4767\left(\frac{1}{10} + \frac{1}{20}\right)}} = 2.031$$

H_0 is rejected. The packages shipped at the end of the month weigh more.

35. H_0: $\mu_1 \leq \mu_2$
H_1: $\mu_1 > \mu_2$
Reject H_0 if $t > 2.567$.

$$s_p^2 = \frac{(8 - 1)(2.2638)^2 + (11 - 1)(2.4606)^2}{8 + 11 - 2} = 5.672$$

$$t = \frac{10.375 - 5.636}{\sqrt{5.672(1/8 + 1/11)}} = 4.28$$

Reject H_0. The mean number of transactions by the young adults is more than for the senior citizens.

37. H_0: $\mu_1 \leq \mu_2$, H_1: $\mu_1 > \mu_2$. Reject H_0 if $t > 2.650$.

$\bar{X}_1 = 125.125$, $s_1 = 15.094$, $\bar{X}_2 = 117.714$, $s_2 = 19.914$

$$s_p^2 = \frac{(8 - 1)(15.094)^2 + (7 - 1)(19.914)^2}{8 + 7 - 2} = 305.708$$

$$t = \frac{125.125 - 117.714}{\sqrt{305.708\left(\frac{1}{8} + \frac{1}{7}\right)}} = 0.819$$

H_0 is not rejected. There is no difference between the mean number sold at the regular price and the mean number sold at the reduced price.

39. H_0: $\mu_d = 0$
H_1: $\mu_d \neq 0$
Reject H_0 if $t < -2.201$ or $t > 2.201$.
$\bar{d} = 0.0833$, $s_d = 5.143$.

$$t = \frac{0.0833}{5.143/\sqrt{12}} = 0.056$$

Do not reject H_0. There is no difference in output between the two.

41. H_0: $\mu_d \leq 0$, H_1: $\mu_d > 0$. Reject H_0 if $t > 1.895$.

$$\bar{d} = 1.75 \qquad s_d = 2.9155$$

$$t = \frac{1.75}{2.9155/\sqrt{8}} = 1.698$$

H_0 is not rejected. There is no difference in the mean number of absences. The p-value is greater than .10.

43. *a.* μ_1 = without pool, μ_2 = with pool. Critical value = ± 2.000, $df = 73$. $\bar{X}_1 = 152.697$, $s_1 = 26.5137$. $\bar{X}_2 = 175.487$, $s_2 = 38.0921$. Computed $t = -2.817$, $p = .006$.
Reject H_0, indicating that the mean selling price of a home with a pool is significantly greater than the price for one without a pool.

b. $\bar{X}_1 = 138.071$ without a garage, 180.135 with garage, critical value = ± 2.000, computed value of $t = 5.680$. Reject H_0. $p = .000$. Home with garage costs more.

c. H_0: $\mu_1 = \mu_2$, H_1: $\mu_1 \neq \mu_2$, $df = n_1 + n_2 - 2 = 12 + 15 - 2 = 25$. Reject H_0 if $t < -2.060$ or $t > 2.060$. $\bar{X}_1 = 148.64$, $s_1 = 24.61$, $\bar{X}_2 = 172.69$, and $s_2 = 34.29$.

$$s_p^2 = \frac{(11)(24.61)^2 + 14(34.29)^2}{12 + 15 - 2} = 924.94$$

$$t = \frac{148.64 - 172.69}{\sqrt{924.94\left(\frac{1}{12} + \frac{1}{15}\right)}} = -2.042$$

Do not reject H_0.

45. *a.* H_0: $\mu_1 = \mu_2$, H_1: $\mu_1 \neq \mu_2$. $df = 25 + 23 - 2 = 46$. Reject H_0 if $t < -2.01$ or $t > 2.01$. $\bar{X}_1 = 37{,}620$, $s_1 = 24{,}527$, $n_1 = 25$. $\bar{X}_2 = 35{,}551$, $s_2 = 21{,}653$, $n_2 = 23$.

$$s_p^2 = \frac{(25-1)(24{,}527)^2 + (23-1)(21{,}653)^2}{25 + 23 - 2} = 538{,}098{,}315.1$$

$$t = \frac{37{,}620 - 35{,}551}{\sqrt{538{,}098{,}315.1\left(\frac{1}{25} + \frac{1}{23}\right)}} = \frac{2{,}069}{6{,}702.20} = 0.309$$

H_0 is not rejected. There is no difference in the mean cost.

b. H_0: $\mu_1 = \mu_2$, H_1: $\mu_1 \neq \mu_2$. Reject if $t < -2.01$ or $t > 2.01$. $\bar{X}_1 = 4{,}142$, $s_1 = 4{,}679$, $n_1 = 25$. $\bar{X}_2 = 1{,}858$, $s_2 = 1{,}850$, $n_2 = 23$.

$$s_p^2 = \frac{(25-1)(4{,}679)^2 + (23-1)(1{,}858)^2}{25 + 23 - 2} = 13{,}073{,}491.13$$

$$t = \frac{4{,}142 - 1{,}858}{\sqrt{13{,}073{,}491.13\left(\frac{1}{25} + \frac{1}{23}\right)}} = \frac{2{,}284.0}{1{,}044.69} = 2.186$$

Reject H_0. There is a difference in mean circulation between the two groups.

CHAPTER 11

Analysis of Variance

1. 9.01 from Appendix G.

3. Reject H_0 if $F > 10.5$, where df is 7 in the numerator and 5 in the denominator. Computed $F = 2.04$, found by:

$$F = \frac{s_1^2}{s_2^2} = \frac{(10)^2}{(7)^2} = 2.04$$

Do not reject H_0. There is no difference in the variations of the two populations.

5. H_0: $\sigma_1^2 = \sigma_2^2$
H_1: $\sigma_1^2 \neq \sigma_2^2$
Reject H_0 where $F > 3.10$. (3.10 is about halfway between 3.14 and 3.07.) Computed $F = 1.44$, found by:

$$F = \frac{(12)^2}{(10)^2} = 1.44$$

Do not reject H_0. There is no difference in the variations of the two populations.

7. *a.* H_0: $\mu_1 = \mu_2 = \mu_3 = \mu_4$
H_1: The treatment means are not the same.

b. Reject H_0 when $F > 3.49$.

c. SST = 63.19, SSE = 13.75, and SS total = 76.94.

d.

Source	SS	df	MS	F
Treatment	63.19	3	21.06	18.38
Error	13.75	12	1.15	
Total	76.94	15		

e. Reject H_0: $18.38 > 3.49$.

9. H_0: $\mu_1 = \mu_2 = \mu_3$; H_1: Not all treatment means are the same. H_0 is rejected if $F > 4.26$.

$$\text{SS total} = 20{,}783 - \frac{(495)^2}{12} = 364.25$$

$$\text{SST} = \frac{(142)^2}{4} + \frac{(164)^2}{4} + \frac{(189)^2}{4} - \frac{(495)^2}{12} = 276.5$$

$$\text{SSE} = 364.25 - 276.50 = 87.75$$

Source	SS	df	MS	F
Treatment	276.50	2	138.25	14.18
Error	87.75	9	9.75	
Total	364.25	11		

Since $14.18 > 4.26$, H_0 is rejected. Not all treatment means are the same.

11. *a.* H_0: $\mu_1 = \mu_2 = \mu_3$
H_1: Not all means are the same.

b. Reject H_0 where $F > 4.26$.

c. SST = 107.20, SSE = 9.47, SS total = 116.67

d.

Source	SS	df	MS	F
Treatment	107.20	2	53.600	50.96
Error	9.47	9	1.052	
Total	116.67	11		

e. Since 50.96 > 4.26, H_0 is rejected. At least one of the means differ.

f. $(\bar{X}_1 - \bar{X}_2) \pm t\sqrt{\text{MSE}(1/n_1 + 1/n_2)} = (9.667 - 2.20) \pm 2.262\sqrt{1.052(1/3 + 1/5)}$

$7.467 \pm 1.69 = [5.777, 9.157]$. Yes, we can conclude that treatments 1 and 2 have different means.

13. H_0: $\mu_1 = \mu_2 = \mu_3 = \mu_4$; H_1: Not all means are equal. H_0 is rejected if $F > 3.71$.

$$\text{SS total} = 2{,}444 - \frac{(182)^2}{14} = 78.00$$

$$\text{SST} = \frac{(48)^2}{4} + \frac{(46)^2}{4} + \frac{(46)^2}{3} + \frac{(42)^2}{3} - \frac{(182)^2}{14} = 32.33$$

$$\text{SSE} = 78.00 - 32.33 = 45.67$$

Source	SS	df	MS	F
Treatment	32.33	3	10.77	2.36
Error	45.67	10	4.567	
Total	78.00	13		

Since 2.36 is less than 3.71, H_0 is not rejected. There is no difference in the mean number of weeks.

15. *a.* H_0: $\mu_1 = \mu_2$
H_1: Not all treatment means are equal.

b. Reject H_0 where $F > 18.5$

c. H_0: $\mu_1 = \mu_2 = \mu_3$; H_1: Not all block means are equal.
H_0 is rejected if $F > 19.0$

d.

$$\text{SST} = \frac{(127)^2}{3} + \frac{(92)^3}{3} - \frac{(219)^2}{6} = 204.167$$

$$\text{SSB} = \frac{(77)^2}{2} + \frac{(63)^2}{2} + \frac{(79)^2}{2} - \frac{(219)^2}{6} = 76$$

$$\text{SS total} = 8{,}283 - (219)^2/6 = 289.5$$

$$\text{SSE} = 289.5 - 204.167 - 76 = 9.333$$

e.

Source	SS	df	MS	F
Treatment	204.167	1	204.167	43.75
Blocks	76.000	2	38.000	8.14
Error	9.333	2	4.667	
Total	289.5000	5		

f. 43.75 > 18.5, so reject H_0. There is a difference in the treatments. 8.14 < 19.0, so fail to reject H_0 for blocks. There is no difference between blocks.

17. For treatments:
H_0: $\mu_1 = \mu_2 = \mu_3$
H_1: Not all means equal
Reject if $F > 4.46$

For blocks:
H_0: $\mu_1 = \mu_2 = \mu_3 = \mu_4 = \mu_5$
H_1: Not all means equal
Reject if $F > 3.84$

SS total = 139.73, SST = 62.53, SSB = 33.73, SSE = 43.47.

Source	SS	df	MS	F
Treatment	62.53	2	31.265	5.75
Blocks	33.73	4	8.4325	1.55
Error	43.47	8	5.4338	
Total	139.73			

There is a difference by shift but not by employee.

19.

Source	SS	df	MS	F
Treatment	320	2	160	8.00
Error	180	9	20	
Total	500	11		

a. 3
b. 12
c. 4.26
d. H_0: $\mu_1 = \mu_2 = \mu_3$; H_1: Not all means are equal.
e. H_0 is rejected. The treatment means differ.

21. H_0: $\mu_1 = \mu_2 = \mu_3$; H_1: Not all treatment means are equal. H_0 is rejected if $F > 3.89$.

$$\text{SS total} = 3{,}868 - \frac{(238)^2}{15} = 91.73$$

$$\text{SST} = \frac{(66)^2}{5} + \frac{(81)^2}{5} + \frac{(91)^2}{5} - \frac{(238)^2}{15} = 63.33$$

$$\text{SSE} = 91.73 - 63.33 = 28.40$$

Source	df	SS	MS	F
Treatment	2	63.33	31.667	13.38
Error	12	28.40	2.367	
Total	14			

H_0 is rejected. There is a difference in the treatment means.

23. H_0: $\mu_1 = \mu_2 = \mu_3 = \mu_4$; H_1: Not all means are equal. Reject H_0 if $F > 3.10$.

Source	df	SS	MS	F
Factor	3	87.79	29.26	9.12
Error	20	64.17	3.21	
Total	23	151.96		

Since computed F of 9.12 > 3.10, the null hypothesis of no difference is rejected at the .05 level. At least one mean differs.

25. *a.* H_0: $\mu_1 = \mu_2$; H_1: $\mu_1 \neq \mu_2$. Critical value of $F = 4.75$. SS total = 333.4286. SST = 219.4286. SSE = 114.0000.

Source	SS	df	MS	F
Treatment	219.4286	1	219.4286	23.10
Error	114.0000	12	9.5	
	333.4286	13		

b.
$$t = \frac{19 - 27}{\sqrt{9.51\left(\frac{1}{6} + \frac{1}{8}\right)}} = -4.80$$

Then $t^2 = F$. That is $(-4.80)^2 \simeq 23.10$. (Actually, 23.04. Difference due to rounding.)

c. H_0 is rejected. There is a difference in the mean scores.

27. H_0: $\mu_1 = \mu_2 = \mu_3 = \mu_4 = \mu_5 = \mu_6$; H_1: The treatment means are not equal. Reject H_0 if $F > 2.76$.

Source	df	SS	MS	F
Treatment	5	0.03478	0.00696	3.86
Error	58	0.10439	0.00180	
Total	63	0.13917		

H_0 is rejected. There is a difference in the mean weight for different colors.

29. For color the critical value of F is 4.76; for size it is 5.14.

Source	SS	df	MS	F
Treatment	25.0	3	8.3333	5.88
Blocks	21.5	2	10.75	7.59
Error	8.5	6	1.4167	
Total	55.0	11		

H_0 for both treatments and blocks (color and size) is rejected. At least one mean differs for color, and at least one mean differs for size.

31. a. Critical value of F is 3.49. Computed F is 0.668. Do not reject H_0.

b. Critical value of F is 3.26. Computed F value is 100.204. Reject H_0 for block means.

33. For gasoline:

H_0: $\mu_1 = \mu_2 = \mu_3$
H_1: Mean mileage is not the same

Reject H_0 if $F > 3.89$.
For automobile:

H_0: $\mu_1 = \mu_2 = \cdots = \mu_7$
H_1: Mean mileage is not the same

Reject H_0 if $F > 3.00$.

Source	df	SS	MS	F
Gasoline	2	44.095	22.048	26.71
Auto	6	77.238	12.873	15.60
Error	12	9.905	0.825	
Total	20			

There is a difference in both autos and gasoline.

35. a. H_0: $\sigma_p^2 = \sigma_{np}^2$, H_1: $\sigma_p^2 \neq \sigma_{np}^2$. Reject H_0 if F is greater than 2.28 based on 45 and 28 degrees of freedom. The computed value of F is 2.064, found by $(38.09)^2/(26.51)^2$. H_0 is not rejected. The sample size and standard deviations are computed as follows using MINITAB.

```
MTB  > table c4;
SUBC > standard c1;
SUBC > n c1.
  ROWS: Pool
       Price   Price
      STD DEV    N
 0     26.51    29
 1     38.09    46
ALL    35.68    75
```

b. H_0: $\sigma_g^2 = \sigma_{ng}^2$, H_1: $\sigma_g^2 \neq \sigma_{ng}^2$. Reject H_0 if $F > 2.50$ (50 and 23 degrees of freedom). The computed F is 2.614, found by $(33.34)^2/(20.62)^2$. H_0 is rejected. There is a difference in the variation of the selling prices of homes with a garage and those without a garage.

```
MTB  > table c7;
SUBC > standard c1;
SUBC > n c1.
  ROWS: Garage
       Price   Price
      STD DEV    N
 0     20.62    24
 1     33.34    51
ALL    35.68    75
```

c. H_0: $\mu_1 = \mu_2 = \mu_3 = \mu_4 = \mu_5$. H_1: means not all equal. Critical value for $F_{4,70} = 2.28$. Computed value of $F = 1.05$. Do not reject H_0. There is no difference in the mean selling price among the five townships.

```
ANALYSIS OF VARIANCE ON Price
SOURCE   DF    SS     MS     F      p
Twnship   4   5322  1330  1.05  0.389
ERROR    70  88895  1270
TOTAL    74  94217
```

CHAPTER 12
Linear Regression and Correlation

1.

X	Y	X^2	XY	Y^2
4	4	16	16	16
5	6	25	30	36
3	5	9	15	25
6	7	36	42	49
10	7	100	70	49
28	29	186	173	175

$$r = \frac{5(173) - (28)(29)}{\sqrt{[5(186) - (28)^2][5(175) - (29)^2]}}$$

$$= \frac{53}{\sqrt{(146)(34)}} = .75$$

The .75 coefficient indicates a rather strong positive correlation between X and Y.

The coefficient of determination is .5625, found by $(.75)^2$. More than 56 percent of the variation in Y is accounted for by X.

3. *a.* Sales

   b.

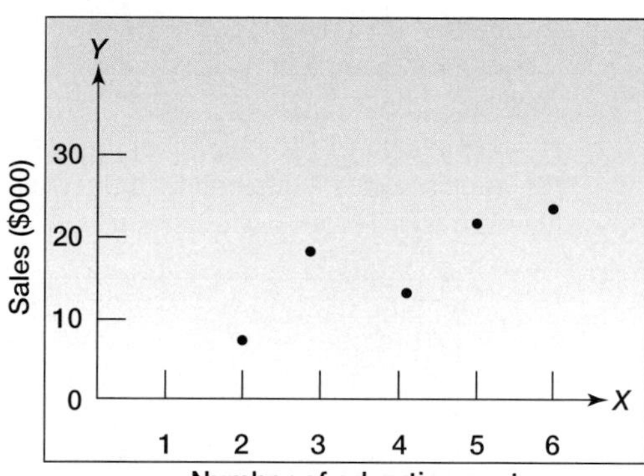

   c. $n = 5$, $\Sigma X = 20$, $\Sigma X^2 = 90$, $\Sigma Y = 85$, $\Sigma Y^2 =$ 1,595, and $\Sigma XY = 376$.

$$r = \frac{5(376) - (20)(85)}{\sqrt{[5(90) - (20)^2][5(1595) - (85)^2]}} = \frac{180}{\sqrt{(50)(750)}} = .93$$

   d. The coefficient of determination is .8649, found by $(.93)^2$.

   e. There is a strong positive association between the variables. About 86 percent of the variation in sales is explained by the number of airings.

5. Reject H_0 if $t > 1.812$.

$$t = \frac{.32\sqrt{12 - 2}}{\sqrt{1 - (.32)^2}} = 1.07$$

   Do not reject H_0.

7. H_0: $\rho \leq 0$
   H_1: $\rho > 0$
   Reject H_0 if $t > 2.552$. $df = 18$.

$$t = \frac{.78\sqrt{20 - 2}}{\sqrt{1 - (.78)^2}} = 5.28$$

   Reject H_0. There is a positive correlation between gallons sold and the pump price.

9. *a.* $Y' = 3.7671 + .3630X$

$$b = \frac{5(173) - (28)(29)}{5(186) - (28)^2} \qquad a = \frac{29}{5} - (0.363)\frac{28}{5}$$

$$= \frac{53}{146} \qquad = 3.7671$$

$$= 0.3630$$

   b. 6.3082, found by $Y' = 3.7671 + 0.3630(7)$.

11. *a.*

$$b = \frac{10(718) - (91)(74)}{10(895) - (91)^2} = \frac{446}{669} = 0.667$$

$$a = \frac{74}{10} - 0.667\left(\frac{91}{10}\right) = 1.333$$

   b. $Y' = 1.333 + 0.667(6) = 5.335$

13. *a.*

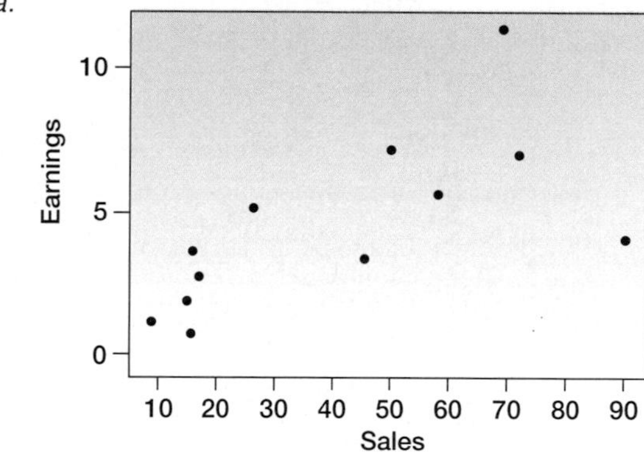

   b.

$$r = \frac{12(3{,}306.35) - (501.10)(64.1)}{\sqrt{[12(28{,}459) - (501.10)^2][12(458.41) - (64.1)^2]}}$$

$$= \frac{7{,}555.69}{\sqrt{(90{,}406.79)(1{,}392.11)}}$$

$$= .673$$

   c. $r^2 = (.673)^2 = .4529$

   d. A strong positive association exists between the variables. About 45 percent of the variation in earnings is accounted for by sales.

   e.

$$b = \frac{12(3{,}306.35) - (501.1)(64.1)}{5(28{,}459) - (501.1)^2} = \frac{7{,}555.69}{90{,}406.79} = 0.0836$$

$$a = \frac{64.1}{12} - 0.0836\left(\frac{501.10}{12}\right) = 1.8507$$

   f. $Y' = 1.8507 + 0.0836(50.0) = 6.0307$ (\$ millions)

15. *a.* .993, found by

$$\sqrt{\frac{175 - 3.767(29) - 0.363(173)}{5 - 2}}$$

   b. $Y' \pm 1s_{y \cdot x} = Y' \pm 1(.993) = Y' \pm .993$

17. *a.* .898, found by

$$\sqrt{\frac{584 - 1.333(74) - 0.667(718)}{10 - 2}}$$

b. $Y' \pm 2(.898) = Y' \pm 1.796$

19. *a.* $6.308 \pm (3.182)(.993)$

$$\sqrt{0.2 + \frac{(7 - 5.6)^2}{186 - (784/5)}}$$

$= 6.308 \pm 1.633$
$= [4.675, 7.941]$

b. $6.3082 \pm (3.182)(.993)\sqrt{1 + 1/5 + 0.0671} =$ [2.751, 9.865]

21. *a.* [4.2939, 6.3721]
b. [2.9854, 7.6806]

23. Coefficient of correlation $r = .8944$, found by:

$$\frac{(5)(340) - (50)(30)}{\sqrt{[(5)(600) - (50)^2][(5)(200) - (30)^2]}}$$

Then $(.8944)^2 = .80$, the coefficient of determination.

25. H_0: $\rho \geq 0$
H_1: $\rho < 0$
Reject H_0 if $t < -1.701$, $df = 28$.

$$t = \frac{-.45\sqrt{30 - 2}}{\sqrt{1 - .2025}} = -2.67$$

Reject H_0. There is a negative correlation between the selling price and the number of miles driven.

27. *a.* From MINITAB, $r = .589$.
b. $r^2 = (.589)^2 = .3469$.
c. H_0: $\rho \leq 0$, H_1: $\rho > 0$. Reject H_0 if $t > 1.860$.

$$t = \frac{.589\sqrt{10 - 2}}{\sqrt{1 - (.589)^2}} = 2.062$$

H_0 is rejected. There is a positive association between family size and the amount spent on food.

29. *a.* From MINITAB, $r = .181$.
b. $r^2 = (.181)^2 = .0327$

31. *a.*

Source	*df*	SS	MS	*F*
Regression	1	50	50	2.5556
Error	23	450	19.5652	
Total	24	500		

b. $n = 25$
c. $s_{y \cdot x} = \sqrt{19.5652} = 4.4233$
d. $r^2 = \dfrac{50}{500} = .10$

33. *a.* $n = 15$, $\Sigma X = 107$, $\Sigma X^2 = 837$, $\Sigma Y = 118.6$, $\Sigma Y^2 = 969.92$, $\Sigma XY = 811.60$, $s_{y \cdot x} = 1.114$.

$$b = \frac{15(811.60) - (107)(118.6)}{15(837.0) - (107)^2} = \frac{-516.2}{1{,}106.0} = -0.4667$$

$$a = \frac{118.6}{15} - (-0.4667)\left(\frac{107}{15}\right) = 11.2358$$

b. $Y' = 11.2358 - 0.4667(7.0) = 7.9689$

c. $$7.9689 \pm (2.160)(1.114)\sqrt{1 + \frac{1}{15} + \frac{(7 - 7.1333)^2}{837 - \frac{(107)^2}{15}}}$$

$= 7.9689 \pm (2.160)(1.114)\sqrt{1.0669}$
$= 7.9689 \pm 2.4854$
$= [5.4835, 10.4543]$

d. $r^2 = 0.499$. Nearly 50 percent of the variation in the amount bid is explained by the number of bidders.

35. *a.*

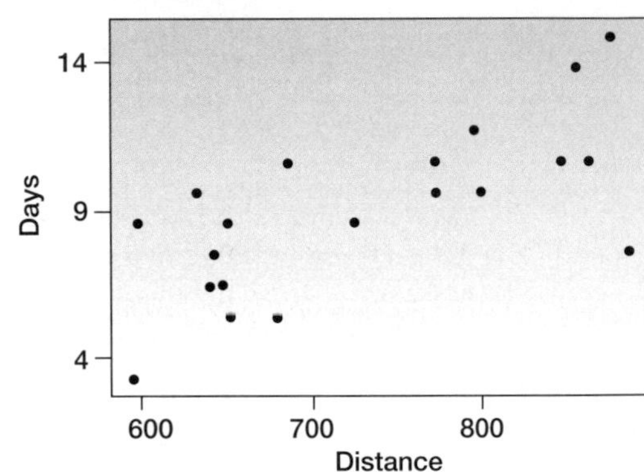

There appears to be a relationship between the two variables. As the distance increases, so does the shipping time.

b. Using the MINITAB system, $r = .692$.
H_0: $\rho \leq 0$, H_1: $\rho > 0$. Reject H_0 if $t > 1.734$.

$$t = \frac{.692\sqrt{20 - 2}}{\sqrt{1 - (.692)^2}} = 4.067$$

H_0 is rejected. There is a positive association between shipping distance and shipping time.

c. $r^2 = .479$
d. From MINITAB, $s_{y \cdot x} = 2.004$.
e, f, g. From the MINITAB system:

```
The regression equation is
Days = -7.13 + 0.0214 Distance

Predictor      Coef        Stdev     t-ratio       p
Constant     -7.126        3.843       -1.85    0.080
Distance   0.021391     0.005258        4.07    0.001

s = 2.004       R-sq = 47.9%        R-sq(adj) = 45.0%

Analysis of Variance

SOURCE       DF        SS         MS        F       p
Regression    1    66.486     66.486    16.55   0.001
Error        18    72.314      4.017
Total        19   138.800

R denotes an obs. with a large st. resid.

    Fit  Stdev.Fit      95.0% C.I.            95.0% P.I.
  7.847     0.468   ( 6.863,   8.831)   ( 3.522,  12.173)
  Estimate          Confidence interval   Prediction interval
```

37. *a.* Using the MINITAB system, the correlation between sales and salary is .488, and between sales and ROE it is .294. The two tests of hypotheses and corresponding *t* values are:

H_0: $\rho \leq 0$
H_1: $\rho > 0$

for salary and sales and

$$t = \frac{.488\sqrt{26-2}}{\sqrt{1-(.488)^2}} = 2.739$$

H_0: $\rho \leq 0$
H_1: $\rho > 0$

for salary and ROE.

$$t = \frac{.294\sqrt{26-2}}{\sqrt{1-(.294)^2}} = 1.507$$

The null hypotheses are rejected if $t > 1.690$. So, we conclude that there is correlation between sales and salary but not between ROE and salary.

b. The coefficients of determination are:

Salary and Sales: $(.488)^2 = .238$
Salary and ROE: $(.294)^2 = .086$

c. Salary seems to be related to the bank sales, but not to ROE.

39. *a.* From the MINITAB system, the output is as follows:

```
MTB > regr c3 1 c2
Regression Analysis
The regression equation is
Area = 0.546 + 0.0227 Employee
Predictor   Coef       Stdev      t-ratio   p
Constant    0.5462     0.6241     0.88      0.392
Employee    0.022719   0.002156   10.54     0.000
s = 2.080      R-sq = 85.4%     R-sq(adj) = 84.6%
```

Each employee cleans an additional .0227 square feet. This is in millions of square feet, so it is actually 22,700 square feet.

b. The coefficient of determination is .854, so the coefficient of correlation is $\sqrt{.854} = .924$.
H_0 $\rho \leq 0$, H_1 $\rho > 0$. Reject H_0 if $t > 1.729$.

$$t = \frac{.924\sqrt{21-2}}{\sqrt{1-(.924)^2}} = 10.532$$

H_0 is rejected. There is a positive correlation between the number of employees and the area cleaned.

41. *a.* H_0: $\rho \leq 0$, H_1: $\rho > 0$. Reject H_0 if $t > 1.706$.
From the MINITAB system the correlation between wins and salary is .301.

$$t = \frac{.301\sqrt{28-2}}{\sqrt{1-(.301)^2}} = 1.609$$

H_0 is not rejected. We have failed to show a correlation between the two variables.

```
The regression equation is
Wins = 68.8 + 0.398 Salary
Predictor      Coef       Stdev    t-ratio       p
Constant     68.829       7.888       8.73   0.000
Salary       0.3979      0.2473       1.61   0.120
s = 11.81        R-sq = 9.1%        R-sq(adj) = 5.6%
Analysis of Variance
SOURCE       DF        SS        MS        F        p
Regression    1     361.0     361.0     2.59    0.120
Error        26    3627.0     139.5
Total        27    3988.0
```

From the regression equation, an increase of 5 in *X*(salary) would result in an increase of 1.9895, or about 2, wins. However, the r^2 value is only 9.1 percent, so salary does not explain much of the variation in wins.

b. The correlation between wins and batting average is .588 and between wins and ERA is −.591. (For those unfamiliar with details of baseball, ERA refers to earned run average. It is a measure of runs per game given up by a team. A lower ERA means more effective pitching.)
Note that there is a positive correlation between batting and wins and a negative association

between wins and ERA, and they are very close in strength.
For wins and batting:
H_0: $\rho \leq 0$, H_1: $\rho > 0$. Reject H_0 if $t > 1.706$.

$$t = \frac{.588\sqrt{28-2}}{\sqrt{1-(.588)^2}} = 3.706$$

For wins and ERA:
H_0: $\rho \geq 0$, H_1: $\rho < 0$. Reject H_0 if $t < -1.706$.

$$t = \frac{-.591\sqrt{28-2}}{\sqrt{1-(.591)^2}} = -3.736$$

In both cases H_0 is rejected. Both variables are correlated with the number of wins.

c. The correlation between the number of games won and attendance is .337.
H_0: $\rho \leq 0$, H_1: $\rho > 0$. Reject H_0 if $t > 1.706$.

$$t = \frac{.337\sqrt{28-2}}{\sqrt{1-(.337)^2}} = 1.825$$

H_0 is rejected. There is a positive association between wins and attendance. Winning teams attract more people. The *p*-value is between .025 and .05.

CHAPTER 13
Multiple Regression and Correlation

1. a. Multiple regression equation.
   b. They Y-intercept.
   c. $374,748, found by:

$$Y' = 64{,}100 + 0.394(796{,}000) + 9.6(6{,}940) - 11{,}600(6.0)$$

3. a. 465.256, found by:

$$Y' = -16.24 + 0.017(18) + 0.0028(26{,}500) + 42(3) + 0.0012(156{,}000) + 0.19(141) + 26.8(2.5)$$

   b. Two more social activities. Income added only 28 to the index; social activities added 53.6.

5. a. $28,000
   b. .5809, found by:

$$R^2 = \frac{\text{SSR}}{\text{SS total}} = \frac{3{,}050}{5{,}250}$$

   c. 9.199, found by $\sqrt{84.62}$.
   d. H_0 is rejected if $F > 2.97$ (approximately).

$$\text{Computed } F = \frac{762.50}{84.62} = 9.01$$

   H_0 is rejected. At least one regression coefficient is not zero.
   e. If computed t is to the left of -2.056 or to the right of 2.056, the null hypothesis in each of these cases is rejected. Computed t for X_2 and X_3 exceeds the critical value. Thus, "population" and "advertising expenses" should be retained and "number of competitors," X_1, dropped.

7. a. $n = 40$
   b. 4
   c. $$R^2 = \frac{750}{1{,}250} = .60$$
   d. $$s_{y \cdot 1234} = \sqrt{500/35} = 3.7796$$
   e. H_0: $\beta_1 = \beta_2 = \beta_3 = \beta_4 = 0$
   H_1: Not all the βs equal zero.
   H_0 is rejected if $F > 2.65$.

$$F = \frac{750/4}{500/35} = 13.125$$

   H_0 is rejected. At least one β_i does not equal zero.

9. a. $n = 26$
   b. $R^2 = 100/140 = .7143$
   c. 1.4142, found by $\sqrt{2}$.
   d. H_0: $\beta_1 = \beta_2 = \beta_3 = \beta_4 = \beta_5 = 0$
   H_1: Not all the βs are 0.
   H_0 is rejected if $F > 2.71$.
   Computed $F = 10.0$. Reject H_0. At least one regression coefficient is not zero.
   e. H_0 is rejected in each case if $t < -2.086$ or $t > 2.086$. X_1 and X_5 should be dropped.

11. a. The strongest correlation is between GPA and legal. No problem with multicollinearity.
   b. $$R^2 = \frac{4.3595}{5.0631} = .8610$$
   c. H_0 is rejected if $F > 5.41$.

$$F = \frac{1.4532}{0.1407} = 10.328.$$

   At least one coefficient is not zero.
   d. Any H_0 is rejected if $t < -2.571$ or $t > 2.571$. It appears that only GPA is significant. Verbal and math could be eliminated.
   e. $$R^2 = \frac{4.2061}{5.0631} = .8307$$

   R^2 has been reduced only .0303.

f. The residuals appear slightly skewed (positive), but acceptable.

g. There does not seem to be a problem with the plot.

13. *a.* Using MINITAB, the correlation matrix is:

	cars	adv	sales
adv	0.808		
sales	0.872	0.537	
city	0.639	0.713	0.389

Size of sales force (0.872) has strongest correlation with cars sold. Fairly strong relationship between location of dealership and advertising (0.713). Could be a problem.

b.

```
The regression equation is: cars = 31.1328
+ 2.1516 adv + 5.0140 sales + 5.6651 city
```

$Y' = 31.1328 + 2.1516(15) + 5.0140(20) + 5.6651(1) = 169.352.$

c. H_0: $\beta_1 = \beta_2 = \beta_3 = 0$; H_1: not all βs are 0. Reject H_0 if computed $F > 4.07$

Analysis of Variance

Source	DF	SS	MS
Regression	3	5504.4	1834.8
Error	8	420.2	52.5
Total	11	5924.7	

$F = 1{,}834.8/52.5 = 34.95$. Reject H_0. At least one regression coefficient is not 0.

d. H_0 is rejected in all cases if $t < -2.306$ or if $t > 2.306$. Advertising and sales force should be retained, city dropped. (Note that dropping city removes the problem with multicollinearity.)

Predictor	Coef	Stdev	t-ratio	P
Constant	31.13	13.40	2.32	0.049
adv	2.1516	0.8049	2.67	0.028
sales	5.0140	0.9105	5.51	0.000
city	5.665	6.332	0.89	0.397

e. The new output is:

```
The regression equation is cars = 25.2952 +
2.6187 adv + 5.0233 sales
```

Predictor	Coef	Stdev	t-ratio
Constant	25.30	11.57	2.19
adv	2.6187	0.6057	4.32
sales	5.0233	0.9003	5.58

s = 7.167   R-sq = .922   R-sq(adj) = .905

Analysis of Variance

Source	DF	SS	MS
Regression	2	5462.4	2731.2
Error	9	462.3	51.4
Total	11	5924.7	

f.

```
Stem-and-leaf of C12    N = 12
Leaf Unit = 1.0
  1    -1  6
  1    -1
  2    -0  5
  5    -0  110
 (5)    0  01224
  2     0  58
```

The normality assumption is reasonable.

g.

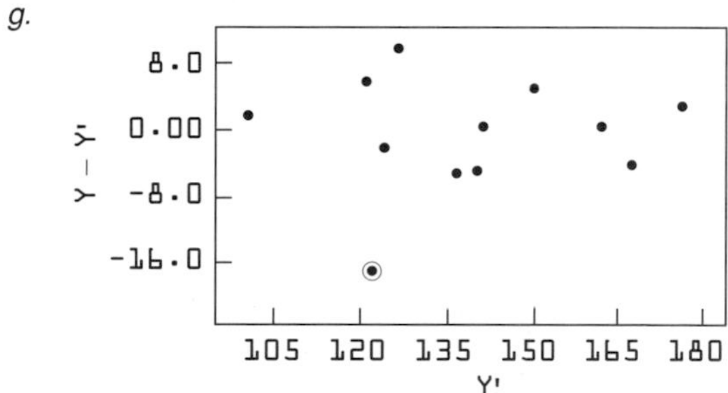

The circled value could be a problem. However, with a small sample the residual plot is acceptable.

15. *a.* Using MINITAB:

```
The regression equation is Profit = 965.2809
+ 2.8653 workers + 6.7538 divid + .2873 inv
```

$2,458,780

b.

Analysis of Variance

Source	DF	SS	MS
Regression	3	45510096	15170032
Error	12	12215892	1017991
Total	15	57725984	

$$F = \frac{15{,}170{,}032}{1{,}017{,}991} = 14.902$$

H_0 is rejected because computed F of 14.9 is greater than the critical value of 3.49. At least one of the regression coefficients is not zero.

c. H_0: $\beta_1 = 0$ $\beta_2 = 0$ $\beta_3 = 0$
H_1: $\beta_1 \neq 0$ $\beta_2 \neq 0$ $\beta_3 \neq 0$
The H_0s are rejected if $t < -2.179$ or $t > 2.179$. Both workers and dividends are not significant variables. Inventory is significant. Stepwise suggests inventory and workers be used.

d. The regression equation (if we used X_1 and X_3) is:
profit = 1,135 + 3.26 workers + 0.310 inv.
If we used only X_3 (inventory), the equation is
$Y' = 1,676.02 + .4738X_3$.

Predictor	Coef	Stdev	t-ratio
Constant	1134.8	418.6	2.71
Workers	3.258	1.434	2.27
inv	0.3099	0.1033	3.00

s = 986.7 R-sq = 78.1% R-sq(adj) = 74.7%

Analysis of Variance

Source	DF	SS	MS	F
Regression	2	45070624	22535312	23.15
Error	13	12655356	973489	
Total	15	57725968		

e.

Histogram of C12 N = 16

Midpoint	Count	
−1500	1	*
−1000	3	***
−500	1	*
0	6	******
500	2	**
1000	2	**
1500	0	
2000	1	*

The normality assumption is reasonable.

f.

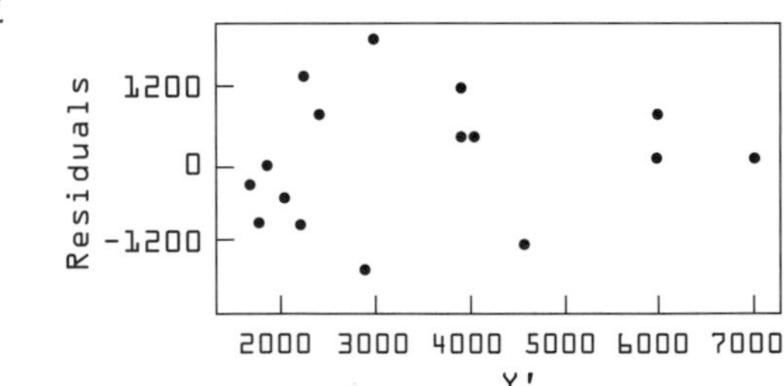

The plot of the residuals is acceptable.

17\. *a.* The MINITAB correlation matrix is:

	Profit	Daily
Daily	0.997	
Sunday	0.995	0.984

The two independent variables are highly correlated.

b. The regression equation is:

$$Y' = -0.643 + 0.401X_1 + 0.269X_2$$
$$Y' = -0.643 + 0.401(50) + 0.269(100) = 46.307$$

About $46.30 per week.

c. From MINITAB, 100 percent of the variation is accounted for by the two variables.

d. Each additional Sunday customer adds $0.269 profit per week, and a daily customer adds $0.401 per week.

e. The large R^2 is expected. There really is no other variable to be added.

19\. The MINITAB output is as follows:

The regression equation is
Salary = 652 + 13.4 Service − 6.71 Age + 206 Gender − 33.5 Job

Predictor	Coef	Stdev	t-ratio	p
Constant	651.9	345.3	1.89	0.071
Service	13.422	5.125	2.62	0.015
Age	−6.710	6.349	−1.06	0.301
Gender	205.65	90.27	2.28	0.032
Job	−33.45	89.55	−0.37	0.712

s = 236.5 R-sq = 43.3% R-sq(adj) = 34.2%

Analysis of Variance

SOURCE	DF	SS	MS	F	p
Regression	4	1066830	266708	4.77	0.005
Error	25	1398651	55946		
Total	29	2465481			

a. The regression equation is:

$$Y' = 651.9 + 13.422X_1 - 6.710X_2 + 205.65X_3 - 33.45X_4$$

b. $R^2 = .433$, which is somewhat low for this type of study.

c. H_0: $\beta_1 = \beta_2 = \beta_3 = \beta_4 = 0$; H_1: Not all β_i equal 0. Reject H_0 if $F > 2.76$.

$$F = \frac{1{,}066{,}830/4}{1{,}398{,}651/25} = 4.77$$

H_0 is rejected. Not all the β_i equal 0.

d. Using the .05 significance level, reject the hypothesis that the regression coefficient is 0 if $t < -2.060$ or $t > 2.060$. Service and gender should remain in the analysis; age and job should be dropped.

e. Following is the MINITAB output using the independent variables service and gender.

```
The regression equation is
Salary = 784 + 9.02 Service + 224 Gender

Predictor    Coef    Stdev   t-ratio       p
Constant    784.2    316.8      2.48   0.020
Service     9.021    3.106      2.90   0.007
Gender     224.41    87.35      2.57   0.016

s = 233.1     R-sq = 40.5%     R-sq(adj) = 36.1%

Analysis of Variance

SOURCE       DF        SS       MS      F       p
Regression    2    998779   499389   9.19   0.001
Error        27   1466703    54322
Total        29   2465481
```

A man earns $224 more per month than a woman, and each additional month of service adds about $9 to the monthly salary. The R^2 value of .405 is somewhat low.

21. From the MINITAB system, the output is as follows:

a.

```
The regression equation is
Wins = -81.3 + 827 Batting + 0.105 Homers + 0.0628
Stolen - 0.127 Errors - 15.3 ERA + 1.81 Turf

Predictor       Coef      Stdev   t-ratio       p
Constant      -81.32      28.62     -2.84   0.010
Batting        827.1      109.1      7.58   0.000
Homers       0.10538    0.04112      2.56   0.018
Stolen       0.06278    0.02583      2.43   0.024
Errors      -0.12689    0.04520     -2.81   0.011
ERA          -15.304      1.830     -8.36   0.000
Turf           1.812      1.964      0.92   0.367

s = 4.551     R-sq = 89.1%     R-sq(adj) = 86.0%

Analysis of Variance

SOURCE       DF        SS       MS       F       p
Regression    6   3553.09   592.18   28.59   0.000
Error        21    434.91    20.71
Total        27   3988.00
```

b. The R^2 value is .891.

c. H_0: $\beta_1 = \beta_2 = \beta_3 = \beta_4 = \beta_5 = \beta_6 = 0$; H_1: Not all β_i = zero. Reject H_0 if $F > 2.57$. The computed value of F is 28.59, so H_0 is rejected. Some of the regression coefficients do not equal zero.

d. The hypothesis that $\beta_i = 0$ is rejected if $t < -2.080$ or $t > 2.080$. H_0 is rejected for all the net regression coefficients except turf. The independent variable turf can be dropped.

e. The regression output for the variables batting, homers, stolen bases, errors, and ERA is as follows.

```
The regression equation is
Wins = -83.6 + 847 Batting + 0.0949 Homers + 0.0682
Stolen - 0.135 Errors - 15.4 ERA

Predictor       Coef      Stdev   t-ratio       p
Constant      -83.62      28.41     -2.94   0.008
Batting        847.3      106.5      7.95   0.000
Homers       0.09488    0.03938      2.41   0.025
Stolen       0.06821    0.02506      2.72   0.012

Errors      -0.13530    0.04412     -3.07   0.006
ERA          -15.426      1.819     -8.48   0.000

s = 4.535     R-sq = 88.7%     R-sq(adj) = 86.1%

Analysis of Variance

SOURCE       DF        SS       MS       F       p
Regression    5   3535.47   707.09   34.38   0.000
Error        22    452.53    20.57
Total        27   3988.00
```

f. The residuals appear to be normally distributed.

```
Histogram of RESI1    N = 28
Midpoint        Count
   -6             4  ****
   -4             4  ****
   -2             3  ***
    0             3  ***
    2             8  ********
    4             4  ****
    6             0
    8             1  *
   10             1  *
```

g. The condition of homoscedasticity is met. See the following diagram.

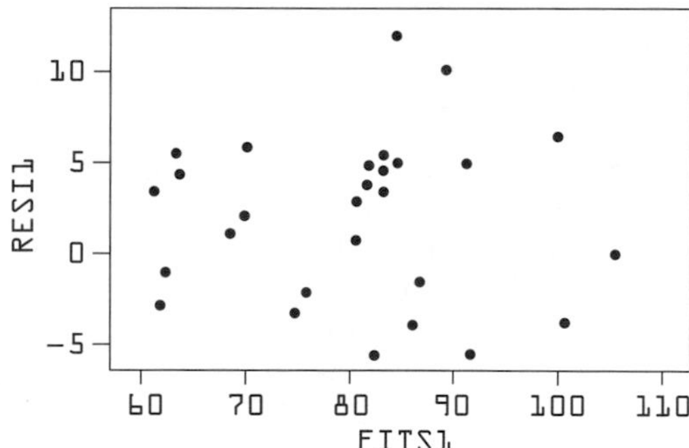

CHAPTER 14
Nonparametric Methods: Chi-Square Applications

1. *a.* There are $k - 1 = 3 - 1 = 2$ degrees of freedom. The critical value is 5.991. Reject H_0 if the computed value of χ^2 is greater than 5.991. Otherwise, do not reject H_0.

b. Computed value of χ^2 is 10.

f_0	f_e	$f_0 - f_e$	$(f_0 - f_e)^2$	$\frac{(f_0 - f_e)^2}{f_e}$
10	20	−10	100	5
20	20	0	0	0
30	20	10	100	5
60	60	0		10 ← χ^2

c. Since 10 > 5.991, reject H_0 and accept H_1.

3. H_0: Shoplifting accounts for half of the loss, employee theft 25 percent, and poor inventory control 25 percent.
H_1: Shoplifting is not as described above.
Computed $\chi^2 = 12.00$.

f_0	f_e	$f_0 - f_e$	$(f_0 - f_e)^2$	$\frac{(f_0 - f_e)^2}{f_e}$
60	50	10	100	2.0
30	25	5	25	1
10	25	−15	225	9.0
100	100	0		12.0 ← χ^2

12.0 is greater than the critical value of 7.824, so H_0 is rejected. Shoplifting does not account for twice the losses compared to theft or inventory control.

5. H_0: There is no difference in the population of opinions.
H_1: There is a difference in the population of opinions.
H_0 is rejected if computed chi-square is greater than 15.086. There are 5 degrees of freedom, found by 6 − 1.
Computed chi-square is 3.400. H_0 is not rejected. The differences are due to chance.

7. H_0: The sample response is representative of the population.
H_1: The response is not representative of the population.
There are 7 − 1 = 6 degrees of freedom. The critical value of chi-square is 12.592. Reject H_0 if the computed value is greater than 12.592.

College	f_0	Proportion	f_e	$\frac{(f_0 - f_e)^2}{f_e}$
A & S	90	.27	81	1.00
Business	45	.14	42	.21
Education	60	.19	57	.16
Engineering	30	.08	24	1.50
Law	15	.05	15	0
Pharmacy	15	.07	21	1.71
University	45	.20	60	3.75
				8.33

Computed $\chi^2 = 8.33$. H_0 is not rejected. The sample is representative of the population since 8.33 < 12.592.

9. There are $k - 1 = 5 - 1 = 4$ degrees of freedom. The critical value is 9.488, and computed chi-square is 19.60.

f_0	f_e	$f_0 - f_e$	$(f_0 - f_e)^2$	$\frac{(f_0 - f_e)^2}{f_e}$
67	56.4	10.6	112.36	1.99
22	37.6	−15.6	243.36	6.47
51	37.6	13.4	179.56	4.78
24	37.6	−13.6	184.96	4.92
24	18.8	5.2	27.04	1.44
188	188	0		19.60

Reject H_0 since 19.60 > 9.488. The observed distribution of M&M colors does not match the expected distribution.

11. Reject H_0 if $\chi^2 > 15.086$.
$df = 5$. To compute f_e:

Commission	z value	Area
Less than $900	Under −2.00	.0228
$900 to $1,200	−2.00 to −1.00	.1359
1,200 to 1,500	−1.00 to 0	.3413
1,500 to 1,800	0 to 1.00	.3413
1,800 to 2,100	1.00 to 2.00	.1359
$2,100 or more	Over 2.00	.0228
		1.000

To compute chi-square:

f_0	f_e	$\frac{(f_0 - f_e)^2}{f_e}$
9	11.40	0.51
63	67.95	0.36
165	170.65	0.19
180	170.65	0.51
71	67.95	0.14
12	11.40	0.03
500	500	1.74

There are $k - 1 = 6 - 1 = 5$ degrees of freedom. Critical value is 15.086. Since 1.74 < 15.086, we fail to reject H_0. The commissions are normally distributed.

13. H_0: Age is not related to the degree of pressure.
H_1: Age is related to the degree of pressure.
$df = (4 - 1)(3 - 1) = 6$. H_0 is rejected if $\chi^2 > 16.812$.

$$\chi^2 = 0.016 + 0.282 + 0.168 + \cdots + 0.178 = 2.191$$

Since 2.191 < 16.812, H_0 is not rejected. Age and pressure are not related.

15. H_0: There is no relationship between the manufacturer and the quality of the light bulbs.
H_1: There is a relationship between the quality of the light bulbs and the manufacturer.

$$df = (r - 1)(c - 1) = (2 - 1)(4 - 1) = 3$$

Reject H_0 if $\chi^2 > 7.815$
$\chi^2 = 3.66$, found by:

$(12 - 9)^2/9 + (8 - 9)^2/9 + \cdots + (89 - 91)^2/91 =$
$1.0 + 0.11 + 1.78 + 0.44 + 0.10 + 0.01 + 0.18 + 0.04$

Do not reject H_0 because $3.66 < 7.815$.

17. *a.* H_0: Unpaid balances are uniformly distributed by size.
H_1: Unpaid balances are not uniformly distributed by size.

b.

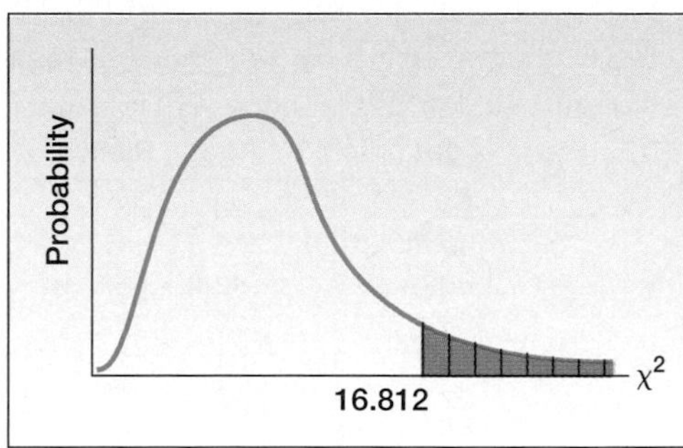

c. $df = 7 - 1 = 6$. H_0 is rejected if $\chi^2 > 16.812$. Computed chi-square = 2.332, found by:

Size	f_0	f_e	$\frac{(f_0 - f_e)^2}{f_e}$
< \$20	13	12	0.083
> \$20 but under \$40	10	12	0.333
> 40 but under 60	15	12	0.750
> 60 but under 80	14	12	0.333
> 80 but under 100	9	12	0.750
> 100 but under 150	12	12	0
150 and over	11	12	0.083
			2.332

Since $2.332 < 16.812$, H_0 is not rejected. The unpaid balances are uniformly distributed by size.

19. *a.* H_0: No relationship between pool and township.
H_1: There is a relationship.

Pool	Township 1	2	3	4	5
0	7	6	6	8	2
1	5	9	13	10	9

$df = 4$. Reject H_0 if $\chi^2 > 9.488$. Computed $\chi^2 = 4.571$. Do not reject H_0. No relationship shown between pool and township.

b. H_0: No relationship between garage and township.
H_1: There is a relationship.

Garage	Township 1	2	3	4	5
0	4	4	7	7	2
1	8	11	12	11	9

$df = 4$. Reject if $\chi^2 > 9.488$. Computed $\chi^2 = 1.768$. Do not reject H_0. No relationship shown between garage and township.

c.

Beds	f_0	z probability	f_e
2	18	.3156	23.67
3	21	.2597	19.48
4	16	.2798	17.24
5	8	.1319	9.89
6	9	.0491	8.68
7 or more.	3	.0139	1.04
	75	1.0000	75.00

$\chi^2 = 13.282$. H_0 is rejected because computed $\chi^2(13.282) >$ critical value of 11.345, $df = 6 - 1 - 2 = 3$. Not normally distributed.

CHAPTER 15
Nonparametric Methods: Analysis of Ranked Data

1. *a.* If the number of pluses (successes) in the sample is 9 or more, reject H_0.
b. Reject H_0 because the cumulative probability associated with nine successes (.073) does not exceed the significance level (.10).

3. *a.* H_0: $p \leq .50$, H_1: $p > .50$; $n = 10$.
b. H_0 is rejected if there are nine or more plus signs. A "+" represents a loss.
c. Reject H_0. It is an effective program, because there were 9 people that lost weight.

5. *a.* H_0: $p \leq .50$ (There is no change in weight).
H_1: $p > .50$ (There is a loss of weight. The program was effective.)
b. Do not reject H_0 if the computed value of z is less than or equal to 1.645. Otherwise, reject H_0. (A weight loss is considered a "+".)
c.

$$z = \frac{(32 - .50) - .50(45)}{.50\sqrt{45}}$$

$$= \frac{31.5 - 22.5}{3.354} = 2.683$$

d. Reject H_0 because 2.683 falls to the right of 1.645. The weight loss program is effective.

7. *a.* H_0: $p \leq .50$, H_1: $p > .50$.
H_0 is rejected if $z > 2.05$.

$$\mu = 81(.50) = 40.5$$

$$\sigma = \sqrt{81(.50)(.50)} = 4.5$$

$$z = \frac{42.5 - 40.5}{4.5} = 0.44$$

Since $0.44 < 2.05$, do not reject H_0. No preference.

9. *a.* H_0: Median $\leq$ \$40,000, H_1: Median > \$40,000.
b. H_0 is rejected if $z > 1.645$.

c.

$$\mu = 200(.50) = 100$$

$$\sigma = \sqrt{200(.50)(.50)} = 7.07$$

$$z = \frac{170 - .5 - 100}{7.07} = 9.83$$

H_0 is rejected. The median income is greater than $40,000.

11.

Absolute difference	Rank	Correctly signed
70	1	−1
90	2	2
120	3	−3
130	4	4
190	5	5
250	6	6
550	7	7

Sums: −4, + 24. So $T = 4$ (the smaller of the two sums). From Appendix J, .05 level, one-tailed test, $N = 7$, the critical value is 3. Since the T of $4 > 3$, do not reject H_0 (one-tailed test). There is no difference in square footage. Yuppies do not live in larger homes.

13. *a.* H_0: The production is the same for the two systems.
H_1: Production using the Mump method is greater.
b. H_0 is rejected if $T \leq 21$, $N = 13$.
c. The calculations for the first three employees are:

Employee	Old	Mump	*d*	Rank	R^+	R^-
A	60	64	4	6	6	
B	40	52	12	12.5	12.5	
C	59	58	−1	2		2

The sum of the negative ranks is 6.5, which is smaller than the sum of the positive ranks. Since 6.5 is less than 21, H_0 is rejected. Production using the Mump method is greater. (*Note:* Answers will vary.)

15. H_0: The distributions are the same.
H_1: The distributions are not the same.
Reject H_0 if $z < -1.96$ or $z > 1.96$.

A		B	
Score	Rank	Score	Rank
38	4	26	1
45	6	31	2
56	9	35	3
57	10.5	42	5
61	12	51	7
69	14	52	8
70	15	57	10.5
79	16	62	13
	86.5		49.5

$$z = \frac{86.5 - \frac{8(8+8+1)}{2}}{\sqrt{\frac{8(8)(8+8+1)}{12}}} = \frac{18.5}{9.5219} = 1.943$$

H_0 is not rejected. There is no difference in the two populations.

17. H_0: The distributions are the same.
H_1: The distribution of Country is skewed to the right.
Reject H_0 if $z > 1.645$.

Country		Rock	
Age	Rank	Age	Rank
26	6	28	8
42	16.5	16	1
65	22	42	16.5
38	13	29	9.5
29	9.5	31	11
32	12	22	3
59	21	50	20
42	16.5	42	16.5
27	7	23	4
41	14	25	5
46	19		94.5
18	2		
	158.5		

$$z = \frac{158.5 - \frac{12(12+10+1)}{2}}{\sqrt{\frac{12(10)(12+10+1)}{12}}} = \frac{20.50}{15.1658} = 1.35$$

H_0 is not rejected. There is no difference in the distributions.

19. ANOVA requires that we have two or more populations, the data be interval-, or ratio-level, the populations be normally distributed, and the population standard deviations be equal. Kruskal-Wallis requires only ordinal-level data, and no assumptions are made regarding the shape of the populations.

21. *a.* H_0: The three population distributions are equal.
b. If the computed value of H is greater than 5.991, reject H_0. If it is 5.991 or less, do not reject H_0. (Use Appendix I, the chi-square distribution.)
c. $H = 8.98$, found by:

Rank	Rank	Rank
8	5	1
11	6.5	2
14.5	6.5	3
14.5	10	4
16	12	9
64	13	19
	53	

$$H = \frac{12}{16(16+1)}\left[\frac{(64)^2}{5} + \frac{(53)^2}{6} + \frac{(19)^2}{5}\right] - 3(16+1)$$
$$= 59.98 - 51 = 8.98$$

d. Reject H_0 because $8.98 > 5.991$. The three distributions are not equal.

23. H_0: The distributions of the lengths of life are the same.
H_1: The distributions of the lengths of life are not the same.
H_0 is rejected if $H > 9.210$. (Refer to the χ^2 table, Appendix I, for the critical value.)

Salt		Fresh		Weeds	
Hours	Rank	Hours	Rank	Hours	Rank
167.3	3	160.6	1	182.7	13
189.6	15	177.6	11	165.4	2
177.2	10	185.3	14	172.9	7
169.4	6	168.6	4	169.2	5
180.3	12	176.6	9	174.7	8
	46		39		35

$H = 0.62$, found by:

$$\frac{12}{15(16)}\left[\frac{(46)^2}{5} + \frac{(39)^2}{5} + \frac{(35)^2}{5}\right] - 3(16)$$

H_0 is not rejected. There is no difference in the three distributions.

25. *a.*

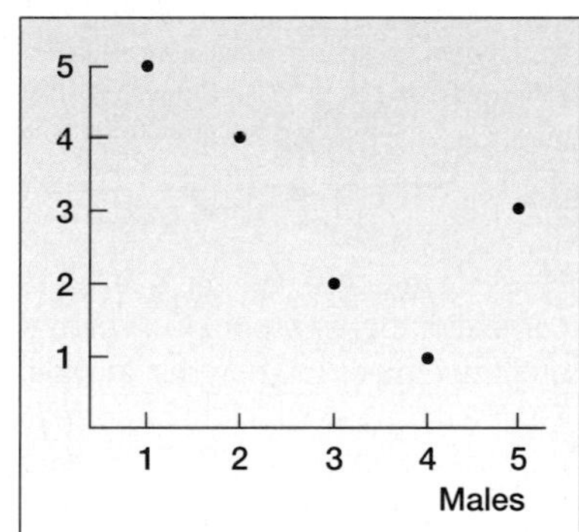

b.

Rank, males	Rank, females	d	d^2
1	5	−4	16
4	1	3	9
3	2	1	1
2	4	−2	4
5	3	2	4
			34

$$r_s = 1 - \frac{6(34)}{5(5^2-1)} = 1 - 1.7 = -.7$$

Fairly strong negative correlation among the ranks.

27.

Representative	Sales	Rank	Training rank	d	d^2
1	319	3	3	0	0
2	150	10	9	1	1
3	175	9	6	3	9
4	460	1	1	0	0
5	348	2	4	−2	4
6	300	4.5	10	−5.5	30.25
7	280	6	5	1	1
8	200	7	2	5	25
9	190	8	7	1	1
10	300	4.5	8	−3.5	12.25
					83.5

a. $r_s = 1 - \frac{6(83.5)}{10(10^2-1)} = 1 - 0.506 = .494.$

b. A moderate positive correlation.

c. H_0: No correlation among the ranks.
H_1: A positive correlation among the ranks.
Reject H_0 if $t > 1.860$.

$$t = .494\sqrt{\frac{10-2}{1-(.494)^2}} = 1.607$$

H_0 is not rejected. We conclude that the correlation in the population among the ranks could be 0.

29. *a.* Two-tailed.

b. $n = 19$. H_0 is rejected if there are either 5 or fewer "+" signs, or 14 or more. The total of 12 "+" signs falls in the acceptance region. H_0 is not rejected. There is no preference between the two shows.

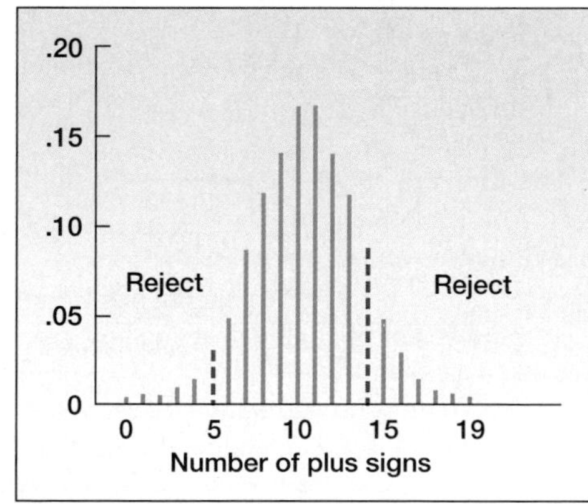

c. The two westerns would be equally popular.

31. H_0: $p = .50$
H_1: $p \neq .50$
H_0 is rejected if there are 12 or more, or 3 or fewer plus signs. Since there are only 8 plus signs, H_0 is not rejected. There is no preference with respect to the two brands of components.

33. H_0: $p = .50$, H_1: $p \neq .50$, $\mu = 100$, $\sigma = 7.071$.
Reject if $z > 1.96$ or $z < -1.96$.
Computed $z = 8.42$, found by $(160 - .5 - 100)/7.071$.
Reject H_0. There is a difference in the preference for the two types of orange juice.
35. H_0: Rates are the same. H_1: The rates are not the same.
H_0 is rejected if $\chi^2 > 5.991$. $H = 0.082$. Do not reject H_0.
37. H_0: The populations are the same.
H_1: The populations differ.
Reject H_0 if $\chi^2 > 7.815$. $H = 14.30$
Reject H_0; accept H_1.
39. $$r_s = 1 - \frac{6(78)}{12(12^2 - 1)} = 1 - 0.273 = .727$$
H_0: There is no correlation between the rankings of the coaches and the sports writers.
H_1: There is a positive correlation between the rankings of the coaches and the sports writers.
Reject H_0 if $t > 1.812$.
$$t = .727\sqrt{\frac{12 - 2}{1 - (.727)^2}} = 3.348$$
H_0 is rejected. There is a positive correlation between the rankings of the sports writers and the coaches.
41. *a.* Using the MINITAB system, the correlation between the starting position and the order of finish is .275.
H_0: There is no correlation between start and finish positions.
H_1: There is a positive correlation between start and finish positions.
Reject H_0 if $t > 1.69$.
$$t = .275\sqrt{\frac{33 - 2}{1 - (.275)^2}} = 1.593$$
H_0 is not rejected. We cannot show a correlation between starting and finishing positions.
b. $r_s = .265$
H_0: There is no correlation between the rank of the number of laps completed and starting position.
H_1: There is a positive correlation between the rank of the number of laps completed and the starting position.
Reject H_0 if $t > 1.69$.
$$t = .265\sqrt{\frac{33 - 2}{1 - (.265)^2}} = 1.530$$
H_0 is not rejected. We cannot reject the hypothesis of no correlation among the ranks.
43. *a.* H_0: The distributions of team salaries are the same.
H_1: The distributions of team salaries are not the same.
Reject H_0 if $z < -1.96$ or $z > 1.96$.
$$z = \frac{224.5 - \dfrac{14(14 + 14 + 1)}{2}}{\sqrt{\dfrac{14(14)(14 + 14 + 1)}{12}}} = \frac{21.5}{21.7639} = 0.989$$
$$P(z < -0.99) + P(z > 0.99) = 2(.5000 - .3389) = .3222$$
Using the *t* distribution:
$$s_p^2 = \frac{(14 - 1)(7.88)^2 + (14 - 1)(10.2)^2}{14 + 14 - 2} = 83.0672$$
$$t = \frac{32.60 - 28.6}{\sqrt{83.0672\left(\dfrac{1}{14} + \dfrac{1}{14}\right)}} = 1.161$$
The MINITAB system reports the *p*-value as .25, so the assumption of a normal distribution yields somewhat different results.
b. H_0: There is no correlation between the rank of wins and the rank of salary.
H_1: There is a positive correlation between the rank of wins and the rank of salary.
Reject H_0 if $t > 1.706$. From MINITAB, $r_s = .238$.
$$t = .238\sqrt{\frac{28 - 2}{1 - (.238)^2}} = 1.249$$
H_0 is not rejected. We have failed to show a correlation between the rank of team salary and the rank of the number of wins.
The Pearson's coefficient of correlation between the two variables is .301. The value of *t* from testing the hypothesis of no correlations is 1.609, found by:
$$t = \frac{.301\sqrt{28 - 2}}{\sqrt{1 - (.301)^2}} = 1.609$$
Both distributions are approximately normal, so using Pearson's coefficient of correlation is reasonable.

CHAPTER 16
Statistical Quality Control

1. Chance variations are usually large in number and random in nature and usually cannot be eliminated.

Assignable variation is usually nonrandom and can be eliminated.

3. *a.* The A_2 factor is 0.729.
   b. The value for D_3 is 0, and for D_4 it is 2.282.

5. *a.*

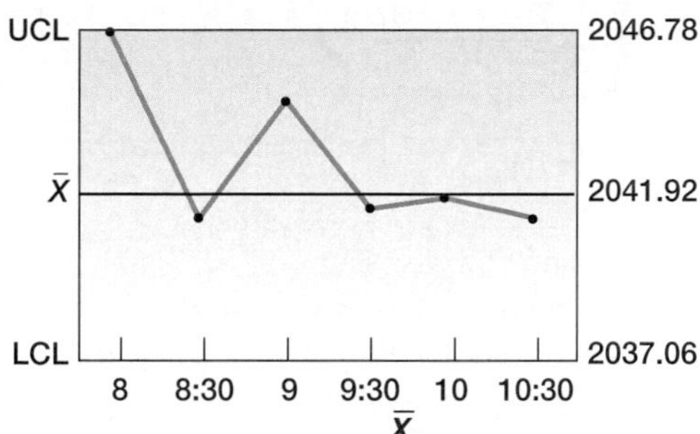

Time	$\bar{X}$, arithmetic mean	*R*, range
8:00 A.M.	46	16
8:30 A.M.	40.5	6
9:00 A.M.	44	6
9:30 A.M.	40	2
10:00 A.M.	41.5	9
10:30 A.M.	39.5	1
	251.5	40

$$\bar{\bar{X}} = \frac{251.5}{6} = 41.92$$

$$\begin{aligned} \text{UCL} &= \bar{\bar{X}} + A_2\bar{R} \\ &= 41.92 + 0.729(6.67) \\ &= 46.78 \\ \text{LCL} &= \bar{\bar{X}} - A_2\bar{R} \\ &= 41.92 - 0.729(6.67) \\ &= 37.06 \end{aligned}$$

   b. Interpreting, the mean reading was 2,041.92 degrees Fahrenheit. If the oven continues operating as evidenced by the first six hourly readings, about 99.7 percent of the mean readings will lie between 2,037.06 degrees and 2,046.78 degrees.

7. *a.* $\bar{p} = \frac{.48}{10} = .048$

$$.048 \pm 3\sqrt{\frac{.048(1 - .048)}{50}} = .048 \pm .091$$

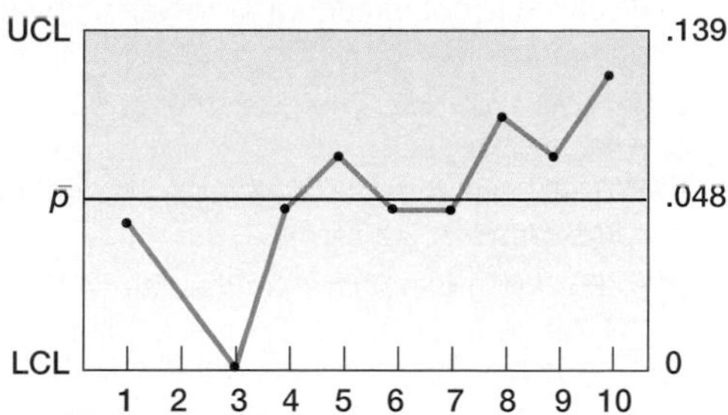

   The limits are from 0 to .139.
   b. 10/50 = .20, so this reading is out of control. The process should be adjusted.

9. *a.* $\bar{c} = \frac{24}{10} = 2.40 \quad 2.40 \pm 3\sqrt{2.40} = 2.40 \pm 4.65$

   The limits are from 0 to 7.05.
   b. The unit that had 6 defects is not out of control because 6 < 7.05; that is, 6 falls below the UCL of 7.05.

11.

Percent defective	Probability of accepting lot
10	.889
20	.558
30	.253
40	.083

13. $P(X \leq 1 \mid n = 10, p = .10) = .736$
    $P(X \leq 1 \mid n = 10, p = .20) = .375$
    $P(X \leq 1 \mid n = 10, p = .30) = .149$
    $P(X \leq 1 \mid n = 10, p = .40) = .046$

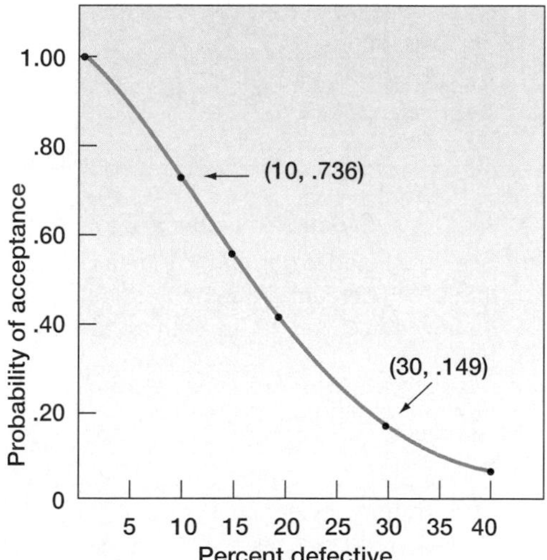

15. *a.* $\bar{\bar{X}} = 10.0, \bar{R} = 0.25$. For mean chart, UCL = 10.0 + 0.577(0.25) = 10.14
    LCL = 9.86. For range chart UCL = 2.115(0.25) = 0.53, LCL = 0.

b. Process is out of control for means, but in control for variation.

17. *a.* $\bar{p} = 93/15 = 6.2$. Then $6.2/200 = .031$.
    b. UCL = .068, LCL = 0.
    c. No. 10 packages = .05, which does not exceed UCL of .068.

19. *a, b.* For the mean chart: central line = 45.2; UCL = 54.3; LCL = 36.1. Control limits computed by $\bar{\bar{X}} \pm A_2\bar{R} = 45.2 \pm 0.729(12.5)$. The factor A_2 is from Appendix B. For the range chart: central line = 12.5; UCL = 28.5; LCL = 0. Control limits computed by:

$$D_4\bar{R} = 2.282(12.5)$$
$$D_3\bar{R} = (0)(12.5)$$

21. *a.*

$$\bar{p} = \frac{.80}{10} = .08$$

To find UCL and LCL:

$$.08 \pm 3\sqrt{\frac{(.08)(.92)}{50}}$$
$$.08 \pm 3(.038)$$
$$\text{UCL} = .1952$$
$$\text{LCL} = 0$$

b.

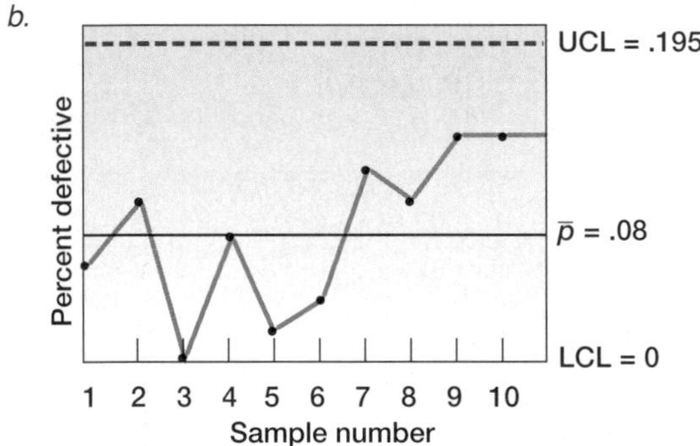

c. The upper and lower control limits indicate that 99.73 percent of the percent defectives will be between 0 and 19.52, with an average of 8 percent.

23. $\bar{c} = 47/20 = 2.35$.
    UCL and LCL $= 2.35 \pm 3\sqrt{2.35} = 0$ and 6.95.

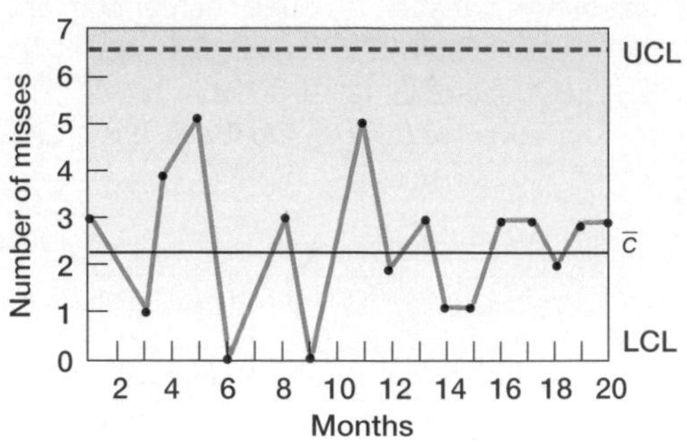

There is no upward trend.

25. $P(x \leq 3 \mid n = 20, p = .10) = .867$
    $P(x \leq 3 \mid n = 20, p = .20) = .412$
    $P(x \leq 3 \mid n = 20, p = .30) = .108$

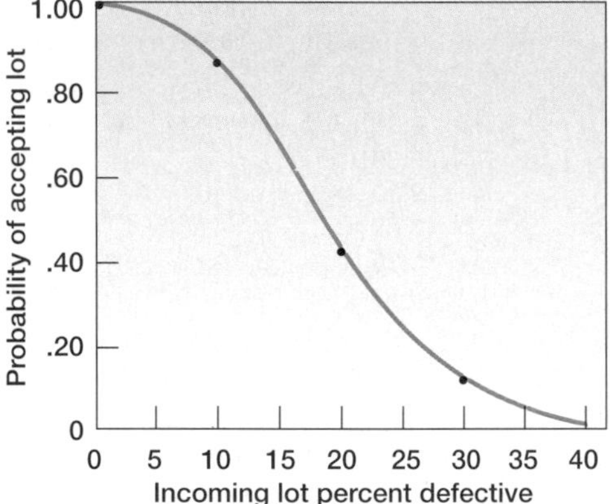

CHAPTER 17
Index Numbers

1. *a.* 127.8, found by (\$115,500/\$90,400)(100). Price increased by 27.8 percent from 1981 to 1994.
   b. 129.1, found by (\$87,200/\$67,550)(100). The loan amount increased 29.1 percent between 1981–82 and 1994.

3. *a.* 121.0, found by (\$97.71/\$80.75)(100).

1983 Price		Amount consumed	1995 Price		
Fruit	p_0	q_0	p_0q_0	p_t	p_0p_t
Bananas	\$0.23	100	\$23.00	\$0.35	\$35.00
Grapefruit	0.29	50	14.50	0.27	13.50
Apples	0.35	85	29.75	0.35	29.75
Strawberries	1.02	8	8.16	1.69	13.52
Oranges	0.89	6	5.34	0.99	5.94
			\$80.75		\$97.71

   b. Prices of fruits in 1995 were 21.0 percent more than they were in 1983.

5. *a.* $Q = 90.4$, found by (\$1,975.92/\$2,186.53)(100).
   $V = 93.8$, found by (\$2,051.81/\$2,186.53)(100).

	p_0	q_0	p_0q_0	p_t	q_t	p_0q_t	p_tq_t
Oats	$1.52	200	$ 304.00	$1.87	214	$ 325.28	$ 400.18
Wheat	2.10	565	1,186.50	2.05	489	1,026.90	1,002.45
Corn	1.48	291	430.68	1.48	203	300.44	300.44
Barley	3.05	87	265.35	3.29	106	323.30	348.74
			$2,186.53			$1,975.92	$2,051.81

Quantity declined 9.6 percent between 1977 and 1995.

b. Value declined 6.2 percent between 1977 and 1995.

7. *a.*

$$\frac{6.8}{5.3}(100)(.20) = 25.66$$

$$\frac{362.26}{265.88}(100)(.40) = 54.50$$

$$\frac{125.0}{109.6}(100)(.25) = 28.51$$

$$\frac{\$622,864}{\$529,917}(100)(.15) = \frac{17.63}{126.3}$$

b. Business activity increased 26.3 percent from 1989 to 1995.

9.

Period	Money income	CPI	Real income
1982–84	$19,800	100	$19,800
1994	32,000	149.7	21,376

The purchasing power has increased since 1982–84 by $1,576, found by $21,376 − $19,800.

11. The real incomes are:

Year	CPI	Mining	Apparel	Printing & publishing	Retail
1989	124.0	459.48	188.98	332.54	152.19
1990	130.7	459.53	183.53	326.23	149.40
1994	146.8	463.62	201.02	333.92	143.26

The weekly salary in mining and printing has stayed about the same. The weekly salary in apparel has increased about $12, while the weekly salary in retail has declined about $9.00.

13. *a.*

Year	International index	Cost index
1983	100.00	100.00
1984	101.14	100.65
1985	102.92	104.98
1986	128.32	106.60
1987	162.79	119.81
1988	187.30	133.33
1989	206.44	140.95
1990	245.77	159.46
1991	262.45	170.27
1992	290.01	189.47
1993	293.61	194.05

b. International sales have gone up nearly threefold and the cost of products sold has doubled during the period.

15. *a.*

Year	Construction	Real estate	Trade	Utilities
1979	100.00	100.00	100.00	100.00
1983	129.15	138.33	132.77	129.26
1987	139.15	166.23	148.07	144.24
1991	149.41	193.85	194.34	154.58
1994	166.58	221.38	187.41	171.33

b. The largest increase was in finance, insurance, and real estate, where the increase was more than 121 percent. There was a 66.58 percent increase in construction, which was the smallest.

17. 1982–84 = 100. Purchasing power of a dollar is $1.00. For November 1994 = $0.67, found by ($1/149.7)100.
Purchasing power of a dollar declined $0.33 between those two periods.

19. *a.* For 1994:

Retail sales	34.01*
Bank deposits	10.46
Industrial production	41.42
Employment	37.09
	122.98

*(1971.0/1,159)(100)(.20)

b. Economy up 22.98 percent from 1983 to 1994.

21.

Item	p_0q_0	p_tq_t	p_tq_0	p_0q_t
Cabbage	$120	$ 75	$100	$ 90
Carrots	20	24	24	20
Peas	80	90	72	100
Endive	15	30	15	30
	$235	$219	$211	$240

a. P = ($211/$235)100 = 89.8. Prices down 10.2 percent from 1977 to 1995.

b. P = ($219/$240)100 = 91.3. Prices down 8.7 percent.

c. Laspeyres uses 1977 quantities for the base; Paasche uses 1995 quantities for the base.

d. Q = ($240/$235)100 = 102.1. Production increased 2.1 percent from 1977 to 1995.

e. V = ($219/$235)100 = 93.2. Value down 6.8 percent from 1977 to 1995.

23. *a.* 686.6, found by ($1,864,912/$271,624.40)100.
b. $721.6, found by ($1,864,912/$258,437)100.

25. Basically, if the CPI increases from 140.5 to 141.0, wages go up 5 cents an hour—or a certain percent.

CHAPTER 18
Time Series and Forecasting

1.

Year	Number of failures	t	Yt	t^2
1990	79	1	79	1
1991	120	2	240	4
1992	138	3	414	9
1993	184	4	736	16
1994	200	5	1,000	25
	721	15	2,469	55

$$b = \frac{2{,}469 - (721)(15)/5}{55 - (15)^2/5} = \frac{306}{10} = 30.6$$

$$a = \frac{721}{5} - 30.6\left(\frac{15}{5}\right) = 52.4$$

For 1997, $t = 8$.

$$Y' = 52.4 + 30.6t = 52.4 + 30.6(8) = 297.2$$

3.

Year	Scrap	t	Yt	t^2
1991	2.0	1	2.0	1
1992	4.0	2	8.0	4
1993	3.0	3	9.0	9
1994	5.0	4	20.0	16
1995	6.0	5	30.0	25
	20.0	15	69.0	55

$$b = \frac{69.0 - (20)(15)/5}{55 - (15)^2/5} = \frac{9}{10} = 0.90$$

$$a = \frac{20.0}{5} - 0.90\left(\frac{15}{5}\right) = 1.30$$

$$Y' = 1.30 + 0.90t = 1.30 + 0.90(7) = 7.6 \text{ (tons)}$$

5. *a.*

Year	Sales	log (sales)	t	Yt	t^2
1990	1.1	0.041393	1	0.041393	1
1991	1.5	0.176091	2	0.352182	4
1992	2.0	0.301030	3	0.903090	9
1993	2.4	0.380211	4	1.520845	16
1994	3.1	0.491362	5	2.456808	25
		1.390087	15	5.274318	55

$$b = \frac{5.274318 - (1.390087)(15)/5}{55 - (15)^2/5} = \frac{1.104057}{10} = 0.1104057$$

$$a = \frac{1.390087}{5} - 0.1104057\left(\frac{15}{5}\right) = -0.0531997$$

b. 28.95 percent, found by 1 − 1.28945 − 1.0.

c. $Y' = -0.0531997 + 0.1104057t$
$= -0.0531997 + 0.1104057(8) = 0.8300459$
Antilog of 0.8300459 = 6.76

7. The output from the CBS system is as follows.

```
Classical Seasonal Indices
Period  Quarter  Value   Trend     S-I
  1        1       4       –        –
           2      10       –        –
           3       7    6.1250   1.1429
           4       3    6.5000   0.4615
  2        1       5    7        0.7143
           2      12    7.3750   1.6271
           3       9    7.6250   1.1803
           4       4    8.2500   0.4848
  3        1       6    9.1250   0.6575
           2      16    9.5000   1.6842
           3      12       –        –
           4       4       –        –
Seasonal Index by Quarter
              Average SI   Seasonal
   Quarter    Component     Index
      1        0.6859       0.6911
      2        1.6557       1.6682
      3        1.1616       1.1704
      4        0.4732       0.4768
```

9.

t	Estimated pairs (millions)	Seasonal index	Quarterly forecast (millions)
21	40.05	110.0	44.055
22	41.80	120.0	50.160
23	43.55	80.0	34.840
24	45.30	90.0	40.770

11.

Row	Qtr.	Index	Absent	Deseason	Time
1	1	0.6911	4	5.7879	1
2	2	1.6682	10	5.9945	2
3	3	1.1704	7	5.9809	3
4	4	0.4768	3	6.2919	4
5	1	0.6911	5	7.2348	5
6	2	1.6682	12	7.1934	6
7	3	1.1704	9	7.6897	7
8	4	0.4768	4	8.3893	8
9	1	0.6911	6	8.6818	9
10	2	1.6682	16	9.5912	10
11	3	1.1704	12	10.2529	11
12	4	0.4768	4	8.3893	12

Using MINITAB, the results are as follows.

```
MTB > regr c4 1 c5;
The regression equation is
Deseason = 5.17 + 0.378 Time

Predictor    Coef      Stdev     t-ratio     P
Constant    5.1658    0.3628      14.24    0.000
Time        0.37805   0.04930      7.67    0.000
```

Using the regression equation $Y' = 5.1658 + 0.37805t$, the following estimates were obtained.

Estimate	Index	Seasonally adjusted
10.080	0.6911	6.966
10.458	1.6682	17.446
10.837	1.1704	12.684
11.215	0.4768	5.343

13\. *a.* $Y' = 18{,}000 - 400t$, assuming the straight line starts at 18,000 in 1975 and goes down to 10,000 in 1995.

b. 400

c. 8,000, found by 18,000 − 400(25).

15\. *a.*

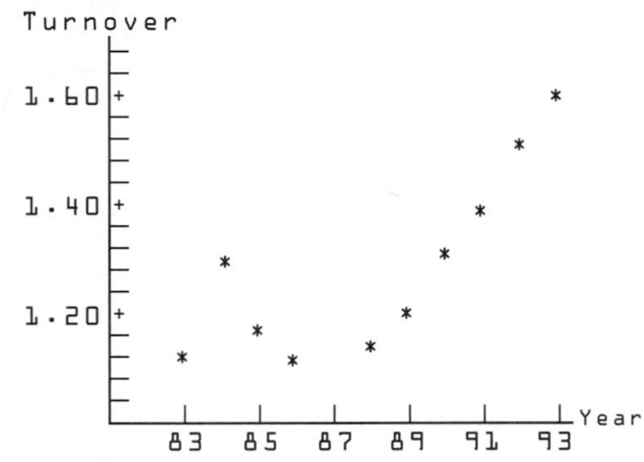

b. Using the MINITAB system, the regression equation using $t = 1$ for 1983 is

$$Y' = 1.00455 + 0.04409t$$

c. The estimates for 1986 and 1991 are:

$$Y' = 1.00455 + 0.04409(4) = 1.18091$$
$$Y' = 1.00455 + 0.04409(9) = 1.40136$$

d. The estimate for 1998 is:

$$Y' = 1.00455 + 0.04409(16) = 1.70999$$

e. Assets turned over an average of 0.044 times per year.

17\. *a.*

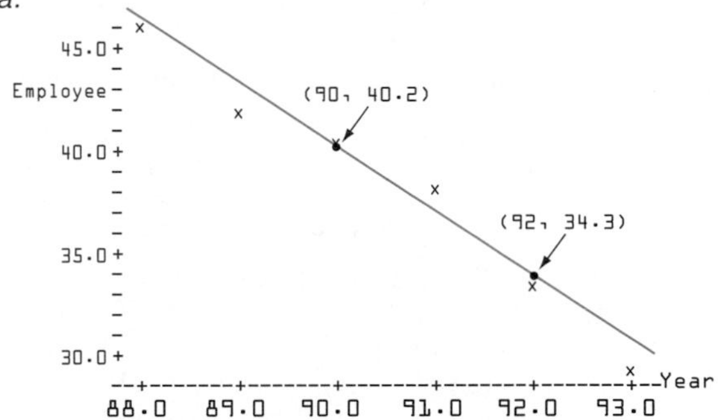

b. From the MINITAB system, the regression equation using $t = 1$ for 1988 is:

$$Y' = 49.140 - 2.9829t$$

c. For 1990:

$$Y' = 49.140 - 2.9829(3) = 40.1913$$

For 1992:

$$Y' = 49.140 - 2.9829(5) = 34.2255$$

d. For 1996:

$$Y' = 49.140 - 2.9829(9) = 22.2939$$

e. The number of employees decreased at a rate of about 3,000 per year (2,983 actual).

19\. *a.* Using the MINITAB system, the equation, in log form, is:

$$Y' = 0.790231 + 0.113669t$$

b. For 1988:

$$Y' = 0.790231 + 0.113669(4) = 1.244907 \qquad \text{antilog is } 17.575$$

For 1993:

$$Y' = 0.79023 + 0.113669(9) = 1.813252 \qquad \text{antilog is } 65.05$$

c. 29.92, found by the antilog of 0.113669 minus 1.

d. $Y' = 0.79023 + 0.113669(12) = 2.154258$ antilog is 142.65

21\. *a.* Using the MINITAB system, the logarithmic equation is:

$$Y' = 0.0109 + 0.16842t$$

b. $Y' = 0.0109 + 0.16842(18) = 3.04246$ antilog is 1102.71

c. 47.4 percent per year, found by antilog of 0.16842 minus 1 (1.47373 − 1.0 = 0.47373).

23\. *a.* July 87.5; August 92.9; September 99.3; October 109.1.

b.

Month	Total	Mean	Corrected
July	348.9	87.225	86.777
Aug.	368.1	92.025	91.552
Sept.	395.0	98.750	98.242
Oct.	420.4	105.100	104.560
Nov.	496.2	124.050	123.412
Dec.	572.3	143.075	142.340
Jan.	333.5	83.375	82.946
Feb.	297.5	74.375	73.993
March	347.3	86.825	86.379
April	481.3	120.325	119.707
May	396.2	99.050	98.541
June	368.1	92.025	91.552
		1,206.200	

Correction = 1,200/1,206.2 = 0.99486

c. April, November, and December are periods of high sales, while February is low.

25\. *a.* The output from the CBS software is as follows.

```
Model: Seasonal Indices
Number of Periods: 24
Classical Seasonal Indices
Period  Quarter  Value   Trend      S-I
  1       1       142     –          –
          2       312     –          –
          3       488    288        1.6944
          4       208    289.2500   0.7191
  2       1       146    293        0.4983
          2       318    296.5000   1.0725
          3       512    298.7500   1.7138
          4       212    302        0.7020
  3       1       160    314.7500   0.5083
          2       330    322.8750   1.0221
          3       602    319.5000   1.8842
          4       187    320.2500   0.5839
  4       1       158    317.5000   0.4976
          2       338    312.3750   1.0820
          3       572    311.5000   1.8363
          4       176    317.2500   0.5548
  5       1       162    321.3750   0.5041
          2       380    323.2500   1.1756
          3       563    326.2500   1.7257
          4       200    324        0.6173
  6       1       162    324.7500   0.4988
          2       362    328.3750   1.1024
          3       587     –          –
          4       205     –          –
          Seasonal Index by Quarter
                Average SI  Seasonal
        Quarter Component    Index
           1     0.5014      0.5027
           2     1.0909      1.0936
           3     1.7709      1.7753
           4     0.6354      0.6370
```

b. The production is the largest in the third quarter; it is 77.5 percent above the average quarter. The second quarter is also above average. The first and fourth quarters are well below average, with the first quarter at about 50 percent of a typical quarter.

27\. *a.* The CBS system was used to determine the seasonal indexes.

```
Model: Seasonal Indices
Number of Periods: 20
Classical Seasonal Indices
Period  Quarter   Value    Trend     S-I
  1       1       4.4000    –         –
          2       6.1000    –         –
          3      11.7000  7.3125   1.6000
          4       7.2000  7.3375   0.9813
  2       1       4.1000  7.3250   0.5597
          2       6.6000  7.4250   0.8889
          3      11.1000  7.5750   1.4653
          4       8.6000  7.5750   1.1353
  3       1       3.9000  7.7125   0.5057
          2       6.8000  7.9625   0.8540
          3      12       8.2375   1.4568
          4       9.7000  8.4125   1.1530
  4       1       5       8.5375   0.5857
          2       7.1000  8.5375   0.8316
          3      12.7000  8.3625   1.5187
          4       9       8.0375   1.1198
  5       1       4.3000  7.5625   0.5686
          2       5.2000  7.1500   0.7273
          3      10.8000    –         –
          4       7.6000    –         –
          Seasonal Index by Quarter
                Average SI  Seasonal
        Quarter Component    Index
           1     0.5549      0.5577
           2     0.8254      0.8296
           3     1.5102      1.5178
           4     1.0973      1.1029
```

b. The MINITAB system was used to determine the trend equation.

```
The regression equation is
Deseason = 7.667 + 0.0023 Code
Predictor    Coef      Stdev    t-ratio     P
Constant   7.6696    0.3196      24.00   0.000
Code       0.00227   0.02876      0.08   0.938
```

c.

Period	Production	Index	Forecast
21	7.7153	0.5577	4.3028
22	7.7176	0.8296	6.4025
23	7.7199	1.5178	11.7173
24	7.7222	1.1029	8.5168

29\. Using the CBS system, the index for each quarter was:

```
      Seasonal Index by Quarter
              Average SI  Seasonal
   Quarter    Component    Index
      1        1.1962     1.2053
      2        1.0135     1.0212
      3        0.6253     0.6301
      4        1.1371     1.1457
```

The MINITAB output is:

```
The regression equation is
Y' = 43.6 + 7.22 C1
```

```
Predictor     Coef      Stdev    t-ratio      P
Constant     43.611     7.600      5.74    0.000
Year          7.2153    0.4579    15.76    0.000
```

Period	Visitors	Index	Forecast
29	252.86	1.2053	304.77
30	260.07	1.0212	265.58
31	267.29	0.6301	168.42
32	274.50	1.1457	314.50

In 1994 there were a total of 928 visitors. A 10 percent increase in 1995 means there will be 1,021 visitors. The quarterly estimates are 1021/4 = 255.25 visitors per quarter.

Period	Visitors	Index	Forecast
Winter	255.25	1.2053	307.65
Spring	255.25	1.0212	260.66
Summer	255.25	0.6301	160.83
Fall	255.25	1.1457	292.44

The regression approach is probably superior because the trend is considered.

CHAPTER 19
An Introduction to Decision Making under Uncertainty

1. $EMV(A_1) = .30(\$50) + .50(\$70) + .20(\$100) = \$70$
   $EMV(A_2) = .30(\$90) + .50(\$40) + .20(\$80) = \$63$
   $EMV(A_3) = .30(\$70) + .50(\$60) + .20(\$90) = \$69$
   Decision: Choose alternative 1.

3.

	Opportunity loss		
	S_1	S_2	S_3
A_1	$40	$ 0	$ 0
A_2	0	30	20
A_3	20	10	10

5. (Answers in $000)

$EOL(A_1) = .30(\$40) + .50(\$0) + .20(\$0) = \$12$
$EOL(A_2) = .30(\$0) + .50(\$30) + .20(\$20) = 19$
$EOL(A_3) = .30(\$20) + .50(\$10) + .20(\$10) = 13$

7. Expected value under conditions of certainty is $82, found by .30($90) + .50($70) + .20($100) = $82

   EVPI = $82 − $70 = $12

9. Yes, it changes the decision. Choose alternative 2. (Answers in $000.)

   $EMV(A_1) = .50(\$50) + .20(\$70) + .30(\$100) = \$69$
   $EMV(A_2) = .50(\$90) + .20(\$40) + .30(\$80) = \$77$
   $EMV(A_3) = .50(\$70) + .20(\$60) + .30(\$90) = \$74$

11. *a.* (Answers in $000)

   EMV(neither) = .30($0) + .50($0) + .20($0) = $0
   EMV(1) = .30($125) + .50($65) + .20($30) = $76.00
   EMV(2) = .30($105) + .50($60) + .20($30) = $67.50
   EMV(both) = .30($220) + .50($110) + .20($40) = $129.00

   b. Choose both.

   c.

	Opportunity loss		
	S_1	S_2	S_3
Neither	$220	$110	$40
1	95	45	10
2	115	50	10
Both	0	0	0

   d. EOL(neither) = .30($220) + .50($110) + .20($40) = $129.00
   EOL(1) = .30($95) + .50($45) + .20($10) = $53.00
   EOL(2) = .30($115) + .50($50) + .20($10) = $61.50
   EOL(both) = .30($0) + .50($0) + .20($0) = $0

   e. EVPI = $0, found by $129 − $129.

   Certainty = .30($220) + .50($110) + .20($40) = $129

13. The payoff table is as follows in $000.

	Recession, S_1	No recession, S_2
Production	$−10.0	$15.0
Stock	−5.0	12.0
CD	6.0	6.0

   a. Purchase a CD.
   b. Increase production.
   c. (Answers in $000)

EMV(Prod.) = .2(−10) + .8(15.0) = 10.0
EMV(Stock) = .2(−5) + .8(12.0) = 8.6
EMV(CD) = .2(6) + .8(6) = 6.0

Expand production.

d. EVPI = [.2(6) + .8(15)] − [10.0] = 13.2 − 10.0 = 3.2

15. *a.*

	Event				
Act	**10**	**11**	**12**	**13**	**14**
10	$500	$500	$500	$500	$500
11	200	550	550	550	550
12	−100	250	600	600	600
13	−400	−50	300	650	650
14	−700	−350	0	350	700

b.

Act	Expected profit
10	$500.00
11	504.50
12	421.50
13	233.50
14	−31.50

Order 11 mobile homes because expected profit of $504.50 is the highest.

c.

	Opportunity loss				
Supply	**10**	**11**	**12**	**13**	**14**
10	$ 0	$ 50	$100	$150	$200
11	300	0	50	100	150
12	600	300	0	50	100
13	900	600	300	0	50
14	1,200	900	600	300	0

d.

	Act				
	10	**11**	**12**	**13**	**14**
Expected opportunity loss	$95.50	$91	$174	$362	$627

Decision: Order 11 homes because the opportunity loss of $91 is the smallest.

e. $91, found by:

$595.50	Profit under certainty
−504.50	Profit under uncertainty
$ 91.00	Value of perfect information

17. *a.*

	Event					
Act	**41**	**42**	**43**	**44**	**45**	**46**
41	$410	$410	$410	$410	$410	$410
42	405	420	420	420	420	420
43	400	415	430	430	430	430
44	395	410	425	440	440	440
45	390	405	420	435	450	450
46	385	400	415	430	445	460

b.

Act	Expected profit
41	$410.00
42	419.10
43	426.70
44	432.20
45	431.70
46	427.45

c. Order 44 because $432.20 is the largest expected profit.

d. Expected opportunity loss:

41	42	43	44	45	46
$28.30	$19.20	$11.60	$6.10	$6.60	$10.85

e. Order 44 because the opportunity loss of $6.10 is the smallest. Yes, it agrees.

f. $6.10, found by:

$438.30	Profit under certainty
−432.20	Profit under uncertainty
$ 6.10	Value of perfect information

The maximum we should pay for perfect information is $6.10.

ANSWERS

TO ODD-NUMBERED REVIEW EXERCISES

A REVIEW OF CHAPTERS 1–4

1. *a.* Sample.
   b. Ratio.
   c. \$11.60, found by \$58/5.
   d. \$11.70. Half of the employees earn below \$11.70 an hour, and the other half earn above \$11.70 an hour.
   e. $$s^2 = \frac{696.18 - \frac{(58)^2}{5}}{5 - 1} = 5.845$$
   f. $$Sk = \frac{3(11.60 - 11.70)}{2.42} = -0.123$$

3. *a.*

Rolls	Frequency
3 up to 6	2
6 up to 9	6
9 up to 12	8
12 up to 15	3
15 up to 18	1

   b.

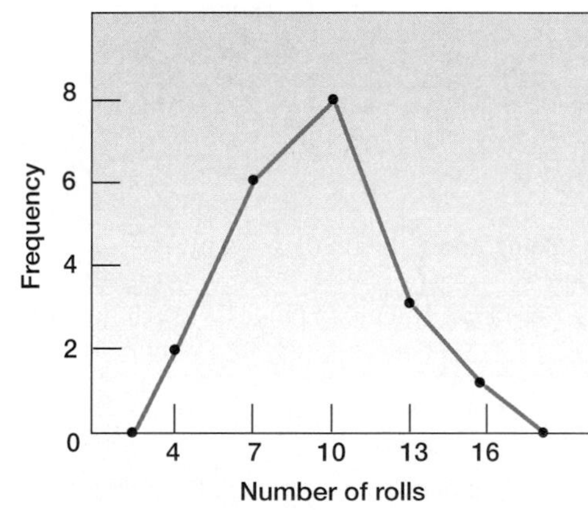

   c. $$\overline{X} = \frac{186}{20} = 9.3$$
   d. $$\text{Median} = 9 + \frac{10 - 8}{8}(3) = 9.75$$
   e. 10
   f. 14 using the frequency distribution, 13 using the actual data.
   g. $$s^2 = \frac{1,906 - \frac{(186)^2}{20}}{20 - 1} = 9.2736$$
   h. $s = \sqrt{9.2736} = 3.045$
   i. $9.30 \pm 2(3.045)$. The limits are 3.21 up to 15.39.

5. *a.* 8.82%, found by 44.1/5.
   b. 7.479%.
   c. Geometric mean since it is not highly influenced by the 19.5%.

7.

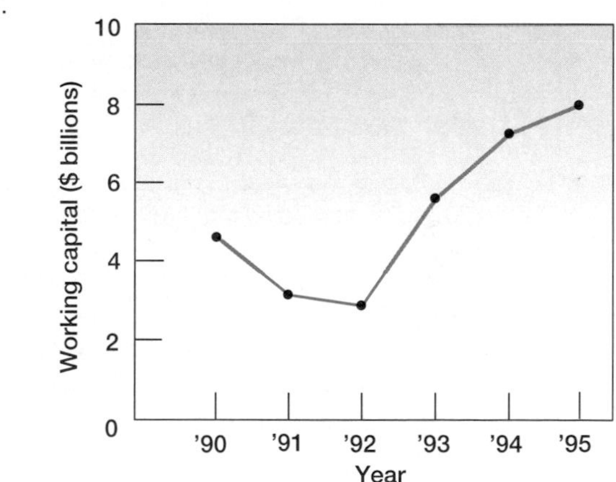

9. Ordinal.
11. Less-than cumulative frequency polygon. About 45; about 35; 10, 5 found by 10/2; 35, found by 55 − 20.
13. 9.375%
15. Coefficient of variation.
17. 92 and 108, found by $100 \pm 2(4)$.
19. *a.* The following histogram is from MINITAB.

```
Histogram of C1      N = 50
Midpoint    Count
      0         1 *
     40         7 *******
     80         3 ***
    120         8 ********
    160        15 ***************
    200        10 **********
    240         3 ***
    280         3 ***
   N   MEAN  MEDIAN  TRMEAN  STDEV  SEMEAN
  50 147.90  148.50  146.11  69.24    9.79
   MIN     MAX      Q1      Q3
 14.00  299.00  106.00  186.25
```

b. and *c.* The distribution is fairly symmetrical because the mean ($147.90) and the median ($148.50) are quite close. The mean ± 2*s* indicates that the middle 95% of the deposits are between $147.90 ± 2($69.24) = $9.42 and $286.38. Range = $299.00 − $14.00 = $285.00. There is a very slight negative skewness (because the mean is less than the median).

21. *a.* From MINITAB:

```
MTB > desc c1
      N   MEAN  MEDIAN  TRMEAN  STDEV  SEMEAN
C1   85  15.06   15.00   14.79   9.63    1.04
     MIN    MAX     Q1     Q3
C1  0.00  36.00   6.00  22.50
```

Typical length of service is about 15 years (mean or median).

b. Range is 36 years, found by 36 (MAX) −0 (MIN).

c. Only slight positive skewness because the mean of 15.06 is slightly larger than the median (15.00).

d.

```
Stem-and-leaf of C1     N = 85
Leaf Unit = 1.0
  12    0  011222333444
  30    0  555555566677788999
  42    1  000133334444
 (16)   1  5555566666788899
  27    2  00001233333
  16    2  6667889
   9    3  00123344
   1    3  6
```

23. Median: Women $15,762, men $24,345.
Mode: Women $12,500, men $37,500.
Lowest 25%: Women $11,053, men $15,732.
Upper 25%: Women $22,231, men $39,858.
The distribution of the annual earnings of men is significantly higher than that for the distribution of the women. Note: Mean cannot be computed because of open-ended class.

A REVIEW OF CHAPTERS 5–7

1. Subjective.
3. An outcome.
5. Complement rule. $1 - P(X) = .999$.
7. Discrete.
9. Discrete.
11. Bell-shaped, symmetrical, asymptotic.
13. *a.* .10, found by 20/200.
    b. .725, found by 145/200.
    c. .925, found by 1 − 15/200.
15. *a.* .1353, found from Appendix C, where $\mu = 2.0$.
    b. 346, found by 400(.1353) = 54. Then 400 − 54 = 346.
    c. .3233, found by 1 − (.1353 + .2707 + .2707).
17. *a.* .417, found by 223/535.
    b. .407, found by 177/435.
    c. .914, found by (435/535) + (312/535) − 258/535.
19. *a.* $1.84 million, found by 0 + .64 + 1.2.
    b. .98.
    c. .20, found by .004/.02.
    d. Yes. The $2 million premium is greater than the expected loss of $1.84 million. Thus the expected profit is $0.16 million.

A REVIEW OF CHAPTERS 8 and 9

1. *b*
3. *c*
5. *d*
7. *e*
9. *a*
11. H_0: $\mu \geq 36$, H_1: $\mu < 36$, Reject H_0 if $z < -1.645$.

    Computed $z = -3.60$, found by $\dfrac{35.5 - 36}{.9/\sqrt{42}}$

    Reject H_0. The mean height is less than 36 inches.

13. *a.* 457, found by $n = .05(1 - .05)\left(\dfrac{1.96}{.02}\right)^2$
    b. Change the level of confidence to 90 percent, or raise the allowable error.
15. *a.* H_0: $\mu_B = \mu_V$; H_1: $\mu_B \neq \mu_V$
    b. Two tailed. No direction given.
    c. $$z = \frac{\overline{X}_B - \overline{X}_V}{\sqrt{\dfrac{s_B^2}{n_B} + \dfrac{s_V^2}{n_V}}}$$

d. $-1.96, +1.96$.

e. Computed $z = -2.0203$, found by

$$\frac{10.92 - 11.05}{\sqrt{\frac{(.78)^2}{180} + \frac{(.39)^2}{200}}}$$

Reject H_0 and accept H_1. The mean wages are not equal.

A REVIEW OF CHAPTERS 10 and 11

1. *b*
3. *a*
5. *d*
7. *d*
9. *b*
11. *e*
13. H_0: $\mu \leq 20$, H_1: $\mu > 20$. Reject H_0 if $t > 1.860$.

$$\bar{X} = 21 \qquad s = 6.185$$
$$t = \frac{21 - 20}{6.185/\sqrt{9}} = 0.485$$

H_0 is not rejected. The mean amount of break time is not more than 20 minutes.

15. H_0: $\mu_d \leq 0$, H_1: $\mu_d > 0$. Reject H_0 if $t > 1.833$.

$$\bar{d} = 0.4 \qquad s_d = 6.11 \qquad t = \frac{0.4}{6.11/\sqrt{10}} = 0.21$$

H_0 is not rejected. There is no difference in the life of the paints.

17. H_0: $\mu_1 = \mu_2 = \mu_3 = \mu_4 = \mu_5$. H_1: Means not equal. Reject if $F > 3.84$.
H_0: $\mu_1 = \mu_2 = \mu_3$. H_1: Means not equal. Reject if $F > 4.46$.

Source	SS	*df*	MS	*F*
Treatments	165.73	4	41.43	11.098
Blocks	22.8	2	11.40	3.054
Error	29.87	8	3.73	
Total	218.40	14		

There is a difference in fertilizer types, but not soil conditions.

A REVIEW OF CHAPTERS 12 and 13

1. Coefficient of correlation or the coefficient of determination.
3. H_0: $\rho \leq 0$, H_1: $\rho > 0$. Critical value of t is 1.671. Computed $t = 3.324$. H_0 is rejected. There is a positive correlation.
5. The independent variables are entered into the equation in the order in which they increase R^2 the fastest.
7. $Y' = a + b_1X_1 + b_2X_2 + b_3X_3 + b_4X_4$
9. About 86 percent of the variation in net profit is explained by the four variables.
11. *a.*

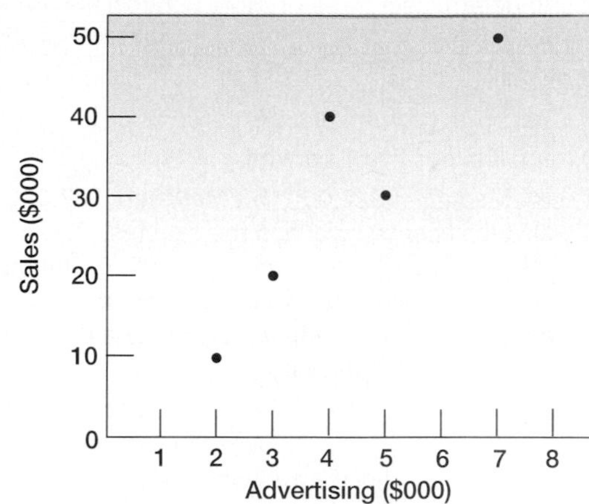

b.

Y	*X*	*XY*	X^2	Y^2
10	2	20	4	100
40	4	160	16	1,600
30	5	150	25	900
50	7	350	49	2,500
20	3	60	9	400
150	21	740	103	5,500

$$r = \frac{5(740) - 21(150)}{\sqrt{[5(103) - (21)^2][5(5{,}500) - (150)^2]}} =$$
$$\frac{550}{\sqrt{(74)(5{,}000)}} = .9042$$

c. $r^2 = (.9042)^2 = .8176$

d.
$$b = \frac{5(740) - 21(150)}{5(103) - (21)^2} = \frac{550}{74} = 7.4324$$
$$a = \frac{150}{5} - (7.4324)\left(\frac{21}{5}\right) = -1.2161$$
$$Y' = -1.2161 + 7.4324X$$

e. $Y' = -1.2161 + 7.4324(4.5) = \$32.23$, in thousands.

f. Strong positive association between amount spent on advertising and monthly sales. For each additional $1,000 spent on advertising, sales increase $7,432.40.

A REVIEW OF CHAPTERS 16 and 17

1. Frequency observed and frequency expected.
3. Chi-square distribution.
5. Not rejected because 11.248 is less than 12.592.
7. There is no difference between the observed and the expected set of frequencies.

9. Nominal level.
11. To determine if two or more independent populations are the same.
13. To determine if three or more populations are the same.
15. Kruskal-Wallis.
17. Yes.
19. No. It is positively skewed.
21. H_0: Median = \$27,000, H_1: Median $\neq$ \$27,000. Use .05 significance level and the sign test. The critical values are $z < -1.96$ and $z > 1.96$. Count the number of values above the median, compute z, assuming a large sample, and make a decision. Note: examples will vary.

INDEX

I–J

K–L

M

Q

R

S

T

U–V

W–Z

PHOTO CREDITS

CHAPTER 1

p. 1: courtesy of Busch Gardens; Williamsburg, Va.; **p. 7:** courtesy of Indianapolis Motor Speedway Corporation.

CHAPTER 2

p. 25: © Bruce Ayres: Tony Stone Images; **p. 34:** courtesy of Cunard; **p. 55:** courtesy of Minitab, Inc.; **p. 65:** courtesy of The University of Toledo.

CHAPTER 3

p. 73: © Zephyr Pictures: West Stock Photography; **p. 89:** courtesy of Navistar International Transportation Corp.; **p. 105:** courtesy of The University of Toledo.

CHAPTER 4

p. 113: courtesy of Blockbuster Entertainment; **p. 115:** Photo courtesy of Hewlett-Packard Company; **p. 133:** courtesy of Northwest Natural Gas.

CHAPTER 5

p. 167: © Nicholas Communications, Inc.; **p. 175:** courtesy of Insurance Institute for Highway Safety; **p. 185:** courtesy of Dean Foods Company; **p. 208:** Sharon Hoogstraten.

CHAPTER 6

p. 217: Sharon Hoogstraten; **p. 221:** courtesy Southern California Edison Company; **p. 235:** *Kellogg's Corn Flakes* ® is a registered trademark of Kellogg Company; © 1994 Kellogg Company. Used with permission; **p. 242:** courtesy of Saturn Corporation.

CHAPTER 7

p. 255: courtesy of American Stock Exchange; **p. 256:** courtesy of Aluminum Company of America; **p. 265:** courtesy of Delta Airlines, Inc.; **p. 277:** courtesy of Del Monte Foods.

CHAPTER 8

p. 293: © J. McGuire: Washington Stock Photo, Inc.; **p. 294:** Sharon Hoogstraten; **p. 301:** courtesy of Wendy's International, Inc.; **p. 327:** courtesy of Aluminum Company of America.

CHAPTER 9

p. 343: courtesy of The Boeing Company; **p. 371:** courtesy of Ford Motor Company; **p. 382:** courtesy of The Manitowoc Company, Inc.

CHAPTER 10

p. 399: courtesy of Airborne Express; **p. 427:** Photo courtesy of Hewlett-Packard Company.

CHAPTER 11

p. 433: © C. Raymond: Photo Researchers, Inc.; **p. 435:** courtesy of USX Corporation; **p. 447:** courtesy of International Business Machines Corporation; **p. 464:** Sharon Hoogstraten.

CHAPTER 12

p. 477: © D. Durrance: Woodfin Camp & Associates, Inc.; **p. 478:** courtesy of Jordache Enterprises, Inc.; **p. 485:** Photo courtesy of Hewlett-Packard Company; **p. 516:** courtesy Florida Department of Commerce, Division of Tourism.

CHAPTER 13

p. 529: © David Pollack: The Stock Market; **p. 531:** courtesy of Minitab, Inc.; **p. 534:** Photo courtesy of Allen-Bradley, a Rockwell International Company; **p. 562:** courtesy of Monsanto Company.

CHAPTER 14

p. 575: © Doug Wilson: MGA/Photri; **p. 577:** Sharon Hoogstraten; **p. 598:** courtesy of the *Chicago Tribune.*

CHAPTER 15

p. 605: © Allen Lee Page: The Stock Market; **p. 606:** courtesy of Nestlé Beverage Company; **p. 626:** courtesy of International Business Machines Company; **p. 633:** courtesy of Saab Scania.

CHAPTER 16

p. 655: © Jeff Zaruba: The Stock Market; **p. 657:** courtesy of Ford Motor Company; **p. 665:** courtesy of George J. Meyer Manufacturing, a Figgie International Company; **p. 667:** courtesy of StatSoft, Inc.; **p. 686:** courtesy of Seiko Corporation of America.

CHAPTER 17

p. 691: courtesy of Nike, Inc.; **p. 709:** courtesy The University of Chicago; **p. 719:** courtesy of Southern California Edison Company.

CHAPTER 18

p. 727: courtesy of Motorola Corporation; **p. 728:** courtesy of SPSS, Inc.; **p. 747:** courtesy of Toys "R" Us.

CHAPTER 19

p. 767: Zenith/Charlie Weterman; **p. 770:** courtesy of Monsanto Company; **p. 784:** Artco Sales, Inc.